Less managing. More teaching. Greater learning.

 INSTRUCTORS...

Would you like your **students** to show up for class more **prepared**? *(Let's face it, class is much more fun if everyone is engaged and prepared...)*

Want ready-made application-level **interactive assignments,** student progress reporting, and auto-assignment grading? *(Less time grading means more time teaching...)*

Want an **instant view of student or class performance** relative to learning objectives? *(No more wondering if students understand...)*

Need to **collect data and generate reports** required for administration or accreditation? *(Say goodbye to manually tracking student learning outcomes...)*

Want to **record and post your lectures** for students to view online?

 With McGraw-Hill's *Connect® Plus Business*,

INSTRUCTORS GET:

- Interactive Applications – **book-specific interactive assignments** that require students to APPLY what they've learned.

- Simple **assignment management**, allowing you to spend more time teaching.

- **Auto-graded** assignments, quizzes, and tests.

- **Detailed Visual Reporting** where student and section results can be viewed and analyzed.

- Sophisticated **online testing** capability.

- A **filtering and reporting** function that allows you to easily assign and report on materials that are correlated to accreditation standards, learning outcomes, and Bloom's taxonomy.

- An easy-to-use **lecture capture** tool.

STUDENTS...

Want an online, **searchable version** of your textbook?

Wish your textbook could be **available online** while you're doing your assignments?

Connect® Plus Business eBook

If you choose to use *Connect® Plus Business*, you have an affordable and searchable online version of your book integrated with your other online tools.

Connect® Plus Business eBook offers features like:

- Topic search
- Direct links from assignments
- Adjustable text size
- Jump to page number
- Print by section

STUDENTS...

Want to get more **value** from your textbook purchase?

Think learning about business should be a bit more **interesting**?

Check out the INTERACTIVE PRESENTATIONS found in *Connect®*.

Interactive Presentations are a great prep tool that teach each chapter's core learning objectives and concepts through a multimedia, professional presentation, which brings the text content to life. Come to class more prepared with knowledge of the chapter material, making you ready to participate in class.

understanding
BUSINESS

understanding

tenth edition

BUSINESS

William G. Nickels
University of Maryland

James M. McHugh
St. Louis Community College at Forest Park

Susan M. McHugh
Applied Learning Systems

McGraw-Hill Irwin

McGraw-Hill
Irwin

UNDERSTANDING BUSINESS

Published by McGraw-Hill/Irwin, a business unit of The McGraw-Hill Companies, Inc., 1221 Avenue of the Americas, New York, NY, 10020. Copyright © 2013, 2010, 2008, 2005, 2002, 1999, 1996, 1993, 1990, 1986 by The McGraw-Hill Companies, Inc. All rights reserved. Printed in the United States of America. No part of this publication may be reproduced or distributed in any form or by any means, or stored in a database or retrieval system, without the prior written consent of The McGraw-Hill Companies, Inc., including, but not limited to, in any network or other electronic storage or transmission, or broadcast for distance learning.

Some ancillaries, including electronic and print components, may not be available to customers outside the United States.

This book is printed on acid-free paper.

1 2 3 4 5 6 7 8 9 0 DOW/DOW 1 0 9 8 7 6 5 4 3 2

ISBN 978-0-07-352459-7
MHID 0-07-352459-X

Vice president and editor-in-chief: *Brent Gordon*
Editorial director: *Paul Ducham*
Executive director of development: *Ann Torbert*
Development editor II: *Kelly L. Delso*
Vice president and director of marketing: *Robin J. Zwettler*
Marketing director: *Amee Mosley*
Senior marketing manager: *Sarah Schuessler*
Vice president of editing, design, and production: *Sesha Bolisetty*
Lead project manager: *Christine A. Vaughan*
Senior buyer: *Carol A. Bielski*
Lead designer: *Matthew Baldwin*
Senior photo research coordinator: *Jeremy Cheshareck*
Photo researcher: *Jen Blankenship*
Lead media project manager: *Brian Nacik*
Typeface: *10/12 New Aster*
Compositor: *Laserwords Private Limited*
Printer: *R. R. Donnelley*

Library of Congress Cataloging-in-Publication Data

Nickels, William G.
    Understanding business / William G. Nickels, James M. McHugh,
Susan M. McHugh.—10th ed.
        p. cm.
    Includes index.
    ISBN-13: 978-0-07-352459-7 (student ed. : alk. paper)
    ISBN-10: 0-07-352459-X (student ed. : alk. paper)
    1. Industrial management. 2. Business. 3. Business—Vocational guidance. I. McHugh, James M.
II. McHugh, Susan M. III. Title.
HD31.N4897 2013
650—dc23
                                                                    2011040783

www.mhhe.com

dedication

To our families—Marsha, Joel, Carrie, Casey, Dan, Molly, Michael, Colin, and Quinn. Thank you for making everything worth doing and giving us the support to do it well!

and

To the team that made this edition possible, especially the instructors and students who gave us such valuable guidance as we developed the text and package.

ABOUT THE
authors

Bill Nickels is emeritus professor of business at the University of Maryland, College Park. He has over 30 years' experience teaching graduate and undergraduate business courses, including introduction to business, marketing, and promotion. He has won the Outstanding Teacher on Campus Award four times and was nominated for the award many other times. He received his M.B.A. degree from Western Reserve University and his Ph.D. from The Ohio State University. He has written a marketing communications text and two marketing principles texts in addition to many articles in business publications. He has taught many seminars to businesspeople on subjects such as power communications, marketing, non-business marketing, and stress and life management. His son, Joel, is a Professor of English at the University of Miami (Florida).

Jim McHugh holds an M.B.A. degree from Lindenwood University and has had broad experience in education, business, and government. As chairman of the Business and Economics Department of St. Louis Community College/ Forest Park, Jim coordinated and directed the development of the business curriculum. In addition to teaching several sections of Introduction to Business each semester for nearly 30 years, Jim taught in the marketing and management areas at both the undergraduate and graduate levels. Jim enjoys conducting business seminars and consulting with small and large businesses. He is actively involved in the public service sector and served as chief of staff to the St. Louis County Executive.

Susan McHugh is a learning specialist with extensive training and experience in adult learning and curriculum development. She holds an M.Ed. degree from the University of Missouri and completed her course work for a Ph.D. in education administration with a specialty in adult learning theory. As a professional curriculum developer, she has directed numerous curriculum projects and educator training programs. She has worked in the public and private sectors as a consultant in training and employee development. While Jim and Susan treasure their participation in writing projects, their greatest accomplishment is their collaboration on their three children. Casey is carrying on the family's teaching tradition as an adjunct professor at Washington University. Molly and Michael are carrying on the family writing tradition by contributing to the development of several supplementary materials for this text.

Understanding Business has long been the MARKET LEADER. We've listened to you and your students and that's helped us offer you:

Resources that were developed based directly on *your* feedback—all geared to make the most of your time and to help students succeed in this course. All the supplemental resources for *Understanding Business* are carefully reviewed by Bill, Jim, and Susan to ensure cohesion with the text.

Technology that leads the way and is consistently being updated to keep up with you and your students. *Connect® Business* offers students a truly interactive and adaptive study arena. *Interactive Presentations, Interactive Applications*, and *LearnSmart* are designed to engage students and have been proven to increase grades by a full letter.

Support that is always available to help you in planning your course, working with technology, and meeting the needs of you and your students.

Go for the GOLD—Over 3 million students have.

KEEPING UP WITH WHAT'S NEW

Users of *Understanding Business* have always appreciated the currency of the material and the large number of examples from companies of all sizes and industries (e.g., service, manufacturing, nonprofit, and profit) in the United States and around the world. A glance at the Chapter Notes will show you that almost all of them are from 2010 or 2011. Accordingly, this edition features the latest business practices and other developments affecting business including:

- Using social media in business (integrated throughout the text and featured in new themed boxes)
- Growing economic importance of China
- European debt crisis and its affect on the U.S. economy
- COMESA, the African trading bloc
- BRIC economies
- Dodd-Frank Wall Street Reform and Consumer Protection Act
- Socially-conscious research organizations
- Recent conflicts between governments and public sector labor unions
- Economic crisis beginning in 2008—its causes, effects, and attempted remedies, including TARP and the stimulus package.
- Web 2.0 and Web 3.0
- Cloud computing
- NYSE Euronext ownership changes
- Patient Protection and Affordable Care Act (PPACA)
- Credit Card Responsibility Accountability and Disclosure Act
- Taxing online purchases
- Millennials in the workplace
- And much, much more

GOLD STANDARD STUDENT RESOURCES

Connect

 McGraw-Hill *Connect*® is the leading online assignment and assessment solution that connects students with the tools and resources they need to achieve success while providing instructors with tools to quickly pick content and assignments according to the learning objectives they want to emphasize.

Connect improves student learning and retention with engaging presentations and activities that prepare students for class, help them master concepts, and review for exams.

Interactive Presentations within *Connect* are designed to reinforce learning by offering a visual presentation of the Learning Goals highlighted in every chapter of the text. Interactive presentations are engaging, online, professional presentations (fully Section 508 compliant) covering the same core concepts directly from the chapter, while offering additional examples and graphics. *Interactive Presentations* teach students Learning Goals in a multimedia format, bringing the course and the book to life. *Interactive Presentations* are a great prep tool for students—when the student is better prepared, they are more engaged and better able to participate in class.

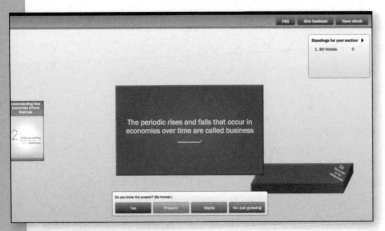

LearnSmart within *Connect* is an adaptive learning system designed to help students learn faster, study more efficiently, and retain more knowledge for greater success. *LearnSmart* adaptively assesses students' skill levels to determine which topics students have mastered and which require further practice. Then it delivers customized learning content based on their strengths and weaknesses. The result: students learn faster and more efficiently because they get the help they need, right when they need it—instead of getting stuck on lessons, or being continually frustrated with stalled progress.

Interactive Applications within *Connect*, offer students a variety of tools to help them assess their understanding. All *Interactive Applications* require students to APPLY what they have learned from the text to these assignments, and other than the Comprehension Cases, are all auto-graded. Some of the *Interactive Application* exercises include: video cases, decision generators, comprehensive cases, and self-assessments (concept checks).

Click and Drag exercises allow students to reinforce key models/processes by requiring students to label key illustrations and models from the text or build a process, and then demonstrate application-level knowledge.

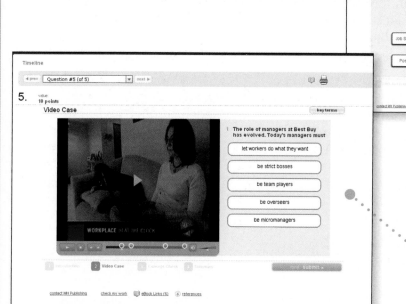

Video cases give students the opportunity to watch case videos and apply chapter concepts to a real-world business scenario as the scenario unfolds.

Decision generators require students to make real business decisions based on specific real-world scenarios and cases.

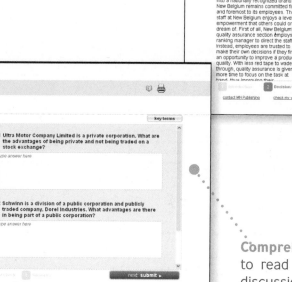

Comprehensive cases encourage students to read a case and answer open-ended discussion questions to demonstrate writing and critical-thinking skills.

Concept Checks integrated with every *Interactive Application* exercise ensure students fully understand the concepts they they are applying.

Manager's Hotseat (*Connect* Library)—short video cases that show 15 real managers applying their years of experience in confronting certain management and organizational behavior issues. Students assume the role of the manager as they watch the video and answer multiple choice questions that pop up during the segment, forcing them to make decisions on the spot. Students learn from the managers' unscripted mistakes and successes, and then do a report critiquing the managers' approach by defending their reasoning.

Integrated Media-Rich eBook

- A Web-optimized eBook is seamlessly integrated within *ConnectPlus*.
- Students can access Interactive Presentations and test their knowledge through self-assessment quizzes provided throughout the chapter to enhance their learning experience.
- Students can highlight, take notes, or even access shared instructor's notations to learn course material.
- The integrated eBook provides students with a cost-saving alternative to the traditional textbook.

Online Learning Center (www.mhhe.com/UB10e)

The Online Learning Center will help students use *Understanding Business* effectively. Some features on the website are:

- Additional Cases—based on interviews with company executives from interesting companies like Redbox, Pillow Pets, and Zappos provide students with an insider view of real business practices. The videos that accompany these cases feature companies in action to which students can relate. These videos are provided in the *Connect* Library for students and on the instructor DVD.
- Casing the Web—short cases that allow students to practice managerial decision-making. These discussion starters are provided for every chapter and are intended to replace comprehensive cases that can consume class time.
- Multiple-choice questions—quizzes focusing on key concepts and providing immediate feedback offer students the opportunity to determine their level of understanding.
- Student Assessment and Learning Guide—questions, key term review, practice tests with answer key, and Internet exercises to help students succeed in their course.

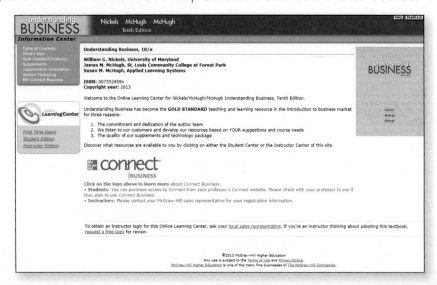

GOLD STANDARD STUDENT-FRIENDLY FEATURES

Learning Goals Everything in the text and supplements package ties back to the chapter learning goals. The learning goals listed throughout the chapter help students preview what they should know after reading the chapter. Chapter summaries test students' knowledge by asking questions related to the learning goals. The Test Bank, Instructor's Manual, PowerPoints, Online Course, and *Connect* are all organized according to the learning goals.

Getting to Know Business Professionals Every chapter in the text opens with the profile of a business professional whose career relates closely to the material in the chapter. These business professionals work for a variety of businesses from small businesses and nonprofit organizations to large corporations. These career profiles are an engaging way to open the chapter and to introduce students to a variety of business career paths.

Name That Company Every text chapter opens with a Name That Company challenge. The answer for the challenge can be found somewhere in the chapter.

Progress Assessments help students understand and retain the material in the chapters. Progress Assessment questions stop them at important points in the chapter to assess what they've learned before they continue reading.

progress assessment

- What is the difference between macroeconomics and microeconomics?
- What is better for an economy than teaching a man to fish?
- What does Adam Smith's term *invisible hand* mean? How does the invisible hand create wealth for a country?

NEW to This Edition! **Social Media in Business** boxes ask students to consider the impact social media have on the way they communicate and the way companies conduct business as a result.

Legal Briefcase boxes give students the opportunity to learn about legal issues involving real companies.

Thinking Green boxes highlight corporate responsibility and help students understand the various ways business activities affect the environment.

Spotlight on Small Business boxes feature how the concepts in the chapter relate to small businesses.

Reaching beyond Our Borders boxes focus on global issues surrounding business.

Making Ethical Decisions boxes offer students ethical dilemmas to consider.

GOLD STANDARD INSTRUCTOR RESOURCES

Connect offers instructors auto-gradable material in an effort to facilitate learning and to save time.

Student Progress Tracking

Connect keeps instructors informed about how each student, section, and class is performing, allowing for more productive use of lecture and office hours. The progress-tracking function enables instructors to:

- View scored work immediately and track individual or group performance with assignment and grade reports.
- Access an instant view of student or class performance relative to learning objectives.
- Collect data and generate reports required by many accreditation organizations, such as AACSB.

Online Learning Center for Instructors www.mhhe.com/ubl0e

The Online Learning Center offers instructors a one-stop, secure site for essential course materials, allowing instructors to save prep time before class. The instructor site offers:

- Instructor's Manual
- *Connect* Instructor's Manual
- PowerPoint Presentations
- Testbank/EZ Test
- Monthly Newsletters
- Videos
- Video Guide

Instructor's Resource CD (IRCD): The authors have carefully reviewed all resources provided on this CD to ensure cohesion with the text. It includes the Instructor's Manual containing everything an instructor needs to prepare a lecture, including lecture outlines, discussion questions, and teaching notes. More than 900 PowerPoint® slides offer material from the text, as well as expanded coverage to supplement discussion. The Test Bank and Computerized Test Bank offer over 8,000 multiple-choice, true/false, short answer, essay, and application questions. The Online Learning Center contains the media-enhanced PowerPoint Presentations that are found on the IRCD. The media-enhanced slides have video and commercials embedded into the presentations and makes for an engaging and interesting classroom lecture.
ISBN: 0077474376

Video/DVD

Video/DVD Chapter-specific videos are provided to complement each chapter of the text. Eleven of the twenty videos have been updated to include interesting companies that students will identify with such as Redbox, Zappos, and Groupon.
ISBN: 0077474473

Video Guide

This guide (available on the Online Learning Center) includes detailed teaching notes to accompany the chapter videos, as well as essay-style and multiple choice questions.

Connect Instructor's Manual

This Instructor's Manual offers instructor what they need to set up *Connect* for their courses. It explains everything from how to get started to suggestions of what to assign and ideas about assigning credit. This tool was developed by instructors who have used and continue to use *Connect* successfully in their course. This Instructor's Manual can be found in *Connect*, on the Instructor's Resource CD, and on the OLC.

GOLD STANDARD TEACHING OPTIONS AND SOLUTIONS

McGraw-Hill Higher Education and Blackboard have teamed up. What does this mean for you?

1. **Your life, simplified. Single Sign-On:** A single login and single environment provide seamless access to all course resources—all McGraw-Hill's resources are available within the Blackboard Learn platform.

2. **Deep integration of content and tools. Deep Integration:** One click access to a wealth of McGraw-Hill content and tools—all from within Blackboard Learn.™

3. **Seamless Gradebooks. One Gradebook:** Automatic grade synchronization with Blackboard gradebook. All grades for McGraw-Hill *Connect* assignments are recorded in the Blackboard gradebook automatically.

4. **A solution for everyone. Openness:** Unique in Higher Education, the partnership of McGraw-Hill Higher Education and Blackboard preserves the spirit of academic freedom and openness. Blackboard remains publisher independent, and McGraw-Hill remains LMS independent. The result makes our content, engines and platform more usable and accessible, with fewer barriers to adoption and use.

5. **100% FERPA**-compliant solution protects student privacy.

6. **McGraw-Hill and Blackboard** can now offer you easy access to industry-leading technology and content, whether your campus hosts it, or we do. Be sure to ask your local McGraw-Hill representative for details.

McGraw-Hill *Connect Plus Understanding Business*

McGraw-Hill reinvents the textbook-learning experience for today's students with *Connect Plus Understanding Business.* A seamless integration of an eBook and *Connect* provides all of the *Connect* features plus the following:

- An integrated eBook, allowing for anytime, anywhere online access to the textbook.
- Dynamic links between the problems or questions assigned to students and the location in the eBook where that problem or question is covered.
- Powerful search function to pinpoint and connect key concepts in a snap.

For more information about *Connect,* go to **connect.mcgraw-hill.com,** or contact your local McGraw-Hill sales representative.

 CourseSmart
LearnSmart. Choose Smart.

CourseSmart is a new way for faculty to find and review eTextbooks. It's also a great option for students who are interested in accessing their course materials digitally, and saving money.

CourseSmart offers thousands of the most commonly adopted textbooks across hundreds of courses from a wide variety of higher education publishers. It is the only place for faculty to review and compare the full text of a textbook online, providing immediate access without the environmental impact of requesting a print exam copy.

With the CourseSmart eTextbook, students can save up to 45 percent off the cost of a printed book, reduce their impact on the environment, and access powerful Web tools for learning. CourseSmart is an online eTextbook, which means users access and view their textbook online when connected to the Internet. Students can also print sections of the book for maximum portability. CourseSmart eTextbooks are available in one standard online reader with full text search, notes, and highlighting, and e-mail tools for sharing notes between classmates. For more information on CourseSmart, go to **http://www.coursesmart.com.**

 CREATE
Instructors can now tailor their teaching resources to match the way they teach! With McGraw-Hill Create, **www.mcgrawhillcreate.com**, instructors can easily rearrange chapters, combine material from other content sources, and quickly upload and integrate their own content, like course syllabi or teaching notes. Find the right content in Create by searching through thousands of leading McGraw-Hill textbooks. Arrange the material to fit your teaching style. Order a Create book and receive a complimentary print review copy in 3–5 business days or a complimentary electronic review copy (eComp) via e-mail within one hour. Go to **www.mcgrawhillcreate.com** today and register.

Tegrity Campus: Lectures 24/7
Tegrity Campus is a service that makes class time available 24/7 by automatically capturing every lecture in a searchable format for students to review when they study and complete assignments. With a simple one-click start-and-stop process, you capture all computer screens and corresponding audio. Students can replay any part of any class with easy-to-use browser-based viewing on a PC or Mac.

Educators know that the more students can see, hear, and experience class resources, the better they learn. In fact, studies prove it. With patented Tegrity "search anything" technology, students instantly recall key class moments for replay online, or on iPods® and mobile devices. Instructors can help turn all their students' study time into learning moments immediately supported by their lecture.

To learn more about Tegrity watch a 2-minute Flash demo at **http://tegritycampus.mhhe.com.**

Assurance of Learning Ready

Many educational institutions today are focused on the notion of *assurance of learning,* an important element of some accreditation standards. *Understanding Business* is designed specifically to support instructors' assurance of learning initiatives with a simple, yet powerful solution.

Each test bank question for *Understanding Business* maps to a specific chapter learning outcome/objective listed in the text. Instructors can use our test bank software, EZ Test and EZ Test Online, to easily query for learning outcomes/objectives that directly relate to the learning objectives for their course. Instructors can then use the reporting features of EZ Test to aggregate student results in similar fashion, making the collection and presentation of assurance of learning data simple and easy.

AACSB Statement

The McGraw-Hill Companies is a proud corporate member of AACSB International. Understanding the importance and value of AACSB accreditation, *Understanding Business* recognizes the curricula guidelines detailed in the AACSB standards for business accreditation by connecting selected questions in the text and the test bank to the six general knowledge and skill guidelines in the AACSB standards.

The statements contained in *Understanding Business* are provided only as a guide for the users of this textbook. The AACSB leaves content coverage and assessment within the purview of individual schools, the mission of the school, and the faculty. While the *Understanding Business* teaching package makes no claim of any specific AACSB qualification or evaluation, we have within *Understanding Business* labeled selected questions according to the six general knowledge and skills areas.

McGraw-Hill Customer Experience Group Contact Information

At McGraw-Hill, we understand that getting the most from new technology can be challenging. That's why our services don't stop after you purchase our products. You can e-mail our Product Specialists 24 hours a day to get product training online. Or you can search our knowledge bank of Frequently Asked Questions on our support website. For Customer Support, call **800-331-5094,** e-mail **hmsupport@mcgraw-hill.com**, or visit **www.mhhe.com/support**. One of our Technical Support Analysts will be able to assist you in a timely fashion.

Our editorial director, Paul Ducham and our Senior Sponsoring Editor, Anke Weekes, led the talented team at Irwin/McGraw-Hill. We appreciate their dedication to the success of the project and their responsiveness to the demands of the market. Kelly Delso served as our developmental editor and kept everyone on task and on schedule. Molly and Michael McHugh contributed several of the new boxes and profiles. Michael Hannon provided much appreciated research assistance. Matt Baldwin created the new fresh, open interior design and extraordinary cover. Jeremy Cheshareck and Jen Blankenship carried out the extensive research for photos that was necessary to effectively reflect the concepts presented in the text. Lead project manager, Christine Vaughan, did a splendid job of keeping the production of the text on schedule. Brian Nacik expertly supervised the supplements and media assets and Chris Nowack assisted in the delivery of *Connect* materials.

Many dedicated educators made extraordinary contributions to the quality and utility of this text and package. For this edition, Pam McElligott of St. Louis Community College and Molly McHugh did an exceptional job in preparing the Test Bank and creating the quizzes for the Online Learning Center and *Connect*. Molly also did a superb job of creating the PowerPoint slides and worked with Gayle Lois Megginson Ross of Circle Publishing to provide a useful and current Instructor's Resource Manual. We also recognize the efforts of Barbara Barrett of St. Louis Community College, Donna Haeger of Monroe Community College, John Striebich of Monroe Community College, Grace McLaughlin of University of California, Irvine, Colette Wolfson of Ivy Tech Community College of Indiana, and Linda Hoffman of Ivy Tech Community College of Indiana who contributed to the creation of *Connect* materials, and to our LearnSmart "team" at Monroe Community College; Judy Bulin, John Striebich, and Donna Haeger who tirelessly worked to review and perfect LearnSmart content. Thank you to Len Davis, Kelly Yee, and the crew of Pure Imagination for the fabulous new videos they produced. We'd also like to thank Kelly Luchtman at Lightfellow for providing two new videos to accompany this edition. Thank you to the Digital Faculty Consultants who have helped to train and support so many instructors in the Introduction to Business course, as well as assist them in successfully implementing *Connect* into their courses: Chris Finnin, Drexel University; Julie Hansen, Grossmont College; Todd Korol, Monroe Community College; John Striebich, Monroe Community College; and Marie Lapidus, Oakton Community College.

Our outstanding marketing manager, Sarah Schuessler, was up to the challenge of once again guiding the text to market leadership. With the assistance of the market's finest sales professionals, she led the text to record highs. We appreciate her commitment and the renowned product knowledge, service, and dedication of the McGraw-Hill/Irwin sales reps. We want to thank the many instructors who contributed to the development of *Understanding Business*.

REVIEWERS

We would like to thank the following instructors for sharing their opinions with us in an effort to improve this new edition:

Ashraf Almurdaah, *Los Angeles City College*

Lydia Anderson, *Fresno City College*

Chi Anyasi-Archibong, *North Carolina A&T*

Maria Aria, *Camden County College*

Michael Aubry, *Cuyamaca College*

Frank Barber, *Cuyahoga Community College*

Richard Bartlett, *Columbus State Community College*

Lorraine P. Bassette, *Prince George's Community College*

Jim Beard, *University of Arkansas–Fort Smith*

Amy Beattie, *Champlain College*

Charles Beem, *Bucks County Community College*

Robert Bennett, *Delaware County Community College*

Michael Bento, *Owens Community College*

George H. Bernard, *Seminole State College of Florida*

Marilyn Besich, *Montana State University–Great Falls*

Dennis Brode, *Sinclair Community College*

Kathy Broneck, *Pima Community College*

Harvey Bronstein, *Oakland Community College*

Jerri Buiting, *Baker College–Flint*

Bonnie Chavez, *Santa Barbara City College*

Savannah Clay, *Central Piedmont Community College*

Paul Coakley, *Community College of Baltimore County*

Patrick Conroy, *Delgado Community College*

James Darling, *Central New Mexico Community College*

Joseph Dutka, *Ivy Tech Community College of Indiana*

MaryBeth Furst, *Howard Community College*

Wayne Gawlik, *Joliet Junior College*

Ross Gittell, *University of New Hampshire*

Constance Golden, *Lakeland Community College*

Doug Greiner, *University of Toledo–Scott Park*

John Guess, *Delgado Community College*

Lisa E. Hadley, *Southwest Tennessee Community College*

Nancy Hernandez, *Howard College*

Maryanne Holcomb, *Oakland Community College*

Russell E. Holmes, *Des Moines Area Community College*

Janice Karlen, *La Guardia Community College*

James W. Marco, *Wake Technical Community College*

Theresa Mastrianni, *Kingsborough Community College*

Michelle Meyer, *Joliet Junior College*

Catherine Milburn, *University of Colorado–Denver*

Mihai Nica, *University of Central Oklahoma*

David Oliver, *Edison Community College*

Dyan Pease, *Sacramento City College*

Vincent Quan, *Fashion Institute of Technology*

David Robinson, *University of California–Berkeley*

Rieann Spence-Gale, *Nova Community College*

Kurt Stanberry, *University of Houston*

Marguerite Teubner, *Nassau Community College*

Rod Thirion, *Pikes Peak Community College*

William J. Wardrope, *University of Central Oklahoma*

David Washington, *North Carolina State University*

We also want to acknowledge those instructors who were willing to pilot test LearnSmart with their students:

Robb Bay, *College of Southern Nevada*

Judy Bulin, *Monroe Community College*

Jose Duran, *Riverside Community College*

Donna Haeger, *Monroe Community College*

Ken Jones, *Ivy Tech Community College of Indiana*

Bob Urell, *Irvine Valley College*

Esther Wood, *Western Michigan University*

We would like to thank the following instructors and students who generously provided the input and advice on which the refinements and enhancements that contributed to the development of this text were based.

Nikolas Adamou, *Borough of Manhattan Community College*

Cathy Adamson, *Southern Union State Community College*

Gary Amundson, *Montana State University–Billings*

Kenneth Anderson, *Borough of Manhattan Community College*

Kenneth Anderson, *Mott Community College*

Lydia Anderson, *Fresno City College*

Narita Anderson, *University of Central Oklahoma*

Roanne Angiello, *Bergen Community College*

Chi Anyansi-Archibong, *North Carolina A&T University*

Michael Atchison, *University of Virginia–Charlottesville*

Andrea Bailey, *Moraine Valley Community College*

Sandra Bailey, *Ivy Tech Community College of Indiana*

Scott Bailey, *Troy University*

Wayne Ballantine, *Prairie View A&M University*

Ruby Barker, *Tarleton State University*

Rosalia (Lia) Barone, *Norwalk Community College*

Barbara Barrett, *St. Louis Community College–Meramec*

Barry Barrett, *University of Wisconsin–Milwaukee*

Lorraine Bassette, *Prince George's Community College*

Robb Bay, *College of Southern Nevada–West Charle*

Charles Beavin, *Miami Dade College North*

Charles Beem, *Bucks County Community College*

Cathleen Behan, *Northern Virginia Community College*

Lori Bennett, *Moorpark College*

Ellen Benowitz, *Mercer Community College*

Patricia Bernson, *County College of Morris*

William Bettencourt, *Edmonds Community College*

Robert Blanchard, *Salem State College*

Mary Jo Boehms, *Jackson State Community College*

James Borden, *Villanova University*

Michael Bravo, *Bentley College*

Dennis Brode, *Sinclair Community College*

Harvey Bronstein, *Oakland Community College–Farmington Hills*

Deborah Brown, *North Carolina State University–Raleigh*

Aaron A. Buchko, *Bradley University*

Laura Bulas, *Central Community College–Hastings*

Judy Bulin, *Monroe Community College*

Barry Bunn, *Valencia Community College–West Campus*

Bill Burton, *Indiana Wesleyan University*

Paul Callahan, *Cincinnati State Technical and Community College*

William Candley, *Lemoyne Owen College*

Nancy Carr, *Community College of Philadelphia*

Ron Cereola, *James Madison University*

Bonnie Chavez, *Santa Barbara City College*

Susan Cisco, *Oakton Community College*

Margaret (Meg) Clark, *Cincinnati State Technical and Community College*

David Clifton, *Ivy Tech Community College of Indiana*

C. Cloud, *Phoenix College*

Doug Cobbs, *JS Reynolds Community College*

Brooks Colin, *University of New Orleans*

Debbie Collins, *Anne Arundel Community College*

Andrew Cook, *Limestone College*

Bob Cox, *Salt Lake Community College*

Susan Cremins, *Westchester Community College*

Julie Cross, *Chippewa Valley Tech College*

Geoffrey Crosslin, *Kalamazoo Valley Community College*

Douglas Crowe, *Bradley University*

John David, *Stark State College of Technology*

Peter Dawson, *Collin County Community College*

Joseph Defilippe, *Suffolk County Community College–Brentwood*

Tim DeGroot, *Midwestern State University*

Len Denault, *Bentley College*

Frances Depaul, *Westmoreland County Community College*

Donna Devault, *Fayetteville Tech Community College*

Sharon Dexter, *Southeast Community College–Beatrice*

John Dilyard, *St. Francis College*

Barbara Dinardo, *Owens Community College*

George Dollar, *St. Petersburg College*

Glenn Doolittle, *Santa Ana College*

Ron Dougherty, *Ivy Tech Community College of Indiana*

Michael Drafke, *College of DuPage*

Karen Eboch, *Bowling Green State University*

Brenda Eichelberger, *Portland State University*

Kelvin Elston, *Nashville State Tech Community College*

Robert Ettl, *Stony Brook University*

Nancy Evans, *Heartland Community College*

Michael Ewens, *Ventura College*

Hyacinth Ezeka, *Coppin State University*

Bob Farris, *Mt. San Antonio College*

Karen Faulkner, *Long Beach City College*

Gil Feiertag, *Columbus State Community College*

Joseph Flack, *Washtenaw Community College*

Lucinda Fleming, *Orange County Community College*

Jackie Flom, *University of Toledo*

Andrea Foster, *John Tyler Community College*

Michael Foster, *Bentley College*

Leatrice Freer, *Pitt Community College*

Alan Friedenthal, *Kingsborough Community College*

Charles Gaiser, *Brunswick Community College*

Ashley Geisewite, *Southwest Tennessee Community College*

Katie Ghahramani, *Johnson County Community College*

Debora Gilliard, *Metropolitan State College-Denver*

James Glover, *Community College of Baltimore County-Essex*

Constance Golden, *Lakeland Community College*

Toby Grodner, *Union County College*

Clark Hallpike, *Elgin Community College*

Geri Harper, *Western Illinois University*

Frank Hatstat, *Bellevue Community College*

Spedden Hause, *University of Maryland-University College*

Karen Hawkins, *Miami-Dade College-Kendall*

Travis Hayes, *Chattanooga State Technical Community College*

Jack Heinsius, *Modesto Junior College*

Charlane Held, *Onondaga Community College*

James Hess, *Ivy Tech Community College of Indiana*

Steve Hester, *Southwest Tennessee Community College-Macon Campus*

William Hill, *Mississippi State University*

Nathan Himelstein, *Essex County College*

Paula Hladik, *Waubonsee Community College*

David Ho, *Metropolitan Community College*

Douglas Hobbs, *Sussex County Community College*

Maryanne Holcomb, *Antelope Valley College*

Mary Carole Hollingsworth, *Georgia Perimeter College*

Russell Holmes, *Des Moines Area Community College*

Scott Homan, *Purdue University-West Lafayette*

Stacy Horner, *Southwestern Michigan College*

Dennis Hudson, *University of Tulsa*

Jo Ann Hunter, *Community College Allegheny County in Pittsburgh*

Kimberly Hurns, *Washtenaw Community College*

Victor Isbell, *University of Nevada-Las Vegas*

Deloris James, *University of Maryland-University College*

Pam Janson, *Stark State College of Technology*

William Jedlicka, *Harper College*

Carol Johnson, *University of Denver*

Gwendolyn Jones, *University of Akron*

Kenneth Jones, *Ivy Tech Community College of Indiana*

Marilyn Jones, *Friends University*

Michael Jones, *Delgado Community College*

Dmitriy Kalyagin, *Chabot College*

Jack Kant, *San Juan College*

Jimmy Kelsey, *Seattle Central Community College*

Robert Kemp, *University of Virginia-Charlottesville*

David Kendall, *Fashion Institute of Technology*

Kristine Kinard, *Shelton State Community College*

Sandra King, *Minnesota State University-Mankato*

John Kurnik, *Saint Petersburg College*

Jeff LaVake, *University of Wisconsin-Oshkosh*

Robert Lewis, *Davenport University*

Byron Lilly, *DeAnza College*

Beverly Loach, *Central Piedmont Community College*

Boone Londrigan, *Mott Community College*

Ladonna Love, *Fashion Institute of Technology*

Ivan Lowe, *York Technical College*

Yvonne Lucas, *Southwestern College*

Robert Lupton, *Central Washington University*

Megan Luttenton, *Grand Valley State University*

Elaine Madden, *Anne Arundel Community College*

Lawrence Maes, *Davenport University*

Niki Maglaris, *Northwestern College*

James Maniki, *Northwestern College*

Martin Markowitz, *College of Charleston*

Fred Mayerson, *Kingsborough Community College*

Stacy McCaskill, *Rock Valley College*

Vershun L. McClain, *Jackson State University*

Gina McConoughey, *Illinois Central College*

Patricia McDaniel, *Central Piedmont Community College*

Pam McElligott, *St. Louis Community College-Meramec*

Tom McFarland, *Mt. San Antonio College*

Bill McPherson, *Indiana University of Pennsylvania*

Ginger Moore, *York Technical College*

Sandy Moore, *Ivy Tech Community College of Indiana*

Jennifer Morton, *Ivy Tech Community College of Indiana*

Peter Moutsatson, *Central Michigan University*

Rachna Nagi-Condos, *American River College*

Darrell Neron, *Pierce College*

Mihia Nica, *University of Central Oklahoma*

Charles Nichols, *Sullivan University*

Frank Novakowski, *Davenport University*

Mark Nygren, *Brigham Young University-Idaho*

Paul Okello, *Tarrant County College*

Faviana Olivier, *Bentley College*

John Olivo, *Bloomsburg University of Pennsylvania*

Teresa O'Neill, *International Institute of the Americas*

Cathy Onion, *Western Illinois University*

Susan Ontko, *Schoolcraft College*

Glenda Orosco, *Oklahoma State University Institute of Technology*

Christopher O'Suanah, *J. S. Reynolds Community College*

Daniel Pacheco, *Kansas City Kansas Community College*

Esther Page-Wood, *Western Michigan University*

Lauren Paisley, *Genesee Community College*

John Pappalardo, *Keene State College*

Ron Pardee, *Riverside Community College*

Jack Partlow, *Northern Virginia Community College*

Jeff Pepper, *Chippewa Valley Tech College*

Sheila Petcavage, *Cuyahoga Community College Western-Parma*

Roy Pipitone, *Erie Community College*

Lana Powell, *Valencia Community College-West Campus*

Dan Powroznik, *Chesapeake College*

Litsa Press, *College of Lake County*

Sally Proffitt, *Tarrant County College-Northeast*

Michael Quinn, *James Madison University*

Anthony Racka, *Oakland Community College*

Larry Ramos, *Miami-Dade Community College*

Greg Rapp, *Portland Community College-Sylvania*

Robert Reese, *Illinois Valley Community College*

David Reiman, *Monroe County Community College*

Gloria Rembert, *Mitchell Community College*

Levi Richard, *Citrus College*

Clinton Richards, *University of Nevada-Las Vegas*

Patricia Richards, *Westchester Community College*

Susan Roach, *Georgia Southern University*

Sandra Robertson, *Thomas Nelson Community College*

Catherine Roche, *Rockland Community College*

Tim Rogers, *Ozark Technical College*

Sam Rohr, *University of Northwestern Ohio*

Pamela Rouse, *Butler University*

Carol Rowey, *Community College of Rhode Island*

Jeri Rubin, *University of Alaska-Anchorage*

Storm Russo, *Valencia Community College*

Mark Ryan, *Hawkeye Community College*

Richard Sarkisian, *Camden County College*

Andy Saucedo, *Dona Ana Community College-Las Cruces*

James Scott, *Central Michigan University*

Janet Seggern, *Lehigh Carbon Community College*

Sashi Sekhar, *Purdue University-Calumet-Hammond*

Pat Setlik, *Harper College*

Swannee Sexton, *University of Tennessee-Knoxville*

Phyllis Shafer, *Brookdale Community College*

Richard Shortridge, *Glendale Community College*

Louise Stephens, *Volunteer State Community College*

Desiree Stephens, *Norwalk Community College*

Clifford Stalter, *Chattanooga State Technical Community College*

Kurt Stanberry, *University of Houston-Downtown*

Martin St. John, *Westmoreland County Community College*

John Striebich, *Monroe Community College*

David Stringer, *DeAnza College*

Ron Surmacz, *Duquesne University*

William Syvertsen, *Fresno City College*

Scott Taylor, *Moberly Area Community College*

Jim Thomas, *Indiana University Northwest*

Deborah Thompson, *Bentley College*

Evelyn Thrasher, *University of Massachusetts–Dartmouth*

Jon Tomlinson, *University of Northwestern Ohio*

Bob Trewartha, *Minnesota School of Business*

Bob Urell, *Irvine Valley College*

Dan Vetter, *Central Michigan University*

Andrea Vidrine, *Baton Rouge Community College*

Daniel Viveiros, *Johnson & Wales University*

Joann Warren, *Community College of Rhode Island–Warwick*

R. Patrick Wehner, *Everest University*

Sally Wells, *Columbia College*

Mildred Wilson, *Georgia Southern University*

Karen Wisniewski, *County College of Morris*

Greg Witkowski, *Northwestern College*

Colette Wolfson, *Ivy Tech Community College of Indiana*

Deborah Yancey, *Virginia Western Community College*

Mark Zarycki, *Hillsborough Community College*

Lisa Zingaro, *Oakton Community College*

Mark Zorn, *Butler County Community College*

This edition continues to be the market's gold standard due to the involvement of these committed instructors and students. We thank them all for their help, support, and friendship.

Bill Nickels   Jim McHugh   Susan McHugh

brief
CONTENTS

contents

Bonus Chapter B

B   Using Technology to Manage Information

Bonus Chapter C

C   Managing Risk

Bonus Chapter D

D   Managing Personal Finances

getting ready for prime time

Top 10 Reasons to Read This Introduction

(Even If It Isn't Assigned)

10 What the heck—you already bought the book, so you might as well get your money's worth.

9 You don't want the only reason you get a raise to be that the government has increased the minimum wage.

8 How else would you find out a spork isn't usually one of the utensils used at a business dinner?

7 You need to know a cover letter isn't a blank sheet of paper used to protect your résumé.

6 Not many successful job interviews start with "Like, you know, this is like, what I want to, like, do, you know."

5 Getting off to a good start in the course can improve your chances of getting a higher grade, and your Uncle Ernie will send you a dollar for every A you get.

4 You don't want to experience the irony of frantically reading the "time management" section at 3 a.m.

3 It must be important because the authors spent so much time writing it.

2 You want to run with the big dogs someday.

And the number one reason for reading this introductory section is . . .

1 It could be on a test.

LEARNING THE SKILLS YOU NEED TO SUCCEED TODAY AND TOMORROW

Your life is full. You're starting a new semester, perhaps even beginning your college career, and you're feeling pulled in many directions. Why take time to read this introduction? We lightheartedly offer our top 10 reasons on page P-1, but the real importance of this section is no joking matter.

Its purpose, and that of the entire text, is to help you learn principles, strategies, and skills for success that will serve you not only in this course but also in your career and your life. Whether you learn them is up to you. Learning them won't guarantee success, but not learning them—well, you get the picture.

We hope you invest the time to read the entire Getting Ready for Prime Time section. However, we realize some parts may be more relevant at a particular time than others. To help you focus on the most important information for your needs, we've divided it into two major categories:

1. **Succeeding in This Course.** An overview of the skills you'll need to succeed in this course and throughout college, as well as the skills you need to succeed in your career after you earn your diploma. READ THIS SECTION BEFORE YOUR FIRST CLASS and make a great first impression!

2. **Getting the Job You Want.** Guidelines to finding and getting the job you want with an emphasis on job search, résumé writing, and interviewing skills.

This is an exciting and challenging time. Success in any venture comes from understanding basic principles and knowing how to apply them effectively. What you learn now could help you be a success—for the rest of your life. Begin applying these skills now to gain an edge on the competition. Good luck. We wish you the best.

Bill Nickels   **Jim McHugh**   **Susan McHugh**

SUCCEEDING IN THIS COURSE

Since you've signed up for this course, we're guessing you already know the value of a college education. The holders of bachelor's degrees make an average of $46,000 per year compared to $30,000 for high school graduates.[1] That's 53 percent more for college graduates than those with just a high school diploma. Compounded over the course of a 30-year career, the average college grad will make nearly a half million dollars more than the high school grad! Thus, what you invest in a college education is likely to pay you back many times. See Figure P.1 for more of an idea of how much salary difference a college degree makes by the end of a 30-year career. That doesn't mean there aren't good careers available to non–college graduates. It just means those with an education are more likely to have higher earnings over their lifetime.

The value of a college education is more than just a larger paycheck. Other benefits include increasing your ability to think critically and communicate your ideas to others, improving your ability to use technology, and preparing yourself to live in a diverse world. Knowing you've met your goals and earned a college degree also gives you the self-confidence to work toward future goals.

Experts say today's college graduates will likely hold seven or eight different jobs (often in several different careers) in their lifetime. Many returning students are changing their careers and their plans for life. In fact, over 30 percent of the people enrolled in college today are 25 or older. In addition, over 60 percent of all part-time college students are 25 or older.[2]

You too may want to change careers someday. It can be the path to long-term happiness and success. That means you'll have to be flexible and adjust your strengths and talents to new opportunities.[3] Learning has become a lifelong job. You'll constantly update your skills to achieve and remain competitive.

If you're typical of many college students, you may not have any idea what career you'd like to pursue. That isn't necessarily a big disadvantage in today's fast-changing job market. After all, many of the best jobs of the future don't even exist today. Figure P.2 lists 10 careers that didn't exist 10 years ago. There are no perfect or certain ways to prepare for the most interesting and challenging jobs of tomorrow. Rather, you should continue your college education, develop strong computer and Internet skills, improve your verbal and written communication skills, and remain flexible while you explore the job market.

The rewards of college are well worth the effort for graduates, who can expect to earn 50 to 55 percent more than high school graduates over the course of their careers. Businesses like graduates too, because the growing needs of a global workplace require knowledgeable workers to fill the jobs of the future. What other benefits do you see from earning a college degree?

figure P.1

SALARY COMPARISON OF HIGH SCHOOL VERSUS COLLEGE GRADUATES

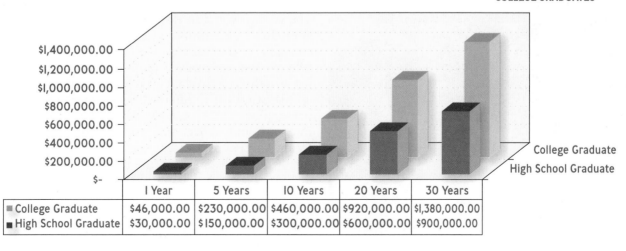

	I Year	5 Years	IO Years	20 Years	30 Years
■ College Graduate	$46,000.00	$230,000.00	$460,000.00	$920,000.00	$1,380,000.00
■ High School Graduate	$30,000.00	$150,000.00	$300,000.00	$600,000.00	$900,000.00

figure P.2

NEW CAREERS

NEW CAREERS

These careers didn't exist 10 years ago

- Bloggers
- Community managers or content managers
- Green funeral directors
- Interior redesigners
- Patient advocates
- Senior *move* management
- Social media strategists
- User experience analyst
- Video journalist
- Virtual business service providers

Source: Rachel Zupek, "10 Careers That Didn't Exist 10 years Ago," www.Careerbuilders.com, accessed June 2011.

USING THIS COURSE TO PREPARE FOR YOUR CAREER

One of the objectives of this class, and this book, is to help you choose an area in which you might enjoy working and have a good chance to succeed. You'll learn about economics, global business, ethics, entrepreneurship, management, marketing, accounting, finance, and more. At the end of the course, you should have a much better idea which careers would be best for you and which you would not enjoy.

But you don't have to be in business to use business principles. You can use marketing principles to get a job and to sell your ideas to others. You can use your knowledge of investments to make money in the stock market. You'll use your management skills and general business knowledge wherever you go and in whatever career you pursue—including government agencies, charities, and social causes.

ASSESSING YOUR SKILLS AND PERSONALITY

Networking provides you with an array of personal contacts on whom you can call for career advice and help. Have you begun creating your network yet? Are you part of someone else's?

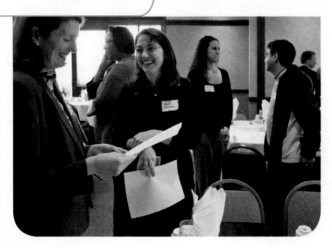

The earlier you can do a personal assessment of your interests, skills, and values, the better it can help you find career direction. Hundreds of schools use software exercises like the System for Interactive Guidance and Information (SIGI) and DISCOVER to offer self-assessment exercises, personalized lists of occupations based on your interests and skills, and information about different careers and the preparation each requires. Visit your college's placement center, career lab, or library soon and learn what programs are available for you. Even if you're a returning student, an assessment of your skills will help you choose the right courses and career path to follow next.

Self-assessment will help you determine the kind of work environment you'd prefer (technical, social service, or business); what values you seek to fulfill in a career (security, variety, or independence); what abilities you have (creative/artistic, numerical, or sales); and what job characteristics matter to you (income, travel, or amount of job pressure versus free time).

USING PROFESSIONAL BUSINESS STRATEGIES RIGHT NOW

Here are two secrets to success you can start practicing now: *networking* and *keeping files on subjects important to you*.

Networking is building a personal array of people you've met, spoken to, or corresponded with who can offer you advice about and even help with your career options. Start with the names of your professors, both as employment references and as resources about fields of interest to you. Add additional contacts, mentors, and resource people, and keep the notes you make when talking with them about careers including salary information and courses you need to take.

All students need a way to retain what they learn. An effective way to become an expert on almost any business subject is to set up your own information system. You can store data on your computer and cell phone (back these files up!), or you can establish a comprehensive filing system on paper, or you can use a combination of the two. Few college students make this effort; those who don't lose much of the information they read in college or thereafter.

Keep as many of your textbooks and other assigned readings as you can, and your course notes. Read a national newspaper such as *The Wall Street Journal*, *The New York Times*, or *USA Today*. Read your local newspaper. Each time you read a story that interests you, save a paper copy or add a link to the story online in your electronic file, under a topic heading like *careers*, *small business*, *marketing*, *economics*, or *management*. You'll easily find the latest data on almost any subject on the Internet. Don't rely on just one site for information (and be especially wary of Wikipedia)! Get familiar with a variety of sources and use them.

Start a file for your résumé. In it, keep a copy of your current résumé along with reference letters and other information about jobs you may have held, including projects accomplished and additions to your responsibilities over time. Soon you'll have a tremendous amount of information to help you prepare a polished résumé and answer challenging job interview questions with ease.

Watching television shows about business, such as *Nightly Business Report* and Jim Cramer's *Mad Money*, is like getting a free graduate education in business. Try viewing some of these shows or listening to similar ones on the radio, and see which ones you like best. Take notes and put them in your files. Keep up with business news in your area so that you know what jobs are available and where. You may also want to join a local business group to begin networking with people and learning the secrets of the local business scene. Many business groups and professional societies accept student members.

LEARNING TO BEHAVE LIKE A PROFESSIONAL

There's a reason good manners never go out of style. As the world becomes increasingly competitive, the gold goes to teams and individuals with that extra bit of polish. The person who makes a good impression will be the one who gets the job, wins the promotion, or clinches the deal. Good manners and professionalism are not difficult to acquire; they're second nature to those who achieve and maintain a competitive edge.

Not even a great résumé or designer suit can substitute for poor behavior, including verbal behavior, in an interview.[4] Say "Please" and "Thank you" when you ask for something. Open doors for others, stand when an older person enters the room, and use a polite tone of voice. You may want to take a class in etiquette to learn the proper way to eat in a nice restaurant, what to do at a formal party, and so on. Of course, it's also critical to be honest, reliable, dependable, and ethical at all times.

Some rules are not formally written anywhere; instead, every successful businessperson learns them through experience. If you follow these rules in college, you'll have the skills for success when you start your career. Here are the basics:

1. **Making a good first impression.** An old saying goes, "You never get a second chance to make a good first impression." You have just a few seconds to make an impression. Therefore, how you dress and how you look are important. Take a clue as to what is appropriate at any specific company by studying the people there who are most successful. What do they wear? How do they act?

2. **Focusing on good grooming.** Be aware of your appearance and its impact. Wear appropriate, clean clothing and a few simple accessories. Revealing shirts, nose rings, and tattoos may not be appropriate in a work setting. Be consistent too; you can't project a good image by dressing well a few times a week and then showing up looking like you're getting ready to mow a lawn.

   Many organizations have adopted "business casual" guidelines, but others still require traditional attire, so ask what the organization's policies are and choose your wardrobe accordingly. Casual doesn't mean sloppy or shabby. Wrinkled clothing, shirttails hanging out, and hats worn indoors are not usually appropriate. For women, business casual attire includes simple skirts and slacks (no jeans), cotton shirts, sweaters (not too tight), blazers, and low-heeled shoes or boots. Men may wear khaki trousers, sport shirts with collars, sweaters or sport jackets, and casual loafers or lace-up shoes.

3. **Being on time.** When you don't come to class or work on time, you're sending this message to your teacher or boss: "My time is more important than your time. I have more important things to do than be here." In addition to showing a lack of respect to your teacher or boss, lateness rudely disrupts the work of your colleagues.

   Pay attention to the corporate culture. Sometimes you have to come in earlier than others and leave later to get that promotion you desire. To develop good work habits and get good grades, arrive in class on time and avoid leaving (or packing up to leave) early.

4. **Practicing considerate behavior.** Listen when others are talking—for example, don't read the newspaper or eat in class. Don't interrupt others when they are speaking; wait your turn. Eliminate profanity from your vocabulary. Use appropriate body language by sitting up attentively and not slouching. Sitting up has the added bonus of helping you stay awake! Professors and managers alike get a favorable impression from those who look and act alert.

5. **Practicing good e-mail etiquette.** The basic rules of courtesy in face-to-face communication also apply to e-mail exchanges. Introduce

Many businesses have adopted business casual as the proper work attire, but others still require traditional clothing styles. How does your appearance at work affect both you and your company?

yourself at the beginning of your first e-mail message. Next, let your recipients know how you got their names and e-mail addresses. Then proceed with your clear but succinct message, and always be sure to type full words (*ur* is not the same thing as *your*). Finally, close the e-mail with a signature. Do not send an attachment unless your correspondent has indicated he or she will accept it. Ask first! You can find much more information about proper Internet etiquette, or netiquette, online—for example, at NetManners.com.

6. **Practicing good cell phone manners.** Your Introduction to Business class is not the place to be arranging a date for tonight. Turn off the phone during class or in a business meeting unless you are expecting a critical call. If you are expecting such a call, let your professor know before class. Turn off your ringer and put the phone on vibrate. Sit by the aisle and near the door. If you do receive a critical call, leave the room before answering it. Apologize to the professor after class and explain the situation.

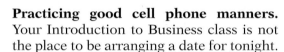

7. **Practicing safe posting on social media.** Be careful what you post on your Facebook page or any other social media. While it may be fun to share your latest adventures with your friends, your boss or future boss may not appreciate your latest party pictures. Be aware that those pictures may not go away even if you delete them from your page. If anyone else downloaded them, they are still out there waiting for a recruiter to discover. Make sure to update your privacy settings frequently. It's a good idea to separate your list of work friends and limit what that group can view. Also be aware that some work colleagues aren't interested in becoming your Facebook friend. To avoid awkwardness, wait for work associates to reach out to you first.[5] Make sure you know your employer's policy on using social media on company time. Obviously, they will probably frown on using it for personal use on company time, but there may be rules about sharing technical matter, etc. Be mindful that social media accounts time-stamp your comments.[6]

Behavior that's taken for granted in other countries might be unusual in the United States. In some cultures bowing is a form of greeting to show respect. How can you learn the appropriate business etiquette for the countries in which you do business?

8. **Being prepared.** A businessperson would never show up for a meeting without having read the appropriate materials and being prepared to discuss the topics on the agenda. For students, acting like a professional means reading assigned materials before class, asking and responding to questions in class, and discussing the material with fellow students.

Just as traffic laws enable people to drive more safely, business etiquette allows people to conduct business with the appropriate amount of consideration. Sharpen your competitive edge by becoming familiar with the rules. If your job or career requires you to travel internationally, learn the proper business etiquette for each country you visit. Customs differ widely for such everyday activities as greeting people, eating, giving gifts, presenting and receiving business cards, and conducting business in general. In Japan, businesspeople typically bow instead of shaking hands, and in some Arab countries it is insulting to sit so as to show the soles of your shoes. Honesty, high ethical standards, and reliability and trustworthiness are important for success in any country.

Having a reputation for integrity will enable you to be proud of who you are and contribute a great deal to your business success. Unethical behavior can ruin your reputation; so think carefully before you act. When in doubt, don't! Ethics is so important to success that we include discussions about it throughout the text.

DOING YOUR BEST IN SCHOOL

The skills you need to succeed in life after college are the same ones that will serve you well in your studies. Career, family, and hobbies all benefit from organizational and time-management skills you can apply right now. Here are some tips for improving your study habits, taking tests, and managing your time.

Study Hints

For the remainder of your college career, consider studying to be your business. Though you may hold another job while enrolled in this class, you're in school because you want to advance yourself. So until you get out of school and into your desired occupation, studying is your business. And like any good businessperson, you aim for success. Follow these strategies:

1. **Go to class.** It's tempting to cut a class on a nice day or when there are other things to do. But nothing is more important to doing well in school than going to class every time. If possible, sit in the front near the instructor. This will help you focus better and avoid distractions in the room.

2. **Listen well.** It's not enough to show up for class if you use the time for a nap. Make eye contact with the instructor. In your mind, form a picture of what he or she is discussing. Include your existing knowledge and past experiences in your picture. This ties new knowledge to what you already know.

3. **Take careful notes.** Make two columns in your notebook or on your laptop. On one side write down important concepts, and on the other examples or more detailed explanations. Use abbreviations and symbols whenever possible and wide spacing to make the notes easier to read. Edit your notes after class to make them easier to read. Rereading and rewriting help store the information in your long-term memory. Learn the concepts in your courses the same way you learn the words to your favorite song: through repetition and review.

The SQ3R study system recommends that you "survey, question, read, recite, and review" to stay up-to-date with assignments and shine in class every day. Have you adopted this system?

4. **Find a good place to study.** Find a place with good lighting and a quiet atmosphere. Some students do well with classical music or other music without lyrics playing in the background. Keep your study place equipped with extra supplies such as pens, pencils, calculator, folders, and paper so you don't have to interrupt studying to hunt for them.

5. **Read the text using a strategy such as "survey, question, read, recite, review" (SQ3R).**

   a. *Survey* or scan the chapter first to see what it is all about. This means looking over the table of contents, learning goals, headings, photo essays, and charts so you get a broad idea of the content. Scanning will provide an introduction and help get your mind in a learning mode.

b. Write *questions*, first by changing the headings into questions. For example, you could change the heading of this section to "What hints can I use to study better?" Read the questions that appear throughout each chapter in the Progress Assessment sections to give yourself a chance to recall what you've read.

c. *Read* the chapter to find the answers to your questions. Be sure to read the boxes as well. They offer extended examples or discussions of the concepts in the text. You've probably asked, "Will the material in the boxes be on the tests?" Even if your instructor chooses not to test over them directly, they are often the most interesting parts of the chapter and will help you retain the concepts better.

d. *Recite* your answers to yourself or to others in a study group. Make sure you say the answers in your own words so that you clearly understand the concepts. Research has shown that saying things is a more effective way to learn them than seeing, hearing, or reading about them. While often used in study groups, recitation is also good practice for working in teams in the work world.

e. *Review* by rereading and recapping the information. The chapter summaries are written in a question-and-answer form, much like a classroom dialogue. They're also tied directly to the learning goals so that you can see whether you've accomplished the chapter's objectives. Cover the written answers and see whether you can answer the questions yourself first.

6. **Use flash cards.** You'll master the course more easily if you know the language of business. To review the key terms in the book, write any terms you don't know on index cards and go through your cards between classes and when you have other free time.

7. **Use this text's Online Learning Center.** Using the Online Learning Center (OLC) on this text's website (www.mhhe.com/ub10e) is a great way to practice your test-taking skills. The OLC contains sample test questions, review work allowing you to gauge what material you have mastered, and other material you may need to review again.

8. **Use *Connect* Introduction to Business** (if your professor has recommended it for your course). *Connect's* online features include interactive presentations, *LearnSmart* (intelligent flashcards that offer feedback and direct you back to the text based on your performance), and interactive applications.

9. **Go over old exams, if possible.** If old exams are not available from your professor, ask how many multiple-choice, true/false, and essay questions will be on your test. It's acceptable to ask your professor's former students what kind of questions are given and what material is usually emphasized. It is unethical, though, to go over exams you obtain illegally.

10. **Use as many of your senses in learning as possible.** If you're an auditory learner—that is, if you learn best by hearing—record yourself reading your notes and answering the questions you've written. Listen to the tape while you're dressing in the morning. You can also benefit from reading or studying aloud. If you're a visual learner, use pictures, charts, colors, and graphs. Your professor has a set of videos that illustrate the concepts in this text. If you're a kinesthetic learner, you remember best by doing, touching, and experiencing. Do some of the

Developing Workplace Skills and Taking It to the Net exercises at the end of each chapter.

Test-Taking Hints

Often students will say, "I know this stuff, but I'm just not good at taking multiple-choice (or essay) tests." Other students find test-taking relatively easy. Here are a few test-taking hints:

1. **Get plenty of sleep and a good meal.** It's better to be alert and awake during an exam than to study all night and be groggy. If you keep up with your reading and your reviews, you won't need to pull an all-nighter. Proper nutrition plays an important part in your brain's ability to function.

2. **Bring all you need for the exam.** Sometimes you'll need No. 2 pencils, erasers, and a calculator. Ask beforehand.

3. **Relax.** At home before the test, take deep, slow breaths. Picture yourself in the testing session, relaxed and confident. Get to class early to settle down. If you start to get nervous during the test, stop and take a few deep breaths. Turn the test over and write down information you remember. Sometimes this helps you connect the information you know to the questions on the test.

4. **Read the directions on the exam carefully.** You don't want to miss anything or do something you're not supposed to do.

5. **Read all the answers in multiple-choice questions.** Even if there is more than one correct-sounding answer to a multiple-choice question, one is clearly better. Read them all to be sure you pick the best. Try covering up the choices while reading the question. If the answer you think of is one of the choices, it is probably correct. If you are still unsure of the answer, start eliminating options you know are wrong. Narrowing the choices to two or three improves your odds.

6. **Answer all the questions.** Unless your instructor takes off more for an incorrect answer than for no answer, you have nothing to lose by guessing. Also, skipping a question could lead to inadvertently misaligning your answers on a scan sheet. You could end up with all your subsequent answers scored wrong!

7. **Read true/false questions carefully.** All parts of the statement must be true or else the entire statement is false. Watch out for absolutes such as *never*, *always*, and *none*. These often make a statement false.

8. **Organize your thoughts before answering essay questions.** Think about the sequence in which to present what you want to say. Use complete sentences with correct grammar and punctuation. Explain or defend your answers.

9. **Go over the test at the end.** Make sure you've answered all the questions, put your name on the exam, and followed all directions.

Time Management Hints

The most important management skill you can learn is how to manage your time. Now is as good an opportunity to practice as any. Here are some hints other students have learned—often the hard way:

1. **Write weekly goals for yourself.** Make certain your goals are realistic and attainable. Write the steps you'll use to achieve each goal. Reward yourself when you reach a goal.

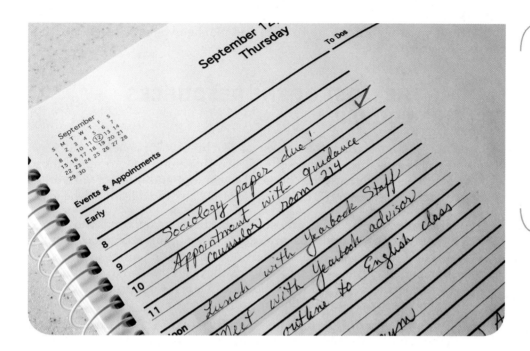

Keeping a daily schedule is only one of the many strategies that will help you manage your time. You should also keep a running list of goals and things you need to do each week. In what other ways can you defend your study time?

2. **Keep a "to do" list.** It's easy to forget things unless you write them down. Jot tasks down as soon as you know of them. That gives you one less thing to do: remembering what you have to do.

3. **Prepare a daily schedule.** Use a commercial printed or electronic daily planner or create your own. Write the days of the week across the top of the page. Write the hours of the day from the time you get up until the time you go to bed down the left side. Draw lines to form columns and rows and fill in all the activities you have planned in each hour. Hopefully, you will be surprised to see how many slots of time you have available for studying.

4. **Prepare for the next day the night before.** Having everything ready to go will help you make a quick, stress-free start in the morning.

5. **Prepare weekly and monthly schedules.** Use a calendar to fill in activities and upcoming assignments. Include both academic and social activities so that you can balance your work and fun.

6. **Space out your work.** Don't wait until the last week of the course to write all your papers and study for your exams. If you do a few pages a day, you can write a 20-page paper in a couple of weeks with little effort. It is really difficult to push out 20 pages in a day or two.

7. **Defend your study time.** Study every day. Use the time between classes to go over your flash cards and read the next day's assignments. Make it a habit to defend your study time so you don't slip.

8. **Take time for fun.** If you have some fun every day, life will be full. Schedule your fun times along with your studying so that you have balance.

"Time is money," the saying goes. Some, however, would argue that time is more valuable than money. If your bank account balance falls, you might be able to build it back up by finding a better-paying job, taking a second job, or even selling something you own. But you only have a limited amount of time and there is no way to make more. Learn to manage your time well, because you can never get it back.

MAKING THE MOST OF THE RESOURCES FOR THIS COURSE

College courses and textbooks are best at teaching you concepts and ways of thinking about business. However, to learn firsthand how to apply those ideas to real business situations, you need to explore and interact with other resources. Here are seven basic resources for the class in addition to the text:

1. **The professor.** One of the most valuable facets of college is the chance to study with experienced professors. Your instructor is a resource who's there to answer some questions and guide you to answers for others. Many professors get job leads they can pass on to you and can provide letters of recommendation too. Thus it's important to develop a friendly relationship with your professors.

2. **The supplements that come with this text.** The Online Learning Center (at www.mhhe.com/ub10e) and *Connect* Introduction to Business online course material (if your professor has recommended it for your course) will help you review and interpret key material and give you practice answering test questions. Even if your professor does not assign these materials, you may want to use them anyhow. Doing so will improve your test scores and help you compete successfully with the other students.

3. **Outside readings.** One secret to success in business is staying current. Review and become familiar with the following magazines and newspapers during the course and throughout your career: *The Wall Street Journal, Forbes, Barron's, Bloomberg Businessweek, Fortune, Money, Hispanic Business, Smart Money, Harvard Business Review, Black Enterprise, BtoB, Inc.,* and *Entrepreneur.* You may also want to read your local newspaper's business section and national news magazines such as *Time* and *Newsweek.* You can find them in your school's learning resource center or the local public library. Some are also available free online.

4. **Your own experience and that of your classmates.** Many college students have had experience working in business or nonprofit organizations. Hearing and talking about those experiences exposes you to many real-life examples that are invaluable for understanding business. Don't rely exclusively on the professor for answers to the cases and other exercises in this book. Often there is no single "right" answer, and your classmates may open up new ways of looking at things for you.

   Part of being a successful businessperson is knowing how to work with others. Some professors let their students work together and build teamwork as well as presentation and analytical skills. Students from other countries can help you learn about different cultures and different approaches to handling business

Your college professors are among the most valuable resources and contacts you'll encounter as you develop your career path. How many of your professors have you gotten to know so far?

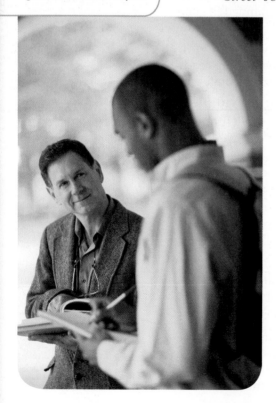

problems. There is strength in diversity, so seek out people different from you to work with on teams.

5. **Outside contacts.** Who can tell you more about what it's like to start a career in accounting than someone who's doing it now? One of the best ways to learn about different businesses is to visit them in person. The world can be your classroom.

     When you go shopping, think about whether you would enjoy working in and managing a store. Think about owning or managing a restaurant, an auto body shop, a health club, or any other establishment you visit. If something looks interesting, talk to the employees and learn more about their jobs and the industry. Be constantly on the alert to find career possibilities, and don't hesitate to talk with people about their careers. Many will be pleased to give you their time.

6. **The Internet.** The Internet offers more material than you could use in a lifetime. Throughout this text we present information and exercises that require you to use the Internet. Information changes rapidly, and it is up to you to stay current.

7. **The library or learning resource center.** The library is a great complement to the Internet and a valuable resource. Work with your librarian to learn how to best access the information you need.

Getting the Most from This Text

Many learning aids appear throughout this text to help you understand the concepts:

1. **List of Learning Goals at the beginning of each chapter.** Reading through these goals will help you set the framework and focus for the chapter material. Since every student at one time or other has found it difficult to get into studying, the Learning Goals are there to provide an introduction and to get your mind into a learning mode.

2. **Opening Profile and Name That Company features.** The opening profiles offer stories that will help you get to know professionals who successfully use the concepts presented in the chapters. The Name That Company feature at the beginning of each chapter challenges you to identify a company discussed in the chapter.

3. **Photo essays.** The photos offer examples of the concepts in the chapter. Looking at the photos and reading the photo essays (captions) before you read the chapter will give you a good idea of what the chapter is all about.

4. **Self-test questions.** Periodically, within each chapter, you'll encounter set-off lists of questions called Progress Assessment. These questions give you a chance to pause, think carefully about, and recall what you've just read.

5. **Key terms.** Developing a strong business vocabulary is one of the most important and useful aspects of this course. To assist you, all key terms in the book are highlighted in boldface type. Key terms are also defined in the margins, and page references to these terms are given at the end of each chapter. A full glossary is located in the back of the book. You should rely heavily on these learning aids in adding new terms to your vocabulary.

6. **Boxes.** Each chapter contains a number of boxed extended examples or discussions that cover major themes of the book: (*a*) ethics (Making

Ethical Decisions); (*b*) small business (Spotlight on Small Business); (*c*) legal environment of business (Legal Briefcase); (*d*) global business (Reaching Beyond Our Borders); (*e*) environmental issues (Thinking Green) and (f) social media (Social Media in Business). They're interesting to read; we hope you enjoy and learn from them.

7. **End-of-chapter summaries.** The chapter summaries are directly tied to the chapter Learning Goals so that you can see whether you've accomplished the chapter's objectives.

8. **Critical Thinking questions.** The end-of-chapter questions help you relate the material to your own experiences.

9. **Developing Workplace Skills exercises.** To really remember something, it's best to do it. That's why Developing Workplace Skills sections at the end of each chapter suggest small projects that help you use resources, develop interpersonal skills, manage information, understand systems, and sharpen computer skills.

10. **Taking It to the Net exercises.** These exercises not only give you practice surfing the Internet but, more important, direct you to dynamic outside resources that reinforce the concepts introduced in the text. You might want to bookmark some of the websites you'll discover. They appear on the Online Learning Center at www.mhhe.com/ub10e.

11. **Video Cases.** These cases feature companies, processes, practices, and managers that bring to life the key concepts in the chapter and give you real-world information to think over and discuss.

12. **Casing the Web cases.** These cases give you another chance to think about the material and apply it in real-life situations. They also appear on the Online Learning Center at www.mhhe.com/ub10e.

If you use the suggestions we've presented here, you'll actively participate in a learning experience that will help you greatly in your chosen career. The most important secret to success may be to enjoy what you're doing and do your best in everything. To do your best, take advantage of all the learning aids available to you.

GETTING THE JOB YOU WANT

One of the more important objectives of this text is to help you get the job you want. First, you have to decide what you want to do. We'll help you explore this decision by explaining what people do in the various business functions: human resource management, marketing, accounting, finance, and so on. There are many good books about finding the job you want, so we can only introduce the subject here to get you thinking about careers as you read the various chapters.

If you are a returning student, you have both blessings and handicaps that younger students do not have. First, you may have had a full-time job already. Second, you are more likely to know what kind of job you don't want. That is a real advantage. By exploring the various business careers in depth, you should be able to choose a career path that will meet your objectives.

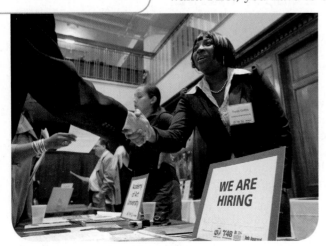

Do you look forward to saying, "I got the job!" after your years of college study? Job fairs are among the many resources that can help you find the right job for you. Is it ever too early to start thinking about your career?

WE ARE HIRING

If you have a full-time job right now, you already know that working while going to school requires juggling school and work responsibilities. Many older students must also balance family responsibilities in addition to those of school and work. But take heart. You have also acquired many skills from these experiences. Even if they were acquired in unrelated fields, these skills will be invaluable as you enter your new career. You should have no trouble competing with younger students because you have more focus and experience. Instructors enjoy having both kinds of students in class because of the different perspectives they have.

So, whether you're beginning your first career or your latest career, it's time to develop a strategy for finding and obtaining a personally satisfying job.

JOB SEARCH STRATEGY

It is never too early to begin thinking about a future career or careers. The following strategies will give you some guidance in that pursuit:

1. **Begin with self-analysis.** You might begin your career quest by completing a self-analysis inventory. You can refer to Figure P.3 for a sample of a simple assessment.

2. **Search for jobs you would enjoy.** Begin at your college's career planning office or placement office, if your school has one. Keep interviewing people in various careers, even after you've found a job. Career progress demands continuous research.

3. **Begin the networking process.** Networking remains the number one way for new job seekers to get their foot in the door, even beating using the Internet. You can start with your fellow students, family, relatives, neighbors, friends, professors, and local businesspeople. Be sure to keep a file with the names, addresses, and phone numbers of contacts—where they work, the person who recommended them to you, and the relationship between the source person and the contact. A great way to make contacts and a good impression on employers is to do part-time work and summer internships at those firms you find interesting. Many professionals use online social-networking sites, like Facebook, Twitter, and LinkedIn, to expand their networks. If you choose to post to these websites, be careful to include only information you would want a potential hiring agent to see and not something that might hurt your chances for landing a job.

4. **Go to the Internet for help.** You will find details about finding jobs on a variety of websites. Many of these sites can help you write your résumé as well as help you search for jobs that meet your interests and skills.

5 **Prepare a good cover letter and résumé.** Once you know what you want to do and where you would like to work, you need to develop a good résumé and cover letter. Your résumé lists your education, work experience, and activities. We'll talk about these key job search tools in more detail. We'll also give you a list of resources you can use.

6. **Develop interviewing skills.** Interviewers will be checking your appearance (clothes,

Professional interview behavior includes writing a follow-up letter to thank the person or persons you met. What are your goals in writing such a letter?

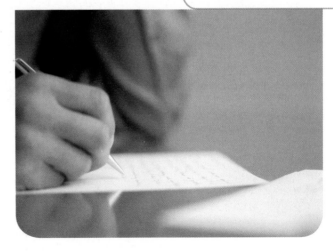

Interests

1. How do I like to spend my time?
2. Do I enjoy being with people?
3. Do I like working with mechanical things?
4. Do I enjoy working with numbers?
5. Am I a member of many organizations?
6. Do I enjoy physical activities?
7. Do I like to read?

Abilities

1. Am I adept at working with numbers?
2. Am I adept at working with mechanical things?
3. Do I have good verbal and written communication skills?
4. What special talents do I have?
5. In which abilities do I wish I were more adept?

Education

1. Have I taken certain courses that have prepared me for a particular job?
2. In which subjects did I perform the best? The worst?
3. Which subjects did I enjoy the most? The least?
4. How have my extracurricular activities prepared me for a particular job?
5. Is my GPA an accurate picture of my academic ability? Why?
6. Do I want a graduate degree? Do I want to earn it before beginning my job?
7. Why did I choose my major?

Experience

1. What previous jobs have I held? What were my responsibilities in each?
2. Were any of my jobs applicable to positions I may be seeking? How?
3. What did I like the most about my previous jobs? Like the least?
4. Why did I work in the jobs I did?
5. If I had to do it over again, would I work in these jobs? Why?

Personality

1. What are my good and bad traits?
2. Am I competitive?
3. Do I work well with others?
4. Am I outspoken?
5. Am I a leader or a follower?
6. Do I work well under pressure?
7. Do I work quickly, or am I methodical?
8. Do I get along well with others?
9. Am I ambitious?
10. Do I work well independently of others?

Desired job environment

1. Am I willing to relocate? Why?
2. Do I have a geographic preference? Why?
3. Would I mind traveling in my job?
4. Do I have to work for a large, nationally known firm to be satisfied?
5. Must I have a job that initially offers a high salary?
6. Must the job I assume offer rapid promotion opportunities?
7. In what kind of job environment would I feel most comfortable?
8. If I could design my own job, what characteristics would it have?

Personal goals

1. What are my short- and long-term goals? Why?
2. Am I career-oriented, or do I have broader interests?
3. What are my career goals?
4. What jobs are likely to help me achieve my goals?
5. What do I hope to be doing in 5 years? In 10 years?
6. What do I want out of life?

figure P.3

A PERSONAL ASSESSMENT

haircut, fingernails, shoes); your attitude (friendliness is desired); your verbal ability (speak clearly); and your motivation (be enthusiastic). Note also that interviewers want you to have been active in clubs and activities and to have set goals. Have someone evaluate you on these scales now to see if you have any weak points. You can then work on those points before you have any actual job interviews. We'll give you some clues on how to do this later.

7. **Follow up.** Write a thank-you note after interviews, even if you think they didn't go well. You have a chance to make a lasting impression

with a follow-up note. Keep in touch with companies in which you have an interest by calling periodically or sending an e-mail and letting the company know you are still interested. Indicate your willingness to travel to be interviewed. Get to know people in the company and learn from them whom to contact and what qualifications to emphasize.

MORE HINTS ON THE JOB SEARCH

The placement bureau at your school is a good place to begin reading about potential employers. On-campus interviewing is often a great source of jobs (see Figure P.4). Your library and the Internet may have annual reports that will give you even more information about your selected companies.

Other good sources of jobs include the want ads, job fairs, summer and other internship programs, placement bureaus, and sometimes walking into firms that appeal to you and asking for an interview. The *Occupational Outlook Quarterly,* produced by the U.S. Department of Labor, says this about job hunting:

> The skills that make a person employable are not so much the ones needed on the job as the ones needed to get the job, skills like the ability to find a job opening, complete an application, prepare the résumé, and survive an interview.

Here are a few printed sources you can use for finding out about jobs, writing résumé and cover letters, and other career information:

1. U.S. Department of Labor, *Occupational Outlook Handbook, 2010–2011.*

2. Howard Greene and Matthew W. Greene, *College Grad Seeks Future* (New York: St. Martin's Press, 2010).

3. Janet Nagle, *How to Use the Internet to Get Your Next Job* (Ocala, FL: Atlantic Publishing Group, 2010).

figure P.4

WHERE COLLEGE STUDENTS FIND JOBS

SOURCE OF JOB	PERCENTAGE OF NEW EMPLOYEES
On-campus interviewing	49.3%
Write-ins	9.8
Current employee referrals	7.2
Job listings with placement office	6.5
Responses from want ads	5.6
Walk-ins	5.5
Cooperative education programs	4.8
Summer employment	4.7
College faculty/staff referrals	4.5
Internship programs	4.5
High-demand major programs	4.4
Minority career programs	2.9
Part-time employment	2.4
Unsolicited referrals from placement	2.1
Women's career programs	2.1
Job listings with employment agencies	1.9
Referrals from campus organizations	1.8

4. Brad and Debra Schepp, *How to Find a Job on LinkedIn, Facebook, Twitter, MySpace and Other Social Media* (Chicago: McGraw-Hill Companies, 2010).

5. Paul Powers, *Winning Job Interviews* (Franklin Lakes, NJ: Career Press, 2010).

6. Richard N. Bolles, *What Color Is Your Parachute?* (Berkeley, CA: Ten Speed Press, Latest Edition).

7. Martin Yate, *Knock 'Em Dead* (Avon, MA: Adams Media, 2011).

8. Carol McClelland, *Green Careers for Dummies* (Indianapolis: Wiley Publishing, 2010).

9. Martin Yate, *Knock 'Em Dead Cover Letters,* 9th ed. (Avon, MA: Adams Media, 2010).

10. Wendy S. Enelow and Louise M. Kursmark, *Expert Resumes for Career Changes* (Indianapolis: Jist Works, 2010.

11. Katherine Brooks, *You Majored in What?* (First Plume Printing, 2010).

12. Brian Davis, *Top Notch Interviews* (Franklin Lakes, NJ: Career Press, 2010).

13. Susan Britton Whitcomb, *Resume Magic,* 4th ed. (Indianapolis: Jist Works, 2010).

Obviously, you can use the Internet to search for job information. To find information about careers or internships, try these sites (though keep in mind that addresses on the Internet are subject to sudden and frequent change):

- www.CareerBuilder.com
- www.Hoovers.com
- www.Job.com
- www.Monster.com
- www.dice.com

It's never too early in your career to begin designing a résumé and thinking of cover letters. Preparing such documents reveals your strengths and weaknesses more clearly than most other techniques. By preparing a résumé now, you may discover that you haven't been involved in enough outside activities to impress an employer. That information may prompt you to join some student groups, to become a volunteer, or to otherwise enhance your social skills.

You may also discover that you're weak on experience, and seek an internship or part-time job to fill in that gap. In any event, it's not too soon to prepare a résumé. It will certainly help you decide what you'd like to see in the area marked Education and, if you haven't already done so, help you choose a major and other coursework. Given that background, let's discuss how to prepare your résumé.

WRITING YOUR RÉSUMÉ

A résumé is a document that lists information an employer would need to evaluate you and your background. It explains your immediate goals and career objectives. This information is followed by an explanation of your educational background, experience, interests, and other relevant data. Having experience working in teams, for example, is important to many companies. If you have exceptional abilities but your résumé doesn't communicate them to the employer, those abilities aren't part of the person he or she will evaluate. Use some of the action words listed in Figure P.5 because companies use them

figure P.5

SAMPLE ACTION WORDS

Managed	Wrote	Budgeted	Improved
Planned	Produced	Designed	Increased
Organized	Scheduled	Directed	Investigated
Coordinated	Operated	Developed	Teamed
Supervised	Conducted	Established	Served
Trained	Administered	Implemented	Handled

as keywords to scan résumés. You must be comprehensive and clear in your résumé if you are to communicate all your attributes.

Your résumé is an advertisement for yourself. If your ad is better than the other person's ad, you're more likely to get the interview. In this case, *better* means that your ad highlights your attributes attractively. In discussing your education, for example, be sure to highlight your extracurricular activities such as part-time jobs, sports, and clubs. If you did well in school, include your grades. The idea is to make yourself look as good on paper as you are in reality.

The same is true for your job experience. Be sure to describe what you did, any special projects in which you participated, and any responsibilities you had. For the interests section, if you include one, don't just list your interests, but describe how deeply you were involved. If you organized the club, volunteered your time, or participated more often than usual in an organization, make sure to say so in the résumé. See Figure P.6 for a sample résumé. Most companies prefer that you keep your résumé to one page unless you have years of experience.

PUTTING YOUR RÉSUMÉ ONLINE

Many larger firms seek candidates online. An online résumé can thus allow you to reach the greatest number of potential employers with the least amount of effort. However, the Internet is not always the most effective job search tool. It may have been more effective a few years ago, but today thousands of other eager job hunters send résumés online and the volume can overwhelm recruiters. That doesn't mean you shouldn't post your résumé online. It does mean, though, that you can't just send a few hundred résumés into cyberspace and then sit back and wait for the phone to ring. Include online résumés as a tool in your job search process, but continue to use the more traditional tools such as networking.

An online résumé is different from a standard one because computers often do the elimination process. Thus, you must understand what the computer is programmed to look for. Listing jobs chronologically may no longer be the best thing to do. Instead, you might emphasize knowledge, skills, and abilities. Organizing and wording content with the key words stated in the job requirement may increase your chance of standing out from the thousands of other resumes. Figure P.7 offers a sample online resume, but you should consult the latest resume handbook to see what the newer resumes should look like.

Here are some hints on preparing your résumé for the Internet:

- Keep it simple. Use text only. Put a summary of your skills and your objective at the top so that the reader can capture as much as possible in the first 30 seconds.

- If you e-mail your résumé, send it in the text of the message; don't send it as an attachment. It takes too long for the receiver to open an attachment.

- Customize each mailing to that specific company. You may use a standard résumé, but add data to customize it and to introduce it.
- Save your cover letter and résumé in one file.
- Use any advertised job title as the subject of your e-mail message, citing any relevant job numbers.

Posting résumés to online job sites can cause privacy nightmares for job seekers, resulting in everything from identity theft to losing their current job when their employers, who use the same job search services, find out that they are looking for new jobs. Sometimes posted résumés are sold to other sites or individuals willing to pay for them. Scam artists posing as recruiters, meanwhile, can download all the résumés they want and do virtually whatever they

figure P.6

SAMPLE RÉSUMÉ

Yann Ng
345 Big Bend Boulevard
Kirkwood, Missouri, 63122
314-555-5385
YNG@STILNET.COM

Job objective: Sales representative in business-to-business marketing

Education:

St. Louis Community College at Meramec
A.A. in Business (3.6 grade point average)
Served on Student Representative Board

University of Missouri, St. Louis
B.S. in Business: Marketing major (3.2 grade point average, 3.5 in major)
Earned 100 percent of college expenses working 35 hours a week.
Member of Student American Marketing Association
Vice President of Student Government Association
Dean's List for two semesters

Work experience:
Schnuck's Supermarket: Worked checkout evenings and weekends for four years while in school. Learned to respond to customer requests quickly, and communicate with customers in a friendly and helpful manner.

Mary Tuttle's Flowers: For two summers, made flower arrangements, managed sales transactions, and acted as assistant to the manager. Also trained and supervised three employees. Often handled customer inquiries and complaints.

Special skills:
Fluent in Vietnamese, French, and English. Proficient at using Word. Developed my own Web site (www.yng@stilnet.com) and use the Internet often to do research for papers and for personal interests.

Other interests:
Cooking: often prepare meals for my family and friends. Reading, especially the classics. Piano playing and aerobics. Traveling: Asia, Europe, and America. Doing research on the Internet.

want with them. At worst, online résumés can give identity thieves a starting point to steal personal information. Here are tips to protect your résumé and your identity:

- *Never* include highly private information, such as Social Security numbers and birthdays.
- Check job boards' privacy policies to see how information is used and resold.
- Post résumés directly to employers if possible.
- Date résumés and remove them promptly after finding a job.
- If possible, withhold confidential information such as telephone numbers and your name and use temporary e-mail addresses for contacts.

figure P.7

SAMPLE ONLINE RÉSUMÉ

Yann Ng
345 Big Bend Boulevard
Kirkwood, Missouri, 63122
314-555-5385
YNG@STILNET.COM

Job objective: Sales representative in business-to-business marketing

Education:
St. Louis Community College at Meramec
A.A. in Business (3.6 grade point average)
Served on Student Representative Board
Courses included introduction to business, accounting, and marketing.

University of Missouri, St. Louis
B.S. in Business: Marketing major
(3.2. grade point average, 3.5 in major)
Earned 100 percent of college expenses working 35 hours a week.
Member of Student American Marketing Association
Vice President of Student Government Association
Dean's List for two semesters

Work experience:
Schnuck's Supermarket: Worked checkout evenings and weekends for four years while in school. Learned to respond to customer requests quickly, and communicate with customers in a friendly and helpful manner.

Mary Tuttle's Flowers: For two summers, made flower arrangements, managed sales transactions, and acted as assistant to the manager. Also trained and supervised three employees. Often handled customer inquiries and complaints.

Special skills: Fluent in Vietnamese, French, and English. Proficient at using MS Word, MS Excel, and MS PowerPoint. Developed my own Web site (www.yng@stilnet.com) and use the Internet often to do research for papers and for personal interests. Sales skills include conducting focus groups, prospecting, making presentations, and customer service.

Other interests: Cooking: often prepare meals for my family and friends. Reading, especially the classics. Piano playing and aerobics. Traveling: Asia, Europe, and America. Doing research on the Internet.

WRITING A COVER LETTER

A cover letter is used to announce your availability and to introduce the résumé. The cover letter is probably one of the most important advertisements anyone will write in a lifetime—so it should be done right.

First, the cover letter should indicate that you've researched the organization in question and are interested in a job there. Let the organization know what sources you used and what you know about it in the first paragraph to get the attention of the reader and show your interest.

You may have heard people say, "What counts is not what you know, but whom you know." This is only partly true—because both knowledge and

figure P.8

SAMPLE COVER LETTER

345 Big Bend Blvd.
Kirkwood, MO 63122
October 10, 2012

Mr. Carl Karlinski
Premier Designs
45 Apple Court
Chicago, IL 60536

Dear Mr. Karlinski: [Note that it's best to know the name of the recipient.]
　　　Recent articles in *Inc.* and *Success* have praised your company for its innovative products and strong customer orientation. I'm familiar with your creative display materials. In fact, we've used them at Mary Tuttle's Flower Shop—my employer for the last two summers. Christie Bouchard, your local sales representative, told me all about your products and your training program at Premier Designs.
　　　Christie mentioned the kind of salespeople you are seeking. Here's what she said and my qualifications.
　　　Requirement: Men and women with proven sales ability.
　　　Qualifications: Success making and selling flower arrangements at Mary Tuttle's and practicing customer relations at Schnuck's Supermarket. As you know, Schnuck's has one of the best customer-oriented training programs in the food industry.
　　　Requirement: Self-motivated people with leadership ability.
　　　Qualifications: Paid my way through college working nights and summers. Selected to be on the Student Representative Board at St. Louis Community College at Meramec and active in student government at the University of Missouri. Paid my own way to Asia, Europe, and the Americas.
　　　Could you use such a successful salesperson at Premier Designs? I will be in the Chicago area the week of January 4–9. What time and date would be most convenient for us to discuss career opportunities at Premier? I'll phone your secretary to set up an appointment.

Sincerely,

Yann Ng

personal contacts are necessary—but it's important nonetheless. If you don't know someone, you can get to know someone. You do this by calling the organization (or better yet, visiting its offices) and talking to people who already have the kind of job you're hoping to get. Ask about training, salary, and other relevant issues. Then, in your cover letter, mention that you've talked with some of the firm's employees and that this discussion increased your interest. You thereby show the letter reader that you "know someone," if only casually, and that you're interested enough to actively pursue the organization. This is all part of networking.

Second, in the description of yourself, be sure to say how your attributes will benefit the organization. For example, don't just say, "I will be graduating with a degree in marketing." Say, "You will find that my college training in marketing and marketing research has prepared me to learn your marketing system quickly and begin making a contribution right away." The sample cover letter in Figure P.8 will give you a better feel for how this looks.

Third, be sure to "ask for the order." That is, say in your final paragraph that you're available for an interview at a time and place convenient for the interviewer. Again, see the sample cover letter in Figure P.8 for guidance. Notice in this letter how the writer subtly shows that she reads business publications and draws attention to her résumé.

Principles to follow in writing a cover letter and preparing your résumé include the following:

- Be confident. List all your good qualities and attributes.

- Don't be apologetic or negative. Write as one professional to another, not as a humble student begging for a job.

- Describe how your experience and education can add value to the organization.

- Research every prospective employer thoroughly before writing anything. Use a rifle approach rather than a shotgun approach. That is, write effective marketing-oriented letters to a few select companies rather than to a general list.

- Have your materials prepared by an experienced keyboarder if you are not highly skilled yourself. Use printing services like FedEx Office if you do not have access to a good quality printer.

- Have someone edit your materials for spelling, grammar, and style. Don't be like the student who sent out a second résumé to correct "some mixtakes." Or another who said, "I am acurite with numbers."

- Don't send the names of references until asked.

PREPARING FOR JOB INTERVIEWS

Companies usually don't conduct job interviews unless they're somewhat certain that the candidate has the requirements for the job. The interview, therefore, is pretty much a make-or-break situation. If it goes well, you have a greater chance of being hired. That's why you must be prepared for your interviews. There are five stages of interview preparation:

1. **Do research about the prospective employers.** Learn what industry the firm is in, its competitors, the products or services it produces and their acceptance in the market, and the title of your desired position. You can find such information in the firm's annual reports, in Standard & Poor's, Hoover's, Moody's manuals, and various business

- How would you describe yourself?
- What are your greatest strengths and weaknesses?
- How did you choose this company?
- What do you know about the company?
- What are your long-range career goals?
- What courses did you like best? Least?
- What are your hobbies?
- Do you prefer a specific geographic location?

- Are you willing to travel (or move)?
- Which accomplishments have given you the most satisfaction?
- What things are most important to you in a job?
- Why should I hire you?
- What experience have you had in this type of work?
- How much do you expect to earn?

figure P.9

FREQUENTLY ASKED QUESTIONS

publications such as *Fortune, Bloomberg Businessweek,* and *Forbes.* Ask your librarian for help or search the Internet. You can look in the *Reader's Guide to Business Literature* to locate the company name and to look for articles about it. This important first step shows you have initiative and interest in the firm.

2. **Practice the interview.** Figure P.9 lists some of the more frequently asked questions (of you) in an interview. Practice answering these questions and more at the placement office and with your roommate(s), parents, or friends. Don't memorize your answers, but do be prepared—know what you're going to say. Review the action words in Figure P.5 and try to fit them into your answers. Interviewers will be impressed if you thought enough to prepare questions for *them* about the products, job, company culture, and so on. Figure P.10 shows sample questions you might ask. Be sure you know whom to contact, and write down the names of everyone you meet.

3. **Be professional during the interview.** You should look and sound professional throughout the interview. Do your homework and find out how managers dress at the firm. Make sure you wear an appropriate outfit. When you meet the interviewers, greet them by name, smile, and maintain good eye contact. Sit up straight in your chair and be alert and enthusiastic. If you have practiced, you should be able to relax and be confident. Other than that, be yourself, answer questions, and be friendly and responsive. (You will learn more about what types of questions job interviewers are legally allowed to ask you in Chapter 11.)

figure P.10

SAMPLE QUESTIONS TO ASK THE INTERVIEWER

- Who are your major competitors, and how would you rate their products and marketing relative to yours?
- How long does the training program last, and what is included?
- How soon after school would I be expected to start?
- What are the advantages of working for this firm?
- How much travel is normally expected?
- What managerial style should I expect in my area?
- How would you describe the working environment in my area?

- How would I be evaluated?
- What is the company's promotion policy?
- What is the corporate culture?
- What is the next step in the selection procedures?
- How soon should I expect to hear from you?
- What other information would you like about my background, experience, or education?
- What is your highest priority in the next six months and how could someone like me help?

figure P.11

TRAITS RECRUITERS SEEK IN JOB PROSPECTS

1. **Ability to communicate.** Do you have the ability to organize your thoughts and ideas effectively? Can you express them clearly when speaking or writing? Can you present your ideas to others in a persuasive way?

2. **Intelligence.** Do you have the ability to understand the job assignment? Learn the details of operation? Contribute original ideas to your work?

3. **Self-confidence.** Do you demonstrate a sense of maturity that enables you to deal positively and effectively with situations and people?

4. **Willingness to accept responsibility.** Are you someone who recognizes what needs to be done and is willing to do it?

5. **Initiative.** Do you have the ability to identify the purpose of work and to take action?

6. **Leadership.** Can you guide and direct others to obtain the recognized objectives?

7. **Energy level.** Do you demonstrate a forcefulness and capacity to make things move ahead? Can you maintain your work effort at an above-average rate?

8. **Imagination.** Can you confront and deal with problems that may not have standard solutions?

9. **Flexibility.** Are you capable of changing and being receptive to new situations and ideas?

10. **Interpersonal skills.** Can you bring out the best efforts of individuals so they become effective, enthusiastic members of a team?

11. **Self-knowledge.** Can you realistically assess your own capabilities? See yourself as others see you? Clearly recognize your strengths and weaknesses?

12. **Ability to handle conflict.** Can you successfully contend with stress situations and antagonism?

13. **Competitiveness.** Do you have the capacity to compete with others and the willingness to be measured by your performance in relation to that of others?

14. **Goal achievement.** Do you have the ability to identify and work toward specific goals? Do such goals challenge your abilities?

15. **Vocational skills.** Do you possess the positive combination of education and skills required for the position you are seeking?

16. **Direction.** Have you defined your basic personal needs? Have you determined what type of position will satisfy your knowledge, skills, and goals?

Source: "So You're Looking for a Job?" The College Placement Council.

Remember, the interview is not one-way communication; don't forget to ask the questions you've prepared before the interview. Do *not* ask about salary, however, until you've been offered a job. When you leave, thank the interviewers and, if you're still interested in the job, tell them so. If they don't tell you, ask them what the next step is. Maintain a positive attitude. Figures P.11 and P.12 outline what the interviewers will be evaluating.

4. **Follow up on the interview.** First, write down what you can remember from the interview: names of the interviewers and their titles, dates for training, and so on. Put the information in your career file. You can send a follow-up letter thanking each interviewer for his or her time. You can also send a letter of recommendation or some other piece of added information to keep their interest. "The squeaky wheel gets the grease" is the operating slogan. Your enthusiasm for working for the company could be a major factor in hiring you.

figure P.12

INTERVIEW RATING SHEET

Candidate: "For each characteristic listed below there is a rating scale of I through 7, where 'I' is generally the most unfavorable rating of the characteristic and '7' the most favorable. Rate each characteristic by *circling* just one number to represent the impression you gave in the interview that you have just completed."

Name of Candidate _____

I. Appearance

| Sloppy | I | 2 | 3 | 4 | 5 | 6 | 7 | Neat |

2. Attitude

| Unfriendly | I | 2 | 3 | 4 | 5 | 6 | 7 | Friendly |

3. Assertiveness/Verbal Ability

a. Responded completely to questions asked

| Poor | I | 2 | 3 | 4 | 5 | 6 | 7 | Excellent |

b. Clarified personal background and related it to job opening and description

| Poor | I | 2 | 3 | 4 | 5 | 6 | 7 | Excellent |

c. Able to explain and sell job abilities

| Poor | I | 2 | 3 | 4 | 5 | 6 | 7 | Excellent |

d. Initiated questions regarding position and firm

| Poor | I | 2 | 3 | 4 | 5 | 6 | 7 | Excellent |

e. Expressed thorough knowledge of personal goals and abilities

| Poor | I | 2 | 3 | 4 | 5 | 6 | 7 | Excellent |

4. Motivation

| Poor | I | 2 | 3 | 4 | 5 | 6 | 7 | High |

5. Subject/Academic Knowledge

| Poor | I | 2 | 3 | 4 | 5 | 6 | 7 | Good |

6. Stability

| Poor | I | 2 | 3 | 4 | 5 | 6 | 7 | Good |

7. Composure

| Ill at ease | I | 2 | 3 | 4 | 5 | 6 | 7 | Relaxed |

8. Personal Involvement/Activities, Clubs, Etc.

| Low | I | 2 | 3 | 4 | 5 | 6 | 7 | Very high |

9. Mental Impression

| Dull | I | 2 | 3 | 4 | 5 | 6 | 7 | Alert |

10. Adaptability

| Poor | I | 2 | 3 | 4 | 5 | 6 | 7 | Good |

II. Speech Pronunciation

| Poor | I | 2 | 3 | 4 | 5 | 6 | 7 | Good |

12. Overall Impression

| Unsatisfactory | I | 2 | 3 | 4 | 5 | 6 | 7 | Highly satisfactory |

13. Would you hire this individual if you were permitted to make a decision right now?

Yes   No

5. **Be prepared to act.** Know what you want to say if you do get a job offer. You may not want the job once you know all the information. Don't expect to receive a job offer from everyone you meet, but do expect to learn something from every interview. With some practice and persistence, you should find a rewarding and challenging job.

BE PREPARED TO CHANGE CAREERS

If you're like most people, you'll find that you'll follow several different career paths over your lifetime. This is a good thing in that it enables you to try different jobs and stay fresh and enthusiastic. The key to moving forward in your career is a willingness to change jobs, always searching for the career that will bring the most personal satisfaction and growth. This means that you'll have to write many cover letters and résumés and go through many interviews. Each time you change jobs, go through the steps in this section of the Prologue to be sure you're fully prepared. Good luck!

All your efforts pay off when you land the job you wanted and take the first big step in your career. Go for it!

Taking Risks and Making Profits within the DYNAMIC BUSINESS Environment

1

LEARNING goals

After you have read and studied this chapter, you should be able to

1 Describe the relationship between profit and risk, and show how businesses and nonprofit organizations can raise the standard of living for all.

2 Compare and contrast being an entrepreneur and working for others.

3 Analyze the effects of the economic environment and taxes on businesses.

4 Describe the effects of technology on businesses.

5 Demonstrate how businesses can meet and beat competition.

6 Analyze the social changes affecting businesses.

7 Identify what businesses must do to meet global challenges, including war and terrorism.

8 Review how past trends are being repeated in the present and what those trends mean for tomorrow's college graduates.

What do you do when you are a full-figured woman and want nice clothes to wear, especially a flattering bathing suit? Few designers offer fashionable clothing in larger sizes, making shopping for clothes very frustrating for plus-sized women. That was the issue facing Monif Clarke. She decided to fill the need for such clothes by designing her own line. Using a $30,000 loan from her father and help from her mother (her business partner), she started Monif C. Contemporary Plus Sizes.

As a plus-sized woman, Clarke understands the need for a new point of view in the plus-size market. "It took me many years to appreciate my curves and recognize them as a plus and NOT a minus . . . I was tired of buying the standard uniform that every woman has, I needed luxurious feminine clothes that make a statement . . . Who says plus size can't be sexy, luxurious, and feminine?" Clarke's designs are heavily inspired by her love of the Caribbean, the glamour of New York City nightlife, and European style. Recognizing the importance of versatility, she makes certain that the clothes work well for day and night . . . dressed up or down. Fabrics, trims, and treatments are carefully selected. The Monif C. collection is targeted to young, contemporary women. You can go to www.Monifc.com to see her collection for yourself.

Clarke earned her degree from Rutgers University where she majored in math and computer science. She signed up for classes at New York's Fashion Institute of Technology and started networking (meeting people) and attending trade shows. She met a manufacturer who she tried to convince to produce her collection, but her order was too small to be profitable for him. However, he was so impressed with Clarke's enthusiasm and persistence that he gave her the contact information of the manufacturer, fabric vendors, and trim vendors who she still works with today. All of her garments are made in New York's garment district. That makes sense for local, new designers because such factories will take lower minimum orders.

Clarke got a lot of good publicity when her outfits appeared on TLC's *What Not to Wear* television show, which featured her clothing as a good option for plus-sized women. Despite the good publicity, Monif C. had trouble getting merchandise into leading department stores since they were looking for more traditional designs (black or tan that try to conceal curves). Clarke turned to the Internet and developed an e-commerce site to distribute her creative collection. She also teamed up with other online retailers such as Overstock.com and Ideeli.com to carry her fashions. Some customers helped her spread the word by modeling her clothes on YouTube.

Monif C. now sells her clothing to retailers throughout the United States and around the world. Like all businesses, Monif C. was affected by the economic downturn, but Clarke was able to set prices and adapt products to meet the changing needs of the market. When her mother died, Clarke was forced to hire new people, and she became even more motivated to succeed. Monifc.com has been around since 2005, so it has proven successful. Be sure to check out the swimsuit models on her website. Swimsuits now make up over 40 percent of sales.

Businesses are constantly trying to adapt to the wants and needs of their customers and to the technologies that those customers are using. This chapter will introduce you to entrepreneurship in general and some of the many changes occurring in businesses today. As you learn more about businesses and non-profit organizations, you will see that adapting to changing times is a constant necessity.

Getting to Know

X **Monif Clarke**

of **Monifc.com**

Sources: Tamara E. Holmes, "Plus-Sized Profits," *Black Enterprise*, April 2011, and www.Monifc.com, accessed April 2011.

This microlending organization provides small loans to entrepreneurs too poor to qualify for traditional loans. The person who started the organization has started 30 of what he calls social businesses that do not have profit as their goal. Name that organization and its founder. (Find the answers in the chapter.)

LEARNING goal 1

Describe the relationship between profit and risk, and show how businesses and nonprofit organizations can raise the standard of living for all.

business
Any activity that seeks to provide goods and services to others while operating at a profit.

goods
Tangible products such as computers, food, clothing, cars, and appliances.

services
Intangible products (i.e., products that can't be held in your hand) such as education, health care, insurance, recreation, and travel and tourism.

entrepreneur
A person who risks time and money to start and manage a business.

revenue
The total amount of money a business takes in during a given period by selling goods and services.

profit
The amount of money a business earns above and beyond what it spends for salaries and other expenses.

loss
When a business's expenses are more than its revenues.

ENTREPRENEURSHIP AND WEALTH BUILDING

One thing you can learn from the chapter-opening Profile is that success in business is based on constantly adapting to the market. A **business** is any activity that seeks to provide goods and services to others while operating at a profit. To earn that profit, you provide desired goods, jobs, and services to people in the area. **Goods** are *tangible* products such as computers, food, clothing, cars, and appliances. **Services** are *intangible* products (i.e., products that can't be held in your hand) such as education, health care, insurance, recreation, and travel and tourism. Once you have developed the right goods and services, based on consumer wants and needs, you need to reach those consumers using whatever media they prefer, including blogs, tweets, Facebook, TV advertising, and more.[1]

Although you don't need to have wealth as a primary goal, one result of successfully filling a market need is that you can make money for yourself, sometimes a great deal, by giving customers what they want. Sam Walton of Walmart began by opening one store in Arkansas and, over time, became one of the richest people in the United States.[2] There are over 11 million millionaires in the world.[3] Maybe you will be one of them some day if you start your own business. An **entrepreneur** is a person who risks time and money to start and manage a business.

Revenues, Profits, and Losses

Revenue is the total amount of money a business takes in during a given period by selling goods and services. **Profit** is the amount of money a business earns above and beyond what it spends for salaries and other expenses needed to run the operation. A **loss** occurs when a business's expenses are more than its revenues. If a business loses money over time, it will likely have to close, putting its employees out of work. About 80,000 businesses in the United States close each year; even more close during a slowdown like the United States experienced starting in 2008.[4]

As noted above, the business environment is constantly changing. What seems like a great opportunity one day—for example, online grocery shopping or SUVs—may become a huge failure when the economy changes. Starting a business may thus come with huge risks.[5] But huge risks often result in huge profits. We'll explore that concept next.

Matching Risk with Profit

Risk is the chance an entrepreneur takes of losing time and money on a business that may not prove profitable. Profit, remember, is the amount of money a business earns *above and beyond* what it pays out for salaries and other expenses. For example, if you were to start a business selling hot dogs from a cart in the summer, you would have to pay for the cart rental. You would also have to pay for the hot dogs and other materials and for someone to run the cart while you were away. After you paid your employee and yourself, paid for the food and materials you used, paid the rent on the cart, and paid your taxes, any money left over would be profit.

Keep in mind that profit is over and above the money you pay yourself in salary. You could use any profit to rent or buy a second cart and hire other employees. After a few summers, you might have a dozen carts employing dozens of workers.

Not all enterprises make the same amount of profit. Those that take the most risk may make the most profit. There is high risk, for example, in making a new kind of automobile.[6] It's also risky to open a business in an inner city, because insurance and rent are usually higher than in suburban areas, but reduced competition makes substantial profit possible. Irish entrepreneur Denis O'Brien, of Digicel, makes billions of dollars selling cell phones in the poorest, most violent countries in the world. Big risk, big profits.

Standard of Living and Quality of Life

Entrepreneurs such as Sam Walton (Walmart) and Bill Gates (Microsoft) not only became wealthy themselves; they also provided employment for many other people. Walmart is currently the nation's largest private employer.

Businesses and their employees pay taxes that the federal government and local communities use to build hospitals, schools, libraries, playgrounds, roads, and other public facilities. Taxes also help to keep the environment clean, support people in need, and provide police and fire protection. Thus, the wealth businesses generate and the taxes they pay help everyone in their communities. A nation's businesses are part of an economic system that contributes to the standard of living and quality of life for everyone in the country (and, potentially, the world). How has the recent economic slowdown affected the standard of living and quality of life in your part of the world?

The term **standard of living** refers to the amount of goods and services people can buy with the money they have. For example, the United States has one of the highest standards of living in the world, even though workers in some other countries, such as Germany and Japan, may on average make more money per hour. How can that be? Prices for goods and services in Germany and Japan are higher than in the United States, so a person in those countries can buy less than what a person in the United States can buy with the same amount of money. For example, a bottle of beer may cost $7 in Japan and $3 in the United States.

risk
The chance an entrepreneur takes of losing time and money on a business that may not prove profitable.

standard of living
The amount of goods and services people can buy with the money they have.

Mary Kate and Ashley Olsen are now the head designers of their company Dualstar which has three clothing lines ranging from the high-end to the more affordable. Today the business is worth over $1 billion. What risks and rewards did the twins face when they started their business?

Often, goods cost more in one country than another because of higher taxes and stricter government regulations. Finding the right level of taxes and regulation is important in making a country or city prosperous. We'll explore that issue more deeply in Chapter 2. At this point, it is enough to understand that the United States enjoys a high standard of living largely because of the wealth created by its businesses.

The term **quality of life** refers to the general well-being of a society in terms of its political freedom, natural environment, education, health care, safety, amount of leisure, and rewards that add to the satisfaction and joy that other goods and services provide. Maintaining a high quality of life requires the combined efforts of businesses, nonprofit organizations, and government agencies. The more money businesses create, the more is potentially available to improve the quality of life for everyone. It's important to be careful, however. Working to build a higher standard of living may lower the quality of life if it means less time with family or more stress.[7]

Responding to the Various Business Stakeholders

Stakeholders are all the people who stand to gain or lose by the policies and activities of a business and whose concerns the business needs to address.[8] They include customers, employees, stockholders, suppliers, dealers (retailers), bankers, people in the surrounding community, the media, environmentalists, and elected government leaders (see Figure 1.1).

A primary challenge for organizations of the 21st century will be to recognize and respond to the needs of their stakeholders. For example, the need for the business to make profits may be balanced against the needs of employees to earn sufficient income or the need to protect the environment.[9] Ignore the media, and they might attack your business with articles that hurt sales. Oppose the local community, and it may stop you from expanding.

quality of life
The general well-being of a society in terms of its political freedom, natural environment, education, health care, safety, amount of leisure, and rewards that add to the satisfaction and joy that other goods and services provide.

stakeholders
All the people who stand to gain or lose by the policies and activities of a business and whose concerns the business needs to address.

figure 1.1

A BUSINESS AND ITS STAKEHOLDERS
Often the needs of a firm's various stakehoders will conflict. For example, paying employees more may cut into stockholders' profits. Balancing such demands is a major role of business managers.

Staying competitive may call for outsourcing. **Outsourcing** means contracting with other companies (often in other countries) to do some or all the functions of a firm, like its production or accounting tasks. Outsourcing has had serious consequences in some states where jobs have been lost to overseas competitors. We discuss outsourcing in more detail in Chapter 3.

outsourcing
Contracting with other companies (often in other countries) to do some or all of the functions of a firm, like its production or accounting tasks.

The other side of the outsourcing coin is *insourcing*.[10] Many foreign companies are setting up design and production facilities here in the United States. For example, Korea-based Hyundai operates design and engineering headquarters in Detroit, Michigan, and produces cars in Montgomery, Alabama. Japanese automakers Honda and Toyota have been producing cars in the United States for years. Insourcing creates many new U.S. jobs and helps offset those being outsourced.[11]

It may be legal and profitable to outsource, but is it best for all the stakeholders? Business leaders must make outsourcing decisions based on all factors. Pleasing stakeholders is not easy and often calls for trade-offs.

Using Business Principles in Nonprofit Organizations

Despite their efforts to satisfy their stakeholders, businesses cannot do everything needed to make a community all it can be. Nonprofit organizations—such as public schools, civic associations, charities like United Way and Salvation Army, and groups devoted to social causes—also make a major contribution to the welfare of society. A **nonprofit organization** is an organization whose goals do not include making a personal profit for its owners or organizers. Nonprofit organizations often do strive for financial gains, but they use them to meet their social or educational goals rather than for personal profit.[12]

nonprofit organization
An organization whose goals do not include making a personal profit for its owners or organizers.

Social entrepreneurs are people who use business principles to start and manage not-for-profits and help address social issues. Muhammad Yunus won the Nobel Prize for starting the Grameen Bank, a microlending organization that provides small loans to entrepreneurs too poor to qualify for traditional loans. Yunus has started 30 of what he calls social businesses that do not have profit as their goal. One, for example, provides cataract operations for a fraction of the usual cost.[13]

The goals of nonprofit organizations are social and educational, not profit-oriented. The Red Cross, for instance provides assistance to around 30 million people annually from refugees to victims of natural disasters. Why do good management principles apply equally to businesses and nonprofit organizations?

Your interests may lead you to work for a nonprofit organization such as those started by Yunus. That doesn't mean, however, that you shouldn't study business in college. You'll still need to learn business skills such as information management, leadership, marketing, and financial management. The knowledge and skills you acquire in this and other business courses are useful for careers in any organization, including nonprofits. We'll explore entrepreneurship in more detail right after the Progress Assessment.

progress assessment

- What is the difference between *revenue* and *profit?*
- What is the difference between *standard of living* and *quality of life?*
- What is risk, and how is it related to profit?
- What do the terms *stakeholders, outsourcing,* and *insourcing* mean?

To create wealth for its citizens, a country requires more than natural resources. It needs the efforts of entrepreneurs and the skill and knowledge to produce goods and services. How can government support entrepreneurship and the spread of knowledge?

LEARNING goal 2

Compare and contrast being an entrepreneur and working for others.

ENTREPRENEURSHIP VERSUS WORKING FOR OTHERS

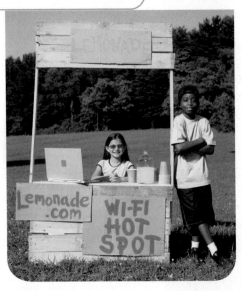

There are two ways to succeed in business. One is to rise through the ranks of large companies. The advantage of working for others is that somebody else assumes the company's entrepreneurial risk and provides you with benefits like paid vacation time and health insurance.[14] It's a good option, and many people choose it.

The other, riskier path is to become an entrepreneur. The national anthem, "The Star Spangled Banner," says that the United States is the "land of the free and the home of the brave." Part of being free is being able to own your own business and reap the profits from it. But freedom to succeed also means freedom to fail, and many small businesses fail each year. It takes a brave person to start one. As an entrepreneur, you don't receive any benefits such as paid vacation time, day care, a company car, or health insurance. You have to provide them for yourself! But what you gain—freedom to make your own decisions, opportunity, and possible wealth—is often worth the effort. Before you take on the challenge, you should study successful entrepreneurs to learn the process. You can talk to them personally and read about them in Chapter 6, as well as in other books and magazines.

Opportunities for Entrepreneurs

Millions of people from all over the world have taken the entrepreneurial challenge and succeeded. For example, the number of Hispanic-owned businesses in the United States has grown dramatically (Hispanics are now the largest ethnic group in the United States). Both Hispanic men and women are doing

Networking of Minority Businesses

The Black Enterprise Entrepreneurs Conference attracts about 2,000 accomplished business owners each year. Earl Graves, the publisher of *Black Enterprise* magazine says, "We cannot build businesses of size, scale and significance in the global marketplace without aggressively and effectively building and leveraging our relationships with others." He goes on to say, "You need to establish mutually beneficial relationships within your industry, with customers, suppliers, other business owners, bankers, lawyers, financiers, and corporate managers to grow your business."

A good example of black entrepreneurs relying on others as vendors, customers, investors, and partners is the story of Carol's Daughter, the hair care and beauty products company founded as an online and mail-order business by Lisa Price. Price started out by experimenting with homemade fragrances and bath products in her Brooklyn kitchen. When she met music industry executive Steve Stoute, he grew so convinced of the potential of her business that he encouraged others like celebrities Will Smith and Shawn "Jay-Z" Carter to invest in her company. Carol's Daughter is now a nationally recognized brand with a store in Harlem and retail partnerships with Sephora, Macy's, and Home Shopping Network.

Sources: Earl G. Graves, "To Build Our Businesses, We Must Leverage Our Relationships," *Black Enterprise,* March 2011; and artgoodiesonline, accessed March 2011.

particularly well. Similar successes are true of businesses owned by Asians, Pacific Islanders, Native Americans, and Alaskan Natives.

Women now own over a third of all businesses. Names you may know include Oprah Winfrey, Donna Karan, and Lillian Vernon. Andrea Jung is the CEO of Avon Products. The world's most powerful women include Ho Ching, the chief executive of Temasek Holdings in Singapore; Indra Nooyi, chief executive of Pepsico, U.S.; and Cynthia Carroll, chief executive of Anglo American in the United Kingdom.

Businesses owned by minority women are growing faster than those owned by men or nonminority women. Women of color are establishing businesses at twice the rate of their male counterparts and more than four times that of nonminority entrepreneurs.[15] Read the nearby Spotlight on Small Business box to learn more about minority entrepreneurs.

The Importance of Entrepreneurs to the Creation of Wealth

Have you ever wondered why some countries are relatively wealthy and others poor? Economists have been studying the issue of wealth creation for many years. They began by identifying five **factors of production** that seemed to contribute to wealth (see Figure 1.2):

1. Land (or natural resources).
2. Labor (workers).

factors of production
The resources used to create wealth: land, labor, capital, entrepreneurship, and knowledge.

3. Capital. (This includes machines, tools, buildings, or whatever else is used in the production of goods. It may not include money; money is used to buy factors of production but is not always considered a factor by itself.)
4. Entrepreneurship.
5. Knowledge.

Traditionally, business and economics textbooks emphasized only four factors of production: land, labor, capital, and entrepreneurship. But the late management expert and business consultant Peter Drucker said the most important factor of production in our economy is and always will be *knowledge.*

What do we find when we compare the factors of production in rich and poor countries? Some poor countries have plenty of land and natural resources. Russia, for example, has vast areas of land with many resources such as timber and oil, but it is not considered a rich country (yet). Therefore, land isn't the critical element for wealth creation.

Most poor countries, such as Mexico, have many laborers, so it's not labor that's the primary source of wealth today. Laborers need to find work to make a contribution; that is, they need entrepreneurs to create jobs for them. Furthermore, capital—machinery and tools—is now fairly easy for firms to find in world markets, so capital isn't the missing ingredient either. Capital is not productive without entrepreneurs to put it to use.

What makes rich countries rich today is a combination of *entrepreneurship* and the effective use of *knowledge.* Entrepreneurs use what they've learned (knowledge) to grow their businesses and increase wealth. Economic and political freedom also matter.

The business environment either encourages or discourages entrepreneurship. That helps explain why some states and cities in the United States grow rich while others remain relatively poor. In the following section, we'll explore what makes up the business environment and how to build an environment that encourages growth and job creation.

figure 1.2

THE FIVE FACTORS OF PRODUCTION

Land

Land and other natural resources are used to make homes, cars, and other products.

Labor

People have always been an important resource in producing goods and services, but many people are now being replaced by technology.

Capital

Capital includes machines, tools, buildings, and other means of manufacturing.

Entrepreneurship

All the resources in the world have little value unless entrepreneurs are willing to take the risk of starting businesses to use those resources.

Knowledge

Information technology has revolutionized business, making it possible to quickly determine wants and needs and to respond with desired goods and services.

- What are some of the advantages of working for others?
- What benefits do you lose by being an entrepreneur, and what do you gain?
- What are the five factors of production? Which ones seem to be the most important for creating wealth?

THE BUSINESS ENVIRONMENT

The **business environment** consists of the surrounding factors that either help or hinder the development of businesses. Figure 1.3 shows the five elements in the business environment:

> **business environment**
> The surrounding factors that either help or hinder the development of businesses.

1. The economic and legal environment.
2. The technological environment.
3. The competitive environment.
4. The social environment.
5. The global business environment.

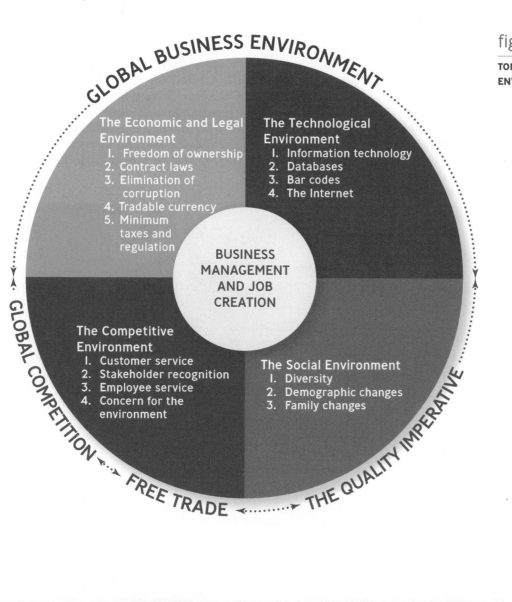

figure I.3

TODAY'S DYNAMIC BUSINESS ENVIRONMENT

Businesses that create wealth and jobs grow and prosper in a healthy environment. Thus, creating the right business environment is the foundation for social benefits of all kinds, including good schools, clean air and water, good health care, and low rates of crime. Businesses normally can't control their environment, but they need to monitor it carefully and do what they can to adapt as it changes.

LEARNING goal 3

Analyze the effects of the economic environment and taxes on businesses.

The Economic and Legal Environment

People are willing to start new businesses if they believe the risk of losing their money isn't too great. The economic system and the way government works with or against businesses can have a strong impact on that level of risk. For example, a government can *minimize spending* and *keep taxes and regulations to a minimum,* policies that tend to favor business. Much of the debate in recent elections has focused on whether or not to raise taxes and how to lower government spending.[16] President Obama is increasing government spending with the idea of getting the economy moving faster. Some economists agree with such a stimulus, but some do not.[17] One way for government to actively promote entrepreneurship is to *allow private ownership of businesses.* In some countries, the government owns most businesses, and there's little incentive for people to work hard or create profit. Around the world today, however, some governments are selling those businesses to private individuals to create more wealth. One of the best things the governments of developing countries can do is to *minimize interference with the free exchange of goods and services.*

The government can further lessen the risks of entrepreneurship by *passing laws that enable businesspeople to write enforceable contracts.* In the United

Starting a business is much harder in some countries than in others. In India, for example, it requires a time-consuming and bureaucratic process to obtain government permission. Nonetheless, new businesses can become a major source of wealth and employment; this sari shop is one small example. What do you think would be the effect of a little more freedom to create business opportunities in this country of over a billion people?

States, the Uniform Commercial Code, for example, regulates business agreements like contracts and warranties so that firms know they can rely on one another. In countries that don't yet have such laws, the risks of starting a business are that much greater. You can read more about business laws in Bonus Chapter A at the end of this book.

The government can also *establish a currency that's tradable in world markets.* That is, the currency lets you buy and sell goods and services anywhere in the world when it is easily exchanged for that of the other countries where you do business. If the Chinese did not want to trade their yuan for the U.S. dollar, for instance, it's hard to imagine how Coca-Cola or Disney would have been able to sell their products and services there.

Finally, the government can help *minimize corruption* in business and in its own ranks. Where governments are corrupt, it's difficult to build a factory or open a store without a government permit, which is obtained largely through bribery of public officials. Among businesses themselves, unscrupulous leaders can threaten their competitors and unlawfully minimize competition.

Many laws in the United States attempt to minimize corruption. Nonetheless, corrupt and illegal activities at some companies do negatively affect the business community and the economy as a whole.[18] The news media widely reports these scandals. Ethics is so important to the success of businesses and the economy as a whole that we feature stories about ethics in most chapters and devote Chapter 4 to the subject.

The capitalist system relies heavily on honesty, integrity, and high ethical standards. Failure of those fundamentals can weaken the whole system. The faltering economy that began in 2008 was due in large part to such failure. Some mortgage lenders, for instance, failed to do the research necessary to ensure their borrowers' creditworthiness. Many subprime borrowers (people with low credit ratings) forfeited their loans. The ripple effects of these unpaid debts not only cost many people their homes but also reduced the value of housing across the world and made it difficult even for business borrowers to get new loans. Part of the blame for this economic disaster can be placed on the borrowers who didn't tell the truth about their income or who otherwise deceived the lenders.

It is easy to see the damage caused by the poor moral and ethical behavior of some businesspeople.[19] What is not so obvious is the damage caused by the moral and ethical lapses of the everyday consumer—that is, you and me. The nearby Making Ethical Decisions box discusses that issue in more depth.

LEARNING goal 4

Describe the effects of technology on businesses.

The Technological Environment

Since prehistoric times, humans have felt the need to create tools that make work easier. Few technological changes have had a more comprehensive and lasting impact on businesses, however, than the emergence of information technology (IT): computers, networks, cell phones, and especially the Internet.

The iPod, iPhone, BlackBerry and other smartphones, as well as social media like MySpace, Facebook, and Twitter, have completely changed the way people communicate with one another. Advertisers and other businesspeople

MAKING ethical decisions

Ethics Begins with You

It is easy to criticize the ethics of people whose names appear in the headlines. It is more difficult to see the moral and ethical misbehavior of your own social group. Do you find some of the behaviors of your friends morally or ethically questionable?

A survey found that the number of employees calling in sick had reached a five-year high, and three-fifths were not sick at all. Other employees have been caught conducting personal business at work, such as doing their taxes. And others play video games on their work computers. We're sure you can add many more examples.

Many companies today are creating ethics codes to guide their employees' behavior. We believe the trend toward improving ethical behavior is so important that we've made it a major theme of this book. Throughout the text you'll see boxes like this one, called Making Ethical Decisions, that pose ethical dilemmas and ask what you would do to resolve them. The idea is for you to think about the moral and ethical dimensions of every decision you make.

Here is your first one: You have become addicted to your electronic gadgets. Some days at work you spend most of the time playing games, watching TV, texting, sending e-mails to friends, or reading a book or magazine on your devices. What is the problem in this situation? What are your alternatives? What are the consequences of each alternative? Which alternative will you choose? Is your choice ethical?

---

technology
Everything from phones and copiers to computers, medical imaging devices, personal digital assistants, and the various software programs that make business processes more effective, efficient, and productive.

have created ways of using these tools to reach their suppliers and customers. Even politicians have harnessed the power of the Internet to advance their causes. See the nearby Social Media in Business box for an example of how a well-established company uses these tools to interact with customers.

IT is such a major force in business today that we discuss its impact on businesses throughout the entire text.

How Technology Benefits Workers and You   One of the advantages of working for others is that the company often provides the tools and technology to make your job more productive. **Technology** means everything from phones and copiers to computers, medical imaging devices, personal digital assistants, and the

Technology makes workers more productive. Instead of spending hours traveling to meet, for instance, this doctor is using teleconferencing to consult with a colleague about diagnosis and treatment options. Are some workers likely to be more comfortable with new technology than others?

JCPenney Keeps in Touch

Nothing highlights the dynamic nature of business more than the number of new electronic devices people carry today, including iPads, iPhones, e-readers, and cell phones of all kinds. People seem to be constantly texting, tweeting, and talking to each other. You cannot help but notice them in restaurants, on buses, and even walking down the street. Hopefully, though, you don't see them doing it while they're driving.

In order to reach the coveted 18-to-35-year-olds, JCPenney ran local ads featuring fashion blogger Geri Hirsh. In the spots, Hirsh showcased the retailer's spring line as she was preparing for an Oscar party. JCPenney's social media team then posted clothing selected by Hirsh to the brand's Facebook page, which includes a shopping app.

During the Oscar broadcast, JCPenny incorporated Twitter and Facebook into the spring campaign using seven commercials. JCPenney was the only retail sponsor for the show and wanted to reach young women. During the show, the company posted mini-blogs with trivia questions about fashion. The first person to send in a correct answer received a $20 gift card from the retailer. Before the show, the company also sent warm-up tweets with questions like, "Which film should win for Best Costume?"

The store also launched a "Shop Like a Celebrity" sweepstakes on Facebook. Winners received a free trip to New York complete with a two-night hotel stay, a $500 JCPenney gift card, and fashion advice from blogger Mia Morgan (The Fashion Alchemist). Other digital components of the campaign included a design contest on social shopping site Polyvore and an original video series on Olsenboye.com. JCPenney is a great example of how successful well-established businesses continue to adapt to the wants and needs of their customers and to the technology they use.

Sources: Christopher Heine, "JCPenney Hopes Twitter Contest Creates Oscar Buzz," *Department Store Retailing News* online, accessed March 3, 2011; and Marilyn Much, "The Changing Face (book) of Internet Commerce," *Investor's Business Daily,* February 2, 2011.

---

various software programs that make business processes more effective, efficient, and productive. *Effectiveness* means producing the desired result. *Efficiency* means producing goods and services using the least amount of resources.

Productivity is the amount of output you generate given the amount of input, such as the number of hours you work. The more you can produce in any given period, the more money you are worth to companies. The average worker in the United States contributes $63,885 to GDP, making U.S. workers some of the world's most productive employees. The problem with productivity today is that workers are so productive that fewer are needed, and that is contributing to the high unemployment rate we are now experiencing.[20]

> **productivity**
> The amount of output you generate given the amount of input (e.g., hours worked).

Technology affects people in all industries. For example, Don Glenn, a farmer in Decatur, Alabama, uses his personal computer to compare data from the previous year's harvest with infrared satellite photos of his farm that show which crops are flourishing. He has a desktop terminal called a DTN that allows him to check the latest grain prices, and he uses AgTalk, a web-based bulletin board, to converse with other farmers from all over the world. He also bids for bulk fertilizer on XSAg.com, an online agricultural exchange. High-tech equipment tells Glenn how and where to spread fertilizer and seed, tracks yields yard by yard, and allows him to maintain high profit margins.

The Growth of E-Commerce **E-commerce** is the buying and selling of goods over the Internet. There are two major types of e-commerce transactions: business-to-consumer (B2C) and business-to-business (B2B). As important as the Internet has been to retailers like Amazon.com in the consumer market, it has become even more important in the B2B market, where businesses sell

> **e-commerce**
> The buying and selling of goods over the Internet.

goods and services to one another, such as IBM selling consulting services to a local bank. Websites have become the new stores.[21]

Traditional businesses must deal with the competition from B2B and B2C firms, and vice versa. Many new parents would just as soon buy used items posted on Craigslist than shop in a baby-goods store. Starting a business on eBay has never been easier. More than 450 million Chinese citizens are using the Internet. This is about double the number of U.S. users.[22] And what did people do before they could google? E-commerce has become so important that we will discuss it throughout the text.

Using Technology to Be Responsive to Customers   A major theme of this text is that those businesses most responsive to customer wants and needs will succeed. That realization points to one way in which even traditional retailers can use Internet technology. For example, businesses use bar codes to identify products you buy and their size, quantity, and color. The scanner at the checkout counter identifies the price but can also put all your purchase information into a **database**, an electronic storage file for information.

Databases enable stores to carry only the merchandise their local population wants. But because companies routinely trade database information, many retailers know what you buy and from whom you buy it. Thus they can send you catalogs and other direct mail advertising offering the kind of products you might want, as indicated by your past purchases. We discuss other ways businesses use technology to be responsive to consumers throughout the text.

Unfortunately, the legitimate collection of personal customer information also opens the door to identity theft. **Identity theft** is the obtaining of individuals' personal information, such as Social Security and credit card numbers, for illegal purposes. The Federal Trade Commission says millions of U.S. consumers are victims of identity theft each year. What you should learn from these examples is to limit those to whom you give personal information. You also need antivirus software on your computer as well as a firewall and antispyware software.[23] You may also want to monitor your credit report. It is important for you to understand identity theft, security, privacy, stability, and other important IT issues.

> **database**
> An electronic storage file for information.

> **identity theft**
> The obtaining of individuals' personal information, such as Social Security and credit card numbers, for illegal purposes.

LEARNING goal 5

Demonstrate how businesses can meet and beat competition.

The Competitive Environment

Competition among businesses has never been greater. Some have found a competitive edge by focusing on quality. The goal for many companies is zero defects—no mistakes in making the product. However, even achieving a rate of zero defects isn't enough to stay competitive in world markets. Companies now have to offer both high-quality products and good value—that is, outstanding service at competitive prices.

Competing by Exceeding Customer Expectations   Today's customers want not only good quality at low prices but great service as well. Every manufacturing and service organization in the world should have a sign over its door telling its workers that the customer is king. Business is becoming customer-driven, not management-driven as often occurred in the past. Successful organizations must now listen more closely to customers to determine their wants and needs, and then adjust the firm's products, policies, and practices accordingly. We will explore these ideas in more depth in Chapter 13.

Competing by Restructuring and Empowerment   To meet the needs of customers, firms must give their frontline workers—for example, office clerks, front-desk people at hotels, and salespeople—the responsibility, authority, freedom, training, and equipment they need to respond quickly to customer requests. They also must allow workers to make other decisions essential to producing high-quality goods and services. The process is called **empowerment**, and we'll be talking about it throughout this book.

As many companies have discovered, it sometimes takes years to restructure an organization so that managers can and will give up some of their authority, and employees will assume more responsibility. We'll discuss such organizational changes in Chapter 8.

empowerment
Giving frontline workers the responsibility, authority, freedom, training, and equipment they need to respond quickly to customer requests.

LEARNING goal 6

Analyze the social changes affecting businesses.

demography
The statistical study of the human population with regard to its size, density, and other characteristics such as age, race, gender, and income.

The Social Environment

Demography is the statistical study of the human population with regard to its size, density, and other characteristics such as age, race, gender, and income. In this text, we're particularly interested in the demographic trends that most affect businesses and career choices. The U.S. population is going through major changes that are dramatically affecting how people live, where they live, what they buy, and how they spend their time. Furthermore, tremendous population shifts are leading to new opportunities for some firms and to declining opportunities for others. For example, there are many more retired workers than in the past, creating new markets for all kinds of goods and services.[24]

Managing Diversity   *Diversity* has come to mean much more than recruiting and keeping minority and female employees. Diversity efforts now include seniors, people with disabilities, homosexuals, atheists, extroverts, introverts, married people, singles, and the devout. It also means dealing sensitively with workers and cultures around the world.

Legal and illegal immigrants have had a dramatic effect on many cities. Schools and hospitals have been especially affected. Some local governments are making every effort to adapt, including changing signs, brochures, websites, and forms to include other languages. Has your city experienced such changes? What are some of the impacts you've noticed?

The U.S. boasts enormous ethnic and racial diversity. Its workforce is also widely diverse in terms of age, which means managers must adopt to the generational demographics of the workplace. What are some challenges of working with someone much younger or much older than yourself?

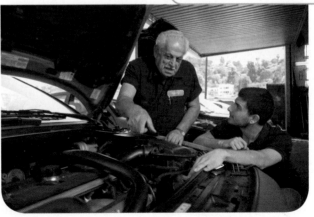

The Increase in the Number of Older Citizens   People ages 65 to 74 are currently the richest demographic group in the United States. They thus represent a lucrative market for companies involved with food service, transportation, entertainment, education, lodging, and so on. By 2020, the percentage of the population over 60 will be 22.8 percent (versus

16 percent in 2000). What do these changes mean for you and for businesses in the future? Think of the products and services that middle-aged and elderly people will need—medicine, nursing homes, assisted-living facilities, adult day care, home health care, recreation, and the like—and you'll see opportunities for successful businesses of the 21st century. Don't rule out computer games and Internet services, even Wii. Businesses that cater to older consumers will have the opportunity for exceptional growth in the near future. The market is huge.[25]

On the other hand, retired people will be draining the economy of wealth. Social Security has become a major issue. The pay-as-you-go system (in which workers today pay the retirement benefits for today's retirees) operated just fine in 1940, when 42 workers supported each retiree; but by 1960, there were only 5 workers per retiree, and today, as the baby-boom generation (born between 1946 and 1964) begins to retire, that number is under 3 and dropping. In addition, the government has been spending the accumulated Social Security money instead of leaving it in a Social Security account.

Soon, less money will be coming into Social Security than will be going out. The government will have to do something to make up for the shortfall: raise taxes, reduce Social Security benefits (e.g., raise the retirement age at which people qualify for payments), reduce spending elsewhere (e.g., in other social programs like Medicare or Medicaid), or borrow on the world market.

In short, paying Social Security to senior citizens in the future will draw huge amounts of money from the working population. That is why there is so much discussion in the media today about what to do with Social Security.

The Increase in the Number of Single-Parent Families   It is a tremendous task to work full-time and raise a family. Thus, the rapid growth of single-parent households has also had a major effect on businesses. Single parents, including those forced by welfare rules to return to work after a certain benefit period, have encouraged businesses to implement programs such as family leave (giving workers time off to attend to a sick child or elder relative) and flextime (allowing workers to arrive or leave at selected times). You will read about such programs in more detail in Chapter 11.

More and more working families consist of single parents who must juggle the demands of a job and responsibilities of raising children. What can managers do to try to retain valued employees who face such challenges?

LEARNING goal 7

Identify what businesses must do to meet global challenges, including war and terrorism.

The Global Environment

The global environment of business is so important that we show it as surrounding all other environmental influences (see again Figure 1.3). Two important changes here are the growth of global competition and the increase of free trade among nations.

World trade, or *globalization,* has grown thanks to the development of efficient distribution systems (we'll talk about these in Chapter 15) and communication advances such as the Internet. Globalization has greatly improved living standards around the world. China and India have become major U.S. competitors. Lenovo, a Chinese firm, bought IBM's PC unit. Shop at Walmart and most other U.S. retail stores, and you can't help but notice the number of "Made in China" stickers you see. Call for computer help, and you are as likely to be talking with someone in India as someone in the United States.

World trade has its benefits and costs. You'll read much more about its importance in Chapter 3 and in the Reaching Beyond Our Borders boxes throughout the text.

War and Terrorism   The wars in Iraq and Afghanistan have drawn billions of dollars from the U.S. economy. Some companies—like those that make bullets, tanks, and uniforms—have benefited greatly. Others, however, have lost workers to the armed forces, and still others (e.g., tourism) have grown more slowly as money has been diverted to the war effort. The threat of other wars and terrorism leads the government to spend even more money on the military. Such expenditures are subject to much debate, especially as the United States responds to an economic recession. Note the increased unrest in the world as people in other nations are demanding more freedom.

The threat of terrorism also adds greatly to organizational costs, including the cost of insurance. In fact, some firms are finding it difficult to get insurance against terrorist attacks. Security, too, is costly. Airlines, for example, have had to install stronger cockpit doors and add more passenger screening devices.

Like all citizens, businesspeople benefit from a peaceful and prosperous world. One way to lessen international tensions is to foster global economic growth among both profit-making and nonprofit organizations.

How Global Changes Affect You   As businesses expand to serve global markets, new jobs will be created in both manufacturing and service industries. Global trade also means global competition. The students who will prosper will be those prepared for the markets of tomorrow. Rapid changes create a need for continuous learning, so be prepared to continue your education throughout your career. You'll have every reason to be optimistic about job opportunities in the future if you prepare yourself well.

The Ecological Environment   Few issues have captured the attention of the international business community more than climate change. **Climate change** is the movement of the temperature of the planet up or down over time. The issue now is global warming, but the issue may become global cooling. Some of the world's largest firms—including General Electric, Coca-Cola, Shell, Nestlé, DuPont, Johnson & Johnson, British Airways, and Shanghai Electric— say the evidence for climate change is overwhelming. Saving energy and producing products that cause less harm to the environment is a trend called **greening**.[26] Greening has become such a pervasive issue that we devote boxes to that subject throughout the text. (See the nearby Thinking Green box for things you can do to contribute to the cause.)

climate change
The movement of the temperature of the planet up or down over time.

greening
The trend toward saving energy and producing products that cause less harm to the environment.

progress assessment

- What are four ways the government can foster entrepreneurship?
- What's the difference between effectiveness, efficiency, and productivity?
- What is *empowerment?*
- What are some of the major issues affecting the economy today?

Getting Involved Personally

There is little doubt humans can take action to protect the environment. What can we do now to start?

It's not necessary to change your lifestyle radically in order to make a difference. Simply heating or cooling your apartment or house more efficiently is a good start. Why not buy a reusable grocery bag? You can recycle paper and containers. You can walk or ride a bike instead of driving. You can reduce your use of electrical equipment and of water (pumping water takes a lot of electricity). Buy produce that is grown locally to save the energy used in shipping food from faraway places. If you're in the market for a car, you could "go green" by buying a hybrid or a small, fuel-efficient car.

The idea is to become more ecologically aware and join others throughout the world in using less energy and emitting less carbon into the atmosphere. Everyone benefits when the air is cleaner. That's part of what the green movement is all about.

LEARNING goal 8

Review how past trends are being repeated in the present and what those trends mean for tomorrow's college graduates.

THE EVOLUTION OF U.S. BUSINESS

Businesses in the United States have become so productive that they need fewer workers than ever before to produce goods. If global competition and improved technology are putting skilled people out of work, should we be concerned about the prospect of high unemployment rates and low incomes? Where will the jobs be when you graduate? These important questions force us all to look briefly at the U.S. economy and its future.

Progress in the Agricultural and Manufacturing Industries

The United States has experienced strong economic development since the 1800s. The agricultural industry led the way, providing food for the United States and much of the world. Cyrus McCormick's invention of the harvester in 1834, other inventions such as Eli Whitney's cotton gin, and modern improvements on such equipment did much to make large-scale farming successful. Technology has made modern farming so efficient that the number of farmers has dropped from about 33 percent of the population to about 1 percent today. However, average farm size is now about 450 acres versus 160 acres in the past.

Agriculture is still a major industry in the United States. What has changed is that the millions of small farms that existed previously have been replaced by some huge farms, some merely large farms, and some small but highly specialized farms. The loss of farm workers over the past century is not a negative sign. It is instead an indication that U.S. agricultural workers are the most productive in the world.

Most farmers who lost their jobs during the 19th and 20th centuries went to work in factories springing up around the country. Manufacturers, like farms, began using technology like tools and machines to become more productive. Eventually the consequence in manufacturing, as in farming, was the elimination of many jobs.

Again, the loss to society is minimized if the wealth created by increased productivity and efficiency creates new jobs elsewhere—and that's exactly what has happened over the past 50 years. Many workers in the industrial sector found jobs in the growing service sector. Most of those who can't find work today are people who need retraining and education to become qualified for jobs that now exist or will exist in the near future, like building wind farms or making electric automobiles. We'll discuss the manufacturing sector and production in more detail in Chapter 9.

Agriculture is one of the largest and most important industries in the US. Technology has increased productivity and made farmers more efficient, allowing for larger farms. This trend has reduced the price of food for consumers, but has also reduced the number of small, family-run farms. Does the new technology also help smaller farms compete? How?

Progress in Service Industries

In the past, the fastest-growing industries in the United States produced goods like steel, automobiles, and machine tools. Today, the fastest-growing firms provide services in areas like law, health, telecommunications, entertainment, and finance.

Together, services make up about 70 percent of the value of the U.S. economy. Since the mid-1980s, the service industry has generated almost all the increases in employment. Although service-sector growth has slowed, it remains the largest area of growth. Chances are very high that you'll work in a service job at some point in your career. Figure 1.4 lists many service-sector jobs; look it over to see where the careers of the future are likely to be. Retailers like American Eagle are part of the service sector. Each new retail store can create managerial jobs for college graduates.

Another bit of good news is that there are *more* high-paying jobs in the service sector than in the goods-producing sector. High-paying service-sector jobs abound in health care, accounting, finance, entertainment, telecommunications, architecture, law, software engineering, and more. Projections are that some areas of the service sector will grow rapidly, while others may have much slower growth. The strategy for college graduates is to remain flexible, find out where jobs are being created, and move when appropriate.[27]

Your Future in Business

Despite the growth in the service sector we've described above, the service era now seems to be coming to a close as a new era is beginning. We're in the midst of an information-based global revolution that will alter all sectors of the economy: agricultural, industrial, and service. It's exciting to think about the role you'll play in that revolution. You may be a leader who will implement the changes and accept the challenges of world competition based on world quality standards. This book will introduce you to some of the concepts that make such leadership possible, not just in business but also in government agencies and nonprofit organizations. Business can't prosper in the future without the cooperation of government and social leaders throughout the world.

There's much talk about the service sector, but few discussions actually list what it includes. Here's a representative list of services as classified by the government:

Lodging Services

Hotels, rooming houses, and other lodging places
Sporting and recreation camps
Trailer parks and camp sites for transients

Personal Services

Laundries	Child care
Linen supply	Shoe repair
Diaper service	Funeral homes
Carpet cleaning	Tax preparation
Photographic studios	Beauty shops
Health clubs	

Business Services

Accounting	Exterminating
Ad agencies	Employment agencies
Collection agencies	Computer programming
Commercial photography	Research & development labs
Commercial art	Management services
Stenographic services	Public relations
Window cleaning	Detective agencies
Consulting	Interior design
Equipment rental	Web design
Tax preparation	Trash collection

Automotive Repair Services and Garages

Auto rental	Tire retreading
Truck rental	Exhaust system shops
Parking lots	Car washes
Paint shops	Transmission repair

Miscellaneous Repair Services

Radio and television	Welding
Watch	Sharpening
Reupholstery	Septic tank cleaning

Motion Picture Industry

Production	Theaters
Distribution	Drive-ins

Amusement and Recreation Services

Restaurants	Racetracks
Symphony orchestras	Golf courses
Pool halls	Amusement parks
Bowling alleys	Carnivals
Fairs	Ice skating rinks
Botanical gardens	Circuses
Video rentals	Infotainment

Health Services

Physicians	Nursery care
Dentists	Medical labs
Chiropractors	Dental labs

Legal Services

Educational Services

Libraries	Computer schools
Schools	Online schools

Social Services

Child care	Family services
Job training	Elder care

Noncommercial Museums, Art Galleries, and Botanical and Zoological Gardens

Selected Membership Organizations

Business associations	Civic associations

Financial Services

Banking	Real estate agencies
Insurance	Investment firms (brokers)

Miscellaneous Services

Architectural	Surveying
Engineering	Utilities
Telecommunications	Lawn care
Vending	Delivery

figure I.4

WHAT IS THE SERVICE SECTOR?

progress assessment

- What major factor caused people to move from farming to manufacturing and from manufacturing to the service sector?
- What does the future look like for tomorrow's college graduates?

summary

Learning Goal 1. Describe the relationship between profit and risk, and show how businesses and nonprofit organizations can raise the standard of living for all.

- **What is the relationship of businesses' profit to risk assumption?**

Profit is money a business earns above and beyond the money that it spends for salaries and other expenses. Businesspeople make profits by taking risks. *Risk* is the chance an entrepreneur takes of losing time and money on a business that may not prove profitable. A loss occurs when a business's costs and expenses are higher than its revenues.

- **Who are stakeholders, and which stakeholders are most important to a business?**

Stakeholders include customers, employees, stockholders, suppliers, dealers, bankers, the media, people in the local community, environmentalists, and elected government leaders. The goal of business leaders is to try to recognize and respond to the needs of these stakeholders and still make a profit.

Learning Goal 2. Compare and contrast being an entrepreneur and working for others.

- **What are the advantages and disadvantages of entrepreneurship?**

Working for others means getting benefits like paid vacations and health insurance. Entrepreneurs take more risks and lose those benefits. They gain the freedom to make their own decisions, more opportunity, and possible wealth.

- **What are the five factors of production?**

The five factors of production are land, labor, capital, entrepreneurship, and knowledge. Of these, the most important are entrepreneurship and knowledge. Entrepreneurs are people who risk time and money to start and manage a business. What makes rich countries rich today is a combination of *entrepreneurship* and the effective use of *knowledge*.

Learning Goal 3. Analyze the effects of the economic environment and taxes on businesses.

- **What can governments in developing countries do to reduce the risk of starting businesses and thus help entrepreneurs?**

The government may allow private ownership of businesses, pass laws that enable businesspeople to write contracts that are enforceable in court, establish a currency that's tradable in world markets, help to lessen corruption in business and government, and keep taxes and regulations to a minimum. From a business perspective, lower taxes mean lower risks, more growth, and thus more money for workers and the government.

Learning Goal 4. Describe the effects of technology on businesses.

- **How has technology benefited workers, businesses, and consumers?**

Technology enables workers to be more effective, efficient, and productive. *Effectiveness* means doing the right thing in the right way. *Efficiency* means producing items using the least amount of resources. *Productivity* is the amount of output you generate given the amount of input (e.g., hours worked).

Learning Goal 5. Demonstrate how businesses can meet and beat competition.

- **What are some ways in which businesses meet and beat competition?**
Some companies have found a competitive edge by focusing on making high-quality products, all the way to zero defects. Companies also aim to exceed customer expectations. Often that means *empowering* frontline workers by giving them more training and more responsibility and authority.

Learning Goal 6. Analyze the social changes affecting businesses.

- **How have social changes affected businesses?**
Diversity has come to mean much more than recruiting and keeping minority and female employees. Diversity efforts now include seniors, disabled people, homosexuals, atheists, extroverts, introverts, married people, singles, and the devout. It also means dealing sensitively with workers and cultures around the world. Providing Social Security benefits to senior citizens in the future will draw huge amounts of money from the working population. That is why there is so much discussion about Social Security in the media today.

Learning Goal 7. Identify what businesses must do to meet global challenges, including war and terrorism.

- **Which countries are creating the greatest challenges?**
China and India are two major competitors.
- **What will be the impacts of future wars and terrorism?**
Some businesses, such as those in the defense industry, may prosper. Others, such as tourism, may suffer. One way to minimize world tensions is to help less developed countries to become more prosperous.

Learning Goal 8. Review how past trends are being repeated in the present and what those trends mean for tomorrow's college graduates.

- **What is the history of our economic development in the United States, and what does it tell us about the future?**
Agricultural workers displaced by improved farm technology went to work in factories. Improved manufacturing productivity and increased competition from foreign firms contributed to the development of a service economy in the United States. The service era is now giving way to an information-based global revolution that will affect all sectors of the economy. The secret to long-term success in such an economy is flexibility and continuing education to be prepared for the opportunities that are sure to arise.
- **What job opportunities for college graduates exist in the service sector?**
Check over Figure 1.4, which outlines the service sector. That is where you are most likely to find the fast-growing firms of the future.

key terms

business 4	**e-commerce** 15	**greening** 19
business environment 11	**empowerment** 17	**identity theft** 16
climate change 19	**entrepreneur** 4	**loss** 4
database 16	**factors of production** 9	**nonprofit organization** 7
demography 17	**goods** 4	**outsourcing** 7

productivity I5

profit 4

quality of life 6

revenue 4

risk 5

services 4

stakeholders 6

standard of living 5

technology I4

critical thinking

Imagine you are thinking of starting a restaurant in your community. Answer the following questions:

1. Who will be the various stakeholders of your business?

2. What are some of the things you can do to benefit your community other than providing jobs and tax revenue?

3. How will you establish good relationships with your suppliers? With your employees?

4. Do you see any conflict between your desire to be as profitable as possible and your desire to pay employees a living wage?

5. Which of the environmental factors outlined in this chapter might have the biggest impact on your business? How?

developing workplace skills

1. Poll the class and determine which students believe that climate change is primarily caused by humans and which believe that other factors, such as climate cycles or sun spots, are the primary cause. Discuss what students can do to minimize human effects on the environment regardless of the primary causes of climate change. Are there any negative consequences to trying to minimize humans' impact on the environment?

2. Imagine you are a local businessperson who has to deal with the issue of outsourcing. You want to begin with the facts. How many, if any, jobs have been lost to outsourcing in your area? Are there any foreign firms in your area that are creating jobs (insourcing)? You may want to use the Internet to find the data you need.

3. What indicates that you and other people in the United States have a high standard of living? What are some signs that maintaining such a high standard of living may have a negative impact on quality of life?

4. Look through your local phone book to find five businesses that provide services in your area. List those businesses and, for each, describe how social trends might affect them in both positive and negative ways. Be prepared to explain your descriptions.

5. Form into teams of four or five and discuss the technological and e-commerce revolutions. How many students now shop for goods and services online? What have been their experiences? What other high-tech equipment do they use (iPhones, iPads, laptops, etc.)?

taking it to the net

Purpose

To learn what changes are occurring in the business environment today and how those changes are affecting businesses.

Exercise

1. Go to the National Taxpayers Union website (www.ntu.org) "Who Pays Income Taxes? See Who Pays What." Study the tables showing what percent of taxes the various income groups pay. Do you think that businesspeople pay their fair share? What percent of taxes does the top 1 percent of earners pay? What about the top 5 percent? The lowest 50 percent? How do such tax rates affect incentives to become a successful entrepreneur?

2. Go to the Census Bureau's website (www.census.gov) and learn what the population of the United States is at this moment. While at the site, you may want to look up the population in your town or city. Explore what other data are available at this site. What trends seem most important to you and to businesspeople in general?

3. Do a Google search for "business blogs" and check out some of the available results. Go to one of the blogs that seems interesting to you and write a brief paragraph about it—including such things as who sponsors it, who contributes the posts, and what other features it has—and how it may help a student in an introductory business course.

casing the web

To access the case "Moving Up the Corporate Ladder," visit **www.mhhe.com/ub10e**

video case

To access the video case featuring Redbox, visit **www.mhhe.com/ub10e**

Understanding
ECONOMICS and How It
AFFECTS Business

2

LEARNING
goals

After you have read and studied this chapter, you should be able to

1 Explain basic economics.

2 Explain what capitalism is and how free markets work.

3 Compare socialism and communism.

4 Analyze the trend toward mixed economies.

5 Describe the economic system of the United States, including the significance of key economic indicators (especially GDP), productivity, and the business cycle.

6 Contrast fiscal policy and monetary policy, and explain how each affects the economy.

profile

If you listened to much of the recent debates about the state of the nation's economy and what to do about it, you've probably heard people mention Keynes or Keynesian economics and wondered what they were talking about. John Maynard Keynes (pronounced *Canes*) was one of the economists who had a great influence on U.S. economic policy. It was Keynes who advocated stabilizing the economy by the use of fiscal policy (policy related to taxes and spending). He believed that if the economy was in a recession, the government should increase *spending* (e.g., on infrastructure—roads, bridges, schools, and utilities) and cut taxes in order to stimulate the economy. The goal of cutting taxes would be to increase consumer spending to revive businesses. Conversely, when the economy seems to be growing too fast and inflation results, Keynesian theory suggests cutting back on government spending and increasing taxes. Such government intervention is supposed to be a short-term solution to wide swings in the business cycle. Once the economy was stabilized, Keynes believed, free economic principles could be restored.

Keynes published his most famous book, *The General Theory of Employment, Interest and Money,* in 1936. Until that time U.S. economic thinking was dominated by Adam Smith's classic economics. Smith believed that the economy would automatically function at full employment if there was minimal government intervention. The depression of the 1930s changed that view, and Keynesian economics took over.

While Keynesian economics has been in and out of favor since the 1930s, it was Keynesian theory that Presidents Bush and Obama had in mind when they attempted to stimulate the economy by spending money. While there are signs that the economy is now on the road to recovery, the $787 billion stimulus package did not lead to the job growth expected, and unemployment stayed about 9 percent.

The economic environment is critical to the success of business. That is what this chapter is all about. You will learn to compare different economic systems to see the benefits and the drawbacks of each. You will learn how the free-market system of the United States works. And you will learn more about what makes some countries rich and other countries poor. By the end of the chapter, you should understand the direct effect economic systems have on the wealth and happiness of communities throughout the world.

Sources: Paul Johnson, "There Is No Keynesian Miracle," *Forbes,* March 1, 2010; Daniel Fisher, "Keynes Who?" *Forbes,* August 9, 2010; Peter Coy, "The Keynes Solution," *Bloomberg Businessweek,* November 1–November 7, 2010; and Peter Coy, "Keynes vs. Alesina; Alesina Who?" *Bloomberg Businessweeek,* July 5–July 11, 2010.

Getting to Know

X *John Maynard Keynes*

Economist

This organization lends small amounts of money to people in poor countries. For example, it loaned a woman in Uganda enough to buy a refrigerator. She was able to sell fresh food from the refrigerator and make enough money for her family to succeed. Name this organization. (The answer is in the chapter.)

LEARNING goal 1

Explain basic economics.

HOW ECONOMIC CONDITIONS AFFECT BUSINESSES

Compared to, say, Mexico, the United States is a relatively wealthy country. Why? Why is South Korea comparatively wealthy and North Korea suffering economically, with many of its people starving?[1] Such questions are part of the subject of economics. In this chapter, we explore the various economic systems of the world and how they either promote or hinder business growth, the creation of wealth, and a higher quality of life for all.

A major part of the United States' business success in the past was due to an economic and social climate that allowed most businesses to operate freely. People were free to start a business anywhere, and just as free to fail and start again. That freedom motivated people to try until they succeeded because the rewards were often so great.[2]

Any change in the U.S. economic or political system has a major influence on the success of the business system. For example, the recent increase in government involvement in business will have an economic effect.[3] What that effect will be in the long run, however, remains to be seen.

Global economics and global politics also have a major influence on businesses in the United States. Therefore, to understand business, you must also understand basic economics and politics.

What Is Economics?

Economics is the study of how society chooses to employ resources to produce goods and services and distribute them for consumption among various competing groups and individuals. There are two major branches of economics: **macroeconomics** looks at the operation of a nation's economy as a whole (the whole United States), and **microeconomics** looks at the behavior of people and organizations in markets for particular products or services. A question in macroeconomics might be: What should the United States do to lower its national debt?[4] Macroeconomic topics in this chapter include gross

economics
The study of how society chooses to employ resources to produce goods and services and distribute them for consumption among various competing groups and individuals.

microeconomics
The part of economics study that looks at the behavior of people and organizations in particular markets.

macroeconomics
The part of economics study that looks at the operation of a nation's economy as a whole.

The economic contrast is remarkable. Business is booming in Seoul, South Korea (pictured on the left). But North Korea, a communist country, is not doing well, as the picture on the right of thousands of workers using old-fashioned tools in a work-for-food program shows. What do you think accounts for the dramatic differences in the economies of these two neighboring countries?

domestic product (GDP), the unemployment rate, and price indexes. A question in microeconomics might be: Why do people buy smaller cars when gas prices go up?

Some economists define economics as the study of the allocation of *scarce* resources. They believe resources need to be carefully divided among people, usually by the government. However, there's no way to maintain peace and prosperity in the world by merely dividing the resources we have today among the existing nations. There aren't enough known resources to do that. **Resource development** is the study of how to increase resources (say, by getting oil from shale and tar sands) and create conditions that will make better use of them (like recycling and conservation).[5]

Businesses can contribute to an economic system by inventing products that greatly increase available resources. For example, they can discover new energy sources (hydrogen fuel for autos), new ways of growing food (hydroponics), and new ways of creating needed goods and services (nanotechnology). Mariculture, or raising fish in pens out in the ocean, could lead to more food for everyone and more employment. It is believed that the United States could monopolize the shrimp industry using aquaculture.[6] Now we import about a billion pounds of shrimp a year.[7] The nearby Thinking Green box explores some new ventures that have been created to help lessen climate change.

The Secret to Creating a Wealthy Economy

Imagine the world when kings and other rich landowners had most of the wealth, and the majority of the people were peasants. The peasants had many children, and it may have seemed a natural conclusion that if things went on as usual there would soon be too many people and not enough food and other

resource development
The study of how to increase resources and to create the conditions that will make better use of those resources.

Bringing in the Green with Green Products

Adjusting to climate changes creates as many opportunities as it does challenges. Companies that help lower carbon emissions can prosper as people become more concerned about climate change. Toyota has had success selling its hybrid Prius, and most automakers now offer similar hybrids, which get better mileage with less pollution than gas-only vehicles. Some all-electric cars are now available. And several firms are offering cars half the size of regular cars—to get better fuel economy.

Farmers are growing more corn and other crops for use as biofuels. That creates more demand for tractors and other farm equipment, and helps the economy grow. It also causes food prices to skyrocket. Given these outcomes, would you recommend an increase in the use of biofuels?

It's amazing what you find when you begin looking for greener businesses There are now "green" tennis shoes and "green" jeans. Have you ever seen hot-dog wrappers blowing around the ballpark? In the future, they'll be recycled. *Reduce. Reuse. Recycle.* These have become the tenets of a greener, more environmentally responsive lifestyle.

Sources: Christina Binkley, "How Green Is My Sneaker?" *The Wall Street Journal*, July 22, 2010; Jason B. White, "The Confusing Shades of Green Cars," *The Wall Street Journal,* October 13, 2010; and Paul H. Rubin, "Why Is the Gulf Cleanup So Slow?" *The Wall Street Journal,* July 2, 2010.

resources. Economist Thomas Malthus made this argument in the late 1700s and early 1800s, leading the writer Thomas Carlyle to call economics "the dismal science."

Followers of Malthus today (who are called neo-Malthusians) still believe there are too many people in the world and that the solution to poverty is radical birth control, including forced abortions and sterilization. The latest world statistics, however, show population growing more slowly than expected. In some industrial countries—like Japan, Germany, Italy, Russia, and the United States—population growth may be so slow that eventually there will be too many old people and too few young people to care for them.[8] In the developing world, on the other hand, population will climb relatively quickly and may lead to greater poverty and more unrest. Studies about the effects of population growth on the economy are part of macroeconomics.

Some macroeconomists believe that a large population, especially an educated one, can be a valuable resource. You've probably heard the saying "Give a man a fish and you feed him for a day, but teach a man to fish and you feed him for a lifetime." You can add to that: "Teach a person to start a fish farm, and he or she will be able to feed a village for a lifetime." *The secret to economic development is contained in this last statement.* Business owners provide jobs and economic growth for their employees and communities as well as for themselves.

The challenge for macroeconomists is to determine what makes some countries relatively wealthy and other countries relatively poor, and then to implement policies and programs that lead to increased prosperity for everyone in all countries. One way to begin understanding this challenge is to consider the theories of Adam Smith.

New ways of producing goods and services add resources to the economy and create more employment. Fish farms, for instance, create both food and jobs. Can you think of other innovations that can help increase economic development?

Adam Smith and the Creation of Wealth

Rather than believing fixed resources had to be divided among competing groups and individuals, Scottish economist Adam Smith envisioned creating more resources so that everyone could become wealthier. Smith's book *An Inquiry into the Nature and Causes of the Wealth of Nations* (often called simply *The Wealth of Nations*) was published in 1776.

Smith believed *freedom* was vital to the survival of any economy, especially the freedom to own land or property and to keep the profits from working the land or running a business.[9] He believed people will work long and hard if they have incentives for doing so—that is, if they know they'll be rewarded. As a result of those efforts, the economy will prosper, with plenty of food and all kinds of products available to everyone.[10] Smith's ideas were later challenged by Malthus and others who believed economic conditions would only get worse, but Smith, not Malthus, is considered the *father of modern economics.*

How Businesses Benefit the Community

In Adam Smith's view, businesspeople don't necessarily deliberately set out to help others. They work primarily for their own prosperity and growth. Yet as people try to improve their own situation in life, Smith said, their efforts serve as an "invisible hand" that helps the economy grow and prosper through the production of needed goods, services, and ideas. Thus, the phrase **invisible hand** is used to describe the process that turns self-directed gain into social and economic benefits for all.

How do people working in their own self-interest produce goods, services, and wealth for others? The only way farmers can become wealthy is to sell some of their crops to others. To become even wealthier, they have to hire workers to produce more food. So the farmers' self-centered efforts to become wealthy lead to jobs for some and food for almost all. Think about that process for a minute, because it is critical to understanding economic growth in the United States and other free countries. The same principles apply to everything from clothing to houses to iPads.

invisible hand
A phrase coined by Adam Smith to describe the process that turns self-directed gain into social and economic benefits for all.

According to Adam Smith's theory, business owners are motivated to work hard because they know they will earn, and keep, the rewards of their labor. When they prosper, as the owner of this store has, they are able to add employees and grow, indirectly helping the community and the larger economy grow in the process. What might motivate you to start your own business?

Smith assumed that as people became wealthier, they would naturally reach out to help the less fortunate in the community. That has not always happened. Today, however, many businesspeople are becoming more concerned about social issues and their obligation to return to society some of what they've earned.[11] As we mentioned in Chapter 1, it is important for businesses to be ethical as well as generous. Unethical practices undermine the whole economic system. The nearby Making Ethical Decisions box explores what universities are now doing about this.

progress assessment

- What is the difference between macroeconomics and microeconomics?
- What is better for an economy than teaching a man to fish?
- What does Adam Smith's term *invisible hand* mean? How does the invisible hand create wealth for a country?

LEARNING goal 2

Explain what capitalism is and how free markets work.

UNDERSTANDING FREE-MARKET CAPITALISM

Basing their ideas on free-market principles such as those of Adam Smith, businesspeople in the United States, Europe, Japan, Canada, and other countries began to create more wealth than ever before. They hired others to work on their farms and in their factories, and their nations began to prosper as a result. Businesspeople soon became the wealthiest people in society.

However, great disparities in wealth remained or even increased. Many businesspeople owned large homes and fancy carriages while most workers lived in humble surroundings. Nonetheless, there was always the promise of better times. One way to be really wealthy was to start a successful business of your own. Of course, it wasn't that easy—it never has been. Then and now, you have to accumulate some money to buy or start a business, and you have to work long hours to make it grow. But the opportunities are there.[12]

The economic system that has led to wealth creation in much of the world is known as capitalism.[13] Under **capitalism** all or most of the factors of production and distribution—such as land, factories, railroads, and stores—are owned by individuals. They are operated for profit, and businesspeople, not government officials, decide what to produce and how much, what to charge, and how much to pay workers. They also decide whether to produce goods in their own countries or have them made in other countries. No country is purely capitalist, however. Often the government gets involved in issues such as determining minimum wages, setting farm prices, and lending money to some failing businesses—as it does in the United States. But capitalism is the *foundation* of the U.S. economic system, and of the economies of England, Australia, Canada, and most other industrialized nations. There have been many suggestions as to how the United States could improve its capitalist system, especially given the recession that began on 2008.[14]

Some countries are practicing state capitalism. *State capitalism* is where the state runs some businesses instead of private owners. The most obvious example is China, but the same concepts are being used in Russia and some of the Arab nations of the Middle East.[15] These countries have experienced some success using capitalist principles, but the future is still uncertain.[16]

The root word of *capitalism* is "capital." The Spotlight on Small Business box on page 36 shows how a little capital can help small businesses grow in the poorest countries in the world.

> **capitalism**
> An economic system in which all or most of the factors of production and distribution are privately owned and operated for profit.

The Foundations of Capitalism

Under free-market capitalism people have four basic rights:

1. *The right to own private property.* This is the most fundamental of all rights under capitalism. Private ownership means that individuals can buy, sell, and use land, buildings, machinery, inventions, and other forms of property. They can also pass property on to their children. Would farmers work as hard if they didn't own the land and couldn't keep the profits from what they earned? More than 90 percent of Egyptians hold their property without legal title. This is one reason they can't build wealth and why they protested in the streets in 2011.[17]

2. *The right to own a business and keep all that business's profits.* Recall from Chapter 1 that profits equal revenues minus expenses (salaries, materials, taxes). Profits act as important incentives for business owners.

3. *The right to freedom of competition.* Within certain guidelines established by the government, individuals are free to compete with other individuals or businesses in selling and promoting goods and services.

4. *The right to freedom of choice.* People are free to choose where they want to work and what career they want to follow. Other choices people are free to make include where to live and what to buy or sell.

The right to own private property and the right to own a business and keep its profits are two of the fundamental rights that exist in the economic system called free-market capitalism. Would either of these rights be viable without the other?

A Small Loan Can Make a Big Difference

One way people in industrialized countries can help people in developing countries is to create a local "bank" that lends money to budding entrepreneurs so they can begin or expand their business. The entrepreneurs must pay the money back, with interest, and often must keep some money in the bank. Such banks don't necessarily have to be in a bank building. Village women often assume the role of banker and decide which women will get the loans. The "bankers" meet in a community building of some sort.

Such banks are sponsored by the Foundation for International Community Assistance (FINCA). In its 10-year history, FINCA has loaned more than $447 million to over 600,000 small-scale entrepreneurs in some of the world's poorest countries. Its borrowers have a 97.6 percent loan repayment rate.

The story of one small entrepreneur will help you understand the process. Pros Magaga lives in Kampala, Uganda. She had a tiny shop in town, but it carried very little inventory. She did not make enough to send her four children to school or to feed them more than once a day. FINCA lent her $50; she used it to buy a refrigerator, which allowed her to carry fresh foods and cold snacks. Later she added a freezer. Now her children are all in school, and the family enjoys two meals a day. Magaga has built a small home with two rooms and plans to add another room soon. She can borrow more money from FINCA because she has already paid back her $50 loan.

Sources: Ruth David, "In a Microfinance Boom, Echoes of Subprime," *Bloomberg Businessweek,* June 21–June 27, 2010; and Daniel Fisher, "Bullish on Harare," *Forbes,* November 22, 2010.

One benefit of the four basic rights of capitalism is that people are willing to take more risks than they might otherwise. President Franklin Roosevelt believed four additional freedoms were essential to economic success: freedom of speech and expression, freedom to worship in your own way, freedom from want, and freedom from fear. Do you see the benefits of these additional freedoms?

Now let's explore how the free market works. What role do consumers play in the process? How do businesses learn what consumers need and want? These questions and more are answered next.

How Free Markets Work

A free market is one in which decisions about what and how much to produce are made by the market—by buyers and sellers negotiating prices for goods and services. You and I and other consumers send signals to tell producers what to make, how many, in what color, and so on. We do that by choosing to buy (or not to buy) certain products and services.

For example, if all of us decided we wanted T-shirts supporting our favorite baseball team, the clothing industry would respond in certain ways. Manufacturers and retailers would increase the price of those T-shirts, because they know people are willing to pay more for the shirts they want. They would also realize they could make more money by making more of those T-shirts. Thus, they have an incentive to pay workers to start earlier and end later. Further, the number of companies making T-shirts would increase. How many T-shirts they make depends on how many we request or buy in the stores. Prices and quantities will continue to change as the number of T-shirts we buy changes.

The same process occurs with most other products. The *price* tells producers how much to produce. If something is wanted but isn't available, the price tends to go up until someone begins making more of that product, sells the ones already on hand, or makes a substitute. As a consequence, there's rarely a long-term shortage of goods in the United States.

How Prices Are Determined

In a free market, prices are not determined by sellers; they are determined by buyers and sellers negotiating in the marketplace. A seller may want to receive $50 for a T-shirt, but the quantity buyers demand at that high price may be quite low. If the seller lowers the price, the quantity demanded is likely to increase. How is a price determined that is acceptable to both buyers and sellers? The answer is found in the microeconomic concepts of supply and demand. We shall explore both next.

The Economic Concept of Supply

Supply refers to the quantities of products manufacturers or owners are willing to sell at different prices at a specific time. Generally speaking, the amount supplied will increase as the price increases, because sellers can make more money with a higher price.

Economists show this relationship between quantity supplied and price on a graph. Figure 2.1 shows a simple supply curve for T-shirts. The price of the shirts in dollars is shown vertically on the left of the graph. The quantity of shirts sellers are willing to supply is shown horizontally at the bottom of the graph. The various points on the curve indicate how many T-shirts sellers would provide at different prices. For example, at a price of $5 a shirt, a T-shirt vendor would provide only 5 shirts, but at $50 a shirt the vendor would supply 50 shirts. The supply curve indicates the relationship between the price and the quantity supplied. All things being equal, the higher the price, the more the vendor will be willing to supply.

The Economic Concept of Demand

Demand refers to the quantity of products that people are willing to buy at different prices at a specific time. Generally speaking, the quantity demanded will increase as the price decreases. Again, we can show the relationship between price and quantity demanded in a graph. Figure 2.2 shows a simple demand curve for T-shirts. The various points on the graph indicate the quantity demanded at various prices. For example, at $45, buyers demand just 5 shirts, but at $5, the quantity demanded would increase to 35 shirts. All things being equal, the lower the price, the more buyers are willing to buy.

The Equilibrium Point, or Market Price

You might realize from Figures 2.1 and 2.2 that the key factor in determining the quantities supplied and demanded is *price*. If you were to lay the two graphs one on top of the other, the supply curve and the demand curve would cross where quantity demanded and quantity supplied are equal. Figure 2.3 illustrates that point. At a price of $15, the quantity of T-shirts demanded and the quantity supplied are equal (25 shirts). That crossing point is known as the *equilibrium point* or *equilibrium price*. In the long run, that price will become the market price. **Market price**, then, is determined by supply and demand. It is the price toward which the market will trend.

supply
The quantity of products that manufacturers or owners are willing to sell at different prices at a specific time.

demand
The quantity of products that people are willing to buy at different prices at a specific time.

market price
The price determined by supply and demand.

figure 2.1

THE SUPPLY CURVE AT VARIOUS PRICES
The supply curve rises from left to right. Think it through. The higher the price of T-shirts goes (the vertical axis), the more sellers will be willing to supply.

figure 2.2

THE DEMAND CURVE AT VARIOUS PRICES
This is a simple demand curve showing the quantity of T-shirts demanded at different prices. The demand curve falls from left to right. It is easy to understand why. The lower the price of T-shirts, the higher the quantity demanded.

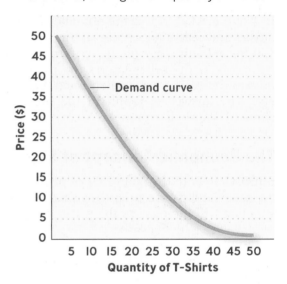

figure 2.3

THE EQUILIBRIUM POINT
The place where quantity demanded and quantity supplied meet is called the equilibrium point. When we put both the supply and demand curves on the same graph, we find that they intersect at a price where the quantity supplied and the quantity demanded are equal. In the long run, the market price will tend toward the equilibrium point.

Proponents of a free market argue that, because supply and demand interactions determine prices, there is no need for the government to set prices. If quantity supplied exceeds quantity demanded, the resulting surplus signals sellers to lower the price. If shortages develop because the quantity supplied is less than quantity demanded, it signals sellers to increase the price. Eventually, supply will again equal demand if nothing interferes with market forces.

When supplies of oil were lower because of the Gulf oil spill, for instance, the price of gasoline went up. When supplies were again plentiful, the price of gas fell a little. The price of gas rose again when there was turmoil in the Middle East (e.g., Libya) and the supply of oil was suspect. Note, too, how many alternative fuel sources (wind, solar, tar sands shale gas, etc.) were tried when the price of gas approached $4 a gallon.[18]

In countries without a free market, there is no mechanism to reveal to businesses (via price) what to produce and in what amounts, so there are often shortages (not enough products) or surpluses (too many products). In such countries, the government decides what to produce and in what quantity, but without price signals it has no way of knowing what the proper quantities are. Furthermore, when the government interferes in otherwise free markets, such as when it subsidizes farm goods, surpluses and shortages may develop. Competition differs in free markets, too. We shall explore that concept next.

The economic concept of demand measures the quantities of goods and services that people are willing to buy. Judging from this photo of people waiting to buy the iPad on the first day it was available for sale, how would you describe the demand for this product? Did the introduction of the iPad 2 generate similar demand?

Competition within Free Markets

Economists generally agree there are four different degrees of competition: (1) perfect competition, (2) monopolistic competition, (3) oligopoly, and (4) monopoly.

Perfect competition exists when there are many sellers in a market and none is large enough to dictate the price of a product. Sellers' products appear to be identical, such as agricultural products like apples, corn, and potatoes. There are no true examples of perfect competition. Today, government price supports and drastic reductions in the number of farms make it hard to argue that even farming represents perfect competition.

Under **monopolistic competition** a large number of sellers produce very similar products that buyers nevertheless perceive as different, such as hot dogs, sodas, personal computers, and T-shirts. Product differentiation—the attempt to make buyers think similar products are different in some way—is a key to success. Think about what that means. Through advertising, branding, and packaging, sellers try to convince buyers that their products are different from competitors', though they may be very similar or even interchangeable. The fast-food industry, with its pricing battles among hamburger offerings and the like, offers a good example of monopolistic competition.[19]

An **oligopoly** is a degree of competition in which just a few sellers dominate a market, as we see in tobacco, gasoline, automobiles, aluminum, and aircraft. One reason some industries remain in the hands of a few sellers is that the initial investment required to enter the business often is tremendous. Think, for example, of how much it would cost to start a new airplane manufacturing facility.

In an oligopoly, products from different companies tend to be priced about the same. The reason is simple: Intense price competition would lower profits for everyone, since a price cut by one producer would most likely be matched by the others. As in monopolistic competition, product differentiation, rather than price, is usually the major factor in market success in an oligopoly. Note, for example, that most cereals are priced about the same, as are soft drinks.

perfect competition
The degree of competition in which there are many sellers in a market and none is large enough to dictate the price of a product.

monopolistic competition
The degree of competition in which a large number of sellers produce very similar products that buyers nevertheless perceive as different.

oligopoly
A degree of competition in which just a few sellers dominate the market.

Thus, advertising is a major factor determining which of the few available brands consumers buy, because often it is advertising that creates the perceived differences.[20]

monopoly
A degree of competition in which only one seller controls the total supply of a product or service, and sets the price.

A **monopoly** occurs when one seller controls the total supply of a product or service, and sets the price. In the United States, laws prohibit the creation of monopolies. Nonetheless, the U.S. legal system has permitted monopolies in the markets for public utilities that sell natural gas, water, and electric power. These companies' prices and profits are usually controlled by public service commissions to protect the interest of buyers. For example, the Florida Public Service Commission is the administering agency over the Florida Power and Light utility company. Legislation ended the monopoly status of utilities in some areas, letting consumers choose among providers. The intention of such *deregulation* is to increase competition among utility companies and, ultimately, lower prices for consumers.

Benefits and Limitations of Free Markets

One benefit of the free market is that it allows open competition among companies. Businesses must provide customers with high-quality products at fair prices with good service. If they don't, they lose customers to businesses that do. Do government services have the same incentives?

The free market—with its competition and incentives—was a major factor in creating the wealth that industrialized countries now enjoy. Some people even talk of the free market as an economic miracle. Free-market capitalism, more than any other economic system, provides opportunities for poor people to work their way out of poverty. Capitalism also encourages businesses to be more efficient so they can successfully compete on price and quality.

Yet, even as free-market capitalism has brought prosperity to the United States and to much of the rest of the world, it has brought inequality as well.[21] Business owners and managers usually make more money and have more wealth than lower-level workers. Yet people who are old, disabled, or sick may not be able to start and manage a business, and others may not have the talent or the drive. What should society do about such inequality? Not everyone in the United States is as generous as Bill Gates, founder of Microsoft, who with his wife has established the Bill and Melinda Gates Foundation to support world health and education.[22] In fact, the desire to create as much wealth as possible has led some business-people throughout history, and still today, to exploit such practices as slavery and child labor.

One of the dangers of free markets is that some people let greed dictate how they act. Criminal charges brought against some big businesses in banking, oil, accounting, telecommunications, insurance, and pharmaceuticals indicate the scope of the potential problem. Some businesspeople have deceived the public about their products; others have deceived stockholders about the value of their stock, all in order to increase executives' personal assets.[23]

Clearly, some government laws and regulations are necessary to protect businesses' stakeholders and make sure people who cannot work get the basic care they need.[24] To overcome some of capitalism's limitations, some countries have adopted an economic system called socialism. It, too, has its good and bad points. We explore these after you review the following Progress Assessment questions.

progress assessment

- What are the four basic rights that people have under free-market capitalism?
- How do businesspeople know what to produce and in what quantity?
- How are prices determined?
- What are the four degrees of competition, and what are some examples of each?

LEARNING goal 3

Compare socialism and communism.

> **socialism**
> An economic system based on the premise that some, if not most, basic businesses should be owned by the government so that profits can be more evenly distributed among the people.

UNDERSTANDING SOCIALISM

Socialism is an economic system based on the premise that some, if not most, basic businesses (e.g., steel mills, coal mines, and utilities) should be owned by the government so that profits can be more evenly distributed among the people. Entrepreneurs often own and run smaller businesses, and individuals are often taxed relatively steeply to pay for social programs. The top federal personal income tax rate in the United States, for example, was 35 percent recently, but in some socialist countries the top rate can be as much as 60 percent. While U.S. shoppers pay sales taxes ranging from over 10 percent in Chicago to zero in Delaware, socialist countries charge a similar value-added tax of 15 to 20 percent or more. Socialists acknowledge the major benefit of capitalism—wealth creation—but believe that wealth should be more evenly distributed than occurs in free-market capitalism. They believe the government should carry out the distribution and be much more involved in protecting the environment and providing for the poor.

The Benefits of Socialism

The major benefit of socialism is supposed to be social equality.[25] Ideally it comes about because the government takes income from wealthier people, in the form of taxes, and redistributes it to poorer people through various government programs. Free education through college, free health care, and free child care are some of the benefits socialist governments, using the money from taxes, may provide to their people. Such education benefits helped Finland become the world leader in student achievement.[26] Workers in socialist countries usually get longer vacations, work fewer hours per week, and have more employee benefits (e.g., generous sick leave) than those in countries where free-market capitalism prevails.

Socialism has been more successful in some countries than in others. This photo shows Denmark's clean and modern public transportation system. In Greece, overspending caused a debt crisis that forced the government to impose austerity measures that many Greeks oppose. What other factors might lead to slower growth in socialist countries?

The Negative Consequences of Socialism

Socialism may create more equality than capitalism, but it takes away some of businesspeople's incentives. For example, tax rates in some socialist nations once reached 83 percent. Today, doctors, lawyers, business owners, and others who earn a lot of money pay very high tax rates. As a consequence, many of them leave socialist countries for capitalistic countries with lower taxes, such as the United States. This loss of the best and brightest people to other countries is called a **brain drain**.

Imagine an experiment in socialism in your own class. Imagine that after the first exam, those with grades of 90 and above have to give some of their points to those who make 70 and below so that everyone ends up with grades in the 80s. Would those who got 90s study as hard for the second exam? What about those who got 70s? Can you see why workers may not work as hard or as well if they all get the same benefits regardless of how hard they work?

Socialism also tends to result in fewer inventions and less innovation, because those who come up with new ideas usually don't receive as much reward as they would in a capitalist system. Communism may be considered a more intensive version of socialism. We shall explore that system next.

brain drain
The loss of the best and brightest people to other countries.

UNDERSTANDING COMMUNISM

Communism is an economic and political system in which the government makes almost all economic decisions and owns almost all the major factors of production. It intrudes further into the lives of people than socialism does. For example, some communist countries have not allowed their citizens to practice certain religions, change jobs, or move to the town of their choice.

One problem with communism is that the government has no way of knowing what to produce, because prices don't reflect supply and demand as they do in free markets. The government must guess what the people need. As a result, shortages of many items, including food and clothing, may develop. Another problem is that communism doesn't inspire businesspeople to work hard because the incentives are not there. Therefore, communism is slowly disappearing as an economic form.

Most communist countries today are suffering severe economic depression. In North Korea, many people are starving. In Cuba, people suffer a lack of goods and services readily available in most other countries, and some fear the government. Even so, there seems to be a movement toward communist principles in Venezuela, following the Cuban model.

While some parts of the former Soviet Union remain under communist ideals, Russia itself now has a flat tax of only 13 percent. Yet this low rate increased the government's tax revenues by nearly 30 percent, because more people were willing to pay. The trend toward free markets is growing in Vietnam and parts of China as well. The regions of China that are most free have prospered rapidly, while the rest of the country has grown relatively slowly. Remnants of China's communist system, such as political and religious oppression, still exist, however.

communism
An economic and political system in which the government makes almost all economic decisions and owns almost all the major factors of production.

LEARNING goal 4

Analyze the trend toward mixed economies.

THE TREND TOWARD MIXED ECONOMIES

The nations of the world have largely been divided between those that followed the concepts of capitalism and those that adopted the concepts of communism or socialism. We can now contrast the two major economic systems as follows:

1. **Free-market economies** exist when the market largely determines what goods and services get produced, who gets them, and how the economy grows. *Capitalism* is the popular term for this economic system.

2. **Command economies** exist when the government largely decides what goods and services will be produced, who gets them, and how the economy will grow. *Socialism* and *communism* are variations on this economic system.

Although all countries actually have some mix of the two systems, neither free-market nor command economies have resulted in optimal economic conditions. Free-market mechanisms don't seem to respond enough to the needs of the poor, the old, or the disabled. Some people also believe that businesses in free-market economies have not done enough to protect the environment. (We shall discuss that issue throughout the text.) Over time, voters in mostly free-market countries, such as the United States, have elected officials who have adopted many social and environmental programs such as Social Security, welfare, unemployment compensation, and various clean air and water acts. What new or enhanced social policies do you know of that are being considered today?

Socialism and communism haven't always created enough jobs or wealth to keep economies growing fast enough. Thus, communist governments are disappearing, and some socialist governments have been cutting back on social programs and lowering taxes on businesses and workers to generate more business growth and more revenue.[27] The Reaching Beyond Our Borders box discusses how the economy of China has been growing despite its communist base.

The trend, then, has been for mostly capitalist countries (like the United States) to move toward socialism (i.e. more government involvement in health care), and for mostly socialist countries, such as France and China, to move toward capitalism

free-market economies
Economic systems in which the market largely determines what goods and services get produced, who gets them, and how the economy grows.

command economies
Economic systems in which the government largely decides what goods and services will be produced, who will get them, and how the economy will grow.

Since the communist system in Russia has largely collapsed, the country has been moving toward a viable market economy. As poverty begins to decline, a middle class is emerging. More jobs are being created like the ones in this Hewlett-Packard manufacturing facility. Do you think the Russian economy will continue to grow?

our borders

China's Changing Economy

It is important, when studying economics, to look at countries throughout the world to see how they are doing economically. One country that has been in the news a lot lately is China. China's economy is growing two or three times faster than the United States. As a consequence of that rapid growth, China is worried about inflation and the possibility of a housing crash and market drop much like the one experienced recently in the U.S.

China is now the world's second largest economy, replacing Japan. China's GDP grew 10.3 percent in 2010, up from 9.2 percent in 2009. The rapid rise in the Chinese economy creates opportunities for companies that sell them goods and services, but the rapid growth in Chinese manufacturing also creates problems for countries trying to compete. There is much discussion in the United States about losing jobs to Chinese workers whose pay is much lower than in the United States.

Although it is known for its socialist and communist foundations, one reason China is growing so rapidly is because it has adopted capitalist principles. This is an interesting time

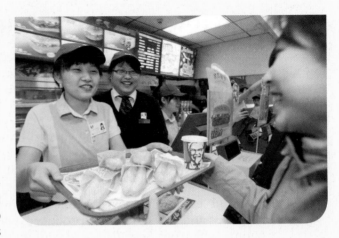

to watch world economies to see what kind of system proves to be the most beneficial to the most people.

Sources: Jason Dean and Aaron Back, "China Growth Shows Contrast with U.S.," *The Wall Street Journal,* January 21, 2011; and Kevin D. Williamson, "The Other National Debt," *National Review,* June 21, 2010.

(more private businesses, lower taxes). All countries have some mix of the two systems. Thus, the long-term global trend is toward a blend of capitalism and socialism. This trend likely will increase with the opening of global markets made easier by the Internet. The net effect is the emergence throughout the world of mixed economies.

Mixed economies exist where some allocation of resources is made by the market and some by the government. Most countries don't have a name for such a system. If free-market mechanisms allocate most resources, the leaders call their system capitalism. If the government allocates most resources, the leaders call it socialism. Figure 2.4 compares the various economic systems.

Like most other nations of the world, the United States has a mixed economy. The U.S. government has now become the largest employer in the country, which means there are more workers in the public sector (government) than in any of the major businesses in the United States. Do you see the government growing or declining in the coming years?

mixed economies
Economic systems in which some allocation of resources is made by the market and some by the government.

progress assessment

- What led to the emergence of socialism?
- What are the benefits and drawbacks of socialism?
- What countries still practice communism?
- What are the characteristics of a mixed economy?

	CAPITALISM* (United States)	SOCIALISM (Sweden)	COMMUNISM (North Korea)	MIXED ECONOMY (Germany)
Social and Economic Goals	Private ownership of land and business. Liberty and the pursuit of happiness. Free trade. Emphasis on freedom and the profit motive for economic growth.	Public ownership of major businesses. Some private ownership of smaller businesses and shops. Government control of education, health care, utilities, mining, transportation, and media. Very high taxation. Emphasis on equality.	Public ownership of all businesses. Government-run education and health care. Emphasis on equality. Many limitations on freedom, including freedom to own businesses and to assemble to protest government actions.	Private ownership of land and business with government regulation. Government control of some institutions (e.g., mail). High taxation for defense and the common welfare. Emphasis on a balance between freedom and equality.
Motivation of Workers	Much incentive to work efficiently and hard because profits are retained by owners. Workers are rewarded for high productivity.	Capitalist incentives exist in private businesses. Government control of wages in public institutions limits incentives.	Very little incentive to work hard or to produce quality goods or services.	Incentives are similar to capitalism except in government-owned enterprises, which may have fewer incentives.
Control over Markets	Complete freedom of trade within and among nations. Some government control of markets.	Some markets are controlled by the government and some are free. Trade restrictions among nations vary and include some free-trade agreements.	Total government control over markets except for illegal transactions.	Some government control of trade within and among nations (trade protectionism).
Choices in the Market	A wide variety of goods and services is available. Almost no scarcity or over-supply exists for long because supply and demand control the market.	Variety in the marketplace varies considerably from country to country. Choice is directly related to government involvement in markets.	Very little choice among competing goods.	Similar to capitalism, but scarcity and oversupply may be caused by government involvement in the market (e.g., subsidies for farms).
Social Freedoms	Freedom of speech, press, assembly, religion, job choice, movement, and elections.	Similar to mixed economy. Governments may restrict job choice, movement among countries, and who may attend upper-level schools (i.e., college).	Very limited freedom to protest the government, practice religion, or change houses or jobs.	Some restrictions on freedoms of assembly and speech. Separation of church and state may limit religious practices in schools.

*The United States is a mixed economy based on a foundation of capitalism.

figure 2.4

COMPARISONS OF KEY ECONOMIC SYSTEMS

gross domestic product (GDP)
The total value of final goods and services produced in a country in a given year.

LEARNING goal 5

Describe the economic system of the United States, including the significance of key economic indicators (especially GDP), productivity, and the business cycle.

UNDERSTANDING THE U.S. ECONOMIC SYSTEM

The following sections will introduce the terms and concepts that you, as an informed citizen, will need to understand in order to grasp the issues facing government and business leaders in the United States.

Key Economic Indicators

Three major indicators of economic conditions are (1) the gross domestic product (GDP), (2) the unemployment rate, and (3) price indexes. Another important statistic is the increase or decrease in productivity. When you read business literature, you'll see these terms used again and again. Let's explore what they mean.

Gross Domestic Product **Gross domestic product (GDP)**, which we mentioned briefly in Chapter 1, is the total value of final goods and services produced in a country in a given year. Both domestic and foreign-owned companies can produce the goods and services included in GDP, as long as the companies are located within the country's boundaries. For example, production values from Japanese automaker Honda's factory in Ohio are included in U.S. GDP. Revenue generated by Ford's factory in Mexico is included in Mexico's GDP, even though Ford is a U.S. company.

Almost every discussion about a nation's economy is based on GDP. If growth in GDP slows or declines, businesses may feel many negative effects, such as the slowdown in retail sales experienced beginning in 2008. A major influence on the growth of GDP is the productivity of the workforce—that is, how much output workers create with a given amount of input. The total U.S. GDP is about $14 trillion. The level of U.S. economic activity is actually larger than the GDP figures show, because those figures don't take into account illicit activities such as sales of illegal drugs. The high GDP in the United States is what enables its citizens to enjoy a high standard of living.

The Unemployment Rate The **unemployment rate** refers to the percentage of civilians at least 16 years old who are unemployed *and tried to find a job within the prior four weeks.* In 2000, the U.S. unemployment rate reached its lowest point in over 30 years, falling as low as 3.9 percent, but by 2010

The overall unemployment rate in the U.S. fluctuates. Over the last decade, it has been as low as less than 5 percent and as high as more than 10 percent. Unemployment insurance goes only so far to relieve the loss of income caused by losing your job. How high is the unemployment rate in your area today?

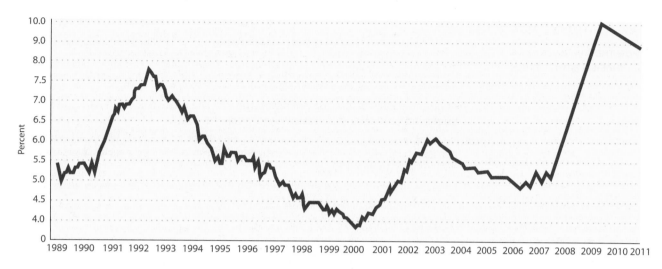

figure 2.5

**U.S. UNEMPLOYMENT RATE
1989–2011**

the rate had risen to over 9.5 percent (see Figure 2.5). The unemployment rate fell to below 9 percent in 2011, but many people had given up looking for jobs (people who are not actively looking for work are not included in the unemployment figures).

Figure 2.6 describes the four types of unemployment: frictional, structural, cyclical, and seasonal. The United States tries to protect those who are unemployed because of recessions (defined later in the chapter), industry shifts, and other cyclical factors. Nonetheless, the *underemployment* figure in 2010 was about 17 percent (this includes those who are working part time and want to work full time and those who stopped looking for work).[28]

If you worry about the U.S. unemployment rate, consider this: the unemployment rate in Zimbabwe is way over 80 percent, and the inflation rate is spectacular. You would enjoy cashing in your dollars in Zimbabwe; one dollar will get you billions of Zimbabwean dollars. Actually, the situation is getting much worse. Do you suppose Zimbabwe is a capitalist economy?

Inflation and Price Indexes　Price indexes help gauge the health of the economy by measuring the levels of inflation, disinflation, deflation, and stagflation. **Inflation** is a general rise in the prices of goods and services over time.

unemployment rate
The number of civilians at least 16 years old who are unemployed and tried to find a job within the prior four weeks.

inflation
A general rise in the prices of goods and services over time.

figure 2.6

**FOUR TYPES OF
UNEMPLOYMENT**

- *Frictional unemployment* refers to those people who have quit work because they didn't like the job, the boss, or the working conditions and who haven't yet found a new job. It also refers to those people who are entering the labor force for the first time (e.g., new graduates) or are returning to the labor force after significant time away (e.g., parents who reared children). There will always be some frictional unemployment because it takes some time to find a first job or a new job.

- *Structural unemployment* refers to unemployment caused by the restructuring of firms or by a mismatch between the skills (or location) of job seekers and the requirements (or location) of available jobs (e.g., coal miners in an area where mines have been closed).

- *Cyclical unemployment* occurs because of a recession or a similar downturn in the business cycle (the ups and downs of business growth and decline over time). This type of unemployment is the most serious.

- *Seasonal unemployment* occurs where demand for labor varies over the year, as with the harvesting of crops.

figure 2.7

HOW THE CONSUMER PRICE INDEX IS PUT TOGETHER

1. 400 data collectors visit stores and gather 80,000 retail price quotes and 5,000 housing rent quotes, transmitting data daily to Washington.
2. 40 commodity analysts at the Bureau of Labor Statistics review about a quarter of this avalanche of price data.
3. About nine days before the release of the CPI, the office is locked down—with bright red RESTRICTED AREA signs posted on all the doors.
4. 90 people—a mix of commodity analysts and other economists who specialize in assembling the CPI—compute basic indexes for 211 item categories, which are divided into 38 index areas.
5. Final results are released at 8:30 a.m., Eastern time, about two weeks after the end of the month in question.

The official definition is "a persistent increase in the level of consumer prices or a persistent decline in the purchasing power of money, caused by an increase in available currency and credit beyond the proportion of goods and services." Thus, it is also described as "too many dollars chasing too few goods." Go back and review the laws of supply and demand to see how that works. Rapid inflation is scary. If the prices of goods and services go up by just 7 percent a year, they will double in about 10 years. Think of how much fear was generated by the rapid increase in the price of gasoline in 2011.

Disinflation occurs when price increases are slowing (the inflation rate is declining). That was the situation in the United States throughout the 1990s. **Deflation** means that prices are declining.[29] It occurs when countries produce so many goods that people cannot afford to buy them all (too few dollars are chasing too many goods). Some experts believed that deflation could occur in 2011.[30] **Stagflation** occurs when the economy is slowing but prices are going up anyhow. Some economists fear the United States may face stagflation in the near future.

The **consumer price index (CPI)** consists of monthly statistics that measure the pace of inflation or deflation. The government computes costs of goods and services—including housing, food, apparel, and medical care—to see whether they are going up or down (see Figure 2.7). The CPI is an important figure because some wages and salaries, rents and leases, tax brackets, government benefits, and interest rates are based on it. You may see the term *core inflation*. That means the CPI minus food and energy costs. Since food and energy have been going up rapidly, the core inflation figure is actually much lower than the real CPI.

The **producer price index (PPI)** measures prices at the wholesale level. Other indicators of the economy's condition include housing starts, retail sales, and changes in personal income. You can learn more about such indicators by reading business periodicals, listening to business broadcasts on radio and television, and exploring business sites on the Internet.

Productivity in the United States

An increase in productivity means a worker can produce more goods and services than before in the same time period, usually thanks to machinery or other equipment. Productivity in the United States has risen because computers and other technology have made production faster and easier. The higher is productivity, the lower are the costs of producing goods and services, and the lower prices can be. Therefore, businesspeople are eager to increase productivity. Remember, however, that high productivity can lead to high unemployment.[31]

disinflation
A situation in which price increases are slowing (the inflation rate is declining).

deflation
A situation in which prices are declining.

stagflation
A situation when the economy is slowing but prices are going up anyhow.

consumer price index (CPI)
Monthly statistics that measure the pace of inflation or deflation.

producer price index (PPI)
An index that measures prices at the wholesale level.

Certainly, that is what the United States in now experiencing.

Now that the U.S. economy is a service economy, productivity is an issue because service firms are so labor-intensive. Spurred by foreign competition, productivity in the manufacturing sector is rising rapidly. In the service sector, productivity is growing more slowly because service workers—like teachers, clerks, lawyers, and barbers—have fewer new technologies available than there are for factory workers.

Productivity in the Service Sector

One problem with the service industry is that an influx of machinery may add to the *quality* of the service provided but not to the *output per worker*. For example, you've probably noticed how many computers there are on college campuses. They add to the quality of education but don't necessarily boost professors' productivity. The same is true of some equipment in hospitals, such as CAT scanners, PET scanners, and MRI scanners. They improve patient care but don't necessarily increase the number of patients doctors can see. In other words, today's productivity measures in the service industry fail to capture the increase in quality caused by new technology.

Clearly, the United States and other countries need to develop new measures of productivity for the service economy that include quality as well as quantity of output. Despite productivity improvement, the economy is likely to go through a series of ups and downs, much as it has over the past few years. We'll explore that process next.

It can be difficult to measure productivity in the service sector. New technology can improve the quality of services without necessarily increasing the number of people served. A doctor can make more accurate diagnoses with scans, for instance, but still can only see so many patients in a day. How can productivity measures capture improvements in the quality of service?

The Business Cycle

Business cycles are the periodic rises and falls that occur in economies over time. Economists look at a number of business cycles, from seasonal cycles that occur within a year to cycles that occur every 48–60 years.

Economist Joseph Schumpeter identified the four phases of long-term business cycles as boom–recession–depression–recovery:

1. An *economic boom* is just what it sounds like—business is booming.

2. **Recession** is two or more consecutive quarters of decline in the GDP. In a recession prices fall, people purchase fewer products, and businesses fail. A recession brings high unemployment, increased business failures, and an overall drop in living standards. The recession that started in 2008 is an example.

3. A **depression** is a severe recession, usually accompanied by deflation. Business cycles rarely go through a depression phase. In fact, while there were many business cycles during the 20th century, there was only one severe depression (1930s). Nonetheless some economists are predicting a depression in the coming years.

4. A *recovery* occurs when the economy stabilizes and starts to grow. This eventually leads to an economic boom, starting the cycle all over again.

One goal of some economists is to predict such ups and downs. That is very difficult to do. Business cycles are identified according to facts, but we can explain those facts only by using theories. Therefore, we cannot predict

business cycles
The periodic rises and falls that occur in economies over time.

recession
Two or more consecutive quarters of decline in the GDP.

depression
A severe recession, usually accompanied by deflation.

with certainty. But one thing is certain: over time, the economy *will* rise and fall as it has done lately.

Since dramatic swings up and down in the economy cause all kinds of disruptions to businesses, the government tries to minimize such changes. It uses fiscal policy and monetary policy to try to keep the economy from slowing too much or growing too rapidly.

LEARNING goal 6

Contrast fiscal policy and monetary policy, and explain how each affects the economy.

Stabilizing the Economy through Fiscal Policy

fiscal policy
The federal government's efforts to keep the economy stable by increasing or decreasing taxes or government spending.

Fiscal policy refers to the federal government's efforts to keep the economy stable by increasing or decreasing taxes or government spending. The first fiscal policy tool is taxation. Theoretically, high tax rates tend to slow the economy because they draw money away from the private sector and put it into the government. High tax rates may discourage small-business ownership because they decrease the profits businesses can earn and make the effort less rewarding.[32] It follows, then, that low tax rates will theoretically give the economy a boost.

In the United States, the percentage of GDP the government takes through taxes at all levels (federal, state, and local) is about 28 percent. When you count all fees, sales taxes, and more, taxes on the highest-earning citizens could exceed 50 percent. Is that figure too high or not high enough in your opinion? Why?

The second fiscal policy tool is government spending on highways, social programs, education, infrastructure (e.g., roads and utilities), defense, and so on. The *national deficit* is the amount of money the federal government spends beyond what it gathers in taxes for a given fiscal year. The deficit is expected to be over $1 trillion for the next several years. Such deficits increase the national debt. The **national debt** is the sum of government deficits over time. Recently, the national debt was over $14 trillion (see Figure 2.8). That is a rather misleading number, however, since the unfunded obligation for Medicare alone is about $34 trillion. The unfunded debt to Social Security is on top of that. If the government takes in more revenue than it spends (i.e., tax revenues exceed expenditures), there is a *national surplus*. That is not likely to happen soon.

One way to lessen deficits is to cut government spending. Many presidents and those in Congress have promised to make the government "smaller," that is, to reduce government spending—but that doesn't happen very often. There seems to be a need for more social programs or more defense spending (such as for the wars in Iraq, Afghanistan, and Libya) each year, and thus the deficits continue and add to the national debt. Some people believe that government spending helps the economy grow. Others believe that the money the government spends comes out of the pockets of consumers and businesspeople, and thus slows growth. What do you think?

national debt
The sum of government deficits over time.

Keynesian economic theory
The theory that a government policy of increasing spending and cutting taxes could stimulate the economy in a recession.

Fiscal Policy in Action during the Economic Crisis that Began in 2008

monetary policy
The management of the money supply and interest rates by the Federal Reserve.

For most of his presidency, George W. Bush followed the basic economic principles of free markets. By the end of his term, however, the economy was facing a dire economic crisis and President Bush approved the spending of almost $1 trillion of government money in an effort to revive the failing economy (including helping out banks, the auto industry, and others). (A trillion dollars

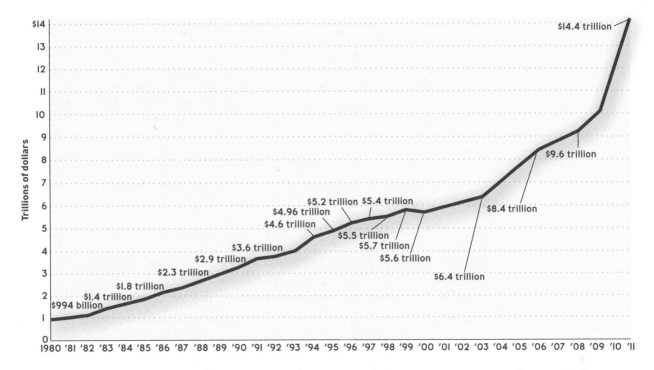

figure 2.8

THE NATIONAL DEBT

is about $3,272 per person in the United States.) President Barack Obama promised to spend additional funds. Both presidents were following the basic economic theory of Keynes discussed in the Profile.[33] As you recall, **Keynesian economic theory** is the theory that a government policy of increasing spending and cutting taxes could stimulate the economy in a recession.

Using Monetary Policy to Keep the Economy Growing

Have you ever wondered what organization adds money to or subtracts money from the economy? The answer is the Federal Reserve Bank (the Fed). The Fed is a semiprivate organization that is not under the direct control of the government but does have members appointed by the president. We will discuss the Fed in detail when we look at banking in Chapter 20. Now we simply introduce monetary policy and the role of the Fed in controlling the economy.

Monetary policy is the management of the money supply and interest rates by the Federal Reserve Bank. The Fed's most visible role is the raising and lowering of interest rates. When the economy is booming, the Fed tends to raise interest rates. This makes money more expensive to borrow. Businesses thus borrow less, and the economy slows as businesspeople spend less money on everything they need to grow, including labor and machinery. The opposite is true when the Fed lowers interest rates. Businesses tend to borrow more, and the economy is expected to grow. Raising and lowering interest rates should therefore help control the rapid ups and downs of the economy.[34] In 2010–2011, the Fed kept interest rates near zero,

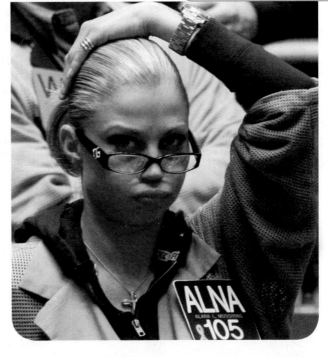

The economic crisis beginning in 2008 caused much anguish among Wall Street workers and people in general. How effective was the government's response?

but the economy remained sluggish. You can imagine the pressure that put on the head of the Federal Reserve.[35]

The Fed also controls the money supply. A simple explanation of this function is that the more money the Fed makes available to businesspeople and others, the faster the economy is supposed to grow. To slow the economy (and prevent inflation), the Fed lowers the money supply. The Fed poured money into the economy in 2008–2011. What would you expect the result to be?

To sum up, there are two major tools for managing the economy of the United States: fiscal policy (government taxes and spending) and monetary policy (the Fed's control over interest rates and the money supply). The goal is to keep the economy growing so that more people can rise up the economic ladder and enjoy a higher standard of living and quality of life.

progress assessment

- Name the three economic indicators and describe how well the United States is doing based on each indicator.
- What's the difference between a recession and a depression?
- How does the government manage the economy using fiscal policy?
- What does the term *monetary policy* mean? What organization is responsible for monetary policy?

summary

Learning Goal 1. Explain basic economics.
- **What is economics?**

Economics is the study of how society chooses to employ resources to produce goods and services and distribute them for consumption among various competing groups and individuals.
- **What are the two branches of economics?**

There are two major branches of economics: macroeconomics studies the operation of a nation's economy as a whole, and microeconomics studies the behavior of people and organizations in particular markets (e.g., why people buy smaller cars when gas prices go up).
- **How can we be assured of having enough resources?**

Resource development is the study of how to increase resources and create the conditions that will make better use of them.
- **How does capitalism create a climate for economic growth?**

Under capitalism, businesspeople don't often deliberately set out to help others; they work mostly for their own prosperity and growth. Yet people's efforts to improve their own situation in life act like an *invisible hand* to help the economy grow and prosper through the production of needed goods, services, and ideas.

Learning Goal 2. Explain what capitalism is and how free markets work.
- **What is capitalism?**

Capitalism is an economic system in which all or most of the means of production and distribution are privately owned and operated for profit.

- **Who decides what to produce under capitalism?**

In capitalist countries, businesspeople decide what to produce, how much to pay workers, and how much to charge for goods and services. They also decide whether to produce certain goods in their own countries, import those goods, or have them made in other countries.

- **What are the basic rights people have under capitalism?**

The four basic rights under capitalism are (1) the right to private property, (2) the right to own a business and to keep all of that business's profits after taxes, (3) the right to freedom of competition, and (4) the right to freedom of choice. President Franklin D. Roosevelt felt that other economic freedoms were also important: the right to freedom of speech and expression, the right to worship in your own way, and freedom from want and fear.

- **How does the free market work?**

The free market is one in which buyers and sellers negotiating prices for goods and services influence the decisions about what gets produced and in what quantities. Buyers' decisions in the marketplace tell sellers what to produce and in what quantity. When buyers demand more goods, the price goes up, signaling suppliers to produce more. The higher the price, the more goods and services suppliers are willing to produce. Price is the mechanism that allows free markets to work.

Learning Goal 3. Compare socialism and communism.

- **What is socialism?**

Socialism is an economic system based on the premise that some businesses should be owned by the government.

- **What are the advantages and disadvantages of socialism?**

Socialism intends to create more social equity. Workers in socialist countries usually receive more education, health care, and other benefits and also work fewer hours, with longer vacations. The major disadvantage of socialism is that it lowers the incentive to start a business or to work hard. Socialist economies tend to have a higher unemployment rate and a slower growth rate than capitalist economies.

- **How does socialism differ from communism?**

Under communism, the government owns almost all major production facilities and dictates what gets produced and by whom. Communism is also more restrictive when it comes to personal freedoms, such as religious freedom.

Learning Goal 4. Analyze the trend toward mixed economies.

- **What is a mixed economy?**

A mixed economy is part capitalist and part socialist. Some businesses are privately owned, but taxes tend to be high to distribute income more evenly among the population.

- **What countries have mixed economies?**

The United States has a mixed economy, as do most other industrialized countries.

- **What are the benefits of mixed economies?**

A mixed economy has most of the benefits of wealth creation that free markets bring plus the benefits of greater social equality and concern for the environment that socialism promises.

Learning Goal 5. Describe the economic system of the United States, including the significance of key economic indicators (especially GDP), productivity, and the business cycle.

- **What are the key economic indicators in the United States?**

Gross domestic product (GDP) is the total value of final goods and services produced in a country in a given year. The *unemployment rate* refers to the percentage of civilians at least 16 years old who are unemployed and tried to find a job within the most recent four weeks. The *consumer price index (CPI)* measures changes in the prices of about 400 goods and services that consumers buy.

- **What are the four phases of business cycles?**

In an *economic boom,* businesses do well. A *recession* occurs when two or more quarters show declines in the GDP, prices fall, people purchase fewer products, and businesses fail. A *depression* is a severe recession. *Recovery* occurs when the economy stabilizes and starts to grow.

Learning Goal 6. Contrast fiscal policy and monetary policy, and explain how each affects the economy.

- **What is fiscal policy?**

Fiscal policy consists of government efforts to keep the economy stable by increasing or decreasing taxes or government spending.

- **What is the importance of monetary policy to the economy?**

Monetary policy is the management of the money supply and interest rates. When unemployment gets too high, the Federal Reserve Bank (the Fed) may put more money into the economy and lower interest rates. That is supposed to provide a boost to the economy as businesses borrow and spend more money and hire more people.

key terms

brain drain 42
business cycles 49
capitalism 35
command
    economies 43
communism 42
consumer price
    index (CPI) 48
deflation 48
demand 37
depression 49
disinflation 48
economics 30
fiscal policy 50

free-market economies 43
gross domestic product
    (GDP) 46
inflation 47
invisible hand 33
Keynesian economic
    theory 50
macroeconomics 30
market price 37
microeconomics 30
mixed economies 44
monetary policy 50
monopolistic
    competition 39

monopoly 40
national debt 50
oligopoly 39
perfect competition 39
producer price index
    (PPI) 48
recession 49
resource
    development 31
socialism 41
stagflation 48
supply 37
unemployment rate 46

critical thinking

U.S. Supreme Court ruled that cities could have school voucher programs that give money directly to parents, who could then choose between competing schools, public or private. The idea was to create competition among schools. Like businesses, schools were expected to improve their services (how effectively they teach) to win students from competitors. The result would be improvement in all schools, private and public, to benefit many students.

1. Do you believe economic principles like competition apply in both private and public organizations? Be prepared to defend your answer.

2. Are there other public functions that might benefit from more competition, including competition from private firms?

3. Many people say that businesspeople do not do enough for society. Some students choose to go into the public sector instead of business because they want to help others. However, businesspeople say that they do more to help others than nonprofit groups do because they provide jobs for people rather than giving them charity. Furthermore, they believe businesses create all the wealth that nonprofit groups distribute.

   a. How can you find some middle ground in this debate to show that both businesspeople and those who work for nonprofit organizations contribute to society and need to work together more closely to help people?

   b. How could you use the concepts of Adam Smith to help illustrate your position?

developing workplace skills

1. In teams, develop a list of the advantages of living in a capitalist society. Then develop lists headed "What are the disadvantages?" and "How could such disadvantages be minimized?" Describe why a poor person in a socialist country might reject capitalism and prefer a socialist state.

2. Show your understanding of the principles of supply and demand by looking at the oil market today. Why does the price of gas fluctuate so greatly? What will happen as more and more people in China and India decide to buy automobiles? What would happen if most U.S. consumers decided to drive electric cars?

3. This exercise will help you understand socialism from different perspectives. Form three groups. Each group should adopt a different role in a socialist economy: one group will be the business owners, another group will be workers, and another will be government leaders. Within your group discuss and list the advantages and disadvantages to you of lowering taxes on businesses. Then have each group choose a representative to go to the front of the class and debate the tax issue with the representatives from the other groups.

4. Draw a line and mark one end "Free-Market Capitalism" and the other end "Central Planning." Mark where on the line the United States is now.

Explain why you marked the spot you chose. Students from other countries may want to do this exercise for their own countries and explain the differences to the class.

5. Break into small groups. In your group discuss how the following changes have affected people's purchasing behavior and attitudes toward the United States and its economy: the wars in Iraq and Afghanistan, the increased amount spent on homeland security, the government involvement in banking and other industries, and the growth of the Internet. Have a group member prepare a short summary for the class.

taking it to the net

Purpose

To familiarize you with the sources of economic information that are important to business decision makers.

Exercise

Imagine that your boss asked you to help her to prepare the company's sales forecast for the coming two years. In the past, she felt that such trends in the nation's GDP, U.S. manufacturing, and manufacturing in Illinois were especially helpful in forecasting sales. She would like you to do the following:

1. Go to the Bureau of Economic Analysis's website (www.bea.gov) and locate the gross domestic product data. Compare the annual figure for the last four years. What do the figures indicate for the next couple of years?

2. At the Bureau of Labor Statistics' website (www.bls.gov) under Industries, click on Industries at a Glance to find the information about the manufacturing industry. What is the employment trend in manufacturing over the last four years (percentage change from preceding period)?

3. Return to the Bureau of Labor Statistics' home page and use the Search feature to find trends in employment for the state of Illinois. Look around the website to see what other information is available. Plot the trend in manufacturing employment in Illinois over the last four years. On your own, discuss what economic changes may have influenced that trend.

4. Based on the information you have gathered, write a brief summary of what may happen to company sales over the next couple of years.

casing the web

To access the case "The Rule of 72," visit **www.mhhe.com/ub10e**

To access the video case featuring Oppurtunity International,
visit **www.mhhe.com/ubl0e**

DOING
Business in GLOBAL
Markets

3

LEARNING
goals

After you have read and studied this chapter, you should be able to

1 Discuss the importance of the global market and the roles of comparative advantage and absolute advantage in global trade.

2 Explain the importance of importing and exporting, and understand key terms used in global business.

3 Illustrate the strategies used in reaching global markets and explain the role of multi-national corporations.

4 Evaluate the forces that affect trading in global markets.

5 Debate the advantages and disadvantages of trade protectionism.

6 Discuss the changing landscape of the global market and the issue of offshore outsourcing.

With a population of more than 1.3 billion people, China has the world's largest media market by far. However, much of the media content, especially television, remains controlled by state authorities. Succeeding in such an environment means walking a tight line between what's interesting for the audience and what's acceptable to the government censors.

Yang Lan, China's biggest television personality, not only managed to flourish in such a restrictive medium, but also used her success to build a massive multimedia empire. It's no wonder why many have dubbed her the Chinese Oprah Winfrey. Still, even that bold claim might be an understatement: Oprah's daily average of 7 million viewers seem modest compared to the 200 million viewers that tune in to each of Lan's shows.

The daughter of a wealthy communications technology engineer and an English literature professor, Lan studied English at Beijing Foreign Studies University. After college she first appeared on TV as a co-host on the Zheng Da Variety Show in 1990. With few other options available to the Chinese viewing audience, the show attracted an immense following that made Lan a household name. But success on the small screen was not Lan's sole ambition at the time. In 1994 she quit the show and enrolled at Columbia University in New York, studying international affairs.

After graduate school, Lan went back to Chinese television with Yang Lan Horizon, later retitled Yang Lan One on One. Lan's proficiency with English and the highly professional style of the program drew a number of foreign guests, including Bill and Hillary Clinton, former British Prime Minister Tony Blair, and Kobe Bryant. The show also made Lan one of the most recognizable media personalities in China, surpassed only by international superstars like Yao Ming and Jackie Chan.

The late 90s found Lan using her rising media clout to purchase various publications and start Chinese language websites on the rapidly expanding Internet. She failed, however, in 2000 with the launch of her own television station, Sun TV. Given Lan's powerful brand and image, investors flocked to the project, anticipating another inevitable success for the broadcaster. The only problem was that almost no one in China could watch the network. With its home base in Hong Kong, Sun TV was banned from mainland cable networks, airing almost solely in luxury hotels. Lan eventually sold the station in 2003.

Though Sun TV's failure hit her hard, Lan bounced back and used her entrepreneurial talents in a number of other areas. Her Sun Media Group now produces other television shows as well as a credit card line and a jewelry brand partnership with Celine Dion.

As Lan continues to push the boundaries of Chinese media, clashes between her enterprises and the state's restrictions seem unavoidable. For instance, in 2008 the government suspended publication of one of her newspapers after it exposed embezzlement at a state-owned bank. Lan shut the paper down entirely in response. As for the future, Lan is confident that the growth of the Chinese media will eventually lead to a more open press. "We see more and more often that public opinions will drive public policies and drive the government to be more transparent and open. So we see the progress of freedom of speech," said Lan. "I just take it as the growing pains of the whole society."

Yang Lan is a prime example of an emerging global businessperson. She has learned to speak different languages, understands cultural and economic differences, and is well schooled in technology. This chapter explains the opportunities and challenges businesspeople like Yang Lan face every day in dealing with the dynamic environment of global business.

profile

Getting to Know
x **Yang Lan**
Co-founder and Chairman of Sun Media Group

Sources: April Rabkin, "Chinese TV Host Stays True to Self to Build Empire," *Fast Company*, September 1, 2010; Michel Martin, "China's Oprah: Yang Lan," *NPR*, October 7, 2010; Caroline Hedley, "'China's Oprah Winfrey' Yang Lan Signs Deal with Hollywood Agent," *The Telegraph*, March 28, 2009.

We franchise 37,000 of our KFC, Taco Bell, and Pizza Hut restaurants in 109 countries around the world. It didn't take us long to learn that customers around the globe have very different tastes when it comes to their food. We found in Japan that a favorite pizza enjoyed by our patrons was topped with squid and sweet mayonnaise. In China it's a must to serve a "dragon twister" with our world-famous chicken. Name our company. (Find the answer in the chapter.)

LEARNING goal 1

Discuss the importance of the global market and the roles of comparative advantage and absolute advantage in global trade.

THE DYNAMIC GLOBAL MARKET

Have you dreamed of traveling to cities like Paris, London, Rio de Janeiro, or Moscow? Today, over 90 percent of the companies doing business globally believe it's important for their employees to have experience working in other countries.[1] The reason is not surprising— although the United States is a market of over 310 *million* people, there are over 6.9 *billion* potential customers in

The Houston Rockets and the New Jersey Nets christened the new Guangzhou International Sports Arena with a preseason game in 2010. The NBA now plays games in several countries around the world. What cultural factors must U.S. sports franchises overcome to increase popularity abroad?

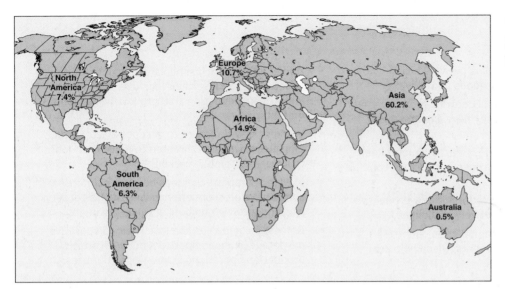

figure 3.1

**WORLD POPULATION
BY CONTINENT**

the 194 countries that make up the global market.[2] That's too many people to ignore! (See Figure 3.1 for a map of the world and important statistics about world population.)

Today U.S. consumers buy billions of dollars' worth of goods from China.[3] United Parcel Service (UPS) has experienced double-digit market growth in its global operations and Walmart is planning to expand into Africa.[4] Major League Baseball opened its 2008 season in Japan and the National Basketball Association (NBA) and the National Football League (NFL) play games in Mexico, Italy, England, and elsewhere. Chinese-born Yao Ming formerly of the NBA's Houston Rockets was a 7-time NBA All-Star and Paul Gasol of Spain helped the L.A. Lakers win championships in 2009–2010.[5] U.S. film stars Johnny Depp, Will Smith, and Julia Roberts draw crowds to movie theaters around the globe.[6]

Because the global market is so large, it is important to understand the language used in global trade. For example, **importing** is buying products from another country. **Exporting** is selling products to another country. As you might suspect, competition among exporting nations is intense. The United States is the largest importing nation in the world and is the third largest exporting nation, behind China and Germany.[7]

This chapter will familiarize you with global business and its many challenges. As competition in global markets intensifies, the demand for students with training in global business is almost certain to grow. If you choose such a career, prepare yourself to work hard and always be ready for new challenges.

importing
Buying products from another country.

exporting
Selling products to another country.

WHY TRADE WITH OTHER NATIONS?

No nation, not even a technologically advanced one, can produce all the products its people want and need. Even if a country did become self-sufficient, other nations would seek to trade with it to meet the needs of their own people. Some nations, like Venezuela and Russia, have an abundance of natural resources but limited technological know-how. Other countries, such as Japan and Switzerland, have sophisticated technology but few natural resources. Global trade enables a nation to produce what it is most capable of producing and buy what it needs from others in a mutually beneficial exchange relationship. This happens through the process called free trade.[8]

PROS	CONS
• The global market contains over 6.9 billion potential customers for goods and services. • Productivity grows when countries produce goods and services in which they have a comparative advantage. • Global competition and less-costly imports keep prices down, so inflation does not curtail economic growth. • Free trade inspires innovation for new products and keeps firms competitively challenged. • Uninterrupted flow of capital gives countries access to foreign investments, which help keep interest rates low.	• Domestic workers (particularly in manufacturing-based jobs) can lose their jobs due to increased imports or production shifts to low-wage global markets. • Workers may be forced to accept pay cuts from employers, who can threaten to move their jobs to lower-cost global markets. • Moving operations overseas because of intense competitive pressure often means the loss of service jobs and growing numbers of white-collar jobs. • Domestic companies can lose their comparative advantage when competitors build advanced production operations in low-wage countries.

figure 3.2

THE PROS AND CONS OF FREE TRADE

free trade
The movement of goods and services among nations without political or economic barriers.

comparative advantage theory
Theory that states that a country should sell to other countries those products that it produces most effectively and efficiently, and buy from other countries those products that it cannot produce as effectively or efficiently.

absolute advantage
The advantage that exists when a country has a monopoly on producing a specific product or is able to produce it more efficiently than all other countries.

Free trade is the movement of goods and services among nations without political or economic barriers. It has become a hotly debated concept.[9] In fact, many in the United States take the position "fair trade, not free trade."[10] Figure 3.2 offers some of the pros and cons of free trade.

The Theories of Comparative and Absolute Advantage

Countries exchange more than goods and services, however. They also exchange art, sports, cultural events, medical advances, space exploration, and labor. Comparative advantage theory, suggested in the early 19th century by English economist David Ricardo, was the guiding principle that supported the idea of free economic exchange.[11]

Comparative advantage theory states that a country should sell to other countries those products it produces most effectively and efficiently, and buy from other countries those products it cannot produce as effectively or efficiently. The United States has a comparative advantage in producing goods and services, such as software and engineering services. In contrast, it lacks a comparative advantage in growing coffee or making shoes; thus, we import most of the shoes and coffee we consume. By specializing and trading, the United States and its trading partners can realize mutually beneficial exchanges.[12]

A country has an **absolute advantage** if it has a monopoly on producing a specific product or is able to produce it more efficiently than all other countries. However, absolute advantage in natural resources does not last forever; for instance, South Africa once had an absolute advantage in diamond production, but that is no longer the case. Global competition also causes other absolute advantages to fade. Today there are very few instances of absolute advantage in global markets.

LEARNING goal 2

Explain the importance of importing and exporting, and understand key terms used in global business.

GETTING INVOLVED IN GLOBAL TRADE

People interested in a job in global business often think they are limited to firms like Boeing, Caterpillar, or IBM, which have large multinational accounts. However, real global job potential may be with small businesses.[13] In the United States, only 1 percent of the 29 million small businesses export yet they account for about 30 percent of the total U.S. exports. President Obama wants small businesses to think big and help double exports by 2015. With the support of the U.S. Department of Commerce, it's expected that almost half of these businesses will become involved in global trade.[14]

Getting started globally is often a matter of observing, being determined, and taking risks. For example, several years ago a U.S. traveler in an African country noticed there was no ice available for drinks or for keeping foods fresh. Research showed there was no ice factory for hundreds of miles, yet the market seemed huge. The man returned to the United States, found some investors, and returned to Africa to build an ice-making plant. The job was tough; much negotiation was necessary with local authorities (much of which was done by local citizens and businesspeople who knew the system). But the plant was built, and this forward-thinking entrepreneur gained a considerable return on his idea, while the people gained a needed product. The nearby Spotlight on Small Business box highlights how a small nonprofit business hopes to bring better sight to the world.

Importing Goods and Services

Students attending colleges and universities abroad often notice that some products widely available in their countries are unavailable or more expensive elsewhere. By working with producers in their native country, finding some start-up financing, and putting in long hours of hard work, many have become major importers while still in school.

Howard Schultz, CEO of Starbucks, found his opportunity while traveling in Italy. Schultz was enthralled with the ambience, the aroma, and especially the sense of community in the 200,000 Italian neighborhood coffee and espresso bars that stretched across the country. He felt such gathering places would be great in the United States. Schultz bought the original Starbucks coffee shop in Seattle and transformed it according to his vision.[15] Because the Italian coffee bars caught his attention, U.S. coffee lovers now know what a grande latte is.

Exporting Goods and Services

Who would think U.S. firms could sell beer in Germany, home of so many good beers? Well, around the corner from a famous beer hall in Munich you can buy Samuel Adams Boston Lager. If this surprises you, imagine selling sand in the Middle East. Meridan Group exports a special kind of sand used in swimming pool filters that sells well there.

The fact is, you can sell just about any good or service used in the United States to other countries—and sometimes the competition is not nearly so intense as it is at home. For example, you can sell snowplows to Saudi Arabians, who use them to clear sand off their driveways. In China,

Things may not have started off "pretty" for Ugly Dolls, a venture founded almost by accident, but the two-person company has grown into a global business selling its products in over 1,000 stores around the world. The original dolls have been joined by books, calendars, action figures, and T-shirts. Does a career in exporting or importing sound appealing to you?

A Small Business with a Big Vision

When optometrist Jordan Kassalow made an aid trip to Mexico, he learned firsthand how the lack of glasses affected the local workers. "Losing eyesight is a silent robber of economic activity," said Kassalow. "Hundreds of millions of poor people lose their livelihood in their prime working years."

Kassalow wanted to help the people he met, but he didn't like the idea of relying solely on donations to achieve his goals. So Kassalow and a partner founded VisionSpring, a business that is part charity and part small franchisor. Kassalow employs mostly women needing additional income to travel around their villages selling glasses. The women buy glasses at cost from VisionSpring for $2.50 a pair and then sell them for $4 to $7 apiece. This way Kassalow is not only giving sight to those who need it most, but he's also stimulating the local economy. So far VisionSpring has sold 600,000 pairs of basic reading glasses in seven countries.

VisionSpring still operates at a loss, however, making charitable donations a necessary part of the company's income. Kassalow is making strides toward profitability though. VisionSpring recently opened its first store that sells higher-priced prescription glasses in El Salvador. A $15 pair of prescription glasses yields about $4.50 in profit, including a $1 finder's fee to Kassalow's local salespeople. The store made money in its first year of operation, putting Kassalow one step closer to his dream of a sustainable, market-driven solution for vision problems in the developing world.

Sources: Helen Coster and Jason Daley, "The Vision Thing," *Entrepreneur*, March 2010; and "New Vision for Nonprofits," *Forbes*, February 14, 2011.

sales of men's cosmetic products is growing at twice the rate of women's due to their desire to project an image of success.[16] Exporting also provides a terrific boost to the U.S. economy. C. Fred Bergsten, director of the Peterson Institute for International Economics, states that U.S. exports of $1.5 trillion goods and services create approximately 10 million well-paid jobs in our economy. He also estimates that every $1 billion in additional U.S. exports generates over 7,000 jobs at home.[17] But selling in global markets and adapting products to global customers are by no means easy tasks. We discuss key forces that affect global trading later in this chapter.

If you are interested in exporting, send for "The Basic Guide to Exporting," a brochure from the U.S. Government Printing Office, Superintendent of Documents, Washington, DC 20402. More advice is available at websites such as those sponsored by the U.S Department of Commerce (www.doc.gov), the Bureau of Export Administration (www.bea.gov), the Small Business Administration (www.sba.gov), and the Small Business Exporters Association (www.sbea.org).

Measuring Global Trade

balance of trade
The total value of a nation's exports compared to its imports measured over a particular period.

trade surplus
A favorable balance of trade; occurs when the value of a country's exports exceeds that of its imports.

trade deficit
An unfavorable balance of trade; occurs when the value of a country's imports exceeds that of its exports.

In measuring global trade, nations rely on two key indicators: balance of trade and balance of payments. The **balance of trade** is the total value of a nation's exports compared to its imports measured over a particular period. A *favorable* balance of trade, or **trade surplus**, occurs when the value of a country's exports exceeds that of its imports. An *unfavorable* balance of trade, or **trade deficit**, occurs when the value of a country's exports is less than its imports. It's easy to understand why countries prefer to export more than they import. If I sell you $200 worth of goods and buy only $100 worth, I have an extra $100 available to buy other things. However, I'm in an unfavorable position if I buy $200 worth of goods from you and sell you only $100.

The United States imports most of its toys from China—and so does the rest of the world. China now produces and exports 80 percent of the toys manufactured in the world. The highest U.S. trade deficit is with China. What products do you use that are imported from China?

The **balance of payments** is the difference between money coming into a country (from exports) and money leaving the country (for imports) plus money flows coming into or leaving a country from other factors such as tourism, foreign aid, military expenditures, and foreign investment. The goal is to have more money flowing into the country than out—a *favorable* balance of payments. Conversely, an *unfavorable* balance of payments exists when more money is flowing out of a country than coming in.

In the past, the United States exported more goods and services than it imported. However, since 1975 it has bought more goods from other nations than it has sold and thus has a trade deficit.[18] Over the past few years, the United States ran its highest trade deficits with China.[19] Still the United States remains one of the world's largest *exporting* nations even though the U.S. exports a much lower *percentage* of its products than other countries, such as China, Japan and Germany. Improving that percentage by expanding exports is a goal the U.S. hopes to achieve by 2015.[20] (Figure 3.3 lists the major trading countries in the world and the leading U.S. trading partners.)

balance of payments
The difference between money coming into a country (from exports) and money leaving the country (for imports) plus money flows from other factors such as tourism, foreign aid, military expenditures, and foreign investment.

figure 3.3

THE LARGEST EXPORTING NATIONS IN THE WORLD AND THE LARGEST U.S. TRADE PARTNERS

World's Largest Exporting Nations

China
Germany
United States
Japan
France
South Korea
Italy
Netherlands
Canada
United Kingdom

Top U.S. Trading Partners	
COUNTRY	2010 TOTAL TRADE (IN BILLIONS)
1. Canada	$525
2. China	$456
3. Mexico	$393
4. Japan	$180
5. Germany	$130
6. U.K.	$98
7. South Korea	$87
8. France	$65
9. Taiwan	$61
10. Brazil	$59

dumping
Selling products in a foreign country at lower prices than those charged in the producing country.

In supporting free trade, the United States, like other nations, wants to make certain global trade is conducted fairly. To ensure a level playing field, countries prohibit unfair practices such as dumping. **Dumping** is selling products in a foreign country at lower prices than those charged in the producing country. This predatory pricing tactic is sometimes used to reduce surplus products in foreign markets or to gain a foothold in a new market. Some governments may offer financial incentives to certain industries to sell goods in global markets for less than they sell them at home. China, Brazil, and Russia, for example, have been penalized for dumping steel in the United States.[21] U.S. laws against dumping are specific and require foreign firms to price their products to include 10 percent overhead costs plus an 8 percent profit margin.

Now that you understand some of the basic terms used in global business, we can look at different strategies for entering global markets. First, let's assess your progress so far.

progress assessment

- What are two of the main arguments favoring the expansion of U.S. businesses into global markets?
- What is comparative advantage, and what are some examples of this concept at work in global markets?
- How are a nation's balance of trade and balance of payments determined?
- What is meant by the term *dumping* in global trade?

LEARNING goal 3

Illustrate the strategies used in reaching global markets and explain the role of multinational corporations.

STRATEGIES FOR REACHING GLOBAL MARKETS

Businesses use different strategies to compete in global markets. The key strategies include licensing, exporting, franchising, contract manufacturing, international joint ventures and strategic alliances, foreign subsidiaries, and foreign direct investment. Each provides different economic opportunities, along with specific commitments and risks. Figure 3.4 places the strategies on a continuum showing the amount of commitment, control, risk, and profit potential associated with each. Take a few minutes to look over Figure 3.4 before you continue.

Licensing

licensing
A global strategy in which a firm (the licensor) allows a foreign company (the licensee) to produce its product in exchange for a fee (a royalty).

A firm (the licensor) may decide to compete in a global market by **licensing** the right to manufacture its product or use its trademark to a foreign company (the licensee) for a fee (a royalty). A company with an interest in licensing generally sends company representatives to the foreign company to help set up operations. The licensor may also assist or work with a licensee in such areas as distribution, promotion, and consulting.

A licensing agreement can benefit a firm in several ways. First, the firm can gain revenues it would not otherwise have generated in its home market. Also, foreign licensees often must purchase start-up supplies, materials, and

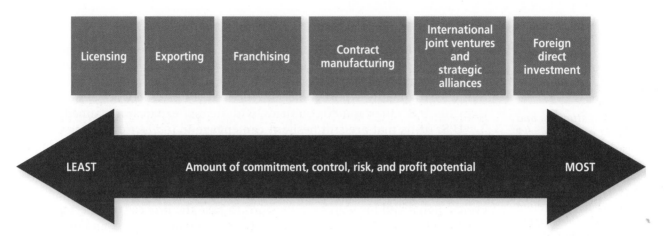

| Licensing | Exporting | Franchising | Contract manufacturing | International joint ventures and strategic alliances | Foreign direct investment |

LEAST   Amount of commitment, control, risk, and profit potential   MOST

figure 3.4

STRATEGIES FOR REACHING GLOBAL MARKETS

consulting services from the licensing firm. Coca-Cola has entered into global licensing agreements with over 300 licensees that have extended into long-term service contracts that sell over $1 billion of the company's products each year.[22] Service-based companies are also active in licensing. For example, retailer Frederick's of Hollywood recently entered into a licensing agreement with Emirates Associated Business Group to build and operate Frederick's of Hollywood stores in the Middle East.[23]

A final advantage of licensing is that licensors spend little or no money to produce and market their products. These costs come from the licensee's pocket. Therefore, licensees generally work hard to succeed. However, licensors may also experience problems. Often a firm must grant licensing rights to its product for an extended period, 20 years or longer. If a product experiences remarkable growth in the foreign market, the bulk of the revenues belong to the licensee. Perhaps even more threatening is that the licensing firm is actually selling its expertise. If a foreign licensee learns the company's technology or product secrets, it may break the agreement and begin to produce a similar product on its own. If legal remedies are not available, the licensing firm may lose its trade secrets, not to mention promised royalties.

Warner Bros, has licensed hundreds of companies to make products related to its series of hit films based on the best-selling Harry Potter books, which have been translated into dozens of languages. Do you think Potter-licensed products will maintain their global popularity with new generations of young readers and viewers?

Exporting

To meet increasing global competition, the U.S. Department of Commerce created Export Assistance Centers (EACs). EACs provide hands-on exporting assistance and trade-finance support for small and medium-sized businesses that wish to directly export goods and services. An EAC network exists in more than 109 U.S. cities and 80 countries, with further expansion planned.[24]

U.S. firms that are still hesitant can engage in *indirect* exporting through specialists called export-trading companies (or export-management companies) that assist in negotiating and establishing trading relationships. An export-trading company not only matches buyers and sellers from different countries but also deals with foreign customs offices, documentation, and even weights and measures conversions to ease the process of entering global markets. It also can assist exporters with warehousing, billing, and insuring. If you are considering a career in global business, export-trading companies often provide internships or part-time opportunities for students.

Tired of studying and want a quick snack? How about a piping hot Pizza Hut pizza with shrimp and mayonnaise? Pizza Hut serves pizzas around the globe that appeal to different tastes. How can franchises ensure their products are appropriate for global markets?

Franchising

맛도, 가격도
더 스페셜
the special
피자

정말 맛있는
5가지 피자

15,900원

크림치킨   까망베르   데이그라스 비프   바질씨푸드   갈릭토마토

Pizza Hut

Franchising is a contractual agreement whereby someone with a good idea for a business sells others the rights to use the business name and sell a product or service in a given territory in a specified manner. Franchising is popular domestically and internationally. (We discuss it in depth in Chapter 5.) Major U.S. franchisors such as Subway, Holiday Inn, and Dunkin' Donuts have many global units operated by foreign franchisees, but global franchising isn't limited to large franchisors. For example, Rocky Mountain Chocolate Factory, a Colorado-based producer of premium chocolates, has franchising agreements with the Al Muhairy Group of the United Arab Emirates, where chocolate is considered a gourmet luxury much like caviar in the United States.[25] Foreign franchisors also may look to expand to the U.S. market. Vietnamese entrepreneur Ly Qui Trung hopes to introduce his Pho24 franchises to the U.S. by 2012.[26]

Franchisors have to be careful to adapt their product or service to the countries they serve. Yum Brands has 37,000 of its KFC, Taco Bell, and Pizza Hut restaurants in 109 countries around the world.[27] They learned quickly that preferences in pizza toppings differ globally. Japanese customers, for example, enjoy squid and sweet mayonnaise pizza. In the company's KFC restaurants in China, the menu is chicken with Sichuan spicy sauce and rice, egg soup, and a "dragon twister" (KFC's version of a traditional Beijing duck wrap).[28] Read the nearby Reaching Beyond Our Borders box that highlights another franchise champion, McDonald's.

Contract Manufacturing

contract manufacturing
A foreign country's production of private-label goods to which a domestic company then attaches its brand name or trademark; part of the broad category of outsourcing.

In **contract manufacturing** a foreign company produces private-label goods to which a domestic company then attaches its own brand name or trademark. For example, contract manufacturers make circuit boards and components

Golden Arches Glowing across the Globe

For decades the undisputed king of global food franchising has been McDonald's. With more than 32,000 restaurants in 117 countries, Mickey D's serves more than 60 million customers every day.

So how did McDonald's become such a global powerhouse? It certainly didn't get there through hamburgers alone. Since it first began expanding overseas, McDonald's has been careful to include regional tastes on its menus along with the usual Big Mac and French fries. For instance, in Thailand patrons can order the Samurai Burger, a pork-patty sandwich marinated in teriyaki sauce and topped with mayonnaise and a pickle. If fish is more your taste, try Norway's salmon burger called the McLaks, or the Ebi Filet-o shrimp sandwich from Japan.

McDonald's is also careful to adapt its menus to local customs and culture. In Israel, all meat served in the chain's restaurants is 100 percent kosher beef. The company also closes many of its restaurants on the Sabbath and religious holidays. McDonald's pays respect to religious sentiments in India as well by not including any beef or pork on its menu. For more examples, go to www.mcdonalds.com and explore the various McDonald's international franchises websites. Notice how the company blends the culture of each country into the restaurant's image.

McDonald's main global market concern as of late has been China. So far McDonald's strategy seems to be working. In Shanghai the company's Hamburger University attracts top-level college graduates to be trained for management positions. Only about eight out of every 1,000 applicants makes it into the program, an acceptance rate even lower than Harvard's. McDonald's also found a boost of prestige in Hong Kong with its so-called McWeddings. Matrimony is a big deal in the city, with many young people saving for years or going deeply into debt to fund lavish ceremonies that cost around $29,000 for the average couple. A McWedding, on the other hand, starts at $1,280 and includes drinks and food for 50 people along with gifts and invitations. The affordable wedding package even comes with a "cake" made out of a stack of McDonald's signature apple pies.

On that note, McDonald's continues to battle controversies over the fat content of its food as well as the safety of its production methods. In 2010, for instance, the company instituted a recall of its promotional line of *Shrek Forever After* glassware after reports of cadmium poisoning surfaced. In the end, one can only hope that McDonald's remains dedicated to quality as it continues adapting and expanding into the global market.

Sources: Bloomberg News, "Getting into Harvard Easier than McDonald's University in China," *Bloomberg,* January 25, 2011; Joyce Hor-Chung Lau, "Raising a Milkshake to the Bride and Groom," *The New York Times,* February 27, 2011; Zach Tropf, "McLobster Sandwich and other McMenu Madness," *Gunaxin,* March 12, 2009; and McDonalds, www.mcdonalds. com, accessed March 20, 2011.

used in computers, printers, cell phones, medical products, airplanes, and consumer electronics for companies such as Dell, Xerox, and IBM.[29] Nike has more than 700 contract factories around the world that manufacture all its footwear and apparel. The worldwide contract manufacturing business is estimated to be a $250 billion industry that's expected to grow to $325 billion by 2013.[30]

Contract manufacturing enables a company to experiment in a new market without incurring heavy start-up costs such as building a manufacturing plant. If the brand name becomes a success, the company has penetrated a new market with relatively low risk. A firm can also use contract manufacturing temporarily to meet an unexpected increase in orders, and, of course, labor costs are often very low. Contract manufacturing falls under the broad category of *outsourcing,* which we defined in Chapter 1 and will discuss in more depth later in this chapter.

International Joint Ventures and Strategic Alliances

A **joint venture** is a partnership in which two or more companies (often from different countries) join to undertake a major project. Joint ventures are often mandated by governments such as China as a condition of doing business in their country. For example, Disney and state-owned Shanghai Shendi Group entered a joint venture to create a Disneyland theme park in Shanghai that is expected to open in 2015.[31]

Joint ventures are developed for many different reasons. Marriott International and AC Hotels in Spain entered a joint venture to create AC Hotels by Marriott to increase their global footprint and future growth.[32] PepsiCo agreed to a joint venture with Tata Global Beverages of India to develop packaged health and wellness beverages for the mass consumer market in India.[33] Joint ventures can also be truly unique, such as the University of Pittsburgh's Medical Center and the Italian government's joint venture that brought a new medical transplant center to Sicily. The transplant center in Palermo called ISMETT recently celebrated its fifteenth year of operation.[34]

The benefits of international joint ventures are clear:

1. Shared technology and risk.
2. Shared marketing and management expertise.
3. Entry into markets where foreign companies are often not allowed unless goods are produced locally.

The drawbacks of joint ventures are not so obvious but are important. One partner can learn the other's technology and business practices and then use what it has learned to its own advantage. Also, a shared technology may become obsolete, or the joint venture may become too large to be as flexible as needed.

The global market is also fueling the growth of strategic alliances. A **strategic alliance** is a long-term partnership between two or more companies established to help each company build competitive market advantages. Unlike joint ventures, strategic alliances don't share costs, risks, management, or even profits. Such alliances provide broad access to markets, capital, and technical expertise. Thanks to their flexibility, strategic alliances can effectively link firms from different countries and firms of vastly different sizes. Hewlett-Packard has strategic alliances with Hitachi and Samsung and Coca-Cola and Nestlé have had an alliance since early 1990 to distribute ready-to-drink tea and coffee.

Foreign Direct Investment

Foreign direct investment (FDI) is the buying of permanent property and businesses in foreign nations. The most common form of FDI is a **foreign subsidiary**, a company owned in a foreign country by another company, called the *parent company.* The subsidiary operates like a domestic firm, with production, distribution, promotion, pricing, and other business functions under the control of the subsidiary's management. The subsidiary also must observe the legal requirements of both the country where the parent firm is located

joint venture
 A partnership in which two or more companies (often from different countries) join to undertake a major project.

strategic alliance
A long-term partnership between two or more companies established to help each company build competitive market advantages.

foreign direct investment (FDI)
The buying of permanent property and businesses in foreign nations.

foreign subsidiary
A company owned in a foreign country by another company, called the *parent company.*

multinational corporation
An organization that manufactures and markets products in many different countries and has multinational stock ownership and multinational management.

sovereign wealth funds (SWFs)
Investment funds controlled by governments holding large stakes in foreign companies.

Religion is an important part of any society's culture and can have a significant impact on business operations. Consider the violent clashes between religious communities in India, Pakistan, and the Middle East—clashes that have wounded these areas' economies. Even successful global companies sometimes ignore religious implications in making business decisions. For example, in honor of nations competing in the World Cup, both McDonald's and Coca-Cola decided to reprint the flags of the countries participating on their packaging. Muslims were offended by putting the Saudi Arabian flag on their packaging because the flag's design contains a passage from the Koran, and Muslims believe their holy writ should never be wadded up and thrown away.

In another classic story, a U.S. manager in Islamic Pakistan toured a new plant under his control. While the plant was in full operation, he went to his office to make some preliminary production forecasts. Suddenly all the machinery in the plant stopped. The manager rushed out, suspecting a power failure, only to find his production workers on their prayer rugs. Upon learning that Muslims are required to pray five times a day, he returned to his office and lowered his production estimates.

Understanding sociocultural differences is also important in managing employees. In some Latin American countries, workers believe managers are in positions of authority to make decisions concerning the well-being of the workers under their control. Consider the U.S. manager in Peru who was unaware of this cultural characteristic and believed workers should participate in managerial functions. He was convinced he could motivate his workers to higher levels of productivity by instituting a more democratic decision-making style. Workers instead began quitting in droves. When asked why, they said the new manager did not know his job and was asking the workers what to do. All stated they wanted to find new jobs, since this company was doomed due to its incompetent management.

Many U.S. companies still fail to think globally. Even something like the color of flowers can have different meanings in different cultures.[38] A sound philosophy is: *Never assume what works in one country will work in another.* Intel, Nike, IBM, Apple, Honda, KFC, and Walmart have developed brand names with widespread global appeal and recognition, but even they often face difficulties. To get an idea of the problems companies have faced with translations of advertising, take a look at Figure 3.6.

- PepsiCo attempted a Chinese translation of "Come Alive, You're in the Pepsi Generation" that read to Chinese customers as "Pepsi Brings Your Ancestors Back from the Dead."
- Coors Brewing Company put its slogan "Turn It Loose" into Spanish and found it translated as "Suffer from Diarrhea."
- Perdue Chicken used the slogan "It Takes a Strong Man to Make a Chicken Tender," which was interpreted in Spanish as "It Takes an Aroused Man to Make a Chicken Affectionate."
- KFC's patented slogan "Finger-Lickin' Good" was understood in Japanese as "Bite Your Fingers Off."
- On the other side of the translation glitch, Electrolux, a Scandinavian vacuum manufacturer, tried to sell its products in the U.S. market with the slogan "Nothing Sucks Like an Electrolux."

figure 3.6

OOPS, DID WE SAY THAT?
A global marketing strategy can be very difficult to implement. Look at the problems these well-known companies encountered in global markets.

When the dollar is "up," foreign goods and travel are a bargain for U.S. consumers. When the dollar trades for less foreign currency, however, foreign tourists like these often flock to U.S. cities to enjoy relatively cheaper vacations and shopping trips. Do U.S. exporters profit more when the dollar is up or when it is down?

Economic and Financial Forces

Economic differences can muddy the water in global markets. It's hard for us to imagine buying chewing gum by the stick. Yet this behavior is commonplace in economically depressed nations like Haiti, where customers can afford only small quantities. You might suspect with over 1 billion people each, India and China would be dream markets for companies like Pepsi-Cola and Procter & Gamble (P&G). Unfortunately, Indians consume an average of three soft drinks per person a year and China's 1.3 billion customers spend just $3 per year on P&G products due to low per-capita income.[39]

Mexicans shop with pesos, Chinese with yuan, South Koreans with won, Japanese with yen, and U.S. consumers with dollars. Globally, the U.S. dollar is considered a dominant and stable currency.[40] However, it doesn't always retain the same market value. In a global transaction today, a dollar may be exchanged for eight pesos; tomorrow you may get seven. The **exchange rate** is the value of one nation's currency relative to the currencies of other countries.

Changes in a nation's exchange rates have effects in global markets. A *high value of the dollar* means a dollar is trading for more foreign currency than previously. Therefore, foreign products become cheaper because it takes fewer dollars to buy them. However, U.S.-produced goods become more expensive because of the dollar's high value. Conversely, a *low value of the dollar* means a dollar is traded for less foreign currency—foreign goods become more expensive because it takes more dollars to buy them, but U.S. goods become cheaper to foreign buyers because it takes less foreign currency to buy them.

Global financial markets operate under a system called *floating exchange rates,* which means that currencies "float" in value according to the supply and demand for them in the global market for currency. This supply and demand is created by global currency traders who develop a market for a nation's currency based on the country's perceived trade and investment potential.

Changes in currency values can cause many problems globally.[41] For instance, labor costs for multinational corporations like Nestlé, General Electric, and Sony can vary considerably as currency values shift, causing them to juggle production from one country to another. The same is true for medium-sized companies like H. B. Fuller of St. Paul, Minnesota, which has 3,100 employees in 38 countries. Like their larger counterparts, H. B. Fuller learned to use currency fluctuations to their advantage in dealing with their global markets.

Currency valuation problems can be especially harsh on developing economies.[42] At times a nation's government will intervene and readjust the value of its currency, often to increase the export potential of its products. **Devaluation** lowers the value of a nation's currency relative to others. Sometimes, due to a nation's weak currency, the only way to trade is *bartering,* the exchange of merchandise for merchandise or service for service with no money traded.

Countertrading is a complex form of bartering in which several countries each trade goods or services for other goods or services. Let's say a developing country such as Jamaica wants to buy vehicles from Ford Motor Company in exchange for bauxite, a mineral compound that is a source of aluminum ore. Ford does not need Jamaican bauxite, but it does need compressors. In a

exchange rate
The value of one nation's currency relative to the currencies of other countries.

devaluation
Lowering the value of a nation's currency relative to other currencies.

countertrading
A complex form of bartering in which several countries may be involved, each trading goods for goods or services for services.

countertrade, Ford may trade vehicles to Jamaica, which trades bauxite to another country, say India, which exchanges compressors with Ford. All three parties benefit and avoid some of the financial problems and currency constraints in global markets. Estimates are that countertrading accounts for over 20 percent of all global exchanges, especially with developing countries.[43]

Legal and Regulatory Forces

In any economy, the conduct and the direction of business are firmly tied to the legal and regulatory environment. In global markets, no central system of law exists, so different systems of laws and regulations may apply in different places. This makes conducting global business difficult as businesspeople navigate a sea of laws and regulations that are often inconsistent. Antitrust rules, labor relations, patents, copyrights, trade practices, taxes, product liability, child labor, prison labor, and other issues are governed differently country by country.

U.S. businesses must follow U.S. laws and regulations in conducting business globally, although legislation such as the Foreign Corrupt Practices Act of 1978 can create competitive disadvantages. This law prohibits "questionable" or "dubious" payments to foreign officials to secure business contracts.[44] That runs contrary to practices in many countries, where corporate or government bribery is not merely acceptable but perhaps the only way to secure a lucrative contract. The Organization for Economic Cooperation and Development (OECD) and Transparency International have led a global effort to fight corruption and bribery in global business, with limited success.[45] Figure 3.7 shows a partial list of countries where bribery or other unethical business practices are most common.

The cooperation and sponsorship of local businesspeople can help a company penetrate the market and deal with laws, regulations, and bureaucratic barriers in their country.

Physical and Environmental Forces

Physical and environmental forces certainly affect a company's ability to conduct global business. Some developing countries have such primitive transportation and storage systems that international distribution is ineffective, if not impossible, especially for perishable food. Add unclean water and lack of effective sewer systems, and you can see the intensity of the problem.

Technological differences also influence the features of exportable products. For example, residential electrical systems in most developing countries do not match those of U.S. homes, in kind or capacity. Computer and Internet use in many developing countries is thin or nonexistent. These facts make for a tough environment for business in general and for e-commerce in particular. After the Progress Assessment, we'll explore how another force, trade protectionism, affects global business.

figure 3.7

COUNTRIES RATED HIGHEST ON CORRUPT BUSINESS

1. Somalia
2. Myanmar
3. Afghanistan
4. Iraq
5. Uzbekistan
6. Turkmenistan
7. Sudan
8. Chad
9. Burundi
10. Angola

Source: Transparency International, 2011.

progress assessment

- What are four major hurdles to successful global trade?
- What does *ethnocentricity* mean, and how can it affect global success?
- How would a low value of the dollar affect U.S. exports?
- What does the Foreign Corrupt Practices Act prohibit?

trade protectionism
The use of government regulations to limit the import of goods and services.

tariff
A tax imposed on imports.

import quota
A limit on the number of products in certain categories that a nation can import.

embargo
A complete ban on the import or export of a certain product, or the stopping of all trade with a particular country.

Some workers believe that too many U.S. jobs have been lost due to the growing number of imported products. Should governments protect their industries by placing tariffs on imported products? Why or why not?

LEARNING goal 5

Debate the advantages and disadvantages of trade protectionism.

TRADE PROTECTIONISM

As we discussed in the previous section, sociocultural, economic and financial, legal and regulatory, and physical and environmental forces are all challenges to global trade. What is often a much greater barrier to global trade, however, is trade protectionism. **Trade protectionism** is the use of government regulations to limit the import of goods and services. Advocates of protectionism believe it allows domestic producers to survive and grow, producing more jobs. Other countries use protectionist measures because they are wary of foreign competition in general. To understand how protectionism affects global business, let's briefly review a bit of global economic history.

Business, economics, and politics have always been closely linked. Economics was once referred to as *political economy,* indicating the close ties between politics (government) and economics. In the 17th and 18th centuries, businesspeople and government leaders endorsed an economic policy called *mercantilism.*[46] The idea was for a nation to sell more goods to other nations than it bought from them, that is, to have a favorable balance of trade. According to mercantilists, this resulted in a flow of money to the country that sold the most globally. The philosophy led governments to implement **tariffs,** taxes on imports, making imported goods more expensive to buy.

There are two kinds of tariffs: protective and revenue. *Protective tariffs* (import taxes) raise the retail price of imported products so that domestic goods are more competitively priced. These tariffs are meant to save jobs for domestic workers and keep industries—especially infant industries that have companies in the early stages of growth—from closing down because of foreign competition. *Revenue tariffs* are designed to raise money for the government.

An **import quota** limits the number of products in certain categories a nation can import. The United States has import quotas on a number of products, including sugar and shrimp, to protect U.S. companies and preserve jobs. Nations also prohibit the export of specific products. Antiterrorism laws and the U.S. Export Administration Act of 1979 prohibit exporting goods such as high-tech weapons that could endanger national security. An **embargo** is a complete ban on the import or export of a certain product, or the stopping of all trade with a particular country. Political disagreements have caused many countries to establish embargoes, such as the U.S. embargo against Cuba, in effect since 1962.[47]

Non-tariff barriers are not as specific or formal as tariffs, import quotas, and embargoes but can be as detrimental to free trade. For example, India imposes a number of restrictive standards like import licensing, burdensome product testing requirements, and lengthy customs procedures that inhibit the sale of imported products. China omits many American-made products from its government catalogs that specify what products may be purchased by its huge government sector. Other countries detail exactly how a product must be sold in a country. South Korea sells almost 450,000 cars to the United States each year but imports fewer than 6,000 due to nontariff barriers such as the size of the engine.[48] Hopefully a pending free trade agreement with South Korea will eliminate such nontariff barriers and open the market to U.S. producers.

Would-be exporters might view such trade barriers as good reasons to avoid global trade, but overcoming constraints creates business opportunities. Next, we'll look at organizations and agreements that attempt to eliminate trade barriers.

The World Trade Organization

In 1948, government leaders from 23 nations formed the **General Agreement on Tariffs and Trade (GATT),** a global forum for reducing trade restrictions on goods, services, ideas, and cultural programs. In 1986, the Uruguay Round of the GATT convened to renegotiate trade agreements. After eight years of meetings, 124 nations voted to lower tariffs an average of 38 percent worldwide and to expand new trade rules to areas such as agriculture, services, and the protection of patents.

The Uruguay Round also established the **World Trade Organization (WTO)** to mediate trade disputes among nations. The WTO, headquartered in Geneva, is an independent entity of 153 member nations whose purpose is to oversee cross-border trade issues and global business practices.[49] Trade disputes are presented by member nations with decisions made within a year, rather than languishing for years as in the past; member nations can appeal a decision.[50]

The WTO has not solved all global trade problems. Legal and regulatory differences (discussed above) often impede trade expansion. Also a wide gap persists between developing nations (80 percent of the WTO membership) and industrialized nations like the United States. The WTO meetings in Doha, Qatar, begun in 2001 to address dismantling protection of manufactured goods, eliminating subsidies on agricultural products, and overturning temporary protectionist measures have still not resulted in any significant agreements.[51]

Common Markets

An issue not resolved by the GATT or the WTO is whether common markets create regional alliances at the expense of global expansion. A **common market** (also called a *trading bloc*) is a regional group of countries with a common external tariff, no internal tariffs, and coordinated laws to facilitate exchange among members. The European Union (EU), Mercosur, the Association of Southeast Asian Nations (ASEAN) Economic Community, and the Common Market for Eastern and Southern Africa (COMESA) are common markets.

The EU began in the late 1950s as an alliance of six trading partners (then known as the Common Market and later the European Economic Community). Today it is a group of 27 nations (see Figure 3.8) with a population of over 500 million and a GDP of $16.4 trillion. France, Germany, Italy, the Netherlands, Poland, Spain, and the U.K. account for almost 80 percent of

General Agreement on Tariffs and Trade (GATT)
A 1948 agreement that established an international forum for negotiating mutual reductions in trade restrictions.

World Trade Organization (WTO)
The international organization that replaced the General Agreement on Tariffs and Trade and was assigned the duty to mediate trade disputes among nations.

This Indian family used to use bullocks to pull their plow, but had to sell them because the cost to maintain the animals is now too high. Do you think a Doha resolution regarding tariff protection would help families like these?

common market
A regional group of countries that have a common external tariff, no internal tariffs, and a coordination of laws to facilitate exchange; also called a *trading bloc*. An example is the European Union.

figure 3.8

**MEMBERS OF THE
EUROPEAN UNION**

Current EU members are
highlighted in dark blue.
Countries that have
applied for membership
are in light blue.

EU GDP.[52] The EU sees continued economic integration as the major way to compete for global business, particularly with the United States, China, and Japan.[53]

European unification was not easy but in 1999 the EU took a significant step by adopting the euro as a common currency. The euro helped EU businesses save billions by eliminating currency conversions. It has also proven to be a worthy challenger to the U.S. dollar's dominance in global markets. In 2010–2011, the EU faced debt, deficit, and growth problems due to financial difficulties in member nations Greece, Ireland, Portugal, and Spain.[54] EU officials are moving forward with a broad economic-policy overhaul to try to ensure the stability of the union.[55]

Mercosur unites Brazil, Argentina, Paraguay, Uruguay, and associate members Bolivia, Chile, Colombia, Ecuador, and Peru in a trading bloc that encompasses more than 250 million people. Its economic goals also include the establishment of a single currency among member nations. Mercosur has expressed an interest in joining a Union of South American Nations that would pave the way for an economic free-trade zone spanning South America much like the EU.[56]

The ASEAN Economic Community was established in 1967 in Thailand to create economic cooperation among its five original members (Indonesia, Malaysia, Philippines, Singapore, and Thailand). ASEAN has expanded to include Brunei, Cambodia, the Lao People's Democratic Republic, Myanmar, and Vietnam, creating a trade association with a population of approximately 600 million and a GDP of $1.8 trillion.[57] COMESA is a 19-member African trading bloc. In 2008, COMESA joined with the Southern African Development

Community (SADC) and the East Africa Community (EAC) to form an expanded free trade zone that has a GDP of $740 billion and a population of 533 million.

The North American and Central American Free Trade Agreements

A widely debated issue of the early 1990s was the **North American Free Trade Agreement (NAFTA),** which created a free-trade area among the United States, Canada, and Mexico. Opponents warned of the loss of U.S. jobs and capital. Supporters predicted NAFTA would open a vast new market for U.S. exports and create jobs and market opportunities in the long term.

NAFTA's objectives were to (1) eliminate trade barriers and facilitate cross-border movement of goods and services, (2) promote conditions of fair competition, (3) increase investment opportunities, (4) provide effective protection and enforcement of intellectual property rights (patents and copyrights), (5) establish a framework for further regional trade cooperation, and (6) improve working conditions in North America. Today, the three NAFTA countries have a combined population of over 450 million and a gross domestic product (GDP) of $17 trillion.[58]

NAFTA promises to remain a hotly debated issue. On the positive side, trade volume in goods and services among the three partners has expanded from $289 billion in 1994 to over $1 trillion today. On the downside, almost 750,000 U.S. jobs have been lost since enacting NAFTA; unfortunately most were in the high paying manufacturing sector. Illegal immigration remains a major problem since annual per capita income in Mexico still lags considerably behind that of the United States.[59] NAFTA critics also argue that working conditions in Mexico are less safe than before NAFTA, especially in southern Mexico.

NAFTA controversies have not changed the U.S. commitment to free-trade agreements. In 2005, the Central American Free Trade Agreement (CAFTA) was signed into law, creating a free-trade zone with Costa Rica, the Dominican Republic, El Salvador, Guatemala, Honduras, and Nicaragua. Again, supporters claimed CAFTA would open new markets, lower tariffs, and ease regulations between the member nations. Critics countered the measure would cost U.S. jobs, especially in the sugar and textile industries. Today, free trade agreements are being negotiated with South Korea, Colombia, and Panama.[60] The United States is also considering an agreement with a nine-nation free trade bloc called the Trans-Pacific Partnership.[61]

Common markets and free-trade areas will be debated far into the future. While some economists resoundingly praise such efforts, others are concerned the world is dividing into major trading blocs (EU, NAFTA, etc.) that will exclude poor and developing nations. After the Progress Assessment, we'll look at the future of global trade and the issue of outsourcing.

North American Free Trade Agreement (NAFTA)
Agreement that created a free-trade area among the United States, Canada, and Mexico.

progress assessment

- What are the advantages and disadvantages of trade protectionism and of tariffs?
- What is the primary purpose of the WTO?
- What is the key objective of a common market like the EU?
- What three nations comprise NAFTA?

LEARNING goal 6

Discuss the changing landscape of the global market and the issue of offshore outsourcing.

THE FUTURE OF GLOBAL TRADE

Global trade opportunities grow more interesting and more challenging each day. After all, 6.9 billion potential customers are attractive.[62] However, terrorism, nuclear proliferation, rogue states, and other issues cast a dark shadow on global markets. Let's conclude this chapter by looking at issues certain to influence global markets, and perhaps your business career.

With more than 1.3 billion people and incredible exporting prowess, China has transformed the world economic map. However, not long ago, foreign direct investment in China was considered risky and not worth the risk. In 2010, China attracted $105 billion in foreign direct investment.[63] Today, 400 of the Fortune 500 companies (the world's largest companies) have invested in over 2000 projects in China. China has dethroned Germany as the world's largest exporter and surpassed Japan as the second largest economy in the world. According to Goldman Sachs Group economist Jim O'Neill, China could overtake the United States as the world's largest economy by 2027.[64]

Since 2009 China has been the largest motor vehicle market in the world with sales and production topping 18 million in 2010. It's estimated that the Chinese car market will grow tenfold during the period 2005–2030, which means there could be more cars on the road in China than all the cars in the world today.[65] Walmart began operations in China in 1996 and now has over 200 stores with plans to open more. Newcomers like Imax Corporation are also expanding in this fast-growing market. Imax plans to open 80 movie theaters in the next few years to get a share of a market that could rival the United States by 2016.[66]

China's economy is booming, and a highly educated middle class with money to spend is emerging, especially in the cities. Many observers believe China will continue its rapid growth and play a major role in the global economy. Are U.S. firms prepared to compete?

Many view China as a free trader's dream, where global investment and entrepreneurship will lead to wealth. However, concerns remain about China's one-party political system, human rights abuses, currency issues, and increasing urban population growth. China's underground economy also generates significant product piracy and counterfeiting, although China has been more responsive to these problems since its admission to the WTO. While the global economic downturn beginning in 2008 slowed China's economy down a bit, it is now a key driver of the world economy along with Japan, the EU, and the United States.

While China attracts most of the attention in Asia, India's population of 1.1 billion presents a tremendous opportunity. With 600 million of its population under 25, India's working age population will continue to grow while the U.S., China, and the EU see a possible decline in the 2020s.[67] Already India has seen huge growth in information technology and biotechnology, and its pharmaceutical business is expected to grow to $30 billion, a jump of over 150 percent by 2020. Still, it remains a nation with difficult trade laws and an inflexible bureaucracy.

Russia is an industrialized nation with large reserves of oil, gas, and gold. Multinationals like Chevron, ExxonMobil, and BP are intent on developing Russia's oil reserves.[68] Other multinationals, including Ford, General Motors, Toyota and Volkswagen, have announced investments to boost auto production in Russia.[69] Unfortunately, Russia is plagued by political, currency, and social problems and is considered by Transparency International as the world's most corrupt major economy.[70]

Brazil is an emerging nation that along with China, India, and Russia is expected to be one of the wealthier global economies by 2030. In fact, the term *BRIC* has been used as an acronym for the economies of Brazil, Russia, India, and China. Expectations are that Brazil and Russia will dominate global business as suppliers of raw materials and China and India will be the leading global suppliers of manufactured goods and services. Today, Brazil is the largest economy in South America and the 7th largest economy in the world with well-developed agriculture, mining, manufacturing, and service sectors. Its rapidly growing consumer market of 200 million people is a target for major exporters like the United States and China.

The *BRIC* economies are certainly not the only areas of opportunity in the global market. The developing nations of Asia, including Indonesia, Thailand, Singapore, the Philippines, Korea, Malaysia, and Vietnam, also offer great potential for U.S. businesses. Africa, especially South Africa, has only begun to emerge as a center for global economic growth. Business today is truly global and your role in it is up to you.

The Challenge of Offshore Outsourcing

Outsourcing, as noted in Chapter 1, is the process whereby one firm contracts with other companies, often in other countries, to do some or all of its functions. In the United States, companies have outsourced payroll functions, accounting, and some manufacturing operations for many years. However, the shift to primarily low-wage global markets, called *offshore outsourcing,* has remained a major issue in the United States. Take a look at the pros and cons of offshore outsourcing in Figure 3.9.

As lower-level manufacturing became more simplified, U.S. companies like Levi Strauss and Nike outsourced manufacturing offshore. Today, economists suggest, we are moving into the "second wave" of offshore outsourcing, shifting from product assembly to design and architecture. This process is proving more disruptive to the U.S. job market than the first, which primarily

figure 3.9

THE PROS AND CONS OF OFFSHORE OUTSOURCING

PROS

1. Less-strategic tasks can be outsourced globally so that companies can focus on areas in which they can excel and grow.

2. Outsourced work allows companies to create efficiencies that in fact let them hire more workers.

3. Consumers benefit from lower prices generated by effective use of global resources and developing nations grow, thus fueling global economic growth.

CONS

1. Jobs may be lost permanently and wages fall due to low-cost competition offshore.

2. Offshore outsourcing may reduce product quality and can therefore cause permanent damage to a company's reputation.

3. Communication among company members, with suppliers, and with customers becomes much more difficult.

affected manufacturing jobs. Today, increasing numbers of skilled, educated, middle-income workers in service-sector jobs such as accounting, law, finance, risk management, health care, and information technology are seeing their jobs outsourced offshore.

While loss of jobs is a major concern it's not the only worry. Nations such as China have a spotty safety record in manufacturing toys, food, and drugs. Today, concerns are mounting about companies like Medtronic and Siemens shifting production of sensitive medical devices such as MRI and CT machines to China. IBM is setting up research facilities in offshore locations. U.S. airlines have even outsourced airline maintenance to countries such as El Salvador. India at one time was the center for telemarketing, data entry, call centers, billing, and low-end software development. Today—with its well-educated deep pool of scientists, software engineers, chemists, accountants, lawyers, and physicians—India is providing more sophisticated services. For example, radiologists from Wipro Health Science read CAT scans and MRIs for many U.S. hospitals. Some medical providers are shifting surgical procedures to India and other nations. The nearby Making Ethical Decisions box offers an interesting ethical question about this process.

As technical talent grows around the globe, offshore outsourcing will increase. To stay competitive, education and training will be critical for U.S. workers to preserve the skill premium they possess today and to stay ahead in the future.

Globalization and Your Future

Whether you aspire to be an entrepreneur, a manager, or some other type of business leader, think globally in planning your career. By studying foreign languages, learning about foreign cultures, and taking business courses (including a global business course), you can develop a global perspective on your future. As you progress through this text, keep two things in mind: globalization is real, and economic competition promises to intensify.

Also keep in mind that global market potential does not belong only to large, multinational corporations. Small and medium-sized businesses have a world of opportunity in front of them. In fact, these firms are often better prepared to leap into global markets and react quickly to opportunities than are large businesses. Finally, don't forget the potential of franchising, which we examine in more detail in Chapter 5.

progress assessment

- What are the major threats to doing business in global markets?
- What key challenges must India and Russia face before becoming global economic leaders?
- What does the acronym *BRIC* stand for?
- What are the two primary concerns associated with offshore outsourcing?

summary

Learning Goal 1. Discuss the importance of the global market and the roles of comparative advantage and absolute advantage in global trade.

- **Why should nations trade with other nations?**

(1) No country is self-sufficient, (2) other countries need products that prosperous countries produce, and (3) natural resources and technological skills are not distributed evenly around the world.

- **What is the theory of comparative advantage?**

The theory of comparative advantage contends that a country should make and then sell those products it produces most efficiently but buy those it cannot produce as efficiently.

- **What is absolute advantage?**

Absolute advantage means that a country has a monopoly on a certain product or can produce the product more efficiently than any other country. There are few examples of absolute advantage in the global market today.

Learning Goal 2. Explain the importance of importing and exporting, and understand key terms used in global business.

- **What kinds of products can be imported and exported?**

Though it is not necessarily easy, just about any kind of product can be imported or exported.

- **What terms are important in understanding world trade?**

Exporting is selling products to other countries. *Importing* is buying products from other countries. The *balance of trade* is the relationship of exports to imports. The *balance of payments* is the balance of trade plus other money flows such as tourism and foreign aid. *Dumping* is selling products for less in a foreign country than in your own country. See the Key Terms list at the end of this chapter to be sure you know the other important terms.

Learning Goal 3. Illustrate the strategies used in reaching global markets and explain the role of multinational corporations.

- **What are some ways in which a company can engage in global business?**

Ways of entering world trade include licensing, exporting, franchising, contract manufacturing, joint ventures and strategic alliances, and direct foreign investment.

- **How do multinational corporations differ from other companies that participate in global business?**

Unlike companies that only export or import, multinational corporations also have manufacturing facilities or other physical presence abroad.

Learning Goal 4. Evaluate the forces that affect trading in global markets.

- **What are some of the forces that can discourage participation in global business?**

Potential stumbling blocks to global trade include sociocultural forces, economic and financial forces, legal and regulatory forces, and physical and environmental forces.

Learning Goal 5. Debate the advantages and disadvantages of trade protectionism.

- **What is trade protectionism?**

Trade protectionism is the use of government regulations to limit the import of goods and services. Advocates believe it allows domestic producers to grow, producing more jobs. The key tools of protectionism are tariffs, import quotas, and embargoes.

- **What are tariffs?**

Tariffs are taxes on foreign products. Protective tariffs raise the price of foreign products and protect domestic industries; revenue tariffs raise money for the government.

- **What is an embargo?**

An embargo prohibits the importing or exporting of certain products.

- **Is trade protectionism good for domestic producers?**

That is debatable. Trade protectionism offers pluses and minuses.

- **Why do governments continue such practices?**

The theory of mercantilism started the practice of trade protectionism and it has persisted, though in a weaker form, ever since.

Learning Goal 6. Discuss the changing landscape of the global market and the issue of offshore outsourcing.

- **What is offshore outsourcing? Why is it a major concern for the future?**

Outsourcing is the purchase of goods and services from outside a firm rather than providing them inside the company. Today, more businesses are outsourcing manufacturing and services offshore. Many fear that growing numbers of jobs in the United States will be lost due to offshore outsourcing and that the quality of products produced could be inferior.

key terms

absolute advantage 62	exchange rate 74	multinational corporation 70
balance of payments 65	exporting 61	North American Free Trade Agreement (NAFTA) 79
balance of trade 64	foreign direct investment (FDI) 70	sovereign wealth funds (SWFs) 70
common market 77	foreign subsidiary 70	strategic alliance 70
comparative advantage theory 62	free trade 62	tariffs 76
contract manufacturing 68	General Agreement on Tariffs and Trade (GATT) 77	trade deficit 64
countertrading 74	importing 61	trade protectionism 76
devaluation 74	import quota 76	trade surplus 64
dumping 66	joint venture 70	World Trade Organization (WTO) 77
embargo 76	licensing 66	

critical thinking

1. About 95 percent of the world's population lives outside the United States, but many U.S. companies, especially small businesses, still do not engage in global trade. Why not? Do you think more small businesses will participate in global trade in the future? Why or why not?

2. Countries like the United States that have a high standard of living are referred to as *industrialized nations*. Countries with a lower standard of living and quality of life are called *developing countries* (or *underdeveloped* or *less developed countries*). What factors prevent developing nations from becoming industrialized nations?

3. What can businesses do to prevent unexpected problems in dealing with sociocultural, economic and financial, legal and regulatory, and physical and environmental forces in global markets?

4. How would you justify the use of revenue or protective tariffs in today's global market?

developing workplace skills

1. Find out firsthand the global impact on your life. How many different countries' names appear on the labels in your clothes? How many languages do your classmates speak? List the ethnic restaurants in your community. Are they family-owned or corporate chains?

2. Call, e-mail, or visit a local business that imports foreign goods (perhaps a wine or specialty foods importer). Ask the owner or manager about the business's participation in global trade, and compile a list of the advantages and disadvantages he or she cites. Compare notes with your classmates about their research.

3. Visit four or five public locations in your community such as schools, hospitals, city/county buildings, or airports. See how many signs are posted in different languages (don't forget the restrooms) and look for other multilingual information, such as brochures or handouts. Do any of the locations fly flags from different nations? In what other ways do they recognize the diversity of employees or students? What does your search tell you about your community?

4. Suppose Representative I. M. Wright delivers a passionate speech at your college on tariffs. He argues tariffs are needed to

   a. Protect our young industries.

   b. Encourage consumers to buy U.S.-made products because it's patriotic.

   c. Protect U.S. jobs and wages.

   d. Achieve a favorable balance of trade and balance of payments.

   Do you agree with Representative Wright? Evaluate each of his major points and decide whether you consider it valid. Be sure to justify your position.

5. Form an imaginary joint venture with three classmates and select a product, service, or idea to market to a specific country. Have each team member select a key global market force in that country (sociocultural, economic and financial, legal and regulatory, or physical and environmental) to research. Have each report his or her findings. Then, as a group, prepare a short explanation of whether the market is worth pursuing.

taking it to the net

Purpose

To compare the shifting exchange rates of various countries and to predict the effects of such exchange shifts on global trade.

Exercise

One of the difficulties of engaging in global trade is the constant shift in exchange rates. How much do exchange rates change over a 30-day period? Research this by choosing five currencies (say, the euro, the British pound, the Japanese yen, the Mexican peso, the Saudi Arabian riyal) and recording their exchange rates relative to the U.S. dollar for 30 days. The rates are available on the Internet at Yahoo Finance's Currency Center (http://finance.yahoo.com/currency). At the end of the tracking period, choose a company and describe what effects the currency shifts you noted might have on this company's trade with each of the countries or areas whose currency you chose.

casing the web

To access the case "Tough Being a Kid," visit **www.mhhe.com/ubl0e**

video case

To access the video case featuring CH2M Hill, visit **www.mhhe.com/ubl0e**

Demanding
Ethical and Socially
Responsible Behavior

4

After you have read and studied this chapter, you should be able to

1 Explain why obeying the law is only the first step in behaving ethically.

2 Ask the three questions you need to answer when faced with a potentially unethical action.

3 Describe management's role in setting ethical standards.

4 Distinguish between compliance-based and integrity-based ethics codes, and list the six steps in setting up a corporate ethics code.

5 Define *corporate social responsibility* and compare corporations' responsibilities to various stakeholders.

6 Analyze the role of U.S. businesses in influencing ethical behavior and social responsibility in global markets.

Although many companies are generous with charities, few include corporate giving in the first draft of their business plans. For TOMS Shoes founder Blake Mycoskie, however, earning a profit and giving were inseparable from the outset. By selling quality footwear at premium prices, the company's profit-driven side is simple enough. But the business part of TOMS exists in order to serve a nobler purpose: to give a free pair of shoes to a child in need for every pair the company sells.

So far TOMS has been wildly successful in its mission, giving away more than 1 million pairs of shoes since its founding in 2006. So why didn't Mycoskie just set up a nonprofit operation instead of a revenue-generating company in order to achieve his charitable goals? In Mycoskie's case, it's because he had no idea how to set up a charity, but he did know a thing or two about starting a business.

Mycoskie's entrepreneurial career began in his college days at Southern Methodist University when he started a door-to-door laundry service company at age 19. After selling the business when it went national, he spent the following years working on a number of ventures. Before TOMS was even a glimmer in his entrepreneurial eye, Mycoskie founded and operated three other companies, including an ad agency and a successful online driver's education school.

Mycoskie's life changed, though, when he visited Argentina while he was a contestant on the reality show The Amazing Race. There he witnessed the extreme poverty of fieldworkers who worked all day without footwear of any kind on rough terrain. After the show wrapped he went back to Argentina, this time visiting villages where children often have to walk barefoot for miles to reach school or water. The heartbreaking scene impelled Mycoskie to want to help in some way, but the way local volunteers simply asked for donations did not provide a long-term solution in his eyes.

"Most people look at problems in the Third World and one word comes to mind: charity," said Mycoskie. "But for me the word entrepreneurship came to mind." So in 2006 he established TOMS Shoes, a play off the company's original slogan, "shoes for tomorrow." Instead of soliciting donations, the retail side of the business would generate the necessary capital for the company's One for One program. TOMS' marketing heavily emphasized the giving program, building the TOMS name into a unique brand within just a few months.

Mycoskie returned to Argentina in 2007 with friends, family, and employees to hand out 10,000 pairs of new shoes. That same year, the company received the People's Design Award from the National Design Museum in the Smithsonian. As the company grew in the following years, so did its stack of accolades. In 2009 Mycoskie and TOMS received the prestigious Award of Corporate Excellence from Secretary of State Hillary Clinton. As for the future, Mycoskie believes his dual roles as both a savvy businessman and humanitarian will become the benchmark of tomorrow's entrepreneurs. "My advice to budding entrepreneurs is, don't try to be an entrepreneur," said Mycoskie. "Try to identify problems in the world that you want to solve. That, often, will lead to a great business idea."

Although they do not receive as much press as their corrupt colleagues do when a scandal is uncovered, ethical entrepreneurs are the backbone of the business world. In this chapter, we explore the responsibility of businesses to their stakeholders: customers, investors, employees, and society. We look at the responsibilities of individuals as well. After all, responsible business behavior depends on responsible behavior of each individual in the business.

Sources: Will Fifeid, "Not Business as Usual," *The Costco Connection,* September 2010; TOMS Shoes, Annual Giving Report; TOMS Shoes, "Bio of Blake Mycoskie," http://www.toms.com/blakes-bio, accessed March 14, 2011.

profile

Getting to Know
X *Blake Mycoskie*
Founder of TOMS Shoes

This company has a program it calls Social Service Leave that allows employees to take up to a year off to work for a nonprofit organization while earning their full salary and benefits, including job security. Name that company. (Find the answer in the chapter.)

Bernie Madoff was once a respected investment manager. He swindled $65 billion from his investors, which included many charities and pension plans. He was sentenced to 150 years behind bars with no chance of parole. What motivates a person to risk everything by committing fraud?

LEARNING goal 1

Explain why obeying the law is only the first step in behaving ethically.

ETHICS IS MORE THAN LEGALITY

In the early 2000s, the U.S. public was shocked to learn that Enron, the giant energy trading company, had created off-the-books partnerships to unlawfully hide its debts and losses. The Enron disgrace soon was followed by more scandals at major companies like WorldCom, Tyco International, ImClone, HealthSouth, and Boeing.[1] (See the nearby Legal Briefcase box for a brief summary of a few of these cases.) In recent years, greedy borrowers and lenders alike were among those who brought the real estate, mortgage, and banking industries to the edge of a financial crisis that threatened the entire U.S. and world economies.[2]

Given the ethical lapses prevalent today, how can we restore trust in the free-market system and in leaders in general? First, those who have broken the law should be punished accordingly. New laws making accounting records more transparent (easy to read and understand) and businesspeople and others more accountable for their actions may also help.[3] But laws alone don't make people honest, reliable, or truthful. If they did, crime would disappear.

One danger in writing new laws to correct behavior is that people may begin to think that any behavior that is within the law is also acceptable. The measure of behavior then becomes "Is it legal?" A society gets into trouble when people consider only what is illegal and not also what is unethical. Ethics and legality are two very different things. Although following the law is an important first step, behaving ethically requires more than that. Ethics reflects people's proper relationships with one another: How should we treat others? What responsibility should we feel for others? Legality is narrower. It refers to laws we have written to protect ourselves from fraud, theft, and violence. Many immoral and unethical acts fall well within our laws. For example gossiping about your neighbor or sharing something told to you in confidence is unethical, but not illegal.

briefcase

Cost of Corruption

News stories of corporate fraud and corruption are all too common. White-collar criminals often assume the complexity of the financial system will hide their crimes, leaving them free to embezzle to their heart's content. But people tend to notice when a few billion dollars suddenly go missing. Eventually, even the most careful corporate criminals must pay for their crimes.

When the credit crunch hit in 2008, it unexpectedly exposed one of history's most shameful financial felons. Since the early 1970s Bernie Madoff ran his exclusive wealth management firm as a gigantic Ponzi scheme. Legitimate money managers invest their client's money in various ventures and pay them back on their returns, minus a commission. With a Ponzi scheme, however, the fraudsters don't invest the money. They simply pass money contributed by new investors on to early investors (minus a healthy sum held back for their own personal use, of course), claiming the money as profits from the existing clients' "investments." The steady income fools the investors into thinking their wealth is growing when in reality it is being siphoned from other people. Obviously the scheme depends upon being able to continuously attract new "investors."

Once the bubble burst on Wall Street, Madoff confessed his crimes to his sons, who then contacted police. Though exact estimates are still uncertain, Madoff swindled approximately $65 billion from his investors, including $20 billion in cash losses that can never be recovered. In June 2009 a judge sentenced Madoff to 150 years behind bars with no chance of parole.

Before Madoff, though, the Enron scandal of the early 2000s was the gold standard of American corporate deception. Former Enron chairman and chief executive officer (CEO) Kenneth Lay, former CEO Jeffery Skilling, and chief accounting officer Richard Causey were convicted of committing accounting fraud by setting up partnerships that the company used to improperly enhance profits while removing billions of dollars of debt from its balance sheet. That made the company's financial picture look better than it was and artificially inflated the company's stock and bond prices.

The company's pension regulations prohibited regular employees from selling their stock, but the executives sold millions of dollars' worth of shares just before the fraud became public. They bankrupted the company, yet made fortunes while the employees and other small investors lost millions.

Skilling is serving a 24-year prison sentence in Minnesota and must pay a $45 million fine. His lawyers are still working to have his conviction overturned. Causey entered a guilty plea and received a shorter sentence than Skilling. He is scheduled to be released from prison in October 2011. Lay suffered a heart attack and passed away before his sentencing. All his convictions were thrown out.

Around the time of the Enron scandal, the communications multinational WorldCom admitted that intentional accounting irregularities made the company look almost $4 billion more profitable than it was. Further scrutiny of the company's books revealed WorldCom's practice of counting revenue twice dated as far back as 1999, that additional debt continued to be undisclosed, and that revenue not received was entered in the books—pushing the irregularities to more than $11 billion.

In 2005, former CEO Bernie Ebbers was convicted of fraud, conspiracy, and making false regulatory filings. He was sentenced to 25 years in federal prison. The company has emerged from bankruptcy and now operates under the name of MCI Inc. Ebbers is in Oakdale Federal Correctional Institution in Louisiana and is expected to be released in July 2028.

Sources: "Top 10 Crooked CEOs," Time.com, accessed March 14, 2011; and Diana B. Henriques, "From Prison, Madoff Says Banks 'Had to Know' of Fraud," *The New York Times,* February 15, 2011.

Ethical Standards Are Fundamental

We define **ethics** as society's accepted standards of moral behavior, that is, behaviors accepted by society as right rather than wrong. Many Americans today have few moral absolutes. Many decide situationally whether it's OK to steal, lie, or drink and drive. They seem to think that what is right is whatever works best for the individual—that each person has to work out for himself or

ethics
Standards of moral behavior, that is, behavior accepted by society as right versus wrong.

herself the difference between right and wrong. Such thinking may be part of the behavior that has led to the recent scandals in government and business.

This isn't the way it always was. When Thomas Jefferson wrote that all men have the right to life, liberty, and the pursuit of happiness, he declared it to be a self-evident truth. Going back even further in time, the Ten Commandments were not called the "Ten Highly Tentative Suggestions."

In the United States, with so many diverse cultures, you might think it is impossible to identify common standards of ethical behavior. However, among sources from many different times and places—such as the Bible, Aristotle's *Ethics*, the Koran, and the *Analects* of Confucius—you'll find the following common statements of basic moral values: Integrity, respect for human life, self-control, honesty, courage, and self-sacrifice are right. Cheating, cowardice, and cruelty are wrong. Furthermore, all the world's major religions support a version of what some call the Golden Rule: Do unto others as you would have them do unto you.[4]

LEARNING goal 2

Ask the three questions you need to answer when faced with a potentially unethical action.

"I don't know what plagiarizing is, so I'm gonna take the easy way out and just copy something off the internet."

Plagiarizing from the Internet is one of the most common forms of cheating in colleges today. Have you ever been tempted to plagiarize a paper or project? What are the possible consequences of copying someone else's material?

Ethics Begins with Each of Us

It is easy to criticize business and political leaders for moral and ethical shortcomings, and in a recent study both managers and workers cited low managerial ethics as a major cause of U.S. businesses' competitive woes.[5] But employees also reported frequently violating safety standards and goofing off as much as seven hours a week. U.S. adults in general are not always as honest or honorable as they should be. Even though volunteerism is at an all-time high according to the U.S. Census Bureau, three of every four citizens do not give any time to the community in which they live.[6]

Plagiarizing material from the Internet, including cutting and pasting information from websites without giving credit, is the most common form of cheating in schools today. To fight this problem, many instructors now use services like TurnItIn.com, which scans students' papers against more than 13 billion online sources to provide evidence of copying in seconds.[7]

In a recent study, most teens said they were prepared to make ethical decisions in the workforce, but an alarming 38 percent felt that lying, cheating, plagiarizing, or behaving violently is sometimes necessary. Studies have found a strong relationship between academic dishonesty among undergraduates and dishonesty at work.[8] In response, many schools are establishing heavier consequences for cheating and requiring students to perform a certain number of hours of community service to graduate. Do you think such policies make a difference in student behavior?

The Making Ethical Decisions boxes throughout the text—like the accompanying one on fake Facebook identities—remind you to keep ethics in mind whenever you are making a business decision. Choices are not always easy, and the

Facebook or Fakebook?

Facebook is so much a part of our culture that many people see their online profiles as extensions of themselves. It only takes an e-mail address to set up a Facebook account. Such accessibility allows for scammers to take advantage of the trust Facebook's users have in the online community.

With the site's massive collection of pictures and data, con artists can set up fake Facebook accounts with little difficulty. For example, a few scammers copied pictures of military servicemen from their profiles and set up dummy accounts. From there they established relationships with women by playing the part of lonely soldiers looking for love. Soon enough, the imposters asked their victims for money to pay for phone calls or visits home. With cash in hand, the scammers then severed contact with their prey and deleted the fake account, likely to start the whole process over again with a new victim.

Other Facebook scams may not be as dastardly, but are just as dangerously creative. In one instance, a banner ad offered an application called "Creeper Tracker" that supposedly lets users know who's looking at their Facebook page the most. Although this method is relatively common among fraudsters, this particular scheme came with an added element. After the victims filled out a survey that generated money for the scammer, they were directed to a new page where they could purchase a toolkit that provided step-by-step instructions on how to create their own scam. So Facebookers beware, because in this social media driven world even acts of fraud can go viral.

Some people create fake Facebook identities for less criminal activities—to prank friends or harass foes. Do you think it is ethical to create such fake online identities? Why or why not?

Sources: Bruce Schreiner and Janet Cappiello Blake, "Soldier Impersonators Hit the Web," Associated Press, February 27, 2011; and Matt Liebowitz, "Malicious Facebook Trick Has Users Create Their Own Scam," MSNBC, February 8, 2011.

obvious ethical solution may have personal or professional drawbacks. Imagine that your supervisor has asked you to do something you feel is unethical. You've just taken out a mortgage on a new house to make room for your first baby, due in two months. Not carrying out your supervisor's request may get you fired. What should you do? Sometimes there is no easy alternative in such *ethical dilemmas* because you must choose between equally unsatisfactory alternatives.

It can be difficult to balance ethics and other goals, such as pleasing stakeholders or advancing in your career. According to management writer Ken Blanchard and religious leader Norman Vincent Peale, it helps to ask yourself the following questions when facing an ethical dilemma.[9]

1. *Is my proposed action legal?* Am I violating any law or company policy? Whether you're thinking about having a drink and driving home, gathering marketing intelligence, designing a product, hiring or firing employees, getting rid of industrial waste, or using a questionable nickname for an employee, think about the legal implications. This is the most basic question in business ethics, but it is only the first.

2. *Is it balanced?* Am I acting fairly? Would I want to be treated this way? Will I win everything at the expense of another? Win–lose situations often become lose–lose situations and generate retaliation from the loser. Not every situation can be completely balanced, but the health of our relationships requires us to avoid major imbalances over time.

An ethical businessperson has a win–win attitude and tries to make decisions that benefit all.

3. *How will it make me feel about myself?* Would I feel proud if my family learned of my decision? My friends? Could I discuss the proposed situation or action with my supervisor? The company's clients? Will I have to hide my actions? Has someone warned me not to disclose them? What if my decision were announced on the evening news? Am I feeling unusually nervous? Decisions that go against our sense of right and wrong make us feel bad—they erode our self-esteem. That is why an ethical businessperson does what is proper as well as what is profitable.

Individuals and companies that develop a strong ethics code and use the three questions above have a better chance than most of behaving ethically. If you would like to know which style of recognizing and resolving ethical dilemmas you favor, fill out the ethical orientation questionnaire in Figure 4.1.

progress assessment

- What are ethics?
- How do ethics differ from legality?
- When faced with ethical dilemmas, what questions can you ask yourself that might help you make ethical decisions?

LEARNING goal 3

Describe management's role in setting ethical standards.

MANAGING BUSINESSES ETHICALLY AND RESPONSIBLY

Ethics is caught more than it is taught. That is, people learn their standards and values from observing what others do, not from hearing what they say. This is as true in business as it is at home. Organizational ethics begins at the top, and the leadership and example of strong managers can help instill corporate values in employees. The majority of CEOs surveyed recently attributed unethical employee conduct to leadership's failure to establish ethical standards and culture.[10]

Trust and cooperation between workers and managers must be based on fairness, honesty, openness, and moral integrity. The same applies to relationships among businesses and between nations. A business should be managed ethically for many reasons: to maintain a good reputation; to keep existing customers and attract new ones; to avoid lawsuits; to reduce employee turnover; to avoid government intervention in the form of new laws and regulations controlling business activities; to please customers, employees, and society; and simply to do the right thing.

Some managers think ethics is a personal matter—either individuals have ethical principles or they don't. These managers feel that they are not responsible for an individual's misdeeds and that ethics has nothing to do with management. But a growing number of people think ethics has everything to do

Please answer the following questions.

1. Which is worse?
   A. Hurting someone's feelings by telling the truth.
   B. Telling a lie and protecting someone's feelings.
2. Which is the worse mistake?
   A. To make exceptions too freely.
   B. To apply rules too rigidly.
3. Which is it worse to be?
   A. Unmerciful.
   B. Unfair.
4. Which is worse?
   A. Stealing something valuable from someone for no good reason.
   B. Breaking a promise to a friend for no good reason.
5. Which is it better to be?
   A. Just and fair.
   B. Sympathetic and feeling.

6. Which is worse?
   A. Not helping someone in trouble.
   B. Being unfair to someone by playing favorites.
7. In making a decision you rely more on
   A. Hard facts.
   B. Personal feelings and intuition.
8. Your boss orders you to do something that will hurt someone. If you carry out the order, have you actually done anything wrong?
   A. Yes.
   B. No.
9. Which is more important in determining whether an action is right or wrong?
   A. Whether anyone actually gets hurt.
   B. Whether a rule, law, commandment, or moral principle is broken.

To score: The answers fall in one of two categories, J or C. Count your number of J and C answers using this key: 1. A = C; B = J; 2. A = J; B = C; 3. A = C; B = J; 4. A = J; B = C; 5. A = J; B = C; 6. A = C; B = J; 7. A = J; B = C; 8. A = C; B = J; 9. A = C; B = J

What your score means: The higher your J score, the more you rely on an ethic of *justice*. The higher your C score, the more you prefer an ethic of core. Neither style is better than the other, but they are different. Because they appear so different, they may seem opposed to one another, but they're actually complementary. In fact, your score probably shows you rely on each style to a greater or lesser degree. (Few people end up with a score of 9 to 0.) The more you can appreciate both approaches, the better you'll be able to resolve ethical dilemmas and to understand and communicate with people who prefer the other style.

An ethic of justice is based on principles like justice, fairness, equality, or authority. People who prefer this style see ethical dilemmas as conflicts of rights that can be solved by the impartial application of some general principle. The advantage of this approach is that it looks at a problem logically and impartially. People with this style try to be objective and fair, hoping to make a decision according to some standard that's higher than any specific individual's interests.

The disadvantage of this approach is that people who rely on it might lose sight of the Immediate interests of particular Individuals. They may unintentionally ride roughshod over the people around them in favor of some abstract ideal or policy. This style is more common for men than women.

An ethic of care is based on a sense of responsibility to reduce actual harm or suffering. People who prefer this style see moral dilemmas as conflicts of duties or responsibilities. They believe that solutions must be tailored to the special details of individual circumstances. They tend to feel constrained by policies that are supposed to be enforced without exception. The advantage of this approach Is that it is responsive to immediate suffering and harm. The disadvantage Is that, when carried to an extreme, this style can produce decisions that seem not simply subjective, but arbitrary. This style is more common for women than men.

To learn more about these styles and how they might relate to gender, go to www.ethicsandbusiness.org/kgl.htm.

Source: Thomas I. White, *Discovering Philosophy—Brief Edition*, 1e, © Copyright 1996. Adapted by permission of Pearson Education, Inc., Upper Saddle River, NJ.

figure 4.1

ETHICAL ORIENTATION QUESTIONNAIRE

with management. Individuals do not usually act alone; they need the implied, if not the direct, cooperation of others to behave unethically in a corporation.

For example, there have been reports of cell phone service sales representatives who actually lie to get customers to extend their contracts—or even extend their contracts without the customers' knowledge. Some phone reps

compliance-based ethics codes
Ethical standards that emphasize preventing unlawful behavior by increasing control and by penalizing wrongdoers.

integrity-based ethics codes
Ethical standards that define the organization's guiding values, create an environment that supports ethically sound behavior, and stress a shared accountability among employees.

intentionally hang up on callers to prevent them from canceling their contracts. Why do these sales reps sometimes resort to overly aggressive tactics? Because poorly designed incentive programs reward them for meeting certain goals, sometimes doubling or tripling their salaries with incentives. Do their managers say directly, "Deceive the customers"? No, but the message is clear. Overly ambitious goals and incentives can create an environment in which unethical actions like this can occur.[11]

LEARNING goal 4

Distinguish between compliance-based and integrity-based ethics codes, and list the six steps in setting up a corporate ethics code.

Setting Corporate Ethical Standards

More and more companies have adopted written codes of ethics. Figure 4.2 offers Johnson & Johnson's as a sample. Although these codes vary greatly, they can be placed into two categories: compliance-based and integrity-based (see Figure 4.3). **Compliance-based ethics codes** emphasize preventing unlawful behavior by increasing control and penalizing wrongdoers. **Integrity-based ethics codes** define the organization's guiding values, create an environment that supports ethically sound behavior, and stress shared accountability.

Here are six steps many believe can improve U.S. business ethics:[12]

1. Top management must adopt and unconditionally support an explicit corporate code of conduct.

2. Employees must understand that expectations for ethical behavior begin at the top and that senior management expects all employees to act accordingly.

3. Managers and others must be trained to consider the ethical implications of all business decisions.

4. An ethics office must be set up with which employees can communicate anonymously. **Whistleblowers** (insiders who report illegal or unethical behavior) must feel protected from retaliation. The Sarbanes-Oxley Act protects whistleblowers by requiring all public corporations to allow employee concerns about accounting and auditing to be submitted confidentially and anonymously. The act also requires reinstatement and back pay to people who were punished by their employers for passing information about fraud on to authorities. (We cover Sarbanes-Oxley in more detail in Chapter 17.) In 2010 the Dodd-Frank Wall Street Reform and Consumer Protection Act was signed into law. The new law includes a "bounty" provision that allows corporate whistleblowers who provide information that leads to a successful enforcement action to collect 10–30 percent of the total penalty for violations that exceed $1 million. In 2011, a whistleblower

H. Dean Steinke blew the whistle on his former employer, drug company Merck, maker of Vioxx and Zocor, charging that it gave doctors excessive financial incentives to prescribe the drugs and discounts unavailable to government health programs. Steinke was awarded $68 million for reporting the misconduct. What motivates whistleblowers?

Written in 1943 by long-time Chairman General Robert Wood Johnson, the Johnson & Johnson Credo serves as a conscious plan that represents and encourages a unique set of values. Our Credo sums up the responsibilities we have to the four important groups we serve:

- Our customers—We have a responsibility to provide high-quality products they can trust, offered at a fair price.

- Our employees—We have a responsibility to treat them with respect and dignity, pay them fairly and help them develop and thrive personally and professionally.

- Our communities—We have a responsibility to be good corporate citizens, support good works, encourage better health and protect the environment.

- Our stockholders—We have a responsibility to provide a fair return on their investment.

The deliberate ordering of these groups—customers first, stockholders last–proclaims a bold business philosophy: If we meet our first three responsibilities, the fourth will take care of itself. . . . To ensure our adherence to Credo values, we periodically ask every employee to evaluate the company's performance in living up to them. We believe that by monitoring our actions against the ethical framework of Our Credo, we will best ensure that we make responsible decisions as a company.

figure 4.2

OVERVIEW OF JOHNSON & JOHNSON'S CODE OF ETHICS

This is an overview of Johnson & Johnson's code of ethics, what it calls its Credo. To see the company's complete Credo, go to www.jnj.com/connect/about=jnj/jnj=credo and click on "Our Credo Values."

FEATURES OF COMPLIANCE-BASED ETHICS CODES		FEATURES OF INTEGRITY-BASED ETHICS CODES	
ideal:	Conform to outside standards (laws and regulations)	Ideal:	Conform to outside standards (laws and regulations) and chosen internal standards
Objective:	Avoid criminal misconduct	Objective:	Enable responsible employee conduct
Leaders:	Lawyers	Leaders:	Managers with aid of lawyers and others
Methods:	Education, reduced employee discretion, controls, penalties	Methods:	Education, leadership, accountability, decision processes, controls, and penalties

figure 4.3

STRATEGIES FOR ETHICS MANAGEMENT

Integrity-based ethics codes move beyond legal compliance to create a "do-it-right" climate that emphasizes core values such as honesty, fair play, good service to customers, a commitment to diversity, and involvement in the community. These values are ethically desirable, but not necessarily legally mandatory.

in the Enron case received a $1 million reward from the IRS (and, yes, it is taxable).

5. Outsiders such as suppliers, subcontractors, distributors, and customers must be told about the ethics program. Pressure to put aside ethical considerations often comes from the outside, and it helps employees resist such pressure when everyone knows what the ethical standards are.

6. The ethics code must be enforced with timely action if any rules are broken. That is the most forceful way to communicate to all employees that the code is serious.

whistleblowers
Insiders who report illegal or unethical behavior.

This last step is perhaps the most critical. No matter how well intended a company's ethics code, it is worthless if not enforced.[13] Enron had a written code of ethics. By ignoring it, Enron's board and management sent employees the message that rules could be shelved when inconvenient. In contrast, Johnson & Johnson's response to a cyanide poisoning crisis in the 1980s shows that enforcing ethics codes can enhance profit. Although not legally required to do so, the company recalled its Tylenol products and won great praise and a reputation of corporate integrity.

An important factor in enforcing an ethics code is selecting an ethics officer. The most effective ethics officers set a positive tone, communicate effectively, and relate well to employees at every level. They are equally comfortable as counselors and investigators and can be trusted to maintain confidentiality, conduct objective investigations, and ensure fairness. They can demonstrate to stakeholders that ethics are important in everything the company does.[14]

progress assessment

- What are compliance-based and integrity-based ethics codes?
- What are the six steps to follow in establishing an effective ethics program in a business?

LEARNING goal 5

Define *corporate social responsibility* and compare corporations' responsibilities to various stakeholders.

CORPORATE SOCIAL RESPONSIBILITY

corporate social responsibility (CSR)
A business's concern for the welfare of society.

Just as you and I need to be good citizens, contributing what we can to society, corporations need to be good citizens as well. **Corporate social responsibility (CSR)** is the concern businesses have for the welfare of society, not just for their owners. CSR goes well beyond being ethical. It is based on a commitment to integrity, fairness, and respect.

You may be surprised to know that not everyone thinks that CSR is a good thing. Some critics of CSR believe that a manager's sole role is to compete and win in the marketplace. U.S. economist Milton Friedman made the famous statement that the only social responsibility of business is to make money for stockholders. He thought doing anything else was moving dangerously toward socialism. Other CSR critics believe that managers who pursue CSR are doing so with other people's money—which they invested to make more money, not to improve society. In this view spending money on CSR activities is stealing from investors.[15]

CSR defenders, in contrast, believe that businesses owe their existence to the societies they serve and cannot succeed in societies that fail. Firms have access to society's labor pool and its natural resources, in which every member of society has a stake. Even Adam Smith, the father of capitalism, believed that self-interested pursuit of profit was wrong and that benevolence was the highest virtue. CSR defenders acknowledge that businesses have deep obligations to investors and should not attempt government-type social responsibility projects. However, they also argue that CSR makes more money for investors in the long run. Studies show that companies with good ethical reputations attract and retain better employees, draw more customers, and enjoy greater employee loyalty.[16]

The social performance of a company has several dimensions:

- **Corporate philanthropy** includes charitable donations to nonprofit groups of all kinds. Eighty percent of the business leaders surveyed in a recent study said that their companies participate in philanthropic activities. Some make long-term commitments to one cause, such as McDonald's Ronald McDonald Houses for families whose critically ill children require treatment away from home. The Bill & Melinda Gates Foundation is by far the nation's largest philanthropic foundation, with assets of more than $34 billion.[17]

- **Corporate social initiatives** include enhanced forms of corporate philanthropy. Corporate social initiatives differ from traditional philanthropy in that they are more directly related to the company's competencies. For example, logistics giant TNT keeps a 50-person emergency-response team on standby to go anywhere in the world at 48 hours' notice to provide support in aviation, warehousing, transportation, reporting and communications. Since 2005, 225 TNT employees have been involved in 17 emergency response activities.[18]

- **Corporate responsibility** includes everything from hiring minority workers to making safe products, minimizing pollution, using energy wisely, and providing a safe work environment—essentially everything that has to do with acting responsibly within society.

- **Corporate policy** refers to the position a firm takes on social and political issues. For example, Patagonia's corporate policy includes this statement: "A love of wild and beautiful places demands participation in the fight to save them, and to help reverse the steep decline in the overall environmental health of our planet. We donate our time, services and at least 1% of our sales to hundreds of grassroots environmental groups all over the world who work to help reverse the tide."[19]

The problems corporations cause get so much news coverage that people tend to get a negative view of their impact on society. But businesses make positive contributions too. Few people know, for example, that a Xerox

corporate philanthropy
The dimension of social responsibility that includes charitable donations.

corporate social initiatives
Enhanced forms of corporate philanthropy directly related to the company's competencies.

corporate responsibility
The dimension of social responsibility that includes everything from hiring minority workers to making safe products.

corporate policy
The dimension of social responsibility that refers to the position a firm takes on social and political issues.

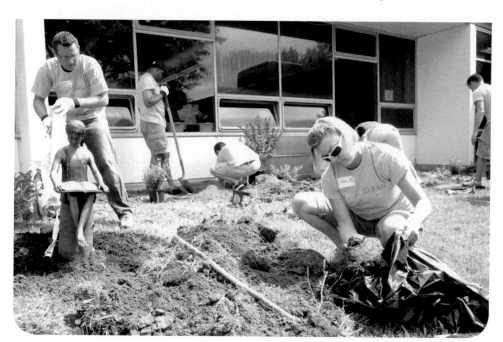

Volunteers in Procter & Gamble's "Make a Clean Difference" program work to improve the learning environments in 30 schools in 20 cities across the country. Do companies have responsibilities to the environment beyond obeying environmental laws?

program called Social Service Leave allows employees to take up to a year to work for a nonprofit organization while earning their full Xerox salary and benefits, including job security.[20] IBM and Wells-Fargo Bank have similar programs.

In fact, many companies allow employees to give part-time help to social agencies of all kinds. The recent recession has changed the way that many corporations approach corporate philanthropy. According to a survey by the Committee Encouraging Corporate Philanthropy, 60 percent of companies cut their philanthropic donations since 2008, most of them by more than 10 percent. That doesn't mean that they stopped giving. Now they are more likely to give time and goods rather than money. When asked how the recession has changed their philanthropy, the largest number said they were encouraging employees to volunteer more.[21] NetworkforGood.org, 1-800-Volunteer.org, and VolunteerMatch.org are web-based services that link volunteers with non-profit and public sector organizations around the country. Volunteers enter a zip code or indicate the geographic area in which they'd like to work, and the programs list organizations that could use their help.

Two-thirds of the MBA students surveyed by a group called Students for Responsible Business said they would take a reduced salary to work for a socially responsible company.[22] But when the same students were asked to define *socially responsible*, things got complicated. Even those who support the idea of social responsibility can't agree on what it is. Let's look at the concept through the eyes of the stakeholders to whom businesses are responsible: customers, investors, employees, and society in general.

Responsibility to Customers

President John F. Kennedy proposed four basic rights of consumers: (1) the right to safety, (2) the right to be informed, (3) the right to choose, and (4) the right to be heard. These rights will be achieved only if businesses and consumers recognize them and take action in the marketplace.

A recurring theme of this book is the importance of pleasing customers by offering them real value. Since three of five new businesses fail, we know this responsibility is not as easy to meet as it seems. One sure way of failing to please customers is to be less than honest with them. The payoff for socially conscious behavior, however, can be new customers who admire the company's social efforts—a powerful competitive edge. Consumer behavior studies show that, all else being equal, a socially conscious company is likely to be viewed more favorably than others.[23]

Given the value customers place on social efforts, how do companies make customers aware of such efforts? One tool many companies use to raise awareness of their social responsibility efforts is social media. More than 70 percent of the executives surveyed report the primary value of using social media to communicate their CSR efforts is that it allows them to reach broad and diverse groups, allows them to connect directly with customers in a low-cost, efficient way, and enables them to interact with specific groups more easily than through more traditional efforts.[24]

It's not enough for companies to brag about their social responsibility efforts; they must live up to the expectations they raise or face the consequences. When herbal tea maker Celestial Seasonings ignored its advertised image of environmental stewardship by poisoning prairie dogs on its property, it incurred customers' wrath. Customers prefer to do business with companies they trust and, even more important, don't want to do business with those they don't trust. Companies earn customers' trust by demonstrating credibility over time; they can lose it at any point.

Responsibility to Investors

Ethical behavior doesn't subtract from the bottom line; it adds to it. In contrast, unethical behavior, even if it seems to work in the short term, does financial damage. Those cheated are the shareholders themselves. For example, in just 11 business days in June 2002, 44 CEOs left U.S. corporations amid accusations of wrongdoing, and the stock prices of their companies plummeted.

Some people believe that you must make money before you can do good; others believe that by doing good, you can also do well. Bagel Works, a New England–based chain of bagel stores, has a dual-bottom-line approach that focuses on the well-being of the planet in addition to profits. Each store not only employs environmentally protective practices such as in-store recycling, composting, and the use of organically grown ingredients and nontoxic cleaners. It also includes donations for community causes in its budget. The company donates 10 percent of its pretax profits to charities each year and has earned national recognition for social responsibility.

insider trading
An unethical activity in which insiders use private company information to further their own fortunes or those of their family and friends.

Many investors believe that it makes financial as well as moral sense to invest in companies that plan ahead to create a better environment. By choosing to put their money into companies whose goods and services benefit the community and the environment, investors can improve their own financial health while improving society's.[25]

A few investors, however, have chosen unethical means to improve their financial health. For example, **insider trading** uses private company information to further insiders' own fortunes or those of their family and friends. In 2011, one of the biggest insider trading cases in history went to trial in New York. Billionaire Raj Rajaratnam was convicted of masterminding an insider trading ring that made his Galleon Group hedge fund $64 million richer. Of course, he didn't do this all by himself. More than three dozen former traders, executives, and lawyers have pled guilty or face charges that they helped Rajaratnam trade illegally on more than 35 stocks, including Intel, Hilton, IBM and eBay.[26]

Insider trading isn't limited to company executives and their friends. Before it was publicly known that IBM was going to take over Lotus Development, an IBM secretary told her husband, who told two co-workers, who told friends, relatives, business associates, and even a pizza delivery man. A total of 25 people traded illegally on the insider tip within a six-hour period. When the deal was announced publicly, Lotus stock soared 89 percent. One of the inside traders, a stockbroker who passed the information to a few customers, made $468,000 in profits. The U.S. Securities and Exchange Commission (SEC) filed charges against the secretary, her husband, and 23 others. Four defendants settled out of court by paying penalties of twice their profits. Prosecutors are increasingly pursuing insider trading cases to ensure that the securities market remains fair and equally accessible to all.

After the deluge of insider trader cases was made public in the early

Billionaire Raj Rajaratnam, co-founder of Galleon Group hedge fund, was found guilty in the largest insider trading case in a generation. Rajaratnam gained $64 million trading on illegal tips from corporate executives, bankers, consultants, traders, and directors of public companies. More than 40 people have pleaded guilty or face criminal charges or civil lawsuits stemming from the case.

2000s, the SEC adopted a new rule called Regulation FD (for "fair disclosure"). The rule doesn't specify what information can and cannot be disclosed. It simply requires companies that release any information to share it with everybody, not just a few select people. In other words, if companies tell anyone, they must tell everyone—at the same time.

Some companies have misused information for their own benefit at investors' expense. When WorldCom admitted to accounting irregularities misrepresenting its profitability, investors who had purchased its stock on the basis of the false financial reports saw share prices free-fall from the mid-teens in January 2002 to less than a dime the following July. The pain was even greater for long-term investors, who had bought the stock at around $60 in 1999.

Responsibility to Employees

It's been said that the best social program in the world is a job. Businesses have a responsibility to create jobs if they want to grow. Once they've done so, they must see to it that hard work and talent are fairly rewarded. Employees need realistic hope of a better future, which comes only through a chance for upward mobility. Studies have shown that what most influences a company's effectiveness and financial performance is responsible human resource management.[27] We'll discuss this in Chapter 11.

If a company treats employees with respect, those employees usually will respect the company as well. Mutual respect can make a huge difference to a company's profit. In their book *Contented Cows Give Better Milk*, Bill Catlette and Richard Hadden compared "contented cow" companies with "common cow" companies. The companies with contented employees outgrew their counterparts by four to one for more than 10 years. They also out-earned the "common cow" companies by nearly $40 billion and generated 800,000 more jobs. Catlette and Hadden attribute this difference in performance to the commitment and caring the outstanding companies demonstrated for their employees.[28]

One way a company can demonstrate commitment and caring is to give employees salaries and benefits that help them reach their personal goals. The wage and benefit packages offered by warehouse retailer Costco are among the best in hourly retail. Even part-time workers are covered by Costco's health plan, and the workers pay less for their coverage than at other retailers such as Walmart. Increased benefits reduce employee turnover, which at Costco is less than a third of the industry average.[29] The U.S. Department of Labor estimates that replacing employees costs between 150 and 250 percent of their annual salaries, so retaining workers is good for business as well as morale.

Getting even is one of the most powerful incentives for good people to do bad things. Few disgruntled workers are desperate enough to commit violence in the workplace, but a great number relieve their frustrations in subtle ways: blaming mistakes on others, not accepting responsibility, manipulating budgets and expenses, making commitments they intend to ignore, hoarding resources, doing the minimum needed to get by, and making results look better than they are.

The loss of employee commitment, confidence, and trust in the company and its management can be costly indeed. Employee fraud costs U.S. businesses approximately 5 percent of annual revenue and causes 30 percent of all business failures,

Campbell's Soup ranked second on a list of "100 Best Corporate Citizens." The companies are judged on environment, climate change, human rights, employee relations, governance, philanthropy, and financial performance. Are companies responsible to their investors to be profitable, or to do good? Can they do both?

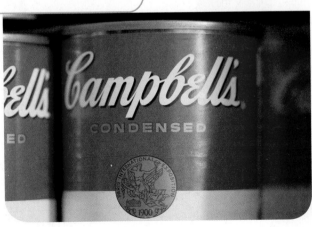

according to the Association of Certified Fraud Examiners.[30] You'll read more about employee–management issues like pay equity, sexual harassment, child and elder care, drug testing, and violence in the workplace in Chapter 12.

Responsibility to Society and the Environment

More than a third of U.S. workers receive salaries from nonprofit organizations that receive funding from others, that in turn receive their money from businesses. Foundations, universities, and other nonprofit organizations own billions of shares in publicly held companies. As stock prices of those firms increase, businesses create more wealth to benefit society.

Businesses are also partly responsible for promoting social justice. Many companies believe they have a role in building communities that goes well beyond simply "giving back." To them, charity is not enough. Their social contributions include cleaning up the environment, building community toilets, providing computer lessons, caring for the elderly, and supporting children from low-income families.

As concern about climate change increased, the green movement emerged in nearly every aspect of daily life. What makes a product green? Some believe that a product's carbon footprint (the amount of carbon released during production, distribution, consumption, and disposal) defines how green it is. Many variables contribute to a product's carbon footprint. The carbon footprint of a package of, say, frozen corn includes not only the carbon released by the fertilizer to grow the corn but also the carbon in the fertilizer itself, the gas used to run the farm equipment and transport the corn to market, the electricity to make the plastic packages and power the freezers, and so on.

No specific guidelines define the carbon footprints of products, businesses, or individuals or outline how to communicate them to consumers. PepsiCo presents carbon information with a label on bags of cheese-and-onion potato chips, for example, that says "75 grams of CO_2." Simple enough, but what does it mean? (We don't know either.)

The green movement has provided consumers with lots of product choices. However, making those choices means sorting through the many and confusing claims made by manufacturers. (See the Thinking Green box for a discussion of misusing the green label.) The noise in the marketplace challenges even the most dedicated green activists, but taking the easy route of buying what's most readily available violates the principles of the green movement.

Environmental efforts may increase a company's costs, but they also allow the company to charge higher prices, increase market share, or both. Ciba Specialty Chemicals, a Swiss textile-dye manufacturer, developed dyes that require less salt than traditional dyes. Since used dye solutions must be treated before being released into rivers or streams, less salt means lower water-treatment costs. Patents protect Ciba's low-salt dyes, so the company can charge more for its dyes than other companies can charge for theirs. Ciba's experience illustrates that, just as a new machine enhances labor productivity, lowering environmental costs can add value to a business.

Not all environmental strategies are as financially beneficial as Ciba's, however. In the early 1990s, tuna producer StarKist responded to consumer concerns about dolphins in the eastern Pacific dying in nets set out for yellow fin tuna. The company announced it would sell only skipjack tuna from the western Pacific, which do not swim near dolphins. Unfortunately, customers were unwilling to pay a premium for dolphin-safe tuna and considered the taste of skipjack inferior. Nor was there a clear environmental gain: for every dolphin saved in the eastern Pacific, thousands of immature tuna and dozens of sharks, turtles, and other marine animals died in the western Pacific fishing process.

Sustainable or Suspect: Greenwashing

With public concern over the environment at an all-time high, companies are constantly looking for more eco-friendly ways of doing business. Some, however, only want to appear green while still maintaining the same business practices.

These corner-cutting companies have been accused of "greenwashing," or using deceptive marketing and advertising that portray their business as environmentally responsible. For example, many paint brands claim to be low in eco-unfriendly volatile organic compounds (VOCs), but when colorant is added to the paint at stores, VOCs are added too and the count jumps to dangerous levels. Other products simply offer irrelevant information to appear green, such as aerosol cans with green dots to show the product has no ozone-depleting chlorofluorocarbons (CFCs). In fact, no aerosol spray contains CFC, because the chemical was banned in 1978.

Since most greenwashed ads are subtle, they fall short of being illegal and are ignored by most consumers. To combat this marketing strategy, independent organizations such as Consumer Reports' greenerchoices.org and the University of Oregon's greenwashingindex.com screen hundreds of ads and determine which are genuinely green and which are greenwashing. For more information, visit these sites, and keep in mind that not everything's as green as it seems.

Sources: Irene Park, "Chicago Shoppers Wary of Green Labeling by Marketers," *Medill Reports Chicago,* March 10, 2011; "Sherwin-Williams Zero-VOC Claim Misleading," *Environmental Building News,* January 21, 2011; and "What Is Greenwashing and How You Can Avoid It," GreenAnswers.com, March 4, 2011.

The green movement can have a positive impact on the U.S. labor force. Emerging renewable-energy and energy-efficiency industries currently account for 9 million jobs and by 2030 may create as many as 40 million more in engineering, manufacturing, construction, accounting, and management, according to a green-collar job report by the American Solar Energy Society.[31]

Environmental quality is a public good; that is, everyone gets to enjoy it regardless of who pays for it. The challenge for companies is to find the public goods that will appeal to their customers. Many corporations are publishing reports that document their net social contribution. To do that, a company must measure its positive social contributions and subtract its negative social impacts. We discuss that process next.

Social Auditing

Can we measure whether organizations are making social responsibility an integral part of top management's decision making? The answer is yes, and the term that represents that measurement is *social auditing.*

social audit
A systematic evaluation of an organization's progress toward implementing socially responsible and responsive programs.

A **social audit** is a systematic evaluation of an organization's progress toward implementing socially responsible and responsive programs. One of the major problems of conducting a social audit is establishing procedures for measuring a firm's activities and their effects on society. What should a social audit measure? Many consider workplace issues, the environment, product safety, community relations, military weapons contracting, international operations and human rights, and respect for the rights of local people.

It remains a question whether organizations should add up positive actions like charitable donations and pollution control efforts, and then subtract negative effects like layoffs and overall pollution created, to get a net social contribution. Or should they just record positive actions? What do you think? However they are conducted, social audits force organizations to consider their social responsibility beyond the level of just feeling good or managing public relations.

In addition to social audits conducted by companies themselves, five types of groups serve as watchdogs to monitor how well companies enforce their ethical and social responsibility policies:

1. *Socially conscious investors* insist that a company extend its own high standards to its suppliers. Social responsibility investing (SRI) is on the rise, with nearly $3 trillion invested in SRI funds in the United States already.[32]

2. *Social conscious research organizations,* such as Ethisphere, analyze and report on corporate social responsibility efforts.[33]

3. *Environmentalists* apply pressure by naming companies that don't abide by environmentalists' standards. After months of protests coordinated by the San Francisco–based Rainforest Action Network (RAN), JPMorgan Chase & Co. adopted guidelines that restrict its lending and underwriting practices for industrial projects likely to have a negative impact on the environment. RAN activists first go after an industry leader, like JPMorgan, then tackle smaller companies. "We call it, 'Rank 'em and spank 'em,'" says RAN's executive director.[34]

4. *Union officials* hunt down violations and force companies to comply to avoid negative publicity.

5. *Customers* make buying decisions based on their social conscience. Half of the companies surveyed recently said that they were adjusting their environmental and social responsibility strategies because of the number of customers that factor these into their buying decisions.[35]

Bob McDonald, Chairman of the Board, President and CEO of Procter and Gamble, described the importance of corporate social responsibility this way: "I don't believe sustainability is optional anymore. The world today is so flat, so transparent with the Internet, and the impact of individuals is so heightened because of the ability to blog and Tweet and other things, that consumers want to know what they're buying into when they buy your brand. They want to know the company behind that brand. They want to know what that company stands for, and they want to know how that company takes care of the environment."[36] As you can see, it isn't enough for a company to be right when it comes to ethics and social responsibility—it also has to convince its customers and society that it's right.

The goal of the Rainforest Action Network, an environmental activist group, is to show companies that it is possible to do well by doing good. It conducts public campaigns designed to put consumer pressure on companies that refuse to adopt responsible environmental policies. RAN has helped convince dozens of corporations including Home Depot, Citigroup, Boise Cascade, and Goldman Sachs to change their practices.

progress assessment

- What is corporate social responsibility, and how does it relate to each of a business's major stakeholders?
- What is a social audit, and what kinds of activities does it monitor?

LEARNING goal 6

Analyze the role of U.S businesses in influencing ethical behavior and social responsibility in global markets.

INTERNATIONAL ETHICS AND SOCIAL RESPONSIBILITY

Ethical problems and issues of social responsibility are not unique to the United States. Influence-peddling or bribery charges have been brought against top officials in Japan, South Korea, China, Italy, Brazil, Pakistan, and Zaire. What is new about the moral and ethical standards by which government leaders are being judged? They are much stricter than in the past. Top leaders are now being held to higher standards.

Many U.S. businesses also demand socially responsible behavior from their international suppliers, making sure they don't violate U.S. human rights and environmental standards. Sears will not import products made by Chinese prison labor. Clothing manufacturer Phillips–Van Heusen will cancel orders from suppliers that violate its ethical, environmental, and human rights code. Dow Chemical expects suppliers to conform to tough U.S. pollution and safety laws rather than just to local laws of their respective countries. McDonald's denied rumors that one of its suppliers grazes cattle on cleared rain-forest land but wrote a ban on the practice anyway.

In contrast are companies criticized for exploiting workers in less developed countries. Nike, the world's largest athletic shoe company, has been accused by human rights and labor groups of treating its workers poorly while lavishing millions of dollars on star athletes to endorse its products. Cartoonist Garry Trudeau featured an anti-Nike campaign in his popular syndicated series *Doonesbury*. In 1998, even Nike CEO Phil Knight acknowledged, "Nike product has become synonymous with slave wages, forced overtime, and arbitrary abuse."[37]

Nike has been working hard to improve its reputation. In the late 1990s, Nike began monitoring efforts to improve labor conditions in its 700 contract factories that are subject to local culture and economic conditions. In 2005, Nike released the names and locations of its factories, both as a show of transparency and to encourage its competitors to work on improving conditions as well. The company shared its audit data with a professor at MIT's Sloan School of Management, who released his findings in 2006. He concluded that despite "significant efforts and investments by Nike . . . workplace conditions in almost 80% of its suppliers have either remained the same or worsened over time."

Why has Nike's monitoring program not been as successful as the company hoped? One reason is that in emerging economies, government regulations tend to be weak, which leaves companies to police their suppliers. That's a major task for a company like Nike, which produces 98 percent of its shoes in hundreds of factories in many different countries. Another reason is that as a buyer, Nike has different degrees of leverage. This leverage is based on how long Nike has worked with a supplier or how much of the factory's revenue depends on Nike alone.

Nike is now trying to change its outsourcing model by helping convert suppliers from using low-skilled assembly lines to lean manufacturing, which organizes workers into multitasking teams (see Chapter 9 for more on lean

Nike has outsourced the manufacture of its products to plants in other countries and has weathered much criticism for operating in low-wage countries where child labor is common. The company has taken many corrective measures, including working with other companies and advocacy groups on a set of common labor standards and factory guidelines. Can a successful firm overcome past ethical errors?

manufacturing). This requires more on-the-job training, which in turn can motivate factory owners to improve conditions in order to hold onto their high-skilled laborers.[38]

The fairness of requiring international suppliers to adhere to U.S. ethical standards is not as clear-cut as you might think. For example, a gift in one culture can be a bribe in another. Is it always ethical for companies to demand compliance with the standards of their own countries? What about countries where child labor is accepted and families depend on children's salaries for survival? Should foreign companies doing business in the United States expect U.S. companies to comply with their ethical standards? Since multinational corporations span different societies, should they conform to any society's standards? Why is Sears applauded for not importing goods made in Chinese prisons when there are many prison-based enterprises in the United States? None of these questions are easy to answer, but they suggest the complexity of social responsibility in international markets. (See the nearby Reaching Beyond Our Borders box for an example of an ethical culture clash.)

In the 1970s, the Foreign Corrupt Practices Act (discussed in Chapter 3) sent a chill throughout the U.S. business community by criminalizing the act of paying foreign business or government leaders to get business. Many U.S. executives complained that this law put their businesses at a competitive disadvantage when bidding against non-U.S. companies, since foreign companies don't have to abide by it.[39]

To identify some form of common global ethic and fight corruption in global markets, partners in the Organization of American States signed the Inter-American Convention Against Corruption.[40] The United Nations adopted a formal condemnation of corporate bribery, as did the European Union and the Organization for Economic Cooperation and Development. The International Organization for Standardization (ISO) plans to publish a standard on social responsibility called ISO 26000, with guidelines on product manufacturing, fair pay rates, appropriate employee treatment, and hiring practices. These standards

Ethical Culture Clash

Now that corporations have expanded into communities all over the globe, it raises the question: For which communities are they responsible?

Take communications and electronics giant Motorola. Almost half its employees live outside the United States, and more than half its revenues come from non-U.S. markets. Is it difficult for Motorola employees to adhere to the company's ethical values while at the same time respecting the values of the host countries in which Motorola manufactures and markets its products?

Here's an example of how corporate ethics can clash with cultural ethics. Joe, the oldest son of a poor South American cloth peddler, managed to move to the United States, earn an engineering degree, and get a job with Motorola. After five years, Joe seemed to have bought into the

Motorola culture and was happy to be granted a transfer back to his home country. He was told that the company expected him to live there in a safe and presentable home of his choice. To help him afford such a residence, Motorola agreed to reimburse him a maximum of $2,000 a month for the cost of his rent and servants. Each month Joe submitted rental receipts for exactly $2,000. The company later found out that Joe was living in what was, by Western standards, a shack in a dangerous area of town. Such a humble home could not have cost more than $200 a month. The company was concerned for Joe's safety as well as for the effect his residence would have on Motorola's image. The human resource manager was also worried about Joe's lack of integrity, given he had submitted false receipts for reimbursement.

Joe was upset with what he considered the company's invasion of his privacy. He argued he should receive the full $2,000 monthly reimbursement all employees received. He explained his choice of housing by saying he was making sacrifices so he could send the extra money to his family and put his younger siblings through school. This was especially important since his father had died and his family had no one else to depend on. "Look, my family is poor," Joe said, "so poor that most Westerners wouldn't believe our poverty even if they saw it. This money means the difference between hope and despair for all of us. For me to do anything less for my family would be to defile the honor of my late father. Can't you understand?"

Often it is difficult to understand what others perceive as ethical. Different situations often turn the clear waters of "rightness" downright muddy. Joe was trying to do the honorable thing for his family. Yet Motorola's wish to have its higher-level people live in safe housing is not unreasonable, given the dangerous conditions of the city in which Joe lived. The policy of housing reimbursement supports Motorola's intent to make its employees' stay in the country reasonably comfortable and safe, not to increase their salaries. If Joe worked in the United States, where he would not receive a housing supplement, it would be unethical for him to falsify expense reports in order to receive more money to send to his family. In South America, though, the issue is not so clear.

Sources: R. S. Moorthy, Robert C. Solomon, William J. Ellos, and Richard T. De George, "Friendship or Bribery?" *Across the Board,* January 1999; Yale Political Union, "Should Corporations Be Responsible to More than Their Shareholders?" *The Huffington Post,* October 27, 2009; and Walter Mosley, "Ten Things to Foster Socially Responsible Corporations," *The Nation,* July 15, 2010.

are advisory only and will not be used for certification purposes. The formation of a single set of international rules governing multinational corporations is unlikely in the near future. In many places "Fight corruption" remains just a slogan, but even a slogan is a start.

progress assessment

- How are U.S. businesses demanding socially responsible behavior from their international suppliers?
- Why is it unlikely that there will be a single set of international rules governing multinational companies soon?

summary

Learning Goal 1. Explain why obeying the law is only the first step in behaving ethically.

- **How is legality different from ethics?**

Ethics goes beyond obeying laws to include abiding by the moral standards accepted by society. Ethics reflects people's proper relationships with one another. Legality is more limiting; it refers only to laws written to protect people from fraud, theft, and violence.

Learning Goal 2. Ask the three questions you need to answer when faced with a potentially unethical action.

- **How can we tell if our business decisions are ethical?**

We can put our business decisions through an ethics check by asking three questions: (1) Is it legal? (2) Is it balanced? and (3) How will it make me feel?

Learning Goal 3. Describe management's role in setting ethical standards.

- **What is management's role in setting ethical standards?**

Managers often set formal ethical standards, but more important are the messages they send through their actions. Management's tolerance or intolerance of ethical misconduct influences employees more than any written ethics codes.

Learning Goal 4. Distinguish between compliance-based and integrity-based ethics codes, and list the six steps in setting up a corporate ethics code.

- **What's the difference between compliance-based and integrity-based ethics codes?**

Whereas compliance-based ethics codes are concerned with avoiding legal punishment, integrity-based ethics codes define the organization's guiding values, create an environment that supports ethically sound behavior, and stress a shared accountability among employees.

Learning Goal 5. Define *corporate social responsibility* and compare corporations' responsibilities to various stakeholders

- **What is corporate social responsibility?**

Corporate social responsibility is the concern businesses have for society.

- **How do businesses demonstrate corporate responsibility toward stakeholders?**

Business is responsible to four types of stakeholders: (1) it must satisfy *customers* with goods and services of real value; (2) it must make money for its *investors;* (3) it must create jobs for *employees,* maintain job security, and see that hard work and talent are fairly rewarded; and (4) it must create new wealth for *society,* promote social justice, and contribute to making its own environment a better place.

- **How are a company's social responsibility efforts measured?**

A corporate social audit measures an organization's progress toward social responsibility. Some people believe the audit should add together the organization's positive actions and then subtract the negative effects to get a net social benefit.

Learning Goal 6. Analyze the role of U.S. businesses in influencing ethical behavior and social responsibility in global markets

- **How can U.S. companies influence ethical behavior and social responsibility in global markets?**

Many U.S. businesses are demanding socially responsible behavior from their international suppliers by making sure their suppliers do not violate U.S. human rights and environmental standards. Companies like Sears, Phillips–Van Heusen, and Dow Chemical will not import products from companies that do not meet their ethical and social responsibility standards.

key terms

compliance-based ethics codes 96	corporate social initiatives 99	integrity-based ethics codes 96
corporate philanthropy 99	corporate social responsibility (CSR) 98	social audit 104
corporate policy 99	ethics 91	whistleblowers 97
corporate responsibility 99	insider trading 101	

critical thinking

Think of a situation that tested your ethical behavior. For example, maybe your best friend forgot about a term paper due the next day and asked if he could copy a paper you wrote for another instructor last semester.

1. What are your alternatives, and what are the consequences of each?

2. Would it have been easier to resolve the dilemma if you had asked yourself the three questions listed in the chapter? Try answering them now and see whether you would have made a different choice.

developing workplace skills

1. What sources have helped shape your personal code of ethics and morality? What influences, if any, have ever pressured you to compromise those standards? Think of an experience you had at work or school that tested your ethical standards. How did you resolve your dilemma? Now that time has passed, are you comfortable with the decision you made? If not, what would you do differently?

2. Do a little investigative reporting of your own. Identify a public interest group in your community and identify its officers, objectives, sources and amount of financial support, and size and characteristics of membership. List some examples of its recent actions and/or accomplishments. You should be able to choose from environmental groups, animal protection groups, political action committees, and so on. Call the local chamber of commerce, the Better Business Bureau, or local government agencies for help. Try using the Internet to help you find more information.

3. You're the manager of a coffeehouse called the Morning Cup. One of your best employees desires to be promoted to a managerial position; however, the owner is grooming his slow-thinking son for the job. The owner's nepotism may hurt a valuable employee's chances for advancement, but complaining may hurt your own chances for promotion. What do you do?

4. Contact a local corporation and ask for a copy of its written ethics code. Would you classify its code as compliance-based or integrity-based? Explain.

5. What effects have the new laws protecting whistleblowers had on the business environment? Use the Internet or the library to research individuals who reported their employers' illegal and/or unethical behavior. Did the companies change their policies? If so, what effect have these policies had on the companies' stakeholders? What effect did reporting the problems have on the whistleblowers themselves?

taking it to the net

Purpose

To demonstrate the level of commitment one business has to social responsibility.

Exercise

Richard Foos of Rhino Records built a multimillion-dollar entertainment experience out of a pile of dusty old records—by sticking to his ideals. Foos fosters ethical practices in Rhino's day-to-day business, supporting numerous charitable groups and promoting community service by Rhino employees. See for yourself how Foos responds to social and environmental issues by going to Rhino's website at www.rhino.com and exploring the "About Rhino" links. Then answer the following questions:

1. What is the social mission of Rhino Records?

2. What does the Social and Environmental Responsibility Team (SERT) do to implement this mission?

3. How does Rhino Records encourage its employees to get involved in community service?

4. How do Rhino employees communicate the company's social mission to their customers?

casing the web

To access the case "Got a Deadline? Click Here," visit **www.mhhe.com/ubI0e**

video case

To access the video case featuring Cell Phones for Soldiers, visit **www.mhhe.com/ubI0e**

HOW to Form a Business

5

LEARNING goals

After you have read and studied this chapter, you should be able to

1 Compare the advantages and disadvantages of sole proprietorships.

2 Describe the differences between general and limited partners, and compare the advantages and disadvantages of partnerships.

3 Compare the advantages and disadvantages of corporations, and summarize the differences between C corporations, S corporations, and limited liability companies.

4 Define and give examples of three types of corporate mergers, and explain the role of leveraged buyouts and taking a firm private.

5 Outline the advantages and disadvantages of franchises, and discuss the opportunities for diversity in franchising and the challenges of global franchising.

6 Explain the role of cooperatives.

profile

Regardless of background or experience, every successful entrepreneur shares at least one thing in common: they each identified a need and filled it. For Mary Ellen Sheets, all she wanted when she started her business was for her sons Brig and Jon Sorber to get out of the house and earn some money during their summer vacation. Sheets gave the boys an old pickup truck and soon they had an ad in the paper that read, "Two men and a truck." The simple slogan eventually became the name of the moving business Sheets' sons ran throughout their high school years.

Once Brig and Jon went off to college, Sheets continued to receive phone calls from customers asking for her sons' services. Recognizing the demand, Sheets purchased a used moving van for $350 and hired two employees to do the lifting. Her minimal initial investment turned out to be the only money Sheets ever had to take out of her own pocket for the business. As Two Men and a Truck steadily grew, Sheets took a big risk and quit her job in state government (forgoing her retirement) to work on the business full time. The gamble paid off within a year when Sheets granted the first Two Men and a Truck franchise to her daughter Melanie in Atlanta, GA.

Since then Sheets and her family have expanded their brand to more than 215 locations across the country, earning $193.3 million annually. The key to the company's success is its simplicity. The name says it all, as does the straightforward stick-figure logo drawn by Sheets when the business was still her sons' summer jobs. The brand is so effective that the company is now expanding overseas with franchises in the United Kingdom.

Besides its financial success, Two Men and a Truck also remains committed to giving back to each community it serves. Every truck in its system sports the slogan, "The Movers Who Care." Two Men and a Truck's record of service goes back to the company's beginnings. After generating a $1,000 profit in its first year, Sheets was so pleased that she gave away the money to 10 different charities, giving each $100. Two Men and a Truck continues to donate generously to those original organizations. The company also contributes a portion of every move completed to the American Cancer Society. With 317,841 moves completed in 2010 alone, that's certainly no small donation. Nevertheless, Sheets and her family see charity and service as integral parts of their business plan. The corporate office even grants a Humanitarian Award each year to the franchisee that performs the most community service. The Omaha, NE, franchise took home the prize in 2010 after donating more than 2,000 hours of service.

Getting to Know

X *Mary Ellen Sheets*

Founder of Two Men and a Truck

Sheets herself is no stranger to accolades. In 2004 she became the first woman to win the International Franchise Association's Entrepreneur of the Year award. She was honored with a number of other recognitions over the years, including a Blue Chip Award and the Michigan Entrepreneur of the Year Award. With her kids in charge of most of the corporate leadership these days, Sheets operates the company's flagship location in Lansing, MI. She now manages 53 employees and completed more than 4,200 moves in 2010. Not bad for a $350 investment.

Just like Sheets, all business owners must decide for themselves which form of business is best for them. Whether you dream of starting a business for yourself, going into business with a partner, forming a corporation, or someday being a leading franchisor, it's important to know that each form of ownership has its advantages and disadvantages. You will learn about them all in this chapter.

Sources: Randy J. Stine, "A Long History of Giving," *The Greater Lansing Business Monthly,* April 2011; "Recent Interview with Mary Ellen Sheets," *Franchise Gator,* accessed April 2011; "Two Men and a Truck Leads the Way as It Arrives in the UK," *The Franchise Magazine,* accessed April 2011; and www.TwoMenAndATruck.com/mary-ellen-sheets, accessed April 2011.

Around April 15th every year, we are a very sought out company. With thousands of locations in the United States we make tax filing much easier. Most people are unaware that we are actually a Canadian franchise even though we have our headquarters in the United States. Who are we? (Find the answer in the chapter.)

BASIC FORMS OF BUSINESS OWNERSHIP

Like Mary Ellen Sheets, hundreds of thousands of people have started new businesses in the United States. In fact, more than 600,000 are started each year.[1] Chances are, you've thought of owning your own business or know someone who has.

How you form your business can make a tremendous difference in your long-term success. The three major forms of business ownership are (1) sole proprietorships, (2) partnerships, and (3) corporations. Each has advantages and disadvantages that we'll discuss.

It can be easy to get started in your own business. You can begin a lawn mowing service, develop a website, or go about meeting other wants and needs of your community. A business owned, and usually managed, by one person is called a **sole proprietorship**. That is the most common form of business ownership.

Many people do not have the money, time, or desire to run a business on their own. When two or more people legally agree to become co-owners of a business, the organization is called a **partnership**.

Sole proprietorships and partnerships are relatively easy to form, but there are advantages to creating a business that is separate and distinct from the owners. This is a **corporation**, a legal entity with authority to act and have liability apart from its owners. The almost 5 million corporations in the United

sole proprietorship
A business that is owned, and usually managed, by one person.

partnership
A legal form of business with two or more owners.

corporation
A legal entity with authority to act and have liability apart from its owners.

figure 5.1

FORMS OF BUSINESS OWNERSHIP

Although corporations make up only 20 percent of the total number of businesses, they make 81 percent of the total receipts. Sole proprietorships are the most common form (72 percent), but they earn only 6 percent of the receipts.
Source: U.S. Internal Revenue Service.

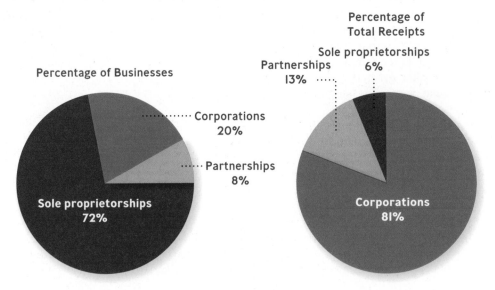

States make up only 20 percent of all businesses, but they earn 81 percent of total U.S. business receipts (see Figure 5.1).

Keep in mind that just because a business starts in one form of ownership, it doesn't have to stay in that form.[2] Many companies start out in one form, then add (or drop) a partner or two, and eventually become corporations, limited liability companies, or franchisors.[3] Let's begin our discussion by looking at the most basic form of ownership—the sole proprietorship.

LEARNING goal 1

Compare the advantages and disadvantages of sole proprietorships.

SOLE PROPRIETORSHIPS

Advantages of Sole Proprietorships

Sole proprietorships are the easiest kind of businesses to explore in your quest for an interesting career. Every town has sole proprietors you can visit and talk with about the joys and frustrations of being in business on their own.[4] Most will mention the benefits of being their own boss and setting their own hours. Other advantages include:

Warren Brown's career is finally "rising." Brown left a promising law career to create Cakelove, a bustling bakery that specializes in making pastries from scratch using natural ingredients. Brown regularly appears on the Food Network. Do you have a passion you would like to pursue as a business?

1. *Ease of starting and ending the business.* All you have to do to start a sole proprietorship is buy or lease the needed equipment (a saw, a laptop, a tractor, a lawn mower) and put up some announcements saying you are in business. You may have to get a permit or license from the local government, but often that is no problem. It is just as easy to get out of business; you simply stop. There is no one to consult or disagree with about such decisions.

2. *Being your own boss.* Working for others simply does not have the same excitement as working for yourself—at least, that's the way sole proprietors feel. You may make mistakes, but they are your mistakes—and so are the many small victories each day.

3. *Pride of ownership.* People who own and manage their own businesses are rightfully proud of their work. They deserve all the credit for taking the risks and providing needed goods or services.

4. *Leaving a legacy.* Owners can leave an ongoing business for future generations.

5. *Retention of company profits.* Owners not only keep the profits earned but also benefit from the increasing value as the business grows.

6. *No special taxes.* All the profits of a sole proprietorship are taxed as the personal income of the owner, and the owner pays the normal income tax on that money.[5] However, owners do have to pay the self-employment tax (for Social Security and Medicare). They also have to estimate their taxes and make quarterly payments to the government or suffer penalties for nonpayment.

Disadvantages of Sole Proprietorships

Not everyone is equipped to own and manage a business. Often it is difficult to save enough money to start a business and keep it going. The costs of inventory, supplies, insurance, advertising, rent, computers, utilities, and so on may be too much to cover alone. There are other disadvantages:

1. *Unlimited liability—the risk of personal losses.* When you work for others, it is their problem if the business is not profitable. When you own your own business, you and the business are considered one. You have **unlimited liability;** that is, any debts or damages incurred by the business are your debts and you must pay them, even if it means selling your home, your car, or whatever else you own. This is a serious risk, and undertaking it requires not only thought but also discussion with a lawyer, an insurance agent, an accountant, and others.

2. *Limited financial resources.* Funds available to the business are limited to what the one owner can gather. Since there are serious limits to how much money one person can raise, partnerships and corporations have a greater probability of obtaining the financial backing needed to start and equip a business and keep it going.

3. *Management difficulties.* All businesses need management; someone must keep inventory, accounting, and tax records. Many people skilled at selling things or providing a service are not so skilled at keeping records. Sole proprietors often find it difficult to attract qualified employees to help run the business because often they cannot compete with the salary and benefits offered by larger companies.

4. *Overwhelming time commitment.* Though sole proprietors say they set their own hours, it's hard to own a business, manage it, train people, and have time for anything else in life when there is no one with whom to share the burden. The owner of a store, for example, may put in 12 hours a day at least six days a week—almost twice the hours worked by a nonsupervisory employee in a large company. Imagine how this time commitment affects the sole proprietor's family life. Many sole proprietors will tell you, "It's not a job, it's not a career, it's a way of life."

5. *Few fringe benefits.* If you are your own boss, you lose the fringe benefits that often come with working for others. You have no paid health insurance, no paid disability insurance, no pension plan, no sick leave, and no vacation pay. These and other benefits may add up to 30 percent or more of a worker's compensation.

6. *Limited growth.* Expansion is often slow since a sole proprietorship relies on its owner for most of its creativity, business know-how, and funding.

7. *Limited life span.* If the sole proprietor dies, is incapacitated, or retires, the business no longer exists (unless it is sold or taken over by the sole proprietor's heirs).

Talk with a few local sole proprietors about the problems they've faced in being on their own. They are likely to have many interesting stories about problems getting loans from the bank, problems with theft, and problems simply keeping up with the business. These are reasons why many sole proprietors choose to find partners to share the load.

Being the sole proprietor of a company, like a dog-walking service, means making a major time commitment to run the business, including constantly seeking out new customers and looking for reliable employees when the time comes to grow. If you were a sole proprietor, what would you need to do if you wanted to take a week's vacation?

unlimited liability
The responsibility of business owners for all of the debts of the business.

progress assessment

- Most people who start businesses in the United States are sole proprietors. What are the advantages and disadvantages of sole proprietorships?
- Why would unlimited liability be considered a major drawback to sole proprietorships?

LEARNING goal 2

Describe the differences between general and limited partners, and compare the advantages and disadvantages of partnerships.

PARTNERSHIPS

A partnership is a legal form of business with two or more owners. There are several types: (1) general partnerships, (2) limited partnerships, and (3) master limited partnerships. In a **general partnership** all owners share in operating the business and in assuming liability for the business's debts. A **limited partnership** has one or more general partners and one or more limited partners. A **general partner** is an owner (partner) who has unlimited liability and is active in managing the firm. Every partnership must have at least one general partner. A **limited partner** is an owner who invests money in the business but does not have any management responsibility or liability for losses beyond his or her investment. **Limited liability** means that the limited partners' liability for the debts of the business is *limited* to the amount they put into the company; their personal assets are not at risk.

One form of partnership, the **master limited partnership (MLP)**, looks much like a corporation (which we discuss next) in that it acts like a corporation and is traded on the stock exchanges like a corporation, but is taxed like a partnership and thus avoids the corporate income tax.[6] Master Limited Partnerships are normally found in the oil and gas industry. For example, Sunoco Inc. formed the MLP Sunoco Logistics Partners (SXL) to acquire, own, and operate a group of crude oil and refined-product pipelines and storage facilities. Income received by SXL is not taxed before it is passed on to investors as dividends as it would be if SXL were a corporation.[7]

Another type of partnership was created to limit the disadvantage of unlimited liability. A **limited liability partnership (LLP)** limits partners' risk of losing their personal assets to the outcomes of only their own acts and omissions and those of people under their supervision. If you are a limited partner in an LLP, you can operate without the fear that one of your partners might commit an act of malpractice resulting in a judgment that takes away your house, car, retirement plan, even your collection of vintage Star Wars action figures, as would be the case in a general partnership. However, in many states this personal protection does not extend to contract liabilities such as bank loans, leases, and business debt the partnership takes on; loss of personal assets is still a risk if these are not paid. In states without additional contract liability protections for LLPs, the LLP is in many ways similar to an LLC (discussed later in the chapter).

All states except Louisiana have adopted the Uniform Partnership Act (UPA) to replace earlier laws governing partnerships. The UPA defines the

general partnership
A partnership in which all owners share in operating the business and in assuming liability for the business's debts.

limited partnership
A partnership with one or more general partners and one or more limited partners.

general partner
An owner (partner) who has unlimited liability and is active in managing the firm.

limited partner
An owner who invests money in the business but does not have any management responsibility or liability for losses beyond the investment.

limited liability
The responsibility of a business's owners for losses only up to the amount they invest; limited partners and shareholders (stockholders) have limited liability.

master limited partnership (MLP)
A partnership that looks much like a corporation (in that it acts like a corporation and is traded on a stock exchange) but is taxed like a partnership and thus avoids the corporate income tax.

limited liability partnership (LLP)
A partnership that limits partners' risk of losing their personal assets to only their own acts and omissions and to the acts and omissions of people under their supervision.

three key elements of any general partnership as (1) common ownership, (2) shared profits and losses, and (3) the right to participate in managing the operations of the business.

Advantages of Partnerships

Often, it is much easier to own and manage a business with one or more partners. Your partner may be skilled at inventory control and accounting, while you do the selling or servicing. A partner can also provide additional money, support, and expertise as well as cover for you when you are sick or on vacation. The Spotlight on Small Business box offers a few tips about choosing a partner.

Partnerships usually have the following advantages:

1. *More financial resources.* When two or more people pool their money and credit, it is easier to pay the rent, utilities, and other bills incurred by a business. A limited partnership is specially designed to help raise money. As mentioned earlier, a limited partner invests money in the business but cannot legally have management responsibility and has limited liability.

2. *Shared management and pooled/complementary skills and knowledge.* It is simply much easier to manage the day-to-day activities of a business with carefully chosen partners. Partners give each other free time from the business and provide different skills and perspectives. Some people find that the best partner is a spouse. Many husband-and-wife teams manage restaurants, service shops, and other businesses.[8]

3. *Longer survival.* One study that examined 2,000 businesses started since 1960 found that partnerships were four times more likely to succeed than sole proprietorships. Being watched by a partner can help a businessperson become more disciplined.

4. *No special taxes.* As with sole proprietorships, all profits of partnerships are taxed as the personal income of the owners, who pay the normal income tax on that money. Similarly, partners must estimate their taxes and make quarterly payments or suffer penalties for nonpayment.

Kate and Andy Spade started a business selling a $155 black nylon handbag in 1993. Their business has grown into a global brand. What makes the pair of Spades such great business partners? It's their differences: Kate is the creative soul who designs the products and Andy is the risk taker who shapes the brand. What problems might partners who share both business and home encounter that other partners might not?

The Ties That Bind

Before plunging into a partnership, ask yourself these questions regarding your potential partner: Do you share the same goals? Do you share the same vision for the company's future? What skills does the person have? Are those skills the same as yours, or do they complement your skills? What contacts, resources, or special attributes will the person bring to the business? What type of decision maker is the person? Is this someone with whom you could happily share authority for all major business decisions? Do you trust each other? How does the person respond to adversity? Does he or she try to solve the problem or try to defend his or her ego? Can the person accept constructive criticism without getting defensive? To what extent can you build fun and excitement into the partnership?

If the answers to many of these questions are negative, this person is not the partner for you. But remember, there's no such thing as a perfect partner, so allow for some imperfection (after all, you aren't going to be the perfect partner either). As in a good marriage, the best way to avoid major conflicts in a business partnership is to begin with an honest discussion of what each partner expects to give to and get from the endeavor.

Disadvantages of Partnerships

Anytime two people must agree, conflict and tension are possible. Partnerships have caused splits between relatives, friends, and spouses. Let's explore the disadvantages of partnerships:

1. *Unlimited liability.* Each *general* partner is liable for the debts of the firm, no matter who was responsible for causing them. You are liable for your partners' mistakes as well as your own. Like sole proprietors, general partners can lose their homes, cars, and everything else they own if the business loses a lawsuit or goes bankrupt.

2. *Division of profits.* Sharing risk means sharing profits, and that can cause conflicts. There is no set system for dividing profits in a partnership, and they are not always divided evenly. For example, if one partner puts in more money and the other puts in more hours, each may feel justified in asking for a bigger share of the profits.

3. *Disagreements among partners.* Disagreements over money are just one example of potential conflict in a partnership. Who has final authority over employees? Who hires and fires employees? Who works what hours? What if one partner wants to buy expensive equipment for the firm and the other partner disagrees? All terms of the partnership should be spelled out in writing to protect all parties and minimize misunderstandings.

4. *Difficulty of termination.* Once you have committed yourself to a partnership, it is not easy to get out of it. Sure, you can just quit. However, questions about who gets what and what happens next are often difficult to resolve when the partnership ends. Surprisingly, law firms often have faulty partnership agreements and find that breaking up is hard to do. How do you get rid of a partner you don't like? It is best to decide such questions up front in the partnership agreement. Figure 5.2 gives you ideas about what to include in partnership agreements.

figure 5.2
_____
HOW TO FORM A PARTNERSHIP

It's not hard to form a partnership, but it's wise for each prospective partner to get the counsel of a lawyer experienced with such agreements. Lawyers' services are usually expensive, so would-be partners should read all about partnerships and reach some basic agreements before calling a lawyer.

For your protection, be sure to put your partnership agreement In writing. The Model Business Corporation Act recommends including the following in a written partnership agreement:

1. The name of the business. Many states require the firm's name to be registered with state and/or county officials if the firm's name is different from the name of any of the partners.

2. The names and addresses of all partners.

3. The purpose and nature of the business, the location of the principal offices, and any other locations where business will be conducted.

4. The date the partnership will start and how long it will last. Will It exist for a specific length of time, or will it stop when one of the partners dies or when the partners agree to discontinue?

5. The contributions made by each partner. Will some partners contribute money, while others provide real estate, personal property, expertise, or labor? When are the contributions due?

6. The management responsibilities. Will all partners have equal voices in management, or will there be senior and junior partners?

7. The duties of each partner.

8. The salaries and drawing accounts of each partner.

9. Provision for sharing of profits or losses.

10. Provision for accounting procedures. Who'll keep the accounts? What bookkeeping and accounting methods will be used? Where will the books be kept?

11. The requirements for taking in new partners.

12. Any special restrictions, rights, or duties of any partner.

13. Provision for a retiring partner.

14. Provision for the purchase of a deceased or retiring partner's share of the business.

15. Provision for how grievances will be handled.

16. Provision for how to dissolve the partnership and distribute the assets to the partners.

The best way to learn about the advantages and disadvantages of partnerships is to interview several people who have experience with them. They will give you insights and hints on how to avoid problems.

One fear of owning your own business or having a partner is the fear of losing everything you own if someone sues the business or it loses a lot of money. Many businesspeople try to avoid this and the other disadvantages of sole proprietorships and partnerships by forming corporations. We discuss this basic form of business ownership in the following section.

progress assessment

- What is the difference between a limited partner and a general partner?
- What are some of the advantages and disadvantages of partnerships?

LEARNING goal 3

Compare the advantages and disadvantages of corporations, and summarize the differences between C corporations, S corporations, and limited liability companies.

conventional (C) corporation
A state-chartered legal entity with authority to act and have liability separate from its owners.

CORPORATIONS

Many corporations—like General Electric, Microsoft, and Walmart—are big and contribute substantially to the U.S. economy. However, it's not necessary to be big to incorporate. Incorporating may be beneficial for small businesses as well.

A **conventional (C) corporation** is a state-chartered legal entity with authority to act and have liability separate from its owners—its *stockholders*. Stockholders are not liable for the debts or other problems of the corporation beyond the money they invest in it by buying ownership shares, or stock, in the company. They don't have to worry about losing their house, car, or other property because of some business problem—a significant benefit. A corporation not only limits the liability of owners but often enables many people to share in the ownership (and profits) of a business without working there or having other commitments to it.[9] Corporations may choose whether to offer ownership to outside investors or remain privately held. (We discuss stock ownership in Chapter 19.) Figure 5.3 on p. 124 describes various types of corporations.

Advantages of Corporations

Most people are not willing to risk everything to go into business. Yet for a business to grow, prosper, and create economic opportunity, many people have to be willing to invest money in it. One way to solve this problem is to create an artificial being, an entity that exists only in the eyes of the law—a corporation. Let's explore some of the advantages of corporations:

1. *Limited liability.* A major advantage of corporations is the limited liability of their owners. Remember, limited liability means that the owners of a business are responsible for its losses only up to the amount they invest in it.
2. *Ability to raise more money for investment.* To raise money, a corporation can sell shares of its stock to anyone who is interested. This means that millions of people can own part of major companies like IBM, Apple, and Coca-Cola, and smaller corporations as well. If a company sells 10 million shares of stock for $50 a share, it will have $500 million available to build plants, buy materials, hire people, manufacture products, and so on. Such a large amount of money would be difficult to raise any other way.

   Corporations can also borrow money by obtaining loans from financial institutions like banks. They can also borrow from individual investors by issuing bonds, which involve paying investor's interest until the bonds are repaid sometime in the future.[10] You can read about how corporations raise funds through the sale of stocks and bonds in Chapter 19.

Burton Baskin and Irvine Robbins ran their ice cream businesses separately for two years. Once they had succeeded apart, Baskin and Robbins became partners and were able to avoid many of the pitfalls of starting a new business from scratch. They flipped a coin to see whose name would come first. What factors besides the partners' individual success do you think contributed to their long-lasting partnership?

figure 5.3

CORPORATE TYPES

Corporations can fit in more than one category.

You may find some confusing types of corporations when reading about them. Here are a few of the more widely used terms:

An *alien corporation* does business in the United States but is chartered (incorporated) in another country.

A *domestic corporation* does business in the state in which it's chartered (incorporated).

A *foreign corporation* does business In one state but is chartered in another. About one-third of all corporations are chartered in Delaware because of its relatively attractive rules for incorporation. A foreign corporation must register in states where it operates.

A *closed (private) corporation* is one whose stock is held by a few people and isn't available to the general public.

An *open (public) corporation* sells stock to the general public. General Motors and ExxonMobil are examples of public corporations.

A *quasi-public corporation* is a corporation chartered by the government as an approved monopoly to perform services to the general public. Public utilities are examples of quasi-public corporations.

A *professional corporation* is one whose owners offer professional services (doctors, lawyers, etc.). Shares in professional corporations aren't publicly traded.

A *nonprofit (or not-for-profit) corporation* is one that doesn't seek personal profit for Its owners.

A *multinational corporation* is a firm that operates in several countries.

3. *Size.* "Size" summarizes many of the advantages of some corporations. Because they can raise large amounts of money to work with, big corporations can build modern factories or software development facilities with the latest equipment. They can hire experts or specialists in all areas of operation. They can buy other corporations in different fields to diversify their business risks. In short, a large corporation with numerous resources can take advantage of opportunities anywhere in the world.

   But corporations do not have to be large to enjoy the benefits of incorporating. Many doctors, lawyers, and individuals, as well as partners in a variety of businesses, have incorporated. The vast majority of corporations in the United States are small businesses.

4. *Perpetual life.* Because corporations are separate from those who own them, the death of one or more owners does not terminate the corporation.

5. *Ease of ownership change.* It is easy to change the owners of a corporation. All that is necessary is to sell the stock to someone else.

6. *Ease of attracting talented employees.* Corporations can attract skilled employees by offering such benefits as stock options (the right to purchase shares of the corporation for a fixed price).

7. *Separation of ownership from management.* Corporations are able to raise money from many different owners/stockholders without getting them involved in management. The corporate hierarchy in Figure 5.4 shows how the owners/stockholders are separate from the managers and employees. The owners/stockholders elect a board of directors, who hire the officers of the corporation and oversee major policy issues. The owners/stockholders thus have some say in who runs the corporation but have no real control over the daily operations.[11]

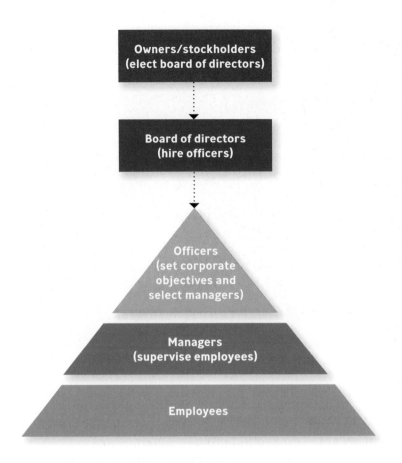

figure 5.4

HOW OWNERS AFFECT MANAGEMENT
Owners have an influence on how a business is managed by electing a board of directors. The board hires the top officers (and fires them if necessary). It also sets the pay for those officers. The officers then select managers and employees with the help of the human resources department.

Disadvantages of Corporations

There are so many sole proprietorships and partnerships in the United States that there must be some disadvantages to incorporating. Otherwise, everyone would do it. The following are a few of the disadvantages:

1. *Initial cost.* Incorporation may cost thousands of dollars and require expensive lawyers and accountants. There are less expensive ways of incorporating in certain states (see the following subsection), but many people do not have the time or confidence to go through this procedure without the help of a potentially expensive lawyer.

2. *Extensive paperwork.* The paperwork needed to start a corporation is just the beginning. A sole proprietor or partnership may keep rather broad accounting records. A corporation, in contrast, must keep detailed financial records, the minutes of meetings, and more. As noted in Figure 5.3, many firms incorporate in Delaware or Nevada because these state's business-oriented laws make the process easier than it is in other states.

3. *Double taxation.* Corporate income is taxed twice. First the corporation pays tax on its income before it can distribute any, as *dividends,* to stockholders. Then the stockholders pay income tax on the dividends they receive.[12] States often tax corporations more heavily than other enterprises, and some special taxes apply only to corporations.

4. *Two tax returns.* An individual who incorporates must file both a corporate tax return and an individual tax return. Depending on the size of the corporation, a corporate return can be quite complex and require the assistance of a certified public accountant (CPA).

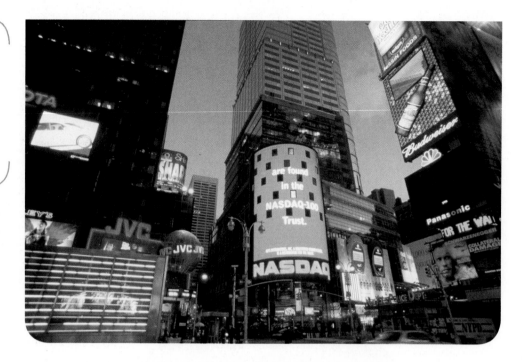

You can be part owner of a corporation by buying shares of the company's stock on exchanges like the NASDAQ. What are the advantages and disadvantages of corporations?

5. *Size*. Size may be one advantage of corporations, but it can be a disadvantage as well. Large corporations sometimes become too inflexible and tied down in red tape to respond quickly to market changes, and their profitability can suffer.

6. *Difficulty of termination*. Once a corporation has started, it's relatively hard to end.

7. *Possible conflict with stockholders and board of directors*. Conflict may brew if the stockholders elect a board of directors who disagree with management. Since the board of directors chooses the company's officers, entrepreneurs serving as managers can find themselves forced out of the very company they founded. This happened to Tom Freston, one of the founders of MTV, and Steve Jobs, a founder of Apple Computer (Jobs of course returned to the company later).

Many businesspeople are discouraged by the costs, paperwork, and special taxes corporations must pay. However, many others believe the advantages of incorporation outweigh the hassles.

Individuals Can Incorporate

Not all corporations are large organizations with hundreds of employees and thousands of stockholders. Truckers, doctors, lawyers, plumbers, athletes, and small-business owners of all kinds can also incorporate. Normally, individuals who incorporate do not issue stock to outsiders; therefore, they do not share all the advantages and disadvantages of large corporations (such as size and more money for investment). Their major advantages are limited liability and possible tax benefits. Although you are not required to file for incorporation through a lawyer, it is usually wise to consult one. In addition to lawyers' fees, the secretary of state's office charges a fee for incorporating a business, varying by state from a low of $50 (in Colorado, Iowa, Kentucky, Mississippi, and Oklahoma) to a high of $300 (in Texas).[13] Like the fee, the length of time it will take to actually have your business incorporated will vary by state. The average

figure 5.5

HOW TO INCORPORATE

The process of forming a corporation varies somewhat from state to state. The articles of incorporation are usually filed with the secretary of state's office in the state in which the company incorporates. The articles contain:

- The corporation's name.
- The names of the people who incorporated it.
- Its purposes.
- Its duration (usually perpetual).
- The number of shares that can be issued, their voting rights, and any other rights the shareholders have.
- The corporation's minimum capital.
- The address of the corporation's office.
- The name and address of the person responsible for the corporation's legal service.
- The names and addresses of the first directors.
- Any other public information the incorporators wish to include.

Before a business can so much as open a bank account or hire employees, it needs a federal tax identification number. To apply for one, get an SS-4 form from the IRS.

In addition to the articles of incorporation listed, a corporation has bylaws. These describe how the firm is to be operated from both legal and managerial points of view. The bylaws include:

- How, when, and where shareholders' and directors' meetings are held, and how long directors are to serve.
- Directors' authority.
- Duties and responsibilities of officers, and the length of their service.
- How stock is Issued.
- Other matters, including employment contracts.

time is approximately 30 days from the date of application. Figure 5.5 outlines how to incorporate.

S Corporations

An **S corporation** is a unique government creation that looks like a corporation but is taxed like sole proprietorships and partnerships. (The name comes from the fact that the rules governing them are in Subchapter S of Chapter 1 of the Internal Revenue Code.) The paperwork and details of S corporations are similar to those of conventional (C) corporations. S corporations have shareholders, directors, and employees, and the benefit of limited liability, but their profits are taxed only as the personal income of the shareholders—thus avoiding the double taxation of C corporations.

Avoiding double taxation is reason enough for approximately 3 million U.S. companies to operate as S corporations. Yet not all businesses can become S corporations. In order to qualify, a company must:

1. Have no more than 100 shareholders. (All members of a family count as one shareholder.)
2. Have shareholders that are individuals or estates, and who (as individuals) are citizens or permanent residents of the United States.
3. Have only one class of stock. (You can read more about the various classes of stock in Chapter 19.)
4. Derive no more than 25 percent of income from passive sources (rents, royalties, interest).

S corporation
A unique government creation that looks like a corporation but is taxed like sole proprietorships and partnerships.

An S corporation that loses its S status may not operate under it again for at least five years. The tax structure of S corporations isn't attractive to all businesses. For one thing, the benefits change every time the tax rules change. The best way to learn all the benefits or shortcomings for a specific business is to go over the tax advantages and liability differences with a lawyer, an accountant, or both.

Limited Liability Companies

A **limited liability company (LLC)** is similar to an S corporation, but without the special eligibility requirements. LLCs were introduced in Wyoming in 1977 and were recognized by the Internal Revenue Service as a partnership for federal income tax purposes in 1988. By 1996, all 50 states and the District of Columbia recognized LLCs.

The number of LLCs has risen dramatically since 1988, when there were fewer than 100 filings to operate them. Today more than half of new business registrations in some states are LLCs. The nearby Legal Briefcase box features a new type of LLC, a virtual company.

Why the drive toward forming LLCs? Advantages include:

1. *Limited liability.* Personal assets are protected. Limited liability was previously available only to limited partners and shareholders of C corporations.

2. *Choice of taxation.* LLCs can choose to be taxed as partnerships or as corporations. Partnership-level taxation was previously a benefit normally reserved for partners or S corporation owners.

3. *Flexible ownership rules.* LLCs do not have to comply with ownership restrictions as S corporations do. Owners can be a person, partnership, or corporation.

4. *Flexible distribution of profits and losses.* Profits and losses don't have to be distributed in proportion to the money each person invests, as in corporations. LLC members agree on the percentage to be distributed to each member.

5. *Operating flexibility.* LLCs do have to submit articles of organization, which are similar to articles of incorporation, but they are not required to keep minutes, file written resolutions, or hold annual meetings. An LLC also submits a written operating agreement, similar to a partnership agreement, describing how the company is to be operated.

Of course, LLCs have their disadvantages as well. These include:

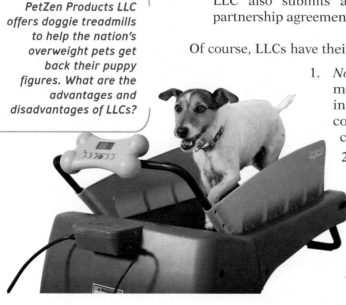

PetZen Products LLC offers doggie treadmills to help the nation's overweight pets get back their puppy figures. What are the advantages and disadvantages of LLCs?

1. *No stock.* LLC ownership is nontransferable. LLC members need the approval of the other members in order to sell their interests in the company. In contrast, regular and S corporation stockholders can sell their shares as they wish.

2. *Limited life span.* LLCs are required to identify dissolution dates in the articles of organization (no more than 30 years in some states). The death of a member can cause LLCs to dissolve automatically. Members may choose to reconstitute the LLC after it dissolves.

3. *Fewer incentives.* Unlike corporations, LLCs can't deduct the cost of fringe benefits for

members owning 2 percent or more of the company. And since there's no stock, they can't use stock options as incentives to employees.

4. *Taxes.* LLC members must pay self-employment taxes—the Medicare/Social Security taxes paid by sole proprietors and partnerships—on their profits. In contrast, S corporations pay self-employment tax on owners' salaries but not on the entire profits.

5. *Paperwork.* While the paperwork required of LLCs is not as great as that required of corporations, it is more than required of sole proprietors.

The start-up cost for an LLC varies. Online legal services such as Legal Zoom (www.legalzoom.com) can file the necessary paperwork for as little as $150. Figure 5.6 on p. 130 summarizes the advantages and disadvantages of the major forms of business ownership.

progress assessment

- What are the major advantages and disadvantages of incorporating a business?
- What is the role of owners (stockholders) in the corporate hierarchy?
- If you buy stock in a corporation and someone gets injured by one of the corporation's products, can you be sued? Why or why not?
- Why are so many new businesses choosing a limited liability company (LLC) form of ownership?

	SOLE PROPRIETORSHIP	Partnerships		Corporations		
		GENERAL PARTNERSHIP	LIMITED PARTNERSHIP	CONVENTIONAL CORPORATION	S CORPORATION	LIMITED LIABILITY COMPANY
Documents Needed to Start Business	None; may need permit or license	Partnership agreement (oral or written)	Written agreement; must file certificate of limited partnership	Articles of incorporation, bylaws	Articles of incorporation, bylaws, must meet criteria	Articles of organization and operating agreement; no eligibility requirements
Ease of Termination	Easy to terminate: just pay debts and quit	May be hard to terminate, depending on the partnership agreement	Same as general partnership	Hard and expensive to terminate	Same as conventional corporation	May be difficult, depending upon operating agreement
Length of Life	Terminates on the death of owner	Terminates on the death or withdrawal of partner	Same as general partnership	Perpetual life	Same as conventional corporation	Varies according to dissolution dates in articles of organization
Transfer of Ownership	Business can be sold to qualified buyer	Must have other partner(s)' agreement	Same as general partnership	Easy to change owners; just sell stock	Can sell stock, but with restrictions	Can't sell stock
Financial Resources	Limited to owner's capital and loans	Limited to partners' capital and loans	Same as general partnership	More money to start and operate; may sell stocks and bonds	Same as conventional corporation	Same as partnership
Risk of Losses	Unlimited liability	Unlimited liability	Limited liability	Limited liability	Limited liability	Limited liability
Taxes	Taxed as personal income	Taxed as personal income	Same as general partnership	Corporate, double taxation	Taxed as personal income	Varies
Management Responsibilities	Owner manages *all* areas of the business	Partners share management	Can't participate in management	Separate management from ownership	Same as conventional corporation	Varies
Employee Benefits	Usually fewer benefits and lower wages	Often fewer benefits and lower wages; promising employee could become a partner	Same as general partnership	Usually better benefits and wages, advancement opportunities	Same as conventional corporation	Varies, but are not tax deductible

figure 5.6

COMPARISON OF FORMS OF BUSINESS OWNERSHIP

LEARNING goal **4**

Define and give examples of three types of corporate mergers, and explain the role of leveraged buyouts and taking a firm private.

CORPORATE EXPANSION: MERGERS AND ACQUISITIONS

The merger mania of the late 1990s reached its peak in 2000, when the total spent on mergers and acquisitions hit a stunning $3.4 trillion and a new deal was being struck every 17 minutes. It seemed as though each deal made was intended to top the one before. Most of the new deals involved companies trying to expand within their own fields to save costs, enter new markets, position for global competition, or adapt to changing technologies or regulations. Those proved to be unattainable goals for many of the merged giants; two-thirds of mergers of the late 1990s failed to meet their goals. By 2009, the bleak U.S. economy caused the volume of mergers and acquisitions to plummet 86 percent. 2010 offered some renewed optimism as mergers increased 14 percent.[14]

What's the difference between mergers and acquisitions? A **merger** is the result of two firms joining to form one company. It is similar to a marriage, joining two individuals as one family. An **acquisition** is one company's purchase of the property and obligations of another company. It is more like buying a house than entering a marriage.

There are three major types of corporate mergers: vertical, horizontal, and conglomerate. A **vertical merger** joins two firms operating in different stages of related businesses. A merger between a soft drink company and an artificial sweetener maker would ensure the merged firm a constant supply of an ingredient the soft drink manufacturer needs. It could also help ensure quality control of the soft drink company's products.

A **horizontal merger** joins two firms in the same industry and allows them to diversify or expand their products. A soft drink company and a mineral water company that merge can now supply a variety of drinking products.

A **conglomerate merger** unites firms in completely unrelated industries in order to diversify business operations and investments. A soft drink company and a snack food company would form a conglomerate merger. Figure 5.7 on p. 132 illustrates the differences among the three types of mergers.

Rather than merge or sell to another company, some corporations decide to maintain, or in some cases regain, control of a firm internally. By *taking a firm private,* management or a group of stockholders obtain all the firm's stock for themselves by buying it back from the other stockholders.[15] Burger King and Gymboree are firms that have been taken private. Suppose employees believe they may lose their jobs, or managers believe they could improve corporate performance if they owned the company. Does either group have an opportunity of taking ownership of the company? Yes—they might attempt a leveraged buyout.

A **leveraged buyout (LBO)** is an attempt by employees, management, or a group of private investors to buy out the stockholders in a company, primarily by borrowing the necessary funds. The

---

merger
The result of two firms forming one company.

acquisition
One company's purchase of the property and obligations of another company.

vertical merger
The joining of two companies involved in different stages of related businesses.

horizontal merger
The joining of two firms in the same industry.

conglomerate merger
The joining of firms in completely unrelated industries.

leveraged buyout (LBO)
An attempt by employees, management, or a group of investors to purchase an organization primarily through borrowing.

Mars, the maker of M&M's, acquired the Wm. Wrigley Jr. Company for $23 billion. What type of merger is this (vertical, horizontal, or conglomerate)?

figure 5.7

TYPES OF MERGERS

Soft drink company Buys Mineral water company = **Horizontal merger** (companies in same industry)

Soft drink company + Buys Artificial sweetener company = **Vertical merger** (companies in different stages in related industries)

Soft drink company + Buys Snack food company = **Conglomerate merger** (companies in unrelated industries)

employees, managers, or investors now become the owners of the firm. LBOs have ranged in size from $50 million to $31 billion and have involved everything from small family businesses to giant corporations like Hertz Corporation, Toys "R" Us, Chrysler and the former RJR Nabisco.[16]

Today, business acquisitions are not limited to U.S. buyers. Foreign companies have found the fastest way to grow is often to buy an established operation that can enhance their technology or expand the number of brands they offer. Swiss drug maker Roche paid $43 billion to take control of biotechnology giant Genentech. Belgium's InBev purchased the largest U.S. brewer, Anheuser-Busch and its Budweiser and Bud Light brands, for $52 billion. Number two brewer Miller Brewing Company was acquired by London-based SAB.[17] In 2010, foreign investors poured over $300 billion into U.S. companies.

However, such deals are not always welcomed. In 2005, U.S. lawmakers feared the proposed purchase of U.S. oil company Unocal by a Chinese oil company might threaten American economic and national security interests. CNOOC, the Chinese company, eventually withdrew its bid.

LEARNING goal 5

Outline the advantages and disadvantages of franchises, and discuss the opportunities for diversity in franchising and the challenges of global franchising.

THINKING green

www.epa.gov

Play Ball but Play Green

Many people think the only type of franchises you can buy is restaurants. Franchising, however, goes beyond a local Subway or KFC. Hotels, schools, even teams in The National Football League and Major League Baseball, are franchises. While these sports franchises compete for fans, one area where both the NFL and MLB have reached common agreement is going green.

Washington, DC decided that the new home for the Nationals baseball team would be the first sports stadium to earn a Leadership in Energy and Environmental Design (LEED) rating from the U.S. Green Building Council. When the Nationals took the field on opening day in 2008, fans may not have noticed that 95 percent of the stadium's steel was recycled or that the low-flow toilets saved millions of gallons of water each season. They also may not have known that the wastewater system screens out organic debris such as peanut shells and hot-dog bits, or that the park's recycling center is large enough to handle glass, metal, and plastic recyclables amassed during a three-game home stand. This was just the beginning.

When the New York Mets finalized a deal for the team's new home they reached an agreement with the U.S. Environmental Protection Agency (EPA) to build their new ballpark using the latest green technologies and practices. The Regional

EPA Administrator boasted that the Mets deserved an environmental MVP award for their effort to reduce the carbon footprint and for the waste system at Citi Field. Not to be outdone, the New York Giants and the New York Jets joined with the EPA to make the New Meadowlands Stadium one of the nation's greenest sport's venues. Let's play ball! But let's play green!

Sources: www.epa.gov, accessed April 2011; www.mlb.com, accessed April 2011; and www.nfl.com, accessed April 2011.

FRANCHISES

In addition to the three basic forms of business ownership, there are two special forms: franchises and cooperatives. Let's look at franchises first. A **franchise agreement** is an arrangement whereby someone with a good idea for a business (the **franchisor**) sells the rights to use the business name and sell a product or service (the **franchise**) to others (the **franchisees**) in a given territory.

Some people, uncomfortable with the idea of starting their own business from scratch, would rather join a business with a proven track record through a franchise agreement. A franchise can be formed as a sole proprietorship, a partnership, or a corporation. The U.S. Census Bureau estimates that one out of every ten businesses in the United States is a franchise.[18] Some of the best-known franchises are McDonald's, Jiffy Lube, 7-Eleven, Weight Watchers, and Holiday Inn.

According to the International Franchising Association, the more than 825,000 franchised businesses operating in the United States create approximately 17.5 million jobs that produce a direct and indirect economic impact of $2.1 trillion in the U.S. economy.[19] The most popular businesses for franchising are restaurants (fast food and full service) and gas stations with convenience stores.[20] McDonald's, the largest restaurant chain in the United States in terms of sales, is often considered the gold standard of franchising.[21] Retail

franchise agreement
An arrangement whereby someone with a good idea for a business sells the rights to use the business name and sell a product or service to others in a given territory.

franchisor
A company that develops a product concept and sells others the rights to make and sell the products.

franchise
The right to use a specific business's name and sell its products or services in a given territory.

franchisee
A person who buys a franchise.

Merry Maids is the largest home cleaning franchise in the U.S. It cleans over 300,000 houses, apartments, and condos a month. The franchise fee includes a comprehensive eight-day training program followed by in-depth interaction with the franchise development team and assistance from an established franchise owner. The training helps new franchisees learn how to select, train, develop and compensate employees. What type of franchise might appeal to you as a business owner?

stores, financial services, health clubs, hotels and motels, and automotive parts and service centers are also popular franchised businesses. Today a fast-growing franchise sector is senior care. In fact, *Entrepreneur Magazine*'s 2011 list of 100 fastest-growing franchises included eight senior care concepts.[22] With roughly 40 million seniors in the United States today and projections the number will double in the next 20 years, it's a market that is not going to disappear.

The nearby Thinking Green box discusses a business that many people don't realize is a franchise system.

Advantages of Franchises

Franchising has penetrated every aspect of U.S. and global business life by offering products and services that are reliable, convenient, and competitively priced. Franchising clearly has some advantages:

1. *Management and marketing assistance.* Compared with someone who starts a business from scratch, a franchisee usually has a much greater chance of succeeding because he or she has an established product to sell, help choosing a location, and assistance in all phases of promotion and operation. It's like having your own store but with full-time consultants when you need them. Franchisors usually provide intensive training. For example, McDonald's sends all new franchisees and managers to Hamburger University in Oak Brook, Illinois.[23]

   Some franchisors help their franchisees with local marketing efforts rather than having them depend solely on national advertising. Franchisees also have a network of fellow franchisees facing similar problems who can share their experiences. The UPS Store provides its more than 4,500 franchisees with a software program that helps them build customer databases along with quick and personal one-on-one phone and e-mail support.

2. *Personal ownership.* A franchise operation is still your business, and you enjoy as much of the incentives and profit as any sole proprietor would. You are still your own boss, although you must follow more rules, regulations, and procedures than with your own privately owned business.

3. *Nationally recognized name.* It is one thing to open a gift shop or an ice cream store. It is quite another to open a new Hallmark store or a Baskin-Robbins. With an established franchise, you get instant recognition and support from a product group with established customers around the world.

4. *Financial advice and assistance.* Two major problems for small-business owners are arranging financing and learning to keep good records. Franchisees often get valuable assistance and periodic advice from people with expertise in these areas. In fact, some franchisors provide financing to potential franchisees they feel will be valuable parts of the franchise system. For example, Merry Maids, a leader in

the maid service business, offers up to 80 percent financial assistance with their franchise fee to promising franchisees.

5. *Lower failure rate.* Historically, the failure rate for franchises has been lower than that of other business ventures. However, franchising has grown so rapidly that many weak franchises have entered the field, so you need to be careful and invest wisely.

Disadvantages of Franchises

There are, however, some potential pitfalls to franchising. Check out any franchise arrangement with present franchisees and discuss the idea with an attorney and an accountant. Disadvantages of franchises include the following:

1. *Large start-up costs.* Most franchises demand a fee for the rights to the franchise. Start-up costs for a Jazzercise franchise range from $3,000, but if it's Dunkin Donuts you're after, you'd better have a lot more dough—approximately $2 million.[24]

2. *Shared profit.* The franchisor often demands either a large share of the profits in addition to the start-up fees or a percentage commission based on sales, not profit. This share is called a *royalty.* For example, if a franchisor demands a 10 percent royalty on a franchise's net sales, 10 cents of every dollar the franchisee collects (before taxes and other expenses) must be paid to the franchisor.

3. *Management regulation.* Management "assistance" has a way of becoming managerial orders, directives, and limitations. Franchisees feeling burdened by the company's rules and regulations may lose the drive to run their own business. Often franchisees will band together to resolve their grievances with franchisors rather than fighting their battles alone. For example, in 2010 the KFC National Council & Advertising Cooperative, which represents all U.S. franchisees, sued KFC to gain control of advertising strategies. The franchisees were angry over Yum Brands (owners of KFC) decision to implement an ad strategy that emphasized a shift to grilled chicken rather than fried chicken. The campaign centered around the slogan "Unthink KFC" which was exactly what customers did. Sales plummeted 7 percent that quarter and franchisees had to throw away up to 50 percent of their grilled chicken supplies.[25] In another case, Burger King franchisees filed suit over whether the franchisor could impose $1 pricing on them for double cheeseburgers they claim lost them money.[26]

4. *Coattail effects.* What happens to your franchise if fellow franchisees fail? The actions of other franchises have an impact on your future growth and profitability. Due to this *coattail effect,* you could be forced out of business even if your particular franchise has been profitable. For example, the customer passion for high-flying franchisor Krispy Kreme in the early 2000s sank as the market became flooded with new stores and the availability of the product at retail locations caused overexposure. McDonald's and Subway franchisees complain that due to the company's relentless growth, some new stores have taken business away from existing locations, squeezing franchisees' profits per outlet.

5. *Restrictions on selling.* Unlike owners of private businesses, who can sell their companies to whomever they choose on their own terms,

Since buying a franchise is a major investment, be sure to check out a company's financial strength before you get involved. Watch out for scams too. Scams called *bust-outs* usually involve people coming to town, renting nice offices, taking out ads, and persuading people to invest. Then they disappear with the investors' money. For example, in San Francisco a company called T.B.S. Inc. sold distributorships for in-home AIDS tests. It promised an enormous market and potential profits of $3,000 for an investment of less than $200. The "test" turned out to be nothing more than a mail-order questionnaire about lifestyle.

A good source of information about evaluating a franchise deal is the handbook *Investigate before Investing,* available from International Franchise Association Publications.

Checklist for Evaluating a Franchise

The Franchise

Did your lawyer approve the franchise contract you're considering after he or she studied it paragraph by paragraph?

Does the franchise give you an exclusive territory for the length of the franchise?

Under what circumstances can you terminate the franchise contract and at what cost to you?

If you sell your franchise, will you be compensated for your goodwill (the value of your business's reputation and other intangibles)?

If the franchisor sells the company, will your investment be protected?

The Franchisor

How many years has the firm offering you a franchise been in operation?

Does it have a reputation for honesty and fair dealing among the local firms holding its franchise?

Has the franchisor shown you any certified figures indicating exact net profits of one or more going firms that you personally checked yourself with the franchisee? Ask for the company's disclosure statement.

Will the firm assist you with
  A management training program?
  An employee training program?
  A public relations program?
  Capital?
  Credit?
  Merchandising ideas?

Will the firm help you find a good location for your new business?

Has the franchisor investigated you carefully enough to assure itself that you can successfully operate one of its franchises at a profit both to itself and to you?

You, the Franchisee

How much equity capital will you need to purchase the franchise and operate it until your income equals your expenses?

Does the franchisor offer financing for a portion of the franchising fees? On what terms?

Are you prepared to give up some independence of action to secure the advantages offered by the franchise? Do you have your family's support?

Does the industry appeal to you? Are you ready to spend much or all of the remainder of your business life with this franchisor, offering its product or service to the public?

Your Market

Have you made any study to determine whether the product or service that you propose to sell under the franchise has a market in your territory at the prices you'll have to charge?

Will the population in the territory given to you increase, remain static, or decrease over the next five years?

Will demand for the product or service you're considering be greater, about the same, or less five years from now than it is today?

What competition already exists in your territory for the product or service you contemplate selling?

Sources: U.S. Department of Commerce, *Franchise Opportunities Handbook;* and Steve Adams, "Buying a Brand," *Patriot Ledger* (Quincy, MA), March 1, 2008.

figure 5.8

BUYING A FRANCHISE

many franchisees face restrictions on the resale of their franchises. To control quality, franchisors often insist on approving the new owner, who must meet their standards.

6. *Fraudulent franchisors.* Most franchisors are not large systems like McDonald's and Subway. Many are small, rather obscure companies that prospective franchisees may know little about. Most are honest, but complaints to the Federal Trade Commission have increased about franchisors that delivered little or nothing of what they promised. Before you buy a franchise, make certain you check out the facts fully and remember the old adage "You get what you pay for." See Figure 5.8 for some tips on evaluating a franchisee.

Judi Sheppard Missett started a dance-fitness program called Jazzercise in 1969. The worldwide franchise company now takes fitness-minded adults and kids in 32 countries through weekly classes blending jazz dance, resistance training, Pilates, yoga and kickboxing moves choreographed to the latest popular music. Jazzercise is consistently listed among Entrepreneur magazine's top 20 franchises. What accounts for its appeal?

Diversity in Franchising

A lingering issue in franchising is the number of women who own franchises. While women own about half of all U.S. companies and are opening businesses at double the rate of men, their ownership of franchises is about 25 percent.[27] Some think there is not so much a glass ceiling for women as a green ceiling— lack of money. Many experts believe more needs to be done to attract educated women business owners about the opportunities and forms of financing available for franchise growth. The International Franchise Association has increased its efforts to attract more women into franchising.[28]

Women are getting the message. In fact, women aren't just franchisees anymore; they're becoming franchisors as well. Think back to the opening Profile of Mary Ellen Sheets of Two Men and a Truck. Women are finding if they face difficulty getting financing for growing their business, turning to franchisees to help carry expansion costs can help. For example, top-rated franchise companies Auntie Anne's, Decorating Den, and Jazzercise are owned by women.

Minority-owned businesses are growing at more than six times the national rate. Franchisors are becoming more focused on recruiting minority franchisees. MinorityFran is an initiative by the International Franchise Association to build awareness of franchising opportunities within minority communities. The U.S. Commerce Department's Federal Minority Business Development Agency provides aspiring minority business owners with training in how to run franchises. Domino's Pizza launched a minority franchisee recruitment program called Delivering the Dream. The company provides financial support and a financing partner to help budding franchisees "realize their dream."

Today over 20 percent of franchises are owned by African Americans, Latinos, Asians, and Native Americans. Franchising opportunities seem perfectly attuned to the needs of aspiring minority businesspeople. For example, Junior Bridgeman was a basketball star in college and enjoyed a stellar career with the Milwaukee Bucks and Los Angeles Clippers in the NBA. He transferred his dedication on the court to dedication to building Bridgeman Foods. His company now owns several Wendy's franchises and runs 162 other Wendy's restaurants.[29]

Home-Based Franchises

Home-based businesses offer many obvious advantages, including relief from the stress of commuting, extra time for family activities, and low overhead expenses. One disadvantage is the feeling of isolation. Compared to home-based entrepreneurs, home-based franchisees feel less isolated. Experienced franchisors often share their knowledge of building a profitable enterprise with other franchisees.

Home-based franchises can be started for as little as $5,000. Today you can be a franchisee in areas ranging from cleaning services to tax preparation, child care, pet care, or direct mail services. But don't get the idea working at home is easy. Home-based franchisee Ralph Santisteban was excited by the challenge when he bought his CruiseOne franchise. What he didn't expect was the 12 to 14 hours per day he put in to get the business going.[30] Before investing in a home-based franchise it is helpful to ask yourself the following questions: Are you willing to put in long hours? Can you work in a solitary environment? Are you motivated and well organized? Does your home have the space you need for the business? Can your home also be the place you work? It's also important to check out the franchisor carefully.

E-Commerce in Franchising

The Internet has changed franchising in many ways. Most brick-and-mortar franchises have expanded their businesses online and created virtual storefronts to deliver increased value to customers. Franchisees like Carole Shutts, a Rocky Mountain Chocolate Factory franchisee in Galena, Illinois, increased her sales by setting up her own website. Many franchisors, however, prohibit franchisee-sponsored websites because conflicts can erupt if the franchisor creates its own website. Sometimes franchisors send "reverse royalties" to franchisees who believe their sales were hurt by the franchisor's Internet sales, but that doesn't always bring about peace. Before buying a franchise, read the small print regarding online sales.

Holiday Inn's InterContinental Amstel hotel in Amsterdam has been celebrated as the Netherlands' most beautiful and luxurious hotel. Holiday Inn franchises try to complement the environment of the area they serve. This hotel is on the crossroads of Amsterdam's financial and exclusive shopping districts. What do you think would have been the reaction if Holiday Inn had built the typical U.S-style Holiday Inn in this area?

Today potential franchisees can make a choice between starting an online business or a business requiring an office or storefront outside of the home.[31] Quite often the decision comes down to financing. Traditional brick-and-mortar franchises require finding real estate and often require a high franchise fee. Online franchises like Printinginabox.com charge no upfront franchise fee and require little training to start a business. Franchisees pay only a set monthly fee. Online franchises also do not set exclusive territories limiting where the franchisee can compete. An online franchisee can literally compete against the world.[32]

Using Technology in Franchising

Franchisors often use technology, including social media, to extend their brands, to meet the needs of both their customers and their franchisees, and even to expand their businesses.[33] For example, Candy Bouquet International, Inc., of Little Rock, Arkansas, offers franchises that sell candies in flowerlike arrangements. Franchisees have brick-and-mortar locations to serve walk-in customers, but they also are provided leads from the company's main website. All franchisees are kept up-to-date daily on company news via e-mail, and they use a chat room to discuss issues and product ideas with each other. The

Franchise Expansion on Facebook

Although social media is still a relatively young medium, companies across the board are using it to reach customers. While many businesses are using social marketing to communicate with customers, some are using the technology to reach out to potential investors and franchisees as well.

The ice cream company Häagen-Dazs, for instance, launched a Facebook game called Ice Cream Boss in 2010. The program simulates the day-to-day operations of a Häagen-Dazs store. Additionally, each week the game challenges users to offer feedback on a new story or situation occurring at the virtual store. The company ultimately hopes that players who become engaged with the game will move on to become franchisees of a real Häagen-Dazs store. Though it's found no new investors from Ice Cream Boss as of this writing, only time will tell if the scheme is a success.

Sources: Jason Ankeny, "Social Climbers," *Entrepreneur,* January 2011; and Lucy Fisher, "Fool's Gold?" *Marketing Week,* April 4, 2011.

company has found the Internet a great way of disseminating information that is revolutionizing franchisor support and franchisee communications. Candy Bouquet plans international expansion in the near future.

Some franchisors use social media not only to reach customers and current franchisees, but also to recruit new franchisees. See the nearby Social Media in Business box for an example of a company using a Facebook game to attract potential franchisees.

Franchising in Global Markets

Franchising today is truly a global effort. U.S. franchisors are counting their profits in euros, yuan, pesos, won, krona, baht, yen, and many other currencies. McDonald's has more than 13,500 restaurants in 117 countries serving over 50 million customers each day.[34]

Because of its proximity and shared language, Canada is the most popular target for U.S.-based franchises. Franchisors are finding it surprisingly easier now to move into China, South Africa, the Philippines, and the Middle East. Plus it's not just the large franchises like Subway and Marriott Hotels making the move. Newer, smaller franchises are going global as well. Auntie Anne's sells hand-rolled pretzels in 22 different countries including Indonesia, Malaysia, the Philippines, Singapore, Venezuela, and Thailand. Build-A-Bear Workshops has 63 franchisees in 12 countries including South Africa and the United Arab Emirates.[35] In 2005, 29-year-old Matthew Corrin launched Freshii, a sandwich, salad, and soup restaurant with fresh affordable food in trendy locations. He already has 45 locations in four countries with a new store in India on the horizon.[36]

What makes franchising successful in global markets is what makes it successful in the United States: convenience and a predictable level of service and quality. Franchisors, though, must be careful and do their homework before entering into global franchise agreements. Three questions to ask before forming a global franchise are: Will your intellectual property be protected? Can you give proper support to global partners? Are you able to adapt to franchise regulations in other countries? If the answer is yes to all three questions, global franchising creates great opportunities. It's also important to remember that adapting products and brand names to different countries creates challenges. In France, people thought a furniture-stripping franchise called Dip 'N' Strip was a bar that featured strippers.

Just as McDonald's and Subway have exported golden arches and sub sandwiches worldwide, foreign franchises see the United States as a popular target. Japanese franchises like Kumon Learning Centers and Canadian franchises like tax preparer H&R Block are very active in the United States.[37] H&R Block even has its headquarters in Kansas City, Missouri. Other franchises are hoping to change our tastes here. Ly Qui Trung would like to see his Pho 24 Noodle Bars become a part of the American landscape and Canada's Yogen Fruz frozen yogurt wants us to eat healthier desserts.

LEARNING goal 6

Explain the role of cooperatives.

COOPERATIVES

> **cooperative**
> A business owned and controlled by the people who use it—producers, consumers, or workers with similar needs who pool their resources for mutual gain.

Some people dislike the notion of owners, managers, workers, and buyers being separate individuals with separate goals. So they have formed cooperatives, a different kind of organization to meet their needs for electricity, child care, housing, health care, food, and financial services. A **cooperative**, or co-op, is owned and controlled by the people who use it—producers, consumers, or workers with similar needs who pool their resources for mutual gain. In many rural parts of the country, for example, the government sells wholesale power to electric cooperatives at rates 40 to 50 percent below the rates nonfederal utilities charge. Electric cooperatives serve 42 million U.S. consumer-members in 47 states—or 12 percent of the population.

Worldwide, some 750,000 cooperatives serve 730 million members—120 million of them in the United States.[38] Members democratically control these businesses by electing a board of directors that hires professional management. Some co-ops ask members/customers to work for a number of hours a month as part of their membership duties. You may have one of the country's 4,000 food co-ops near you. If so, stop by and chat to learn more about this growing aspect of the U.S. economy. If you are interested in knowing more about cooperatives, contact the National Cooperative Business Association at 202-638-6222 or visit its website at www.ncba.coop.

Another kind of cooperative in the United States is formed to give members more economic power as a group than they have as individuals.[39] The best example is a farm cooperative. The goal at first was for farmers to join together to get better prices for their food products. Eventually the idea expanded, and farm cooperatives now buy and sell fertilizer, farm equipment, seed, and other products in a multibillion-dollar industry. Cooperatives have an advantage in the marketplace because they don't pay the same kind of taxes corporations pay.

Cooperatives are still a major force in agriculture and other industries today. Some top co-ops have familiar names such as Land O Lakes, Sunkist, Ocean Spray, Blue Diamond, Associated Press, Ace Hardware, True Value Hardware, Riceland Foods, and Welch's.

WHICH FORM OF OWNERSHIP IS FOR YOU?

You can build your own business in a variety of ways. You can start your own sole proprietorship, partnership, corporation, LLC, or cooperative—or you can buy a franchise and be part of a larger corporation. There are advantages and disadvantages to each. Before you decide which form is for you, evaluate all the alternatives carefully.

The miracle of free enterprise is that the freedom and incentives of capitalism make risks acceptable to many people who go on to create the great corporations of America. You know many of their names and companies: James Cash Penney (JCPenney), Steve Jobs (Apple Computer), Sam Walton (Walmart), Levi Strauss (Levi Strauss), Henry Ford (Ford Motor Company), Thomas Edison (General Electric), Bill Gates (Microsoft), and so on. They started small, accumulated capital, grew, and became industrial leaders. Could you do the same?

progress assessment

- What are some of the factors to consider before buying a franchise?
- What opportunities are available for starting a global franchise?
- What is a cooperative?

summary

Learning Goal 1. Compare the advantages and disadvantages of sole proprietorships.

• What are the advantages and disadvantages of sole proprietorships?
The advantages of sole proprietorships include ease of starting and ending, ability to be your own boss, pride of ownership, retention of profit, and no special taxes. The disadvantages include unlimited liability, limited financial resources, difficulty in management, overwhelming time commitment, few fringe benefits, limited growth, and limited life span.

Learning Goal 2. Describe the differences between general and limited partners, and compare the advantages and disadvantages of partnerships.

• What are the three key elements of a general partnership?
The three key elements of a general partnership are common ownership, shared profits and losses, and the right to participate in managing the operations of the business.

• What are the main differences between general and limited partners?
General partners are owners (partners) who have unlimited liability and are active in managing the company. Limited partners are owners (partners) who have limited liability and are not active in the company.

- **What does *unlimited liability* mean?**

Unlimited liability means that sole proprietors and general partners must pay all debts and damages caused by their business. They may have to sell their houses, cars, or other personal possessions to pay business debts.

- **What does *limited liability* mean?**

Limited liability means that corporate owners (stockholders) and limited partners are responsible for losses only up to the amount they invest. Their other personal property is not at risk.

- **What is a master limited partnership?**

A master limited partnership is a partnership that acts like a corporation but is taxed like a partnership.

- **What are the advantages and disadvantages of partnerships?**

The advantages include more financial resources, shared management and pooled knowledge, and longer survival. The disadvantages include unlimited liability, division of profits, disagreements among partners, and difficulty of termination.

Learning Goal 3. Compare the advantages and disadvantages of corporations, and summarize the differences between C corporations, S corporations, and limited liability companies.

- **What is the definition of a corporation?**

A corporation is a state-chartered legal entity with authority to act and have liability separate from its owners.

- **What are the advantages and disadvantages of corporations?**

The advantages include more money for investment, limited liability, size, perpetual life, ease of ownership change, ease of drawing talented employees, and separation of ownership from management. The disadvantages include initial cost, paperwork, size, difficulty in termination, double taxation, and possible conflict with a board of directors.

- **Why do people incorporate?**

Two important reasons for incorporating are special tax advantages and limited liability.

- **What are the advantages of S corporations?**

S corporations have the advantages of limited liability (like a corporation) and simpler taxes (like a partnership). To qualify for S corporation status, a company must have fewer than 100 stockholders (members of a family count as one shareholder), its stockholders must be individuals or estates and U.S. citizens or permanent residents, and the company cannot derive more than 25 percent of its income from passive sources.

- **What are the advantages of limited liability companies?**

Limited liability companies have the advantage of limited liability without the hassles of forming a corporation or the limitations imposed by S corporations. LLCs may choose whether to be taxed as partnerships or corporations.

Learning Goal 4. Define and give examples of three types of corporate mergers, and explain the role of leveraged buyouts and taking a firm private.

- **What is a merger?**

A merger is the result of two firms forming one company. The three major types are vertical mergers, horizontal mergers, and conglomerate mergers.

- **What are leveraged buyouts, and what does it mean to take a company private?**

Leveraged buyouts are attempts by managers and employees to borrow money and purchase the company. Individuals who, together or alone, buy all the stock for themselves are said to take the company private.

Learning Goal 5. Outline the advantages and disadvantages of franchises, and discuss the opportunities for diversity in franchising and the challenges of global franchising.

- **What is a franchise?**

An arrangement to buy the rights to use the business name and sell its products or services in a given territory is called a franchise.

- **What is a franchisee?**

A franchisee is a person who buys a franchise.

- **What are the benefits and drawbacks of being a franchisee?**

The benefits include getting a nationally recognized name and reputation, a proven management system, promotional assistance, and pride of ownership. Drawbacks include high franchise fees, managerial regulation, shared profits, and transfer of adverse effects if other franchisees fail.

- **What is the major challenge to global franchises?**

It is often difficult to transfer an idea or product that worked well in the United States to another culture. It is essential to adapt to the region.

Learning Goal 6. Explain the role of cooperatives.

- **What is the role of a cooperative?**

Cooperatives are organizations owned by members/customers. Some people form cooperatives to acquire more economic power than they would have as individuals. Small businesses often form cooperatives to gain more purchasing, marketing, or product development strength.

key terms

acquisition 131	**general partner** 119	**limited partnership** 119
conglomerate merger 131	**general partnership** 119	**master limited partnership (MLP)** 119
conventional (C) corporation 123	**horizontal merger** 131	**merger** 131
cooperative 140	**leveraged buyout (LBO)** 131	**partnership** 116
corporation 116	**limited liability** 119	**S corporation** 127
franchise 133	**limited liability company (LLC)** 128	**sole proprietorship** 116
franchise agreement 133	**limited liability partnership (LLP)** 119	**unlimited liability** 118
franchisee 133	**limited partner** 119	**vertical merger** 131
franchisor 133		

critical thinking

Imagine you are considering starting your own business.

1. What kinds of products or services will you offer?

2. What talents or skills do you need to run the business?

3. Do you have all the skills and resources to start the business, or will you need to find one or more partners? If so, what skills would your partners need to have?

4. What form of business ownership would you choose—sole proprietorship, partnership, C corporation, S corporation, or LLC? Why?

developing workplace skills

1. Research businesses in your area and identify sole proprietorships, partnerships, corporations, and franchises. Arrange interviews with managers using each form of ownership and get their impressions, hints, and warnings. (If you are able to work with a team of fellow students, divide the interviews among team members.) How much does it cost to start? How many hours do they work? What are the specific benefits? Share the results with your class.

2. Have you thought about starting your own business? What opportunities seem attractive? Think of a friend or friends whom you might want for a partner or partners in the business. List all the financial resources and personal skills you will need to launch the business. Then make separate lists of the personal skills and the financial resources that you and your friend(s) might bring to your new venture. How much capital and what personal skills will be needed beyond those you already have? Develop an action plan for needed capital.

3. Let's assume you want to open one of the following new businesses. What form of business ownership would you choose for each? Why?

   a. Video game rental store.

   b. Wedding planning service.

   c. Software development firm.

   d. Online bookstore.

4. Successful businesses continually change hands. Methods of change discussed in this chapter include mergers, acquisitions, taking a firm private, and using leveraged buyouts. Search for an article online that illustrates how one of these methods changed an organization. What led to the change? How did this change affect the company's stakeholders? What benefits did the change provide? What new challenges were created?

5. Find information online about a business cooperative (i.e. Welch's, Land O Lakes, Sunkist). Research how it was formed, who can belong to it, and how it operates.

taking it to the net

Purpose

To explore franchising opportunities and to evaluate the strengths and weaknesses of a selected franchise.

Exercise

Go to Franchise Expo (www.franchiseexpo.com).

1. Take the self-test to see if franchising is a good personal choice for you. Find the test by clicking on Resources, then on Introduction to Franchising. Then, under Franchising Basics, click on Franchising—An Interactive Self-Test.

2. Go back to the home page and use the search tool to find a franchise that has the potential of fulfilling your entrepreneurial dreams. Navigate to the profile of the franchise you selected. Explore the franchise's website if a link is available. Refer to the questions listed in Figure 5.8 in this chapter and assess the strengths and weaknesses of your selected franchise. (Hint: The website also contains tips for evaluating a franchise listing.)

3. Did your search give you enough information to answer most of the questions in Figure 5.8? If not, what other information do you need, and where can you obtain it?

casing the web

To access the case "Stopped Cold," visit **www.mhhe.com/ubl0e**

video case

To access the video case featuring PODS, visit **www.mhhe.com/ubl0e**

Entrepreneurship and STARTING A Small Business

LEARNING goals

After you have read and studied this chapter, you should be able to

1 Explain why people take the risks of entrepreneurship; list the attributes of successful entrepreneurs; and describe entrepreneurial teams, intrapreneurs, and home- and web-based businesses.

2 Discuss the importance of small business to the American economy and summarize the major causes of small-business failure.

3 Summarize ways to learn about how small businesses operate.

4 Analyze what it takes to start and run a small business.

5 Outline the advantages and disadvantages small businesses have in entering global markets.

profile

Shawn Carter, aka Jay-Z, should be no stranger to hip hop fans. The 10-time Grammy winning artist has sold more than 45 million albums worldwide. He's bested only by the Beatles in terms of No. 1 albums on the Billboard charts. Although Jay-Z still releases an album from time to time, today he's more concerned with his business ventures than with rap. For good reason, too: his businesses have earned him a net worth of $450 million.

But Jay-Z didn't turn from rapper to media mogul overnight. Many musicians attempt to translate their artistic success into a business empire only to fail from either a lack of knowledge or unwillingness to adapt to the system. Jay-Z, on the other hand, used his entrepreneurial cunning along with his complete control over the Jay-Z brand to become one of the world's richest musicians. In fact, in a few years Jay-Z's fortune may exceed $1 billion, making him one of the richest people in the world.

Part of the reason Jay-Z has been so successful is that he's been involved in the business side of music almost as long as he's been rapping. In 1996 no labels wanted to sign a 26-year-old low profile personality known mostly through New York's local hip hop scene. Out of necessity, he and two others founded Roc-A-Fella Records. The risk of starting his own business paid off big both for his career and his brand. Since he owned the company he rapped for, that made him more attractive to cost-cutting labels wanting to avoid traditional contracts. He eventually entered a joint venture with Def Jam Recordings and together the two companies made millions from albums like *Reasonable Doubt* and *The Blueprint*.

As his stardom rose, Jay-Z did endorsements like any other pop star would. But unlike his industry peers, Jay-Z carefully considered which products he promoted all while obtaining creative control over each ad. In a spot for HP computers, for instance, Jay-Z played the role of a professional commanding his empire in a sharp suit with his trusty computer. Each ad that played up his business side slowly wore down his Brooklyn bad boy image from his rap days and replaced it with that of a slick corporate player. By the time Jay-Z took up the mantle of CEO at Def Jam, few questioned the abilities of this rapper to take over the reins of a major company.

Jay-Z's branding expertise has served him as well in his clothing line. In the late 1990s he noticed that sales of Iceberg apparel rose after he mentioned the company in his raps. Jay-Z once again took the entrepreneurial route and started his own clothing brand called Rocawear. The line took off and in 2006 Jay-Z sold it to a brand licensing company for $204 million. Jay-Z continues to own a stake in the Rocawear name.

Today Jay-Z's business holdings are almost too numerous to count. The international 40/40 night-club chain, a partial ownership in the New Jersey Nets basketball team, and a footwear line with Reebok account for just a portion of his wide portfolio. His most ambitious entrepreneurial venture at the moment is his role as the CEO of Roc Nation, a joint project with concert giant Live Nation.

As a testament to his success as a businessman, Jay-Z has talked shop with global leaders such as Bill Gates, Warren Buffett and former President Bill Clinton. Although his popularity as a rapper helped launch his valuable brand, Jay-Z wouldn't be the success he is today without the entrepreneurial risks he took throughout his career. As you read about such risk-takers in this chapter, maybe you'll be inspired to become an entrepreneur yourself.

Getting to Know

Jay-Z

Rapper and Founder of Roc Nation

Sources: Daniel Gross, "Jay-Z's $450 Million Business Empire," *Yahoo Finance: The Daily Ticker,* March 25, 2011; John Jurgensen, "The State of Jay-Z's Empire," *The Wall Street Journal,* October 29, 2010; Lisa Taddeo, "Jay-Z: It Takes a Harmless, Hand-Built Gangster to Run this Town," *Esquire,* February 2010.

When this company's founder had financial problems in the business's early days, he asked his suppliers to help him out. They did and they were well rewarded for their risk. Today these suppliers still service this mammoth company that has franchises all over the world. Name that company. (Find the answer in the chapter.)

THE AGE OF THE ENTREPRENEUR

Today most young people know it's unlikely they will get a job in a large corporation and stay 30 years. For those who want more control over their destiny, working in or starting a small business makes sense. **Entrepreneurship** is accepting the risk of starting and running a business. Explore this chapter and think about the possibility of entrepreneurship in your future.

Mark Pincus is the founder and CEO of Zynga, maker of popular Facebook games FarmVille and Mafia Wars. The company pocketed $835 million in 2010 and has more than 100 million users. Zynga is by far the most successful company built on the Facebook platform. Do you have any ideas for other businesses that might be successful on Facebook?

THE JOB-CREATING POWER OF ENTREPRENEURS IN THE UNITED STATES

Well before the recent economic turmoil, one of the major issues in the United States has been the need to create more jobs. With the current high unemployment rate, job creation is even more critical. You can begin to understand the job-creating power of entrepreneurs when you look at some of the great U.S. entrepreneurs from the past and the present. The history of the United States is the history of its entrepreneurs. Consider just a few of the many who have helped shape the U.S. economy:[1]

- DuPont, which manufactures thousands of products under such brand names as Teflon and Lycra, was started in 1802 by French immigrant Éleuthère Irénée du Pont de Nemours. Some 18 shareholders provided $36,000 in start-up money.

- Avon, the familiar beauty products retailer, started in 1886 with $500 David McConnell borrowed from a friend.

- George Eastman launched photographic giant Kodak in 1880 with a $3,000 investment.

- Procter & Gamble, now a multinational marketer of household products, was formed in 1837 by William Procter, James Gamble, and a total of $7,000 in capital.

- Ford Motor Company began with an investment of $28,000 by Henry Ford and 11 associates.

business

Success Knows No Age

Although fortunes are amassed over time, that doesn't mean they are exclusive to older people. Here are just a few examples of young entrepreneurs who found success in their college years:

Derek Johnson came up with the idea for his company, Tatango, during a lunch with a fellow undergrad. As the chair of communications for her sorority, his friend complained that even with Facebook and e-mail she couldn't get important announcements to her entire chapter quickly. Within months Johnson established a mass-texting business that generated more than $500,000 in sales in 2010.

Peter Findley stumbled into the business program of his college after trying a number of different majors. Inspired in an entrepreneurship class, Findley began writing the business plan for Giant Campus. The company organizes summer camps for middle- and high school age kids on college campuses where they learn new media skills like web design. Five years after his initial spark, Giant Campus grew to more than 70 colleges located across the world.

Sam Hogg opened his wallet one day after Christmas and stared at all the plastic gift cards he received. Troubled at the waste of plastic, Hogg was shocked when he learned that 75 million pounds of gift card plastic end up in landfills each year. In 2008 he started GiftZip.com, an electronic gift card aggregator site. With 275 retailers now onboard, use of the site has increased 2,100 percent since the company launched.

John Goscha lived in a dorm for student entrepreneurs in his freshman year at Babson College. He and his friends spent many nights in his room brainstorming on enormous sheets of paper spread across the wall. After a while Goscha wondered if it would be possible simply to write all their ideas directly on the wall. After years of development, he finally devised a paint that can turn any wall into a dry erase board. With help from his friends he launched IdeaPaint in 2002, and six years later the company won the Innovation Award at NeoCon, one of the design industry's largest showcases.

Sources: Joel Holland, "What's Your Problem?" *Entrepreneur,* May 2010; Jason Daley, "A Charter for New Courses," *Entrepreneur,* April 2010; Ivy Hughes, "Guilt Free Gifting," *Entrepreneur,* April 2010; Kasey Wehrum, "30 Under 30: IdeaPaint," *Inc.,* October 1, 2009.

- Amazon.com began with investments by founder Jeff Bezos's family and friends. Bezos's parents invested $300,000, a huge portion of their retirement account. Today they are billionaires.

entrepreneurship
Accepting the risk of starting and running a business.

These stories have much in common. One or a couple of entrepreneurs had a good idea, borrowed some money from friends and family, and started a business. That business now employs thousands of people and helps the country prosper.

The United States has plenty of entrepreneurial talent. Names such as Steve Jobs (Apple Computer), Mark Zuckerberg (Facebook), Michael Dell (Dell Inc.), Bill Gates (Microsoft), Howard Schultz (Starbucks), Jack Dorsey (Twitter), and Chad Hurley and Steve Chen (YouTube) have become as familiar as those of the great entrepreneurs of the past. The nearby Spotlight on Small Business box highlights several young entrepreneurs who started businesses while still in school.

Explain why people take the risks of entrepreneurship; list the attributes of successful entrepreneurs; and describe entrepreneurial teams, intrapreneurs, and home- and web-based businesses.

WHY PEOPLE TAKE THE ENTREPRENEURIAL CHALLENGE

Taking the risks of starting a business can be scary and thrilling at the same time. One entrepreneur described it as almost like bungee jumping. You might be scared, but if you watch six other people do it and they survive, then you're more likely to do it yourself. Here are some reasons people are willing to take the entrepreneurial risk:

- *Opportunity.* The opportunity to share in the American dream is a tremendous lure. Many people, including those new to this country, may not have the skills for today's complex organizations, but they do have the initiative and drive to work the long hours demanded by entrepreneurship. The same is true of many corporate managers who leave corporate life (by choice or after downsizing) to run businesses of their own. Others, including an increasing number of women, minorities, older people, and people with disabilities, find that starting their own businesses offers them more opportunities than working for others.[2]

- *Profit.* Profit is another important reason to become an entrepreneur. Bill Gates, who cofounded Microsoft, is the richest man in the United States and one of the richest men in the world.[3]

- *Independence.* Many entrepreneurs simply do not enjoy working for someone else. Melissa Harvey, whose company Will n' Roses LLC produces all-natural nut and whole-grain Kizo bars, says one of the best things about being an entrepreneur is the freedom to pursue your passion: "It's about independence. You can take something that motivates you, that inspires you and act on it without roadblocks."[4]

- *Challenge.* Some people believe that entrepreneurs are excitement junkies who thrive on risk. Entrepreneurs take moderate, calculated risks; they don't just gamble. In general, though, entrepreneurs seek achievement more than power.[5]

What Does It Take to Be an Entrepreneur?

Would you succeed as an entrepreneur? You can learn about the managerial and leadership skills needed to run a firm. However, you may not have the personality to assume the risks, take the initiative, create the vision, and rally others to follow your lead. Such personality traits are harder to learn or acquire than academic skills are. A list of entrepreneurial attributes to look for in yourself includes:[6]

- *Self-directed.* You should be self-disciplined and thoroughly comfortable being your own boss. You alone will be responsible for your success or failure.

- *Self-nurturing.* You must believe in your idea even when no one else does, and be able to replenish your own enthusiasm. When Walt Disney suggested the possibility of a full-length animated feature film, *Snow White,* the industry laughed. His personal commitment and enthusiasm caused the Bank of America to back his venture. The rest is history.

- *Action-oriented.* Great business ideas are not enough. Most important is a burning desire to realize, actualize, and build your dream into reality.

- *Highly energetic.* It's your business, and you must be emotionally, mentally, and physically able to work long and hard. Employees have weekends and vacations; entrepreneurs often work seven days a week and don't take vacations for years. Working 18-hour days in your own business can be exhausting, but most entrepreneurs think it is better than working long hours for someone else.

- *Tolerant of uncertainty.* Successful entrepreneurs take only calculated risks (if they can help it). Still, they must be able to take *some* risks. Remember, entrepreneurship is not for the squeamish or those bent on security. You can't be afraid to fail. Many well-known entrepreneurs failed several times before achieving success. The late football coach Vince Lombardi summarized the entrepreneurial philosophy when he said, "We didn't lose any games this season, we just ran out of time twice." New entrepreneurs must be prepared to run out of time a few times before they succeed.

Turning Your Passions and Problems into Opportunities

As a young man in Queens, a borough of New York City, Russell Simmons channeled his passion for hip-hop culture into Def Jam Records. Today, his multimillion-dollar empire also includes Phat Farm clothing and Rush Management. Simmons used his time, money, and energy to turn his passion into a sustainable business.[7]

While many entrepreneurs' business ideas are inspired by their passions, many see business opportunities in their problems. For example, Anita Roddick started The Body Shop, which recycles its bottles and jars, because she hated paying for expensive packaging when she bought makeup.[8]

Most entrepreneurs don't get ideas for products and services from some flash of inspiration. The source of innovation is more like a *flashlight.* Imagine a search party walking in the dark, shining lights, looking around, asking questions, and looking some more. "That's how most creativity happens," says business author Dale Dauten. "Calling around, asking questions, saying 'What if?' till you get blisters on your tongue."

To look at problems and/or passions and see opportunities in them, ask yourself these questions: What do I want, but can never find? What product or service would improve my life? What really irritates me and what product or service would help?

Paula Deen had a dream that she could grow a business based on her passion for good country cooking. Her home-based catering business grew from a small family operation into multiple television shows, countless cookbooks, several restaurants, a bi-monthly magazine, and an ever-expanding product line. Do you have a passion that you could turn into a profitable business?

Keep in mind, however, that not all ideas are opportunities. If your idea doesn't meet anyone else's needs, the business won't succeed. You may have a business idea that is a good opportunity if:[9]

- It fills customers' needs.
- You have the skills and resources to start a business.
- You can sell the product or service at a price customers are willing and able to pay—and still make a profit.
- You can get your product or service to customers before your window of opportunity closes (before competitors with similar solutions beat you to the marketplace).
- You can keep the business going.

If you think you may have the entrepreneurial spirit in your blood, complete the Entrepreneurial Readiness Questionnaire on pages 153–154.

Entrepreneurial Teams

entrepreneurial team
A group of experienced people from different areas of business who join together to form a managerial team with the skills needed to develop, make, and market a new product.

An **entrepreneurial team** is a group of experienced people from different areas of business who join to form a managerial team with the skills to develop, make, and market a new product. A team may be better than an individual entrepreneur because team members can combine creative skills with production and marketing skills right from the start. Having a team also can ensure more cooperation and coordination later among functions in the business.

While Steve Jobs was the charismatic folk hero and visionary of Apple Computers, it was Steve Wozniak who invented the first personal computer model and Mike Markkula who offered business expertise and access to venture capital. The key to Apple's early success was that it was built around this "smart team" of entrepreneurs. The team wanted to combine the discipline of a big company with an environment in which people could feel they were participating in a successful venture. The trio of entrepreneurs recruited seasoned managers with similar desires. Everyone worked together to conceive, develop, and market products.[10]

Micropreneurs and Home-Based Businesses

micropreneurs
Entrepreneurs willing to accept the risk of starting and managing the type of business that remains small, lets them do the kind of work they want to do, and offers them a balanced lifestyle.

Not everyone who starts a business wants to grow a mammoth corporation. Some are interested in maintaining a balanced lifestyle while doing the kind of work they want to do. Such business owners are called **micropreneurs**. While other entrepreneurs are committed to the quest for growth, micropreneurs know they can be happy even if their companies never appear on a list of top-ranked businesses.

Many micropreneurs are home-based business owners. More than half of all small businesses are run from owners' homes.[11] Micropreneurs include consultants, video producers, architects, and bookkeepers. Many with professional skills such as graphic design, writing, and translating have found that one way of starting a freelance business is through websites such as Elance (www.elance.com) and oDesk (www.odesk.com) that link clients and freelancers. The sites post job openings and client feedback and serve as secure intermediaries for clients' payments.

ENTREPRENEUR READINESS QUESTIONNAIRE

Each of the following items describes something that you may or may not feel represents your personality or other characteristics about you. Read each item and then circle the response (1, 2, 3, 4, or 5) that most nearly reflects the extent to which you agree or disagree that the item seems to fit you.

Response

Looking at My Overall Philosophy of Life and Typical Behavior, I Would Say That . . .	AGREE COMPLETELY (1)	MOSTLY AGREE (2)	PARTIALLY AGREE (3)	MOSTLY DISAGREE (4)	DISAGREE COMPLETELY (5)
1. I am generally optimistic.	1	(2)	3	4	5
2. I enjoy competing and doing things better than someone else.	(1)	2	(3)	4	5
3. When solving a problem, I try to arrive at the best solution first without worrying about other possibilities.	1	2	(3)	4	5
4. I enjoy associating with co-workers after working hours.	1	2	3	4	(5)
5. If betting on a horse race I would prefer to take a chance on a high-payoff "long shot."	1	2	3	(4)	5
6. I like setting my own goals and working hard to achieve them.	(1)	2	3	4	5
7. I am generally casual and easy-going with others.	(1)	2	3	4	5
8. I like to know what is going on and take action to find out.	(1)	2	3	4	5
9. I work best when someone else is guiding me along the way.	1	2	(3)	4	5
10. When I am right I can convince others.	1	2	3	(4)	5
11. I find that other people frequently waste my valuable time.	1	2	(3)	4	5
12. I enjoy watching football, baseball, and similar sports events.	1	2	3	(4)	5
13. I tend to communicate about myself very openly with other people.	(1)	2	3	4	5
14. I don't mind following orders from superiors who have legitimate authority.	(1)	2	3	4	5
15. I enjoy planning things more than actually carrying out the plans.	(1)	2	3	4	5
16. I don't think it's much fun to bet on a "sure thing."	1	2	3	(4)	5
17. If faced with failure, I would shift quickly to something else rather than sticking to my guns.	1	2	(3)	4	5
18. Part of being successful in business is reserving adequate time for family.	(1)	2	3	4	5
19. Once I have earned something, I feel that keeping it secure is important.	1	2	(3)	4	5
20. Making a lot of money is largely a matter of getting the right breaks.	(1)	2	3	4	5
21. Problem solving is usually more effective when a number of alternatives are considered.	1	(2)	3	4	5
22. I enjoy impressing others with the things I can do.	1	2	(3)	4	5
23. I enjoy playing games like tennis and handball with someone who is slightly better than I am.	1	2	3	4	(5)
24. Sometimes moral ethics must be bent a little in business dealings.	1	2	3	4	(5)
25. I think that good friends would make the best subordinates in an organization.	1	2	3	(4)	5

(continued)

Micropreneur Jane Mason, of Virtuous Bread, teaches small bread-making classes in her home kitchen. She also created a network of "Bread Angels," people she taught to start their own home-based bread businesses. Her website contains a blog, a newsletter and recipes. Mason is more concerned with building positive relationships within communities than with building a huge baking company. Can you see why Mason is considered a micropreneur?

Many home-based businesses are owned by people combining career and family. Don't picture just moms with young children; nearly 60 percent are men. Here are more reasons for the growth of home-based businesses:[12]

- Computer technology has leveled the competitive playing field, allowing home-based businesses to look and act as big as their corporate competitors. Broadband Internet connections, smart phones such as the BlackBerry and the iPhone, and other technologies are so affordable that setting up a business takes a much smaller initial investment than it once did.

- Corporate downsizing has led many to venture out on their own. Meanwhile, the work of the downsized employees still needs to be done, and corporations are outsourcing much of it to smaller companies.

- Social attitudes have changed. Whereas home-based entrepreneurs used to be asked when they were going to get a "real" job, they are now likely to be asked for how-to-do-it advice.

- New tax laws have loosened restrictions on deducting expenses for home offices.

Working at home has its challenges, of course. Here are a few:[13]

- *Getting new customers.* Getting the word out can be difficult because you don't have a retail storefront.

- *Managing time.* You save time by not commuting, but it takes self-discipline to use that time wisely.

- *Keeping work and family tasks separate.* It's great to be able to throw a load of laundry in the washer in the middle of the workday if you need to, but you have to keep such distractions to a minimum. It also takes self-discipline to leave your work at the office if the office is at home.

- *Abiding by city ordinances.* Government ordinances restrict the types of businesses allowed in certain parts of the community and how much traffic a home-based business can attract to the neighborhood.

figure 6.1

POTENTIAL HOME-BASED BUSINESSES

Many businesses can be started at home. Listed below are 10 businesses that have low start-up costs, don't require an abundance of administrative tasks, and are in relatively high demand:

1. Cleaning service.
2. Gift-basket business.
3. Web merchant.
4. Mailing list service.
5. Microfarming (small plots of land for such high-value crops as mushrooms, edible flowers, or sprouts).
6. Tutoring.
7. Résumé service.
8. Web design.
9. Medical claims assistance.
10. Personal coaching.

Look for a business that meets these important criteria: (1) The job is something you truly enjoy doing; (2) you know enough to do the job well or you are willing to spend time learning it while you have another job; and (3) you can identify a market for your product or service.

- *Managing risk.* Home-based entrepreneurs should review their homeowner's insurance policy, since not all policies cover business-related claims. Some even void the coverage if there is a business in the home.

Home-based entrepreneurs should focus on finding opportunity instead of accepting security, getting results instead of following routines, earning a profit instead of earning a paycheck, trying new ideas instead of avoiding mistakes, and creating a long-term vision instead of seeking a short-term payoff. Figure 6.1 lists 10 ideas for potentially successful home-based businesses, and Figure 6.2 highlights clues for avoiding home-based business scams. You can find a wealth of online information about starting a home-based business at *Entrepreneur* magazine's website (www.entrepreneur.com).

figure 6.2

WATCH OUT FOR SCAMS

You've probably read many newspaper and magazine ads selling home-based businesses. You may have even received unsolicited e-mail messages touting the glory of particular work-at-home opportunities. Beware of work-at-home scams! Here are a few clues that tell you a home business opportunity is a scam:

1. The ad promises that you can earn hundreds or even thousands of dollars a week working at home.
2. No experience is needed.
3. You only need to work a few hours a week.
4. There are loads of CAPITAL LETTERS and exclamation points!!!!!
5. You need to call a 900 number for more information.
6. You're asked to send in some money to receive a list of home-based business opportunities.
7. You're pressured to make a decision NOW!!!!

Do your homework before investing in a business opportunity. Call and ask for references. Contact the Better Business Bureau (www.bbb.org), county and state departments of consumer affairs, and the state attorney general's office. Conduct an Internet search and ask people in forums or on social networking sites if they've dealt with the company. Visit Web sites such as Friends In Business (www.friendsinbusiness.com) to find advice on specific online scams. Most important, don't pay a great deal of money for a business opportunity until you've talked to an attorney.

Web-Based Businesses

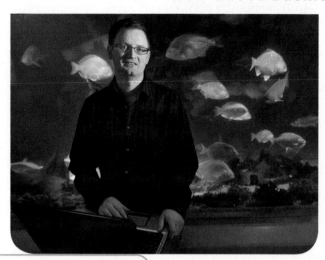

Markus Frind operates his dating website, Plenty of Fish, out of his apartment. Apparently there really are plenty of fish since his site brings in $10 million a year.

affiliate marketing
An Internet-based marketing strategy in which a business rewards individuals or other businesses (affiliates) for each visitor or customer the affiliate sends to its website.

The Internet has sprouted a world of small web-based businesses selling everything from staplers to refrigerator magnets to wedding dresses. In 2010, online retail sales reached $172.9 billion, or approximately 7 percent of all retail sales. Online retail sales were up 11 percent in 2010, compared to just 2.5 percent for all retail sales. Forrester Research predicts that online retail sales will reach $250 billion by 2014.[14]

Web-based businesses have to offer more than the same merchandise customers can buy at stores—they must offer unique products or services. For example, Marc Resnik started his web-based distribution company after waking up one morning laughing about his business idea. Now ThrowThings.com makes money for him—he's shipped products to more than 44 countries. Although the company's offerings seem like a random collection of unrelated items, everything it sells can be thrown. You can buy promotional products in the "Throw Your Name Around!" section, ventriloquist dummies in the "Throw Your Voice!" section, and sporting equipment in the "Things to Throw!" section. Stranger products include fake vomit ("Throw Up!") and a $3.50 certificate that says you wasted your money ("Throw Your Money Away!"). Resnik doesn't sell very many of those certificates, but he does sell more dummies than anyone else in the United States. About two-thirds of the company's revenue comes from the promotional products section, which allows customers to add a logo to thousands of products. Why is Resnik's business so successful? As one frequent customer said, it's because of Resnik's exceptional service and quick turn-around time.[15]

One of the easiest ways to start a web-based business is through affiliate marketing. **Affiliate marketing** is an Internet-based marketing strategy in which a business rewards individuals or other businesses (affiliates) for each visitor or customer the affiliate sends to its website. For example, imagine you discovered a backpack online made of an extremely lightweight, amazingly strong fabric that holds everything you need for the day, is easy to carry, and looks great. You want to tell all your friends about it, so you register as an affiliate on the seller's website and download to your Facebook page a *widget*, a tiny application that links your page to the seller's site. Whenever anyone clicks on the widget (an image of the product) and buys a backpack, the seller pays you a commission.

If you can make a little money in commissions from sales of a single backpack, imagine setting up an online store with many products you love. Building such a store has become easier with the advent of social commerce services such as Lemonade Inc.'s Lemonade Stand (www.lemonade.com). Once partnered, an online retailer typically provides Lemonade Stand access to product information and images. Lemonade Stand then funnels that information through its website so that users can select which products they would like to appear in their widget product galleries on their websites, Facebook pages, or blogs. Widget users get commissions on sales generated through the widgets. Using social commerce services like Lemonade Stand saves users from the time-consuming task of registering as an affiliate with multiple sellers. Such services are allowing Internet users to become what amounts to peer-to-peer affiliates for e-retailers where the users can make money.

A web-based business isn't always a fast road to success.[16] It can sometimes be a shortcut to failure. Hundreds of high-flying dot-coms crashed after promising to revolutionize the way we shop. That's the bad news. The good news is that you can learn from someone else's failure and spare yourself some pain.

intrapreneurs
Creative people who work as entrepreneurs within corporations.

Entrepreneurship within Firms

Entrepreneurship in a large organization is often reflected in the efforts and achievements of **intrapreneurs,** creative people who work as entrepreneurs within corporations. The idea is to use a company's existing resources—human, financial, and physical—to launch new products and generate new profits.[17] At 3M, which produces a wide array of products from adhesives like Scotch tape to nonwoven materials for industrial use, managers are expected to devote 15 percent of their work time to thinking up new products or services.[18] You know those bright-colored Post-it Notes people use to write messages on just about everything? That product was developed by Art Fry, a 3M employee. He needed to mark the pages of his hymnal with something that wouldn't damage the book or fall out. He came up with the idea of the self-stick, repositionable paper slips. The labs at 3M produced a sample, but distributors were unimpressed and market surveys were inconclusive. Nonetheless, 3M kept sending samples to secretaries of top executives. Eventually, after a major sales and marketing program, the orders began pouring in, and Post-it Notes became a big winner. The company continues to update the product; making it from recycled paper is one of many innovations. Post-it Notes have gone international as well—the notepads sent to Japan are long and narrow to accommodate vertical writing. You can even use Post-it Notes electronically—the Post-it Software Notes program allows you to type messages onto brightly colored notes and store them on memo boards, embed them in documents, or send them through e-mail.

A classic intrapreneurial venture is Lockheed Martin Corporation's Skunkworks, a research and development center that turned out such monumental products as the United States' first fighter jet in 1943 and the Stealth fighter in 1991.[19]

When you come up with a winning idea, stick with it. That's certainly been the motto of 3M, the maker of Post-It Notes. The company encourages intrapreneurship among its employees by requiring them to devote at least 15 percent of their time to think about new products. How has this commitment to innovation paid off for 3M and its employees?

Encouraging Entrepreneurship: What Government Can Do

Part of the Immigration Act passed by Congress in 1990 was intended to encourage more entrepreneurs to come to the United States. The act created a category of "investor visas" that allows 10,000 people to come to the United States each year if they invest $1 million in an enterprise that creates or preserves 10 jobs. Some people are promoting the idea of increasing the allowed number of such immigrants. They believe the more entrepreneurs that can be drawn to the United States, the more jobs will be created and the more the economy will grow.[20]

Another way to encourage entrepreneurship is **enterprise zones,** specific geographic areas to which governments attract private business investment by offering lower taxes and other government support. (These are also sometimes

enterprise zones
Specific geographic areas to which governments try to attract private business investment by offering lower taxes and other government support.

Incubators, such as this one in Alabama, offer new businesses low-cost offices with basic business services such as accounting, legal advice, and secretarial help. Do you have such incubators in your area?

incubators
Centers that offer new businesses low-cost offices with basic business services.

called *empowerment zones* or *enterprise communities*.) The government could have a significant effect on entrepreneurship by offering tax breaks to businesses that make investments to create jobs.[21]

States are becoming stronger supporters of entrepreneurs and are creating programs that invest directly in new businesses. Often, state commerce departments serve as clearinghouses for such programs. States are also creating incubators and technology centers to reduce start-up capital needs. **Incubators** offer new businesses in the critical stage of early development low-cost offices with basic services such as accounting, legal advice, and secretarial help. According to a recent study conducted by the National Business Incubator Association (NBIA), 87 percent of incubator graduates remain in business.[22] To learn more about what incubators offer and to find links to incubators in your area, visit the NBIA's website (www.nbia.org).

There are a few states that offer assistance to qualified candidates under the Self-Employment Assistance (SEA) program. The program allows participants to collect unemployment checks while they build their businesses. Participants often get training and counseling as well. Unemployment checks may not seem like much, but many business owners say they are enough to help them launch their companies without depleting savings to pay for living expenses until their businesses are strong enough to support them. Rose Rios entered the New Jersey SEA program in 2007 when she was laid off from her job in market research. She collected benefits of about $450 while she started a medical communications and market research company. Since then she has brought in over $2.5 million in revenue and hired three full-time employees and several freelancers.[23]

The government can also join with private entities to promote entrepreneurship. For example, Startup America is a White House initiative to "celebrate, inspire, and accelerate high-growth entrepreneurship throughout the nation."[24] It is a public and private effort to bring together the country's most innovative entrepreneurs, corporations, universities, foundations, and other leaders, to work with federal agencies to increase the number and success of U.S. entrepreneurs. One of the core goals is to empower more Americans not just to get a job, but to create jobs. Learn more about the resources offered by Startup America at www.startupamericapartnership.org.[25]

progress assessment

- Why are people willing to take the risks of entrepreneurship?
- What are the advantages of entrepreneurial teams?
- How do micropreneurs differ from other entrepreneurs?
- What are some opportunities and risks of web-based businesses?

LEARNING goal 2

Discuss the importance of small business to the American economy and summarize the major causes of small-business failure.

GETTING STARTED IN SMALL BUSINESS

Let's suppose you have a great idea for a new business, you have the attributes of an entrepreneur, and you're ready to take the leap into business for yourself. How do you start? That's what the rest of this chapter is about.

It may be easier to identify with a small neighborhood business than with a giant global firm, yet the principles of management are similar for each. The management of charities, government agencies, churches, schools, and unions is much the same as the management of small and large businesses. So, as you learn about small-business management, you will take a giant step toward understanding management in general. All organizations demand capital, good ideas, planning, information management, budgets (and financial management in general), accounting, marketing, good employee relations, and good overall managerial know-how. We shall explore these areas as they relate to small businesses and then, later in the book, apply the concepts to large firms and even global organizations.

Small versus Big Business

The Small Business Administration (SBA) defines a **small business** as one that is independently owned and operated, is not dominant in its field of operation, and meets certain standards of size in terms of employees or annual receipts (such as under $2 million a year for service businesses). A small business is considered "small" only in relationship to other businesses in its industry. A wholesaler may sell up to $22 million and still be considered a small business by the SBA. In manufacturing, a plant can have 1,500 employees and still be considered small. Let's look at some interesting statistics about small businesses:[26]

small business
A business that is independently owned and operated, is not dominant in its field of operation, and meets certain standards of size (set by the Small Business Administration) in terms of employees or annual receipts.

- There are 27.8 million small businesses in the United States.
- Of all nonfarm businesses in the United States, almost 97 percent are considered small by SBA standards.
- Small businesses account for more than 50 percent of the gross domestic product (GDP).
- Nearly 600,000 tax-paying, employee-hiring businesses are started every year.
- Small businesses generate 60–80 percent of the new jobs each year.
- Small businesses employ about half of all private-sector employees.
- About 80 percent of U.S. workers find their first jobs in small businesses.

As you can see, small business is really a big part of the U.S. economy. How big? Let's find out.

Importance of Small Businesses

Since 60–80 percent of the nation's new jobs are in small businesses, there's a very good chance you'll either work in a small business someday or start one. In addition to providing employment opportunities, small firms believe they offer other advantages over larger companies—more personal customer service and the ability to respond quickly to opportunities.

Bigger is not always better. Picture a hole in the ground. If you fill it with boulders, there are many empty spaces between them. If you fill it with sand, there is no space between the grains. That's how it is in business. Big businesses don't serve all the needs of the market. There is plenty of room for small companies to make a profit filling those niches.

Small-Business Success and Failure

You can't be naïve about business practices, or you'll go broke. It's been reported that half of new businesses don't last five years.[27] Yet a study by economist Bruce Kirchhoff showed that the failure rate is only 18 percent over the first eight years. Kirchhoff contends that other reported failure rates are misinterpretations of Dun & Bradstreet statistics. When small-business owners closed down one business to start another, for instance, they were included in the "failure" category—even though they hadn't failed at all. Similarly, when a business changed its form of ownership or a sole proprietor retired, it was counted as a failure. The good news for entrepreneurs is that business failures are much lower than traditionally reported.[28]

Figure 6.3 lists reasons for small-business failures, among them managerial incompetence and inadequate financial planning. Keep in mind that when a business fails, it is important that the owners learn from their mistakes. Some entrepreneurs who have suffered flops are more realistic than novice entrepreneurs. Because of the lessons they've learned, they may be more successful in their future ventures.[29]

Choosing the right type of business is critical. Many businesses with low failure rates require advanced training to start—veterinary services, dental practices, medical practices,

Thirteen-year-old Madison Waldrop developed her own dress collection called Designs by Malyse, specializing in evening and bridal gowns. One of the young entrepreneur's bridal gowns was featured on the runway at the 2010 Bridal Fashion Week in New York City.

figure 6.3

CAUSES OF SMALL-BUSINESS FAILURE

The following are some of the causes of small-business failure:

- Plunging in without first testing the waters on a small scale.
- Underpricing or overpricing goods or services.
- Underestimating how much time it will take to build a market.
- Starting with too little capital.
- Starting with too much capital and being careless in its use.
- Going into business with little or no experience and without first learning something about the industry or market.
- Borrowing money without planning just how and when to pay it back.
- Attempting to do too much business with too little capital.

- Not allowing for setbacks and unexpected expenses.
- Buying too much on credit.
- Extending credit too freely.
- Expanding credit too rapidly.
- Failing to keep complete, accurate records, so that the owners drift into trouble without realizing it.
- Carrying habits of personal extravagance into the business.
- Not understanding business cycles.
- Forgetting about taxes, insurance, and other costs of doing business.
- Mistaking the freedom of being in business for oneself for the liberty to work or not, according to whim.

figure 6.4

SITUATIONS FOR
SMALL-BUSINESS SUCCESS

The following factors increase the chances of small-business success:

- The customer requires a lot of personal attention, as in a beauty parlor.

- The product is not easily made by mass-production techniques (e.g., custom-tailored clothes or custom auto-body work).

- Sales are not large enough to appeal to a large firm (e.g., a novelty shop).

- The neighborhood is not attractive because of crime or poverty. This provides a unique opportunity for small grocery stores and laundries.

- A large business sells a franchise operation to local buyers. (Don't forget franchising as an excellent way to enter the world of small business.)

- The owner pays attention to new competitors.

- The business is in a growth industry (e.g., computer services or web design).

and so on. While training and degrees may buy security, they do not tend to produce much growth—one dentist can fill only so many cavities. If you want to be both independent and rich, you need to go after growth. Often high-growth businesses, such as technology firms, are not easy to start and are even more difficult to keep going.

The easiest businesses to start have the least growth and greatest failure rate (like restaurants). The easiest to keep alive are difficult to get started (like manufacturing). And the ones that can make you rich are both hard to start and hard to keep going (like automobile assembly). See Figure 6.4 to get an idea of the business situations most likely to lead to success.

When you decide to start your own business, think carefully. You're unlikely to find everything you want—easy entry, security, and reward—in one business. Choose those characteristics that matter most to you; accept the absence of the others; plan, plan, plan; and then go for it!

LEARNING goal 3

Summarize ways to learn about how small businesses operate.

LEARNING ABOUT SMALL-BUSINESS OPERATIONS

Hundreds of would-be entrepreneurs ask the same question: "How can I learn to run my own business?" Here are some hints.

Learn from Others

Investigate your local community college for classes on small business and entrepreneurship; there are thousands of such programs throughout the United States. Many bring together entrepreneurs from diverse backgrounds who form helpful support networks. Talk to others who have already

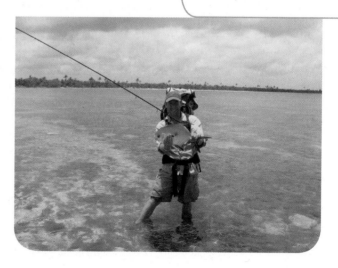

Jason White, owner of Crested Butte Angler, turned his love of fishing into a successful guide business. He learned to fish in the Ozarks of Missouri and Arkansas and now leads fishing excursions in Colorado, Mexico, and Thailand. What experiences do you have that would help you start and run a successful business?

Going Down with the Ship

Suppose you've worked for two years in a company and you see signs that it is beginning to falter. You and a co-worker have ideas about how to make a company like your boss's succeed. Rather than share your ideas with your boss, you and your friend are considering quitting your jobs and starting your own company together. Should you approach other co-workers about working for your new venture? Will you try to lure your old boss's customers to your own business? What are your alternatives? What are the consequences of each alternative? What's the most ethical choice?

done it. They'll tell you that location is critical and caution you not to be undercapitalized, that is, not to start without enough money. They'll warn you about the problems of finding and retaining good workers. And, most of all, they'll tell you to keep good records and hire a good accountant and lawyer before you start. Free advice like this is invaluable.

Get Some Experience

There is no better way to learn small-business management than by becoming an apprentice or working for a successful entrepreneur. Many small-business owners got the idea for their businesses from their prior jobs. The rule of thumb is: Have three years' experience in a comparable business first.[30]

Back in 1818, Cornelius Vanderbilt sold his own sailing vessels and went to work for a steamboat company so that he could learn the rules of the new game of steam. After learning what he needed to know, he quit, started his own steamship company, and became the first U.S. business owner to accumulate $100 million.

Running a small business part-time, during your off hours or on weekends, can bring the rewards of working for yourself while still enjoying a regular paycheck at another job. It may save you money too, because you're then less likely to make "rookie mistakes" when you start your own business. The Making Ethical Decisions box presents ethical questions about using the knowledge you've gained as an employee to start your own business.

Take Over a Successful Firm

Small-business owners work long hours and rarely take vacations. After many years, they may feel stuck and think they can't get out because they have too much time and effort invested. Thus millions of small-business owners are eager to get away, at least for a long vacation.

This is where you come in. Find a successful businessperson who owns a small business. Tell him or her you are eager to learn the business and would like to serve an apprenticeship, that is, a training period. Say that at the end of the training period (one year or so), you would like to help the owner or manager by becoming assistant manager. Thus you can free the owner to take off weekends and holidays and have a long vacation—a good deal for him or her. For another year or so, work very hard to learn all about the business—suppliers, inventory, bookkeeping, customers, promotion. At the end of two years, make this offer: The owner can retire or work only part-time, and you will take over management of the business. You can establish a profit-sharing plan with the owner plus pay yourself a salary. Be generous with yourself; you'll earn it if you manage the business. You can even ask for 40 percent or more of the profits.

The owner benefits by keeping ownership in the business and making 60 percent of what he or she earned before—without having to work. You benefit by making 40 percent of the profits of a successful firm. This is an excellent deal for an owner about to retire—he or she is able to keep the firm and a healthy profit flow. It is also a clever and successful way to share in the profits of a successful small business without making any personal monetary investment.

If profit sharing doesn't appeal to the owner, you may want to buy the business outright. How do you determine a fair price for a business? Value is based on (1) what the business owns, (2) what it earns, and (3) what makes it unique. Naturally, an accountant will need to help you determine the business's value.[31]

If you fail at your efforts to take over the business through either profit sharing or buying, you can quit and start your own business fully trained.

LEARNING goal 4

Analyze what it takes to start and run a small business.

MANAGING A SMALL BUSINESS

According to the Small Business Administration, one of the major causes of small business failures is poor management. Keep in mind, though, that *poor management* covers a number of faults. It could mean poor planning, record keeping, inventory control, promotion, or employee relations. Most likely it includes poor capitalization. To help you succeed as a business owner, in the following sections we explore the functions of business in a small-business setting:

- Planning your business.
- Financing your business.
- Knowing your customers (marketing).
- Managing your employees (human resource development).
- Keeping records (accounting).

Although all the functions are important in both the start-up and management phases of the business, the first two—planning and financing—are the primary concerns when you start your business. The others are the heart of your operations once the business is under way.

Begin with Planning

Many people eager to start a small business come up with an idea and begin discussing it with professors, friends, and other businesspeople. At this stage the entrepreneur needs a business plan. A **business plan** is a detailed written statement that describes the nature of the business, the target market, the

business plan
A detailed written statement that describes the nature of the business, the target market, the advantages the business will have in relation to competition, and the resources and qualifications of the owner(s).

advantages the business will have over competition, and the resources and qualifications of the owner(s). A business plan forces potential small-business owners to be quite specific about the products or services they intend to offer. They must analyze the competition, calculate how much money they need to start, and cover other details of operation. A business plan is also mandatory for talking with bankers or other investors.

Lenders want to know everything about an aspiring business. First, pick a bank that serves businesses the size of yours. Have a good accountant prepare a complete set of financial statements and a personal balance sheet. Make an appointment before going to the bank and go to the bank with an accountant and all the necessary financial information. Demonstrate to the banker that you're a person of good character: civic minded and respected in business and community circles.[32] Finally, ask for *all* the money you need, be specific, and be prepared to personally guarantee the loan.

Writing a Business Plan

A good business plan takes a long time to write, but you've got only five minutes, in the *executive summary,* to convince readers not to throw it away. Since bankers receive many business plans every day, the summary has to catch their interest quickly. There's no such thing as a perfect business plan, but prospective entrepreneurs do think out the smallest details. An outline of a comprehensive business plan is shown on pages 165–166.

Many computer software programs can help you get organized. One highly rated business-plan program is Business Plan Pro by Palo Alto Software. To see samples of successful business plans for a variety of businesses go to www.bplans.com/sample_business_plans. You can also learn more about writing business plans on the Small Business Administration website at www.sba.gov/starting.

Madcloth co-founders Susan and Eric Koger started selling vintage clothes when they were in college. They entered a hastily written business plan in a school competition— and lost. While discouraging at first, the loss taught them that they needed to refocus and create a solid business plan if they were going to attract investors. Today their company has 100 full-time employees.

Getting the completed business plan into the right hands is almost as important as getting the right information into the plan. Finding funding requires research. Next we discuss sources of money available to new business ventures. All require a comprehensive business plan. The time and effort you invest before starting a business will pay off many times later. The big payoff is survival.

Getting Money to Fund a Small Business

An entrepreneur has several potential sources of capital: personal savings; relatives; former employers; banks; finance companies; venture capitalists; and government agencies such as the Small Business Administration (SBA), the Farmers Home Administration, the Economic Development Authority, and the Minority Business Development Agency. The most common source of funding after personal savings is friends and family.[33]

You may even want to consider borrowing from a potential supplier to your future business. Helping you get started may be in the supplier's interest if there is a chance you will be a big customer later. This is what Ray Kroc did in the early years of McDonald's. When Kroc didn't have the funds available to keep the company going, he asked his suppliers to help him with the necessary funds. These suppliers grew along with McDonalds. It's usually not a

OUTLINE OF A COMPREHENSIVE BUSINESS PLAN

A good business plan is between 25 and 50 pages long and takes at least six months to write.

Cover Letter

Only one thing is certain when you go hunting for money to start a business: You won't be the only hunter out there. You need to make potential funders want to read *your* business plan instead of the hundreds of others on their desks. Your cover letter should summarize the most attractive points of your project in as few words as possible. Be sure to address the letter to the potential investor by name. "To whom it may concern" or "Dear Sir" is not the best way to win an investor's support.

Section 1—Executive Summary

Begin with a two-page or three-page management summary of the proposed venture. Include a short description of the business, and discuss major goals and objectives.

Section 2—Company Background

Describe company operations to date (if any), potential legal considerations, and areas of risk and opportunity. Summarize the firm's financial condition, and include past and current balance sheets, income and cash flow statements, and other relevant financial records (you will read about these financial statements in Chapter 17). It is also wise to include a description of insurance coverage. Investors want to be assured that death or other mishaps do not pose major threats to the company.

Section 3—Management Team

Include an organization chart, job descriptions of listed positions, and detailed résumés of the current and proposed executives. A mediocre idea with a proven management team is funded more often than a great idea with an inexperienced team. Managers should have expertise in all disciplines necessary to start and run a business. If not, mention outside consultants who will serve in these roles and describe their qualifications.

Section 4—Financial Plan

Provide five-year projections for income, expenses, and funding sources. Don't assume the business will grow in a straight line. Adjust your planning to allow for funding at various stages of the company's growth. Explain the rationale and assumptions used to determine the estimates. Assumptions should be reasonable and based on industry/historical trends. Make sure all totals add up and are consistent throughout the plan. If necessary, hire a professional accountant or financial analyst to prepare these statements.

Stay clear of excessively ambitious sales projections; rather, offer best-case, expected, and worst-case scenarios. These not only reveal how sensitive the bottom line is to sales fluctuations but also serve as good management guides.

Section 5—Capital Required

Indicate the amount of capital needed to commence or continue operations, and describe how these funds are to be used. Make sure the totals are the same as the ones on the cash-flow statement. This area will receive a great deal of review from potential investors, so it must be clear and concise.

Section 6—Marketing Plan

Don't underestimate the competition. Review industry size, trends, and the target market segment. Sources like *American Demographics* magazine and the *Rand McNally Commercial Atlas and Marketing Guide* can help you put a plan together. Discuss strengths and weaknesses of the product or service. The most important things investors want to know are what makes the product more desirable than what's already available and whether the product can be patented. Compare pricing to the competition's. Forecast sales in dollars and units. Outline sales, advertising, promotion, and public relations programs. Make sure the costs agree with those projected in the financial statements.

Section 7—Location Analysis

In retailing and certain other industries, the location of the business is one of the most important factors. Provide a comprehensive demographic analysis of consumers in the area of the proposed business as well as a traffic-pattern analysis and vehicular and pedestrian counts.

(continued)

Section 8—Manufacturing Plan

Describe minimum plant size, machinery required, production capacity, inventory and inventory-control methods, quality control, plant personnel requirements, and so on. Estimates of product costs should be based on primary research.

Section 9—Appendix

Include all marketing research on the product or service (off-the-shelf reports, article reprints, etc.) and other information about the product concept or market size. Provide a bibliography of all the reference materials you consulted. This section should demonstrate that the proposed company won't be entering a declining industry or market segment.

If you would like to see sample business plans that successfully secured funding, go to Bplans.com (www.bplans .com). You can also learn more about writing business plans on the Small Business Administration website at www.sba.gov/starting.

Wouldn't it be great if money grew on trees? Unfortunately it doesn't, so prospective entrepreneurs must find other sources of capital such as personal savings, relatives, former employers, banks, finance companies, venture capitalists, and government agencies. What is the most common source of funding after personal savings?

good idea to ask such an investor for money at the outset. Begin by asking for advice; if the supplier likes your plan, he or she may be willing to help you with funding too.

The credit crunch spurred by the recent financial crisis made it necessary for small-business owners to do a little extra shopping to find a friendly lender. Many found that smaller community banks were more likely to grant loans than larger regional banks. Since small banks do business in a single town or cluster of towns, they know their customers better. They have more flexibility to make lending decisions based on everything they know about their customers, rather than on a more automated basis as larger banks must.[34]

Community development financial institutions (CDFIs) may be a source of funding for businesses in lower-income communities. Today CDFIs are playing a big role in the economic recovery. CDFIs were first formed in the early 1980s by socially motivated investors such as nuns investing their retirement funds. However, in 2009 more than $1 billion flowed into CDFIs from big investment companies and another $247 million from the government. CDFIs succeeded even after the credit bubble because they maintained the financial discipline other lenders lacked. They have the incentive to make sure their clients succeed because, if borrowers don't repay their loans, the CDFIs take the hit, not investors. Only 1 percent of their loans were not paid back in the last three decades. CDFIs don't just loan money. More importantly, they provide business counseling such as helping owners learn how to develop marketing strategies, manage inventory, and improve cash flow.[35]

Individual investors are also a frequent source of capital for most entrepreneurs. *Angel investors* are private individuals who invest their own money in potentially hot new companies before they go public.[36] A number of websites match people who want money with those willing to lend it; they include Prosper Marketplace, Zopa, Lending Club, Kiva, Virgin Money, CircleLending, and GlobeFunder. Other sites, such as GreenNote and People Capital, specialize in lending to students. This form of individual investing is called peer-to-peer (P2P) lending.[37] A creditworthy borrower often gets such money faster and easier than going to the bank. And the cost is often less than a bank

SOCIAL MEDIA IN
business

Social Lending

For aspiring entrepreneurs, having a good idea is only half the battle. The next hurdle is gathering enough capital to turn a business plan into reality. But bank loans are hard to come by these days. The failed speculation that spurred the financial crisis remains a vivid memory for many investors, making them reluctant to lend funds.

Although traditional avenues of investment may be closed to some, a number of new ventures online can help entrepreneurs acquire cash. Kickstarter.com, for instance, helps potential business owners, as well as musicians and artists, gather funds from a variety of backers. Instead of dealing in interest rates and equity, however, contributors pledge to give as little as $1 in exchange for free products or just a thank-you for helping make the project a reality. Although these may seem like small contributions, a little money from a lot of people can go a long way. Vidam Akimenko posted a $15,000 investment goal on Kickstarter in order to establish a Boston-area butcher shop specializing in meat from local farms. After donations from 201 different people, he surpassed his investment cap by $1,405 and soon opened Akimenko Meats.

For those investors wanting a larger return than a T-bone steak, peer-to-peer lending sites like Lending Club

act as a sort of Facebook of money. But instead of collecting online friends, loan-seekers look for people who are willing to lend them money. Individuals set up a profile that outlines their credit history, how much cash they need, and what they intend to do with it. Administrators at Lending Club then assign an interest rate between 6.78 percent and 24.95 percent based on the criteria above. Many users, such as Karla Brazelton of Detroit, use the money to pay down debt. After facing rejection from banks across the board, Brazelton signed up to Lending Club in order to reduce her $7,000 credit card debt. After investment from a small collection of lenders, Brazelton eventually secured a 36-month personal loan at 7.74 percent interest. Not only does the loan help Brazelton, it also provides investors with a much higher rate of return on their money than any standard savings account could offer.

Sources: John Tozzi, "Eight Companies Kick-Started by Fans," *Bloomberg Businessweek,* June 28–July 4, 2010; and John Simons, "How to Get a Loan the Web 2.0 Way," *Black Enterprise,* December 1, 2010.

---

loan. The Social Media in Business box offers a number of examples of companies that started with P2P loans.

Venture capitalists may finance your project—for a price. Venture capitalists may ask for a hefty stake in your company (as much as 60 percent) in exchange for the cash to start your business. If the venture capitalist takes too large a stake, you could lose control of the business. Since the widespread failure of early web startups, venture capitalists have been willing to invest less and expect more return on their investment if the new company is sold.[38] Therefore, if you're a very small company, you don't have a very good chance of getting venture capital. You'd have a better chance finding an angel investor.

If your proposed venture does require millions of dollars to start, experts recommend that you talk with at least five investment firms and their clients in order to find the right venture capitalist. You may able to connect with potential investors through Angellist.com, a nonprofit service that helps entrepreneurs and venture capitalist get to know each other.[39] To learn more about how to find venture capitalists, visit the National Venture Capital Association's website (www.nvca.org).

venture capitalists
Individuals or companies that invest in new businesses in exchange for partial ownership of those businesses.

The Small Business Administration (SBA)

Small Business Administration (SBA)
A U.S. government agency that advises and assists small businesses by providing management training and financial advice and loans.

The **Small Business Administration (SBA)** is a U.S. government agency that advises and assists small businesses by providing management training and financial advice and loans (see Figure 6.5). The SBA started a microloan demonstration program in 1991. The program provides very small loans (up to $50,000) and technical assistance to small-business owners. It is administered through a nationwide network of nonprofit organizations chosen by the SBA. Rather than award loans based on collateral, credit history, or previous business success, the program judges worthiness on belief in the borrowers' integrity and the soundness of their business ideas.[40]

The SBA microloan program helps people like Ted Cooper, who owns Fresh Look Remodeling, a New York–based energy-audit business. Faced with laying off his six workers, Cooper searched for a loan to keep the business going. Before Cooper received a $10,000 SBA microloan, he applied to a few big banks, one of which asked for $15,000 worth of collateral. "If I had that, I wouldn't have needed to borrow it," Cooper said.[41]

Small Business Investment Company (SBIC) Program
A program through which private investment companies licensed by the Small Business Administration lend money to small businesses.

You may also want to consider requesting funds from the **Small Business Investment Company (SBIC) Program.** SBICs are private investment companies licensed by the SBA to lend money to small businesses. An SBIC must have a minimum of $5 million in capital and can borrow up to $2 from the SBA for each $1 of capital it has. It lends to or invests in small businesses that meet its criteria. Often SBICs are able to keep defaults to a minimum by identifying a business's trouble spots early, giving entrepreneurs advice, and in some cases rescheduling loan payments.[42]

Perhaps the best place for young entrepreneurs to start shopping for an SBA loan is a Small Business Development Center (SBDC). SBDCs are funded jointly by the federal government and individual states, and are usually associated with state and community colleges and universities. SBDCs can help you evaluate the feasibility of your idea, develop your business plan, and complete your funding application—all for no charge.

figure 6.5

TYPES OF SBA FINANCIAL ASSISTANCE

The SBA may provide the following types of financial assistance:

- *Guaranteed loans*—loans made by a financial institution that the government will repay if the borrower stops making payments. The maximum individual loan guarantee is capped at $5 million.

- *Microloans*—amounts ranging from $100 to $50,000 to people such as single mothers and public housing tenants.

- *Export Express*—loans made to small businesses wishing to export. The maximum guaranteed loan amount is $500,000.

- *Community Adjustment and Investment Program (CAIP)*—loans to businesses to create new, sustainable jobs or to preserve existing jobs in eligible communities that have lost jobs due to changing trade patterns with Mexico and Canada following the adoption of NAFTA.

- *Pollution control loans*—loans to eligible small businesses for the financing of the planning, design, or installation of a pollution control facility. This facility must prevent, reduce, abate, or control any form of pollution, including recycling.

- *504 certified development company (CDC) loans*—loans for purchasing major fixed assets, such as land and buildings for businesses in eligible communities, typically rural communities or urban areas needing revitalization. The program's goal is to expand business ownership by minorities, women, and veterans. The maximum guaranteed loan amount is $1.5 million.

The SBA reduced the size of its application from 150 pages to one page for loans under $50,000. In February 2011, the SBA introduced a new program called Community Advantage and Small Loan Advantage program, which is aimed at providing a simpler and easier way for lenders to make smaller loans to businesses in underserved areas. However, a month later the House Small Business Committee recommended the SBA budget be cut and that no money be used for the new program.[43] Confused? Since government regulations are constantly changing, you may want to go to the SBA's website (www.sba.gov) for the latest information about SBA programs and other business services.

Obtaining money from banks, venture capitalists, and government sources is very difficult for most small businesses. (You will learn more about financing in Chapter 18.) Those who do survive the planning and financing of their new ventures are eager to get their businesses up and running. Your success in running a business depends on many factors, especially knowing your customers, managing your employees, and keeping good records.

Knowing Your Customers

One of the most important elements of small-business success is knowing the **market**, which consists of consumers with unsatisfied wants and needs who have both resources and willingness to buy. Most of our students have the willingness to own a brand-new Maserati sports car. However, few have the resources necessary to satisfy this want. Would they be a good market for a luxury car dealer?

market
People with unsatisfied wants and needs who have both the resources and the willingness to buy.

Once you have identified your market and its needs, you must set out to fill those needs. How? Offer top quality at a fair price with great service. Remember, it isn't enough to get customers—you have to *keep* them. As Victoria Jackson, founder of the $50 million company Victoria Jackson Cosmetics, says of the stars who push her products on television infomercials, "All the glamorous faces in the world wouldn't mean a thing if my customers weren't happy with the product and didn't come back for more." Everything must be geared to bring customers the satisfaction they deserve.

One of the greatest advantages small businesses have is the ability to know their customers better and adapt quickly to their ever-changing needs. You will gain more insights about markets in Chapters 13–16. Now let's consider effectively managing the employees who help you serve your market.

Managing Employees

As a business grows, it becomes impossible for an entrepreneur to oversee every detail, even by putting in 60 hours per week. This means that hiring, training, and motivating employees are critical.

It is not easy to find good help when you offer less money, skimpier benefits, and less room for advancement than larger firms do. That's one reason employee relations is important for small-business management. Employees of small companies are often more satisfied with their jobs than are their counterparts in big business. Why? Quite often they find their jobs more challenging, their ideas more accepted, and their bosses more respectful.[44]

Often entrepreneurs are reluctant to recognize that to keep growing, they must delegate authority to others. Who should have this delegated authority, and how much?

This can be a particularly touchy issue in small businesses with long-term employees, and in family businesses. As you might expect, entrepreneurs who have built their companies from scratch often feel compelled to promote employees who have been with them from the start—even when they aren't qualified to serve as managers. Common sense tells you this could hurt the business. The idea that you must promote or can't fire people because "they're family" can also hinder growth. Entrepreneurs best serve themselves and the business if they gradually recruit and groom employees for management positions, enhancing trust and support between them. You'll learn more about managing employees in Chapters 7–12.

Keeping Records

Small-business owners often say the most important assistance they received in starting and managing their business was in accounting.[45] A businessperson who sets up an effective accounting system early will save much grief later. Computers simplify record keeping and enable a small-business owner to daily follow sales, expenses, and profits. An inexpensive computer system can also help owners with inventory control, customer records, and payroll.

Many business failures are caused by poor accounting practices that lead to costly mistakes. A good accountant can help you decide whether to buy or lease equipment and whether to own or rent a building. He or she may also help you with tax planning, financial forecasting, choosing sources of financing, and writing requests for funds.

Other small-business owners may tell you where to find an accountant experienced in small business. It pays to shop around for advice. You'll learn more about accounting in Chapter 17.

Looking for Help

Small-business owners have learned, sometimes the hard way, that they need outside consulting advice early in the process. This is especially true of legal, tax, and accounting advice but also of marketing, finance, and other areas. Most small and medium-sized firms cannot afford to hire such experts as employees, so they must turn to outside assistance.

A necessary and invaluable aide is a competent, experienced lawyer who knows and understands small businesses. Lawyers can help with leases, contracts, partnership agreements, and protection against liabilities.[46] They don't have to be expensive. In fact, several prepaid legal plans offer services such as drafting legal documents for a low annual rate. Of course, you can find plenty of legal services online. The SBA offers plain-English guides and mini-tutorials that will help you gain a basic understanding of the laws that affect each phase of the life of a small business. FindForms.com offers a search tool that helps you find free legal forms from all over the web as well as advice, links, books, and more. Remember, "free" isn't a bargain if the information isn't correct, so check the sources carefully and double-check any legal actions with an attorney.

Make your marketing decisions long before you introduce a product or open a store. An inexpensive marketing research study may help you determine where to locate, whom to select as your target market, and what is an effective strategy for reaching it.

Not all small businesses stay small; some become business superstars. Take Mattel, for example. Mattel founders Ruth and Elliot Handler started their business in their garage—making picture frames. When they found that the dollhouse furniture they made with the wood scraps sold better than the frames, they changed their business. Today toys like Barbie helped Mattel grow into a $6.4 billion business.

Small business owner Michelle Matta received several microloans from the SBA to start and expand her promotional products business. In addition to financing, what other forms of business assistance do entrepreneurs like Matta need?

Thus a marketing consultant with small-business experience can be of great help to you, especially one who has had experience with the Internet and social media.

Two other invaluable experts are a commercial loan officer and an insurance agent. The commercial loan officer can help you design an acceptable business plan and give you valuable financial advice as well as lend you money when you need it. An insurance agent will explain all the risks associated with a small business and how to cover them most efficiently with insurance and other means like safety devices and sprinkler systems.

An important source of information for small businesses is the **Service Corps of Retired Executives (SCORE)**. This SBA office has more than 10,500 volunteers from industry, trade associations, and education who counsel small businesses at no cost (except for expenses).[47] You can find a SCORE counselor by logging on to www.score.org. The SBA also offers a free, comprehensive online entrepreneurship course for aspiring entrepreneurs.

Often business professors from local colleges will advise small-business owners free or for a small fee. Some universities have clubs or programs that provide consulting services by master of business administration (MBA) candidates for a nominal fee. The University of Maryland and Virginia Tech have internship programs that pair MBA students with budding companies in local incubator programs. The incubator companies pay half the intern's salary, which is around $20 an hour.

It is also wise to seek the counsel of other small-business owners. The website YoungEntrepreneur.com offers experienced entrepreneurs and young start-ups an open forum to exchange advice and ideas. Visitors have access to articles on marketing, business planning, incorporation, and financial management.

Other sources of counsel include local chambers of commerce, the Better Business Bureau, national and local trade associations, the business reference section of your library, and many small-business-related sites on the Internet. Some can match your consulting needs with the proper consultant, like Company Expert (www.4consulting-services.com).

Service Corps of Retired Executives (SCORE)
An SBA office with volunteers from industry, trade associations, and education who counsel small businesses at no cost (except for expenses).

- A business plan is probably the most important document a small business owner will ever create. There are nine sections in the business plan outline on pages I65–I66. Can you describe at least five of those sections now?

LEARNING goal 5

Outline the advantages and disadvantages small businesses have in entering global markets.

GOING GLOBAL: SMALL-BUSINESS PROSPECTS

As we noted in Chapter 3, there are over 310 million people in the United States but more than 6.9 billion people in the world.[48] Obviously, the world market is a much larger, more lucrative market for small businesses than the United States alone. In spite of that potential, many small businesses still do not think globally. Only 1 percent of small businesses now export, but half are expected to engage in global trade by 2015. Small businesses are well on their way to meeting those expectations; small and medium-sized business accounted for 99 percent of the growth in exporting firms in recent years.[49]

Technological advances have helped increase small business exporting. PayPal makes it possible for small businesses to get paid automatically when they conduct global business online. The Internet also helps small businesses find customers without the expense of international travel. As people acquire more wealth, they often demand specialized products that are not mass-produced and are willing to pay more for niche goods that small businesses offer. Dave Hammond, inventor and founder of Wizard Vending, began to push his gumball machines into the global market via a website. In the site's first year, he sold machines in Austria, Belgium, and Germany. The nearby Reaching Beyond Our Borders box offers examples of entrepreneurs who are thriving in emerging markets.

Still, many small businesses have difficulty getting started in global business. Why are so many missing the boat to the huge global markets? Primarily, because the voyage includes a few major hurdles: (1) Financing is often difficult to find, (2) would-be exporters don't know how to get started and do not understand the cultural differences between markets, and (3) the bureaucratic paperwork can threaten to bury a small business.

Beside the fact that most of the world's market lies outside the United States, there are other good reasons for going global. Exporting can absorb excess inventory, soften downturns in the domestic market, and extend product lives. It can also spice up dull routines.

Small businesses have several advantages over large businesses in international trade:

- Overseas buyers often enjoy dealing with individuals rather than with large corporate bureaucracies.
- Small companies can usually begin shipping much faster.

Emerging Markets, Emerging Entrepreneurship

A good entrepreneur finds a need in the market and fills it with a new business. For emerging markets, entire industries and services are wide open for innovation. Given the technological advances of the past few decades, the amount of resources required to start a business venture in emerging markets is often lower now than in the past.

These factors are contributing to an entrepreneurial revolution in many developing nations. And the growth isn't just occurring in markets that economists have been watching for years like India and Brazil. In Lebanon's capital of Beirut, for instance, Christine Sfeir opened the country's first Dunkin' Donuts at age 22. More than 10 years later, Sfeir now owns 30 locations throughout Lebanon. Stories like Sfeir's are becoming more common as educated professionals hailing from the Middle East, Africa, and Southeast Asia return home with global experience and credentials. Many entrepreneurs in the developing world hold degrees and have worked at high-level companies like Toyota and Pepsi.

Opportunities for growth are so vast in emerging markets that entrepreneurs must often expand into different areas of business in order for their first venture to grow. When Aisha Natto wanted to expand her high-end eyewear chain in Saudi Arabia, the company first had to build a lens manufacturing plant just to keep up with demand. Not only did this help grow the business, it also provided Natto and her employees with knowledge about several fields of business. Such a wide range of expertise almost ensures that entrepreneurial expansion in the developing world should continue for years to come.

Sources: Anne S. Habiby and Deirdre M. Coyle, Jr., "The High-Intensity Entrepreneur," *Harvard Business Review,* September 2010; and Dayananda Yumlembam, "Foreigners Get Incubation Tips at EDI," *The Times of India,* April 4, 2011.

- Small companies can provide a wide variety of suppliers.
- Small companies can give customers personal service and undivided attention, because each overseas account is a major source of business to them.

A good place to start finding information about exporting is the Department of Commerce's Bureau of Industry and Security (www.bis.doc.gov). Other sources include the SBA's list of international business resources (www.sba.gov/hotlist/internat.html). The SBA's Export Express loan program provides export financing opportunities for small businesses. The program is designed to finance a variety of needs of small-business exporters, including participation in foreign trade shows, catalog translations for use in foreign markets, lines of credit for export purposes, and real estate and equipment for the production of goods or services to be exported.

progress assessment

- Why do many small businesses avoid doing business globally?
- What are some of the advantages small businesses have over large businesses in selling in global markets?

summary

Learning Goal 1. Explain why people take the risks of entrepreneurship; list the attributes of successful entrepreneurs; and describe entrepreneurial teams, intrapreneurs, and home- and web-based businesses.

- **What are a few of the reasons people start their own businesses?**

Reasons include profit, independence, opportunity, and challenge.

- **What are the attributes of successful entrepreneurs?**

Successful entrepreneurs are self-directed, self-nurturing, action-oriented, highly energetic, and tolerant of uncertainty.

- **What have modern entrepreneurs done to ensure longer terms of management?**

They have formed entrepreneurial teams with expertise in the many skills needed to start and manage a business.

- **What is a micropreneur?**

Micropreneurs are people willing to accept the risk of starting and managing the type of business that remains small, lets them do the kind of work they want to do, and offers them a balanced lifestyle.

- **What is intrapreneuring?**

Intrapreneuring is the establishment of entrepreneurial centers within a larger firm where people can innovate and develop new product ideas internally.

- **Why has there been such an increase in the number of home-based and web-based businesses in the last few years?**

The increase in power and decrease in price of computer technology have leveled the field and made it possible for small businesses to compete against larger companies—regardless of location.

Learning Goal 2. Discuss the importance of small business to the American economy and summarize the major causes of small business failure.

- **Why are small businesses important to the U.S. economy?**

Small business accounts for almost 50 percent of gross domestic product (GDP). Perhaps more important to tomorrow's graduates, 80 percent of U.S. workers' first jobs are in small businesses.

- **What does the *small* in small business mean?**

The Small Business Administration defines a small business as one that is independently owned and operated and not dominant in its field of operation, and that meets certain standards of size in terms of employees or sales (depending on the size of others in the industry).

- **Why do many small businesses fail?**

Many small businesses fail because of managerial incompetence and inadequate financial planning. See Figure 6.3 for a list of causes of small-business failure.

Learning Goal 3. Summarize ways to learn about how small businesses operate.

- **What hints would you give someone who wants to learn about starting a small business?**

First, learn from others. Take courses and talk with some small-business owners. Second, get some experience working for others. Third, take over a successful firm. Finally, study the latest in small-business management techniques, including the use of computers for functions like payroll, inventory control, and mailing lists.

Learning Goal 4. Analyze what it takes to start and run a small business.

- **What goes into a business plan?**

See the Business Plan on pages 165–166.

- **What sources of funds should someone wanting to start a new business consider investigating?**

A new entrepreneur has several potential sources of capital: personal savings, relatives, former employers, banks, finance companies, venture capital organizations, government agencies, and more.

- **What are some of the special problems that small-business owners have in dealing with employees?**

Small-business owners often have difficulty finding competent employees and grooming employees for management responsibilities.

- **Where can budding entrepreneurs find help in starting their businesses?**

Help can come from many sources: accountants, lawyers, marketing researchers, loan officers, insurance agents, the SBA, SBDCs, SBICs, and even college professors.

Learning Goal 5. Outline the advantages and disadvantages small businesses have in entering global markets.

- **What are some advantages small businesses have over large businesses in global markets?**

Foreign buyers enjoy dealing with individuals rather than large corporations because (1) small companies provide a wider variety of suppliers and can ship products more quickly and (2) small companies give more personal service. •

- **Why don't more small businesses start trading globally?**

There are several reasons: (1) financing is often difficult to find, (2) many people don't know how to get started and do not understand the cultural differences in foreign markets, and (3) the bureaucratic red tape is often overwhelming.

key terms

affiliate marketing 156
business plan 163
enterprise zones 157
entrepreneurial team 152
entrepreneurship 149
incubators 158

intrapreneurs 157
market 169
micropreneurs 152
Service Corps of Retired Executives (SCORE) 171
small business 159

Small Business Administration (SBA) 168
Small Business Investment Company (SBIC) Program 168
venture capitalists 167

critical thinking

1. Do you have the entrepreneurial spirit? What makes you think that?

2. Are there any similarities between the characteristics demanded of an entrepreneur and those of a professional athlete? Would an athlete be a good prospect for entrepreneurship? Why or why not? Could teamwork be important in an entrepreneurial effort? Why or why not?

3. Imagine yourself starting a small business. What kind of business would it be? How much competition is there? What could you do to make your business more attractive than those of competitors? Would you be willing to work 60 to 70 hours a week to make the business successful?

developing workplace skills

1. Find issues of *Entrepreneur, Black Enterprise,* and *Inc.* magazines in the library or on the Internet. Read about the entrepreneurs who are heading today's dynamic new businesses. Write a profile about one.

2. Select a small business that looks attractive as a career possibility for you. Talk to at least one person who manages such a business. Ask how he or she started it. Ask about financing; human resource management (hiring, firing, training, scheduling); accounting issues; and other managerial matters. Prepare a summary of your findings, including whether the person's job was rewarding, interesting, and challenging—and why or why not.

3. Contact the Small Business Administration by visiting a local office or the organization's website at www.sba.gov. Write a brief summary of the services the SBA offers.

4. Select a small business in your area or a surrounding area that has failed. List the factors you think led to its failure. Compile a list of actions the business owners might have taken to keep the company in business.

5. Choose a partner from among your classmates and put together a list of factors that might mean the difference between success and failure of a new company entering the business technology industry. Can small start-ups realistically hope to compete with companies such as Microsoft and Intel? Discuss the list and your conclusions in class.

taking it to the net

Purpose

To assess your potential to succeed as an entrepreneur and to evaluate a sample business plan.

Exercise

1. Go to www.bizmove.com/other/quiz.htm and take the interactive entrepreneurial quiz to find out whether you have the qualities to be a successful entrepreneur.

2. If you have entrepreneurial traits and decide you would like to start your own business, you'll need to develop a business plan. Go to www.bplans.com/sample_business_plans.cfm and click on Coffee Shops. Review the sample business plan for Internet Café. Although the plan may not follow the same format as the business plan outline on pages 165–166, does it contain all the necessary information listed in the outline? If not, what is missing?

casing the web

To access the case "BMOC; Starting a Small Business at School," visit **www.mhhe.com/ubl0e**

video case

To access the video case featuring Pillow Pets, visit **www.mhhe.com/ubl0e**

MANAGEMENT
and
Leadership

John Mackey has become one of the more controversial and successful entrepreneurs and managers in America. After attending the University of Texas, Mackey went to work in a vegetarian co-op in Austin where he thought he could "meet some interesting women." Soon he became the co-op's food buyer and later went to work in a natural foods store.

Mackey and his girlfriend, Renee Lawson Hardy, borrowed $45,000 from friends and family and eventually opened their own store called SaferWay Natural Foods. (The name was a spoof of Safeway, which had several stores in Austin at the time.) Shortly after the store opened the couple was kicked out of their apartment for storing food there and they decided to move into the store. Since the building was zoned commercial, there was no shower so they bathed in the Hobart dishwasher that had an attached hose. (Nobody said entrepreneurship is easy!)

In 1980 SaferWay merged with a competitor and became Whole Foods Market. The first Whole Foods store opened with only 19 employees. There were less than a half dozen natural food stores in all of the United States at the time. Today Whole Foods Market is a world leader in natural and organic foods with over 300 stores in North America and the United Kingdom. Whole Foods Market is consistently listed as one of *Fortune* magazine's "100 Best Companies to Work For." Let's see why.

You would expect someone like Mackey to have a different view of management, and you would be right. At Whole Foods, titles don't count as much as the ability to get along with others and make decisions collectively. As a consequence, decisions may take longer to make, but implementation is faster. All the executives of the company make the same compensation. Mackey now shares leadership of the company with Walter Robb as co-CEOs (Chief Executive Officers).

Mackey and his team say that their success is due largely to their focus on the company's mission: Whole Foods, Whole people, Whole planet. As you can see, one of the core values at Whole Foods is the happiness and excellence of its people. Whole Foods recruits the best people and empowers them to make their own decisions. They believe that their decentralized self-directed team culture creates a respectful workplace where people are treated fairly and are highly motivated to succeed. Mackey believes that business can be a "win–win" situation. For example, if Whole Foods hires good people and trains them well, then those people will treat customers well, and both will be happier as a result: win–win.

This chapter is all about leadership and management. You will learn that shared leadership is more widespread than you might have imagined. You will also learn about the functions of management and how management differs from leadership. All in all, you should get a better idea of what leaders and managers do and how they do it.

Sources: John Mackey, "What Is It That Only I Can Do?" *Harvard Business Review,* January–February 2011; and www.wholefoods.com, accessed March 2011.

profile

Getting to Know

X *John Mackey*

Founder of Whole Foods Market

Like many companies today, this company uses social media to communicate with customers. In one case, a customer complained on Twitter when the company sent a Blackberry to replace an iPhone that had failed. The company responded quickly with a replacement iPhone. The customer then tweeted about the company's great customer service. Name that company. (The answer is in the chapter.)

LEARNING goal 1

Describe the changes occurring today in the management function.

MANAGERS' ROLES ARE EVOLVING

Managers, like John Mackey, must practice the art of getting things done through organizational resources, which include workers, financial resources, information, and equipment. At one time, managers were called "bosses" and their job consisted of telling people what to do, watching over them to be sure they did it, and reprimanding those who didn't. Many managers still behave that way. Perhaps you've witnessed such behavior; some coaches use this style.

Today, however, some managers tend to be more progressive. For example, they emphasize teams and team building; they create drop-in centers, team

Here a Best Buy manager rallies his employees just before opening the store's doors. Rather than telling employees exactly what to do, managers today tend to give their employees enough independence to make their own informed decisions about how best to please customers. How do you think most employees respond to this empowerment on the job?

spaces, and open work areas.[1] They may change the definition of *work* from a task you do for a specified period in a specific place to something you do anywhere, anytime. They tend to guide, train, support, motivate, and coach employees rather than tell them what to do.[2] Managers of high-tech firms, for instance, realize that many workers often know more about technology than they do.[3] Thus most modern managers emphasize teamwork and cooperation rather than discipline and order giving. They may also open their books to employees to share the company's financials.[4]

The years 2008–2011 were particularly hard on managers and workers. The financial crisis forced many leading firms—like Boeing, IBM, and Caterpillar— to fire managers and lower-level workers. PepsiCo's CEO Indra Nooyi won praise for rallying employees amid the gloom. But she too announced plans to cut some 3,000 employees. Furthermore, it became more difficult to get financing for new ventures or to modernize existing plants. Managers tended to be cautious in starting new ventures as they waited to see what the economy would do. That hesitancy contributed to the high unemployment the U.S. experienced in 2010–2011.[5]

The people entering management today are different from those who entered in the past.[6] Leaders of Fortune 100 companies tend to be younger, more of them are female, and fewer of them were educated at elite universities. Managers in the future are more likely to be working in teams and assuming completely new roles in the firm. For one thing, they'll be doing more expansion overseas. Further, they will be taking a leadership role in adapting to climate change. They will also be more concerned with recycling and other "green" issues.[7]

What these changes mean for you is that management will demand a new kind of person: a skilled communicator and team player as well as a planner, organizer, motivator, and leader. Future managers will need to be more globally prepared; that is, they need skills such as adaptability, foreign language skills, and ease in other cultures.[8] We'll address these trends in the next few chapters to help you decide whether management is the kind of career you would like.

Ursula Burns, for example, is the new CEO of Xerox. She is a mechanical engineer, and the first African-American woman to run a Fortune 500 company. She was outspoken and blunt in a culture that was probably overly genteel.[9] Burns was just one of the women who inspired an article called "The Year of the Business Woman" in *U.S. News and World Report*.[10] You will read more about Burns in the next chapter. In the following sections, we shall discuss management in general and the functions that Ursula Burns and other new managers are performing.

LEARNING goal 2

Describe the four functions of management.

THE FOUR FUNCTIONS OF MANAGEMENT

The following definition of management provides the outline of this chapter: **Management** is the process used to accomplish organizational goals through planning, organizing, leading, and controlling people and other organizational resources (see Figure 7.1 on p. 182).

management
The process used to accomplish organizational goals through planning, organizing, leading, and controlling people and other organizational resources.

figure 7.1

WHAT MANAGERS DO
Some modern managers perform all of these tasks with the full cooperation and participation of workers. Empowering employees means allowing them to participate more fully in decision making.

Planning
- Setting organizational goals.
- Developing strategies to reach those goals.
- Determining resources needed.
- Setting precise standards.

Organizing
- Allocating resources, assigning tasks, and establishing procedures for accomplishing goals.
- Preparing a structure (organization chart) showing lines of authority and responsibility.
- Recruiting, selecting, training, and developing employees.
- Placing employees where they'll be most effective.

Leading
- Guiding and motivating employees to work effectively to accomplish organizational goals and objectives.
- Giving assignments.
- Explaining routines.
- Clarifying policies.
- Providing feedback on performance.

Controlling
- Measuring results against corporate objectives.
- Monitoring performance relative to standards.
- Rewarding outstanding performance.
- Taking corrective action when necessary.

planning
A management function that includes anticipating trends and determining the best strategies and tactics to achieve organizational goals and objectives.

organizing
A management function that includes designing the structure of the organization and creating conditions and systems in which everyone and everything work together to achieve the organization's goals and objectives.

Planning is what helps managers understand the environment in which their business must operate. When people's tastes and preferences for restaurant meals change, food services managers need to be ready to respond with menu alternatives. What changes have occurred in your own preferences?

Planning includes anticipating trends and determining the best strategies and tactics to achieve organizational goals and objectives. One of the major objectives of organizations is to please customers.[11] The trend today is to have *planning teams* to help monitor the environment, find business opportunities, and watch for challenges. *Planning* is a key management function because accomplishing the other functions depends heavily on having a good plan.

Organizing includes designing the structure of the organization and creating conditions and systems in which everyone and everything works together to achieve the organization's goals and objectives. Many of today's organizations are being designed around pleasing the customer at a profit. Thus they must remain flexible and adaptable, because when customer needs change, firms must change with them. Whole Foods Market, for example, is known for its high-quality, high-priced food items.[12] But it has introduced many lower-cost items to adjust to the financial losses of its customer base. General Motors lost much of its customer base to manufacturers of more fuel-efficient cars. It hopes to win back market share by offering hydrogen-powered or electric vehicles that cost less to run.[13] GM has had some success in doing that.

Leading means creating a vision for the organization and communicating, guiding, training, coaching, and motivating others to achieve goals and objectives in a timely manner. The trend is to empower employees, giving them as much freedom as possible to become self-directed and self-motivated. This function was once known as *directing;* that is, telling employees exactly what to do. In many smaller firms, that is still the manager's role. In most large firms, however, managers no longer tell people exactly what to do because knowledge workers and others often know how to do their jobs better than the manager does. Nonetheless, leadership is still necessary to keep employees focused on the right tasks at the right time.

Controlling establishes clear standards to determine whether an organization is progressing toward its goals and objectives, rewarding people for doing a good job, and taking corrective action if they are not. Basically, it means measuring whether what actually occurs meets the organization's goals.

Planning, organizing, leading, and controlling are the heart of management, so let's explore them in more detail. The process begins with planning; we'll look at that right after the Progress Assessment.

progress assessment

- What are some of the changes happening in management today?
- What's the definition of *management* used in this chapter?
- What are the four functions of management?

LEARNING goal **3**

Relate the planning process and decision making to the accomplishment of company goals.

PLANNING AND DECISION MAKING

Planning, the first managerial function, is setting the organization's vision (including its mission statement), goals, and objectives. Executives find planning to be their most valuable tool. A **vision** is more than a goal; it's a broad explanation of why the organization exists and where it's trying to go. It gives the organization a sense of purpose and a set of values that unite workers in a common destiny. Managing an organization without first establishing a vision is like getting everyone in a rowboat excited about going somewhere, but not telling them exactly where. The boat will just keep changing directions rather than speeding toward an agreed-on goal.[14]

Top management usually sets the vision for the organization and then often works with others in the firm to establish a mission statement. A **mission statement** outlines the organization's fundamental purposes. It should address:

- The organization's self-concept.
- Its philosophy.
- Long-term survival needs.
- Customer needs.
- Social responsibility.
- Nature of the product or service.

The mission statement becomes the foundation for setting specific goals and objectives. **Goals** are the broad, long-term accomplishments an organization

leading
Creating a vision for the organization and guiding, training, coaching, and motivating others to work effectively to achieve the organization's goals and objectives.

controlling
A management function that involves establishing clear standards to determine whether or not an organization is progressing toward its goals and objectives, rewarding people for doing a good job, and taking corrective action if they are not.

vision
An encompassing explanation of why the organization exists and where it's trying to head.

mission statement
An outline of the fundamental purposes of an organization.

goals
The broad, long-term accomplishments an organization wishes to attain.

objectives
Specific, short-term statements detailing how to achieve the organization's goals.

wishes to attain. Because workers and management need to agree on them, setting goals is often a team process. **Objectives** are specific, short-term statements detailing *how to achieve* the organization's goals. One of your goals for reading this chapter, for example, may be to learn basic concepts of management. An objective you could use to achieve this goal is to answer the chapter's Progress Assessment questions.

Planning is a continuous process. A plan that worked yesterday may not be successful in today's market.[15] Most planning also follows a pattern. The procedure you'll follow in planning your life and career is basically the same as the one businesses use. It answers several fundamental questions:

1. *What is the situation now?* What are the success factors affecting the industry participants and how do we compare? What is the state of the economy and other environments?[16] What opportunities exist for meeting people's needs? What products and customers are most profitable? Who are our major competitors?[17] What threats are there to our business? These questions are part of **SWOT analysis,** which analyzes the organization's **s**trengths and **w**eaknesses, and the **o**pportunities and **t**hreats it faces, usually in that order. Opportunities and threats are often external to the firm and cannot always be anticipated.[18] See the Reaching Beyond Our Borders box for an example of how environmental threats affect businesses.

SWOT analysis
A planning tool used to analyze an organization's strengths, weaknesses, opportunities, and threats.

Weaknesses and strengths are more often internal and therefore more within reach of being measured and fixed. Figure 7.2 lists some of the general issues companies consider when conducting a SWOT analysis: What external success factors affect the industry? How does our firm measure up to other firms? What are our social objectives? What are our personal development objectives? What can we do to survive and prosper during a recession? For more on SWOT analysis, see the Taking It to the Net exercise at the end of this chapter.

2. *How can we get to our goal from here?* Answering this question is often the most important part of planning. It takes four forms: strategic, tactical, operational, and contingency (see Figure 7.3).

figure 7.2

SWOT MATRIX

This matrix identifies potential strengths, weaknesses, opportunities, and threats organizations may consider in a SWOT analysis.

Potential Internal STRENGTHS	Potential Internal WEAKNESSES
• Core competencies in key areas • An acknowledged market leader • Well-conceived functional area strategies • Proven management • Cost advantages • Better advertising campaigns	• No clear strategic direction • Obsolete facilities • Subpar profitability • Lack of managerial depth and talent • Weak market image • Too narrow a product line
Potential External OPPORTUNITIES	Potential External THREATS
• Ability to serve additional customer groups • Expand product lines • Ability to transfer skills/technology to new products • Falling trade barriers in attractive foreign markets • Complacency among rival firms • Ability to grow due to increases in market demand	• Entry of lower-cost foreign competitors • Rising sales of substitute products • Slower market growth • Costly regulatory requirements • Vulnerability to recession and business cycles • Changing buyer needs and tastes

The Japanese Crisis, Terrorism, and American Business

Few catastrophes can compare to the one that occurred in Japan in March 2011. A 9.0 magnitude earthquake followed by a tsunami completely devastated whole cities and ports. The looming failure of nuclear power plants only added to the devastation. Such disasters point out the need for contingency planning and for disaster planning. It will take a long time for Japanese companies to recover from the crisis. What about U.S. companies and other companies throughout the world that rely on Japan for parts and products?

Over 30 U.S. corporations (e.g., Rambus, Coach, Callaway, and Tiffany) get at least 15 percent of their sales from Japan. About 75 percent of Aflac's 2010 sales came from Japan. Texas Instruments had a silicon wafer plant in Japan that experienced substantial damage. Furthermore, the damage in Japan may disrupt the flow of auto and tech supplies from Japan to U.S. and other foreign producers. Japanese companies supply 35 percent of Boeing's new 787 Dreamliner, for example.

The global supply chain not only is affected by natural disasters such as the one in Japan, but is constantly threatened by man-made and other disasters, such as the consequences of war and terrorism. You can see how strategic planning and contingency planning are critical to the long-term success of firms. That often means cooperating with companies across the globe and making plans for what to do when disasters happen.

Sources: Janet Napolitano, "How to Secure the Global Supply Chain," *The Wall Street Journal,* January 6, 2011; Thomas Black, "The Impact on American Companies," *Bloomberg Businessweek,* March 21–March 27, 2011; and Joseph Sternberg, "Now Comes the Global Revolution in Services," *The Wall Street Journal,* February 10, 2011.

Strategic planning is done by top management and determines the major goals of the organization and the policies, procedures, strategies, and resources it will need to achieve them. *Policies* are broad guidelines for action, and *strategies* determine the best way to use resources. At the strategic planning stage, top managers of the company decide which customers to serve, when to serve them, what products or services to sell, and the geographic areas in which to compete.[19] Take Taco Bell, for example. Recognizing the economic slump, the company introduced a "value menu" of items like cheese roll-ups and bean burritos with prices starting at 79 cents. It also went after the "fourth-meal" (late-night) crowd and introduced several low-calorie, low-fat Fresco items.

> **strategic planning**
> The process of determining the major goals of the organization and the policies and strategies for obtaining and using resources to achieve those goals.

FORMS OF PLANNING

STRATEGIC PLANNING
The setting of broad, long-range goals by top managers

TACTICAL PLANNING
The identification of specific, short-range objectives by lower-level managers

CONTINGENCY PLANNING
Backup plans in case primary plans fail

OPERATIONAL PLANNING
The setting of work standards and schedules

figure 7.3

PLANNING FUNCTIONS
Very few firms bother to make contingency plans. If something changes the market, such companies may be slow to respond. Most organizations do strategic, tactical, and operational planning.

This strategy resulted in an 8 percent increase in sales. Blockbuster was not as successful in fighting off the introduction of new technology, making the company seemingly obsolete.[20]

In today's rapidly changing environment, strategic planning is becoming more difficult because changes are occurring so fast that plans—even those set for just months into the future—may soon be obsolete. Think of how the amusement park company Six Flags had to change its plans when gas went from a couple of dollars per gallon to over four dollars and then dropped back to the three-dollar range again. Think too of how Japanese companies had to respond to the earthquake and tsunami that created such devastation in a short period of time in 2011.[21]

Clearly, some companies are making shorter-term plans that allow for quick responses to customer needs and requests. The goal is to be flexible and responsive to the market.

Tactical planning is the process of developing detailed, short-term statements about what is to be done, who is to do it, and how. Managers or teams of managers at lower levels of the organization normally make tactical plans. Such plans can include setting annual budgets and deciding on other activities necessary to meet strategic objectives. If the strategic plan of a truck manufacturer, for example, is to sell more trucks in the South, the tactical plan might be to fund more research of southern truck drivers' wants and needs, and to plan advertising to reach them.

Operational planning is the process of setting work standards and schedules necessary to implement the company's tactical objectives. Whereas strategic planning looks at the organization as a whole, operational planning focuses on specific supervisors, department managers, and individual employees. The operational plan is the department manager's tool for daily and weekly operations. An operational plan may include, for example, the specific dates for certain truck parts to be completed and the quality specifications they must meet.

Contingency planning is the process of preparing alternative courses of action the firm can use if its primary plans don't work out. The economic and competitive environments change so rapidly that it's wise to have alternative

tactical planning
The process of developing detailed, short-term statements about what is to be done, who is to do it, and how it is to be done.

operational planning
The process of setting work standards and schedules necessary to implement the company's tactical objectives.

contingency planning
The process of preparing alternative courses of action that may be used if the primary plans don't achieve the organization's objectives.

Organizations of all kinds need contingency plans for unexpected events. Here Memphis firefighters help mock wounded during a drill preparing for a possible terrorist attack. What contingency plans are you aware of on your campus or at work?

plans of action ready in anticipation of such changes.[22] For example, if an organization doesn't meet its sales goals by a certain date, the contingency plan may call for more advertising or a cut in prices at that time. Crisis planning is a part of contingency planning that anticipates sudden changes in the environment. For example, many cities and businesses have developed plans to respond to terrorist attacks. You can imagine how important such plans would be to hospitals, airlines, the police, and public transportation authorities.

Instead of creating detailed strategic plans, the leaders of market-based companies (companies that respond quickly to changes in competition or to other environmental changes) often simply set direction. They want to stay flexible, listen to customers, and seize opportunities—expected or not. Think of how stores selling to teenagers must adapt to style changes.

The opportunities, however, must fit into the company's overall goals and objectives; if not, the company could lose its focus. Clearly, then, much of management and planning requires decision making.

Decision Making: Finding the Best Alternative

Planning and all the other management functions require decision making. **Decision making** is choosing among two or more alternatives, which sounds easier than it is. In fact, decision making is the heart of all the management functions.

The *rational decision-making model* is a series of steps managers often follow to make logical, intelligent, and well-founded decisions. Think of the steps as the seven Ds of decision making:

1. Define the situation.
2. Describe and collect needed information.
3. Develop alternatives.
4. Develop agreement among those involved.
5. Decide which alternative is best.
6. Do what is indicated (begin implementation).
7. Determine whether the decision was a good one, and follow up.

Managers don't always go through this seven-step process. Sometimes they have to make decisions *on the spot*—with little information available. They still must make good decisions in all such circumstances. **Problem solving** is less formal than decision making and usually calls for quicker action to resolve everyday issues. Both decision making and problem solving call for a lot of judgment.

Problem-solving teams are two or more workers assigned to solve a specific problem (e.g., Why aren't customers buying our service contracts?). Problem-solving techniques include **brainstorming**, that is, coming up with as many solutions as possible in a short period of time with no censoring of ideas. Another technique is called **PMI**, or listing all the **p**luses for a solution in one column, all the **m**inuses in another, and the **i**mplications in a third. The idea is to make sure the pluses exceed the minuses.

You can try using the PMI system on some of your personal decisions to get some practice. For example, should you stay home and study tonight? List all the pluses in one column: better grades, more self-esteem, more responsible behavior, and so on. In the other column, put the minuses: boredom, less fun, and so on. We hope the pluses outweigh the minuses most of the time and that you study often. But sometimes it's best to go out and have some fun, as long as doing so won't hurt your grades or job prospects.

decision making
Choosing among two or more alternatives.

problem solving
The process of solving the everyday problems that occur. Problem solving is less formal than decision making and usually calls for quicker action.

brainstorming
Coming up with as many solutions to a problem as possible in a short period of time with no censoring of ideas.

PMI
Listing all the Pluses for a solution in one column, all the Minuses in another, and the Implications in a third column.

- What's the difference between goals and objectives?
- What does a company analyze when it does a SWOT analysis?
- What are the differences between strategic, tactical, and operational planning?
- What are the seven Ds in decision making?

LEARNING goal 4

Describe the organizing function of management.

organization chart
A visual device that shows relationships among people and divides the organization's work; it shows who reports to whom.

ORGANIZING: CREATING A UNIFIED SYSTEM

After managers have planned a course of action, they must organize the firm to accomplish their goals. That means allocating resources (such as funds for various departments), assigning tasks, and establishing procedures. An **organization chart** is a visual device that shows relationships among people and divides the organization's work; it shows who reports to whom (see Figure 7.4).[23]

Top management, the highest level, consists of the president and other key company executives who develop strategic plans. Job titles and abbreviations you're likely to see often are chief executive officer (CEO), chief operating officer (COO), chief financial officer (CFO), and chief information officer (CIO) or

top management
Highest level of management, consisting of the president and other key company executives who develop strategic plans.

figure 7.4

LEVELS OF MANAGEMENT
This figure shows the three levels of management. In many firms, there are several levels of middle management. Recently, however, firms have been eliminating middle-level managers because fewer are needed to oversee self-managed teams of employees.

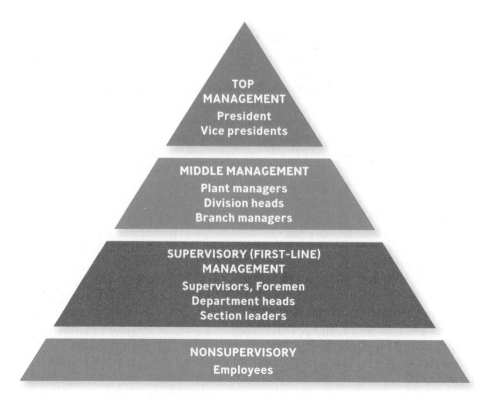

TOP MANAGEMENT
President
Vice presidents

MIDDLE MANAGEMENT
Plant managers
Division heads
Branch managers

SUPERVISORY (FIRST-LINE) MANAGEMENT
Supervisors, Foremen
Department heads
Section leaders

NONSUPERVISORY
Employees

in some companies chief knowledge officer (CKO). The CEO is often also the president of the firm and is responsible for all top-level decisions. The CEO and president are the same person in 65 percent of the S&P 500 companies, including big companies like United Parcel Service, John Deere, and General Electric.

CEOs are responsible for introducing change into an organization. The COO is responsible for putting those changes into effect. His or her tasks include structuring work, controlling operations, and rewarding people to ensure that everyone strives to carry out the leader's vision. Many companies today are eliminating the COO function as a cost-cutting measure and assigning that role to the CEO. Often, the CFO participates in the decision to cut the COO position. The CFO is responsible for obtaining funds, planning budgets, collecting funds, and so on. The CIO or CKO is responsible for getting the right information to other managers so they can make correct decisions. CIOs are more important than ever to the success of their companies given the crucial role that information technology has come to play in every aspect of business.[24]

Middle management includes general managers, division managers, and branch and plant managers (in colleges, deans and department heads) who are responsible for tactical planning and controlling. Many firms, as a result of the recession that began in 2008, have eliminated some middle managers through downsizing and have given their remaining managers more employees to supervise.[25] Nonetheless, middle managers are still considered very important to most firms.[26]

Supervisory management includes those directly responsible for supervising workers and evaluating their daily performance; they're often known as first-line managers (or supervisors) because they're the first level above workers. This is the first management position you are most likely to acquire after college.

middle management
The level of management that includes general managers, division managers, and branch and plant managers who are responsible for tactical planning and controlling.

supervisory management
Managers who are directly responsible for supervising workers and evaluating their daily performance.

Tasks and Skills at Different Levels of Management

Few people are trained to be good managers. Usually a person learns how to be a skilled accountant or sales representative or production-line worker, and then—because of her or his skill—is selected to be a manager. Such managers tend to become deeply involved in showing others how to do things, helping them, supervising them, and generally being active in the operating task.

The further up the managerial ladder a person moves, the less important his or her original job skills become. At the top of the ladder, the need is for people who are visionaries, planners, organizers, coordinators, communicators, morale builders, and motivators.[27] Figure 7.5 shows that a manager must have three categories of skills:

figure 7.5

SKILLS NEEDED AT VARIOUS LEVELS OF MANAGEMENT

All managers need human relations skills. At the top, managers need strong conceptual skills and rely less on technical skills. First-line managers need strong technical skills and rely less on conceptual skills. Middle managers need to have a balance between technical and conceptual skills.

1. **Technical skills** are the ability to perform tasks in a specific discipline (such as selling a product or developing software) or department (such as marketing or information systems).

2. **Human relations skills** include communication and motivation; they enable managers to work through and with people. Skills associated with leadership—coaching, morale building, delegating, training and development, and supportiveness—are also human relations skills.

3. **Conceptual skills** let the manager picture the organization as a whole and see the relationships among its various parts. They are needed in planning, organizing, controlling, systems development, problem analysis, decision making, coordinating, and delegating.

Looking at Figure 7.5, you'll notice that first-line managers need to be skilled in all three areas. However, they spend most of their time on technical and human relations tasks, like assisting operating personnel and giving directions, and less time on conceptual tasks. Top managers, in contrast, need to use few technical skills. Instead, they spend almost all their time on human relations and conceptual tasks. A person who is competent at a low level of management may not be competent at higher levels, and vice versa. Different skills are needed at different levels.

Staffing: Getting and Keeping the Right People

To get the right kind of people to staff an organization, the firm has to offer the right kind of incentives. For example, Google's gourmet chefs cook up free lunches, dinners, and snacks for employees. Would such an incentive appeal to you? How important to you is pay relative to other incentives?

Staffing is recruiting, hiring, motivating, and retaining the best people available to accomplish the company's objectives. Today, staffing is critical, especially in the Internet and high-tech areas. At most high-tech companies, like Google, Sony, and Microsoft, the primary capital equipment is brainpower. A firm with innovative and creative workers can go from start-up to major competitor in just a few years.[28]

Many people are not willing to work at companies unless they are treated well and get fair pay. They may leave to find a better balance between work and home. Staffing is becoming a greater part of each manager's assignment, and all managers need to cooperate with human resource management to win and keep good workers. Chapter 11 is devoted to human resource issues, including staffing.

LEARNING goal 5

Explain the differences between leaders and managers, and describe the various leadership styles.

LEADING: PROVIDING CONTINUOUS VISION AND VALUES

One person might be a good manager but not a good leader. Another might be a good leader without being a good manager. Managers strive to produce order and stability, whereas leaders embrace and manage change. Leadership is creating a

MAKING ethical decisions

To Share or Not to Share

First-line managers assist in the decisions made by their department heads. The department heads retain full responsibility for the decisions—if a plan succeeds, it's their success; if a plan fails, it's their failure. Now imagine this: As a first-line manager, you have new information that your department head hasn't seen yet. The findings in this report indicate that your manager's recent plans are sure to fail. If the plans do fail, the manager will probably be demoted and you're the most likely candidate to fill the vacancy. Will you give your department head the report? What is the ethical thing to do? What might be the consequences of your decision?

vision for others to follow, establishing corporate values and ethics, and transforming the way the organization does business in order to improve its effectiveness and efficiency.[29] Good leaders motivate workers and create the environment for them to motivate themselves. Management is carrying out the leader's vision.[30]

Leaders must therefore:

- *Communicate a vision and rally others around that vision.* The leader should be openly sensitive to the concerns of followers, give them responsibility, and win their trust. A successful leader must influence the actions of others. Ellen Kullman took the reins at Dupont in the middle of a crisis. Nonetheless, she set the tone for growth and prosperity in the future.[31]

- *Establish corporate values.* These include concern for employees, for customers, for the environment, and for the quality of the company's products. When companies set their business goals, they're defining the company's values as well. The number one trait that others look for in a leader is honesty. The second requirement is that the leader be forward looking.

- *Promote corporate ethics.* Ethical behavior includes an unfailing demand for honesty and an insistence that everyone in the company gets treated fairly (see the Making Ethical Decisions box). That's why we stress ethical decision making throughout this text. Many businesspeople have made the news by giving away huge amounts to charity, thus setting a model of social concern for their employees and others.[32]

- *Embrace change.* A leader's most important job may be to transform the way the company does business so that it's more effective (does things better) and more efficient (uses fewer resources to accomplish the same objectives).[33]

- *Stress accountability and responsibility.* If there is anything we have learned from the failures of banking managers and other industry and government managers during the recession that began in 2008, it is that leaders need to be held accountable and need to

> *When Ellen Kullman took the reins at Dupont, the company was in crisis. Immediately Kullman oversaw two restructurings, dismissed thousands of employees, and asked the remaining employees to take a two- to three-week holiday without pay. Throughout it all Kullman never lost her ready sense of humor and set the tone for the company going forward.*

transparency
The presentation of a company's facts and figures in a way that is clear and apparent to all stakeholders.

feel responsible for their actions. A key word that has emerged from the crisis is transparency. **Transparency** is the presentation of a company's facts and figures in a way that is clear and apparent to all stakeholders. Clearly it is time to make businessess and the government more transparent so that everyone is more aware of what is happening to the economy and to specific businesses and government agencies.[34]

All organizations need leaders, and all employees can help lead. You don't have to be a manager to perform a leadership function. That is, any employee can motivate others to work well, add to a company's ethical environment, and report ethical lapses when they occur. Some employees today are taking a leadership position through the use of social media. (You can read about them in the nearby Social Media in Business box.)

Leadership Styles

Nothing has challenged management researchers more than the search for the best leadership traits, behaviors, or styles. Thousands of studies have tried to identify characteristics that make leaders different from other people. Intuitively, you might conclude the same thing they did: leadership traits are hard to pin down. Some leaders are well groomed and tactful, while others are unkempt and abrasive—yet both may be just as effective.

Just as no one set of traits describes a leader, no one style of leadership works best in all situations. Even so, we can look at a few of the most commonly recognized leadership styles and see how they may be effective (see Figure 7.6):

autocratic leadership
Leadership style that involves making managerial decisions without consulting others.

1. **Autocratic leadership** means making managerial decisions without consulting others. This style is effective in emergencies and when absolute followership is needed—for example, when fighting fires. Autocratic leadership is also effective sometimes with new, relatively unskilled workers who need clear direction and guidance. Coach Phil Jackson used an autocratic leadership style to take the Los Angeles Lakers to three consecutive National Basketball Association championships in his first three seasons. By following his leadership,

figure 7.6

VARIOUS LEADERSHIP STYLES

Source: Reprinted by permission of the *Harvard Business Review.* An exhibit from "How to Choose a Leadership Pattern" by Robert Tannenbaum and Warren Schmidt (May/June 1973). Copyright © 1973 by the Harvard Business School Publishing Corporation. All rights reserved.

Using Social Media to Build Customer Support

You probably know someone who has used social media to complain about products and services. One woman, for example, tweeted to complain about her Maytag washer. Another man expressed his irritation with an airline's baggage handling through a music video on YouTube that reached some 8 million viewers.

Of course, many companies use that same technology to proactively and reactively communicate with the public. Best Buy, for example, has 2,500 employees who can see consumer complaints and respond to them on Twitter. The system used at Best Buy is called Twelpforce. Here's an example of how it works. One person bought a cell phone and an insurance plan. When the iPhone stopped working, the customer was offered a BlackBerry as a loaner. The consumer was unhappy with that solution and began tweeting about his experience. A customer service rep from Best Buy quickly tweeted a reply and arranged to get a replacement iPhone to

the customer. As a result, the customer got back on Twitter to talk about the good service at Best Buy. In another example, one person posted Best Buy's TV commercials on his blog before they were aired. After one customer complained about a commercial he saw on the blog, the spot was never aired.

Twitter, Facebook, blogs, YouTube, etc. have made it possible for companies to be proactive in reaching customers. Sadly, many companies with IT departments have been slow to implement such programs. As a result, there seem to be many more complaints on social media than positive support for companies. That is likely to change as more and more companies realize the importance and benefits of the two-way communication that is simplified by social media.

Sources: Josh Bernoff and Ted Schadler, "Empowered," *Harvard Business Review,* July–August 2010; and Sonya A. Donaldson, "Social Media: Things That Make You Go 'Oops?'" *Black Enterprise,* December 2010.

---

a group of highly skilled individuals became a winning team. How is the team doing now? What kind of leadership do you see being used most successfully in baseball, football, and other areas?

2. **Participative (democratic) leadership** involves managers and employees working together to make decisions. Research has found that employee participation in decisions may not always increase effectiveness, but it usually does increase job satisfaction.[35] Many large organizations like Google, Apple, IBM, Cisco, and AT&T, and most smaller firms have been highly successful using a democratic style of leadership that values traits such as flexibility, good listening skills, and empathy. Employees meet to discuss and resolve management issues by giving everyone some opportunity to contribute to decisions.

3. In **free-rein leadership** managers set objectives and employees are free to do whatever is appropriate

Mike Krzyewski, coach of Duke University's basketball team, has been successful as an autocratic leader. That makes sense, since you don't want basketball players deciding whether or not to play as a team. On the other hand, can you see why it is not so good to use autocratic leadership with a team of doctors?

participative (democratic) leadership
Leadership style that consists of managers and employees working together to make decisions.

free-rein leadership
Leadership style that involves managers setting objectives and employees being relatively free to do whatever it takes to accomplish those objectives.

to accomplish those objectives. Free-rein leadership is often the most successful leadership style in certain organizations, such as those in which managers supervise doctors, professors, engineers, or other professionals. The traits managers need in such organizations include warmth, friendliness, and understanding. More and more firms are adopting this style of leadership with at least some of their employees.

Individual leaders rarely fit neatly into just one of these categories. We can think of leadership as a continuum along which employee participation varies, from purely boss-centered leadership to subordinate-centered leadership.

Which leadership style is best? Research tells us that it depends largely on what the goals and values of the firm are, who's being led, and in what situations.[36] A manager may be autocratic but friendly with a new trainee, democratic with an experienced employee, and free-rein with a trusted long-term supervisor.

enabling
Giving workers the education and tools they need to make decisions.

There's no such thing as a leadership trait that is effective in all situations, or a leadership style that always works best. A successful leader in one organization may not be successful in another organization. For example, there was a question recently about whether or not Meg Whitman, eBay's former CEO, would make a good governor for California even though she oversaw eBay's growth from $4 million annual revenue and 30 employees to $8 billion and 15,000 employees in her ten-year tenure. In 2010, voters of California decided not to elect her.[37] A truly successful leader has the ability to adopt the leadership style most appropriate to the situation and the employees.

Empowering Workers

Many leaders in the past gave explicit instructions to workers, telling them what to do to meet the goals and objectives of the organization. The term for this process is *directing*. In traditional organizations, directing includes giving assignments, explaining routines, clarifying policies, and providing feedback on performance. Many organizations still follow this model, especially

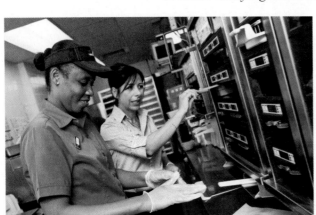

Fast-food restaurant employees often don't have the skill and experience to make empowerment work very well. Instead their managers generally have to supervise and direct them fairly closely. What do you think are some of the consequences for managers of not being able to empower their staff with decision-making authority?

fast-food restaurants and small retail establishments where the employees don't have the skill and experience needed to work on their own, at least at first.

Progressive leaders, such as those in some high-tech firms and Internet companies, empower employees to make decisions on their own. *Empowerment* means giving employees the authority to make a decision without consulting the manager and the responsibility to respond quickly to customer requests. Managers are often reluctant to give up their decision-making power and often resist empowerment. In firms that implement the concept, however, the manager's role is less that of a boss and director and more that of a coach, assistant, counselor, or team member.[38]

Enabling means giving workers the education and tools they need to make decisions. Clearly, it's the key to the success of empowerment. Without the right education, training, coaching, and tools, workers cannot assume the responsibilities and decision-making roles that make empowerment work.[39]

Managing Knowledge

"Knowledge is power." Empowering employees means giving them knowledge—that is, the information they need to do the best job they can. Finding the right information, keeping it in a readily accessible place, and making it known to everyone in the firm together constitute the tasks of **knowledge management.**

The first step to developing a knowledge management system is determining what knowledge is most important. Do you want to know more about your customers? Do you want to know more about competitors? What kind of information would make your company more effective or more efficient or more responsive to the marketplace? Once you've decided what you need to know, you set out to find answers to those questions.

Knowledge management tries to keep people from reinventing the wheel—that is, duplicating the work of gathering information—every time a decision must be made. A company really progresses when each person continually asks, "What do I still not know?" and "Whom should I be asking?" It's as important to know what's *not* working as it is to know what *is* working. Employees and managers now have texting, tweeting, and other means of keeping in touch with one another, with customers, and with other stakeholders. The key to success is learning how to process information effectively and turn it into knowledge that everyone can use to improve processes and procedures. The benefits are obvious.

> **knowledge management**
> Finding the right information, keeping the information in a readily accessible place, and making the information known to everyone in the firm.

LEARNING goal 6

Summarize the five steps of the control function of management.

CONTROLLING: MAKING SURE IT WORKS

The control function measures performance relative to the planned objectives and standards, rewards people for work well done, and takes corrective action when necessary. Thus the control process (see Figure 7.7) provides the feedback that lets managers and workers adjust to deviations from plans and to changes in the environment that have affected performance.

figure 7.7

THE CONTROL PROCESS
The whole control process is based on clear standards. Without such standards, the other steps are difficult, if not impossible. With clear standards, performance measurement is relatively easy and the proper action can be taken.

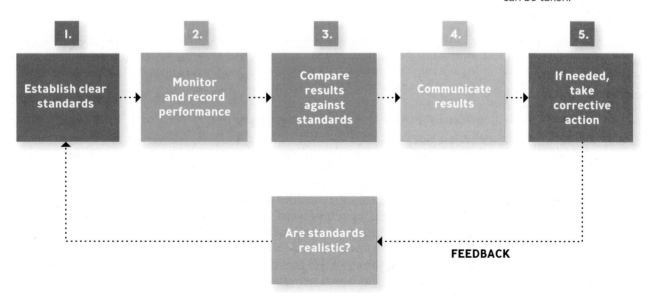

1. Establish clear standards
2. Monitor and record performance
3. Compare results against standards
4. Communicate results
5. If needed, take corrective action

Are standards realistic?

FEEDBACK

One way colleges and universities measure their performance is to track the number of students who complete their degrees or who graduate within a certain number of years. What are some of the factors that could affect the achievement of this performance standard, and how do college administrators take corrective action when necessary?

Controlling consists of five steps:

1. Establishing clear performance standards. This ties the planning function to the control function. Without clear standards, control is impossible.
2. Monitoring and recording actual performance or results.
3. Comparing results against plans and standards.
4. Communicating results and deviations to the appropriate employees.
5. Taking corrective action when needed and providing positive feedback for work well done.

For managers to measure results, the standards must be specific, attainable, and measurable. Setting such clear standards is part of the planning function. Vague goals and standards such as "better quality," "more efficiency," and "improved performance" aren't sufficient because they don't describe in enough detail what you're trying to achieve. For example, let's say you're a runner and you have made the following statement: "My goal is to improve my distance." When you started your improvement plan last year, you ran 2.0 miles a day; now you run 2.1 miles a day. Did you meet your goal? Well, you did increase your distance, but certainly not by very much.

A more appropriate statement would be "My goal is to increase my running distance from two miles a day to four miles a day by January 1." It's important to establish a time period for reaching goals. The following examples of goals and standards meet these criteria:

- Cutting the number of finished product rejects from 10 per 1,000 to 5 per 1,000 by March 31.
- Increasing the number of times managers praise employees from 3 per week to 12 per week by the end of the quarter.
- Increasing sales of product X from 10,000 per month to 12,000 per month by July.

One way to make control systems work is to establish clear procedures for monitoring performance. Accounting and finance are often the foundations for control systems because they provide the numbers management needs to evaluate progress.

A Key Criterion for Measurement: Customer Satisfaction

Traditional measures of success are usually financial; that is, they define success in terms of profits or return on investment. Certainly these measures are still important, but they're not the whole purpose of the firm. Other purposes may include pleasing employees, stakeholders, and customers—including both external and internal customers.

External customers include dealers, who buy products to sell to others, and ultimate customers (also known as end users) such as you and me, who buy products for their own personal use. **Internal customers** are individuals

external customers
Dealers, who buy products to sell to others, and ultimate customers (or end users), who buy products for their own personal use.

internal customers
Individuals and units within the firm that receive services from other individuals or units.

and units within the firm that receive services from other individuals or units. For example, the field salespeople are the internal customers of the marketing research people who prepare market reports for them.

One goal today is to go beyond simply satisfying customers to "delighting" them with unexpectedly good products and services. We'll discuss management in more detail in the next few chapters. Let's pause now, review, and do some exercises. Management is doing, not just reading.

progress assessment

- How does enabling help achieve empowerment?
- What are the five steps in the control process?
- What's the difference between internal and external customers?

summary

Learning Goal 1. Describe the changes occurring today in the management function.
- **What does management look like today?**
At one time, managers were called bosses, and their job consisted of telling people what to do, watching over them to be sure they did it, and reprimanding those who didn't. Many, if not most, managers still behave that way. Today, however, some managers tend to be more progressive. For example, they emphasize teams and team building; they create drop-in centers, team spaces, and open work areas. They tend to guide, train, support, motivate, and coach employees rather than tell them what to do.
- **What reasons can you give to account for changes in management?**
Leaders of Fortune 100 companies today tend to be younger, more of them are female, and fewer of them were educated at elite universities. They know that many of their employees know more about technology and other practices than they do. Therefore, they tend to put more emphasis on motivation, teamwork, and cooperation. Managers in the future are likely to be assuming completely new roles in the firm. For one thing, they will be taking a leadership role in adapting to climate change. Further, they'll be doing more expansion overseas.

Learning Goal 2. Describe the four functions of management.
- **What are the primary functions of management?**
The four primary functions are (1) planning, (2) organizing, (3) leading, and (4) controlling.
- **How do you define each of these functions?**
Planning includes anticipating trends and determining the best strategies and tactics to achieve organizational goals and objectives. Organizing includes designing the structure of the organization and creating conditions and systems in which everyone and everything works together to achieve the organization's goals and objectives. Leading means creating a vision for the organization, and communicating, guiding, training, coaching, and motivating others to achieve goals and objectives. Controlling means measuring whether what actually occurs meets the organization's goals.

Learning Goal 3. Relate the planning process and decision making to the accomplishment of company goals.

- **What's the difference between goals and objectives?**

Goals are broad, long-term achievements that organizations aim to accomplish, whereas objectives are specific, short-term plans made to help reach the goals.

- **What is a SWOT analysis?**

Managers look at the **S**trengths and **W**eaknesses of the firm and the **O**pportunities and **T**hreats facing it.

- **What are the four types of planning, and how are they related to the organization's goals and objectives?**

Strategic planning is broad, long-range planning that outlines the goals of the organization. *Tactical planning* is specific, short-term planning that lists organizational objectives. *Operational planning* is part of tactical planning and sets specific timetables and standards. *Contingency planning* is developing an alternative set of plans in case the first set doesn't work out.

- **What are the steps involved in decision making?**

The seven Ds of decision making are (1) define the situation; (2) describe and collect needed information; (3) develop alternatives; (4) develop agreement among those involved; (5) decide which alternative is best; (6) do what is indicated (begin implementation); and (7) determine whether the decision was a good one, and follow up.

Learning Goal 4. Describe the organizing function of management.

- **What is an organization chart?**

An organization chart is a visual device that shows relationships among people and divides the organization's work; it shows who is accountable for the completion of specific work and who reports to whom.

- **What are the three levels of management in the corporate hierarchy?**

The three levels of management are (1) top management (highest level consisting of the president and other key company executives who develop strategic plans); (2) middle management (general managers, division managers, and plant managers who are responsible for tactical planning and controlling); and (3) supervisory management (first-line managers/supervisors who evaluate workers' daily performance).

- **What skills do managers need?**

Managers must have three categories of skills: (1) technical skills (ability to perform specific tasks such as selling products or developing software), (2) human relations skills (ability to communicate and motivate), and (3) conceptual skills (ability to see organizations as a whole and how all the parts fit together).

- **Are these skills equally important at all management levels?**

Managers at different levels need different skills. Top managers rely heavily on human relations and conceptual skills and rarely use technical skills, while first-line supervisors need strong technical and human relations skills but use conceptual skills less often. Middle managers need to have a balance of all three skills (see Figure 7.5).

Learning Goal 5. Explain the differences between leaders and managers, and describe the various leadership styles.

- **What's the difference between a manager and a leader?**

A manager plans, organizes, and controls functions within an organization. A leader has vision and inspires others to grasp that vision, establishes corporate values, emphasizes corporate ethics, and doesn't fear change.

- **Describe the various leadership styles.**

Figure 7.6 shows a continuum of leadership styles ranging from boss-centered to subordinate-centered leadership.

- **Which leadership style is best?**

The most effective leadership style depends on the people being led and the situation. The challenge of the future will be to empower self-managed teams.

- **What does empowerment mean?**

Empowerment means giving employees the authority and responsibility to respond quickly to customer requests. Enabling is giving workers the education and tools they need to assume their new decision-making powers.

- **What is knowledge management?**

Knowledge management is finding the right information, keeping the information in a readily accessible place, and making the information known to everyone in the firm.

Learning Goal 6. Summarize the five steps of the control function of management.

- **What are the five steps of the control function?**

Controlling incorporates (1) setting clear standards, (2) monitoring and recording performance, (3) comparing performance with plans and standards, (4) communicating results and deviations to employees, and (5) providing positive feedback for a job well done and taking corrective action if necessary.

- **What qualities must standards possess to measure performance results?**

Standards must be specific, attainable, and measurable.

key terms

autocratic
  leadership 192
brainstorming 187
conceptual skills 190
contingency planning 186
controlling 183
decision making 187
enabling 194
external customers 196
free-rein leadership 194
goals 183
human relations
  skills 190
internal customers 196

knowledge
  management 195
leading 183
management 181
middle management 189
mission statement 183
objectives 184
operational
  planning 186
organization chart 188
organizing 182
participative
  (democratic)
  leadership 193

planning 182
PMI 187
problem solving 187
staffing 190
strategic
  planning 185
supervisory
  management 189
SWOT analysis 184
tactical planning 186
technical skills 190
top management 188
transparency 192
vision 183

critical thinking

Many students say they would like to be a manager someday. Here are some questions to get you started thinking like a manager:

1. Would you like to work for a large firm or a small business? Private or public? In an office or out in the field? Give your reasons for each answer.

2. What kind of leader would you be? Do you have evidence to show that?

3. Do you see any problems with a participative (democratic) leadership style? Can you see a manager getting frustrated when he or she can't control others?

4. Can someone who's trained to give orders (like a military sergeant) be retrained to be a participative leader? How? What problems may emerge?

developing workplace skills

1. Allocate time to do some career planning with a SWOT analysis of your present situation. Choose one career you are interested in and answer the following questions: What does the marketplace for your chosen career look like today? What skills do you have that will make you a winner in that type of career? What weaknesses might you target to correct? What are the threats to your career choice? What are the opportunities? Prepare a two-minute presentation to the class.

2. Bring several decks of cards to class and have the class break up into teams of four or so members. Each team should then elect a leader. Each leader should be assigned a leadership style and learn how to perform that style: autocratic, participative (democratic), or free rein. Have each team try to build a house of cards by stacking them on top of each other. The team with the tallest house wins. Each team member should report his or her experience under the selected style of leadership.

3. In class, discuss the advantages and disadvantages of becoming a manager. Does the size of the business make a difference? What are the advantages of a career in a profit-seeking business versus a career in a nonprofit organization?

4. Review Figure 7.6 and discuss managers you have known, worked for, or read about who have practiced each management style. Students from other countries may have interesting experiences to add. Which managerial style did you like best? Why? Which was or were most effective? Why?

5. Because of the illegal and unethical behavior of a few managers, managers in general are under suspicion for being greedy and dishonest. Discuss the fairness of such charges, and suggest what could be done to improve the opinion of managers among the students in your class.

taking it to the net

Purpose

To perform a simple SWOT analysis.

Exercise

Go to www.marketingteacher.com, locate the list of SWOT analyses, and click the link to go to the SWOT for Toys "R" Us.

1. What are Toys "R" Us's strengths, weaknesses, opportunities, and threats?

2. Analyze Toys "R" Us's weaknesses. How do you think the company's strengths might be used to overcome some of its weaknesses?

3. Analyze Toys "R" Us's opportunities and threats. What additional opportunities can you suggest? What additional threats can you identify?

casing the web

To access the case "Leading in a Leaderless Company," visit **www.mhhe.com/ubl0e**

video case

To access the video case featuring Zappos, visit **www.mhhe.com/ubl0e**

Structuring
Organizations
for Today's
Challenges

8

LEARNING goals

After you have read and studied this chapter, you should be able to

1 Outline the basic principles of organization management.

2 Compare the organizational theories of Fayol and Weber.

3 Evaluate the choices managers make in structuring organizations.

4 Contrast the various organizational models.

5 Identify the benefits of interfirm cooperation and coordination.

6 Explain how organizational culture can help businesses adapt to change.

W hen Ursula Burns replaced Anne Mulcahy as CEO of Xerox in 2009, she had big shoes to fill. Mulcahy was one of the few women to run a top public company and the first woman to be chosen CEO of the Year by *Chief Executive* magazine. Mulcahy took Xerox back to the foundations of its corporate culture—innovation and customer care. "You need to change and adapt," she said.

Burns was certainly up to the task of taking the reins from Mulcahy and more. Recently *Forbes* magazine named Burns as the 14th most powerful woman in the world! She not only is the CEO at Xerox, but she's also on many boards, including the boards of American Express and MIT. President Obama named her to help lead the White House national program on STEM (science, technology, engineering and math), and V.P. Biden placed her on the Export Council in 2010. Burns is the only female African-American chief executive among the Fortune 500's top 150 companies.

Burns was born and raised in New York City. She earned her bachelor's degree from Polytechnic Institute of NYU and received her Master's degree from Columbia. She started with Xerox as a summer intern and joined the company a year later. From 1992 to 2000, she led several business teams including the office color and fax business and the office network printing business. She worked as an executive assistant for a while and eventually became president for global manufacturing in 1999. She worked closely with Mulcahy as executive vice president until Mulcahy left in 2009.

When Burns took over as CEO, Xerox had to cut its employee ranks to 50,000. Around the same time, however, the company bought ACS, an IT services company with 80,000 employees. That acquisition took Xerox into a new services market and created a new challenge for Burns. Using ACS's base in IT and business process outsourcing, Xerox hopes to persuade its customers to give them a bigger slice of their document-related work.

This chapter is about changing and adapting organizations to today's markets, as Ursula Burns is doing at Xerox. Most managers never face challenges that big, but there are plenty of opportunities in every firm to use the principles of organizing to manage—and benefit from—change, especially today as firms adapt to the recent economic crisis.

profile

Getting to Know

X *Ursula Burns*

CEO of Xerox

Sources: Diane Brady, "Hard Choices," *Bloomberg Businessweek,* April 26–May 2, 2010; Richard Waters, "Xerox Chief Sets Out the Big Picture," *Financial Times,* May 6, 2010; and Xerox Newsroom Bios, accessed online March 2011.

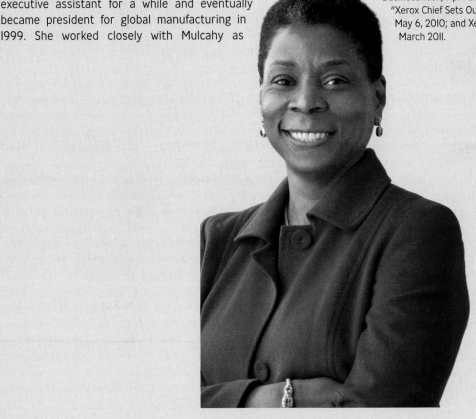

This sports equipment company studied the compact-disc industry and learned to use ultraviolet inks to print graphics on skis. It went to the cable television industry to learn how to braid layers of fiberglass and carbon, and adapted that knowledge to make its products. Name that company. (The answer can be found in this chapter.)

LEARNING goal 1

Outline the basic principles of organization management.

EVERYONE'S REORGANIZING

The principles of organization apply to businesses of all sizes. Structuring the business, making an appropriate division of labor using job specialization and departmentalization, establishing procedures, and assigning authority are tasks found in most firms. How do these principles operate at your current or most recent job?

You don't have to look far to find examples of companies reorganizing.[1] Xerox is just one of many—and sometimes the process is quite painful. A. G. Lafley, former CEO of legendary Procter & Gamble, transformed the company into one of the most innovative firms in the United States. Some entrepreneurial companies are organizing globally from the start and succeeding. Other organizations have been declining, including automobile makers, homebuilders, and banks. You have been hearing about such failures in the news. Clearly the challenge to reorganize is strong.

Few firms have established as strong an image in the United States as Starbucks, but even that company had to restructure to keep its customer base.[2] As the company expanded its menu to include more sandwiches, one of the unexpected results was a change in the smell of the stores (the odor of burning cheese was overwhelming the smell of coffee). The company restored the stores' aroma by cutting back on sandwiches for a while.[3] Many stores had to be closed and other stores were remodeled to recapture the feel of a Milan coffee bar. In the end, Starbucks regained its market image and is prospering again.[4]

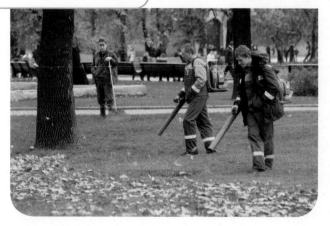

You may be wondering what has happened to U.S. producers—so many seem to be failing. But adjusting to changing markets is a normal function in a capitalist economy. There will be big winners, like Google and Facebook, and big losers as well. The key to success is remaining flexible enough to adapt to the changing times.[5] Often that means going back to basic organizational principles and rebuilding the firm on a sound foundation. This chapter will discuss such basic principles.

Safety versus Profit

Imagine you have begun a successful lawn-mowing service in your neighborhood. Other lawn-mowing services in the area seem to hire untrained workers, many from other countries. They pay only the minimum wage or slightly more. Most obviously, however, they often provide no safety equipment. Workers don't have ear protection against the loud mowers and blowers. Most don't wear goggles when operating the shredder. Very few wear masks when spraying potentially harmful fertilizers.

You are aware there are many hazards connected with yard work, but safety gear can be expensive and workers often prefer to work without it. You are interested in making as much money as possible, but you also are concerned about the safety and welfare of your workers. You know yard maintenance equipment creates noise pollution, but quiet equipment is expensive.

The corporate culture you create as you begin your service will last a long time. If you emphasize safety and environmental concern from the start, your workers will adopt your values. On the other hand, you can see the potential for making faster profits by ignoring safety rules and paying little attention to the environment as your competitors seem to do. What are the consequences?

Building an Organization from the Bottom Up

No matter the size of the business, the principles of organization are much the same. Let's say you and two friends plan to start a lawn-mowing business. One of the first steps is to organize your business. *Organizing,* or structuring, begins with determining what work needs to be done (mowing, edging, trimming) and then dividing up the tasks among the three of you; this is called a *division of labor.* One of you might have a special talent for trimming bushes, while another is better at mowing. The success of a firm often depends on management's ability to identify each worker's strengths and assign the right tasks to the right person. Many jobs can be done quickly and well when each person specializes. Dividing tasks into smaller jobs is called *job specialization.* For example, you might divide the mowing task into mowing, trimming, and raking.

If your business is successful, you'll probably hire more workers to help. You might organize them into teams or departments to do the various tasks. One team might mow while another uses blowers to clean up leaves and debris. If you're really successful over time, you might hire an accountant to keep records, various people to handle advertising, and a crew to maintain the equipment.

You can see how your business might evolve into a company with several departments: production (mowing and everything related to that), marketing, accounting, and maintenance. The process of setting up individual departments to do specialized tasks is called *departmentalization.* Finally, you'll assign authority and responsibility to people so that you can control the whole process. If something went wrong in the accounting department, for example, you would know who was responsible.

Structuring an organization, then, consists of devising a division of labor (sometimes resulting in specialization); setting up teams or departments to do specific tasks (like production and accounting); and assigning responsibility and authority to people. It also includes allocating resources (such as funds for various departments), assigning specific tasks, and establishing procedures for accomplishing the organizational objectives. From the start, you have to make ethical decisions about how you'll treat your workers and how you will benefit the community (see the nearby Making Ethical Decisions box).[6]

You may develop an *organization chart* that shows relationships among people: who is accountable for the completion of specific work, and who reports to whom. Finally, you'll monitor the environment to see what competitors are doing and what customers are demanding. Then you must adjust to the new realities. For example, a major lawn care company may begin promoting itself in your area. You might have to make some organizational changes to offer even better service at competitive prices. What would you do first if you began losing business to competitors?

LEARNING goal 2

Compare the organizational theories of Fayol and Weber.

THE CHANGING ORGANIZATION

Never before in the history of business has so much change been introduced so quickly—sometimes too quickly, as we saw with the earthquake and tsunami in Japan. Think of the effects these disasters have had on the nuclear power industry.[7] As we noted in earlier chapters, much change is due to the evolving business environment—more global competition, a declining economy, faster technological change, and pressure to preserve the natural environment.[8] Equally important to many businesses is the change in customer expectations. Consumers today expect high-quality products and fast, friendly service—at a reasonable cost.[9]

Managing change, then, has become a critical managerial function. That sometimes includes changing the whole organization structure. Such change may occur in nonprofit and government organizations as well as businesses.[10] Many organizations in the past were designed more to facilitate management than to please the customer. Companies designed many rules and regulations to give managers control over employees. As you'll learn later in this chapter, this reliance on rules is called *bureaucracy*. When Hurricane Katrina hit New Orleans in August 2005, the government seemed paralyzed and didn't respond quickly. The victims placed blame on federal, state, and local *bureaucracy*. Meanwhile, more flexible businesses in the area and in other states adjusted to the new conditions, reopened, and waited for the government to catch up. The local, state, and federal responses to the Gulf oil spill in 2010 were not much better. Yes, the government has to wrestle with bureaucracy as well as businesses.

To understand where we are in organization design, it helps to know where we've been. We'll look at that subject next.

The Development of Organization Design

Until the 20th century, most businesses were rather small, the processes for producing goods were relatively simple, and organizing workers was fairly easy. Organizing workers is still not too hard in most small firms, such as a lawn-mowing service or a small shop that produces custom-made boats. Not until the 1900s and the introduction of *mass production* (methods for efficiently producing large quantities of goods) did production processes and business organization become so complex. Usually, the bigger the plant, the more efficient production becomes.

Business growth led to **economies of scale**. This term refers to the fact that companies can reduce their production costs by purchasing raw

economies of scale
The situation in which companies can reduce their production costs if they can purchase raw materials in bulk; the average cost of goods goes down as production levels increase.

materials in bulk. The average cost of goods decreases as production levels rise. The cost of building a car, for example, declined sharply when automobile companies adopted mass production and GM, Ford, and others introduced their huge factories. Over time, such innovations became less meaningful as other companies copied the processes. You may have noticed the benefits of mass production in housing and computers.

During the era of mass production, organization theorists emerged. Two influential thinkers were Henri Fayol and Max Weber. Many of their principles are still being used in businesses throughout the world. Let's explore these principles.

Fayol's Principles of Organization   In France, economic theoretician Henri Fayol published his book *Administration industrielle et générale* in 1919. It was popularized in the United States in 1949 under the title *General and Industrial Management*. Fayol introduced such principles as the following:

- *Unity of command.* Each worker is to report to one, and only one, boss. The benefits of this principle are obvious. What happens if two different bosses give you two different assignments? Which one should you follow? To prevent such confusion, each person should report to only one manager. (Later we'll discuss an organizational plan that seems to violate this principle.)

- *Hierarchy of authority.* All workers should know to whom they report. Managers should have the right to give orders and expect others to follow. (As we discussed in Chapter 7, this concept has changed over time, and empowerment is often more important now.)

- *Division of labor.* Functions are to be divided into areas of specialization such as production, marketing, and finance. (This principle too is being modified, as you'll read later, and cross-functional teamwork is getting more emphasis.)

- *Subordination of individual interests to the general interest.* Workers are to think of themselves as a coordinated team. The goals of the team are more important than the goals of individual workers. (This concept is still very much in use.) Have you heard this concept being applied to football and basketball teams?

- *Authority.* Managers have the right to give orders and the power to enforce obedience. Authority and responsibility are related: whenever authority is exercised, responsibility arises. (This principle is also being modified as managers are beginning to empower employees.)

- *Degree of centralization.* The amount of decision-making power vested in top management should vary by circumstances. In a small organization, it's possible to centralize all decision-making power in the top manager. In a larger organization, however, some decision-making power, for both major and minor issues, should be delegated to lower-level managers and employees.

- *Clear communication channels.* All workers should be able to reach others in the firm quickly and easily.

- *Order.* Materials and people should be placed and maintained in the proper location.

- *Equity.* A manager should treat employees and peers with respect and justice. (That includes, of course, the treatment of women. Note, for

Henri Fayol introduced several management principles still followed today, including the idea that each worker should report to only one manager and that managers, in turn, should have the right to give orders for others to follow and the power to enforce them. Which of Fayol's principles have you observed?

example, the Walmart class-action lawsuit where women have claimed that the company did not treat them equally.)[11]

- *Esprit de corps.* A spirit of pride and loyalty should be created among people in the firm.

Management courses in colleges throughout the world taught Fayol's principles for years, and they became synonymous with the concept of management. Organizations were designed so that no person had more than one boss, lines of authority were clear, and everyone knew to whom to report. Naturally, these principles tended to be written down as rules, policies, and regulations as organizations grew larger.

That process of rule making has often led to rather rigid organizations that haven't always responded quickly to consumer requests. For example, in various cities, the Department of Motor Vehicles (DMV) and auto repair facilities have been slow to adapt to the needs of their customers. So where did the idea of *bureaucracy* come from? We talk about that next.

Max Weber and Organizational Theory   Max Weber's book *The Theory of Social and Economic Organizations,* like Fayol's, appeared in the United States in the late 1940s. Weber, a German sociologist and economist, promoted the pyramid-shaped organization structure that became popular in large firms. Weber put great trust in managers and felt the firm would do well if employees simply did what they were told. The less decision making they had to do, the better. Clearly, this is a reasonable way to operate if you're dealing with relatively uneducated and untrained workers. Such was generally the case at the time Weber was writing. Most employees today, however, have considerably more education and technical skills.

Weber's principles of organization resembled Fayol's. In addition, Weber emphasized:

- Job descriptions.
- Written rules, decision guidelines, and detailed records.
- Consistent procedures, regulations, and policies.
- Staffing and promotion based on qualifications.

Weber believed that large organizations demanded clearly established rules and guidelines to be followed precisely. In other words, he was in favor of *bureaucracy.* Although his principles made sense at the time, rules and procedures became so rigid in some companies that they grew counterproductive. Some organizations today still thrive on Weber's theories. United Parcel Service (UPS), for example, maintains strict written rules and decision guidelines. Those rules enable the firm to deliver packages quickly because employees don't have to pause to make decisions—procedures are clearly spelled out for them.

Some organizations that follow Weber's principles are less effective than UPS because they don't allow employees to respond quickly to new challenges. That has clearly been the case with disaster relief agencies in many areas. Later, we explore how to make organizations more responsive. First, let's look at some basic terms and concepts.

Turning Principles into Organization Design

Following theories like Fayol's and Weber's, managers in the latter 1900s began designing organizations so that managers could *control* workers. Many companies are still organized that way, with everything set up in a hierarchy. A **hierarchy** is a system in which

hierarchy
A system in which one person is at the top of the organization and there is a ranked or sequential ordering from the top down of managers who are responsible to that person.

Max Weber promoted an organizational structure composed of middle managers who implement the orders of top managers. He believed less-educated workers were best managed if managers or supervisors gave them strict rules and regulations to follow and monitored their performance. What industries or businesses today would benefit by using such controls?

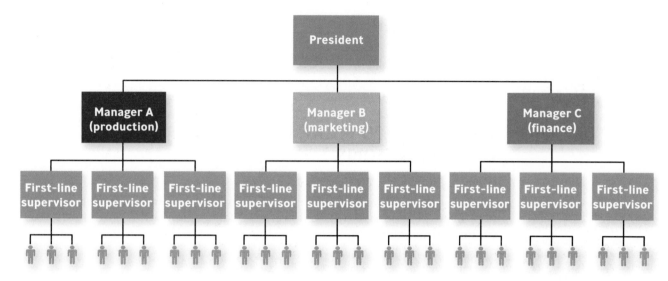

figure 8.1

TYPICAL ORGANIZATION CHART
This is a rather standard chart with managers for major functions and supervisors reporting to the managers. Each supervisor manages three employees.

one person is at the top of the organization and there is a ranked or sequential ordering from the top down of managers and others who are responsible to that person. Since one person can't keep track of thousands of workers, the top manager needs many lower-level managers to help. The **chain of command** is the line of authority that moves from the top of the hierarchy to the lowest level. Figure 8.1 shows a typical hierarchy.

Some organizations have a dozen or more layers of management between the chief executive officer (CEO) and the lowest-level employees. If employees want to introduce work changes, they ask a supervisor (the first level of management), who asks his or her manager, who asks a manager at the next level up, and so on. It can take weeks or months for a decision to be made and passed from manager to manager until it reaches employees.

Max Weber used the word *bureaucrat* to describe a middle manager whose function was to implement top management's orders. Thus, **bureaucracy** came to be the term for an organization with many layers of managers.

When employees in a bureaucracy of any size have to ask managers for permission to make a change, the process may take so long that customers become annoyed. Has this happened to you in a department store or other organization? Since customers want efficient service—and they want it *now*—slow service is simply not acceptable in today's competitive firms.[12]

Some companies are therefore reorganizing to let employees make decisions in order to please customers no matter what. Home Depot has adopted this approach to win more customers from competitors. Nordstrom employees can accept a return from a customer without managerial approval, even if the item was not originally sold at that store. As you read earlier in this book, giving employees such authority is called *empowerment*. Remember that empowerment works only when employees are given the proper training and resources to respond. Can you see how such training would help first responders in crisis conditions?

chain of command
The line of authority that moves from the top of a hierarchy to the lowest level.

bureaucracy
An organization with many layers of managers who set rules and regulations and oversee all decisions.

progress assessment

- What do the terms *division of labor* and *job specialization* mean?
- What are the principles of management outlined by Fayol?
- What did Weber add to the principles of Fayol?

Evaluate the choices managers make in structuring organizations.

centralized authority
An organization structure in which decision-making authority is maintained at the top level of management.

decentralized authority
An organization structure in which decision-making authority is delegated to lower-level managers more familiar with local conditions than headquarters management could be.

span of control
The optimal number of subordinates a manager supervises or should supervise.

A broad span of control allows one supervisor to be responsible for many workers whose work tasks are predictable and standardized. In addition to assembly lines, can you think of other management situations that might benefit from a broad span of control? What about in a service industry?

DECISIONS TO MAKE IN STRUCTURING ORGANIZATIONS

When designing responsive organizations, firms have to make decisions about several organizational issues: (1) centralization versus decentralization, (2) span of control, (3) tall versus flat organization structures, and (4) departmentalization.

Choosing Centralized or Decentralized Authority

Centralized authority occurs when decision making is concentrated at the top level of management. The retailing giant Target, for example, has a very centralized form of management. *Fortune* magazine commented that Target is so top-down that the CEO personally interviews candidates for the top 600 positions. That doesn't mean Target hasn't adapted to different circumstances, however, as you'll see later in this chapter.

McDonald's believes that purchasing, promotion, and other such decisions are best handled centrally. There's usually little need for each McDonald's restaurant in the United States to carry different food products. McDonald's thus leans toward centralized authority. However, today's rapidly changing markets, added to global differences in consumer tastes, tend to favor some decentralization and thus more delegation of authority, even at McDonald's.[13] Its restaurants in England offer tea, those in France offer a Croque McDo (a hot ham-and-cheese sandwich), those in Japan sell rice, and Chinese McDonald's offer taro and red bean desserts.

Decentralized authority occurs when decision making is delegated to lower-level managers and employees more familiar with local conditions than headquarters management could be. JCPenney customers in California, for example, demand clothing styles different from what customers in Minnesota or Maine like. It makes sense to delegate to store managers in various cities the authority to buy, price, and promote merchandise appropriate for each area. In response to the economic crisis that began in 2008, Macy's department store is also shifting to local tastes. The plan, called "My Macy's," proved successful in test markets. Both Home Depot and Lowe's also responded to the financial crisis with similar moves toward catering to local markets. Figure 8.2 lists some advantages and disadvantages of centralized and decentralized authority.

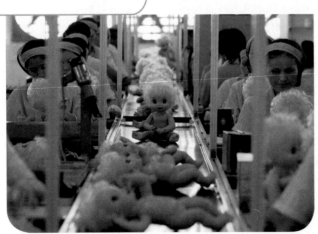

Choosing the Appropriate Span of Control

Span of control describes the optimal number of subordinates a manager supervises or should supervise. What is the "right" span of control? At

figure 8.2

ADVANTAGES AND
DISADVANTAGES OF
CENTRALIZED VERSUS
DECENTRALIZED
MANAGEMENT

ADVANTAGES	DISADVANTAGES
Centralized	
• Greater top-management control	• Less responsiveness to customers
• More efficiency	• Less empowerment
• Simpler distribution system	• Interorganizational conflict
• Stronger brand/corporate image	• Lower morale away from headquarters
Decentralized	
• Better adaptation to customer wants	• Less efficiency
• More empowerment of workers	• Complex distribution system
• Faster decision making	• Less top-management control
• Higher morale	• Weakened corporate image

lower levels, where work is standardized, it's possible to implement a broad span of control (15 to 40 workers). For example, one supervisor can be responsible for 20 or more workers assembling computers or cleaning movie theaters. The appropriate span gradually narrows at higher levels of the organization, because work becomes less standardized and managers need more face-to-face communication.

The trend today is to expand the span of control as organizations adopt empowerment, reduce the number of middle managers, and hire more talented and better educated lower-level employees. Information technology also allows managers to handle more information, so the span can be broader still.[14]

At Rowe Furniture in Salem, Virginia, the manufacturing chief dismantled the assembly line and empowered the people who had had limited functions—like sewing, gluing, and stapling—with the freedom to make sofas as they saw fit. Productivity and quality soared.

Choosing between Tall and Flat Organization Structures

In the early 20th century, organizations grew even bigger, adding layer after layer of management to create **tall organization structures**. Some had as many as 14 levels, and the span of control was small (few people reported to each manager).

Imagine how a message might be distorted as it moved up the organization and back down through managers, management assistants, secretaries, assistant secretaries, supervisors, trainers, and so on. The cost of all these managers and support people was high, the paperwork they generated was enormous, and the inefficiencies in communication and decision making were often intolerable.

More recently, organizations have adopted **flat organization structures** with fewer layers of management (see Figure 8.3) and a broad span of control

tall organization structure
An organizational structure in which the pyramidal organization chart would be quite tall because of the various levels of management.

flat organization structure
An organization structure that has few layers of management and a broad span of control.

figure 8.3

A FLAT ORGANIZATION
STRUCTURE

ADVANTAGES	DISADVANTAGES
Narrow	
• More control by top management	• Less empowerment
• More chances for advancement	• Higher costs
• Greater specialization	• Delayed decision making
• Closer supervision	• Less responsiveness to customers
Broad	
• Reduced costs	• Fewer chances for advancement
• More responsiveness to customers	• Overworked managers
• Faster decision making	• Loss of control
• More empowerment	• Less management expertise

(many people report to each manager).[15] Flat structures can respond readily to customer demands because lower-level employees have authority and responsibility for making decisions, and managers can be spared some day-to-day tasks. In a bookstore with a flat organization structure, employees may have authority to arrange shelves by category, process special orders for customers, and so on.

Large organizations use flat structures to try to match the friendliness of small firms, whose workers often know customers by name. The flatter organizations become, the broader their spans of control, which means some managers lose their jobs. Figure 8.4 lists advantages and disadvantages of narrow and broad spans of control.

Weighing the Advantages and Disadvantages of Departmentalization

departmentalization
The dividing of organizational functions into separate units.

Departmentalization divides organizations into separate units. The traditional way to departmentalize is by *function*—such as design, production, marketing, and accounting. Departmentalization groups workers according to their skills, expertise, or resource use so that they can specialize and work together more effectively. It may also save costs and thus improve efficiency. Other advantages include the following:

1. Employees can develop skills in depth and progress within a department as they master more skills.

2. The company can achieve economies of scale by centralizing all the resources it needs and locate various experts in that area.

3. Employees can coordinate work within the function, and top management can easily direct and control various departments' activities.

Disadvantages of departmentalization by function include the following:

1. Departments may not communicate well. For example, production may be so isolated from marketing that it does not get needed feedback from customers.

2. Employees may identify with their department's goals rather than the organization's. The purchasing department may find a good value somewhere and buy a huge volume of goods. That makes purchasing look good, but the high cost of storing the goods hurts overall profitability.

3. The company's response to external changes may be slow.

4. People may not be trained to take different managerial responsibilities; rather, they tend to become narrow specialists.

5. Department members may engage in groupthink (they think alike) and may need input from outside to become more creative.

Looking at Alternative Ways to Departmentalize   Functional separation isn't always the most responsive form of organization. So what are the alternatives? Figure 8.5 shows five ways a firm can departmentalize. One way is by product. A book publisher might have a trade book department (for books sold to the general public), a textbook department, and a technical book department, each with separate development and marketing processes. Such product-focused departmentalization usually results in good customer relations.

Some organizations departmentalize by customer group. A pharmaceutical company might have one department for the consumer market, another that calls on hospitals (the institutional market), and another that targets doctors. You can see how customer groups can benefit from having specialists satisfying their needs.

Some firms group their units by geographic location because customers vary so greatly by region. Japan, Europe, and South America may deserve separate departments, with obvious benefits.

The decision about how to departmentalize depends on the nature of the product and the customers. A few firms find that it's most efficient to separate activities by process. For example, a firm that makes leather coats may have one department cut the leather, another dye it, and a third sew the coat together. Such specialization enables employees to do a better job because they can focus on learning a few critical skills.

Some firms use a combination of departmentalization techniques to create *hybrid forms.* For example, a company could departmentalize by function, geographic location, *and* customer groups.

After the material for footballs has been cut and sewn in the Wilson Sporting Goods factory, it moves on to the lacing department where workers like this one open up the deflated balls and prepare them for lacing. What are the advantages and disadvantages of departmentalizing by process like this?

figure 8.5

WAYS TO DEPARTMENTALIZE
A computer company may want to departmentalize by geographic location (countries), a manufacturer by function, a pharmaceutical company by customer group, a leather manufacturer by process, and a publisher by product. In each case the structure must fit the firm's goals.

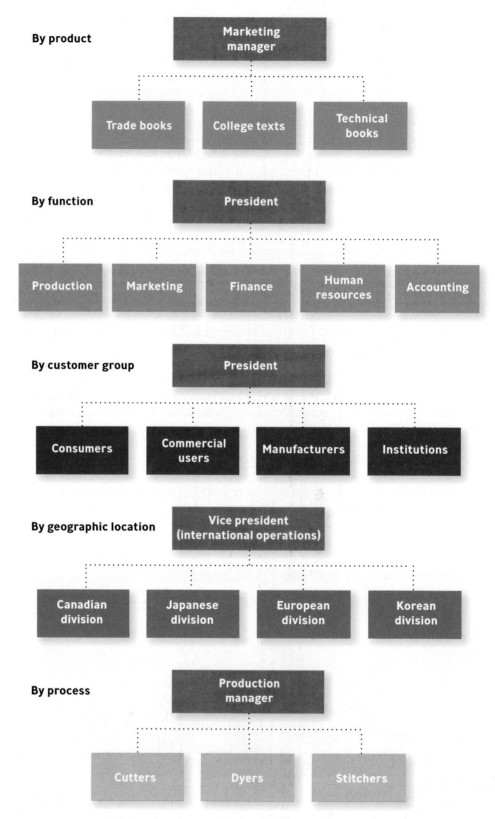

progress assessment

- Why are organizations becoming flatter?
- What are some reasons for having a narrow span of control in an organization?
- What are the advantages and disadvantages of departmentalization?
- What are the various ways a firm can departmentalize?

LEARNING goal **4**

Contrast the various organizational models.

ORGANIZATIONAL MODELS

Now that we've explored the basic choices in organization design, let's look in depth at four ways to structure an organization: (1) line organizations, (2) line-and-staff organizations, (3) matrix-style organizations, and (4) cross-functional self-managed teams. You'll see that some of these models violate traditional management principles. The business community is in a period of transition, with some traditional organizational models giving way to new structures. Such transitions can be not only unsettling to employees and managers but also fraught with problems and errors.

Line Organizations

A **line organization** has direct two-way lines of responsibility, authority, and communication running from the top to the bottom of the organization, with everyone reporting to only one supervisor. The military and many small businesses are organized this way. For example, a locally owned pizza parlor might have a general manager and a shift manager. All the general employees report to the shift manager, and he or she reports to the general manager or owner.

A line organization does not have any specialists who provide managerial support. There is no legal department, accounting department, human resources department, or information technology (IT) department. Line organizations follow all of Fayol's traditional management rules. Line managers can issue orders, enforce discipline, and adjust the organization as conditions change.

In large businesses, a line organization may have the disadvantages of being too inflexible, of having few specialists or experts to advise people along the line, and of having lengthy lines of communication.[16] Thus they may be unable to handle complex decisions relating to thousands of products and tons of paperwork. Such organizations usually turn to a line-and-staff form of organization.

Line-and-Staff Organizations

To minimize the disadvantages of simple line organizations, many organizations today have both line and staff personnel. **Line personnel** are responsible for directly achieving organizational goals, and include production workers, distribution people, and marketing personnel. **Staff personnel** advise and assist line personnel in meeting their goals, and include those in marketing research, legal advising, information technology, and human resource management.

line organization
An organization that has direct two-way lines of responsibility, authority, and communication running from the top to the bottom of the organization, with all people reporting to only one supervisor.

line personnel
Employees who are part of the chain of command that is responsible for achieving organizational goals.

staff personnel
Employees who advise and assist line personnel in meeting their goals.

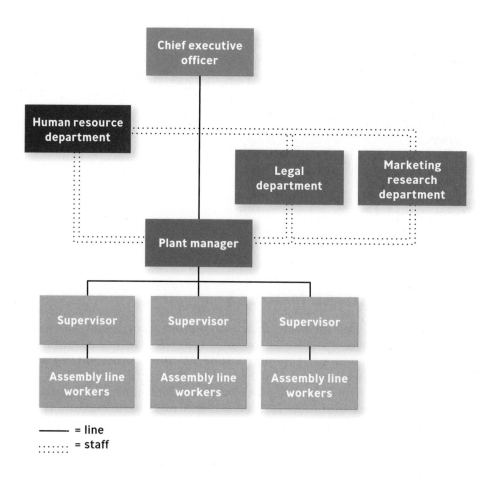

See Figure 8.6 for a diagram of a line-and-staff organization. One important difference between line and staff personnel is authority. Line personnel have formal authority to make policy decisions. Staff personnel have authority to advise line personnel and influence their decisions, but they can't make policy changes themselves. The line manager may seek or ignore the advice from staff personnel.

Many organizations benefit from expert staff advice on safety, legal issues, quality control, database management, motivation, and investing. Staff personnel strengthen the line positions and are like well-paid consultants on the organization's payroll.

Matrix-Style Organizations

Both line and line-and-staff organization structures may suffer from inflexibility. Both allow for established lines of authority and communication and work well in organizations with stable environments and slow product development (such as firms selling household appliances). In such firms, clear lines of authority and relatively fixed organization structures are assets that ensure efficient operations.

Today's economy, however, is dominated by high-growth industries like telecommunications, nanotechnology, robotics, biotechnology, and aerospace, where competition is stiff and the life cycle of new ideas is short.[17] Emphasis is on product development, creativity, special projects, rapid communication, and interdepartmental teamwork. From those changes grew the popularity of the **matrix organization**, in which specialists from different parts of the organization work together temporarily on specific projects, but still remain part of a line-and-staff structure (see Figure 8.7). In other words, a project manager

matrix organization
An organization in which specialists from different parts of the organization are brought together to work on specific projects but still remain part of a line-and-staff structure.

figure 8.7

A MATRIX ORGANIZATION
In a matrix organization, project managers are in charge of teams made up of members of several departments. In this case, project manager 2 supervises employees A, B, C, and D. These employees are accountable not only to project manager 2 but also to the head of their individual departments. For example, employee B, a market researcher, reports to project manager 2 *and* to the vice president of marketing.

can borrow people from different departments to help design and market new product ideas.

The matrix structure was developed in the aerospace industry and is now familiar in areas such as banking, management consulting firms, accounting firms, ad agencies, and school systems. Among its advantages:

- It gives managers flexibility in assigning people to projects.
- It encourages interorganizational cooperation and teamwork.
- It can produce creative solutions to product development problems.
- It makes efficient use of organizational resources.

As for disadvantages:

- It's costly and complex.
- It can confuse employees about where their loyalty belongs—with the project manager or with their functional unit.
- It requires good interpersonal skills as well as cooperative employees and managers to avoid communication problems.
- It may be only a temporary solution to a long-term problem.

If you're thinking that matrix organizations violate some traditional managerial principles, you're right. Normally a person can't work effectively for two bosses. Who has the real authority? Whose directive has first priority?

In reality, however, the system functions more effectively than you might imagine. To develop a new product, a project manager may be given temporary authority to "borrow" line personnel from production, marketing, and other line functions. The employees work together to complete the project and then return to their regular positions. Thus, no one actually reports to more than one manager at a time.

A potential real problem with matrix management, however, is that the project teams are not permanent. They form to solve a problem and then break

In matrix organizations, specialists from different parts of the organization work together temporarily on specific projects. For example, a team developing a new product may have members from production, marketing, and finance who report to the team's project manager. When the project is over, the team members return to their regular positions.

up. There is little chance for cross-functional learning, because teams work together so briefly.

Decision making in the future will be distributed throughout the organization so that people can respond rapidly to change, says the *Harvard Business Review.* Global teams will collaborate on the Internet for a single project and then disband. Young people who play online games will feel quite comfortable working in such groups.

Cross-Functional Self-Managed Teams

One solution to the temporary nature of matrix teams is to establish long-lived teams and empower them to work closely with suppliers, customers, and others to quickly and efficiently bring out new, high-quality products while giving great service. *BusinessWeek* reports that some 82 percent of white-collar workers partner with co-workers. Over 80 percent say they prefer working in groups of three or more. Most work in groups to learn from others, but 30 percent use groups to accomplish a specific task.

Cross-functional self-managed teams are groups of employees from different departments who work together on a long-term basis (as opposed to the temporary teams established in matrix-style organizations). *Self-managed* means that they are empowered to make decisions without management approval. The barriers among design, engineering, marketing, distribution, and other functions fall when interdepartmental teams are created. Sometimes the teams are interfirm; that is, the members come from two or more companies.

Cross-functional teams work best when leadership is shared. An engineer may lead the design of a new product, but a marketing expert may take the leadership position once it's ready for distribution.

Going Beyond Organizational Boundaries

Cross-functional teams work best when the voice of the customer is brought in, especially in product development tasks. Suppliers and distributors should be on the team as well. A cross-functional team that includes customers,

cross-functional self-managed teams
Groups of employees from different departments who work together on a long-term basis.

suppliers, and distributors goes beyond organizational boundaries. When suppliers and distributors are in other countries, cross-functional teams may share market information across national boundaries.[18] Government coordinators may assist such projects, letting cross-functional teams break the barriers between government and business.

Cross-functional teams are only one way businesses can interact with other companies. Next we look at others.

progress assessment

- What is the difference between line and staff personnel?
- What management principle does a matrix-style organization challenge?
- What is the main difference between a matrix-style organization's structure and the use of cross-functional teams?

LEARNING goal 5

Identify the benefits of interfirm cooperation and coordination.

MANAGING THE INTERACTIONS AMONG FIRMS

Whether it involves customers, suppliers, distributors, or the government, **networking** uses communications technology and other means to link organizations and allow them to work together on common objectives.[19] Let's explore this concept further.

networking
Using communications technology and other means to link organizations and allow them to work together on common objectives.

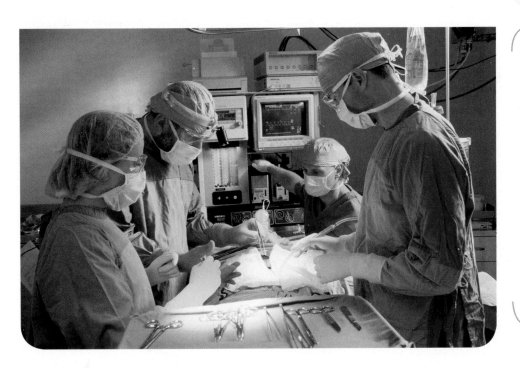

You can think of a team of medical specialists in an operating room as a cross-functional, self-managed team. Doctors, nurses, technicians, and anesthesiologists from different departments and areas in the hospital work together to complete successful operations. What kinds of tasks do cross-functional, self-managed teams complete in an office or retail environment?

Transparency and Virtual Organizations

Networked organizations are so closely linked by the Internet that each can find out what the others are doing in real time. **Real time** simply means the present moment or the actual time in which an event takes place. The Internet has allowed companies to send real-time data to organizational partners as they are developed or collected. The result is transparency (see Chapter 7), which occurs when a company is so open to other companies that electronic information is shared as if the companies were one. With this integration, two companies can work as closely as two departments in traditional firms.

Can you see the implications for organizational design? Most organizations are no longer self-sufficient or self-contained. Rather, they are part of a vast network of global businesses that work closely together. An organization chart showing what people do within any one organization is simply not complete, because the organization is part of a much larger system of firms. A modern chart would show people in different organizations and indicate how they are networked. This is a relatively new concept, however, so few such charts are yet available. The nearby Spotlight on Small Business box offers an example of how a small business works with another company that performs production, fulfillment and shipping functions.

Networked organization structures tend to be flexible. A company may work with a design expert from another company in Italy for a year and then not need that person anymore. It may hire an expert from a company in another country for the next project. Such a temporary network, made of replaceable firms that join and leave as needed, is a **virtual corporation** (see Figure 8.8).[20] This is quite different from a traditional organization structure; in fact, traditional managers sometimes have trouble adapting to the speed of change and the impermanence of relationships in networking. We discuss adaptation to change below; first, we describe how organizations use benchmarking and outsourcing to manage their interactions with other firms.

real time
The present moment or the actual time in which something takes place.

virtual corporation
A temporary networked organization made up of replaceable firms that join and leave as needed.

figure 8.8

A VIRTUAL CORPORATION
A virtual corporation has no permanent ties to the firms that do its production, distribution, legal, and other work. Such firms are flexible enough to adapt to changes in the market quickly.

When Your Workers Work for Someone Else

It was rather noisy where Douglas Pick lived near the University of Southern California. He found that earplugs were a great help. In fact, he decided that he could profit from making earplugs himself, so he launched DAP World from his apartment. After a few years, Pick found that he could not keep up with demand. His home-based office was simply not big enough to produce as many units as he needed.

Pick was hesitant to take on the overhead necessary to house and run his own manufacturing facility. About that time, however, he learned about an organization called New Horizons that assists and employs developmentally disabled adults. New Horizons not only could produce his earplugs, but could handle fulfillment and shipping as well. The organization was cost-competitive because the State of California and private contributions helped to subsidize the labor costs. Now Pick sells millions of pairs of earplugs to major outlets such as Walgreens and Rite Aid and supports some 200 workers. Can you see the benefit of being creative when planning, organizing, and structuring a business?

Source: Gwen Moran, "Sound Principles," *Entrepreneur*, April 2011; and www.dapworld.com, accessed April 2011.

Benchmarking and Core Competencies

Organizations historically tried to do all functions themselves. Each had its own department for accounting, finance, marketing, production, and so on. As we've noted, today's organizations look to other organizations for help in areas where they do not generate world-class quality.

Benchmarking compares an organization's practices, processes, and products against the world's best. As one example, K2 Skis is a company that makes skis, snowboards, in-line skates, and related products. It studied the compact-disc industry and learned to use ultraviolet inks to print graphics on skis. It went to the aerospace industry to get piezoelectric technology to reduce vibration in its snowboards (the aerospace industry uses the technology for wings on planes). It learned from the cable television industry how to braid layers of fiberglass and carbon, and adapted that knowledge to make skis. As another example, Wyeth, a pharmaceutical company, benchmarked the aerospace industry for project management, the shipping industry for standardization of processes, and computer makers to learn the most efficient way to make prescription drugs.

Benchmarking also has a more directly competitive purpose. In retailing, Target may compare itself to Walmart to see what, if anything, Walmart does better. Target will then try to improve its practices or processes to become even better than Walmart.

If an organization can't do as well as the best in, say, shipping, it will try to outsource the function to an organization like UPS or FedEx that specializes in shipping. Outsourcing, remember, means assigning one or more

benchmarking
Comparing an organization's practices, processes, and products against the world's best.

Nike's core competencies are designing and marketing athletic shoes. The company outsources other functions (i.e. manufacturing) to other companies that assemble shoes better and cheaper than Nike could do on its own. What are the advantages of focusing on the company's core competencies? What are the disadvantages?

functions—such as accounting, production, security, maintenance, and legal work—to outside organizations. Even small firms are getting involved in outsourcing. We've already discussed some problems with outsourcing, especially when companies outsource to other countries. Some functions, such as information management and marketing, may be too important to assign to outside firms. In that case, the organization should benchmark the best firms and restructure its departments to try to be equally good. It is important to remember that companies in other countries often outsource their functions to companies in the United States. We call that *insourcing* and it is the source of many jobs.[21]

When a firm has completed its outsourcing process, the remaining functions are its **core competencies**, those functions it can do as well as or better than any other organization in the world.[22] For example, Nike is great at designing and marketing athletic shoes. Those are its core competencies. It outsources manufacturing, however, to other companies that assemble shoes better and less expensively than Nike can. Similarly, Dell is best at marketing computers and outsources most other functions, including manufacturing and distribution.

After you have structured an organization, you must keep monitoring the environment (including customers) to learn what changes are needed. Dell, for example, recently reversed its practice of outsourcing customer support and now offers a premium service that allows U.S. customers to reach tech support in North America. The following section discusses organizational change in more detail.

ADAPTING TO CHANGE

core competencies
Those functions that the organization can do as well as or better than any other organization in the world.

Once you have formed an organization, you must be prepared to adapt the structure to changes in the market.[23] That's not always easy to do. Over time, an organization can get stuck in its ways. Employees have a tendency to say, "That's the way we've always done things. If it isn't broken, don't fix it." Managers also get complacent. They may say they have 20 years' experience when in fact they've had 1 year's experience 20 times. Do you think that slow adaptation to change was a factor in the decline of the manufacturing sector in the United States?

Introducing change is thus one of the hardest challenges facing any manager. Nonetheless, change is what's happening at General Motors (GM), Ford, Facebook, and other companies eager to become more competitive. If you have old facilities that are no longer efficient, you have to get rid of them. That's exactly what GM and other companies are doing. In fact, they have asked the government to lend them billions of dollars to help. You may have to cut your labor force to lower costs.

digital natives
Young people who have grown up using the Internet and social networking.

The Internet has created whole new opportunities, not only to sell to customers directly but also to ask them questions and provide them with any information they want. To win market share, companies must coordinate the efforts of their traditional departments and their Internet staff to create friendly, easy-to-manage interactions. Young people today are called **digital natives** because they grew up with the Internet. To reach them, companies are retraining older employees to be more tech-savvy. That means becoming

When Twitter and Facebook Are Old School

There was a day when many people were eager to hear about microchips and how they worked. Today, there aren't many people talking about microprocessors or other old high-tech innovations. Today, the focus is on Facebook, Twitter, cloud computing, and the like. People are still debating which eBook reader is the best. But soon people will become so accustomed to having these tools at their fingertips that they will no longer be newsworthy. Matt Ridley writes, "The very notion that we discussed the relative merits of text, email, social network messaging, and tweeting will seem quaint. In the future, my part of the cloud will get a message to a friend's part of the cloud by whichever method works best, and I will not even know which way it went."

There will be dozens of new high-tech gadgets to try. Many of them will be slight improvements on what is available today (just as the iPad 2 was a slight improvement on the original iPad), while others may be revolutionary. What is most relevant to this chapter is how social media will affect organizations in the future. There is likely to be an even greater increase in working from home. There will be closer and better relationships with customers and suppliers and dealers. All in all, social media will continue to have a major influence on how business gets done and where it gets done and who does it. The moral of the story for managers is: Keep up with the latest technology or be left behind.

Sources: Matt Ridley, "Microchips Are Old Hat, Can Tweets Be Far Behind?" *The Wall Street Journal,* March 5–6, 2011; and B. L. Ochman, " 3 Things You Need to Know about Social Media," www.mashable.com, accessed April 2011.

familiar with YouTube, Facebook, Wikis, Skype, Twitter, RSS, and more. The Social Media in Business box explores the future of such high-tech devices.

We've seen that Target is highly centralized. Nonetheless, the company reacts effectively to changes in consumer preferences throughout the country, in part by keeping in touch with an enormous web of people of all ages, interests, and nationalities—its "creative cabinet"—via the Internet. The members of the "cabinet," who never meet so they cannot influence each other, evaluate various new initiatives and recommend new programs to help Target figure out what belongs on store shelves.

Restructuring for Empowerment

To empower employees, firms often must reorganize dramatically to make frontline workers their most important people. **Restructuring** is redesigning an organization so it can more effectively and efficiently serve its customers.[24]

Until recently, department store clerks, bank tellers, and front-desk staff in hotels weren't considered key employees. Instead, managers were considered more important, and they were responsible for directing the work of the frontline people. The organization chart in a typical firm looked much like the pyramid in Figure 8.1.

A few service-oriented organizations have turned the traditional organization structure upside down. An **inverted organization** has contact people (like nurses) at the top and the chief executive officer at the bottom. Management layers are few, and the manager's job is to *assist and support* frontline people, not boss them around. Figure 8.9 illustrates the difference between an inverted and a traditional organizational structure.

restructuring
Redesigning an organization so that it can more effectively and efficiently serve its customers.

inverted organization
An organization that has contact people at the top and the chief executive officer at the bottom of the organization chart.

Traditional Organization   Inverted Organization

figure 8.9

COMPARISON OF AN INVERTED ORGANIZATIONAL STRUCTURE AND A TRADITIONAL ORGANIZATIONAL STRUCTURE

Companies based on this organization structure support frontline personnel with internal and external databases, advanced communication systems, and professional assistance. Naturally, this means frontline people have to be better educated, better trained, and better paid than in the past. It takes a lot of trust for top managers to implement such a system—but when they do, the payoff in customer satisfaction and profits is often well worth the effort.[25]

In the past, managers controlled information—and that gave them power. In more progressive organizations today, everyone shares information, often through an elaborate database system, and *among* firms as well as *within* them. No matter what organizational model you choose or how much you empower your employees, the secret to successful organization change is to focus on customers and give them what they want.

LEARNING goal 6

Explain how organizational culture can help businesses adapt to change.

Creating a Change-Oriented Organizational Culture

Any organizational change is bound to cause some stress and resistance among members. Firms adapt best when their culture is already change-oriented. **Organizational (or corporate) culture** is the widely shared values within an organization that foster unity and cooperation to achieve common goals. Usually the culture of an organization is reflected in its stories, traditions, and myths.

Each McDonald's restaurant has the same feel, look, and atmosphere; in short, each has a similar organizational culture. It's obvious from visiting almost any McDonald's that the culture emphasizes quality, service, cleanliness, and value.

An organizational culture can also be negative. Have you ever been in an organization where you feel no one cares about service or quality? The clerks may seem uniformly glum, indifferent, and testy. Their mood pervades the atmosphere, and patrons become unhappy or upset. It may be hard to believe

organizational (or corporate) culture
Widely shared values within an organization that provide unity and cooperation to achieve common goals.

an organization, especially a profit-making one, can be run so badly and still survive. Clearly then, when you search for a job, study the organizational culture to see whether you will thrive in it.

Some of the best organizations have cultures that emphasize service to others, especially customers. The atmosphere reflects friendly, caring people who enjoy working together to provide a good product at a reasonable price. Companies that have such cultures have less need for close supervision of employees. That usually means fewer policy manuals; organization charts; and formal rules, procedures, and controls. The key to a productive culture is mutual trust.[26] You get such trust by giving it. The very best companies stress high moral and ethical values such as honesty, reliability, fairness, environmental protection, and social involvement.

Empowering employees who deal directly with customers to solve problems without needing a manager's approval makes a higher level of customer service possible and helps employees grow as well. What kind of guest issues do you think a frontline hotel employee should be allowed to solve on his or her own?

We've been talking as if organizational matters were mostly controllable by management. In fact, the formal structure is just one element of the total organizational system, including its culture. The informal organization is of equal or even greater importance. Let's explore this notion next.

Managing the Informal Organization

All organizations have two organizational systems. The **formal organization** details lines of responsibility, authority, and position. It's the structure shown on organization charts. The other system is the **informal organization**, the system that develops spontaneously as employees meet and form cliques, relationships, and lines of authority outside the formal organization. It's the human side of the organization that doesn't show on any organization chart.

No organization can operate effectively without both types of organization. The formal system is often too slow and bureaucratic to let the organization adapt quickly, although it does provide helpful guides and lines of authority for routine situations.

The informal organization is often too unstructured and emotional to allow careful, reasoned decision making on critical matters. It's extremely effective, however, in generating creative solutions to short-term problems and creating camaraderie and teamwork among employees.[27]

In any organization, it's wise to learn quickly who is important in the informal organization. Following formal rules and procedures can take days. Who in the organization knows how to obtain supplies immediately without the normal procedures? Which administrative assistants should you see if you want your work given first priority? Answers to these questions help people work effectively in many organizations.

The informal organization's nerve center is the *grapevine*, the system through which unofficial information flows between and among managers and employees. Key people in the grapevine usually have considerable influence.

In the old "us-versus-them" system of organizations, where managers and employees were often at odds, the informal system hindered effective management. In more open organizations, managers and employees work together to set objectives and design procedures. The informal organization is an invaluable managerial asset that can promote harmony among workers and establish the corporate culture.

formal organization
The structure that details lines of responsibility, authority, and position; that is, the structure shown on organization charts.

informal organization
The system that develops spontaneously as employees meet and form cliques, relationships, and lines of authority outside the formal organization.

The informal organization is the system that develops as employees meet and form relationships. The grapevine, the unofficial flow of information among employees, is the nerve center of the informal organization. How does the informal organization affect the work environment?

As effective as the informal organization may be in creating group cooperation, it can still be equally powerful in resisting management directives. Employees may form unions, go on strike together, and generally disrupt operations. Learning to create the right corporate culture and work within the informal organization is thus a key to managerial success.[28]

progress assessment

- What is an inverted organization?
- Why do organizations outsource functions?
- What is organizational culture?

summary

Learning Goal 1. Outline the basic principles of organization management.
- **What is happening today to American businesses?**
They are adjusting to changing markets. That is a normal function in a capitalist economy. There will be big winners, like Google and Facebook, and big losers as well. The key to success is remaining flexible and adapting to the changing times.
- **What are the principles of organization management?**
Structuring an organization means devising a division of labor (sometimes resulting in specialization), setting up teams or departments, and assigning responsibility and authority. It includes allocating resources (such as funds), assigning specific tasks, and establishing procedures for accomplishing the organizational objectives. Managers also have to make ethical decisions about how to treat workers.

Learning Goal 2. Compare the organizational theories of Fayol and Weber.
- **What were Fayol's basic principles?**

Fayol introduced principles such as unity of command, hierarchy of authority, division of labor, subordination of individual interests to the general interest, authority, clear communication channels, order, and equity.
- **What principles did Weber add?**

Weber added principles of bureaucracy such as job descriptions, written rules and decision guidelines, consistent procedures, and staffing and promotions based on qualifications.

Learning Goal 3. Evaluate the choices managers make in structuring organizations.
- **What are the four major choices in structuring organizations?**

Choices to make in structuring and restructuring organizations cover (1) centralization versus decentralization, (2) breadth of span of control, (3) tall versus flat organization structures, and (4) type of departmentalization.
- **What are the latest trends in structuring?**

Departments are often replaced or supplemented by matrix organizations and cross-functional teams that decentralize authority. The span of control becomes larger as employees become self-directed. Another trend is to eliminate managers and flatten organizations.

Learning Goal 4. Contrast the various organizational models.
- **What are the two major organizational models?**

Two traditional forms of organization are (1) line organizations and (2) line-and-staff organizations. A line organization has clearly defined responsibility and authority, is easy to understand, and provides each worker with only one supervisor. The expert advice of staff assistants in a line-and-staff organization helps in areas such as safety, quality control, computer technology, human resource management, and investing.
- **What are the key alternatives to the major organizational models?**

Matrix organizations assign people to projects temporarily and encourage interorganizational cooperation and teamwork. Cross-functional self-managed teams have all the benefits of the matrix style and are long-term.

Learning Goal 5. Identify the benefits of interfirm cooperation and coordination.
- **What are the major concepts involved in interfirm communications?**

Networking uses communications technology and other means to link organizations and allow them to work together on common objectives. A virtual corporation is a networked organization of replaceable firms that join and leave as needed. Benchmarking tells firms how their performance measures up to that of their competitors in specific functions. The company may then *outsource* to companies that perform its weaker functions more effectively and efficiently. The functions that are left are the firm's *core competencies*.
- **What is an inverted organization?**

An inverted organization places employees at the top of the hierarchy; managers are at the bottom to train and assist employees.

Learning Goal 6. Explain how organizational culture can help businesses adapt to change.

- **What is organizational culture?**

Organizational (or corporate) culture consists of the widely shared values within an organization that foster unity and cooperation to achieve common goals.

- **What is the difference between the formal and informal organization of a firm?**

The formal organization details lines of responsibility, authority, and position. It's the structure shown on organization charts. The informal organization is the system that develops spontaneously as employees meet and form cliques, relationships, and lines of authority outside the formal organization. It's the human side of the organization. The informal organization is an invaluable managerial asset that often promotes harmony among workers and establishes the corporate culture. As effective as the informal organization may be in creating group cooperation, it can still be equally powerful in resisting management directives.

key terms

benchmarking 221
bureaucracy 209
centralized
  authority 210
chain of command 209
core competencies 222
cross-functional
  self-managed teams 218
decentralized
  authority 210
departmentalization 212

digital natives 222
economies of scale 206
flat organization
  structure 211
formal organization 225
hierarchy 208
informal
  organization 225
inverted organization 223
line organization 215
line personnel 215

matrix organization 216
networking 219
organizational (or
  corporate) culture 224
real time 220
restructuring 223
span of control 210
staff personnel 215
tall organization
  structure 211
virtual corporation 220

critical thinking

Now that you have learned some of the basic principles of organization, pause and think about where you have already applied such concepts yourself or when you have been part of an organization that did.

1. Did you find a division of labor necessary and helpful?

2. Were you assigned specific tasks or left on your own to decide what to do?

3. Were promotions based strictly on qualifications, as Weber suggested? What other factors may have been considered?

4. What problems seem to emerge when an organization gets larger?

5. What organizational changes might you recommend to the auto companies? The airline industry?

developing workplace skills

1. There is no better way to understand the effects of having many layers of management on communication accuracy than the game of Message Relay. Choose seven or more members of the class and have them leave the classroom. Then choose one person to read the following paragraph and another student to listen. Call in one of the students from outside and have the "listener" tell him or her what information was in the paragraph. Then bring in another student and have the new listener repeat the information to him or her. Continue the process with all those who left the room. Do not allow anyone in the class to offer corrections as each listener becomes the storyteller in turn. In this way, all the students can hear how the facts become distorted over time. The distortions and mistakes are often quite humorous, but they are not so funny in organizations such as Ford, which once had 22 layers of management.

Here's the paragraph:

Dealers in the midwest region have received over 130 complaints about steering on the new Commander and Roadhandler models of our mini-vans. Apparently, the front suspension system is weak and the ball joints are wearing too fast. This causes slippage in the linkage and results in oversteering. Mr. Berenstein has been notified, but so far only 213 of 4,300 dealers have received repair kits.

2. Describe some informal groups within an organization with which you are familiar at school or work. What have you noticed about how those groups help or hinder progress in the organization?

3. Imagine you are working for Kitchen Magic, an appliance manufacturer that produces dishwashers. A competitor introduces a new dishwasher that uses sound waves not only to clean even the worst burned-on food but also to sterilize dishes and silverware. You need to develop a similar offering fast, or your company will lose market share. Write an e-mail to management outlining the problem and explaining your rationale for recommending use of a cross-functional team to respond quickly.

4. Divide the class into teams of five. Each team should imagine your firm, a producer of athletic shoes, has been asked to join a virtual network. How might you minimize the potential problems of joining? Begin by defining a virtual corporation and listing its advantages and disadvantages. Each team should report its solutions to the class.

5. Many work groups of the future, including management, will be cross-functional and self-managed. To practice working in such an organization, break into groups of five or so students, preferably with different backgrounds and interests. Each group must work together to prepare a report on the advantages and disadvantages of working in teams. Many of the problems and advantages of cross-functional, self-managed teams should emerge in your group as you try to complete this assignment. Each group should report to the class how it handled the problems and benefited from the advantages.

taking it to the net

Purpose

To learn more about the process of organizational change.

Exercise

Xerox is a very familiar corporate name in the United States. There was a time, however, when the company was faltering and needed to adapt to foreign competition. This exercise will help you see how complex such change can be.

1. Do an online search for Xerox Corporation.

2. Read through the history of the company and describe its current strengths, weaknesses, opportunities, and threats (a SWOT analysis; see Chapter 7).

3. Describe Xerox's reasons for success.

casing the web

To access the case "IBM Is Both an Outsourcer and a Major Outsource for Others," visit **www.mhhe.com/ubl0e**

video case

To access the video case featuring New Belgium Brewery, visit **www.mhhe.com/ubl0e**

PRODUCTION and Operations Management

9

LEARNING goals

After you have read and studied this chapter, you should be able to

1 Describe the current state of U.S. manufacturing and what manufacturers have done to become more competitive.

2 Describe the evolution from production to operations management.

3 Identify various production processes and describe techniques that improve productivity, including computer-aided design and manufacturing, flexible manufacturing, lean manufacturing, and mass customization.

4 Describe operations management planning issues including facility location, facility layout, materials requirement planning, purchasing, just-in-time inventory control, and quality control.

5 Explain the use of PERT and Gantt charts to control manufacturing processes.

ew companies in the world are more familiar than IBM. What many people do not know is that although the company still produces servers and storage devices, IBM has shifted its emphasis from products to services. The person in charge of that dramatic change was Sam Palmisano.

Palmisano was born to a large Italian family in Baltimore, Maryland in 1951. He earned a degree in history from Johns Hopkins University and started working as a salesperson for IBM in 1973. He became senior vice president and group executive of global services in 1998, and chairman in 2002. Under Palmisano, earnings have quadrupled and the stock is up 57 percent. Its 5,896 patents in 2010—more than any other company in the world—help explain why IBM is number 12 on *Fortune*'s annual list of the World's Most Admired Companies. Did you see the IBM computer beat the champs on Jeopardy?

An international company like IBM must always look toward the future and project what its strengths will be relative to competitors. When IBM looked at the PC market, for example, it decided making and selling PCs was not its strength. It sold its PC business to a Chinese firm and turned to other areas for growth. It turned out IBM had a major advantage in selling software and services. It had also established good relationships with customers in emerging markets like Brazil, Russia, India, and China. By turning toward software and services, IBM began growing much more rapidly. Palmisano believes the company will continue that pace into the future.

With Smarter Planet, IBM is selling the idea that many of the systems that power our cities—electric grids, transportation, buildings, factories—can be made to run more efficiently if you can better monitor them, analyze the information you collect, and use it to make improvements.

No company offers more information technology (IT) services than IBM. Its employees are able to help customers use less energy for the same or more computing. IBM also helps manage its customers' complex computing systems and integrates the information technologies of merging companies.

By switching IBM's focus from production to services, software, and customer support, Sam Palmisano has led his company into the fastest-growing segment of the global market—emerging markets. This chapter will explore what is occurring in the manufacturing sector now, and how the United States generally is moving from a production-based economy to a service economy.

profile

Getting to Know

X *Samuel J. Palmisano*

of IBM

Sources: Jessi Hempel, "IBM's Super Second Act," *Fortune*, March 21, 2011; and various online sources accessed March 2011.

This company's robots manufacture, test, and package motor starters—all untouched by human hands. The machines can fill special orders, even for a single item, without slowing down the process. Name that company. (Find the answer in the chapter.)

LEARNING goal **1**

Describe the current state of U.S. manufacturing and what manufacturers have done to become more competitive.

MANUFACTURING AND SERVICES IN PERSPECTIVE

In November 2008, *The Washington Post* reported, "Activity in the nation's manufacturing sector . . . declined last month to the lowest level in more than two decades, offering economists more evidence that the country is entering a deep recession."[1] Soon after that, on January 29, 2009, *The Wall Street Journal* reported, "Joblessness was worst in the West and Midwest, indicating that the industries hit first by the recession—housing and manufacturing—continue to lose jobs."[2] Another *Wall Street Journal* article went on to say that unemployment could reach double-digit levels, home values could plunge a total of 36 percent, and stocks could fall a total of 55 percent.[3] Such events led President Obama and Congress to propose a stimulus package that would spend about a trillion dollars (including interest) to "create or save" millions of jobs and get the economy moving again—including manufacturing.[4] Much of this chapter is devoted to showing you what manufacturers and service providers can and are doing to revive the U.S. economy to become world-class competitors.

Sure, there has been lots of bad news about the manufacturing sector, but the story may not be as bad as you think. Data from the United Nations on global output from 1970 to 2009 show that America's manufacturing output has continued to increase since the 1970s. In fact, output is about twice as much as it was in the 1970s. On its own, U.S. manufacturing would rank as the sixth largest economy in the world. In 2009, U.S. manufacturing output was over $2 trillion (including mining and utilities). That's more than 45 percent higher than China's.[5] So, how can we reconcile the facts that so many workers in manufacturing are unemployed while manufacturing output continues to increase? The answer is that today's workers are so productive that the U.S. needs fewer workers to produce more goods.[6] An article in *The Wall Street Journal* says that we should not go back to a less

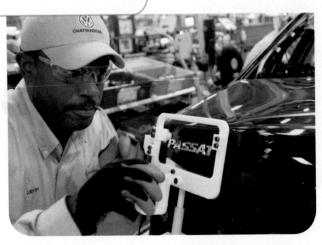

Volkswagen is just one of many auto manufacturers that have insourced jobs to the United States like this one in the VW Chattanooga, Tennessee plant. Why do you suppose so many news reports emphasize outsourcing when thousands of jobs are created by insourcing?

Key Word: Sustainability

Imagine a world that is populated by 9 billion people. In order to maintain our current quality of life, such a world would require 2.3 planets worth of resources. Given the rate of population growth, you can see how it would be important now to plan for such a world. A word you would use to describe what would be necessary is *sustainability*. In order to sustain the U.S. way of life, businesses and the government must plan for 30 percent more people living across the globe. Most of those people will be in developing countries, and the demand will be great for energy, food, water, and health care.

The challenges are great. More people mean more carbon dioxide emitted into the atmosphere. Many questions thus emerge: What does a sustainable world look like? How can manufacturers and others produce those results? What technologies and processes will make it possible to provide for so many new people needing so many new resources?

Procter & Gamble and Kaiser Permanente are issuing their own mandatory sustainability scorecards to their supply chains. They will be monitoring things like water use, recyclables, waste, and greenhouse gases. The message is, "Green up your act today lest you lose huge clients tomorrow." There are many more companies, like DuPont, Michelin, Chevron, and Nokia, that are working on sustainability projects. Such businesses are looking to cooperate with other businesses to create a sustainable future. This may or may not include electric cars, wind farms and the like. Some would suggest that there is a road map. Forces that have shaped the competitive landscape in recent decades suggest a megatrend toward sustainability. Studying such megatrends from the past will help companies learn how to adjust to the new realities. The focus will be, for example, on quality and efficiency and information technology. All the concepts discussed in this chapter will be used to make firms more competitive, less energy dependent, more efficient, and more responsive to environmental dangers. That is, their firms hope to be ready to implement sustainability in the near future.

Sources: David A. Lubin and Daniel C. Estey, "The Sustainability Imperative," *Harvard Business Review,* May 2010; Damian Joseph, "Score Two for Sustainability," *Fast Company,* November 2010; and Alan Cohen, "A Sustainable Future," *Fortune,* July 26, 2010.

---

efficient economy, but should instead retrain the workforce to participate in this dynamic new economy.[7] A reader replied to the positive article in *The Wall Street Journal* with a letter of his own. He pointed out that the U.S. share of production declined from 31 percent in 1980 to 24 percent in 2008. He also pointed out that the U.S. may be the world's largest manufacturer, but it is also the world's largest importer.[8] Many manufacturing jobs could come back to the United States as wages increase dramatically in other countries.[9]

Some areas of the country are enjoying economic growth from manufacturing while others are experiencing declines. One key to ending such declines is to adapt to the new realities and attract new manufacturers. Boston did that when it attracted many high-tech firms and became another Silicon Valley. Foreign companies add much to the U.S. economy when they outsource their activities to the United States. In 2007, for example, foreign U.S. manufacturing operations spent $63.7 billion in capital investments and exported over $125 billion in goods. They employed nearly 2 million Americans at an average compensation of nearly $80,000.[10] Later in this chapter, we shall discuss how to draw even more manufacturers to the U.S. It is important at this point to note that many U.S. firms are thinking more about producing in the United States since the earthquake, tsunami, and resulting nuclear industry problems in Japan made it a less reliable source for auto parts.[11]

American industry is doing what it can to rebuild. The construction industry is ready to build homes that are easier to heat and cool, and U.S.

automakers are scrambling to stage a comeback with more competitive vehicles.[12] The nearby Thinking Green box discusses how U.S. firms are implementing the concept called *sustainability* to stay competitive in world markets.[13]

Don't expect a comeback to result in the same number of jobs as were available before the recession. Just as U.S. productivity gains in agriculture lowered the number of farmers needed, today's productivity gains in manufacturing have lowered the number of manufacturing workers companies require. *The U.S. economy is no longer manufacturing-based.* Over 70 percent of U.S. GDP and 85 percent of U.S. jobs now come from the *service sector*. In fact, the majority of college graduates are likely to be employed in the service sector. Top-paying jobs already exist in legal services; medical services; entertainment; broadcasting; and business services such as accounting, finance, and management consulting. In fact, the service sector in general has suffered along with manufacturing as a result of the economic slowdown, but not nearly as much.[14]

Manufacturers and Service Organizations Become More Competitive

U.S. producers no longer strike fear in the heart of foreign competitors. In fact, they have much to learn from them, although one reason foreign producers have become so competitive is that they are using U.S. technology and concepts to increase effectiveness and efficiency. Overall, that's a good thing because it helps reduce poverty and hunger in developing countries and opens new markets to the developed world. IBM and other major companies are growing by providing needed goods and services to those developing markets.

Foreign producers are also streaming to the United States to take advantage of its labor force and opportunities. The United States is still the leader in nanotechnology, biotechnology, and other areas. Its workforce is creative and dynamic. Nonetheless, U.S. business cannot stand still; it must keep up with the latest production techniques and processes. The Reaching Beyond Our Borders box looks at Germany and how some companies there have found a competitive advantage that could be applied in the United States.

As the U.S. service sector becomes a larger part of the overall economy, managers will be more occupied with service productivity, and with blending services and manufacturing through the Internet. How can U.S. manufacturers and service organizations maintain a competitive edge? Most of them are:

- Focusing more on customers.
- Maintaining closer relationships with suppliers and other companies to satisfy customer needs.
- Practicing continuous improvement.[15]
- Focusing on quality.
- Saving on costs through site selection.
- Relying on the Internet to unite companies that work together.
- Adopting production techniques such as enterprise resource planning, computer integrated manufacturing, flexible manufacturing, and lean manufacturing.

This chapter explores these and other operations management techniques in both the service and the manufacturing sectors. We'll begin by going over a few key terms.

Learning from Germany

Ten years ago, Germany's economy was faltering much like the U.S. economy. One thing we can learn from other countries is how to compete with something other than cheap labor. Let's see what we can learn from Germany.

German manufacturer Stihl sells high-quality, high-cost chainsaws throughout the world. How can the company compete with chainsaws made in China and other low-wage countries? After all, a chainsaw is really just plastic and metal parts screwed together with old-fashioned nuts and bolts.

Surprisingly, one thing Stihl did was to invest in highly trained workers by offering full-time employment until 2015. Stihl even added specialists to its product-development team during the downturn. The result was high-quality products that commanded price tags large enough to make manufacturing profitable in Germany, even with the country's high wages. Stihl's chairman doesn't think U.S. companies try hard enough to keep production inside the country.

Another thing that the German companies have done is to stay away from producing high-tech smart phones and iPads and focus on heavy equipment. One consequence is that unemployment fell from 8.6 percent to 6.9 percent. Much like China, Germany sits in the center of a network of regional suppliers that feed its export industries with parts and other resources. Could that be done in the U.S.? Of course, German

industries poured money into research and development and cut expenses. Unions helped in the process, making it easier to hire and fire workers. That too could happen in the United States. Manufacturers in the United States have often led the world in quality and productivity. After all, Cadillacs were the Cadillac of cars, meaning high quality. The U.S. could once again be the world leader in manufacturing. This chapter outlines some of the steps that must be taken to regain that lead.

Sources: Michael Schuman, "How Germany Became the China of Europe," *Time*, March 7, 2011; and "German Manufacturing Rebounds," www.WSJ.com, accessed April 2011.

LEARNING goal 2

Describe the evolution from production to operations management.

FROM PRODUCTION TO OPERATIONS MANAGEMENT

Production is the creation of finished goods and services using the factors of production: land, labor, capital, entrepreneurship, and knowledge (see Chapter 1). Production has historically meant *manufacturing,* and the term **production management** has described the management activities that helped firms create goods. But the nature of business has changed significantly over the last 20 years as the service sector, including Internet services, has grown dramatically. *The United States has become a service economy—that is, one dominated by the service sector.*

production
The creation of finished goods and services using the factors of production: land, labor, capital, entrepreneurship, and knowledge.

production management
The term used to describe all the activities managers do to help their firms create goods.

operations management
A specialized area in management that converts or transforms resources (including human resources) into goods and services.

Operations management is a term that is used in both manufacturing and service organizations. **Operations management** is a specialized area in management that converts or transforms resources, including human resources like technical skills and innovation, into goods and services. It includes inventory management, quality control, production scheduling, follow-up services, and more. In an automobile plant, operations management transforms raw materials, human resources, parts, supplies, paints, tools, and other resources into automobiles. It does this through the processes of fabrication and assembly.

In a college or university, operations management takes inputs such as information, professors, supplies, buildings, offices, and computer systems—and creates services that transform students into educated people. It does this through a process called education. For a more extensive discussion, see the Free Management Library's entry on operations management (www.managementhelp.org/ops_mgnt/ops_mgnt.htm).

Some organizations—such as factories, farms, and mines—produce mostly goods. Others—such as hospitals, schools, and government agencies—produce mostly services. Still others produce a combination of goods and services. For example, an automobile manufacturer not only makes cars but also provides services such as repairs, financing, and insurance. At Wendy's you get goods such as hamburgers and fries, but you also get services such as order taking, order filling, food preparation, and cleanup.

Operations Management in the Service Sector

Operations management in the service industry is all about creating a good experience for those who use the service. In a Ritz-Carlton hotel, for example, operations management includes restaurants that offer the finest in service, elevators that run smoothly, and a front desk that processes people quickly. It may include fresh-cut flowers in the lobbies and dishes of fruit in every room. More important, it may mean spending thousands of dollars to provide training in quality management for every new employee.

Ritz-Carlton's commitment to quality is apparent in the many innovations and changes the company has initiated over the years. These innovations included installation of a sophisticated computerized guest-recognition program and a quality management program designed to ensure that all employees are "certified" in their positions.

Hotel customers today want in-room Internet access and a help center with toll-free telephone service. Executives traveling on business may need video equipment and a host of computer hardware and other aids. At the International House in New Orleans, 16 rooms have Apple TV boxes so that iPod and iPad-dependent clients can easily stream live video.[16]

Foreign visitors would like multilingual customer-support services. Hotel shops need to carry more than souvenirs, newspapers, and some drugstore and food items to serve today's high-tech travelers: the shops may also carry laptop computer supplies, electrical adapters, and the like. Operations management is responsible for locating and providing such amenities to make customers happy. Ritz-Carlton uses an internal measurement system to assess the performance results of its service delivery system.

In short, delighting customers by anticipating their needs has become the quality standard for luxury hotels, as it has for most other service businesses.[17] But knowing customer needs and satisfying them are two different things.

That's why operations management is so important: it is the implementation phase of management. Can you see the need for better operations management in airports, hospitals, government agencies, schools, and nonprofits like the Red Cross? The opportunities seem almost unlimited. Much of the future of U.S. growth is in these service areas, but growth is also needed in manufacturing. Next we'll explore production processes and what companies are doing to keep the United States competitive in that area.

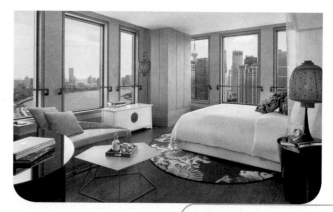

progress assessment

- What have U.S. manufacturers done to regain a competitive edge?
- What must U.S. companies do to continue to strengthen the country's manufacturing base?
- What led companies to focus on operations management rather than production?

LEARNING goal 3

Identify various production processes and describe techniques that improve productivity, including computer-aided design and manufacturing, flexible manufacturing, lean manufacturing, and mass customization.

> *Operations management for services is all about enriching the customer experience. Hotels, for instance, have responded to the needs of business travelers with in-room Internet access and other kinds of office-style support, as well as stored information about the preferences of frequent guests. How important do you think guest-recognition programs are to business travelers?*

PRODUCTION PROCESSES

Common sense and some experience have already taught you much of what you need to know about production processes. You know what it takes to write a term paper or prepare a dinner. You need money to buy the materials, you need a place to work, and you need to be organized to get the task done. The same is true of the production process in industry. It uses basic inputs to produce outputs (see Figure 9.1). Production adds value, or utility, to materials or processes.

Form utility is the value producers add to materials in the creation of finished goods and services, such as by transforming silicon into computer chips or putting services together to create a vacation package. Form utility can exist at the retail level as well. For example, a butcher can produce a specific cut of beef from a whole cow, or a baker can make a specific type of cake from basic ingredients. We'll be discussing utility in more detail in Chapter 15.

form utility
The value producers add to materials in the creation of finished goods and services.

figure 9.1

THE PRODUCTION PROCESS
The production process consists of taking the factors of production (land, etc.) and using those inputs to produce goods, services, and ideas. Planning, routing, scheduling, and the other activities are the means to accomplish the objective—output.

INPUTS	PRODUCTION CONTROL	OUTPUTS
Land	Planning	Goods
Labor	Routing	Services
Capital	Scheduling	Ideas
Entrepreneurship	Dispatching	
Knowledge	Follow-up	

process manufacturing
That part of the production process that physically or chemically changes materials.

assembly process
That part of the production process that puts together components.

continuous process
A production process in which long production runs turn out finished goods over time.

Bakers, like Duff Goldman of Ace of Cakes, add form utility to materials by transforming basic ingredients into special customized cakes. Can you see how the production of such cakes involves both process manufacturing and assembly process?

Manufacturers use several different processes to produce goods. Andrew S. Grove, the former chairman of computer chip manufacturer Intel, uses this analogy to explain production:

Imagine that you're a chef . . . and that your task is to serve a breakfast consisting of a three-minute soft-boiled egg, buttered toast, and coffee. Your job is to prepare and deliver the three items simultaneously, each of them fresh and hot.

Grove says this task encompasses the three basic requirements of production: (1) to build and deliver products in response to the demands of the customer at a scheduled delivery time, (2) to provide an acceptable quality level, and (3) to provide everything at the lowest possible cost.

Let's use the breakfast example to understand process and assembly. **Process manufacturing** physically or chemically changes materials. For example, boiling physically changes the egg. Similarly, process manufacturing turns sand into glass or computer chips. The **assembly process** puts together components (eggs, toast, and coffee) to make a product (breakfast). Cars are made through an assembly process that puts together the frame, engine, and other parts.

Production processes are either continuous or intermittent. A **continuous process** is one in which long production runs turn out finished goods over time. As a chef, you could have a conveyor belt that continuously lowers eggs into boiling water for three minutes and then lifts them out. A three-minute egg would be available whenever you wanted one. A chemical plant, for example, is run on a continuous process.

It usually makes more sense when responding to specific customer orders to use an **intermittent process**. Here the production run is short (one or two eggs) and the producer adjusts machines frequently to make different products (like the oven in a bakery or the toaster in the diner). Manufacturers of custom-designed furniture would use an intermittent process.

Today many manufacturers use intermittent processes. Computers, robots, and flexible manufacturing processes allow firms to turn out custom-made goods almost as fast as mass-produced goods were once produced.[18] We'll discuss how they do that in more detail in the next few sections as we explore advanced production techniques and technology.

The Need to Improve Production Techniques and Cut Costs

The ultimate goal of operations management is to provide high-quality goods and services instantaneously in response to customer demand. As we stress throughout this book, traditional organizations were simply not designed to be so responsive to the customer. Rather, they were designed to make goods efficiently (inexpensively). The idea behind mass production was to make a large number of a limited variety of products at very low cost.

Over the years, low cost often came at the expense of quality and flexibility. Furthermore, suppliers didn't always deliver when they said they would, so manufacturers had to carry large inventories of raw materials and components to keep producing. Such inefficiencies made U.S. companies vulnerable to foreign competitors who were using more advanced production techniques.

As a result of new global competition, companies have had to make a wide variety of high-quality custom-designed products at very low cost.[19] Clearly, something had to change on the production floor to make that possible. Several major developments have made U.S. companies more competitive: (1) computer-aided design and manufacturing, (2) flexible manufacturing, (3) lean manufacturing, and (4) mass customization.

Computer-Aided Design and Manufacturing

One development that has changed production techniques is the integration of computers into the design and manufacturing of products. The first thing computers did was help in the design of products, in a process called **computer-aided design (CAD)**. Today CAD systems allow designers to work in three dimensions.

The next step was to bring computers directly into the production process with **computer-aided manufacturing (CAM)**. CAD/CAM, the use of both computer-aided design and computer-aided manufacturing, makes it possible to custom-design products to meet the needs of small markets with very little increase in cost. A manufacturer programs the computer to make a simple design change, and that change is readily incorporated into production. In the clothing industry, a computer program establishes a pattern and cuts the cloth automatically, even adjusting to a specific person's dimensions to create custom-cut clothing at little additional cost. In food service, CAM supports on-site, small-scale, semiautomated, sensor-controlled baking in fresh-baked cookie shops to make consistent quality easy to achieve.

CAD has doubled productivity in many firms. But in the past CAD machines couldn't talk to CAM machines directly. Today, however, software programs unite CAD and CAM: the result is **computer-integrated manufacturing (CIM)**. The software is expensive, but it cuts as much as 80 percent of the time needed to program machines to make parts. The printing company Johns-Byrne uses CIM in its Niles, Illinois, plant and has noticed decreased overhead, reduced outlay of resources, and fewer errors. Consult the *International Journal of Computer-Integrated Manufacturing* for other examples.

Flexible Manufacturing

Flexible manufacturing means designing machines to do multiple tasks so they can produce a variety of products. Allen-Bradley uses flexible manufacturing to build motor starters. Orders come in daily, and within 24 hours the company's 26 machines and robots manufacture, test, and package the starters—which are untouched by human hands. Allen-Bradley's machines are so flexible that managers can include a special order, even a single item, in the assembly without slowing

intermittent process
A production process in which the production run is short and the machines are changed frequently to make different products

computer-aided design (CAD)
The use of computers in the design of products.

computer-aided manufacturing (CAM)
The use of computers in the manufacturing of products.

computer-integrated manufacturing (CIM)
The uniting of computer-aided design with computer-aided manufacturing.

3-D CAD tools allow designers to create cloth prototypes without a pattern's traditional stages: seaming, trying on, alterations, etc. What advantages might this technology offer to smaller manufacturing companies?

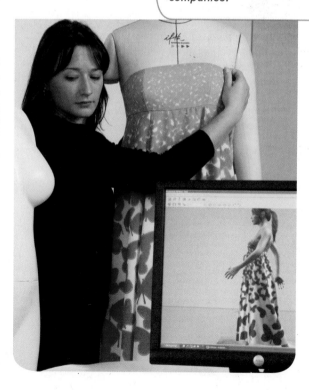

flexible manufacturing
Designing machines to do multiple tasks so that they can produce a variety of products.

lean manufacturing
The production of goods using less of everything compared to mass production.

mass customization
Tailoring products to meet the needs of individual customers.

down the process. Did you notice that these products were made without any labor? One way to compete with cheap overseas labor is to have as few workers as possible.

Lean Manufacturing

Lean manufacturing is the production of goods using less of everything than in mass production: less human effort, less manufacturing space, less investment in tools, and less engineering time to develop a new product. Consulting firm RSM McGladrey found that 65 percent of the more than 900 manufacturing and wholesale distribution companies it surveyed nationwide planned to use lean manufacturing.[20] A company becomes lean by continuously increasing its capacity to produce high-quality goods while decreasing its need for resources. Here are some characteristics of lean companies:

- They take half the human effort.
- They have half the defects in the finished product or service.
- They require one-third the engineering effort.
- They use half the floor space for the same output.
- They carry 90 percent less inventory.

Technological improvements are largely responsible for the increase in productivity and efficiency of U.S. plants. That technology made labor more productive and made it possible to pay higher wages. On the other hand, employees can get frustrated by innovations (e.g., they must learn new processes), and companies must constantly train and retrain employees to stay competitive. The need for more productivity and efficiency has never been greater. The solution to the economic crisis depends on such innovations. One step in the process is to make products more individualistic. The next section discusses how that happens.

Not only can you customize the colors of your M & Ms, you can also have personal messages and/or images imprinted on them. What other customized products can you think of?

Mass Customization

To *customize* means to make a unique product or provide a specific service to specific individuals. Although it once may have seemed impossible, **mass customization**, which means tailoring products to meet the needs of a large number of individual customers, is now practiced widely. The National Bicycle Industrial Company in Japan makes 18 bicycle models in more than 2 million combinations, each designed to fit the needs of a specific customer. The customer chooses the model, size, color, and design. The retailer takes various measurements from the buyer and faxes the data to the factory, where robots handle the bulk of the assembly.

More and more manufacturers are learning to customize their products. Some colleges, even, are developing promotions for individual students. Some General Nutrition Center (GNC) stores feature machines that enable shoppers to custom-design their own vitamins, shampoo, and lotions. The Custom Foot stores use infrared scanners to precisely measure each foot so that shoes can be made to fit perfectly. Adidas can make each shoe fit perfectly for each customer. InterActive Custom Clothes offers a wide variety of options in

Mass Customization of Candy

Students today understand the problems that new graduates have with getting a good job in the industry they desire. Eric Heinbockel wanted a career in finance, but an unpaid internship in New York didn't lead to the job he wanted.

He was getting his political science degree at Columbia University when he and two friends decided that entrepreneurship might be the way to go. It seemed that selling chocolate would be a good thing to do. After all, people don't give up their chocolate just because they have less money. Therefore, the three started Chocomize, an online shop that lets chocolate lovers customize their candy bars with ingredients ranging from graham crackers to gold flakes.

Yes, you can mass customize chocolate bars. For example, you can choose between dark, milk, or white chocolate.

You can also choose up to five inserts—choosing from 100 different selections.

So, how do you find the money to start such a business? The banks are not lending money to such entrepreneurs. Heinbockel's grandparents offered to help with the funding and one of the owners sold his car. The net proceeds were $100,000, enough to get started.

Chocomize now has three full-time chocolate makers and two who come in when needed. Chocomize is expected to be a success even though it has a European competitor. Big companies are not likely to compete in such a niche market. Sounds like a yummy business, doesn't it?

Sources: Zachary Tracer, "A Sweet Dream for Young Entrepreneurs," *Bloomberg Businessweek*, September 6–September 12, 2010; and www.chocomize.com, accessed March 2011.

custom-made jeans, including four different rivet colors. BMW can build a car exactly the way you want it.[21] You can even buy custom-made M&M's in colors of your choice. See the Spotlight on Small Business box for a unique way of using mass customization.

Mass customization exists in the service sector as well. Capital Protective Insurance (CPI) uses the latest computer software and hardware to sell customized risk-management plans to companies. Health clubs offer unique fitness programs for individuals, travel agencies provide vacation packages that vary according to individual choices, and some colleges allow students to design their own majors. It is much easier to custom-design service programs than to custom-make goods, because there is no fixed tangible good to adapt. Each customer can specify what he or she wants, within the limits of the service organization—limits that seem to be ever-widening.

As you learned in the opening Profile, manufacturing companies may become service companies over time. As you shall see, operations management concepts are applicable in both situations.

progress assessment

- What is form utility?
- Define and differentiate the following: process manufacturing, assembly process, continuous process, and intermittent process.
- What do you call the integration of CAD and CAM?
- What is mass customization?

LEARNING goal 4

Describe operations management planning issues including facility location, facility layout, materials requirement planning, purchasing, just-in-time inventory control, and quality control.

OPERATIONS MANAGEMENT PLANNING

Operations management planning helps solve many of the problems in the service and manufacturing sectors. These include facility location, facility layout, materials requirement planning, purchasing, inventory control, and quality control. The resources used may be different, but the management issues are similar.

Facility Location

facility location
The process of selecting a geographic location for a company's operations.

Facility location is the process of selecting a geographic location for a company's operations. In keeping with the need to focus on customers, one strategy is to find a site that makes it easy for consumers to use the company's services and to communicate about their needs. Flower shops and banks have placed facilities in supermarkets so that their products and services are more accessible than in freestanding facilities. You can find a McDonald's inside some Walmart stores and gas stations. Customers order and pay for their meals at the pumps, and by the time they've filled their tanks, it's time to pick up their food.

The ultimate in convenience is never having to leave home to get services. That's why there is so much interest in Internet banking, Internet shopping, online education, and other services. Internet commerce is now using Facebook and other social media to make transactions even easier.[22] For brick-and-mortar retailers to beat such competition, they have to choose good locations and offer outstanding service.[23] Study the location of service-sector businesses—such as hotels, banks, athletic clubs, and supermarkets—and you'll see that the most successful are conveniently located. Google is building large data centers in the United States where states give out tax breaks and cheap electricity is readily available in large quantities. They are also located near bodies of water for cooling their servers.

Facility Location for Manufacturers

Volkswagen's factory in Bratislava, Slovakia, turns out 250,000 cars a year, including Audi's SUV, that used to be made in Western European plants. Geographic shifts in production sometimes result in pockets of unemployment in some geographic areas and tremendous growth in others. We are witnessing such changes in the United States, as automobile and tractor production has shifted to more southern cities.[24]

Why would companies spend millions of dollars to move their facilities from one location to another? In their decisions they consider labor costs; availability of resources, including labor; access to transportation that can reduce time to market; proximity to suppliers; proximity to customers; crime rates; quality of life for employees; cost of living; and the need to train or retrain the local workforce.

Even though labor is becoming a smaller percentage of total cost in highly automated industries, availability of low-cost labor or the right kind of skilled labor remains a key reason many producers move their plants to Malaysia, China, India, Mexico, and other countries.[25] In general, however, U.S. manufacturing firms tend to pay more and offer more benefits than local firms elsewhere in the world. One result of the financial crisis that began in 2008 is that U.S. workers may be forced to take less pay and receive fewer benefits in order to stay competitive.

Facility location is a major decision for manufacturing and other companies. The decision involves taking into account the availability of qualified workers; access to suppliers, customers, and transportation; and local regulations including zoning and taxes. How has the growth of commerce on the Internet affected company location decisions?

Inexpensive resources are another major reason for moving production facilities. Companies usually need water, electricity, wood, coal, and other basic resources. By moving to areas where these are inexpensive and plentiful, firms can significantly lower not only the cost of buying such resources but also the cost of shipping finished products.[26] Often the most important resource is people, so companies tend to cluster where smart and talented people are. Witness Silicon Valley in California and similar areas in Colorado, Massachusetts, Virginia, Texas, Maryland, and other states.

Time-to-market is another decision-making factor. As manufacturers attempt to compete globally, they need sites that allow products to move quickly, at the lowest costs, so they can be delivered to customers fast. Access to highways, rail lines, waterways, and airports is thus critical. Information technology (IT) is also important to quicken response time, so many firms are seeking countries with the most advanced information systems.[27]

Another way to work closely with suppliers to satisfy customers' needs is to locate production facilities near supplier facilities. That cuts the cost of distribution and makes communication easier.

Many businesses are building factories in foreign countries to get closer to their international customers. That's a major reason the Japanese automaker Honda builds cars in Ohio and the German company Mercedes builds them in Alabama. When U.S. firms select foreign sites, they consider whether they are near airports, waterways, and highways so that raw and finished goods can move quickly and easily.

Businesses also study the quality of life for workers and managers. Are good schools nearby? Is the weather nice? Is the crime rate low? Does the local community welcome new businesses? Do the chief executive and other key managers want to live there? Sometimes a region with a high quality of life is also an expensive one, which complicates the decision. In short, facility location has become a critical issue in operations management. The Making Ethical Decisions box looks at the kinds of decisions companies must make when it comes to locating.

Taking Operations Management to the Internet

Many rapidly growing companies do very little production themselves. Instead, they outsource engineering, design, manufacturing, and other tasks to companies such as Flextronics and Sanmina-SCI that specialize in those functions. They create new relationships with suppliers over the Internet, making operations management an *interfirm* process in which companies work closely together to design, produce, and ship products to customers.

Manufacturing companies are developing Internet-focused strategies that will enable them and others to compete more effectively in the future. These changes are having a dramatic effect on operations managers as they adjust from a one-firm system to an *interfirm* environment and from a relatively stable environment to one that is constantly changing and evolving.

Facility Location in the Future

Information technology (IT)—that is computers, modems, e-mail, voice mail, text messaging, teleconferencing, etc.—is giving firms and employees increased flexibility to choose locations while staying in the competitive mainstream. **Telecommuting**, working from home via computer, is a major trend in business. Companies that no longer need to locate near sources of labor will be able to move to areas where land is less expensive and the quality of life may be higher.[28] Furthermore, more salespeople are keeping in touch with the company and its customers through teleconferencing, using computers to talk with and show images to others.

One big incentive to locate in a particular city or state is the tax situation there and degree of government support. Some states and local governments have higher taxes than others, yet many compete fiercely by offering companies tax reductions and other support, such as zoning changes and financial aid, so they will locate there. Some people would like the federal government to offer financial incentives—beyond what is already being offered by state and local agencies—to various manufacturing companies to build factories in the United States.[29]

telecommuting
Working from home via computer.

Facility Layout

Facility layout is the physical arrangement of resources, including people, to most efficiently produce goods and provide services for customers. Facility layout depends greatly on the processes that are to be performed. For services, the layout is usually designed to help the consumer find and buy things, including on the Internet. Some stores have kiosks that enable customers to search for goods online and place orders or make returns and credit payments in the store. In short, the facilities and Internet capabilities of service organizations are becoming more customer-oriented.

facility layout
The physical arrangement of resources (including people) in the production process.

At Cisco Systems, work spaces in some offices are fluid and unassigned, so employees with laptops and mobile phones can choose where to sit when they arrive each day. What do you think are some of the advantages of such nontraditional facility layouts? Are there any disadvantages?

Some service-oriented organizations, such as hospitals, use layouts that improve efficiency, just as manufacturers do. For manufacturing plants, facilities layout has become critical because cost savings of efficient layouts are enormous.

Many companies are moving from an *assembly-line layout,* in which workers do only a few tasks at a time, to a *modular layout,* in which teams of workers combine to produce more complex units of the final product. There may have been a dozen or more workstations on an assembly line to complete an automobile engine in the past, but all that work might be done in one module today.

When working on a major project, such as a bridge or an airplane, companies use a *fixed-position layout* that allows workers to congregate around the product to be completed.

A *process layout* is one in which similar equipment and functions are grouped together. The order in which the product visits a function depends on the design of the item. This allows for flexibility. The Igus manufacturing plant in Cologne, Germany, can shrink or expand in a flash. Its flexible design keeps it competitive in a fast-changing market. Because the layout of the plant changes so often, some employees use scooters in order to more efficiently provide needed skills, supplies, and services to multiple workstations. A fast-changing plant needs a fast-moving employee base to achieve maximum productivity. Figure 9.2 illustrates typical layout designs.

Materials Requirement Planning

Materials requirement planning (MRP) is a computer-based operations management system that uses sales forecasts to make sure needed parts and materials are available at the right time and place. **Enterprise resource planning (ERP),** a newer version of MRP, combines the computerized functions of all the divisions and subsidiaries of the firm—such as finance, human resources, and order fulfillment—into a single integrated software program that uses a single database. The result is shorter time between orders and payment, less staff needed to do ordering and order processing,

materials requirement planning (MRP)
A computer-based operations management system that uses sales forecasts to make sure that needed parts and materials are available at the right time and place.

enterprise resource planning (ERP)
A newer version of materials requirement planning (MRP) that combines the computerized functions of all the divisions and subsidiaries of the firm—such as finance, human resources, and order fulfillment—into a single integrated software program that uses a single database.

PRODUCT LAYOUT (also called Assembly Line Layout)
Used to produce large quantities of a few types of products.

PROCESS LAYOUT
Frequently used in operations that serve different customers' different needs.

CELLULAR or MODULE LAYOUT
Can accommodate changes in design or customer demand.

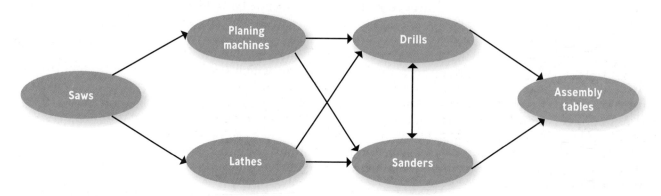

FIXED-POSITION LAYOUT
A major feature of planning is scheduling work operations.

figure 9.2

TYPICAL LAYOUT DESIGNS

reduced inventories, and better customer service. For example, the customer can place an order, either through a customer service representative or online, and immediately see when the order will be filled and how much it will cost. The representative can instantly see the customer's credit rating and order history, the company's inventory, and the shipping schedule. Everyone else in the company can see the new order as well; thus when one department finishes its portion, the order is automatically routed via the ERP system to the next department. The customer can see exactly where the order is at any point by logging into the system.

Purchasing

Purchasing is the function that searches for high-quality material resources, finds the best suppliers, and negotiates the best price for quality goods and services. In the past, manufacturers dealt with many suppliers so that if one couldn't deliver, the firm could get materials from someone else. Today, however, manufacturers rely more heavily on just one or two suppliers, because the relationship between suppliers and manufacturers is much closer than before. Producers share so much information that they don't want too many suppliers knowing their business.

purchasing
The function in a firm that searches for high-quality material resources, finds the best suppliers, and negotiates the best price for goods and services.

The Internet has transformed the purchasing function. A business looking for supplies can contact an Internet-based purchasing service and find the best items at the best price. Similarly, a company wishing to sell supplies can use the Internet to find all the companies looking for such supplies. The time and dollar cost of purchasing items has thus been reduced tremendously.

Just-in-Time Inventory Control

One major cost of production is the expense of holding parts, motors, and other items in storage for later use. Storage not only subjects items to obsolescence, pilferage, and damage but also requires construction and maintenance of costly warehouses. To cut such costs, many companies have implemented a concept called **just-in-time (JIT) inventory control**. JIT systems keep a minimum of inventory on the premises—and deliver parts, supplies, and other needs just in time to go on the assembly line. To work effectively, however, the process requires an accurate production schedule (using ERP) and excellent coordination with carefully selected suppliers, who are usually connected electronically so they know what will be needed and when. Sometimes the suppliers build new facilities close to the main producer to minimize distribution time. JIT runs into problems when suppliers are farther away. Weather may delay shipments, for example. You saw the problems that emerged when weather (earthquakes and the resulting tsunami) disrupted the supply chain of materials from Japan to the United States. JIT systems make sure the right materials are at the right place at the right time at the cheapest cost to meet both customer and production needs. That's a key step in modern production innovation.

just-in-time (JIT) inventory control
A production process in which a minimum of inventory is kept on the premises and parts, supplies, and other needs are delivered just in time to go on the assembly line.

Quality Control

Maintaining **quality** means consistently producing what the customer wants while reducing errors before and after delivery. In the past, firms often conducted quality control at the end of the production line. Products were completed first and then tested for quality. This resulted in several problems:

quality
Consistently producing what the customer wants while reducing errors before and after delivery to the customer.

1. The need to inspect work required extra people and resources.
2. If an error was found, someone had to correct the mistake or scrap the product. This, of course, was costly.
3. If the customer found the mistake, he or she might be dissatisfied and might even buy from another firm thereafter.

Such problems led to the realization that quality is not an outcome; it is a never-ending process of continually improving what a company produces. Quality control should thus be part of the operations management planning process rather than simply an end-of-the-line inspection.[30]

Companies have turned to the use of modern quality-control standards such as Six Sigma. **Six Sigma quality**, which sets a benchmark of just 3.4 defects per million opportunities, detects potential problems to prevent their occurrence. That's important to a company that makes 4 million transactions a day, like some banks.

Statistical quality control (SQC) is the process some managers use to continually monitor all phases of the production process and assure quality is being built into the product from the beginning. **Statistical process control (SPC)** is the process of testing statistical samples of product components at each stage of production and plotting the test results on a graph. Managers can thus see and correct any deviation from quality standards. Making sure products meet standards all along the production process reduces the need for a quality-control inspection at the end because mistakes are caught much earlier in the process. SQC and SPC thus save companies much time and money.

Some companies use a quality-control approach called the Deming cycle (after the late W. Edwards Deming, the father of the movement toward quality). Its steps are Plan, Do, Check, Act (PDCA). Again, the idea is to find potential errors *before* they happen.

U.S. businesses are getting serious about providing top customer service, and many are already doing it. Service organizations are finding it difficult to provide outstanding service every time because the process is so labor-intensive. Physical goods (e.g., a gold ring) can be designed and manufactured to near perfection. However, it is hard to reach such perfection when designing and providing a service experience such as a dance on a cruise ship or a cab drive through New York City.

The Baldrige Awards

In the United States in 1987, a standard was set for overall company quality with the introduction of the Malcolm Baldrige National Quality Awards, named in honor of the late U.S. secretary of commerce. Companies can apply for these awards in each of the following areas: manufacturing, services, small businesses, nonprofit/government, education, and health care. The 2011–2012 Criteria for Performance (also called the Business/Nonprofit Criteria) are now available.

To qualify, an organization has to show quality in seven key areas: leadership, strategic planning, customer and market focus, information and analysis, human resources focus, process management, and business results. Major criteria for earning the award include whether customer wants and needs are being met and whether customer satisfaction ratings are better than those of competitors. As you can see, the focus is shifting away from just making quality goods and services to providing top-quality customer service in all respects.

Six Sigma quality
A quality measure that allows only 3.4 defects per million opportunities.

statistical quality control (SQC)
The process some managers use to continually monitor all phases of the production process to assure that quality is being built into the product from the beginning.

statistical process control (SPC)
The process of testing statistical samples of product components at each stage of the production process and plotting those results on a graph. Any variances from quality standards are recognized and can be corrected if beyond the set standards.

ISO 9000 and ISO 14000 Standards

The International Organization for Standardization (ISO) is a worldwide federation of national standards bodies from more than 140 countries that set global measures for the quality of individual products. ISO is a nongovernmental organization established in 1947 to promote the development of world standards to facilitate the international exchange of goods and services. (ISO is not an acronym. It comes from the Greek word *isos,* meaning "oneness.") **ISO 9000** is the common name given to quality management and assurance standards. Some of the latest standards are called ISO 9001: 2008.

The standards require that a company determine what customer needs are, including regulatory and legal requirements, and make communication arrangements to handle issues such as complaints. Other standards cover process control, product testing, storage, and delivery.

What makes ISO 9000 so important is that the European Union (EU) demands that companies that want to do business with the EU be certified by ISO standards. Some major U.S. companies are also demanding suppliers meet these standards. Several accreditation agencies in Europe and the United States will certify that a company meets the standards for all phases of its operations, from product development through production and testing to installation.

ISO 14000 is a collection of the best practices for managing an organization's impact on the environment. As an environmental management system, it does not prescribe a performance level. Requirements for certification include having an environmental policy, having specific improvement targets, conducting audits of environmental programs, and maintaining top management review of the processes.

Certification in both ISO 9000 and ISO 14000 would show that a firm has a world-class management system in both quality and environmental standards. In the past, firms assigned employees separately to meet each set of standards. Today, ISO 9000 and 14000 standards have been blended so that an organization can work on both at once. ISO is now compiling social responsibility guidelines to go with the other standards.

The Nestle Purina PetCare Company, headquartered in St. Louis, received the 2010 Malcolm Baldrige National Quality Award in the manufacturing category. What quality criteria do you think the award was based on?

ISO 9000
The common name given to quality management and assurance standards.

ISO 14000
A collection of the best practices for managing an organization's impact on the environment.

progress assessment

- What are the major criteria for facility location?
- What is the difference between MRP and ERP?
- What is just-in-time inventory control?
- What are Six Sigma quality, the Baldrige Award, ISO 9000, and ISO 14000?

LEARNING goal 5

Explain the use of PERT and Gantt charts to control manufacturing processes.

CONTROL PROCEDURES: PERT AND GANTT CHARTS

figure 9.3

PERT CHART FOR A MUSIC VIDEO

The minimum amount of time it will take to produce this video is 15 weeks. To get that number, you add the week it takes to pick a star and a song to the four weeks to design a set, the two weeks to purchase set materials, the six weeks to construct the set, the week before rehearsals, and the final week when the video is made. That's the critical path. Any delay in that process will delay the final video.

Operations managers must ensure products are manufactured and delivered on time, on budget, and to specifications. How can managers be sure all will go smoothly and be completed by the required time? One popular technique for monitoring the progress of production was developed in the 1950s for constructing nuclear submarines: the **program evaluation and review technique (PERT)**. PERT users analyze the tasks to complete a given project, estimate the time needed to complete each, and compute the minimum time needed to complete the whole project.

The steps used in PERT are (1) analyzing and sequencing tasks that need to be done, (2) estimating the time needed to complete each task, (3) drawing a PERT network illustrating the information from steps 1 and 2, and (4) identifying the critical path. The **critical path** is the sequence of tasks that takes the longest time to complete. We use the word *critical* because a delay anywhere along this path will cause the project or production run to be late.

Figure 9.3 illustrates a PERT chart for producing a music video. The squares indicate completed tasks, and the arrows indicate the time needed to complete each. The path from one completed task to another illustrates the relationships among tasks; the arrow from "set designed" to "set materials purchased" indicates we must design the set before we can purchase the materials. The critical path, indicated by the bold black arrows, shows producing the set takes more time than auditioning dancers, choreographing dances, or designing and making costumes. The project manager now knows it's critical that set construction remain on schedule if the project is to be completed on time, but short delays in dance and costume preparation are unlikely to delay it.

A PERT network can be made up of thousands of events over many months. Today, this complex procedure is done by computer. Another, more basic strategy manufacturers use for measuring production progress is a Gantt chart. A **Gantt chart** (named for its developer, Henry L. Gantt) is a bar graph, now also prepared by computer, that clearly shows what projects are being worked on and how much has been completed at any given time. Figure 9.4, a Gantt chart for a doll manufacturer, shows that the dolls' heads and bodies should be

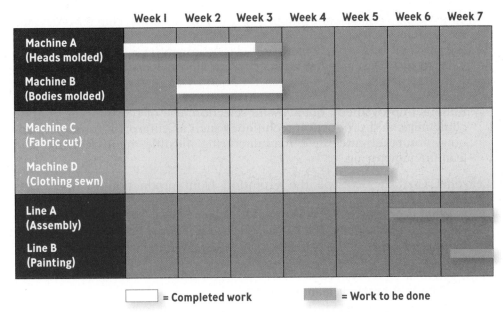

figure 9.4

GANTT CHART FOR A DOLL MANUFACTURER
A Gantt chart enables a production manager to see at a glance when projects are scheduled to be completed and what the status is now. For example, the dolls' heads and bodies should be completed before the clothing is sewn, but they could be a little late as long as everything is ready for assembly in week 6. This chart shows that at the end of week 3, the dolls' bodies are ready, but the heads are about half a week behind.

completed before the clothing is sewn. It also shows that at the end of week 3, the dolls' bodies are ready, but the heads are about half a week behind. Using a Gantt-like computer program, a manager can trace the production process minute by minute to determine which tasks are on time and which are behind, so that adjustments can be made to allow the company to stay on schedule.

PREPARING FOR THE FUTURE

The United States remains a major industrial country, but competition grows stronger each year. Tremendous opportunities exist for careers in operations management as both manufacturing and service companies fight to stay competitive. Students who can see future trends and have the skills to own or work in tomorrow's highly automated factories and modern service facilities will benefit.

progress assessment

- Draw a PERT chart for making a breakfast of three-minute eggs, buttered toast, and coffee. Define the critical path.
- How could you use a Gantt chart to keep track of production?

summary

Learning Goal 1. Describe the current state of U.S. manufacturing and what manufacturers have done to become more competitive.
- **What is the current state of manufacturing in the United States?**
Activity in the nation's manufacturing sector has declined. The result has been an increase in joblessness. One cause of that increase is the fact that companies have become more productive, meaning that they need fewer

employees to do the same amount of work. Much of this chapter is devoted to showing you what manufacturers and service providers can do to revive the U.S. economy to become world-class competitors.

- **What have U.S. manufacturers done to achieve increased output?**

U.S. manufacturers have increased output by emphasizing close relationships with suppliers and other companies to satisfy customer needs; continuous improvement; quality; site selection; use of the Internet to unite companies; and production techniques such as enterprise resource planning, computer integrated manufacturing, flexible manufacturing, and lean manufacturing.

Learning Goal 2. Describe the evolution from production to operations management.

- **What is production management?**

Production management consists of all the activities managers do to help their firms create goods. To reflect the change in importance from manufacturing to services, the term *production* is often replaced by the term *operations*.

- **What is operations management?**

Operations management is the specialized area in management that converts or transforms resources, including human resources, into goods and services.

- **What kind of firms use operations managers?**

Firms in both the manufacturing and service sectors use operations managers.

Learning Goal 3. Identify various production processes and describe techniques that improve productivity, including computer-aided design and manufacturing, flexible manufacturing, lean manufacturing, and mass customization.

- **What is process manufacturing, and how does it differ from assembly processes?**

Process manufacturing physically or chemically changes materials. Assembly processes put together components.

- **How do CAD/CAM systems work?**

Design changes made in computer-aided design (CAD) are instantly incorporated into the computer-aided manufacturing (CAM) process. The linking of CAD and CAM is computer-integrated manufacturing (CIM).

- **What is flexible manufacturing?**

Flexible manufacturing means designing machines to produce a variety of products.

- **What is lean manufacturing?**

Lean manufacturing is the production of goods using less of everything than in mass production: less human effort, less manufacturing space, less investment in tools, and less engineering time to develop a new product.

- **What is mass customization?**

Mass customization means making custom-designed goods and services for a large number of individual customers. Flexible manufacturing makes mass customization possible. Given the exact needs of a customer, flexible machines can produce a customized good as fast as mass-produced goods were once made. Mass customization is also important in service industries.

Learning Goal 4. Describe operations management planning issues including facility location, facility layout, materials requirement planning, purchasing, just-in-time inventory control, and quality control.

- **What is facility location and how does it differ from facility layout?**

Facility location is the process of selecting a geographic location for a company's operations. Facility layout is the physical arrangement of resources, including people, to produce goods and services effectively and efficiently.

- **How do managers evaluate different sites?**

Labor costs and land costs are two major criteria for selecting the right sites. Other criteria include whether resources are plentiful and inexpensive, skilled workers are available or are trainable, taxes are low and the local government offers support, energy and water are available, transportation costs are low, and the quality of life and of education are high.

- **What relationship do materials requirement planning (MRP) and enterprise resource planning (ERP) have with the production process?**

MRP is a computer-based operations management system that uses sales forecasts to make sure the needed parts and materials are available at the right time and place. Enterprise resource planning (ERP), a newer version of MRP, combines the computerized functions of all the divisions and subsidiaries of the firm—such as finance, material requirements planning, human resources, and order fulfillment—into a single integrated software program that uses a single database. The result is shorter time between orders and payment, less staff to do ordering and order processing, reduced inventories, and better customer service for all the firms involved.

- **What is just-in-time (JIT) inventory control?**

JIT requires suppliers to deliver parts and materials just in time to go on the assembly line so they don't have to be stored in warehouses.

- **What is Six Sigma quality?**

Six Sigma quality sets standards at just 3.4 defects per million opportunities and detects potential problems before they occur. Statistical quality control (SQC) is the process some managers use to continually monitor all processes in the production process and ensure quality is being built into the product from the beginning. Statistical process control (SPC) tests statistical samples of product components at each stage of the production process and plots the results on a graph so managers can recognize and correct deviations from quality standards.

- **What quality standards do firms use in the United States?**

To qualify for the Malcolm Baldrige National Quality Awards, a company must demonstrate quality in seven key areas: leadership, strategic planning, customer and market focus, information and analysis, human resources focus, process management, and business results. International standards U.S. firms strive to meet include ISO 9000 and ISO 14000. The first is a world standard for quality and the second is a collection of the best practices for managing an organization's impact on the environment.

Learning Goal 5. Explain the use of PERT and Gantt charts to control manufacturing processes.

- **Is there any relationship between a PERT chart and a Gantt chart?**

Figure 9.3 shows a PERT chart. Figure 9.4 shows a Gantt chart. Whereas PERT is a tool used for planning, a Gantt chart is a tool used to measure progress.

key terms

assembly process 240
computer-aided design (CAD) 241
computer-aided manufacturing (CAM) 241
computer-integrated manufacturing (CIM) 241
continuous process 240
critical path 252
enterprise resource planning (ERP) 247
facility layout 246
facility location 244
flexible manufacturing 242

form utility 239
Gantt chart 252
intermittent process 241
ISO 14000 251
ISO 9000 251
just-in-time (JIT) inventory control 249
lean manufacturing 242
mass customization 242
materials requirement planning (MRP) 247
operations management 238
process manufacturing 240

production 237
production management 237
program evaluation and review technique (PERT) 252
purchasing 249
quality 249
Six Sigma quality 250
statistical process control (SPC) 250
statistical quality control (SQC) 250
telecommuting 246

critical thinking

1. Workers on the manufacturing floor are being replaced by robots and other machines. On the one hand, this lets companies compete with cheap labor from other countries. On the other hand, automation eliminates many jobs. Are you concerned that automation may increase unemployment or underemployment in the United States and around the world? Why or why not?

2. Computer-integrated manufacturing (CIM) has revolutionized the production process. What will such changes mean for the clothing industry, the shoe industry, and other fashion-related industries? What will they mean for other consumer and industrial goods industries? How will you benefit as a consumer?

3. One way to create new jobs in the United States is to increase innovation among new graduates from engineering and the sciences. How can the United States motivate more students to major in those areas?

developing workplace skills

1. Choosing the right location for a manufacturing plant or a service organization is often critical to its success. Form small groups and have each group member pick one manufacturing plant or one service organization in town and list at least three reasons why its location helps or hinders its success. If its location is not ideal, what would be a better one?

2. In teams of four or five, discuss the need for better operations management in the airline industry. Have the team develop a report listing (*a*) problems team members have encountered in traveling by air and (*b*) suggestions for improving operations so such problems won't occur in the future.

3. Discuss some of the advantages and disadvantages of producing goods overseas using inexpensive labor. Summarize the moral and ethical dimensions of this practice.

4. Think of any production facility at your school, such as a sandwich shop, library, or copy center, and redesign the layout (make a pencil sketch) to more effectively serve customers and allow employees to be more effective and efficient.

5. Think about recent experiences you have had with service organizations and select one in which you had to wait for an unreasonable length of time to get what you wanted. Describe what happens when customers are inconvenienced, and explain how management could make the operation more efficient and customer-oriented.

taking it to the net

Purpose

To illustrate production processes.

Exercise

Take a virtual tour of the Hershey Foods Corporation's chocolate factory by going to www.hersheys.com/discover/tour_video.asp.

1. Does Hershey use process manufacturing or the assembly process? Is the production of Hershey's chocolate an intermittent or continuous production process? Justify your answers.

2. What location factors might go into the selection of a manufacturing site for Hershey's chocolate?

casing the web

To access the case "Griffin Hospital," visit **www.mhhe.com/ub10e**

video case

To access the video case featuring Ball Corporation, visit **www.mhhe.com/ub10e**

Motivating
Employees

10

After you have read and studied this chapter, you should be able to

1 Explain Taylor's theory of scientific management.

2 Describe the Hawthorne studies and their significance to management.

3 Identify the levels of Maslow's hierarchy of needs and apply them to employee motivation.

4 Distinguish between the motivators and hygiene factors identified by Herzberg.

5 Differentiate among Theory X, Theory Y, and Theory Z.

6 Explain the key principles of goal-setting, expectancy, reinforcement, and equity theories.

7 Show how managers put motivation theories into action through such strategies as job enrichment, open communication, and job recognition.

8 Show how managers personalize motivation strategies to appeal to employees across the globe and across generations.

profile

Although the recession dealt a major blow to the restaurant industry, there's no sign of a downturn at Panda Express. In 2010 the nation's largest Chinese food chain posted $1.4 billion in sales from its 1,350 privately owned locations. Founder and Co-CEO Andrew Cherng hopes to have 2,300 American stores by 2015. Cherng is also expanding Panda Express into Mexico and, as strange as it may seem, China.

In order to earn the capital for such an expansion, Cherng wants annual sales at his best locations to rise from $1.4 million to $2 million. To reach his goal, he is doing a lot more than just number crunching. A fan of self-help manuals, like Steven Covey's *Seven Habits of Highly Effective People,* Cherng sees the wellness of his staff as an important key to the company's success. According to Cherng, employees' personal growth will lead to Panda Express's financial growth. Managers are urged to eat a healthy diet, exercise regularly, and attend company motivational seminars. With his energetic, upbeat personality, Cherng himself attends many of these meetings with a friendly smile, hugs, or whatever else employees need to improve their well-being.

Born in China and raised in Taiwan and Japan, Cherng moved to the United States in 1966 to attend college in the Midwest. He relocated to Los Angeles after earning a master's degree in applied mathematics at the University of Missouri. When he arrived in California, he couldn't help but notice the overwhelming number of Chinese restaurants. Even more surprising to him than the popularity of Chinese cuisine was the poor quality of that food. Cherng was managing a Chinese restaurant when his parents moved to America in 1973. He and his master chef father decided to open their own restaurant and offer a high quality menu. Cherng borrowed $20,000 from the bank and $10,000 from one of his waiters to open the Panda Inn (which eventually became Panda Express).

Even in the early days employees knew of Cherng's devotion to self-improvement texts and audiobooks. Today, his passion lies in the Landmark Forum, a motivational program about which *Psychology Today* said, "Tore you down and put you back together." The system stresses the importance of openness and the destruction of obstacles that can harm personal growth. Panda Express managers are required to attend Landmark seminars and actively participate in company gatherings based on the program. "Business is a playground," said Cherng. "Business is where you practice your human skills. It's where you grow. You have to grow! You grow as a person, and then you will grow in business. That's how you go forward."

Cherng doesn't just motivate employees with intensive sharing sessions and positive thinking. Panda Express pays 80 percent of health insurance costs for all employees, including part-timers, and 50 percent for dependants. The company also pays its employees $1 to $2 more per hour than other fast food chains. Part of the reason for the increased pay is that it is more difficult to work at Panda Express than at McDonald's. After all, fried rice needs to be stirred constantly and vegetables need to be cut uniformly, which are both far more labor-intensive tasks than flipping burgers. To Cherng, the only way to ensure the kind of quality Panda Express prides itself upon is to have employees who actually care about their jobs.

In this chapter, you'll learn about the theories and practices managers like Andrew Cherng use in motivating their employees to focus on goals common to them and the organization.

Sources: Karl Taro Greenfeld, "General Tso, Meet Steven Covey," *Bloomberg Businessweek,* November 18, 2010; Russell Flannery, "Biggest Chinese Restaurant Chain in U.S. Eyes Investment in Motherland," *Forbes,* April 11, 2011; www.pandaexpress.com, accessed April 2011.

Getting to Know

X *Andrew Cherng*

Founder and Co-CEO of Panda Express

THE VALUE OF MOTIVATION

"If work is such fun, how come the rich don't do it?" quipped comedian Groucho Marx. Well, the rich do work—Bill Gates didn't make his billions playing computer games. And workers can have fun, if managers make the effort to motivate them.

It's difficult to overstate the importance of workers' job satisfaction. Happy workers usually lead to happy customers, and happy customers lead to successful businesses. On the other hand, unhappy workers are likely to leave. When that happens, the company usually loses more than an experienced employee. It can also lose the equivalent of 6 to 18 months' salary to cover the costs of recruiting and training a replacement.[1] The "soft" costs of losing employees are even greater: loss of intellectual capital, decreased morale of remaining workers, increased employee stress, decreased customer service, interrupted product development, and a poor reputation.

While it is costly to recruit and train new workers, it's also expensive to retain those who are disengaged. The word *engagement* is used to describe employees' level of motivation, passion, and commitment. Engaged employees work with passion and feel a connection to their company.[2] Disengaged workers have essentially checked out; they plod through their day putting in time, but not energy. Not only do they act out their unhappiness at work, but disengaged employees undermine the efforts of engaged co-workers. A Gallup survey estimated that the lower productivity of actively disengaged workers costs the U.S. economy about $300 billion a year. This number may increase in the near future considering the effect the recent recession has had on employee loyalty. In 2011, only 47 percent of employees surveyed said that they felt a very strong loyalty to their employer, down from 59 percent just three years earlier. While employers reported increased productivity (doing more with less), this gain came at the expense of employee loyalty. It is important that managers turn the tide around.[3]

Motivating the right people to join the organization and stay with it is a key function of managers. Top-performing managers are usually surrounded by top-performing employees. It is no coincidence that geese fly faster in formation than alone. Although the desire to perform well ultimately comes from within, good managers stimulate people and bring out their natural drive to do a good job. People are willing to work, and work hard, if they feel their work makes a difference and is appreciated.[4]

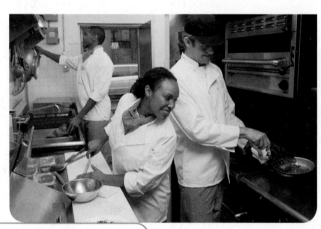

One important type of motivator is intrinsic (inner) rewards, which include the personal satisfaction you feel for a job well done. People who respond to such inner promptings often enjoy their work and share their enthusiasm with others. Are you more strongly motivated by your own desire to do well, or by extrinsic rewards like pay and recognition?

People are motivated by a variety of things, such as recognition, accomplishment, and status. An **intrinsic reward** is the personal satisfaction you feel when you perform well and complete goals. The belief that your work makes a significant contribution to the organization or to society is a form of intrinsic reward. An **extrinsic reward** is given to you by someone else as recognition for good work. Pay increases, praise, and promotions are extrinsic rewards.

This chapter will help you understand the concepts, theories, and practice of motivation. We begin with a look at some traditional theories of motivation. Why should you bother to know about these theories? Because sometimes "new" approaches aren't really new; variations of them have been tried in the past. Knowing what has gone before will help you see what has worked and what hasn't. First, we discuss the Hawthorne studies because they created a new interest in worker satisfaction and motivation. Then we look at some assumptions about employees that come from the traditional theorists. You will see the names of these theorists over and over in business literature and future courses: Taylor, Mayo, Maslow, Herzberg, and McGregor. Finally, we'll introduce modern motivation theories and show you how managers apply them.

LEARNING goal 1

Explain Taylor's theory of scientific management.

Frederick Taylor: The Father of Scientific Management

Several 19th-century thinkers presented management principles, but not until the early 20th century did any work with lasting implications appear. *The Principles of Scientific Management* was written by U.S. efficiency engineer Frederick Taylor and published in 1911, earning Taylor the title "father of scientific management." Taylor's goal was to increase worker productivity to benefit both the firm and the worker. The solution, he thought, was to scientifically study the most efficient ways to do things, determine the one "best way" to perform each task, and then teach people those methods. This approach became known as **scientific management**. Three elements were basic to Taylor's approach: time, methods, and rules of work. His most important tools were observation and the stopwatch. Taylor's thinking lies behind today's measures of how many burgers McDonald's expects its cooks to flip.

A classic Taylor story describes his study of men shoveling rice, coal, and iron ore with the same type of shovel. Believing different materials called for different shovels, he proceeded to invent a wide variety of sizes and shapes of shovels and, stopwatch in hand, measured output over time in what were called **time-motion studies**. These were studies of the tasks performed in a job and the time needed for each. Sure enough, an average person could shovel 25 to 35 tons more per day using the most efficient motions and the proper shovel. This finding led to time-motion studies of virtually every factory job. As researchers determined the most efficient ways of doing things, efficiency became the standard for setting goals.

Taylor's scientific management became the dominant strategy for improving productivity in the early 1900s. One follower of Taylor was Henry L. Gantt, who developed charts by which managers plotted the work of employees a day in advance down to the smallest detail. (See Chapter 9 for a discussion of Gantt charts.) U.S. engineers Frank and Lillian Gilbreth used Taylor's ideas in

intrinsic reward
The personal satisfaction you feel when you perform well and complete goals.

extrinsic reward
Something given to you by someone else as recognition for good work; extrinsic rewards include pay increases, praise, and promotions.

scientific management
Studying workers to find the most efficient ways of doing things and then teaching people those techniques.

time-motion studies
Studies, begun by Frederick Taylor, of which tasks must be performed to complete a job and the time needed to do each task.

UPS tells drivers how to get out of their trucks, how fast to walk, how many packages to pick up and deliver a day, and even how to hold their keys. Can you see how UPS follows the principles of scientific management by teaching people the one "best way" to perform each task?

principle of motion economy
Theory developed by Frank and Lillian Gilbreth that every job can be broken down into a series of elementary motions.

a three-year study of bricklaying. They developed the **principle of motion economy**, showing how every job could be broken into a series of elementary motions called a *therblig* (*Gilbreth* spelled backward with the *t* and *h* transposed). They then analyzed each motion to make it more efficient.

Scientific management viewed people largely as machines that needed to be properly programmed. There was little concern for the psychological or human aspects of work. Taylor believed that workers would perform at a high level of effectiveness—that is, be motivated—if they received high enough pay.[5]

Some of Taylor's ideas are still in use. Some companies continue to emphasize conformity to work rules rather than creativity, flexibility, and responsiveness. For example, United Parcel Service (UPS) tells drivers how to get out of their trucks (with right foot first), how fast to walk (three feet per second), how many packages to pick up and deliver a day (an average of 400), and how to hold their keys (teeth up, third finger). Drivers wear ring scanners, electronic devices on their index fingers wired to a small computer on their wrists. The devices shoot a pattern of photons at a bar code on a package to let a customer check the Internet and know exactly where a package is at any given moment. If a driver is considered slow, a supervisor rides along, prodding the driver with stopwatches and clipboards. UPS has a training center in Landover, Maryland, with simulators that teach employees how to properly lift and load boxes, drive their trucks proficiently, and even lessen the risk of slipping and falling when carrying a package.

The benefits of relying on workers to come up with solutions to productivity problems have long been recognized, as we shall discover next.

LEARNING goal 2

Describe the Hawthorne studies and their significance to management.

Elton Mayo and the Hawthorne Studies

Hawthorne effect
The tendency for people to behave differently when they know they are being studied.

One study, inspired by Frederick Taylor's research, began at the Western Electric Company's Hawthorne plant in Cicero, Illinois, in 1927 and ended six years later. Let's see why it is one of the major studies in management literature.

Elton Mayo and his colleagues from Harvard University came to the Hawthorne plant to test the degree of lighting associated with optimum productivity. In this respect, their study was a traditional scientific management study. The idea was to keep records of the workers' productivity under different levels of illumination. But the initial experiments revealed what seemed to be a problem. The researchers had expected productivity to fall as the lighting was dimmed. Yet the experimental group's productivity went up regardless of whether the lighting was bright or dim, and even when it was reduced to about the level of moonlight.

In a second series of 13 experiments, a separate test room was set up where researchers could manipulate temperature, humidity, and other environmental factors. Productivity went up each time; in fact, it increased by 50 percent overall. When the experimenters repeated the original condition (expecting productivity to fall to original levels), productivity increased yet again. The experiments were considered a total failure at this point. No matter what the experimenters did, productivity went up. What was causing the increase?

In the end, Mayo guessed that some human or psychological factor was at play. He and his colleagues interviewed the workers, asking about their feelings and attitudes toward the experiment. The answers began a profound change in management thinking that still has repercussions today. Here is what the researchers concluded:

- The workers in the test room thought of themselves as a social group. The atmosphere was informal, they could talk freely, and they interacted regularly with their supervisors and the experimenters. They felt special and worked hard to stay in the group. This motivated them.

- The workers were included in planning the experiments. For example, they rejected one kind of pay schedule and recommended another, which was adopted. They believed their ideas were respected and felt engaged in managerial decision making. This, too, motivated them.

- No matter the physical conditions, the workers enjoyed the atmosphere of their special room and the additional pay for being more productive. Job satisfaction increased dramatically.

Researchers now use the term **Hawthorne effect** to refer to people's tendency to behave differently when they know they're being studied. The Hawthorne study's results encouraged researchers to study human motivation and the managerial styles that lead to higher productivity. Research emphasis shifted from Taylor's scientific management toward Mayo's new human-based management.

Mayo's findings led to completely new assumptions about employees. One was that pay is not the only motivator. In fact, money was found to be a relatively ineffective motivator. New assumptions led to many theories about the human side of motivation. One of the best-known motivation theorists was Abraham Maslow, whose work we discuss next.

Little did Elton Mayo and his research team from Harvard University know they would forever change managers' beliefs about employee motivation. Their research at the Hawthorne plant of Western Electric in Cicero, Illinois (pictured here), gave birth to the concept of human-based motivation by showing that employees behaved differently simply because they were involved in planning and executing the experiments.

LEARNING goal 3

Identify the levels of Maslow's hierarchy of needs and apply them to employee motivation.

MOTIVATION AND MASLOW'S HIERARCHY OF NEEDS

Psychologist Abraham Maslow believed that to understand motivation at work, we must understand human motivation in general. It seemed to him that motivation arises from need. That is, people are motivated to satisfy unmet needs. Needs that have already been satisfied no longer provide motivation.

Figure 10.1 shows **Maslow's hierarchy of needs,** whose levels are:

Maslow's hierarchy of needs
Theory of motivation based on unmet human needs from basic physiological needs to safety, social, and esteem needs to self-actualization needs.

Physiological needs: Basic survival needs, such as the need for food, water, and shelter.

Safety needs: The need to feel secure at work and at home.

Social needs: The need to feel loved, accepted, and part of the group.

Esteem needs: The need for recognition and acknowledgment from others, as well as self-respect and a sense of status or importance.

Self-actualization needs: The need to develop to one's fullest potential.

When one need is satisfied, another, higher-level need emerges and motivates us to satisfy it. The satisfied need is no longer a motivator. For example, if you just ate a full-course dinner, hunger would not be a motivator (at least for several hours), and your attention may turn to your surroundings (safety needs) or family (social needs). Of course, lower-level needs (perhaps thirst) may reemerge at any time they are not being met and take your attention away from higher-level needs.

Most of the world's workers struggle all day simply to meet the basic physiological and safety needs. In more developed countries, such needs no longer dominate, and workers seek to satisfy growth needs—social, esteem, and self-actualization needs.

To compete successfully, U.S. firms must create a work environment that includes goals such as social contribution, honesty, reliability, service, quality, dependability, and unity—for all levels of employees. Chip Conley of Joie de Vivre, a chain of 30 boutique hotels, thinks about higher-level needs such as meaning (self-actualization) for all employees, including lower-level workers. Half his employees are housekeepers who clean toilets all day. How does he help them feel they're doing meaningful work? One technique is what he calls the George Bailey exercise, based on the main character in the movie *It's a Wonderful Life*. Conley asks small groups of housekeepers what would happen if they weren't there every day. Trash would pile up, bathrooms would be full of wet towels, and let's not even think about the toilets. Then he asked them to come up with some other name for housekeeping. They offered suggestions like "serenity keepers," "clutter busters," or "the peace-of-mind police." In the end, these employees had a sense of how the customer's experience wouldn't be the same without them. This gave meaning to their work that helped satisfy higher-level needs.[6]

figure 10.1

MASLOW'S HIERARCHY OF NEEDS

Maslow's hierarchy of needs is based on the idea that motivation comes from need. If a need is met, it's no longer a motivator, so a higher-level need becomes the motivator. Higher-level needs demand the support of lower-level needs. This chart shows the various levels of need. Do you know where you are on the chart right now?

LEARNING goal **4**

Distinguish between the motivators and hygiene factors identified by Herzberg.

HERZBERG'S MOTIVATING FACTORS

Another direction in managerial theory explores what managers can do with the job itself to motivate employees. In other words, some theorists ask: Of all the factors controllable by managers, which are most effective in generating an enthusiastic work effort?

In the mid-1960s, psychologist Frederick Herzberg conducted the most discussed study in this area. Herzberg asked workers to rank various job-related factors in order of importance relative to motivation. The question was: What creates enthusiasm for workers and makes them work to full potential? The most important factors were:

1. Sense of achievement.
2. Earned recognition.
3. Interest in the work itself.
4. Opportunity for growth.
5. Opportunity for advancement.
6. Importance of responsibility.
7. Peer and group relationships.
8. Pay.
9. Supervisor's fairness.
10. Company policies and rules.
11. Status.
12. Job security.
13. Supervisor's friendliness.
14. Working conditions.

Factors receiving the most votes all clustered around job content. Workers like to feel they contribute to the company (sense of achievement was number 1). They want to earn recognition (number 2) and feel their jobs are important (number 6). They want responsibility (which is why learning is so important) and to earn recognition for that responsibility by having a chance for growth and advancement. Of course, workers also want the job to be interesting. Do you feel the same way about your work?

Workers did not consider factors related to job environment to be motivators. It was interesting to find that one of those factors was pay. Workers felt the *absence* of good pay, job security, and friendly supervisors could cause dissatisfaction, but their presence did not motivate employees to work harder; it just provided satisfaction and contentment. Would you work harder if you were paid more?

Herzberg concluded that certain factors, which he called **motivators**, made employees productive and gave them satisfaction. These factors, as you have seen, mostly related to job content. Herzberg called other elements of the job **hygiene factors** (or maintenance factors). These related to the job environment and could cause dissatisfaction if missing but would not necessarily motivate employees if increased. See Figure 10.2 for a list of motivators and hygiene factors.

Herzberg's motivating factors led to this conclusion: The best way to motivate employees is to make their jobs interesting, help them achieve their objectives, and recognize their achievement through advancement and added

motivators
In Herzberg's theory of motivating factors, job factors that cause employees to be productive and that give them satisfaction.

hygiene factors
In Herzberg's theory of motivating factors, job factors that can cause dissatisfaction if missing but that do not necessarily motivate employees if increased.

figure IO.2

**HERZBERG'S MOTIVATORS
AND HYGIENE FACTORS**
There's some controversy over Herzberg's results. For example, sales managers often use money as a motivator. Recent studies have shown that money can be a motivator if used as part of a recognition program.

MOTIVATORS	HYGIENE (MAINTENANCE) FACTORS
(These factors can be used to motivate workers.)	(These factors can cause dissatisfaction, but changing them will have little motivational effect.)
Work itself	Company policy and administration
Achievement	Supervision
Recognition	Working conditions
Responsibility	Interpersonal relations (co-workers)
Growth and advancement	Salary, status, and job security

responsibility.[7] A review of Figure 10.3 shows the similarity between Maslow's hierarchy of needs and Herzberg's theory.

Look at Herzberg's motivating factors, identify those that motivate you, and rank them in order of importance to you. Keep them in mind as you consider jobs and careers. What motivators do your job opportunities offer you? Are they the ones you consider important? Evaluating your job offers in terms of what's really important to you will help you make a wise career choice.

progress assessment

- What are the similarities and differences between Taylor's time-motion studies and Mayo's Hawthorne studies?
- How did Mayo's findings influence scientific management?
- Draw a diagram of Maslow's hierarchy of needs. Label and describe the parts.
- Explain the distinction between what Herzberg called motivators and hygiene factors.

figure IO.3

**COMPARISON OF MASLOW'S
HIERARCHY OF NEEDS AND
HERZBERG'S THEORY OF
FACTORS**

LEARNING goal 5

Differentiate among Theory X, Theory Y, and Theory Z.

MCGREGOR'S THEORY X AND THEORY Y

The way managers go about motivating people at work depends greatly on their attitudes toward workers. Management theorist Douglas McGregor observed that managers' attitudes generally fall into one of two entirely different sets of managerial assumptions, which he called Theory X and Theory Y.

Theory X

The assumptions of Theory X management are:

- The average person dislikes work and will avoid it if possible.
- Because of this dislike, workers must be forced, controlled, directed, or threatened with punishment to make them put forth the effort to achieve the organization's goals.
- The average worker prefers to be directed, wishes to avoid responsibility, has relatively little ambition, and wants security.
- Primary motivators are fear and money.

The natural consequence of these assumptions is a manager who is very busy and watches people closely, telling them what to do and how to do it. Motivation is more likely to take the form of punishment for bad work than reward for good work. Theory X managers give workers little responsibility, authority, or flexibility. Taylor and other theorists who preceded him would have agreed with Theory X. Time-motion studies calculated the one best way to perform a task and the optimal time to devote to it. Researchers assumed workers needed to be trained and carefully watched to see that they conformed to standards.

Many managers and entrepreneurs still suspect that employees cannot be fully trusted and need to be closely supervised. No doubt you have seen such managers in action. How did they make you feel? Were these managers' assumptions accurate regarding workers' attitudes?

Theory X managers do not come in one-size-fits-all packages. Take Salina Lo of Ruckus Wireless, for example. On the job this graduate of University of California at Berkeley is a tough and exacting Theory X manager. Her in-your-face style has earned her a reputation as one of the industry's toughest managers. Would you prefer to work for a Theory X or a Theory Y manager?

Theory Y

Theory Y makes entirely different assumptions about people:

- Most people like work; it is as natural as play or rest.
- Most people naturally work toward goals to which they are committed.
- The depth of a person's commitment to goals depends on the perceived rewards for achieving them.
- Under certain conditions, most people not only accept but also seek responsibility.
- People are capable of using a relatively high degree of imagination, creativity, and cleverness to solve problems.

- In industry, the average person's intellectual potential is only partially realized.
- People are motivated by a variety of rewards. Each worker is stimulated by a reward unique to him or her (time off, money, recognition, and so on).

Rather than authority, direction, and close supervision, Theory Y managers emphasize a relaxed managerial atmosphere in which workers are free to set objectives, be creative, be flexible, and go beyond the goals set by management. A key technique here is *empowerment*, giving employees authority to make decisions and tools to implement the decisions they make. For empowerment to be a real motivator, management should follow these three steps:

1. Find out what people think the problems in the organization are.
2. Let them design the solutions.
3. Get out of the way and let them put those solutions into action.

Often employees complain that although they're asked to engage in company decision making, their managers fail to actually empower them to make decisions. Have you ever worked in such an atmosphere? How did that make you feel?

OUCHI'S THEORY Z

One reason many U.S. companies choose a more flexible managerial style is to meet competition from firms in Japan, China, and the European Union. In the 1980s, Japanese companies seemed to be outperforming U.S. businesses. William Ouchi, management professor at the University of California–Los Angeles, wondered whether the reason was the way Japanese companies managed their workers. The Japanese approach, which Ouchi called Type J, included lifetime employment, consensual decision making, collective responsibility for the outcomes of decisions, slow evaluation and promotion, implied control mechanisms, nonspecialized career paths, and holistic concern for employees. In

Google has its own state-of-the-art gym and resistance swimming pool to help employees work off the extra pounds. Large and colorful exercise balls are everywhere to remind employees to take care of their bodies. Can you think of any other examples of the kind of holistic concern for employees suggested by William Ouchi's Theory Z style of management?

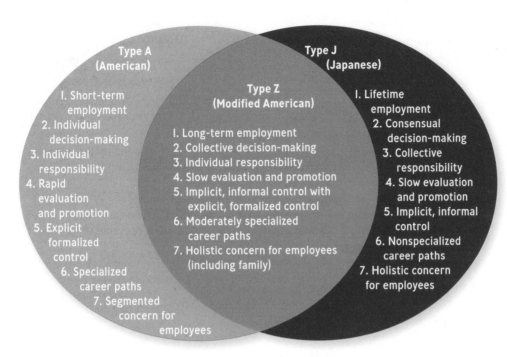

figure 10.4

THEORY Z: A BLEND OF AMERICAN AND JAPANESE MANAGEMENT APPROACHES

contrast, the U.S. management approach, which Ouchi called Type A, relied on short-term employment, individual decision making, individual responsibility for the outcomes of decisions, rapid evaluation and promotion, explicit control mechanisms, specialized career paths, and segmented concern for employees.

Type J firms are based on the culture of Japan, which includes a focus on trust and intimacy within the group and family. Conversely, Type A firms are based on American culture, which includes a focus on individual rights and achievements. Ouchi wanted to help U.S. firms adopt successful Japanese strategies, but he realized it wouldn't be practical to expect U.S. managers to accept an approach based on the culture of another country. Judge for your-self. A job for life may sound good until you think of the implications: no chance to change jobs and no opportunity to move quickly through the ranks.

Ouchi recommended a hybrid approach, Theory Z (see Figure 10.4). Theory Z includes long-term employment, collective decision making, indi-vidual responsibility for the outcomes of decisions, slow evaluation and pro-motion, moderately specialized career paths, and holistic concern for employees (including family). Theory Z views the organization as a family that fosters cooperation and organizational values.

In recent years, demographic and social changes, fierce global competition, and the worst recession in their country's history have forced Japanese managers to reevaluate the way they conduct business. The effects of the 2011 earthquake on Japanese businesses reinforced the need to change. They now need to become both more dynamic and more efficient in order to compete effectively.

Electronics giant Hitachi was the first major Japanese company to quit requiring corporate calisthenics. Having everyone start the day with group exercises had symbolized doing the same thing the same way, and reinforced the cultural belief that employees should not take risks or think for them-selves. Many managers think such conformity is what hurt Japanese business. Will Japanese managers move toward the hybrid Theory Z in the future? We'll have to wait and see. An appropriate managerial style matches the culture, situation, and specific needs of the organization and its employees. (See Figure 10.5 for a summary of Theories X, Y, and Z.)

figure 10.5

**A COMPARISON OF
THEORIES X, Y, AND Z**

THEORY X	THEORY Y	THEORY Z
1. Employees dislike work and will try to avoid it.	1. Employees view work as a natural part of life.	1. Employee involvement is the key to increased productivity.
2. Employees prefer to be controlled and directed.	2. Employees prefer limited control and direction.	2. Employee control is implied and informal.
3. Employees seek security, not responsibility.	3. Employees will seek responsibility under proper work conditions.	3. Employees prefer to share responsibility and decision making.
4. Employees must be intimidated by managers to perform.	4. Employees perform better in work environments that are nonintimidating.	4. Employees perform better in environments that foster trust and cooperation.
5. Employees are motivated by financial rewards.	5. Employees are motivated by many different needs.	5. Employees need guaranteed employment and will accept slow evaluations and promotions.

LEARNING goal **6**

Explain the key principles of goal-setting, expectancy, reinforcement, and equity theories.

GOAL-SETTING THEORY AND MANAGEMENT BY OBJECTIVES

goal-setting theory
The idea that setting ambitious but attainable goals can motivate workers and improve performance if the goals are accepted, accompanied by feedback, and facilitated by organizational conditions.

Goal-setting theory says setting ambitious but attainable goals can motivate workers and improve performance if the goals are accepted and accompanied by feedback, and if conditions in the organization pave the way for achievement. All organization members should have some basic agreement about both overall goals and specific objectives for each department and individual. Thus there should be a system to engage everyone in the organization in goal setting and implementation.

The late management expert Peter Drucker developed such a system in the 1960s. "Managers cannot motivate people; they can only thwart people's motivation because people motivate themselves," he said. Called **management by objectives (MBO)**, Drucker's system of goal setting and implementation includes a cycle of discussion, review, and evaluation of objectives among top and middle-level managers, supervisors, and employees. It calls on managers to formulate goals in cooperation with everyone in the organization, to commit employees to those goals, and to monitor results and reward accomplishment. Government agencies like the Department of Defense use MBO.

management by objectives (MBO)
A system of goal setting and implementation; it involves a cycle of discussion, review, and evaluation of objectives among top and middle-level managers, supervisors, and employees.

MBO is most effective in relatively stable situations when managers can make long-range plans and implement them with few changes.[8] Managers must also understand the difference between helping and coaching subordinates. *Helping* means working with the subordinate and doing part of the work if necessary. *Coaching* means acting as a resource—teaching, guiding, and recommending—but not participating actively or doing the task. The central idea of MBO is that employees need to motivate themselves.

Employee input and expectations are important.[9] Problems can arise when management uses MBO as a strategy for forcing managers and workers to commit to goals that are not agreed on together, but are instead set by top management.[10]

Victor Vroom identified the importance of employee expectations and developed a process called expectancy theory. Let's examine this concept next.

MEETING EMPLOYEE EXPECTATIONS: EXPECTANCY THEORY

According to Victor Vroom's **expectancy theory**, employee expectations can affect motivation. That is, the amount of effort employees exert on a specific task depends on their expectations of the outcome. Vroom contends that employees ask three questions before committing their maximum effort to a task: (1) Can I accomplish the task? (2) If I do accomplish it, what's my reward? (3) Is the reward worth the effort? (See Figure 10.6.)

Think of the effort you might exert in class under the following conditions: Suppose your instructor says that to earn an A in the course, you must achieve an average of 90 percent on coursework plus jump eight feet high. Would you exert maximum effort toward earning an A if you knew you could not possibly jump eight feet high? Suppose your instructor said any student can earn an A in the course, but you know this instructor has not awarded an A in 25 years of teaching. If the reward of an A seems unattainable, would you exert significant effort in the course? Better yet, let's say you read online that businesses prefer hiring C-minus students to A-plus students. Does the reward of an A seem worth it? Now think of similar situations that may occur on the job.

Expectancy theory does note that expectation varies from individual to individual. Employees establish their own views of task difficulty and the value of the reward.[11] Researchers David Nadler and Edward Lawler modified Vroom's theory and suggested that managers follow five steps to improve employee performance:[12]

1. Determine what rewards employees value.
2. Determine each employee's desired performance standard.
3. Ensure that performance standards are attainable.
4. Guarantee rewards tied to performance.
5. Be certain that employees consider the rewards adequate.

expectancy theory
Victor Vroom's theory that the amount of effort employees exert on a specific task depends on their expectations of the outcome.

figure IO.6

EXPECTANCY THEORY
The amount of effort employees exert on a task depends on their expectations of the outcome.

figure 10.7

REINFORCEMENT THEORY
Managers can either add or subtract stimuli (positive reinforcement, negative reinforcement, or punishers) to increase desired behavior or decrease undesired behavior.
Source: Casey Limmer, MSW, LCSW, Washington University.

	ADD STIMULI	SUBTRACT STIMULI
Increase Behavior	Positive Reinforcement: Jill gets praise (the reinforcement added) for turning in her reports on time (target behavior to increase).	Negative Reinforcement: Jack is on probation (punishment that will be removed) until such time as he can turn in 3 reports on time (target behavior to increase).
Decrease Behavior	Punishment: Jack gets written up (the punisher) for turning in his reports late (target behavior to decrease).	Extinction: Jill does not get praise (reinforcement is removed) when her reports are turned in late (target behavior to decrease), no matter how well done they are.

REINFORCING EMPLOYEE PERFORMANCE: REINFORCEMENT THEORY

reinforcement theory
Theory that positive and negative reinforcers motivate a person to behave in certain ways.

According to **reinforcement theory**, positive reinforcers, negative reinforcers and punishers motivate a person to behave in certain ways. In other words, motivation is the result of the carrot-and-stick approach: individuals act to receive rewards and avoid punishment. Positive reinforcements are rewards such as praise, recognition, and a pay raise. Punishment includes reprimands, reduced pay, and layoffs or firing. Negative reinforcement occurs when people work to escape the punishers. Escaping the punishment reinforces or rewards the positive behavior. A manager might also try to stop undesirable behavior by not responding to it. This response is called extinction because managers hope the unwanted behavior will become extinct. Figure 10.7 illustrates how a manager can use reinforcement theory to motivate workers.

TREATING EMPLOYEES FAIRLY: EQUITY THEORY

equity theory
The idea that employees try to maintain equity between inputs and outputs compared to others in similar positions.

Equity theory looks at how employees' perceptions of fairness affect their willingness to perform. It assumes employees ask, "If I do a good job, will it be worth it?" and "What's fair?" Employees try to maintain equity between what they put into the job and what they get out of it, comparing those inputs and outputs to those of others in similar positions. Workers find comparative information through personal relationships, professional organizations, and other sources.

When workers perceive inequity, they will try to reestablish fairness in a number of ways. For example, suppose you compare the grade you earned on a term paper with your classmates' grades. If you think you received a lower grade than someone who put out the same effort as you, you may (1) reduce your effort on future class projects or (2) rationalize the difference by saying, "Grades are overvalued anyway!" If you think your paper received a higher grade than comparable papers, you will probably (1) increase your effort to justify the higher reward in the future or (2) rationalize by saying, "I'm worth it!"

In the workplace, perceived inequity may lead to lower productivity, reduced quality, increased absenteeism, and voluntary resignation.

Remember that equity judgments are based on perception and are therefore subject to error. When workers overestimate their own contributions—as happens often—they feel *any* rewards given out for performance are inequitable. Sometimes organizations try to deal with this by keeping employee salaries secret, but secrecy may make things worse. Employees are likely to overestimate the salaries of others, in addition to overestimating their own contribution. The best remedy is generally clear and frequent communication. Managers must communicate as clearly as possible both the results they expect and the outcomes that will occur.[13]

progress assessment

- Briefly describe the managerial attitudes behind Theories X, Y, and Z.
- Explain goal-setting theory.
- Evaluate expectancy theory. When could expectancy theory apply to your efforts or lack of effort?
- Explain the principles of equity theory.

LEARNING goal 7

Show how managers put motivation theories into action through such strategies as job enrichment, open communication, and job recognition.

PUTTING THEORY INTO ACTION

Now that you know what a few theorists have to say about motivation, you might be asking yourself "So what? What do all those theories have to do with what really goes on in the workplace today?" Fair question. Let's look at how companies put the theories into action through job enrichment, open communication, and job recognition.

Motivation through Job Enrichment

Managers have extended both Maslow's and Herzberg's theories through **job enrichment**, a strategy that motivates workers through the job itself. Work is assigned so that individuals can complete an identifiable task from beginning to end and are held responsible for successful achievement. Job enrichment is based on Herzberg's higher motivators, such as responsibility, achievement, and recognition. It stands in contrast to *job simplification*, which produces task efficiency by breaking a job into simple steps and assigning people to each. Review Maslow's and Herzberg's work to see how job enrichment grew from those theories.

Those who advocate job enrichment believe that five characteristics of work are important in motivation and performance:

1. *Skill variety*. The extent to which a job demands different skills.
2. *Task identity*. The degree to which the job requires doing a task with a visible outcome from beginning to end.
3. *Task significance*. The degree to which the job has a substantial impact on the lives or work of others in the company.

job enrichment
A motivational strategy that emphasizes motivating the worker through the job itself.

Here a worker in Baccarat's factory puts the finishing touches on a crystal vase. One of the hallmarks of job enrichment is the worker's ability to perform a complete task from beginning to end. Why do you think this might be more motivating than simply adding a few parts to an assembly on a production line?

job enlargement
A job enrichment strategy that involves combining a series of tasks into one challenging and interesting assignment.

job rotation
A job enrichment strategy that involves moving employees from one job to another.

4. *Autonomy.* The degree of freedom, independence, and discretion in scheduling work and determining procedures.

5. *Feedback.* The amount of direct and clear information given about job performance.

Variety, identity, and significance contribute to the meaningfulness of the job. Autonomy gives people a feeling of responsibility; feedback contributes to a feeling of achievement and recognition.[14]

One type of job enrichment is **job enlargement**, which combines a series of tasks into one challenging and interesting assignment. Maytag, the home appliance manufacturer, redesigned its washing machine production process so that employees could assemble an entire water pump instead of just adding one part. **Job rotation** also makes work more interesting and motivating by moving employees from one job to another. One problem, of course, is the need to train employees to do several different operations. However, the resulting increase in motivation and the value of having flexible, cross-trained employees usually offsets the costs.[15]

Motivating through Open Communication

Communication and information must flow freely throughout the organization when employees are empowered to make decisions—they can't make them in a vacuum. Procedures for encouraging open communication include the following:

- *Create an organizational culture that rewards listening.* Top managers must create places to talk and show employees that talking with superiors counts—by providing feedback, adopting employee suggestions, and rewarding upward communication—even if the discussion is negative. Employees must feel free to say anything they deem appropriate and believe their opinions are valued.[16]

- *Train supervisors and managers to listen.* Most people receive no training in how to listen, in school or anywhere else, so organizations must do such training themselves or hire someone to do it.

- *Use effective questioning techniques.* We get information through questioning. Different kinds of questions yield different kinds of information. Closed questions that generate yes/no answers don't encourage the longer, more thoughtful responses that open questions do. Appropriate personal questions can create a sense of camaraderie between employee and manager.

- *Remove barriers to open communication.* Separate offices, parking areas, bathrooms, and dining rooms for managers only set up barriers. Other barriers are different dress codes and different ways of addressing one another (like calling workers by their first names and managers by their last). Removing such barriers may require imagination and managers' willingness to give up special privileges.

- *Avoid vague and ambiguous communication.* Passive voice appears weak and tentative. Statements such as "Mistakes were made" leave you wondering who made the mistakes. Hedging is another way managers send garbled messages. Terms like *possibly* and *perhaps* sound wishy-washy to employees who need more definitive direction.

- *Make it easy to communicate.* Encouraging organization members to eat together at large lunch tables, allowing employees to gather in conference rooms, having organizational picnics and athletic teams, and so on can help workers at all levels mix with one another.

- *Ask employees what is important to them.* Managers shouldn't wait until the exit interview to ask an employee, "What can I do to keep you?" Then it's too late. Instead they should have frequent *stay interviews* to find out what matters to employees and what they can do to keep them on the job.[17]

The nearby Social Media in Business box offers advice on using open communication strategies in businesses.

Applying Open Communication in Self-Managed Teams

Before the recent economic crisis, the auto companies were often cited for good practices. At Ford Motor Company, for example, a group known as Team Mustang set the guidelines for how production teams should be formed. Given the challenge to create a car that would make people dust off their old "Mustang Sally" records and dance into showrooms, the 400-member team was also given the freedom to make decisions without waiting for approval from headquarters. Everyone worked under one roof in an old warehouse where drafting experts sat next to accountants, engineers next to stylists. Budgetary walls between departments were knocked down too as department managers were persuaded to surrender some control over their subordinates on the team.

When the resulting Mustang convertible displayed shaking problems, engineers were so motivated to finish on time and under budget that they worked late into the night, sleeping on the floor when necessary. Senior Ford executives were tempted to intervene, but they stuck with their promise not to meddle. Working with suppliers, the team solved the shaking problem and still came in under budget and a couple of months early. The new car was a hit with drivers, and sales soared.[18]

To implement such teams, managers at most companies must reinvent work. This means respecting workers, providing interesting work, developing workers' skills, allowing autonomy, decentralizing authority, and rewarding good work. Next we'll take a look at some of the ways companies recognize and reward good work.

In the car business nothing works like the "wow" factor. At Ford, the 400-member Team Mustang group was empowered to create the "wow" response for the company's sleek Mustang convertible. The work team, suppliers, company managers, and even customers worked together to make the Mustang a winner in the very competitive automobile market.

Recognizing a Job Well Done

Letting people know you appreciate their work is usually more powerful than giving a raise or bonus alone.[19] When asked in a recent survey their reason for changing jobs, only 42 percent of the participants listed increased compensation and benefits, while 83 percent said they left for increased responsibilities and/or a more senior role.[20] Clearly, providing advancement opportunity is important in retaining valuable employees.

Promotions aren't the only way to celebrate a job well done. Recognition can be as simple as noticing positive actions out loud, making employees feel their efforts are worthwhile and valued enough to be noticed. For example: "Sarina, you didn't say much in the meeting today. Your ideas are usually so valuable; I missed hearing them." This comment lets Sarina know her ideas are appreciated, and she'll be more apt to participate fully in the next meeting.

Here are just a few examples of ways managers have raised employee spirits without raising paychecks:

- A Los Angeles law firm sent 400 employees and their families to Disneyland for the day. FedEx Office did something similar, but it sent high-achieving employees to Disneyland *and* put the company's top executives in those employees' place while they were gone.

- Accounting firm KPMG gave employees a sundae surprise of gourmet ice cream and toppings.

- Give More Media offers perks like Netflix and XM Satellite Radio memberships. It also encourages participation in its Smile and Give program, which gives employees three paid days off to work for a nonprofit of their choice.

- Lotus Public Relations in New York City has an annual "Lotus Day." One year employees sailed the Hudson, ate in an expensive restaurant, and enjoyed a comedy show and drinks. Other everyday perks include a free snack cabinet, free coffee, and free unlimited city commuting.

- Walt Disney World offers more than 200 employee recognition programs. The Spirit of Fred Award is named after an employee named Fred, who makes each award (a certificate mounted and varnished on a plaque) himself. Fred's name became an acronym for Friendly, Resourceful, Enthusiastic, and Dependable.

- Maritz Inc., in Fenton, Missouri, has a Thanks a Bunch program that gives flowers to a selected employee in appreciation of a job well done. That employee passes the bouquet to someone else who helped. The idea is to see how many people are given the flowers throughout the day. The bouquet comes with thank-you cards that are entered into a drawing for awards like binoculars and jackets.

- Hewlett-Packard (HP) bestows its Golden Banana Award for a job well done. The award started when an engineer burst into his manager's office saying he'd found the solution to a long-standing problem. In his haste to find something to give the employee to show his appreciation, the manager grabbed a banana from his lunch and said, "Well done! Congratulations!" The Golden Banana is now one of the most prestigious honors given to an inventive HP employee.

Yahoo honors employees who have worked at the company for at least five years with this gumball machine service award. What part do you think awards like this play in motivating the winners to continue their outstanding performance?

The nearby Spotlight on Small business box offers examples of what a number of small businesses have done to motivate employees.

Giving valued employees prime parking spots, more vacation days, or more flexible schedules may help them feel their work is appreciated, but sometimes nothing inspires workers like the prospect of a payout down the road. Companies that offer a small equity stake or stock options often have a good chance of developing loyal employees

The same things don't motivate all employees. Next we'll explore how employees from different cultures and generations are motivated in different ways.

LEARNING goal 8

Show how managers personalize motivation strategies to appeal to employees across the globe and across generations.

PERSONALIZING MOTIVATION

Managers cannot use one motivational formula for all employees. They have to get to know each worker personally and tailor the motivational effort to the individual. This is further complicated by the increase in global business and the fact that managers now work with employees from a variety of cultural backgrounds. Cultural differences also exist between generations raised in the same country. Let's look at how managers personalize their strategies to appeal to employees across the globe and across generations.

Small Incentives Can be Big Motivators

How can small businesses motivate their workers to perform their best when they can't offer their employees the financial incentives larger businesses can? Many strive to create an upbeat, relaxed company culture to encourage employees to bond with one another. For example, at Blurb, a San Francisco–based specialty publishing company, at the end of every Friday the conference room is transformed into a concert venue as employees play the video game Rock Band. The boss provides refreshments along with the game, allowing the staff to relax and let the stress of the workweek pass into memory. Sprout Group, a small marketing firm based in Utah, uses a similarly laid-back strategy with weekly company trips to the movie theater where tickets and popcorn are on the boss.

Employee motivation isn't just about morale-boosting leisure activities like video games and movie nights. Besides providing social interaction, management needs to communicate clearly with the staff in order to give purpose and direction. At the small consulting firm Sonoma Partners, veteran employees mentor new hires to acquaint them with the work environment and show them how to excel. Not only does this method help new employees bond with their colleagues; it also sets them on the path to becoming productive workers.

Small businesses have a greater opportunity to motivate with open communication and broad responsibility. Individual workers can have more say in the company and not feel like just another drone in the great corporate beehive. As long as management encourages innovation from employees (and throws an occasional video game party), small businesses should have no trouble motivating their employees.

Sources: Sarah E. Needleman, "Business Owners Try to Motivate Employees," *The Wall Street Journal,* January 14, 2010; and Toddi Gutner, "Motivate Employees with Goal-Setting," www.smallbusiness.foxbusiness.com, April 13, 2011.

Motivating Employees across the Globe

Different cultures experience motivational approaches differently; therefore, managers study and understand these cultural factors in designing a reward system. In a *high-context culture,* workers build personal relationships and develop group trust before focusing on tasks. In a *low-context culture,* workers often view relationship building as a waste of time that diverts attention from the task. Koreans, Thais, and Saudis tend to be high-context workers who often view their U.S. colleagues as insincere due to their need for data and quick decision making.

Dow Chemical solved a cross-cultural problem with a recognition program for its 52,000 employees in over 37 countries who use a wide variety of languages and currencies. Globoforce Ltd. created a Web-based program for Dow called Recognition@Dow that automatically adjusts for differences created by cultural preferences, tax laws, and even local standards of living. Thus a U.S. employee might receive a gift certificate for Macy's, whereas a Chinese employee receives one for online retailer Dangdang.com. The system even allows employees to nominate colleagues for recognition using an "award wizard" to help determine the appropriate award.[21]

Understanding motivation in global organizations and building effective global teams is still a new task for most companies. Developing group leaders who are culturally astute, flexible, and able to deal with ambiguity is a challenge businesses face in the 21st century. See the Reaching Beyond Our Borders box for more about managing culturally diverse employees.

Importance of Cultural Competency

Managers of employees from different cultural and geographic backgrounds have unique opportunities to reach out to new markets and understand ways to extend their products to new markets. A better understanding of other cultures' customs and concerns helps managers increase customer satisfaction and customer loyalty.

Part of cultural competency is not only understanding different languages, but also understanding different food choices, customs, how people want to be addressed, and even how much space should be between people. In some cultures, people are taught not to interrupt or not to look someone in the eye. So managers need to understand how to work with all

people. Often the formality of a culture is tied to the age of that culture. The older the culture the more formal it usually is.

United Parcel Service has employees in 200 countries and territories around the world. Emphasizing diversity is strategically important because it allows them to tap into differences. Danny Torian, Learning and Development manager at UPS Air Operations in Louisville, Kentucky, says, "Not emphasizing diversity and inclusion in a workforce are threefold. It impacts your brand, it hurts recruiting . . . it will create a decline in business growth."

Sources: Rachel Reynolds, "Corporate Champions See Many Advantages in Diverse Workforce," *Business First,* February 2, 2011.

Motivating Employees across Generations

Baby boomers (born between 1946 and 1964), Generation X members (born between 1965 and 1980), and Generation Y members, also known as Millennials or echo boomers (born between 1980 and 2000), are linked through experiences they shared in their formative years—usually the first 10 years of life. The beliefs you accept as a child affect how you view risk, challenge, authority, technology, relationships, and economics. When you're in a management position, they can even affect whom you hire, fire, or promote.

In general, boomers were raised in families that experienced unprecedented economic prosperity, secure jobs, and optimism about the future. Gen Xers were raised in dual-career families with parents who focused on work. As children, they attended day care or became latchkey kids. Their parents' layoffs added to their insecurity about a lifelong job. Millennials were raised by indulgent parents, and most don't remember a time without cell phones, computers, and electronic entertainment. The main constant in the lives of Gen Xers and Millennials is inconstancy. Consider the unprecedented change in the past 10–20 years in every area (i.e. economic, technological, scientific, social, and political). Gen Xers and Millennials expect change. It is the absence of change that they find questionable.[22]

How do generational differences among these groups affect motivation in the workplace? Boomer managers need to be flexible with their Gen X and Millennial employees, or they will lose them. Gen X employees need to use their enthusiasm for change and streamlining to their advantage.[23] Although many are unwilling to pay the same price for success their parents and grandparents did, their concern about undue stress and long hours doesn't mean they lack ambition. They want economic security as much as older workers, but

> *Millennials tend to be skeptical, outspoken, and image-driven as well as adaptable, tech-savvy employees with a sense of fun and tolerance. It is important for managers of all ages to be aware that employees of different generations communicate differently. How do you think generational differences will affect this manager and employee?*

Gary Kelly, CEO of Southwest Airlines, shocked his co-workers the year he showed up at the company Halloween party dressed as Gene Simmons, front man for the rock group Kiss. Now each year in his blog he asks Southwest employees to suggest his next costume. How do you think Kelly's Halloween antics help develop happy, productive, and loyal employees?

they have a different approach to achieving it. Rather than focusing on job security, Gen Xers tend to focus on career security instead and are willing to change jobs to find it.[24]

Many Gen Xers are now managers themselves, responsible for motivating other employees. What kind of managers are they? In general, they are well equipped to motivate people. They usually understand that there is more to life than work, and they think a big part of motivating is letting people know you recognize that fact. Gen X managers tend to focus more on results than on hours in the workplace. They tend to be flexible and good at collaboration and consensus building. They often think in broader terms than their predecessors because the media have exposed them to problems around the world. They also have a big impact on their team members. They are more likely to give them the goals and outlines of the project and leave them alone to do their work.[25]

Perhaps the best asset of Gen X managers is their ability to give employees feedback, especially positive feedback. One reason might be that they expect more of it themselves. One new employee was frustrated because he hadn't received feedback from his boss since he was hired—two weeks earlier. In short, managers need to realize that young workers demand performance reviews and other forms of feedback more than the traditional one or two times a year.

As Millennials continue to enter the job market, they are creating a workplace four generations deep. As a group, they tend to share a number of characteristics: they're impatient, skeptical, blunt and expressive, image-driven, and inexperienced. Like any other generation, they can transform their characteristics into unique skills. For example, Millennials tend to be adaptable, tech-savvy, able to grasp new concepts, practiced at multitasking, efficient, and tolerant. Perhaps the most surprising attribute they share is a sense of commitment.[26] Millennials place a higher value on work-life balance, expect their employers to adapt to them (not the other way around), and are more likely to rank fun and stimulation in their top five ideal-job requirements.[27] What do you think are the most effective strategies managers can use to motivate Millennial workers?

Many Millennials aren't rushing to find lifetime careers after graduation. They're "job surfing" and aren't opposed to living with their parents while they test out jobs. Some of this career postponement isn't by choice as much as a result of the state of the economy. The recession hurt younger workers more deeply than other workers. In July 2010, the unemployment rate was 15.3 percent for those aged 20 to 24, while the overall unemployment rate was 9.5 percent. Unemployment for 18- to 29-year-olds was the highest it's been in more than three decades. In fact, today Millennials are less likely to be employed than Gen Xers or boomers were at the same age. The recession has increased the competition for jobs as younger workers struggle to enter the job market, boomers try to make up lost retirement savings, and Gen Xers fight to pay mortgages and raise families.[28]

As Millennials assume more responsibilities in the workplace, they sometimes must manage and lead others far older than themselves. How can young managers lead others who may have more experience than they do? Perhaps the three most important things to keep in mind are to be confident, be open minded, and solicit feedback regularly. Just remember that asking for input and advice is different from asking for permission or guidance.[29]

It is important for managers of all ages to be aware that employees of different generations communicate differently. The traditionalists, the generation that lived through the Great Depression and World War II, prefer to communicate face-to-face. Their second choice is by phone, but recordings often frustrate them. Boomers prefer to communicate in meetings or conference calls. Gen Xers generally prefer email and will choose meetings only if there are no other options. Millennials most often use technology to communicate, particularly through social media.[30]

In every generational shift, the older generation tends to say the same thing about the new: "They break the rules." The traditionalists said it of the baby boomers. Boomers look at Gen Xers and say, "Why are they breaking the rules?" And now Gen Xers are looking at Millennials and saying, "What's wrong with these kids?"

One thing in business is likely to remain constant: much motivation will come from the job itself rather than from external punishments or rewards. Managers need to give workers what they require to do a good job: the right tools, the right information, and the right amount of cooperation. Motivation doesn't have to be difficult. It begins with acknowledging a job well done—and especially doing so in front of others. After all, as we said earlier, the best motivator is frequently a sincere "Thanks, I really appreciate what you're doing."

progress assessment

- What are several steps firms can take to increase internal communications and thus motivation?
- What problems may emerge when firms try to implement participative management?
- Why is it important to adjust motivational styles to individual employees? Are there any general principles of motivation that today's managers should follow?

summary

Learning Goal 1. Explain Taylor's theory of scientific management.

- **What is Frederick Taylor known for?**

Human efficiency engineer Frederick Taylor was one of the first people to study management and has been called the father of scientific management. He conducted time-motion studies to learn the most efficient way of doing a job and then trained workers in those procedures. He published his book The *Principles of Scientific Management* in 1911. Henry L. Gantt and Frank and Lillian Gilbreth were followers of Taylor.

Learning Goal 2. Describe the Hawthorne studies and their significance to management.

- **What led to the more human-based managerial styles?**

The greatest impact on motivation theory was generated by the Hawthorne studies in the late 1920s and early 1930s. In these studies, Elton Mayo found that human factors such as feelings of involvement and participation led to greater productivity gains than did physical changes in the workplace.

Learning Goal 3. Identify the levels of Maslow's hierarchy of needs and apply them to employee motivation.

- **What did Abraham Maslow find human motivation to be based on?**

Maslow studied basic human motivation and found that motivation was based on needs. He said that a person with an unfilled need would be motivated to satisfy it and that a satisfied need no longer served as motivation.

- **What levels of need did Maslow identify?**

Starting at the bottom of Maslow's hierarchy and going to the top, the levels of need are physiological, safety, social, esteem, and self-actualization.

- **Can managers use Maslow's theory?**

Yes, they can recognize what unmet needs a person has and design work so that it satisfies those needs.

Learning Goal 4. Distinguish between the motivators and hygiene factors identified by Herzberg.

- **What is the difference between Frederick Herzberg's motivator and hygiene factors?**

Herzberg found that while some factors motivate workers (motivators), others cause job dissatisfaction if missing but are not motivators if present (hygiene or maintenance factors).

- **What are the factors called motivators?**

The work itself, achievement, recognition, responsibility, growth, and advancement.

- **What are the hygiene (maintenance) factors?**

Company policies, supervision, working conditions, interpersonal relationships, and salary.

Learning Goal 5. Differentiate among Theory X, Theory Y, and Theory Z.

- **Who developed Theory X and Theory Y?**

Douglas McGregor held that managers have one of two opposing attitudes toward employees. He called them Theory X and Theory Y.

- **What is Theory X?**

Theory X assumes the average person dislikes work and will avoid it if possible. Therefore, people must be forced, controlled, and threatened with punishment to accomplish organizational goals.

- **What is Theory Y?**

Theory Y assumes people like working and will accept responsibility for achieving goals if rewarded for doing so.

- **What is Theory Z?**

William Ouchi based Theory Z on Japanese management styles and stresses long-term employment; collective decision making; individual responsibility; slow evaluation and promotion; implicit, informal control with explicit, formalized control; moderately specialized career paths; and a holistic concern for employees (including family).

Learning Goal 6. Explain the key principles of goal-setting, expectancy, reinforcement, and equity theories.

- **What is goal-setting theory?**

Goal-setting theory is based on the notion that setting ambitious but attainable goals will lead to high levels of motivation and performance if the goals are accepted and accompanied by feedback, and if conditions in the organization make achievement possible.

- **What is management by objectives (MBO)?**

MBO is a system of goal setting and implementation; it includes a cycle of discussion, review, and evaluation of objectives among top and middle-level managers, supervisors, and employees.

- **What is the basis of expectancy theory?**

According to Victor Vroom's expectancy theory, employee expectations can affect an individual's motivation.

- **What are the key elements of expectancy theory?**

Expectancy theory centers on three questions employees often ask about performance on the job: (1) Can I accomplish the task? (2) If I do accomplish it, what's my reward? and (3) Is the reward worth the effort?

- **What are the variables in reinforcement theory?**

Positive reinforcers are rewards like praise, recognition, or raises that a worker might strive to receive after performing well. Negative reinforcers are punishments such as reprimands, pay cuts, or firing that a worker might be expected to try to avoid.

- **According to equity theory, employees try to maintain equity between inputs and outputs compared to other employees in similar positions. What happens when employees perceive that their rewards are not equitable?**

If employees perceive they are under-rewarded, they will either reduce their effort or rationalize that it isn't important. If they perceive that they are over-rewarded, they will either increase their effort to justify the higher reward in the future or rationalize by saying, "I'm worth it!" Inequity leads to lower productivity, reduced quality, increased absenteeism, and voluntary resignation.

Learning Goal 7. Show how managers put motivation theories into action through such strategies as job enrichment, open communication, and job recognition.

- **What characteristics of work affect motivation and performance?**

The job characteristics that influence motivation are skill variety, task identity, task significance, autonomy, and feedback.

- **Name two forms of job enrichment that increase motivation.**

Job enlargement combines a series of tasks into one challenging and interesting assignment. Job rotation makes work more interesting by moving employees from one job to another.

- **How does open communication improve employee motivation?**

Open communication helps both top managers and employees understand the objectives and work together to achieve them.

- **How can managers encourage open communication?**

Managers can create an organizational culture that rewards listening, train supervisors and managers to listen, use effective questioning techniques, remove barriers to open communication, avoid vague and ambiguous communication, and actively make it easier for all to communicate.

Learning Goal 8. Show how managers personalize motivation strategies to appeal to employees across the globe and across generations.

- **What is the difference between high-context and low-context cultures?**

In high-context cultures people build personal relationships and develop group trust before focusing on tasks. In low-context cultures, people often view relationship building as a waste of time that diverts attention from the task.

- **How are Generation X managers likely to be different from their baby boomer predecessors?**

Baby boomers tend to be willing to work long hours to build their careers and often expect their subordinates to do likewise. Gen Xers may strive for a more balanced lifestyle and are likely to focus on results rather than on how many hours their teams work. Gen Xers tend to be better than previous generations at working in teams and providing frequent feedback. They are not bound by traditions that may constrain those who have been with an organization for a long time and are willing to try new approaches to solving problems.

- **What are some common characteristics of Millennials?**

Millennials tend to be adaptable, tech-savvy, able to grasp new concepts, practiced at multitasking, efficient, and tolerant. They often place a higher value on work-life balance, expect their employers to adapt to them, and are more likely to rank fun and stimulation in their top five ideal job requirements.

key terms

equity theory 272
expectancy theory 271
extrinsic reward 261
goal-setting theory 270
Hawthorne effect 262
hygiene factors 265
intrinsic reward 261

job enlargement 274
job enrichment 273
job rotation 274
management by
  objectives (MBO) 270
Maslow's hierarchy of
  needs 263

motivators 265
principle of motion
  economy 262
reinforcement theory 272
scientific
  management 261
time-motion studies 261

critical thinking

Your job right now is to finish reading this chapter. How strongly would you be motivated to do that if you were sweating in a room at 105 degrees Fahrenheit? Imagine your roommate has turned on the air-conditioning. Once you are more comfortable, are you more likely to read? Look at Maslow's hierarchy of needs to see what need would be motivating you at both times. Can you see how helpful Maslow's theory is in understanding motivation by applying it to your own life?

developing workplace skills

1. Talk with several of your friends about the subject of motivation. What motivates them to work hard or not work hard in school and on the job? How important to them is self-motivation as opposed to external reward?

2. Look over Maslow's hierarchy of needs and try to determine where you are right now on the hierarchy. What needs of yours are not being met? How could a company go about meeting those needs and thus motivate you to work more effectively?

3. One recent managerial idea is to let employees work in self-managed teams. There is no reason why such teams could not be formed in colleges as well as businesses. Discuss the benefits and drawbacks of dividing your class into self-managed teams for the purpose of studying, doing cases, and so forth.

4. Think of all the groups with which you have been associated over the years—sports groups, friendship groups, and so on—and try to recall how the leaders of those groups motivated the group to action. Did the leaders assume a Theory X or a Theory Y attitude? How often was money a motivator? What other motivational tools were used and to what effect?

5. Herzberg concluded that pay was not a motivator. If you were paid to get better grades, would you be motivated to study harder? In your employment experiences, have you ever worked harder to obtain a raise or as a result of receiving a large raise? Do you agree with Herzberg about the effects of pay?

taking it to the net

Purpose

To assess your personality type using the Jung-Myers-Briggs typology test and to evaluate how well the description of your personality type fits you.

Exercise

Sometimes understanding differences in employees' personalities helps managers understand how to motivate them. Find out about your personality by going to the Human Metrics website (www.humanmetrics.com) and take the Jung Typology Test (based on Carl Jung's and Isabel Myers-Briggs's approaches to typology). (Disclaimer: The test, like all other personality tests, is only a rough and preliminary indicator of personality.)

1. After you identify your personality type, read the corresponding personality portrait. How well or how poorly does the identified personality type fit?

2. Sometimes a personality test does not accurately identify your personality, but it may give you a place to start looking for a portrait that fits. After you have read the portraits on the website, ask a good friend or relative which one best describes you.

casing the web

To access the case "Making Teams Work in a Changing Market," visit **www.mhhe.com/ubl0e**

video case

To access the video case featuring The Container Store, visit **www.mhhe.com/ubl0e**

Human
Resource
Management

FINDING AND KEEPING THE BEST EMPLOYEES

11

LEARNING goals

After you have read and studied this chapter, you should be able to

1 Explain the importance of human resource management, and describe current issues in managing human resources.

2 Illustrate the effects of legislation on human resource management.

3 Summarize the five steps in human resource planning.

4 Describe methods that companies use to recruit new employees, and explain some of the issues that make recruitment challenging.

5 Outline the six steps in selecting employees.

6 Illustrate employee training and development methods.

7 Trace the six steps in appraising employee performance.

8 Summarize the objectives of employee compensation programs, and evaluate pay systems and fringe benefits.

9 Demonstrate how managers use scheduling plans to adapt to workers' needs.

10 Describe how employees can move through a company: promotion, reassignment, termination, and retirement.

Sometimes the relationship between managers and employees has an "us vs. them" quality. Wary staff may not respect superiors they view as out of touch with the day-to-day operations of the business. After all, many of today's upper managers did not work their way to the top of the companies they now lead. Moving from high-level positions at a number of different firms is common practice in some industries. Nevertheless, there are loyal veterans with decades of technical experience who run many of the world's most successful companies.

Such is the case for Nike's CEO Mark Parker. As a champion marathoner at Penn State, Parker often modified his running shoes to increase their performance. After graduating in 1977 he was hired by Nike's research and development department to turn his hobby into a career in footwear design. During his first years at the company, though, Nike R&D was little more than a shoe shop instead of a hotbed of innovation. By the mid-1980s the company's footwear division was in dire straits as Reebok's increasing market dominance caused Nike's net income to fall 75 percent.

In an effort to turn its fortunes around, the company turned to the R&D department for ideas. Parker and his design team worked feverishly on a project called Visible Air, a technology that placed a hole in the sole that showed Nike's unique cushioning at work. By 1986 the new line of Air shoes soon became a hit, not only with athletes but casual consumers too. Over the following decade Parker played an integral part in the development of other Nike footwear mainstays, such as the Air Jordan and Air Force One brands. Although admittedly remaining a designer at heart, he steadily ascended the corporate ladder until finally assuming the title of CEO in 2006. Parker's business goals for Nike are ambitious. By 2015 he hopes to increase revenues by more than 40 percent to $27 billion a year.

In order to hit his financial targets Parker knows he needs to keep the company's 33,000 employees motivated and thinking creatively. While he appreciates the respect the employees have for his own accomplishments at Nike, he wants to provide a work environment that helps employees flourish as well. Parker has certainly taken care of the latter for the 7,000 workers employed at Nike's world headquarters in Beaverton, Oregon. The sprawling 17-building campus is home to two employee gyms for the exercise-obsessed Nike staff. The Lance Armstrong gym alone is home to an Olympic-size pool as well as workout spaces for yoga, spinning classes and Pilates. Besides its ample exercise facilities, the headquarters also hosts five restaurants where employees can eat lunch and watch the big games of the day. Nike also offers free on-site childcare, paid leave and a 50 percent discount on its products to all employees. It's no wonder why Nike was named one of the 100 Best Places to Work by *Fortune* magazine in 2006, 2007, and 2008.

Still, it's impossible to talk about labor at Nike without recalling accusations of inhumane working conditions at the factories of the company's contractors overseas. Parker has taken active strides toward fixing the problem. Nike now employees more than 130 people to keep constant watch on the safety and energy impact of the 20 percent of its contractors who produce 80 percent of the company's goods. Parker and his team have made progress, although he admits that the process is a "never-ending challenge."

Really, though, the same thing could be said for almost every aspect of the manager-employee relationship. In this chapter, you'll learn how businesses that succeed like Nike recruit, manage, and make the most of their employees.

profile

Getting to Know

X *Mark Parker*

CEO of Nike

Sources: Ellen McGirt, "How Nike's CEO Shook Up the Shoe Industry," *Fast Company,* September 1, 2010; Jessica Flint, "Inside the Swoosh," *Bloomberg Businessweek,* November 29–December 5, 2010; and "Company Overview—Awards and Recognition," Nikebiz.com, accessed May 2011.

This company is one of the largest U.S. steel producers. It pays its teams bonuses that are calculated on quality—tons of steel that go out the door with no defects. There are no limits on bonuses a team can earn; they usually average around $20,000 per employee each year. Name that company. (Find the answer in the chapter.)

LEARNING goal **1**

> Explain the importance of human resource management, and describe current issues in managing human resources.

WORKING WITH PEOPLE IS JUST THE BEGINNING

Students often say they want to go into human resource management because they want to "work with people." Human resource managers do work with people, but they are also deeply involved in planning, record keeping, and other administrative duties. To begin a career in human resource management, you need a better reason than "I want to work with people." This chapter will tell you what else human resource management is all about.

Human resource management (HRM) is the process of determining human resource needs and then recruiting, selecting, developing, motivating, evaluating, compensating, and scheduling employees to achieve organizational goals (see Figure 11.1). For many years, human resource management was called "personnel" and involved clerical functions such as screening applications, keeping records, processing the payroll, and finding new employees when necessary. The roles and responsibilities of HRM have evolved primarily because of two key factors: (1) organizations' recognition of employees as their ultimate resource and (2) changes in the law that rewrote many traditional practices. Let's explore both.

Developing the Ultimate Resource

One reason human resource management is receiving increased attention now is that the U.S. economy has experienced a major shift—from traditional manufacturing industries to service and high-tech manufacturing industries that require highly technical job skills. This shift means that many workers must be retrained for new, more challenging jobs. They truly are the ultimate resource. People develop the ideas that eventually become products to satisfy consumers' wants and needs. Take away their creative minds, and leading firms such as Disney, Apple, Procter & Gamble, Google, and General Electric would be nothing.

human resource management (HRM)
The process of determining human resource needs and then recruiting, selecting, developing, motivating, evaluating, compensating, and scheduling employees to achieve organizational goals.

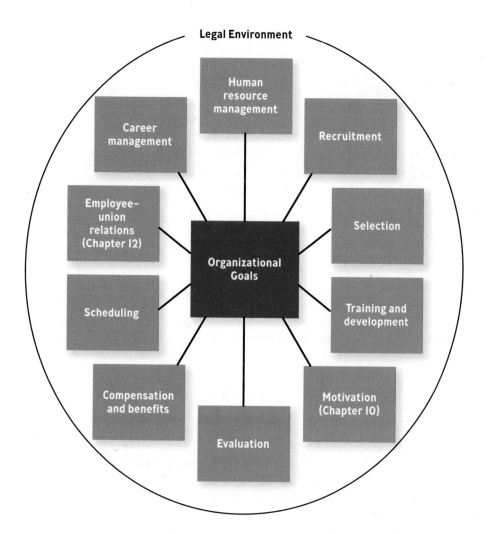

Legal Environment

Human resource management

Career management

Recruitment

Employee-union relations (Chapter 12)

Selection

Scheduling

Organizational Goals

Training and development

Compensation and benefits

Motivation (Chapter 10)

Evaluation

figure II.I

HUMAN RESOURCE MANAGEMENT
As this figure shows, human resource management is more than hiring and firing personnel. All activities are designed to achieve organizational goals within the laws that affect human resource management. (Note that human resource management includes motivation, as discussed in Chapter 10, and employee-union relations, as discussed in Chapter 12.)

In the past, human resources were plentiful, so there was little need to nurture and develop them. If you needed qualified people, you simply hired them. If they didn't work out, you fired them and found others. Most firms assigned the job of recruiting, selecting, training, evaluating, compensating, motivating, and, yes, firing people to the functional departments that employed them, like accounting, manufacturing, and marketing. Today the job of human resource management has taken on an increased role in the firm since *qualified* employees are much scarcer, which makes recruiting and retaining people more important and more difficult.[1]

In the future, human resource management may become the firm's most critical function, responsible for dealing with all aspects of a business's most critical resource—people. In fact, the human resource function has become so important that it's no longer the job of just one department; it's a responsibility of *all* managers. What are some human resource challenges all managers face? We'll outline a few next.

The Human Resource Challenge

Many of the changes that have had the most dramatic impact on U.S. business are those in the labor force. The ability to compete in global markets depends on new ideas, new products, and new levels of productivity—in other words, on people with good ideas. These are some of the challenges and opportunities in human resources:[2]

U.S. firms face a shortage of workers skilled in areas like science, green technology, and the development of clean energy sources like this wind turbine. What other job markets do you think will grow as companies focus more on environmentally friendly policies? Which ones appeal to you?

- Shortages of trained workers in growth areas, such as computer technology, biotechnology, robotics, green technology, and the sciences.

- An increasing number of skilled and unskilled workers from declining industries, such as steel and automobiles, who are unemployed or underemployed and need retraining. *Underemployed workers* are those who have more skills or knowledge than their current jobs require or those with part-time jobs who want to work full time.

- A growing percentage of new workers who are undereducated and unprepared for jobs in the contemporary business environment.

- A shortage of workers in skilled trades due to retirement of aging baby boomers.

- An increasing number of baby boomers who, due to the recession, delay retirement (preventing the promotion of younger workers) or move to lower-level jobs (increasing the supply of workers for such jobs).

- An increasing number of both single-parent and two-income families, resulting in a demand for job sharing, maternity leave, and special career advancement programs for women.

- A shift in employee attitudes toward work. Leisure time has become a much higher priority, as have flextime and a shorter workweek.

- A recession that took a toll on employee morale and increased the demand for temporary and part-time workers.

- A challenge from overseas labor pools whose members work for lower wages and are subject to fewer laws and regulations than U.S. workers. This results in many jobs being outsourced overseas.

- An increased demand for benefits tailored to the individual yet cost-effective to the company.

- Growing concerns over health care, elder care, child care, drug testing, workplace violence (all discussed in Chapter 12), and opportunities for people with disabilities.

- Changes in health care laws that have added a large number of new regulations that employers must read, interpret, implement, and track.

- A decreased sense of employee loyalty, which raises employee turnover and the cost of replacing lost workers.

Given these issues, you can see why human resource management has taken a central place in management thinking. However, significant changes in laws covering hiring, safety, unionization, equal pay, and affirmative action have also had a major influence. Let's look at their impact on human resource management.

LEARNING goal 2

Illustrate the effects of legislation on human resource management.

LAWS AFFECTING HUMAN RESOURCE MANAGEMENT

Until the 1930s, the U.S. government had little to do with human resource decisions. Since then, legislation and legal decisions have greatly affected all areas of human resource management, from hiring to training to monitoring working conditions (see Figure 11.2). These laws were passed because many businesses did not exercise fair labor practices voluntarily.

One of the more important pieces of social legislation passed by Congress was the Civil Rights Act of 1964. This act generated much debate and was amended 97 times before final passage. Title VII of that act brought the

National *Labor Relations Act of 1935.* Established collective bargaining in labor–management relations and limited management interference in the right of employees to have a collective bargaining agent.

Fair Labor Standards Act of 1938. Established a minimum wage and overtime pay for employees working more than 40 hours a week. Amendments expanded the classes of workers covered, raised the minimum wage, redefined regular-time work, raised overtime payments, and equalized pay scales for men and women.

Manpower Development and Training Act of 1962. Provided for the training and retraining of unemployed workers.

Equal Pay Act of 1963. Specified that men and women doing equal jobs must be paid the same wage.

Civil Rights Act of 1964. For firms with 15 or more employees, outlawed discrimination in employment based on sex, race, color, religion, or national origin.

Age Discrimination in Employment Act of 1967. Outlawed employment practices that discriminate against people 40 and older. An amendment outlaws requiring retirement by a specific age.

Occupational Safety and Health Act of 1970. Regulated the degree to which employees can be exposed to hazardous substances and specified the safety equipment the employer must provide.

Equal Employment Opportunity Act of 1972. Strengthened the Equal Employment Opportunity Commission (EEOC) and authorized the EEOC to set guidelines for human resource management.

Comprehensive Employment and Training Act of 1973 (CETA). Provided funds for training unemployed workers.

Employee Retirement Income Security Act of 1974 (ERISA). Regulated and insured company retirement plans.

Immigration Reform and Control Act of 1986. Required employers to verify employment eligibility of all new hires including U.S. citizens.

Supreme Court ruling against set-aside programs (affirmative action), 1989. Declared that setting aside 30 percent of contracting jobs for minority businesses was reverse discrimination and unconstitutional.

Older Workers Benefit Protection Act, 1990. Protects older people from signing away their rights to pensions and protection from illegal age discrimination.

Civil Rights Act of 1991. For firms with over 15 employees, extends the right to a jury trial and punitive damages to victims of intentional job discrimination.

Americans with Disabilities Act of 1990 (1992 implementation). Prohibits employers from discriminating against qualified individuals with disabilities in hiring, advancement, or compensation and requires them to adapt the workplace if necessary.

Family and Medical Leave Act of 1993. Businesses with 50 or more employees must provide up to 12 weeks of unpaid leave per year upon birth or adoption of an employee's child or upon serious illness of a parent, spouse, or child.

Americans with Disabilities Amendments Act of 2008 (ADA). Provides broader protection for disabled workers and reverses Supreme Court decisions deemed too restrictive. Adds disabilities such as epilepsy and cancer to ADA coverage.

figure 11.2

GOVERNMENT LEGISLATION AFFECTING HUMAN RESOURCE MANAGEMENT

affirmative action
Employment activities designed to "right past wrongs" by increasing opportunities for minorities and women.

reverse discrimination
Discrimination against members of a dominant or majority group (e.g. whites or males) usually as a result of policies designed to correct previous discrimination against minority or disadvantaged groups.

The Americans with Disabilities Act guarantees that all U.S. workers have equal opportunity in employment. This legislation requires businesses to make "reasonable accommodations" on the job for people with disabilities. What required accommodations do you think would be reasonable?

government directly into the operations of human resource management. Title VII prohibits discrimination in hiring, firing, compensation, apprenticeships, training, terms, conditions, or privileges of employment based on race, religion, creed, sex, or national origin. Age was later added to the conditions of the act. The Civil Rights Act of 1964 was expected to stamp out discrimination in the workplace, but specific language in it made enforcement quite difficult. Congress took on the task of amending the law.

In 1972, the Equal Employment Opportunity Act (EEOA) was added as an amendment to Title VII. It strengthened the Equal Employment Opportunity Commission (EEOC), which was created by the Civil Rights Act, by giving it rather broad powers. For example, it permitted the EEOC to issue guidelines for acceptable employer conduct in administering equal employment opportunity. The EEOC also mandated specific record-keeping procedures, and Congress vested it with the power of enforcement to ensure these mandates were carried out. The EEOC became a formidable regulatory force in the administration of human resource management.

Perhaps the most controversial policy enforced by the EEOC was **affirmative action**, designed to "right past wrongs" by increasing opportunities for minorities and women. Interpretation of the affirmative action law led employers to actively recruit, and in some cases give preference to, women and minority group members. Questions persist about the legality of affirmative action and the effect it may have in creating a sort of reverse discrimination in the workplace. **Reverse discrimination** has been defined as discriminating against members of a dominant or majority group (e.g. whites or males) usually as a result of policies designed to correct previous discrimination against minority or disadvantaged groups. The issue has generated much heated debate as well as many lawsuits.[3]

The Civil Rights Act of 1991 expanded the remedies available to victims of discrimination by amending Title VII of the Civil Rights Act of 1964. Now victims of discrimination have the right to a jury trial and punitive damages. Human resource managers must follow court decisions closely to see how the law is enforced.[4] The Legal Briefcase box discusses a case that may change the way class action discrimination disputes are handled in the future.

The Office of Federal Contract Compliance Programs (OFCCP) ensures that employers comply with nondiscrimination and affirmative action laws and regulations when doing business with the federal government.

Laws Protecting Employees with Disabilities and Older Employees

As you read above, laws prohibit discrimination related to race, sex, or age in hiring, firing, and training. The Vocational Rehabilitation Act of 1973 extended protection to people with any physical or mental disability.

The Americans with Disabilities Act of 1990 (ADA) requires employers to give applicants with physical or mental disabilities the same consideration for employment as people without disabilities. It also requires making "reasonable accommodations" for employees with disabilities, such as modifying equipment or widening doorways. Accommodations are not always expensive; an inexpensive headset can allow someone with cerebral

The Million Woman Suit against Walmart

From the late 1990s until 2004, the retail giant Walmart relied on a "tap-on-the-shoulder" policy for management promotion. Rather than posting openings and accepting applications, it is charged that managers simply promoted their colleagues and friends from within. And since most of the company's upper staff consisted of men, the new crop of managers remained overwhelmingly male.

Such alleged unchecked gender dominance led to widespread bias, according to the plaintiffs of a class action discrimination suit filed by more than one million women. (Class-action lawsuits pool individual claims into a single case that creates the potential for a large judgment and increases the pressure on businesses to settle.) The case charges that not only did the company leapfrog over women for leadership roles, it engaged in pay inequality and harassment.

Walmart argued that with such a large field of plaintiffs it would be impossible for them to verify each individual claim. Those in the business community who supported Walmart agreed that a ruling in favor of the women would have led to a flood of class-action lawsuits based on vague evidence. Supporters of the women, on the other hand, maintained that the huge number of litigants reflected the scope of Walmart's discriminatory policies.

On June 11, 2011, the U.S. Supreme Court (on a 5–4 vote) dismissed the enormous class-action suit that sought billions of dollars on behalf of the over one million women. The Court did not decide whether Walmart had, in fact, discriminated against the women, only that they could not proceed as a class. Walmart and business groups applauded the court's decision, while consumer groups strongly criticized it. Both sides agreed, however, that the decision was momentous.

Sources: Greg Stohr, "Wal-Mart Faces the Big Box of Bias Suits," *Bloomberg Businessweek,* March 24, 2011; James Oliphant and David G. Savage, "Supreme Court Appears Poised to Reject Class Action in Wal-Mart Sex-bias Case," *Los Angeles Times,* March 30, 2011; and Adam Liptak, "Justices Rule for Walmart in Class-Action Bias Case," *New York Times,* June 20, 2011.

palsy to talk on the phone.[5] The ADA also protects individuals with disabilities from discrimination in public accommodations, transportation, and telecommunications.[6]

Most companies have no trouble making structural changes to be accommodating. Some, however, find cultural changes difficult. Employers used to think that being fair meant treating everyone the same, but *accommodation* in fact means treating people *according to their specific needs.* That can include putting up barriers to isolate people readily distracted by noise, reassigning workers to new tasks, and making changes in supervisors' management styles.

In 2008, Congress passed the Americans with Disabilities Amendments Act, which overturned Supreme Court decisions that had reduced protections for certain people with disabilities such as diabetes, epilepsy, heart disease, autism, major depression, and cancer.[7] In 2011, the EEOC issued new regulations that widen the range of disabilities covered by the ADA and shifted the burden of proof of disability in labor disputes from employees to business owners.[8] Enforcement promises to be a continuing issue for human resource management. [9]

The Age Discrimination in Employment Act of 1967 (ADEA) protects individuals 40 or older from employment and workplace discrimination in hiring, firing, promotion, layoff, compensation, benefits, job assignments, and training. The ADEA is enforced by the EEOC, applies to employers with 20 or more employees, and protects both employees and job applicants. It also outlaws mandatory retirement in most organizations. It does, however, allow age restrictions for certain job categories such as airline pilot or bus driver if evidence shows that the ability to perform significantly diminishes with age or that age imposes a danger to society.

Effects of Legislation

Clearly, laws ranging from the Social Security Act of 1935 to the 2008 Americans with Disabilities Amendments Act require human resource managers to keep abreast of laws and court decisions to effectively perform their jobs. Choosing a career in human resource management offers a challenge to anyone willing to put forth the effort. Remember:

- Employers must know and act in accordance with the legal rights of their employees or risk costly court cases.
- Legislation affects all areas of human resource management, from hiring and training to compensation.
- Court cases demonstrate that it is sometimes legal to go beyond providing equal rights for minorities and women to provide special employment (affirmative action) and training to correct discrimination in the past.
- New court cases and legislation change human resource management almost daily; the only way to keep current is to read the business literature and stay familiar with emerging issues.

progress assessment

- What is human resource management?
- What did Title VII of the Civil Rights Act of 1964 achieve?
- What is the EEOC, and what was the intention of affirmative action?
- What does *accommodations* mean in the Americans with Disabilities Act of 1990?

LEARNING goal 3

Summarize the five steps in human resource planning.

DETERMINING A FIRM'S HUMAN RESOURCE NEEDS

All management, including human resource management, begins with planning. The five steps in the human resource planning process are:

1. *Preparing a human resource inventory of the organization's employees.* This inventory should include ages, names, education, capabilities, training, specialized skills, and other relevant information (such as languages spoken). It reveals whether the labor force is technically up-to-date and thoroughly trained.

2. *Preparing a job analysis.* A **job analysis** is a study of what employees do who hold various job titles. It's necessary in order to recruit and train employees with the necessary skills to do the job. The results of job analysis are two written statements: job descriptions and job specifications. A **job description** specifies the objectives of the job, the type of work, the responsibilities and duties, working conditions, and the job's relationship to other functions. **Job specifications** are a written summary of the minimal education and skills to do a particular job. In short, job descriptions are about the job, and job specifications are about the person who does the job. Visit the Occupational Information Network (O*NET) at www.onetcenter.org for detailed information about job analyses and job descriptions. See Figure 11.3 for a hypothetical job description and job specifications.

3. *Assessing future human resource demand.* Because technology changes rapidly, effective human resource managers are proactive; that is, they forecast the organization's requirements and train people ahead of time or ensure trained people are available when needed.

4. *Assessing future labor supply.* The labor force is constantly shifting: getting older, becoming more technically oriented, attracting more women. Some workers will be scarcer in the future, like computer and robotic repair workers, and others will be oversupplied, like assembly-line workers.

5. *Establishing a strategic plan.* The human resource strategic plan must address recruiting, selecting, training, developing, appraising, compensating, and scheduling the labor force. Because the first four steps lead up to this one, we'll focus on them in the rest of the chapter.

job analysis
A study of what employees do who hold various job titles.

job description
A summary of the objectives of a job, the type of work to be done, the responsibilities and duties, the working conditions, and the relationship of the job to other functions.

job specifications
A written summary of the minimum qualifications required of workers to do a particular job.

JOB ANALYSIS

Observe current sales representatives doing the job.

Discuss job with sales managers.

Have current sales reps keep a diary of their activities.

JOB DESCRIPTION

Primary objective is to sell company's products to stores in Territory Z. Duties include servicing accounts and maintaining positive relationships with clients. Responsibilities include:

- Introducing the new products to store managers in the area.
- Helping the store managers estimate the volume to order.
- Negotiating prime shelf space.
- Explaining sales promotion activities to store managers.
- Stocking and maintaining shelves in stores that wish such service.

JOB SPECIFICATIONS

Characteristics of the person qualifying for this job include:

- Two years' sales experience.
- Positive attitude.
- Well-groomed appearance.
- Good communication skills.
- High school diploma and two years of college credit.

figure 11.3

JOB ANALYSIS
A job analysis yields two important statements: job descriptions and job specifications. Here you have a job description and job specifications for a sales representative.

Some companies use advanced technology to perform the human resource planning process more efficiently. IBM manages its global work-force of about 100,000 employees and 100,000 subcontractors with a data-base that matches employee skills, experiences, schedules, and references with jobs available. If a client in Quebec, Canada, has a month-long project requiring a consultant who speaks English and French, has an advanced degree in engineering, and is experienced with Linux programming, IBM's database can find the best-suited consultant available and put him or her in touch with the client.

LEARNING goal 4

Describe methods that companies use to recruit new employees, and explain some of the issues that make recruitment challenging.

RECRUITING EMPLOYEES FROM A DIVERSE POPULATION

recruitment
The set of activities used to obtain a sufficient number of the right employees at the right time.

Recruitment is the set of activities for obtaining the right number of quali-fied people at the right time. Its purpose is to select those who best meet the needs of the organization. You might think a continuous flow of new people into the workforce makes recruiting easy. On the contrary, it's become very challenging for several reasons:

- Some organizations have policies that demand promotions from within, operate under union regulations, or offer low wages, which makes recruiting and keeping employees difficult or subject to outside influence and restrictions.

- The emphasis on corporate culture, teamwork, and participative management makes it important to hire people who not only are skilled but also fit in with the culture and leadership style of the

Human resource managers today have the opportunity to recruit people from a wide range of cultural and ethnic backgrounds. What are some of the advantages of a diverse workforce?

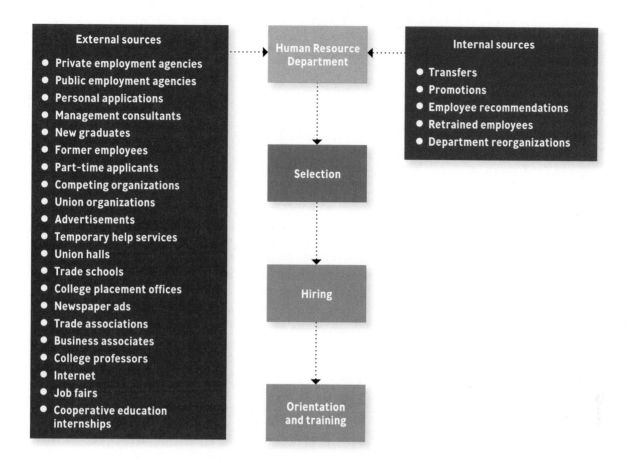

External sources

- Private employment agencies
- Public employment agencies
- Personal applications
- Management consultants
- New graduates
- Former employees
- Part-time applicants
- Competing organizations
- Union organizations
- Advertisements
- Temporary help services
- Union halls
- Trade schools
- College placement offices
- Newspaper ads
- Trade associations
- Business associates
- College professors
- Internet
- Job fairs
- Cooperative education internships

Human Resource Department

Selection

Hiring

Orientation and training

Internal sources

- Transfers
- Promotions
- Employee recommendations
- Retrained employees
- Department reorganizations

organization.[10] Wegmans Food Markets (a perennial member of *Fortune* magazine's list of best companies to work for) encourages employees to do whatever they think is necessary to make a customer happy. For example, they don't have to ask a supervisor if they need to cook a Thanksgiving turkey at the store for a customer whose oven is too small or go to a customer's home to check a food order.

- Sometimes people with the necessary skills are not available; then workers must be hired and trained internally.

Human resource managers can turn to many sources for recruiting assistance (see Figure 11.4). *Internal sources* include current employees who can be transferred or promoted or who can recommend others to hire. Using internal sources is less expensive than recruiting from outside and helps maintain employee morale. However, it isn't always possible to find qualified workers within the company, so human resource managers also use *external sources* such as advertisements, public and private employment agencies, college placement bureaus, management consultants, Internet sites, professional organizations, referrals, and online and walk-in applications.

Recruiting qualified workers may be particularly difficult for small businesses with few staff members and less-than-competitive compensation to attract external sources. CareerBuilder.com and Monster.com have helped such firms. They attract more than 80 million visitors per month.[11] The Spotlight on Small Business box on p. 300 offers additional ways small businesses can recruit.

figure II.4

EMPLOYEE SOURCES

Internal sources are often given first consideration, so it's useful to get a recommendation from a current employee of the firm for which you want to work. College placement offices are also an important source. Be sure to learn about such facilities early so that you can plan a strategy throughout your college career.

It's Not Easy Being Small

To survive, it's critical for small businesses to recruit and retain qualified workers. However, competing for top talent is difficult when you can't afford corporate-level benefits or expensive recruiters to hunt down the best people. Despite these hurdles, small-business management consultants say there are many ways to lure desirable workers:

- *Transform ads into promotional tools.* Ecoprint, a small print shop in Maryland, touts the benefits of working for this collegial company in its regular advertisements.

- *Post job openings on the Internet.* Running an ad on an online service like CareerBuilder.com or Monster.com for 30 days costs about one-fourth the price of a comparable ad in the *New York Times* that runs for one week.

- *Let your staff help recruit and select hires.* The more staff is engaged in the search and interview process, the better chance to find recruits with the right personality and skills.

- *Create a dynamic workplace that attracts local, energetic applicants.* Sometimes word-of-mouth is the most effective recruiting tool.

- *Test-drive an employee.* Hiring contingent workers allows you to test candidates for a few months before deciding whether to make an offer of permanent employment.

- *Hire customers.* Loyal customers sometimes make the smartest employees. Build-A-Bear Workshop often hires customers who come into its stores and exhibit a real interest in the company and its products.

- *Check community groups and local government agencies.* Don't forget to check state-run employment agencies. Many nonprofit organizations serve immigrants new to a region or people in need of a job who become excellent candidates you can train.

- *Work hard for publicity in local media.* Publicity is more believable than advertising.

- *Lure candidates with a policy of promotions and raises.* Most employees want to know they can move up. Give employees an incentive for learning the business.

- *Outsource fringe benefit management to a professional employer organization (PEO).* It's tough to build a benefits program equivalent to those offered by large companies, but PEOs may offer lower insurance rates due to economies of scale. Face it, any way you can close the gap may help attract qualified workers.

Sources: "7 Tips for Motivating Employees," *Inc.,* April 20, 2010; Leigh Buchanan, "Opening the Books and Motivating the Workers," *Inc.,* June 8, 2010; and Lou DuBois, "How to Build a Corporate Culture of Trust," *Inc.,* August 2, 2010.

LEARNING goal 5

Outline the six steps in selecting employees.

SELECTING EMPLOYEES WHO WILL BE PRODUCTIVE

selection
The process of gathering information and deciding who should be hired, under legal guidelines, to serve the best interests of the individual and the organization.

Selection is the process of gathering information and deciding who should be hired, under legal guidelines, to serve the best interests of the individual and the organization. Selecting and training employees are extremely expensive processes in some firms. Just think what's involved: advertising or recruiting agency fees, interview time, medical exams, training costs, unproductive time spent learning the job, possible travel and moving expenses, and more. It can cost one and a half times the employee's annual salary to recruit, process, and train even an entry-level worker, and over six figures for a top manager. A typical selection process has six steps:

1. *Obtaining complete application forms.* Although equal employment laws limit the kinds of questions that can appear, applications help reveal the applicant's educational background, work experience, career objectives, and other qualifications directly related to the job.

   Large retail employers like Winn-Dixie and Finish Line make the application process more efficient by using an automated program called Workforce Acquisition. An applicant sits at a computer and answers questions about job experience, time available to work, and personality. The software e-mails a report to the hiring manager recommending whether to interview the applicant and, if so, suggesting questions to ask. Mike Marchetti, executive vice president of store operations for Finish Line, says his company processed 330,000 applications, eliminating 60,000 interview hours and reducing turnover 24 percent.[12]

2. *Conducting initial and follow-up interviews.* A staff member from the human resource department often screens applicants in a first interview. If the interviewer considers the applicant a potential hire, the manager who will supervise the new employee may interview the applicant as well. It's important that managers prepare adequately for the interview to avoid selection decisions they may regret.[13] No matter how innocent the intention, missteps such as asking about pregnancy or child care could later be evidence if the applicant files discrimination charges.

3. *Giving employment tests.* Organizations often use tests to measure basic competency in specific job skills like welding or firefighting, and to help evaluate applicants' personalities and interests. The tests should always be directly related to the job. Employment tests have been legally challenged as potential means of discrimination.[14] Many companies test potential employees in assessment centers where they perform actual job tasks. Such testing can make the selection process more efficient and will generally satisfy legal requirements.

4. *Conducting background investigations.* Most organizations now investigate a candidate's work record, school record, credit history, and references more carefully than in the past to help identify those most likely to succeed. It is simply too costly to hire, train, and motivate people only to lose them and have to start the process over. Services such as LexisNexis allow prospective employers not only to conduct speedy background checks of criminal records, driving records, and credit histories but also to verify work experience and professional and educational credentials.[15]

Choosing qualified employees is a challenge. Psychologist Turhan Canli believes he can tell what makes some people better suited to a job than others by using human physiology mechanisms. Canli uses brain scans to see how people react to certain word-image combinations and believes you can read personalities from them. What do you think are key criteria for evaluating job candidates?

5. *Obtaining results from physical exams.* There are obvious benefits to hiring physically and mentally healthy people. However, according to the Americans with Disabilities Act, medical tests cannot be given just to screen out individuals. In some states, physical exams can be given only after an offer of employment has been accepted. In states that allow pre-employment physical exams, they must be given to everyone applying for the same position. Pre-employment testing to detect drug or alcohol abuse has been controversial, as has screening to detect carriers of HIV, the virus that causes AIDS.

6. *Establishing trial (probationary) periods.* Often an organization will hire an employee conditionally to let the person prove his or her value on the job. After a specified probationary period (perhaps six months or a year), the firm can either permanently hire or discharge that employee on the basis of supervisors' evaluations. Although such systems make it easier to fire inefficient or problem employees, they do not eliminate the high cost of turnover.

contingent workers
Employees that include part-time workers, temporary workers, seasonal workers, independent contractors, interns, and co-op students.

The selection process is often long and difficult, but it is worth the effort to select new employees carefully because of the high cost of replacing them.[16] Care helps ensure that new employees meet all requirements, including communication skills, education, technical skills, experience, personality, and health.

Hiring Contingent Workers

A company with employment needs that vary—from hour to hour, day to day, week to week, or season to season—may find it cost-effective to hire contingent workers. **Contingent workers** include part-time workers (anyone who works 1 to 34 hours per week), temporary workers (workers paid by temporary employment agencies), seasonal workers, independent contractors, interns, and co-op students.

Companies may also hire contingent workers when full-timers are on some type of leave (such as maternity leave), when there is a peak demand for labor or products (like the holiday shopping season), or when quick service to customers is a priority. Companies also tend to hire more contingent workers in an uncertain economy, particularly when they are available and qualified, and when the jobs require minimal training.

Seasonal businesses, such as Halloween stores and haunted houses, depend on hiring contingent (temporary) workers to help them through the limited times they are operational. What are the advantages and disadvantages of hiring contingent workers? What are the advantages and disadvantages of being a contingent worker?

Contingent workers receive few benefits; they are rarely offered health insurance, vacation time, or company pensions. They also tend to earn less than permanent workers do. On the positive side, many on temporary assignments are eventually offered full-time positions. Managers see using temporary workers as a way of weeding out poor workers and finding good hires. Although exact numbers are difficult to gather, the Bureau of Labor Statistics estimates there are approximately 5.7 million contingent workers in the United States, with the majority under age 25.[17] Experts say temps are filling openings in an increasingly broad range of jobs, from unskilled manufacturing and distribution positions to middle management. Increasing numbers of contingent workers are educated professionals such as accountants, attorneys, and engineers.

Many companies include college students in their contingent workforce plan. Working with temporary staffing agencies, companies have easier access to workers who have already been screened. Of course, temp agencies benefit college students as well. Once the agencies have assessed the workers, their information is entered into their databases. Then when students are coming back in town for vacations or whatever, they can call the agency and ask them to put their names into the system for work assignments. No need to spend time searching for openings or running around town for interviews. Randstad USA, a global staffing services giant with over 350 branches in the United States, welcomes college students primarily because of their computer skills and familiarity with many of the popular software programs companies use.[18]

College interns can be considered temporary workers. However, when these internships are unpaid, ethical questions could arise (see the nearby Making Ethical Decisions box).

In an era of rapid change and economic uncertainty, some contingent workers have even found that temping can be more secure than full-time employment.

progress assessment

- What are the five steps in human resource planning?
- What factors make it difficult to recruit qualified employees?
- What are the six steps in the selection process?
- Who is considered a contingent worker, and why do companies hire such workers?

LEARNING goal 6

Illustrate employee training and development methods.

TRAINING AND DEVELOPING EMPLOYEES FOR OPTIMUM PERFORMANCE

As technology and other innovations change the workplace, companies must offer training programs that often are quite sophisticated. The term **training and development** includes all attempts to improve productivity by increasing an employee's ability to perform. A well-designed training program often leads to higher retention rates, increased productivity, and greater job satisfaction. Employers in the United States generally find that money for training is well spent. *Training* focuses on short-term skills, whereas *development* focuses on long-term abilities. Both include three steps: (1) assessing organization needs and employee skills to determine training needs; (2) designing training activities to meet identified needs; and (3) evaluating the training's effectiveness. Some common training and development activities are employee orientation, on-the-job training, apprenticeships, off-the-job training, vestibule training, job simulation, and management training.

- **Orientation** is the activity that initiates new employees into the organization; to fellow employees; to their immediate supervisors; and to the policies, practices, and objectives of the firm. Orientation programs

training and development
All attempts to improve productivity by increasing an employee's ability to perform. Training focuses on short-term skills, whereas development focuses on long-term abilities.

orientation
The activity that introduces new employees to the organization; to fellow employees; to their immediate supervisors; and to the policies, practices, and objectives of the firm.

MAKING ethical decisions

Are Unpaid Interns Too Interred?

Traditionally, unpaid internships have been a great way for young people to transition from college to the workforce. The sacrifice of financial benefits usually pays off in practical experience the interns otherwise would not get in a classroom. Businesses in turn risk nothing financially, but could end up benefiting in the long run if an intern eventually becomes a key paid employee. However, with entry-level positions scarce in today's job market, interns can end up in an unpaid position for as long as six months with no chance of advancement. At that point, interns may wonder if they are improving their chances for a rewarding career or simply performing free services for the company.

In order to distinguish a quality internship from a dead end, simply look at the tasks you're asked to do every day. If your central duties include keeping the coffee pot full or running errands, chances are that those jobs will not translate into valuable experience down the line. Interns should be taught about the day-to-day duties of a business, not how to

be professional gofers. Management must also be sure to outline an intern's responsibilities explicitly and provide regular feedback. Even without a regular paycheck, internships can be beneficial as long as the person is compensated in experience.

Some businesses are quite willing to give interns plenty of professional responsibility. For example, one Toronto newspaper fired all of its paid staff writers and replaced them with unpaid interns.

Is it ethical for companies to use unpaid interns if they know they will not have any jobs to offer at the end of the internships or if the unpaid internships replace paid jobs? Why or why not?

Source: Knight Kiplinger, "Are Unpaid Interns Exploited by Employers?" *Kiplinger,* April 2011; Diane Brady, "Turmoil Strategies," *Bloomberg Businessweek,* February 10, 2009; and Bruce Weinstein, "Dos and Don'ts of Unpaid Internships," *Bloomberg Businessweek,* May 28, 2010.

range from informal talks to formal activities that last a day or more and often include scheduled visits to various departments and required reading of handbooks. For example, at Zappos every new employee in the online retailer's Henderson, Nevada, headquarters must spend two weeks answering customer calls, two weeks learning in a classroom, and a week shipping boxes in the company's Kentucky fulfillment center.[19]

on-the-job training
Training at the workplace that lets the employee learn by doing or by watching others for a while and then imitating them.

- **On-the-job training** lets the employee learn by doing, or by watching others for a while and then imitating them, right at the workplace. Salespeople, for example, are often trained by watching experienced salespeople perform (often called *shadowing*). Naturally, this can be either quite effective or disastrous, depending on the skills and habits of the person being observed. On-the-job training is the easiest kind of training to implement when the job is relatively simple (such as clerking in a store) or repetitive (such as collecting refuse, cleaning carpets, or mowing lawns). More demanding or intricate jobs require a more intense training effort. Intranets and other forms of technology make cost-effective on-the-job training programs available 24 hours a day. Computer systems can monitor workers' input and give them instructions if they become confused about what to do next.

apprentice programs
Training programs during which a learner works alongside an experienced employee to master the skills and procedures of a craft.

- In **apprentice programs** a learner works alongside an experienced employee to master the skills and procedures of a craft. Some apprentice programs include classroom training. Trade unions in skilled crafts, such as bricklaying and plumbing, require a new worker to serve as an apprentice for several years to ensure excellence as well as to limit entry to the union. Workers who successfully complete an apprenticeship earn the classification *journeyman*. As baby boomers retire from skilled trades such as pipefitting, welding, and carpentry, shortages of trained workers will result. Apprentice programs may be shortened to prepare people for skilled jobs in changing industries such as auto repair and aircraft maintenance that require increased knowledge of computer technology. About 450,000 apprentices are registered with the U.S. Department of Labor.[20]

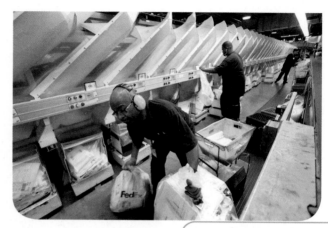

- **Off-the-job training** occurs away from the workplace and consists of internal or external programs to develop any of a variety of skills or to foster personal development. Training is becoming more sophisticated as jobs become more sophisticated. Furthermore, training is expanding to include education (through the Ph.D.) and personal development. Subjects may include time management, stress management, health and wellness, physical education, nutrition, and even art and languages.

- **Online training** demonstrates how technology is improving the efficiency of many off-the-job training programs. Most colleges and universities now offer a wide variety of online classes, sometimes called *distance learning,* including introductory business courses. Both nonprofit and profit-seeking businesses make extensive use of online training. The Red Cross offers an online tutorial called "Be Red Cross Ready" to help citizens prepare for disasters such as floods, tornadoes, or hurricanes.[21] Technology giants like EMC and large manufacturers like Timken use the online training tool GlobeSmart to teach employees how to operate in different cultures.[22] Online training's key advantage is the ability to provide a large number of employees with consistent content tailored to specific training needs at convenient times.

- **Vestibule training** (or near-the-job training) is done in classrooms with equipment similar to that used on the job so that employees learn proper methods and safety procedures before assuming a specific job assignment. Computer and robotics training is often completed in a vestibule classroom.

- **Job simulation** is the use of equipment that duplicates job conditions and tasks so that trainees can learn skills before attempting them on the job. It differs from vestibule training in that it duplicates the *exact* combination of conditions that occur on the job. This is the kind of training given to astronauts, airline pilots, army tank operators, ship captains, and others who must learn difficult procedures off the job.

Management Development

Managers often need special training. To be good communicators, they need to learn listening skills and empathy. They also need time management,

At FedEx, time is money. That's why the company spends six times more on employee training than the average firm. Does the added expense pay off? You bet. FedEx enjoys a remarkably low 4 percent employee turnover rate. Should other companies follow FedEx's financial commitment to training? Why?

off-the-job training
Internal or external training programs away from the workplace that develop any of a variety of skills or foster personal development.

online training
Training programs in which employees complete classes via the Internet.

vestibule training
Training done in schools where employees are taught on equipment similar to that used on the job.

job simulation
The use of equipment that duplicates job conditions and tasks so trainees can learn skills before attempting them on the job.

NASA's KC-I35 aircraft helps astronauts like these train for space missions. After the plane makes a fast and steep ascent, it suddenly free-falls for 20 to 30 seconds enabling the passengers to experience "apparent weightlessness." (For obvious reasons the plane is also known as the Vomit Comet.) Do you think simulation training is effective for jobs like this? Why or why not?

management development
The process of training and educating employees to become good managers, and then monitoring the progress of their managerial skills over time.

planning, and human relations skills. **Management development**, then, is the process of training and educating employees to become good managers, and then monitoring the progress of their managerial skills over time. Management development programs are widespread, especially at colleges, universities, and private management development firms. Managers may participate in role-playing exercises, solve various management cases, and attend films and lectures.[23]

Management development is increasingly being used as a tool to accomplish business objectives. General Electric's and Motorola's management teams were built with significant investment in their development. Most management training programs include several of the following:

- *On-the-job coaching.* A senior manager assists a lower-level manager by teaching needed skills and providing direction, advice, and helpful feedback. E-coaching is being developed to coach managers electronically, though it will take time and experimentation before firms figure out how to make coaches come to life online.[24]

- *Understudy positions.* Job titles such as *undersecretary* and *assistant* are part of a relatively successful way of developing managers. Selected employees work as assistants to higher-level managers and participate in planning and other managerial functions until they are ready to assume such positions themselves.

- *Job rotation.* So that they can learn about different functions of the organization, managers are often given assignments in a variety of departments. Such job rotation gives them the broad picture of the organization they need to succeed.[25]

- *Off-the-job courses and training.* Managers periodically go to classes or seminars for a week or more to hone technical and human relations skills. Major universities like the University of Michigan, MIT, and the University of Chicago offer specialized short courses to assist managers in performing their jobs more efficiently. McDonald's Corporation has its own Hamburger University. Managers and potential franchisees attend six days of classes and complete a course of study equivalent to 36 hours of college business-school credit.[26]

Networking

Networking is the process of establishing and maintaining contacts with key managers in your own and other organizations, and using those contacts to weave strong relationships that serve as informal development systems. Of equal or greater importance may be a **mentor**, a corporate manager who supervises, coaches, and guides selected lower-level employees by introducing them to the right people and generally acting as their organizational sponsor. In most organizations informal mentoring occurs as experienced employees assist less experienced workers. However, many organizations formally assign mentors to employees considered to have strong potential.[27]

It's also important to remember that networking and mentoring go beyond the business environment. For example, college is a perfect place to begin networking. Associations you nurture with professors, with local businesspeople through internships, and especially with your classmates can provide a valuable network to turn to for the rest of your career.

Informal networking gatherings like this help professionals make new connections with people in their fields. Why do you think younger workers prefer such informal gatherings?

networking
The process of establishing and maintaining contacts with key managers in and outside the organization and using those contacts to weave strong relationships that serve as informal development systems.

mentor
An experienced employee who supervises, coaches, and guides lower-level employees by introducing them to the right people and generally being their organizational sponsor.

Diversity in Management Development

As more women moved into management, they learned the importance of networking and of having mentors. Unfortunately, women often have more difficulty than men in networking or finding mentors, since most senior managers are male. Women, however, won a major legal victory when the U.S. Supreme Court ruled it illegal to bar women from certain clubs, long open to men only, where business activity flows and contacts are made. This decision allowed more women to enter established networking systems or, in some instances, create their own.

Similarly, African American and Hispanic managers learned the value of networking. Both groups are forming pools of capital and new opportunities helping many individuals overcome traditional barriers to success. *Black Enterprise* magazine sponsors several networking forums each year for African American professionals. The Hispanic Alliance for Career Enhancement (HACE) is committed to building career opportunities and career advancement for Hispanics. Monte Jade is an association that helps Taiwanese and Chinese assimilate in U.S. business. Sulekha is an Indian networking group that unites Indians in the United States and around the world.

Companies that take the initiative to develop female and minority managers understand three crucial principles: (1) grooming women and minorities for management positions isn't about legality, morality, or even morale but rather about bringing more talent in the door, the key to long-term profitability; (2) the best women and minorities will become harder to attract and retain, so companies that commit to development early have an edge; and (3) having more women and minorities at all levels lets businesses serve their increasingly female and minority customers better. If you don't have a diversity of people working in the back room, how are you going to satisfy the diversity of people coming in the front door?

LEARNING goal 7

Trace the six steps in appraising employee performance.

APPRAISING EMPLOYEE PERFORMANCE TO GET OPTIMUM RESULTS

performance appraisal
An evaluation that measures employee performance against established standards in order to make decisions about promotions, compensation, training, or termination.

Managers must be able to determine whether their workers are doing an effective and efficient job, with a minimum of errors and disruptions. They do so by using a **performance appraisal**, an evaluation that measures employee performance against established standards in order to make decisions about promotions, compensation, training, or termination. Performance appraisals have six steps:

1. *Establishing performance standards.* This step is crucial. Standards must be understandable, subject to measurement, and reasonable. Both manager and subordinate must accept them.
2. *Communicating those standards.* It's dangerous to assume that employees know what is expected of them. They must be told clearly and precisely what the standards and expectations are, and how to meet them.
3. *Evaluating performance.* If the first two steps are done correctly, performance evaluation is relatively easy. It is a matter of evaluating the employee's behavior to see whether it matches standards.
4. *Discussing results with employees.* Employees often make mistakes and fail to meet expectations at first. It takes time to learn a job and do it well. Discussing an employee's successes and areas that need improvement can provide managers an opportunity to be understanding and helpful and guide the employee to better performance. The performance appraisal can also allow employees to suggest how a task could be done better.
5. *Taking corrective action.* As part of performance appraisal, a manager can take corrective action or provide feedback to help the employee perform better. The key word is *perform*. The primary purpose of an appraisal is to improve employee performance if possible.
6. *Using the results to make decisions.* Decisions about promotions, compensation, additional training, or firing are all based on performance evaluations. An effective performance appraisal system is also a way of satisfying legal requirements about such decisions.

Managing effectively means getting results through top performance. That's what performance appraisals are for at all levels of the organization, including at the top where managers benefit from reviews by their subordinates and peers.

In the *360-degree review*, management gathers opinions from all around the employee, including those under, above, and on the same level, to get an accurate, comprehensive idea of the worker's abilities. Figure 11.5 illustrates how managers can make performance appraisals more meaningful.

progress assessment

- Name and describe four training techniques.
- What is the primary purpose of a performance appraisal?
- What are the six steps in a performance appraisal?

1. **DON'T** attack the employee personally. Critically evaluate his or her work.
2. **DO** allow sufficient time, without distractions, for appraisal. (Take the phone off the hook or close the office door.)
3. **DON'T** make the employee feel uncomfortable or uneasy. *Never* conduct an appraisal where other employees are present (such as on the shop floor).
4. **DO** include the employee in the process as much as possible. (Let the employee prepare a self-improvement program.)
5. **DON'T** wait until the appraisal to address problems with the employee's work that have been developing for some time.
6. **DO** end the appraisal with positive suggestions for employee improvement.

figure II.5

CONDUCTING EFFECTIVE APPRAISALS AND REVIEWS

LEARNING goal 8

Summarize the objectives of employee compensation programs, and describe various pay systems and fringe benefits.

COMPENSATING EMPLOYEES: ATTRACTING AND KEEPING THE BEST

Companies don't just compete for customers; they also compete for employees. Compensation is one of the main tools companies use to attract qualified employees, and one of their largest operating costs. The long-term success of a firm—perhaps even its survival—may depend on how well it can control employee costs and optimize employee efficiency. Service organizations like hospitals and airlines struggle with high employee costs since these firms are *labor-intensive* (the primary cost of operations is the cost of labor). Manufacturing firms in the auto and steel industries have asked employees to take reductions in wages (called *givebacks*) to make the firms more competitive. (We discuss this in Chapter 12.) Those are just a few reasons compensation and benefit packages require special attention. In fact, some experts believe determining how best to compensate employees is today's greatest human resources challenge.[28]

A carefully managed and competitive compensation and benefit program can accomplish several objectives:

- Attracting the kinds of people the organization needs, and in sufficient numbers.
- Providing employees with the incentive to work efficiently and productively.
- Keeping valued employees from going to competitors or starting competing firms.
- Maintaining a competitive position in the marketplace by keeping costs low through high productivity from a satisfied workforce.
- Providing employees with some sense of financial security through fringe benefits such as insurance and retirement benefits.

Pay Systems

The way an organization chooses to pay its employees can have a dramatic effect on efficiency and productivity. Managers thus look for a system that compensates employees fairly.

Many companies still use the pay system known as the Hay system, devised by Edward Hay. This plan is based on job tiers, each of which has a strict pay range. The system is set up on a point basis with three key factors considered: know-how, problem solving, and accountability.

Firms like San Francisco–based Skyline Construction let workers pick their own pay system. They can earn a fixed salary or collect a lower salary with potential for a bonus. John Whitney, author of *The Trust Factor*, believes that companies should set pay at the market level or better and then award all employees the same percentage merit raise. Doing so, he says, sends the message that everyone in the company is important. Figure 11.6 outlines some of the most common pay systems. Which do you think is the fairest?

Compensating Teams

Thus far, we've talked about compensating individuals. What about teams? Since you want your teams to be more than simply a group of individuals, would you compensate them like individuals? If you can't answer that question immediately, you're not alone. Most managers believe in using teams, but fewer are sure about how to pay them. Team-based pay programs are not as effective or as fully developed as managers would hope. Measuring and rewarding individual performance on teams, while at the same time rewarding team performance, is tricky—but it can be done. Professional football players, for example, are rewarded as a team when they go to the playoffs and to the Super Bowl, but they are paid individually as well. Companies are now experimenting with and developing similar incentive systems.

Jim Fox, founder and senior partner of compensation and human resource specialist firm Fox Lawson & Associates, insists that setting up the team right in the first place is the key element to designing an appropriate team compensation plan. He believes the pay model to enhance performance will be a natural outcome of the team's development process. Jay Schuster, coauthor of a study of team pay, found that when pay is based strictly on individual performance, it erodes team cohesiveness and makes the team less likely meet its goals as a collaborative effort. Workplace studies indicate over 50 percent of team compensation plans are based on team goals. Skill-based pay and gain-sharing systems are the two most common compensation methods for teams.

Skill-based pay rewards the growth of both the individual and the team. Base pay is raised when team members learn and apply new skills. Baldrige Award winner Eastman Chemical Company rewards its teams for proficiency in technical, social, and business knowledge skills. A cross-functional compensation policy team defines the skills. The drawbacks of skill-based pay are twofold: the system is complex, and it is difficult to relate the acquisition of skills directly to profit gains.

Most *gain-sharing systems* base bonuses on improvements over previous performance. Nucor Steel, one of the largest U.S. steel producers, calculates bonuses on quality—tons of steel that go out the door with no defects. There are no limits on bonuses a team can earn; they usually average around $20,000 per employee each year.[29]

Competitive compensation and benefit programs can have a tremendous impact on employee efficiency and productivity. Sometimes businesses reward exceptional performance by awarding bonuses. Does your instructor ever award bonuses for exceptional performance in class?

Some of the different pay systems are as follows:

- **Salary:** Fixed compensation computed on weekly, biweekly, or monthly pay periods (e.g., $1,600 per month or $400 per week). Salaried employees do not receive additional pay for any extra hours worked.
- **Hourly wage or daywork:** Wage based on number of hours or days worked, used for most blue-collar and clerical workers. Often employees must punch a time clock when they arrive at work and when they leave. Hourly wages vary greatly. The federal minimum wage is $7.25, and top wages go as high as $40 per hour or more for skilled craftspeople. This does not include benefits such as retirement systems, which may add 30 percent or more to the total package.
- **Piecework system:** Wage based on the number of items produced rather than by the hour or day. This type of system creates powerful incentives to work efficiently and productively.
- **Commission plans:** Pay based on some percentage of sales. Often used to compensate salespeople, commission plans resemble piecework systems.
- **Bonus plans:** Extra pay for accomplishing or surpassing certain objectives. There are two types of bonuses: monetary and cashless. Money is always a welcome bonus. Cashless rewards include written thank-you notes, appreciation notes sent to the employee's family, movie tickets, flowers, time off, gift certificates, shopping sprees, and other types of recognition.
- **Profit-sharing plans:** Annual bonuses paid to employees based on the company's profits. The amount paid to each employee is based on a predetermined percentage. Profit sharing is one of the most common forms of performance-based pay.
- **Gain-sharing plans:** Annual bonuses paid to employees based on achieving specific goals such as quality measures, customer satisfaction measures, and production targets.
- **Stock options:** Right to purchase stock in the company at a specific price over a specific period. Often this gives employees the right to buy stock cheaply despite huge increases in the price of the stock. For example, if over the course of his employment a worker received options to buy 10,000 shares of the company stock at $10 each and the price of the stock eventually grows to $100, he can use those options to buy the 10,000 shares (now worth $1 million) for $100,000.

figure 11.6

PAY SYSTEMS
Competitive compensation and benefit programs can have a tremendous impact on employee efficiency and productivity. Sometimes businesses reward exceptional performance by awarding bonuses. Does your instructor ever award bonuses for exceptional performance in class?

It is important to reward individual team players also. Outstanding team players—who go beyond what is required and make an outstanding individual contribution—should be separately recognized, with cash or noncash rewards. A good way to compensate for uneven team participation is to let the team decide which members get what type of individual award. After all, if you really support the team process, you need to give teams freedom to reward themselves.

Fringe Benefits

Fringe benefits include sick-leave pay, vacation pay, pension plans, and health plans that provide additional compensation to employees beyond base wages. Benefits in recent years grew faster than wages and can't really be considered fringe anymore. In 1929, such benefits accounted for less than 2 percent of payroll; today they account for about 30 percent. Health care costs have soared, forcing employees to pay a larger share of their own health insurance bill. Since 2000, the cost to the employee for employee-only coverage has increased 86 percent; the cost of family coverage premiums has increased 80

fringe benefits
Benefits such as sick-leave pay, vacation pay, pension plans, and health plans that represent additional compensation beyond base wages.

The workers at DreamWorks Studios who helped create the popular Shrek movies enjoy perks like free breakfast and lunch, afternoon yoga classes, free movie screenings, on-campus art classes, and monthly parties. How might fringe benefits like these affect employee performance?

percent.[30] Employees often request more fringe benefits instead of salary, in order to avoid higher taxes. This has resulted in increased debate and government investigation.

Fringe benefits can include recreation facilities, company cars, country club memberships, discounted massages, special home-mortgage rates, paid and unpaid sabbaticals, day care services, and executive dining rooms. Employees often want dental care, mental health care, elder care, legal counseling, eye care, and even short workweeks.[31]

Understanding that it takes many incentives to attract and retain the best employees, dozens of firms among *Fortune* magazine's "100 Best Companies to Work For" list offer so-called soft benefits. *Soft benefits* help workers maintain the balance between work and family life that is often as important to hardworking employees as the nature of the job itself.[32] These perks include onsite haircuts and shoe repair, concierge services, and free breakfasts.[33] Freeing employees from errands and chores gives them more time for family—and work. Biotechnology firm Genentech even offers doggie day care and an onsite farmer's market.[34]

At one time, most employees sought benefits that were similar. Today, however, some may seek childcare benefits while others prefer attractive pension plans. To address such growing demands, over half of all large firms offer **cafeteria-style fringe benefits**, in which employees can choose the benefits they want up to a certain dollar amount. Such plans let human resource managers equitably and cost-effectively meet employees' individual needs by allowing them choice.

As the cost of administering benefits programs has accelerated, many companies have chosen to outsource this function. Managing benefits can be especially complicated when employees are located in other countries. The Reaching Beyond Our Borders box discusses the human resource challenges faced by global businesses. To put it simply, benefits are often as important to recruiting top talent as salary and may even become more important in the future.

cafeteria-style fringe benefits
Fringe benefits plan that allows employees to choose the benefits they want up to a certain dollar amount.

LEARNING goal 9

Demonstrate how managers use scheduling plans to adapt to workers' needs.

SCHEDULING EMPLOYEES TO MEET ORGANIZATIONAL AND EMPLOYEE NEEDS

Workplace trends and the increasing costs of transportation have led employees to look for scheduling flexibility. Flextime, in-home employment, and job sharing are becoming important benefits employees seek.

Working Worldwide

Human resource management of a global workforce begins with an understanding of the customs, laws, and local business needs of every country in which the organization operates. Country-specific cultural and legal standards can affect a variety of human resource functions:

- *Compensation.* Salaries must be converted to and from foreign currencies. Often employees with international assignments receive special allowances for relocation, children's education, housing, travel, and other business-related expenses.

- *Health and pension standards.* There are different social contexts for benefits in other countries. In the Netherlands the government provides retirement income and health care.

- *Paid time off.* Four weeks of paid vacation is the standard of many European employers. But many other countries lack the short-term and long-term absence policies offered in the United States, including sick leave, personal leave, and family and medical leave. Global companies need a standard definition of *time off.*

- *Taxation.* Different countries have varying taxation rules, and the payroll department is an important player in managing immigration information.

- *Communication.* When employees leave to work in another country, they often feel disconnected from their home country. Wise companies use their intranet and the Internet to help these faraway employees keep in direct contact.

Human resource policies at home are influenced more and more by conditions and practices in other countries and cultures. Human resource managers need to sensitize themselves and their organizations to overseas cultural and business practices.

Sources: Anne Vo and Pauline Stanton, "The Transfer of HRM Policies and Practices to a Transitional Business System," *The Journal of Human Resource Management,* April I, 2011; and Liisa Mäkelä and Vesa Suutari, "Coping with Work-Family Conflicts in the Global Career Context," *International Business Review,* April 14, 2011.

Flextime Plans

A **flextime plan** gives employees some freedom to choose which hours to work, as long as they work the required number of hours or complete their assigned tasks. The most popular plans allow employees to arrive between 7:00 and 9:00 a.m. and leave between 4:00 and 6:00 p.m. Flextime plans generally incorporate core time. **Core time** is the period when all employees are expected to be at their job stations. An organization may designate core time as 9:00 to 11:00 a.m. and 2:00 to 4:00 p.m. During these hours all employees are required to be at work (see Figure 11.7 on p. 314). Flextime allows employees to adjust to work/life demands. Two-income families find them especially helpful. Companies that use flextime say that it boosts employee productivity and morale.[35]

flextime plan
Work schedule that gives employees some freedom to choose when to work, as long as they work the required number of hours or complete their assigned tasks.

core time
In a flextime plan, the period when all employees are expected to be at their job stations.

figure 11.7

A FLEXTIME CHART
At this company, employees can start work anytime between 6:30 and 9:30 a.m. They take a half hour for lunch anytime between 11:00 a.m. and 1:30 p.m. and can leave between 3:00 and 6:30 p.m. Everyone works an eight-hour day. The blue arrows show a typical employee's flextime day.

compressed workweek
Work schedule that allows an employee to work a full number of hours per week but in fewer days.

Flextime is not for all organizations, however. It doesn't suit shift work like fast-food or assembly processes like manufacturing, where everyone on a given shift must be at work at the same time. Another disadvantage is that managers often have to work longer days to assist and supervise in organizations that may operate from 6:00 a.m. to 6:00 p.m. Flextime also makes communication more difficult since certain employees may not be there when others need to talk to them. Furthermore, if not carefully supervised, some employees could abuse the system, causing resentment among others.[36]

Another option that about one in four companies uses is a **compressed workweek**. An employee works the full number of hours, but in fewer than the standard number of days. For example, an employee may work four 10-hour days and then enjoy a long weekend, instead of working five 8-hour days with a traditional weekend. There are obvious advantages of compressed workweeks, but some employees get tired working such long hours, and productivity can decline. Others find the system a great benefit, however, and are enthusiastic about it. Nurses often work compressed weeks.

Home-Based Work

Nearly 10 million U.S. workers now telecommute, working at home at least several days per month. Approximately 12 percent of businesses use some home-based work.[37] Home-based workers can choose their own hours, interrupt work for child care or other tasks, and take time out for personal reasons. Working at home isn't for everyone. It requires discipline to stay focused on the job and not be easily distracted.

Home-based work can be a cost saver for employers. For example, Bank of America introduced a program it calls My Work that saves an estimated $5,500 per enrolled employee every year (this adds up to a $100 million a year savings). Employees in the program work remotely about 60 percent of the time. When they do come into the office, they work in communal areas or plug laptops into mobile workstations on a first-come, first-served basis. Bank of America was able to terminate leases and sublease space it no longer needed.[38] Many other large companies offer "hot-desking," or sharing a desk with other employees who work at different times.

Many companies are hiring U.S. home-based call agents rather than using either more expensive in-house operators or less-qualified offshore call centers. Office Depot shifted to home-based call agents and saved 30 or 40 percent on the cost of each call by not providing workspace (or benefits) for its home-based call-center workers. Figure 11.8 outlines the benefits and challenges of home-based work to organizations, individuals, and society.

	BENEFITS	CHALLENGES
To Organization	• Increases productivity due to fewer sick days, fewer absences, higher job satisfaction, and higher work performance ratings • Broadens available talent pool • Reduces costs of providing on-site office space	• Makes it more difficult to appraise job performance • Can negatively affect the social network of the workplace and can make it difficult to promote team cohesiveness • Complicates distribution of tasks (should office files, contact lists, and such be allowed to leave the office?)
To Individual	• Makes more time available for work and family by reducing or eliminating commute time • Reduces expenses of buying and maintaining office clothes • Avoids office politics • Helps balance work and family • Expands employment opportunities for disabled individuals	• Can cause feeling of isolation from social network • Can raise concerns regarding promotions and other rewards due to being out of sight, out of mind • May diminish individual's influence within company due to limited opportunity to learn the corporate culture
To Society	• Decreases traffic congestion • Discourages community crime that might otherwise occur in bedroom communities • Increases time available to build community ties	• Increases need to resolve zoning regulations forbidding business deliveries in residential neighborhoods • May reduce ability to interact with other people in a personal, intimate manner

Job-Sharing Plans

Job sharing lets two or more part-time employees share one full-time job. Students and parents with small children, for instance, may work only during school hours, and older workers can work part-time before fully retiring or after retiring. Benefits of job sharing include:

- Employment opportunities for those who cannot or prefer not to work full-time.

- An enthusiastic and productive workforce.

- Reduced absenteeism and tardiness.

- Ability to schedule part-time workers into peak demand periods (e.g., banks on payday).

- Retention of experienced employees who might otherwise have retired.

Disadvantages include the need to hire, train, motivate, and supervise at least twice as many people and perhaps prorate some fringe benefits. But firms are finding that the advantages generally outweigh the disadvantages.

LEARNING goal 10

Describe how employees can move through a company: promotion, reassignment, termination, and retirement.

figure II.8

BENEFITS AND CHALLENGES OF HOME-BASED WORK
Home-based work (also known as telecommuting) offers many benefits and challenges to organizations, individuals, and society as a whole.

job sharing
An arrangement whereby two part-time employees share one full-time job.

Working from home gives workers the flexibility to choose their own hours and to take time out for personal tasks. It requires self-discipline in order to stay focused on the job and not allow yourself to be distracted. Do you think you have the discipline to be a home-based worker?

MOVING EMPLOYEES UP, OVER, AND OUT

Employees don't always stay in the position they were hired to fill. They may excel and move up the corporate ladder or fail and move out the door. Employees can also be reassigned or retire. Of course, some choose to move themselves by going to another company.

Promoting and Reassigning Employees

Many companies find that promotion from within the company improves employee morale. It's also cost-effective in that the promoted employees are already familiar with the corporate culture and procedures and don't need to spend valuable time on basic orientation.

In the new, flatter corporate structures (see Chapter 8), there are fewer levels for employees to reach than in the past. Thus they often move *over* to a new position rather than *up*. Such lateral transfers allow employees to develop and display new skills and learn more about the company overall. Reassignment is one way of motivating experienced employees to remain in a company with few advancement opportunities.[39]

Terminating Employees

We've seen that the relentless pressure of global competition, shifts in technology, increasing customer demands for greater value, and uncertain economic conditions have human resource managers struggling to manage layoffs and firings. Even if the economy is booming, many companies are hesitant to hire or rehire workers full-time. Why is that the case? One reason is that the cost of terminating employees is prohibitively high in terms of lost training costs and possible damages and legal fees for wrongful discharge suits. That's why many companies are either using temporary employees or outsourcing certain functions.

At one time the prevailing employment doctrine in the United States was "employment at will." This meant managers had as much freedom to fire workers as workers had to leave voluntarily. Most states now limit the at-will doctrine to protect employees from wrongful firing. An employer can no longer fire someone for exposing the company's illegal actions or refusing to violate a law. Employees who are members of a minority or other protected group also may have protections under equal employment law. In some cases, workers fired for using illegal drugs have sued on the ground that they have an illness (addiction) and are therefore protected by laws barring discrimination under the Americans with Disabilities Act (ADA). Well-intended legislation has in some ways restricted management's ability to terminate employees as it increased workers' rights to their jobs. See Figure 11.9 for advice about how to minimize the chance of wrongful discharge lawsuits.

Retiring Employees

Companies looking to downsize sometimes offer early retirement benefits to entice older (and more expensive) workers to retire. Such benefits can include one-time cash payments, known in some companies as *golden handshakes*. The advantage early retirement benefits have over layoffs or firing is the increased morale of surviving employees. Retiring senior workers earlier also increases promotion opportunities for younger employees.

Losing Valued Employees

In spite of a company's efforts to retain them, some talented employees will choose to pursue opportunities elsewhere. Knowing their reasons for leaving can be invaluable in preventing the loss of other good people in the future. One way to learn the reasons is to have an outside expert conduct an *exit interview*. Outsiders can provide confidentiality and anonymity that earns more honest feedback than employees are comfortable giving in face-to-face interviews with their bosses. Web-based systems can capture, track, and statistically analyze employee exit interview data to generate reports that identify trouble areas. Such programs can also coordinate exit interview data with employee satisfaction surveys to predict which departments should expect turnover to occur.

As the economic crisis grew, managers had to terminate a growing number of employees. Do you think they will rehire full-time employees when the economy recovers? Why or why not? What alternatives do employers have?

Consultants offer this advice to minimize the chance of a lawsuit for wrongful discharge:

- Prepare before hiring by requiring recruits to sign a statement that retains management's freedom to terminate at will.

- Don't make unintentional promises by using such terms as *permanent employment*.

- Document reasons before firing and make sure you have an unquestionable business reason for the firing.

- Fire the worst first and be consistent in discipline.

- Buy out bad risk by offering severance pay in exchange for a signed release from any claims.

- Be sure to give employees the true reasons they are being fired. If you do not, you cannot reveal it to a recruiter asking for a reference without risking a defamation lawsuit.

- Disclose the reasons for an employee's dismissal to that person's potential new employers. For example, if you fired an employee for dangerous behavior and you withhold that information from your references, you can be sued if the employee commits a violent act at his or her next job.

figure II.9

HOW TO AVOID WRONGFUL-DISCHARGE LAWSUITS

Sources: "In Economics Old and New, Treatment of Workers Is Paramount," *The Washington Post*, February II, 200I, p. LI; and U.S. Law, www.uslaw.com.

Attracting and retaining the best employees is the key to success in the competitive global business environment. Dealing with controversial issues employees have on the job is challenging and never-ending. Chapter 12 discusses such issues.

progress assessment

- Can you name and describe five alternative compensation techniques?
- What advantages do compensation plans such as profit sharing offer an organization?
- What are the benefits and challenges of flextime? Telecommuting? Job sharing?

summary

Learning Goal 1. Explain the importance of human resource management, and describe current issues in managing human resources.

- **What are current challenges and opportunities in the human resource area?**

Many current challenges and opportunities arise from changing demographics: more women, minorities, immigrants, and older workers in the workforce. Others include a shortage of trained workers and an abundance of unskilled workers, skilled workers in declining industries requiring retraining, changing employee work attitudes, and complex laws and regulations.

Learning Goal 2. Illustrate the effects of legislation on human resource management.

- **What are some of the key laws?**

See the Legal Briefcase box on page 295 and review the text section on laws.

Learning Goal 3. Summarize the five steps in human resource planning.

- **What are the steps in human resource planning?**

The five steps are (1) preparing a human resource inventory of the organization's employees; (2) preparing a job analysis; (3) assessing future demand; (4) assessing future supply; and (5) establishing a plan for recruiting, hiring, educating, appraising, compensating, and scheduling employees.

Learning Goal 4. Describe methods that companies use to recruit new employees, and explain some of the issues that make recruitment challenging.

- **What methods do human resource managers use to recruit new employees?**

Recruiting sources are classified as either internal or external. Internal sources include those hired from within (transfers, promotions, reassignments) and employees who recommend others to hire. External recruitment sources include advertisements, public and private employment agencies, college placement bureaus, management consultants, professional organizations, referrals, walk-in applications, and the Internet.

- **Why has recruitment become more difficult?**

Legal restrictions complicate hiring and firing practices. Finding suitable employees can be more difficult if companies are considered unattractive workplaces.

Learning Goal 5. Outline the six steps in selecting employees.

- **What are the six steps in the selection process?**

The steps are (1) obtaining complete application forms, (2) conducting initial and follow-up interviews, (3) giving employment tests, (4) conducting background investigations, (5) obtaining results from physical exams, and (6) establishing a trial period of employment.

Learning Goal 6. Illustrate employee training and development methods.

- **What are some training activities?**

Training activities include employee orientation, on- and off-the-job training, apprentice programs, online training, vestibule training, and job simulation.

- **What methods help develop managerial skills?**

Management development methods include on-the-job coaching, understudy positions, job rotation, and off-the-job courses and training.

- **How does networking fit in this process?**

Networking is the process of establishing contacts with key managers within and outside the organization to get additional development assistance.

Learning Goal 7. Trace the six steps in appraising employee performance.

- **How do managers evaluate performance?**

The steps are (1) establish performance standards; (2) communicate those standards; (3) compare performance to standards; (4) discuss results; (5) take corrective action when needed; and (6) use the results for decisions about promotions, compensation, additional training, or firing.

Learning Goal 8. Summarize the objectives of employee compensation programs, and describe various pay systems and fringe benefits.

- **What are common types of compensation systems?**

They include salary systems, hourly wages, piecework, commission plans, bonus plans, profit-sharing plans, and stock options.

- **What types of compensation are appropriate for teams?**

The most common are gain-sharing and skill-based compensation programs. Managers also reward outstanding individual performance within teams.

- **What are fringe benefits?**

Fringe benefits include sick leave, vacation pay, company cars, pension plans, and health plans that provide additional compensation to employees beyond base wages. Cafeteria-style fringe benefits plans let employees choose the benefits they want, up to a certain dollar amount.

Learning Goal 9. Demonstrate how managers use scheduling plans to adapt to workers' needs.

- **What scheduling plans can adjust work to employees' need for flexibility?**

Such plans include job sharing, flextime, compressed workweeks, and working at home.

Learning Goal 10. Describe how employees can move through a company: promotion, reassignment, termination, and retirement.

• **How can employees move within a company?**

Employees can be moved up (promotion), over (reassignment), or out (termination or retirement) of a company. They can also choose to leave a company to pursue opportunities elsewhere.

key terms

affirmative action 294
apprentice programs 304
cafeteria-style fringe benefits 312
compressed workweek 314
contingent workers 302
core time 313
flextime plan 313
fringe benefits 311
human resource management (HRM) 290

job analysis 297
job description 297
job sharing 315
job simulation 305
job specifications 297
management development 306
mentor 307
networking 307
off-the-job training 305
online training 305

on-the-job training 304
orientation 303
performance appraisal 308
recruitment 298
reverse discrimination 294
selection 300
training and development 303
vestibule training 305

critical thinking

1. Does human resource management interest you as a career? What are your experiences working with human resource professionals?

2. What effects have dual-career families had on the human resource function?

3. What problems can arise when family members work together in the same firm?

4. If you were a human resource manager, how would you address the brain drain that occurs as knowledgeable workers retire?

5. Imagine you must fire an employee. What effect might the dismissal have on remaining employees? Explain how you would tell the employee and your other subordinates.

developing workplace skills

1. Look in the classified ads in your local newspaper or on the Internet and find at least two positions you might like to have when you graduate. List the qualifications specified in each of the ads and identify methods the companies might use to determine how well applicants meet them.

2. Read several current business periodicals to find information about the latest court rulings on benefits, affirmative action, and other human resource issues. Summarize your findings. Is there a trend in these decisions? If so, what is it, and what will it mean for tomorrow's college graduates?

3. Recall any on-the-job and off-the-job training sessions you've experienced. Write a brief critique of each. How would you improve them? Share your ideas with the class.

4. Consider the following occupations: doctor, computer salesperson, computer software developer, teacher, and assembly worker. Identify the method of compensation you think is appropriate for each. Explain your answer.

5. Choose one of these positions: a human resource manager notifying employees of mandatory drug testing or an employee representative protesting such testing. Write a memorandum supporting your position.

taking it to the net

Purpose

The two purposes here are to illustrate the types of questions managers typically ask during interviews and practice answering such questions in a safe environment.

Exercise

Go to Monster.com's virtual interview page at http://resources.monster.com/tools/quiz_section2.asp. This page offers links to virtual interviews for jobs in a variety of fields. Select the one in the field that most interests you and then answer the sample interview questions. This interactive section gives you the opportunity to test your answers so that when you do go on an actual interview you are less likely to fumble for an answer.

casing the web

To access the case "Dual-Career Planning," visit **www.mhhe.com/ubl0e**

video case

To access the video case featuring SAS, visit **www.mhhe.com/ubl0e**

Dealing with Union and Employee–Management Issues

12

LEARNING goals

After you have read and studied this chapter, you should be able to

1 Trace the history of organized labor in the United States.

2 Discuss the major legislation affecting labor unions.

3 Outline the objectives of labor unions.

4 Describe the tactics used by labor and management during

conflicts, and discuss the role of unions in the future.

5 Assess some of today's controversial employee–management issues, such as executive compensation, pay equity, child care and elder care, drug testing, and violence in the workplace.

The relationship between management and employees is a delicate one. While both have a vested interest in seeing their particular business thrive, the needs and desires of each party can sometimes be wholly different. Few people understand this better than National Basketball Association Commissioner David Stern. During his nearly three-decade-long term, Stern has presided over five employee lockouts. And as of this writing, if contract negotiations for the 2011–2012 season continue to sour, Stern may have to face his sixth lockout soon.

A native New Yorker with a law degree from Columbia University, Stern has never been the type to shy away from an argument. He first joined the NBA in 1966 as an outside legal counselor before becoming the league's General Counsel in 1978. By the beginning of the 1980s, he was promoted to the role of Executive Vice President. In those early years Stern served as a central participant in several matters that changed the shape of the NBA. He spearheaded settlements between players and coaches that led to the implementation of free agency, salary caps, and revenue sharing.

It's that last item that has caused so much trouble for Stern and the NBA as of late. As commissioner since 1984, Stern led the league to unprecedented growth. Income from ticket sales, TV contracts, video games and merchandise is more than 15 times larger than before he came on the scene. Stern also transformed the NBA into a global phenomenon, with games televised in 215 countries and in 43 languages. Still, even with this worldwide athletic empire, in 2009 the NBA lost $380 million despite $4 billion in revenues. How could such a powerful brand post such immense losses? According to Stern, one need not look further than the players themselves, who get 57 percent of all revenue earned.

To offset losses and generate a profit, Stern wants $750–800 million to pass from the players' union to the league itself. By some estimates, that could mean cutting as much as 35 percent of players' salaries and benefits. Naturally, the athletes have resisted the cuts and a bitter collective bargaining

debate has ensued. If the stalemate continues, management could lock out the players and suspend games during the 2011–2012 season indefinitely.

But none of this is new territory to Stern. The NBA faced similar labor issues in 1998, as a player lockout canceled all games during October, November, December, and January of 1999. Stalled talks almost cut the rest of the season as well, before a last-minute compromise finally ended the standoff. Insiders credit Stern himself with leveraging the deal as he painted the protesting players in the press as a bunch of rich, spoiled athletes. Still, the stakes are even higher in this latest labor deadlock. Since NBA revenues have never been higher, the public might have a problem stomaching the theory that the owners are the victims in this situation. And with steady losses predicted for the foreseeable future, NBA management might not be able to afford a prolonged lockout. Stay tuned, sports fans, because one thing's certain: Stern and company won't be able to solve this problem quickly.

Professional sports, of course, is not the only industry that has problems dealing with labor–management relations, employee compensation, and other work-related issues. This chapter discusses such issues and other employee–management concerns, including executive pay, pay equity, child and elder care, drug testing, and violence in the workplace.

Sources: Steve Moore, "The Global Basketball Association," *The Wall Street Journal,* October 23, 2010; Tommy Craggs, "David Stern vs. Roger Goodell," *The New York Times,* March 25, 2011; Mike Bresnahan, "David Stern Says Change Is Needed," *The Los Angeles Times,* February 19, 2011; and Amy Shipley, "NBA Players, Owners Closely Watching NFL Labor Case," *The Washington Post,* April 7, 2011.

profile

Getting to Know

X *David Stern*

Commissioner of the National Basketball Association (NBA)

EMPLOYEE–MANAGEMENT ISSUES

union
An employee organization whose main goal is representing its members in employee–management negotiation of job-related issues.

A good starting point in discussing employee–management relations in the United States is a discussion of labor unions. A **union** is an employee organization whose main goal is representing its members in employee–management negotiations over job-related issues. Recently labor unions have been in the news more than they have been for years. The conflicts between management and various sports teams is just one issue making headlines.

Another major issue in the news has to do with public sector labor unions (those employees who work for governments, such as teachers, firefighters, police officers, etc.). With many states facing serious debt problems, state governments are trying to find ways of cutting costs, particularly labor costs. However, states with public sector unions have limited ability to cut labor costs because of prior agreements with the unions that represent public workers. The Governor of Wisconsin recently decided to challenge public sector labor unions on the issue of collective bargaining. We shall discuss collective bargaining in depth later in the chapter. For now, it is enough to say that public sector labor unions have been in the news because of such conflicts between the governments of various states and public sector labor unions. Before we get into such issues, however, let's explore the nature of unions in general and what the issues have been over time.

The relationship between managers and employees isn't always smooth. Management's responsibility to produce a profit by maximizing productivity sometimes necessitates hard decisions, which limit managers' chances to win popularity contests with workers. Labor (the collective term for nonmanagement workers) is interested in fair and competent management, human dignity, and a reasonable share in the wealth its work generates. Like other managerial challenges, employee–management issues require open discussion, goodwill, and compromise.

Workers originally formed unions to protect themselves from intolerable work conditions and unfair treatment. They also secured some say in the operation of their jobs. As the number of private union members grew, workers gained more negotiating power with managers and more political power. For example, labor unions were largely responsible for the establishment of minimum-wage laws, overtime rules, workers'

Protesters fill the streets in front of the Wisconsin state capitol in March 2011 to protest Governor Scott Walker's elimination of union bargaining rights for state and public employees. Do you think public employees such as teachers and firefighters should have union bargaining rights? Why or why not? Do public employees in your state have such rights?

compensation, severance pay, child-labor laws, job safety regulations, and more.[1]

Union strength among private workers, however, has waned as private labor unions have lost the economic and political power they once had, and membership has declined.[2] Economists suggest that increased global competition, shifts from manufacturing to service and high-tech industries that are less heavily unionized, growth in part-time work, and changes in management philosophies are some of the reasons for private labor's decline. Others contend the decline is a result of labor's success in seeing the issues it championed become law.[3]

Many insist that private unions have seen their brightest days; others insist that the role and influence of unions—particularly in selected regions—will continue to arouse emotions and opinions that contrast considerably.[4] Let's briefly look at labor unions and then analyze some key issues affecting employee–management relations.

LEARNING goal 1

Trace the history of organized labor in the United States.

LABOR UNIONS FROM DIFFERENT PERSPECTIVES

Are labor unions necessary in the U.S. economy today? Yes, says a teacher protesting at the state capitol building in Wisconsin, as does a plumber carrying a picket sign in New York City. Both elaborate on the dangers to workers if employers continue to try to weaken or break apart unions.[5] Wisconsin's budget-strapped governor and a small manufacturer in New York would disagree, and complain about being restricted by union wage and benefit obligations in an increasingly competitive global economy.[6]

Historians generally agree that today's unions are an outgrowth of the economic transition caused by the Industrial Revolution of the 19th and early 20th centuries. Workers who once toiled in the fields, dependent on the mercies of nature for survival, found themselves relying on the continuous roll of factory presses and assembly lines for their living. Making the transition from an agricultural economy to an industrial economy was quite difficult.[7] Over time, workers in businesses learned that strength through unity (unions) could lead to improved job conditions, better wages, and job security.

While the technological achievement of the Industrial Revolution brought countless new products to market and reduced the need for physical labor in many industries, it also put pressure on workers to achieve higher productivity in factory jobs that called for long hours and low pay. Can you see how these conditions made it possible for labor unions to take hold by the turn of the 20th century?

Today's critics of organized labor maintain that few of the inhuman conditions once dominant in U.S. industry exist in the modern workplace. They argue that labor is an industry in itself, and protecting workers has become secondary. Some analysts maintain that the current legal system and changing management philosophies minimize the possibility that sweatshops (workplaces of the late 19th and early 20th centuries with unsatisfactory, unsafe, or oppressive labor conditions) could reappear in the United States.[8] Let's look at the history of labor unions to see how we got to where we are today.

The History of Organized Labor

Formal labor organizations in the United States date to the time of the American Revolution. As early as 1792, cordwainers (shoemakers) in Philadelphia met to discuss fundamental work issues of pay, hours, conditions, and job security—pretty much the same issues that dominate labor negotiations today. The cordwainers were a **craft union**, an organization of skilled specialists in a particular craft or trade, typically local or regional.[9] Most craft unions were established to achieve some short-range goal, such as curtailing the use of convict labor as an alternative to available free labor. Often, after attaining their goal, the union disbanded. This situation changed dramatically in the late 19th century with the expansion of the Industrial Revolution in the United States. The Industrial Revolution brought enormous productivity increases, gained through mass production and job specialization, that made the United States an economic world power. This growth, however, created problems for workers in terms of productivity expectations, hours of work, wages, job security, and unemployment.

Workers were faced with the reality that productivity was vital. Those who failed to produce, or who stayed home because they were ill or had family problems, lost their job. Over time, the increased emphasis on production led firms to expand the hours of work. The length of the average workweek in 1900 was 60 hours, compared to 36-40 today, but an 80-hour week was not uncommon for some industries.[10] Wages were low, and child labor was widespread.[11] Minimum-wage laws and unemployment benefits were nonexistent, which made periods of unemployment hard on families who earned subsistence wages. The nearby Spotlight on Small Business box highlights the severity of these conditions and the tragedy that resulted.

The first truly national labor organization was the **Knights of Labor**, formed by Uriah Smith Stephens in 1869. The Knights offered membership to all private working people, including employers, and promoted social causes as well as labor and economic issues. By 1886, the organization claimed a membership of 700,000. The Knights' intention was to gain significant *political* power and eventually restructure the U.S. economy. The organization fell from prominence, however, after being blamed for a bomb that killed eight policemen during a labor rally at Haymarket Square in Chicago in 1886.

A rival group, the **American Federation of Labor (AFL)**, was formed that same year. By 1890, the AFL, under the dynamic leadership of Samuel Gompers, stood at the forefront of the labor movement. The AFL was never one big union, but rather an organization of craft unions that championed fundamental labor issues. It intentionally limited membership to skilled workers (craftspeople), assuming they would have better bargaining power than unskilled workers in obtaining concessions from employers. As a federation, its many individual unions can become members yet keep their separate union status.

Over time, an unauthorized AFL group called the Committee of Industrial Organizations began to organize **industrial unions**, which consisted of unskilled and semiskilled workers in mass-production industries such as automobile manufacturing and mining. John L. Lewis, president of the United Mine Workers, led this committee. His objective was to organize both craftspeople and unskilled workers under one banner.

When the AFL rejected his proposal in 1935, Lewis broke away to form the **Congress of Industrial Organizations (CIO)**. The CIO soon rivaled the AFL in membership, partly because of the passage of the National Labor Relations Act (also called the Wagner Act) that same year (see the next section).[12] For 20 years, the two organizations struggled for power. It wasn't until passage of the

craft union
An organization of skilled specialists in a particular craft or trade.

Knights of Labor
The first national labor union; formed in 1869.

American Federation of Labor (AFL)
An organization of craft unions that championed fundamental labor issues; founded in 1886.

industrial unions
Labor organizations of unskilled and semiskilled workers in mass-production industries such as automobiles and mining.

Congress of Industrial Organizations (CIO)
Union organization of unskilled workers; broke away from the American Federation of Labor (AFL) in 1935 and rejoined it in 1955.

The Triangle Fire

On March 25, 1911, a warm spring day in New York City, hundreds of young women (the youngest 14 years old) were busy at work at the Triangle Shirtwaist Company when the unthinkable happened. A fire raced from the eighth floor to the ninth and then the tenth. As the panic-stricken women tried to race to safety they found that a crucial door was locked, trapping them within the fire. It was suggested at a later trial that the door was kept locked to prevent theft. In the blaze that lasted about 18 minutes, 146 workers were killed. Many of the workers burned to death, while others jumped to their fate holding hands with their clothes burning. The fire became the touchstone for organized labor and raised support for changes in the workplace.

Prior to the tragedy at Triangle Shirtwaist, workers had struck for higher pay, shorter hours (average workweek was often 60 hours), and safer workplace conditions. Unfortunately public opinion was strongly against them. After the tragedy, the International Ladies Garment Workers Union (now called Workers United) grew in numbers and in public support. Today labor leaders say that the Triangle fire is proof of why labor unions are crucial to maintain workplace balance in the United States. At a ceremony in New York City commemorating the 100th anniversary of the fire, labor leaders encouraged workers to not let the modern labor movement die.

The 100th anniversary of the Triangle Shirtwaist fire came at a time when *public* union workers in Wisconsin, Ohio, and other states battled to retain their right to collectively bargain. In Wisconsin, 150,000 people protested the limits placed on collective bargaining rights of state employees, fearing this could spread to union busting across the nation. Several states are also considering becoming Right-to-Work states, a move that would limit the power of labor unions in general. It's hard to imagine that in the 1950s, unions represented 36 percent of the private sector workers in the U.S. compared to just 6.9 percent today. It's uncertain if private labor will be Big Labor again, remain Little Labor, or fall to Mini Labor. What is certain, however, is that *public sector* unions are likely to be in the news for a long time to come—certainly until the debt crisis has subsided, which may be a long time coming.

Sources: Bill Singer, "The Triangle Fire: Remembered a Century Later," *Forbes,* March 9, 2011; "100 Years After Triangle Fire Killed 146 in NYC and Galvanized Labor, the Horror Resonates, "*The Washington Post,* March 22, 2011; and Beth Fouhy, "NYC Marks 100th Anniversary of Deadly Factory Fire," *Bloomberg Businessweek,* March 25, 2011.

Taft-Hartley Act in 1947 (see Figure 12.1 on p. 329) that they saw the benefits of a merger. In 1955, 16 million union members united to form the AFL-CIO. Today, the AFL-CIO is trying to regain influence after suffering problems in the early 2000s.

In 2005, seven member unions, including the Service Employees International Union (the AFL-CIO's largest union with 2.2 million members) left the AFL-CIO to form a coalition with six other unions called Change to Win (CtW). By 2010, three of the unions in CtW (Carpenters, UNITE, and Laborers) decided to return to the AFL-CIO.[13] The AFL-CIO today maintains affiliations with 56 national and international labor unions and has about 12.2 million members.[14]

Public Sector Union Membership

Many people today think of union workers as people who work in construction and manufacturing. In other words, they think that union people work in the private sector of the economy. Today, however, for the first time in U.S. history, 7.6 million of the 14.7 million workers in unions work in government, not the private sector.[15] What this means is taxpayers, not stockholders, are paying the cost of union workers' wages and benefits.[16] Unfortunately for the unions, the huge state and local government revenue losses caused by the economic crisis of 2008–2011 have put pressure on governments to reduce wage and benefit costs.[17] Today, at least 17 states are trying to restrict union rights and cut labor costs.[18]

LEARNING goal 2

Discuss the major legislation affecting labor unions.

LABOR LEGISLATION AND COLLECTIVE BARGAINING

Much of the growth and influence of organized labor in the United States has depended primarily on two major factors: the law and public opinion.[19] Figure 12.1 outlines five major federal laws with a significant impact on the rights and operations of labor unions. Take a few moments to read it before going on. Note that such laws govern private workers.

The Norris-LaGuardia Act paved the way for union growth in the United States. This legislation prohibited employers from using contracts that forbid union activities such as a yellow-dog contract.[20] A **yellow-dog contract** required employees to agree, as a condition of employment, not to join a union. The National Labor Relations Act (or Wagner Act) passed three years later provided labor with clear legal justification to pursue key issues that were strongly supported by Samuel Gompers and the AFL. One of these issues, **collective bargaining**, is the process whereby union and management representatives negotiate a contract for workers. Gompers believed collective bargaining was critical to workers obtaining a fairer share of the economic pie and improving work conditions on the job. The Wagner Act expanded labor's right to collectively bargain by obligating employers to meet at reasonable times and bargain in good faith with respect to wages, hours, and other terms and conditions of employment.[21]

It is collective bargaining among *public* union workers that has become the key issue today. Many public employees are not given the privilege of collective bargaining, but many employees at the state level do have such privileges. One of the issues is the fact that public employees are paid by the state (read you and me). Thus we all have an interest in how much such workers are being paid and what privileges they have won in collective bargaining. When it is perceived that public employees are winning more or better health care, more or better hours of work, and so on, some have questioned whether or not such negotiations should be allowed to continue. That is the issue in states like Wisconsin and Ohio where public and private union members have joined together to fight any efforts to take away collective bargaining among public employees.

yellow-dog contract
A type of contract that required employees to agree as a condition of employment not to join a union; prohibited by the Norris-LaGuardia Act in 1932.

collective bargaining
The process whereby union and management representatives form a labor–management agreement, or contract, for workers.

Norris-LaGuardia Act, 1932	Prohibited courts from issuing injunctions against nonviolent union activities; outlawed contracts forbidding union activities; outlawed the use of yellow-dog contracts by employers. (Yellow-dog contracts were contractual agreements forced on workers by employers whereby the employee agreed not to join a union as a condition of employment.)
National Labor Relations Act (Wagner Act), 1935	Gave employees the right to form or join labor organizations (or to refuse to form or join); the right to collectively bargain with employers through elected union representatives; and the right to engage in labor activities such as strikes, picketing, and boycotts. Prohibited certain unfair labor practices by the employer and the union, and established the National Labor Relations Board to oversee union election campaigns and investigate labor practices. This act gave great impetus to the union movement.
Fair Labor Standards Act, 1938	Set a minimum wage and maximum basic hours for workers in interstate commerce industries. The first minimum wage set was 25 cents an hour, except for farm and retail workers.
Labor-Management Relations Act (Taft-Hartley Act), 1947	Amended the Wagner Act; permitted states to pass laws prohibiting compulsory union membership (right-to-work laws); set up methods to deal with strikes that affect national health and safety; prohibited secondary boycotts, closed-shop agreements, and featherbedding (the requiring of wage payments for work not performed) by unions. This act gave more power to management.
Labor-Management Reporting and Disclosure Act (Landrum-Griffin Act), 1959	Amended the Taft-Hartley Act and the Wagner Act; guaranteed individual rights of union members in dealing with their union, such as the right to nominate candidates for union office, vote in union elections, attend and participate in union meetings, vote on union business, and examine union records and accounts; required annual financial reports to be filed with the U.S. Department of Labor. One goal of this act was to clean up union corruption.

figure 12.1

MAJOR LEGISLATION AFFECTING LABOR–MANAGEMENT RELATIONS

Union Organizing Campaigns

The Wagner Act established an administrative agency (discussed in bonus chapter A), the National Labor Relations Board (NLRB), to oversee labor–management relations.[22] The NLRB consists of five members appointed by the U.S. president and is authorized to investigate and remedy unfair labor practices. It also provides workplace guidelines and legal protection to workers seeking to vote on organizing a union to represent them. **Certification** is the formal process whereby the NLRB recognizes a labor union as the authorized bargaining agent for a group of employees. Figure 12.2 on p. 330 describes the steps in a union-organizing campaign leading to certification. After the election, both the union and company have five days to contest the results with the NLRB. Workers also have a clear process to remove a union as its workplace representative. **Decertification**, also described in Figure 12.2, is the process by which workers can take away a union's right to represent them.

certification
Formal process whereby a union is recognized by the National Labor Relations Board (NLRB) as the bargaining agent for a group of employees.

decertification
The process by which workers take away a union's right to represent them.

figure 12.2

STEPS IN UNION-ORGANIZING AND DECERTIFICATION CAMPAIGNS

Note that the final vote in each case requires that the union receive over 50 percent of the *votes cast*. Note, too, that the election is secret.

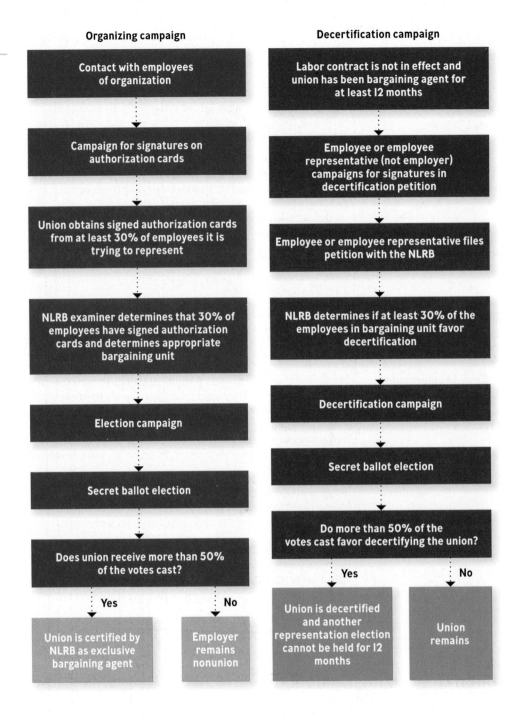

Organizing campaign

Contact with employees of organization

↓

Campaign for signatures on authorization cards

↓

Union obtains signed authorization cards from at least 30% of employees it is trying to represent

↓

NLRB examiner determines that 30% of employees have signed authorization cards and determines appropriate bargaining unit

↓

Election campaign

↓

Secret ballot election

↓

Does union receive more than 50% of the votes cast?

Yes → Union is certified by NLRB as exclusive bargaining agent

No → Employer remains nonunion

Decertification campaign

Labor contract is not in effect and union has been bargaining agent for at least 12 months

↓

Employee or employee representative (not employer) campaigns for signatures in decertification petition

↓

Employee or employee representative files petition with the NLRB

↓

NLRB determines if at least 30% of the employees in bargaining unit favor decertification

↓

Decertification campaign

↓

Secret ballot election

↓

Do more than 50% of the votes cast favor decertifying the union?

Yes → Union is decertified and another representation election cannot be held for 12 months

No → Union remains

negotiated labor–management agreement (labor contract)
Agreement that sets the tone and clarifies the terms under which management and labor agree to function over a period of time.

Unions have strongly urged Congress to pass the Employee Free Choice Act (EFCA), which would make it much easier for unions to organize workers. The EFCA would replace the secret ballot now used in union certification with a *card check* whereby workers could openly approve union representation simply by signing a card.[23] If a majority of workers sign the cards, the union would be certified. Unfortunately for unions, this legislation failed to receive the needed support in the U.S. Congress and seems unlikely to pass in the near future.

LEARNING goal 3

Outline the objectives of labor unions.

Objectives of Organized Labor over Time

The objectives of labor unions shift with social and economic trends. In the 1980s, job security and union recognition were the key focus. In the 1990s and into the 2000s, unions again focused on job security mainly due to the growth of global competition and outsourcing. The AFL-CIO, for example, was a major opponent of NAFTA (see Chapter 3) and other free trade agreements, fearing its members would lose jobs to low-wage workers in other nations. Labor unions have strongly opposed the increase in offshore outsourcing for the same reason.

The **negotiated labor–management agreement**, informally referred to as the labor contract, sets the tone and clarifies the terms and conditions under which management and the union will function over a specific period. Unions attempt to address their most pressing concerns in the labor contract. Negotiations cover a wide range of work topics, and it can take a long time to reach an agreement. Figure 12.3 lists topics commonly negotiated by management and labor.

Labor unions generally insist that a contract contain a **union security clause** stipulating that employees who reap union benefits either officially join or at least pay dues to the union. After passage of the Wagner Act, labor unions sought strict security in the form of the **closed shop agreement**, which specified that workers had to be members of a union before being hired for a job. To labor's dismay, the Labor–Management Relations Act (Taft-Hartley Act) outlawed this practice in 1947 (see Figure 12.4 on p. 332).

Today, unions favor the **union shop agreement**, under which workers do not have to be members of a union to be hired but must agree to join within a prescribed period (usually 30, 60, or 90 days). However, under a contingency called an **agency shop agreement**, employers may hire workers who are not required to join the union but must pay a special union fee or regular union dues. Labor leaders believe that such fees or dues are justified because the union represents all workers in collective bargaining, not just its members.

union security clause
Provision in a negotiated labor–management agreement that stipulates that employees who benefit from a union must either officially join or at least pay dues to the union.

closed shop agreement
Clause in a labor–management agreement that specified workers had to be members of a union before being hired (was outlawed by the Taft-Hartley Act in 1947).

union shop agreement
Clause in a labor–management agreement that says workers do not have to be members of a union to be hired, but must agree to join the union within a prescribed period.

agency shop agreement
Clause in a labor–management agreement that says employers may hire nonunion workers; employees are not required to join the union but must pay a union fee.

1. Management rights
2. Union recognition
3. Union security clause
4. Strikes and lockouts
5. Union activities and responsibilities
   a. Dues checkoff
   b. Union bulletin boards
   c. Work slowdowns
6. Wages
   a. Wage structure
   b. Shift differentials
   c. Wage incentives
   d. Bonuses
   e. Piecework conditions
   f. Tiered wage structures
7. Hours of work and time-off policies
   a. Regular hours of work
   b. Holidays
   c. Vacation policies

d. Overtime regulations
e. Leaves of absence
f. Break periods
g. Flextime
h. Mealtime allotments
8. Job rights and seniority principles
   a. Seniority regulations
   b. Transfer policies and bumping
   c. Promotions
   d. Layoffs and recall procedures
   e. Job bidding and posting
9. Discharge and discipline
   a. Suspension
   b. Conditions for discharge
10. Grievance procedures
    a. Arbitration agreement
    b. Mediation procedures
11. Employee benefits, health, and welfare

figure 12.3

ISSUES IN A NEGOTIATED LABOR–MANAGEMENT AGREEMENT
Labor and management often meet to discuss and clarify the terms that specify employees' functions within the company. The topics listed in this figure are typically discussed during these meetings.

figure 12.4

DIFFERENT FORMS OF UNION
AGREEMENTS

TYPE OF AGREEMENT	DESCRIPTION
Closed shop	The Taft-Hartley Act made this form of agreement illegal. Under this type of labor agreement, employers could hire only current union members for a job.
Union shop	The majority of labor agreements are of this type. In a union shop, the employer can hire anyone, but as a condition of employment, employees hired must join the union to keep their jobs.
Agency shop	Employers may hire anyone. Employees need not join the union, but are required to pay a union fee. A small percentage of labor agreements are of this type.
Open shop	Union membership is voluntary for new and existing employees. Those who don't join the union don't have to pay union dues. Few union contracts are of this type.

right-to-work laws
Legislation that gives workers the right, under an open shop agreement, to join or not join a union if it is present.

open shop agreement
Agreement in right-to-work states that gives workers the option to join or not join a union, if one exists in their workplace.

The Taft-Hartley Act recognized the legality of the union shop but granted individual states the power to outlaw such agreements through **right-to-work laws**.[24] To date, 22 states have passed such legislation (see Figure 12.5).[25] In a right-to-work state, an **open shop agreement** gives workers the option to join or not join a union if one exists. A worker who does not join cannot be forced to pay a fee or dues.[26]

Future contract negotiations will likely focus on evolving workplace issues such as child and elder care, worker retraining, two-tiered wage plans, drug testing, and other such work-related issues. Job security will remain a top union priority due to the threat of job losses from offshore outsourcing and free trade agreements. For public union employees, the major issue may be collective bargaining in general.

Resolving Labor–Management Disagreements

The negotiated labor–management agreement becomes a guide to work relations between management and the union. However, it doesn't necessarily end negotiations between them because there are sometimes differences concerning

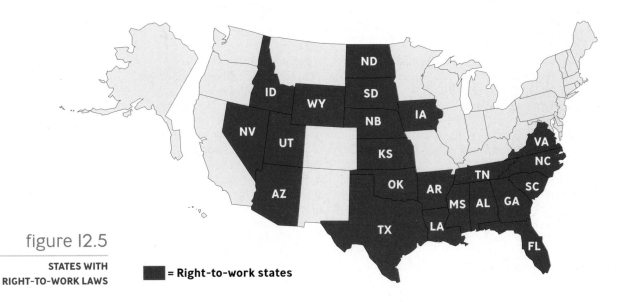

figure 12.5

STATES WITH
RIGHT-TO-WORK LAWS

■ = Right-to-work states

interpretations of the agreement. For example, managers may interpret a certain clause in the agreement to mean they are free to select who works overtime. Union members may interpret the same clause to mean that managers must select employees for overtime on the basis of seniority. If the parties can't resolve such controversies, employees may file a grievance.

A **grievance** is a charge by employees that management is not abiding by or fulfilling the terms of the negotiated labor–management agreement as they perceive it. Overtime rules, promotions, layoffs, transfers, and job assignments are generally sources of employee grievances. Handling them demands a good deal of contact between union officials and managers. Grievances, however, do not imply that a company has broken the law or the labor agreement. In fact, the vast majority of grievances are negotiated and resolved by **shop stewards** (union officials who work permanently in an organization and represent employee interests on a daily basis) and supervisory-level managers. However, if a grievance is not settled at this level, formal grievance procedures will begin. Figure 12.6 illustrates the steps a formal grievance procedure could follow.

Mediation and Arbitration

During the negotiation process, there is generally a **bargaining zone**, which is the range of options between the initial and final offers that each party will consider before negotiations dissolve or reach an impasse. If labor and

grievance
A charge by employees that management is not abiding by the terms of the negotiated labor–management agreement.

shop stewards
Union officials who work permanently in an organization and represent employee interests on a daily basis.

bargaining zone
The range of options between the initial and final offer that each party will consider before negotiations dissolve or reach an impasse.

figure 12.6

THE GRIEVANCE RESOLUTION PROCESS
The grievance process may move through several steps before the issue is resolved. At each step, the issue is negotiated between union officials and managers. If no resolution comes internally, an outside arbitrator may be mutually agreed on. If so, the decision by the arbitrator is binding (legally enforceable).

mediation
The use of a third party, called a mediator, who encourages both sides in a dispute to continue negotiating and often makes suggestions for resolving the dispute.

arbitration
The agreement to bring in an impartial third party (a single arbitrator or a panel of arbitrators) to render a binding decision in a labor dispute.

Writer/actor Tina Fey joined about 12,000 movie and television writers in a strike against the Alliance of Motion Picture and Television Producers, delaying the production of dozens of new TV episodes and movies. Can the public impartially evaluate job actions supported by celebrities?

management negotiators aren't able to agree on alternatives within this bargaining zone, mediation may be necessary.

Mediation is the use of a third party, called a *mediator*, who encourages both sides in a dispute to continue negotiating and often makes suggestions for resolving the matter. Keep in mind that mediators evaluate facts in the dispute and then make suggestions, not decisions. Elected officials (both current and past), attorneys, and college professors often serve as mediators in labor disputes. The National Mediation Board provides federal mediators when requested in a labor dispute.[27] In 2011, the National Football League and National Football League Players Association asked for the assistance of a federal mediator in their attempt to forge a new contract between the players and the league.[28]

A more extreme option used to resolve conflicts is **arbitration**—an agreement to bring in an impartial third party—a single arbitrator or arbitration panel—to render a binding decision in a labor dispute.[29] The arbitrator(s) must be acceptable to both labor and management. You may have heard of professional baseball players filing for arbitration to resolve a contract dispute with their teams.[30] Many negotiated labor–management agreements in the United States call for the use of arbitration to end labor disputes. The nonprofit American Arbitration Association is the dominant organization used in dispute resolution.[31]

LEARNING goal 4

Describe the tactics used by labor and management during conflicts, and discuss the role of unions in the future.

TACTICS USED IN LABOR–MANAGEMENT CONFLICTS

If labor and management cannot reach an agreement through collective bargaining, and negotiations break down, either side, or both, may use specific tactics to enhance its negotiating position and perhaps sway public opinion. Unions primarily use strikes and boycotts, as well as pickets and work slowdowns. Management may implement lockouts, injunctions, and even strikebreakers. The following sections explain each tactic briefly.

Union Tactics

A **strike** occurs when workers collectively refuse to go to work. Strikes have been the most potent union tactic. They attract public attention to a labor dispute and can cause operations in a company to slow down or totally cease. Besides refusing to work, strikers may also picket the company, walking around carrying signs and talking with the public and the media about the issues in the dispute. Unions also often use picketing as an informational tool before going on strike. The purpose is to alert the public to an issue stirring labor unrest, even though a strike has not yet been approved by the union's membership. Strikes sometimes lead to the resolution of a labor dispute; however, they also have generated violence and extended bitterness. Often after a strike is finally settled, labor and management remain openly hostile toward each other and mutual complaints of violations of the negotiated labor–management agreement continue.

The public often realizes how important a worker is when he or she goes on strike. Imagine the economic and social disaster if a town's police force or firefighters went on strike. That's why many states prohibit such public safety workers from striking, even though they can be unionized. Employees of the federal government, such as postal workers, can unionize but are also denied the right to strike. When strikes are prohibited, however, workers sometimes display their frustrations by engaging in sickouts (often called the *blue flu*). That is, they arrange as a group to be absent from work and claim illness as the reason. You may have witnessed such a sickout during the Wisconsin union dispute.

Under the Taft-Hartley Act, the U.S. president can ask for a **cooling-off period**, during which workers return to their jobs while negotiations continue, to prevent a strike in a critical industry such as airlines or railroads.[32] The cooling-off period can last up to 80 days.

Today, both labor and management seek to avoid strikes. Still, you may recall the 100-day screenwriters' strike in 2007–2008 that shut down some television shows and moved many famous faces to picket lines. As technological change, offshore outsourcing, and reductions in worker benefits such as health insurance and pensions continue, it's unlikely that strikes will disappear. Strikes in entertainment, health care, transportation, professional sports, and other industries prove the strike is not dead as a labor tactic.

Unions also attempt boycotts as a means to obtain their objectives in a labor dispute. Boycotts can be classified as primary or secondary. A **primary boycott** occurs when labor encourages both its members and the general public not to buy the products or services of a firm engaged in a labor dispute. A **secondary boycott** is an attempt by labor to convince others to stop doing business with a firm that is the subject of a primary boycott. Labor unions can legally authorize primary boycotts, but the Taft-Hartley Act prohibits using secondary boycotts. For example, a union could not initiate a secondary boycott against a retail chain because its stores carry products of a company that's the target of a primary boycott.

Management Tactics

Like labor unions, management also uses specific tactics to achieve its workplace goals. A **lockout** is an attempt by management to put pressure on union workers by temporarily closing the business. When workers don't work, they don't get paid. Though management rarely uses lockouts to achieve its objectives, the high-profile lockout of National Football League players in 2011 shows that this tactic is still used.[33] Management, however, most often uses injunctions and strikebreakers to counter labor demands it sees as excessive.

An **injunction** is a court order directing someone to do something or to refrain from doing something. Management has sought

strike
A union strategy in which workers refuse to go to work; the purpose is to further workers' objectives after an impasse in collective bargaining.

cooling-off period
When workers in a critical industry return to their jobs while the union and management continue negotiations.

primary boycott
When a union encourages both its members and the general public not to buy the products of a firm involved in a labor dispute.

secondary boycott
An attempt by labor to convince others to stop doing business with a firm that is the subject of a primary boycott; prohibited by the Taft-Hartley Act.

lockout
An attempt by management to put pressure on unions by temporarily closing the business.

injunction
A court order directing someone to do something or to refrain from doing something.

The 2011 conflict between NFL players and owners resulted in the owners locking the players out of team facilities for many months. How did the lockout affect the 2011–12 season? What effect did the lockout have on fans?

injunctions to order striking workers back to work, limit the number of pickets during a strike, or otherwise deal with any actions that could be detrimental to the public welfare. For a court to issue an injunction, management must show a just cause, such as the possibility of violence or destruction of private property.

Employers have had the right to replace striking workers since a 1938 Supreme Court ruling, but this tactic was used infrequently until the 1980s. The use of strikebreakers since then has been a particular source of hostility and violence in labor relations. **Strikebreakers** (called scabs by unions) are workers hired to do the jobs of striking employees until the labor dispute is resolved. The National Football League, for example, used strikebreakers to replace striking players in 1987.[34] Be sure to read the nearby Making Ethical Decisions box, which deals with this issue.

strikebreakers
Workers hired to do the jobs of striking workers until the labor dispute is resolved.

The Future of Unions and Labor–Management Relations

Organized labor is at a crossroads. As noted earlier, only about 7 percent of workers in the private sector are unionized and more than half of all union members work in the public sector, with union membership varying considerably by state (see Figure 12.7).[35] Once powerful unions like the United Auto Workers (UAW) have lost three-fourths of their membership since 1979.[36] This loss has occurred despite unions like the UAW granting management concessions, or **givebacks**, of previous gains in attempts to save jobs.[37] Both public and private sector union members now face challenges as they try to maintain remaining wage and fringe benefit gains achieved in past negotiations. Perhaps what's even more concerning to labor unions is that union membership is highest among workers 55–64 years old and lowest among workers 18–25 years old.[38]

givebacks
Concessions made by union members to management; gains from labor negotiations are given back to management to help employers remain competitive and thereby save jobs.

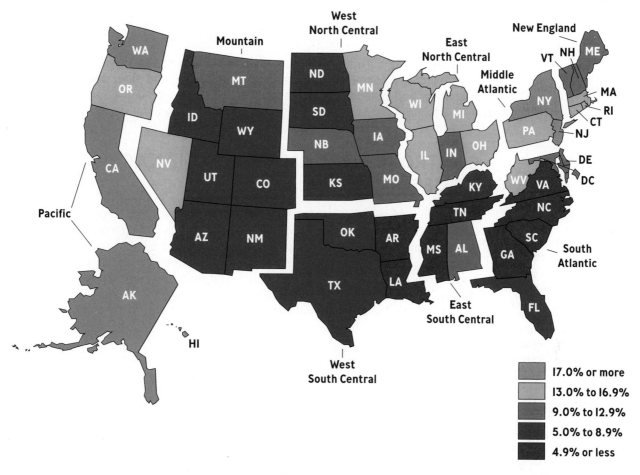

17.0% or more
13.0% to 16.9%
9.0% to 12.9%
5.0% to 8.9%
4.9% or less

figure 12.7

UNION MEMBERSHIP BY STATE

Source: www.bls
.gov,accessednovember2011.

Unions in the future will undoubtedly be quite different from those in the past. Today the largest union in the United States is the Service Employees International Union (SEIU) with 2.2 million members. Notice the emphasis is on services. To grow, unions will have to include more white-collar, female, and foreign-born workers than they have traditionally included. The traditional manufacturing base that unions depended on for growth needs to give way to organizing efforts in industries like health care (over 12 million workers), and information technology (over 3 million workers).[39] Unions will also need to take on a new role in assisting management in training workers, redesigning jobs, and assimilating the changing workforce to the job requirements of the new service and knowledge-work economy. How organized labor and management handle these challenges may well define the future for labor unions. After the Progress Assessment, we will look at other issues facing employees and managers in the 21st century.

progress assessment

- What are the major laws that affected union growth, and what does each one cover?
- How do changes in the economy affect the objectives of unions?
- What are the major tactics used by unions and by management to assert their power in contract negotiations?
- What types of workers do unions need to organize in the future?

LEARNING goal 5

Assess some of today's controversial employee–management issues, such as executive compensation, pay equity, child care and elder care, drug testing, and violence in the workplace.

CONTROVERSIAL EMPLOYEE–MANAGEMENT ISSUES

This is an interesting time in the history of employee–management relations. Organizations are active in global expansion, offshore outsourcing, and technology change. The United States economy is on the road to recovery from the worst recession in many decades. The government has been taking a more active role in mandating what benefits and assurances businesses must provide to workers. Employees are raising questions of fairness and workplace security. Let's look at several key workplace issues, starting with executive compensation.

Executive Compensation

LeBron James dribbles his way to $43 million a year, Johnny Depp acts his way to $75 million a year, Beyonce Knowles sings her way to $87 million a year, and Oprah Winfrey still talks her way to over $315 million a year.[40] Is it out of line, then, for Lawrence Ellison, CEO of Oracle, to make $67 million a year?[41] Chapter 2 explained that the U.S. free-market system is built on incentives that allow top executives to make such large amounts—or more. Today, however, the government, boards of directors, stockholders, unions, and employees are challenging this principle and arguing that executive compensation has gotten out of line. In fact, the average total CEO compensation (salary, bonuses, and incentives) at a major company was $9.2 million, compared to just over $40,000 for the average worker.[42]

In theory, CEO compensation and bonuses were determined by the firm's profitability or an increase in its stock price. The logic of this assumption was that as the fortunes of a company and its stockholders grew, so would the rewards of the CEO. Today, however, executives generally receive stock options (the ability to buy company stock at a set price at a later date) and restricted stock (stock issued directly to the CEO that can't be sold usually for three or four years) as part of their compensation.[43] Stock options account for over 50 percent of a CEO's compensation, and restricted stock makes up almost 25 percent. The decline in the stock prices during the financial crisis in 2008–2009 allowed executives to obtain stock options at very low prices. The market's recovery in 2010–2011 made the options very lucrative, causing executive pay to skyrocket 27 percent in 2010 compared to 2.1 percent for average workers.[44]

What's even more frustrating to those who question how much executives are paid, is that CEOs are often rewarded richly even if their company does not meet expectations, or they leave under pressure. Regulators approved a combined $17 million to the CEOs of taxpayer-backed mortgage giants Fannie Mae and Freddie Mac even

While average workers saw their salary rise 2.1 percent, Disney's CEO Robert Iger enjoyed a 35 percent pay boost in 2010. Iger's salary plus bonus jumped from $12 million to $16.3 million. He also received additional stock awards making his total compensation for the year a hefty $28 million. Corporate boards of directors determine executive compensation. Do you think this is a fair system of compensation for CEOs? Do you think workers should have input?

briefcase

Executive Pay Remains on the Rise

Perhaps no other aspect of the recent economic crisis angered Americans more than the high pay awarded to some of the executives who contributed to the cause of the crisis. High-ranking officers of the nation's biggest financial institutions walked away with millions even as the banking industry and the real estate market crumbled around them.

Stanley O'Neal of Merrill Lynch, for instance, earned a salary of $87 million during five years of service as he engaged in risky investments in mortgage markets. After the company posted $8 billion in losses, O'Neal jumped ship in September 2008 with a $165 million severance package to comfort him. A few months earlier, the founder of Countrywide Financial and one of the architects of the subprime mortgage fiasco, Angelo Mozilo, left the company after Bank of America assumed control. He took home $188 million for his trouble and immediately retired.

These "golden parachutes" enraged a public that was already making sacrifices to survive in the downturned economy. President Obama and other political leaders criticized executives during stump speeches, but were relatively unable to rein in lavish compensation through direct government action. Still, the government could regulate those companies who borrowed money through TARP, the $700 billion bailout bill. Under the legislation, executive salaries, including bonuses, stock options and severance packages, would be kept under a cap as long as a company still used taxpayer money. Even outside the circle of TARP-aided businesses, executive pay from 2008 to 2009 was lower than it had been in years.

But as the economy turned, CEO pay shot back up to unprecedented levels. In the fourth quarter of 2010, profits at American businesses increased by 29.2 percent, the fastest recorded growth in more than 60 years. As annual corporate profits grew to $1.678 trillion, median pay for top executives rose as well by 12 percent to an average of $9.2 million. At the very top, Philippe Dauman of Verizon took in a whopping $84.5 million in just nine months. Occidental Petroleum's Ray

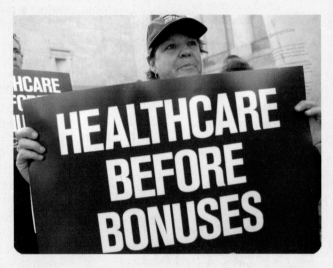

Irani saw his salary skyrocket 142 percent with $76.1 million in bonuses and stock. Executive pay is on the rise even at former TARP beneficiaries like Goldman Sachs, where CEO Lloyd C. Blankfein saw his annual income rise from $.9 million to $14.1 million once the company paid off its government debt.

With unemployment still high, would companies be better off using their newfound profits to hire workers? Weaning companies off excessive compensation won't be easy, though, since the practice is deeply ingrained in the fabric of many companies. After all, many executives create their own compensation committees and stack them with sympathetic peers with similarly "generous" intentions. As the legendary investor Warren Buffet put it, executives "aren't looking for Dobermans; they're looking for cocker spaniels."

Sources: Michael Baron, "TARP Czar Holds Line on CEO Pay," *The Street*, April 1, 2011; Liz Wolgemuth, "Warren Buffet on Executive Compensation," *U.S. New and World Report Money*, May 4, 2009; Daniel Costello, "The Drought Is Over (At Least for C.E.O.'s)," *The New York Times*, April 9, 2011; and "The Pay at the Top," *The New York Times*, April 9, 2011.

though the companies required $153 billion in taxpayer subsidies to keep operating.[45] Mark Hurd walked away with a $40 million severance package after he resigned as CEO at Hewlett-Packard following a sexual harassment violation.[46] Many CEOs are also awarded fat retainers, consulting contracts, and lavish perks when they retire. Make sure to read the Legal Briefcase box for further discussion of this controversial trend.

Management consultant Peter Drucker (1909–2005) long criticized executive pay levels. He suggested CEOs should not earn more than 20 times the

Women have made important strides in business, politics, and sports. They still, however, are behind when it comes to getting paid. Today women earn only 81 percent of what men earn. Such disparities cause many to support the case for comparable worth and a more equitable workplace. What's your opinion concerning this issue?

WE NEED TO GET AN EQUAL PAY EXPERT IN...

LET'S GET A **GIRL** – IT'LL BE CHEAPER!

JOHN BYRNE

salary of the company's lowest-paid employee.[47] Not many companies have placed such limits on executive compensation. Today the average CEO makes over 400 times what the lowest-paid employee earns.[48] Some numbers can be staggering. For example, a custodian earning just over minimum wage at Liberty Media would have to work approximately 4,400 years to make what CEO Gregory Maffei earned in 2010 ($87 million).[49]

As global competition intensifies, executive paychecks in Europe have increased, but European CEOs typically earn less than 50 percent what U.S. CEOs make. In some European countries, such as Germany, by law workers have a say in company management and are entitled to seats on the board of directors of major firms. Since boards set executive pay, this could be a reason why pay imbalances are less in Germany. This process, called *co-determination*, calls for cooperation between management and workers in decision making. In Japan, few Japanese CEOs take home super-sized paychecks like in the United States.[50]

Today, government and shareholder pressure for full disclosure of executive compensation is putting U.S. boards of directors on notice that they are not there simply to enrich CEOs. The recent financial crisis strengthened shareholders' desire to overhaul executive compensation. The passage of the Dodd-Frank Wall Street Reform and Consumer Protection Act was intended to give shareholders more say in compensation decisions.

Still, it's important to remember that most U.S. executives are responsible for multibillion-dollar corporations, work 70-plus hours a week, and often travel excessively. Many have turned potential problems at companies into successes and reaped huge benefits for employees and stockholders as well as themselves. Furthermore, there are few seasoned, skilled professionals who can manage large companies, especially troubled companies looking for the right CEO to accomplish a turnaround. There's no easy answer to the question of what is fair compensation for executives, but it's a safe bet the controversy will not go away.

Pay Equity

The Equal Pay Act of 1963 requires companies to give equal pay to men and women who do the same job. For example, it's illegal to pay a female nurse less than a male nurse unless factors such as seniority, merit pay, or performance incentives are involved.[51] But *pay equity* goes beyond the concept of equal pay for equal work; it says people in jobs that require similar levels of education, training, or skills should receive equal pay. Pay equity compares the value of a job like a hair stylist or librarian (traditionally women's jobs) with jobs like a plumber or truck driver (traditionally men's jobs). Such a comparison shows that "women's" jobs tend to pay less—sometimes much less. This disparity caused a brief reconsideration of a 1980s concept called *comparable worth* that suggested people in jobs requiring similar levels of education, training, or skills should receive equal pay. Evidence did not support that comparable worth would lead to better market equilibrium, only more chaos and inequity.

In the United States today, women earn 81 percent of what men earn, although the disparity varies by profession, job experience and tenure, and level of education.[52] In the past, the primary explanation for this disparity was that women worked only 50 to

60 percent of their available years once they left school, whereas men normally worked all those years. This explanation doesn't have much substance today because fewer women leave the workforce for an extended time. Other explanations suggest many women devote more time to their families than men do and thus accept lower-paying jobs with more flexible hours.

Today women are competing financially with men in fields such as health care, biotechnology, information technology, and other knowledge-based jobs. Younger women seem to be faring better than older women financially. Recent reports suggest that young urban women actually earn 8 percent more than their male counterparts due to their higher college graduation rates. Today women earn almost 60 percent of the bachelor's and master's degrees awarded.[53] With more women earning business degrees, the number of women in management and high paying finance jobs has also increased considerably over the past 10 years.[54] Still, Heather Boushey, a senior economist at the Center for American Progress, believes that the government puts too much faith in the idea that education will automatically close the pay gap. She and other critics claim that women, especially women with children, still earn less, are less likely to go into business, and are more likely to live in poverty than men.[55] There is no question that pay equity promises to remain a challenging employee–management issue.

Sexual Harassment

Sexual harassment refers to unwelcome sexual advances, requests for sexual favors, and other verbal or physical conduct of a sexual nature that creates a hostile work environment.[56] Conduct on the job can be considered illegal under specific conditions:

- An employee's submission to such conduct is explicitly or implicitly made a term or condition of employment, or an employee's submission to or rejection of such conduct is used as the basis for employment decisions affecting the worker's status. A threat like "Go out with me or you're fired" or "Go out with me or you'll never be promoted here" constitutes *quid pro quo sexual harassment.*

- The conduct unreasonably interferes with a worker's job performance or creates an intimidating, hostile, or offensive work environment. This type of harassment is *hostile work environment sexual harassment.*

The Civil Rights Act of 1991 governs sexual harassment of both men and women.[57] In 1997, the Supreme Court reinforced this fact when it said same-sex harassment also falls within the purview of sexual harassment law. Managers and workers are now much more sensitive to sexual comments and behavior than they were in the past. The number of complaints filed to the Equal Employment Opportunity Commission (EEOC) declined to its lowest number since 1993. Still, EEOC statistics show sexual harassment remains a persistent employee complaint.

The Supreme Court in 1996 broadened the scope of what can be considered a hostile work environment; the key word seemed to be *unwelcome,* a term for behavior that would offend a reasonable person. Companies have found that the U.S. justice system means business in enforcing sexual

sexual harassment
Unwelcome sexual advances, requests for sexual favors, and other conduct (verbal or physical) of a sexual nature that creates a hostile work environment.

Unwelcome sexual advances, requests for sexual favors, and other verbal or physical conduct are prohibited under the Civil Rights Act of 1991. While most employees are aware of sexual harassment policies in the workplace, they are often not certain what sexual harassment actually means. Should companies train employees about the dos and don'ts of acceptable sexual conduct on the job?

harassment laws. In a highly publicized case, Madison Square Garden lost a judgment of $11.6 million to a former executive who sued New York Knicks' basketball coach Isiah Thomas and other team executives for sexual harassment. The Ivy League's Yale University has been the subject of an ongoing investigation of sexual harassment by the Department of Education's Civil Rights Office.[58] Foreign companies doing business in the United States are also not immune to sexual harassment charges as both Toyota and Nissan discovered.

A key problem is that workers and managers often know a policy concerning sexual harassment exists, but have no idea what it says. To remedy this, some states have taken the lead. California and Connecticut require all companies with 50 employees or more to provide sexual harassment prevention training to supervisors. Maine requires such training for companies with 15 or more employees. Many companies have set up rapid, effective grievance procedures and react promptly to allegations of harassment. Such efforts may save businesses millions of dollars in lawsuits and make the workplace more productive and harmonious. Nonetheless, there is a long way to go before sexual harassment as a key employee–management issue disappears.

Child Care

Today for the first time in U.S. history women outnumber men in the workforce.[59] Approximately three-fourths of the women with children under 18 (including over 60 percent of the mothers with children under age 3) are in the workforce. Such statistics concern employers for two reasons: (1) absences related to child care cost U.S. businesses billions of dollars annually, and (2) the issue of who should pay for employee child care raises a question that often divides employees. Many co-workers oppose child care benefits for parents or single parents, arguing that single workers and single-income families should not subsidize child care. Others contend that employers and the government have the responsibility to create child care systems to assist employees. Unfortunately federal assistance has not increased since passage of the Welfare Reform Act many years ago and few expect new government spending for child care due to the current federal deficit problems. Thus, child care remains an important workplace issue.

A number of large companies offer child care as an employee benefit. *Working Mother* magazine compiles an annual list of the 100 best companies for working mothers. IBM and Johnson & Johnson have made the list every year for the past 25 years.[60] Both companies are praised as particularly sympathetic and cooperative with working mothers. Other large firms with extensive child care programs include American Express, Bristol-Myers Squibb, and Intel, which provides online homework assistance for employees' children.[61] Some additional child care benefits provided by employers include:

On-site day care is still a relatively uncommon employee benefit in the United States today. Although it is often expensive to operate, it can pay big dividends in employee satisfaction and productivity. Who should pay for employee benefits like child care and elder care, the employee or the company?

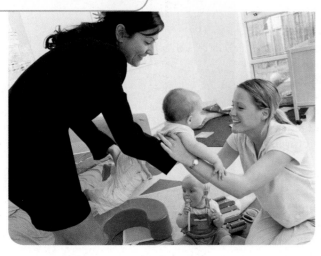

- Discount arrangements with national child care chains.
- Vouchers that offer payments toward child care the employee selects.

- Referral services that help identify high-quality child care facilities to employees.

- On-site child care centers at which parents can visit children at lunch or during lag times throughout the workday.

- Sick-child centers to care for moderately ill children.

Unfortunately, small businesses with fewer than 100 employees cannot compete with big companies in providing assistance with child care. Some small companies, however, have found that implementing creative child care programs can help them compete with larger organizations in hiring and retaining qualified employees. Haemonetics, located in Braintree, Massachuetts, is a leading company in blood processing technology that believes creating a work-life balance is the key to keeping valued workers. The company operates "Kid's Space" at its corporate headquarters staffed by highly qualified early childhood educators who develop planned and spontaneous daily activities. Kid's Space also provides emergency child care services for employees whose children are ill or whose regular child care arrangements are disrupted.[62]

Twenty-five years ago, entrepreneurs Roger Brown and Linda Mason recognized the emerging need for child care as a benefit in the workplace. The husband-and-wife team started Bright Horizons Family Solutions Inc. to provide child care at worksites for employers. Today, their company is the leading provider in the corporate-sponsored child care market and runs nearly 700 child care centers for about 400 companies including 90 Fortune 500 companies. Increasing numbers of two-income households and the over 13 million single-parent households in the United States ensure that child care will remain a key employee–management issue even as businesses face the growing challenge of elder care.

Elder Care

Currently, there are approximately 40 million Americans over the age of 65.[63] Over the next 20 years, the number of Americans over 65 is expected to grow to over 70 million; that will be approximately 20 percent of the U.S. population in 2030. The likelihood that an American age 65 will live to age 90 has also increased significantly. What this means is that many workers will be confronted with how to care for older parents and other relatives. Today in the United States 65.7 million caregivers constituting 29 percent of the adult population are providing some care to an elderly person.[64] According to the National Alliance for Caregiving, such caregiving obligations cause employees to miss approximately 15 million days of work per year. Companies are losing an estimated $35 billion a year in reduced productivity, absenteeism, and turnover from employees responsible for aging relatives. Elder care is becoming a key workplace issue.

The U.S. Office of Personnel Management (OPM) found that employees with elder care responsibilities need information about medical, legal, and insurance issues, as well as the full support of their supervisors and company. The OPM also suggests such caregivers may require flextime, telecommuting, part-time employment, or job sharing. Some firms offer employee assistance programs. Du Pont and JPMorgan Chase provide elder care management services that provide a needs assessment program for the employee. AAA and UPS offer health-spending accounts in which employees can put aside pretax income for elder care expenses. The number of companies offering an elder care benefit program are small, however, compared to child care. A Hewitt

Associates survey found that only 49 percent of companies either currently had an elder care program or planned to introduce one in the near future. Unfortunately, the government does not provide much relief since both Medicare and Medicaid place heavy financial burdens for care on family caregivers.

According to the American Association of Retired Persons (AARP), as more experienced and high-ranking employees care for older parents and relatives, the costs to companies will rise even higher. This argument makes sense, since older, more experienced workers often hold jobs more critical to a company than those held by younger workers (who are most affected by child care issues). Many firms now face the fact that transfers and promotions are often out of the question for employees whose elderly parents need ongoing care. Unfortunately, as the nation gets older, the elder care situation will grow considerably worse, meaning this employee–management issue will persist well into the future.

Drug Testing

Not long ago, acquired immunodeficiency syndrome (AIDS) caused great concern in the workplace. Many companies called for pre-employment testing for AIDS. Thankfully, the spread of AIDS has declined in the United States—good news for all citizens and for business. However, alcohol and drug abuse are serious workplace issues that touch far more workers and stretch from factory floors to construction sites to the locker rooms of professional sports teams.

Alcohol is the most widely used drug in the workplace, with an estimated 6.5 percent of full-time U.S. employees believed to be heavy drinkers.[65] Approximately 40 percent of industrial injuries and fatalities can be linked to alcohol consumption. According to the Department of Health and Human Services' Substance Abuse & Mental Health Services Association more than 8 percent of full-time workers ages 18–49 use illegal drugs. In some industries, such as food services and construction, the percentage of workers using illegal drugs is much higher.

Individuals who use illegal drugs are three and a half times more likely to be in workplace accidents and five times more likely to file a workers' compensation claim than other employees.[66] According to the National Institute on Drug Abuse, employed drug users cost their employers about twice as much in medical and workers' compensation claims as do their drug-free co-workers. The U.S. Department of Labor projects that over a one-year period, drug abuse costs the U.S. economy $414 billion in lost work, health care costs, crime, traffic accidents, and other expenses, and over $150 billion in lost productivity. The National Institutes of Health estimates each drug abuser can cost an employer approximately $10,000 annually. Drug abusers are associated with 50 percent on-the-job accident rates, 10 percent higher absenteeism, 30 percent more turnover, and more frequent workplace violence incidents. Today, over 80 percent of major companies drug test new employees and 40 percent conduct random drug testing.[67]

Drug abuse costs the U.S. economy hundreds of billions of dollars in lost work, health care costs, crime, traffic accidents, and productivity. It is estimated that each drug abuser can cost an employer approximately $10,000 a year. Today, over 80 percent of major companies drug test new employees and 40 percent conduct random drug testing. Do you think these efforts are successful in reducing drug abuse in the workplace? Why or why not?

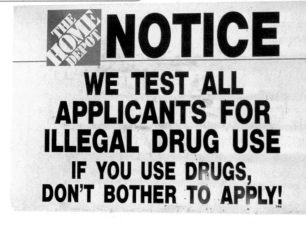

Violence in the Workplace

Even though workplace violence has declined since the 1990s, the threat has in no way disappeared.[68] Employers must be vigilant about potential violence in the workplace. The Bureau of Labor Statistics reports that more than 2 million Americans are impacted by workplace violence annually.[69] The Occupational Safety and Health Administration (OSHA) reports that homicides account for 16 percent of all workplace deaths and are the number one cause of death for women in the workplace. In fact, one in six violent crimes in the United States occurs at work.

Many companies have taken action to prevent problems before they occur. They have held focus groups that invite employee input, hired managers with strong interpersonal skills, and employed skilled consultants to deal with any growing potential for workplace violence. State Farm Insurance and Verizon Wireless are among companies that have initiated policies to deal with this growing threat. At software firm Mindbridge, based in Worchester, Pennsylvania, two company officials must be present whenever an employee is disciplined or fired. In many states employers can seek a temporary restraining order on behalf of workers experiencing threats or harassment.

Some companies believe that the media exaggerates reports of workplace violence. According to the Bureau of Labor Statistics, 70 percent of U.S. workplaces neither provide any formal training for dealing with prevention of violence at work nor have a policy that addresses workplace violence.[70] Unfortunately, organizations such as the U.S. Postal Service and Xerox can attest that workplace violence is all too real and is likely to be an issue for the foreseeable future.

Firms that have healthy employee–management relations have a better chance to prosper than those that don't. Taking a proactive approach is the best way to ensure positive employee–management work environments. The proactive manager anticipates potential issues and works toward resolving them before they get out of hand—a good lesson for any manager.

progress assessment

- How does top-executive pay in the United States compare with top-executive pay in other countries?
- What's the difference between pay equity and equal pay for equal work?
- How is the term *sexual harassment* defined, and when does sexual behavior become illegal?
- What are some of the issues related to child care and elder care, and how are companies addressing those issues?

summary

Learning Goal 1. Trace the history of organized labor in the United States.
- **What was the first union?**

The cordwainers (shoemakers) organized a craft union of skilled specialists in 1792. The Knights of Labor, formed in 1869, was the first national labor organization.

- **How did the AFL-CIO evolve?**

The American Federation of Labor (AFL), formed in 1886, was an organization of craft unions. The Congress of Industrial Organizations (CIO), a group of unskilled and semiskilled workers, broke off from the AFL in 1935. Over time, the two organizations saw the benefits of joining and became the AFL-CIO in 1955. The AFL-CIO is a federation of labor unions, not a national union.

Learning Goal 2. Discuss the major legislation affecting labor unions.
- **What are the provisions of the major legislation affecting labor unions?**

See Figure 12.1 on page 329.

Learning Goal 3. Outline the objectives of labor unions.
- **What topics typically appear in labor–management agreements?**

See Figure 12.3 on page 331.

Learning Goal 4. Describe the tactics used by labor and management during conflicts, and discuss the role of unions in the future.
- **What are the tactics used by unions and management in conflicts?**

Unions can use strikes and boycotts. Management can use strikebreakers, injunctions, and lockouts.

- **What will unions have to do to cope with declining membership?**

Unions are facing a changing workplace. The Service Employees International Union (SEIU) with 2.2 million members is the now the largest union. Going forward, unions must adapt to an increasingly white-collar, female, and culturally diverse workforce. To help keep U.S. businesses competitive in global markets, many have taken on a new role in assisting management in training workers, redesigning jobs, and assimilating the changing workforce.

Learning Goal 5. Assess some of today's controversial employee–management issues, such as executive compensation, pay equity, child care and elder care, drug testing, and violence in the workplace.
- **What is a fair wage for managers?**

The market and the businesses in it set managers' salaries. What is fair is open to debate.

- **How are equal pay and pay equity different?**

The Equal Pay Act of 1963 provides that workers receive equal pay for equal work (with exceptions for seniority, merit, or performance). Pay equity is the demand for equivalent pay for jobs requiring similar levels of education, training, and skills.

- **How are some companies addressing the child care issue?**

Responsive companies are providing child care on the premises, emergency care when scheduled care is interrupted, discounts with child care chains, vouchers to be used at the employee's chosen care center, and referral services.

- **What is elder care, and what problems do companies face with regard to this growing problem?**

Workers who need to provide elder care for dependent parents or others are generally more experienced and vital to the mission of the organization than younger workers are. The cost to business is very large and growing.

- **Why are more and more companies now testing workers and job applicants for substance abuse?**

Drug abuse costs the U.S. economy $414 billion in lost work, health care costs, crime, traffic accidents, and other expenses, and over $150 billion in lost productivity. Individuals who use drugs are three and a half times more likely to be in workplace accidents and five times more likely to file a workers' compensation claim than those who do not use drugs.

key terms

agency shop
  agreement 331
American Federation of
  Labor (AFL) 326
arbitration 334
bargaining zone 333
certification 329
closed shop
  agreement 331
collective
  bargaining 328
Congress of Industrial
  Organizations
  (CIO) 326
cooling-off period 335

craft union 326
decertification 329
givebacks 336
grievance 333
industrial unions 326
injunction 336
Knights of Labor 326
lockout 335
mediation 334
negotiated
  labor–management
  agreement (labor
  contract) 330
open shop
  agreement 332

primary boycott 335
right-to-work
  laws 332
secondary boycott 335
sexual
  harassment 341
shop stewards 333
strike 335
strikebreakers 336
union 324
union security clause 331
union shop
  agreement 331
yellow-dog
  contract 328

critical thinking

1. Do you believe that union shop agreements are violations of a worker's freedom of choice in the workplace? Do you think open shop agreements unfairly penalize workers who pay dues to unions they have elected to represent them in the workplace?

2. Some college football and basketball coaches earn huge incomes. Should college volleyball and swimming coaches be paid comparably? Should players in the Women's National Basketball Association (WNBA) be paid the same as their male counterparts in the National Basketball Association (NBA)? What role should market forces and government play in determining such wages?

3. If a company provides employer-paid child care services to workers with children, should those who don't have children or don't need child care services be paid extra?

developing workplace skills

1. Check whether your state supports the right of public employees (police, firefighters, teachers) to unionize and collectively bargain. If not, should it? Should such workers be allowed to strike?

2. Evaluate the following statement: "Labor unions are dinosaurs that have outlived their usefulness in today's knowledge-based economy." After your evaluation, take the position on this statement that differs from your own point of view and defend that position. Be sure to consider such questions as: Do unions serve a purpose in some industries? Do unions make the United States less competitive in global markets?

3. Research federal and state legislation related to child care, parental leave, and elder care benefits for employees. Are specific trends emerging? Should companies be responsible for providing such workplace benefits, or should the government share some responsibility? Why?

4. Compile a list of two or three employee–management issues not covered in the chapter. Compare your list with those of several classmates and see which issues you selected in common and which are unique to each individual. Pick an issue you all agree will be important in the future and discuss its likely effects and outcomes.

5. Do businesses and government agencies have a duty to provide additional benefits to employees beyond fair pay and good working conditions? Should benefits like health care be mandatory? Propose a system you consider fair and equitable for employees and employers.

taking it to the net

Purpose

To understand why workers choose to join unions and how unions have made differences in certain industries.

Exercise

Visit the AFL-CIO website (www.aflcio.org) and find information about why workers join unions and what the benefits have been.

1. What percentage of workers in your state are members of a union? If it is higher or lower than the national average, explain why unions do or do not have strength in your state.

2. Explain how union membership has affected minorities, women, older workers, and part-time workers.

3. The AFL-CIO site presents the union's perspective on labor issues. Look at the key issues and check sources such as the National Association of Manufacturers (www.nam.org) and the National Right to Work Legal Defense Foundation (www.righttowork.org) that support management's perspectives and compare their positions on these issues.

casing the web

To access the case "The Unions versus Walmart," visit **www.mhhe.com/ubl0e**

video case

To access the video case featuring Screen Actors Guild, visit **www.mhhe.com/ubl0e**

MARKETING:
HELPING
Buyers Buy

13

LEARNING goals

After you have read and studied this chapter, you should be able to

1 Define *marketing*, and apply the marketing concept to both for-profit and nonprofit organizations.

2 Describe the four Ps of marketing.

3 Summarize the marketing research process.

4 Show how marketers use environmental scanning to learn about the changing marketing environment.

5 Explain how marketers apply the tools of market segmentation, relationship marketing, and the study of consumer behavior.

6 Compare the business-to-business market and the consumer market.

Joseph (Joe) Jimenez was a collegiate all-American swimmer and captain of the swim team at Stanford University. He credits competitive swimming with helping him build an inner strength that sustains him to this day. Today Jimenez is CEO of Novartis, one of the world's largest pharmaceutical companies.

After earning an M.B.A. from the University of California, Berkeley, Jimenez began his career in marketing as a brand manager at Clorox. Success in marketing at Clorox led him to ConAgra Foods where he became a division head and finally to H.J. Heinz Company where he became President and CEO of Heinz Europe and Heinz North America. In 2010, he became the first American CEO of Swiss-based Novartis.

On assuming the CEO job at Novartis, Jimenez put his marketing experience to good use. Instead of lamenting the problems faced in the pharmaceutical industry, such as the uncertain Food & Drug Administration (FDA) approval process in the United States, he decided Novartis "was not going to complain—but was going to change." One decision Jimenez made was to "geo tailor" the sales force at Novartis to fit particular markets. He restructured the sales force to address specific trends in individual markets where payer organizations (i.e. insurance companies) have a great influence on what pharmaceutical products are purchased. In other areas where physicians make decisions, a more traditional sales model was retained. His intention was to focus on the individual needs of specific customers and develop better relationships with them as they make purchasing decisions. In other words, he wanted to help buyers buy.

Like all good marketers, Jimenez sees Novartis as more than just a pharmaceutical company. He understands that to exemplify marketing at its best, social

responsibility needs to be part of the Novartis mission. For example, Novartis teamed with Americas's VetDogs to train and provide guide dogs for veterans who are blind or visually impaired, and service dogs for those with disabilities other than blindness—at no cost to the veteran. The program trains over 1,000 dogs a year.

Novartis and Jimenez are also proud of the company's access-to-medicine program that has reached more than 80 million patients worldwide. The company offers discounts and support programs to patients who lack medical insurance or cannot afford treatment. Such strategies emphasize Jimenez's belief that marketing is a multidimensional discipline and is not just centered on issues of selling and advertising.

This chapter and the following three chapters are about marketing. You will learn about traditional marketing practices, but you will also learn about new marketing practices, including the use of social media. Joseph Jimenez is a role model for other progressive managers who see marketing from a broader perspective.

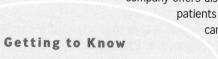

Getting to Know

X *Joseph Jimenez*

CEO of Novartis

profile

Sources: David Bach and David Bruce Allen, "What Every CEO Needs to Know about Nonmarket Strategy," *MIT Sloan Management Review*, Spring 2010; www.forbes.com, accessed April 2011; www.youtube, accessed in April 2011; www.novartis.com; and Dominic Barton, "Capitalism for the Long Term," *Harvard Business Review*, May 2011.

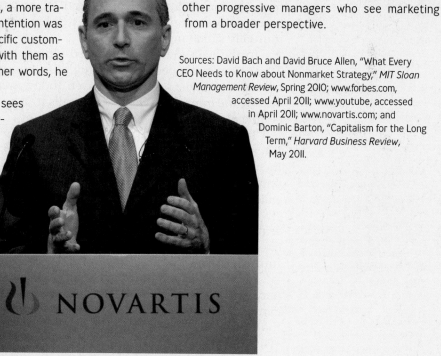

LEARNING goal 1

> Define *marketing,* and apply the marketing concept to both for-profit and nonprofit organizations.

WHAT IS MARKETING?

marketing
The activity, set of institutions, and processes for creating, communicating, delivering, and exchanging offerings that have value for customers, clients, partners, and society at large.

The term marketing means different things to different people. Many think of marketing as simply "selling" or "advertising."[1] Yes, selling and advertising are part of marketing, but it's much more. The American Marketing Association has defined **marketing** as the activity, set of institutions, and processes for creating, communicating, delivering, and exchanging offerings that have value for customers, clients, partners, and society at large. We can also think of marketing, more simply, as the activities buyers and sellers perform to facilitate mutually satisfying exchanges.

In the past marketing focused almost entirely on helping the seller sell. That's why many people still think of it as mostly selling, advertising, and distribution *from the seller to the buyer.* Today, much of marketing is instead about *helping the buyer buy.* One author calls it "The Power of Pull."[2] Let's examine a couple of examples.

Today, when people want to buy a new or used car, they often turn to the Internet first. They go to a website like Vehix (www.vehix.com) to search for the vehicle they want and even take a virtual ride.[3] At other websites they compare prices and features. By the time they go to the dealer, they may know exactly which car they want and the best price available.

The websites have *helped the buyer buy.* Not only are customers spared searching one dealership after another to find the best price, but manufacturers and dealers are eager to participate so that they don't lose customers. The future of marketing is doing everything you can to help the buyer buy.[4]

Let's look at another case. In the past, one of the few ways students and parents could find the college with the right "fit" was to travel from campus to campus, a grueling and expensive process. Today, colleges use podcasts, virtual tours, live chats, and other interactive technologies to make on-campus visits less necessary. Such virtual tours help students and their parents buy.

Of course, helping the buyer buy also helps the seller sell. Think about that for a minute.

Here's an example from *The Wall Street Journal:* In the vacation market, many people find the holiday they want themselves. They use the Internet to find the right spot, and then make choices, sometimes questioning potential sellers online. In industries like this, the role of marketing is to make sure that a company's products or services are easily found online, and that the company responds effectively to potential customers.[5]

These are only a few examples of the marketing trend toward helping buyers buy. Consumers today spend hours searching the Internet for good deals. Wise marketers provide a wealth of information online and even cultivate customer relationships using blogs and social networking sites such as Facebook and Twitter.[6]

Online communities provide an opportunity to observe people (customers and others) interacting with one another, expressing their own opinions, forming relationships, and commenting on various goods and services.[7] It is important for marketers to track what relevant bloggers are writing by doing blog searches using key terms that define their market. Vendors who have text-mining tools can help companies measure conversations about their products and their personnel. Much of the future of marketing lies in mining such online conversations and responding appropriately.[8]

Retailers and other marketers who rely solely on *traditional* advertising and selling are losing out to the new ways of marketing. The Spotlight on Small Business box on p. 354 discusses how some theaters are being creative with their marketing efforts.[9]

The Evolution of Marketing

What marketers do at any particular time depends on what they need to do to fill customers' needs and wants, which continually change. Let's take a brief look at how those changes have influenced the evolution of marketing. Marketing in the United States has passed through four eras: (1) production, (2) selling, (3) marketing concept, and (4) customer relationship (see Figure 13.1).

The Production Era   From the time the first European settlers began their struggle to survive in America until the early 1900s, the general philosophy of business was "Produce as much as you can, because there is a limitless market for it." Given the limited production capability and vast demand for products in those days, a production philosophy was both logical and profitable. Business owners were mostly farmers, carpenters, and trade workers. They needed to produce more and more, so their goals centered on

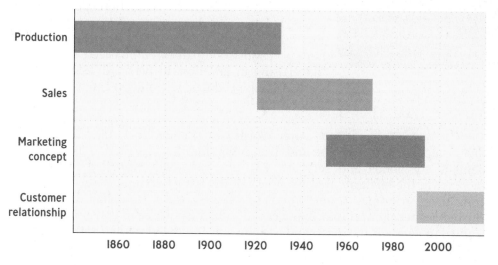

figure 13.1

MARKETING ERAS
The evolution of marketing in the United States involved four eras: (1) production, (2) selling, (3) marketing concept, and (4) customer relationship.

SPOTLIGHT ON SMALL
business

Let's Go to the Movies

Imagine you own a small movie theater. How can you differentiate your theater from the others in your town? Some theaters have had success with 3D movies. Others offer bigger and more screens. For many theaters today, the answer is to provide food with the movie. In fact, about 400 of the 5,750 theaters are doing just that. In-theater dining is said to be one of the biggest bets for increasing the theater-going audience. Thus, you should expect to see more such theaters in the future.

It is a risk to offer an eat-in experience. For example, it is more difficult than you might imagine to keep such theaters clean. After all, there isn't that much time between showings. You can imagine the difficulty some theaters have had trying to create a menu that allows people to eat in the dark. You can also imagine the work it takes to add a kitchen and luxury facilities to an old theater. Nonetheless, theater owners have decided that to fill a need they would have to go to such lengths. It may turn out that such theaters only appeal to a niche market and may not prove profitable.

To further enhance the experience, some theaters are offering alcohol, luxury seats, footrests, blankets, pillows, and the like. Have you experienced these theaters yet? What did you think? Was the additional cost worth it? Do you have other suggestions for how to improve the movie-going experience?

Sources: Lauren A. E. Schuker, "Double Feature: Dinner and a Movie," *The Wall Street Journal*, January 5, 2011; and Judy Hedding, "iPic Theatres—A Scottsdale Luxury Theatre Experience," About.com, accessed April 2011.

In the selling era, the focus of marketing was on selling, with little service afterward and less customization. What economic and social factors made this approach appropriate for the times?

production. You can see this same process occurring in the oil industry today, where producers can often sell as much oil as they can produce. For a long time, GE thought that they would sell all the products they produced.[10] Now they know better, of course. The greatest marketing need in this industry is for more production and less expensive distribution and storage.

The Selling Era By the 1920s, businesses had developed mass-production techniques (such as automobile assembly lines), and production capacity often exceeded the immediate market demand. Therefore, the business philosophy turned from producing to *selling.*[11] Most companies emphasized selling and advertising in an effort to persuade consumers to buy existing products; few offered extensive service after the sale.

The Marketing Concept Era After World War II ended in 1945, returning soldiers starting new careers and beginning families sparked a tremendous demand for goods and services. The postwar years launched the sudden increase in the birthrate that we now call the baby boom, and also a boom in consumer spending. Competition for the consumer's dollar was fierce. Businesses recognized that they needed to be responsive to consumers if they wanted to get their business, and a philosophy emerged in the 1950s called the marketing concept.

The **marketing concept** had three parts:

1. *A customer orientation.* Find out what consumers want and provide it for them. (Note the emphasis on meeting consumer needs rather than on promotion or sales.)
2. *A service orientation.* Make sure everyone in the organization has the same objective: customer satisfaction. This should be a total and integrated organizational effort. That is, everyone from the president of the firm to the delivery people should be customer-oriented. Does that seem to be the norm today?
3. *A profit orientation.* Focus on those goods and services that will earn the most profit and enable the organization to survive and expand to serve more consumer wants and needs.

It took a while for businesses to implement the marketing concept. The process went slowly during the 1960s and 70s. During the 1980s, businesses began to apply the marketing concept more aggressively than they had done over the preceding 30 years. That led to a focus on customer relationship management (CRM) that has become very important today. We explore that concept next.

The Customer Relationship Era　In the 1990s and early 2000s managers extended the marketing concept by adopting the practice of customer relationship management. **Customer relationship management (CRM)** is the process of learning as much as possible about present customers and doing everything you can over time to satisfy them—or even to exceed their expectations—with goods and services. The idea is to enhance customer satisfaction and stimulate long-term customer loyalty.[12] For example, most airlines offer frequent-flier programs that reward loyal customers with free flights. The newest in customer relationship building, as mentioned earlier, involves social networks, online communities, tweets, and blogs.[13]

Clearly, the degree of consumer dissatisfaction that exists, especially with services such as airlines and phone companies, shows that marketers have a long way to go to create customer satisfaction and loyalty. According to a recent study, only 6.8 percent of marketers said they have excellent knowledge of their customers when it comes to demographic, behavioral, and psychographic (how they think) data.

The newest in CRM efforts is customer-managed relationships (CMR). The idea is to give the customer the power to build relationships with suppliers and consumers. Websites like Expedia, Travelocity, and Priceline allow customers to find the best price or set their own.[14] Since consumers are interested in green marketing today, relationship building also means responding to that desire. The Thinking Green box on p. 356, for example, explores "going green" in the apparel industry.

Nonprofit Organizations and Marketing

Even though the marketing concept emphasizes a profit orientation, marketing is a critical part of almost all organizations, including nonprofits. Charities use marketing to raise funds for combating world hunger, for instance, or to obtain other resources.[15] The Red Cross uses promotion to encourage people to donate blood when local or national supplies run low. Greenpeace uses marketing to promote ecologically safe technologies. Environmental groups use marketing to try to cut

---

marketing concept
A three-part business philosophy: (1) a customer orientation, (2) a service orientation, and (3) a profit orientation.

customer relationship management (CRM)
The process of learning as much as possible about customers and doing everything you can to satisfy them—or even exceed their expectations—with goods and services.

The Ad Council sponsors many public service ads like this one. The idea is to make the public more aware of various needs that only nonprofit organizations are meeting. The ads then encourage the public to get engaged in the issue somehow, if only by donating money. Have you reponded to any Ad Council advertisements?

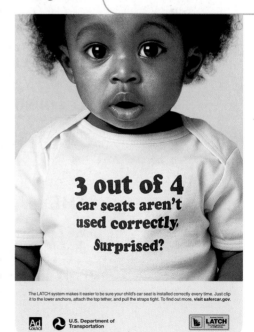

3 out of 4
car seats aren't
used correctly.
Surprised?

The LATCH system makes it easier to be sure your child's car seat is installed correctly every time. Just clip it to the lower anchors, attach the top tether, and pull the straps tight. To find out more, **visit safercar.gov.**

U.S. Department of Transportation

carbon emissions. Churches use marketing to attract new members and raise funds. Politicians use marketing to get votes.

States use marketing to attract new businesses and tourists. Many states, for example, have competed to get automobile companies from other countries to locate plants in their area.[16] Schools use marketing to attract new students. Other organizations, such as arts groups, unions, and social groups, also use marketing.[17] The Ad Council, for example, uses public service ads to create awareness and change attitudes on such issues as drunk driving and fire prevention.

Organizations use marketing, in fact, to promote everything from environmentalism and crime prevention ("Take A Bite Out Of Crime") to social issues ("Choose Life").

LEARNING goal 2

Describe the four Ps of marketing.

THE MARKETING MIX

We can divide much of what marketing people do into four factors, called the four Ps to make them easy to remember. They are:

1. Product
2. Price
3. Place
4. Promotion

356

Marketing manager

Marketing mix

Product   Price   Place   Promotion

figure 13.2

MARKETING MANAGERS AND THE MARKETING MIX
Marketing managers must choose how to implement the four Ps of the marketing mix: product, price, place, and promotion. The goals are to please customers and make a profit.

Managing the controllable parts of the marketing process means (1) designing a want-satisfying *product*, (2) setting a *price* for the product, (3) putting the product in a *place* where people will buy it, and (4) *promoting* the product, including how "green" it is. These four factors are called the **marketing mix** because businesses blend them together in a well-designed marketing program (see Figure 13.2).

marketing mix
The ingredients that go into a marketing program: product, price, place, and promotion.

Applying the Marketing Process

The four Ps are a convenient way to remember the basics of marketing, but they don't necessarily include everything that goes into the marketing process for all products. One of the best ways to understand the entire marketing process is to take a product or a group of products and follow the process that led to their development and sale (see Figure 13.3 on p. 358).

Imagine, for example, that you and your friends want to start a money-making business near your college. You've noticed a lot of vegetarians among your acquaintances. You do a quick survey in a few dorms, sororities, and fraternities and find many vegetarians—and other students who like to eat vegetarian meals once in a while.[18] Your preliminary research indicates some demand for a vegetarian restaurant nearby. You check the fast-food stores in the area and find that none offer more than one or two vegetarian meals. In fact, most don't have any, except salads and some soups.

Further research identifies a number of different kinds of vegetarians. Lacto-ovo vegetarians eat dairy products and eggs. Lacto-vegetarians eat dairy products but no eggs. Fruitarians eat mostly raw fruits, grains, and nuts. Vegans eat neither eggs nor dairy products. Flexitarians eat the occasional cheesecake, hamburger, or whatever.

Your research identifies vegan farmers who don't use any synthetic chemical fertilizers, pesticides, herbicides, or genetically modified ingredients. You also find that KFC Canada offers a vegan version of its chicken sandwich in 500 of its 750 outlets. Is the Colonel on to something? He may be, since there are successful vegetarian restaurants even in Argentina, where the per-capita consumption of beef is the highest in the world. You conclude that a vegetarian restaurant would have to appeal to all kinds of vegetarians to be a success.

figure 13.3

THE MARKETING PROCESS WITH THE FOUR PS

```
┌─────────────────────┐
│  Find opportunities │
└─────────────────────┘
           ↓
┌─────────────────────┐
│  Conduct research   │
└─────────────────────┘
           ↓
┌─────────────────────┐
│     Identify a      │
│    target market    │
└─────────────────────┘
           ↓
Product
┌─────────────────────┐
│  Design a product to│
│  meet the need based│
│     on research     │
└─────────────────────┘
           ↓
┌─────────────────────┐
│  Do product testing │
└─────────────────────┘
           ↓
Price
┌─────────────────────┐
│  Determine a brand  │
│   name, design a    │
│ package, and set a price │
└─────────────────────┘
           ↓
Place
┌─────────────────────┐
│ Select a distribution│
│      system         │
└─────────────────────┘
           ↓
Promotion
┌─────────────────────┐
│ Design a promotional│
│      program        │
└─────────────────────┘
           ↓
┌─────────────────────┐
│ Build a relationship│
│   with customers    │
└─────────────────────┘
```

product
Any physical good, service, or idea that satisfies a want or need plus anything that would enhance the product in the eyes of consumers, such as the brand.

test marketing
The process of testing products among potential users.

brand name
A word, letter, or group of words or letters that differentiates one seller's goods and services from those of competitors.

You've just performed the first few steps in the marketing process. You noticed an opportunity (a need for vegetarian food near campus). You conducted some preliminary research to see whether your idea had any merit. And then you identified groups of people who might be interested in your product. They will be your *target market* (the people you will try to persuade to come to your restaurant).

Designing a Product to Meet Consumer Needs

Once you've researched consumer needs and found a target market (which we'll discuss in more detail later) for your product, the four Ps of marketing come into play. You start by developing a product or products. A **product** is any physical good, service, or idea that satisfies a want or need, plus anything that would enhance the product in the eyes of consumers, such as the brand name. In this case, your proposed product is a restaurant that would serve different kinds of vegetarian meals.

It's a good idea at this point to do *concept testing*. That is, you develop an accurate description of your restaurant and ask people, in person or online, whether the idea of the restaurant and the kind of meals you intend to offer appeals to them. If it does, you might go to a supplier, like Amy's Kitchen, that makes vegetarian meals, to get samples you can take to consumers to test their reactions. The process of testing products among potential users is called **test marketing**.

If consumers like the products and agree they would buy them, you have the information you need to find investors and look for a convenient location to open a restaurant. You'll have to think of a catchy name. (For practice, stop for a minute and try to think of one.) We'll use Very Vegetarian in this text, although we're sure you can think of a better name. Meanwhile, let's continue with the discussion of product development.

You may want to offer some well-known brand names to attract people right away. A **brand name** is a word, letter, or group of words or letters that differentiates one seller's goods and services from those of competitors. Brand names of vegetarian products include Tofurky, Mori-Nu, and Yves Veggie Cuisine. We'll discuss the product development process in detail in Chapter 14, and follow the Very Vegetarian case to show you how all marketing and other business decisions tie together. For now, we're simply sketching the whole marketing process to give you an overall picture. So far, we've covered the first P of the marketing mix: product. Next comes price.

Setting an Appropriate Price

After you've decided what products and services you want to offer consumers, you have to set appropriate prices.[19] Those depend on a number of factors. In the restaurant business, the price could be close to what other restaurants charge to stay competitive. Or you might charge less to attract business, especially at the beginning. Or you may offer high-quality products for which customers are willing to pay a little more (as Starbucks does). You also have to consider the costs of producing, distributing, and promoting the product, which all influence your price. We'll discuss pricing issues in more detail in Chapter 14.

Getting the Product to the Right Place

There are several ways you can serve the market for vegetarian meals. You can have people come in, sit down, and eat at the restaurant, but that's not the only alternative—think of pizza. You could deliver the food to customers' dorms, apartments, and student unions. You may want to sell your products in supermarkets or health-food stores, or through organizations that specialize in distributing food products. Such *intermediaries* are the middle links in a series of organizations that distribute goods from producers to consumers. (The more traditional word for them is *middlemen*.) Getting the product to consumers when and where they want it is critical to market success.[20] Don't forget to consider the Internet as a way to reach consumers. We'll discuss the importance of marketing intermediaries and distribution in detail in Chapter 15.

promotion
All the techniques sellers use to inform people about and motivate them to buy their products or services.

Developing an Effective Promotional Strategy

The last of the four Ps of marketing is promotion. **Promotion** consists of all the techniques sellers use to inform people about and motivate them to buy their products or services. Promotion includes advertising; personal selling; public relations; publicity; word of mouth (viral marketing); and various sales promotion efforts, such as coupons, rebates, samples, and cents-off deals.[21] We'll discuss promotion in detail in Chapter 16.

Promotion often includes relationship building with customers. Among other activities, that means responding to suggestions consumers make to improve the products or their marketing, including price and packaging. For Very Vegetarian, postpurchase, or after-sale, service may include refusing payment for meals that weren't satisfactory and stocking additional vegetarian products customers say they would like. Listening to customers and responding to their needs is the key to the ongoing process that is marketing. The Social Media in Business box on p. 360 discusses how businesses can use social media and smartphones to build relationships with customers.

A vegetarian restaurant might fill a popular need in the neighborhood of many college campuses today. Is there one near your school? What can you tell about its manager's application of the four Ps of marketing – product, price, place, and promotion?

Calling All Businesses!

In this digital age, setting up shop online is vital for most retail businesses. But having only an online presence that customers can access at home isn't enough anymore. Now consumers have an array of smartphones and digital tablets that can get them online from anywhere. For social networks and retailers alike, the mobile market has already enjoyed tremendous growth. Amazon, for instance, earned more than $1 billion from purchases made on phones in 2009. The online auction house eBay predicts that its mobile sales will double in 2011 to $4 billion.

Translating a company's current online presence into something suited for a smartphone isn't difficult for large retailers with vast resources. For small businesses, however, migrating to the mobile medium can be tricky. The array of devices available and lack of uniform design standards present a challenge to web designers, thus increasing the cost of going mobile. But as Amazon's mobile sales suggests, making the leap from laptop to touchscreen may become essential for the survival of small retailers.

Boulder-based company mShopper is helping small retailers break into the mobile market with the introduction of the Mobile Commerce Platform, or mStore. The service takes the guesswork out of constructing a mobile site by providing design and search engine tools along with an analytics dashboard to track traffic and sales. It also streamlines records and retains customer service processes. mShopper charges a licensing fee on a sliding scale ranging from $99 to $999, depending on web traffic. Since mShopper doesn't get paid if their clients' stores don't get hits, the company also offers a marketing system that sends out promotional texts and discounts to customers on an mStore's mailing list.

Some retailers are hoping to use social media to enter the mobile market. Although many companies use social media to create awareness, there is a trend now of setting up direct outlets on social platforms. JCPenney and Delta Airlines have been in talks for months about obtaining a direct presence on Facebook. In three to five years, economists estimate that as much as 15 percent of total consumer spending may go through social networking sites. That means that many companies could be poised for a fortune if all those friends turn into customers.

Sources: Jason Ankeny, "Setting Sale on Smartphones," *Entrepreneur*, December 2010; and Sarah Shannon, "Fashion Retailer ASOS Sets Up Shop on Facebook," *Bloomberg Businessweek*, February 17, 2011.

---

progress assessment

- What does it mean to "help the buyer buy"?
- What are the three parts of the marketing concept?
- What are the four Ps of the marketing mix?

LEARNING goal 3

Summarize the marketing research process.

---

marketing research
The analysis of markets to determine opportunities and challenges, and to find the information needed to make good decisions.

PROVIDING MARKETERS WITH INFORMATION

Every decision in the marketing process depends on information. When they conduct **marketing research**, marketers analyze markets to determine opportunities and challenges, and to find the information they need to make good decisions.

Marketing research helps identify what products customers have purchased in the past, and what changes have occurred to alter what they want now and what they're likely to want in the future. Marketers also conduct research on business trends, the ecological impact of their decisions, global trends, and more. Businesses need information to compete effectively, and marketing research is the activity that gathers it. Besides listening to customers, marketing researchers also pay attention to what employees, shareholders, dealers, consumer advocates, media representatives, and other stakeholders have to say. As noted earlier, some of that research is now being gathered online through blogs and social networks.

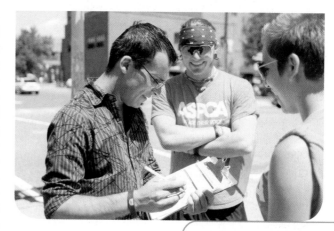

Personal interviews are one way of collecting primary research data about customers' needs, wants, and buying habits. Perhaps someone has stopped you in a shopping mall recently to ask you some questions about a product or product category you use. What might contribute to the difficulty of collecting information through such interviews, and how can marketers improve the process?

The Marketing Research Process

A simplified marketing research process consists of at least four key steps:

1. Defining the question (the problem or opportunity) and determining the present situation.
2. Collecting research data.
3. Analyzing the research data.
4. Choosing the best solution and implementing it.

The following sections look at each of these steps.

Defining the Question and Determining the Present Situation Marketing researchers need the freedom to discover what the present situation is, what the problems or opportunities are, what the alternatives are, what information they need, and how to go about gathering and analyzing data.

Collecting Data Usable information is vital to the marketing research process. Research can become quite expensive, however, so marketers must often make a trade-off between the need for information and the cost of obtaining it. Normally the least expensive method is to gather information already compiled by others and published in journals and books or made available online.

Such existing data are called **secondary data**, since you aren't the first one to gather them. Figure 13.4 on p. 362 lists the principal sources of secondary marketing research information. Despite its name, *secondary* data is what marketers should gather *first* to avoid incurring unnecessary expense. To find secondary data about vegetarians, go to the website for *Vegetarian Times* (www.vegetariantimes.com) or search other websites on vegetarianism.

Often, secondary data don't provide all the information managers need for important business decisions. To gather additional in-depth information, marketers must do their own research. The results of such *new studies* are called **primary data**. One way to gather primary data is to conduct a survey.

Telephone surveys, online surveys, mail surveys, and personal interviews are the most common forms of primary data collection. Focus groups (defined below) are another popular method of surveying individuals. What do you think would be the best way to survey students about your potential new restaurant? Would you do a different kind of survey after it had been open a few months? How could you help vegetarians find your restaurant? That is, how

secondary data
Information that has already been compiled by others and published in journals and books or made available online.

primary data
Data that you gather yourself (not from secondary sources such as books and magazines).

PRIMARY SOURCES	SECONDARY SOURCES		

PRIMARY SOURCES

Interviews

Surveys

Observation

Focus groups

Online surveys

Questionnaires

Customer comments

Letters from customers

SECONDARY SOURCES

Government Publications

Statistical Abstract of the United States	*Census of Transportation*
Survey of Current Business	*Annual Survey of Manufacturers*
Census of Retail Trade	

Commercial Publications

ACNielsen Company studies on retailing and media

Marketing Research Corporation of America studies on consumer purchases

Selling Areas—Marketing Inc. reports on food sales

Magazines

Entrepreneur	*Journal of Retailing*	*Journal of Advertising Research*
Bloomberg Businessweek	*Journal of Consumer Research*	
Fortune		Trade magazines appropriate to your industry such as *Progressive Grocer*
Inc.	*Journal of Advertising*	
Advertising Age	*Journal of Marketing Research*	
Forbes	*Marketing News*	Reports from various chambers of commerce
Harvard Business Review	*Hispanic Business*	
Journal of Marketing	*Black Enterprise*	

Newspapers

The Wall Street Journal, Barron's, your local newspapers

Internal Sources

| Company records | Income statements |
| Balance sheets | Prior research reports |

General Sources

| Internet searches | Commercial databases |
| Google-type searches | |

figure 13.4

SELECTED SOURCES OF PRIMARY AND SECONDARY INFORMATION

You should spend a day or two at the library becoming familiar with these sources. You can read about primary research in any marketing research text from the library.

focus group

A small group of people who meet under the direction of a discussion leader to communicate their opinions about an organization, its products, or other given issues.

could you help your buyers buy? One question researchers pay close attention to is: "Would you recommend this product to a friend?"

A **focus group** is a group of people who meet under the direction of a discussion leader to communicate their opinions about an organization, its products, or other given issues. This textbook is updated periodically using many focus groups made up of faculty and students. They tell us, the authors, what subjects and examples they like and dislike, and the authors follow their suggestions for changes.

Marketers can now gather both secondary and primary data online. The authors of this text, for example, do much research online, but they also gather data from books, articles, interviews, and other sources.

Analyzing the Research Data   Marketers must turn the data they collect in the research process into useful information. Careful, honest interpretation of the data can help a company find useful alternatives to specific marketing challenges. For example, by doing primary research, Fresh Italy, a small Italian

The authors of this text enjoy the benefits of using focus groups. College faculty and students come to these meetings and tell us how to improve this book and its support material. We listen carefully and make as many changes as we can in response. Suggestions have included adding more descriptive captions to the photos in the book and making the text as user-friendly as possible. How are we doing so far?

pizzeria, found that its pizza's taste was rated superior to that of the larger pizza chains. However, the company's sales lagged behind the competition. Secondary research on the industry revealed that free delivery (which Fresh Italy did not offer) was more important to customers than taste. Fresh Italy now delivers—and has increased its market share.

Choosing the Best Solution and Implementing It   After collecting and analyzing data, market researchers determine alternative strategies and make recommendations about which may be best and why. This final step in a research effort also includes following up on actions taken to see whether the results were what was expected. If not, the company can take corrective action and conduct new studies in its ongoing attempt to provide consumer satisfaction at the lowest cost. You can see, then, that marketing research is a *continuous process* of responding to changes in the marketplace and in consumer preferences.

LEARNING goal 4

Show how marketers use environmental scanning to learn about the changing marketing environment.

THE MARKETING ENVIRONMENT

Marketing managers must be aware of the surrounding environment when making marketing mix decisions. **Environmental scanning** is the process of identifying factors that can affect marketing success. As you can see in Figure 13.5 on p. 364, they include global, technological, sociocultural,

environmental scanning
The process of identifying the factors that can affect marketing success.

figure 13.5

**THE MARKETING
ENVIRONMENT**

competitive, and economic influences. We discussed these factors in some detail in Chapter 1, but now let's review them from a strictly marketing perspective.

Global Factors

Using the Internet, businesses can reach many of the world's consumers relatively easily and carry on a dialogue with them about the goods and services they want. By 2018, half of all small businesses will be engaged in global trade.

The globalization process puts more pressure on those whose responsibility it is to deliver products. Many marketers outsource delivery to companies like FedEx, UPS, and DHL, which have a solid reputation for shipping goods quickly.[22]

Technological Factors

The most important technological changes also relate to the Internet. Using consumer databases, blogs, social networking, and the like, companies can develop products and services that closely match consumers' needs. As you read in Chapter 9, firms can now produce customized goods and services for about the same price as mass-produced goods. Thus flexible manufacturing and mass customization are also major influences on marketers. You can imagine, for example, using databases to help you devise custom-made fruit mixes and various salads for your customers at Very Vegetarian.

Sociocultural Factors

Marketers must monitor social trends to maintain their close relationship with customers, since population growth and changing demographics can have an effect on sales. One of the fastest-growing segments of the U.S. population in the 21st century is people over 65. The increase in the number of older adults creates growing demand for nursing homes, health care, prescription drugs, recreation, continuing education, and more.

Other shifts in the U.S. population are creating new challenges for marketers as they adjust their products to meet the tastes and preferences of Hispanic, Asian, and other growing ethnic groups.[23] To appeal to diverse groups, marketers must listen better and be more responsive to unique ethnic needs. What might you do to appeal to specific ethnic groups with Very Vegetarian?

Competitive Factors

Of course, marketers must pay attention to the dynamic competitive environment. Many brick-and-mortar companies must be aware of new competition from the Internet, including firms that sell automobiles, insurance, music, and clothes. In the book business, Barnes & Noble is still adjusting to the new reality of Amazon.com's huge selection of books at good prices. Borders Books went out of business.[24] What will the challenge from Kindle and other eReaders provide? Now that consumers can literally search the world for the best buys through the Internet, marketers must adjust their pricing, delivery, and services accordingly. Can you see any opportunities for Very Vegetarian to make use of the Internet and social media?

Economic Factors

Marketers must pay close attention to the economic environment. As we began the new millennium, the United States was experiencing unparalleled growth, and customers were eager to buy even the most expensive automobiles, watches, and vacations. But as the economy slowed, marketers had to adapt by offering products that were less expensive and more tailored to consumers with modest incomes.[25]

The economic collapse beginning in 2008 really slowed sales and became global in scope. You can see why environmental scanning is critical to a company's success during rapidly changing economic times. What economic changes are occurring around your school that might affect a new restaurant? How have the economic crisis, the wars in Iraq, Afghanistan, and Libya, or natural disasters affected your area?

TWO DIFFERENT MARKETS: CONSUMER AND BUSINESS-TO-BUSINESS (B2B)

Marketers must know as much as possible about the market they wish to serve. As we defined it in Chapter 6, a *market* consists of people with unsatisfied wants and needs who have both the resources and the willingness to buy. There are two major markets in business: the *consumer market* and the *business-to-business market*. The **consumer market** consists of all the individuals or households that want goods and services for personal consumption or use and have the resources to buy them.

The **business-to-business (B2B) market** consists of all the individuals and organizations that want goods and services to use in producing other goods and services or to sell, rent, or supply goods to others. Oil-drilling bits, cash registers, display cases, office desks, public accounting audits, and business software are B2B goods and services. Traditionally, they have been known

consumer market
All the individuals or households that want goods and services for personal consumption or use.

business-to-business (B2B) market
All the individuals and organizations that want goods and services to use in producing other goods and services or to sell, rent, or supply goods to others.

as *industrial* goods and services because they are used in industry.

The important thing to remember is that the buyer's reason for buying—that is, the end use of the product—determines whether a product is a consumer product or a B2B product. A cup of yogurt that a student buys for breakfast is a consumer product. However, when Very Vegetarian purchases the same cup of yogurt to sell to its breakfast customers, it has purchased a B2B product. The following sections outline consumer and B2B markets.

The B2B market consists of individuals and organizations that sell goods and services to other businesses. For example, manufacturer E.G.O. makes components for appliances and supplies them to virtually every stove, washing machine, and dishwasher manufacturer. How many ways can you think of in which B2B products differ from those you buy, like toothpaste and laundry detergent?

progress assessment

- What are the four steps in the marketing research process?
- What is environmental scanning?
- What factors are included in environmental scanning?

LEARNING goal 5

Explain how marketers apply the tools of market segmentation, relationship marketing, and the study of consumer behavior.

THE CONSUMER MARKET

The total potential consumer market consists of the 7 billion or so people in global markets. Because consumer groups differ greatly by age, education level, income, and taste, a business usually can't fill the needs of every group. It must decide which groups to serve, and then develop products and services specially tailored to their needs.

Take the Campbell Soup Company, for example. You know Campbell for its traditional soups such as chicken noodle and tomato. You may also have noticed that Campbell has expanded its U.S. product line to appeal to a number of different tastes. Aware of population growth in the South and in Latino communities in cities across the nation, it introduced a Creole soup for the southern market and a red bean soup for the Latino market. In Texas and California, where people like their food with a bit of kick, Campbell makes its nacho cheese soup spicier than in other parts of the country. It's just one company that has had some success studying the consumer market, breaking it down into categories, and developing products for separate groups.

The process of dividing the total market into groups with similar characteristics is called **market segmentation**. Selecting which groups or segments an organization can serve profitably is **target marketing**. For example, a shoe store may choose to sell only women's shoes, only children's shoes, or only athletic shoes. The issue is finding the right *target market*—the most profitable segment—to serve.

market segmentation
The process of dividing the total market into groups whose members have similar characteristics.

target marketing
Marketing directed toward those groups (market segments) an organization decides it can serve profitably.

figure 13.6

MARKET SEGMENTATION

This table shows some of the methods marketers use to divide the market. The aim of segmentation is to break the market into smaller units.

MAIN DIMENSION	SAMPLE VARIABLES	TYPICAL SEGMENTS
Geographic segmentation	Region	Northeast, Midwest, South, West
	City or county size	Under 5,000; 5,000–10,999; 20,000–49,000; 50,000 and up
	Density	Urban, suburban, rural
Demographic segmentation	Gender	Male, female
	Age	Under 5; 5–10; 11–18; 19–34; 35–49; 50–64; 65 and over
	Education	Some high school or less, high school graduate, some college, college graduate, postgraduate
	Race	Caucasian, African American, Indian, Asian, Hispanic
	Nationality	American, Asian, Eastern European, Japanese
	Life stage	Infant, preschool, child, teenager, collegiate, adult, senior
	Income	Under $15,000; $15,000–$24,999; $25,000–$44,999; $45,000–$74,999; $75,000 and over
	Household size	1; 2; 3–4; 5 or more
	Occupation	Professional, technical, clerical, sales supervisors, farmers, students, home-based business owners, retired, unemployed
Psychographic segmentation	Personality	Gregarious, compulsive, extroverted, aggressive, ambitious
	Values	Actualizers, fulfillers, achievers, experiencers, believers, strivers, makers, strugglers
	Lifestyle	Upscale, moderate
Benefit segmentation	Comfort	(Benefit segmentation divides an already established market into smaller, more homogeneous segments. Those people who desire economy in a car would be an example. The benefit desired varies by product.)
	Convenience	
	Durability	
	Economy	
	Health	
	Luxury	
	Safety	
	Status	
Volume segmentation	Usage	Heavy users, light users, nonusers
	Loyalty status	None, medium, strong

Segmenting the Consumer Market

A firm can segment the consumer market several ways (see Figure 13.6). Rather than selling your product throughout the United States, you might focus on just one or two regions where you can be most successful, say southern states such as Florida, Texas, and South Carolina. Dividing a market by cities, counties, states, or regions is **geographic segmentation**.

Alternatively, you could aim your product's promotions toward people ages 25 to 45 who have some college education and above-average incomes.

geographic segmentation
Dividing a market by cities, counties, states, or regions.

demographic segmentation
Dividing the market by age, income, and education level.

psychographic segmentation
Dividing the market using groups' values, attitudes, and interests.

benefit segmentation
Dividing the market by determining which benefits of the product to talk about.

volume (or usage) segmentation
Dividing the market by usage (volume of use).

niche marketing
The process of finding small but profitable market segments and designing or finding products for them.

The Internet has dramatically increased the ways in which companies can reach out to customers and conduct relationship marketing. For example, it can assist marketers in customizing products like photo books and calendars shown here. What appeals to you about these firms?

Automobiles such as Lexus are often targeted to this audience. Age, income, and education level are criteria for **demographic segmentation**. So are religion, race, and occupation. Demographics are the most widely used segmentation variable, but not necessarily the best.

You may want your ads to portray a target group's lifestyle. To do that, you would study the group's values, attitudes, and interests in a strategy called **psychographic segmentation**. If you decide to target Generation Y, you would do an in-depth study of members' values and interests, like which TV shows they watch and which personalities they like best. With that information you would develop advertisements for those TV shows using those stars.

In marketing for Very Vegetarian, what benefits of vegetarianism might you talk about? Should you emphasize freshness, heart-healthiness, taste, or something else? Determining which product benefits your target market prefers and using those benefits to promote a product is **benefit segmentation**.

You can also determine who are the big eaters of vegetarian food. Does your restaurant seem to attract more men or more women? More students or more faculty members? Are your repeat customers from the local community or are they commuters? Separating the market by volume of product use is called **volume (or usage) segmentation**. Once you know who your customer base is, you can design your promotions to better appeal to that specific group or groups.

The best segmentation strategy is to use all the variables to come up with a consumer profile that represents a sizable, reachable, and profitable target market. That may mean not segmenting the market at all and instead going after the total market (everyone). Or it may mean going after ever-smaller segments. We'll discuss that strategy next.

Reaching Smaller Market Segments

Niche marketing is identifying small but profitable market segments and designing or finding products for them. Because it so easily offers an unlimited choice of goods, the Internet is transforming a consumer culture once based on big hits and best-sellers into one that supports more specialized niche products.[26] Just how small such a segment can be is illustrated by FridgeDoor.com. This company sells refrigerator magnets on the Internet. It keeps some 1,500 different magnets in stock and sells as many as 400 a week.

One-to-one marketing means developing a unique mix of goods and services for *each individual customer*. Travel agencies often develop such packages, including airline reservations, hotel reservations, rental cars, restaurants, and admission to museums and other attractions for individual customers. This is relatively easy to do in B2B markets where each customer may buy in huge volume. But one-to-one marketing is now becoming possible in consumer markets as well. Dell produces a unique computer system for each customer. Can you envision designing special Very Vegetarian menu items for individual customers?

Moving toward Relationship Marketing

In the world of mass production following the Industrial Revolution, marketers responded by practicing mass marketing. **Mass marketing** means developing products and promotions to please large groups of people. That is, there is little market segmentation. The mass marketer tries to sell the same products to as many people as possible. That means using mass media, such as TV, radio, and newspapers to reach them. Although mass marketing led many firms to success, marketing managers often got so caught up with their products and competition that they became less responsive to the market. Airlines, for example, are so intent on meeting competition that they often annoy their customers.

Relationship marketing tends to lead away from mass production and toward custom-made goods and services. The goal is to keep individual customers over time by offering them new products that exactly meet their requirements. The latest in technology enables sellers to work with individual buyers to determine their wants and needs and to develop goods and services specifically designed for them, like hand-tailored shirts and unique vacations.

Understanding consumers is so important to marketing that a whole area of marketing emerged called consumer behavior. We explore that area next.

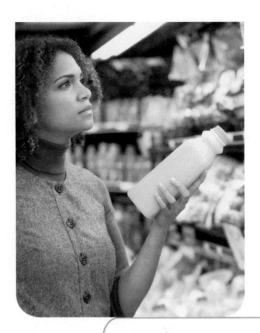

The Consumer Decision-Making Process

Figure 13.7 on p. 370 shows the consumer decision-making process and some outside factors that influence it. The five steps in the process are often studied in courses on consumer behavior.

The first step is *problem recognition,* which may occur when your washing machine breaks down and you realize you need a new one. This leads to an *information search*—you look for ads and brochures about washing machines. You may consult a secondary data source like *Consumer Reports* or other information, perhaps online. And you'll likely seek advice from other people who have purchased washing machines.

After compiling all this information, you *evaluate alternatives* and make a *purchase decision.* But your buying process doesn't end here. After the purchase, you may ask the people you spoke to previously how their machines perform and then do other comparisons to your new washer.

Marketing researchers investigate these consumer thought processes and behavior at each stage in a purchase to determine the best way to help the buyer buy. This area of study is called *consumer behavior.*

Consumer behavior researchers also study the influences that affect consumer behavior. Figure 13.7 shows several: marketing mix variables (the four Ps); psychological influences, such as perception and attitudes; situational influences, such as the type of purchase and the physical surroundings; and sociocultural influences, such as reference groups and culture. Other important factors include these:

- *Learning* creates changes in an individual's behavior resulting from previous experiences and information. If you've tried a particular brand of shampoo and don't like it, you've learned not to buy it again.

- *Reference group* is the group an individual uses as a reference point in forming beliefs, attitudes, values, or behavior. A college student who carries a briefcase instead of a backpack may see businesspeople as his or her reference group.

- *Culture* is the set of values, attitudes, and ways of doing things transmitted from one generation to another in a given society. The U.S. culture emphasizes and transmits the values of education, freedom, and diversity.

Consumer behavior researchers investigate people's buying decisions and the factors that influence their choices. Social, psychological, and marketing-mix factors are important when we decide what to buy. So are the store environment and our previous buying experiences. What influences the choices you make in your local supermarket?

one-to-one marketing
Developing a unique mix of goods and services for each individual customer.

mass marketing
Developing products and promotions to please large groups of people.

relationship marketing
Marketing strategy with the goal of keeping individual customers over time by offering them products that exactly meet their requirements.

figure 13.7

THE CONSUMER DECISION-MAKING PROCESS AND OUTSIDE INFLUENCES

There are many influences on consumers as they decide which goods and services to buy. Marketers have some influence, but it's not usually as strong as sociocultural influences. Helping consumers in their information search and their evaluation of alternatives is a major function of marketing.

- *Subculture* is the set of values, attitudes, and ways of doing things that results from belonging to a certain ethnic group, racial group, or other group with which one closely identifies (e.g., teenagers).

- *Cognitive dissonance* is a type of psychological conflict that can occur after a purchase. Consumers who make a major purchase may have doubts about whether they got the best product at the best price. Marketers must reassure such consumers after the sale that they made a good decision. An auto dealer, for example, may send positive press articles about the particular car a consumer purchased, offer product guarantees, and provide certain free services.

Many universities have expanded the marketing curriculum to include courses in business-to-business marketing. As you'll learn below, that market is huge.

LEARNING goal 6

Compare the business-to-business market and the consumer market.

THE BUSINESS-TO-BUSINESS MARKET

Business-to-business (B2B) marketers include manufacturers; intermediaries such as retailers; institutions like hospitals, schools, and charities; and the government. The B2B market is larger than the consumer market because items are often sold and resold several times in the B2B process before they reach the final consumer. B2B marketing strategies also differ from consumer marketing because business buyers have their own decision-making process. Several factors make B2B marketing different, including these:

1. Customers in the B2B market are relatively few; there are just a few construction firms or mining operations compared to the 70 million or so households in the U.S. consumer market.

2. Business customers are relatively large; that is, big organizations account for most of the employment and production of various goods and services. Nonetheless, there are many small- to medium-sized firms in the United States that together make an attractive market.

3. B2B markets tend to be geographically concentrated. For example, oilfields are found in the Southwest and Alaska. Thus B2B marketers can concentrate their efforts on a particular area and minimize distribution problems by locating warehouses near industrial centers.

4. Business buyers are generally more rational and less emotional than ultimate consumers; they use product specifications to guide buying choices and often more carefully weigh the total product offer, including quality, price, and service.

5. B2B sales tend to be direct, but not always. Tire manufacturers sell directly to auto manufacturers but use intermediaries, such as wholesalers and retailers, to sell to ultimate consumers.

6. Whereas consumer promotions are based more on *advertising*, B2B sales are based on *personal selling*. There are fewer customers and they usually demand more personal service.

Figure 13.8 shows some of the differences between buying behavior in the B2B and consumer markets. B2B buyers also use the Internet to make purchases. You'll learn more about the business-to-business market in advanced marketing courses.

figure 13.8

COMPARING BUSINESS-TO-BUSINESS AND CONSUMER BUYING BEHAVIOR

	BUSINESS-TO-BUSINESS MARKET	CONSUMER MARKET
Market Structure	Relatively few potential customers Larger purchases Geographically concentrated	Many potential customers Smaller purchases Geographically dispersed
Products	Require technical, complex products Frequently require customization Frequently require technical advice, delivery, and after-sale service	Require less technical products Sometimes require customization Sometimes require technical advice, delivery, and after-sale service
Buying Procedures	Buyers are trained Negotiate details of most purchases Follow objective standards Formal process involving specific employees Closer relationships between marketers and buyers Often buy from multiple sources	No special training Accept standard terms for most purchases Use personal judgment Informal process involving household members Impersonal relationships between marketers and consumers Rarely buy from multiple sources

YOUR PROSPECTS IN MARKETING

There is a wider variety of careers in marketing than in most business disciplines. If you major in marketing, an array of career options will be available to you. You could become a manager in a retail store like Saks or Target. You could do marketing research or work in product management. You could go into selling, advertising, sales promotion, or public relations. You could work in transportation, storage, or international distribution. You could design interactive websites to implement CRM. These are just a few of the possibilities. Think, for example, of the many ways to use Facebook, Google, and other new technologies in marketing. As you read through the following marketing chapters, consider whether a marketing career would interest you.

progress assessment

- Can you define the terms *consumer market and business-to-business market?*
- Can you name and describe five ways to segment the consumer market?
- What is niche marketing, and how does it differ from one-to-one marketing?
- What are four key factors that make B2B markets different from consumer markets?

summary

Learning Goal 1. Define *marketing,* and apply the marketing concept to both for-profit and nonprofit organizations.

- **What is marketing?**

Marketing is the activity, set of institutions, and processes for creating, communicating, delivering, and exchanging offerings that have value for customers, clients, partners, and society at large.

- **How has marketing changed over time?**

During the *production era,* marketing was largely a distribution function. Emphasis was on producing as many goods as possible and getting them to markets. By the early 1920s, during the *selling era,* the emphasis turned to selling and advertising to persuade customers to buy the existing goods produced by mass production. After World War II, the tremendous demand for goods and services led to the *marketing concept era,* when businesses recognized the need to be responsive to customers' needs. During the 1990s, marketing entered the *customer relationship era,* focusing on enhancing customer satisfaction and stimulating long-term customer loyalty. The newest in customer relationship building involves social networks, online communities, and blogs.

- **What are the three parts of the marketing concept?**

The three parts of the marketing concept are (1) a customer orientation, (2) a service orientation, and (3) a profit orientation (that is, marketing goods and services that will earn a profit and enable the firm to survive and expand).

- **What kinds of organizations are involved in marketing?**

All kinds of organizations use marketing, including for-profit and nonprofit organizations like states, charities, churches, politicians, and schools.

Learning Goal 2. Describe the four Ps of marketing.

- **How do marketers implement the four Ps?**

The idea behind the four Ps is to design a *product* people want, *price* it competitively, *place* it where consumers can find it easily, and *promote* it so consumers know it exists.

Learning Goal 3. Summarize the marketing research process.

- **What are the steps in conducting marketing research?**

(1) Define the problem or opportunity and determine the present situation, (2) collect data, (3) analyze the data, and (4) choose the best solution.

Learning Goal 4. Show how marketers use environmental scanning to learn about the changing marketing environment.

- **What is environmental scanning?**

Environmental scanning is the process of identifying factors that can affect marketing success. Marketers pay attention to all the environmental factors that create opportunities and threats.

- **What are some of the more important environmental trends in marketing?**

The most important global and technological change is probably the growth of the Internet. Another is the growth of consumer databases, with which companies can develop products and services that closely match consumers' needs. Marketers must monitor social trends like population growth and shifts to maintain their close relationship with customers. They must also monitor the dynamic competitive and economic environments.

Learning Goal 5. Explain how marketers apply the tools of market segmentation, relationship marketing, and the study of consumer behavior.

- **What are some of the ways marketers segment the consumer market?**

Geographic segmentation means dividing the market into different regions. Segmentation by age, income, and education level is *demographic segmentation*. We study a group's values, attitudes, and interests using *psychographic segmentation*. Determining which benefits customers prefer and using them to promote a product is *benefit segmentation*. Separating the market by usage is called *volume segmentation*. The best segmentation strategy is to use all the variables to come up with a consumer profile for a target market that's sizable, reachable, and profitable.

- **What is the difference between mass marketing and relationship marketing?**

Mass marketing means developing products and promotions to please large groups of people. Relationship marketing tends to lead away from mass production and toward custom-made goods and services. Its goal is to keep individual customers over time by offering them products or services that meet their needs.

- **What are some of the factors that influence the consumer decision-making process?**

See Figure 13.7 on p. 370 for some of the major influences on consumer decision-making. Other factors are learning, reference group, culture, subculture, and cognitive dissonance.

Learning Goal 6. Compare the business-to-business market and the consumer market.

- **What makes the business-to-business market different from the consumer market?**

Customers in the B2B market are relatively few and large. B2B markets tend to be geographically concentrated, and industrial buyers generally are more rational than ultimate consumers in their selection of goods and services. B2B sales tend to be direct, and there is much more emphasis on personal selling than in consumer markets.

key terms

benefit
   segmentation 368

brand name 358

business-to-business
   (B2B) market 365

consumer market 365

customer relationship
   management (CRM) 355

demographic
   segmentation 368

environmental
   scanning 363

focus group 362

geographic
   segmentation 367

marketing 352

marketing concept 355

marketing mix 357

marketing research 360

market
   segmentation 366

mass marketing 369

niche marketing 368

one-to-one marketing 369

primary data 361

product 358

promotion 359

psychographic
   segmentation 368

relationship
   marketing 369

secondary data 361

target marketing 366

test marketing 358

volume (or usage)
   segmentation 368

critical thinking

1. When businesses buy goods and services from other businesses, they usually buy in large volume. Salespeople in the business-to-business area usually are paid on a commission basis; that is, they earn a certain percentage of each sale they make. Why might B2B sales be a more financially rewarding career area than consumer sales?

2. Industrial companies sell goods such as steel, lumber, computers, engines, parts, and supplies. Name three such companies in your region.

3. What environmental changes are occurring in your community? What has been the impact of the recent economic crisis? What environmental changes in marketing are most likely to change your career prospects in the future? How can you learn more about those changes? What might you do to prepare for them?

4. Which of your needs are not being met by businesses and/or nonprofit organizations in your area? Are there enough people with similar needs to attract an organization that would meet those needs? How would you find out?

developing workplace skills

1. Think of an effective marketing mix for a new electric car or a brushless car wash for your neighborhood. Be prepared to discuss your ideas in class.

2. Working in teams of five (or on your own), think of a product or service your friends want but cannot get on or near campus. You might ask your friends at other schools what's available there. What kind of product would fill that need? Discuss your results in class and how you might go about marketing that new product or service.

3. Business has fallen off greatly at your upscale restaurant because of the economic crisis. List four things you can do to win back the loyalty of your past customers.

4. Working in teams of four or five (or on your own), list as many brand names of pizza as you can, including from pizza shops, restaurants, supermarkets, and so on. Merge your list with the lists from other groups or classmates. Then try to identify the target market for each brand. Do they all seem to be after the same market, or are there different brands for different markets? What are the separate appeals?

5. Take a little time to review the concepts in this chapter as they apply to Very Vegetarian, the restaurant we used as an example throughout. Have an open discussion in class about (a) a different name for the restaurant, (b) a location for the restaurant, (c) a promotional program, and (d) a way to establish a long-term relationship with customers.

taking it to the net

Purpose

To demonstrate how the Internet can be used to enhance marketing relationships.

Exercise

Nike wants to help its customers add soul to their soles and express their individuality by customizing their own shoes. See for yourself at www.nike.com. Enter "customize" in the search box and build a shoe that fits your style.

1. What if you're in the middle of your shoe design and have questions about what to do next? Where can you go for help?

2. How does Nike's website help the company strengthen its relationships with its stakeholders? Give examples to support your answer.

3. How do the elements of the website reflect Nike's target market?

4. Does Nike invite comments from visitors to its website? If so, how does this affect its attempt to build positive relationships with its customers?

casing the web

To access the case "Measuring Marketing Effectiveness," visit **www.mhhe.com/ub10e**

video case

To access the video case featuring Energizer, visit **www.mhhe.com/ub10e**

DEVELOPING AND
Pricing
Goods and
Services

14

LEARNING
goals

After you have read and studied this chapter, you should be able to

1 Describe a total product offer.

2 Identify the various kinds of consumer and industrial goods.

3 Summarize the functions of packaging.

4 Contrast *brand, brand name,* and *trademark*, and show the value of brand equity.

5 Explain the steps in the new-product development process.

6 Describe the product life cycle.

7 Identify various pricing objectives and strategies.

When General Motors (GM) faced bankruptcy in 2009, the government invested $50 billion in the company. That means that U.S. citizens now have an ownership interest in the carmaker. With our money on the line, we certainly have an interest in what the company plans to do to regain profitability. Many of the most important decisions will involve developing new products that consumers will want to buy. The new GM senior vice president of global product development is Mary Barra. Barra was already GM's highest-ranking woman, having served as vice president for global human resources. She has also been vice president for global manufacturing engineering and manager of an assembly plant in Detroit.

Barra earned her undergraduate degree in electrical engineering at Kettering University and her MBA at Stanford. The GM chairman and CEO said that Barra will bring a fresh perspective to the critically important job of managing global vehicle programs for GM. She will focus on the customer in the areas of global design, vehicle and power train engineering, program management, and quality with the goal of delivering the world's best vehicles. With more than 36,000 members, her team will also manage global strategic product alliances. GM is working to gain market share in highly competitive segments like small fuel-efficient cars, and it plans to expand its lineup of plug-in hybrids beyond the Chevy Volt.

profile

Getting to Know

X *Mary Barra*

GM Senior Vice President

Barra doesn't emphasize her status as the first female to head product development for an American automaker. But, "If it encourages more young girls in junior high to stick with math and science, that's great," she said. "We need more women in engineering in general." Perhaps there are women in college today who will be inspired by Barra's success.

Barra faces a substantial task: figuring out how to cut the time it takes to design, engineer, and build new vehicles while turning out cars and trucks that respond to consumer needs from all nations. GM's new-vehicle development process was slowed leading up to the company's bankruptcy reorganization and is now entering a period in which few new models will be introduced. About 12 percent of GM's U.S. vehicle sales in 2011 was from "new" or heavily redesigned vehicles. That number is expected to rise to 30 percent in 2012. The automaker's sales rose 7 percent in 2010 (from a year earlier) despite removing eight brands from its lineup.

Developing and pricing goods and services will be a major goal of firms around the world as they begin to dig themselves out of the financial problems they are now facing. This chapter will introduce you to the many facets of new product development in both goods and services. You will also learn about packaging, branding, and the other elements of a total product offer. It will be interesting to follow the auto industry as it introduces new electric cars, the new, smaller, fuel-efficient cars, and the like. With people like Mary Barra leading the charge, we would expect the U.S. auto industry to be right up with the global leaders in the coming years.

Sources: Sharon Terlep, "GM Product Chief's Job: New Cars Fast," *The Wall Street Journal*, January 21, 2011; LinkedIn profile accessed March 2011; and "GM Appoints Mary Barra to Lead Global Product Development," *GM News*, accessed March 2011.

It's no secret that the airline industry is extremely competitive and many airlines have cut basic services like free baggage and food. In order to set itself apart from its competitors, this company takes a different path by offering door-to-door limousine service and in-flight massages. What is the name of this company? (Find the answer in the chapter.)

LEARNING goal 1

Describe a total product offer.

PRODUCT DEVELOPMENT AND THE TOTAL PRODUCT OFFER

value
Good quality at a fair price. When consumers calculate the value of a product, they look at the benefits and then subtract the cost to see if the benefits exceed the costs.

Global managers will be challenging U.S. managers with new products at low prices.[1] The best way to compete is to design and promote better products, meaning products that customers perceive to have the best **value**—good quality at a fair price.[2] You may have noticed that many restaurants were pushing "value meals" when the economy slowed from 2008 to 2011. Have you tried, for example, the new, smaller Blizzard from Dairy Queen?[3]

One of the American Marketing Association's definitions of marketing says it's "a set of processes for creating, communicating, and delivering *value* to customers." When consumers calculate the value of a product, they look at the benefits and then subtract the cost (price) to see whether the benefits exceed the costs, including the cost of driving to the store (or shipping fees if they buy the product online). Note that L.L. Bean eliminated shipping charges. That lowers the cost for consumers and makes their products more desirable (valuable).[4]

Whether consumers perceive a product as the best value depends on many factors, including the benefits they seek and the service they receive. To satisfy consumers, marketers must learn to listen better and constantly adapt to changing market demands. For example, traditional phone companies must now compete with Voice over Internet Protocol (VoIP)—a system that allows people to make very inexpensive phone calls through the Internet. And U.S. automobile companies must adapt to foreign producers by offering more competitive cars, or face extinction.[5]

Marketers have learned that adapting products to new competition and new markets is an ongoing need. We're sure you've noticed menu changes at your local fast-food restaurant over time. An organization can't do a one-time survey of consumer wants and needs, design a group of products to meet those needs, put them in the stores, and then just relax. It must constantly monitor changing consumer wants and needs, and adapt products, policies, and services accordingly. Did you know that McDonald's sells as much chicken as beef these days?[6] Some is being sold as a Chicken Biscuit for breakfast. Those double cheeseburgers fast-food restaurants were serving for $1.00 turned out to be a money loser, even though they were popular with consumers. You can't give consumers *too* good a deal or you can go out of business.

McDonald's and other restaurants are constantly trying new ideas. It added smoothies and oatmeal with fruit.[7] In Kokomo, Indiana, McDonald's tried waiter service and a more varied menu. In New York, it offered McDonuts to compete with Krispy Kreme. In Atlanta and other cities, McDonald's had computer stations linked to the Internet. In Hawaii, it tried a Spam breakfast platter, and in Columbus, Ohio, a mega-McDonald's had a karaoke booth. McDonald's has a McCafé in Chicago's Loop that sells premium coffee, pastries, and wrapped sandwiches. It has more than 300 such cafés in other countries and most McDonald's in the United States are putting in something similar. Watch out Starbucks. Some McDonald's even have digital-media kiosks that allow customers to burn custom CDs from a catalog of 70,000 songs, print digital photos, and download ringtones for mobile phones.

What was Starbucks' answer to the new challenges from McDonald's, Dunkin' Donuts, Target, and others? It began offering more food products. Oatmeal has become a huge success at Starbucks as well. The new menu also includes fruit smoothies and more—like regular coffee at lower prices.

All fast-food organizations must constantly monitor all sources of information for new-product ideas. McDonald's isn't alone in that. Look at those baguettes and cream cheese croissants at 7-Eleven—they're right next to the cappuccino machine. KFC put in a line of chicken sandwiches. Burger King tried an X-treme Double Cheeseburger. Wendy's is trying a major coffee program in Mississippi, including iced coffee, and introducing a whole new lineup of other products.

Offerings may differ in various locations according to the wants of the local community. In Iowa pork tenderloin is big, but in Oklahoma City it's tortilla scramblers. Globally, companies must adapt to local tastes. At Bob's Big Boy in Thailand, you can get Tropical Shrimp; at Carl's Junior in Mexico, you can order the Machaca Burrito; and at Shakey's Pizza in the Philippines, you can get Cali Shandy, a Filipino beer. Product development, then, is a key activity in any modern business, anywhere in the world.

You can imagine what could happen when your product loses some of its appeal. Zippo lighters, for example, may lose some market as people turn away from smoking. Zippo, therefore, tried offering products such as key holders, tape measures and belt buckles. They are no longer being sold, but Zippo has recently introduced a new men's fragrance and a clothing line that includes hoodies, ball caps and jeans.[8]

How would you like a beer or glass of wine with your Big Mac? You can get both at this McDonald's in Paris. Notice how the restaurant's architecture fits the style of the city. The same is true of the food in McDonald's other restaurants outside the United States. In Europe, the menus and interior designs are frequently adapted to fit the tastes and cultural preferences of each country.

Distributed Product Development

The increase in outsourcing and alliance building has resulted in innovation efforts that often require using multiple organizations separated by cultural, geographic and legal boundaries. **Distributed product development** is the

distributed product development
Handing off various parts of your innovation process—often to companies in other countries.

figure 14.1

POTENTIAL COMPONENTS OF A TOTAL PRODUCT OFFER

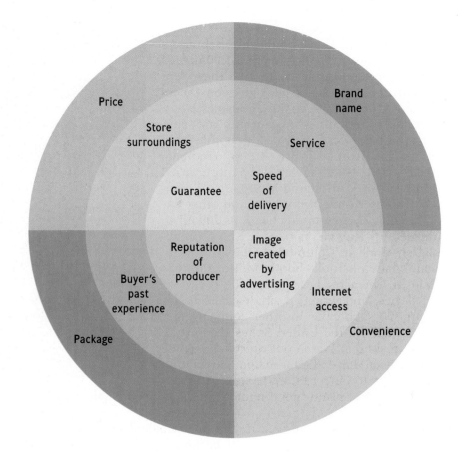

total product offer
Everything that consumers evaluate when deciding whether to buy something; also called a value package.

Apple's iPhone offers a range of features and functions, including the ability to make video calls, take photos, check e-mail, browse websites, get directions, tell time, keep a shopping list, record appointments in your calendar, download songs, sync with your other devices, and even make and receive phone calls. The product will likely continue to evolve and improve. What would you like Apple to add to the iPhone's total product offer?

term used to describe handing off various parts of your innovation process—often to companies in other countries. It is difficult enough to coordinate processes within a firm; it becomes substantially more difficult when trying to coordinate multifirm processes.[9] Great care must be taken to establish goals and procedures and standards before any such commitment is made.[10] One company that has collaborated with many other firms to make innovative products is 3M Company. It has developed some 55,000 products from Scotch tape to Thinsulate, and many of those products are embedded in other products such as the iPhone.[11]

Developing a Total Product Offer

From a strategic marketing viewpoint, a product is more than just the physical good or service. A **total product offer** consists of everything consumers evaluate when deciding whether to buy something. Thus, the basic product or service may be a washing machine, an insurance policy, or a beer, but the total product offer includes some or all the *value* enhancers in Figure 14.1. You may hear some people call the basic product the "core product" and the total product offer the "augmented product." Can you see how sustainability can be part of the augmented product? The nearby Thinking Green box discusses quality and sustainability.

When people buy a product, they may evaluate and compare total product offers on many dimensions. Some are tangible (the product itself and its package); others are intangible (the producer's reputation

Quality and Sustainability

One product that concerns consumers for both its health benefits and environmental aspects is fish. Trident Seafoods is one company that brings customers the freshest and healthiest fish possible and still assures sustainability by staying well within catch limits.

Trident Seafoods started with one boat. It focused on Alaska, fishing for salmon, pollock, crab, halibut and cod. Ignoring the cries that "It can't be done," Chuck Bundrant, the owner, decided to build a boat that both caught and processed crab. Despite that focus, the boat still catches salmon and bottom fish for diversity's sake. Bundrant and his partners now supply wild-caught salmon to warehouse giant Costco and have 40 vessels and 16 shore-based plants.

One focus of the firm is on quality. Quality control includes everything from temperature control to X-raying the fish for bones. Everything is carefully weighed to make sure that weights are honest and accurate.

Quality control goes hand in hand with sustainability. The company works with the North Pacific Fishery Management Council and the Marine Stewardship Council, which promote world sustainability practices. One part of its sustainability practices is to use all of the fish. That results in fish oil, fishmeal, and byproducts used in fertilizer and fishmeal. Bundrant says that none of what he does will amount to anything if there are no fish to catch.

Sources: Stephanie E. Ponder, "Success at Sea," *The Costco Connection,* February 2011; and Trident Seafoods Corporation, tridentseafoods.com, accessed April 2011.

and the image created by advertising). A successful marketer must begin to think like a consumer and evaluate the total product offer as a collection of impressions created by all the factors listed in Figure 14.1. It is wise to talk with consumers to see which features and benefits are most important to them and which value enhancers they want or don't want in the final offering. Frito-Lay, for example, had to drop biodegradable bags because they were "too noisy."

What questions might you ask consumers when developing the total product offer for Very Vegetarian? (Recall the business idea we introduced in Chapter 13.) Remember, store surroundings are important in the restaurant business, as are the parking lot and the condition of bathrooms. When designing services, some have even suggested the importance of things like trust and feelings in general.[12]

Sometimes an organization can use low prices to create an attractive total product offer. For example, outlet stores offer brand-name goods for less. Shoppers like getting high-quality goods and low prices, but they must be careful. Outlets also carry lower-quality products with similar but not exactly the same features as goods carried in regular stores. Different consumers may want different total product offers, so a company must develop a variety of offerings.

Product Lines and the Product Mix

Companies usually don't sell just one product. A **product line** is a group of products that are physically similar or intended for a similar market. They usually face similar competition. In one product line, there may be several competing brands. Notice, for example, Diet Coke, Diet Coke with Splenda, Coke Zero, Diet Coke with Lemon, Diet Coke with Lime, Diet Vanilla Coke, and Diet Cherry Coke. Makes it kind of hard to choose, doesn't it? Even Coke

product line
A group of products that are physically similar or are intended for a similar market.

commercials have product managers who can't tell the difference between Coke and Coke Zero. Have you seen the new aluminum Coke bottle? It's recyclable, resealable, less costly to make than a plastic or glass bottle, and feels cooler to the touch. Both Coke and Pepsi have added water and sports drinks to their product lines to meet new consumer tastes.

Procter & Gamble (P&G) has many brands in its laundry detergent product line, including Tide, Era, Downy, and Bold. P&G's product lines together make up its **product mix**, the combination of all product lines offered by a manufacturer. Have you noticed that there are some 352 distinct types of toothpastes available in stores?[13] Do you think that is too many or not?

Service providers have product lines and product mixes as well. A bank or credit union may offer a variety of services from savings accounts, automated teller machines, and computer banking to money market funds, safety deposit boxes, car loans, mortgages, traveler's checks, online banking, and insurance. AT&T combines services (communications) with goods (phones) in its product mix, with special emphasis on wireless.

> **product mix**
> The combination of product lines offered by a manufacturer.

LEARNING goal 2

Identify the various kinds of consumer and industrial goods.

PRODUCT DIFFERENTIATION

Product differentiation is the creation of real or perceived product differences. Actual product differences are sometimes quite small, so marketers must use a creative mix of pricing, advertising, and packaging (value enhancers) to create a unique, attractive image. Various bottled water companies, for example, have successfully attempted product differentiation. The companies made their bottled waters so attractive through pricing and promotion that now restaurant customers often order water by brand name.

There's no reason why you couldn't create a similar attractive image for Very Vegetarian, your vegetarian restaurant. Small businesses can often win market share with creative product differentiation. Yearbook photographer Charlie Clark competes by offering multiple clothing changes, backgrounds, and poses along with special allowances, discounts, and guarantees. His small business has the advantage of being more flexible in adapting to customer needs and wants, and he's able to offer attractive product options. Clark has been so successful that companies use him as a speaker at photography conventions. How could you respond creatively to the consumer wants of vegetarians?

> **product differentiation**
> The creation of real or perceived product differences.

> **convenience goods and services**
> Products that the consumer wants to purchase frequently and with a minimum of effort.

> **shopping goods and services**
> Those products that the consumer buys only after comparing value, quality, price, and style from a variety of sellers.

> **specialty goods and services**
> Consumer products with unique characteristics and brand identity. Because these products are perceived as having no reasonable substitute, the consumer puts forth a special effort to purchase them.

Marketing Different Classes of Consumer Goods and Services

One popular classification of consumer goods and services has four general categories—convenience, shopping, specialty, and unsought.

1. **Convenience goods and services** are products the consumer wants to purchase frequently and with a minimum of effort, like candy, gum,

milk, snacks, gas, and banking services. One store that sells mostly convenience goods is 7-Eleven. Location, brand awareness, and image are important for marketers of convenience goods and services. The Internet has taken convenience to a whole new level, especially for banks and other service companies. Companies that don't offer such services are likely to lose market share to those that do unless they offer outstanding service to customers who visit in person.

2. **Shopping goods and services** are products the consumer buys only after comparing value, quality, price, and style from a variety of sellers. Shopping goods and services are sold largely through *shopping centers* where consumers can make comparisons of products like clothes, shoes, appliances, and auto repair services. Target is one store that sells mostly shopping goods. Because many consumers carefully compare such products, marketers can emphasize price differences, quality differences, or some combination of the two. Think of how the Internet has helped you find the right shopping goods..

3. **Specialty goods and services** are consumer products with unique characteristics and brand identity. Because consumers perceive that specialty goods have no reasonable substitute, they put forth a special effort to purchase them. Examples include fine watches, expensive wine, fur coats, jewelry, imported chocolates, and services provided by medical specialists or business consultants.

   Specialty goods are often marketed through specialty magazines. Specialty skis may be sold through sports magazines and specialty foods through gourmet magazines. Again, the Internet helps buyers find specialty goods. In fact, some specialty goods can be sold exclusively on the Internet.

4. **Unsought goods and services** are products consumers are unaware of, haven't necessarily thought of buying, or suddenly find they need to solve an unexpected problem. They include emergency car-towing services, burial services, and insurance.

The marketing task varies according to the category of product; convenience goods are marketed differently from specialty goods. The best way to promote convenience goods is to make them readily available and create the proper image. Some combination of price, quality, and service is the best appeal for shopping goods. Specialty goods rely on reaching special market segments through advertising. Unsought goods such as life insurance often rely on personal selling. Car towing relies heavily on Yellow Pages advertising.

Whether a good or service falls into a particular class depends on the individual consumer. Coffee can be a shopping good for one consumer, while flavored gourmet roast is a specialty good for another. Some people shop around to compare different dry cleaners, so dry cleaning is a shopping service for them. Others go to the closest store, making it a convenience service. Marketers must carefully monitor their customer base to determine how consumers perceive their products.[14]

Tap the "Gift a Drink" button on Pepsi's new Social Vending Machine, enter your info, choose a drink, record an optional video message, enter your friends' info, and instantly they'll receive a text message with a code to redeem their drink at another sociable machine. Do you think this new machine will be popular with your friends?

unsought goods and services
Products that consumers are unaware of, haven't necessarily thought of buying, or find that they need to solve an unexpected problem.

Marketing Industrial Goods and Services

Many goods could be classified as consumer goods or industrial goods, based on their uses. A computer kept at home for personal use is clearly a consumer good. But in a commercial setting, such as an accounting firm or manufacturing plant, the same computer is an industrial good.

Industrial goods (sometimes called business goods or B2B goods) are products used in the production of other products. They are sold in the business-to-business (B2B) market. Some products can be both consumer and industrial goods. We've just mentioned how personal computers fit in both categories. As a consumer good, a computer might be sold through electronics stores like Best Buy or computer magazines. Most of the promotion would be advertising. As an industrial good, personal computers are more likely to be sold through salespeople or on the Internet. Advertising is less of a factor when selling industrial goods. Thus, you can see that classifying goods by user category helps marketers determine the proper marketing-mix strategy.

Figure 14.2 shows some categories of both consumer goods and industrial goods and services. *Installations* consist of major capital equipment such as new factories and heavy machinery. *Capital items* are expensive products that last a long time. A new factory building is both a capital item and an installation. *Accessory equipment* consists of capital items that are not quite as long-lasting or expensive as installations—like computers, copy machines, and various tools. Various categories of industrial goods are shown in the figure.

industrial goods
Products used in the production of other products. Sometimes called business goods or B2B goods.

Many goods could be classified as consumer goods or industrial goods, based on their uses. For example, a computer that a person uses at home for personal use would clearly be a consumer good. But that same computer used in a commercial setting, such as a hospital, would be classified as an industrial good. What difference does it make how a good is classified?

progress assessment

- What value enhancers may be included in a total product offer?
- What's the difference between a product line and a product mix?
- Name the four classes of consumer goods and services, and give examples of each.
- Describe three different types of industrial goods.

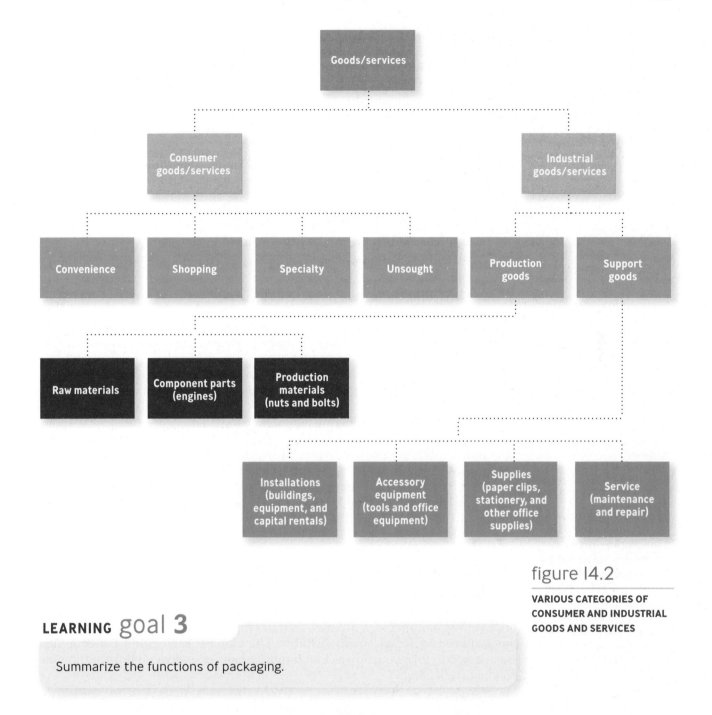

figure 14.2

VARIOUS CATEGORIES OF CONSUMER AND INDUSTRIAL GOODS AND SERVICES

LEARNING goal 3

Summarize the functions of packaging.

PACKAGING CHANGES THE PRODUCT

We've said that consumers evaluate many aspects of the total product offer, including the brand. It's surprising how important packaging can be in such evaluations. Many companies have used packaging to change and improve their basic product. We have squeezable ketchup bottles that stand upside down; square paint cans with screw tops and integrated handles; plastic bottles for motor oil that eliminate the need for funnels; toothpaste pumps; packaged dinners and other foods, like popcorn, that can be cooked in a microwave oven; single-use packets of spices; and so forth. Another interesting innovation is aromatic packaging. Arizona Beverage Company now has aromatic caps on its flavored iced teas.

In each case, the package changed the product in consumers' minds and opened large new markets. Do you sometimes have difficulty opening plastic packaging? Which packaging innovations do you like best? Can you see some market potential in developing better packaging? Packaging has even become a profession. Check out the Michigan State University School of Packaging, for example. Packages must perform the following functions:

1. Attract the buyer's attention.
2. Protect the goods inside, stand up under handling and storage, be tamperproof, and deter theft.
3. Be easy to open and use.
4. Describe and give information about the contents.
5. Explain the benefits of the good inside.
6. Provide information on warranties, warnings, and other consumer matters.
7. Give some indication of price, value, and uses.

Packaging can also make a product more attractive to retailers. The Universal Product Codes (UPCs) on many packages help stores control inventory. They combine a bar code and a preset number that gives the retailer information about the product's price, size, color, and other attributes. In short, packaging changes the product by changing its visibility, usefulness, or attractiveness.

One relatively new packaging technology for tracking products is the radio frequency identification (RFID) chip, especially the ones made with nanoparticle powder. When attached to a product, the chip sends out signals telling a company where the product is at all times. RFID chips carry more information than bar codes, don't have to be read one at a time (whole pallets can be read in an instant), and can be read at a distance. Walmart has been a leader in using RFID technology.

bundling
Grouping two or more products together and pricing them as a unit.

The Growing Importance of Packaging

Packaging has always been an important aspect of the product offer, but today it's carrying more of the promotional burden than in the past. Many products once sold by salespersons are now sold in self-service outlets, and the package has acquired more sales responsibility. The Fair Packaging and Labeling Act was passed to give consumers much more quantity and value information on product packaging.

Even industrial products can benefit from innovative packaging. The new Heinz Dip & Squeeze ketchup package allows restaurant owners to offer their customers a choice of peeling off the lid for dipping or tearing off the top for squeezing. The new package contains 3 times the ketchup of traditional sachets and uses less packaging. Shaped like the iconic bottles, the packets reinforce the Heinz Ketchup brand.

Packaging may make use of a strategy called **bundling**, which combines goods and/or services for a single price. Virgin Airlines has bundled door-to-door limousine service and in-flight massages in its total product offer. Financial institutions are offering everything from financial advice to help in purchasing insurance, stocks, bonds, mutual funds, and more. When combining goods or services into one package, marketers must not include so much that the price gets too high. It's best to work with customers to develop value enhancers that meet their individual needs.[15]

LEARNING goal **4**

Contrast *brand, brand name,* and *trademark,* and show the value of brand equity.

> **brand**
> A name, symbol, or design (or combination thereof) that identifies the goods or services of one seller or group of sellers and distinguishes them from the goods and services of competitors.

BRANDING AND BRAND EQUITY

A **brand** is a name, symbol, or design (or combination thereof) that identifies the goods or services of one seller or group of sellers and distinguishes them from the goods and services of competitors. The word *brand* includes practically all means of identifying a product. As we noted in Chapter 13, a *brand name* consists of a word, letter, or group of words or letters that differentiates one seller's goods and services from those of competitors. Brand names you may be familiar with include Red Bull, Sony, Del Monte, Campbell, Levi's, Google, Borden, Michelob, and of course many more. Brand names give products a distinction that tends to make them attractive to consumers. The Reaching Beyond Our Borders box on p. 388 discusses product names in more depth.

A **trademark** is a brand that has exclusive legal protection for both its brand name and its design. Trademarks like McDonald's golden arches are widely recognized and help represent the company's reputation and image. McDonald's might sue to prevent a company from selling, say, McDonnel hamburgers. Did you know there are Starsbuck coffee shops in China? (Look closely at that name.)

> **trademark**
> A brand that has exclusive legal protection for both its brand name and its design.

People are often impressed by certain brand names, even though they say there's no difference between brands in a given product category. For example, even when people say that all aspirin is alike, if you put two aspirin bottles in front of them—one with the Anacin label and one with an unknown name—most choose the one with the well known brand name. Gasoline buyers often choose a brand name (e.g., Exxon) over price.

For the buyer, a brand name ensures quality, reduces search time, and adds prestige to purchases. For the seller, brand names facilitate new-product introductions, help promotional efforts, add to repeat purchases, and differentiate products so that prices can be set higher. What brand names do you prefer?

> *Whether its contained in a name like Cheerios, a symbol like Nike's swoosh, a design like Coca-Cola's logo, or a combination of those, a brand distinguishes one marketer's goods and services from everyone else's. How do familiar brands influence consumers' choices of products every day?*

Brand Categories

Several categories of brands are familiar to you. **Manufacturers' brands** represent manufacturers that distribute products nationally—Xerox, Kodak, Sony, and Dell, for example.

Dealer (private-label) brands are products that don't carry the manufacturer's name but carry a distributor or retailer's name instead. Kenmore and Diehard are dealer brands sold by Sears. These brands are also known as *house brands* or *distributor brands.*

Many manufacturers fear having their brand names become generic names. A *generic name* is the name for a whole product category. Did you know that aspirin and linoleum were once brand names? So were nylon, escalator,

> **manufacturers' brands**
> The brand names of manufacturers that distribute products nationally.

> **dealer (private-label) brands**
> Products that don't carry the manufacturer's name but carry a distributor or retailer's name instead.

The Name Game

So, you've developed a product and you're ready to take it on the market. So what should you call it? America's favorite cookie, Oreo, is said to be a great name because the two O's nicely mirror the shape of the cookie itself. Could the name be part of the charm? Twitter has become the most-used word in the English language according to Global Language Monitor data. Think of the names that come to your mind when you think of American products: Coke, Pepsi, Häagen-Dazs (yes, an American product) and so on.

At one time, finding a name for a product was relatively simple. Now, with a couple hundred countries on the cyber-platform, choosing the right name is a global issue. For example, a Web development company in New Zealand chose the name hairyLemon. It has been estimated that at least a third of hairyLemon's business came from its name. Not all do-it-yourself names have been successful. For example, when Russian gas company Gazprom formed a joint venture with Nigeria's NNPC, the company was called NiGaz. Not a great name, we'd say.

Every once in a while, a successful name is created by accident. For example, the popular search engine was supposed to be called Googol (a scientific name for I followed by one hundred zeros). However, the founders made a typo when registering the domain name. The error resulted in a warm, catchy, human-sounding name.

In the marketing chapter, we chose the name Very Vegetarian for our new vegetarian restaurant. Have you come up with a better name? Would it help to brainstorm names with others? Would it be worthwhile to bring in an expert?

What if you wanted to build vegetarian restaurants at schools around the world? Would that make a difference? Can you see why names are critical to the long-run success of many firms?

Sources: Susan Purcell and Jay Jurisich, "Enter the Lexicon," *Bloomberg Businessweek*, October 25–October 31, 2010; and Igor International Naming and Branding Agency, www.igorinternational.com, accessed April 2011.

---

kerosene, and zipper. All those names became so popular, so identified with the product, that they lost their brand status and became generic. (Such issues are decided in the courts.) Their producers then had to come up with new names. The original Aspirin, for example, became Bayer aspirin. Companies working hard to protect their brand names today include Xerox and Rollerblade (in-line skates).

Generic goods are nonbranded products that usually sell at a sizable discount compared to national or private-label brands. They feature basic packaging and are backed with little or no advertising. Some are of poor quality, but many come close to the same quality as the national brand-name goods they copy. There are generic tissues, generic cigarettes, generic drugs, and so on. Consumers today are buying large amounts of generic products because their overall quality has improved so much in recent years. What has been your experience trying generic products?

Knockoff brands are illegal copies of national brand-name goods. If you see an expensive brand-name item such as a Polo shirt or a Rolex watch for

generic goods
Nonbranded products that usually sell at a sizable discount compared to national or private-label brands.

knockoff brands
Illegal copies of national brand-name goods.

sale at a ridiculously low price, you can be pretty sure it's a knockoff. Often the brand name is just a little off, too, like Palo (Polo) or Bolex (Rolex). Look carefully. Zippo has taken to calling counterfeit copies "Rippos."[16]

Generating Brand Equity and Loyalty

A major goal of marketers in the future will be to reestablish the notion of brand equity. **Brand equity** is the value of the brand name and associated symbols. Usually, a company cannot know the value of its brand until it sells it to another company. Brand names with high reported brand equity ratings include Reynolds Wrap aluminum foil and Ziploc food bags. What's the most valuable brand name today? It's Apple. Microsoft is not far behind.[17]

The core of brand equity is **brand loyalty**, the degree to which customers are satisfied, like the brand, and are committed to further purchases. A loyal group of customers represents substantial value to a firm, and that value can be calculated. One way manufacturers are trying to create more brand loyalty is by lowering the carbon footprint of their products.

In the past, companies tried to boost their short-term performance by offering coupons and price discounts to move goods quickly. This eroded consumers' commitment to brand names, especially of grocery products. Many consumers complain when companies drop brand names like Carnation Breakfast Bars or Flex shampoo.[18] Such complaints show the power of brand names.[19] Now companies realize the value of brand equity and are trying harder to measure the earning power of strong brand names.

Brand awareness refers to how quickly or easily a given brand name comes to mind when someone mentions a product category. Advertising helps build strong brand awareness. Established brands, such as Coca-Cola and Pepsi, are usually among the highest in brand awareness. Sponsorship of events, like football's Orange Bowl and NASCAR's Cup Series, helps improve brand awareness. Simply being there over and over also increases brand awareness. That's one way Google became such a popular brand..

Perceived quality is an important part of brand equity. A product that's perceived as having better quality than its competitors can be priced accordingly. The key to creating a perception of quality is to identify what consumers look for in a high-quality product, and then to use that information in every message the company sends out. Factors influencing the perception of quality include price, appearance, and reputation.

Consumers often develop *brand preference*—that is, they prefer one brand over another—because of such cues. When consumers reach the point of *brand insistence*, the product becomes a specialty good. For example, a consumer may insist on Goodyear tires for his or her car.

It's now so easy to copy a product's benefits that off-brand products can draw consumers away from brand-name goods. Brand-name manufacturers like Intel Corporation have to develop new products and new markets faster and promote their names better than ever before to hold off challenges from competitors.

Creating Brand Associations

The name, symbol, and slogan a company uses can assist greatly in brand recognition for that company's products. **Brand association** is the linking of a brand to other favorable images, like famous product users, a popular celebrity, or a particular geographic area. Note, for example, how ads for Mercedes-Benz associate its company's cars with successful people who live luxurious lives. The person responsible for building brands is known as a brand manager or product manager. We'll discuss that position next.

---

brand equity
The value of the brand name and associated symbols.

brand loyalty
The degree to which customers are satisfied, like the brand, and are committed to further purchases.

brand awareness
How quickly or easily a given brand name comes to mind when a product category is mentioned.

brand association
The linking of a brand to other favorable images.

Brand Management

A **brand manager** (known as a *product manager* in some firms) has direct responsibility for one brand or product line, and manages all the elements of its marketing mix: product, price, place, and promotion. Thus, you might think of the brand manager as the president of a one-product firm.

One reason many large consumer-product companies created this position was to have greater control over new-product development and product promotion. Some companies have brand-management *teams* to bolster the overall effort. In B2B companies, brand managers are often known as product managers.

progress assessment

- What six functions does packaging now perform?
- What's the difference between a brand name and a trademark?
- Can you explain the difference between a manufacturer's brand, a dealer brand, and a generic brand?
- What are the key components of brand equity?

LEARNING goal 5

Explain the steps in the new-product development process.

THE NEW-PRODUCT DEVELOPMENT PROCESS

The odds a new product will fail are high.[20] Over 80 percent of products introduced in any year fail to reach their business objectives. Not delivering what is promised is a leading cause of new-product failure. Other causes include getting ready for marketing too late, poor positioning, too few differences from competitors, and poor packaging. Small firms especially may experience a low success rate unless they do proper product planning and new product development. As Figure 14.3 shows, new-product development for producers consists of six stages.

New products continue to pour into the market every year, and their profit potential looks tremendous. Think, for example, of the potential of home video conferencing, interactive TV, Wii games and products, smart phones, iPads, and other innovations.[21] Where do these ideas come from? How are they tested? What's the life span for an innovation? Let's look at these issues.

Generating New-Product Ideas

It now takes about seven ideas to generate one commercial product. Most ideas for new industrial products come from employee suggestions rather than research and development. Research and development, nonetheless, is a major source of new products. Employees are a major source for new consumer-goods ideas. Firms should also listen to their suppliers for new-product ideas because suppliers are often exposed to new ideas. Present customers are also a good source for new product ideas.[22]

Product Screening

Product screening reduces the number of new-product ideas a firm is working on at any one time so it can focus on the most promising. *Screening* applies criteria to determine whether the product fits well with present products, has good profit potential, and is marketable. The company may assign each of these factors a weight and compute a total score for each new product so that it can compare their potentials.

Product Analysis

After product screening comes **product analysis**, or making cost estimates and sales forecasts to get a feeling for the profitability of new-product ideas. Products that don't meet the established criteria are withdrawn from consideration.

Product Development and Testing

If a product passes the screening and analysis phase, the firm begins to develop it further, testing many different product concepts or alternatives. A firm that makes packaged meat products may develop the concept of a chicken dog—a hot dog made of chicken that tastes like an all-beef hot dog. It will develop a prototype, or sample, so that consumers can try the taste. The Spotlight on Small Business box on p. 392 discusses some new ideas for products.

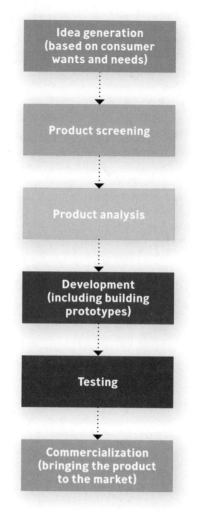

Idea generation (based on consumer wants and needs)

Product screening

Product analysis

Development (including building prototypes)

Testing

Commercialization (bringing the product to the market)

figure 14.3

THE NEW-PRODUCT DEVELOPMENT PROCESS
Product development is a six-stage process. Which stage do you believe to be the most important?

product screening
A process designed to reduce the number of new-product ideas being worked on at any one time.

product analysis
Making cost estimates and sales forecasts to get a feeling for profitability of new-product ideas.

Tom Szaky of TerraCycle makes new products such as plant food, planters, pencil cases, and tote bags from discarded products made by other companies. (To see his bags made from drink pouches and Oreo cookie wrappers, go to www.terracycle.net.) What products do you own that are made of recycled material?

Don't Come to Me; I'll Come to You

In many cities, street vendors hawking hot dogs and other traditional fare is part of Americana. They are American icons. But that icon is changing. Not only is their menu changing from greasy hot dogs and salty pretzels to crème brulee and organic drinks, but also how customers find them is becoming more high tech. Some vendors now use Twitter and other social media to reveal their current locations and build customer relationships.

There are some cities, like Chicago, where legislation restricts food trucks for health and sanitary reasons. But in cities like New York and Portland and Austin, you can find these mobile units selling hot dogs and, often, more gourmet offerings. French rotisserie Roli Roti in San Francisco, Vietnamese bahn mi at Nom Nom in L.A., and Gruyere grilled cheese in Austin are offering gourmet food items not usually found in standard street vendor carts. Here are just a few of the mobile units you can find online:

- Clover Food Truck in Boston/Cambridge offers a rotating menu of local organic materials.

- Sugar Philly Truck in Philadelphia offers crème brulee hot off the truck.

- Dim and Den Sum in Cleveland has some of the best food truck art in America.

- Koi Fusion PDX in Portland is one of the few mobile eateries in that town.

You may enjoy looking online for a mobile unit near you. Such exploring may give you an idea about how you may start your own small business on a truck. The possibilities seem endless. You should be able to put into practice all of the product concepts you learned in this chapter. Say, how about a vegetarian truck?

Sources: Leslie Robarge, "Gourmet Food Truck Smackdown," *Bloomberg Businessweek*, March 14–March 20, 2011; Matt Vilano, "The Secret Sauce Part II," *Entrepreneur*, April 2011; and Cloverfoodlab.com, DimandDenSum.com, accessed in April 2011.

---

concept testing
Taking a product idea to consumers to test their reactions.

Concept testing takes a product idea to consumers to test their reactions. Do they see the benefits of this new product? How frequently would they buy it? At what price? What features do they like and dislike? What changes in it would they make? The firm tests samples using different packaging, branding, and ingredients until a product emerges that's desirable from both production and marketing perspectives. Some new hotels are being built to match the trendy W chain. They are said to have "hipness." Such innovations must be tried on consumers to see if they indeed recognize and appreciate the new "hip" design.[23] As you plan for Very Vegetarian, can you see the importance of concept testing for new vegetarian dishes?

How do firms test services? American Airlines conducted a six-month trial of a new self-tagging system that allowed customers to print and put the tags on their own checked bags. What features and benefits was American Airlines probably testing for?

Commercialization

Even if a product tests well, it may take quite a while to achieve success in the market. Take the zipper, for example, the result of one of the longest development efforts on record for a consumer product. After Whitcomb Judson received the first patents for his clothing fastener in the early 1890s, it took more than 15 years to perfect the product—and even then consumers weren't interested. Judson's company suffered numerous financial setbacks, name changes, and relocations before settling in Meadville, Pennsylvania. Finally, the U.S. Navy started using zippers during World War I. Today, Talon Inc. is the leading U.S. maker of zippers, producing some 500 million of them a year.

The example of the zipper shows why the marketing effort must include **commercialization**, which includes (1) promoting the product to distributors and retailers to get wide distribution, and (2) developing strong advertising and sales campaigns to generate and maintain interest in the product among distributors and consumers. New products are now getting rapid exposure to global markets through commercialization on the Internet and social media. Websites enable consumers to view new products, ask questions, and make purchases easily and quickly.[24]

commercialization
Promoting a product to distributors and retailers to get wide distribution, and developing strong advertising and sales campaigns to generate and maintain interest in the product among distributors and consumers.

LEARNING goal 6

Describe the product life cycle.

product life cycle
A theoretical model of what happens to sales and profits for a product class over time; the four stages of the cycle are introduction, growth, maturity, and decline.

THE PRODUCT LIFE CYCLE

Once a product has been developed and tested, it goes to market. There it may pass through a **product life cycle** of four stages: introduction, growth, maturity, and decline (see Figure 14.4). This cycle is a *theoretical* model of what happens

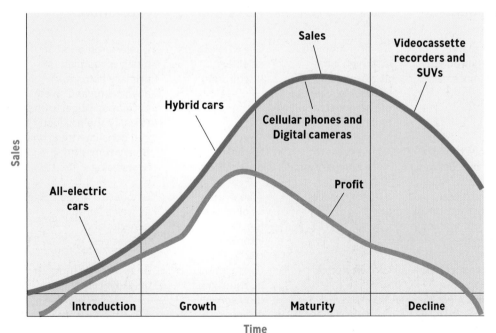

figure 14.4

SALES AND PROFITS DURING THE PRODUCT LIFE CYCLE
Note that profit levels start to fall *before* sales reach their peak. This is due to increasing price competition. When profits and sales start to decline, it's time to come out with a new product or to remodel the old one to maintain interest and profits.

to sales and profits for a *product class* over time. However, not all individual products follow the life cycle, and particular brands may act differently. For example, while frozen foods as a generic class may go through the entire cycle, one brand may never get beyond the introduction stage. Some product classes, such as microwave ovens, stay in the introductory stage for years. Some products, like catsup, become classics and never experience decline. Others, such as fad clothing, may go through the entire cycle in a few months. Still others may be withdrawn from the market altogether. Nonetheless, the product life cycle may provide some basis for anticipating future market developments and for planning marketing strategies.

Example of the Product Life Cycle

The product life cycle can give marketers valuable clues to successfully promoting a product over time. Some products, like crayons and sidewalk chalk, have very long product life cycles, change very little, and never seem to go into decline. Crayola Crayons has been successful for 100 years! How long do you think the new virtual video games will last?[25]

You can see how the theory works by looking at the product life cycle of instant coffee. When it was introduced, most people didn't like it as well as "regular" coffee, and it took several years for instant coffee to gain general acceptance (introduction stage). At one point, though, instant coffee grew rapidly in popularity, and many brands were introduced (growth stage). After a while, people became attached to one brand and sales leveled off (maturity stage). Sales then went into a slight decline when freeze-dried coffees were introduced (decline stage). Now freeze-dried coffee is, in turn, at the decline stage as consumers are buying bags of coffee from Starbucks and brewing them at home. It's extremely important for marketers to recognize what stage a product is in so that they can make intelligent and efficient marketing decisions about it.

figure 14.5

SAMPLE STRATEGIES FOLLOWED DURING THE PRODUCT LIFE CYCLE

	MARKETING MIX ELEMENTS			
LIFE CYCLE STAGE	PRODUCT	PRICE	PLACE	PROMOTION
Introduction	Offer market-tested product; keep mix small	Go after innovators with high introductory price (skimming strategy) or use penetration pricing	Use wholesalers, selective distribution	Dealer promotion and heavy investment in primary demand advertising and sales promotion to get stores to carry the product and consumers to try it
Growth	Improve product; keep product mix limited	Adjust price to meet competition	Increase distribution	Heavy competitive advertising
Maturity	Differentiate product to satisfy different market segments	Further reduce price	Take over wholesaling function and intensify distribution	Emphasize brand name as well as product benefits and differences
Decline	Cut product mix; develop new-product ideas	Consider price increase	Consolidate distribution; drop some outlets	Reduce advertising to only loyal customers

LIFE CYCLE STAGE	SALES	PROFITS	COMPETITORS
Introduction	Low sales	Losses may occur	Few
Growth	Rapidly rising sales	Very high profits	Growing number
Maturity	Peak sales	Declining profits	Stable number, then declining
Decline	Falling sales	Profits may fall to become losses	Declining number

Using the Product Life Cycle

Different stages in the product life cycle call for different marketing strategies. Figure 14.5 outlines the marketing mix decisions you might make. As you go through the figure, you'll see that each stage calls for multiple marketing mix changes. Remember, these concepts are largely theoretical and you should use them only as guidelines. We'll discuss the price strategies mentioned in the figure later in this chapter.

Figure 14.6 shows in theory what happens to sales volume, profits, and competition during the product life cycle. Compare it to Figure 14.4. Both figures show that a product at the mature stage may reach the top in sales growth while profit is decreasing. At that stage, a marketing manager may decide to create a new image for the product to start a new growth cycle. You may have noticed how Arm & Hammer baking soda gets a new image every few years to generate new sales. One year it's positioned as a deodorant for refrigerators and the next as a substitute for harsh chemicals in swimming pools. Knowing what stage in the cycle a product has reached helps marketing managers decide when such strategic changes are needed.

Theoretically, all products go through these stages at various times in their life cycle. What happens to sales as a product matures?

progress assessment

- What are the six steps in the new-product development process?
- What is the difference between product screening and product analysis?
- What are the two steps in commercialization?
- What is the theory of the product life cycle?

LEARNING goal 7

Identify various pricing objectives and strategies.

COMPETITIVE PRICING

Pricing is so important to marketing and the development of total product offers that it has been singled out as one of the four Ps in the marketing mix, along with product, place, and promotion. It's one of the most difficult of the four Ps for a manager to control, however, because price is such a critical ingredient in consumer evaluations of the product. In this section, we'll explore price both as an ingredient of the total product offer and as a strategic marketing tool.

Pricing Objectives

A firm may have several objectives in mind when setting a pricing strategy. When pricing a new vegetarian offering, we may want to promote the product's image. If we price it *high* and use the right promotion, maybe we can make it the Evian of vegetarian meals. We also might price it high to achieve a certain profit objective or return on investment. We could also price our product *lower* than its competitors, because we want low-income people to afford this healthy meal. That is, we could have some social or ethical goal in mind. Low pricing may also discourage competition because it reduces the profit potential, but it may help us capture a larger share of the market.

Thus a firm may have several pricing objectives over time, and it must formulate these objectives clearly before developing an overall pricing strategy. Popular objectives include the following:

1. *Achieving a target return on investment or profit.* Ultimately, the goal of marketing is to make a profit by providing goods and services to others. Naturally, one long-run pricing objective of almost all firms is to optimize profit. One way companies have tried to increase profit is by reducing the amount provided to customers. Thus cereal companies have cut the amount of cereal in a box, toilet paper companies are making their products smaller, and so on.[26] Have you noticed this happening for products you buy?

2. *Building traffic.* Supermarkets often advertise certain products at or below cost to attract people to the store. These products are called *loss leaders.* The long-run objective is to make profits by following the short-run objective of building a customer base. The Internet portal Yahoo once provided a free auction service to compete with eBay. Why give such a service away? To increase advertising revenue on the Yahoo site and attract more people to Yahoo's other services.

3. *Achieving greater market share.* One way to capture a larger part of the market is to offer lower prices, low finance rates (like 0 percent financing), low lease rates, or rebates.

4. *Creating an image.* Certain watches, perfumes, and other socially visible products are priced high to give them an image of exclusivity and status.

5. *Furthering social objectives.* A firm may want to price a product low so people with little money can afford it. The government often subsidizes the price of farm products to keep basic necessities like milk and bread easily affordable.

A firm may have short-run objectives that differ greatly from its long-run objectives. Managers should understand both types at the beginning and put both into their strategic marketing plan. They should also set pricing objectives in the context of other marketing decisions about product design, packaging, branding, distribution, and promotion. All these marketing decisions are interrelated.

Intuition tells us the price charged for a product must bear some relationship to the cost of producing it. Prices usually *are*

Some products are priced high to create a high-status image of exclusivity and desirability. Salvatore Ferragamo shoes fall into this category. What is the total product offer for a product like this?

set somewhere above cost. But as we'll see, price and cost aren't always related. In fact, there are three major approaches to pricing strategy: cost-based, demand-based (target costing), and competition-based.

Cost-Based Pricing

Producers often use cost as a primary basis for setting price. They develop elaborate cost accounting systems to measure production costs (including materials, labor, and overhead), add in a margin of profit, and come up with a price. Picture the process in terms of producing a car. You add up all the various components—engine parts, body, tires, radio, door locks and windows, paint, and labor—add a profit margin, and come up with a price. The question is whether the price will be satisfactory to the market as well. How has the market responded to the prices of U.S. cars lately? In the long run, the market—not the producer—determines what the price will be (see Chapter 2). Pricing should take into account costs, but it should also include the expected costs of product updates, the marketing objectives for each product, and competitor prices.

Demand-Based Pricing

Unlike cost-based pricing, **target costing** is demand-based. That means we design a product so it not only satisfies customers but also meets the profit margins we've set. Target costing makes the final price an *input* to the product development process, not an outcome of it. You first estimate the selling price people would be willing to pay for a product and then subtract your desired profit margin. The result is your target cost of production, or what you can spend to profitably produce the item. Imagine how you would use this process to make custom-made jewelry.

target costing
Designing a product so that it satisfies customers and meets the profit margins desired by the firm.

Competition-Based Pricing

Competition-based pricing is a strategy based on what all the other competitors are doing. The price can be at, above, or below competitors' prices. Pricing depends on customer loyalty, perceived differences, and the competitive climate. **Price leadership** is the strategy by which one or more dominant firms set pricing practices all competitors in an industry follow. You may have noticed that practice among oil companies.

competition-based pricing
A pricing strategy based on what all the other competitors are doing. The price can be set at, above, or below competitors' prices.

price leadership
The strategy by which one or more dominant firms set the pricing practices that all competitors in an industry follow.

Break-Even Analysis

Before you begin selling a new vegetarian sandwich, it may be wise to determine how many sandwiches you'd have to sell before making a profit. You'd then determine whether you could reach such a sales goal. **Break-even analysis** is the process used to determine profitability at various levels of sales. The break-even point is the point where revenues from sales equal all costs. The formula for calculating the break-even point is as follows:

$$\text{Break-even point (BEP)} = \frac{\text{Total fixed costs (FC)}}{\text{Price of one unit (P)} - \text{Variable costs (VC) of one unit}}$$

Total fixed costs are all the expenses that remain the same no matter how many products are made or sold. Among the expenses that make up fixed costs are the amount paid to own or rent a factory or warehouse and the amount paid for business insurance. **Variable costs** change according to the level of production. Included are the expenses for the materials used in making products and

break-even analysis
The process used to determine profitability at various levels of sales.

total fixed costs
All the expenses that remain the same no matter how many products are made or sold.

variable costs
Costs that change according to the level of production.

the direct costs of labor used in making those goods. For producing a specific product, let's say you have a fixed cost of $200,000 (for mortgage interest, real estate taxes, equipment, and so on). Your variable cost (e.g., labor and materials) per item is $2. If you sold the products for $4 each, the break-even point would be 100,000 items. In other words, you wouldn't make any money selling this product unless you sold more than 100,000 of them:

$$BEP = \frac{FC}{P-VC} = \frac{\$200,000}{\$4.00-\$2.00} = \frac{\$200,000}{\$2.00} = 100,000 \text{ boxes}$$

Other Pricing Strategies

skimming price strategy
Strategy in which a new product is priced high to make optimum profit while there's little competition.

Let's say a firm has just developed a new line of products, such as Blu-ray players. The firm has to decide how to price these sets at the introductory stage of the product life cycle. A **skimming price strategy** prices a new product high to recover research and development costs and make as much profit as possible while there's little competition. Of course, those large profits will eventually attract new competitors.

penetration strategy
Strategy in which a product is priced low to attract many customers and discourage competition.

A second strategy is to price the new players low. Low prices will attract more buyers and discourage other companies from making sets because profits are slim. This **penetration strategy** enables the firm to penetrate or capture a large share of the market quickly.

everyday low pricing (EDLP)
Setting prices lower than competitors and then not having any special sales.

Retailers use several pricing strategies. **Everyday low pricing (EDLP)** is the choice of Home Depot and Walmart. They set prices lower than competitors and don't usually have special sales. The idea is to bring consumers to the store whenever they want a bargain rather than having them wait until there is a sale.

high–low pricing strategy
Setting prices that are higher than EDLP stores, but having many special sales where the prices are lower than competitors'.

Department stores and some other retailers most often use a **high–low pricing strategy**. Regular prices are higher than at stores using EDLP, but during special sales they're lower. The problem with such pricing is that it encourages consumers to wait for sales, thus cutting into profits. As online shopping continues to grow, you may see fewer stores with a high–low strategy because consumers will be able to find better prices on the Internet.

Retailers can use price as a major determinant of the goods they carry. Some promote goods that sell only for 99 cents, or only for $10. Some of those 99-cent stores have raised their prices to over a dollar because of rising costs.

You learned earlier in this chapter that bundling means grouping two or more products together and pricing them as a unit. For example, a store might price washers and dryers as a unit. Jiffy Lube offers an oil change and lube, checks your car's fluid levels and air pressure, and bundles all these services into one price. Research suggests that a discount will increase sales more effectively if it's offered on an attractive, pleasurable item.[27]

Psychological pricing means pricing goods and services at price points that make the product appear less expensive than it is. A house might be priced at $299,000 because that sounds like a lot less than $300,000. Gas stations almost always use psychological pricing.

psychological pricing
Pricing goods and services at price points that make the product appear less expensive than it is.

How Market Forces Affect Pricing

Recognizing that different consumers may be willing to pay different prices, marketers sometimes price on the basis of consumer demand rather than cost or some other calculation. That's called *demand-oriented pricing,* and you can observe it at movie theaters with low rates for children and drugstores with discounts for senior citizens. The Washington Opera Company in Washington, DC, raised prices on prime seating and lowered them on less-attractive seats. This strategy raised the company's revenues 9 percent.

Marketers are facing a new pricing problem: Customers can now compare prices of many goods and services on the Internet, at websites like DealTime. com and MySimon.com. Priceline.com introduced consumers to a "demand collection system," in which buyers post the prices they are willing to pay and invite sellers to accept or decline the price. Consumers can get great prices on airlines, hotels, and other products by naming their price. They can also buy used goods online. Clearly, price competition is going to heat up as consumers have more access to price information from all around the world.[28] As a result, nonprice competition is likely to increase.

NONPRICE COMPETITION

Marketers often compete on product attributes other than price. You may have noted that price differences are small for products like gasoline, candy bars, and even major products such as compact cars and private colleges.

You won't typically see price as a major promotional appeal on television. Instead, marketers tend to stress product images and consumer benefits such as comfort, style, convenience, and durability.

Many small organizations promote the services that accompany basic products rather than price in order to compete with bigger firms. Good service will enhance a relatively homogeneous product. Danny O'Neill, for example, is a small wholesaler who sells gourmet coffee to upscale restaurants. He has to watch competitors' prices *and* the services they offer so that he can charge the premium prices he wants. To charge high prices, he has to offer and then provide superior service. Larger companies often do the same thing. Some airlines stress friendliness, large "sleeping" seats, promptness, abundant flights, and other such services. Many hotels stress "no surprises," business services, health clubs, and other extras.

progress assessment

- Can you list two short-term and two long-term pricing objectives? Can the two be compatible?
- What are the limitations of a cost-based pricing strategy?
- What is psychological pricing?

summary

Learning Goal 1. Describe a total product offer.

- **What's included in a total product offer?**

A total product offer consists of everything consumers evaluate when deciding whether to buy something. It includes price, brand name, and satisfaction in use.

- **What's the difference between a product line and a product mix?**

A product line is a group of physically similar products with similar competitors. A product line of gum may include bubble gum and sugarless gum. A product mix is a company's combination of product lines. A manufacturer may offer lines of gum, candy bars, and breath mints in its product mix.

- **How do marketers create product differentiation for their goods and services?**

Marketers use a combination of pricing, advertising, and packaging to make their products seem unique and attractive.

Learning Goal 2. Identify the various kinds of consumer and industrial goods.

- **What are consumer goods?**

Consumer goods are sold to ultimate consumers like you and me for personal use.

- **What are the four classifications of consumer goods and services, and how are they marketed?**

There are convenience goods and services (requiring minimum shopping effort); shopping goods and services (for which people search and compare price and quality); specialty goods and services (which consumers go out of their way to get, and for which they often demand specific brands); and unsought goods and services (products consumers are unaware of, haven't thought of buying, or need to solve an unexpected problem). Convenience goods and services are best promoted by location, shopping goods and services by some price/quality appeal, and specialty goods and services by specialty magazines and interactive websites.

- **What are industrial goods, and how are they marketed differently from consumer goods?**

Industrial goods are products sold in the business-to-business (B2B) market and used in the production of other products. They're sold largely through salespeople and rely less on advertising.

Learning Goal 3. Summarize the functions of packaging.

- **What are the seven functions of packaging?**

Packaging must (1) attract the buyer's attention; (2) protect the goods inside, stand up under handling and storage, be tamperproof, and deter theft; (3) be easy to open and use; (4) describe the contents; (5) explain the benefits of the good inside; (6) provide information about warranties, warnings, and other consumer matters; and (7) indicate price, value, and uses. Bundling means grouping two or more products into a unit, through packaging, and charging one price for them.

Learning Goal 4. Contrast *brand*, *brand name*, and *trademark*, and show the value of brand equity.

- **Can you define brand, brand name, and trademark?**

A *brand* is a name, symbol, or design (or combination thereof) that identifies the goods or services of one seller or group of sellers and distinguishes them from the goods and services of competitors. The word *brand* includes all means of identifying a product. A *brand name* consists of a word, letter, or group of words or letters that differentiates one seller's goods and services from those of competitors. A *trademark* is a brand that has exclusive legal protection for both its brand name and design.

- **What is brand equity, and how do managers create brand associations?**

Brand equity is the value of a brand name and associated symbols. Brand association is the linking of a brand to other favorable images such as product users, a popular celebrity, or a geographic area.

- **What do brand managers do?**

Brand managers coordinate product, price, place, and promotion decisions for a particular product.

Learning Goal 5. Explain the steps in the new-product development process.

- **What are the six steps of the product development process?**

The steps of product development are (1) generation of new-product ideas, (2) product screening, (3) product analysis, (4) development, (5) testing, and (6) commercialization.

Learning Goal 6. Describe the product life cycle.

- **What is the product life cycle?**

The product life cycle is a theoretical model of what happens to sales and profits for a product class over time.

- **What are the four stages in the product life cycle?**

The four product life cycle stages are introduction, growth, maturity, and decline.

Learning Goal 7. Identify various pricing objectives and strategies.

- **What are pricing objectives?**

Pricing objectives include achieving a target profit, building traffic, increasing market share, creating an image, and meeting social goals.

- **What strategies can marketers use to determine a product's price?**

A skimming strategy prices the product high to make big profits while there's little competition. A penetration strategy uses low price to attract more customers and discourage competitors. Demand-oriented pricing starts with consumer demand rather than cost. Competition-oriented pricing is based on all competitors' prices. Price leadership occurs when all competitors follow the pricing practice of one or more dominant companies.

- **What is break-even analysis?**

Break-even analysis is the process used to determine profitability at various levels of sales. The break-even point is the point where revenues from sales equal all costs.

- **Why do companies use nonprice strategies?**

Pricing is one of the easiest marketing strategies to copy. It's often not a good long-run competitive tool.

key terms

brand 387
brand association 389
brand awareness 389
brand equity 389
brand loyalty 389
brand manager 390
break-even analysis 397

bundling 386
commercialization 393
competition-based
 pricing 397
concept testing 392
convenience goods
 and services 382

dealer (private-label)
 brands 387
distributed product
 development 379
everyday low pricing
 (EDLP) 398
generic goods 388

critical thinking

1. What value enhancers affected your choice of the school you attend? Did you consider size, location, price, reputation, WiFi services, library and research services, sports, and courses offered? What factors were most important? Why? What schools were your alternatives? Why didn't you choose them?

2. What could you do to enhance the product offer of Very Vegetarian, other than changing the menu from time to time?

3. How could you use psychological pricing when making up the menu at Very Vegetarian?

4. Are you impressed by the use of celebrities in product advertisements? What celebrity could you use to promote Very Vegetarian?

developing workplace skills

1. Look around your classroom and notice the different types of shoes students are wearing. What product qualities were they looking for when they chose their shoes? How important were price, style, brand name, and color? Describe the product offerings you would feature in a new shoe store designed to appeal to college students.

2. A total product offer consists of everything consumers evaluate when choosing among products, including price, package, service, and reputation. Working in teams, compose a list of factors consumers might consider when evaluating the total product offer of a vacation resort, a cell phone, and a rental apartment.

3. How important is price to you when buying the following: clothes, milk, computers, haircuts, rental cars? What nonprice factors, if any, are more important than price? How much time do you spend evaluating factors other than price when making such purchases?

4. Go through several local stores of different types and note how often they use psychological pricing. Discuss the practice with the class to see whether students recognize the influence psychological pricing has upon them.

taking it to the net

Purpose

To assess how consumers can use the Internet to shop for various goods.

Exercise

Shopbots are Internet sites for finding the best prices on goods you need. No shopbot searches the entire Internet, so it's a good idea to use more than one to get the best deals. Furthermore, not all shopbots quote shipping and handling costs. Here are some to try: MySimon.com, PriceGrabber.com, PriceSCAN. com, and YahooShopping.com.

1. Which of the shopbots offers the most goods and the most information? How helpful are the consumer reviews? The product descriptions?

2. Which shopbot is easiest to use? The hardest? Why?

3. Write down some of the prices you find on the Internet and then go to a local store, such as Walmart or Target, and compare prices. Does either source (online or brick-and-mortar) consistently offer the best price?

4. Compare shopping on the Internet to shopping in stores. What are the advantages and disadvantages of each? Which has the best total product offer?

casing the web

To access the case, "Everyday Low Pricing," visit a **www.mhhe.com/ubl0e**

video case

To access the video case featuring Dream Dinners, visit **www.mhhe.com/ubl0e**

DISTRIBUTING
PRODUCTS

LEARNING
goals

After you have read and studied this chapter, you should be able to

1 Explain the concept of marketing channels and their value.

2 Demonstrate how intermediaries perform the six marketing utilities.

3 Identify the types of wholesale intermediaries in the distribution system.

4 Compare the distribution strategies retailers use.

5 Explain the various kinds of nonstore retailing.

6 Explain the various ways to build cooperation in channel systems.

7 Describe logistics and outline how intermediaries manage the transportation and storage of goods.

Although many online shopping sites have been extremely successful, e-tailers often fall short of their brick-and-mortar rivals in terms of customer service. After all, dealing with an issue face-to-face with a salesperson is usually easier than negotiating an issue over a series of e-mails. At the online shoe store Zappos, however, a unique company culture demonstrates that online shoppers need not sacrifice quality service for convenience.

When Tony Hsieh sold his first company to Microsoft for $265 million, he joined Zappos as CEO. One of the first things he wanted to do was change the company's corporate work environment. To set Zappos apart from the pack of online retailers, he wanted his service representatives to wow customers with their energy and expertise. Accomplishing that task meant keeping employees upbeat and motivated through the love of their work. He gave his call-center staffers remarkable freedom, allowing them to talk to customers for hours at a time or send flowers and thank-you notes on the company dime. In Hsieh's mind, a customer may only call Zappos once in their lifetime, but the experience is guaranteed to stick with them.

Hsieh's commitment to a fun work environment and quality service helped grow Zappos from a $32 million company to a $1.2 billion powerhouse. Nevertheless, Zappos didn't become the success it is today based on Hsieh's freewheeling managerial style alone. Hsieh also decided that the company needed total control of its supply chain. Up until 2003 Zappos earned 25 percent of its annual revenue through a drop shipping system (passing the customer orders to producers who would ship the products directly to the customers). While this saved the company the hassle of handling, stocking, or delivering the products, it also prevented the company from knowing exactly what it had in stock at any given time, thus impeding its customer service

capabilities. In order to provide the top-notch service it promised, Zappos needed to control the whole process from beginning to end.

After assuming total control over its inventory, Zappos' service department knows exactly what is in stock and what is out. If a customer wants a pair of shoes Zappos doesn't have, an employee may even direct the customer to a competitor that does. Maintaining its own inventory and order fulfillment gives Zappos' company culture the independence it needs to succeed by getting the products its customers want where they want them.

The four Ps of marketing are product, place, promotion, and price. This chapter is all about place. The place function goes by many other names as well, including shipping, warehousing, distribution, logistics, and supply-chain management. We'll explore all these concepts in this chapter. At the end, you will have a much better understanding of the many steps required to get products from the producer to the consumer.

profile

Getting to Know
X   *Tony Hsieh*
CEO of Zappos

Sources: Christopher Palmeri, "Now For Sale, The Zappos Culture," *Bloomberg Businessweek,* January 11, 2010; Brian Solis, "Zappos' Tony Hsieh Delivers Happiness Through Service and Innovation," *Fast Company,* April 12, 2011; Adam Bryant, "On a Scale of 1 to 10, How Weird Are You?" *The New York Times,* January 9, 2010; and Paul B. Carroll, "Getting a Foothold Online," *The Wall Street Journal,* June 7, 2010.

Although this automobile manufacturer builds its cars in South Korea, the 30,000 components come from all over the world. For example, the airbags come from a Swedish company that makes them in Utah. Its supply chain is truly interfirm and international. What is the name of this company? (Find the answer in the chapter.)

marketing intermediaries
Organizations that assist in moving goods and services from producers to businesses (B2B) and from businesses to consumers (B2C).

channel of distribution
A whole set of marketing intermediaries, such as agents, brokers, wholesalers, and retailers, that join together to transport and store goods in their path (or channel) from producers to consumers.

LEARNING goal **1**

Explain the concept of marketing channels and their value.

THE EMERGENCE OF MARKETING INTERMEDIARIES

It's easy to overlook distribution and storage in marketing, where the focus is often on advertising, selling, marketing research, and other functions. But it doesn't take much to realize how important distribution is. Imagine the challenge Timberland faces of getting raw materials together, making 12 million pairs of shoes, and then distributing those shoes to stores throughout the world. That's what thousands of manufacturing firms—making everything from automobiles to toys—have to deal with every day. Imagine further that there has been a major volcano eruption or tsunami that has caused a disruption in the supply of goods. Such issues are commonplace for distribution managers.[1]

Fortunately there are hundreds of thousands of companies and individuals whose job it is to help move goods from the raw-material state to producers and then on to consumers. Then, as is often the case, the products are sent from consumers to recyclers and back to manufacturers or assemblers. Did you know that only 20 percent of plastic water bottles are recycled? See the Thinking Green box for more on sustainability and the distribution process.[2]

Managing the flow of goods has become one of the most important managerial functions for many organizations. Let's look at how this function is carried out.

Marketing intermediaries (once called *middlemen*) are organizations that assist in moving goods and services from producers to businesses (B2B) and from businesses to consumers (B2C). They're called intermediaries because they're in the middle of a series of organizations that join together to help distribute goods from producers to consumers. A **channel of distribution** consists of a whole set of marketing intermediaries, such as agents, brokers, wholesalers, and retailers, that

Distribution warehouses store goods until they are needed. Have you ever thought about the benefits of having food, furniture, clothing, and other needed goods close at hand?

Distribution and Sustainability

Throughout this text we've talked about companies that have adopted a "greener" attitude toward producing and selling goods and services. But such companies will not be successful in implementing a "green" strategy without the cooperation and participation of other companies in their supply chain. Thus environmentally aware companies are pushing their supply chain partners to work with them to come up with a distribution plan that would minimize pollution and optimize profits. Such a plan is good to not only halt negative publicity, but to make the whole system more profitable.

Recently, transportation accounted for over 28 percent of U.S. energy consumption and over 33 percent of carbon dioxide emissions. Motor transportation is four times less fuel efficient per ton-mile than rail, and emissions from airfreight are 600 times higher than rail or ocean shipping. Clearly, the decision of what distribution mode to use is more complex than first imagined—if you keep the environment in mind. Companies throughout the world are taking such measurements and are responding accordingly. The era of sustainability has entered into distribution as well as the other aspects of marketing.

Sources: Michael S. Hopkins, "How Sustainability Creates New Opportunity," *MIT Sloan Management Review,* Summer 2010; Susan L. Golicic, Courtney N. Boerstler and Lisa M. Ellram, " 'Greening' in the Supply Chain," *MIT Sloan Management Review,* Winter 2010; and Todd W. Price, "Making Resource Management Work: Sustainability and the Supply Chain," *Harvard Business Review,* March 2011.

---

join together to transport and store goods in their path (or channel) from producers to consumers. **Agents/brokers** are marketing intermediaries who bring buyers and sellers together and assist in negotiating an exchange but don't take title to the goods—that is, at no point do they own the goods. Think of real estate agents as an example.

A **wholesaler** is a marketing intermediary that sells to other organizations, such as retailers, manufacturers, and hospitals. Wholesalers are part of the B2B system. Because of high distribution costs, Walmart has been trying to eliminate independent wholesalers from its system and do the job itself. That is, Walmart provides its own warehouses and has its own trucks. It has over 120 distribution centers and 53,000 trailers to distribute goods to its stores.[3] Finally, a **retailer** is an organization that sells to ultimate consumers (people like you and me).

Channels of distribution help ensure communication flows *and* the flow of money and title to goods. They also help ensure that the right quantity and assortment of goods will be available when and where needed. Figure 15.1 on p. 408 shows selected channels of distribution for both consumer and industrial goods.

You can see the distribution system in the United States at work when you drive down any highway and see the thousands of trucks and trains moving goods from here to there. Less visible, however, are the many distribution warehouses that store goods until they are needed. Have you ever thought about the benefits of having food, furniture, and other needed goods close at hand? Have you seen distribution warehouses along the road as you drive from town to town?

Why Marketing Needs Intermediaries

Figure 15.1 shows that some manufacturers sell directly to consumers. So why have marketing intermediaries at all? The answer is that intermediaries perform certain marketing tasks—such as transporting, storing, selling, advertising, and

agents/brokers
Marketing intermediaries who bring buyers and sellers together and assist in negotiating an exchange but don't take title to the goods.

wholesaler
A marketing intermediary that sells to other organizations.

retailer
An organization that sells to ultimate consumers.

Channels for consumer goods

Channels for industrial goods

This channel is used by craftspeople and small farmers.

This channel is used for cars, furniture, and clothing.

This channel is the most common channel for consumer goods such as groceries, drugs, and cosmetics.

This is a common channel for food items such as produce.

This is a common channel for consumer services such as real estate, stocks and bonds, insurance, and nonprofit theater groups.

This is a common channel for nonprofit organizations that want to raise funds. Included are museums, government services, and zoos.

This is the common channel for industrial products such as glass, tires, and paint for automobiles.

This is the way that lower-cost items such as supplies are distributed. The wholesaler is called an industrial distributor.

Manufacturer | Manufacturer | Manufacturer | Farmer | Service organization | Nonprofit organization | Manufacturer | Manufacturer

Retailer | Wholesaler | Broker | Broker | Store | Wholesaler

Retailer | Wholesaler

Retailer | Retailer

Consumers

Industrial users

figure 15.1

SELECTED CHANNELS OF DISTRIBUTION FOR CONSUMER AND INDUSTRIAL GOODS AND SERVICES

relationship building—faster and more cheaply than most manufacturers could.[4] Here's a simple analogy: You could personally deliver packages to people anywhere in the world, but usually you don't. Why not? Because it's generally cheaper and faster to have them delivered by the U.S. Postal Service or a private firm such as UPS.[5]

Similarly, you could sell your home by yourself or buy stock directly from individual companies, but you probably wouldn't. Why? Again, because agents and brokers are marketing intermediaries who make the exchange process easier and more efficient and profitable.[6] In the next section, we'll explore how intermediaries improve the efficiency of various exchanges.

How Intermediaries Create Exchange Efficiency

Here is an easy way to see the benefits of using marketing intermediaries. Suppose five manufacturers of various food products each tried to sell directly to five retailers. The number of exchange relationships needed to create this market is 5 times 5, or 25.

figure 15.2

HOW INTERMEDIARIES CREATE EXCHANGE EFFICIENCY

This figure shows that adding a wholesaler to the channel of distribution cuts the number of contacts from 25 to 10. This improves the efficiency of distribution.

Manufacturers   **Retailers**   **Manufacturers**   **Retailers**

But picture what happens when a wholesaler enters the system. The five manufacturers each contact the wholesaler, establishing five exchange relationships. The wholesaler then establishes contact with the five retailers, creating five more exchange relationships. The wholesaler's existence reduces the number of exchanges from 25 to only 10. Figure 15.2 shows this process.

Some economists have said that intermediaries add *costs* and should be eliminated. Marketers say intermediaries add *value,* and that the *value greatly exceeds the cost.* Let's explore this debate and see what value intermediaries provide.[7]

The Value versus the Cost of Intermediaries

The public has often viewed marketing intermediaries with a degree of suspicion. Some surveys show about half the cost of what we buy is marketing costs that go largely to pay for the work of intermediaries. If we could only get rid of intermediaries, people reason, we could greatly reduce the cost of everything we buy. Sounds good, but is the solution really that simple?

Take a box of cereal that sells for $4. How could we, as consumers, get the cereal for less? Well, we could all drive to Michigan, where some cereal is produced, and save shipping costs. But imagine millions of people getting in their cars and driving to Michigan just to buy cereal. No, it doesn't make sense. It's much cheaper to have intermediaries bring the cereal to major cities. That might make transportation and warehousing by wholesalers necessary. These steps add cost, don't they? Yes, but they add value as well—the value of not having to drive to Michigan.

The cereal is now in a warehouse somewhere on the outskirts of the city. We could all drive down to the wholesaler and pick it up. But that still isn't the most economical way to buy cereal. If we figure in the cost of gas and time, the cereal will again be too expensive. Instead, we prefer to have someone

figure 15.3

DISTRIBUTION'S EFFECT ON YOUR FOOD DOLLAR

Note that the farmer gets only 25 cents of your food dollar. The bulk of your money goes to intermediaries to pay distribution costs. Their biggest cost is labor (truck drivers, clerks), followed by warehouses and storage.

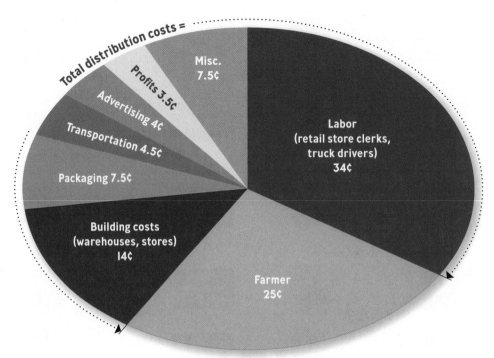

move the cereal from the warehouse to a truck, drive it to the corner supermarket, unload it, unpack it, price it, shelve it, and wait for us to come in to buy it. To make it even more convenient, the supermarket may stay open for 24 hours a day, seven days a week. Think of the costs. But think also of the value! For $4, we can get a box of cereal *when* we want it, and with little effort.

If we were to get rid of the retailer, we could buy a box of cereal for slightly less, but we'd have to drive farther and spend time in the warehouse looking through rows of cereals. If we got rid of the wholesaler, we could save a little more money, not counting our drive to Michigan. But a few cents here and there add up—to the point where distribution (marketing) may add up to 75 cents for every 25 cents in manufacturing costs. Figure 15.3 shows where your money goes in the distribution process. The largest percentage goes to people who drive trucks and work in wholesale and retail organizations. Note that only 3.5 cents goes to profit.

Here are three basic points about intermediaries:

1. Marketing intermediaries can be eliminated, but their activities can't; that is, you can eliminate some wholesalers and retailers, but then consumers or someone else would have to perform the intermediaries' tasks, including transporting and storing goods, finding suppliers, and establishing communication with suppliers.

2. Intermediary organizations have survived because they perform marketing functions faster and more cheaply than others can. To maintain their competitive position in the channel, they now must adopt the latest technology. That includes search engine optimization, social networking (on sites like Facebook), and analyzing website statistics to understand their customers better.

3. Intermediaries add costs to products, but these costs are usually more than offset by the values they create.

LEARNING goal 2

Demonstrate how intermediaries perform the six marketing utilities.

THE UTILITIES CREATED BY INTERMEDIARIES

Utility, in economics, is the want-satisfying ability, or value, that organizations add to goods or services by making them more useful or accessible to consumers than they were before. The six kinds of utility are form, time, place, possession, information, and service. Although producers provide some utilities, marketing intermediaries provide most. Let's look at how.

Form Utility

Traditionally, producers rather than intermediaries have provided form utility (see Chapter 9) by changing raw materials into useful products. Thus, a farmer who separates the wheat from the chaff and the processor who turns the wheat into flour are creating form utility. Retailers and other marketers sometimes provide form utility as well. For example, retail butchers cut pork chops from a larger piece of meat and trim off the fat. The servers at Starbucks make coffee just the way you want it. Dell assembles computers according to customers' wishes.

Time Utility

Intermediaries, such as retailers, add **time utility** to products by making them available when consumers need them. Devar Tennent lives in Boston. One winter evening while watching TV with his brother, Tennent suddenly got the urge for a hot dog and a Coke. The problem was there were no hot dogs or Cokes in the house.

Devar ran down to the corner delicatessen and bought some hot dogs, buns, Cokes, and potato chips. He also bought some frozen strawberries and ice cream. Devar was able to get these groceries at midnight because the local deli was open 24 hours a day. That's time utility. You can buy goods at any time on the Internet, but you can't beat having them available right around the corner *when you want them*. On the other hand, note the value an Internet company provides by staying accessible 24 hours a day.

Place Utility

Intermediaries add **place utility** to products by placing them *where* people want them. While traveling through the badlands of South Dakota, Juanita Ruiz got hungry and thirsty. There are no stores for miles in this part of the country, but Juanita saw signs along the road saying a 7-Eleven was ahead. Following the signs, she stopped at the store for refreshments. She also bought some sunglasses and souvenir items there. The goods and services provided by 7-Eleven are in a convenient place for vacationers. Throughout the United States, 7-Eleven stores remain popular because they are usually in easy-to-reach locations. They provide place utility. As more and more sales become global, place utility will grow in importance.

utility
In economics, the want-satisfying ability, or value, that organizations add to goods or services.

time utility
Adding value to products by making them available when they're needed.

place utility
Adding value to products by having them where people want them.

Think of how many stores provide time utility by making goods and services available to you 24 hours a day, seven days a week. Have you ever needed to renew a prescription late at night or needed a late night snack? Can you see how time utility offers added value?

Possession Utility

possession utility
Doing whatever is necessary to transfer ownership from one party to another, including providing credit, delivery, installation, guarantees, and follow-up service.

Intermediaries add **possession utility** by doing whatever is necessary to transfer ownership from one party to another, including providing credit. Activities associated with possession utility include delivery, installation, guarantees, and follow-up service. Larry Rosenberg wanted to buy a nice home in the suburbs. He found just what he wanted, but he didn't have the money he needed. So he went with the real estate broker to a local savings and loan and borrowed money to buy the home. Both the real estate broker and the savings and loan are marketing intermediaries that provide possession utility. For those who don't want to own goods, possession utility makes it possible for them to use goods through renting or leasing.

Information Utility

information utility
Adding value to products by opening two-way flows of information between marketing participants.

Intermediaries add **information utility** by opening two-way flows of information between marketing participants. Jerome Washington couldn't decide what kind of TV set to buy. He looked at various ads in the newspaper, talked to salespeople at several stores, read material at the library and on the Internet, and tweeted his friends. Newspapers, salespeople, libraries, websites, and government publications are all information sources made available by intermediaries. They provide information utility.

Service Utility

service utility
Adding value by providing fast, friendly service during and after the sale and by teaching customers how to best use products over time.

Service after the sale is one of the contributing factors to Apple's success. Customers can call to make an appointment with an Apple Genius who will help them learn how to use their computers, iPhones, or iPads. How does this service add value to Apple's products?

Intermediaries add **service utility** by providing fast, friendly service during and after the sale and by teaching customers how to best use products over time. Sze Leung bought a personal computer for his home office. Both the computer manufacturer and the retailer Leung used continue to offer help whenever he needs it. He also gets software updates for a small fee to keep his computer up-to-date. What attracted Leung to the retailer in the first place was the helpful, friendly service he received from the salesperson in the store. Service utility is rapidly becoming the most important utility for many retailers, because without it they would lose business to direct marketing (e.g., marketing by catalog or on the Internet). Can you see how the Internet can provide some forms of service utility?

progress assessment

- What is a channel of distribution, and what intermediaries participate in it?
- Why do we need intermediaries? Illustrate how intermediaries create exchange efficiency.
- How would you defend intermediaries to someone who said getting rid of them would save consumers millions of dollars?
- Can you give examples of the utilities intermediaries create and how they provide them?

LEARNING goal 3

Identify the types of wholesale intermediaries in the distribution system.

WHOLESALE INTERMEDIARIES

Let's distinguish wholesaling from retailing and clearly define the functions of each. Some producers deal only with wholesalers and won't sell directly to retailers or to end users (consumers). Some producers deal with both wholesalers and retailers, but give wholesalers a bigger discount. In turn, some wholesalers sell to both retailers and consumers. The office superstore Staples is a good example. It sells office supplies to small businesses and to consumers as well. Warehouse clubs such as Sam's Club and Costco are other companies with both wholesale and retail functions.

The difference is this: A *retail sale* is the sale of goods and services to consumers *for their own use*. A *wholesale sale* is the sale of goods and services to businesses and institutions, like schools or hospitals, *for use in the business*, or to wholesalers or retailers *for resale*.

Wholesalers make business-to-business sales. Most people are not as familiar with the various kinds of wholesalers as they are with retailers. Let's explore some of these helpful wholesale intermediaries. Most of them provide a lot of marketing jobs and offer you a good opportunity.

Merchant Wholesalers

Merchant wholesalers are independently owned firms that take title to the goods they handle. About 80 percent of wholesalers fall in this category. There are two types of merchant wholesalers: full-service and limited-function. *Full-service wholesalers* perform all the distribution functions (see Figure 15.4 on p. 414). *Limited-function wholesalers* perform only selected functions, but try to do them especially well. Three common types of limited-function wholesalers are rack jobbers, cash-and-carry wholesalers, and drop shippers.

Rack jobbers furnish racks or shelves full of merchandise, like music, toys, hosiery, and health and beauty aids, to retailers. They display the products and sell them on consignment, meaning they keep title to the goods until they're sold and then share the profits with the retailer. Have you seen shelves at the supermarket full of CDs and related items? Rack jobbers likely put them there.

Cash-and-carry wholesalers serve mostly smaller retailers with a limited assortment of products. Traditionally, retailers went to such wholesalers, paid cash, and carried the goods back to their stores—thus the term *cash-and-carry*. Today, stores such as Staples allow retailers and others to use credit cards for wholesale purchases. Thus the term *cash-and-carry* is becoming obsolete for wholesalers.

Drop shippers solicit orders from retailers and other wholesalers and have the merchandise shipped directly from a producer to a buyer. They own the merchandise but don't handle, stock, or deliver it. That's done by the producer. Drop shippers tend to handle bulky products such as coal, lumber, and chemicals.

merchant wholesalers
Independently owned firms that take title to the goods they handle.

rack jobbers
Wholesalers that furnish racks or shelves full of merchandise to retailers, display products, and sell on consignment.

cash-and-carry wholesalers
Wholesalers that serve mostly smaller retailers with a limited assortment of products.

drop shippers
Wholesalers that solicit orders from retailers and other wholesalers and have the merchandise shipped directly from a producer to a buyer.

figure 15.4

A FULL-SERVICE WHOLESALER

A FULL-SERVICE WHOLESALER WILL:	THE WHOLESALER MAY PERFORM THE FOLLOWING SERVICES FOR CUSTOMERS:
1. Provide a sales force to sell the goods to retailers and other buyers.	1. Buy goods the end market will desire and make them available to customers.
2. Communicate manufacturers' advertising deals and plans.	2. Maintain inventory, thus reducing customers' costs.
3. Maintain inventory, thus reducing the level of the inventory suppliers have to carry.	3. Transport goods to customers quickly.
4. Arrange or undertake transportation.	4. Provide market information and business consulting services.
5. Provide capital by paying cash or quick payments for goods.	5. Provide financing through granting credit, which is especially critical to small retailers.
6. Provide suppliers with market information they can't afford or can't obtain themselves.	6. Order goods in the types and quantities customers desire.
7. Undertake credit risk by granting credit to customers and absorbing any bad debts, thus relieving the supplier of this burden.	
8. Assume the risk for the product by taking title.	

Source: Thomas C. Kinnear, *Principles of Marketing,* 4th ed., © 1995, p. 394. Reprinted by permission of Pearson Education, Inc., Upper Saddle River, NJ.

Agents and Brokers

Agents and brokers bring buyers and sellers together and assist in negotiating an exchange. However, unlike merchant wholesalers, agents and brokers never own the products they distribute. Usually they do not carry inventory, provide

Agents and brokers are a familiar type of intermediary. Typically they don't take possession of the goods they sell. A real estate broker, for instance, facilitates the transaction between seller and buyer but never holds title to the house. What functions does a realtor provide in a home sale?

credit, or assume risks. While merchant wholesalers earn a profit from the sale of goods, agents and brokers earn commissions or fees based on a percentage of the sales revenues. Agents maintain long-term relationships with the people they represent, whereas brokers are usually hired on a temporary basis.

Agents who represent producers are either *manufacturer's agents* or *sales agents*. As long as they do not carry competing products, manufacturer's agents may represent several manufacturers in a specific territory. They often work in the automotive supply, footwear, and fabricated steel industries. Sales agents represent a single producer in a typically larger territory.

Brokers have no continuous relationship with the buyer or seller. Once they negotiate a contract between the parties, their relationship ends. Producers of seasonal products like fruits and vegetables often use brokers, as does the real estate industry.

LEARNING goal 4

Compare the distribution strategies retailers use.

RETAIL INTERMEDIARIES

A retailer, remember, is a marketing intermediary, like a supermarket, that sells to ultimate consumers. The United States boasts approximately 2.3 million retail stores, not including retail websites. Retail organizations employ more than 11 million people and are one of the major employers of marketing graduates. The recent recession has affected retailers, forcing many to cut back on employees, but large retailers like Macy's and Sears have been making a comeback.[8] Figure 15.5 lists, describes, and gives examples of various kinds of retailers. Have you shopped in each kind of store? What seem to be the

figure 15.5

TYPES OF RETAIL STORES

TYPE	DESCRIPTION	EXAMPLE
Department store	Sells a wide variety of products (clothes, furniture, housewares) in separate departments	Sears, JCPenney, Nordstrom
Discount store	Sells many different products at prices generally below those of department stores	Walmart, Target
Supermarket	Sells mostly food with other nonfood products such as detergent and paper products	Safeway, Kroger, Albertson's
Warehouse club	Sells food and general merchandise in facilities that are usually larger than supermarkets and offer discount prices; membership may be required	Costco, Sam's Club
Convenience store	Sells food and other often-needed items at convenient locations; may stay open all night	7-Eleven
Category killer	Sells a huge variety of one type of product to dominate that category of goods	Toys "R" Us, Bass Proshops, Office Depot
Outlet store	Sells general merchandise directly from the manufacturer at a discount; items may be discontinued or have flaws ("seconds")	Nordstrom Rack, Liz Claiborne, Nike, TJ Maxx
Specialty store	Sells a wide selection of goods in one category	Jewelry stores, shoe stores, bicycle shops

Pop Goes the Retail Store

With online shopping sites like Amazon continuing to gather market share, brick-and-mortar retailers have had to step up their game in order to compete. In the early 2000s, companies experimented with so-called "pop-up stores" to create a new shopping experience for consumers. These temporary outlets remained open for a short amount of time in small spaces and offered promotional offers and/or items not found in traditional stores. Though some excused the strategy as too gimmicky at the time, many are now willing to give the pop-up experience another shot.

While the decline of the American mall dealt a major blow to retailers, the empty storefronts provide lots of space for pop-up stores. In fact, this past holiday season Toys 'R' Us opened more than 600 pop-up stores with many of them in malls that used to house the bankrupt KB Toys. Of the 25 pop-ups that Borders opened last year, the majority were placed in malls where the retailer used to have a presence itself.

Still, pop-up stores aren't guaranteed to bring a company out of the doldrums, as evidenced by Borders' recent closing.

The most ambitious pop-ups don't even sell items. Instead, they try to create a unique experience between the consumers and the company's products, often opting to give products away rather than sell them. For instance, Procter & Gamble recently opened a pop-up in New York solely for promotion. Visitors could get a free Cover Girl makeover or take home complimentary samples of Febreeze candles and Head & Shoulders shampoo. The idea was to engage in a different conversation with customers and let them interact with the products. The aim of these types of pop-ups is to create lasting relationships with customers rather than just distribute products quickly. And if the strategy works, people will talk, text and tweet about the experience they had, giving the company invaluable exposure.

Sources: Matt Townsend, "The Staying Power of Pop-Up Stores," *Bloomberg Businessweek,* November 11, 2010; and Jason DelRay, "Shop Now Before It All Disappears," *Inc.,* July–August 2010.

advantages of each? Would you enjoy working in a retail store of some kind? Some retailers seem to compete mostly on price, but others, such as specialty stores, use variety as a competitive tool. The nearby Spotlight on Small Business box describes a new innovation in retail stores popping up across the country. Marketers use several strategies for retail distribution. We explain them next.

Retail Distribution Strategy

Because different products call for different retail distribution strategies, a major decision marketers must make is selecting the right retailers to sell their products. There are three categories of retail distribution: intensive, selective, and exclusive.

Intensive distribution puts products into as many retail outlets as possible, including vending machines. Products that need intensive distribution include convenience goods such as candy, cigarettes, gum, and popular magazines.

intensive distribution
Distribution that puts products into as many retail outlets as possible.

Selective distribution uses only a preferred group of the available retailers in an area. Such selection helps ensure producers of quality sales and service. Manufacturers of appliances, furniture, and clothing (shopping goods) use selective distribution.

Exclusive distribution is the use of only one retail outlet in a given geographic area. The retailer has exclusive rights to sell the product and is therefore likely to carry a large inventory, give exceptional service, and pay more attention to this brand than to others. Luxury auto manufacturers often use exclusive distribution, as do producers of specialty goods such as skydiving equipment and fly-fishing products.

selective distribution
Distribution that sends products to only a preferred group of retailers in an area.

exclusive distribution
Distribution that sends products to only one retail outlet in a given geographic area.

progress assessment

- Describe the activities of rack jobbers and drop shippers.
- What kinds of products would call for each of the different distribution strategies: intensive, selective, exclusive?

LEARNING goal 5

Explain the various kinds of nonstore retailing.

NONSTORE RETAILING

Nothing else in retailing has received more attention recently than electronic retailing. Internet retailing is just one form of nonstore retailing. Other categories are telemarketing; vending machines, kiosks, and carts; direct selling; multilevel marketing; and direct marketing. Small businesses can use nonstore retailing to open up new channels of distribution for their products.

Electronic Retailing

Electronic retailing consists of selling goods and services to ultimate consumers over the Internet. Thanks to website improvements and discounting, online retail sales have risen dramatically over the last few years.[9] But getting customers is only half the battle. The other half is delivering the goods, providing helpful service, and keeping your customers. When electronic retailers lack sufficient inventory or fail to deliver goods on time (especially at holidays and other busy periods), customers often give up and go back to brick-and-mortar stores.

Most Internet retailers now offer e-mail order confirmation. But sometimes they are less good at handling complaints, accepting returns, and providing personal help. Some are improving customer service by adding help buttons that lead customers to real-time online assistance from a human employee.

Old brick-and-mortar stores that add online outlets are sometimes called brick-and-click stores. They allow customers to choose which shopping technique suits them best. Most companies that want to compete in the future will probably need both a real store and an online presence to provide consumers with all the options they want. Walmart has added same-day in-store pickup of online purchases to its services.[10]

electronic retailing
Selling goods and services to ultimate customers (e.g., you and me) over the Internet.

Many brick-and-mortar stores have added Internet services for the added convenience of their customers. Some people shop online and then go to the store to buy the merchandise. Others both shop and buy on the Internet. What are the advantages and disadvantages of shopping and buying online?

telemarketing
The sale of goods and services by telephone.

Traditional retailers like Sears have learned that selling on the Internet calls for a new kind of distribution. Sears's warehouses were accustomed to delivering truckloads of goods to the company's retail outlets. But they were not prepared to deliver to individual consumers, except for large orders like furniture and appliances. It turns out, therefore, that both traditional and Internet retailers have to develop new distribution systems to meet the demands of today's Internet-savvy shoppers. It's often easy to sell goods and services on eBay, but there is always the need to distribute those goods. Most people outsource that function to FedEx or UPS, which have the needed expertise.

Telemarketing

Telemarketing is the sale of goods and services by telephone. Some 80,000 companies use it to supplement or replace in-store selling and complement online selling. Many send a catalog to consumers, who order by calling a toll-free number. Many electronic retailers provide a help feature online that serves the same function.

Vending Machines, Kiosks, and Carts

Vending machines dispense convenience goods when consumers deposit sufficient money. They carry the benefit of location—they're found in airports, office buildings, schools, service stations, and other areas where people want convenience items. In Japan, they sell everything from bandages and face cloths to salads and spiced seafood. Vending by machine will be an interesting area to watch as more innovations are introduced in the United States. U.S. vending machines are already selling iPods, Bose headphones, sneakers, digital cameras, and DVD movies. You can even find earthworms, medical marijuana, and Chardonnay in vending machines.[11] An ATM machine in Abu Dhabi dispenses gold.[12]

Carts and kiosks have lower overhead costs than stores do, so they can offer lower prices on items such as T-shirts, purses, watches, and cell phones. You often see vending carts outside stores or along walkways in malls. Many mall owners love them because they're colorful and create a marketplace atmosphere. Kiosk workers often dispense coupons and helpful product information. You may have noticed airlines are using kiosks to speed the process of getting on the plane. Most provide a boarding pass and allow you to change your seat. Many kiosks serve as gateways to the Internet, so in one place consumers can shop at a store and still have access to all the products available on the Internet. What's your reaction to such kiosks?

Direct Selling

Direct selling reaches consumers in their homes or workplaces. Because so many men and women work outside the home and aren't in during the day, companies that use direct selling are sponsoring parties at workplaces or evenings and weekends. Major users of this sales category include cosmetics producers and vacuum cleaner manufacturers. Trying to copy their success, other businesses are venturing into direct selling with lingerie, artwork, and candles sold at house parties they sponsor. Some companies, however, such as those in encyclopedia sales, have dropped most of their direct selling efforts in favor of Internet selling.

Vending machines and kiosks are convenient and easy for customers to use. They also have lower overhead than stores do. What do stores provide that kiosks and vending machines don't?

Multilevel Marketing

Over 1,000 U.S. companies have had success using multilevel marketing (MLM) and salespeople who work as independent contractors. One of the most successful MLM firms today is called Team. It sells MonaVie, a fruit juice in a wine bottle for $39. Salespeople earn commissions on their own sales, create commissions for the "upliners" who recruited them, and receive commissions from any "downliners" they recruit to sell. When you have hundreds of downliners—people recruited by the people you recruit—your commissions can be sizable. Some people make tens of thousands of dollars a month this way. That doesn't mean you should get involved with such schemes. More often than not, people at the bottom buy the products themselves and sell a bare minimum to others.

The main attraction of multilevel marketing for employees, other than the potential for making money, is the low cost of entry. For a small investment, the average person can start up a business and begin recruiting others. Many people question MLM because some companies using it have acted unethically. Potential employees must be very careful to examine the practices of such firms. Nonetheless, MLM's sales of $30 billion a year demonstrate the potential for success in this form of marketing.

direct selling
Selling to consumers in their homes or where they work.

Direct Marketing

Direct marketing includes any activity that directly links manufacturers or intermediaries with the ultimate consumer. One of the fastest-growing types of retailing, it includes direct mail, catalog sales, and telemarketing as well as online marketing. Popular consumer catalog companies that use direct marketing include Coldwater Creek, L.L. Bean, and Lands' End (now owned by Sears). Direct marketing has created tremendous competition in some high-tech areas as well.

Direct marketing has become popular because shopping from home or work is more convenient for consumers than going to stores. Instead of driving to a mall, people can shop in catalogs and advertising supplements in the newspaper and then buy by phone, mail, or computer. Interactive online selling

direct marketing
Any activity that directly links manufacturers or intermediaries with the ultimate consumer.

is expected to provide increasing competition for retail stores. Recently, L.L. Bean put pressure on rivals by eliminating shipping charges. That made L.L. Bean even more attractive to people who like to shop by catalog or online.[13]

Direct marketing took on a new dimension with *interactive video*. Producers now provide all kinds of information on websites. Consumers can ask questions, seek the best price, and order goods and services—all online. Companies that use interactive video have become major competitors for those who market through paper catalogs.

To offer consumers the maximum benefit, marketing intermediaries must work together to ensure a smooth flow of goods and services. There hasn't always been total harmony in the channel of distribution. As a result, channel members have created systems to make the flows more efficient. We'll discuss those next.

> **corporate distribution system**
> A distribution system in which all of the organizations in the channel of distribution are owned by one firm.

> **contractual distribution system**
> A distribution system in which members are bound to cooperate through contractual agreements.

LEARNING goal 6

Explain the various ways to build cooperation in channel systems.

BUILDING COOPERATION IN CHANNEL SYSTEMS

One way traditional retailers can compete with online retailers is to be so efficient that online retailers can't beat them on cost—given the need for customers to pay for delivery. That means manufacturers, wholesalers, and retailers must work closely to form a unified system. How can manufacturers get wholesalers and retailers to cooperate in such a system? One way is to link the firms in a formal relationship. Four systems have emerged to tie firms together: corporate systems, contractual systems, administered systems, and supply chains.

Corporate Distribution Systems

In a **corporate distribution system** one firm owns all the organizations in the channel of distribution. If the manufacturer owns the retail firm, clearly it can maintain a great deal of control over its operations. Sherwin Williams, for example, owns its own retail stores and coordinates everything: display, pricing, promotion, inventory control, and so on.

Franchisors like Chocolate Chocolate Chocolate Company use a contractual distribution system that requires franchisees to follow the franchisors' rules and procedures. How does such a system ensure consistent quality and level of service?

Contractual Distribution Systems

If a manufacturer can't buy retail stores, it can try to get retailers to sign a contract to cooperate with it. In a **contractual distribution system** members are bound to cooperate through contractual agreements. There are three forms of contractual systems:

1. *Franchise systems* such as McDonald's, KFC, Baskin-Robbins, and AAMCO. The franchisee agrees to all the rules, regulations, and procedures established by the franchisor. This results in the consistent quality and level of service you find in most franchised organizations.

2. *Wholesaler-sponsored chains* such as Ace Hardware and IGA food stores. Each store signs an agreement to use the same name, participate in chain promotions, and cooperate as a unified system of stores, even though each is independently owned and managed.

3. *Retail cooperatives* such as Associated Grocers. This arrangement is much like a wholesaler-sponsored chain except it is initiated by the retailers. The same degree of cooperation exists, and the stores remain independent. Normally in such a system, retailers agree to focus their purchases on one wholesaler, but cooperative retailers could also purchase a wholesale organization to ensure better service.

Administered Distribution Systems

If you were a producer, what would you do if you couldn't get retailers to sign an agreement to cooperate? You might manage all the marketing functions yourself, including display, inventory control, pricing, and promotion. A system in which producers manage all the marketing functions at the retail level is called an **administered distribution system**. Kraft does that for its cheeses. Scott does it for its seed and other lawn care products. Retailers cooperate with producers in such systems because they get a great deal of free help. All the retailer has to do is ring up the sale.

Supply Chains

A **supply chain** (or **value chain**) consists of all the linked activities various organizations must perform to move goods and services from the source of raw materials to ultimate consumers. A supply chain is longer than a channel of distribution because it includes links from suppliers to manufacturers, whereas the channel of distribution begins with manufacturers.[14] Channels of distribution are part of the overall supply chain (see Figure 15.6).

Included in the supply chain are farmers, miners, suppliers of all kinds (parts, equipment, supplies), manufacturers, wholesalers, and retailers. **Supply-chain management** is the process of managing the movement of raw materials, parts, work in progress, finished goods, and related information through all the organizations in the supply chain; managing the return of such goods if necessary; and recycling materials when appropriate.[15]

One complex supply chain is that for the automaker Kia's Sorento model. The Sorento is assembled in South Korea and made of over 30,000 components from all over the world. The shock and front-loading system is from AF Sachs AG, the front-wheel drive is from BorgWarner, and the tires are from Michelin. Airbags are sometimes flown in from Swedish company Autoliv Inc., which makes them in Utah. As you can see, supply-chain management is

administered distribution system
A distribution system in which producers manage all of the marketing functions at the retail level.

supply chain (value chain)
The sequence of linked activities that must be performed by various organizations to move goods from the sources of raw materials to ultimate consumers.

supply-chain management
The process of managing the movement of raw materials, parts, work in progress, finished goods, and related information through all the organizations involved in the supply chain; managing the return of such goods, if necessary; and recycling materials when appropriate.

figure 15.6

THE SUPPLY CHAIN

REACHING BEYOND
our borders

The Global Supply Chain for Services

It is easy to imagine the supply chain for parts and materials that go into goods. For example, you can easily imagine components traveling from Thailand, the Philippines, Malaysia, and Taiwan to a factory in China where they are assembled before being sold as iPods or iPad 2s in an Apple store in New York. In the future, it may be more important to study and understand the supply chain for services. Imagine call centers as part of the service supply chain. They are relatively easy to establish and most of us have experienced talking to someone on the phone from Asia when we've had technology problems. Now imagine outsourcing other services such as the programming of software, reviewing legal documents, processing expense reports and the like.

Much movie animation is now taking place in the Philippines, and companies in China are providing research and development services. One article stated, "We're heading for a day when a Malaysian architect will sketch out a new office tower for London, a Philippine architect will prepare detailed renderings, and a Chinese engineer will assess the structural soundness of the design. Or a specialist firm in Bangalore will administer health benefits for a Kansas company." The competition among foreign suppliers is intense, including the need to find workers with strong language skills. Those countries that excel in providing supply chains for goods (e.g., China) may not be the same as those providing expertise in services (e.g., India). Of course, one of the countries that could become a leader in supplying supply-chain services is the United States. One important step is to make supply chains secure. The 2011 disasters in Japan showed people that the supply chain is only as good as the weakest link.

Sources: Joseph Sternberg, "Now Comes the Global Revolution in Services," *The Wall Street Journal,* February 10, 2011; Janet Napolitano, "How to Secure the Global Supply Chain," *The Wall Street Journal,* January 6, 2011; and Bruce Einhorn, Tim Culpan and Alan Ohnsman, "Now, A Weak Link in the Supply Chain," *Bloomberg Businessweek,* March 21–March 27, 2011.

---

interfirm and international.[16] Increasingly, it also involves services. To learn about supply chains and services, see the nearby Reaching Beyond Our Borders box.

Companies like SAP, i2, and Oracle have developed software to coordinate the movement of goods and information so that producers can translate consumer wants into products with the least amount of materials, inventory, and time. Firms can move parts and information so smoothly, they look like one firm.

Computers make such links possible. Naturally, the systems are quite complex and expensive, but they can pay for themselves in the long run because of inventory savings, customer service improvement, and responsiveness to market changes. Because such systems are so effective and efficient, they are sometimes called *value chains* instead of supply chains.[17]

Not all supply chains are as efficient as they can be. Some companies have struggled with high distribution costs, including the cost of gas, inefficient truck routes, and excess inventory.[18] The complexity of supply-chain management often leads firms to outsource the whole process to experts that know how to integrate it. Richardson Electronics of La Fox, Illinois, does business in 125 countries with 37 different currencies. It relies on Oracle's PeopleSoft Supply Chain Management and Financial Management solutions. Oracle's PeopleSoft also provides financial help, making it easier and less expensive to ship goods anywhere in the world and be sure of payment. Outsourcing is on the rise as more firms realize how complex distribution is.

Outsourcing this function can have serious consequences as companies learned when they found lead paint in toys and contaminants in the drug Heparin.[19] Cardinal Health, the nation's second largest drug distributor, became much more successful when the CEO reorganized the supply chain.[20] All companies must be careful to evaluate each of the components of the supply chain to make sure the whole system is sustainable.[21] Emphasis today is focused on "green" technology because so much of what affects the environment is caused by distribution.[22]

LEARNING goal **7**

Describe logistics and outline how intermediaries manage the transportation and storage of goods.

LOGISTICS: GETTING GOODS TO CONSUMERS EFFICIENTLY

Shipping costs have risen dramatically in recent years. When shipping from country to country, it is often impossible to use trucks or trains because the goods have to travel over water. Shipping by air is often prohibitively expensive, which sometimes narrows the choice to moving goods by ship. But how do you get the goods to the ship—and from the ship to the buyer? How do you keep costs low enough to make exchanges beneficial for you and your customers? And how do you handle foreign trade duties and taxes? Distributing goods globally is complicated. As transportation and distribution have grown more complex, marketers have responded by developing more sophisticated systems.

To better manage customs problems, for instance, many turn to web-based trade compliance systems. Firms like TradePoint and Xporta determine what paperwork is needed, cross-checking their databases for information about foreign trade duties and taxes, U.S. labor law restrictions, and federal regulations from the Food and Drug Administration or the Bureau of Alcohol, Tobacco, and Firearms. In other words, they manage logistics.[23]

Logistics is the planning, implementing, and controlling of the physical flow of materials, final goods, and related information from points of origin to

logistics
The marketing activity that involves planning, implementing, and controlling the physical flow of materials, final goods, and related information from points of origin to points of consumption to meet customer requirements at a profit.

How do you move heavy raw materials like timber from one country to another? This photo shows some of the firms engaged in the logistics process. A trucking firm brings the logs to a dock where huge cranes lift them into the hold of a ship. The ship must be unloaded and the logs put on another truck to travel to a processing plant. Why is managing the logistics process a key to survival in some industries?

inbound logistics
The area of logistics that involves bringing raw materials, packaging, other goods and services, and information from suppliers to producers.

materials handling
The movement of goods within a warehouse, from warehouses to the factory floor, and from the factory floor to various workstations.

outbound logistics
The area of logistics that involves managing the flow of finished products and information to business buyers and ultimate consumers (people like you and me).

reverse logistics
The area of logistics that involves bringing goods back to the manufacturer because of defects or for recycling materials.

points of consumption to meet customer requirements at a profit. **Inbound logistics** brings raw materials, packaging, other goods and services, and information from suppliers to producers.

Materials handling is the movement of goods within a warehouse, from warehouses to the factory floor, and from the factory floor to various workstations. *Factory processes* change raw materials and parts and other inputs into outputs, such as finished goods like shoes, cars, and clothes.

Outbound logistics manages the flow of finished products and information to business buyers and ultimately to consumers like you and me. **Reverse logistics** brings goods back to the manufacturer because of defects or for recycling materials.[24]

Logistics is as much about the movement of *information* as it is about the movement of goods. Customer wants and needs must flow through the system all the way to suppliers and must do so in real time. Information must also flow down through the system with no delay. That, of course, demands sophisticated hardware and software. One company in India, Fabindia (a seller of hand-woven garments and home furnishings), ensures close relationships with its suppliers by having its suppliers become shareholders.

Third-party logistics is the use of outside firms to help move goods from here to there. It is part of the trend to outsource functions your firm cannot do more efficiently than outside firms.[25] The 3PLs (third-party logistics providers) that have superior capability in business intelligence and are proactively sharing that knowledge are the ones who will grow in the future.[26] Greatwide Logistics Services, for example, does business with six of the top 10 grocery retailers and wholesalers in the United States.[27]

Texas Instruments (TI) is one of the world's largest makers of silicon chips. About 75 percent of its semiconductor products move through its distribution network. The company uses a regional distribution center in Singapore to serve customers in Asia; one in Dallas to serve North America; one in Utrecht, the Netherlands, to serve Europe; and one in Tsubuka, Japan, to serve markets in that country. TI uses a 3PL service to handle the day-to-day operations of those warehouses. Moving goods from one place to another is a major part of logistics.

How do you get products to people around the world after the sale? What are your options? You could send goods by truck, by train, ship, or pipeline. You could use a shipping specialist, such as UPS, FedEx, or the U.S. Postal Service, but often that is expensive, especially for large items. Nonetheless, some of the most sophisticated marketers outsource the distribution process to such specialists.[28] All transportation modes can be evaluated on basic service criteria: cost, speed, dependability, flexibility, frequency, and reach. Figure 15.7 compares the various transportation modes on these criteria.

figure 15.7

COMPARING TRANSPORTATION MODES
Combining trucks with railroads lowers cost and increases the number of locations reached. The same is true when combining trucks with ships. Combining trucks with airlines speeds goods over long distances and gets them to almost any location.

MODE	COST	SPEED	ON-TIME DEPENDABILITY	FLEXIBILITY HANDLING PRODUCTS	FREQUENCY OF SHIPMENTS	REACH
Railroad	Medium	Slow	Medium	High	Low	High
Trucks	High	Fast	High	Medium	High	Highest
Pipeline	Low	Medium	Highest	Lowest	Highest	Lowest
Ships (water)	Lowest	Slowest	Lowest	Highest	Lowest	Low
Airplane	Highest	Fastest	Low	Low	Medium	Medium

Railroads carry over a third of all goods shipped within the United States and are expected to remain a dominant transportation mode. What are some of the advantages of shipping by rail, for both large and small producers?

Trains Are Great for Large Shipments

The largest percentage of goods in the United States (by volume) is shipped by rail. As a whole, the rail industry carries about 43 percent of all freight (as measured in ton miles), but uses only 7 percent of the total energy used to move freight.[29] Railroad shipment is best for bulky items such as coal, wheat, automobiles, and heavy equipment. In *piggyback* shipping, a truck trailer is detached from the cab, loaded onto a railroad flatcar, and taken to a destination where it will be offloaded, attached to a truck, and driven to the customer's plant. Railroads should continue to hold their own in competition with other modes of transportation. They offer a relatively energy-efficient way to move goods and could experience significant gains if fuel prices climb.

A company may not ship enough goods to think of using a railroad. Such smaller manufacturers or marketers can get good rates and service by using a **freight forwarder**, which puts many small shipments together to create a single large one that can be transported cost-effectively by truck or train. Some freight forwarders also offer warehousing, customs assistance, and other services along with pickup and delivery. You can see the benefits of such a company to a smaller seller. A freight forwarder is just one of many distribution specialists that have emerged to help marketers move goods from one place to another.

freight forwarder
An organization that puts many small shipments together to create a single large shipment that can be transported cost-effectively to the final destination.

Trucks Are Good for Small Shipments to Remote Locations

The second largest surface transportation mode is motor vehicles (trucks and vans). As Figure 15.7 shows, trucks reach more locations than trains and can deliver almost any commodity door-to-door.

You could buy your own truck to make deliveries, but for widespread delivery you can't beat trucking specialists. Like freight forwarders, they have emerged to supply one important marketing function—transporting goods. Railroads have joined with trucking firms to further the process of piggybacking with 20-foot-high railroad cars, called double stacks, that carry two truck trailers, one on top of the other.

When fuel prices rise, trucking companies look for ways to cut costs. The newest measure of transportation from farm to consumer is the *carbon cost*. Some argue that the fewer miles food travels, the better for the environment, but that may not always be true.

Water Transportation Is Inexpensive but Slow

When sending goods overseas, often the least expensive way is by ship. Obviously, ships are slower than ground or air transportation, so water transportation isn't appropriate for goods that need to be delivered quickly. There was a huge dropoff in shipping when oil prices skyrocketed, improved somewhat when oil prices came down, and dropped off again when oil prices rose again. Water transport is local as well as international. If you live near the Mississippi River, you've likely seen towboats hauling as many as 30 barges at a time, with a cargo of up to 35,000 tons. On smaller rivers, towboats can haul about eight barges, carrying up to 20,000 tons—that's the equivalent of four 100-car railroad trains. Add to that Great Lakes shipping, shipping from coast to coast and along the coasts, and international shipments, and water transportation takes on a new dimension as a key transportation mode. When truck trailers are placed on ships to travel long distances at lower rates, it's called *fishyback* (see the explanation of piggyback above). When they are placed in airplanes, by the way, that's *birdyback*.

Pipelines Are Fast and Efficient

One transportation mode we don't often observe is pipeline. Pipelines primarily transport water, petroleum, and petroleum products—but a lot more products than you may imagine are shipped by pipelines. For example, coal can be sent by pipeline by first crushing it and mixing it with water.

Air Transportation Is Fast but Expensive

Today, only a small proportion of shipping goes by air. Nonetheless, air transportation is a critical factor in many industries, carrying everything from small packages to luxury cars and elephants. Its primary benefit is speed. No firms know this better than FedEx and UPS. As just two of several competitors vying for the fast-delivery market, FedEx and UPS have used air transport to expand into global markets.

The air freight industry is starting to focus on global distribution. Emery has been an industry pioneer in establishing specialized sales and operations teams aimed at serving the distribution needs of specific industries. KLM Royal Dutch Airlines has cargo/passenger planes that handle high-profit items such as diplomatic pouches and medical supplies. Specializing in such cargo has enabled KLM to compete with FedEx, TNT, and DHL.

Intermodal Shipping

intermodal shipping
The use of multiple modes of transportation to complete a single long-distance movement of freight.

Intermodal shipping uses multiple modes of transportation—highway, air, water, rail—to complete a single long-distance movement of freight. Services that specialize in intermodal shipping are known as intermodal marketing companies. Today, railroads are merging with each other and with other transportation companies to offer intermodal distribution.

Picture an automobile made in Japan for sale in the United States. It's shipped by truck to a loading dock, and from there moved by ship to a port in the United States. It may be placed on another truck and then taken to a railroad station for loading on a train that will take it across the country, to again be loaded on a truck for delivery to a local dealer. No doubt you've seen automobiles being hauled across the country by train and by truck. Now imagine that one integrated shipping firm handled all that movement. That's what intermodal shipping is all about.

The Storage Function

The preceding sections detailed the various ways of shipping goods once the company has sold them. But that's only the first step in understanding the system that moves goods from one point to another. Another important part of a complex logistics system is storage.

Buyers want goods delivered quickly. That means marketers must have goods available in various parts of the country ready to be shipped locally when ordered. A good percentage of the total cost of logistics is for storage. This includes the cost of the storage warehouse (distribution facility) and its operation, plus movement of goods within the warehouse.

There are two major kinds of warehouses: storage and distribution. A *storage warehouse* holds products for a relatively long time. Seasonal goods such as lawn mowers are kept in such a warehouse. *Distribution warehouses* are facilities used to gather and redistribute products. You can picture a distribution warehouse for FedEx or UPS handling thousands of packages in a very short time. The packages are picked up at places throughout the country and then processed for reshipment at these centers. General Electric's combination storage and distribution facility in San Gabriel Valley, California, gives you a feel for how large such buildings can be. It is nearly half a mile long and 465 feet wide—that's enough to hold almost 27 football fields.

Tracking Goods

How do producers keep track of where their goods are at any given time? As we noted in Chapter 14, companies use Universal Product Codes—the familiar black-and-white bar codes and a preset number—to keep track of inventory. Bar codes got a big lift when camera phone apps made it possible to compare prices and read reviews about products from different suppliers.[30]

RFID tags are being used in all kinds of situations, from the movement of goods to the tracking of livestock. RFID tags in products like these jeans helps retailers and producers track products from the suppliers' docks through the retailers' doors. How can RFID tags help you avoid losing your luggage, car keys, and other things?

Radio frequency identification (RFID), which we also mentioned earlier, is newer technology that tags merchandise so that it can be tracked from its arrival on the supplier's docks to its exit through the retailer's door. Walmart, Target, and other organizations all plan to require suppliers to use RFID. Currently, RFID tags cost about 10 cents each, but the goal is to get the cost down to about 1 cent.

Few companies are more interested in tracking items than UPS, which now uses a mix of Bluetooth's short-range radio capability and wireless receivers to track merchandise. It claims the system is even better than RFID. The U.S. State Department is producing an electronic passport card as a substitute for booklet passports to be used by U.S. citizens who travel often to Canada, Mexico, and the Caribbean. It uses an RFID chip to provide data about the user. The card is very controversial, however, because some people believe it can be easily altered.

WHAT ALL THIS MEANS TO YOU

The life or death of a firm often depends on its ability to take orders, process orders, keep customers informed about the progress of their orders, get the goods out to customers quickly, handle returns, and manage any recycling issues. Some of the most exciting firms in the marketplace are those that assist in some aspect of supply-chain management.

What all this means to you is that many new jobs are becoming available in the exciting area of supply-chain management. These include jobs in distribution: trains, airplanes, trucks, ships, and pipelines. It also means jobs handling information flows between and among companies, including website development. Other jobs include processing orders, keeping track of inventory, following the path of products as they move from seller to buyer and back, recycling goods, and much more.

progress assessment

- What four systems have evolved to tie together members of the channel of distribution?
- How does logistics differ from distribution?
- What are inbound logistics, outbound logistics, and reverse logistics?

summary

Learning Goal 1. Explain the concept of marketing channels and their value.

- **What is a channel of distribution?**

A channel of distribution consists of a whole set of marketing intermediaries, such as agents, brokers, wholesalers, and retailers, that join together to transport and store goods in their path (or channel) from producers to consumers.

- **How do marketing intermediaries add value?**

Intermediaries perform certain marketing tasks—such as transporting, storing, selling, advertising, and relationship building—faster and more cheaply than most manufacturers could. Channels of distribution ensure communication flows and the flow of money and title to goods. They also help ensure that the right quantity and assortment of goods will be available when and where needed.

- **What are the principles behind the use of such intermediaries?**

Marketing intermediaries can be eliminated, but their activities can't. Without wholesalers and retailers, consumers would have to perform the tasks of transporting and storing goods, finding suppliers, and establishing communication with them. Intermediaries add costs to products, but these costs are usually more than offset by the values they create.

Learning Goal 2. Demonstrate how intermediaries perform the six marketing utilities.

- **How do intermediaries perform the six marketing utilities?**

A retail grocer may cut or trim meat, providing some form utility. But marketers are more often responsible for the five other utilities. They provide time utility by having goods available *when* people want them, and place utility by having goods *where* people want them. Possession utility makes it possible for people to own things and includes credit, delivery, installation, guarantees, and anything else that completes the sale. Marketers also inform consumers of the availability of goods and services with advertising, publicity, and other means. That provides information utility. Finally, marketers provide fast, friendly, and efficient service during and after the sale (service utility).

Learning Goal 3. Identify the types of wholesale intermediaries in the distribution system.

- **What is a wholesaler?**

A wholesaler is a marketing intermediary that sells to organizations and individuals, but not to final consumers.

- **What are some wholesale organizations that assist in the movement of goods from manufacturers to consumers?**

Merchant wholesalers are independently owned firms that take title to the goods they handle. *Rack jobbers* furnish racks or shelves full of merchandise to retailers, display products, and sell on consignment. *Cash-and-carry wholesalers* serve mostly small retailers with a limited assortment of products. *Drop shippers* solicit orders from retailers and other wholesalers and have the merchandise shipped directly from a producer to a buyer.

Learning Goal 4. Compare the distribution strategies retailers use.

- **What is a retailer?**

A retailer is an organization that sells to ultimate consumers. Marketers develop several strategies based on retailing.

- **What are three distribution strategies marketers use?**

Marketers use three basic distribution strategies: intensive (putting products in as many places as possible), selective (choosing only a few stores in a chosen market), and exclusive (using only one store in each market area).

Learning Goal 5. Explain the various kinds of nonstore retailing.

- **What are some of the forms of nonstore retailing?**

Nonstore retailing includes online marketing; telemarketing (marketing by phone); vending machines, kiosks, and carts (marketing by putting products in convenient locations, such as in the halls of shopping centers); direct selling (marketing by approaching consumers in their homes or places of work); multilevel marketing (marketing by setting up a system of salespeople who recruit other salespeople and help them to sell directly to customers); and direct marketing (direct mail and catalog sales). Telemarketing and online marketing are also forms of direct marketing.

Learning Goal 6. Explain the various ways to build cooperation in channel systems.

- **What are the four types of distribution systems?**

The four distribution systems that tie firms together are (1) *corporate systems,* in which all organizations in the channel are owned by one firm; (2) *contractual systems,* in which members are bound to cooperate through contractual agreements; (3) *administered systems,* in which all marketing functions at the retail level are managed by manufacturers; and (4) *supply chains,* in which the various firms in the supply chain are linked electronically to provide the most efficient movement of information and goods possible.

Learning Goal 7. Describe logistics and outline how intermediaries manage the transportation and storage of goods.

- **What is logistics?**

Logistics includes planning, implementing, and controlling the physical flow of materials, final goods, and related information from points of origin to points of consumption to meet customer requirements at a profit.

- **What is the difference between logistics and distribution?**

Distribution generally means transportation. Logistics is more complex. *Inbound logistics* brings raw materials, packaging, other goods and services, and information from suppliers to producers. *Materials handling* is the moving of goods from warehouses to the factory floor and to various workstations. *Outbound logistics* manages the flow of finished products and information to business buyers and ultimate consumers (people like you and me). *Reverse logistics* brings goods back to the manufacturer because of defects or for recycling materials.

- **What are the various transportation modes?**

Transportation modes include rail (for heavy shipments within the country or between bordering countries); trucks (for getting goods directly to consumers); ships (for slow, inexpensive movement of goods, often internationally); pipelines (for moving water and oil and other such goods); and airplanes (for shipping goods quickly).

- **What is intermodal shipping?**

Intermodal shipping uses multiple modes of transportation—highway, air, water, rail—to complete a single long-distance movement of freight.

- **What are the different kinds of warehouses?**

A storage warehouse stores products for a relatively long time. Distribution warehouses are used to gather and redistribute products.

key terms

critical thinking

1. Imagine that we have eliminated marketing intermediaries, and you need groceries and shoes. How would you find out where the shoes and groceries are? How far would you have to travel to get them? How much money do you think you'd save for your time and effort?

2. Which intermediary do you think is most important today and why? What changes are happening to companies in that area?

3. One scarce item in the future will be water. If you could think of an inexpensive way to get water from places of abundance to places where it is needed for drinking, farming, and other uses, you could become a wealthy marketing intermediary. Pipelines are an alternative, but could you also freeze the water and ship it by train or truck? Could you use ships to tow icebergs to warmer climates? What other means of transporting water might there be?

developing workplace skills

1. The six utilities of marketing are form, time, place, possession, information, and service. Give examples of organizations in your area that perform each of these functions.

2. Form small groups and diagram how Dole might get pineapples from a field in Thailand to a canning plant in California to a store near your college. Include the intermediaries and the forms of transportation each one might use.

3. Compare the merits of buying and selling goods in stores and over the Internet. What advantages do stores have? Has anyone in the class tried to sell anything on the Internet? How did he or she ship the product?

4. In class, discuss the differences between wholesaling and retailing and why retailing has more appeal for students considering jobs. Since fewer students seek jobs in wholesaling than in retailing, do you think wholesaling jobs may be easier to get?

5. One part of retailing is using auction sites like eBay to sell new and used merchandise. Form small groups and discuss group members' experiences using eBay. What tips have they learned? How do eBay users minimize the problems associated with shipping?

taking it to the net

Purpose

To examine how small businesses can learn to use the Internet to distribute their products directly to customers.

Exercise

Many small-business owners have no idea how to begin selling goods over the Internet. Several free websites have been developed to help them get started with tasks from setting up their site to doing online marketing, handling credit purchases, and more. Go to Homestead.com or BlueVoda.com and listen to the presentations they make. Search the Web to find other sources of help in designing your own website. Then answer the following questions:

1. How long do the websites say that it takes to get started?

2. Does the process seem easier or harder than you imagined?

3. Do you have questions that the websites did not answer?

4. What help are you given, if any, in planning how to ship your goods?

casing the web

To access the case "Multilevel Marketing," visit **www.mhhe.com/ubl0e**

video case

To access the video case featuring Netflix, visit **www.mhhe.com/ubl0e**

USING Effective Promotions

LEARNING goals

After you have read and studied this chapter, you should be able to

1 Identify the new and traditional tools that make up the promotion mix.

2 Contrast the advantages and disadvantages of various advertising media, including the Internet and social media.

3 Illustrate the steps of the B2B and B2C selling processes.

4 Describe the role of the public relations department, and show how publicity fits in that role.

5 Assess the effectiveness of various forms of sales promotion, including sampling.

6 Show how word of mouth, e-mail marketing, viral marketing, blogging, podcasting, and mobile marketing work.

After falling out of fashion in the free-spending 1990s and early 2000s, deal hunting returned with a vengeance when the recession hit. In this digital age, cost-conscious shoppers have far more options than just print coupons to aid them in their quest for value. Deal sites like Groupon combine aspects of social networking with clearance-level discounts, driving foot traffic to local businesses and giving consumers more bang for their buck.

Founded in 2008 by Andrew Mason, Groupon posts a single local deal every day. Typical promotions include coupons for $40 worth of food at an area restaurant for only $20. In order for the coupon to become valid, Groupon requires that a certain number of people first buy into the deal. Businesses hope that in the long run the deal will convert bargain hunters into lifelong customers, all while bringing in a healthy number of immediate sales. Groupon splits the revenue from the purchased coupons with merchants, claiming as much as 40 to 50 percent of each deal.

Such high commissions turned Groupon into a dot-com goldmine. In fact, it grew faster than any Web company in history, ballooning from $740 million in revenue in 2010 to approximately $4 billion in 2011. The company was valued at $1.4 billion at the start of 2010 and quickly grew to $3 billion by November. Google offered to buy the company for $6 billion in December 2010, but Mason astonished the market by rejecting the offer. Now with talks of an initial public offering (first public sale of stock) on the rise, Groupon could be worth as much as $25 billion when it finally reaches the open market.

The one constant throughout Groupon's turbulently successful initial years has been its founder and CEO Andrew Mason. As an idealistic public policy grad student at University of Chicago, Mason first tried his hand at crowdsourcing (an open call to interested people to contribute ideas or perform tasks) with a website called The Point. The idea of the site was to gather large groups of consumers to lobby companies and government officials for various policy changes, such as making Election Day a national holiday. Although The Point attracted few users, Mason recognized that he could harness the same technology to bring clusters of bargain hunting customers to local businesses' doorsteps. Within 13 months of The Point's conversion to Groupon, Mason attracted $1.3 billion of venture capital investment.

Much of Mason's success can be attributed to Groupon's simplicity. Unfortunately, that simplicity is also responsible for Groupon's increasing number of competitors. Several high profile startups such as Tippr and the Amazon-backed LivingSocial basically mirror the Groupon model. While these sites haven't experienced the same explosive popularity, they nevertheless command a big enough share of the market to worry Mason.

In response to competitors, Mason and his staff introduced a new venture dubbed Groupon Now. As opposed to the regular site's single daily deal, Groupon Now offers a variety of discounts filtered through a smartphone app. When users activate the app they are greeted with two buttons: "I'm bored" and "I'm hungry." If they select the latter, a map will pop up with a selection of restaurants in the area offering deals. The catch is that the coupons are only valid at certain times during the day. This way, restaurants can fill up tables during off times when they aren't busy. Mason is optimistic about Groupon Now, predicting that it will bring in $1 billion in revenue by the end of its first year. On the other hand, some skeptical insiders wonder if merchants will want to handle even more discount-related hassles. Still, as with all forms of promotion, only time will tell whether or not Mason's service will succeed.

In this chapter, we explore all the traditional and new elements of promotion. We'll explain how marketers use different media for promotion and the advantages and disadvantages of each. We'll compare B2C and B2B promotions and look at the role of public relations. Throughout the chapter we'll pay particular attention to promotional uses of electronic media like blogging, social networking, and podcasts.

Getting to Know

X *Andrew Mason*

CEO of Groupon

Sources: Brad Stone and Douglas MacMillan, "Are Four Words Worth $25 Billion for Groupon?" *Bloomberg Businessweek,* March 17, 2011; Christopher Steiner, "The Next Web Phenom," *Forbes,* September 9, 2010; Jayne O'Donnell and Rachel Huggins, "Crave Coupons, Bargains? Group-Buying Sites Offer Deals," *USA Today,* May 14, 2010; Brad Stone and Douglas MacMillan, "When Groupon Dodged Google," *Bloomberg Businessweek,* December 8, 2010.

profile

LEARNING goal **1**

Identify the new and traditional tools that make up the promotion mix.

PROMOTION AND THE PROMOTION MIX

Promotion is one of the four Ps of marketing. As noted in Chapter 13, promotion consists of all the techniques sellers use to motivate people to buy their products or services. Both profit-making and nonprofit organizations use promotional techniques to communicate with people in their target market about goods and services, and to persuade them to participate in a marketing exchange.[1] Marketers use many different tools to promote their products.[2] Traditionally, those tools were advertising, personal selling, public relations, and sales promotion. Today they also include e-mail promotions, mobile promotions (those that use cell phones), social networking, blogging, podcasting, tweets, and more.[3] The Spotlight on Small Business box explores what happens when a small business seems too busy to do traditional marketing.

The combination of promotional tools an organization uses is called its **promotion mix;** see Figure 16.1. We show the product in the middle of the

promotion mix
The combination of promotional tools an organization uses.

figure 16.1

THE TRADITIONAL PROMOTION MIX

Fresh-Baked Promotion

Many entrepreneurs have little time for marketing because they spend nearly all of their time just keeping the business running. One of those entrepreneurs is Amy Scherber. She owns Amy's Bread in New York City. She has more than 100 employees in three retail stores. Baking bread is labor-intensive and doesn't leave much time for traditional marketing. Scherber says that she doesn't use a marketing company or a public relations firm. She does, however, build relationships with people—a major goal of promotion.

Scherber generates media attention by pitching story ideas to the *New York Times* and other publications. She doesn't send them press releases. Instead, she calls the editors who assign articles to see if they would be interested in a particular story. Why would the editors listen to her? Because some of them shop at her stores and she has developed relationships with them. She also attends food industry events where she mingles with reporters. Such contacts enable Scherber to know what editors would be interested in what stories.

Scherber has no advertising budget, but she invests $2,000 to $3,000 a year for printed materials such as T-shirts. Her employees also wear T-shirts, and customers sometimes buy them. Selling T-shirts is one more aspect of marketing. Selected as Alumnus of the Year by her high school, Scherber maintains contact with that community. She also maintains contact with her college alumni to build relationships. As Scherber shows us, building customer relationships doesn't require fancy PR firms or expensive advertising to stay close to your customers.

Sources: Morey Stettner, "Do-It-Yourself Marketing Creates Surprising Results," *Investors Business Daily,* July 7, 2008; Craig Matsuda, "Yes, I Blog at the Office," *Entrepreneur,* March 2010; and www.amysbread.com, accessed April 2011.

figure to illustrate that the product itself can also be a promotional tool, such as when marketers give away free samples.

Integrated marketing communication (IMC) combines the promotional tools into one comprehensive, unified promotional strategy. With IMC, marketers can create a positive brand image, meet the needs of the consumer, and meet the strategic marketing and promotional goals of the firm. Emphasis today is on integrating traditional media, like TV, with social media[4] or integrating print media with online sites.[5]

integrated marketing communication (IMC)
A technique that combines all the promotional tools into one comprehensive, unified promotional strategy.

1. Identify a target market. (Refer back to Chapter 13 for a discussion of segmentation and target marketing.)
2. Define the objectives for each element of the promotion mix. Goals should be clear and measurable.
3. Determine a promotional budget. The budgeting process will clarify how much can be spent on advertising, personal selling, and other promotional efforts.
4. Develop a unifying message. The goal of an integrated promotional program is to have one clear message communicated by advertising, public relations, sales, and every other promotional effort.
5. Implement the plan. Advertisements, blogs, and other promotional efforts must be scheduled to complement efforts being made by public relations and sales promotion. Salespeople should have access to all materials to optimize the total effort.
6. Evaluate effectiveness. Measuring results depends greatly on clear objectives. Each element of the promotional mix should be evaluated separately, and an overall measure should be taken as well. It is important to learn what is working and what is not.

figure 16.2

STEPS IN A PROMOTIONAL CAMPAIGN

Figure 16.2 on p. 437 shows the six steps in a typical promotional campaign. Let's begin exploring promotional tools by looking at advertising—the most visible tool.

Figure 16.2 on p. 437

LEARNING goal 2

Contrast the advantages and disadvantages of various advertising media, including the Internet and social media.

ADVERTISING: INFORMING, PERSUADING, AND REMINDING

advertising
Paid, nonpersonal communication through various media by organizations and individuals who are in some way identified in the advertising message.

Advertising is paid, nonpersonal communication through various media by organizations and individuals who are in some way *identified in the message.* Identification of the sender separates advertising from *propaganda,* which is nonpersonal communication that *does not have an identified sponsor.* Propaganda is often distributed by the government in various countries. Figure 16.3 lists various categories of advertising. Take a minute to look it over; you'll see there's a lot more to advertising than just television commercials.

It's also easy to appreciate the impact of advertising spending on the U.S. economy; see Figure 16.4. Total ad volume exceeds $241 billion yearly. Note that direct mail is the number one medium, with expenditures over $52

Figure 16.3

MAJOR CATEGORIES OF ADVERTISING
Different kinds of advertising are used by various organizations to reach different market targets.

- *Retail advertising*—advertising to consumers by various retail stores such as supermarkets and shoe stores.
- *Trade advertising*—advertising to wholesalers and retailers by manufacturers to encourage them to carry their products.
- *Business-to-business advertising*—advertising from manufacturers to other manufacturers. A firm selling motors to auto companies would use business-to-business advertising.
- *Institutional advertising*—advertising designed to create an attractive image for an organization rather than for a product. "We Care about You" at Giant Food is an example. "Virginia Is for Lovers" and "I ❤ New York" were two institutional campaigns by government agencies.
- *Product advertising*—advertising for a good or service to create interest among consumer, commercial, and industrial buyers.
- *Advocacy advertising*—advertising that supports a particular view of an issue (e.g., an ad in support of gun control or against nuclear power plants). Such advertising is also known as cause advertising.
- *Comparison advertising*—advertising that compares competitive products. For example, an ad that compares two different cold care products' speed and benefits is a comparative ad.
- *Interactive advertising*—customer-oriented communication that enables customers to choose the information they receive, such as interactive video catalogs that let customers select which items to view.
- *Online advertising*—advertising messages that appear on computers as people visit different websites.
- *Mobile advertising*—advertising that reaches people on their cell phones.

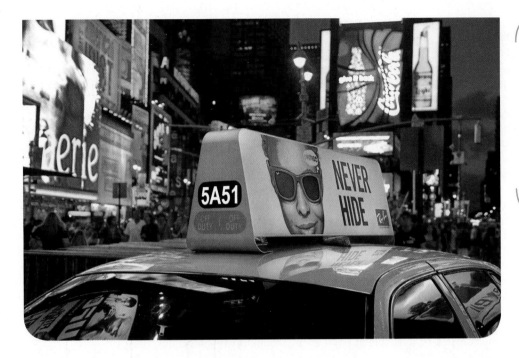

Advertising seems to be everywhere as we go about our daily lives. How many advertisements can you spot in this photo? Can the noise created by so many ads interfere with the messages the advertisers are trying to communicate?

billion. Would you have guessed that direct mail is number one? Broadcast TV is number two, with expenditures of over $36 billion. Cable networks bring in another $27 billion. Note that the Internet is at $25 billion. That's double what it was in 2005. The leading advertising agencies still take the bulk of promotional dollars and still have a major impact on consumers.[6]

How do we, as consumers, benefit from these advertising expenditures? First, ads are informative. Direct mail is full of information about products, prices, features, store policies, and more; so is newspaper advertising. Newspaper advertising is down because more and more people are getting their news on mobile devices.[7]

Second, not only does advertising inform us, but the money advertisers spend for commercial time pays the production costs of TV and radio programs. Advertising also covers the major costs of producing newspapers and magazines. Subscriptions and newsstand revenues cover only mailing and promotional costs. Figure 16.5 compares the advantages and disadvantages

RANK	MEDIUM	PROJECTED ADVERTISING SPENDING
1	Direct mail	52.3
2	Broadcast TV (network, spot, synd.)	36.8
3	Newspaper	23.4
4	Cable TV networks	27.0
5	Radio	15.9
6	Yellow Pages	11.9
7	Consumer magazine	9.1
8	Internet	25.3
9	All other	39.7
Total		241.4 billion

Source: www.businessinsider.com, 2011.

figure 16.4

ESTIMATED U.S ADVERTISING SPENDING BY MEDIUM, 2010 (IN BILLIONS OF DOLLARS)

MEDIUM	ADVANTAGES	DISADVANTAGES
Newspapers	Good coverage of local markets; ads can be placed quickly; high consumer acceptance; ads can be clipped and saved.	Ads compete with other features in paper; poor color; ads get thrown away with paper (short life span).
Television	Uses sight, sound, and motion; reaches all audiences; high attention with no competition from other material.	High cost; short exposure time; takes time to prepare ads. Digital video recorders skip over ads.
Radio	Low cost; can target specific audiences; very flexible; good for local marketing.	People may not listen to ad; depends on one sense (hearing); short exposure time; audience can't keep ad.
Magazines	Can target specific audiences; good use of color; long life of ad; ads can be clipped and saved.	Inflexible; ads often must be placed weeks before publication; cost is relatively high.
Outdoor	High visibility and repeat exposures; low cost; local market focus.	Limited message; low selectivity of audience.
Direct mail	Best for targeting specific markets; very flexible; ad can be saved.	High cost; consumers may reject ad as junk mail; must conform to post office regulations.
Yellow Pages–type advertising	Great coverage of local markets; widely used by consumers; available at point of purchase.	Competition with other ads; cost may be too high for very small businesses.
Internet	Inexpensive global coverage; available at any time; interactive.	Customers may leave the site before buying.
Mobile advertising	Great reach among younger shoppers.	Easy to ignore, avoid.
Social media	Wonderful communication tools.	Time drain.

figure 16.5

ADVANTAGES AND DISADVANTAGES OF VARIOUS ADVERTISING MEDIA
The most effective media are often very expensive. The inexpensive media may not reach your market. The goal is to use the medium that can reach your desired market most effectively and efficiently.

for marketers of various advertising media. Notice that newspapers, radio, and the Yellow Pages are especially attractive to local advertisers.

Marketers must choose which media will best reach the audience they desire. Radio advertising, for example, is less expensive than TV advertising and often reaches people when they have few other distractions, such as while they're driving. Radio is thus especially effective at selling *services* people don't usually read about in print media—banking, mortgages, continuing education, and brokerage services, to name a few. On the other hand, radio has become so commercial-ridden that many people are paying to switch to commercial-free satellite radio. Marketers also search for other places to put advertising, such as on video screens mounted in elevators. Have you noticed ads on park benches and grocery carts? You've certainly seen them on websites you visit.

Mobile marketing via cell phones started out mostly as text messages, but now Starbucks can send signals to your phone as you approach the store, reminding you to stop in for a latte. Kraft Foods developed the iPhone Assistant, an iPhone application that serves up recipes for users—recipes made with Kraft products. Other retailers use e-mail advertisements to build brand awareness and drive people to their stores or websites.[8] Social media in general is growing so fast that marketers can hardly keep up.[9] Take the restaurant industry for example. Starbucks is number one in social media with 12 million Twitter followers. It registers 19.3 million "likes" on Facebook. McDonald's has over 80,000 followers with Twitter and 7 million friends on Facebook.[10]

Another way to get more impact from advertising is to appeal to the interest in green marketing among consumers and businesses.[11] A brief glance through magazines and the business press reveals all kinds of new appeals to sustainability and carbon-cutting measures. In the next sections, we'll look in more depth at some other popular advertising media.

Television Advertising

Television offers many advantages to national advertisers, but it's expensive. Thirty seconds of advertising during the Super Bowl telecast cost about $3 million.[12] How many bottles of beer or automobiles must a company sell to pay for such commercials? A lot, but few media besides television allow advertisers to reach so many people with such impact, although not all ads are equally effective.[13]

Despite what you may read about the growth of alternative promotional tools, TV advertising is still a dominant medium.[14] Digital video recorders (DVRs) enable consumers to skip the ads on TV. This may make TV less attractive to advertisers unless commercials get so much better that people *want* to watch them. New program delivery systems, such as video on demand, make it even more difficult for TV advertisers to catch consumers' eyes. Thus marketers are demanding better and more accurate measures of TV advertising's effectiveness, and many are switching to social media as a result.[15]

Product Placement

TV advertising isn't limited to traditional commercials; sometimes the products appear in the programs themselves. With **product placement**, advertisers pay to put their products into TV shows and movies where the audience will see them. One classic example of product placement is the trail of Reese's Pieces in the movie E.T.[16] Did you ever notice the Coca-Cola cups on the judges' table on *American Idol?* Many placements are more subtle, like the wheeled luggage from Zuca Inc. that appeared on the TV show *CSI.*

The latest wrinkle in product placement puts virtual products into video games. If you're a gamer, you've seen in-game ads, like ads around the court in

product placement
Putting products into TV shows and movies where they will be seen.

Product placement is often subtle. You can see it in the products used in movies like the ones shown on the table in this one. The goal is to influence you to want that product yourself. What product placements have you noticed in your favorite TV shows and movies?

basketball games. New technology allows vending machines in racing games to be branded and rebranded over time, depending on whether Coke, Pepsi, Exxon, or Shell has purchased ad time.[17]

Infomercials

An **infomercial** is a full-length TV program devoted exclusively to promoting a particular good or service. Infomercials have been successful because they show the product and how it works in great detail. They are the equivalent of sending your very best salespeople to a person's home and having them use all of their techniques to make the sale: drama, demonstration, testimonials, graphics, and more. Because of their success, infomercials are expected to rise to over $170 billion in 2014.[18]

Products that have earned over $1 billion in sales through infomercials include Proactiv (acne cream), Soloflex, Total Gym, Bowflex (exercise machines), the George Foreman Grill, and Ron Popeil's Rotisserie and Grill. Some products, such as personal development seminars, real estate programs, and workout tapes, are hard to sell without showing people a sample of their contents and using testimonials. Have you purchased any products that you saw in an infomercial?

Online Advertising

When marketers advertise on an online search engine such as Google or Bing, they can reach the people they most want to reach—consumers researching vacations, exploring the car market, or checking stocks. One goal of online advertising is to get potential customers to a website where they can learn more about the company and its products—and the company can learn more about them.[19] If users click through an ad to get to the website, the company has an opportunity to gather their names, addresses, opinions, and preferences.[20] Online advertising thus brings customers and companies together. Another advantage is that it enables advertisers to see just how many people have clicked on a commercial and how much of it each potential customer has read or watched. It has been one of the fastest-growing parts of advertising. Spending on online advertising and social media is expected to increase greatly in the next three years.[21]

E-mail marketing has become a big component of online advertising. However, advertisers have to be careful not to overuse it because customers don't like to see too many promotional e-mails in their in-boxes. Thus some companies use e-mail as an alert to send users to other social media such as Facebook and Twitter. The nearby Social Media in Business box discusses the link between social media and other promotional tools in more depth.[22]

Interactive promotion allows marketers to go beyond a *monologue,* in which sellers try to persuade buyers to buy things, to a *dialogue,* in which buyers and sellers work together to create mutually beneficial exchange relationships. Garden.com is an online retailer of garden products and services.[23] Dionn Schaffner, the company's vice president of marketing, once said that gardening is an information-intensive activity. Customers obviously want to learn about gardening, but they also seek inspiration by communicating with fellow gardeners and experts. Garden.com's answer to such customers has been to include a forum on its website where people can chat with each other and ask gardening questions.

Technology has greatly improved customer communications.[24] Many companies provide online videos, chat rooms, and other services in a *virtual*

Social Media Complements Other Promotions

store where customers are able to talk to each other, ask questions of salespeople, examine goods and services, and buy products. The Internet is fundamentally changing the way marketers are working with customers. Notice we said *working with* rather than *promoting to*. Marketers now want to *build relationships* with customers over time. That means carefully listening to what consumers want, tracking their purchases, providing them with excellent service, and giving them access to a full range of information.[25]

Here's how online interactive promotion helped one traditional marketer stay competitive. Vita-Mix Corporation makes expensive food blenders. In the beginning, when there was little competition, the company relied mostly on 140 independent contractors to sell the blenders at state fairs, food events, and

Online advertising is the fastest-growing type of advertising and can offer more than just a list of products and their features. For example, Tissot will introduce a new 3-D reality application on its website that allows customers to try on a 3-D virtual watch and interact with its features. Do you think some types of products or services are promoted more effectively online than others?

stores. Eventually Vita-Mix began using infomercials, and sales passed $100 million. Then commercial blender maker K-Tec in Orem, Utah, began going after Vita-Mix's consumer market. K-Tec promoted its new product on a website that showed the CEO blending things like golf balls, a rotisserie chicken, and, believe it or not, an Apple iPhone. The video eventually got on YouTube, and sales of this new competitor took off. Vita-Mix successfully responded by creating its own site called Vita-Village, showing how to create healthy meals and snacks, and a social network that enables blender fans to share recipes.[26] Online marketers should strive to make sure that their efforts fit into an overall multimedia strategy.

Using Social Media to Monitor Ad Effectiveness

Dr Pepper has an 8.5 million fan base on Facebook. Now the company can track and test users who say they "like" the soft drink. The company posts two messages daily on a Facebook fan page and then monitors the results. The company can thus measure how many times a message is reviewed, how many times it is shared, and what the fan response is. The company believes that if it is to engage in social media, it has to listen and understand the nature of the conversation, the volume, and the topics being discussed. In short, social media, such as Facebook and Twitter, have made it possible for organizations to test ads before airing them on traditional media like TV and to listen to the reasons why people like and dislike some messages.

It is best, if a company wants to establish a base with customers, to include top managers in the dialogue. For example, Richard Branson of Virgin Group Ltd and Tony Hsieh of Zappos tweet their customers.[27] Sherry Chris of Better Homes & Gardens Real Estate LLC spends two hours each day reading and contributing to Twitter, Facebook, LinkedIn, and Foursquare. Such involvement with customers has become a major part of many company's listening strategy. It may take time, but there is not a better way to learn about what customers are thinking and saying about your firm.

Many firms are allowing employees to use their personal phones for business purposes. That includes, of course, using Facebook, Twitter, and other social media. The nearby Making Ethical Decisions box explores some issues that may come up as a result.

Global Advertising

Global advertising requires the marketer to develop a single product and promotional strategy it can implement worldwide, like MasterCard's "Priceless" campaign. Certainly global advertising that's the same everywhere can save companies money in research and design. In some cases, however, promotions tailored to specific countries or regions may be more successful since each country or region has its own culture, language, and buying habits.

Some problems do arise when marketers use one campaign in all countries. When a Japanese company tried to use English words to name a popular drink, it came up with Pocari Sweat, not a

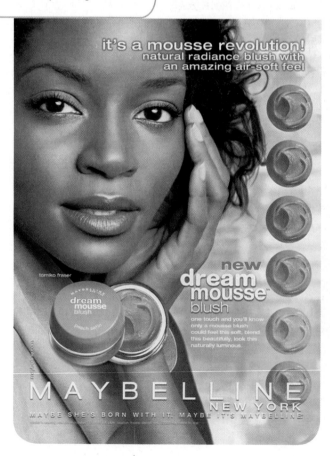

This Maybelline ad is designed for African-American women. There are many ads directed toward the Latina and Asian markets as well. What other groups are attractive candidates for targeted ads?

Electronic Ethics

Many companies let employees use their personal gadgets such as their smartphones to do their jobs. What happens, though, when a phone loaded with sensitive business documents gets lost? Most companies insist that workers use the password feature found in every smartphone. The password prevents other users from accessing any of the phone's basic functions. This is important because employees often store e-mails and attachments with company data on their phones.

Imagine that you have received personal information about fellow workers, including some of your bosses, on your phone. You know that the information could lead to discipline or firing of many of those workers and managers. You also know that other workers have received the same information. You are wondering what would be the ethical thing to do with such information. Should you pass it along to your immediate supervisor or not? What are the ethical issues involved? What would you do? What do you expect to be the consequences of your actions?

good image for most English-speaking people.[28] In England, the Ford Probe didn't go over too well because the word *probe* made people think of doctors' waiting rooms and medical examinations.[29] People in the United States may have difficulty with Krapp toilet paper from Sweden. But perhaps worse was the translation of Coors' slogan "Turn it loose," which became "Suffer from diarrhea." Clairol introduced its curling iron, the Mist Stick, to the German market, not realizing *mist* in German can mean "manure." A T-shirt promoting the Pope's visit to Miami read *la papa,* which in Spanish means "the potato." (It should have said *el Papa.*) As you can see, getting the words right in international advertising is tricky and critical. So is understanding the culture, which calls for researching each country, designing appropriate ads, and testing them.

In the United States, some groups are large enough and different enough to call for specially designed promotions. Masterfoods USA, for example, tried to promote dulce de leche (caramel) M&M's to the Hispanic market in cities like Los Angeles, Miami, and San Antonio. The promotion was not successful, however. Knowing the market had potential, Masterfoods changed course and bought a candy company called the Lucas Group, which has had success selling such candies as Felix Sour Fruit and Lucas Hot and Spicy in Mexico. Masterfoods had much more success selling those candies in the United States.[30]

Many marketers today are moving from globalism (one ad for everyone in the world) to regionalism (specific ads for each country or for specific groups within a country). In the future, marketers will prepare more custom-designed promotions to reach even smaller audiences—audiences as small as one person.[31] The Reaching Beyond Our Borders box on p. 446 presents an example of how advertising is done in remote areas such as rural villages in India.

LEARNING goal 3

Illustrate the steps of the B2B and B2C selling processes.

Promotion in Rural India

While advertisers in the United States use the latest technology to promote their products, global advertising agencies in India can't rely on even the most traditional media such as TV, radio or newspapers to reach the country's 700 million rural consumers. So they use traveling performers like Sandeep Sharma. The former wedding singer cracks jokes, gives demonstrations, and stages game shows in order to bring the world's biggest brands to small audiences in the remotest areas of India.

Insulated from the worst of the global recession, India's rural consumers are spending more than ever. International brands are sending out armies of salesmen like Sharma to reach these customers. Overall advertising spending climbed about 10 percent in India last year; while rural advertising grew at more than four times that rate. Sharma gives free Castrol oil changes for tractors, passes out bowls of Nestlé noodles in village schools, and sells Unilever soaps, creams, and promotes tooth powder. He starts by asking the village elders for permission to set up his mobile stage. He then rouses the villagers by driving around with music blaring and passes out candy to the children telling them to bring their neighbors. The crowds are all male. Selling takes a lot of interaction—but very little with women. When Sharma does talk to women about the wonders of Unilever soaps and skin creams, he does so from behind flip charts so there is no direct eye contact that could offend the men. Usually a husband or brother stands nearby and asks all the questions, even for women's products.

Sharma has been working the circuit for five years for Linterland Rural Communication, the rural outreach company connected to Lowe Worldwide, an agency owned by Interpublic Group PLC. He earns about $350 a month, a higher-than-average rural wage. Sharma is on the road more than 5,000 miles a month, visiting as many as three villages a day. He sleeps in cheap hotel rooms with the four others on his team, or in his truck. He can't go home for months at a time. No, this isn't as good as his dream of singing in the best hotels, but Sharma makes a lot more money than he made singing at weddings.

Sources: Eric Bellman, "The Infomercial Comes to Life in India's Remotest Villages," *The Wall Street Journal,* June 10, 2009; and Interpublic Group, www.interpublic.com, accessed May 2011.

PERSONAL SELLING: PROVIDING PERSONAL ATTENTION

personal selling
The face-to-face presentation and promotion of goods and services

Personal selling is the face-to-face presentation and promotion of goods and services, including the salesperson's search for new prospects and follow-up service after the sale. Effective selling isn't simply a matter of persuading others to buy. In fact, it's more accurately described today as helping others satisfy their wants and needs (again, helping the buyer buy).

Given that perspective, you can see why salespeople use the Internet, laptop computers, iPads, and other technology to help customers search for information, design custom-made products, look over prices, and generally do everything it takes to complete the order. The benefit of personal selling is having a person help you complete a transaction. The salesperson should listen to your needs, help you reach a solution, and do everything possible to make accomplishing it smoother and easier.

It's costly for firms to provide customers with personal attention, so those companies that retain salespeople must train them to be especially effective, efficient, and helpful. To attract new salespeople, companies are paying them quite well. The average cost of a single sales call to a potential business-to-business (B2B) buyer is about $400. Surely no firm would pay that much to send anyone but a skillful and highly trained professional salesperson and consultant.

Steps in the Selling Process

The best way to understand personal selling is to go through the selling process. Imagine you are a software salesperson whose job is to show business users the advantages of various programs your firm markets. One product critically important to establishing long-term relationships with customers is customer relationship management (CRM) software, particularly social CRM that integrates social media to create a community-based relationship with customers.[32] Let's go through the seven steps of the selling process to see what you can do to sell social CRM software.

Although this is a business-to-business (B2B) example, the process in consumer selling is similar but less complex. In both cases the salesperson must have deep *product* knowledge—that is, he or she must know the product—and competitors' products—thoroughly.

1. Prospect and Qualify   The first step in the selling process is **prospecting**, researching potential buyers and choosing those most likely to buy. The selection process is called **qualifying**. To qualify people means to make sure they have a need for the product, the authority to buy, and the willingness to listen to a sales message. Some people call prospecting and qualifying the process of *lead generation*.

A person who meets the qualifying criteria is called a **prospect**. You often meet prospects at trade shows, where they come to booths sponsored by manufacturers and ask questions. Others may visit your website seeking information. But often the best prospects are people recommended to you by others who use or know about your product. Salespeople often e-mail prospects with proposals to see whether there is any interest before making a formal visit.

2. Preapproach   The selling process may take a long time, and gathering information before you approach the customer is critical. Before making a sales call, you must do some further research. In the preapproach phase, you learn as much as possible about customers and their wants and needs.[33] Before you try to sell the social CRM software, you'll want to know which people in the company are most likely to buy or use it. What kind of customers do they deal with? What kind of relationship strategies are they using now? How is their system set up, and what kind of improvements are they looking for? All that information should be in a database so that, if one representative leaves the firm, the company can carry information about customers to the new salesperson.

3. Approach   "You don't have a second chance to make a good first impression." That's why the approach is so important. When you call on a customer for the first time, you want to give an impression of friendly professionalism, create rapport, build credibility, and start a business relationship.[34] Often a company's decision to use a new software package is based on the buyer's perception of reliable service from the salesperson. In selling social CRM products, you can make it known from the start that you'll be available to help your customer train its employees and to upgrade the package when necessary.

You're familiar with all kinds of situations in which people do personal selling. They work in local stores such as the one shown here. They also sell all kinds of goods and services like automobiles, insurance, and real estate. What could they do to be more helpful to you, the customer?

prospecting
Researching potential buyers and choosing those most likely to buy.

qualifying
In the selling process, making sure that people have a need for the product, the authority to buy, and the willingness to listen to a sales message.

prospect
A person with the means to buy a product, the authority to buy, and the willingness to listen to a sales message.

trial close
A step in the selling process that consists of a question or statement that moves the selling process toward the actual close.

Making the sale isn't the end of the salesperson's relationship with the customer. The salesperson should follow up on the sale to make sure the customer is happy and perhaps suggest something to complement what the customer purchased. Have salespeople been able to sell you more because they used effective follow-up procedures? How did they do it?

4. Make a Presentation   In your actual presentation of the software, you'll match the benefits of your value package to the client's needs. Companies such as Ventaso Inc. and the Sant Group now provide sales proposal software that includes everything from PowerPoint presentations to competitive analysis. Since you've done your homework and know the prospect's wants and needs, you can tailor your sales presentation accordingly.[35] The presentation is a great time to use testimonials showing potential buyers that they're joining leaders in other firms who are using the product.

5. Answer Objections   You should anticipate any objections the prospect may raise and determine the proper responses. Think of questions as opportunities for creating better relationships, not as challenges to what you're saying. Customers may have legitimate doubts, and you are there to resolve them. Successfully and honestly working with others helps you build relationships based on trust. Often you can introduce the customer to others in your firm who can answer their questions and provide them with anything they need. Using a laptop computer, you may set up a virtual meeting in which the customer can chat with your colleagues and begin building a relationship.

6. Close the Sale   After you've answered questions and objections, you may present a **trial close**, a question or statement that moves the selling process toward the actual purchase. You might ask, "When would be the best time to train your staff to use the new software?" The final step is to ask for the order and show the client where to sign. Once you've established a relationship, the goal of your sales call may be to get a testimonial from the customer.

7. Follow Up   The selling process isn't over until the order is approved and the customer is happy. Salespeople need to be providers of solutions for their customers and to think about what happens after the sale. The follow-up step includes handling customer complaints, making sure the customer's questions are answered, and quickly supplying what the customer wants. Often, customer service is as important to the sale as the product itself. That's why most manufacturers have websites where customers can find information and get questions answered. You can see why we describe selling as a process of *establishing relationships,* not just exchanging goods or services. The sales relationship may continue for years as you respond to new requests for information and provide new services.

The selling process varies somewhat among different goods and services, but the general idea stays the same. Your goals as a salesperson are to help the buyer buy and make sure the buyer is satisfied after the sale. Sales force automation (SFA) includes hundreds of software programs that help salespeople design products, close deals, tap into company intranets, and more. Some salespeople use it to conduct virtual reality tours of the manufacturing plant for the customer. An IBM salesperson may rely on everything from a BlackBerry and sales management software to wikis (collaborative websites that users can edit), blogs, podcasts, IBM's intranet, and more.

The Business-to-Consumer Sales Process

Most sales to consumers take place in retail stores, where the role of the salesperson differs somewhat from that in B2B selling. In both cases, knowing the product comes first.[36] However, in business-to-consumer (B2C) sales, the salesperson does not have to do much prospecting or qualifying. The seller assumes most people who come to the store are qualified to buy the merchandise (except in sales of expensive products such as automobiles and furniture, during which salespeople may have to ask a few questions to qualify prospective customers before spending too much time with them).

Similarly, retail salespeople don't usually have to go through a preapproach step, although they should understand as much as possible about the type of people who shop at a given store. The salesperson does need to focus on the customer and refrain from talking to fellow salespeople, however—or, worse, to friends on the phone. Have you ever experienced such rude behavior from salespeople? What did you think?

The first formal step in the B2C sales process is the approach. Too many salespeople begin with a line like "May I help you?" but the answer too often is "No." A better approach is "How can I help you?" or, simply, "Welcome to our store." The idea is to show the customer you are there to help and are friendly and knowledgeable.

Discover what the customer wants first, and then make a presentation. Show customers how your products meet their needs and answer questions that help them choose the right products for them.

As in B2B selling, it is important to make a trial close, like "Would you like me to put that on hold?" or "Will you be paying for that with your store credit card?" Selling is an art, and a salesperson must learn how to walk the fine line between being helpful and being pushy. Often individual buyers need some time alone to think about the purchase. The salesperson must respect that need but still be clearly available when needed.

After-sale follow-up is an important but often neglected step in B2C sales. If the product is to be delivered, the salesperson should follow up to be sure it is delivered on time. The same is true if the product has to be installed. There is often a chance to sell more merchandise when a salesperson follows up on a sale. Figure 16.6 shows the whole B2C selling process. Compare it to the seven-step process we outlined earlier for B2B selling.

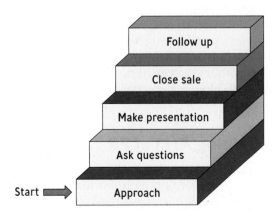

figure 16.6

STEPS IN THE BUSINESS-TO-CONSUMER (B2C) SELLING PROCESS

progress assessment

- What are the four traditional elements of the promotion mix?
- What are the three most important advertising media in order of dollars spent?
- What are the seven steps in the B2B selling process?

LEARNING goal **4**

Describe the role of the public relations department, and show how publicity fits in that role.

PUBLIC RELATIONS: BUILDING RELATIONSHIPS

public relations (PR)
The management function that evaluates public attitudes, changes policies and procedures in response to the public's requests, and executes a program of action and information to earn public understanding and acceptance.

Public relations (PR) is the management function that evaluates public attitudes, changes policies and procedures in response to the public's requests, and executes a program of action and information to earn public understanding and acceptance. In other words, a good public relations program has three steps:

1. *Listen to the public.* Public relations starts with good marketing research to evaluate public attitudes.

2. *Change policies and procedures.* Businesses earn understanding not by bombarding the public with propaganda but by creating programs and practices in the public interest. The best way to learn what the public wants is to listen to people often—in different forums, including on the Internet. That includes being able to handle a crisis by communicating online.

3. *Inform people you're responsive to their needs.* It's not enough to simply have programs in the public interest. You have to *tell* the public about those programs. Public relations has more power to influence consumers than other corporate communications because the message comes via the media, a source usually perceived as trustworthy.

Recent events have emphasized the need for good public relations. Such events include Toyota Motor's safety problems, Apple's iPhone antenna problems, BPs oil spill, Japan's nuclear power problems, and the issues surrounding some key actors and sports personalities.[37]

The PR department maintains close ties with company stakeholders (customers, media, community leaders, government officials, and other corporate stakeholders). Marketers are looking for alternatives to advertising. Public relations is a good alternative. As newspapers cut back on their reporting staff, people are looking for other sources of news information, including publicity releases. Linking up with bloggers has become an important way to keep company names in the news.

Publicity: The Talking Arm of PR

Publicity is the talking arm of public relations and one of the major functions of almost all organizations. Here's how it works: Suppose you want to introduce your store, Very Vegetarian, to consumers, but you have little money to promote it. You need to get some initial sales to generate funds. One effective way to reach the public is through publicity.

Publicity is any information about an individual, product, or organization that's distributed to the public through the media and is not paid for or controlled by the seller. It takes skill to write interesting or newsworthy press releases that the media will want to publish. You may need to write different stories for different media. One may introduce the new owners. Another may describe the unusual product offerings. If the stories are published, news about your store will reach many potential consumers (and investors, distributors, and dealers), and you may be on your way to becoming a successful marketer. John D. Rockefeller once remarked, "Next to doing the right thing, the most important thing is to *let people know* that you are doing the right thing." What might Very Vegetarian do to help the community and thus create more publicity?

Besides being free, publicity has several further advantages over other promotional tools like advertising. It may reach people who wouldn't read an ad. It may appear on the front page of a newspaper or in some other prominent position, or be given air time on a television news show. Perhaps the greatest advantage of publicity is its believability. When a newspaper or magazine publishes a story as news, the reader treats that story as news—and news is more believable than advertising.

Publicity has several disadvantages as well. For example, marketers have no control over whether, how, and when the media will use the story. The media aren't obligated to use a publicity release, most of which are thrown away. Furthermore, the media may alter the story so that it's not positive. There's good publicity (iPod sales are taking off) and bad publicity (GM is going bankrupt). Also, once a story has run, it's not likely to be repeated. Advertising, in contrast, can be repeated as often as needed. One way to see that the media handle your publicity well is to establish a friendly relationship with media representatives and be open with them. Then, when you want their support, they're more likely to cooperate.

Some companies will race to extremes to generate publicity. This streaker avoided Super Bowl XXXVIII security to show off a tattooed message for Internet casino GoldenPalace. com. Which do you think attracts more attention for a firm, an appealing news story or a paid ad?

LEARNING goal 5

Assess the effectiveness of various forms of sales promotion, including sampling.

SALES PROMOTION: GIVING BUYERS INCENTIVES

Sales promotion is the promotional tool that stimulates consumer purchasing and dealer interest by means of short-term activities. These activities include such things as displays, trade shows and exhibitions, event sponsorships, and contests. Figure 16.7 lists some B2B sales promotion techniques.

publicity
Any information about an individual, product, or organization that's distributed to the public through the media and that's not paid for or controlled by the seller.

sales promotion
The promotional tool that stimulates consumer purchasing and dealer interest by means of short-term activities

Trade shows	Catalogs
Portfolios for salespeople	Conventions
Deals (price reductions)	

figure 16.7

BUSINESS-TO-BUSINESS SALES PROMOTION TECHNIQUES

figure 16.8

**CONSUMER SALES
PROMOTION TECHNIQUES**

Coupons	Bonuses (buy one, get one free)
Cents-off promotions	Catalogs
Sampling	Demonstrations
Premiums	Special events
Sweepstakes	Lotteries
Contests	In-store displays

For consumer sales promotion activities, think of those free samples you get in the mail, cents-off coupons you clip from newspapers, contests that various retail stores sponsor, and prizes in cereal boxes (see Figure 16.8). You can stimulate sales at Very Vegetarian by putting half-off coupons in the school paper and home mailers. Do you see any problems that might emerge by using Groupon to bring in customers?

Sales promotion programs are designed to supplement personal selling, advertising, public relations, and other promotional efforts by creating enthusiasm for the overall promotional program. There was a big increase in such promotions as the 21st century began, especially online. The recent financial crisis has people looking more closely for coupons and other promotional deals.

Sales promotion can take place both within and outside the company. The most important internal sales promotion efforts are directed at salespeople and other customer-contact people, such as customer service representatives and clerks. Internal sales promotion efforts include (1) sales training; (2) the development of sales aids such as flip charts, portable audiovisual displays, and videos; and (3) participation in trade shows where salespeople can get leads. Other employees who deal with the public may also receive special training to improve their awareness of the company's offerings and make them an integral part of the total promotional effort.

After generating enthusiasm internally, marketers want to make distributors and dealers eager to help promote the product. Trade shows allow marketing intermediaries to see products from many different sellers and make comparisons among them. Today, virtual trade shows on the Internet, called

The International Manufacturing Trade Show in Chicago featured 4,000 booths, giving buyers for other businesses thousands of new products to explore and purchase. Can you see why trade shows in many industries are an efficient and necessary way to stay abreast of the latest developments, competitors, and consumer reactions and needs?

Webinars, enable buyers to see many products without leaving the office. Such promotions are usually interactive, so buyers can ask questions, and the information is available 24 hours a day, seven days a week.

After the company's employees and intermediaries have been motivated with sales promotion efforts, the next step is to promote to final consumers using samples, coupons, cents-off deals, displays, store demonstrations, premiums, contests, rebates, and so on. Sales promotion is an ongoing effort to maintain enthusiasm, so sellers use different strategies over time to keep the ideas fresh. You could put food displays in your Very Vegetarian store to show customers how attractive the products look. You could also sponsor in-store cooking demonstrations to attract new vegetarians. You can imagine the success of a promotion using Groupon or LivingSocial.

One popular sales promotion tool is **sampling**—letting consumers have a small sample of the product for no charge. Because many consumers won't buy a new product unless they've had a chance to see it or try it, grocery stores often have people standing in the aisles handing out small portions of food and beverage products. Sampling is a quick, effective way of demonstrating a product's superiority when consumers are making a purchase decision. Standing outside Very Vegetarian and giving out samples would surely attract attention.

Pepsi introduced its SoBe (herbal fortified drinks) product line with a combination of sampling, event marketing, and a new website. *Event marketing* means sponsoring events such as rock concerts or being at various events to promote your products. In the case of SoBe, Pepsi first sent samples to beach cities during spring break where students got samples of the drinks. Similar sampling and event marketing efforts had been successful with Snapple (fruit drinks and iced teas).

Everyone likes a free sample. Sampling is a promotional strategy that lets people try a new product, often in a situation when they can buy it right away if they like it. What are some advantages of sampling food products that advertising can't duplicate?

sampling
A promotional tool in which a company lets consumers have a small sample of a product for no charge.

progress assessment

- What are the three steps in setting up a public relations program?
- What are the sales promotion techniques used to reach consumers?
- What sales promotion techniques are used to reach businesses?

LEARNING goal 6

Show how word of mouth, e-mail marketing, viral marketing, blogging, podcasting, and mobile marketing work.

WORD OF MOUTH AND OTHER PROMOTIONAL TOOLS

Although word of mouth was not traditionally listed as one of the major promotional efforts (it was not considered to be manageable), it is now one of the most effective, especially on the Internet. In **word-of-mouth promotion**, people tell other people about products they've purchased.

When James and Ann Scaggs started a company that repairs iPods, customers were hesitant to part with their units without assurance they would be fixed properly. The Scaggs went to RatePoint, a Web 2.0 system for collecting

word-of-mouth promotion
A promotional tool that involves people telling other people about products they've purchased.

and displaying word of mouth in the form of customer feedback. Sales immediately went up.

Anything that encourages people to talk favorably about an organization can be effective word of mouth. Notice, for example, how stores use clowns, banners, music, fairs, and other attention-getting devices to create word of mouth. Clever commercials can also generate word of mouth. The more that people talk about your products and your brand name, the more easily customers remember them when they shop. You might enjoy brainstorming strategies for creating word of mouth about Very Vegetarian.

Viral Marketing

A number of companies have begun creating word of mouth by rewarding customers for promoting their products to others. One such strategy encourages people to go into Internet chat rooms and hype bands, movies, video games, and sports teams. People who agree to promote products in this way may get what the industry calls *swag*—free tickets, backstage passes, T-shirts, and other such merchandise. What do you think of the ethics of rewarding people to promote goods and services? What do you think of people sending messages to friends on Facebook and Twitter talking about products?

Viral marketing describes everything from paying customers to say positive things on the Internet (e.g., using Twitter) to setting up multilevel selling schemes whereby consumers get commissions for directing friends to specific websites.

One especially effective strategy for spreading positive word of mouth is to send testimonials to current customers. Most companies use these only in promoting to new customers, but testimonials are also effective in confirming customers' belief that they chose the right company. Therefore, some companies make it a habit to ask customers for referrals.

Word of mouth is so powerful that negative word of mouth can hurt a firm badly. Criticism of a product or company can spread through online forums, social media, and websites. Addressing consumer complaints quickly and effectively is one of the best ways to reduce the effects of negative word of mouth.

Blogging

A **blog**—short for web log—is an online diary that looks like a web page but is easier to create and update by posting text, photos, or links to other sites. There are millions of blogs on the Internet, and thousands of new ones are added each day. How do blogs affect marketing? When a book called *Freakonomics* was about to be released, the publisher sent advance copies to 100 bloggers. These bloggers sent reviews to other bloggers (word of mouth), and soon *Freakonomics* was number three on Amazon.com's list of most-ordered books. You can imagine what blogging can do to promote movies, TV shows, and more.

Podcasting

Podcasting is a means of distributing audio and video programs via the Internet. It lets users subscribe to a number of files, also known as feeds, and then hear or view the material when they choose. Podcasting allows you to become your own newscaster, since—besides giving broadcast radio and TV a new distribution medium—it enables independent producers to create self-published, syndicated "radio shows." Many companies have also found success in creating video for YouTube.

viral marketing
The term now used to describe everything from paying customers to say positive things on the Internet to setting up multilevel selling schemes whereby consumers get commissions for directing friends to specific websites.

blog
An online diary (Web log) that looks like a Web page but is easier to create and update by posting text, photos, or links to other sites.

podcasting
A means of distributing audio and video programs via the Internet that lets users subscribe to a number of files, also known as feeds, and then hear or view the material at the time they choose.

E-Mail Promotions

Armstrong, the flooring manufacturer, has an e-mail marketing program designed to increase brand awareness among commercial suppliers. At one time it sent out monthly e-mails to announce new products and product updates and to keep people loyal to the brand. Over time, however, those e-mails lost their power. Armstrong then turned to an e-mail service provider that completely revamped the program. The provider divided the market into four separate segments and tracked the success of the e-mails much more closely.

E-mail promotions are gaining in popularity. Most marketers make sure their e-newsletters are also viewable on mobile devices like BlackBerrys or iPhones. One key to success, therefore, is to keep the message brief, because mobile users don't want to go through much text.

Mobile Media

With mobile media, marketers make use of the cell phone, using text messaging to promote sweepstakes, send customers news or sports alerts, and give them company information. We've seen that companies can now determine where you are and send you messages about restaurants and other services in your vicinity. Despite some technological glitches to work through, mobile marketing is catching on.[38]

Are you getting the idea that traditional promotional methods are slowly but surely being replaced by new technology? If so, you're getting the right idea. By keeping up with the latest trends, you may be able to grab a good job in promotion while traditionalists are still wondering what happened. [39]

Mobile media allow marketers to reach customers through text messaging. Have you received such promotional messages? For which products are they most effective?

MANAGING THE PROMOTION MIX: PUTTING IT ALL TOGETHER

Each target group calls for a separate promotion mix. Advertising is most efficient for reaching large groups of consumers whose members share similar traits. Personal selling is best for selling to large organizations. To motivate people to buy now rather than later, marketers use sales promotions like sampling, coupons, discounts, special displays, and premiums. Publicity supports other efforts and can create a good impression among all consumers. Word of mouth is often the most powerful promotional tool. Generate it by listening, being responsive, and creating an impression worth passing on to others that you spread through blogging, podcasting, and tweeting.

Promotional Strategies

How do producers move products to consumers? In a **push strategy**, the producer uses advertising, personal selling, sales promotion, and all other promotional tools to convince wholesalers and retailers to stock and sell merchandise, *pushing* it through the distribution system to the stores. If the push strategy works, consumers will walk into a store, see the product, and buy it.

A **pull strategy** directs heavy advertising and sales promotion efforts toward *consumers*. If the pull strategy works, consumers will go to the store and ask for the products. The store owner will order them from the wholesaler, who in turn will order them from the producer. Products are thus *pulled* through the distribution system.

push strategy
Promotional strategy in which the producer uses advertising, personal selling, sales promotion, and all other promotional tools to convince wholesalers and retailers to stock and sell merchandise.

pull strategy
Promotional strategy in which heavy advertising and sales promotion efforts are directed toward consumers so that they'll request the products from retailers.

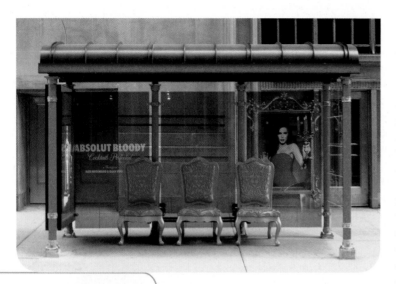

Ads in bus shelters are nothing new, but Absolut furnished this shelter with seating that reflects the style and luxury it attributes to its products. Do you think giving consumers experiences (like luxury seating) is an effective way to remind them of a product?

pick economy
Customers who pick out their products from online outlets or who do online comparison shopping.

Dr Pepper has used TV advertising in a pull strategy to increase distribution. Tripledge, a maker of windshield wipers, also tried to capture the interest of retail stores through a pull strategy. Of course, a company could use both strategies in a major promotional effort. The latest pull and push strategies are being conducted on the Internet, with companies sending messages to both consumers and businesses.

It has been important to make promotion part of a total systems approach to marketing. That is, promotion was part of supply-chain management. In such cases, retailers would work with producers and distributors to make the supply chain as efficient as possible. Then a promotional plan would be developed for the whole system. The idea would be to develop a total product offer that would appeal to everyone: manufacturers, distributors, retailers, and consumers.

Today push and pull strategies have lost some of their effectiveness. Still, customers are interested in searching online outlets like Drugstore.com or Zappos and doing online comparison shopping as they pick the products that appeal to them. Some leading marketers sell directly to consumers with products that really stand out because of their design, packaging, price, or color, like the Dyson vacuum. The idea is to help the consumer distinguish your product from the competitors. The term **pick economy** refers to those consumers who pick out their products from online outlets or who do online comparison shopping.

progress assessment

- What is viral marketing?
- What are blogging and podcasting?
- Describe a push strategy, a pull strategy, and the pick economy.

summary

Learning Goal 1. Identify the new and traditional tools that make up the promotion mix.

- **What is promotion?**

Promotion is an effort by marketers to inform and remind people in the target market about products and to persuade them to participate in an exchange.

- **What are the four traditional promotional tools that make up the promotion mix?**

The four traditional promotional tools are advertising, personal selling, public relations, and sales promotion. The product itself can also be a promotional tool—that's why it is shown in the middle of Figure 16.1.

- **What are some of the newer tools used in promotion?**

Today's promotional tools include e-mail promotions, mobile promotions (those that use cell phones), social networks. blogging, podcasts, and YouTube.

Learning Goal 2. Contrast the advantages and disadvantages of various advertising media, including the Internet and social media.

- **What is advertising?**

Advertising is limited to paid, nonpersonal (not face-to-face) communication through various media by organizations and individuals who are in some way identified in the advertising message.

- **What are the advantages of using the various media?**

Review the advantages and disadvantages of the various advertising media in Figure 16.5.

- **Why the growing use of infomercials?**

Infomercials are growing in importance because they show products in use and present testimonials to help sell goods and services.

Learning Goal 3. Illustrate the steps of the B2B and B2C selling processes.

- **What is personal selling?**

Personal selling is the face-to-face presentation and promotion of products and services. It includes the search for new prospects and follow-up service after the sale.

- **What are the seven steps of the B2B selling process?**

The steps of the selling process are (1) prospect and qualify, (2) preapproach, (3) approach, (4) make presentation, (5) answer objections, (6) close sale, and (7) follow up.

- **What are the steps in the B2C selling process?**

The steps are the approach, which includes asking questions; the presentation, which includes answering questions; the close; and the follow-up.

Learning Goal 4. Describe the role of the public relations department, and show how publicity fits in that role.

- **What is public relations?**

Public relations (PR) is the function that evaluates public attitudes, changes policies and procedures in response to the public's requests, and executes a program of action and information to earn public understanding and acceptance.

- **What are the three major steps in a good public relations program?**

(1) Listen to the public; (2) develop policies and procedures in the public interest; and (3) tell people you're being responsive to their needs.

- **What is publicity?**

Publicity is the talking part of sales promotion; it is information distributed by the media that's not paid for, or controlled by, the seller. Publicity's greatest advantage is its believability.

Learning Goal 5. Assess the effectiveness of various forms of sales promotion, including sampling.

- **How are sales promotion activities used both within and outside the organization?**

Internal sales promotion efforts are directed at salespeople and other customer-contact people to keep them enthusiastic about the company. Internal sales promotion activities include sales training, sales aids, audiovisual displays, and trade shows. External sales promotions to consumers rely on samples, coupons, cents-off deals, displays, store demonstrators, premiums, and other incentives.

Learning Goal 6. Show how word of mouth, e-mail marketing, viral marketing, blogging, podcasting, and mobile marketing work.

- **Is word of mouth a major promotional tool?**

Word of mouth was not one of the traditional forms of promotion because it was not considered to be manageable, but it has always been an effective way of promoting goods and services.

- **How is word of mouth used in promotion today?**

Some companies reward people to blog or go into Internet chat rooms and talk enthusiastically about bands, movies, video games, and sports teams. People who agree to hype products in this way get *swag*—free tickets, backstage passes, T-shirts, and other merchandise. *Viral marketing* is everything from paying people to say positive things on the Internet to setting up multilevel selling schemes whereby consumers get commissions for directing friends to specific websites. Podcasting is like blogging with an audiovisual focus.

- **What are the major promotional strategies?**

In a *push strategy*, the producer uses advertising, personal selling, sales promotion, and all other promotional tools to convince wholesalers and retailers to stock and sell merchandise. In a *pull strategy*, heavy advertising and sales promotion efforts are directed toward consumers so they'll request the products from retailers. The term *pick economy* refers to those consumers who pick out their products from online outlets such as Drugstore.com or Zappos or who do online comparison shopping.

key terms

advertising 438	**pick economy** 456	**pull strategy** 455
blog 454	**podcasting** 454	**push strategy** 455
infomercial 442	**product placement** 441	**qualifying** 447
integrated marketing communication (IMC) 437	**promotion mix** 436	**sales promotion** 451
	prospect 447	**sampling** 453
interactive promotion 442	**prospecting** 447	**trial close** 448
	publicity 451	**viral marketing** 454
personal selling 446	**public relations (PR)** 450	**word-of-mouth promotion** 453

critical thinking

1. What kinds of problems can emerge if a firm doesn't communicate with environmentalists, the news media, and the local community? Do you know of any firms that aren't responsive to your community? What are the consequences?

2. How often do you buy online? If you don't actually buy, do you use the Internet to compare goods and prices? Do you or your friends take advantage of low prices on used goods at eBay or other online sites like Craig's List? Do you look at ads on the Internet? Do they seem to be effective? Do you think you will use the Internet for more purchases over time?

3. As interactive communications between companies and customers grow, do you think traditional advertising will grow or decline? What will be the

effect of growth or decline on the price we pay for TV programs, newspapers, and magazines?

4. How have blogging, podcasting, and social media affected other media you use, like news sites, newspapers, or television? Do you think blogging is an influential word-of-mouth promotional tool? Do you read newspapers now or do you get your news some other way?

developing workplace skills

1. Using at least two different media—a newspaper, magazine, television, radio, the Internet—choose two ads you consider effective and two you find ineffective. Be prepared to rationalize your choices.

2. Scan your local newspaper for examples of publicity (stories about new products) and sales promotion (coupons, contests, sweepstakes). Share your examples and discuss the effectiveness of such promotional efforts with the class.

3. Many students shy away from careers in selling, often because they think they are not outgoing enough or that salespeople are dishonest or pushy. Prepare a one-page document about your experience with salespeople and what you think of selling as a career.

4. In small groups, discuss whether you are purchasing more goods using catalogs and/or the Internet and why. Do you look up information on the Internet before buying goods and services? How helpful are such searches? Present your findings to the class.

5. In small groups or individually, list six goods and services most students own or use and discuss promotional techniques that prompt you to buy them: advertising, personal selling, social media, publicity, sales promotion, or word of mouth. Which seems most effective for your group? Why?

taking it to the net

Purpose

To learn about business blogs.

Exercise

Go to www.google.com/blogger to learn how easy it is to start your own blog. Then go to the following business-oriented blogs: VentureBlog.com (www .ventureblog.com) and PatentPending.blogs.com (http://patentpending.blogs. com).

1. What kind of subjects are covered in each blog?

2. What are the advantages and disadvantages of reading such blogs?

3. Would you like to see a blog for this course? For your school?

casing the web

To access the case "Developing a Promotional Strategy for Biltmore Estate," visit **www.mhhe.com/ubl0e**

video case

To access the video case featuring Groupon, visit **www.mhhe.com/ubl0e**

UNDERSTANDING

Accounting

& Financial

Information

17

LEARNING goals

After you have read and studied this chapter, you should be able to

1 Demonstrate the role that accounting and financial information play for a business and for its stakeholders.

2 Identify the different disciplines within the accounting profession.

3 List the steps in the accounting cycle, distinguish between accounting and bookkeeping, and explain how computers are used in accounting.

4 Explain how the major financial statements differ.

5 Demonstrate the application of ratio analysis in reporting financial information.

When Siggi Hilmarsson left his native Iceland at age 25 to pursue a business degree at Columbia University, he was certain of one thing: working for a large corporation was not the way he wanted to go. However, after graduation he accepted a job with accounting giant Deloitte. Hilmarsson knew he was an entrepreneur at heart and had trouble adjusting to life in corporate America. He also had problems adjusting to sugar-laden American food, and particularly missed an Icelandic treat called skyr—a thick, strained, protein-rich yogurt. Armed with a 1913 recipe his mother found in the Reykjavik library in Iceland, he set about to prepare his own skyr in his kitchen sink.

According to Hilmarsson, his first few batches of skyr were sometimes okay and sometimes awful. One of his problems was that proper skyr requires preparation in specific and exact temperatures, something his small kitchen could not provide. So Hilmarsson took a vacation from his job and traveled to upstate New York to a dairy plant that he could rent that was attached to an agricultural college. It was there that he made his first professional batch of yogurt that he thought tasted wonderful. He resigned from Deloitte to make his own yogurt full time.

With his recipe perfected, he was ready for his friends to try his yogurt. His colleagues gave the taste a unanimous thumbs-up. Then Hilmarsson got his first break. A friend who tried the yogurt brought a sample to a staff tasting at Murray's Cheese in New York City. Impressed with his product Murray's Cheese became his first client.

Knowing he needed financing, Hilmarsson contacted a professor from Columbia University who had tried his yogurt. The professor agreed to invest a small amount in the company if Hilmarsson was investing his own money as well. His next step was to search for a small dairy plant where he could start production. He found an underused dairy plant in Norwich, New York, that had been producing cheese, yogurt, and goat's milk for several years.

After donating skyr to a fundraising event, a Whole Foods employee tasted the yogurt and loved it. Before he knew it Hilmarsson was at Whole Foods' headquarters signing a contract to supply his yogurt to half the Whole Food stores in America. Unfortunately, the company couldn't make the yogurt and cool it fast enough to meet the jump from 15 to 100 stores. The plant shut down for three months to expand, creating a cash flow problem. Hilmarsson worried the company would not be able to recover from the setback. However, his education and work experience at Deloitte helped him face the financial challenge head on. Using careful financial and logistics control, he restarted production in three months.

Going forward, Hilmarsson faces continued cost issues. The core of his product is skim milk from grass-fed cows that's completely strained of whey that requires three times the milk of regular yogurt. This causes the price of his yogurt to approach $3 for a 6-ounce cup in an industry where price competition can be intense. Distribution of a product that must be continuously refrigerated also raises cost problems that can affect cash flow. Hilmarsson knows that all companies have to face such financial challenges. He is, fortunately, familiar with measures of business health—like financial analysis, cost control, financial statements, and return on equity and assets.

Controlling costs, managing cash flows, understanding profit margins and taxes, and financial reporting are keys to growth and survival for large yogurt producers like Dannon and Yoplait, as well as small producers like Siggi's Yogurt. This chapter will introduce you to the accounting fundamentals and financial information critical to business success. It also briefly explores financial ratios that businesses use to measure performance in a large or small business.

profile

Getting to Know

X *Siggi Hilmarsson*

Founder of Siggi's Yogurt

Sources: Jill Priluck, "The Yogurt Chronicles," *Slate,* August 13, 2010; Alexandra Wolfe, "Learning to Milk a Profit," *Bloomberg Businessweek,* August 12, 2010; and Courtney Rubin, "The Sugar Made Him Do It," *Inc.,* February 15, 2011.

Until the development of accounting software simplified the accounting process, accountants had to enter all financial information by hand. Today accounting software makes it possible for businesses to have financial information available whenever they need it. Name two companies that provide accounting software for small businesses. (Find the answer in the chapter.)

LEARNING goal 1

Demonstrate the role that accounting and financial information play for a business and for its stakeholders.

THE ROLE OF ACCOUNTING INFORMATION

Stories like Siggi's Yogurt are repeated every day throughout the business community. Small and large businesses often survive or fail according to how well they handle financial procedures. Financial management is the heartbeat of competitive businesses, and accounting information helps keep the heartbeat stable.

Accounting reports and financial statements reveal as much about a business's health as pulse and blood pressure readings tell us about a person's health. Thus, you have to know something about accounting if you want to succeed in business. It's almost impossible to understand business operations without being able to read, understand, and analyze accounting reports and financial statements.

By the end of the chapter, you should have a good idea what accounting is, how it works, and the value it offers businesses. You should also know some accounting terms and understand the purpose of accounting statements. Your new understanding will pay off as you become more active in business or will help you in simply understanding what's going on in the world of business and finance.

What Is Accounting?

accounting
The recording, classifying, summarizing, and interpreting of financial events and transactions to provide management and other interested parties the information they need to make good decisions.

Accounting is the recording, classifying, summarizing, and interpreting of financial events and transactions in an organization to provide management and other interested parties the financial information they need to make good decisions about its operation. Financial transactions include buying and selling goods and services, acquiring insurance, paying employees, and using supplies. Usually we group all purchases together, and all sales transactions together. The method we use to record and summarize accounting data into reports is an *accounting system* (see Figure 17.1).

A major purpose of accounting is to help managers make well-informed decisions. Another is to report financial information about the firm to interested stakeholders, such as employees, owners, creditors, suppliers, unions, community activists, investors, and the government (for tax purposes) (see Figure 17.2). Accounting is divided into several major disciplines. Let's look at those next.

figure 17.1

THE ACCOUNTING SYSTEM
The inputs to an accounting system include sales documents and other documents. The data are recorded, classified, and summarized. They're then put into summary financial statements such as the income statement and balance sheet and statement of cash flows.

LEARNING goal 2

Identify the different disciplines within the accounting profession.

ACCOUNTING DISCIPLINES

You may think accounting is only for profit-seeking firms. Nothing could be further from the truth. Accounting, often called the language of business, allows us to report financial information about nonprofit organizations such as churches, schools, hospitals, fraternities, and government agencies.[1] The accounting profession is divided into five key working areas: managerial accounting, financial accounting, auditing, tax accounting, and governmental and not-for-profit accounting.[2] All five are important, and all create career opportunities.[3] Let's explore each.

Managerial Accounting

Managerial accounting provides information and analysis to managers *inside* the organization to assist them in decision making. Managerial accounting is concerned with measuring and reporting costs of production, marketing, and other functions; preparing budgets (planning); checking whether or not units are staying within their budgets (controlling); and designing strategies to minimize taxes.

    If you are a business major, you'll probably take a course in managerial accounting. You may even pursue a career as a certified management

managerial accounting
Accounting used to provide information and analyses to managers inside the organization to assist them in decision making.

figure 17.2

USERS OF ACCOUNTING INFORMATION AND THE REQUIRED REPORTS
Many types of organizations use accounting information to make business decisions. The reports needed vary according to the Information each user requires. An accountant must prepare the appropriate forms.

USERS	TYPE OF REPORT
Government taxing authorities (e.g., the Internal Revenue Service)	Tax returns
Government regulatory agencies	Required reports
People interested in the organization's income and financial position (e.g., owners, creditors, financial analysts, suppliers)	Financial statements found in annual reports (e.g., income statement, balance sheet, statement of cash flows)
Managers of the firm	Financial statements and various internally distributed financial reports

Assembling an airplane engine requires many tools, parts, raw materials, and other components, as well as labor costs. Keeping these costs at a minimum and setting realistic production schedules is critical to a business's survival. What other internal departments must management accountants team with to ensure company competitiveness?

certified management accountant (CMA)
A professional accountant who has met certain educational and experience requirements, passed a qualifying exam, and been certified by the Institute of Certified Management Accountants.

financial accounting
Accounting information and analyses prepared for people outside the organization.

annual report
A yearly statement of the financial condition, progress, and expectations of an organization.

private accountant
An accountant who works for a single firm, government agency, or nonprofit oranization.

public accountant
An accountant who provides accounting services to individuals or businesses on a fee basis.

accountant.[4] A **certified management accountant (CMA)** is a professional accountant who has met certain educational and experience requirements, passed a qualifying exam, and been certified by the Institute of Certified Management Accountants.[5] With the growing emphasis on global competition, outsourcing, and organizational cost-cutting, managerial accounting is one of the most important areas you may study in your college career.

Financial Accounting

Financial accounting differs from managerial accounting in that the financial information and analyses it generates are for people primarily *outside* the organization. The information goes not only to company owners, managers, and employees, but also to creditors and lenders, employee unions, customers, suppliers, government agencies, and the general public. External users are interested in questions like: Is the organization profitable? Is it able to pay its bills? How much debt does it owe? These questions and others are often answered in the company's **annual report**, a yearly statement of the financial condition, progress, and expectations of an organization. As pressure from stakeholders for detailed financial information has grown, companies have poured more information than ever into their annual reports.

It's critical for firms to keep accurate financial information. Therefore, many organizations employ a **private accountant** who works for a single firm, government agency, or nonprofit organization. However, not all firms or nonprofit organizations want or need a full-time accountant. Fortunately, thousands of accounting firms in the United States provide the accounting services an organization needs through public accountants.[6]

For a fee, a **public accountant** provides accounting services to individuals or businesses. Such services can include designing an accounting system, helping select the correct software to run the system, and analyzing an organization's financial performance. An accountant who passes a series of examinations established by the American Institute of Certified Public Accountants (AICPA) and meets the state's requirement for education and experience is recognized as a **certified public accountant (CPA)** . CPAs find careers as private or public accountants and are often sought to fill other financial positions within organizations.[7] Today, there are over 650,000 CPAs in the United States, 370,000 of whom are members of the AICPA.[8]

Accountants know it's vital for users of a firm's accounting information to be assured the information is accurate. The independent Financial Accounting Standards Board (FASB) defines the *generally accepted accounting principles (GAAP)* that accountants must follow. If accounting reports are prepared in accordance with GAAP, users can expect the information to meet standards upon which accounting professionals have agreed.

The accounting profession suffered a dark period in the early 2000s when accounting scandals at WorldCom, Enron, and Tyco raised public suspicions about the profession and corporate integrity in general. Arthur Andersen, one of the nation's leading accounting firms, was forced out of business after being convicted of obstruction of justice for shredding records in the Enron case (the conviction was later overturned by the U.S. Supreme Court).

Scrutiny of the accounting industry intensified, and resulted in the U.S. Congress's passage of the Sarbanes-Oxley Act (called Sarbox). This legislation created new government reporting standards for publicly traded companies. It also created the Public Company Accounting Oversight Board (PCAOB), which is charged with overseeing the AICPA.[9] Prior to the passage of Sarbox, the accounting profession was self-regulated.[10] Figure 17.3 lists some of the major provisions of Sarbanes-Oxley.

The financial crisis beginning in 2008 led Congress to pass the Dodd-Frank Wall Street Reform and Consumer Protection Act. The Dodd-Frank Act increased financial regulation affecting accounting by increasing the power of the PCAOB to oversee auditors of brokers and dealers in securities markets.[11] We'll discuss the Dodd-Frank Act in more depth in Chapter 19.

The accounting profession understands that to be effective, accountants must be considered as professional as doctors or lawyers. Besides completing more than 150 hours of intense training and a rigorous exam, CPAs on

certified public accountant (CPA)
An accountant who passes a series of examinations established by the American Institute of Certified Public Accountants (AICPA).

- Prohibits accounting firms from providing certain non-auditing work (such as consulting services) to companies they audit.

- Strengthens the protection for whistle-blowers who report wrongful actions of company officers.

- Requires company CEOs and CFOs to certify the accuracy of financial reports and imparts strict penalties for any violation of securities reporting (e.g., earnings misstatements).

- Prohibits corporate loans to directors and executives of the company.

- Establishes the five-member Public Company Accounting Oversight Board (PCAOB) under the Securities and Exchange Commission (SEC) to oversee the accounting industry.

- Stipulates that altering or destroying key audit documents will result in felony charges and significant criminal penalties.

figure 17.3

KEY PROVISIONS OF THE SARBANES-OXLEY ACT

Fighting Accounting Fraud Line-by-Line

According to the Association of Certified Fraud Examiners, it is likely many companies are losing money in the worst way possible—through fraud. Sam E. Antar, a CPA, agrees with that assessment and he should know. While he was Chief Financial Officer (CFO) of Crazy Eddie, a consumer electronics retailer, Antar was convicted of inflating sales figures, money laundering, and inventory fraud in a corporate scam that cost investors and creditors hundreds of millions of dollars. Today, he lectures companies concerning fraud and how to prevent it from occurring and is a strong proponent of training auditors in forensic accounting.

According to Mr. Antar, auditors are trained to look for bookkeeping errors while forensic accountants are trained as crime-scene investigators. Steve Pedneault of Forensic Accounting Services suggests that more fraud and embezzlement exist in businesses today than there was 10 years ago when Enron, WorldCom, and Tyco were in the news. When a company suspects financial wrongdoings, companies like Mr. Pedneault's are called in to search out fraud by analyzing computer hard drives, financial papers, bank records, e-mail, and billing receipts. *Accounting Today* magazine estimates almost 80 percent of the nation's top CPA firms use forensic accounting in fraud and litigation.

If you think accountants are just glorified pencil pushers think again. Forensic accountants see their job as investigative. In most cases internal informants who have concerns about supervisors encouraging them to falsify financial records or hide some costs are their first line of investigation. With financial problems like the subprime mortgage crisis of the late 2000s and the Bernie Madoff Ponzi scheme that cost investors billions of dollars, forensic accountants won't have any trouble keeping busy in the future.

Sources: Marie Leone, "Something Wicked This Way Comes," *CFO,* June 1, 2010; Laton McCartney, "Where There's Smoke, There's Fraud," *CFO,* March 1, 2011; and "AICPA Adds More Options for Specialty Credentials," *Accounting Today,* April 27, 2011.

---

average take 40 hours of continuing education training a year, are subject to recertification, undergo ethics training requirements, and must pass an ethics exam.

Auditing

auditing
The job of reviewing and evaluating the information used to prepare a company's financial statements.

independent audit
An evaluation and unbiased opinion about the accuracy of a company's financial statements.

Reviewing and evaluating the information used to prepare a company's financial statements is referred to as **auditing**. Private accountants within an organization often perform internal audits to guarantee that it is carrying out proper accounting procedures and financial reporting.[12] Public accountants also conduct independent audits of accounting information and related records. An **independent audit** is an evaluation and unbiased opinion about the accuracy of a company's financial statements. Annual reports often include an auditor's unbiased written opinion.

After the accounting scandals of the early 2000s, questions surfaced about the ethics of allowing an accounting firm to do both auditing and consulting work for the same company. In response, the Sarbanes-Oxley Act put in place new rules about auditing and consulting to ensure the integrity of the auditing process. Auditing procedures again came under fire in 2011.[13] Many called for stricter controls over auditing procedures after analyzing the failure of Lehman Brothers in 2008 and the financial crisis that followed.[14] The nearby Legal Briefcase discusses the problem of accounting fraud and how companies can help prevent it.

In doing their job, auditors not only examine the financial health of an organization but also its operational efficiencies and effectiveness.[15] Accountants who have a bachelor's degree and two years of experience in internal auditing, and who pass an exam administered by the Institute of Internal Auditors, can earn professional accreditation as a **certified internal auditor (CIA)**.[16]

Tax Accounting

Taxes enable governments to fund roads, parks, schools, police protection, the military, and other functions. Federal, state, and local governments require individuals and organizations to file tax returns at specific times and in a precise format. A **tax accountant** is

trained in tax law and is responsible for preparing tax returns or developing tax strategies. Since governments often change tax policies according to specific needs or objectives, the job of the tax accountant is always challenging.[17] And as the burden of taxes grows in the economy, the role of the tax accountant becomes increasingly valuable to the organization, individual, or entrepreneur.[18]

Government and Not-for-Profit Accounting

Government and not-for-profit accounting supports organizations whose purpose is not generating a profit, but serving ratepayers, taxpayers, and others according to a duly approved budget. Federal, state, and local governments require an accounting system that helps taxpayers, special interest groups, legislative bodies, and creditors ensure that the government is fulfilling its obligations and making proper use of taxpayers' money. Government accounting standards are set by an organization called the Governmental Accounting Standards Board (GASB).[19] The Federal Bureau of Investigation, the Internal Revenue Service, the Missouri Department of Natural Resources, and the Cook County Department of Revenue are just a few of the many government agencies that offer career possibilities to accountants seeking to work in government accounting.

Not-for-profit organizations also require accounting professionals. Charities like the Salvation Army, Red Cross, museums, and hospitals all hire accountants to show contributors how their money is spent. In fact, their need for trained accountants is growing since donors to nonprofits want to see exactly how and where the funds they contribute are being spent. During the deep recession beginning in 2008, many businesses and individuals cut back on donations making it more important than ever to account for every dollar contributed.[20]

As you can see, managerial and financial accounting, auditing, tax accounting, and governmental and not-for-profit accounting each require specific training and skill. After the Progress Assessment, we will clarify the difference between accounting and bookkeeping.

The National Park Service, with its workforce of over 26,000 employees, maintains and protects places special to the people of the United States, like the faces on Mount Rushmore. Such government organizations employ accountants, auditors, and financial managers.

certified internal auditor (CIA)
An accountant who has a bachelor's degree and two years of experience in internal auditing, and who has passed an exam administered by the Institute of Internal Auditors.

tax accountant
An accountant trained in tax law and responsible for preparing tax returns or developing tax strategies.

government and not-for-profit accounting
Accounting system for organizations whose purpose is not generating a profit but serving ratepayers, taxpayers, and others according to a duly approved budget.

progress assessment

- What is the key difference between managerial and financial accounting?
- How is the job of a private accountant different from that of a public accountant?
- What is the job of an auditor? What's an independent audit?

List the steps in the accounting cycle, distinguish between accounting and bookkeeping, and explain how computers are used in accounting.

THE ACCOUNTING CYCLE

accounting cycle
A six-step procedure that results in the preparation and analysis of the major financial statements.

bookkeeping
The recording of business transactions.

journal
The record book or computer program where accounting data are first entered.

double-entry bookkeeping
The practice of writing every business transaction in two places.

ledger
A specialized accounting book or computer program in which information from accounting journals is accumulated into specific categories and posted so that managers can find all the information about one account in the same place.

The **accounting cycle** is a six-step procedure that results in the preparation and analysis of the major financial statements (see Figure 17.4). It relies on the work of both a bookkeeper and an accountant. **Bookkeeping**, the recording of business transactions, is a basic part of financial reporting. Accounting, however, goes far beyond the mere recording of financial information. Accountants classify and summarize financial data provided by bookkeepers, and then interpret the data and report the information to management. They also suggest strategies for improving the firm's financial condition and prepare financial analyses and income tax returns.

A bookkeeper's first task is to divide all the firm's transactions into meaningful categories such as sales documents, purchasing receipts, and shipping documents, being very careful to keep the information organized and manageable. Bookkeepers then record financial data from the original transaction documents (sales slips and so forth) into a record book or computer program called a **journal**. The word *journal* comes from the French word *jour*, which means "day." Therefore, a journal is where the day's transactions are kept.

It's quite possible to make a mistake when recording financial transactions, like entering $10.98 as $10.89. That's why bookkeepers record all transactions in two places so they can check one list of transactions against the other to make sure both add up to the same amount. If the amounts are not equal, the bookkeeper knows there is a mistake. The practice of writing every transaction in two places is called **double-entry bookkeeping**. It requires two entries in the journal and in the ledgers (discussed next) for each transaction.

Suppose a business wanted to determine how much it paid for office supplies in the first quarter of the year. Without a specific bookkeeping tool, that would be difficult—even with accurate accounting journals. Therefore, bookkeepers use a specialized accounting book or computer program called a **ledger**. In the ledger, they transfer (or post) information from accounting journals into specific categories so managers can find all the information about a single account, like office supplies or cash, in one place.

figure 17.4

STEPS IN THE ACCOUNTING CYCLE

| 1 Analyze source documents (sales slips, travel records, etc.) | 2 Record transactions in journals | 3 Transfer (post) journal entries to ledger | 4 Take a trial balance | 5 Prepare financial statements | 6 Analyze financial statements |

Balance sheet   Income statement   Statement of cash flows

The next step in the accounting cycle is to prepare a **trial balance**, a summary of all the financial data in the account ledgers that ensures the figures are correct and balanced. If the information in the account ledgers is not accurate, the accountant must correct it before preparing the firm's financial statements. Using the correct information, the accountant then prepares the firm's financial statements—including a balance sheet, an income statement, and a statement of cash flows—according to generally accepted accounting principles.

> **trial balance**
> A summary of all the financial data in the account ledgers that ensures the figures are correct and balanced.

Accounting Technology

Not long ago, accountants and bookkeepers needed to enter all of a firm's financial information by hand. Today, technology has simplified the accounting process considerably.[21] Computerized accounting programs post information from journals instantaneously, even from remote locations, so that financial information is readily available whenever the organization needs it. Such assistance frees accountants' time for more important tasks such as financial analysis. Computerized accounting programs are particularly helpful to small-business owners who often lack the strong accounting support within their companies that larger firms enjoy. Accounting software—such as Intuit's QuickBooks and Sage's Peachtree—addresses the specific needs of small businesses, often significantly different from the needs of a major corporation.[22] Small business owners, however, need to understand exactly which computer systems and programs are best suited for their particular company needs.[23] That's one reason why entrepreneurs planning to start a business should either hire or consult with an accountant to identify the particular needs of their firm. They can then develop a specific computer accounting system that works with the accounting software they've chosen.

With sophisticated accounting software available, you might wonder why you need to study and understand accounting. Without question a computer is a wonderful tool for businesspeople and certainly helps ease the monotony of bookkeeping and accounting work. Unfortunately the work of an accountant requires training and very specific competencies that computers are not programmed to handle. It's the partnership of technology and an accountant's knowledge that helps a firm make the right financial decisions. After the Progress Assessment, we'll explore the balance sheet, income statement, and statement of cash flows. It's from the information contained in these financial statements that the accountant analyzes and evaluates the financial condition of the firm.

progress assessment

- How is the job of the bookkeeper different from that of an accountant?
- What's the purpose of accounting journals and of a ledger?
- Why does a bookkeeper prepare a trial balance?
- How has computer software helped businesses in maintaining and compiling accounting information?

LEARNING goal 4

Explain how the major financial statements differ.

UNDERSTANDING KEY FINANCIAL STATEMENTS

An accounting year is either a calendar or fiscal year. A calendar year begins January 1st and ends December 31st. A fiscal year can begin at any date designated by the business. A **financial statement** is a summary of all the financial transactions that have occurred over a particular period. Financial statements indicate a firm's financial health and stability and are key factors in management decision making.[24] That's why stockholders (the owners of the firm), bondholders and banks (people and institutions that lend money to the firm), labor unions, employees, and the Internal Revenue Service are all interested in a firm's financial statements. The key financial statements of a business are:

1. The *balance sheet*, which reports the firm's financial condition *on a specific date.*

2. The *income statement*, which summarizes revenues, cost of goods, and expenses (including taxes), for a specific period and highlights the total profit or loss the firm experienced *during that period.*

3. The *statement of cash flows*, which provides a summary of money coming into and going out of the firm. It tracks a company's cash receipts and cash payments.

The differences among the financial statements can best be summarized this way: The balance sheet details what the company owns and owes on a certain day; the income statement shows the revenue a firm earned selling its products compared to its selling costs (profit or loss) over a specific period of time; and the statement of cash flows highlights the difference between cash coming in and cash going out of a business. To fully understand this important financial information, you need to know the purpose of an organization's financial statements.[25] To help with this task, we'll explain each statement in more detail next.

The Fundamental Accounting Equation

Imagine you don't owe anybody money. That is, you have no liabilities (debts). In this case, your assets (cash and so forth) are equal to what you *own* (your equity). However, if you borrow some money from a friend, you have incurred a liability. Your assets are now equal to what you *owe* plus what you own. Translated into business terms, Assets = Liabilities + Owners' equity.

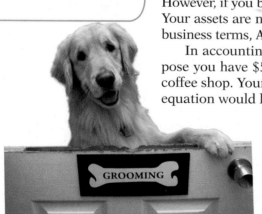

Service businesses like dog groomers rely on the same set of financial statements as manufacturers like Ford and retail sales firms like Macy's. What are some of the assets and liabilities a typical service business, like this, one would carry on its balance sheet?

In accounting, this equation must always be balanced. For example, suppose you have $50,000 in cash and decide to use that money to open a small coffee shop. Your business has assets of $50,000 and no debts. The accounting equation would look like this:

$$\text{Assets} = \text{Liabilities} + \text{Owner's equity}$$
$$\$50{,}000 = \$0 \qquad + \$50{,}000$$

You have $50,000 cash and $50,000 owners' equity (the amount of your investment in the business—sometimes referred to as net worth). However, before opening the business, you borrow $30,000 from a local bank; now the equation changes. You have $30,000 of additional cash, but you also have a debt (liability) of $30,000. (Remember, in double-entry bookkeeping we record each business transaction in two places.)

Your financial position within the business has changed. The equation is still balanced but we change it to reflect the borrowing transaction:

$$\text{Assets} = \text{Liabilities} + \text{Owner's equity}$$
$$\$80{,}000 = \$30{,}000 \quad + \$50{,}000$$

This **fundamental accounting equation** is the basis for the balance sheet.

The Balance Sheet

A **balance sheet** is the financial statement that reports a firm's financial condition at a specific time. As highlighted in the sample balance sheet in Figure 17.5 (for our hypothetical vegetarian restaurant Very Vegetarian introduced in Chapter 13), assets are listed in a separate column from liabilities and owners' (or stockholders') equity. The assets are equal to, or *balanced* with, the liabilities and owners' (or stockholders') equity. The balance sheet is that simple.

balance sheet
Financial statement that reports a firm's financial condition at a specific time and is composed of three major accounts: assets, liabilities, and owners' equity.

VERY VEGETARIAN
Balance Sheet
December 31, 2012

Assets
① Current assets
Cash	$ 15,000	
Accounts receivable	200,000	
Notes receivable	50,000	
Inventory	335,000	
Total current assets		$600,000

② Fixed assets
Land		$ 40,000	
Building and improvements	$200,000		
Less: Accumulated depreciation	−90,000		
		110,000	
Equipment and vehicles	$ 120,000		
Less: Accumulated depreciation	−80,000		
		40,000	
Furniture and fixtures	$ 26,000		
Less: Accumulated depreciation	−10,000		
		16,000	
Total fixed assets			206,000

③ Intangible assets
Goodwill	$ 20,000	
Total intangible assets		20,000
Total assets		$ 826,000

Liabilities and Owners' Equity
④ Current liabilities
Accounts payable	$ 40,000	
Notes payable (due June 2011)	8,000	
Accrued taxes	150,000	
Accrued salaries	90,000	
Total current liabilities		$ 288,000

⑤ Long-term liabilities
Notes payable (due Mar. 2015)	$ 35,000	
Bonds payable (due Dec. 2020)	290,000	
Total long-term liabilities		325,000
Total liabilities		$ 613,000

⑥ Owners' equity
Common stock (1,000,000 shares)	$ 100,000	
Retained earnings	113,000	
Total owners' equity		213,000
Total liabilities & owners' equity		$ 826,000

figure 17.5

SAMPLE VERY VEGETARIAN BALANCE SHEET

① Current assets: Items that can be converted to cash within one year.

② Fixed assets: Items such as land, buildings, and equipment that are relatively permanent.

③ Intangible assets: Items of value such as patents and copyrights that don't have a physical form.

④ Current liabilities: Payments that are due in one year or less.

⑤ Long-term liabilities: Payments not due for one year or longer.

⑥ Owner's equity: The value of what stockholders own in a firm (also called stockholder's equity).

Let's say you want to know what your financial condition is at a given time. Maybe you want to buy a house or car and therefore need to calculate your available resources. One of the best measuring sticks is your balance sheet. First, add up everything you own—cash, property, and money owed you. These are your assets. Subtract from that the money you owe others—credit card debt, IOUs, car loan, and student loan. These are your liabilities. The resulting figure is your net worth, or equity. This is fundamentally what companies do in preparing a balance sheet: they follow the procedures set in the fundamental accounting equation. In that preparation, it's important to follow generally accepted accounting principles (GAAP).

Since it's critical that you understand the financial information on the balance sheet, let's take a closer look at what is in a business's asset account and what is in its liabilities and owners' equity accounts.

Classifying Assets

assets
Economic resources (things of value) owned by a firm.

liquidity
The ease with which an asset can be converted into cash.

current assets
Items that can or will be converted into cash within one year.

fixed assets
Assets that are relatively permanent, such as land, buildings, and equipment.

intangible assets
Long-term assets (e.g., patents, trademarks, copyrights) that have no real physical form but do have value.

liabilities
What the business owes to others (debts).

accounts payable
Current liabilities are bills the company owes to others for merchandise or services purchased on credit but not yet paid for.

Assets are economic resources (things of value) owned by a firm. Assets include productive, tangible items such as equipment, buildings, land, furniture, and motor vehicles that help generate income, as well as intangible items with value like patents, trademarks, copyrights, and goodwill. Goodwill represents the value attached to factors such as a firm's reputation, location, and superior products. Goodwill is included on a balance sheet when one firm acquires another and pays more for it than the value of its tangible assets. Intangible assets like brand names can be among the firm's most valuable resources. Think of the value of brand names such as Starbucks, Coca-Cola, McDonald's, and Apple. Not all companies, however, list intangible assets on their balance sheets.

Accountants list assets on the firm's balance sheet in order of their **liquidity**, or the ease with which they can convert them to cash. Speedier conversion means higher liquidity. For example, an *account receivable* is an amount of money owed to the firm that it expects to receive within one year. It is considered a liquid asset because it can be quickly converted to cash. Land, however, is not considered a liquid asset because it takes time, effort, and paperwork to sell. It is considered as a fixed or long-term asset. Assets are thus divided into three categories, according to how quickly they can be turned into cash:

1. **Current assets** are items that can or will be converted into cash within one year. They include cash, accounts receivable, and inventory.
2. **Fixed assets** are long-term assets that are relatively permanent such as land, buildings, and equipment. (On the balance sheet we also refer to these as property, plant, and equipment.)
3. **Intangible assets** are long-term assets that have no physical form but do have value. Patents, trademarks, copyrights, and goodwill are intangible assets.

Liabilities and Owners' Equity Accounts

Liabilities are what the business owes to others—its debts. *Current liabilities* are debts due in one year or less. *Long-term liabilities* are debts not due for one year or more. The following are common liability accounts recorded on a balance sheet (look at Figure 17.5 again):

1. **Accounts payable** are current liabilities or bills the company owes others for merchandise or services it purchased on credit but has not yet paid for.

2. **Notes payable** can be short-term or long-term liabilities (like loans from banks) that a business promises to repay by a certain date.

3. **Bonds payable** are long-term liabilities; money lent to the firm that it must pay back. (We discuss bonds in depth in Chapters 18 and 19.)

As you saw in the fundamental accounting equation, the value of things you own (assets) minus the amount of money you owe others (liabilities) is called *equity*. The value of what stockholders own in a firm (minus liabilities) is called *stockholders' equity* or *shareholders' equity*. Because stockholders are the owners of a firm, we also call stockholders' equity **owners' equity**, or the amount of the business that belongs to the owners, minus any liabilities the business owes. The formula for owners' equity, then, is assets minus liabilities.

The owners' equity account will differ according to the type of organization. For sole proprietors and partners, owners' equity means the value of everything owned by the business minus any liabilities of the owner(s), such as bank loans. Owners' equity in these firms is called the *capital account*.

For corporations, the owners' equity account records the owners' claims to funds they have invested in the firm (such as stock), as well as retained earnings. **Retained earnings** are accumulated earnings from the firm's profitable operations that are reinvested in the business and not paid out to stockholders in distributions of company profits. (Distributions of profits, called dividends, are discussed in Chapter 19.) Take a few moments to look again at Figure 17.5 and see what facts you can determine about the vegetarian restaurant, Very Vegetarian, from its balance sheet. After the Progress Assessment, have some fun and estimate your own personal net worth, following the directions in Figure 17.6.

notes payable
Short-term or long-term liabilities that a business promises to repay by a certain date.

bonds payable
Long-term liabilities that represent money lent to the firm that must be paid back.

owners' equity
The amount of the business that belongs to the owners minus any liabilities owed by the business.

retained earnings
The accumulated earnings from a firm's profitable operations that were reinvested in the business and not paid out to stockholders in dividends.

progress assessment

- What do we call the formula for the balance sheet? What three accounts does it include?
- What does it mean to list assets according to liquidity?
- What's the difference between long-term and short-term liabilities on the balance sheet?
- What is owners' equity and how do we determine it?

ASSETS		LIABILITIES	
Cash	$ _____	Installment loans & interest	$ _____
Savings account	_____	Other loans & interest	_____
Checking account	_____	Credit card accounts	_____
Home	_____	Mortgage	_____
Stocks & bonds	_____	Taxes	_____
Automobile	_____	Cell phone service	_____
IRA or Keogh	_____		
Personal property	_____		
Other assets	_____		
Total assets	$ _____	Total liabilities	$ _____

Determine your net worth:

Total assets	$ _____
Total liabilities	− _____
Net worth	$ _____

figure 17.6.

YOU INCORPORATED
How do you think You Inc. stacks up financially? Let's take a little time to find out. You may be pleasantly surprised, or you may realize that you need to think hard about planning your financial future. Remember, your net worth is nothing more than the difference between what you own (assets) and what you owe (liabilities). Be honest, and do your best to give a fair evaluation of your private property's value.

The Income Statement

The financial statement that shows a firm's bottom line—that is, its profit after costs, expenses, and taxes—is the **income statement**. The income statement summarizes all the resources, called *revenue,* that have come into the firm from operating activities, money resources the firm used up, expenses it incurred in doing business, and resources it has left after paying all costs and expenses, including taxes. The resources (revenue) left over or depleted are referred to as **net income or net loss** (see Figure 17.7).

The income statement reports the firm's financial operations over a particular period of time, usually a year, a quarter of a year, or a month. It's the financial statement that reveals whether the business is actually earning a profit or losing money. The income statement includes valuable financial information for stockholders, lenders, potential investors, employees, and of course the government. Because it's so valuable, let's take a quick look at how to compile the income statement. Then we will discuss what each element in it means.

Revenue
− Cost of goods sold
= Gross Profit (gross margin)
− Operating expenses
= Net income before taxes
− Taxes
= Net income or loss

Revenue

Revenue is the monetary value of what a firm received for goods sold, services rendered, and other payments (such as rents received, money paid to the firm for use of its patents, interest earned, etc.). Be sure not to confuse the terms *revenue* and *sales;* they are not the same thing. True, most revenue the firm earns does come from sales, but companies can also have other sources of revenue. Also, a quick glance at the income statement shows you that *gross sales* refers to the total of all sales the firm completed. *Net sales* are gross sales minus returns, discounts, and allowances.

Drew Albert owns popular CJ's All-American Grill in Walnut Creek, California. The restaurant earns revenue by selling American fare like this "danger dog." What is the difference between revenue and gross profit? Between gross profit and net income before taxes?

Cost of Goods Sold

The **cost of goods sold (or cost of goods manufactured)** measures the cost of merchandise the firm sells or the cost of raw materials and supplies it used in producing items for resale. It makes sense to compare how much a business earned by selling merchandise and how much it spent to make or buy the merchandise. The cost of goods sold includes the purchase price plus any freight charges paid to transport goods, plus any costs associated with storing the goods.

In financial reporting, it doesn't matter when a firm places a particular item in its inventory, but it does matter how an accountant records the cost of the item when the firm sells it. To find out why, read the Spotlight on Small Business box on p. 478 about two different inventory valuation methods.

When we subtract the cost of goods sold from net sales, we get gross profit or gross margin. **Gross profit (or gross margin)** is how much a firm earned

VERY VEGETARIAN
Income Statement
For the Year Ended December 31, 2012

① Revenues
Gross sales		$720,000
Less: Sales returns and allowances	$ 12,000	
Sales discounts	8,000	−20,000
Net sales		$700,000

② Cost of goods sold
Beginning inventory, Jan. 1		$200,000
Merchandise purchases	$400,000	
Freight	40,000	
Net purchases		440,000
Cost of goods available for sale	$640,000	
Less ending inventory, Dec. 31		−230,000
Cost of goods sold		−410,000

③ Gross profit $290,000

④ Operating expenses
Selling expenses
Salaries for salespeople	$ 90,000	
Advertising	18,000	
Supplies	2,000	
Total selling expenses		$ 110,000

General expenses
Office salaries	$ 67,000	
Depreciation	1,500	
Insurance	1,500	
Rent	28,000	
Light, heat, and power	12,000	
Miscellaneous	2,000	
		112,000

Total operating expenses	222,000
Net income before taxes	$ 68,000
Less: Income tax expense	19,000

⑤ Net income after taxes $ 49,000

figure 17.7

SAMPLE VERY VEGETARIAN INCOME STATEMENT

① Revenue: Value of what's received from goods sold, services rendered, and other financial sources.

② Cost of goods sold: Cost of merchandise sold or cost of raw materials or parts used for producing items for resale.

③ Gross profit: How much the firm earned by buying or selling merchandise.

④ Operating expenses: Cost incurred in operating a business.

⑤ Net income after taxes: Profit or loss over a specific period after subtracting all costs and expenses, including taxes.

by buying (or making) and selling merchandise. In a service firm, there may be no cost of goods sold; therefore, gross profit could *equal* net sales. Gross profit does not tell you everything you need to know about the firm's financial performance. To get that, you must also subtract the business's expenses.

Operating Expenses

In selling goods or services, a business incurs certain **operating expenses** such as rent, salaries, supplies, utilities, and insurance. Other operating expenses that appear on an income statement, like depreciation, are a bit more complex. For example, have you ever heard that a new car depreciates in market value as soon as you drive it off the dealer's lot? The same principle holds true for assets such as equipment and machinery. **Depreciation** is the systematic write-off of the cost of a tangible asset over its estimated useful life. Under accounting rules set by GAAP and the Internal Revenue Service (which are beyond the scope of this chapter), companies are permitted to recapture the cost of these assets over time by using depreciation as an operating expense.

gross profit (or gross margin)
How much a firm earned by buying (or making) and selling merchandise.

operating expenses
Costs involved in operating a business, such as rent, utilities, and salaries.

depreciation
The systematic write-off of the cost of a tangible asset over its estimated useful life.

What's Coming and Going at the College Bookstore?

Generally accepted accounting principles (GAAP) sometimes permit an accountant to use different methods of accounting for a firm's inventory. Let's look at two possible treatments—FIFO and LIFO.

Say a college bookstore buys 100 copies of a particular textbook in July at $100 a copy. When classes begin, the bookstore sells 50 copies of the text to students at $120 each. Since the book will be used again next term, the store places the 50 copies it did not sell in its inventory until then.

In late December, when the bookstore orders 50 additional copies of the text to sell for the coming term, the publisher's price has increased to $110 a copy due to inflation and other production and distribution costs. The bookstore now has in its inventory

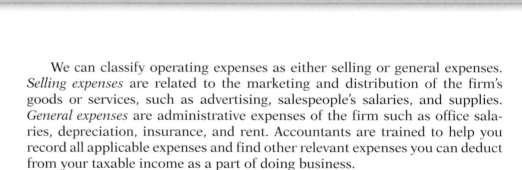

100 copies of the same textbook from different purchase cycles. If it sells 50 copies to students at $120 each at the beginning of the new term, what's the bookstore's cost of the book for accounting purposes? Actually, it depends.

The books are identical, but the accounting treatment could be different. If the bookstore uses a method called first in, first out (FIFO), the cost of goods sold is $100 for each textbook, because the textbook the store bought first—the *first in*—cost $100. The bookstore could use another method, however. Under last in, first out (LIFO), its *last* purchase of the textbooks, at $110 each, determines the cost of each of the 50 textbooks sold.

If the book sells for $120, what is the difference in gross profit (margin) between using FIFO and using LIFO? As you can see, the inventory valuation method used makes a difference.

We can classify operating expenses as either selling or general expenses. *Selling expenses* are related to the marketing and distribution of the firm's goods or services, such as advertising, salespeople's salaries, and supplies. *General expenses* are administrative expenses of the firm such as office salaries, depreciation, insurance, and rent. Accountants are trained to help you record all applicable expenses and find other relevant expenses you can deduct from your taxable income as a part of doing business.

Net Profit or Loss

After deducting all expenses, we can determine the firm's net income before taxes, also referred to as net earnings or net profit (see Figure 17.7 again). After allocating for taxes, we get to the *bottom line,* which is the net income (or perhaps net loss) the firm incurred from revenue minus sales returns, costs, expenses, and taxes over a period of time. We can now answer the question "Did the business earn or lose money in the specific reporting period?"

As you can see, the basic principles of the balance sheet and income statement are already familiar to you. You know how to keep track of costs and expenses when you prepare your own budget. If your rent and utilities exceed your earnings, you know you're in trouble. If you need more money, you may need to sell some of the things you own to meet your expenses. The same is true in business. Companies need to keep track of how much money they earn

Most businesses incur operating expenses including rent, salaries, utilities, supplies, and insurance. What are some of the likely operating expenses for this firm?

and spend, and how much cash they have on hand. The only difference is that they tend to have more complex problems and a good deal more information to record than you do.

Users of financial statements are interested in how a firm handles the flow of cash coming into a business and the cash flowing out of the business. Cash flow problems can plague both businesses and individuals. Keep this in mind as we look at the statement of cash flows next.

The Statement of Cash Flows

The **statement of cash flows** reports cash receipts and cash disbursements related to the three major activities of a firm:

- *Operations* are cash transactions associated with running the business.

- *Investments* are cash used in or provided by the firm's investment activities.

- *Financing* is cash raised by taking on new debt, or equity capital or cash used to pay business expenses, past debts, or company dividends.

Accountants analyze all changes in the firm's cash that have occurred from operating, investing, and financing in order to determine the firm's net cash position. The statement of cash flows also gives the firm some insight into how to handle cash better so that no cash-flow problems occur—such as having no cash on hand for immediate expenses.[26]

Figure 17.8 on p. 480 shows a sample statement of cash flows, again using the example of Very Vegetarian. As you can see, the statement of cash flows answers such questions as: How much cash came into the business from current operations, such as buying and selling goods and services? Did the firm use cash to buy stocks, bonds, or other investments? Did it sell some investments that brought in cash? How much money did the firm take in from issuing stock?

statement of cash flows
Financial statement that reports cash receipts and disbursements related to a firm's three major activities: operations, investments, and financing.

figure 17.8

SAMPLE VERY VEGETARIAN STATEMENT OF CASH FLOWS

① Cash receipts from sales, commissions, fees, interest, and dividends. Cash payments for salaries, inventories, operating expenses, interest, and taxes.

② Includes cash flows that are generated through a company's purchase or sale of long-term operational assets, investments in other companies, and its lending activities.

③ Cash inflows and outflows associated with the company's own equity transactions or its borrowing activities.

VERY VEGETARIAN
Statement of Cash Flows
For the Year Ended December 31, 2012

① Cash flows from operating activities

Cash received from customers	$700,000	
Cash paid to suppliers and employees	(567,000)	
Interest paid	(64,000)	
Income tax paid	(19,000)	
Interest and dividends received	2,000	
Net cash provided by operating activities		$52,000

② Cash flows from investing activities

Proceeds from sale of plant assets	$ 4,000	
Payments for purchase of equipment	(23,000)	
Net cash provided by investing activities		(19,000)

③ Cash flows from financing activities

Proceeds from issuance of short-term debt	$ 2,000	
Payment of long-term debt	(8,000)	
Payment of dividends	(15,000)	
Net cash inflow from financing activities		(21,000)
Net change in cash and equivalents		$ 12,000
Cash balance (beginning of year)		3,000
Cash balance (end of year)		$ 15,000

Cash flow is the difference between money coming into and going out of a business. Careful cash flow management is a must for a business of any size, but it's particularly important for small businesses and for seasonal businesses like ski resorts. Have you read of any firms that were forced into bankruptcy because of cash flow problems?

We analyze these and other financial transactions to see their effect on the firm's cash position. Managing cash flow can mean success or failure of any business, which is why we analyze it in more depth in the next section.

The Need for Cash Flow Analysis

Cash flow, if not properly managed, can cause a business much concern. Understanding cash flow analysis is important and not difficult to understand.[27] Let's say you borrow $100 from a friend to buy a used bike and agree to pay her back at the end of the week. You then sell the bike for $150 to someone else, who also agrees to pay you by the end of the week. Unfortunately, by the weekend your buyer does not have the money as promised, and says he will have to pay you next month. Meanwhile, your friend wants the $100 you agreed to pay her by the end of the week!

What seemed a great opportunity to make an easy $50 profit is now a cause for concern. You owe $100 and have no cash. What do you do? If you were a business, you might default on the loan and possibly go bankrupt, even though you had the potential for profit.

It's possible for a business to increase its sales and profits yet still suffer cash flow problems.[28] **Cash flow** is simply the difference between cash coming in and cash going out of a business. Poor cash flow constitutes a major operating problem for many companies and is particularly difficult for small and seasonal businesses.[29] Accountants sometimes face tough ethical challenges in reporting the flow of funds into a business. Read the Making Ethical Decisions box to see how such an ethical dilemma can arise.

How do cash flow problems start? Often in order to meet the growing demands of customers, a business buys goods on credit (using no cash). If it then sells a large number of goods on credit (getting no cash), the company needs more credit from a lender (usually a bank) to pay its immediate bills. If a firm has reached its credit limit and can borrow no more, it has a severe cash flow problem. It has cash coming in at a later date, but no cash to pay current expenses. That problem could, unfortunately, force the firm into bankruptcy, even though sales may be strong—all because no cash was available when it was most needed. Cash flow analysis shows that a business's relationship with its lenders is critical to preventing cash flow problems. Accountants can provide valuable insight and advice to businesses in managing cash flow, suggesting whether they need cash and how much.[30] After the Progress Assessment, we will see how accountants analyze financial statements using ratios.

> **cash flow**
> The difference between cash coming in and cash going out of a business.

progress assessment

- What are the key steps in preparing an income statement?
- What's the difference between revenue and income on the income statement?
- Why is the statement of cash flows important in evaluating a firm's operations?

LEARNING goal 5

Demonstrate the application of ratio analysis in reporting financial information.

ANALYZING FINANCIAL PERFORMANCE USING RATIOS

ratio analysis
The assessment of a firm's financial condition using calculations and interpretations of financial ratios developed from the firm's financial statements.

The firm's financial statements—its balance sheet, income statement, and statement of cash flows—form the basis for financial analyses performed by accountants inside and outside the firm. **Ratio analysis** is the assessment of a firm's financial condition, using calculations and financial ratios developed from the firm's financial statements. Financial ratios are especially useful in comparing the company's performance to its financial objectives and to the performance of other firms in its industry. You probably are already familiar with the use of ratios. For example, in basketball, we express the number of shots made from the foul line with a ratio: shots made to shots attempted. A player who shoots 85 percent from the foul line is considered an outstanding foul shooter; you don't want to foul this player in a close game.

Whether ratios measure an athlete's performance or the financial health of a business, they provide valuable information. Financial ratios provide key insights into how a firm compares to other firms in its industry on liquidity, amount of debt, profitability, and overall business activity. Understanding and interpreting business ratios is important to sound financial analysis. Let's look briefly at four key types of ratios businesses use to measure financial performance.

Liquidity Ratios

We've discussed that *liquidity* refers to how fast an asset can be converted to cash. Liquidity ratios measure a company's ability to turn assets into cash to pay its short-term debts (liabilities that must be repaid within one year). These short-term debts are of particular importance to the firm's lenders who expect to be paid on time. Two key liquidity ratios are the current ratio and the acid-test ratio.[31]

The *current ratio* is the ratio of a firm's current assets to its current liabilities. This information appears on the firm's balance sheet. Look back at Figure 17.5, which details Very Vegetarian's balance sheet. The company lists current assets of $600,000 and current liabilities of $288,000, yielding a current ratio of 2.08, which means Very Vegetarian has $2.08 of current assets for every $1 of current liabilities. See the following calculation:

$$\text{Current ratio} = \frac{\text{Current assets}}{\text{Current liabilities}} = \frac{\$600,000}{\$288,000} = \$2.08$$

The question the current ratio attempts to answer is: Is Very Vegetarian financially secure for the short term (less than one year)? It depends! Usually a company with a current ratio of 2 or better is considered a safe risk for lenders granting short-term credit, since it appears to be performing in line with market expectations. However, lenders will also compare Very Vegetarian's current ratio to that of competing firms in its industry and to its current ratio from the previous year to note any significant changes.

Another key liquidity ratio, called the *acid-test* or *quick ratio,* measures the cash, marketable securities (such as stocks and bonds), and receivables of a firm, compared to its current liabilities. Again, this information is on a firm's balance sheet.

$$\text{Acid-test ratio} = \frac{\text{Cash} + \text{Accounts receivable} + \text{Marketable securities}}{\text{Current liabilities}}$$

$$= \frac{\$265,000}{\$288,000} = 0.92$$

This ratio is particularly important to firms with difficulty converting inventory into quick cash. It helps answer such questions as: What if sales drop off and we can't sell our inventory? Can we still pay our short-term debt? Though ratios vary among industries, an acid-test ratio between 0.50 and 1.0 is usually considered satisfactory, but bordering on cash-flow problems. Therefore, Very Vegetarian's acid-test ratio of 0.92 could raise concerns that perhaps the firm may not meet its short-term debt and may have to go to a high-cost lender for financial assistance.

Leverage (Debt) Ratios

Leverage (debt) ratios measure the degree to which a firm relies on borrowed funds in its operations. A firm that takes on too much debt could experience problems repaying lenders or meeting promises made to stockholders. The *debt to owners' equity ratio* measures the degree to which the company is financed by borrowed funds that it must repay. Again, let's use Figure 17.5 to measure Very Vegetarian's level of debt:

$$\text{Debt to owners' equity ratio} = \frac{\text{Total liabilities}}{\text{Owners' equity}}$$

$$= \frac{\$613,000}{\$213,000} = 288\%$$

Anything above 100 percent shows a firm has more debt than equity. With a ratio of 288 percent, Very Vegetarian has a rather high degree of debt compared to its equity, which implies that lenders and investors may perceive the firm to be quite risky. However, again *it's important to compare a firm's debt ratios to those of other firms in its industry,* because debt financing is more acceptable in some industries than in others. Comparisons with the same firm's past debt ratios can also identify possible trends within the firm or industry.

Profitability (Performance) Ratios

Profitability (performance) ratios measure how effectively a firm's managers are using its various resources to achieve profits. Three of the more important ratios are earnings per share (EPS), return on sales, and return on equity.

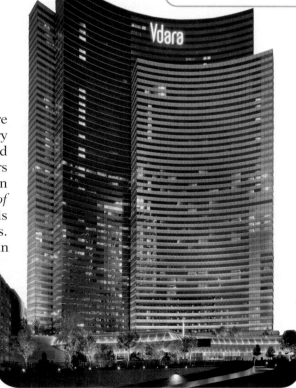

Building luxury hotels, like the Vdara at City Center in Las Vegas, generally requires taking on a high degree of debt before the hotel ever earns its first dollar. Once opened, the company incurs heavy expenses daily just to keep the business functioning efficiently. Would monitoring the four key accounting ratios be a major part of the accountant's job at the Vdara?

EPS is a revealing ratio because earnings help stimulate the firm's growth and provide for stockholders' dividends. The Financial Accounting Standards Board requires companies to report their quarterly EPS in two ways: basic and diluted. The *basic earnings per share (basic EPS) ratio* helps determine the amount of profit a company earned for each share of outstanding common stock.[32] The *diluted earnings per share (diluted EPS) ratio* measures the amount of profit earned for each share of outstanding common stock, but also considers stock options, warrants, preferred stock, and convertible debt securities the firm can convert into common stock. For simplicity's sake, we will compute only the basic EPS for Very Vegetarian:

$$\text{Basic earnings per share} = \frac{\text{Net income after taxes}}{\text{Number of common stock shares outstanding}}$$

$$= \frac{\$49,000}{\$1,000,000} = \$.049 \text{ per share}$$

Another reliable indicator of performance is *return on sales*, which tells us whether the firm is doing as well as its competitors in generating income from sales. We calculate it by comparing net income to total sales. Very Vegetarian's return on sales is 7 percent, a figure we must measure against similar numbers for competing firms to judge Very Vegetarian's performance:

$$\text{Return on sales} = \frac{\text{Net income}}{\text{Net sales}} = \frac{\$49,000}{\$700,000} = 7\%$$

The higher the risk of failure or loss in an industry, the higher the return investors expect on their investment; they expect to be well compensated for shouldering such odds. *Return on equity* indirectly measures risk by telling us how much a firm earned for each dollar invested by its owners. We calculate it by comparing a company's net income to its total owners' equity. Very

Inventory turnover is critical to just about any business, particularly restaurants that serve perishable items and that must turn over tables to keep the flow of food moving and profits up. Can you think of other businesses that need to watch their inventory turnover closely?

Balance Sheet Accounts		
ASSETS	**LIABILITIES**	**OWNERS' EQUITY**
Cash	Accounts payable	Capital stock
Accounts receivable	Notes payable	Retained earnings
Inventory	Bonds payable	Common stock
Investments	Taxes payable	Treasury stock
Equipment		
Land		
Buildings		
Motor vehicles		
Goodwill		

Income Statement Accounts			
REVENUES	**COST OF GOODS SOLD**	**EXPENSES**	
Sales revenue	Cost of buying goods	Wages	Interest
Rental revenue	Cost of storing goods	Rent	Donations
Commissions revenue		Repairs	Licenses
Royalty revenue		Travel	Fees
		Insurance	Supplies
		Utilities	Advertising
		Entertainment	Taxes
		Storage	

figure 17.9

ACCOUNTS IN THE BALANCE SHEET AND INCOME STATEMENT

Vegetarian's return on equity looks reasonably sound since some believe anything over 15 percent is considered a reasonable return:

$$\text{Return on equity} = \frac{\text{Net income after tax}}{\text{Total owners' equity}} = \frac{\$49,000}{\$213,000} = 23\%$$

Remember that profits help companies like Very Vegetarian grow. That's why profitability ratios are such closely watched measurements of company growth and management performance.

Activity Ratios

Converting the firm's inventory to profits is a key function of management. Activity ratios tell us how effectively management is turning over inventory.

The *inventory turnover ratio* measures the speed with which inventory moves through the firm and gets converted into sales. Idle inventory sitting in a warehouse earns nothing and costs money. The more efficiently a firm sells or turns over its inventory, the higher its revenue. We can measure the inventory turnover ratio for Very Vegetarian as follows:

$$\text{Inventory turnover} = \frac{\text{Costs of goods sold}}{\text{Average inventory}} = \frac{\$410,000}{\$215,000} = 1.19 \text{ times}$$

A lower-than-average inventory turnover ratio often indicates obsolete merchandise on hand or poor buying practices. Managers need to be aware of proper inventory control and anticipated inventory turnover to ensure proper performance. For example, have you ever worked as a food server in a restaurant like Very Vegetarian? How many times did your employer expect you to *turn over* a table (keep changing customers at the table) in an evening? The more times a table turns, the higher the return to the owner. Of course, like other ratios, rates of inventory turnover vary from industry to industry.

Accountants of the World United

Throughout this text you've read about the tremendous impact the global market has on business. U.S. companies like Coca-Cola earn the majority of their revenues from global markets, which helps their profitability but creates considerable accounting headaches. Since no global accounting system exists, multinationals like Coca-Cola must adapt their accounting procedures to different countries' rules. However, if the Financial Accounting Standards Board (FASB) in the United States and the London-based International Accounting Standards Board (IASB) get their way, that situation could change.

The governing bodies of the accounting profession have made significant progress toward integrating the U.S. accounting code with the International Financial Reporting Standards (IFRS) used around the world. The U.S. Securities and Exchange Commission (SEC) seems to support such a change and has suggested the IFRS replace the long standing generally accepted accounting principles (GAAP) in the near future. However, moving to one accounting standard is not likely to

happen before 2015 in order to allow companies and auditors in the United States ample time to prepare for the change. Many accountants also question if the international standards under IFRS would provide the same quality of financial reporting as the GAAP.

James Quigley, chief executive officer of Deloitte Touche Tohmatsu, one of the Big Four accounting firms in the United States, favors the move to IFRS. He believes that since we have global capital markets, we need global standards for accounting. Colleges and accounting firms across the country are waiting to see if they need to get ready for implementation of IFRS. Like it or not, it appears that IFRS is coming sooner or later to an accounting department near you.

Sources: Doug DeLoach, "IFRS: International Methods on Convergent Path," *Atlanta Business Chronicle*, January 14, 2011; "Global Accounting Standards Move Forward," *South Florida Business Journal*, April 21, 2011; and Adam Jones, "IASB Optimistic on U.S. Rules Timing, *The Financial Times*, April 22, 2011.

Accountants and other finance professionals use several other specific ratios, in addition to the ones we've discussed. To review where the accounting information in ratio analysis comes from, see Figure 17.9 on p. 485 for a quick reference. Remember, financial analysis begins where the accounting financial statements end.

Like other business disciplines, accounting is subject to change. Currently, the accounting profession is feeling the impact of the global market. The Reaching Beyond Our Borders box discusses a movement taking hold to globalize accounting procedures. It's something that accountants will be following closely. Before leaving this chapter, it's worth saying once more that, as the language of business, accounting is a worthwhile language to learn.

progress assessment

- What is the primary purpose of performing ratio analysis using the firm's financial statements?
- What are the four main categories of financial ratios?

summary

Learning Goal 1. Demonstrate the role that accounting and financial information play for a business and for its stakeholders.

- **What is accounting?**

Accounting is the recording, classifying, summarizing, and interpreting of financial events and transactions that affect an organization. The methods we use to record and summarize accounting data into reports are called an accounting system.

Learning Goal 2. Identify the different disciplines within the accounting profession.

- **How does managerial accounting differ from financial accounting?**

Managerial accounting provides information and analyses to managers within the firm to assist them in decision making. Financial accounting provides information and analyses to external users of data such as creditors and lenders.

- **What is the job of an auditor?**

Auditors review and evaluate the standards used to prepare a company's financial statements. An independent audit is conducted by a public accountant and is an evaluation and unbiased opinion about the accuracy of a company's financial statements.

- **What is the difference between a private accountant and a public accountant?**

A public accountant provides services for a fee to a variety of companies, whereas a private accountant works for a single company. Private and public accountants do essentially the same things with the exception of independent audits. Private accountants do perform internal audits, but only public accountants supply independent audits.

Learning Goal 3. List the steps in the accounting cycle, distinguish between accounting and bookkeeping, and explain how computers are used in accounting.

- **What are the six steps of the accounting cycle?**

The six steps of the accounting cycle are (1) analyzing documents; (2) recording information into journals; (3) posting that information into ledgers; (4) developing a trial balance; (5) preparing financial statements—the balance sheet, income statement, and statement of cash flows; and (6) analyzing financial statements.

- **What is the difference between bookkeeping and accounting?**

Bookkeeping is part of accounting and includes the systematic recording of data. Accounting includes classifying, summarizing, interpreting, and reporting data to management.

- **What are journals and ledgers?**

Journals are the first place bookkeepers record transactions. Bookkeepers then summarize journal entries by posting them to ledgers. Ledgers are specialized accounting books that arrange the transactions by homogeneous groups (accounts).

- **How do computers help accountants?**

Computers can record and analyze data and provide financial reports. Software can continuously analyze and test accounting systems to be sure they are functioning correctly. Computers can help decision making by providing appropriate information, but they cannot themselves make good financial decisions. Accounting applications and creativity are still human functions.

Learning Goal 4. Explain how the major financial statements differ.

* **What is a balance sheet?**

A balance sheet reports the financial position of a firm on a particular day. The fundamental accounting equation used to prepare the balance sheet is Assets = Liabilities + Owners' equity.

* **What are the major accounts of the balance sheet?**

Assets are economic resources owned by the firm, such as buildings and machinery. Liabilities are amounts the firm owes to creditors, bondholders, and others. Owners' equity is the value of everything the firm owns— its assets—minus any liabilities; thus, Owners' equity = Assets − Liabilities.

* **What is an income statement?**

An income statement reports revenues, costs, and expenses for a specific period of time (say, the year ended December 31, 2012). The formulas we use in preparing the income statement are:

* **Revenue − Cost of goods sold = Gross margin**
* **Gross margin − Operating expenses = Net income before taxes**
* **Net income before taxes − Taxes = Net income (or net loss)**

Net income or loss is also called the bottom line.

* **What is a statement of cash flows?**

Cash flow is the difference between cash receipts (money coming in) and cash disbursements (money going out). The statement of cash flows reports cash receipts and disbursements related to the firm's major activities: operations, investments, and financing.

Learning Goal 5. Demonstrate the application of ratio analysis in reporting financial information.

* **What are the four key categories of ratios?**

The four key categories of ratios are liquidity ratios, leverage (debt) ratios, profitability (performance) ratios, and activity ratios.

* **What is the major value of ratio analysis to the firm?**

Ratio analysis provides the firm with information about its financial position in key areas *for comparison to other firms in its industry and its own past performance.*

key terms

accounting 464
accounting cycle 470
accounts
  payable 474
annual report 466
assets 474
auditing 468
balance sheet 473
bonds payable 475
bookkeeping 470
cash flow 481
certified internal
  auditor (CIA) 469

certified management
  accountant (CMA) 466
certified public
  accountant (CPA) 467
cost of goods sold
  (or cost of goods
  manufactured) 476
current assets 474
depreciation 477
double-entry
  bookkeeping 470
financial accounting 466
financial statement 472

fixed assets 474
fundamental accounting
  equation 472
government and not-
  for-profit
  accounting 469
gross profit (or gross
  margin) 477
income statement 476
independent audit 468
intangible assets 474
journal 470
ledger 470

critical thinking

1. As a potential investor in a firm or perhaps the buyer of a particular business, would it be advisable to evaluate the company's financial statements? Why or why not? What key information would you seek from a firm's financial statements?

2. Why must accounting reports be prepared according to specific procedures (GAAP)? Should we allow businesses some flexibility or creativity in preparing financial statements? Why or why not?

3. What value do financial ratios offer investors in reviewing the financial performance of a firm?

4. Why is it important to remember financial ratios can differ from industry to industry?

developing workplace skills

1. Contact a CPA at a firm in your area, or talk with a CPA in your college's business department. Ask what challenges, changes, and opportunities he or she foresees in the accounting profession in the next five years. List the CPA's forecasts on a sheet of paper and then compare them with the information in this chapter.

2. Go to the websites of the American Institute of Certified Public Accountants (www.aicpa.org) and the Institute of Management Accountants (www.imanet.org). Browse the sites and find the requirements for becoming a certified public accountant (CPA) and a certified management accountant (CMA). Compare the requirements of the programs and decide which program is more appealing to you.

3. Suppose you are a new board member for an emerging not-for-profit organization hoping to attract new donors. Contributors want to know how efficiently not-for-profit organizations use their donations. Unfortunately, your fellow board members see little value in financial reporting and analysis and believe the good works of the organization speak for themselves. Prepare a fact sheet convincing the board of the need for effective financial reporting with arguments about why it helps the organization's fund-raising goals.

4. Obtain a recent annual report for a company of your choice. (Hints: *The Wall Street Journal* has a free annual reports service, and virtually all major companies post their annual reports on their websites.) Look over the firm's financial statements and see whether they match the information in

this chapter. Read the auditor's opinion (usually at the end of the report) and evaluate what you think are the most important conclusions of the auditors.

5. Obtain a recent annual report for a company of your choice (see the hints just above in exercise 4) and try your hand at computing financial ratios. Compute the current ratio, debt to owners' equity ratio, and basic earnings per share ratio. Then request an annual report from one of the firm's major competitors and compute the same ratios for that company. What did you find?

taking it to the net

Purpose

To calculate and analyze the current and quick (acid-test) ratios of different businesses.

Exercise

Potz and Pans, a small gift shop, has current assets of $45,000 (including inventory valued at $30,000) and $9,000 in current liabilities. WannaBees, a specialty clothing store, has current assets of $150,000 (including inventory valued at $125,000) and $85,000 in current liabilities. Both businesses have applied for loans. Click the calculators box on the tool bar at www.bankrate.com and then go to small business to answer the following questions:

1. Calculate the current ratio for each company. Which company is more likely to get the loan? Why?

2. The acid-test ratio subtracts the value of the firm's inventory from its total current assets. Because inventory is often difficult to sell, this ratio is considered an even more reliable measure of a business's ability to repay loans than the current ratio. Calculate the acid-test ratio for each business and decide whether you would give either the loan? Why or why not?

casing the web

To access the case "Between a Rock and a Hard Rock," visit **www.mhhe.com/ubl0e**

video case

To access the video case featuring Goodwill, visit **www.mhhe.com/ubl0e**

Financial
MANAGEMENT

LEARNING
goals

After you have read and studied this chapter, you should be able to

1 Explain the role and responsibilities of financial managers.

2 Outline the financial planning process, and explain the three key budgets in the financial plan.

3 Explain why firms need operating funds.

4 Identify and describe different sources of short-term financing.

5 Identify and describe different sources of long-term financing.

profile

In the business world, just because you're on top today doesn't mean you'll be there tomorrow. Uncertainty abounds even at the nation's largest companies as the commercial landscape constantly changes. The savviest businesspeople are always on the lookout for new avenues of opportunity. After all, it's either that or get swept up in the tide.

Carol Tomé, Chief Financial Officer (CFO) at Home Depot, knows a thing or two about adapting to unforeseen circumstances. She first learned about the ins and outs of finance in her hometown of Jackson, Wyoming, where her father owned the Jackson State Bank. Tomé grew up assuming that one day she would become the first female CEO of the family business. Fate dropped a bombshell, however, while she was studying for an MBA at the University of Denver. Tomé's father informed her that after 27 years of marriage he would be divorcing her mother and selling the bank.

Though the news devastated Tomé, she didn't let it destroy her ambition. "When I calmed down, I said to myself, 'Carol, you are going to be a banker. So be a banker.'" She did exactly that, landing a job at the United Bank of Denver after graduation. She then moved on to a series of corporate finance jobs before ending up at Home Depot in 1995. By the time she worked her way up to CFO in 2001, the company was caught up in a store building frenzy. With Tomé in control of the expansion committee, Home Depot added more than 100 locations a year through 2005. "We were very much like that Kevin Costner movie: 'Build a store, and they will come,'" says Tomé.

But the company's obsession with expansion led it to neglect other key areas, primarily technology. Up until 2010 most Home Depot stores kept track of stock with 15-year-old computers, some powered by motorboat batteries set on bulky carts. The company was also slow to offer customers the option of ordering online and picking up the merchandise at a store, as its chief competitor Lowe's did. Even the product information the company offered on its website was minimal. With studies showing that 7 out of 10 consumers first check out products online before buying, Home Depot executives realized that their reliance on aged technology was hurting sales and growth. It was clearly time for a change at the home improvement giant.

By focusing on improving its technological foothold rather than opening new stores, Home Depot's entire business plan shifted to improving sales at existing outlets. As CFO, Tomé was at the center of this transition. In 2010 she oversaw the distribution of $350 million in tech spending, $60 million of that money going to purchasing 40,000 handheld devices to replace the company's outdated in-store computers. The rest went toward beefing up online sales. Digital purchases accounted for a mere 1.5 percent of the $68 billion Home Depot made in 2010. By the end of that year Tomé unveiled a new purchasing app for iPhones and iPads, a technological triumph that not even Lowe's could match at the time. Still, to succeed in the future Tomé will need to strike a middle ground between Home Depot's new customers who shop online and the old contractors who prefer to shop in a store. Tomé will continue working to close that gap and ensure Home Depot's future dominance but, as she knows well already, nothing is certain.

Risk and uncertainty clearly define the role of financial management. In this chapter, you'll explore the role of finance in business. We'll discuss the challenges as well as the tools top managers like Carol Tomé use to attain financial stability and growth.

Getting to Know

X *Carol Tomé*

CFO of Home Depot

Sources: Chris Burritt, "Home Depot's Fix-It Lady," *Bloomberg Businessweek*, January 13, 2011; "Senior Leadership Team: Carol Tomé," Home Depot, corporate.homedepot.com, accessed May 2011; and Maxwell Murphy, "Home Depot Beats Sales, EPS Views, Raises Guidance," *The Wall Street Journal*, February 22, 2011.

At one time this company was the largest automobile maker in the world. Due to severe financial problems in 2009, the company came very close to extinction. A $7 billion government-backed loan and an additional $43 billion government investment in the company helped it survive. It is now attempting a comeback as a much smaller company. What is the name of this company? (Find the answer in the chapter.)

LEARNING goal 1

Explain the role and responsibilities of financial managers.

THE ROLE OF FINANCE AND FINANCIAL MANAGERS

finance
The function in a business that acquires funds for the firm and manages those funds within the firm.

financial management
The job of managing a firm's resources so it can meet its goals and objectives.

financial managers
Managers who examine financial data prepared by accountants and recommend strategies for improving the financial performance of the firm.

The goal of this chapter is to answer two major questions: "What is finance?" and "What do financial managers do?" **Finance** is the function in a business that acquires funds for the firm and manages them within the firm. Finance activities include preparing budgets; doing cash flow analysis; and planning for the expenditure of funds on such assets as plant, equipment, and machinery. **Financial management** is the job of managing a firm's resources to meet its goals and objectives. Without a carefully calculated financial plan, a firm has little chance for survival, regardless of its product or marketing effectiveness. Let's briefly review the roles of accountants and financial managers.

We can compare an accountant to a skilled laboratory technician who takes blood samples and other measures of a person's health and writes the findings on a health report (in business, this process is the preparation of financial statements). A financial manager is like the doctor who interprets the report and makes recommendations that will improve the patient's health. In short, **financial managers** examine financial data prepared by accountants and recommend strategies for improving the financial performance of the firm.

Clearly financial managers can make sound financial decisions only if they understand accounting information. That's why we examined accounting in Chapter 17. Similarly, a good accountant needs to understand finance. Accounting and finance go together like peanut butter and jelly. In large and medium-sized organizations, both the accounting and finance functions are generally under the control of a chief financial officer (CFO).[1] However, financial management could also be in the hands of a person who serves as company treasurer or vice president of finance. A comptroller is the chief *accounting* officer.

Figure 18.1 highlights a financial manager's tasks. As you can see, two key responsibilities are to obtain funds and to effectively control the use of those funds. Controlling funds includes managing the firm's cash, credit accounts (accounts receivable), and inventory. Finance is a critical activity in both profit-seeking and nonprofit organizations.

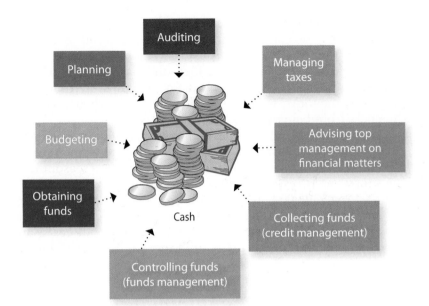

figure 18.1

**WHAT FINANCIAL
MANAGERS DO**

*Michael Miller
overhauled the
underperforming
Goodwill Industries
operation in Portland,
Oregon, by treating
the nonprofit like a
for-profit business.
He trimmed operating
expenses 30 percent by
comparing sales by
store, closing weak
outlets and opening
new ones in better
locations, and cutting
distribution costs. Sales
soared from $4 million
to over $50 million.*

Finance is important, no matter what the firm's size. As you may remember from Chapter 6, financing a small business is essential if the firm expects to survive its important first five years. But the need for careful financial management remains a challenge that any business, large or small, must face throughout its existence.[2] This is a lesson the U.S. businesses learned the hard way in the late 2000s when a financial crisis threatened the economy.[3]

General Motors, once the world's dominant automaker, faced extinction in 2009 because of severe financial problems. The company survived due to a direct government loan of $7 billion and an additional $43 billion in bailout funds provided by the U.S. Treasury.[4] (The $43 billion gave the government a 60 percent ownership stake in the company.) That same year, the government also approved an $85 billion loan to save insurance giant American International Group (AIG) and passed the $700 billion Troubled Assets Relief Program (TARP) to help restore confidence in the financial system.[5]

The Value of Understanding Finance

Three of the most common reasons a firm fails financially are:

1. Undercapitalization (insufficient funds to start the business).
2. Poor control over cash flow.
3. Inadequate expense control.

You can see all three in the following classic story: Two friends, Elizabeth Bertani and Pat Sherwood, started a company called Parsley Patch on what can best be described as a shoestring budget. It began when Bertani prepared

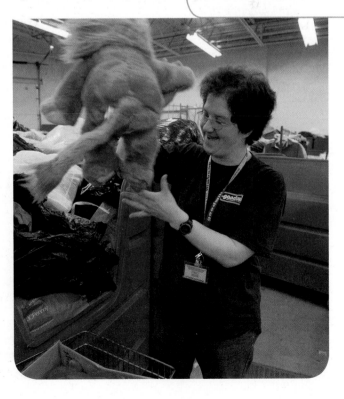

salt-free seasonings for her husband, who was on a no-salt diet. Her friend Sherwood thought the seasonings were good enough to sell. Bertani agreed, and Parsley Patch Inc. was born. The business began with an investment of $5,000 that was rapidly depleted on a logo and label design. Bertani and Sherwood quickly learned about the need for capital in getting a business going. Eventually, they invested more than $100,000 of their own money to keep the business from being undercapitalized.

Everything started well, and hundreds of gourmet shops adopted the product line. But when sales failed to meet expectations, the women decided the health-food market offered more potential because salt-free seasonings were a natural for people with restricted diets. The choice was a good one. Sales soared, approaching $30,000 a month. Still, the company earned no profits.

Bertani and Sherwood weren't trained in monitoring cash flow or in controlling expenses. In fact, they were told not to worry about costs, and they hadn't. They eventually hired a certified public accountant (CPA) and an experienced financial manager, who taught them how to compute the costs of their products, and how to control expenses as well as cash moving in and out of the company (cash flow). Soon Parsley Patch was earning a comfortable margin on operations that ran close to $1 million a year. Luckily, the owners were able to turn things around before it was too late. Eventually, they sold the firm to spice and seasonings giant McCormick.[6]

If Bertani and Sherwood had understood finance before starting their business, they might have been able to avoid the problems they encountered. The key word here is *understood*. You do not have to pursue finance as a career to understand it. Financial understanding is important to anyone who wants to start a small business, invest in stocks and bonds, or plan a retirement fund. In short, finance and accounting are two areas everyone in business should study. Since we discussed accounting in Chapter 17, let's look more closely at what financial management is all about.

What Is Financial Management?

Financial managers are responsible for paying the company's bills at the appropriate time, and for collecting overdue payments to make sure the company does not lose too much money to bad debts (people or firms that don't pay their bills). Therefore, finance functions, such as buying merchandise on credit (accounts payable) and collecting payment from customers (accounts receivable), are key components of the financial manager's job.[7] While these functions are vital to all types of businesses, they are particularly critical to small and medium-sized businesses, which typically have smaller cash or credit cushions than large corporations.

It's essential that financial managers stay abreast of changes or opportunities in finance, such as changes in tax law, since taxes represent an outflow of cash from the business.[8] Financial managers must also analyze the tax implications of managerial decisions to minimize the taxes the business must pay. Usually a member of the firm's finance department, the internal auditor, also checks the journals, ledgers, and financial statements the accounting department prepares, to make sure all transactions are in accordance with generally accepted accounting principles (GAAP). Without such audits, accounting statements would be less reliable. Therefore, it is

Most businesses have predictable day-to-day needs, like the need to buy supplies, pay for fuel and utilities and pay employees. Financial management is the function that helps ensure firms have the funds they need when they need them. What would happen to the company providing the work in this photo if it couldn't buy fuel for its trucks?

important that internal auditors be objective and critical of any improprieties or deficiencies noted in their evaluation.[9] Thorough internal audits assist the firm in financial planning, which we'll look at next.[10]

LEARNING goal **2**

> Outline the financial planning process, and explain the three key budgets in the financial plan.

FINANCIAL PLANNING

Financial planning means analyzing short-term and long-term money flows to and from the firm.[11] Its overall objective is to optimize the firm's profitability and make the best use of its money. It has three steps: (1) forecasting the firm's short-term and long-term financial needs, (2) developing budgets to meet those needs, and (3) establishing financial controls to see whether the company is achieving its goals (see Figure 18.2). Let's look at each step and the role it plays in improving the organization's financial health.

Forecasting Financial Needs

Forecasting is an important part of any firm's financial plan.[12] A **short-term forecast** predicts revenues, costs, and expenses for a period of one year or less. Part of the short-term forecast may be a **cash flow forecast**, which predicts the cash inflows and outflows in future periods, usually months or quarters. The

short-term forecast
Forecast that predicts revenues, costs, and expenses for a period of one year or less.

cash flow forecast
Forecast that predicts the cash inflows and outflows in future periods, usually months or quarters.

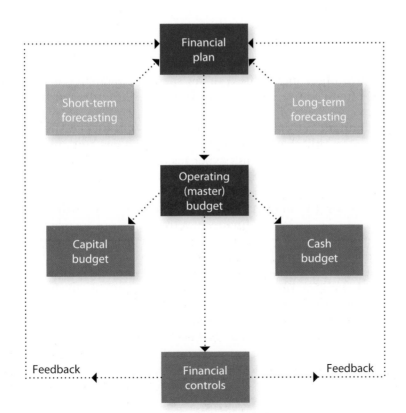

figure 18.2

FINANCIAL PLANNING
Note the close link between financial planning and budgeting.

inflows and outflows of cash recorded in the cash flow forecast are based on expected sales revenues and various costs and expenses incurred, as well as when they are due for payment. The company's sales forecast estimates projected sales for a particular period. A business often uses its past financial statements as a basis for projecting expected sales and various costs and expenses.

A **long-term forecast** predicts revenues, costs, and expenses for a period longer than 1 year, sometimes as long as 5 or 10 years. This forecast plays a crucial part in the company's long-term strategic plan, which asks questions such as: What business are we in? Should we be in it five years from now? How much money should we invest in technology and new plant and equipment over the next decade? Will we have cash available to meet long-term obligations? Innovations in Web-based software help financial managers address these long-term forecasting questions.

The long-term financial forecast gives top management, as well as operations managers, some sense of the income or profit potential of different strategic plans.[13] It also helps in preparing company budgets.

Working with the Budget Process

A **budget** sets forth management's expectations for revenues and, on the basis of those expectations, allocates the use of specific resources throughout the firm. As a financial plan, it depends heavily on the accuracy of the firm's balance sheet, income statement, statement of cash flows, and short-term and long-term financial forecasts, which all need to be as accurate as possible. To prepare budgets, financial managers must therefore take their forecasting responsibilities seriously.[14] A budget becomes the primary guide for the firm's financial operations and expected financial needs.

There are usually several types of budgets in a firm's financial plan:

- A capital budget.
- A cash budget.
- An operating or master budget.

Let's look at each.

A **capital budget** highlights a firm's spending plans for major asset purchases that often require large sums of money, like property, buildings, and equipment.

A **cash budget** estimates cash inflows and outflows during a particular period, like a month or a quarter. It helps managers anticipate borrowing needs, debt repayment, operating expenses, and short-term investments, and is often the last budget prepared. A sample cash budget for our example company, Very Vegetarian, is provided in Figure 18.3.

The **operating (or master) budget** ties together the firm's other budgets and summarizes its proposed financial activities. More formally, it estimates costs and expenses needed to run a business, given projected revenues. The firm's spending on supplies, travel, rent, technology, advertising, and salaries is determined in the operating budget, generally the most detailed a firm prepares.

Financial planning obviously plays an important role in the firm's operations and often determines what long-term investments it makes, when it will need specific funds, and how it will generate them. Once a company forecasts its short-term and long-term financial needs and compiles budgets to show how it will allocate funds, the final step in financial planning is to establish financial controls. Before we talk about those, however, Figure 18.4 on p. 500 challenges you to check your personal financial-planning skill by developing a monthly budget for "You Incorporated."

---

long-term forecast
Forecast that predicts revenues, costs, and expenses for a period longer than 1 year, and sometimes as far as 5 or 10 years into the future.

budget
A financial plan that sets forth management's expectations and, on the basis of those expectations, allocates the use of specific resources throughout the firm.

capital budget
A budget that highlights a firm's spending plans for major asset purchases that often require large sums of money.

cash budget
A budget that estimates cash inflows and outflows during a particular period like a month or a quarter.

operating (or master) budget
The budget that ties together the firm's other budgets and summarizes its proposed financial activities.

VERY VEGETARIAN
Monthly Cash Budget

	January	February	March
Sales forecast	$50,000	$45,000	$40,000
Collections			
Cash sales (20%)		$ 9,000	$ 8,000
Credit sales (80% of past month)		$40,000	$36,000
Monthly cash collection		$49,000	$44,000
Payments schedule			
Supplies and material		$ 11,000	$ 10,000
Salaries		12,000	12,000
Direct labor		9,000	9,000
Taxes		3,000	3,000
Other expenses		7,000	6,000
Monthly cash payments		$42,000	$39,000
Cash budget			
Cash flow		$ 7,000	$ 5,000
Beginning cash		−1,000	6,000
Total cash		$ 6,000	$ 11,000
Less minimum cash balance		−6,000	−6,000
Excess cash to market securities		$ 0	$ 5,000
Loans needed for minimum balance		0	0

figure 18.3

A SAMPLE CASH BUDGET FOR VERY VEGETARIAN

Establishing Financial Controls

Financial control is a process in which a firm periodically compares its actual revenues, costs, and expenses with its budget. Most companies hold at least monthly financial reviews as a way to ensure financial control. Such control procedures help managers identify variances to the financial plan and allow them to take corrective action if necessary. Financial controls also help reveal which specific accounts, departments, and people are varying from the financial plan. Finance managers can judge whether these variances are legitimate and thereby merit adjustments to the plan. Shifts in the economy or unexpected global events can also alter financial plans. For example, unrest in the Middle East and the spike in oil prices in 2011 caused many companies to consider adjusting their financial plans.[15] The Legal Briefcase box on p. 501 highlights how one state is implementing financial control to deal with severe financial problems. After the Progress Assessment, we'll see why firms need readily available funds.

financial control
A process in which a firm periodically compares its actual revenues, costs, and expenses with its budget.

progress assessment

- Name three finance functions important to the firm's overall operations and performance.
- What three primary financial problems cause firms to fail?
- How do short-term and long-term financial forecasts differ?
- What is the purpose of preparing budgets in an organization? Can you identify three different types of budgets?

	EXPECTED	ACTUAL	DIFFERENCE
Monthly income			
Wages (net pay after taxes)	_____	_____	_____
Savings account withdrawal	_____	_____	_____
Family support	_____	_____	_____
Loans	_____	_____	_____
Other sources	_____	_____	_____
Total monthly income	_____	_____	_____
Monthly expenses			
Fixed expenses			
Rent or mortgage	_____	_____	_____
Car payment	_____	_____	_____
Health insurance	_____	_____	_____
Life insurance	_____	_____	_____
Tuition or fees	_____	_____	_____
Other fixed expenses	_____	_____	_____
Subtotal of fixed expenses	_____	_____	_____
Variable expenses			
Food	_____	_____	_____
Clothing	_____	_____	_____
Entertainment	_____	_____	_____
Transportation	_____	_____	_____
Phone	_____	_____	_____
Utilities	_____	_____	_____
Publications	_____	_____	_____
Internet connection	_____	_____	_____
Cable television	_____	_____	_____
Other expenses	_____	_____	_____
Subtotal of variable expenses	_____	_____	_____
Total expenses	_____	_____	_____
Total income − Total expenses = Cash on hand/(Cash deficit)	_____	_____	_____

figure 18.4

YOU INCORPORATED MONTHLY BUDGET

In Chapter 17, you compiled a sample balance sheet for You Inc. (see p. 475). Now, let's develop a monthly budget for You Inc. Be honest and think of everything that needs to be included for an accurate monthly budget for You!

LEARNING goal 3

Explain why firms need operating funds.

THE NEED FOR OPERATING FUNDS

In business, the need for operating funds never seems to end. That's why sound financial management is essential to all businesses. And like our personal financial needs, the capital needs of a business change over time. Remember the example of Parsley Patch to see why a small business's financial requirements can shift considerably. The same is true for large corporations such as Apple, Johnson & Johnson, and Nike when they venture into new-product

Financial Order or Financial Martial Law?

The recession that began in 2008 not only brought tough economic times to millions of Americans; it also exposed severe economic problems in many of the governments of the states and cities where they live. Perhaps nowhere has the economic fallout been more severe than in Michigan where half of the state's communities are in financial distress. These severe financial problems led the state to pass the Local Government and School District Fiscal Accountability Act that allows cities, towns, and school districts to be taken over by state-appointed emergency financial managers (EFMs) selected by the Governor. The emergency managers have broad and far-reaching powers that allow them to void union contracts and in some instances remove elected officials. Supporters of the program insist that a number of struggling communities have been saved from bankruptcy by the actions of the EFMs. Others claim the Governor has become a dictator and has imposed nothing short of martial law.

According to the Governor's office the intention of the law is to protect the health, welfare, and safety of local government. In many instances it blames the financial shortcomings facing many communities on elected officials who were unwilling or unable to address the financial problems they faced. Michael Imber, of accounting firm Grant Thornton, supports the law and believes that many of the same techniques and processes used to bring private sector businesses back on firm financial footing can be used to get communities back on track as well. Directors of big public pension funds in Detroit are not so sure and have filed a lawsuit testing the law's constitutionality.

It's likely that EFMs will expand beyond Michigan. Indiana is considering similar legislation to create its own version of EFMs. In New York and several other states, receivers and oversight boards have been given similar power to EFMs to bring financial stability back to local communities. Whether EFMs are the financial solutions distressed communities need remains to be seen. One thing is for certain: responsible financial management is something that cannot be ignored.

Sources: "Bankrupt Cities Using Emergency Financial Managers to Recover," ABCNews.com, accessed May 2011; Jeff Green and Jonathan Keehner, "Muni Bankruptcy Threat Makes Michigan Train Financial SWAT Team," *Bloomberg Businessweek,* April 18, 2011; John E. Mogk, "Emergency Manager Law No Mistake," *The Detroit News,* April 15, 2011; and Susan Berfield, "Michigan's Extreme Measures," *Bloomberg Businessweek,* May 8, 2011.

areas or new markets. Virtually all organizations have operational needs for which they need funds. Key areas include:

- Managing day-by-day needs of the business.
- Controlling credit operations.
- Acquiring needed inventory.
- Making capital expenditures.

Let's look carefully at the financial needs of these key areas, which affect both the smallest and the largest of businesses.

Managing Day-by-Day Needs of the Business

If workers expect to be paid on Friday, they don't want to wait until Monday for their paychecks. If tax payments are due on the 15th of the month, the government expects the money on time. If the interest payment on a business loan is due on the 30th of this month, the lender doesn't mean the 1st of next month. As you can see, funds have to be available to meet the daily operational costs of the business.

Financial managers must ensure that funds are available to meet daily cash needs without compromising the firm's opportunities to invest money for its future.[16] Money has a *time value*. In other words, if someone offered to give you $200 either today or one year from today, you would benefit by taking the $200 today. Why? It's very simple. You could invest the $200 you receive today and over a year's time it would grow. The same is true in business; the interest a firm gains on its investments is important in maximizing the profit it will gain. That's why financial managers often try to minimize cash expenditures to free up funds for investment in interest-bearing accounts. They suggest the company pay its bills as late as possible (unless a cash discount is available for early payment). They also advise companies to try to collect what's owed them as fast as possible, to maximize the investment potential of the firm's funds.[17] Efficient cash management is particularly important to small firms since their access to capital is much more limited than larger businesses. Software from companies like Peachtree can assist small firms in handling day-to-day cash management.

Controlling Credit Operations

Financial managers know that in today's highly competitive business environment making credit available helps keep current customers happy and helps attract new ones. Credit for customers can be especially important during tough financial times like the recession that began in 2008 when lenders were hesitant to make loans.

The problem with selling on credit is that as much as 25 percent of the business's assets could be tied up in its credit accounts (accounts receivable). This forces the firm to use its own funds to pay for goods or services sold to customers who bought on credit. Financial managers in such firms often develop efficient collection procedures, like offering cash or quantity discounts to buyers who pay their accounts by a certain time. They also scrutinize old and new credit customers to see whether they have a history of meeting credit obligations on time.

One convenient way to decrease the time and expense of collecting accounts receivable is to accept bank credit cards such as MasterCard or Visa. The banks that issue these cards have already established the customer's creditworthiness, which reduces the business's risk. Businesses must pay a fee to accept credit cards, but they are usually offset by the benefits.[18]

It's difficult to think of a business that doesn't make credit available to its customers. However, collecting accounts receivable can be time-consuming and expensive. Accepting credit cards such as Visa, MasterCard, and American Express can simplify transactions for sellers and guarantee payment. What types of products do you regularly purchase with a credit card?

Acquiring Needed Inventory

As we saw in Chapter 13, effective marketing requires focusing on the customer and providing high-quality service and readily available goods. A carefully constructed inventory policy helps manage the firm's available funds and maximize profitability. Doozle's, an ice cream parlor in St. Louis, Missouri, deliberately ties up fewer funds in its inventory of ice cream in winter. It's obvious why: demand for ice cream is lower in winter.

Just-in-time inventory control (see Chapter 9) and other such methods can reduce the funds a firm must tie up in inventory. Carefully evaluating its inventory turnover ratio (see Chapter 17) can also help a firm control the outflow of cash for inventory. A business of any size must understand that poorly managed inventory can seriously affect cash flow and drain its finances dry.[19] The nearby Making Ethical Decisions box raises an interesting question about sound financial management and inventory control in a critical industry.

Making Capital Expenditures

Capital expenditures are major investments in either tangible long-term assets such as land, buildings, and equipment, or intangible assets such as patents, trademarks, and copyrights. In many organizations the purchase of major assets—such as land for future expansion, manufacturing plants to increase production capabilities, research to develop new-product ideas, and equipment to maintain or exceed current levels of output—is essential. Expanding into new markets can be expensive with no guarantee of success. Therefore, it's critical that companies weigh all possible options before committing a large portion of available resources.

Consider a firm that needs to expand its production capabilities due to increased customer demand. It could buy land and build a new plant, purchase an existing plant, or rent space. Can you think of financial and accounting considerations at play in this decision?

The need for operating funds raises several questions for financial managers: How does the firm obtain funds to finance operations and other business needs? Will it require specific funds in the long or the short term? How much will it cost (i.e. interest) to obtain these funds? Will they come from internal or external sources? We address these questions next.

capital expenditures
Major investments in either tangible long-term assets such as land, buildings, and equipment or intangible assets such as patents, trademarks, and copyrights.

Alternative Sources of Funds

We described finance earlier as the function in a business responsible for acquiring and managing funds. Sound financial management determines the amount of money needed and the most appropriate sources from which to obtain it. A firm can raise needed capital by borrowing money (debt), selling

figure 18.5

WHY FIRMS NEED FUNDS

SHORT-TERM FUNDS	LONG-TERM FUNDS
Monthly expenses	New-product development
Unanticipated emergencies	Replacement of capital equipment
Cash flow problems	Mergers or acquisitions
Expansion of current inventory	Expansion into new markets (domestic or global)
Temporary promotional programs	New facilities

debt financing
Funds raised through various forms of borrowing that must be repaid.

equity financing
Money raised from within the firm, from operations or through the sale of ownership in the firm (stock or venture capital).

short-term financing
Funds needed for a year or less.

long-term financing
Funds needed for more than a year (usually 2 to 10 years).

ownership (equity), or earning profits (retained earnings).[20] **Debt financing** refers to funds raised through various forms of borrowing that must be repaid. **Equity financing** is money raised from within the firm, from operations or through the sale of ownership in the firm (stock). Firms can borrow funds either short-term or long-term. **Short-term financing** refers to funds needed for a year or less. **Long-term financing** covers funds needed for more than a year (usually 2 to 10 years). Figure 18.5 highlights why firms may need short-term and long-term funds.

We'll explore the different sources of short- and long-term financing next. Let's first pause to check your understanding by doing the Progress Assessment.

progress assessment

- Money has time value. What does this mean?
- Why is accounts receivable a financial concern to the firm?
- What's the primary reason an organization spends a good deal of its available funds on inventory and capital expenditures?
- What's the difference between debt and equity financing?

LEARNING goal **4**

Identify and describe different sources of short-term financing.

OBTAINING SHORT-TERM FINANCING

The bulk of a finance manager's job does not relate to obtaining *long-term* funds. In small businesses, for example, long-term financing is often out of the question. Instead, day-to-day operations call for the careful management of *short-term* financial needs. Firms may need to borrow short-term funds for purchasing additional inventory or for meeting bills that come due unexpectedly. Like an individual, a business, especially a small business, sometimes needs to secure short-term funds when its cash reserves are low. Let's see how it does so.

Trade Credit

trade credit
The practice of buying goods and services now and paying for them later.

Trade credit is the practice of buying goods or services now and paying for them later. It is the most widely used source of short-term funding, the least expensive, and the most convenient.[21] Small businesses rely heavily on trade credit from firms such as United Parcel Service, as do large firms such as Kmart or Macy's. When a firm buys merchandise, it receives an invoice (a bill) much like the one you receive when you buy something with a credit card. As you'll see, however, the terms businesses receive are often different from those on your monthly statement.

Business invoices often contain terms such as *2/10, net 30*. This means the buyer can take a 2 percent discount for paying the invoice within 10 days. Otherwise the total bill (net) is due in 30 days. Finance managers pay close attention to such discounts because they create opportunities to reduce the firm's costs. Think about it for a moment: If the terms are 2/10, net 30, the customer will pay 2 percent more by waiting an extra 20 days to pay the invoice. If the firm *can* pay its bill within 10 days, it is needlessly increasing its costs by not doing so.

Some suppliers hesitate to give trade credit to an organization with a poor credit rating, no credit history, or a history of slow payment. They may insist the customer sign a **promissory note**, a written contract with a promise to pay a supplier a specific sum of money at a definite time. Promissory notes are negotiable. The supplier can sell them to a bank at a discount (the amount of the promissory note less a fee for the bank's services in collecting the amount due) and the business is then responsible to pay the bank.

promissory note
A written contract with a promise to pay a supplier a specific sum of money at a definite time.

Family and Friends

As we discussed in Chapter 17, firms often have several bills coming due at the same time with no sources of funds to pay them. Many small firms obtain short-term funds by borrowing money from family and friends. Such loans can create problems, however, if all parties do not understand cash flow. That's why it's sometimes better, when possible, to go to a commercial bank that fully understands the business's risk and can help analyze its future financial needs rather than borrow from friends or relatives.

Entrepreneurs appear to be listening to this advice. According to the National Federation of Independent Business, entrepreneurs today are relying less on family and friends as a source of borrowed funds than they have in the past.[22] If an entrepreneur decides to ask family or friends for financial assistance, it's important that both parties (1) agree to specific loan terms, (2) put the agreement in writing, and (3) arrange for repayment in the same way they would for a bank loan. Such actions help keep family relationships and friendships intact.[23]

One thing you can never have too much of is cash. Financial managers must make certain there is enough cash available to meet daily financial needs and still have funds to invest in its future. What does it mean when we say cash has time value?

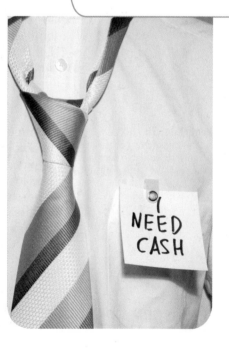

Commercial Banks

Banks, being sensitive to risk, generally prefer to lend short-term money to larger, established businesses. Imagine the different types of businesspeople who go to banks for a loan, and you'll get a better idea of the requests bankers evaluate. Picture, for example, a farmer going to the bank in spring to borrow funds for seed, fertilizer, equipment, and other needs that will be repaid after the fall harvest. Or consider a local toy store buying merchandise for Christmas sales. The store borrows the money for such purchases in the summer and plans to pay it back after Christmas. Restaurants often borrow funds at the beginning of the month and pay at the end of the month.

How much a business borrows and for how long depends on the kind of business it is, and how quickly it can resell the merchandise

Did you ever wonder how retail stores get the money to buy all the treasures we splurge on during the holidays? Department stores and other large retailers make extensive use of commercial banks and other lenders to borrow the funds they need to buy merchandise and stock their shelves. How do the stores benefit from using this type of financing?

it purchases with a bank loan or use it to generate funds. In a large business, specialists in a company's finance and accounting departments do a cash flow forecast.[24] Small-business owners generally lack such specialists and must monitor cash flow themselves.

The financial crisis beginning in 2008 severely curtailed bank lending to small businesses. It was difficult for even a promising and well-organized small business to obtain a bank loan. Fortunately, the situation seems to be changing.[25] What's important for a small firm to remember is if it gets a bank loan, the owner or person in charge of finance should keep in close touch with the bank and send regular financial statements to keep the bank up-to-date on its operations. The bank may spot cash flow problems early or be more willing to lend money in a crisis if the business has established a strong relationship built on trust and sound management. The Spotlight on Small Business highlights the problems and opportunities small businesses face in attempting to secure financing.

Different Forms of Short-Term Loans

secured loan
A loan backed by collateral, something valuable such as property.

Commercial banks offer different types of short-term loans. A **secured loan** is backed by *collateral*, something valuable such as property. If the borrower fails to pay the loan, the lender may take possession of the collateral. An automobile loan is a secured loan. If the borrower doesn't repay it, the lender will repossess the car. Inventory of raw materials like coal and steel often serves as collateral for business loans. Collateral removes some of the bank's risk in lending the money.

Accounts receivable are company assets often used as collateral for a loan; this process is called *pledging* and works as follows: A percentage of the value of a firm's accounts receivable pledged (usually about 75 percent) is advanced to the borrowing firm.[26] As customers pay off their accounts, the funds received are forwarded to the lender in repayment of the funds that were advanced.

Exploring the Financing Universe

Many small businesses had limited access to financing during the recession that began in 2008. Unfortunately, small businesses across the nation are still in a death struggle to stay afloat as many don't qualify for bank loans and financing through alternative sources is very expensive. Estimates are that less than one-third of small business owners qualify for traditional bank or SBA loans. Over 55 percent of small-business owners seek financing through a patchwork of sources such as factoring, unsecured lines of credit, and credit cards that can cost 20 percent or higher. The remaining 15 percent of small businesses are often ineligible for any financing at all.

Securing capital is the lifeblood to launching and expanding a small business. While often attempts at securing financing can be frustrating and fruitless, with some research and dedicated effort small businesses may find unexpected sources of financing. *Peer-to-peer lending* sites like Lending Club match small businesses with lenders and receive a fee for their services. Lending Club borrowers apply on line through a free application process in which they supply information about the company and explain exactly why the funds they are requesting are needed. Unfortunately, only about 10 percent of the requests receive funding, but those that do receive their financing quickly. *Crowdfunding* pools a large number of small loans (or some may say donations) from backers who do not expect to get interest or even their investment back. Instead they receive some type of "reward" if the business succeeds.

Small businesses can also turn to *fee-based services* like Lendio to seek a financing match for their business. Lendio claims to have developed a technology that matches business owners with the right type of business loan and lender. The company also offers services such as a business plan makeover and website design for a fee. Lendio does not guarantee funding for its clients. Small businesses are advised to carefully research fee-based companies before paying for services. With 50 percent of GDP and 60 to 80 percent of new jobs created by small business, the need for small business financing remains critical to the economy.

Sources: Laura Petrecca, "Crowdfunding and Peer-to-Peer Lending Help Small Businesses," *USA Today,* May 9, 2011; Emily Maltby, "Costly Financing Only Choice for Most Small Firms," *The Wall Street Journal,* May 6, 2011; and Helen Coster, "Pay to Play," *Forbes,* March 14, 2011.

An **unsecured loan** is more difficult to obtain because it doesn't require any collateral. Normally, lenders give unsecured loans only to highly regarded customers—long-standing businesses or those considered financially stable.

If a business develops a strong relationship with a bank, the bank may open a **line of credit** for the firm, a given amount of unsecured short-term funds a bank will lend to a business, provided the funds are readily available. A line of credit is *not* guaranteed to a business. However, it speeds up the borrowing process since a firm does not have to apply for a new loan every time it needs funds. As businesses mature and become more financially secure, banks will often increase their line of credit. Some even offer a **revolving credit agreement**, a line of credit that's guaranteed but usually comes with a fee. Both lines of credit and revolving credit agreements are particularly good sources of funds for unexpected cash needs.[27]

If a business is unable to secure a short-term loan from a bank, the financial manager may seek short-term funds from **commercial finance companies**. These non-deposit-type organizations make short-term loans to borrowers who offer tangible assets like property, plant, and equipment as collateral. Commercial finance companies will often make loans to businesses that cannot get short-term funds elsewhere. Since commercial finance companies assume higher degrees of risk than commercial banks, they usually charge higher interest rates. General Electric Capital is one of the world's

unsecured loan
A loan that doesn't require any collateral.

line of credit
A given amount of unsecured short-term funds a bank will lend to a business, provided the funds are readily available.

revolving credit agreement
A line of credit that's guaranteed but usually comes with a fee.

commercial finance companies
Organizations that make short-term loans to borrowers who offer tangible assets as collateral.

Managing Financial Resources

PART 6   *   Managing Financial Resources

A secured loan is backed by collateral, a tangible item of value. A car loan, for instance, is a secured loan in which the car itself is the collateral. What is the collateral in a mortgage loan?

largest commercial finance companies, with $576 billion in assets and operations in over 50 countries around the world.[28]

Factoring Accounts Receivable

factoring
The process of selling accounts receivable for cash.

One relatively expensive source of short-term funds for a firm is **factoring**, the process of selling accounts receivable for cash. Factoring dates as far back as 4,000 years, during the days of ancient Babylon. Here's how it works: Let's say a firm sells many of its products on credit to consumers and other businesses, creating a number of accounts receivable. Some buyers may be slow in paying their bills, so a large amount of money is due the firm. A *factor* is a market intermediary (usually a financial institution or a commercial bank) that agrees to buy the firm's accounts receivable, at a discount, for cash.[29] The discount depends on the age of the accounts receivable, the nature of the business, and the condition of the economy. When it collects the accounts receivable that were originally owed to the firm, the factor keeps them.

While factors charge more than banks' loan rates, remember many small businesses cannot qualify for a loan. So even though factoring is an expensive way of raising short-term funds, it is popular among small businesses.[30] A company can often reduce its factoring cost if it agrees to reimburse the factor for slow-paying accounts, or to assume the risk for customers who don't pay at all. Remember factoring is not a loan; it is the sale of a firm's asset (accounts receivable). Factoring is common in the clothing and furniture businesses, and in growing numbers of global trade ventures.[31]

Commercial Paper

commercial paper
Unsecured promissory notes of $100,000 and up that mature (come due) in 270 days or less.

Often a corporation needs funds for just a few months and prefers not to have to negotiate with a commercial bank. One strategy available to larger firms is to sell commercial paper. **Commercial paper** consists of *unsecured* promissory notes, in amounts of $100,000 and up, that mature or come due in 270 days or less. Commercial paper states a fixed amount of money the business agrees to repay to the lender (investor) on a specific date at a specified rate of interest.

Because commercial paper is unsecured, only financially stable firms (mainly large corporations with excellent credit reputations) are able to sell it. Commercial paper can be a quick path to short-term funds at lower interest than charged by commercial banks. Even very stable firms, however, had trouble selling commercial paper during the financial crisis. The Federal Reserve stepped in and assisted many companies with their short-term financing by purchasing their short-term commercial paper. Since most commercial paper matures in 30 to 90 days, it can be an investment opportunity for buyers who can afford to put up cash for short periods to earn some interest on their money.

Credit Cards

According to the National Small Business Association (NSBA), nearly half of all small firms now use credit cards to finance their businesses. Even though more businesses are turning to credit cards for financing, two-thirds believe the terms of their cards are getting worse and it's very likely they are correct. When the Credit Card Responsibility Accountability and Disclosure Act of 2009 was passed, it reduced consumer interest rates and approved many protections for consumers against card-company abuses. Unfortunately rates for small business credit cards increased almost 30 percent since small businesses did not fall under the protection of the law.[32] Still with many traditional financing options closed to them, entrepreneurs are being forced to finance their firms with credit cards.

Credit cards provide a readily available line of credit that can save time and the likely embarrassment of being rejected for a bank loan. Of course, in contrast to the convenience they offer, credit cards are extremely risky and costly. Interest rates can be exorbitant, and there can be considerable penalties if users fail to make their payments on time. Savvy businesspersons study the perks that are offered with many cards and determine which might be the most beneficial to their companies. Joe Speiser, of pet-food distributor Petflow.com, found a cash-back card that helped put additional dollars back into his business.[33] Still, when dealing with credit cards remember it's an expensive way to borrow money and credit cards are probably best used as a last resort.

After checking your progress below, we'll look into long-term financing options.

progress assessment

- What does an invoice containing the terms *2/10, net 30* mean?
- What's the difference between trade credit and a line of credit?
- What's the key difference between a secured and an unsecured loan?
- What is factoring? What are some of the considerations factors consider in establishing their discount rate?

LEARNING goal 5

Identify and describe different sources of long-term financing.

OBTAINING LONG-TERM FINANCING

In a financial plan, forecasting determines the amount of funding the firm will need over various periods and the most appropriate sources for obtaining those funds. In setting long-term financing objectives, financial managers generally ask three questions:

1. What are our organization's long-term goals and objectives?
2. What funds do we need to achieve the firm's long-term goals and objectives?
3. What sources of long-term funding (capital) are available, and which will best fit our needs?

Firms need long-term capital to purchase expensive assets such as plant and equipment, to develop new products, or perhaps finance their expansion. In major corporations, the board of directors and top management usually make decisions about long-term financing, along with finance and accounting executives. Pfizer, one of the world's largest research-based biomedical and pharmaceutical company, spends over $9 billion a year researching and developing new products. The development of a single new drug could take 10 years and cost the firm close to $1.3 billion before it brings in any profit.[34] It's easy to see why high-level managers make the long-term financing decisions at Pfizer. Owners of small- and medium-sized businesses are almost always actively engaged in analyzing their long-term financing decisions.

As we noted earlier, long-term funding comes from two major sources, debt financing and equity financing. Let's look at these sources next.

Debt Financing

Debt financing is borrowing money the company has a legal obligation to repay. Firms can borrow by either getting a loan from a lending institution or issuing bonds.

term-loan agreement
A promissory note that requires the borrower to repay the loan in specified installments.

Debt Financing by Borrowing from Lending Institutions   Long-term loans are usually due within 3 to 7 years but may extend to 15 or 20 years. A **term-loan agreement** is a promissory note that requires the borrower to repay the loan with interest in specified monthly or annual installments. A major advantage is that the interest is tax deductible.

Long-term loans are both larger and more expensive to the firm than short-term loans. Since the repayment period can be quite long, lenders assume more risk and usually require collateral, which may be real estate, machinery, equipment, company stock, or other items of value. Lenders may also require certain restrictions to force the firm to act responsibly. The interest rate is based on the adequacy of collateral, the firm's credit rating, and the general level of market interest rates. The greater the risk a lender takes in making a loan, the higher the rate of interest. This principle is known as the **risk/return trade-off**.

risk/return trade-off
The principle that the greater the risk a lender takes in making a loan, the higher the interest rate required.

indenture terms
The terms of agreement in a bond issue.

Debt Financing by Issuing Bonds   If an organization is unable to obtain its long-term financing needs by getting a loan from a lending institution it may try to issue bonds. To put it simply, a bond is like an IOU with a promise to repay the amount borrowed, with interest, on a certain date. The terms of the agreement in a bond issue are the **indenture terms**. The types of organizations that can issue bonds include federal, state, and local governments; federal government agencies; foreign governments; and corporations.

You may already be familiar with bonds. You may own investments like U.S. government savings bonds, or perhaps you volunteered your time to help a local school district pass a bond issue. If your community is building a new stadium or cultural center, it may sell bonds to finance the project. Businesses and governments compete when issuing bonds. Potential investors (individuals and institutions) measure the risk of purchasing a bond against the return the bond promises to pay—the interest—and the issuer's ability to repay when promised.

Like other forms of long-term debt, bonds can be secured or unsecured. A **secured bond** is issued with some form of collateral, such as real estate, equipment, or other pledged assets. If the bond's indenture terms are violated (e.g., not paying interest payments), the bondholder can issue a claim on the collateral. An **unsecured bond**, called a debenture bond, is backed only by the reputation of the issuer. Investors in such bonds simply trust that the organization issuing the bond will make good on its financial commitments.

Bonds are a key means of long-term financing for many organizations. They can also be valuable investments for private individuals or institutions. Given this importance, we will discuss bonds in depth in Chapter 19.

Equity Financing

If a firm cannot obtain a long-term loan from a lending institution or is unable to sell bonds to investors, it may seek equity financing. Equity financing makes funds available when the owners of the firm sell shares of ownership to outside investors in the form of stock, when they reinvest company earnings in the business, or obtain funds from venture capitalists.

Equity Financing by Selling Stock   The key thing to remember about stock is that stockholders become owners in the organization. Generally, the corporation's board of directors decides the number of shares of stock that will be offered to investors for purchase. The first time a company offers to sell its stock to the general public is called an *initial public offering (IPO).*[35] Selling stock to the public to obtain funds is by no means easy or automatic. U.S.

secured bond
A bond issued with some form of collateral.

unsecured bond
A bond backed only by the reputation of the issuer; also called a debenture bond.

John Krech created an inventory management product that he believed would sell well if he could find the money to bring it to market. When credit grew tight in the recent financial crisis, Krech sold his home and tapped his retirement funds to obtain start-up money for his new venture. Why is this financing strategy considered risky?

venture capital
Money that is invested in new or emerging companies that are perceived as having great profit potential.

companies can issue stock for public purchase only if they meet requirements set by the U.S. Securities and Exchange Commission (SEC) and various state agencies. They can offer different types of stock such as common and preferred. We'll discuss IPOs and common and preferred stock in depth in Chapter 19.

Equity Financing from Retained Earnings   You probably remember from Chapter 17 that the profits the company keeps and reinvests in the firm are called *retained earnings*. Retained earnings often are a major source of long-term funds, especially for small businesses. They often have fewer financing alternatives, such as selling stock or bonds, than large businesses do. However, large corporations also depend on retained earnings for needed long-term funding. In fact, retained earnings are usually the most favored source of meeting long-term capital needs. A company that uses them saves interest payments, dividends (payments for investing in stock), and any possible underwriting fees for issuing bonds or stock. Retained earnings also create no new ownership in the firm, as stock does.

Suppose you wanted to buy an expensive personal asset such as a new car. Ideally you would go to your personal savings account and take out the necessary cash. No hassle! No interest! Unfortunately, few people have such large amounts of cash available. Most businesses are no different. Even though they would like to finance long-term needs from operations (retained earnings), few have the resources available to accomplish this.

Equity Financing from Venture Capital   The hardest time for a business to raise money is when it is starting up or just beginning to expand. A start-up business typically has few assets and no market track record, so the chances of borrowing significant amounts of money from a bank are slim. **Venture capital** is money invested in new or emerging companies that some investors—venture capitalists—believe have great profit potential. Venture capital helped firms like Intel, Apple, and Cisco Systems get started and let Facebook and Google expand and grow. Venture capitalists invest in a business in return for part ownership of the business. They expect higher-than-average returns and competent management performance for their investment.

The venture capital industry originally began as an alternative investment vehicle for wealthy families. The Rockefeller family, for example (whose vast fortune came from John D. Rockefeller's Standard Oil Company, started in the 19th century), financed Sanford McDonnell when he was operating his company from an airplane hangar. That small venture eventually grew into McDonnell Douglas, a large aerospace and defense contractor that merged with Boeing Corporation in 1997. The venture capital industry grew significantly in the 1990s, especially in high-tech centers like California's Silicon Valley, where venture capitalists concentrated on Internet-related companies. In the early 2000s, problems in the technology industry and a slowdown in the overall economy reduced venture capital expenditures. The recent financial crisis caused venture capital spending to drop to new lows. However, as the economy began to grow in 2011, venture capital again returned to the market.[36]

Comparing Debt and Equity Financing

Figure 18.6 compares debt and equity financing options. Raising funds through borrowing to increase the firm's rate of return is referred to as **leverage**. Though debt increases risk because it creates a financial obligation that must be repaid, it also enhances the firm's ability to increase profits. Recall that two key jobs of the financial manager or CFO are forecasting the firm's need for borrowed funds and planning how to manage these funds once they are obtained.

Firms are very concerned with the cost of capital. **Cost of capital** is the rate of return a company must earn in order to meet the demands of its lenders and expectations of its equity holders (stockholders or venture capitalists). If the firm's earnings are larger than the interest payments on borrowed funds, business owners can realize a higher rate of return than if they used equity financing. Figure 18.7 on p. 514 describes an example, again involving our vegetarian restaurant, Very Vegetarian (introduced in Chapter 13). If Very Vegetarian needed $200,000 in new financing, it could consider debt by selling bonds or equity through offering stock. Comparing the two options in this situation, you can see that Very Vegetarian would benefit by selling bonds since the company's earnings are greater than the interest paid on borrowed funds (bonds). However, if the firm's earnings were less than the interest paid on borrowed funds (bonds), Very Vegetarian could lose money. It's also important to remember that bonds, like all debt, have to be repaid at a specific time.

Individual firms must determine exactly how to balance debt and equity financing by comparing the costs and benefits of each. Leverage ratios (discussed in Chapter 17) can also give companies an industry standard for this balance, to which they can compare themselves. Still debt varies considerably among major companies and industries. For example, automaker Ford Motor Company has almost $100 billion of debt on its balance sheet. This seems mild compared to General Electric that has over $400 billion of debt on theirs.[37] Leisure industry giants Sands and Trump Hotels and Casinos carry billions of dollars of debt to finance their hotels, condos, and golf courses. In contrast, tech leaders Apple and Microsoft have no long-term debt and both have had almost $50 billion in cash available at times. According to Standard & Poor's and Moody's Investor Services (firms that provide corporate and financial research), the debt of a large industrial corporation typically ranges between 33 and 40 percent of its total assets. The amount of small-business debt obviously varies considerably from firm to firm.

leverage
Raising needed funds through borrowing to increase a firm's rate of return

cost of capital
The rate of return a company must earn in order to meet the demands of its lenders and expectations of its equity holders.

figure 18.6
DIFFERENCES BETWEEN DEBT AND EQUITY FINANCING

	Type of Financing	
CONDITIONS	**DEBT**	**EQUITY**
Management influence	There's usually none unless special conditions have been agreed on.	Common stockholders have voting rights.
Repayment	Debt has a maturity date. Principal must be repaid.	Stock has no maturity date. The company is never required to repay equity.
Yearly obligations	Payment of interest is a contractual obligation.	The firm isn't legally liable to pay dividends.
Tax benefits	Interest is tax deductible.	Dividends are paid from after-tax income and aren't deductible.

figure 18.7

**USING LEVERAGE (DEBT)
VERSUS EQUITY FINANCING**
Very Vegetarian wants to
raise $200,000 in new
capital. Compare the firm's
debt and equity options.

ADDITIONAL DEBT		ADDITIONAL EQUITY	
Stockholders' equity	$500,000	Stockholders' equity	$500,000
Additional equity	—	Additional equity	$200,000
Total equity	$500,000	Total equity	$700,000
Bond @ 8% interest	200,000	Bond interest	—
Total shareholder equity	$700,000	Total shareholder equity	$700,000

YEAR-END EARNINGS			
Gross profit	$100,000	Gross profit	$100,000
Less bond interest	−16,000	Less interest	—
Operating profit	$84,000	Operating profit	$100,000
Return on equity	16.6%	Return on equity	14.2%
($84,000 ÷ $500,000 = 16.6%)		($100,000 ÷ $700,000 = 14.2%)	

Lessons from the Financial Crisis

The financial crisis that started in 2008 caused financial markets to suffer their worst fall since the Great Depression of the 1920s and 1930s. The collapse of financial markets could be laid at the feet of financial managers for failing to do their job effectively. Poor investment decisions and risky financial dealings (especially in real estate) caused long-standing financial firms such as Lehman Brothers to close their doors.[38] The multibillion-dollar Ponzi scheme of once respected financial manager Bernie Madoff further caused the public's trust in financial managers to disappear.[39] Unfortunately, it also caused many investors' funds to disappear as well.

The financial meltdown of the late 2000s led the U.S. Congress to pass sweeping financial regulatory reform. The Dodd-Frank Wall Street Reform and Consumer Protection Act affects almost every aspect of the U.S. financial services industry.[40] As the government increases its involvement and intervention in financial markets, the requirements of financial institutions and financial managers have become more stringent. This means that the job of the financial manager promises to become even more challenging. The events in late 2000s questioned the integrity and good judgment of financial managers much like events in the early 2000s questioned the integrity and judgment of the accounting industry (see Chapter 17). Without a doubt, financial managers have a long road back to earning the trust of the public.

Chapter 19 takes a close look at securities markets as a source of securing long-term financing for businesses and as a base for investment options for private investors. You will learn how securities exchanges work, how firms issue stocks and bonds, how to choose the right investment strategy, how to buy and sell stock, where to find up-to-date information about stocks and bonds, and more. Finance takes on a new dimension when you see how you can participate in financial markets yourself.

progress assessment

- What are the two major forms of debt financing available to a firm?
- How does debt financing differ from equity financing?
- What are the three major forms of equity financing available to a firm?
- What is leverage, and why do firms choose to use it?

summary

Learning Goal 1. Explain the role and responsibilities of financial managers.

- **What are the most common ways firms fail financially?**

The most common financial problems are (1) undercapitalization, (2) poor control over cash flow, and (3) inadequate expense control.

- **What do financial managers do?**

Financial managers plan, budget, control funds, obtain funds, collect funds, conduct audits, manage taxes, and advise top management on financial matters.

Learning Goal 2. Outline the financial planning process, and explain the three key budgets in the financial plan.

- **What are the three budgets in a financial plan?**

The capital budget is the spending plan for expensive assets such as property, plant, and equipment. The cash budget is the projected cash balance at the end of a given period. The operating (master) budget summarizes the information in the other two budgets. It projects dollar allocations to various costs and expenses given various revenues.

Learning Goal 3. Explain why firms need operating funds.

- **What are firms' major financial needs?**

Businesses need financing for four major tasks: (1) managing day-by-day operations, (2) controlling credit operations, (3) acquiring needed inventory, and (4) making capital expenditures.

- **What's the difference between debt financing and equity financing?**

Debt financing raises funds by borrowing. Equity financing raises funds from within the firm through investment of retained earnings, sale of stock to investors, or sale of part ownership to venture capitalists.

- **What's the difference between short-term and long-term financing?**

Short-term financing raises funds to be repaid in less than a year, whereas long-term financing raises funds to be repaid over a longer period.

Learning Goal 4. Identify and describe different sources of short-term financing.

- **Why should businesses use trade credit?**

Trade credit is the least expensive and most convenient form of short-term financing. Businesses can buy goods today and pay for them sometime in the future.

- **What is meant by a line of credit and a revolving credit agreement?**

A line of credit is an agreement by a bank to lend a specified amount of money to the business at any time, if the money is available. A revolving credit agreement is a line of credit that guarantees a loan will be available—for a fee.

- **What's the difference between a secured loan and an unsecured loan?**

An unsecured loan has no collateral backing it. Secured loans have collateral backed by assets such as accounts receivable, inventory, or other property of value.

- **Is factoring a form of secured loan?**

No, factoring means selling accounts receivable at a discounted rate to a factor (an intermediary that pays cash for those accounts and keeps the funds it collects on them).

- **What's commercial paper?**

Commercial paper is a corporation's unsecured promissory note maturing in 270 days or less.

Learning Goal 5. Identify and describe different sources of long-term financing.

- **What are the major sources of long-term financing?**

Debt financing is the sale of bonds to investors and long-term loans from banks and other financial institutions. Equity financing is obtained through the sale of company stock, from the firm's retained earnings, or from venture capital firms.

- **What are the two major forms of debt financing?**

Debt financing comes from two sources: selling bonds and borrowing from individuals, banks, and other financial institutions. Bonds can be secured by some form of collateral or unsecured. The same is true of loans.

- **What's leverage, and how do firms use it?**

Leverage is borrowing funds to invest in expansion, major asset purchases, or research and development. Firms measure the risk of borrowing against the potential for higher profits.

key terms

budget 498
capital budget 498
capital expenditures 503
cash budget 498
cash flow forecast 497
commercial finance
  companies 507
commercial paper 508
cost of capital 513
debt financing 504
equity financing 504
factoring 508

finance 494
financial control 499
financial management 494
financial managers 494
indenture terms 510
leverage 513
line of credit 507
long-term financing 504
long-term forecast 498
operating (or master)
  budget 498
promissory note 505

revolving credit
  agreement 507
risk/return trade-off 510
secured bond 511
secured loan 506
short-term financing 504
short-term forecast 497
term-loan agreement 510
trade credit 504
unsecured bond 511
unsecured loan 507
venture capital 512

critical thinking

1. What are the primary sources of short-term funds for new business owners? What are their sources of long-term funds?

2. Why does a finance manager need to understand accounting information if the firm has a trained accountant on its staff?

3. Why do firms generally prefer to borrow funds to obtain long-term financing rather than issue shares of stock?

developing workplace skills

1. Go to your college's website and see whether its operating budget is online. If not, go to the campus library and see whether the reference librarian has a copy of your college's operating budget for the current year. Try to identify major capital expenditures your college has planned for the future.

2. One of the most difficult concepts to get across to small-business owners is the need to take all the trade credit they can get. For example, the credit terms 2/10, net 30 can save businesses money if they pay their bills in the first 10 days. Work with a group of classmates to build a convincing argument for using trade credit.

3. Go online and check the capitalization required to open a franchise of your choice, like Subway or McDonald's. Does the franchisor offer financial assistance to prospective franchisees? Evaluate the cost of the franchise versus its business potential using the risk/return trade-off discussed in the chapter.

4. Contact a lending officer at a local bank in your community, or visit the bank's website, to check the bank's policies on providing a business a line of credit and a revolving line of credit. Evaluate the chances that this bank will give a small business either form of short-term loan.

5. Factoring accounts receivable is a form of financing used since the days of Babylonian King Hammurabi 4,000 years ago. Today it's still a source of short-term funds used by small businesses. Visit www.21stfinancialsolutions. com to get more in-depth information about factoring and be prepared to discuss the pros and cons of factoring.

taking it to the net

Purpose

To identify which types of companies qualify for financing through the Small Business Administration.

Exercise

Many small-business owners have a difficult time finding financing to start or expand their business. The Small Business Administration is one potential source of financing for many types of small businesses, but there are also some businesses that do not qualify for SBA loans. Go to www.sba.gov/content/businesses-eligible-ineligible-sba-assistance and see whether the following businesses are eligible to apply for SBA financing:

1. Growing Like a Weed is a lawn care business that needs funding to buy additional equipment in order to expand. Does it meet SBA criteria? Why or why not?

2. Glamour Galore is a cosmetic company that pays sales commissions based on a system that depends upon salespeople recruiting additional salespeople. It needs funding to build a marketing campaign. Does it meet SBA criteria? Why or why not?

3. Bells'n'Whistles is a pinball refurbishing company. Its founding partners need funding to buy inventory. Do they meet SBA criteria? Why or why not?

4. Lettuce Entertain You is a company needing funding to remodel an old warehouse to house its latest restaurant. Does it meet SBA criteria? Why or why not?

casing the web

To access the case "Surviving Financially in the Nonprofit World," visit **www.mhhe.com/ub10e**

video case

To access the video case featuring Tom & Eddie's, visit **www.mhhe.com/ub10e**

USING Securities Markets for Financing & Investing Opportunities

19

LEARNING goals

After you have read and studied this chapter, you should be able to

1 Describe the role of securities markets and of investment bankers.

2 Identify the stock exchanges where securities are traded.

3 Compare the advantages and disadvantages of equity financing by issuing stock, and detail the differences between common and preferred stock.

4 Compare the advantages and disadvantages of obtaining debt financing by issuing bonds, and identify the classes and features of bonds.

5 Explain how to invest in securities markets and set investment objectives such as long-term growth, income, cash, and protection from inflation.

6 Analyze the opportunities stocks offer as investments.

7 Analyze the opportunities bonds offer as investments.

8 Explain the investment opportunities in mutual funds and exchange-traded funds (ETFs).

9 Describe how indicators like the Dow Jones Industrial Average affect the market.

profile

In some ways, investing has become almost too easy today. Anybody with an e-mail address and a bank account can open an account with an online brokerage like E-Trade or Schwab and instantly start trading stocks from around the world. At the same time, though, the tangle of toxic investments that fueled the economic meltdown beginning in 2008 taught many investors just how complicated the financial world can be.

Many people hoping to find ways to better understand investing have turned to media such as CNBC to help guide them through the sea of easily available information. CNBC's multiple Emmy Award–winning Maria Bartiromo's accessible analysis of the day-to-day intricacies of Wall Street has made her the face of investing for millions of Americans. A recent study of Bartiromo's CNBC peers, both men and women, found that many are inclined to stir up media stunts that cause investors to sell their stocks. Bartiromo, on the other hand, uses her well-earned "street cred" wisely and incites far fewer sells than her colleagues. And in a 24-hour news cycle that sometimes resembles a circus more than actual journalism, Bartiromo's integrity is all the more valuable.

Getting to Know
X *Maria Bartiromo*
CNBC Financial Analyst

Born and raised in Brooklyn, Bartiromo spent her youth working in the coat checkroom of her family's Italian restaurant. Eventually she made it to the kitchen, where she closely observed her father's dogged work ethic as head chef. "Every day, I witnessed my father dedicate himself and his life to his family," said Bartiromo. "He'd regularly work long hours, day after day and he never complained." After graduating from New York University, Bartiromo brought that same dedication to her work as an overnight producer at CNN. Though her responsibilities were limited strictly to behind the camera, she quietly began gathering taped segments of herself as anchor in her off hours. None of these pieces ever made it to air, but they were promising enough to land her a job at CNBC.

After working for two years at the network, Bartiromo distinguished herself by becoming the first journalist to broadcast directly from the hectic floor of the New York Stock Exchange. By the late 1990s she was a CNBC fixture, earning the nickname the "Money Honey." But Bartiromo is far more than a pretty face in an anchor's chair. Her dislike for

sensationalism and her candid interviews with everyone from former General Electric CEO Jack Welch to Bono made her a top draw at the station. By the 2000s she was lead anchor at two of the network's biggest shows, *Closing Bell* and *The Wall Street Journal Report with Maria Bartiromo.* She has written several books and numerous columns and articles in publications such as *Businessweek, Milano Finanza, Individual Investor, Ticker, Financial Times, Newsweek,* and the *New York Post.* In 2009, the *Financial Times* named her one of the "50 Who Shaped the Decade." In 2011 she was the first journalist to be inducted into the Cable Hall of Fame.

When the stock market tanked in 2008, Bartiromo provided front-line insight on the extent of the crisis. Her lengthy relationship with the NYSE gave her a unique perspective on events.

Also, her years of experience helped translate the complicated technical language and concepts of the financial sector into more digestible terms. As she watched Wall Street burn around her, Bartiromo felt saddened for her investment friends who were losing their jobs in droves. Still, she did not fail to recognize those unethical individuals who managed to profit from the crisis. "At the heart of everything on Wall Street has to be integrity," said Bartiromo. "I am outraged to see some of these executives walk away with giant pay packages . . . however, I also believe that an across-the-board, blanket statement that all business is 'bad' is just not true." To be a successful investor, you need a little education. In this chapter you'll learn about the many ways that money can be invested in securities markets.

Sources: Michael Martin, "How Maria Bartiromo May Become the Best Teacher You've Ever Had," *The Huffington Post,* April 15, 2010; Kristina Peterson , "CNBC CEO Chats Seldom Break News: Study," *The Wall Street Journal,* February 17, 2011; and "Maria Bartiromo" CNBC TV Profiles, http://www.cnbc.com/id/15838253, accessed May 2011.

When the price of their stock rises to a certain level, many companies will split the stock (i.e., exchanging two shares worth $50 for each original share worth $100) in order to make the stock appear more affordable. However, this company, run by America's most successful investor, has never split its stock even when the price of the company's stock reached $150,000 a share (that's right $150,000 for one share). What is the name of this company? (Find the answer in the chapter.)

initial public offering (IPO)
The first public offering of a corporation's stock.

David and Tom Gardner, the Motley Fools, are passionate about spreading the message that securities markets can provide opportunities for all. The brothers have built their careers on providing high-quality financial information to investors regardless of education or income. Visit their web site at www.fool.com for more information.

LEARNING goal 1

Describe the role of securities markets and of investment bankers.

THE FUNCTION OF SECURITIES MARKETS

Securities markets—financial marketplaces for stocks, bonds, and other investments—serve two major functions. First, they assist businesses in finding long-term funding to finance capital needs, such as expanding operations, developing new products, or buying major goods and services. Second, they provide private investors a place to buy and sell securities (investments) such as stocks and bonds that can help them build their financial future. In this chapter, we look at securities markets first from the perspective of funding for businesses and second as markets for private investors to buy and trade investments.

Securities markets are divided into primary and secondary markets. *Primary markets* handle the sale of *new* securities. This is an important point to understand. Corporations make money on the sale of their securities (stock) only once—when they sell it on the primary market. The first public offering of a corporation's stock is called an **initial public offering (IPO)**. After that, the *secondary market* handles the trading of these securities between investors, with the proceeds of the sale going to the investor selling the stock, not to the corporation whose stock is sold. For example, imagine your vegetarian restaurant, Very Vegetarian, has grown into a chain and your products are available in many retail stores throughout the country. You want to raise additional funds to expand further. If you offer 1 million shares of stock in your company at $10 a share, you can raise $10 million at this initial offering. However, after the initial sale, if Shareholder Jones decides to sell 100 shares of her Very Vegetarian stock to Investor Smith, Very Vegetarian collects nothing from that transaction. Smith buys the stock from Jones, not from Very Vegetarian. It is possible, however, for companies like Very Vegetarian to offer additional shares of stock for sale to raise additional capital.

As mentioned in Chapter 18, we can't overemphasize the importance of long-term funding to businesses. Given a choice, businesses normally prefer to meet their long-term financial needs by using retained earnings or borrowing funds either from a lending institution (bank, pension fund, insurance company) or corporate bond issue. However, if long-term funds are not available from retained earnings or lenders, a company may be able to raise capital by issuing corporate stock. (Recall from Chapter 18 that selling stock in the corporation is a form of *equity financing* and issuing corporate bonds is a form of *debt financing*.) Social networking giants Groupon and Facebook are expected to have initial public offerings in 2011 that will raise billions for the companies.[1] Visa, the world's largest processor of debit and credit cards, raised $18 billion from its IPO in 2008; Facebook is expected to dwarf that amount.[2] These sources of equity and bond financing are not available to all companies, especially small businesses.

Let's imagine you need further long-term financing to *expand* operations at Very Vegetarian. Your chief financial officer (CFO) says the company lacks sufficient retained earnings and she doesn't think it can secure the needed funds from a lending institution. She suggests that you offer shares of stock or issue corporate bonds to private investors to secure the funding. She warns, however, that issuing shares of stock or corporate bonds is not simple or automatic. To get approval for stock or bond issues you must make extensive financial disclosures and undergo detailed scrutiny by the U.S. Securities and Exchange Commission (SEC). Because of these requirements, your CFO recommends that the company turn to an investment banker for assistance. Let's see why.

The Role of Investment Bankers

Investment bankers are specialists who assist in the issue and sale of new securities. These large financial firms can help companies like Very Vegetarian prepare the extensive financial analyses necessary to gain SEC approval for bond or stock issues. Investment bankers can also *underwrite* new issues of stocks or bonds. That is, the investment banking firm buys the entire stock or bond issue at an agreed-on discount, which can be quite sizable, and then sells the issue to private or institutional investors at full price.[3]

Institutional investors are large organizations—such as pension funds, mutual funds, and insurance companies—that invest their own funds or the funds of others. Because of their vast buying power, institutional investors are a powerful force in securities markets.

Before we look at stocks and bonds as long-term financing and investment opportunities in more depth, it's important to understand stock exchanges—the places where stocks and bonds are traded.

> **investment bankers**
> Specialists who assist in the issue and sale of new securities.

> **institutional investors**
> Large organizations—such as pension funds, mutual funds, and insurance companies—that invest their own funds or the funds of others.

LEARNING goal 2

Identify the stock exchanges where securities are traded.

STOCK EXCHANGES

As the name implies, a **stock exchange** is an organization whose members can buy and sell (exchange) securities on behalf of companies and individual investors. The New York Stock Exchange (NYSE) was founded in 1792 and was primarily a floor-based exchange, which means trades physically took place on the floor of the stock exchange. Things changed in 2005 when the NYSE

> **stock exchange**
> An organization whose members can buy and sell (exchange) securities for companies and individual investors.

The NYSE Euronext was the largest floor-based exchange. Stock trades were made on the crowded floor of the exchange. Today stocks are bought and sold primarily on electronic networks. The illustration (on the right) of the exchange floor that will be completed in 2012 seems deserted compared to the old days.

over-the-counter (OTC) market
Exchange that provides a means to trade stocks not listed on the national exchanges.

NASDAQ
A nationwide electronic system that links dealers across the nation so that they can buy and sell securities electronically.

merged with Archipelago, a securities trading company that specialized in electronic trades. Two years later, it merged with Europe's Euronext exchange, and became the NYSE Euronext. In 2011, the NYSE Euronext agreed to be acquired by Deutsche Borse AG of Germany in a deal valued at approximately $10 billion.[4]

Today, the floor of the NYSE Euronext is now largely symbolic.[5] Most trading takes place on computers that can transact thousands of stock trades within seconds.[6] In fact, trading stocks has become a very small part of the exchange's revenue. The bulk of the company's revenue comes from selling complex financial contracts and market information to companies like Yahoo and Google that offer stock quotes as a service on their websites.[7] They also earn revenue from fees paid by over 8,000 companies to be listed on the NYSE Euronext.[8]

Not all securities are traded on registered stock exchanges. The **over-the-counter (OTC) market** provides companies and investors with a means to trade stocks not listed on the large securities exchanges. The OTC market is a network of several thousand brokers who maintain contact with one another and buy and sell securities through a nationwide electronic system. Trading is conducted between two parties directly, instead of through an exchange like the NYSE Euronext.

The **NASDAQ** (originally known as the National Association of Securities Dealers Automated Quotations) was the world's first electronic stock market. It evolved from the OTC market but is no longer part of it. The NASDAQ is an electronic-based network that links dealers so they can buy and sell securities electronically rather than in person. In 2007, the NASDAQ purchased the Swedish OMX Group and is now the NASDAQ OMX Group.[9] It is the largest U.S. electronic stock trading market and has more trading volume than any electronic exchange in the world. The NASDAQ originally dealt mostly with smaller firms, but today well-known companies such as Microsoft, Intel, Google, Starbucks, Cisco, and Dell trade their stock on the NASDAQ. The NASDAQ also handles federal, state, and city government bonds and lists approximately 3,000 companies.

Adding a company to an exchange is a highly competitive undertaking, and the battle between the stock exchanges for a stock listing is often fierce.[10] If a company fails to meet the requirements of an exchange, the stock can be de-listed from the exchange.[11] You can find the requirements for registering (listing) stocks on the NYSE Euronext and NASDAQ in their websites www.nyse.com and www.nasdaq.com. The nearby Spotlight on Small Business box presents an interesting idea of adding a new exchange for smaller businesses to the securities landscape.

SPOTLIGHT ON SMALL business

A Place for Small Companies to Call Home

Since the beginning of the financial crisis in 2008, small businesses have found it difficult, if not impossible, to secure financing from banks. Even the old "air-ball loans" that banks would grant to businesses they had a personal relationship with disappeared. David Weild, former vice-chairman of NASDAQ, thinks he has a solution to this problem. He would like to see the creation of a new stock exchange where small companies can raise needed capital.

Weild's suggested exchange would move slower than the large exchanges that rely on electronic trading, and it would cost more to buy and sell a stock. It would also involve a larger role for stockbrokers who would go back to the old days of calling clients about new companies they have discovered that offer investment potential. To lure stockbrokers into the exchange, he would consider setting minimum and maximum brokerage commissions to make their efforts worthwhile. He also feels the exchange would be a source for attracting venture capitalists.

While Weild's proposed exchange is a new idea in the United States, it's important to note that China recently established the ChiNext stock exchange that is designed for start-up companies. The ChiNext was created as part of the Shenzhen exchange with the purpose of making it easier for "strategically important emerging companies" to gain access to capital. Liu Zehui, executive director of Legend Capital, feels the ChiNext exchange is doing exactly what it's intended to do. "The ChiNext market has released the pent-up passion for innovation and entrepreneurship in China," he says. "It tells everyone that you don't have to have a powerful dad to get rich."

Sources: Kevin Hamlin, Eva Woo, Dexter Roberts, and Frances Liu, "In China, a Stock Market Where Start-Ups Thrive," *Bloomberg Businessweek,* November 28, 2010; Reinhardt Krause, "China, Emerging-Market Stocks Rising, but Experts Still Cautious," *Investor's Business Daily,* April 7, 2011; and Emily Lambert, "Trading Places," *Forbes,* April 11, 2011.

Securities Regulations and the Securities and Exchange Commission

The **Securities and Exchange Commission (SEC)** is the federal agency responsible for regulating the various stock exchanges. The Securities Act of 1933 helps protect investors by requiring full disclosure of financial information by firms selling bonds or stock. The U.S. Congress passed this legislation to deal with the free-for-all atmosphere that existed in the securities markets during the 1920s and the early 1930s that helped cause the Great Depression. The Securities and Exchange Act of 1934 created the SEC.

Companies trading on the national exchanges must register with the SEC and provide it with annual updates. The 1934 act also established specific guidelines that companies must follow when issuing financial securities such as stocks or bonds. For example, before issuing either stocks or bonds for sale to the public, a company must file a detailed registration statement with the SEC that includes extensive economic and financial information. The condensed version of that registration document—called a **prospectus**—must be sent to prospective investors.

The 1934 act also established guidelines to prevent insiders within the company from taking advantage of privileged information they may have. *Insider trading* is using knowledge or information that individuals gain through

Securities and Exchange Commission (SEC)
The federal agency that has responsibility for regulating the various stock exchanges.

prospectus
A condensed version of economic and financial information that a company must file with the SEC before issuing stock; the prospectus must be sent to prospective investors.

525

figure 19.1

IS IT INSIDER TRADING
OR NOT?

Insider trading involves buying or selling a stock on the basis of company information not available to the investing public. It's sometimes difficult to identify insider trading. The following hypothetical examples will give you an idea of what's legal and what's illegal. See how many of the questions you can answer. The answers are at the end of this box.

1. You work in research and development at a large company and have been involved in a major effort that should lead to a blockbuster new product coming to the market. News about the product is not public, and very few other workers even know about it. Can you purchase stock in the company?

2. Pertaining to the above situation, you are in a local coffee bar and mention to a friend about what's going on at the company. Another customer seated at an adjoining table overhears your discussion. Can this person legally buy stock in the company before the public announcement?

3. You work as an executive secretary at a major investment banking firm. You are asked to copy documents that detail a major merger about to happen that will keenly benefit the company being taken over. Can you buy stock in the company before the announcement is made public?

4. Your stockbroker recommends that you buy shares in a little-known company. The broker seems to have some inside information, but you don't ask any questions about his source. Can you buy stock in this company?

5. You work as a cleaning person at a major securities firm. At your job you come across information from the trash cans and computer printers of employees of the firm that provide detailed information about several upcoming deals the firm will be handling. Can you buy stock in the companies involved?

Answers: 1. No; 2. Yes; 3. No; 4. Yes; 5. No.

their position that allows them to benefit unfairly from fluctuations in security prices. The key words here are *benefit unfairly*. Insiders within a firm are permitted to buy and sell stock in the company they work for, so long as they do not take unfair advantage of information unknown to the public.

Originally, the SEC defined the term *insider* rather narrowly as covering a company's directors and employees and their relatives. Today the term has been broadened to include just about anyone with securities information not available to the general public. Let's say the CFO of Very Vegetarian tells her next-door neighbor she is finalizing paperwork to sell the company to a large corporation, and the neighbor buys the stock based on this information. A court may well consider the purchase an insider trade. Penalties for insider trading can include fines or imprisonment. For example, billionaire hedge fund manager Raj Rajaratnam was convicted of insider trading in a high-profile case in 2011 and could face up to 200 years in prison.[12] Look at Figure 19.1 and test your skill in identifying insider trading.

Foreign Stock Exchanges

Thanks to expanded communications and the relaxation of many legal barriers, investors can buy securities from companies almost anywhere in the world. If you uncover a foreign company you feel has great potential for growth, you can purchase shares of its stock with little difficulty from U.S. brokers who have access to foreign stock exchanges. Foreign investors can also invest in U.S. securities, and large foreign stock exchanges, like those in London and Tokyo, trade large amounts of U.S. securities daily. The number of U.S. companies listed on foreign stock exchanges is growing. In addition to the London and Tokyo exchanges, other major stock exchanges are located in Shanghai, Sydney, Hong Kong, São Paolo, and Toronto. There are stock exchanges in Africa as well.[13]

Raising long-term funds using equity financing by issuing stock is an option many companies pursue. After the Progress Assessment, let's look in more depth at how firms raise capital by issuing stock.

progress assessment

- What is the primary purpose of a securities exchange?
- What does NASDAQ stand for? How does this exchange work?

LEARNING goal 3

Compare the advantages and disadvantages of equity financing by issuing stock, and detail the differences between common and preferred stock.

HOW BUSINESSES RAISE CAPITAL BY SELLING STOCK

Stocks are shares of ownership in a company. A **stock certificate** represents stock ownership. It specifies the name of the company, the number of shares owned, and the type of stock it represents. Today, companies are not required to issue paper stock certificates to owners since stock is generally held electronically.

Stock certificates sometimes indicate a stock's *par value,* which is a dollar amount assigned to each share of stock by the corporation's charter. Today, since par values do not reflect the market value of the stock (what the stock is actually worth), most companies issue *no-par* stock. **Dividends** are part of a firm's profits that the firm may (but is not required to) distribute to stockholders as either cash payments or additional shares of stock. Dividends are declared by a corporation's board of directors and are generally paid quarterly.

Advantages and Disadvantages of Issuing Stock

Some advantages to a firm of issuing stock include:

- As owners of the business, stockholders never have to be repaid their investment.
- There's no legal obligation to pay dividends to stockholders; therefore, the firm can reinvest income (retained earnings) to finance future needs.
- Selling stock can improve the condition of a firm's balance sheet since issuing stock creates no debt. (A corporation may also buy back its stock to improve its balance sheet and make the company appear stronger financially.)

Disadvantages of issuing stock include:

- As owners, stockholders (usually only common stockholders) have the right to vote for the company's board of directors. (Typically, one vote

stocks
Shares of ownership in a company.

stock certificate
Evidence of stock ownership that specifies the name of the company, the number of shares it represents, and the type of stock being issued.

dividends
Part of a firm's profits that the firm may distribute to stockholders as either cash payments or additional shares of stock.

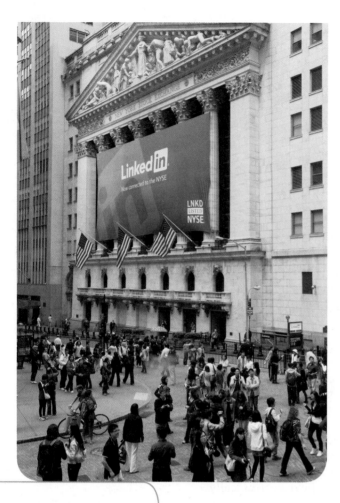

When LinkedIn issued its initial public offering (IPO), the company gained more than $4 billion from the sale. Can you see why issuing stock can be an appealing option for financing a company's growth?

common stock
The most basic form of ownership in a firm; it confers voting rights and the right to share in the firm's profits through dividends, if approved by the firm's board of directors.

preferred stock
Stock that gives its owners preference in the payment of dividends and an earlier claim on assets than common stockholders if the company is forced out of business and its assets sold.

is granted for each share of stock.) Issuing new shares of stock can thus alter the control of the firm.

- Dividends are paid from profit after taxes and are not tax-deductible.
- The need to keep stockholders happy can affect managers' decisions.

Companies can issue two classes of stock: common and preferred. Let's see how these two forms of equity financing differ.

Issuing Shares of Common Stock

Common stock is the most basic form of ownership in a firm. In fact, if a company issues only one type of stock, by law it must be common stock. Holders of common stock have the right to (1) elect members of the company's board of directors and vote on important issues affecting the company and (2) share in the firm's profits through dividends, if approved by the firm's board of directors. Having voting rights in a corporation allows common stockholders to influence corporate policy because the board members they elect choose the firm's top management and make major policy decisions. Common stockholders also have a *preemptive right* to purchase new shares of common stock before anyone else. This allows common stockholders to maintain their proportional share of ownership in the company.

Issuing Shares of Preferred Stock

Owners of **preferred stock** are given preference in the payment of company dividends and must be paid their dividends in full before any common stock dividends can be distributed (hence the term *preferred*). They also have a prior claim on company assets if the firm is forced out of business and its assets sold.[14] Normally, however, preferred stockholders do not get voting rights in the firm.

Preferred stock may be issued with a par value that becomes the base for a fixed dividend the firm is willing to pay. For example, if a preferred stock's par value is $50 a share and its dividend rate is 4 percent, the dividend is $2 a share. An owner of 100 preferred shares receives a fixed yearly dividend of $200 if dividends are declared by the board of directors.

Preferred stock can have other special features that common stock doesn't have. For example it can be *callable*, which means preferred stockholders could be required to sell their shares back to the corporation. Preferred stock can also be converted to shares of common stock (but not the other way around), and it can be *cumulative*. That is, if one or more dividends are not paid when promised, they accumulate and the corporation must pay them in full at a later date before it can distribute any common stock dividends.

Companies often prefer to raise capital by debt financing. One debt funding option frequently used by larger firms is issuing corporate bonds. Let's look at what's involved with issuing corporate bonds and how they differ from issuing stock.

progress assessment

- Name at least two advantages and two disadvantages of a company's issuing stock as a form of equity financing.
- What are the major differences between common stock and preferred stock?

LEARNING goal 4

Compare the advantages and disadvantages of obtaining debt financing by issuing bonds, and identify the classes and features of bonds.

HOW BUSINESSES RAISE CAPITAL BY ISSUING BONDS

A **bond** is a corporate certificate indicating that an investor has lent money to a firm (or a government). An organization that issues bonds has a legal obligation to make regular interest payments to investors and to repay the entire bond principal amount at a prescribed time.[15] Let's further explore the language of bonds so you understand exactly how they work.

Learning the Language of Bonds

Corporate bonds are usually issued in units of $1,000 (government bonds can be in much larger amounts). The *principal* is the face value (dollar value) of a bond, which the issuing company is legally bound to repay in full to the bondholder on the **maturity date**. **Interest** is the payment the bond issuer makes to the bondholders to compensate them for the use of their money. If Very Vegetarian issues a $1,000 bond with an interest rate of 5 percent and a maturity date of 2022, it is agreeing to pay the bondholder a total of $50 interest each year until a specified date in 2022, when it must repay the full $1,000. Maturity dates can vary. Firms such as Disney, IBM and Coca-Cola have issued bonds with 100-year maturity dates.[16]

Bond interest is sometimes called the *coupon rate,* a term that dates back to when bonds were issued as *bearer* bonds. The holder, or bearer, was considered the bond's owner. Back then, the company issuing the bond kept no record of changes in ownership. Bond interest was paid to whoever clipped coupons attached to the bond and sent them to the issuing company for payment. Today, bonds are registered to specific owners and changes in ownership are recorded electronically.

The interest rate paid by U.S. government bonds influences the bond interest rate businesses must pay. U.S. government bonds are considered safe investments, so they can pay lower interest. Figure 19.2 on p. 530 describes several types of government bonds that compete with U.S. corporate bonds in securities markets. Bond interest rates also vary according to the state of the economy, the reputation of the issuing company, and the interest rate for bonds of similar companies. Though bond interest is quoted for an entire year, it is usually paid in two installments, and the rate generally cannot be changed.

bond
A corporate certificate indicating that a person has lent money to a firm (or a government).

maturity date
The exact date the issuer of a bond must pay the principal to the bondholder.

interest
The payment the issuer of the bond makes to the bondholders for use of the borrowed money.

figure 19.2

TYPES OF GOVERNMENT SECURITIES THAT COMPETE WITH CORPORATE BONDS

BOND	DESCRIPTION
U.S. government bond	Issued by the federal government; considered the safest type of bond investment
Treasury bill (T-bill)	Matures in less than a year; issued with a minimum denomination of $1,000
Treasury note	Matures in 10 years or less; sold in denominations of $1,000 and $5,000
Treasury bond	Matures in 25 years or more; sold in denominations of $1,000 and $5,000
Municipal bond	Issued by states, cities, counties, and other state and local government agencies; usually exempt from federal taxes
Yankee bond	Issued by a foreign government; payable in U.S. dollars

Bond rating organizations access the creditworthiness of a corporation's bond issues. Independent rating firms such as Standard & Poor's, Moody's Investors Service, and Fitch Ratings rate bonds according to their degree of risk. Bonds can range from the highest quality to junk bonds (which we discuss later in this chapter).[17] Figure 19.3 gives an example of the range of bond ratings.

Advantages and Disadvantages of Issuing Bonds

Bonds offer long-term financing advantages to an organization:

- Bondholders are creditors of the firm, not owners. They seldom vote on corporate matters; thus, management maintains control over the firm's operations.
- Bond interest is a business expense and tax-deductible to the firm (see Chapter 17).
- Bonds are a temporary source of funding. They're eventually repaid and the debt obligation is eliminated.
- Bonds can be repaid before the maturity date if they contain a *call provision*. They can also be converted to common stock. (We discuss both features below.)

Bonds also have drawbacks:

- Bonds increase debt (long-term liabilities) and may adversely affect the market's perception of the firm.
- Paying interest on bonds is a legal obligation. If interest is not paid, bondholders can take legal action to force payment.
- The face value of the bond must be repaid on the maturity date. Without careful planning, this obligation can cause cash flow problems when the repayment comes due.

debenture bonds
Bonds that are unsecured (i.e., not backed by any collateral such as equipment).

Different Classes of Bonds

Corporations can issue two different classes of corporate bonds. *Unsecured bonds,* usually called **debenture bonds**, are not backed by any specific collateral (such as land or equipment). Only firms with excellent reputations and

BOND RATING AGENCIES			
MOODY'S	**STANDARD & POOR'S**	**FITCH RATINGS**	**DESCRIPTIONS**
Aaa	AAA	AAA	Highest quality (lowest default risk)
Aa	AA	AA	High quality
A	A	A	Upper medium grade
Baa	BBB	BBB	Medium grade
Ba	BB	BB	Lower medium grade
B	B	B	Speculative
Caa	CCC, CC	CCC	Poor (high default risk)
Ca	C	DDD	Highly speculative
C	D	D	Lowest grade

figure 19.3

BOND RATINGS: MOODY'S INVESTORS SERVICE, STANDARD & POOR'S INVESTOR SERVICE, AND FITCH RATINGS

credit ratings can issue debenture bonds, due to the lack of security they provide investors. *Secured bonds,* sometimes called mortgage bonds, are backed by collateral such as land or buildings that is pledged to bondholders if interest or principal isn't paid when promised. A corporate bond issuer can choose to include different bond features. Let's look at some special features.

Special Bond Features

By now you should understand that bonds are issued with an interest rate, are unsecured or secured by some type of collateral, and must be repaid at their maturity date. This repayment requirement often leads companies to establish a reserve account called a **sinking fund**. Its primary purpose is to ensure that enough money will be available to repay bondholders on the bond's maturity date. Firms issuing sinking-fund bonds periodically *retire* (set aside) some part of the principal prior to maturity so that enough funds will accumulate by the maturity date to pay off the bond. Sinking funds are generally attractive to both issuing firms and investors for several reasons:

sinking fund
A reserve account in which the issuer of a bond periodically retires some part of the bond principal prior to maturity so that enough capital will be accumulated by the maturity date to pay off the bond.

- They provide for an orderly retirement (repayment) of a bond issue.
- They reduce the risk the bond will not be repaid.
- They support the market price of the bond because they reduce the risk the bond will not be repaid.

A *callable bond* permits the bond issuer to pay off the principal before its maturity date. This gives companies some discretion in their long-term forecasting. Suppose Very Vegetarian issued $10 million in 20-year bonds at 10 percent interest. Its yearly interest expense is $1 million ($10 million times 10 percent). If market conditions change and bonds of the same quality now pay only 7 percent, Very Vegetarian will be paying 3 percent, or $300,000 ($10 million times 3 percent), in excess interest yearly. The company could benefit by calling in (paying off) the old bonds and issuing new bonds at the lower rate. If a company calls a bond before maturity, it often pays investors a price above the bond's face value.

Investors can convert *convertible bonds* into shares of common stock in the issuing company.[18] This can be an incentive for an investor because common stock value tends to grow faster than a bond. Therefore, if the value of the firm's common stock grows sizably over time, bondholders can compare the value of continued bond interest earned with the potential profit of a specified number of shares of common stock.[19]

Now that you understand the advantages and disadvantages of stocks and bonds as a financing tool from a company's perspective, let's explore the opportunities stocks and bonds provide for *investors*. First, though, let's check your progress.

progress assessment

- Why are bonds considered a form of debt financing?
- What does it mean if a firm issues a 9 percent debenture bond due in 2025?
- Explain the difference between an unsecured and a secured bond.
- Why are convertible bonds attractive to investors?

LEARNING goal 5

Explain how to invest in securities markets and various investment objectives such as long-term growth, income, cash, and protection from inflation.

stockbroker
A registered representative who works as a market intermediary to buy and sell securities for clients.

HOW INVESTORS BUY SECURITIES

Investing in stocks and bonds is not difficult. First, you decide what stock or bond you want to buy. After that, you find a brokerage firm authorized to trade securities to execute your order. A **stockbroker** is a registered representative who works for a brokerage firm as a market intermediary to buy and sell securities for clients. Stockbrokers place an order and negotiate a price. After the transaction is completed, the trade is reported to your broker, who notifies you. Today, large brokerage firms maintain automated order systems that allow brokers to enter your order the instant you make it. The order can be confirmed in seconds.

A stockbroker can also be a source of information about what stocks or bonds would best meet your financial objectives, but it's still important to learn about stocks and bonds on your own.[20] Investment analysts' advice may not always meet your specific expectations and needs.

Online brokers like Scottrade and E*Trade specialize in providing information for investors. What are some of the features of this website (www.scottrade.com) that are designed to provide investment information?

Investing through Online Brokers

Today, investors can choose from multiple online trading services to buy and sell stocks and bonds. Ameritrade, E*Trade, Scottrade, and Fidelity are among the leaders.[21] Investors who trade online are willing to do their own research and make investment decisions without the direct assistance of a broker. This allows online brokers the ability to charge much lower trading fees than traditional stockbrokers. The leading online services do provide important market information, such as company financial data, price histories of a stock, and analysts' reports. Often the level of information services you receive depends on the size of your account and your level of trading.

Money Going Up in Smoke

You recently received news that your Uncle Alex passed away after a long battle with lung cancer. To your surprise, he left you $25,000 in his will, saying you were his favorite nephew. You remember your uncle as a hard-working man who loved baseball and liked nothing better than to watch you pitch for your college team. Unfortunately, your uncle started smoking as a young man and eventually became a heavy chain smoker. His doctors said that smoking was the primary cause of his lung cancer.

After receiving the inheritance, you wonder where to invest the money. Your old teammate Jack, who is now a financial advisor, recommends that you buy stock in a well-known multinational firm that offers a good dividend and has solid growth potential. He tells you the firm's primary product is tobacco, but assures you it produces many other products as well. You know Jack has your best interests at heart. You also believe Uncle Alex would like to see the money he left you grow. However, you wonder if a company that markets tobacco is an appropriate place to invest your inheritance. What are the ethical alternatives in this situation? What are the consequences of the alternatives? What will you do?

Whether you decide to use an online broker or to invest through a traditional stockbroker, remember that investing means committing your money with the hope of making a profit. The dot-com bubble in the early 2000s and the financial crisis beginning in 2008 proved again that investing is a risky business. Therefore, the first step in any investment program is to analyze your level of risk tolerance. Other factors to consider include your desired income, cash requirements, and need to hedge against inflation, along with the investment's growth prospects. The Making Ethical Decisions box describes an interesting stock investment decision.

You are never too young or too old to invest, but you should first ask questions and consider investment alternatives. Let's take a look at several strategies.

Choosing the Right Investment Strategy

Investment objectives change over the course of a person's life. A young person can better afford to invest in high-risk investment options such as stocks than a person nearing retirement. Younger investors generally look for significant growth in the value of their investments over time. If stocks go into a tailspin and decrease in value, as they did in 2008, a younger person has time to wait for stock values to rise again. Older people, perhaps on a fixed income, lack the luxury of waiting and may be more inclined to invest in bonds that offer a steady return as a protection against inflation.

Consider five key criteria when selecting investment options:

1. *Investment risk.* The chance that an investment will be worth less at some future time than it's worth now.
2. *Yield.* The expected return on an investment, such as interest or dividends, usually over a period of one year.
3. *Duration.* The length of time your money is committed to an investment.

4. *Liquidity.* How quickly you can get back your invested funds in cash if you want or need them.
5. *Tax consequences.* How the investment will affect your tax situation.

What's important in any investment strategy is the risk/return trade-off. Setting investment objectives such as *growth* (choosing stocks you believe will increase in price) or *income* (choosing bonds that pay consistent interest) should set the tone for your investment strategy.

Reducing Risk by Diversifying Investments

diversification
Buying several different investment alternatives to spread the risk of investing.

Diversification involves buying several different types of investments to spread the risk of investing. An investor may put 25 percent of his or her money into U.S. stocks that have relatively high risk but strong growth potential, another 25 percent in conservative government bonds, 25 percent in dividend-paying stocks that provide income, 10 percent in an international mutual fund (discussed later), and the rest in the bank for emergencies and other possible investment opportunities. By diversifying with such a *portfolio strategy* or *allocation model,* investors decrease the chance of losing everything they have invested.[22]

Both stockbrokers and certified financial planners (CFPs) are trained to give advice about the investment portfolio that would best fit each client's financial objectives. However, the more investors themselves read and study the market, the higher their potential for gain.[23] A short course in investments can also be useful. Stocks and bonds are investment opportunities individuals can use to enhance their financial future. The Reaching Beyond our Borders box discusses growing opportunities investors can find in global stocks. Before we look at stocks and bonds in depth, let's check your understanding with the Progress Assessment.

Mad Money - Main Event (CNBC) 2008
Shown: Jim Cramer
Credit: CNBC/Photofest © CNBC

Mad mad-time. EDITORIAL use only, unless otherwise negotiated. Please inform us about usage or non-usage as soon as possible. Research fees may apply if no images are used.

Please Credit:
PHOTOFEST
(212) 633-6

Securities markets are like financial supermarkets—there are lots of investment options to choose from. That's why it's important to determine what investment strategy is right for you. Watching investment programs like CNBC's Mad Money with Jim Cramer could be a good starting point. How do you think your investment objectives will change over your lifetime?

progress assessment

- What is the key advantage of investing through online brokers? What is the key disadvantage?
- What is the primary purpose of diversifying investments?

LEARNING goal 6

Analyze the opportunities stocks offer as investments.

INVESTING IN STOCKS

Buying stock makes investors part owners of a company. This means that as stockholders they can participate in its success. Unfortunately, they can also lose money if a company does not do well or the overall stock market declines. The stock market fall beginning in 2008 was proof of that.

Stock investors are often called bulls or bears according to their perceptions of the market. *Bulls* believe that stock prices are going to rise; they buy stock in anticipation of the increase. A bull market is when overall stock prices are rising. *Bears* expect stock prices to decline and sell their stocks in anticipation of falling prices. That's why when stock prices are declining steadily, the market is called a bear market.

The market price and growth potential of most stock depends heavily on how well the corporation is meeting its business objectives. A company that achieves its objectives offers great potential for **capital gains**, the positive difference between the price at which you bought a stock and what you sell it for.[24] For example, an investment of $2,250 in 100 shares of McDonald's when the company first offered its stock to the public in 1965 would have grown to 74,360 shares (after the company's 12 stock splits) worth approximately $5.7 million as of year-end market close on December 31, 2010.[25] Now that's a lot of Big Macs!

Investors often select stocks depending on their investment strategy. Stocks issued by higher-quality companies such as Coca-Cola, Johnson & Johnson,

capital gains
The positive difference between the purchase price of a stock and its sale price.

stock splits
An action by a company that gives stockholders two or more shares of stock for each one they own.

and Procter & Gamble are referred to as *blue-chip stocks* (a term derived from poker where the highest value chip was the blue chip). These stocks generally pay regular dividends and experience consistent price appreciation.

Stocks of corporations in emerging fields such as technology, biotechnology, or Internet-related firms, whose earnings are expected to grow at a faster rate than other stocks, are referred to as *growth stocks*. While riskier, growth stocks offer the potential for higher returns. Stocks of public utilities are considered *income stocks* because they usually offer investors a high dividend yield that generally keeps pace with inflation. There are even *penny stocks,* representing ownership in companies that compete in high-risk industries like oil exploration. Penny stocks sell for less than $2 (some analysts say less than $5) and are considered risky investments.

When purchasing stock, investors have choices when placing buy orders. A *market order* tells a broker to buy or to sell a stock immediately at the best price available. A *limit order* tells the broker to buy or sell a stock at a specific price, if that price becomes available. Let's say a stock is selling for $40 a share. You believe the price will eventually go higher but could drop to $36 first. You can place a limit order at $36, so your broker will buy the stock at $36 if it drops to that price. If the stock never falls to $36, the broker will not purchase it for you.

Stock Splits

Brokers prefer stock purchases in *round lots* of 100 shares at a time. Investors, however, often cannot afford to buy 100 shares, which may sell for as much as $100 each, and therefore often buy in *odd lots,* or fewer than 100 shares at a time. High per-share prices can induce companies to declare **stock splits**, in which they issue two or more shares for every one that's outstanding. If Very Vegetarian stock were selling for $100 a share, the firm could declare a two-for-one stock split. Investors who owned one share of Very Vegetarian would now own two, each worth only $50 (half as much as before the split).

Stock splits cause no change in the firm's ownership structure and no immediate change in the investment's value. Investors generally approve of stock splits, however, because demand for a stock may be greater at $50 than at $100, and the price may then go up in the near future. A company cannot be forced to split its stock, and today stock splits are becoming less common.[26] Legendary American investor Warren Buffett's firm, Berkshire Hathaway, has never split its Class A stock even when its per-share price surpassed $150,000.[27]

Buying Stock on Margin

Buying stock on margin means borrowing some of the stocks' purchase cost from the brokerage firm. The margin is the portion of the stocks' purchase price that investors must pay with their own money. The board of governors of the Federal Reserve System sets *margin rates* in the U.S. market. Briefly, if the margin rate is 50 percent, an

If you stroll through Times Square in New York City, you never have to wonder how stocks on the NASDAQ exchange are performing. The NASDAQ price wall continuously updates prices and the number of shares being traded. Originally, the NASDAQ dealt primarily with small companies; today, it competes with the NYSE Euronet for new stock listings.

investor who qualifies for a margin account may borrow up to 50 percent of the stock's purchase price from the broker.

Although buying on margin sounds like an easy way to buy more stocks, the downside is that investors must repay the credit extended by the broker, plus interest. If the investor's account goes down in value, the broker may issue *a margin call,* requiring the investor to come up with funds to cover the losses the account has suffered.[28] If the investor is unable to fulfill the margin call, the broker can legally sell off shares of the investor's stock to reduce the broker's chance of loss. Margin calls can force an investor to repay a significant portion of his or her account's loss within days or even hours. Buying on margin is thus a risky way to invest in stocks.

> **buying stock on margin**
> Purchasing stocks by borrowing some of the purchase cost from the brokerage firm.

Understanding Stock Quotations

Publications like *The Wall Street Journal, Barron's,* and *Investor's Business Daily* carry a wealth of information concerning stocks and other investments. Your local newspaper may carry similar information as well. Financial websites like MSN Money, Yahoo! Finance, and CNBC carry up-to-the-minute information about companies that is much more detailed and only a click away. Take a look at Figure 19.4 to see an example of a stock quote from MSN Money for Microsoft. Microsoft trades on the NASDAQ exchange under the symbol MSFT. Preferred stock is identified by the letters *pf* following the company symbol. Remember, corporations can have several different preferred stock issues.

The information provided in the quote is easy to understand. It includes the highest and lowest price the stock traded for that day, the stock's high and low over the past 52 weeks, the dividend paid (if any), the stock's dividend yield (annual dividend as a percentage of the stock's price per share), important ratios like the price/earnings (P/E) ratio (the price of the stock divided by the firm's per-share earnings), and the return on equity. Investors can also see the number of shares outstanding and the total market capitalization of the firm. More technical features, such as the stock's beta (which measures the degree of the stock's risk), may also appear. Figure 19.4 illustrates the stock's intraday trading (trading throughout the current day), but you can also click to see charts for different time periods. Similar information about bonds, mutual funds, and other investments is also available online.

You might want to follow the market behavior of specific stocks that catch your interest, even if you lack the money to invest in them. Many successful investors started in college by building hypothetical portfolios of stocks and tracking their performance. The more you know about investing before you

figure 19.4

UNDERSTANDING STOCK QUOTATIONS

actually risk your money, the better. (The Developing Workplace Skills and Taking It to the Net exercises at the end of this chapter have exercises you can use for practice.)

LEARNING goal **7**

Analyze the opportunities bonds offer as investments.

INVESTING IN BONDS

Investors looking for guaranteed income and limited risk often turn to U.S. government bonds for a secure investment. These bonds have the financial backing and full faith and credit of the federal government. Municipal bonds are offered by local governments and often have advantages such as tax-free interest.[29] Some may even be insured. Corporate bonds are a bit more risky and challenging.

First-time corporate bond investors often ask two questions. The first is, "If I purchase a corporate bond, do I have to hold it until the maturity date?" No, you do not. Bonds are bought and sold daily on major securities exchanges (the secondary market we discussed earlier). However, if you decide to sell your bond to another investor before its maturity date, you may not get its face value (usually $1,000). If your bond does not have features that make it attractive to other investors, like a high interest rate or early maturity, you may have to sell at a *discount,* that is, a price less than the bond's face value. But if other investors do highly value it, you may be able to sell your bond at a *premium,* a price above its face value. Bond prices generally fluctuate inversely with current market interest rates. This means *as interest rates go up, bond prices fall, and vice versa.* Like all investments, however, bonds have a degree of risk.

The second question is, "How can I evaluate the investment risk of a particular bond issue?" Standard & Poor's, Moody's Investors Service, and Fitch Ratings rate the risk of many corporate and government bonds (look back at Figure 19.3). In evaluating the ratings, recall the risk/return trade-off: The higher the risk of a bond, the higher the interest rate the issuer must offer. Investors will invest in a bond considered risky only if the potential return (interest) is high enough. In fact, some will invest in bonds considered junk.

Investing in High-Risk (Junk) Bonds

junk bonds
High-risk, high-interest bonds.

Although bonds are considered relatively safe investments, some investors look for higher returns through riskier bonds called **junk bonds**. Standard & Poor's, Moody's Investors Service, and Fitch Ratings define junk bonds as those with high risk *and* high default rates. Junk bonds pay investors interest as long as the value of the company's assets remains high and its cash flow stays strong.[30] Although the interest rates are attractive and often tempting, if the company can't pay off the bond, the investor is left with an investment that isn't worth more than the paper it's written on—in other words, junk.

Understanding Bond Quotations

Bond prices are quoted as a percentage of $1,000, and their interest rate is often followed by an *s* for easier pronunciation. For example, 9 percent bonds due in 2022 are called 9s of 22. Figure 19.5 is an example of a bond

GOLDMAN SACHS GROUP INC

OVERVIEW	
Price:	104.32
Coupon (%):	7.350
Maturity Date:	1-Oct-2012
Yield to Maturity (%):	-3.289
Current Yield (%):	7.045
Fitch Ratings:	A
Coupon Payment Frequency:	Semi-Annual
First Coupon Date:	1-Apr-2000
Type:	Corporate
Callable:	No

figure 19.5

UNDERSTANDING BOND QUOTATIONS

quote for Goldman Sachs from Yahoo! Finance. The quote highlights the bond's interest rate (coupon rate), maturity date, rating, current price, and whether it's callable. The more you know about bonds, the better prepared you will be to discuss with investment advisers and brokers your financial objectives and be sure their advice is consistent with your best interests and objectives.

LEARNING goal 8

Explain the investment opportunities in mutual funds and exchange-traded funds (ETFs).

INVESTING IN MUTUAL FUNDS AND EXCHANGE-TRADED FUNDS

A **mutual fund** buys stocks, bonds, and other investments and then sells shares in those securities to the public. A mutual fund is like an investment company that pools investors' money and then buys stocks or bonds (for example) in many companies in accordance with the fund's specific purpose.[31] Mutual fund managers are specialists who pick what they consider to be the best stocks and bonds available and help investors diversify their investments.

Mutual funds range from very conservative funds that invest only in government securities to others that specialize in emerging biotechnology firms, Internet companies, foreign companies, precious metals, and other investments with greater risk. Some funds will have a mix of investments like stocks and bonds. The number of mutual funds available today is staggering. For example, there were 3,286 stock mutual funds investing in U.S. stocks in 2011.[32] Investors have invested over $11 trillion in mutual funds. Figure 19.6 on p. 540 gives you a list of some mutual fund investment options.

Young or new investors are often advised to buy shares in *index funds* that invest in a certain kind of stocks or bonds or in the market as a whole. An index fund may focus on large companies, small companies, emerging countries, or real estate (real estate investment trusts, or REITs). One way to diversify your investments is by investing in a variety of index funds. A stockbroker, certified financial planner (CFP), or banker can help you find the option that best fits your investment objectives. The *Morningstar Investor* newsletter is an

mutual fund
An organization that buys stocks and bonds and then sells shares in those securities to the public.

AB	Investment-grade corporate bonds	MP	Stock and bond fund
AU	Gold oriented	MT	Mortgage securities
BL	Balanced	MV	Mid-cap value
EI	Equity income	NM	Insured municipal bonds
EM	Emerging markets	NR	Natural resources
EU	European region	PR	Pacific region
GL	Global	SB	Short-term corporate bonds
GM	General municipal bond	SC	Small-cap core
GT	General taxable bonds	SE	Sector funds
HB	Health/biotech	SG	Small-cap growth
HC	High-yield bonds	SM	Short-term municipal bonds
HM	High-yield municipal bonds	SP	S&P 500
IB	Intermediate-term corporate bonds	SQ	Specialty
IG	Intermediate-term government bonds	SS	Single-state municipal bonds
IL	International	SU	Short-term government bonds
IM	Intermediate-term municipal bonds	SV	Small-cap value
LC	Large-cap core	TK	Science & technology
LG	Large-cap growth	UN	Unassigned
LT	Latin America	UT	Utility
LU	Long-term U.S. bonds	WB	World bonds
LV	Large-cap value	XC	Multi-cap core
MC	Mid-cap core	XG	Multi-cap growth
MG	Mid-cap growth	XV	Multi-cap value

Sources: *The Wall Street Journal* and *Investor's Business Daily*.

excellent resource for evaluating mutual funds, as are business publications such as *Bloomberg Businessweek, The Wall Street Journal, Money, Forbes, Investor's Business Daily* and many others.

With mutual funds it's simple to change your investment objectives if your financial objectives change. For example, moving your money from a bond fund to a stock fund is no more difficult than making a phone call or clicking a mouse. Another advantage of mutual funds is that you can generally buy directly from the fund and avoid broker fees or commissions. However, check for fees and charges of the mutual fund because they can differ significantly. A *load fund,* for example, charges investors a commission to buy or sell its shares; a *no-load fund* charges no commission.[33]

It's important to check the long-term performance of the fund's managers; the more consistent the performance of the fund's management, the better.[34] Mutual funds called *open-end funds* will accept the investments of any interested investors. *Closed-end funds,* however, limit the number of shares; once the fund reaches its target number, no new investors can buy into the fund.

Exchange-traded funds (ETFs) resemble both stocks and mutual funds. They are collections of stocks, bonds, and other investments that are traded on securities exchanges but are traded more like individual stocks than like mutual funds. Mutual funds, for example, permit investors to buy and sell shares only at the close of the trading day. ETFs can be purchased or sold at any time during the trading day just like individual stocks.

The key points to remember about mutual funds and ETFs is that they offer small investors a way to spread the risk of stock and bond ownership and have their investments managed by a financial specialist for a fee. Financial advisers put mutual funds and ETFs high on the list of recommended investments, particularly for small or first-time investors.[35]

exchange-traded funds (ETFs)
Collections of stocks, bonds, and other investments that are traded on exchanges but are traded more like individual stocks than like mutual funds.

Understanding Mutual Fund Quotations

You can investigate the specifics of various mutual funds by contacting a broker or contacting the fund directly by phone or through its website. Business publications and online sources also provide information about mutual funds.

Look at the example of the T. Rowe Price Blue Chip Growth fund from Yahoo! Finance in Figure 19.7. The fund's name is listed in large letters. The net asset value (NAV) is the price per share of the mutual fund. The NAV is calculated by dividing the market value of the mutual fund's portfolio by the number of shares it has outstanding. The chart also shows the fund's year-to-date (YTD) return, the change in the NAV from the previous day's trading, and the fund's net assets.

Figure 19.8 evaluates bonds, stocks, mutual funds, and ETFs according to risk, income, and possible investment growth (capital gain).

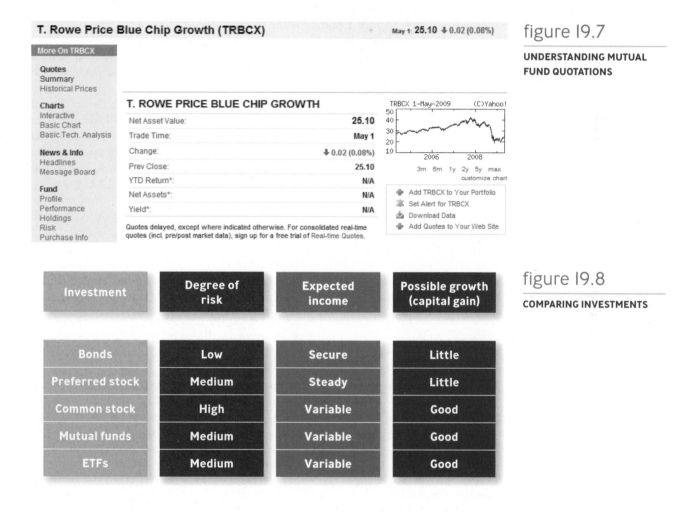

figure 19.7

UNDERSTANDING MUTUAL FUND QUOTATIONS

figure 19.8

COMPARING INVESTMENTS

Investment	Degree of risk	Expected income	Possible growth (capital gain)
Bonds	Low	Secure	Little
Preferred stock	Medium	Steady	Little
Common stock	High	Variable	Good
Mutual funds	Medium	Variable	Good
ETFs	Medium	Variable	Good

progress assessment

- What is a stock split? Why do companies sometimes split their stock?
- What does buying stock on margin mean?
- What are mutual funds and ETFs?
- What is the key benefit to investors in investing in a mutual fund or ETF?

LEARNING goal 9

Describe how stock market indicators like the Dow Jones Industrial Average affect the market.

UNDERSTANDING STOCK MARKET INDICATORS

Investors today have an enormous wealth of investment information available to them. Newspapers like *The Wall Street Journal, Barron's, Investor's Business Daily,* and *USA Today* provide vast amounts of information about companies and global markets. Television networks like MSNBC and CNBC offer daily investment analysis and different viewpoints to assist investors. Websites like MSN Money and Yahoo! Finance offer financial information to investors free of charge that not long ago was only available to brokers for a hefty fee. But keep in mind that investing is an inexact science. Every time someone sells a stock, believing it will fall, someone else is buying it, believing its price will go higher.

You often hear news reports end with a comment like, "The Dow was up 190 points today in active trading." Ever wonder what that's all about? The **Dow Jones Industrial Average (the Dow)** is the average cost of 30 selected industrial stocks. The financial industry uses it to give an indication of the direction (up or down) of the stock market over time. Charles Dow began the practice of measuring stock averages in 1884, using the prices of 12 key stocks. In 1982, the Dow was broadened to include 30 stocks. The 12 original and the 30 current stocks in the Dow are illustrated in Figure 19.9. Do you recognize any of the 12 original companies?

Today, Dow Jones & Company substitutes new stocks in the Dow when it's deemed appropriate. In 1991, Disney was added to reflect the increased economic importance of the service sector. In 1999, the Dow added Home Depot and SBC Communications along with its first NASDAQ stocks, Intel and

Dow Jones Industrial Average (the Dow)
The average cost of 30 selected industrial stocks, used to give an indication of the direction (up or down) of the stock market over time.

figure 19.9

THE ORIGINAL DOW AND CURRENT DOW

THE ORIGINAL DOW 12	THE 30 CURRENT DOW COMPANIES	
American Cotton Oil	Alcoa	Intel
American Sugar Refining Co.	American Express	Johnson & Johnson
American Tobacco	AT&T	JPMorgan Chase
Chicago Gas	Bank of America	Kraft
Distilling & Cattle Feeding Co.	Boeing	McDonald's
General Electric Co.	Caterpillar	Merck
Laclede Gas Light Co.	Chevron	Microsoft
National Lead	Cisco	Pfizer
North American Co.	Coca-Cola	Procter & Gamble
Tennessee Coal, Iron & Railroad Co.	DuPont	3M
U.S. Leather	ExxonMobil	United Technologies
U.S. Rubber Co.	General Electric	Travelers
	Hewlett-Packard	Verizon
	Home Depot	Wal-Mart Stores
	IBM	Walt Disney

Microsoft. In 2004, American International Group (AIG), Pfizer, and Verizon replaced AT&T, International Paper, and Eastman Kodak. (In 2005, AT&T rejoined the Dow when it merged with SBC.) In 2008, Chevron, Bank of America, and Kraft Foods replaced Altria Group, Honeywell, and AIG. In 2009, Travelers and Cisco replaced Citigroup and General Motors.

Critics argue that the 30-company Dow sample is too small to get a good statistical representation of the direction of the market over time. Many investors and analysts prefer to follow stock indexes like the Standard & Poor's 500 (S&P 500), which tracks the performance of 400 industrial, 40 financial, 40 public utility, and 20 transportation stocks. Investors also closely follow the NASDAQ average, which is quoted each trading day to show trends in this important exchange.

Staying abreast of the market will help you decide what investments seem most appropriate to your needs and objectives. Remember two key investment realities: Your personal financial objectives and needs change over time, and markets can be volatile. Let's look at market volatility and the challenges that present investors with new risks and opportunities.

Riding the Market's Roller Coaster

Throughout the 1900s, the stock market had its ups and downs, spiced with several major tremors. The first major crash occurred on Tuesday, October 29, 1929 (called Black Tuesday), when the stock market lost almost 13 percent of its value in a single day. This day, and the deep depression that followed, reinforced the reality of market volatility, especially to those who bought stocks heavily on margin. On October 19, 1987, the stock market suffered the largest one-day drop in its history, losing over 22 percent of its value. On October 27, 1997, investors again felt the market's fury. Fears of an impending economic crisis in Asia caused panic and widespread losses. Luckily, the market regained its strength after a short downturn.

After regaining strength in the late 1990s, the market again suffered misfortune in the early 2000s. All told, investors lost $7 trillion in market value

Investing in the stock market has never been for the weak-hearted. The market seems to have continuous steep climbs and sharp falls. Do you have the risk tolerance to survive the wild market swings?

from 2000 through 2002. A recovery that started in the mid-2000s was cut short in 2008, when the financial crisis fueled a massive exodus from the stock market, resulting in record losses.

What caused the market turmoil of 1987, 1997, 2000–2002, and 2008? In 1987, analysts agreed it was **program trading**, in which investors give their computers instructions to sell automatically to avoid potential losses if the price of their stock dips to a certain point. On October 19, 1987, computers' sell orders caused many stocks to fall to unbelievable depths. The crash prompted the U.S. exchanges to create mechanisms called *curbs* and *circuit breakers* to restrict program trading whenever the market moves up or down by a large number of points in a trading day. A key computer is turned off and program trading is halted. If you watch programming on CNBC or MSNBC, you'll see the phrase *curbs in* appear on the screen.

> **program trading**
> Giving instructions to computers to automatically sell if the price of a stock dips to a certain point to avoid potential losses.

Circuit breakers are more drastic than curbs and are triggered when the Dow falls 10, 20, or 30 percent in a day. That happened on October 27, 1997, when the market suffered an approximate 7 percent decline and the market closed for the day at 3:30 p.m. instead of 4:00. Many believe the 1997 market drop (caused by the financial crisis in Asia) could have been much worse without the trading restrictions. Depending on the rate of decline and the time of day, circuit breakers will halt trading for half an hour to two hours so traders have time to assess the situation.

In the late 1990s the stock market reached unparalleled heights only to collapse into a deep decline in 2000–2002. The bursting of the dot-com bubble was the primary reason. A bubble is caused when too many investors drive the price of something (in this case dot-com stocks) unrealistically high.

The dot-com crash was, unfortunately, accompanied by disclosures of financial fraud at companies such as WorldCom, Enron, Global Crossing, and Tyco. Investors had trusted that the real value of these companies was fairly reflected in their financial statements. This trust was shattered when they found investment analysts often provided clients with wildly optimistic evaluations and recommendations about companies they knew were not worth their current prices.

After the financial downturn caused by the dot-com bubble, the stock market surged in the mid-2000s with the Dow setting a record high in October 2007. The market's growth was dramatic, especially in the real estate sector. From 2000 to 2006 prices of existing homes rose 50 percent; however, between 2006 and 2011, housing values fell $6.3 trillion.[36] The real estate bubble was like the dot-com bubble before it: Investors believed that home prices would increase forever. Financial institutions reduced their lending requirements for buyers, homebuilders overbuilt, and buyers overspent, all sharing blame for the crisis. The government also contributed to the problem by requiring more mortgages be given to low- and moderate-income buyers, many with weak credit scores or no verification of income or assets. These *subprime* loans were pooled together and repackaged as mortgage-backed securities that were sold to investors (discussed in Chapter 20). What followed was huge numbers of foreclosures, the failure of government-sponsored mortgage giants Fannie Mae and Freddie Mac, and more than 350 bank failures.[37]

The collapse of the real estate market caused the economy a combined loss of $8 trillion in

> *The economic crisis that began in 2008 caused much anguish among Wall Street workers and people in general. How effective has the government's response been thus far?*

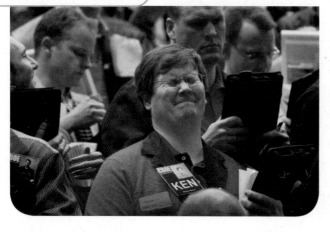

briefcase

Cleaning Up the Street

In response to a historic economic meltdown, Congress passed the Dodd-Frank Financial Reform and Consumer Protection Act into law on July 21, 2010. While the bill is far from the miracle cure that many politicians and consumers demanded, Dodd-Frank nevertheless represents the most sweeping change in financial regulation since the Great Depression. Its provisions will affect every layer of the economy from home buyers and merchants to giant investment banks.

The articles included in Dodd-Frank will have a dramatic effect on the future of American commerce. First of all, the new legislation gives the government power to seize and shutter large financial institutions on the verge of collapse in an effort to prevent further bailouts. It also subjects derivatives, complicated financial deals (including those that packaged subprime mortgages that helped fuel the crisis), to strict governmental oversight. Hedge funds will have to register with the SEC as investment advisers and provide information about trades and portfolio holdings. Perhaps most important to the general public, however, is the law's formation of an independent consumer protection agency housed within the Federal Reserve. The new agency protects borrowers against a host of financial abuses associated with payday loans, mortgages, and credit cards.

Still, the bill is far from perfect. Some advocates worry about the Consumer Financial Protection Bureau's location within the Federal Reserve. Also, a number of entities, such as car dealers, are exempt from regulation by the agency. In the law's most controversial move, it leaves all of the nation's largest financial institutions almost completely intact, even those that remain on taxpayer support. For all its faults, though, the Dodd-Frank Act at least resolves some of the most pressing issues facing our economy today while setting the stage for a stronger financial future.

Sources: Brady Dennis, "Congress Passes Financial Reform Bill," *The Washington Post,* July 16, 2010; Paul Davidson, Paul Wiseman and John Waggoner, "Will New Financial Regulations Prevent Future Meltdowns?" *USA Today,* June 28, 2010; and Phil Mattingly, "Dodd-Frank Consumer Protection Bureau Changes Approved by U.S. House Panel," *Bloomberg Businessweek,* May 13, 2011.

housing and commercial property (more than the GDP of China).[38] Financial institutions, like Lehman Brothers, went out of business and Wall Street icon Merrill Lynch was purchased by Bank of America. With financial markets in the worst condition since the Great Depression and the economy in a deep recession, the federal government took action. Congress passed a $700 billion financial package called the Troubled Assets Relief Program (TARP) that allowed the Treasury Department to purchase or insure "troubled assets" to bolster banks and bail out the automotive industry and insurer American International Group (AIG). Unfortunately in 2009, the economy continued to decline and unemployment grew to double digits causing President Obama to encourage passage of an $800 billion economic stimulus package—a blend of tax cuts and increased government spending—that was intended to reduce unemployment and provide a "significant boost" to the crippled economy.

As the economy slowly moves to recovery today from the financial crisis beginning in 2008, a few positive economic signs have surfaced. The amount of TARP funds spent did not approximate the $700 billion Congress allocated. Plus troubled banks have repaid most of the money they received through TARP, and AIG and General Motors expect to repay the government in full. However, unemployment and slow economic growth continue to be major causes for concern. It's very likely the financial crisis will affect the economy for a long time.[39]

Investing Challenges in the 21st-Century Market

As you can see from the previous section, in the stock market, what goes up also goes down. Financial markets will likely experience changes in the future that will only heighten investor risk. The financial crisis also reinforced that the world's economies are closely linked. The United States was not the only nation affected by the financial crisis; financial markets in Europe, Asia, and South America felt the pain as well. Persistent challenges and even political and social change promise to make securities markets exciting but not stable places to be in the 21st century. The nearby Legal Briefcase box on p. 545 discusses new government regulations designed to address some of these challenges.

Diversify your investments, and be mindful of the risks of investing. Taking a long-term perspective is also a wise idea. There's no such thing as easy money or a sure thing. If you carefully research companies and industries, keep up with the news, and make use of investment resources—such as newspapers, magazines, newsletters, the Internet, and TV programs—the payoff can be rewarding over time.

progress assessment

- What does the Dow Jones Industrial Average measure? Why is it important?
- Why do the 30 companies comprising the Dow change periodically?
- Explain program trading and the problems it can create.

summary

Learning Goal 1. Describe the role of securities markets and of investment bankers.

- **What opportunities do securities markets provide businesses and individual investors?**

By issuing securities businesses are able to raise much-needed funding to help finance their major expenses. Individual investors can share in the success and growth of emerging or established firms by investing in them.

- **What role do investment bankers play in securities markets?**

Investment bankers are specialists who assist in the issue and sale of new securities.

Learning Goal 2. Identify the stock exchanges where securities are traded.

- **What are stock exchanges?**

Stock exchanges are securities markets whose members are engaged in buying and selling securities such as stocks and bonds.

- **What are the different exchanges?**

The NYSE Euronext lists the stock of over 8,000 companies. The NASDAQ is a telecommunications network that links dealers across the nation so that they can buy and sell securities electronically rather than in person. It is the largest U.S. electronic stock trading market. There are stock exchanges all over the world.

- **What is the over-the-counter (OTC) market?**

The OTC market is a system for exchanging stocks not listed on the national exchanges.

- **How are securities exchanges regulated?**

The Securities and Exchange Commission (SEC) regulates securities exchanges and requires companies that intend to sell bonds or stock to provide a prospectus to potential investors.

- **What is insider trading?**

Insider trading is the use of information or knowledge individuals gain that allows them to benefit unfairly from fluctuations in security prices.

Learning Goal 3. Compare the advantages and disadvantages of equity financing by issuing stock, and detail the differences between common and preferred stock.

- **What are the advantages and disadvantages to a firm of selling stock?**

The advantages of selling stock include the following: (1) the stock price never has to be repaid to stockholders, since they become owners in the company; (2) there is no legal obligation to pay stock dividends; and (3) the company incurs no debt, so it may appear financially stronger. Disadvantages of selling stock include the following: (1) stockholders become owners of the firm and can affect its management by voting for the board of directors; (2) it is more costly to pay dividends since they are paid in after-tax profits; and (3) managers may be tempted to make stockholders happy in the short term rather than plan for long-term needs.

- **What are the differences between common and preferred stock?**

Holders of common stock have voting rights in the company. In exchange for having no voting rights, preferred stockholders receive a fixed dividend that must be paid in full before common stockholders receive a dividend. Preferred stockholders are also paid back their investment before common stockholders if the company is forced out of business.

Learning Goal 4. Compare the advantages and disadvantages of obtaining debt financing by issuing bonds, and identify the classes and features of bonds.

- **What are the advantages and disadvantages of issuing bonds?**

The advantages of issuing bonds include the following: (1) management retains control since bondholders cannot vote; (2) interest paid on bonds is tax-deductible; (3) bonds are only a temporary source of financing, and after they are paid off the debt is eliminated; (4) bonds can be paid back early if they are issued with a call provision; and (5) sometimes bonds can be converted to common stock. The disadvantages of bonds include the following: (1) because bonds are an increase in debt, they may adversely affect the market's perception of the company; (2) the firm must pay interest on its bonds; and (3) the firm must repay the bond's face value on the maturity date.

- **What are the different types of bonds?**

Unsecured (debenture) bonds are not supported by collateral, whereas secured bonds are backed by tangible assets such as mortgages, buildings, and equipment.

Learning Goal 5. Explain how to invest in securities markets and set investment objectives such as long-term growth, income, cash, and protection from inflation.

- **How do investors normally make purchases in securities markets?**

Investors purchase investments through market intermediaries called stockbrokers, who provide many different services. Online investing has become increasingly popular.

- **What are the criteria for selecting investments?**

Investors should determine their overall financial objectives and evaluate investments according to (1) risk, (2) yield, (3) duration, (4) liquidity, and (5) tax consequences.

- **What is diversification?**

Diversification means buying several different types of investments (government bonds, corporate bonds, preferred stock, common stock, global stock) with different degrees of risk. The purpose is to reduce the overall risk an investor would assume by investing in just one type of security.

Learning Goal 6. Analyze the opportunities stocks offer as investments.

- **What is a market order?**

A market order tells a broker to buy or to sell a security immediately at the best price available.

- **A limit order?**

A limit order tells the broker to buy or sell if the stock reaches a specific price.

- **What does it mean when a stock splits?**

When a stock splits, stockholders receive two (or more) shares of stock for each share they own. Each is worth half (or less) of the original share, so while the number of the shares increases, the total value of stockholders' holdings stays the same. The lower per-share price that results may increase demand for the stock.

- **What does buying on margin mean?**

An investor buying on margin borrows part (the percentage allowed to be borrowed is set by the Federal Reserve) of the cost of a stock from the broker to get shares of stock without immediately paying the full price.

- **What type of information do stock quotations give you?**

Stock quotations provide the highest and lowest price in the last 52 weeks; the dividend yield; the price/earnings ratio; the total shares traded that day; and the closing price and net change in price from the previous day.

Learning Goal 7. Analyze the opportunities bonds offer as investments.

- **What is the difference between a bond selling at a discount and a bond selling at a premium?**

In the secondary market a bond selling at a premium is priced above its face value. A bond selling at a discount sells below its face value.

- **What is a junk bond?**

Junk bonds are high-risk (rated BB or below), high-interest debenture bonds that speculative investors often find attractive.

- **What information does a bond quotation give you?**

A bond quotation gives the bond's interest rate (coupon rate), maturity date, rating, current price, and whether it's callable.

Learning Goal 8. Explain the investment opportunities in mutual funds and exchange-traded funds (ETFs).

- **How can mutual funds help individuals diversify their investments?**

A mutual fund is an organization that buys stocks and bonds and then sells shares in those securities to the public, enabling individuals to invest in many more companies than they could otherwise afford.

- **What are ETFs?**

Like mutual funds ETFs are collections of stocks that are traded on securities exchanges, but they are traded more like individual stocks.

Learning Goal 9. Describe how stock market indicators like the Dow Jones Industrial Average affect the market.

- **What is the Dow Jones Industrial Average?**

The Dow Jones Industrial Average is the average price of 30 specific stocks that analysts use to track the direction (up or down) of the stock market.

key terms

bond 529
buying stock on margin 537
capital gains 535
common stock 528
debenture bonds 530
diversification 534
dividends 527
Dow Jones Industrial Average (the Dow) 542
exchange-traded funds (ETFs) 540

initial public offering (IPO) 522
institutional investors 523
interest 529
investment bankers 523
junk bonds 538
maturity date 529
mutual fund 539
NASDAQ 524
over-the-counter (OTC) market 524

preferred stock 528
program trading 544
prospectus 525
Securities and Exchange Commission (SEC) 525
sinking fund 531
stockbroker 532
stock certificate 527
stock exchange 523
stocks 527
stock splits 536

critical thinking

1. Imagine you inherited $50,000 and you want to invest it to meet two financial goals: (a) to save for your wedding, which you plan to have in two years, and (b) to save for your retirement a few decades from now. How would you invest the money? Explain your answer.

2. If you are considering investing in the bond market, how could information provided by Standard & Poor's, Moody's Investors Service, and Fitch Ratings help you?

3. Why do companies like callable bonds? Why are investors generally not very fond of them?

4. If you were thinking about investing in the securities market, would you prefer individual stocks, mutual funds, or ETFs? Explain your choice by comparing the advantages and disadvantages of each.

5. Consider the companies added and subtracted from the Dow Jones Industrial Average over the past five years. (Go to www.djaverages.com to learn more about these companies.) What types of companies were added and deleted? Why do you think the changes were made? Do you think new changes will be made in the next five years? Why?

developing workplace skills

1. Go to the websites of Charles Schwab (www.schwab.com), E*Trade (www.etrade.com), and Ameritrade (www.ameritrade.com). Investigate each of these brokerage companies to compare their fees and what they offer in terms of research and advice. Which firm seems most appropriate to your investment objectives? Be prepared to defend your choice to the class.

2. Visit MSN Money or Yahoo! Finance and select six stocks for your portfolio—three from the NYSE and three from the NASDAQ. Track the stocks daily for three weeks using the graphs provided on the websites to see how

market trends and information affected your stock's performance. Report your observations.

3. U.S. government bonds compete with corporations for investors' dollars. Check out the different types of bonds the federal government offers and list the types most appealing to you. Be sure to check out TIPs.

4. See whether anyone in class is interested in forming an investment group. If so, each member should choose one stock and one mutual fund or ETF. Record each student's selections and the corresponding prices. In two weeks measure the percentage of change in the investments and discuss the results.

5. Go to the websites of Charles Schwab (www.schwab.com), E*Trade (www.etrade.com), or Ameritrade (www.ameritrade.com) and find two IPOs offered in the past year or so. Track the performance of each from its introduction to its present market price. Report your observations.

taking it to the net

Purpose

To evaluate and understand the advantages and disadvantages of ETFs.

Exercise

Exchange-traded funds (ETFs) are a low-cost, flexible way to diversify a portfolio. To learn more, go to Yahoo! Finance (www.finance.yahoo.com) and click on investing, then on the ETFs tab.

1. What are the pros and cons of investing in ETFs?

2. What are the five most actively traded ETFs?

3. Which ETFs grew the most in the last three years?

4. In which industry sectors or countries do these high-growth ETFs specialize?

casing the web

To access the case "Making Dreams Come True," visit **www.mhhe.com/ubl0e**

video case

To access the video case featuring Morningstar, visit **www.mhhe.com/ubl0e**

Money,
Financial INSTITUTIONS, AND
the Federal Reserve

20

LEARNING
goals

After you have read and studied this chapter, you should be able to

1 Explain what money is and what makes money useful.

2 Describe how the Federal Reserve controls the money supply.

3 Trace the history of banking and the Federal Reserve System.

4 Classify the various institutions in the U.S. banking system.

5 Briefly trace the causes of the banking crisis starting in 2008 and explain how the government protects your funds during such crises.

6 Describe how technology helps make banking more efficient.

7 Evaluate the role and importance of international banking, the World Bank, and the International Monetary Fund.

Ben Bernanke (pronounced ber-*nan*-kee) is the head of the Federal Reserve. As you will learn in this chapter, the Federal Reserve is in charge of the U.S. monetary policy (managing the money supply and interest rates). Lately, the Fed has flooded the world with dollars, which many believe caused stock and other asset prices to rise, eliminated the risk of deflation, and prevented a double-dip recession. Many other people, however, believe that the Fed's actions created more inflation and put the United States deeper into a debt crisis that may never be resolved. In short, Ben Bernanke is the center of much attention when it comes to monetary issues. No doubt it was this attention that led *Time* magazine to name Bernanke as "Person of the Year" in 2010.

Bernanke was born in Augusta, Georgia. He taught himself calculus in high school, scored 1590 of a possible 1600 on his college entrance exams, and graduated from Harvard summa cum laude with a bachelor's degree in economics. After earning a PhD from MIT, he was an economics professor and department chair at Princeton. He then served as chair of the President's Council of Economic Advisors in 2005 and was a member of the Board of Governors at the Federal Reserve from 2002 to 2005.

Former president George W. Bush appointed Bernanke to the Fed, making him one of the most powerful people in the United States. The Senate approved a second term for Bernanke as Fed chief under President Obama. It was Bernanke, along with former Treasury secretary Henry Paulson, who convinced Congress to commit about $700 billion to try to end the banking collapse. Bernanke lowered interest rates for banks to near zero and kept them there for a couple of years, and was among the group of advisers who made billions of dollars available to banks in an effort to ease the credit crisis.

Bernanke's challenges today include keeping inflation in check, increasing the value of the dollar, and getting the economy moving upward again. Part of that plan includes credit easing and buying more than a trillion dollars in debt and mortgage-backed securities. As you can see, almost everything about the economy is affected by the choices Bernanke makes.

You will learn more about the Federal Reserve and the banking system in general in this chapter. Using that information, you can better understand Bernanke's decisions. Keep up with what he is doing by reading the business press and listening to business reports. His successes and failures will be making headlines for a long time.

profile

Getting to Know

X Ben S. Bernanke

Chairman of the Federal Reserve

Sources: "Bernanke's Inflation Paradox," *The Wall Street Journal,* April 26, 2011; J. Alex Tarquinio, "When QE2 Weighs Anchor," *Smart Money,* May 2011; George Melloan, "The Fed Can Create Money, Not Confidence," *The Wall Street Journal,* August 24, 2010; Sean Fieler and Jeffrey Bell, "Our Unaccountable Fed," *The Wall Street Journal,* April 6, 2011; David J. Lynch and Craig Torres, "Lifting the Veil at the Fed—Sort of," *Bloomberg Businessweek,* April 4–April 10, 2011; Steve Stanek, "It's Inflation When More Dollars Are Needed to Print More Dollars," *Washington Examiner,* March 24, 2011; Neil Irwin, "Bernanke Defends U.S. Policies," *The Washington Post,* February 19, 2011; Patrice Hill, "Senate OKs 2nd Term for Bernanke as Fed Chief," *The Washington Times,* January 29, 2011; and "How the Fed Works," *Time,* January 4, 2010.

This bank-like store in Austin, Texas, was designed to serve low-income clients who don't have traditional bank accounts. Customers pay a one-time $10 fee that allows them to cash checks and put the money onto debit cards. What is the name of this company? (The answer can be found in the chapter.)

LEARNING goal 1

Explain what money is and what makes money useful.

WHY MONEY IS IMPORTANT

The Federal Reserve, or the Fed, is the organization in charge of money in the United States. You will be hearing a lot about it and its head, Ben Bernanke, in the coming years. That is why we chose him to be the subject of the Profile for this chapter. The banking crisis and the moves being made globally by the Fed and other banks to halt a global financial crisis are too complex to discuss in detail here. Our goal in this chapter is simply to introduce you to the world of banking and the role of the Federal Reserve.

Two of the most critical issues in the United States today, economic growth and the creation of jobs, depend on the ready availability of money. Money is so important to the economy that many institutions have evolved to manage it and make it available when you need it. Today you can get cash from an automated teller machine (ATM) almost anywhere in the world, and most organizations will also accept a check, credit card, debit card, or smart card for purchases.[1] Behind the scenes is a complex system of banking that makes the free flow of money possible. Each day, about $4 trillion is exchanged in the world's currency markets. Therefore, what happens to any major country's economy has an effect on the U.S. economy and vice versa. That's why the financial crisis in the United States affected economies throughout the world.

New engraved bills make counterfeiting much more difficult than in the past. The bills look a little different from older ones and are different colors. If you owned a store, what would you do to make sure employees don't accept counterfeit bills?

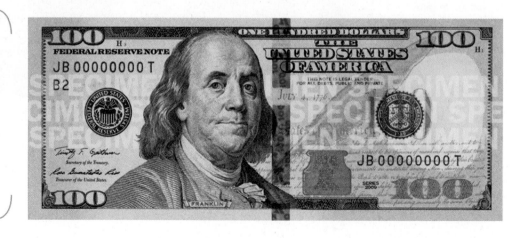

554

There's no way to understand the U.S. economy without understanding global money exchanges and the institutions involved in the creation and management of money. Let's start at the beginning by discussing exactly what the word *money* means and how the supply of money affects the prices you pay for goods and services.

What Is Money?

Money is anything people generally accept as payment for goods and services. In the past, objects as diverse as salt, feathers, fur pelts, stones, rare shells, tea, and horses have served as money. In fact, until the 1880s, cowrie shells were one of the world's most popular currencies.

Barter is the direct trading of goods or services for other goods or services. Though barter may sound like something from the past, many people have discovered the benefits of bartering online.[2] Others barter goods and services the old-fashioned way—face-to-face. In Siberia people have bought movie tickets with two eggs, and in Ukraine people have paid their energy bills with sausages and milk. Today you can go to a *barter exchange* where you can put goods or services into the system and get trade credits for other goods and services that you need. The barter exchange makes it easier to barter because you don't have to find people with whom to barter. The exchange does that for you.

The problem with traditional barter is that eggs and milk are difficult to carry around. Most people need some object that's portable, divisible, durable, and stable so that they can trade goods and services without carrying the actual goods around with them. One solution is coins and paper bills. The five standards for a useful form of money are:

- *Portability*. Coins and paper money are a lot easier to take to market than pigs or other heavy products.
- *Divisibility*. Different-sized coins and bills can represent different values. Prior to 1963, a U.S. quarter had half as much silver content as a half-dollar coin, and a dollar had four times the silver of a quarter. Because silver is now too expensive, today's coins are made of other metals, but the accepted values remain.
- *Stability*. When everybody agrees on the value of coins, the value of money is relatively stable. In fact, U.S. money has become so stable that much of the world has used the U.S. dollar as the measure of value. If the value of the dollar fluctuates too rapidly, the world may turn to some other form of money, such as the euro, for the measure of value.
- *Durability*. Coins last for thousands of years, even when they've sunk to the bottom of the ocean, as you've seen when divers find old coins in sunken ships.
- *Uniqueness*. It's hard to counterfeit, or copy, elaborately designed and minted coins. With the latest color copiers, people are able to duplicate the look of paper money relatively easily. Thus, the government has had to go to extra lengths to make sure *real* dollars are readily identifiable. That's why you have newer paper money with the picture slightly off center and with invisible lines that quickly show up when reviewed by banks and stores. The new $100 bill has features such as a three dimensional ribbon as well as ink that contains microscopic

Although people have long used barter to exchange goods without money, one problem is that objects like chickens and eggs are harder to carry around than a ten-dollar bill. What other drawbacks does bartering have?

money
Anything that people generally accept as payment for goods and services.

barter
The direct trading of goods or services for other goods or services.

flakes that shift color with movement.[3] The new bill had its problems, however, and the Bureau of Engraving and Printing had to sort through millions of bills to eliminate faulty ones.[4]

Coins and paper money simplified exchanges. Most countries have their own currencies, and they're all about equally portable, divisible, and durable. However, they're not always equally stable.[5]

Electronic cash (e-cash) is one of the newest forms of money. You can make online payments using Quicken or Microsoft Money or e-mail e-cash using PayPal. Recipients can choose automatic deposit to their bank, e-dollars for spending online, or a traditional check in the mail. Bitcoin is a digital version of money that is tougher to forge, cuts across international boundaries, and can be stored on your hard drive instead of in a bank. However, the Bitcoin is not yet generally accepted and some of the transactions may be illegal.[6] Nonetheless, efforts will be made in the future to create a cashless society using some other form of currency than the bills and coins we now use.[7]

LEARNING goal 2

Describe how the Federal Reserve controls the money supply.

What Is the Money Supply?

As Fed chairman, Ben Bernanke is in control of the U.S. money supply. Two questions emerge from that sentence. What is the money supply? Why does it need to be controlled?

The **money supply** is the amount of money the Federal Reserve makes available for people to buy goods and services. And, yes, the Federal Reserve, in tandem with the U.S. Treasury, can print more money if it is needed. For example, some of the trillions of dollars that are being spent over the next few years to get the economy moving again were printed with authorization from the Federal Reserve. The terms QE 1 and QE 2 literally mean quantitative easing one and two, but the real meaning is that the Fed is creating more money because it believes that money is needed to get the economy moving again.[8]

There are several ways of referring to the U.S. money supply. They're called M-1, M-2, and M-3. The *M* stands for money, and the 1, 2, and 3 stand for different definitions of the money supply.

M-1 includes coins and paper bills, money that's available by writing checks (demand deposits and share drafts), and money held in traveler's checks—that is, money that can be accessed quickly and easily. **M-2** includes everything in M-1 plus money in savings accounts, and money in money market accounts, mutual funds, certificates of deposit, and the like—that is, money that may take a little more time to obtain than coins and paper bills. M-2 is the most commonly used definition of money.[9] **M-3** is M-2 plus big deposits like institutional money market funds..

Managing Inflation and the Money Supply

Imagine what would happen if governments (or in the case of the United States, the Federal Reserve, a nongovernmental organization) were to generate twice as much money as exists now.[10] There would be twice as much money available, but still the same amount of goods and services. What would

money supply
The amount of money the Federal Reserve Bank makes available for people to buy goods and services.

M-1
Money that can be accessed quickly and easily (coins and paper money, checks, traveler's checks, etc.)

M-2
Money included in M-1 plus money that may take a little more time to obtain (savings accounts, money market accounts, mutual funds, certificates of deposit, etc.).

M-3
M-2 plus big deposits like institutional money market funds.

happen to prices? (Hint: Remember the laws of supply and demand from Chapter 2.) Prices would go up, because more people would try to buy goods and services with their money and bid up the price to get what they wanted. This rise in price is called *inflation,* which some people call "too much money chasing too few goods."

Now think about the opposite: What would happen if the Fed took money out of the economy? Prices would go down because there would be an over-supply of goods and services compared to the money available to buy them; this decrease in prices is called *deflation.*

Now we come to our second question about the money supply: Why does it need to be controlled? The reason is that doing so allows us to manage, somewhat, the prices of goods and services. The size of the money supply also affects employment and economic growth or decline. That's why the Fed and Ben Bernanke are so important.[11]

The Global Exchange of Money

A *falling dollar value* means that the amount of goods and services you can buy with a dollar decreases. A *rising dollar value* means that the amount of goods and services you can buy with a dollar goes up. Thus, the price in euros you pay for a German car will be lower if the U.S. dollar rises relative to the euro.[12] However, if the euro rises relative to the dollar, the cost of cars from Germany will go up and U.S. consumers may buy fewer German cars.

What makes the dollar weak (falling value) or strong (rising value) is the position of the U.S. economy relative to other economies. When the economy is strong, the demand for dollars is high and the value of the dollar rises. When the economy is perceived as weakening, however, the demand for dollars declines and the value of the dollar falls. The value of the dollar thus depends on a relatively strong economy. (See Chapter 3 for further discussion of effects of changes in currency values or exchange rates.) In the following section, we'll discuss in more detail the money supply and how it's managed. Then we'll explore the U.S. banking system and how it lends money to businesses and individuals, like you and me.

CONTROL OF THE MONEY SUPPLY

Theoretically, with the proper monetary policy in place to control the money supply, one can keep the economy growing without causing inflation. (See Chapter 2 to review monetary policy.) Again, the organization in charge of monetary policy is the Federal Reserve.

Basics about the Federal Reserve

The Federal Reserve System consists of five major parts: (1) the board of governors; (2) the Federal Open Market Committee (FOMC); (3) 12 Federal Reserve banks; (4) three advisory councils; and (5) the member banks of the system. Figure 20.1 shows where the 12 Federal Reserve banks are located.[13]

The board of governors administers and super-vises the 12 Federal Reserve banks. The seven members of the board are appointed by the presi-dent and confirmed by the senate. The board's primary function is to set monetary policy. The

The Federal Reserve system includes 12 member banks (see Figure 20.1). This is the Federal Reserve Bank in New York City. What special role in the Fed does the president of this particular bank play?

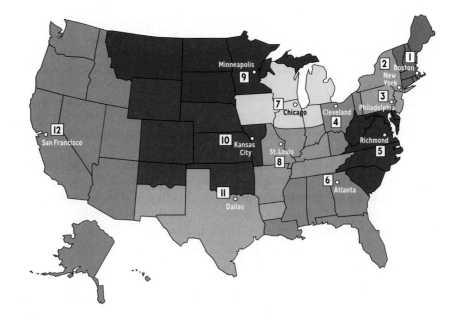

figure 20.1

**THE 12 FEDERAL RESERVE
DISTRICT BANKS**

Federal Open Market Committee (FOMC) has 12 voting members and is the policymaking body. The committee is made up of the seven-member board of governors plus the president of the New York reserve bank and four members who rotate in from the other reserve banks. The advisory councils represent the various banking districts, consumers, and member institutions, including banks, savings and loan institutions, and credit unions. They offer suggestions to the board and to the FOMC.

The Fed buys and sells foreign currencies, regulates various types of credit, supervises banks, and collects data on the money supply and other economic activity. As part of monetary policy, the Fed determines the reserve requirement, that is, the level of reserve funds all financial institutions must keep at one of the 12 Federal Reserve banks.[14] It buys and sells government securities

figure 20.2

**HOW THE FEDERAL RESERVE
CONTROLS THE
MONEY SUPPLY**

CONTROL METHOD	IMMEDIATE RESULT	LONG-TERM EFFECT
Reserve Requirements		
A. Increase.	Banks put more money into the Fed, *reducing* money supply; thus, there is less money available to lend to customers.	Economy slows.
B. Decrease.	Banks put less money into the Fed, *increasing* the money supply; thus, there is more money available to lend to customers.	Economy speeds up.
Open-Market Operations		
A. Fed sells bonds.	Money flows from the economy to the Fed.	Economy slows.
B. Fed buys bonds.	Money flows into the economy from the Fed.	Economy speeds up.
Managing the Discount Rate		
A. Rate increases.	Banks borrow less from the Fed; thus, there is less money to lend.	Economy slows.
B. Rate decreases.	Banks borrow more from the Fed; thus, there is more money to lend.	Economy speeds up.

in *open-market operations*. Finally, it lends money to member banks at an interest rate called the *discount rate*.

As noted, the three basic tools the Fed uses to manage the money supply are reserve requirements, open-market operations, and the discount rate (see Figure 20.2). Let's explore how it administers each.

The Reserve Requirement

The **reserve requirement** is a percentage of commercial banks' checking and savings accounts they must keep in the bank (as cash in the vault) or in a non-interest-bearing deposit at the local Federal Reserve district bank.[15] The reserve requirement is one of the Fed's most powerful tools. When it increases the reserve requirement, money becomes scarcer, which in the long run tends to reduce inflation. For instance, if Omaha Security Bank holds deposits of $100 million and the reserve requirement is, say, 10 percent, then the bank must keep $10 million on reserve. If the Fed were to increase the reserve requirement to 11 percent, then the bank would have to put an additional $1 million on reserve, reducing the amount it could lend out. Since this increase in the reserve requirement would affect all banks, the money supply would be reduced and prices would likely fall.

A decrease of the reserve requirement, in contrast, *increases* the funds available to banks for loans, so they make more loans and money becomes more readily available. An increase in the money supply can *stimulate the economy* to achieve higher growth rates, but it can also create inflationary pressures. That is, the prices of goods and services may go up. Can you see why the Fed may want to decrease the reserve requirement when the economy is in a recession?

> **reserve requirement**
> A percentage of commercial banks' checking and savings accounts that must be physically kept in the bank.

Open-Market Operations

Open-market operations consist of the buying and selling of government bonds. To decrease the money supply, the federal government sells U.S. government bonds to the public. The money it gets as payment is no longer in circulation, decreasing the money supply. If the Fed wants to increase the money supply, it buys government bonds back from individuals, corporations, or organizations that are willing to sell. The money the Fed pays for these securities enters circulation, increasing the money supply. That's why the Fed's Bernanke bought bonds during the recent recession. The idea was to get the economy growing again.[16]

> **open-market operations**
> The buying and selling of U.S. government bonds by the Fed with the goal of regulating the money supply.

The Discount Rate

The Fed has often been called the bankers' bank, because member banks can borrow money from the Fed and pass it on to their customers in the form of loans. The **discount rate** is the interest rate the Fed charges for loans to member banks. An increase in the discount rate discourages banks from borrowing and reduces the number of available loans, decreasing the money supply. In contrast, lowering the discount rate encourages member banks to borrow money and increases the funds they have available for loans, which increases the money supply. For many months, the Fed lowered the discount rate to almost zero, hoping to increase bank lending. Nonetheless, many banks still seemed reluctant to make loans.[17]

> **discount rate**
> The interest rate that the Fed charges for loans to member banks.

The discount rate is one of two interest rates the Fed controls. The other is the rate banks charge each other, called the *federal funds rate*.

The Federal Reserve's Check-Clearing Role

If you write a check to a local retailer that uses the same bank you do, it is a simple matter to reduce your account by the amount of the check and increase the amount in the retailer's account. But what happens if you write a check to a retailer in another state? That's where the Fed's check-clearing function comes into play.

That retailer will take the check to its bank. That bank will deposit the check for credit in the closest Federal Reserve bank. That bank will send the check to your local Federal Reserve bank for collection. The check will then be sent to your bank and the amount of the check will be withdrawn. Your bank will authorize the Federal Reserve bank in your area to deduct the amount of the check. That bank will pay the Federal Reserve bank that began the process in the first place. It will then credit the deposit account in the bank where the retailer has its account. That bank will then credit the account of the retailer. (See Figure 20.3 for a diagram of such an interstate transaction.) This long

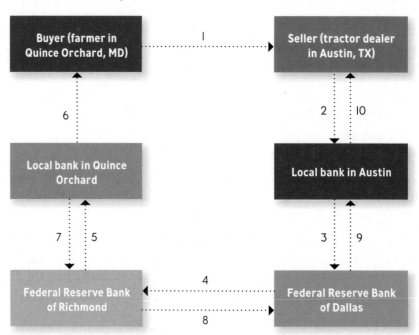

Suppose Mr. Brown, a farmer from Quince Orchard, Maryland, purchases a tractor from a dealer in Austin, Texas.

I. Mr. Brown sends his check to the tractor dealer.
2. The dealer deposits the check in his account at a local bank in Austin.
3. The Austin bank deposits the check for credit in its account at the Federal Reserve Bank of Dallas.
4. The Federal Reserve Bank of Dallas sends the check to the Federal Reserve Bank of Richmond for collection.
5. The Federal Reserve Bank of Richmond forwards the check to the local bank in Quince Orchard, where Mr. Brown has his account.
6. The local bank in Quince Orchard deducts the check amount from Mr. Brown's account.
7. The Quince Orchard bank authorizes the Federal Reserve Bank of Richmond to deduct the check amount from its deposit account with the Federal Reserve Bank.
8. The Federal Reserve Bank of Richmond pays the Federal Reserve Bank of Dallas.
9. The Federal Reserve Bank of Dallas credits the Austin bank's deposit account.
I0. The Austin bank credits the tractor dealer's account.

figure 20.3

CHECK-CLEARING PROCESS
THROUGH THE FEDERAL
RESERVE BANK SYSTEM

and involved process is a costly one; therefore, banks take many measures to lessen the use of checks. Such efforts include the use of credit cards, debit cards, and other electronic transfers of money.[18]

As you can see, the whole economy is affected by the Federal Reserve System's actions. Next we'll briefly discuss the history of banking to give you some background about why the Fed came into existence. Then we'll explore what's happening in banking today.

progress assessment

- What is money?
- What are the five characteristics of useful money?
- What is the money supply, and why is it important?
- How does the Federal Reserve control the money supply?
- What are the major functions of the Federal Reserve? What other functions does it perform?

LEARNING goal 3

Trace the history of banking and the Federal Reserve System.

THE HISTORY OF BANKING AND THE NEED FOR THE FED

At first, there were no banks in the United States. Strict laws in Europe limited the number of coins people could bring to the colonies in the New World. Thus, colonists were forced to barter for goods; for example, they might trade cotton and tobacco for shoes and lumber.

The demand for money was so great that Massachusetts issued its own paper money in 1690, and other colonies soon followed suit. But continental money, the first paper money printed in the United States, became worthless after a few years because people didn't trust its value.

Land banks were established to lend money to farmers. But Great Britain, still in charge of the colonies at that point, ended land banks by 1741. The colonies rebelled against these and other restrictions on their freedom, and a new bank was formed in Pennsylvania during the American Revolution to finance the war against England.

In 1791, after the United States gained independence, Alexander Hamilton persuaded Congress to form a *central bank* (a bank at which other banks could keep their funds and borrow funds if needed). This first version of a federal bank closed in 1811, only to be replaced in 1816 because state-chartered banks couldn't support the War of 1812. The battle between the Second (Central) Bank of the United States and state banks got hot in the 1830s. Several banks in Tennessee were hurt by pressure from the Central Bank. The fight ended when the Central Bank was closed in 1836. You can see that there was great resistance to a central bank, like the Federal Reserve, through much of U.S. history.

By the time of the Civil War, the U.S. banking system was a mess. Different banks issued different kinds of currencies. People hoarded gold and silver coins because they were worth more as precious metal than as money. That may be happening again today. In any case, the chaos continued long after the war ended, reaching something of a climax in 1907, when many banks failed. People got nervous about the safety of banks and in a run on the banks attempted to withdraw their funds. Soon the cash was depleted and some banks had to refuse money to depositors. This caused people to distrust the banking system in general.

Despite the long history of opposition to a central bank, the cash shortage problems of 1907 led to the formation of an organization that could lend money to banks—the Federal Reserve System. It was to be a "lender of last resort" in such emergencies. Under the Federal Reserve Act of 1913, all federally chartered banks had to join the Federal Reserve. State banks could also join. The Federal Reserve became the bankers' bank. If banks had excess funds, they could deposit them in the Fed; if they needed extra money, they could borrow from the Fed. The Federal Reserve System has been intimately related to banking ever since, but never more than now.

Banking and the Great Depression

The Federal Reserve System was designed to prevent a repeat of the 1907 panic. Nevertheless, the stock market crash of 1929 led to bank failures in the early 1930s. When the stock market began tumbling, people hurried to banks to withdraw cash. In spite of the Federal Reserve System, the banks ran out of money and states were forced to close them. President Franklin D. Roosevelt extended the period of bank closings in 1933, to gain time to come up with a solution to the problem. In 1933 and 1935, Congress passed legislation to strengthen the banking system. The most important move was to establish federal deposit insurance to further protect the public from bank failures. As you can see, bank crises are nothing new; they often occur during a recession. From 1945 to 2007, the United States experienced 10 recessions. The average duration was 10 months.

The Federal Reserve System was designed in 1913 to prevent the kind of run on banks that occurred in 1907. Yet the stock market crash of 1929 caused depositors to make another run on their banks and take big withdrawals. Federal deposit insurance was established in 1933 to protect depositors' money. Do you think these protections are enough?

Classify the various institutions in the U.S. banking system.

THE U.S. BANKING SYSTEM

The U.S. banking system consists of commercial banks, savings and loan associations, and credit unions. In addition, there are various financial organizations, or nonbanks, that accept no deposits but offer many of the services of regular banks. Let's discuss the activities and services of each, starting with commercial banks.

Commercial Banks

A **commercial bank** is a profit-seeking organization that receives deposits from individuals and corporations in the form of checking and savings accounts and uses these funds to make loans. It has two types of customers— depositors and borrowers—and is equally responsible to both. A commercial bank makes a profit by efficiently using depositors' funds as inputs (on which it pays interest) to invest in interest-bearing loans to other customers.[19] If the revenue generated by loans exceeds the interest paid to depositors plus operating expenses, the bank makes a profit.

commercial bank
A profit-seeking organization that receives deposits from individuals and corporations in the form of checking and savings accounts and then uses some of these funds to make loans.

Services Provided by Commercial Banks

Individuals and corporations that deposit money in a checking account can write personal checks to pay for almost any purchase or transaction. The technical name for a checking account is a **demand deposit** because the money is available on demand from the depositor. Typically, banks impose a service charge for check-writing privileges or demand a minimum deposit. They might also charge a small handling fee for each check written. For corporate depositors, the amount of the service charge depends on the average daily balance in the checking account, the number of checks written, and the firm's credit rating and credit history.

In the past, checking accounts paid no interest to depositors, but interest-bearing checking accounts have experienced phenomenal growth in recent years. Commercial banks also offer a variety of savings account options. A savings account is technically a **time deposit** because the bank can require a prior notice before you make a withdrawal. Compare online and neighborhood banks to find where your money can earn the most interest.

A **certificate of deposit (CD)** is a time-deposit (savings) account that earns interest, to be delivered on the certificate's maturity date. The depositor agrees not to withdraw any of the funds until then. CDs are now available for periods of months to years; usually the longer the period, the higher the interest rate. The interest rates also depend on economic conditions. At the present time, interest rates are very low because the economy is not robust.

Commercial banks also offer credit cards to creditworthy customers, life insurance, inexpensive brokerage services, financial counseling, automatic payment of bills, safe-deposit boxes, individual retirement accounts (IRAs), traveler's checks, trust departments, automated teller machines, and overdraft checking account privileges. The latter means preferred customers can automatically get loans when they've written checks exceeding their account balance. The Social Media in Business box on p. 564 discusses how banks are using social media to reach new market segments.

demand deposit
The technical name for a checking account; the money in a demand deposit can be withdrawn anytime on demand from the depositor.

time deposit
The technical name for a savings account; the bank can require prior notice before the owner withdraws money from a time deposit.

certificate of deposit (CD)
A time-deposit (savings) account that earns interest to be delivered at the end of the certificate's maturity date.

Banking on Social Media

Just like any other business, banks must know who their customers are and how to best meet their needs. When it comes to reaching Gen Y customers (those born between 1980 and 2000) banks know that to converse and interact with this valued customer group, they have to do it online. That's one reason why banks are committing more resources to using social media.

Take Bank of America (BofA) for example. BofA introduced its mobile banking platform four years ago as cell phones got "smarter" with GPS capabilities and faster Internet access. Today 29 million BofA's customers use online banking, including 6.5 million who use their cell phones for banking. An additional 1.1 million of the bank's customers use text messages on their phones to access account information. This cultural shift led the bank to understand it needs to talk in real time with its customers online. In 2012, the bank plans to introduce two-way text alerts that allow customers to transfer funds between accounts if they receive a text message warning them that one of their account balances is low. BofA admits that it's Gen Y's expectation that banks be accessible by social media that is driving the company's social media focus.

Banks were slow to adapt to social media due to regulatory and privacy concerns, but that's all changing. Reaching the coveted Gen Y demographic requires tweeting or texting rather than hoping they visit a local bank branch. Banks are following the lead of consumer products companies like Starbucks, Adidas, and Victoria's Secret that have used social media to get more customers. As Karen Gutierrez, social media manager for US Bank commented, "It's where our customers are, and we can better meet their needs if we are there."

Sources: Maryann Omidi, "Banks Spooked by Social Media," *Financial News,* May 4, 2011; Meghna Kothari, "Playing a Role in Social Websites," *CPI Financial,* May 11, 2011; and Lisa Brown, "Banks Woo Youth with Social Media," *St. Louis Post Dispatch,* April 17, 2011.

ATMs can dispense maps and directions, phone cards, and postage stamps. They can sell tickets to movies, concerts, and sporting events and show movie trailers, news tickers, and video ads. Some can take orders for flowers and DVDs and download music and games.

Services to Borrowers

Commercial banks offer a variety of services to individuals and corporations in need of a loan. Generally, loans are given on the basis of the recipient's creditworthiness, although the real estate collapse beginning in 2008 was partially due to banks' ignoring that rule. Banks want to manage their funds effectively and are supposed to screen loan applicants carefully to ensure that the loan plus interest will be paid back on time. Clearly banks failed to do that in the period leading up to the banking crisis. We will discuss why that happened later in the chapter. The nearby Making Ethical Decisions box explores a more minor issue that could occur in your banking efforts.

Savings and Loan Associations (S&Ls)

savings and loan association (S&L)
A financial institution that accepts both savings and checking deposits and provides home mortgage loans.

A **savings and loan association (S&L)** is a financial institution that accepts both savings and checking deposits and provides home mortgage loans. S&Ls are often known as thrift institutions because their original purpose (starting in 1831) was to promote consumer thrift and home ownership. To help them encourage home ownership, thrifts were permitted for many years to offer slightly higher interest rates on savings deposits than banks. Those rates attracted a large pool of funds, which S&Ls used to offer long-term fixed-rate mortgages. They no longer offer better rates than banks, however.

Between 1979 and 1983, about 20 percent of the nation's S&Ls failed. Perhaps the biggest reason is that capital gains taxes were raised, making it less attractive to invest in real estate (because the added tax reduced profits). Investors therefore walked away from their real estate loans, leaving S&Ls with lots of properties worth less than the outstanding loans on them. When they sold those properties, the S&Ls lost money. The recent drop in real estate prices has caused similar problems for banks and S&Ls.

In the 1980s, the government stepped in to strengthen S&Ls, permitting them to offer higher interest rates, allocate up to 10 percent of their funds to commercial loans, and offer mortgages with adjustable interest rates based on market conditions. You can learn more about this by looking up the Glass-Steagall Act.[20] In addition, S&Ls were permitted to offer a variety of new banking services, such as financial counseling to small businesses and credit cards. As a result, they became much more similar to commercial banks.

credit unions
Nonprofit, member-owned financial cooperatives that offer the full variety of banking services to their members.

Credit Unions

Credit unions are nonprofit, member-owned financial cooperatives that offer the full variety of banking services to their members—interest-bearing checking accounts at relatively high rates, short-term loans at relatively low rates, financial counseling, life insurance policies, and a limited number of home mortgage loans. They are organized by government agencies, corporations, unions, and professional associations.

As nonprofit institutions, credit unions enjoy an exemption from federal income taxes. You might want to visit a local credit union to see whether you are eligible to belong, and then compare the rates to those at local banks. Ed Mierzwinski, a consumer program director for the U.S. Public Interest Research Group says, "The average consumer does much better at a credit union than a bank. Credit unions have lower requirements for waiving fees, offer better deals on car loans, and are generally more flexible in responding to customer's problems."[21]

Credit unions are member-owned financial cooperatives that offer their members a wide range of banking services and, because they are nonprofits, are exempt from federal income tax. Which credit unions are available in your area?

565

Credit unions often have fewer branches than banks and less access to ATMs. It's best to determine what services you need and then compare those services to the same services offered by banks.

Other Financial Institutions (Nonbanks)

nonbanks
Financial organizations that accept no deposits but offer many of the services provided by regular banks (pension funds, insurance companies, commercial finance companies, consumer finance companies, and brokerage houses).

Nonbanks are financial organizations that accept no deposits but offer many of the services provided by regular banks. Nonbanks include life insurance companies, pension funds, brokerage firms, commercial finance companies, and corporate financial services (like GE Capital). Nonbanks cut back their lending considerably during the banking crisis beginning in 2008. Such a drop-off in lending contributed to slowing the economy greatly.

As competition between banks and nonbanks has increased, the dividing line between them has become less apparent. This is equally true in Europe, where U.S. companies compete with European banks. The diversity of financial services and investment alternatives nonbanks offer has led banks to expand their own services. In fact, many banks have merged with brokerage firms to offer full-service financial assistance.

Life insurance companies provide financial protection for policyholders, who periodically pay premiums. In addition, insurers invest the funds they receive from policyholders in corporate and government bonds. In recent years, more insurance companies have begun to provide long-term financing for real estate development projects. Do you think that was a wise decision?

pension funds
Amounts of money put aside by corporations, nonprofit organizations, or unions to cover part of the financial needs of members when they retire.

Pension funds are monies put aside by corporations, nonprofit organizations, or unions to help fund their members' financial needs when they retire. Contributions to pension funds are made by employees, employers, or both. To generate additional income, pension funds typically invest in low-return but safe corporate stocks or other conservative investments such as government securities and corporate bonds.

Many financial services organizations that provide retirement and health benefits, such as TIAA-CREF, are becoming a major force in U.S. financial markets. They also lend money directly to corporations.

Brokerage firms have traditionally offered investment services in stock exchanges in the United States and abroad. They have also made serious inroads into regular banks' domain by offering high-yield combination savings and checking accounts. In addition, they offer money market accounts with check-writing privileges and allow investors to borrow, using their securities as collateral.

Commercial and consumer finance companies offer short-term loans to those who cannot meet the credit requirements of regular banks, such as new businesses, or who have exceeded their credit limit and need more funds. College students with no credit history often turn to consumer finance companies for education loans. Be careful when borrowing from such institutions because their interest rates can be quite high. The nearby Spotlight on Small Business box offers an example of a newer type of nonbank that offers services to people who do not have traditional checking accounts.

progress assessment

- Why did the United States need a Federal Reserve Bank?
- What's the difference between a bank, a savings and loan association, and a credit union?
- What is a consumer finance company?

business

The Rise of the Nonbank

About a fourth of American households don't have a bank account. That creates a huge market for alternative banking such as that provided by Mango Store. It is a banklike facility in Austin, Texas. Clients pay a one-time $10 fee that lets them cash as many checks as they want by putting the money onto debit cards. More sophisticated services cost extra. Nonetheless, Mango's fees are much less than a typical local bank.

Mango hopes its customers will increase their earning power and remain customers over time. First, however, the company must get customers through the door and onto its system. Because the majority of Mango's cash is stored in the outside ATM, the interior can emphasize open spaces and security cameras. Customers can use self-serve kiosks to check card balances and transfer funds. Bilingual counselors help customers understand the system. To help customers

better understand the services available and the costs, the store has banners clearly displaying fees.

Sources: Dan Macsai, "The Mango Store Lets You Bank without Commitment," *Fast Company*, July 1, 2010; "Mango Financial, Inc., Debuts First U.S. Store in Austin," PR Newswire.com, accessed May 2011; and mangomoney.com, accessed May 2011.

LEARNING goal 5

Briefly trace the causes of the banking crisis starting in 2008 and explain how the government protects your funds during such crises.

THE RECENT BANKING CRISIS AND HOW THE GOVERNMENT PROTECTS YOUR MONEY

What led to the recent banking crisis? There is no simple answer. Some people believe the Federal Reserve is partly responsible because it kept the cost of borrowing so low that people were tempted to borrow more than they could afford to pay back. Congress, very interested in creating more "affordable housing," prodded banks to lend to people with minimal assets. The Community Reinvestment Act further encouraged loans to families with questionable ability to repay.

Other organizations pressured banks, normally quite risk-averse, to make risky loans. Banks learned they could avoid much of the risk by dividing their portfolios of mortgages up and selling the mortgage-backed securities (MBSs) to other banks and other organizations all over the world. These securities seemed quite safe because they were backed by the homes that were mortgaged. Fannie Mae and Freddie Mac are both quasi-government agencies that seemed to guarantee the value of MBSs. Banks sold more and more of such seemingly safe

The bursting of the housing bubble forced a sharp decline in home values. When homeowners discovered they owed more on their mortgages than their homes were worth, many stopped paying off their loans and the banks foreclosed on their homes. This forced home prices to fall lower still and put even more people in jeopardy of losing their homes. What can the government do to help homeowners?

Federal Deposit Insurance Corporation (FDIC)
An independent agency of the U.S. government that insures bank deposits.

securities, hoping to make lots of money. Bankers were also accused of pushing loans onto naive consumers.

Meanwhile, the Federal Reserve and the Securities and Exchange Commission failed to issue sufficient warnings. That is, they failed in their regulatory duties. When the value of homes began to decline, people began defaulting on their loans (not paying them) and turned the properties back over to the banks. Since the banks owned the mortgages on those homes, their profits declined dramatically, leading to the recent banking crisis—and the need for the government to help the banks out. Not doing so was considered too risky because the whole economy might fail. The long-term effects of that process are not yet known.

So whom do we blame for the banking crisis? The answer is that we could blame the Fed for suppressing interest rates, the Congress for promoting questionable loans, the banks for making such loans and creating mortgage-backed securities that were not nearly as safe as promoted, government regulatory agencies for not doing their job, and people who took advantage of low interest rates to borrow money they couldn't reasonably hope to repay. No matter who was to blame, the crisis still needed to be solved.

Toward the end of George W. Bush's presidency, the Treasury Department proposed a $700 billion "bailout" package, known as the Troubled Assets Relief Program (TARP). The program was enacted in October 2008. President Barack Obama, who took office in January 2009, proposed over $800 billion in additional government spending plus a stimulus package. We are just now seeing the results of that spending.

Protecting Your Funds

The recent banking crisis is nothing new. The government had seen similar problems during the Great Depression of the 1930s. To prevent investors from ever again being completely wiped out during an economic downturn, it created three major organizations to protect your money: the Federal Deposit Insurance Corporation (FDIC); the Savings Association Insurance Fund (SAIF); and the National Credit Union Administration (NCUA). All three insure deposits in individual accounts up to a certain amount. Because these organizations are so important to the safety of your money, let's explore them individually in more depth.

The Federal Deposit Insurance Corporation (FDIC)

The **Federal Deposit Insurance Corporation (FDIC)** is an independent agency of the U.S. government that insures bank deposits. If a bank were to fail, the FDIC would arrange to have that bank's accounts transferred to another bank or reimburse depositors up to $250,000. The FDIC covers about 13,000 institutions, mostly commercial banks.

The Savings Association Insurance Fund (SAIF)

The **Savings Association Insurance Fund (SAIF)** insures holders of accounts in savings and loan associations. A brief history will show why it was created. Some 1,700 bank and thrift institutions had failed during the early 1930s, and people were losing confidence in them. The FDIC and the Federal Savings and Loan Insurance Corporation (FSLIC) were designed (in 1933 and 1934, respectively) to create more confidence in banking institutions by protecting people's savings from loss. In the 1980s, to get more control over the banking system in general, the government placed the FSLIC under the FDIC and gave it a new name: the Savings Association Insurance Fund (SAIF).

Savings Association Insurance Fund (SAIF)
The part of the FDIC that insures holders of accounts in savings and loan associations.

The National Credit Union Administration (NCUA)

The National Credit Union Administration (NCUA) provides up to $250,000 coverage per individual depositor per institution. This coverage includes all accounts—checking accounts, savings accounts, money market accounts, and certificates of deposit. Depositors qualify for additional protection by holding accounts jointly or in trust. Individual retirement accounts (IRAs) are also separately insured up to $250,000. Credit unions, like banks, suffered from the banking crisis beginning in 2008 and got money from the federal government to make more loans.

electronic funds transfer (EFT) system
A computerized system that electronically performs financial transactions such as making purchases, paying bills, and receiving paychecks.

LEARNING goal 6

Describe how technology helps make banking more efficient.

Smartphone apps, such as FaceCash, allow users to pay for purchases with their phones. What problems could there be with such capabilities?

USING TECHNOLOGY TO MAKE BANKING MORE EFFICIENT

Imagine the cost to a bank of approving a written check, physically processing it through the banking system, and mailing it back to you. It's expensive. Bankers have long looked for ways to make the system more efficient.

One solution was to issue credit cards to reduce the flow of checks, but they too have their costs: there's still paper to process. Accepting Visa and MasterCard costs retailers about $2 per $100 purchase; Amex costs them about $2.50. In the future we'll see much more electronic rather than physical exchange of money, because it is the most efficient way to transfer funds.

If you must use a credit card, be sure to search for one that offers the best deal for you. Some offer cash back, others offer free travel, and so forth. Don't just sign up for whatever card is offering free T-shirts on campus. Do your research.

In an **electronic funds transfer (EFT) system**, messages about a transaction are sent from one computer to another. Thus, organizations can transfer funds more quickly and economically than

Need to pass the security check in your office building, put gas in your car, and get cash at the ATM? No problem. Smart cards with embedded RFID chips can take care of these tasks and then some. Has cash become a thing of the past?

debit card
An electronic funds transfer tool that serves the same function as checks: it withdraws funds from a checking account.

smart card
An electronic funds transfer tool that is a combination credit card, debit card, phone card, driver's license card, and more.

with paper checks. EFT tools include electronic check conversion, debit cards, smart cards, direct deposits, and direct payments. The latest technology, developed by information commerce company First Data, is the GO-Tag, a pea-shaped chip with a radio transmitter inside that can stick to a cell phone or ID badge to make payments fast and easy. It takes only a second to complete a transaction with a GO-Tag, much faster than even a credit card.

A **debit card** serves the same function as a check—it withdraws funds from a checking account. It looks like a credit card but withdraws (debits) money that is already in your account. When the sale is recorded, the debit card sends an electronic signal to the bank, automatically transferring funds from your account to the store's. A record of transactions immediately appears online. Debit transactions surpassed credit years ago and continue to grow twice as fast.[22]

Payroll debit cards are an efficient way for some firms to pay their workers and an alternative to cash for those who don't qualify for a credit or debit card—the so-called unbanked. Employees can access funds in their accounts immediately after they are posted, withdraw them from an ATM, pay bills online, or transfer funds to another cardholder. The system is much cheaper for companies than issuing checks and more convenient for employees. On the other hand, debit cards don't offer the same protection as credit cards. If someone steals your credit card, you are liable only for a certain amount. You are liable for everything when someone steals your debit card.

A **smart card** is an electronic funds transfer tool that combines a credit card, debit card, phone card, driver's license card, and more. Smart cards replace the typical magnetic strip on a credit or debit card with a microprocessor. The card can then store a variety of information, including the holder's bank balance. Merchants can use this information to check the card's validity and spending limits, and transactions can debit up to the amount on the card.

Some smart cards have embedded radio-frequency identification (RFID) chips that make it possible to enter buildings and secure areas and to buy gas and other items with a swipe of the card. A biometric function lets you use your fingerprint to boot up your computer. Students are using smart cards to open locked doors to dorms and identify themselves to retailers near campus and online. The cards also serve as ATM cards.

For many, the ultimate convenience in banking is automatic transactions such as direct deposit and direct payments. A *direct deposit* is a credit made directly to a checking or savings account in place of a paycheck. The employer contacts the bank and orders it to transfer funds from the employer's account to the worker's account. Individuals can use direct deposits to transfer funds to other accounts, such as from a checking account to a savings or retirement account.

A *direct payment* is a preauthorized electronic payment. Customers sign a separate form for each company whose bill they would like to automatically pay from their checking or savings account on a specified date. The customer's bank completes each transaction and records it on the customer's monthly statement.

Online Banking

All top U.S. retail banks now allow customers to access their accounts online, and most have bill-paying capacity. Thus, you can complete all your financial transactions from home, using your telephone or your computer to transfer funds from one account to another, pay your bills, and check the balance in each of your accounts. You can apply for a car loan or mortgage and get a response while you wait. Buying and selling stocks and bonds is equally easy.

Internet banks such as E*Trade Bank offer online banking only, not physical branches. They can offer customers higher interest rates and lower fees because they do not have the overhead costs traditional banks have. While many consumers are pleased with the savings and convenience, not all are happy with the service. Why? Some are nervous about security. People fear putting their financial information into cyberspace, where others may see it despite all the assurances of privacy. Further, some people want to be able to talk to a knowledgeable person one-on-one when they have banking problems.

The future thus seems to be with traditional banks that offer both online services and brick-and-mortar facilities. Even small, local banks offer online services now.

LEARNING goal 7

Evaluate the role and importance of international banking, the World Bank, and the International Monetary Fund.

INTERNATIONAL BANKING AND BANKING SERVICES

Banks help companies conduct business in other countries by providing three services: letters of credit, banker's acceptances, and money exchange. If a U.S. company wants to buy a product from Germany, the company could pay a bank to issue a letter of credit. A **letter of credit** is a promise by the bank to pay the seller a given amount if certain conditions are met. For example, the German company may not be paid until the goods have arrived at the U.S. company's warehouse. A **banker's acceptance** promises that the bank will pay some specified amount at a particular time. No conditions are imposed. Finally, a company can go to a bank and exchange U.S. dollars for euros to use in Germany; that's called *currency* or *money exchange*.

Banks are making it easier than ever for travelers and businesspeople to buy goods and services overseas. Automated teller machines now provide yen, euros, and other foreign currencies through your personal Visa, MasterCard, Cirrus, or American Express card.

letter of credit
A promise by the bank to pay the seller a given amount if certain conditions are met.

banker's acceptance
A promise that the bank will pay some specified amount at a particular time.

Leaders in International Banking

It would be shortsighted to discuss the U.S. economy apart from the world economy. If the Federal Reserve decides to lower interest rates, within minutes foreign investors can withdraw their money from the United States and put it in countries with higher rates. Of course, the Fed's increasing of interest rates can draw money to the United States equally quickly.

World Bank
The bank primarily responsible for financing economic development; also known as the International Bank for Reconstruction and Development.

International Monetary Fund (IMF)
Organization that assists the smooth flow of money among nations.

Today's money markets thus form a global market system of which the United States is just a part. International bankers make investments in any country where they can get a maximum return for their money at a reasonable risk. That's how about $4 trillion is traded daily! The net result of international banking and finance has been to link the economies of the world into one interrelated system with no regulatory control. U.S. firms must compete for funds with firms all over the world. An efficient firm in London or Tokyo is more likely to get international financing than a less efficient firm in Detroit or Chicago. Global markets mean that banks do not necessarily keep their money in their own countries. They make investments where they get the maximum return.

What this means for you is that banking is no longer a domestic issue; it's a global one. To understand the U.S. financial system, you must learn about the global financial system. To understand the state of the U.S. economy, you need to learn about the economic condition of countries throughout the world. In the new world economy financed by international banks, the United States is just one player. To be a winner, it must stay financially secure and its businesses must stay competitive in world markets. Is that happening today?

The World Bank and the International Monetary Fund (IMF) are intergovernmental organizations that help support the global banking community. Both draw protests for their actions. Why?

The World Bank and the International Monetary Fund (IMF)

The bank primarily responsible for financing economic development is the International Bank for Reconstruction and Development, or the **World Bank**.[23] After World War II, it lent money to countries in Western Europe so they could rebuild. Today, it lends most of its money to developing nations to improve their productivity and help raise standards of living and quality of life. That includes working to eliminate diseases that kill millions of people each year.

The World Bank has faced considerable criticism and protests around the world. Environmentalists charge that it finances projects damaging to the ecosystem. Human rights activists and unionists say the bank supports countries that restrict religious freedoms and tolerate sweatshops. AIDS activists complain that it does not do enough to get low-cost AIDS drugs to developing nations.

Despite its efforts to improve, the World Bank still has many critics. Some want it to forgive the debts of developing countries and others want it to stop making such loans until the countries institute free markets and the right to own property. Some changes in World Bank policy may lie ahead.[24]

In contrast to the World Bank, the **International Monetary Fund (IMF)** was established to foster cooperative monetary policies that stabilize the exchange of one national currency for another.[25] About 185 countries are voluntary members of the IMF and allow their money to be freely exchanged for foreign money, keep the IMF informed about

New Issues Facing the World Bank and the IMF

In the past, the World Bank and the IMF have had to face major crises throughout the world. Today, the issues seem to be as great as ever. For example, the United States has very high unemployment and a debt crisis that exceeds anything in the past. A similar debt crisis is occurring in many European countries. Japan is trying to recover from its earthquake and tsunami and other disasters (e.g., the nuclear problems). There are major disruptions occurring in the Middle East, and the United States is uncertain as to what to do. Emerging nations such as China and Brazil are having problems with high inflation, and food prices are rising all over the planet. Poorer nations are having a particularly hard time because of the high food prices.

The Chair of the IMF's governing body says, "There are significant vulnerabilities still in the global financial and economic systems. That reflects the legacy of an international monetary system that is still not in what we consider satisfactory shape."

The IMF and the World Bank are both trying to come up with answers to the global issues that have become very serious. The United States is a major contributor to those organizations, but there is not enough money to pay down the U.S. debt, much less solve the problems of the rest of the world.

Sources: Neil Irwin, "World Bank, IMF Leaders: Recovery Still a Shaky One," *The Washington Post,* April 17, 2011; and Howard Schneider, "IMF Panel Seeks a New Consensus," *The Washington Post,* March 8, 2011.

changes in monetary policy, and modify those policies on the advice of the IMF to accommodate the needs of the entire membership.

The IMF is designed to oversee member countries' monetary and exchange rate policies. Its goal is to maintain a global monetary system that works best for all nations and enhances world trade. While it is not primarily a lending institution like the World Bank, its members do contribute funds according to their ability, and those funds are available to countries in financial difficulty.[26] The IMF saw a slowing in the global economy in 2010 and was prepared to give certain countries a boost if necessary.[27] The IMF is usually in favor of free capital inflows, but recently it has allowed countries to put up barriers to protect their economies from inflation or bubbles in their stock markets. Countries included in this effort included Brazil, South Korea, and Turkey.[28] The nearby Reaching Beyond Our Borders box discusses what is happening today at the World Bank and the IMF.

progress assessment

- What are some of the causes for the banking crisis that began in 2008?
- What is the role of the FDIC?
- How does a debit card differ from a credit card?
- What is the World Bank and what does it do?
- What is the IMF and what does it do?

summary

Learning Goal 1. Explain what money is and what makes money useful.
- **What is money?**

Money is anything people generally accept as payment for goods and services.
- **What are the five standards for a useful form of money?**

The five standards for a useful form of money are portability, divisibility, stability, durability, and uniqueness.

Learning Goal 2. Describe how the Federal Reserve controls the money supply.
- **How does the Federal Reserve control the money supply?**

The Federal Reserve makes financial institutions keep funds in the Federal Reserve System (reserve requirement), buys and sells government securities (open-market operations), and lends money to banks (the discount rate). To increase the money supply, the Fed can cut the reserve requirement, buy government bonds, and lower the discount rate.

Learning Goal 3. Trace the history of banking and the Federal Reserve System.
- **How did banking evolve in the United States?**

Massachusetts issued its own paper money in 1690; other colonies followed suit. British land banks lent money to farmers but ended such loans by 1741. After the American Revolution, there was much debate about the role of banking, and heated battles between the Central Bank of the United States and state banks. Eventually, a federally chartered and state-chartered system was established, but chaos continued until many banks failed in 1907. The system was revived by the Federal Reserve only to fail again during the Great Depression. There have been 10 recessions since then, including the recession starting in 2008. The Federal Reserve is doing all it can to solve the banking crisis again.

Learning Goal 4. Classify the various institutions in the U.S. banking system.
- **What institutions make up the banking system?**

Savings and loans, commercial banks, and credit unions are all part of the banking system.
- **How do they differ from one another?**

Before deregulation in 1980, commercial banks were unique in that they handled both deposits and checking accounts. At that time, savings and loans couldn't offer checking services; their main function was to encourage thrift and home ownership by offering high interest rates on savings accounts and providing home mortgages. Deregulation closed the gaps between banks and S&Ls and they now offer similar services.
- **What kinds of services do they offer?**

Banks and thrifts offer such services as savings accounts, checking accounts, certificates of deposit, loans, individual retirement accounts (IRAs), safe-deposit boxes, online banking, life insurance, brokerage services, and traveler's checks.
- **What is a credit union?**

A credit union is a member-owned cooperative that offers everything a bank does—it takes deposits, allows you to write checks, and makes loans. It also may sell life insurance and offer mortgages. Credit union interest rates are sometimes higher than those from banks, and loan rates are often lower.
- **What are some of the other financial institutions that make loans and perform banklike operations?**

Nonbanks include life insurance companies that lend out their funds, pension funds that invest in stocks and bonds and make loans, brokerage firms that offer investment services, and commercial finance companies.

Learning Goal 5. Briefly trace the causes of the banking crisis starting in 2008 and explain how the government protects your funds during such crises.

- **What caused the banking crisis that began in 2008?**

The goal was to have affordable housing, so the government urged banks to make loans to some who could not afford to repay. The banks wanted to minimize the risk of such loans, so they created mortgage-backed securities and sold them to other banks and organizations throughout the world. The government did not regulate these transactions well, and many banks failed because housing values fell and people defaulted on their loans. Many have been blamed for the loss: the Fed, Congress, bank managers, Fannie Mae, and Freddie Mac among them.

- **What agencies insure the money you put into a bank, S&L, or credit union?**

Money deposited in banks is insured by the Federal Deposit Insurance Corporation (FDIC). Money in S&Ls is insured by another agency connected to the FDIC, the Savings Association Insurance Fund (SAIF). Money in credit unions is insured by the National Credit Union Administration (NCUA). Accounts are now insured to $250,000.

Learning Goal 6. Describe how technology helps make banking more efficient.

- **What are debit cards and smart cards?**

A debit card looks like a credit card but withdraws money that is already in your account. When the sale is recorded, the debit card sends an electronic signal to the bank, automatically transferring funds from your account to the store's. A smart card is an electronic funds transfer tool that combines a credit card, debit card, phone card, driver's license card, and more. Smart cards replace the typical magnetic strip on a credit or debit card with a microprocessor.

- **What is the benefit of automatic transactions and online banking?**

A *direct deposit* is a credit made directly to a checking or savings account in place of a paycheck. A *direct payment* is a preauthorized electronic payment. Customers sign a separate form for each company whose bill they would like to automatically pay from their checking or savings account on a specified date. The customer's bank completes each transaction and records it on the customer's monthly statement. All top U.S. retail banks now allow customers to access their accounts online, and most have bill-paying capacity.

Learning Goal 7. Evaluate the role and importance of international banking, the World Bank, and the International Monetary Fund.

- **What do we mean by global markets?**

Global markets mean that banks do not necessarily keep their money in their own countries. They make investments where they get the maximum return. What this means for you is that banking is no longer a domestic issue; it's a global one.

- **What roles do the World Bank and the IMF play?**

The World Bank (also called the International Bank for Reconstruction and Development) is primarily responsible for financing economic development. The International Monetary Fund (IMF), in contrast, was established to assist the smooth flow of money among nations. It requires members (who join voluntarily) to allow their own money to be exchanged for foreign money freely, to keep the IMF informed about changes in monetary policy, and to modify those policies on the advice of the IMF to accommodate the needs of the entire membership. Lately the IMF has been lending money to countries affected by the U.S. banking crisis, and the U.S. has promised more money to the IMF.

key terms

banker's acceptance 571	Federal Deposit Insurance Corporation (FDIC) 568	open-market operations 559
barter 555		pension funds 566
certificate of deposit (CD) 563	International Monetary Fund (IMF) 572	reserve requirement 559
commercial bank 563	letter of credit 571	savings and loan association (S&L) 564
credit unions 565	M-1 556	Savings Association Insurance Fund (SAIF) 569
debit card 570	M-2 556	
demand deposit 563	M-3 556	smart card 570
discount rate 559	money 555	time deposit 563
electronic funds transfer (EFT) system 569	money supply 556	World Bank 572
	nonbanks 566	

critical thinking

1. If you were Ben Bernanke, chairman of the Federal Reserve, what economic figures might you use to determine how well you were doing? What role did Bernanke play in the recent banking crisis?

2. How much cash do you usually carry with you? What other means do you use to pay for items at the store or on the Internet? What trends do you see in such payments? How might those trends make your purchase experience more satisfactory?

3. If the value of the dollar declines relative to the euro, what will happen to the price of French wine sold in U.S. stores? Will people in France be more or less likely to buy a U.S.-made car? Why or why not?

4. Do you keep your savings in a bank, an S&L, a credit union, or some combination? Have you compared the benefits you could receive from each? Where would you expect to find the best loan values?

developing workplace skills

1. In a small group, discuss the following: What services do you use from banks and S&Ls? Does anyone use online banking? What seem to be its pluses and minuses? Use this opportunity to compare the rates and services of various local banks and S&Ls.

2. Poll the class to see who uses a bank and who uses a credit union. Have class members compare the services at each (interest rates on savings accounts, services available, loan rates). If anyone uses an online service, see how those rates compare. If no one uses a credit union or online bank, discuss the reasons.

3. One role of the Federal Reserve is to help process your checks. In small groups discuss when and where you use checks, credit cards, debit cards, and cash. Do you often write checks for small amounts? Would you stop if

you calculated how much it costs to process such checks? Have you switched to debit cards as a result? Discuss your findings with the class.

4. Form several smaller groups and discuss the recent banking crisis. How has it affected the people in the class? What has happened to banks and the economy in general since the start of the banking crisis? What have been the political implications of recent economic changes?

5. Write a one-page paper on the role of the World Bank and the International Monetary Fund in providing loans to countries. Is it important for U.S. citizens to lend money to people in other countries through such organizations? Why or why not? Be prepared to debate the value of these organizations in class.

taking it to the net

Purpose

To learn more about the banking crisis that began in 2008 and what has happened since.

Exercise

1. Do an Internet search to find the latest articles on the global financial crisis. What has happened to banking in the United States and around the world since 2009? What role has the Fed played in trying to end the crisis in the United States?

2. How many search items have appeared covering this issue? What does the number of articles tell you about the importance of this issue?

3. Develop your own story about the causes of the banking crisis. Talk to others in the class and compare stories. What organizations share the blame for the crisis?

casing the web

To access the case "Learning about the Federal Reserve System," visit **www.mhhe.com/ubl0e**

video case

To access the video case featuring the Financial Crisis-Banking Disaster, visit **www.mhhe.com/ubl0e**

WORKING within the Legal ENVIRONMENT

LEARNING goals

After you have read and studied this chapter, you should be able to

1 Define *business law*, distinguish between statutory and common law, and explain the role of administrative agencies.

2 Define *tort law* and explain the role of product liability in tort law.

3 Identify the purposes and conditions of patents, copyrights, and trademarks.

4 Describe warranties and negotiable instruments as covered in the Uniform Commercial Code.

5 List and describe the conditions necessary to make a legally enforceable contract, and describe the possible consequences if such a contract is violated.

6 Summarize several laws that regulate competition and protect consumers in the United States.

7 Explain the role of tax laws in generating income for the government and as a method of discouraging or encouraging certain behaviors among taxpayers.

8 Distinguish among the various types of bankruptcy as outlined by the Bankruptcy Code.

9 Explain the role of deregulation as a tool to encourage competition.

The pharmaceutical companies rely on big, risky investments in new drugs in order to grow. Although a successful drug can bring in as much as $5 billion a year, the cost of research required to bring the drug to market in the first place often doubles that. Even after medicine hits the pharmacy counters there's still a risk that all those studies could have missed an unforeseen side effect, inevitably leading to lawsuits. As former general counsel for the pharmaceutical giant Merck, Kenneth Frazier knows the defendant's position well and uses that experience in his new role as the company's CEO.

Hailing from a tough area of Philadelphia, the death of Frazier's mother at age 12 left him in the care of his exacting father, a janitor who "demanded excellence" from his son. Heeding his father's guidance, Frazier graduated from high school at 16 and attended Pennsylvania State University. After college his admiration of legal pioneers like Supreme Court Justice Thurgood Marshall and civil rights leaders led Frazier to law school. Despite receiving acceptance letters from other elite schools like Stanford, Cornell, and Columbia, Frazier only had eyes for Harvard University.

After he earned his law degree, Frazier took a job at the Philadelphia firm Drinker, Biddle & Reath. He soon gained a reputation as a ferocious litigator. In 1991 Frazier and two colleagues were able to secure a new trial for Willie "Bo" Cochran, a man who had spent nearly 20 years on death row for murder. Although a court eventually acquitted Cochran in 1997, by that time Frazier had moved on to Merck defending the company in liability suits. His work caught the attention of executives who promoted Frazier to Merck's general counsel in 1999.

Frazier's greatest challenge appeared in 2004 after Merck discovered that its blockbuster drug Vioxx actually doubled the risk of heart attack and stroke. A sea of lawsuits swept against Merck when the company pulled the pill off the market. With annual sales for Vioxx at $2.5 billion, Frazier was faced with a monumental decision. Either he could follow the industry standard and settle all complaints out of court, or he could take the risky route and fight each case in front of a judge. Frazier opted for the latter. He ended up winning 11 of 16 lawsuits at trial before agreeing to set up a $4.85 billion settlement fund in 2007. Although the final legal bill totaled $7.7 billion, Frazier nevertheless managed to greatly reduce the $18 billion that analysts estimated Merck would lose.

Frazier's success in the Vioxx case earned him a promotion to the head of human health business, Merck's largest unit. Three years later he was appointed CEO. As Merck's leader, Frazier has made in-depth drug research a top priority. Perhaps dreading another Vioxx situation, Frazier allocated $8.5 billion to research in 2011 alone. Although Merck's stock tumbled the day Frazier announced his plan, the long-term payoff of that research could be huge. After all, the last thing Frazier wants to see is the inside of another courtroom.

Legal issues affect almost every area of our lives and of business too. The United States has more lawyers than any other developed nation in the world and is clearly the world's most litigious society. In this bonus chapter, we will briefly discuss the history and structure of the U.S. legal system. Then we will take a look at key areas of business law such as torts, patents, copyrights, and trademarks as well as sales law, contract law, laws to protect competition and consumers, tax law, and bankruptcy law. We will also discuss the controversial topic of deregulation. You probably won't be ready to go head-to-head with Kenneth Frazier after reading this chapter, but if you use it as a foundation to the study of law, who knows what your future may be?

profile

Getting to Know
X *Kenneth C. Frazier*
CEO of Merck

Sources: Tom Randall, "Merck's Risky Bet on Research," *Bloomberg Businessweek*, April 21, 2011; Nathan Koppel, "Another Lawyer Done Good: Merck Names Frazier CEO," *The Wall Street Journal*, November 30, 2010; Christopher K. Hepp, "New Merck CEO Kenneth C. Frazier Has Philadelphia Roots," *The Philadelphia Inquirer*, December 1, 2010; and Melly Alazraki, "Merck Appoints Kenneth Frazier as CEO to Succeed Richard Clark," *Daily Finance*, November 30, 2010.

NAME THAT company

This automaker sells more cars in the United States than any other auto producer. In 2010–2011, however, the company was forced to recall 3 million cars due to sudden acceleration incidents. It's likely the company will face years of litigation from customers who were affected by the product problem. Name that company. (Find the answer in the chapter.)

LEARNING goal 1

Define *business law,* distinguish between statutory and common law, and explain the role of administrative agencies.

THE CASE FOR LAWS

Imagine a society without laws. Just think: no speed limits, no age restrictions on the consumption of alcohol, no limitations on who can practice law or medicine—a society where people are free to do whatever they choose, with no interference. Obviously, the more we consider this possibility, the more unrealistic we realize it is. Laws are an essential part of a civilized nation. Over time, though, the depth and scope of the body of laws must change to continue reflecting the needs of society. The **judiciary** is the branch of government chosen to oversee the legal system through a system of courts.

The U.S. court system is organized at the federal, state, and local levels. At both the federal and state levels, trial courts hear cases involving criminal and civil law. *Criminal law* defines crimes, establishes punishments, and regulates the investigation and prosecution of people accused of committing crimes. *Civil law* proceedings cover noncriminal acts—marriage, personal injury suits, and so on. Both federal and state systems have appellate courts that hear appeals from the losing party about decisions made at the trial-court level. Appellate courts can review and overturn these decisions.

The judiciary also governs the activities and operations of business, including hiring and firing practices, unpaid leave for family emergencies, environmental protection, worker safety, freedom from sexual harassment at work, and more. As you may suspect, businesspeople prefer to set their own standards of behavior and often complain that the government is overstepping its bounds in governing business. Unfortunately, as was evident in the economic crisis that began in 2008, the U.S. business community did not implement acceptable standards—particularly in financial markets—causing government to expand its control and enforcement procedures.[1] This chapter will look at specific laws and regulations and how they affect businesses.

Business law refers to the rules, statutes, codes, and regulations that provide a legal framework for the conduct of business and that are enforceable by court action. A businessperson must be familiar with laws regarding product liability, sales, contracts, fair competition, consumer protection, taxes, and

judiciary
The branch of government chosen to oversee the legal system through a system of courts.

business law
The rules, statutes, codes, and regulations that provide a legal framework for the conduct of business and that are enforceable by court action.

statutory law
State and federal constitutions, legislative enactments, treaties of the federal government, and ordinances—in short, written law.

bankruptcy. Let's start by discussing the foundations of law and what the legal system is all about.

Statutory and Common Law

Two major fields of law are important to businesspeople: statutory law and common law.

Statutory law includes state and federal constitutions, legislative enactments, treaties of the
federal government, and ordinances—in short,
written law. You can read the statutes that make
up this body of law, but they are often written in
language whose meaning must be determined in
court. With more than 1.1 million lawyers, the
United States has more lawyers per citizen than
any country in the world.

Common law is the body of law that comes
from decisions handed down by courts. We often
call it *unwritten law* because it does not appear in
any legislative enactment, treaty, or other written
document. Under common law principles, what
judges have decided in previous cases is very
important in deciding today's cases. Such decisions are called **precedent**, and
they guide judges in the handling of new cases. Common law evolves through
decisions made in trial courts, appellate courts, and special courts (e.g., pro-
bate courts or bankruptcy courts). Lower courts (trial courts) must abide by
the precedents set by higher courts (e.g., appellate courts) such as the U.S.
Supreme Court.

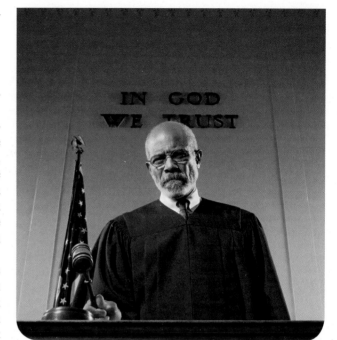

In the U.S. judicial system, judges are guided in their decisions by the precepts of common law (often called unwritten law because it is based on previous court decisions). Such decisions become precedent and assist other judges in making legal rulings. What are some practical benefits of this process?

Administrative Agencies

Administrative agencies are federal or state institutions and other government organizations created by Congress or state legislatures with delegated
power to create rules and regulations within their given area of authority.

Legislative bodies can create administrative agencies and also terminate
them. Some administrative agencies hold quasi-legislative, quasi-executive,
and quasi-judicial powers. This means that an agency is allowed to pass rules
and regulations within its area of authority, conduct investigations in cases of
suspected rules violations, and hold hearings if it feels rules and regulations
have been violated.

Administrative agencies issue more rulings affecting business and settle
more business disputes than courts do. Such agencies include the Securities
and Exchange Commission (SEC), the Federal Communication's Commission,
and the Equal Employment Opportunity Commission (EEOC). Figure A.1 on
p. A-4 lists and describes the powers and functions of several administrative
agencies at the federal, state, and local levels of government.

common law
The body of law that comes
from decisions handed down
by courts; also referred to
as unwritten law.

precedent
Decisions judges have made
in earlier cases that guide
the handling of new cases.

administrative agencies
Federal or state institutions
and other government
organizations created by
Congress or state
legislatures with delegated
power to create rules and
regulations within their
mandated area of authority.

progress assessment

- What is business law?
- What's the difference between statutory and common law?
- What is an administrative agency?

figure A.I

EXAMPLES OF FEDERAL,
STATE, AND LOCAL
ADMINISTRATIVE AGENCIES

EXAMPLES	POWERS AND FUNCTIONS
Federal Agencies	
Federal Trade Commission	Enforces laws and guidelines regarding unfair business practices and acts to stop false and deceptive advertising and labeling.
Food and Drug Administration	Enforces laws and regulations to prevent distribution of adulterated or misbranded foods, drugs, medical devices, cosmetics, and veterinary products, as well as any hazardous consumer products.
State Agencies	
Public utility commissions	Set rates that can be charged by various public utilities to prevent unfair pricing by regulated monopolies (e.g., natural gas, electric power companies).
State licensing boards	License various trades and professions within a state (e.g., state cosmetology board, state real estate commission).
Local Agencies	
Maricopa County Planning Commission	Oversees land-use proposals, long-term development objectives, and other long-range issues in Maricopa County, Arizona.
City of Chesterfield Zoning Board	Sets policy regarding zoning of commercial and residential property in the city of Chesterfield, Missouri.

LEARNING goal 2

Define *tort law* and explain the role of product liability in tort law.

TORT LAW

tort
A wrongful act that causes injury to another person's body, property, or reputation.

A **tort** is a wrongful act that causes injury to another person's body, property, or reputation. Although torts often are noncriminal acts, courts can award victims compensation if the conduct that caused the harm is considered intentional. Legally, an *intentional* tort is a willful act that results in injury. The question of intent was a major factor in the lawsuits against the U.S. tobacco industry. Courts had to decide whether tobacco makers intentionally withheld information from the public about the harmful effects of their products.

negligence
In tort law, behavior that causes unintentional harm or injury.

Negligence, in tort law, describes behavior that causes *unintentional* harm or injury. A court's finding of negligence can lead to huge judgments against businesses. In a classic case, McDonald's lost a lawsuit to an elderly woman severely burned by hot coffee bought at a drive-through window. The jury felt that McDonald's failed to provide an adequate warning on the cup. Product liability is a controversial area of tort law, so let's take a closer look at this issue.

Product Liability

product liability
Part of tort law that holds businesses liable for harm that results from the production, design, or use of products they market.

Few issues in business law raise as much debate as product liability.[2] Critics believe product liability laws have gone too far; others feel these laws should be expanded. **Product liability** holds businesses liable for harm that results from the production, design, or inadequate warnings of products they market. The average product liability case costs businesses $5 million, including defense costs, out-of-court settlements, and jury awards.

At one time the legal standard for measuring product liability was whether a producer knowingly placed a hazardous product on the market. Today, many states have extended product liability to the level of **strict product liability**— legally meaning liability without regard to fault. That is, a company that places a defective product on the market can be held liable for damages—a monetary settlement awarded to a person injured by another's actions—even if the company did not know of the defect at the time of sale.[3]

Strict product liability is a major concern for businesses. More than 70 companies have been forced into bankruptcy due to asbestos litigation and the issue is not yet closed. About 3,000 new cases of mesothelioma (a cancer linked to asbestos exposure) are diagnosed every year keeping the legal docket busy.[4] Lead-based paint producers continue to face expensive lawsuits even though lead-based paint has been banned in the United States since 1978.[5] Mattel was forced to recall 500,000 toy cars produced in China due to lead paint concerns. Toyota Motors recalled 3 million cars in 2010 and 2011 due to sudden acceleration incidents.[6] The company now faces years of litigation from consumers affected by the problem.[7]

Kenneth Frazier, the CEO of Merck and the subject of the Profile of this chapter, knows all too well that manufacturers of chemicals and drugs are vulnerable to lawsuits under strict product liability.[8] Even if a product has gone through the lengthy testing and evaluation process and has been approved by the Food and Drug Administration (FDA), the product's manufacturer is still subject to strict product liability if a side effect or other health problem emerges.[9]

Some product liability cases have raised intriguing questions about responsibility.[10] Handgun manufacturers were unsuccessfully sued by cities

strict product liability
Legal responsibility for harm or injury caused by a product regardless of fault.

COMPANY	YEAR	SETTLEMENT
Ford Motor Company	1978	$125 million in punitive damages awarded in the case of a 13-year-old boy severely burned in a rear-end collision involving a Ford Pinto
A. H. Robins	1987	Dalkon Shield intrauterine birth-control devices recalled after eight separate punitive-damage awards
Playtex Company	1988	Considered liable and suffered a $10 million damage award in the case of a toxic shock syndrome fatality in Kansas; removed certain types of tampons from the market
Jack in the Box	1993	Assessed large damages after a two-year-old child who ate at Jack in the Box died of E. coli poisoning and others became ill
Sara Lee Corporation	1998	Costly company recall necessitated when tainted hot dogs caused food-poisoning death of 15 people
General Motors	1999	Suffered $4.8 billion punitive award in faulty fuel-tank case
Major Tobacco Firms	2004	$130 billion sought by the federal government for smoking cessation programs (settled for $10 billion)

Sources: U.S. Department of Justice; and American Trial Lawyers Association.

figure A.2

MAJOR PRODUCT LIABILITY CASES

including Chicago and Miami for the costs of police work and medical care necessitated by gun violence. McDonald's faced a product liability suit (later dismissed) claiming that its food caused obesity, diabetes, and other health problems in children.[11] Some communities, however, have reacted by banning transfats in food, regulating menu information, and eliminating toys in children's products like McDonald's Happy Meals. Many schools are replacing soft drinks in vending machines with fruit juice and water.

Tort and product liability reform has been a key objective of business for many years. Congress took action with passage of the Class Action Fairness Act in 2005, which expanded federal jurisdiction over many large class-action lawsuits.[12] Businesses and insurance companies argue that more needs to be done to assist companies with product liability. Consumer protection groups disagree and feel not enough is being done to protect consumers. Figure A.2 on p. A-5 highlights several major product liability awards that have cost companies dearly.

LEARNING goal 3

Identify the purposes and conditions of patents, copyrights, and trademarks.

LEGALLY PROTECTING IDEAS: PATENTS, COPYRIGHTS, AND TRADEMARKS

Have you ever invented a product you think may have commercial value? Many people have, and to protect their ideas they took the next step and applied for a patent. A **patent** is a document that gives inventors exclusive rights to their inventions for 20 years from the date they file the patent applications.[13]

patent
A document that gives inventors exclusive rights to their inventions for 20 years.

The 6,200 examiners in the U.S. Patent and Trademark Office (USPTO) review over 350,000 patent requests each year and grant more than 150,000. The agency has a current backlog of 1,200,000 patents that are pending and 700,000 awaiting initial review; the approval process generally takes almost three years.[14] To reduce the backlog, the U.S. Supreme Court imposed stricter standards of "obviousness" on the process, which means that a patent cannot be granted for an invention that is an obvious extension of an existing product. The court, however, has not offered legal clarity on exactly what can be patented.[15]

Patent applicants must make sure a product is truly unique and should seek the advice of an attorney; in fact, fewer than 2 percent of product inventors file on their own. How good are your chances of receiving a patent if you file for one? About 50 percent of patent applications are approved, with fees that vary according to the complexity of the patent. A patent dealing with complex technology can cost anywhere from $10,000 to $30,000.[16] A patent dealing with simpler concepts will cost the inventor about $7,000 to $10,000.

Patent owners have the right to sell or license the use of their patent to others. Foreign companies are also eligible to file for U.S. patents. They account for nearly half the U.S. patents issued. Penalties for violating a patent (patent infringement) can be costly.[17] Dr. Gary Michelson received a settlement of $1.35 billion from Medtronic Inc. to end litigation and license patents covering a range of back-surgery products. The USPTO does not take action on behalf of patent holders if patent infringement occurs. The defense of patent rights is solely the job of the patent holder and can be quite expensive.[18]

The American Inventor's Protection Act requires that patent applications be made public after 18 months regardless of whether a patent has been awarded. This law was passed in part to address critics who argued that some inventors intentionally delayed or dragged out a patent application because they expected others to eventually develop similar products or technology. Then when someone (usually a large company) filed for a similar patent, the inventor surfaced to claim the patent—referred to as a *submarine patent*—and demanded large royalties (fees) for its use. The late engineer Jerome Lemelson, for example, reportedly collected more than $1.3 billion in patent royalties for a series of long-delayed patents—including forerunners of the fax machine, the Walkman, and the bar-code scanner—from auto, computer, retailer, and electronics companies.

Technology companies like Verizon, Google, and Cisco have taken action to defend themselves against patent infringement suits by joining Allied Security Trust, a not-for-profit firm that acquires intellectual property of interest to its members. The idea is to buy up patents that could impact their companies before they fall into the hands of others (mainly law firms and venture capitalists) looking to pursue settlements or legal damages against the tech firms.

Just as a patent protects an inventor's right to a product or process, a **copyright** protects a creator's rights to materials such as books, articles, photos, paintings, and cartoons. Copyrights are filed with the Library of Congress and require a minimum of paperwork. They last for the lifetime of the author or artist plus 70 years and can be passed on to the creator's heirs. The Copyright Act of 1978, however, gives a special term of 75 years from publication to works published before January 1, 1978, whose copyrights had not expired by that date. The holder of a copyright can either prevent anyone from using the copyrighted material or charge a fee for using it. Author J. K. Rowling won a copyright violation suit against a fan who wanted to publish an unauthorized Harry Potter encyclopedia. If a work is created by an employee in the normal course of a job, the copyright belongs to the employer and lasts 95 years from publication or 120 years from creation, whichever comes first.

A *trademark* is a legally protected name, symbol, or design (or combination of these) that identifies the goods or services of one seller and distinguishes them from those of competitors. Trademarks generally belong to the owner forever, as long as they are properly registered and renewed every 10 years. Some well-known trademarks include the Aflac duck, Disney's Mickey Mouse, the Nike swoosh, and the golden arches of McDonald's. Like a patent, a trademark is protected against infringement. Businesses fight hard to protect trademarks, especially in global markets where trademark pirating can be extensive.[19] (Chapter 14 discusses trademarks in more detail.)

Media companies have sued YouTube for carrying videos of their popular television shows on their website. YouTube says that it makes every effort to remove any copyrighted video that users download to the site. Do you think YouTube should be held liable for copyrighted video downloaded by others? Why or why not?

copyright
A document that protects a creator's rights to materials such as books, articles, photos, paintings, and cartoons.

progress assessment

- What is tort law?
- What is product liability? What is strict product liability?
- How many years is a patent protected from infringement?
- What is a copyright?

Uniform Commercial Code (UCC)
A comprehensive commercial law adopted by every state in the United States that covers sales laws and other commercial laws.

LEARNING goal 4

Describe warranties and negotiable instruments as covered in the Uniform Commercial Code.

Would you buy a new car if the dealer offered no warranty? How about an iPhone or a major kitchen appliance with no guarantee of performance? Warranties are an important part of a product and are generally of major concern to purchasers. It's important to check whether a product's warranty is full or limited. Should colleges offer students warranties with their degree programs?

SALES LAW: THE UNIFORM COMMERCIAL CODE

At one time, laws governing businesses varied from state to state, making interstate trade extremely complicated. Today, all states have adopted the same commercial law. The **Uniform Commercial Code (UCC)** is a comprehensive commercial law that covers sales laws and other commercial laws. Since all 50 states have adopted the law (although it does not apply in certain sections of Louisiana), the UCC simplifies commercial transactions across state lines.

The UCC has 11 articles, which contain laws covering sales; commercial paper such as promissory notes and checks; bank deposits and collections; letters of credit; bulk transfers; warehouse receipts, bills of lading, and other documents of title; investment securities; and secured transactions. We do not have space in this text to discuss all 11 articles, but we will discuss two: Article 2, which regulates warranties, and Article 3, which covers negotiable instruments.

Warranties

A *warranty* guarantees that the product sold will be acceptable for the purpose for which the buyer intends to use it. There are two types of warranties. **Express warranties** are specific representations by sellers that buyers rely on regarding the goods they purchase. The warranty you receive in the box with an iPad or a toaster is an express warranty.

Implied warranties are legally imposed on the seller, who implies that a product will conform to the customary standards of the trade or industry in which it competes. An implied warranty entitles you to expect that a toaster will toast your bread to your desired degree (light, medium, dark) or that food you buy for consumption off an establishment's premises is fit to eat.[20]

Warranties can be either full or limited. A full warranty requires a seller to replace or repair a product at no charge if the product is defective; whereas a limited warranty typically limits the defects or mechanical problems the seller covers. Companies often offer extended warranties that provide more coverage, but for a price, of course.[21] Many of the rights of buyers, including the right to accept or reject goods, are spelled out in Article 2 of the UCC.

Negotiable Instruments

Negotiable instruments are forms of commercial paper (such as checks) that are transferable among businesses and individuals; they represent a promise to pay a specified amount. Article 3 of the Uniform Commercial Code requires negotiable instruments to follow four conditions. They must (1) be written and signed by the maker or drawer, (2) be made payable on demand or at a certain time, (3) be made payable to the bearer (the person holding the instrument) or to specific order, and (4) contain an unconditional promise to pay a specified amount of money. Checks or other forms of negotiable instruments are transferred (negotiated for payment) when the payee signs the back. The payee's signature is called an *endorsement.*

LEARNING goal 5

> List and describe the conditions necessary to make a legally enforceable contract, and describe the possible consequences if such a contract is violated.

CONTRACT LAW

If I offer to sell you my bike for $50 and later change my mind, can you force me to sell the bike by saying we had a contract? If I lose $120 to you in a poker game, can you sue in court to get your money? If I agree to sing at your wedding for free and back out at the last minute, can you claim I violated a contract? These are the kinds of questions contract law answers.

A **contract** is a legally enforceable agreement between two or more parties. **Contract law** specifies what constitutes a legally enforceable agreement. Basically, a contract is legally binding if the following conditions are met:

1. *An offer is made.* An offer to do something or sell something can be oral or written. If I agree to sell you my bike for $50, I have made an offer. That offer is not legally binding, however, until the following other conditions are met.

2. *There is a voluntary acceptance of the offer.* The principle of *mutual acceptance* means that both parties to a contract must agree on the terms. If I use duress—coercion through force or threat of force—in getting you to agree to buy my bike, the contract will not be legal. You couldn't use duress to get me to sell my bike, either. Even if we both agree, though, the contract is still not legally binding without the next four conditions.

3. *Both parties give consideration.* **Consideration** means something of value. If I agree to sell you my bike for $50, the bike and the $50 are consideration, and we have a legally binding contract. If I agree to sing at your wedding and you do not give me anything in return (consideration), we have no contract.

4. *Both parties are competent.* A person under the influence of alcohol or drugs, or a person of unsound mind (one who has been legally declared incompetent), cannot be held to a contract. In many cases, a minor may not be held to a contract either. If a 15-year-old agrees to pay $10,000 for a car, the seller will not be able to enforce the contract due to the buyer's lack of competence.

---

express warranties
Specific representations by the seller that buyers rely on regarding the goods they purchase.

implied warranties
Guarantees concerning products legally imposed on the seller.

negotiable instruments
Forms of commercial paper (such as checks) that are transferable among businesses and individuals and represent a promise to pay a specified amount.

contract
A legally enforceable agreement between two or more parties.

contract law
Set of laws that specify what constitutes a legally enforceable agreement.

consideration
Something of value; consideration is one of the requirements of a legal contract.

5. *The contract covers a legal act.* A contract covering the sale of illegal drugs or stolen merchandise is unenforceable since such sales are violations of criminal law. (If gambling is prohibited by state law in your state, you cannot sue to collect the poker debt.)

6. *The contract is in proper form.* An agreement for the sale of goods worth $500 or more must be in writing. Contracts that cannot be fulfilled within one year also must be put in writing. Contracts regarding real property (land and everything attached to it) must be in writing.

Breach of Contract

breach of contract
When one party fails to follow the terms of a contract.

Both parties in a contract may voluntarily choose to end the agreement. **Breach of contract** occurs when one party fails to follow the terms of a contract. If that happens the following may occur:

1. *Specific performance.* The party who violated the contract may be required to live up to the agreement if money damages would not be adequate. If I legally offered to sell you a rare painting, I would have to sell you that painting.

damages
The monetary settlement awarded to a person who is injured by a breach of contract.

2. *Payment of damages.* If I fail to live up to a contract, you can sue me for **damages**, usually the amount you would lose from my nonperformance. If we had a legally binding contract for me to sing at your wedding, for example, and I failed to come, you could sue me for the cost of hiring a new singer.

3. *Discharge of obligation.* If I fail to live up to my end of a contract, you can agree to drop the matter. Generally you would not have to live up to your end of the agreement either.

Lawyers would not be paid so handsomely if contract law were as simple as implied in these rules. That's why it's always best to put a contract in writing even though oral contracts can be enforceable under contract law. The contract should clearly specify the offer and consideration, and the parties to the contract should sign and date it. A contract does not have to be complicated as long as (1) it is in writing, (2) it specifies mutual consideration, and (3) it contains a clear offer and agreement.

progress assessment

- What is the purpose of the Universal Commercial Code (UCC)?
- Compare express and implied warranties.
- What are the four elements of a negotiable instrument specified in the UCC?
- What are the six conditions for a legally binding contract? What could happen if a contract is breached?

LEARNING goal 6

Summarize several laws that regulate competition and protect consumers in the United States.

CASE	OUTCOME
United States v. *Standard Oil* 1911	Standard Oil broken up into 34 companies; Amoco, Chevron, and ExxonMobil are results of the breakup
United States v. *American Tobacco* 1911	American Tobacco split into 16 companies; British Tobacco and R. J. Reynolds are results of the breakup
United States v. *E. I. du Pont de Nemours* 1961	DuPont ordered to divest its 23 percent ownership stake in General Motors
United States v. *AT&T* 1982	Settled after Ma Bell agreed to spin off its local telephone operations into seven regional operating companies
United States v. *Microsoft* 2000	Microsoft ordered to halt prior anticompetitive practices

Source: U.S. Department of Justice.

figure A.3

HISTORY OF HIGH-PROFILE ANTITRUST CASES

PROMOTING FAIR AND COMPETITIVE BUSINESS PRACTICES

Competition is a cornerstone of the free-market system (see Chapter 2). A key responsibility of legislators is to pass laws that ensure a competitive atmosphere among businesses and promote fair business practices. The U.S. Justice Department's antitrust division and other government agencies serve as watchdogs to guarantee competition in markets flows freely, and new competitors have open access to the market. The government's power here is broad. The Justice Department's antitrust division has investigated the competitive practices of market giants such as Microsoft, Apple, Visa, and Google. Figure A.3 highlights several high-profile antitrust cases.

Antitrust oversight was not always the rule, however. Big businesses were once able to force smaller competitors out of business with little government resistance. The following brief history details how government responded to past problems. We'll also look at new challenges government regulators face today.

The History of Antitrust Legislation

In the late 19th century, big oil companies, railroads, steel companies, and other industrial firms dominated the U.S. economy. Some feared that such large and powerful companies would be able to crush any competitors and then charge high prices. In that atmosphere, Congress passed the Sherman Antitrust Act in 1890 to prevent large organizations from stifling the competition of smaller or newer firms. The Sherman Act forbids (1) contracts, combinations, or conspiracies in restraint of trade, and (2) the creation of actual monopolies or attempts to monopolize any part of trade or commerce.

Because some of the language in the Sherman Act was vague, there was doubt about just what practices it prohibited. To clarify its intentions Congress enacted the following laws.

- *The Clayton Act of 1914.* The Clayton Act prohibits exclusive dealing, tying contracts, and interlocking directorates. It also prohibits buying large amounts of stock in competing corporations. *Exclusive dealing* is selling goods with the condition that the buyer will not buy from a competitor (when the effect lessens competition). A *tying contract* requires a buyer to purchase unwanted items in order to purchase desired ones. Let's say I wanted to purchase 20 cases of Pepsi-Cola per week to sell in my restaurant. Pepsi, however, says it will sell me the 20 cases only if I also agree to buy 10 cases each of its Mountain Dew and Diet Pepsi products. My purchase of Pepsi-Cola would be *tied* to the purchase of the other two products. An *interlocking directorate* occurs when a company's board of directors includes members of the boards of competing corporations.

- *The Federal Trade Commission Act of 1914.* The Federal Trade Commission Act prohibits unfair methods of competition in commerce. This legislation set up the five-member Federal Trade Commission (FTC) to enforce compliance with the act. The FTC deals with a wide range of competitive issues—everything from preventing companies from making misleading "Made in the USA" claims to insisting funeral providers give consumers accurate, itemized price information about funeral goods and services.[22] The activity level of the FTC typically depends on its commission members at the time. It has the added responsibility for overseeing mergers and acquisitions (Chapter 5) in the health care, energy, computer hardware, automotive, and biotechnology industries. The Wheeler-Lea Amendment of 1938 gave the FTC additional jurisdiction over false or misleading advertising, along with the power to increase fines if its requirements are not met within 60 days.

- *The Robinson-Patman Act of 1936.* The Robinson-Patman Act prohibits price discrimination and applies to both sellers and buyers who knowingly induce or receive price discrimination. Certain types of price-cutting are criminal offenses punishable by fine and imprisonment. That includes price differences that "substantially" weaken competition unless they can be justified by lower selling costs associated with larger purchases. The law also prohibits advertising and promotional allowances unless they are offered to all retailers, large and small. Remember that this legislation applies to business-to-business transactions and not to business-to-consumer transactions.

The change in U.S. business from manufacturing to knowledge-based technology has created new regulatory challenges for federal agencies. In the early 2000s, Microsoft's competitive practices were the focus of an intense antitrust investigation by the Justice Department. The government charged that Microsoft hindered competition by refusing to sell its Windows operating system to computer manufacturers that refused to sell Windows-based computers exclusively.[23] The case ended with a settlement between the Justice Department and Microsoft that expired in 2011. Many antitrust advocates believe the case broadened the definition of anticompetitive behavior and proved the government's resolve in enforcing antitrust laws.[24] The NASDAQ OMX and Intercontinental Exchange Inc., for example, withdrew their bid for the NYSE Euronext when the Justice Department threatened an antitrust lawsuit in 2011.[25] Google and Yahoo dropped a proposed agreement whereby Google would have provided some search advertising for Yahoo, when the Justice Department promised legal action. It's safe to conclude antitrust issues will persist in the future.

LAWS TO PROTECT CONSUMERS

Consumerism is a social movement that seeks to increase and strengthen the rights and powers of buyers in relationship to sellers. It is the people's way of getting a fair share and equitable treatment in marketing exchanges. The Public Company Accounting Reform and Investor Protection Act (better known as the Sarbanes/Oxley Act) was passed to allay concerns about falsified financial statements from companies like Enron and WorldCom in the early 2000s. The financial crisis beginning in 2008 again fueled consumer anger, this time against the Treasury Department, Federal Reserve, and Securities and Exchange Commission (SEC) for their lack of oversight of the financial markets. The collapse of the real estate market, crisis in the banking industry, and failure of quasi-governmental mortgage agencies such as Fannie Mae and Freddie Mac led to passage of the Dodd-Frank Wall Street Reform and Consumer Protection Act.[26] This legislation created the Consumer Financial Protection Bureau that provides government oversight involving consumers in areas such as online banking, home mortgage loans, and high-interest payday loans.[27] Figure A.4 lists other major consumer protection laws.

consumerism
A social movement that seeks to increase and strengthen the rights and powers of buyers in relation to sellers.

figure A.4

CONSUMER PROTECTION LAWS

Fair Packaging and Labeling Act (1966)	Makes unfair or deceptive packaging or labeling of certain consumer commodities illegal.
Child Protection Act (1966)	Removes from sale potentially harmful toys and allows the FDA to pull dangerous products from the market.
Truth-in-Lending Act (1968)	Requires full disclosure of all finance charges on consumer credit agreements and in advertisements of credit plans.
Child Protection and Toy Safety Act (1969)	Protects children from toys and other products that contain thermal, electrical, or mechanical hazards.
Fair Credit Reporting Act (1970)	Requires that consumer credit reports contain only accurate, relevant, and recent information and are confidential unless a proper party requests them for an appropriate reason.
Consumer Product Safety Act (1972)	Created an independent agency to protect consumers from unreasonable risk of injury arising from consumer products and to set safety standards.
Magnuson-Moss Warranty–Federal Trade Commission Improvement Act (1975)	Provides for minimum disclosure standards for written consumer products warranties and allows the FTC to prescribe interpretive rules and policy statements regarding unfair or deceptive practices.
Alcohol Labeling Legislation (1988)	Provides for warning labels on liquor saying that women shouldn't drink when pregnant and that alcohol impairs a person's abilities.
Nutrition Labeling and Education Act (1990)	Requires truthful and uniform nutritional labeling on every food the FDA regulates.
Consumer Credit Reporting Reform Act (1997)	Increases responsibility of credit issuers for accurate credit data and requires creditors to verify that disputed data are accurate. Consumer notification is necessary before reinstating the data.
Children's Online Privacy Protection Act (2000)	Gives parents control over what information is collected online from their children under age 13; requires website operators to maintain the confidentiality, security, and integrity of the personal information collected from children.
Country of Origin Labeling Law (2009)	Requires that the product label on most food products sold in U.S. supermarkets gives the product's country of origin.
Credit Card Act (2009)	Designed to Protect Consumers from Unfair Credit Card Practices.

LEARNING goal 7

Explain the role of tax laws in generating income for the government and as a method of discouraging or encouraging certain behaviors among taxpayers.

TAX LAWS

taxes
How the government (federal, state, and local) raises money.

Mention taxes and most people frown. **Taxes** are the way federal, state, and local governments raise money. They affect almost every individual and business in the United States.

Governments primarily use taxes as a source of funding for their operations and programs. Taxes can also help discourage or encourage certain behaviors among taxpayers. If the government wishes to reduce consumer use of certain classes of products like cigarettes or liquor, it can pass *sin taxes* on them to raise their cost. Since the financial crisis began in 2008, increasing sin taxes (i.e., taxes on things like liquor and cigarettes) has also become a popular way for cash-starved states to raise revenue.[28] In other situations, the government may encourage businesses to hire new employees or purchase new equipment by offering a *tax credit,* an amount firms can deduct from their tax bill.

Taxes are levied from a variety of sources. Income taxes (personal and business), sales taxes, and property taxes are the major bases of tax revenue. The federal government receives its largest share of taxes from income.[29] States and local communities make extensive use of sales taxes. School districts generally depend on property taxes.

The tax policies of states and cities are important considerations when businesses seek to locate operations. They also affect personal decisions such as retirement. As government revenues at all levels dwindle, new tax issues are sure to be debated. States claim they are losing billions in sales taxes by not collecting from Internet sales transactions.[30] States like Illinois, Arkansas, Connecticut and New York have already taken action.[31] New York, for example, passed a law that requires out-of-state online companies to collect sales

figure A.5

TYPES OF TAXES

TYPE	PURPOSE
Income taxes	Taxes paid on the income received by businesses and individuals. Income taxes are the largest source of tax income received by the federal government.
Property taxes	Taxes paid on real and personal property. *Real property* is real estate owned by individuals and businesses. *Personal property* is a broader category that includes any movable property such as tangible items (wedding rings, equipment, etc.) or intangible items (stocks, checks, mortgages, etc.). Taxes are based on their assessed value.
Sales taxes	Taxes paid on merchandise sold at the retail level.
Excise taxes	Taxes paid on selected items such as tobacco, alcoholic beverages, airline travel, gasoline, and firearms. These are often referred to as *sin taxes.* Income generated from the tax goes toward a specifically designated purpose. For example, gasoline taxes often help the federal government and state governments pay for highway construction or improvements.

taxes from New York shoppers. Other states are petitioning Congress to pass a law permitting them to collect sales taxes from e-commerce transactions.[32] The European Union levies certain Internet taxes, so expect the U.S. debate to intensify. Figure A.5 highlights the primary types of taxes levied on individuals and businesses.

LEARNING goal 8

Distinguish among the various types of bankruptcy as outlined by the Bankruptcy Code.

BANKRUPTCY LAWS

Bankruptcy is the legal process by which a person, business, or government entity, unable to meet financial obligations, is relieved of those debts by a court. Courts divide any of the debtor's assets among creditors, allowing them to recover at least part of their money and freeing the debtor to begin anew. The U.S. Constitution gives Congress the power to establish bankruptcy laws, and legislation has existed since the 1890s. Major amendments to the bankruptcy code include the Bankruptcy Amendments and Federal Judgeships Act of 1984, the Bankruptcy Reform Acts of 1994, and the Bankruptcy Abuse Prevention and Consumer Protection Act of 2005.

The 1984 law allows a person who is bankrupt to keep part of the equity (ownership) in a house and car, and some other personal property. The 1994 Act amended more than 45 sections of the bankruptcy code and created reforms to speed up and simplify the process. The Bankruptcy Reform Act of 2005 was passed to reduce the total number of bankruptcy filings and to eliminate the perceived ease of filing. The legislation increased the cost of filing and made it difficult for people (especially those with high incomes) to escape overwhelming debt from credit cards, medical bills, student loans, or other loans not secured through a home or other asset. It also requires debtors to receive credit counseling.

Bankruptcies started growing in the late 1980s and have increased tremendously since. Many attribute the increase to a lessening of the stigma of bankruptcy, an increase in understanding of bankruptcy law and its protections, and increased advertising by bankruptcy attorneys. Some suggest that the ease with which certain consumers could get credit contributed to the number of filings by allowing people to readily overspend. The 2005 reform helped reduce the annual number of bankruptcy filings to 600,000 from an average of 1.5 million between 2001 and 2004. However, the financial crisis beginning in 2008 pushed the number of bankruptcies again to over a million. As the economy continues to come back slowly, bankruptcies are expected to reach almost 1.5 million in 2011. Although high-profile bankruptcies of businesses—such as Blockbuster, Circuit City, Borders, and General Motors—tend to dominate the news, over 90 percent of bankruptcy filings each year are by individuals.

Bankruptcy can be either voluntary or involuntary. In **voluntary bankruptcy**, the debtor applies for bankruptcy; in **involuntary bankruptcy**, the creditors start legal action against the debtor. Most bankruptcies are voluntary, since creditors usually wait in hopes they will be paid all the money due them rather than settle for only part of it.

bankruptcy
The legal process by which a person, business, or government entity unable to meet financial obligations is relieved of those obligations by a court that divides any assets among creditors, allowing creditors to get at least part of their money and freeing the debtor to begin anew.

voluntary bankruptcy
Legal procedures initiated by a debtor.

involuntary bankruptcy
Bankruptcy procedures filed by a debtor's creditors.

Bankruptcy procedures begin when a petition is filed with the court under one of the following sections of the Bankruptcy Code:

Chapter 7—"straight bankruptcy" or liquidation (used by businesses and individuals).

Chapter 11—reorganization (used almost exclusively by businesses).

Chapter 13—repayment (used by individuals).

Chapter 7 is the most popular form of bankruptcy among individuals; it requires the sale of nonexempt assets.[33] Under federal exemption statutes, a debtor may be able to retain (exempt) up to $21,625 of equity in a home; up to $3,225 of equity in an automobile; up to $11,525 in household furnishings, apparel, and musical instruments; and up to $1,450 in jewelry.[34] States can choose different exemption statutes. When the sale of assets is over, creditors, including the government if taxes are owed, divide the remaining cash as stipulated by law. First, creditors with secured claims receive the collateral for their claims or repossess the claimed asset (such as an automobile or home); then unsecured claims (backed by no asset) are paid in this order:

1. Costs of the bankruptcy case.
2. Any business costs incurred after bankruptcy was filed.
3. Wages, salaries, or commissions owed (limited to $2,000 per creditor).
4. Contributions to employee benefit plans.
5. Refunds to consumers who paid for products that weren't delivered (limited to $900 per claimant).
6. Federal and state taxes.

Figure A.6 outlines the steps used in liquidating assets under Chapter 7.

In Chapter 11 bankruptcy, a company sued by creditors continues to operate under court protection while it tries to work out a plan for paying off its debts. Under certain conditions it may sell assets, borrow money, and change company

figure A.6

HOW ASSETS ARE DIVIDED IN BANKRUPTCY

This figure shows that the creditor (the person owed money) selects the trustee (the person or organization that handles the sale of assets). Note that the process may be started by the debtor or the creditors.

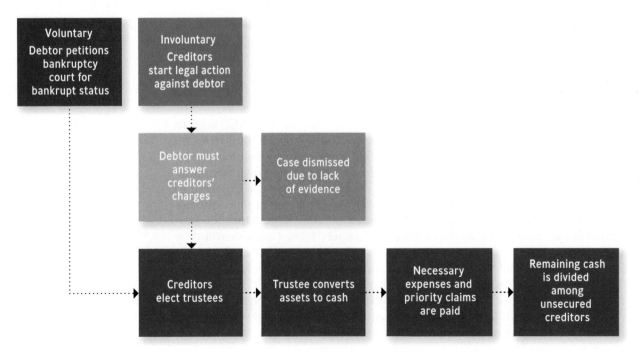

officers to strengthen its market position. A court-appointed trustee supervises the proceedings and protects the creditors' interests.

A company does not have to be insolvent to file for relief under Chapter 11. In theory, it is a way for sick companies to recover, designed to help both debtors and creditors find the best solution. In reality, however, less than one-third of Chapter 11 companies survive—usually those with lots of cash available. The Bankruptcy Reform Act of 1994 provides a fast-track procedure for small businesses filing under Chapter 11. Individuals can also file under Chapter 11, but it's uncommon.

Chapter 13 permits individuals, including small-business owners, to pay back creditors over three to five years. Chapter 13 proceedings are less complicated and less expensive than Chapter 7 proceedings. The debtor files a proposed plan with the court for paying off debts. If the plan is approved, the debtor pays a court-appointed trustee in monthly installments as agreed on in the repayment plan. The trustee then pays each creditor.

Under Chapter 11 bankruptcy law, the mighty can fall. Borders, the second largest U.S. book store chain, filed for bankruptcy after management changes, job cuts, and debt restructuring failed to make up for declining book sales. Do you know other companies forced into bankruptcy due to the recent recession?

LEARNING goal 9

Explain the role of deregulation as a tool to encourage competition.

DEREGULATION VERSUS REGULATION

Under article 1, section 8, clause 3 of the U.S. Constitution, the Commerce Clause gives Congress the right "to regulate commerce." The debate concerning the degree of regulation, however, has been a source of disagreement for many years.[35] At one time, the United States had laws and regulations covering almost every aspect of business. Some felt there were too many laws and regulations, costing the public too much money (see Figure A.7 on p. A-18). A movement toward deregulation took hold. **Deregulation** means that the government withdraws certain laws and regulations that seem to hinder competition. The most publicized examples of deregulation first occurred in the airline and telecommunications industries.

Consumers clearly benefited from the Airline Deregulation Act of 1978 that ended federal control of commercial airlines. Before passage of the act, the government restricted where airlines could land and fly. When the restrictions were lifted, airlines began competing for different routes and charging

deregulation
Government withdrawal of certain laws and regulations that seem to hinder competition.

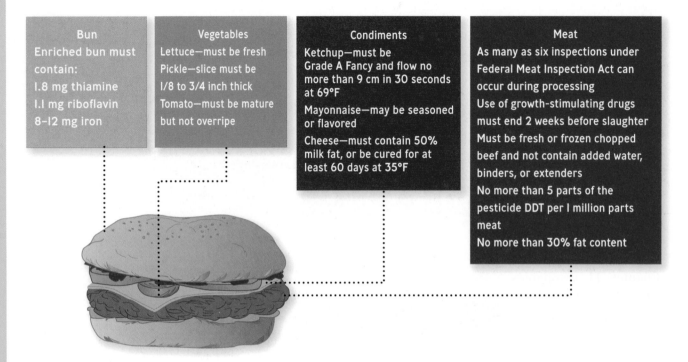

Bun
Enriched bun must contain:
1.8 mg thiamine
1.1 mg riboflavin
8–12 mg iron

Vegetables
Lettuce—must be fresh
Pickle—slice must be 1/8 to 3/4 inch thick
Tomato—must be mature but not overripe

Condiments
Ketchup—must be Grade A Fancy and flow no more than 9 cm in 30 seconds at 69°F
Mayonnaise—may be seasoned or flavored
Cheese—must contain 50% milk fat, or be cured for at least 60 days at 35°F

Meat
As many as six inspections under Federal Meat Inspection Act can occur during processing
Use of growth-stimulating drugs must end 2 weeks before slaughter
Must be fresh or frozen chopped beef and not contain added water, binders, or extenders
No more than 5 parts of the pesticide DDT per 1 million parts meat
No more than 30% fat content

figure A.7

HAMBURGER REGULATIONS
Does this amount of regulation seem just right, too little, or too much for you?

lower prices. The skies were also opened to new competitors, such as Southwest, to take advantage of new opportunities.[36] Today some believe the airline industry could use more government intervention since passenger services have decreased, delays and flight cancellations have increased, and charges, such as bag fees, have become common.

Passage of the Telecommunications Act in 1996 brought similar deregulation to telecommunications and gave consumers a flood of options in local telephone service markets. There was also a significant increase in retail video competition. In the past, most households received only four TV channels (the three major networks—NBC, CBS, and ABC—and public broadcasting). Today most households receive a dozen or more over-the-air stations and hundreds more on cable, satellite, and the Internet.

Deregulation efforts have also been attempted in the electric power industry. Twenty-two states have passed utility deregulation laws intended to increase competition and provide consumers with lower price options. California became the first state to deregulate electric power in the late 1990s and experienced significant problems especially with large-scale blackouts (loss of power). Blackouts also occurred on the east coast. Still some utility deregulation programs have been somewhat successful. Time will tell whether utility deregulation will survive and prosper.

Unfortunately, deregulation has not always worked as desired. The financial market crisis beginning in 2008 reopened the question of how much deregulation is too much. New regulations in the banking and investments industries changed the nature of financial and mortgage markets and created huge problems. For example, the Federal Reserve System's reluctance to toughen mortgage regulations and the government's insistence on providing more home loans to high-risk borrowers contributed to the collapse in the real estate market.[37] The financial crisis that followed led to passage of the most sweeping regulation of financial markets since the Great Depression.[38]

In 2010, the U.S. Congress passed the Patient Protection and Affordable Care Act (PPACA) that introduced a comprehensive system of mandated health insurance for 32 million Americans not covered under an insurance plan.[39] The bill also provides for increased government regulation of the insurance industry. While the bill is to be phased in over a four-year period, court challenges and proposed adjustments to the legislation promise to keep the PPACA in the news.[40]

Most agree some regulation of business seems necessary to ensure fair and honest dealings with the public. Corporate scandals in the early 2000s and the financial crisis led consumers and investors to call for increased government regulation in the financial sector. While the final resolution of the government's health care bill remains to be seen, most agree that businesses will need to deal with some form of health care regulation. With increasing global competition, U.S. business will need to work with government to create a competitive environment that is fair and open and accept responsibilities to all stakeholders.

progress assessment

- What is the primary purpose of antitrust law?
- Describe the different bankruptcy provisions under Chapters 7, 11, and 13.
- What is deregulation? Give examples of successful and unsuccessful deregulation.

summary

Learning Goal 1. Define *business law,* distinguish between statutory and common law, and explain the role of administrative agencies.

- **What is the difference between statutory law and common law?**

Statutory law includes state and federal constitutions, legislative enactments, treaties of the federal government, and ordinances—in short, written law. Common law is the body of unwritten law that comes from decisions handed down by judges.

- **What are administrative agencies?**

Administrative agencies are federal or state institutions and other government organizations created by Congress or state legislatures with power to create rules and regulations within their area of authority.

Learning Goal 2. Define *tort law* and explain the role of product liability in tort law.

- **What is an intentional tort?**

An intentional tort is a willful act that results in injury.

- **What is negligence?**

Negligence, in tort law, is behavior that causes *unintentional* harm or injury. Findings of negligence can lead to huge judgments against businesses.

Learning Goal 3. Identify the purposes and conditions of patents, copyrights, and trademarks.

- **What are patents and copyrights?**

A patent is a document that gives inventors exclusive rights to their inventions for 20 years from the date they file the patent applications. A copyright protects a creator's rights to materials such as books, articles, photos, paintings, and cartoons.

- **What is a trademark?**

A trademark is a legally protected name, symbol, or design (or combination of these) that identifies the goods or services of one seller and distinguishes them from those of competitors.

Learning Goal 4. Describe warranties and negotiable instruments as covered in the Uniform Commercial Code.

- **What does Article 2 of the UCC cover?**

Article 2 contains laws regarding warranties. Express warranties are guarantees made by the seller, whereas implied warranties are guarantees imposed on the seller by law.

- **What does Article 3 of the UCC cover?**

Article 3 covers negotiable instruments such as checks. A negotiable instrument must (1) be written and signed by the maker or drawer, (2) be made payable on demand or at a certain time, (3) be made payable to the bearer (the person holding the instrument) or to specific order, and (4) contain an unconditional promise to pay a specified amount of money.

Learning Goal 5. List and describe the conditions necessary to make a legally enforceable contract, and describe the possible consequences if such a contract is violated.

- **What makes a contract enforceable under the law?**

An enforceable contract must meet six conditions: (1) an offer must be made, (2) the offer must be voluntarily accepted, (3) both parties must give consideration, (4) both parties must be competent, (5) the contract must be legal, and (6) the contract must be in proper form.

- **What are the possible consequences if a contract is violated?**

If a contract is violated, one of the following may be required: (1) specific performance, (2) payment of damages, or (3) discharge of obligation.

Learning Goal 6. Summarize several laws that regulate competition and protect consumers in the United States.

- **What does the Sherman Act cover?**

The Sherman Act forbids contracts, combinations, or conspiracies in restraint of trade and actual monopolies or attempts to monopolize any part of trade or commerce.

- **What does the Clayton Act add?**

The Clayton Act prohibits exclusive dealing, tying contracts, interlocking directorates, and buying large amounts of stock in competing corporations.

- **Which act regulates false and deceptive advertising?**

The Federal Trade Commission Act prohibits unfair methods of competition in commerce, including deceptive advertising.

- **Which act prohibits price discrimination and demands proportional promotional allowances?**

The Robinson-Patman Act applies to both sellers and buyers who knowingly induce or receive an unlawful discrimination in price.

Learning Goal 7. Explain the role of tax laws in generating income for the government and as a method of discouraging or encouraging certain behaviors among taxpayers.

- **How does the government use taxes to encourage or discourage certain behavior among taxpayers?**

If the government wishes to change citizens' behavior, it can reduce their use of certain classes of products (cigarettes, liquor) by passing *sin taxes* to raise their cost. In other situations, the government may offer tax credits to encourage businesses to hire new employees or purchase new equipment.

Learning Goal 8. Distinguish among the various types of bankruptcy as outlined by the Bankruptcy Code.

- **What are the bankruptcy laws?**

Chapter 7 calls for straight bankruptcy, in which all assets are divided among creditors after exemptions. Chapter 11 allows a firm to reorganize and continue operation after paying only a limited portion of its debts. Chapter 13 allows individuals to pay their creditors over an extended period of time.

Learning Goal 9. Explain the role of deregulation as a tool to encourage competition.

- **What are a few of the most publicized examples of deregulation?**

Perhaps the most publicized examples of deregulation have been those in the airline and telecommunications industries.

key terms

administrative
  agencies A-3
bankruptcy A-15
breach of contract A-10
business law A-2
common law A-3
consideration A-9
consumerism A-13
contract A-9
contract law A-9
copyright A-7

damages A-10
deregulation A-17
express warranties A-9
implied warranties A-9
involuntary
  bankruptcy A-15
judiciary A-2
negligence A-4
negotiable
  instruments A-9
patent A-6

precedent A-3
product liability A-4
statutory law A-2
strict product
  liability A-5
taxes A-14
tort A-4
Uniform Commercial
  Code (UCC) A-8
voluntary
  bankruptcy A-15

critical thinking

1. Supporters of tort reform say it's unfair that plaintiffs (the parties bringing lawsuits) don't have to pay damages to the defendants (the parties subject to the lawsuits) if they lose the case. Should plaintiffs pay damages if they lose a case? Why or why not?

2. Go to the website of the U.S. Patent and Trademark Office (www.uspto. gov) and view the information about obtaining a patent. See whether you can estimate how long the process will take and what your cost will be.

3. Call your local real estate board or visit a realtor and obtain a copy of a real estate contract. Read it carefully to see how it meets the six requirements stated in the chapter for a contract to be legal and binding.

4. Twenty-two states have implemented utility deregulation. Has your state or a neighboring state implemented utility deregulation? How does it seem to be working?

developing workplace skills

1. Do you think the laws that promote fair and competitive practices are effective in the United States? Why or why not? Provide evidence for your view.

2. Increasing numbers of individuals file for bankruptcy each year. Do you think the U.S. Congress was correct in toughening the bankruptcy laws?

3. Pick a side: Should government action to deal with deceptive business practices increase, or should we count on business to regulate itself to prevent deceptive practices? Which solution is better for society and business in the long run?

4. Does your state have an income tax? What percentage of your income do you have to pay in state income tax? What about property taxes and sales taxes? How do these taxes in your area compare to those in three other states and communities of your choice?

5. In 2005, Congress passed bankruptcy reform legislation that makes it more difficult for individuals to file for bankruptcy under Chapter 7 and limits certain debts that cannot now be eliminated. Research the law and offer reasons why you support or oppose it. You might want to go to www. bankruptcyaction.com for help.

taking it to the net

You and several of your musician friends decide to start a band you want to call the Subprimes. You want to protect the band name and the new songs you've written so that other groups can't use them. Go to the U.S. Patent and Trademark Office's website (www.uspto.gov) to find out how to get the protection you seek.

1. Do you need to apply for patents, copyrights, or trademarks, or some combination of these to protect your band name and songs?

2. When can you use the trademark symbols™ and®?

3. How can you secure a copyright for your songs?

4. What are the advantages of registering copyrights?

Using Technology to Manage Information

LEARNING goals

After you have read and studied this chapter, you should be able to

1 Outline the changing role of business technology.

2 List the types of business information, identify the characteristics of useful information, and discuss how data are stored and mined.

3 Compare the scope of the Internet, intranets, extranets, and virtual private networks and explain how broadband technology enabled the evolution to Web 2.0 and 3.0.

4 Review the computer hardware most frequently used in business.

5 Classify the types of computer software most frequently used in business.

6 Evaluate the human resource, security, privacy, and stability issues affected by information technology.

profile

Technology has become so much a part of life that it can be difficult to remember that tech is still a young industry full of pioneers who are creating ever-changing ways to communicate and manage information through the use of hardware, software, and the Internet. Tech experts often move freely from company to company, hoping that one of their new ventures turns into the "next big thing."

Social media expert Chris Hughes helped create "the next big thing"—twice. Although he is still in his twenties, Hughes' name is attached to two of the biggest tech triumphs of the past decade—Facebook and the social networking arm of Barack Obama's presidential campaign. Now running his own charitable and nonprofit social network called Jumo, Hughes has become one of the tech world's most respected online community architects.

Born in the small town of Hickory, NC, to modest means, Hughes worked hard to earn a number of scholarships to attend an elite boarding school in Massachusetts. From there he went on to Harvard where he met Mark Zuckerberg, then just a freshman with a good idea for a website that could help students find out what other students are up to (i.e., who they're dating, etc.). Hughes joined the early Facebook team, but not as a code writer. Hughes' strength was his ability to detect the features that bring people closer together and that could develop Facebook as a brand. For instance, when Zuckerberg wanted to expand Facebook outside the Harvard campus, Hughes suggested that different schools should still have their own networks. The idea allowed Facebook to retain its users' feeling of intimacy and community even as the site grew larger. After graduating with a degree in French literature and history, Hughes headed off to Palo Alto, CA, to work for Facebook full time.

In 2006 Facebook introduced a system that allowed political candidates to set up modified profile pages, much like the ones that celebrities and musicians use today. One of the first users was a freshman senator from Illinois named Barack Obama. After meeting with the senator over coffee in Washington, DC, Hughes was hired just weeks before Obama's campaign was officially announced. Hughes worked closely with Obama's staff to set up the page that could unite people through social networks.

The day the campaign went live, so did Hughes' big project: My.BarackObama.com, or MyBO for short. The website allowed supporters to create groups, raise funds, and organize events in their area. Hughes faced many challenges in getting the social network off the ground. First of all, though the site's software was considered top of the line for politics, its quality couldn't compare to the ease of a site like Facebook. Though he lacked the resources and the manpower, once Obama started winning key primary elections it became apparent just how much MyBO had contributed to those successes. By the time the campaign ended, MyBO volunteers had created more than 2 million profiles, planned 200,000 offline events, and raised $30 million on 70,000 funding pages.

Although he's flush with Facebook money and already a tech icon for his contribution to the Obama campaign, Hughes is still working to find ways to use social networking to effect change. In 2010 he launched Jumo, a website that connects nonprofits and charities with prospective donors. Getting attention from the public can be very difficult for the nation's 1.5 million nonprofits. Aside from the challenge of finding a way to stand out from the crowd, many charities do not have the budget to pay for a consulting firm to manage a website and social network. Jumo provides an easy, free platform for all those tasks, allowing nonprofits to tell their own stories and connect with the more than 600 million Facebook users across the globe.

As developers and tech companies continue to change the face of the digital landscape, it's possible that even the most entrenched technologies could become obsolete in a few years. In this bonus chapter you'll learn all about how this ever-changing tech world affects business.

Getting to Know

X Chris Hughes

Co-founder of Facebook

Sources: Kerry A. Dolan, "Chris Hughes on What's Next for Nonprofit Social Site Jumo," *Forbes,* April 21, 2011; Ellen McGirt, "How Chris Hughes Helped Launch Facebook and the Barack Obama Campaign," *Fast Company,* April 1, 2009; Jenna Wortham, "A Facebook Founder Begins a Social Network Focused on Charities," *The New York Times,* November 30, 2010; and Greg Ferenstein, "In a Cutthroat World, Some Web Giants Thrive by Cooperating," *The Washington Post,* February 19, 2011.

This company used social media to build its business. Its customers design new products, name them, and enter them in the company's database. Customers may even make YouTube commercials that are featured on the company's video wall. If other customers buy the new product, the creator gets a small store credit. Name that company. (Find the answer in the chapter.)

LEARNING goal 1

Outline the changing role of business technology.

THE ROLE OF INFORMATION TECHNOLOGY

The importance of business knowledge is nothing new—what is newer is the recognition of the need to manage it like any other asset. To manage knowledge, a company needs to share information throughout the organization and to implement systems for creating new knowledge. This need is constantly leading to new technologies that support the exchange of information among staff, suppliers, and customers. Studies have shown that data-driven decision making (i.e., collecting data, analyzing it, and using it to make crucial decisions, like whether to create a new product or service) lifts productivity 5 to 6 percent higher than traditional decision making based on experience and intuition.[1]

Evolution from Data Processing to Business Intelligence

data processing (DP)
Name for business technology in the 1970s; included technology that supported an existing business and was primarily used to improve the flow of financial information.

information systems (IS)
Technology that helps companies do business; includes such tools as automated teller machines (ATMs) and voice mail.

In the 1970s, business technology was known as **data processing (DP)**. (Although many people use the words *data* and *information* interchangeably, they mean different things. *Data* are raw, unanalyzed, and unorganized facts and figures. *Information* is processed and organized data that managers can use for decision making.) The primary purpose of data processing was to improve the flow of financial information. Data processing employees were support staff who rarely came in contact with customers.

In the 1980s, business technology became known as **information systems (IS)** when it moved out of the back room and into the center of the business. Its role changed from supporting the business to doing business. Customers began to interact with a wide array of technological tools, from automated teller machines (ATMs) to voice mail. As business increased its use of information systems, it became more dependent on them.

Until the late 1980s, business technology was just an addition to the existing way of doing business. Keeping up-to-date was a matter of using new technology on old methods. But things started to change when businesses applied new technology to new methods. Business technology then became known as **information technology (IT)**, and its role became to change business.

Knowledge is information charged with enough intelligence to make it relevant and useful. Knowledge technology adds a layer of intelligence to filter appropriate information and deliver it when it is needed. In the 2000s, as this technology became more sophisticated, it became better known as **business intelligence (BI)** or *analytics*. BI refers to a variety of software applications that analyze an organization's raw data and take useful insights from it. BI activities include data mining (which we discuss later in this chapter), online analytical processes, querying, and reporting.[2]

BI changes the traditional flow of information. Instead of an individual going to the database, the database comes to the individual. Managers can put a new employee at a workstation using BI training software and let the system take over everything from laying out a checklist of the tasks required on a shift to providing answers and insights that once would have taken up a supervisor's time.

BI helps businesspeople focus on what's important: deciding how to react to problems and opportunities. Imagine you're a sales rep who just closed a big deal. While you celebrate your success, the finance department is upset because your customer never pays on time, which costs the company a lot of money. BI could provide you that insight so that you could negotiate different payment terms with the customer, thus connecting sales activity to financial requirements in a seamless process.

Technology changes react with one another to create more change. Maintaining the flexibility to successfully integrate these changes is crucial to business survival. Packard Bell and RCA once dominated their industries but failed to compete effectively and lost market share. They had size and money, but not flexibility. Knowledge sharing is at the heart of keeping pace with change. Of course, it can be difficult to predict which new technologies will be successful. For a fun look at the worst tech predictions of all time, see Figure B.1 on p. B-4.

Obviously, the role of the IT staff has changed as technology itself has improved and evolved. The chief information officer (CIO) has moved out of the back room and into the boardroom and now spends less time worrying about keeping systems running and more time finding ways to boost business by applying technology to purchasing decisions, operational strategy, and marketing and sales. Today the role of the CIO is to help the business use technology to communicate better with others while offering better service and lower costs.[3]

How Information Technology Changes Business

Time and place have always been at the center of business. Customers once had to go to the business during certain hours to satisfy their needs. For example, we went to the store to buy clothes. We went to the bank to arrange for a loan. Businesses decided when and where we did business with them.

information technology (IT)
Technology that helps companies change business by allowing them to use new methods.

business intelligence (BI)
Any of a variety of software applications that analyze an organization's raw data and take out useful insights from it.

Tablets like the popular iPad offer hundreds of downloadable applications and functions, including the ability to watch your favorite movies and other videos. What do you think will be the next big development in consumer technology?

figure B.1

THE 7 WORST TECH PREDICTIONS OF ALL TIME
You can't be right all the time. Here are a few quotes from technology leaders who got it wrong—*way* wrong.

"Inventions have long since reached their limit, and I see no hope for further developments."

—Roman engineer Julius Sextus Frontinus, 10 A.D.

"Do not bother to sell your gas shares. The electric light has no future."

—Professor John Henry Pepper, scientist, 1870s

"This 'telephone' has too many shortcomings to be seriously considered as a means of communication."

— Western Union internal memo, 1876

"Who the hell wants to hear actors talk?"

—H. M. Warner, Warner Brothers, 1927

"I think there is a world market for maybe five computers."

—Thomas Watson, president of IBM, 1943

"Television won't be able to hold on to any market it captures after the first six months. People will soon get tired of staring at a plywood box every night."

—Darryl Zanuck, Executive at 20th Century Fox, 1946

"There is no reason anyone would want a computer in their home."

—Ken Olsen, founder of Digital Equipment Corporation, 1977

"I predict the Internet will soon go spectacularly supernova and in 1996 catastrophically collapse."

—Robert Metcalfe, founder of 3Com, 1995

Sources: Trader Mark, "The 10 Worst Technology Predictions of All Time," *International Business Times*, December 2009 and Cody Willard, "Top 10 Dumbest Tech Predictions of All Time," *The Wall Street Journal*, January 4, 2011.

Today, IT allows businesses to deliver goods and services whenever and wherever the customer wants them. You can order books and clothes, arrange a home mortgage loan, and buy music or a car online, anytime you choose.

Consider how IT has changed the entertainment industry. Forty years ago, you had to go to a movie theater if you wanted to see a movie. Thirty-five years ago, you could wait for it to be on television. Twenty-five years ago, you could wait for it to be on cable television. Twenty years ago, you went to a video store and rented it. Now you can order video on demand by satellite or cable, or download it to watch on your TV, computer, cell phone, iPad, or other device whenever and wherever you wish.

As IT broke time and location barriers, it created new organizations and services that are independent of location. For example, **NASDAQ** is an electronic stock exchange without trading floors where buyers and sellers make trades by computer. Smart phones, laptops, and tablets allow you access to people and information as if you were in the office. That independence brings work to people instead of people to work.

The way people do business drastically changes when companies increase their technological capabilities. Electronic communications can provide substantial time savings. E-mail and texting have put an end to tedious games of telephone tag and is far faster than paper-based correspondence. Internet and intranet communications using shared documents and other methods allow contributors to work on a common document without time-consuming meetings. See Figure B.2 for other examples of how information technology is changing business.

Organization	Technology is breaking down corporate barriers, allowing functional departments or product groups (even factory workers) to share critical information instantly.
Operations	Technology shrinks cycle times, reduces defects, and cuts waste. Service companies use technology to streamline ordering and communication with suppliers and customers.
Staffing	Technology eliminates layers of management and cuts the number of employees. Companies use computers and telecommunication equipment to create "virtual offices" with employees in various locations.
New products	Information technology cuts development cycles by feeding customer and marketing comments to product development teams quickly so that they can revive products and target specific customers.
Customer relations	Customer service representatives can solve customers' problems instantly by using companywide databases to complete tasks from changing addresses to adjusting bills. Information gathered from customer service interactions can further strengthen customer relationships.
New markets	Since it is no longer necessary for customers to walk down the street to get to stores, online businesses can attract customers to whom they wouldn't otherwise have access.

figure B.2

HOW INFORMATION TECHNOLOGY IS CHANGING BUSINESS
This table shows a few ways that information technology is changing businesses, their employees, suppliers, and customers.

progress assessment

- How has the role of information technology changed since the days when it was known as data processing?
- How has information technology changed the way we do business?

LEARNING goal 2

List the types of business information, identify the characteristics of useful information, and discuss how data are stored and mined.

TYPES OF INFORMATION

Today, information flows into and through an organization from many different directions. The types of information available to businesses today include:

- *Business process information.* This includes all transaction data gathered at the point of sale as well as information gained through operations like enterprise resource planning, supply chain management, and customer relationship management systems.
- *Physical-world observations.* These result from the use of radio frequency identification (RFID) devices, miniature cameras, wireless access, global

Fingerprints can serve as a form of identification using a biometric device such as this one. Such technology is used mainly for security purposes today, but in the future it might serve to customize products and provide key services. What ways can you think of for businesses to make use of biometric technology?

positioning systems, and sensor technology—all of which have to do with where people or items are located and what they are doing. Computer chips cost pennies apiece and can be found in a wide range of products, including credit cards, printer ink cartridges, baseballs, tire valves, running shoes, vacuum cleaners, and even beer mugs. That's right—Mitsubishi has produced a "smart" beer mug that senses when it is time for a refill and sends a signal to the bartender.

- *Biological data.* Forms of identification include improved fingerprinting technology and biometric devices that scan retinas, recognize faces and voices, and analyze DNA. Although such information usually serves security purposes, it may customize products and services in the future.

- *Public data.* Free and accessible, public data include the electronic traces we leave when posting to the Internet, sending e-mail, and using instant messaging. More and more, public data are being stored, shared, or sold.

- *Data that indicate personal preferences or intentions.* Internet shoppers leave a trail of information that can reveal personal likes and dislikes.

The volume and complexity of all these data and information are staggering. Computing systems can search through text, numbers, audio, and video and identify, categorize, and refine relevant opinions on any topic imaginable.

Managing Information

Even before the use of computers, managers had to sift through mountains of information to find what they needed to help them make decisions. Today, businesspeople are faced with *infoglut,* an overabundance of data. Have you seen the classic episode of TV's *I Love Lucy* with Lucy and Ethel working in a factory on the candy line? Everything was going OK until the candy started coming too fast for them. Then mayhem broke loose. That's what's happening to many managers today, with information instead of candy. Too much information can confuse issues rather than clarify them.

How can managers keep from getting buried in the infoglut? Stepping back to gain perspective is the key. Identify the four or five key goals you wish to reach, and eliminate information not related to them. That can cut the information flow by half. As we were gathering information for this chapter, we collected hundreds of print journal articles and found thousands more online. Feeling the pressure of information overload, we identified the goals we wanted the chapter to accomplish and eliminated all the articles that didn't address those goals. As we further refined our goals, the huge file gradually dropped to a manageable size.

Obviously, not all the information that ends up on your desk will be useful. The usefulness of management information depends on four characteristics:

1. *Quality.* Quality means that the information is accurate and reliable. When the clerk at a fast-food restaurant enters your order into the cash register, it may be automatically fed to a computer that calculates the day's sales and profits as soon as the store closes. The sales and expense data must be accurate, or the rest of the calculations will be wrong. Quality can be a real problem when a large number of calculations are based on questionable sales forecasts rather than actual sales.

2. *Completeness.* There must be enough information to allow you to make a decision, but not so much as to confuse the issue. Today, as we have noted, the problem is often too much information rather than too little.

3. *Timeliness.* Information must reach managers quickly. E-mail and texting can let marketing, engineering, and production know about a problem with a product the same day the salesperson hears about it, so customer complaints can be handled instantly if possible, or certainly within a day. Product changes can be made on the spot using computer-integrated manufacturing, as discussed in Chapter 9.

4. *Relevance.* Different managers have different information needs. Since information systems often provide too much data, managers must learn which questions to ask to get the answers they seek.

Remember, though, that you can never read everything available. Set goals for yourself, and do the best you can.

Organizing E-Mail and Electronic Files

Today's information management tools make it easier than ever for individuals and small businesses to organize information. Here are some tips for sorting e-mail and electronic files so that you can find what you need easily and quickly:[4]

1. *Use your e-mail program's organizing tools.* Most e-mail programs allow you to create folders for specific topics, projects, or clients. As you work through your in-box, move the messages you want to keep to the appropriate folders. Archive your old e-mail monthly. Figure B.3 offers suggestions for ways to reduce the number of distractions caused by sending and receiving e-mail.

- Turn off all alerts that announce new mail.
- Limit the number of times you check e-mail to no more than once an hour.
- Delete garbage messages [i.e., spam, junk mail, etc.) first.
- Only reply immediately to urgent messages and to messages that take less than 2 minutes to write a response and save the rest for later.
- Set a specific time (i.e., at the end of the work day) to respond to remaining messages.
- Limit use of the reply-all button.
- Use an automatic out-of-office message such as "I will be offline until after 5 p.m." This will give you time to focus on work while letting others know not to expect a reply soon.
- Don't limit your communication to e-mail or texting. Communicating by phone or in person can sometimes save time and build relationships

Source: Joe Robinson, "E-mail Is Making You Stupid," *Entrepreneur,* March 2010; and Robert Strohmeyer, "Master Your E-mail (So It Doesn't Master You)," *PC World,* December 10, 2010.

figure B.3

TAMING E-MAIL INTERRUPTIONS
The typical office worker checks e-mail 50 times and uses instant messaging 77 times a day. Such interruptions undermine workers' attention spans, increase stress, and decrease job satisfaction and creativity. Here are a few hints to reduce the number of e-mail distractions:

2. *Use consistent file names.* Save related materials across multiple software programs under the same name, and file them together. Perhaps you've been assigned to work with a team of other students to create a sample business plan for this course. You could save all files (whether e-mail, spreadsheets, PowerPoint, or Word documents) with a file name that begins "Business Plan Project" and store them in one folder in "My Documents."

3. *Use online backup services.* Backup, backup, backup—we've all heard how important it is to back up our files, but we often forget to follow through. Don't risk an avoidable loss. Some online services like Mozy will do the job for you for only a few dollars a month. Small and midsized companies that need more storage space use vendors such as E-Vault and Iron Mountain.

4. *Use desktop search software.* Finding files can be easier with a desktop search software program like Google Desktop or Windows Live Search. Google Desktop has an enterprise version for midsize companies. Larger companies also have access to Google but may need to pay for additional tech support.

Storing and Mining Data

It doesn't matter how interesting your information is if people can't find it or aren't paying attention to it. How do businesses organize a data glut so that it becomes useful information? The answer for many companies is a *data warehouse* that stores data on a single subject over a specific period.

The whole purpose of having a data warehouse is to get data out. *Data mining* is a technique for looking for hidden patterns and previously unknown relationships among the data. The legendary example is a study by a retail chain that revealed a spike in beer sales coinciding with a spike in diaper sales on weekdays between 5:00 and 7:00 p.m. The conclusion that thirsty dads pick up diapers on the way home from work prompted store managers to consider moving the diapers next to the beer to boost sales. The retailer never did pair the Heineken with the Huggies, but the story led to a new science of tracking what's selling where and who's buying it.

Walmart has massive data warehouses that track sales on a minute-by-minute basis in order to reveal regional and local sales trends. The retail giant thus customizes each store's offerings on the basis of local demand, keeping its suppliers informed about how each of the 70,000 products in the stores is selling and what managers anticipate will sell next. Because data mining showed Walmart that U.S. consumers like to buy Pop-Tarts (particularly strawberry) just before a hurricane hits, the company makes sure they're available in the right place at the right time. The lesson here is that companies can gain a competitive advantage with high-quality data that supports management decisions.[5]

Today innovative companies are using data-mining techniques that treat the Internet itself as a huge database. Tools like Yahoo Pipes can help companies mine the Web and separate the data from the noise.[6]

progress assessment

- What types of information are available to businesses today?
- What are the four characteristics of information that make it useful?
- What is data mining and how do businesses use it?

LEARNING goal 3

Compare the scope of the Internet, intranets, extranets, and virtual private networks and explain how broadband technology enabled the evolution to Web 2.0 and 3.0.

THE HEART OF KNOWLEDGE MANAGEMENT: THE INTERNET

You already know the Internet is a network of computer networks that evolved from a one-to-one communications tool to a one-to-many broadcast communication tool. Today it is the heart of *knowledge management.*[7]

Internet users can point and click their way from site to site with complete freedom. But what if you don't want just anybody to have access to your website? You might create an intranet. An **intranet** is a companywide network, closed to public access that uses Internet-type technology. To prevent unauthorized outsiders (particularly the competition) from accessing their sites, companies can construct a firewall between themselves and the outside world. A firewall can consist of hardware, software, or both. Firewalls allow only authorized users to access the intranet. Some companies use intranets only to publish employee phone lists and policy manuals, while others create interactive applications that fully exploit the technology's possibilities. They allow employees to update their addresses or submit company forms such as supply requisitions, time sheets, or payroll forms online, eliminating paper handling and speeding decision making.

Many businesses choose to open their intranets to other, selected companies and even customers through the use of extranets. An **extranet** is a semiprivate network that lets more than one company access the same information or allows people on different servers to collaborate. Now almost all companies can use extranets for electronic data interchange (EDI) functions like sharing data and processing orders, specifications, invoices, and payments.[8]

Notice that we described an extranet as a semiprivate network. This means that outsiders cannot access the network easily, but since an extranet does use public lines, knowledgeable hackers can gain unauthorized access. Most companies want a network as private and secure as possible, so they use dedicated lines (lines reserved solely for the network).

Dedicated lines are expensive, however, and they limit extranet use only to computers directly linked to those lines. What if your company needs to link securely with another firm or an individual for just a short time? Installing dedicated lines in this case would be too expensive and time-consuming. Virtual private networks are a solution.

A **virtual private network (VPN)** is a private data network that creates secure connections, or "tunnels," over regular Internet lines. It gives users the same capabilities as an extranet at much lower cost by using shared public resources rather than private ones. Just as phone companies provide secure shared resources for voice messages, VPNs provide the same secure sharing of public resources for data. This allows for on-demand networking: An authorized user can join the network for any desired function at any time, for any length of time, while keeping the corporate network secure. If you don't have access to a corporate VPN, you can easily set up an account at a public VPN provider like WiTopia or StrongVPN.[9]

intranet
A companywide network, closed to public access, that uses Internet-type technology.

extranet
A semiprivate network that uses Internet technology and allows more than one company to access the same information or allows people on different servers to collaborate.

virtual private network (VPN)
A private data network that creates secure connections, or "tunnels," over regular Internet lines.

How do users log on to an organization's network? They do so through an *enterprise portal* that centralizes information and transactions and serves as an entry point to a variety of resources, such as e-mail, financial records, schedules, and employment and benefits files. Portals can even include streaming video of the company's day-care center. They are more than simply web pages with links. They identify users and allow them access to areas of the intranet according to their roles: customers, suppliers, employees, and so on. They make information available in one place so that users don't have to deal with a dozen different web interfaces.

The challenge to the CIO is to integrate resources, information, reports, and so on—all of which may be in a variety of places—so that they appear seamless to the user.

Broadband Technology

broadband technology
Technology that offers users a continuous connection to the Internet and allows them to send and receive mammoth files that include voice, video, and data much faster than ever before.

The more traffic on the Internet, the slower connections become. Tools to unlock these traffic jams include **broadband technology**, a continuous connection to the Internet that allows users to send and receive mammoth video, voice, and data files faster than ever before. Even though broadband in the United States is dramatically faster than old dial-up connections, its average speed of 3 megabits per second is snail-like compared to the 14.6 and 7.9 averages of South Korea and Japan.[10] President Obama has made improving and expanding broadband technology a priority of his administration.[11] As people use more and more bandwidth to stream videos on services like Netflix or music on apps like Pandora, Internet Service Providers have begun to place caps on the amount of broadband consumers can use. Right now this isn't a problem for most users since average usage is well below the current caps, but as more mobile devices and services come online, the more likely broadband will become a consumption-based service (i.e., you pay for the broadband you use).[12]

Internet2
The private Internet system that links government supercomputer centers and a select group of universities; it runs more than 22,000 times faster than today's public infrastructure and supports heavy-duty applications.

Even with broadband technology, scientists and other scholars who access, transmit, and manipulate complex mathematical models, data sets, and other digital elements need a faster solution. Their answer? Create a private Internet reserved for research purposes only. **Internet2** runs more than 22,000 times faster than today's public infrastructure, and supports heavy-duty applications such as videoconferencing, collaborative research, distance education, digital libraries, and full-body simulations known as teleimmersion. A key element of Internet2 is a network called very-high-speed backbone network service (vBNS), which was set up in 1995 as a way to link government supercomputer centers and a select group of universities. The power of Internet2 makes it possible for a remote medical specialist to assist in a medical operation over the Internet without having the connection deteriorate as, say, home users check sports scores.[13]

Internet2 became available to only a few select organizations in late 1997, but there are now more than 400 member universities, government agencies, corporations, and laboratories in over 50 countries.[14] Whereas the public Internet divides bandwidth equally among users (if there are 100 users, they each get to use 1 percent of the available bandwidth), Internet2 is more capitalistic. Users who are willing to pay more can use more bandwidth.

Some fear that Internet2 may soon be overrun by undergrads engaged in music swapping and other resource-hogging pursuits. But the designers of Internet2 are thinking ahead. Not only do they expect Internet history to repeat itself; they are counting on it. They are planning to filter Internet2 technology out to the wider Internet community in such a way that there is plenty of room on the road for all of us—at a price, of course.

Social Media and Web 2.0

For businesses, social media provide an array of opportunities and challenges. It's an inexpensive way to gain exposure. Most important, it gives businesses tools to collaborate with consumers on product development, service enhancement, and promotion. Until now, using social media has been optional for most businesses. However, many believe that businesses that do not have a social media presence soon (within the next 3 to 5 years) will not survive. We're not talking just about a Facebook page with an occasional update. Successful businesses will have a social media ecosystem where every part of the organization collaborates and where customers are part of the conversation instantly.[15]

Social networking sites have made posting messages a daily routine for millions of people. Are there any social or other downsides to these activities?

Adam Kidron, co-founder of Manhattan hamburger restaurant 4food, says he wouldn't be in business if it were not for social media. The restaurant is based on customization. Customers choose the type of bun (i.e., bagel, multi-grain, brioche, pumpernickel, etc.), donut-shaped burger (i.e., beef, lamb, egg, turkey, salmon, veggie, sausage, etc.), "scoop" to fill the donut hole (i.e., avocado and chili mango, potato and chorizo hash, etc.), and then finally the cheese, and condiments. Social media become part of the fundamental product when a customer creates a new product and they use their own mobile device or one of the iPads placed around the restaurant to create a name for their burger and save it in 4food's database. If they like the burger, they post their creation directly to Twitter or Facebook. If they *really* like the burger, they create a YouTube commercial that is shown on the restaurant's giant video wall along with Twitter feeds. If another customer buys the burger, the creator gets a 25-cent credit added to his or her 4food account.[16] Figure B.4 offers suggestions to consider when using social media in business. The most important thing to remember is that the social media have to serve a unique purpose and not be just a gimmicky add-on.

While increasing numbers of companies are using social media to woo customers, their employees' productivity may go down as they succumb to social media's many time-wasting aspects. Another challenge is that a single disparaging remark on a social networking forum can have devastating effects on the company's reputation. What happens when an employee posts a derogatory

---

- **Let the network mature.** Don't just set up a network and immediately begin exploiting it. For example, when the list of online supporters started to grow, the Obama fundraisers wanted to immediately tap them for contributions. They were persuaded to wait until his e-mail team created an environment that let people know they were part of the campaign.

- **If your competition is using social media, you better be using it to.** More than 50 percent of Twitter users say that they follow companies, brands or products on social networks.

- **Take customers' comments seriously.** People expect to be listened to. If you respond, they'll keep coming back.

- **Be authentic.** You have to talk directly with your customers, not just make an announcement as you would in a press release. Keep it authentic and you'll build a personality around your company and your brand.

Source: Ellen McGirt, "Boy Wonder," *Fast Company,* April 2009; Max Chafkin, "Social Media Grows Up," *Inc.,* September 2010; and "Social Shopping," *Entrepreneur,* December 2010.

figure B.4

TIPS FOR USING SOCIAL MEDIA TO PARTNER WITH CUSTOMERS
Using social media is about trusting your brand and identity to your customers, partners, and the world at large. The world is going to do things with your brand, whether or not you participate in the process. Here are some tips to keep in mind.

remark about her supervisor on her own Facebook page? In one woman's case, she was fired. The National Labor Relations Board eventually said her comments were "protected speech" under federal law. Obviously, the lesson to be learned here is to not post comments you don't want your boss to see. Some companies ban employees from using social networking sites at work.[17]

For all its strengths and weaknesses, social networking is the best example of what tech publisher Tim O'Reilly in 2004 dubbed "Web 2.0." **Web 2.0** is the set of tools that allow people to build social and business connections, share information, and collaborate on projects online with user-generated sites like blogs, wikis, social networking sites and other online communities, and virtual worlds. (In this context, *Web 1.0* refers to corporate-generated sites like Google and Amazon.) YouTube and the microblogging site Twitter are among the largest Web 2.0 businesses, where ordinary people create all the content.

Web 3.0

Another generation of Web innovators has expanded the utility of the Web so that it enables an unprecedented level of intelligence in almost all applications. The goal is to pull data in real time, as needed. As you pull data, the system learns about you and your interests and pushes information it "thinks" you might like toward you. Known as Web 3.0, this technology represents a shift in how people interact with the Web, and vice versa.[18] Those that describe Web 1.0 as the Static Web and Web 2.0 as the Social Web, describe Web 3.0 as the Personal Web. You could think of Web 3.0 as Web 2.0 with a brain. **Web 3.0** technology is made up of three basic components: semantic Web, mobile Web, and immersive Internet.

The *semantic Web* refers to powerful intelligent decision-making applications. For example, Amdocs is a company that interacts with customers on behalf of its clients in service industries such as telecom, health care, utilities and insurance. This requires the Amdocs representatives to have real-time knowledge from internal sources—such as service disruptions and policy management—and external forces, such as social trends and competitive offers. Using Web 3.0 semantic technologies, Amdocs combines information from a

Web 2.0
The set of tools that allow people to build social and business connections, share information, and collaborate on projects online (including blogs, wikis, social networking sites and other online communities, and virtual worlds).

Web 3.0
A combination of technologies that adds intelligence and changes how people interact with the Web, and vice versa (consists of the semantic Web, mobile Web, and immersive Internet).

Wireless technology lets us stay connected everywhere all of the time. What other functions would you like to be able to perform with wireless technology?

variety of sources in real time to anticipate the reason for a customer's call. Responses can be made 30 percent faster, which makes customers happy.[19]

The *mobile Web* allows users to use the Web as they move from one device to another and one location to another. Location-based services are tied to devices that can track a user's whereabouts and suggest places, like restaurants or shops, in the area. If you happen to have a GPS device in your car, this location-based technology is not new to you, but now that same location-tracking power is used in portable devices like your cell phone. You can now get a message from Starbucks offering you a discount on a latte as you walk by their door. If you do drop in the store, you can even use an app on your smart phone to pay for your drink.[20]

The *immersive Internet* includes virtual worlds, augmented reality, and 3-D environments. The use of virtual worlds, simulations, augmented reality, and multiplayer gaming technologies is expected to increase dramatically for learning in the next few years.[21]

progress assessment

- How do computer networks change the way employees gather information?
- What is an enterprise portal?

LEARNING goal 4

Review the computer hardware most frequently used in business.

THE ENABLING TECHNOLOGY: HARDWARE

Gordon E. Moore, chairman of Intel Corporation, once predicted that the capacity of computer chips would double every year or so, a projection now called Moore's law.[22] In fact, the million-dollar vacuum-tube computers that awed people in the 1950s couldn't keep up with a pocket calculator today. A greeting card that plays "Happy Birthday" contains more computing power than existed before 1950. So rather than add potentially outdated facts to your information overload, we offer a simple overview of current hardware technology. Hardware includes computers, laptops, smart phones, tablets, printers, GPS, and scanners.[23]

Mobile Devices

We are moving away from a computer-dominant environment toward an array of post-PC appliances designed to connect us to the Internet. These include smart phones like the iPhone, tablets like the iPad, laptops, and in-dash computers for cars. Users have the mobility and flexibility to work anywhere they can tap into a wireless network, using technology called wi-fi, from *wireless fidelity.*

Smart phones account for nearly half of the mobile devices in the U.S. today. This means that employees and customers already have mobile computing power in their hands. Smart managers will harness this power to their advantage. For instance, Disney Store launched a service that lets customers use their own smart phones to combine the store and online experiences, and even pay for goods using their own phones anywhere in the store so there's no waiting in line at the cash register. Customers and employees can search Disney's global inventory. If an item isn't in stock in the store, employees can add it to an in-store transaction and have the item shipped directly to the customer's home. Disney realizes that customers are going to compare prices online while they're in the store anyway, so they need to make it as easy as possible for them to stick with Disney.[24]

While the flexibility and utility created by mobile devices is tremendous, the technology does expose businesses to certain risks. With so many employees having the ability to access company networks anytime and anywhere, one of the biggest challenges for businesses is to find ways to keep their networks and the information on them secure.[25] We will discuss security later in the chapter.

Some store employees can now use their smart phones to process customers' credit card purchases anywhere in the store. What are the advantages of using smart phones to make transactions? Can you think of any potential problems this process might create?

Computer Networks

In older systems, mainframe computers performed all the information processing tasks and sent the results to a "dumb" terminal that could not perform them. A few companies in data-intensive industries such as finance and insurance still use mainframes.[26]

Many companies today maintain a **network computing system** (or **client/server computing**) that uses personal computers, or "clients," that obtain needed information from huge databases in a central computer, or "server." Networks have drawbacks as well. Maintaining a fleet of PCs can be expensive. The cost of the computer itself is just the down payment. Computing costs, and productivity losses, go up as you upgrade and troubleshoot equipment and software and train employees to use them. By the time you've recouped your costs, it's time for another upgrade.[27] Many companies that tried networking PCs have moved to other options.

One option was to rent software and hardware access by way of the Internet as needed, instead of trying to maintain a proprietary network. Back in the Web boom, companies called application service providers (ASPs) ran software at data centers and rented access to these functions to customers who didn't want to buy expensive servers and software. Most ASPs went out of business because chief intelligence officers were slow to hand over their critical data to companies with no track record or little experience in their specific industries. But the fall of little ASPs didn't stop the flow of outsourcing IT functions to big service providers like IBM. In fact, the trend today is toward two types of outsourced networking that look like highly developed descendants of earlier forms of networking and ASPs: virtualization and cloud computing. We'll discuss those next.

Virtualization and Cloud Computing

For every computer a company has in its network, an array of potential problems lurks in the shadows, from time-wasting crashes to crippling viruses. To remedy this, many companies have turned to **virtualization**, a process that allows networked computers to run multiple operating systems and programs through one central computer at the same time.[28]

Virtualization's centralized storage system gives companies ready access to update system software and fix problems, a practice as cost-effective as it is convenient. Virtual desktops are also safer from thieves or hackers since the hub can cut off access to the computer if it becomes compromised.

Companies that want to virtualize but not to store all that data in their own offices need only look to the sky for a solution called **cloud computing**. This technology stores a company's data and applications at offsite data centers,

network computing system (client/server computing) Computer systems that allow personal computers (clients) to obtain needed information from huge databases in a central computer (the server).

virtualization A process that allows networked computers to run multiple operating systems and programs through one central computer at the same time.

cloud computing A form of virtualization in which a company's data and applications are stored at offsite data centers that are accessed over the Internet (the cloud).

accessed over the Internet. The data aren't necessarily stored in a single data center; portions could be in a series of centers anywhere in the world. The data are easily accessible from any computer with an Internet connection.[29] Vendors like Amazon, Google, Apple, and IBM offer cloud computing for a monthly pay-as-you-go fee.

This might be an easier way to understand what cloud computing is: imagine that everything you need is in a file cabinet and that whenever you need something, you can pull it out of the cabinet and take it to your desk and when you're finished with it you just put it back. The file cabinet with everything you need is in the cloud and the desk is any computer you happen to be using anywhere in the world with Internet access. Since you have so many things to store, you need a really big cabinet—a cabinet that would be way too big to fit in your office. The cloud gives you all the storage space you need.

Sometimes your computer may not be powerful enough to handle something like a very big multimedia presentation for a class. You don't want to buy a big expensive computer since you aren't going to use it for long. You could rent someone else's powerful computer for the times you need it. Of course, you wouldn't want to lug it back and forth every time you needed it. Instead, with cloud computing, you connect to the power you need when it is somewhere else. It's just like when you connect to your Facebook page that's not on your computer. It's somewhere else. The cloud allows you to rent the extra computing power when you need it. You just pay for what you use.[30]

There are three types of cloud computing: (1) *private* clouds (wholly behind a firewall), *public* clouds (run on remote computers), and (3) *hybrid* clouds (consist of a private cloud for essential tasks, but use a public cloud as needed).[31]

In short, the advantages of cloud computing are:[32]

1. **Reduced software costs.** Most software is free because the service provider supplies it. No more paying for upgrades or spending time installing all those patches since they're installed in the cloud.

2. **Improved security.** Off-site centers provide full and regular backups of data, etc., which is something many small businesses fail to do regularly.

3. **Capacity.** Sometimes businesses need large chunks of capacity during peak demand periods, but much less at other times. Cloud computing allows the company to rent only what it needs when it needs it. If its needs increase, it just rents more. This is especially important to growing businesses that don't know what their needs will be.

4. **Equipment.** Since applications run in the cloud and not on your desk, you don't need to buy expensive equipment.

5. **Access.** Since you access all of your documents in the cloud via the Internet, it is much easier to share documents and make sure that everyone is working with the latest version.

Cloud computing changes the way people and businesses use technology. Since their data is stored in the cloud rather than locked on their computers, users are free to access the data from anywhere with any device rather than only from their own personal computers. Has cloud computing changed the way you access your programs and files?

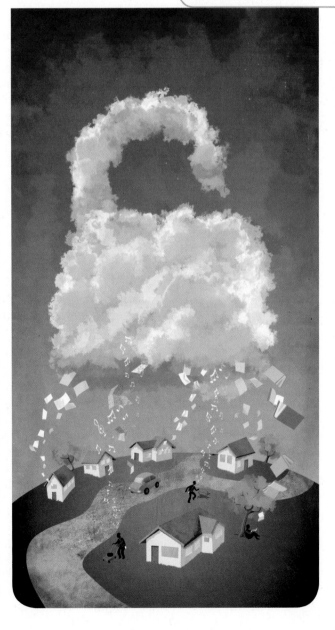

Of course, cloud computing has its disadvantages as well. Primarily these involve concerns about security, stability, and control of data. (We'll discuss these issues in more detail later in the chapter.) An Amazon outage in 2011 demonstrated that cloud services can fail, and customers can lose data.[33] Popular Dropbox file-sharing service was accused of misleading users about the security and privacy of their files.[34] VMware introduced a service that lets IT managers control the data on private and public clouds so that they can enjoy the cost savings and flexibility of cloud services, but still maintain control over security.[35]

LEARNING goal 5

Classify the types of computer software most frequently used in business.

shareware
Software that is copyrighted but distributed to potential customers free of charge.

public domain software (freeware)
Software that is free for the taking.

SOFTWARE

Computer software provides the instructions that tell your computer what to do. Although most software is distributed commercially through suppliers like retail stores or electronic retailers, some software, called **shareware**, is copyrighted but distributed free of charge. Users are asked to send a specified fee to the developer if the program meets their needs and they decide to use it. **Public domain software (freeware)** is free for the taking. The quality of shareware and freeware varies greatly. To learn more, find a website that rates such programs. SharewareJunkies.com lists the programs downloaded most often, editors' picks, and links to downloadable programs.

Businesspeople most frequently use software for writing (word processors), manipulating numbers (spreadsheets), filing and retrieving data (databases), presenting information visually (graphics), communicating (e-mail and instant messaging), collaborating, and accounting. Integrated software, or a software suite such as Microsoft Office, can perform many of these functions. The top business *social/collaboration software* includes Cisco's WebEx, Microsoft Sharepoint, Socialtext, Jive Mobile Module, SAP StreamWork, Salesforce Chatter, SuccessFactors's CubeTree, and Chatter.[36]

As anyone with a smart phone knows, there is an app (application) for just about everything.[37] Keeping up with all the changing technology can be stressful for some. Worried about the effect of all the stress on your health? Sure, there's an app for that. Ford is testing an app that measures a driver's stress levels through heart-rate detection sensors built into the car's seats. Higher stress can be reduced through the app suggesting a change, such as playing soothing music, or having cell calls automatically routed to voice mail.[38]

Collaboration software, such as Cisco's WebEx, allows multiple users to work on the same document at the same time. It also facilitates videoconferencing so that participants can see and hear each other regardless of where they are. What are the advantages of using such software?

progress assessment

- How do computer networks change the way employees gather information?
- What are the major types of computer software used in business?

LEARNING goal 6

Evaluate the human resource, security, privacy, and stability issues affected by information technology.

EFFECTS OF INFORMATION TECHNOLOGY ON MANAGEMENT

The increase of information technology has affected management greatly and will continue to do so. Four major issues today are human resource changes, security threats, privacy concerns, and stability.

Human Resource Issues

We talked in Chapter 8 about tall versus flat organization structures. Computers often eliminate middle-management functions and thus flatten organization structures.

Human resource managers need to recruit employees who know how to use the new technology or train those who already work in the company. Companies often hire consultants instead of internal staff to address these concerns. Outsourcing technical training allows them to concentrate on their core businesses.

Perhaps the most revolutionary effect of computers and the Internet is telecommuting. Using computers linked to the company's network, mobile employees can transmit their work to the office from anywhere as easily as they can walk to the boss's office. Naturally, that decreases travel time and overall costs and often increases productivity. Having fewer employees in the office also means that a company can get by with smaller, and therefore less expensive, office space than before.

Telecommuting enables men and women to work while staying home with small children or elders. It has also been a tremendous boon for workers with disabilities. Employees who can work after hours on their home computers, rather than staying late at the office, report lowered stress and improved morale. Telecommuting is most successful among people who are self-starters, who don't have home distractions, and whose work doesn't require face-to-face interaction with co-workers.

Electronic communication can never replace face-to-face communication for creating enthusiasm and team spirit, however. Even as telecommuting has grown in popularity, some telecommuters report that a consistent diet of long-distance work leaves them feeling dislocated or left out of the loop. Some miss the energy of social interaction or dislike the intrusion of work into what is normally a personal setting. Often people working from home don't know when to turn the work off. Some companies are therefore using telecommuting only as a part-time alternative. In fact, industry now defines telecommuting as working at home a minimum of two days a week.

Today a new class of mobile worker has emerged: nearly autonomous, not in the office, doing business in their own time staff (or *nanobots,* for short). These aren't your typical laptop-toting, texting-from-the-road mobile workers, but highly skilled, high achievers who thrive on the personal freedom to meet the organization's goals in their own way. Nanobots must be technologically self-sufficient, but they also have to have the maturity to use their autonomy in

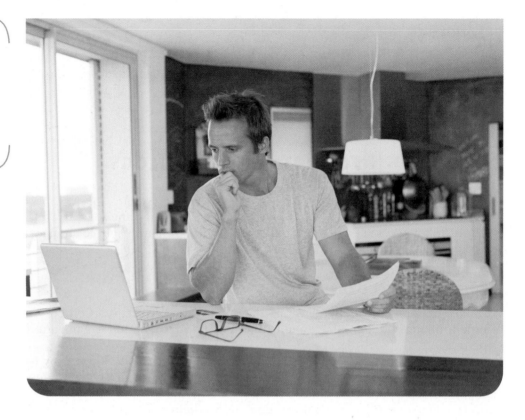

Telecommuting is one of the biggest human resource boons of the wireless age, but some employees are better suited to its demands than others. Do you have what it takes?

the best interest of their employers and clients. They must have personal networks, knowledge, and experience to handle tasks, situations, and problems on their own. Managers have found that it is best to "macro-manage" nanobots, that is, to set goals without telling them specifically how to achieve them. For instance, the manager could instruct the nanobot to complete a project within a set budget by a certain time and leave him or her to get it done. The challenge for managers is to recognize who can be a nanobot. Autonomy can increase productivity and work satisfaction in the right people, but in the wrong hands it can waste resources or damage organizational relationships.

Figure B.5 illustrates how information technology changes the way managers and workers interact. For additional information about telecommuting and home-based workers, review Chapters 6 and 11.

Security Issues

"Secure" information may be at risk from hackers who break into companies' networks; from employees who steal it; or from companies' own incompetence, poor gatekeeping, or sloppy procedures. Computer security is more complicated today than ever, as web-enabled smart phones and the 3G networks they run on, social networks and online games, and USB storage devices (flash drives and memory cards) become hackers' latest targets.[39] When information was processed on mainframes, the single data center was easier to control because there was limited access to it. Today, however, computers are accessible not only in all areas within the company but also in all areas of other companies with which the firm does business.

An ongoing security threat is the spread of computer viruses over the Internet. A **virus** is a piece of programming code inserted into other programming that usually lies dormant until triggered to cause some unexpected and, for the victim, usually undesirable event. Users pick up viruses by unknowingly

virus
A piece of programming code inserted into other programming to cause some unexpected and, for the victim, usually undesirable event.

MANAGERS MUST	WORKERS MUST
• Instill commitment in subordinates rather than rule by command and control.	• Become initiators, able to act without management direction.
• Become coaches, training workers in necessary job skills, making sure they have resources to accomplish goals, and explaining links between a job and what happens elsewhere in the company.	• Become financially literate so that they can understand the business implications of what they do and changes they suggest.
• Give greater authority to workers over scheduling, priority setting, and even compensation.	• Learn group interaction skills, including how to resolve disputes within their work group and how to work with other functions across the company.
• Use new information technologies to measure workers' performance, possibly based on customer satisfaction or the accomplishment of specific goals.	• Develop new math, technical, and analytical skills to use newly available information on their jobs.

figure B.5

WHEN INFORMATION TECHNOLOGY ALTERS THE WORKPLACE

downloading infected programming over the Internet or sharing an infected USB storage device. Often the source of the infected file is unaware of the virus. Some viruses are playful messages ("Kilroy was here!"), but some can be quite harmful, erasing data or causing your hard drive to crash. Programs such as Norton's AntiVirus inoculate your computer so that it doesn't catch a known virus. But because new viruses are being developed constantly, antivirus programs may have only limited success. Keep your antivirus protection up-to-date and, more important, practice safe computing by not downloading files from unknown sources.[40]

Computer viruses can erase your hard drive or make your computer crash. Keeping your anti-virus software up-to-date is essential. When was the last time you updated your anti-virus software?

If a business stores customer data, it is subject to laws and regulations regarding the proper protection of these data.[41] Many smaller businesses that don't have the manpower to handle security concerns might consider hiring a managed security services provider (MSSP). MSSPs can install and manage firewalls, virtual private networks, web filtering and antispam programs, security intelligence services, and wireless and mobile functions. Even with all of this security protection, it is still possible that hackers can get through. Perhaps you were one of the millions who lost access to their PlayStation games in 2011 when Sony's security was breached exposing the account information of more than 100 million people.[42]

Phishing is another type of online security threat. A scammer will embellish an e-mail message with a stolen logo for a well-recognized brand such as eBay, PayPal, or Citibank that makes the message look authentic. Phishing messages often state something like "Account activation required" or "Your account will be canceled if you do not verify." When the victims click the link contained in the message, they are sent to a phony Web site that takes their personal information and uses it to commit fraud. The best way to avoid a phishing scam is never to access a website through a link in an e-mail message. Instead, open a new window and go to the home page of the company's website directly.[43]

As more people log on to the Internet, the number of legal issues surrounding its use will likely increase. Today, copyright and pornography laws are crashing into the virtual world. Other legal questions relate to intellectual property and contract disputes, online sexual and racial harassment, and the use of electronic communication to promote crooked sales schemes. Cybercrimes cost the United States billions of dollars a year.[44]

Until September 11, 2001, corporate and government security officials worried mostly about online theft, credit card fraud, and hackers. Today, however, they are most concerned about *cyberterrorism.* Terrorist hackers could shut down the entire communications, money supply, electricity, and transportation systems. An attempt to shut down web browsing occurred in 2002 when a powerful electronic attack crippled 9 of the 13 computers that manage Internet traffic globally. If one more of the critical computers had been hit, it would have disrupted e-mails and web browsing across many parts of the Internet. Officials considered it the most sophisticated large-scale assault against crucial computers in the history of the Internet. Although most users didn't notice the attack (it lasted only one hour, and most Internet providers routinely store, or cache, popular web directory information), the attack demonstrated the Internet's vulnerability.

The Senate Commerce Subcommittee on Consumer Protection held hearings on consumer protection and privacy in the mobile marketplace. How many of the mobile apps that you use track your whereabouts (both your physical location and where you go online) and share that information with third parties? Probably more than you think.

The Critical Infrastructure Protection Board, a part of the U.S. Department of Homeland Security, was created after September 11, 2001, to devise a plan for improving the security of the United States' critical infrastructure. The agency needs the cooperation of businesses across the country, because 85 percent of the system it needs to protect is in the private sector. Companies have been reluctant to file reports about security breaches, however, for fear the public will lose faith in their ability to protect their assets. To encourage the sharing of such information, Congress passed the Critical Infrastructure Information Act of 2002, assuring businesses that any information they provide the Department of Homeland Security will remain secret through an exemption from the Freedom of Information Act.[45] This is only a start on what is likely to be a long effort to improve security technologies.

Privacy Issues

The increasing use of technology creates major concerns about privacy. You don't need to be the target of a criminal investigation to have your e-mail snooped; it's no more private than a postcard. Many U.S. companies scan employee e-mail regularly, and it's legal. They look for trade secrets, non-work-related traffic, harassing messages, and conflicts of interest. Any hacker with a desire to read your thoughts can also trap and read your messages, most of which are unencrypted. Some e-mail systems, such as Lotus Notes, can encrypt e-mail to keep corporate messages private. If you use browser-based e-mail, you can obtain a certificate that has an encryption key from a company such as VeriSign. Legitimate users who want to decrypt your mail need to get an unlocking key.

The Internet presents increasing threats to your privacy, as more personal information is stored in computers and more people are able to access it, legally or not. Some websites allow people to search for vehicle ownership from a license number or to find other individuals' real estate property records. One key question in the debate over protecting our privacy is "Isn't this personal information already public anyway?" Civil libertarians have long fought to keep certain kinds of information available to the public. If access to such data is restricted on the Internet, wouldn't we have to reevaluate our policies on all public records? Privacy advocates don't think so. After all, the difference is that the Internet makes obtaining personal information *too* easy. Would your neighbors or friends even consider going to the appropriate local agency and sorting through public documents for hours to find your driving records or to see your divorce settlement? Probably not. But they might dig into your background if all it takes is a few clicks of a button.

Many web servers track the online movements of users willing to swap such personal details for free access to online information. Site owners can share your data with others without your permission. Websites also often send **cookies** to your computer that stay on your hard drive. These are pieces of information such as registration data (name and password) or user preferences that the browser sends back to the server whenever you return to that website. Other cookies track your movements around the web and then blend that information with a database so that a company can tailor the ads it sends you. Some software, known as spyware, can be installed on your computer without your knowledge. The spyware can then infect your system with viruses and track your online behavior.

Do you mind someone watching over your shoulder while you're on the Web? Tim Berners-Lee, the researcher who invented the World Wide Web, led the development of a way to prevent you from receiving cookies without your permission. His Platform for Privacy Preferences, or P3, allows a website to automatically send information on its privacy policies.[46] With P3 you can set up your web browser to communicate only with those websites that meet certain criteria. You need to decide how much information about yourself you are willing to give away. Remember, we are living in an information economy, and information is a commodity—that is, an economic good with a measurable value.[47]

cookies
Pieces of information, such as registration data or user preferences, sent by a website over the Internet to a web browser that the browser software is expected to save and send back to the server whenever the user returns to that website.

Stability Issues

Although technology can provide significant increases in productivity and efficiency, instability has a significant impact on business. Candy maker Hershey discovered the Halloween trick was on it one year when the company couldn't get its treats to stores on time. Failure of its new $115 million computer system disrupted shipments, and retailers were forced to order Halloween candy from other companies, leaving Hershey with a 12 percent decrease in sales that quarter.

What's to blame? Experts say it is a combination of computer error; human error; malfunctioning software; and an overly complex marriage of software, hardware, and networking equipment. Some systems are launched too quickly to be bug-proof, and some executives don't have the technical knowledge to challenge computer specialists. As critical as technology is to business, some of it is not built for rigorous engineering, and some people aren't properly trained to use it. As things get more complex, we will probably be prone to more errors.

TECHNOLOGY AND YOU

If you're beginning to think being computer illiterate may be occupational suicide, you're getting the point. As information technology eliminates old jobs while creating new ones, it will be up to you to learn and maintain the skills you need to be certain you aren't left behind. And, who knows, maybe you can find a job like Gabi Gregg did. MTV appreciated so much the trust and passion she shared with her many Twitter followers that it offered her a job. It made her MTV's first "TJ" in order to help them "amplify the voice of our audience as part of the global conversation." She loves her new job, and the $100,000 a year salary isn't bad either![48]

progress assessment

- How has information technology changed the way people work?
- What management issues have been affected by the growth of information technology?

summary

Learning Goal 1. Outline the changing role of business technology.

- **What have been the various names and roles of business technology since 1970?**

In the 1970s, business technology was called data processing (DP) and its role was to support existing business. In the 1980s, its name became information systems (IS) and its role changed to doing business. In the 1990s, business technology became information technology (IT) and its role now is to change business.

- **How does information technology change business?**

Information technology has minimized the importance of time and place to businesses. Firms that are independent of time and location can deliver products and services whenever and wherever convenient for the customer. See Figure B.5 for examples of how information technology changes business.

- **What is business intelligence?**

Business intelligence refers to a variety of software applications that analyze an organization's raw data and take out useful insights from it.

Learning Goal 2. List the types of business information, identify the characteristics of useful information, and discuss how data are stored and mined.

- **What types of information are available to businesses today?**

The types of information available to businesses today include (1) business process information, (2) physical-world observations, (3) biological data, (4) public data, and (5) data that indicate personal preferences or intentions.

- **How can you deal with information overload?**

The most important step in dealing with information overload is to identify your four or five key goals. Eliminate information that will not help you meet them.

- **What makes information useful?**

The usefulness of management information depends on four characteristics: quality, completeness, timeliness, and relevance.

- **What are data storage and data mining?**

Data storage lets businesses organize data into useful information. A *data warehouse* stores data about a single subject over a specific period of time. *Data mining* seeks hidden patterns and relationships among data in a data warehouse.

Learning Goal 3. Compare the scope of the Internet, intranets, extranets, and virtual private networks and explain how broadband technology enabled the evolution to Web 2.0 and 3.0.

- **What information technology is available to help business manage information?**

The heart of information technology involves the Internet, intranets, extranets, and virtual private networks. The Internet is a massive network of thousands of smaller networks open to everyone with a computer and a modem. An intranet is a companywide network protected from unauthorized entry by outsiders. An extranet is a semiprivate network that allows more than one company to access the same information. A virtual private network is a private data network that creates secure connections, or "tunnels," over regular Internet lines.

- **What is Web 2.0?**

Web 2.0 is the set of tools that allows people to build social and business connections, share information, and collaborate on projects online with user-generated sites like blogs, wikis, social networking sites and other online communities, and virtual worlds. YouTube and Twitter are among the largest Web 2.0 businesses, where ordinary people create all the content.

- **What is Web 3.0?**

Web 3.0 is technology that adds a level of intelligence to interacting with the Web. It could be described as the Personal Web, whereas Web 1.0 can be thought of as the Static Web and Web 2.0 as the Social Web. Web 3.0 is made up of three basic components: The semantic Web, the mobile Web, and immersive Internet.

Learning Goal 4. Review the computer hardware most frequently used in business.

- **What was one of the most dynamic changes in computer hardware in the past decade?**

One of the most dynamic changes was the move away from mainframe computers that serve as the center of information processing and toward network systems that allow many users to access information at the same time. The trend today is toward cloud computing that connects users to needed data via the Internet.

• **What are the major benefits of networks?**

Networks' major benefits are (1) saving time and money, (2) providing easy links across functional boundaries, and (3) allowing employees to see complete information.

Learning Goal 5. Classify the types of computer software most frequently used in business.

• **What types of software do managers use most frequently?**

Managers most often use word processing, electronic spreadsheet, database, graphics, e-mail and instant messaging, and accounting programs. Another class of software, called groupware, allows people to work collaboratively and share ideas.

Learning Goal 6. Evaluate the human resource, security, privacy, and stability issues affected by information technology.

• **What effect has information technology had on business management?**

Computers eliminate some middle management functions and thus flatten organization structures. Computers also allow employees to work from their own homes. On the negative side, computers sometimes allow information to fall into the wrong hands. Concern for privacy is an issue affected by the vast store of information available on the Internet. Finding the balance between freedom to access private information and individuals' right to maintain privacy will require continued debate.

key terms

broadband technology B-10

business intelligence(BI) B-3

cloud computing B-14

cookies B-21

data processing (DP) B-2

extranet B-9

information systems (IS) B-2

information technology (IT) B-3

Internet2 B-10

intranet B-9

network computing system (client/server computing) B-14

public domain software (freeware) B-16

shareware B-16

virtual private network (VPN) B-9

virtualization B-14

virus B-18

Web 2.0 B-12

Web 3.0 B-12

critical thinking

1. What information, either for your personal life or for your job, would you like to receive exactly when and where you need it?

2. If you could design a system to provide the information you identified in question 1, what might it look like and what would it do?

3. What are the implications for world trade given the ability firms and government organizations now have to communicate across borders so easily?

developing workplace skills

1. Imagine you have $2,000 to buy or upgrade a computer system. Research hardware and software in computer magazines and on websites such as ZDNet (www.zdnet.com). Visit a computer store or shop online to find the best value. List what you would buy, and write a summary explaining your choices.

2. Interview someone who bought a computer system to use in his or her business. Ask why he or she bought that specific computer and how it is used. Ask about any problems that occurred during the purchase process or in installing and using the system. What would the buyer do differently next time? What software does he or she find especially useful?

3. Describe one computer glitch you've experienced and what you did to resolve it. Discuss the consequences of the interruption (lost data, decreased productivity, increased stress). What steps have you taken to prevent a recurrence of the problem you faced? If you haven't had a problem with a personal computer, talk with a friend or classmate who has.

4. Choose a topic that interests you and use two search engines to find information about it online. Narrow your search using the tips offered by the search engine. Did both search engines find the same websites? If not, how were their results different? Which engine found the most appropriate information?

5. How has technology changed your relationship with specific businesses or organizations such as your bank, your school, and your favorite places to shop? Has it strengthened or weakened your relationship? Has technology affected your relationship with your family, friends, and community? Take a sheet of paper and write down how technology has helped build your business and personal relationships on one side. On the other side, list how technology has weakened those relationships. What can you and others do to use technology more effectively to reduce any negative impact?

taking it to the net

Purpose

To experience the functions and benefits of an enterprise portal.

Exercise

Log on to Dynamic Intranet (www.dynamicintranet.com) and try the demo site to see what an enterprise portal can do and how it can help businesses and their employees. (Click through the demo to get a general idea of the benefits of enterprise portals; don't try to understand the technical descriptions—you can save that for another course.) Business-to-employee (B2E) portals are not accessible to outsiders, but you can see what one looks like and experiment using some of its tools.

1. Using the calendar feature in the demo portal, schedule a meeting with three other employees. (Hint: Click "Calendar" and then "Search Public

Calendar" to get started.) What are the benefits of using this tool rather than calling a meeting personally?

2. Suppose you want to work from home one day a week, but you aren't sure what Toasters' policy is on telecommuting. Find the policy in the human resources directory.

3. You're a team leader for Project 996. What's your reward if your team meets its goal?

4. Some of the folks in marketing have a sick sense of humor. See whether you can find why office humor isn't reserved for the water cooler anymore. Obviously, Toasters Inc. allows individual employees to post information to the portal without supervisor approval. What are the advantages and disadvantages of unmoderated postings?

Managing RISK

LEARNING goals

After you have read and studied this chapter, you should be able to

1 Identify the environmental changes that have made risk management important.

2 Explain the four ways of managing risk, and distinguish between insurable and uninsurable risk.

3 Define insurance policies, and explain the law of large numbers and the rule of indemnity.

4 Discuss the various types of insurance businesses can buy to manage risk.

One of the most publicized disasters of recent history was the earthquake, tsunami, and nuclear meltdown that occurred in Japan. Another major catastrophe was the series of tornadoes that devastated the South in the United States. After that, there was major flooding along the Mississippi. Before that, there was a major volcano that erupted in Iceland. In each case, we were amazed at the cost of the damage. As noted earlier in this text, such damage affects all aspects of business, including the global supply chain. So, how do businesses protect themselves against such losses? Usually, the answer is to buy insurance, although in this chapter you will learn alternative ways to protect companies.

When you see that losses may be in the billions of dollars, one has to wonder how insurance companies can afford to pay such huge damages. The answer is that insurance companies share the risk with other insurance companies. That process is called *reinsurance*. What that means is that insurance companies transfer portions of their risk portfolios to other insurance companies in order to share the risk—thus the term reinsurance. The financial risk is so huge that insurance companies tend to go global to spread the risk as widely as possible. One of those reinsurance companies is called Munich Re. Its U.S. division is called Munich American Reinsurance Company. It was founded in Atlanta in 1959.

Munich Re is the world's largest reinsurer. Munich Re's chief risk officer is Joachim Oechslin. He notes that the damage caused by an earthquake or volcano is not limited to the immediate damage, but spreads throughout the supply chain. It is one thing to know the probability that Los Angeles will suffer a major earthquake in the next three decades (97 percent) and the odds that an American man will die from a heart attack by age 70 (3.2 percent

if he doesn't smoke). It is quite another to predict with accuracy what those events will mean to the family and the community and how much insurance companies will have to pay.

Oechslin is a Swiss citizen. He studied electro-technics and mathematics in Zurich and Winterthur. He then went on to teach at HTL Winterthur. He started his business career in 1998 as a consultant at McKinsey & Company in Zurich. After that, he joined Winterthur Life & Pensions, and was appointed Chief Risk Officer. In 2007, he became the Deputy Chief Risk Officer of the AXA Group in Paris. Munich Re, where he is now, is known for its holistic approach to risk management. It evaluates financial market risks as well as insurance risks for its clients.

In this bonus chapter, you will learn something about risk management. There is so much to learn that we can only touch the surface. Nonetheless, risk management has become such a huge part of every manager's responsibilities that you need to know the basics of risk management before you become involved in any kind of business.

profile

Getting to Know

X *Joachim Oechslin*

Chief Risk Officer of Munich Re

Sources: Carol Marlack, "The Growing Peril of a Connected World," *Bloomberg Businessweek*, December 6–December 12, 2010; Stephanie Simon, Scott Kilman and Cameron McWhirter, "Storms Take a Deadly Toll," *The Wall Street Journal*, April 27, 2011; www.investopedia.com/terms/reinsurance, accessed April 2011; and Cameron McWhirter and Mike Esterl, "Floodwaters Spill into Memphis," *The Wall Street Journal*, May 10, 2011.

NAME THAT company

Every business faces risks that can affect the health of the company. When the government suspected some of our hens had been exposed to bird flu, we killed and buried some 15,000 hens in northwestern Arkansas. Who are we? (Find the answer in the chapter.)

Julian Assange, founder of WikiLeaks, posted unfiltered classified documents online. The documents include classified information regarding the wars in Afghanistan and Iraq, as well as U.S. State Department diplomatic cables. Assange admits that such information could lead to the deaths of innocents. What strategies can help firms and even governments protect themselves against this type of pure risk?

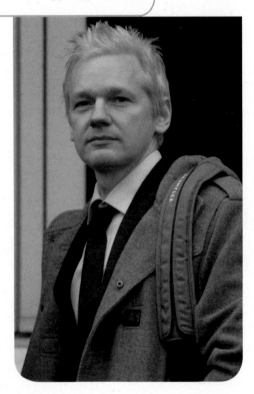

LEARNING goal 1

Identify the environmental changes that have made risk management important.

UNDERSTANDING BUSINESS RISKS

No one knows better than Joachim Oechslin at Munich Re that managing risk is a challenge for businesses throughout the world. Almost every day we hear of a tornado, hurricane, earthquake, flood, fire, airplane crash, terrorist threat, or car accident that destroyed property or injured or killed someone.[1] Over 300 people died from the series of tornadoes that hit the U.S. South in the spring of 2011.[2]

Hackers and viruses are an increasing threat to computers, and identity theft is commonplace.[3] Theft and fraud can destroy a small business. Business lawsuits in recent years have covered everything from job-related accidents to product liability.

Such reports are so much a part of the news that we tend to accept these events as part of everyday life. But the losses of property, equipment, transportation, communications, security, energy, and other resources mean a great deal to the people and organizations injured by them.[4] In some states, insurance against such loss is not available or is too expensive for high-risk businesses. New legislation in some areas aims to lessen some of these risks so that companies can obtain insurance coverage again at a reasonable price.

A survey of executives in *Quality Digest* found more than 90 percent were building or want to build enterprise risk management (ERM) into their organizations. An ERM program usually has a few well-defined goals, such as defining (1) which risks the program will manage; (2) what risk management processes, technologies, and investments will be required; and (3) how risk-management efforts will be coordinated across the firm.[5]

How Rapid Change Affects Risk Management

Risk goes beyond the obvious dangers of fire, theft, or accident. It is inherent in every decision a manager makes, and the prudent company assesses its exposure in all of them.[6] Risk managers are expanding their expertise into human resources, IT, security, legal, site construction, and more. Change is occurring so fast that it is difficult to identify new risks until they are upon us.[7] Who can evaluate the risks of buying or selling products through the Internet? How will currencies fluctuate in a financial crisis, and how will their daily ups and downs affect the profits of global trade? How will climate change affect farms, raising cattle, and the price of food? What would happen to the economy if there were a new terrorist attack or a flu epidemic? What can we do to manage the risks of financial failure at home and social unrest abroad? Could Boeing have anticipated the hole that was torn in the roof of a plane due to structural cracks?[8]

Let's explore how companies go about managing risk. We'll begin by going over a few key terms.

LEARNING goal 2

Explain the four ways of managing risk, and distinguish between insurable and uninsurable risk.

MANAGING RISK

Risk is the chance of loss, the degree of probability of loss, and the amount of possible loss. There are two different kinds of risk:

- **Speculative risk** can result in *either* profit or loss. A firm takes on speculative risk by buying new machinery, acquiring more inventory or a new plant, and making other potentially profitable decisions in which the probability of loss may be relatively low and the amount of loss known. An entrepreneur's chance to make a profit is a speculative risk. Banks that bought mortgage-backed securities were taking a speculative risk.

- **Pure risk** is the threat of loss with *no* chance for profit, such as the threat of fire, accident, or theft. If such events occur, a company loses money, but if they don't, the company gains nothing.

The risk that most concerns businesspeople is pure risk. It threatens the very existence of some firms. Once they identify pure risks, firms have several options:

1. Reduce the risk.
2. Avoid the risk.
3. Self-insure against the risk.
4. Buy insurance against the risk.

We'll discuss the option of buying insurance in detail later in this chapter. First we'll discuss each of the other alternatives for managing risk, which reduce the need for outside insurance.

Reducing Risk

A firm can reduce risk by establishing loss-prevention programs such as fire drills, health education, safety inspections, equipment maintenance, accident prevention programs, and so on. Many retail stores use mirrors, video cameras, and other devices to prevent shoplifting. Water sprinklers and smoke

risk
The chance of loss, the degree of probability of loss, and the amount of possible loss.

speculative risk
A chance of either profit or loss.

pure risk
The threat of loss with no chance for profit.

detectors minimize fire loss. Most industrial machines have safety devices to protect workers' fingers, eyes, and so on. After a terrorist attack in Mumbai, India, one hotel owner added luggage scanners, metal detectors, and more security cameras to his 20 hotels in India.

Tyson Foods killed and buried some 15,000 hens in northwestern Arkansas because the government suspected they had been exposed to bird flu. When an estimated 400 deaths in traffic accidents were blamed on faulty tires a few years ago, Firestone and Ford recalled thousands of tires before more people could be killed or hurt. Quick response to such threats is critical to risk management.

Employees as well as managers can reduce risk. Truck drivers can wear seat belts to minimize injuries from accidents, operators of loud machinery can wear earplugs to reduce the chance of hearing loss, and those who lift heavy objects can wear back braces. The beginning of an effective risk management strategy is a good loss-prevention program. However, high insurance rates have forced some firms to go beyond merely preventing risks to avoiding them, in extreme cases by going out of business.

Avoiding Risk

We can't avoid every risk. There is always the chance of fire, theft, accident, or injury. But some companies are avoiding risk by not accepting hazardous jobs and by outsourcing shipping and other functions. The threat of lawsuits has driven some drug companies to stop manufacturing vaccines, and some consulting engineers refuse to work on hazardous sites. Some companies are losing outside members of their boards of directors who don't have liability coverage protecting them from legal action against the firms they represent. Many companies have cut back on their investments to avoid the risk of financial losses, especially since the market fell in 2008.

Self-Insurance

self-insurance
The practice of setting aside money to cover routine claims and buying only "catastrophe" policies to cover big losses.

Self-insurance is the practice of setting aside money to cover routine claims and buying only "catastrophe" insurance policies to cover big losses. It is most appropriate when a firm has several widely distributed facilities. Firms with a

This is what remained of a Lowe's Home Improvement Center after a tornado passed through Sanford, N.C. in 2011. Businesses cannot accurately estimate damage from natural disasters like tornadoes beforehand. That's the reason for having insurance. Do you think Lowe's insurance covered most of the damage caused by the storm?

TYPE OF INSURANCE	WHAT IT DOES
Unemployment Compensation	Provides financial benefits, job counseling, and placement services for unemployed workers.
Social Security	Provides retirement benefits, life insurance, health insurance, and disability income insurance.
Federal Housing Administration (FHA)	Provides mortgage insurance to lenders to protect against default by home buyers.
National Flood Insurance Association	Provides compensation for damage caused by flooding and mud slides to properties located in flood-prone areas.
Federal Crime Insurance	Provides insurance to property owners in high-crime areas.
Federal Crop Insurance	Provides compensation for damaged crops.
Pension Benefit Guaranty Corporation	Insures pension plans to prevent loss to employees if the company declares bankruptcy or goes out of business.

figure C.1

PUBLIC INSURANCE
State or federal government agencies that provide insurance protection.

single huge facility, in which a major fire or earthquake could destroy the entire operation, usually turn to insurance companies to cover the risk of loss.

One of the riskier self-insurance strategies is for a company to "go bare," paying claims from its operating budget instead of from a special fund. The whole firm could go bankrupt over one claim if the damages are high enough. A less risky alternative is to form group-insurance pools that share similar risks.

Buying Insurance to Cover Risk

Although well-designed and enforced risk-prevention programs reduce the probability of claims, accidents do happen. Insurance is the armor individuals, businesses, and nonprofit organizations use to protect themselves from various financial risks. Together they spend about 10 percent of gross domestic product (GDP) on insurance premiums. The federal government provides some insurance protection (see Figure C.1), but individuals and businesses must cover most on their own.

To reduce the cost of insurance, some companies buy a business ownership policy (BOP)—a package that includes property and liability insurance. We will continue our discussion of insurance by identifying the types of risks that are uninsurable and insurable.

What Risks Are Uninsurable?   Not all risks are insurable. An **uninsurable risk** is one that no insurance company will cover. Examples of things that you cannot insure include market risks (e.g., losses that occur because of price changes, style changes, or new products that make your product obsolete); political risks (e.g., losses from war or government restrictions on trade); some personal risks (such as loss of a job); and some risks of operation (e.g., strikes or inefficient machinery).

What Risks Are Insurable?   An **insurable risk** is one the typical insurance company will cover, using the following guidelines:

1. The policyholder must have an **insurable interest,** which means the policyholder is the one at risk to suffer a loss. You cannot buy fire insurance on your neighbor's house and collect if it burns down.

uninsurable risk
A risk that no insurance company will cover.

insurable risk
A risk that the typical insurance company will cover.

insurable interest
The possibility of the policyholder to suffer a loss.

2. The loss must be measurable.

3. The chance of loss must be measurable.

4. The loss must be accidental.

5. The insurance company's risk should be dispersed; that is, spread among different geographical areas so a flood or other natural disaster in one area will not bankrupt the insurance company.

6. The insurance company must be able to set standards for accepting the risk.

progress assessment

- Why are companies more aware now of the need to manage risk?
- What is the difference between pure risk and speculative risk?
- What are the four major options for handling risk?
- What are some examples of uninsurable risk?

LEARNING goal 3

Define insurance policies, and explain the law of large numbers and the rule of indemnity.

insurance policy
A written contract between the insured and an insurance company that promises to pay for all or part of a loss.

premium
The fee charged by an insurance company for an insurance policy.

UNDERSTANDING INSURANCE POLICIES

An **insurance policy** is a written contract between the insured, whether an individual or organization, and an insurance company that promises to pay for all or part of a loss by the insured. A **premium** is the fee the insurance

Almost everyone who drives is exposed to the risk of having an accident at some point. Insurance companies use the law of large numbers to predict the losses such accidents will cause and set their policy premiums high enough to cover the losses while earning a profit. How much do you pay for your auto policy?

company charges, the cost of the policy to the insured. A **claim** is a statement of loss that the insured sends to the insurance company to request payment.

Like all private businesses, insurance companies are designed to make a profit. They therefore gather data to determine the extent of various risks. What makes it possible for insurance companies to accept risk and profit is the law of large numbers.

The **law of large numbers** says that if a large number of people or organizations are exposed to the same risk, a predictable number of losses will occur during a given period of time. (For your information, the figures for homes are as follows: Over the course of a 30-year mortgage, a home has a 9 percent chance of catching fire and a 26 percent chance of flooding.)[9] Once the insurance company predicts the number of losses likely to occur, it can determine the appropriate premiums for each policy it issues against that loss. The premium will be high enough to cover expected losses and yet earn a profit for the firm and its stockholders. Today, many insurance companies are charging high premiums not for expected losses but for the costs they anticipate from the increasing number of court cases and high damage awards.

Rule of Indemnity

The **rule of indemnity** says an insured person or organization cannot collect more than the actual loss from an insurable risk. Nor can you buy two insurance policies, even from two insurance companies, and collect from both for the same loss. You cannot gain from risk management; you can only minimize losses.

Types of Insurance Companies

There are two major types of insurance companies. A **stock insurance company** is owned by stockholders, just like any other investor-owned company. A **mutual insurance company** is an organization owned by its policyholders. It is a nonprofit organization, and any excess funds (over losses, expenses, and growth costs) go to the policyholders/investors in the form of dividends or premium reductions.

progress assessment

- What is the law of large numbers?
- What is the rule of indemnity?

LEARNING goal 4

Discuss the various types of insurance businesses can buy to manage risk.

INSURANCE COVERAGE FOR VARIOUS KINDS OF RISK

There are many types of insurance to cover various losses: property and liability insurance, health insurance, and life insurance. Property losses result from fires, accidents, theft, or other perils. Liability losses result from property

claim
A statement of loss that the insured sends to the insurance company to request payment.

law of large numbers
Principle that if a large number of people are exposed to the same risk, a predictable number of losses will occur during a given period of time.

rule of indemnity
Rule saying that an insured person or organization cannot collect more than the actual loss from an insurable risk.

stock insurance company
A type of insurance company owned by stockholders.

mutual insurance company
A type of insurance company owned by its policyholders.

figure C.2

PRIVATE INSURANCE

TYPES OF INSURANCE	WHAT IT DOES
Property and Liability	
Fire	Covers losses to buildings and their contents from fire.
Automobile	Covers property damage, bodily injury, collision, fire, theft, vandalism, and other related vehicle losses.
Homeowner's	Covers the home, other structures on the premises, home contents, expenses if forced from the home because of an insured peril, third-party liability, and medical payments to others.
Computer coverage	Covers loss of equipment from fire, theft, and sometimes spills, power surges, and accidents.
Professional liability	Protects from suits stemming from mistakes made or bad advice given in a professional context.
Business interruption	Provides compensation for loss due to fire, theft, or similar disasters that close a business. Covers lost income, continuing expenses, and utility expenses.
Nonperformance loss protection	Protects from failure of a contractor, supplier, or other person to fulfill an obligation.
Criminal loss protection	Protects from loss due to theft, burglary, or robbery.
Commercial credit insurance	Protects manufacturers and wholesalers from credit losses due to insolvency or default.
Public liability insurance	Provides protection for businesses and individuals against losses resulting from personal injuries or damage to the property of others for which the insured is responsible.
Extended product liability insurance	Covers potentially toxic substances in products; environmental liability; and, for corporations, director and officer liability.
Fidelity bond	Protects employers from employee dishonesty.
Surety bond	Covers losses resulting from a second party's failure to fulfill a contract.
Title insurance	Protects buyers from losses resulting from a defect in title to property.
Health Insurance	
Basic health insurance	Covers losses due to sickness or accidents.
Major medical insurance	Protects against catastrophic losses by covering expenses beyond the limits of basic policies.
Hospitalization insurance	Pays for most hospital expenses.
Surgical and medical insurance	Pays costs of surgery and doctor's care while recuperating in a hospital.
Dental insurance	Pays a percentage of dental expenses.
Disability income insurance	Pays income while the insured is disabled as a result of accident or illness.
Life Insurance	
Group life insurance	Covers all the employees of a firm or members of a group.
Owner or key executive insurance	Enables businesses of sole proprietors or partnerships to pay bills and continue operating, saving jobs for the employees. Enables corporations to hire and train or relocate another manager with no loss to the firm.
Retirement and pension plans	Provides employees with supplemental retirement and pension plans.
Credit life insurance	Pays the amount due on a loan if the debtor dies.

damage or injuries suffered by others for which the policyholder is held responsible. Figure C.2 on p. C-8 lists the types of insurance available. Let's begin our exploration of insurance by looking at health insurance.

Health Insurance

The United States is going through a period of major changes in health insurance. Recent legislation has the government much more involved in the health insurance process. Some states have protested this new government involvement and have sued the government to stop the implementation of the health insurance program. As this text is being written, there is still much dispute about what will happen with health insurance in the United States. Because it is so important to your future, you should keep up with this debate and get involved if you think that one means of health care would be better for you than another. Some companies have decided to self-insure against health care costs.[10] We are likely to see many variations of health coverage in the future, but the whole subject in now open for debate.

Until any new government insurance program is enforced, businesses and nonprofit organizations continue to offer their employees an array of health care benefits to choose from. Everything from hospitalization to physician fees, eye exams, dental exams, and prescriptions can be covered. Often, employees may choose between options from health care providers (e.g., Blue Cross/Blue Shield); health maintenance organizations (HMOs, e.g., Kaiser Permanente); preferred provider organizations (PPOs); or Health Savings Accounts (HSAs).

Health Maintenance Organizations (HMOs)   **Health maintenance organizations (HMOs)** offer a full range of health care benefits, with emphasis on helping members stay healthy through preventive care. Members do not receive bills for medical care and do not have to fill out insurance claim forms to be reimbursed for routine service. HMOs employ or contract with particular doctors, hospitals, and other systems of health care, and members must use providers from the approved list to be their primary care physician. That doctor will then recommend specialists, if necessary. The HMO system is called managed care.

health maintenance organizations (HMOs)
Health care organizations that require members to choose from a restricted list of doctors.

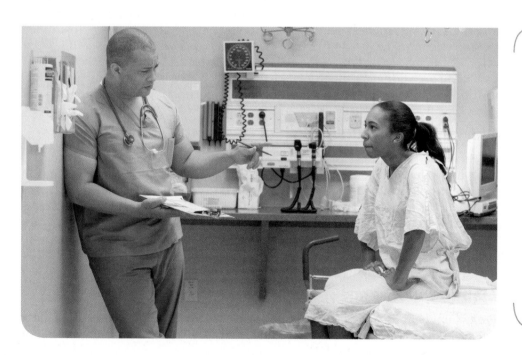

In the United States most people who have health insurance, whether an HMO, a PPO, or another type of coverage, obtain it through their employers and lose it if they are laid off or fired. In contrast, many European countries offer continuous medical coverage to all their citizens through government-sponsored programs. Do you think access to medical care is a privilege, or a right?

HMOs are less expensive than other health insurance providers, but members sometimes complain about not being able to choose doctors or get the care they want or need. Some physicians also feel they lack freedom to do what is needed to make people well and often receive less compensation than they feel is appropriate for their services. To save money, HMOs usually approve treatment before it can be given. Patients who prefer to have their doctor make such decisions often choose a PPO, as we shall see next.

preferred provider organizations (PPOs)
Health care organizations similar to HMOs except that they allow members to choose their own physicians (for a fee).

Preferred Provider Organizations (PPOs) **Preferred provider organizations (PPOs)** also contract with hospitals and physicians, and members usually pay some part of the bill, called co-insurance. However, members can also use outside providers (for which they pay more). They usually must meet a *deductible*, or out-of-pocket minimum, before the PPO will pay any bills. Some people feel that the added expense of PPOs over HMOs is worth it for the freedom to select their own physicians.

Since both HMOs and PPOs can cost 80 percent less than individual health insurance policies, most businesses and individuals choose to join one. Large businesses tend to choose PPOs, but they are more expensive to firms, so smaller businesses often choose HMOs.

health savings accounts (HSAs)
Tax-deferred savings accounts linked to low-cost, high-deductible health insurance policies.

Health Savings Accounts **Health savings accounts (HSAs)** (formerly called medical savings accounts) are tax-deferred savings accounts linked to low-cost, high-deductible health insurance policies. The idea is for your employer (or you) to take the money currently spent on high-cost, low-deductible health insurance and deposit it into a health savings account. You would use the money only for needed health care services. At the end of the year, you get to keep the money you don't spend in the account for future medical coverage. One major benefit to you is that the money grows tax-free until you take it out. Surely there will be other such plans proposed to compete with a comprehensive national health care system.

Disability Insurance

Disability insurance replaces part of your income—usually 50 to 70 percent—if you become disabled and unable to work. You must usually be disabled for a certain period, such as 60 days, before you can begin collecting. Insurance experts recommend getting disability insurance if your employer does not offer it, because the chances of becoming disabled by a disease or accident when you are young are much higher than the chance of dying. The premiums for disability insurance vary according to age, occupation, and income.

Workers' Compensation

Workers' compensation insurance guarantees payment of wages, medical care, and rehabilitation services such as retraining for employees injured on the job. Employers in every state are required to provide this insurance. It also pays benefits to the survivors of those who die as a result of work-related injuries. The cost of workers' compensation varies by the company's safety record, the size of its payroll, and the types of hazards its workers face. It costs more to insure a steelworker than an accountant because the risk of injury is greater.

Liability Insurance

Professional liability insurance covers people found liable for professional negligence. If a lawyer gives advice carelessly and the client loses money, the client may sue the lawyer for an amount equal to that lost, and liability insurance will cover the lawyer's loss. Professional liability insurance is also known as *malpractice insurance.* That term may bring doctors and dentists to mind, but many other professionals, including mortgage brokers and real estate appraisers, are buying professional liability insurance because of large lawsuits their colleagues have faced.

Product liability insurance covers liability arising out of products sold. A person injured by, say, a ladder or some other household good may sue the manufacturer for damages. Insurance usually covers such losses.

Life Insurance for Businesses

Regardless of how careful we are, we all face the prospect of death. To ensure that those left behind will be able to continue the business, entrepreneurs often buy life insurance that will pay partners and others what they need to keep the firm going. We discuss life insurance for individuals and families in Bonus Chapter D. Everything said there applies to life insurance for business executives as well. The best kind of insurance to cover executives in the firm is term insurance, but dozens of new policies with interesting features are now available.

Insurance Coverage for Home-Based Businesses

Homeowner's policies usually don't have adequate protection for a home-based business. For example, they may have a limit for business equipment. For more coverage, you may need to add an endorsement, sometimes called a *rider,* to your homeowner's policy. If clients visit your office or if you receive deliveries regularly, you may need home-office insurance. It protects you from slip-and-fall lawsuits and other risks associated with visitors. For more elaborate businesses, such as custom cabinetry shops and other types of manufacturing or inventory-keeping businesses, you may need a business-owner policy. Unless you are an expert on insurance, you will need to consult an insurance agent about the best insurance for your home-based business needs.[11]

The Risk of Damaging the Environment

Risk management now goes far beyond the protection of individuals, businesses, and nonprofit organizations from known risks. It means the evaluation of worldwide risks with many unknowns, such as climate change. It also means prioritizing these risks so that international funds can be spent where they can do the most good. No insurance company can protect humanity from all such risks. These risks are the concern of businesses and governments throughout the world, with the assistance of the international scientific community.[12] They should also be your concern as you study risk management in all its dimensions.

The benefits of adopting a global environmental outlook in risk management are becoming more obvious. According to Green Marketing International Inc., a recent survey found that 94 percent of all consumers prefer to do business with companies that demonstrate that they care about the environment. About 80 percent said that they would pay more for environmentally friendly products.

progress assessment

- Why should someone buy disability insurance?
- How many different kinds of private insurance can you name?

summary

Learning Goal 1. Identify the environmental changes that have made risk management important.

- **What changes have made risk management more important?**

Hurricanes, floods, terrorist threats, identity theft, and an unstable economy have all contributed to additional risk and the need for more risk management.

Learning Goal 2. Explain the four ways of managing risk, and distinguish between insurable and uninsurable risk.

- **What are the four major ways of managing risk?**

The major ways of managing risk are (1) reduce risk, (2) avoid risk, (3) self-insure, and (4) buy insurance.

- **What's the difference between insurable and uninsurable risk?**

Uninsurable risk is risk that no insurance company will cover. Examples of things that you cannot insure include market risks, political risks, some personal risks (such as loss of a job), and some risks of operation (e.g., strikes or inefficient machinery).

An insurable risk is one the typical insurance company will cover. Generally, insurance companies use the following guidelines when evaluating whether a risk is insurable: (1) the policyholder must have an insurable interest, (2) the amount of loss should be measurable, (3) the chance of loss should be measurable, (4) the loss should be accidental, (5) the risk should be dispersed, and (6) the insurance company can set standards for accepting risks.

Learning Goal 3. Define insurance policies, and explain the law of large numbers and the rule of indemnity.

- **What is the rule of indemnity?**

The rule of indemnity says an insured person or organization cannot collect more than the actual loss from an insurable risk.

Learning Goal 4. Discuss the various types of insurance businesses can buy to manage risk.

- **What are the two kinds of insurance companies?**

A stock insurance company is owned by stockholders, just like any other investor-owned company. A mutual insurance company is owned by its policyholders.

- **What kind of policies cover health risks?**

The United States is going through a period where government involvement with health care is being debated and tested in the courts. It is too early to tell what the final outcome will be. Health maintenance organizations (HMOs) offer a full range of health care benefits and emphasize helping members stay healthy. Like HMOs, preferred provider organizations (PPOs) contract with hospitals and physicians, but unlike an HMO, a PPO does not require its members to choose from only those physicians. Health savings accounts (HSAs) enable you to pay for your doctors from a tax-deferred savings account and buy insurance for catastrophes.

- **What is workers' compensation insurance?**

Workers' compensation insurance guarantees payment of wages, medical care, and rehabilitation services like retraining for employees injured on the job. Employers in every state are required to provide this insurance. Professional liability insurance covers people found liable for professional negligence. Product liability insurance provides coverage against liability arising out of products sold. Most businesses also have some kind of life insurance for their executives. If you conduct business from home, you should also have some form of home-office insurance to cover liabilities.

- **What are businesses doing to cover the risks of harming the environment?**

Many businesses are doing what they can to minimize damage to the environment. Such risks, however, are often beyond what businesses can manage. They are also the concern of governments around the world.

key terms

claim C-7

health maintenance organizations (HMOs) C-9

health savings accounts (HSAs) C-10

insurable interest C-5

insurable risk C-5

insurance policy C-6

law of large numbers C-7

mutual insurance company C-7

preferred provider organizations (PPOs) C-10

premium C-6

pure risk C-3

risk C-3

rule of indemnity C-7

self-insurance C-4

speculative risk C-3

stock insurance company C-7

uninsurable risk C-5

critical thinking

1. Are you self-insuring your residence and your assets?

What have you done to reduce your risk? Have you done anything to avoid risk? How much would it cost to buy insurance for your dwelling and the contents?

2. What risks do you take that insurance cannot cover?

3. What actions have you taken to avoid risk?

4. What can you do to lower your personal risk of loss from natural disasters such as floods, hurricanes, and tornadoes?

developing workplace skills

1. Write a one-page paper about ways you could reduce risk in your life (such as not driving above the speed limit). Form into small groups and share what you have written. Which of your classmates' suggestions can you adopt in your life?

2. You cannot insure yourself against speculative risk. However, you can minimize the risks you take when investing. Compare and contrast the risks of investing in stocks versus investing in bonds for the long term.

3. Much of risk management consists of reducing risky behavior. What kinds of risky behavior have you observed among fellow college students? How can college students learn about and minimize these risks? Are they doing so? Discuss the merits of having a risk manager for education facilities.

4. Form into small groups and discuss liability insurance, automobile insurance, renter's insurance, life insurance, and disability insurance. Develop a list of questions to discuss openly in class so that everyone is more informed about these issues. Do your fellow students understand all of these types of insurance?

5. Write a two-page essay on the risks of a terrorist attack, a natural disaster, climate change, or a major health disaster. Which risk do you perceive as most likely? Most dangerous? Discuss what you could do to warn others of such risks and motivate them to do something about them.

taking it to the net

Purpose

To learn about insurance for your dwelling and property, and to examine the issue of liability.

Exercise

Go to the Information Insurance Institute's website (www.iii.org). Explore the site and then answer the following questions:

1. What is homeowner's insurance?

2. What is in a standard policy?

3. What different types of homeowner's policies are there?

4. What is renter's insurance?

5. Is an umbrella policy a wise purchase? Why or why not?

Managing
PERSONAL
FINANCES

LEARNING goals

After you have read and studied this chapter, you should be able to

1 Outline the six steps for controlling your assets.

2 Explain how to build a financial base, including investing in real estate, saving money, and managing credit.

3 Explain how buying the appropriate insurance can protect your financial base.

4 Outline a strategy for retiring with enough money to last a lifetime.

No matter how many articles you may read about how the world economy is struggling, also making the news is the large number of millionaires in the United States and throughout the world. There's no reason you couldn't be one of them if you want to. One of the best ways to learn how to become a millionaire is to do what companies do: copy those who are successful. Find out what all those millionaires did to make their money.

One of those millionaires is Nathan Myhrvold. He is an exceptional person and few could match what he has done. Myhrvold made his money as chief technology officer at Microsoft. He graduated from high school at 14 and earned two masters degrees and a Ph.D in theoretical and mathematical physics. Obviously, he is not your typical college graduate. What makes him so interesting is what he has done since he left Microsoft in 1999. He has pursued his interests in skydiving, car racing, scuba diving, volcanology, and UFOlogy. On top of that, he has interests in wildlife photography, dinosaur bone hunting, and inventing (he has some 250 patents). His latest project is a cookbook called *Modernist Cuisine*. It is a five-volume, 2,400-page book, and costs $625. As you can see, the money Myhrvold earned during his working career allows him to pursue his passions in his retirement.

You may think that Myhrvold is your typical millionaire: brilliant, educated, and unbelievably talented, but you would be wrong. Thomas Stanley and William Danko have been studying millionaires for years. Their research is available in a book called *The Millionaire Next Door: The Surprising Secrets of America's Wealthy*. Stanley and Danko found that the majority of millionaires are *entrepreneurs* who own one or more small businesses. Self-employed people are about five times as likely to be millionaires as people who earn a paycheck working for others. Yet the average income of U.S. millionaires is only about $131,000 a year. So how did they get to be millionaires? They didn't win their money on a game show. They saved it! To become a millionaire by the time you are 50 or so, you have to save about 15 percent of your income every year—starting when you are in your 20s. If you start later, you have to save an even larger percentage. The secret is to put your money in a place where it will grow without your having to pay taxes on it. You'll learn how to do that in this chapter.

To save that 15 percent a year, you have to spend less than you earn. That is getting more and more difficult as the cost of living rises. Discipline in spending must begin with your first job and stay with you all your life. The millionaires Stanley studied tended to own modest homes and buy used cars. In short, becoming a millionaire has as much or more to do with thrift as with how much you earn. To become a millionaire, you need to get an education, work hard, save your money, and make purchases carefully. You don't have to be as exceptional as Nathan Myhrvold to be a millionaire. You simply need to understand personal finance and to put that knowledge to work. This chapter will get you started. It is all about getting and keeping enough money to make you a millionaire.

Sources: Thomas J. Stanley, "Millionaires," *Bottom Line Personal*, March 1, 2010; Paul J. Lim and George Mannes, "How to Reach $1 Million," *Money*, April 2011; and David Hochman, "Nathan Myhrvold," *Forbes*, March 14, 2011.

profile

Getting to Know

X *Nathan Myhrvold and Other Millionaires*

How to Become a Millionaire

MODERNIST CUISINE

NAME THAT company

One way to save money is to use your credit cards wisely. There are organizations that can help you compare credit cards to get the most out of them. What is the name of one of those organizations? (You can find the answer in this chapter.)

LEARNING goal 1

Outline the six steps for controlling your assets.

THE NEED FOR PERSONAL FINANCIAL PLANNING

The United States is largely a capitalist country. It follows, then, that the secret to success in such a country is to have capital, or money. With capital, you can take nice vacations, raise a family, invest in stocks and bonds, buy the goods and services you want, give generously to others, and retire with enough money to see you through. Money management, however, is not easy. You have to earn the money in the first place. Your chances of becoming wealthy are much greater if you choose to become an entrepreneur. That's one of the reasons why we have put so much emphasis on entrepreneurship throughout the text, including a whole chapter on the subject. Of course, there are risks in starting a business, but the best time to take risks is when you are young. Would it help you to be more motivated if you knew that there are over a thousand billionaires in the world and they average some $4.5 billion in wealth?[1]

After you earn the money, you have to learn to spend some wisely, save the rest, and insure yourself against the risks of serious accidents, illness, or death. With a little bit of luck, you may be one of the millionaires Stanley and Danko interview for their next book.[2]

You'll likely need some help. Recently high school seniors averaged a grade of 48.3 percent on questions having to do with financial concepts. Another report found that college students are also poorly educated about financial matters such as IRAs and 401(k) plans. Even people who are retired are finding that they don't know enough about such plans.[3] This bonus chapter will give you the basics so that you'll be ahead of the game. Financial management is so important to your fiscal health that you may enjoy taking an entire class on it.

Financial Planning Begins with Making Money

You already know one of the secrets to finding a good-paying job is having a good education. Throughout history, an investment in education has paid off regardless of the state of the economy or political ups and downs. Benjamin Franklin said, "If a man empties his purse into his head, no one can take it away from him. An investment in knowledge always pays the best interest."

Education has become even more important since we entered the information age. A typical full-time worker in the United States with a four-year college degree earns about $50,000—62 percent more than one with only a high school diploma. The lifetime income of families headed by individuals with a bachelor's degree will be about $1.6 million more than the incomes of families headed by those with a high school diploma. One way to start to become a millionaire, therefore, is to finish college. The government is eager for you to go to college and is willing to help you with tax breaks like tax-free education savings accounts. Make sure you investigate all the financial help available to you.

Making money is one thing; saving, investing, and spending it wisely is something else.[4] Following the advice in the next section will help you become one of those with enough to live in comfort throughout your life.

Six Steps to Controlling Your Assets

The only way to save enough money to do all the things you want to do in life is to spend less than you make.[5] Although you may find it hard to save today, it is not only possible but imperative if you want to accumulate enough to be financially secure.[6] Fewer than 1 in 10 U.S. adults has accumulated enough money by retirement age to live comfortably, and 36 percent of U.S. households don't have a retirement account. Don't become one of them. The following are six steps you can take today to get control of your finances.

Step 1: Take an Inventory of Your Financial Assets   To take inventory, you need to develop a balance sheet for yourself, like the one in Chapter 17. Remember, a balance sheet starts with the fundamental accounting equation: Assets = Liabilities + Owner's equity. List your tangible assets (such as TV, DVR player, iPod, iPad, computer, cell phone, bicycle, car, jewelry, clothes, and savings account) on one side, and your liabilities (including mortgage, credit card debt, and auto and education loans) on the other.

Assign a dollar figure to each of your assets based on its current value, not what you originally paid for it. If you have debts, subtract them from your assets to get your net worth. If you have no debts, your assets equal your net worth. If your liabilities exceed the value of your assets, you aren't on the path to financial security. You may need more financial discipline in your life.

Let's also create an income statement for you. At the top of the statement is revenue (all the money you take in from your job, investments, and so on). Subtract all your costs and expenses (rent or mortgage, credit card and other loan payments, utilities, commuting costs, and so on) to get your net income or profit. Software programs like Quicken and websites like Dinkytown.net have a variety of tools that can easily help you with these calculations.

Now is also an excellent time to think about how much money you will need to accomplish all your goals. The more clearly you can visualize your goals, the easier it is to begin saving for them.

Step 2: Keep Track of All Your Expenses   Do you occasionally find yourself running out of cash? If you experience a cash flow problem, the only way to trace where the money is going is to keep track of every cent you spend. Keeping records of your expenses can be tedious, but it's a necessary step if you want to learn discipline. Actually, it could turn out to be enjoyable because it gives you such a feeling of control.

Here's what to do: List *everything* you spend as you go through the day. That list is your journal. At the end of the week, transfer your journal entries into a record book or computerized accounting program.

Develop spending categories (accounts) to make your task easier and more informative. You can have a category called "Food" for all food you bought from the grocery or convenience store during the week. You might want a separate account for meals eaten away from home, because you can dramatically cut these costs if you make your meals at home.

Other accounts could include rent, insurance, automobile repairs and gasoline, clothing, utilities, toiletries, entertainment, and donations to charity. Most people also like to have a category called "Miscellaneous" for impulse items like latte and candy. You won't believe how much you fritter away on miscellaneous items unless you keep a *detailed* record for at least a couple of months.

Develop your accounts on the basis of what's most important to you or where you spend the most money.[7] Once you have recorded all your expenses for a few months, you'll easily see where you are spending too much and what you have to do to save more. A venti mocha frappuccino at a coffee specialty shop costs about $4.25. If you cut back from five to one a week, you'll save $17 a week, or over $850 a year. Over 10 years, that could mean an extra $12,000 for retirement, if you invest the money wisely.

Step 3: Prepare a Budget   Once you know your financial situation and your sources of revenue and expenses, you're ready to make a personal budget. Remember, budgets are financial plans. A household budget includes mortgage or rent, utilities, food, clothing, vehicles, furniture, life insurance, car insurance, medical care, and taxes.[8]

You'll need to choose how much to allow for such expenses as eating out, entertainment, cell phone use, and so on. Keep in mind that what you spend now reduces what you can save later. Spending $3.50 or more a day for cigarettes adds up to about $25 a week, $100 a month, $1,200 a year. If you can save $4 or $5 a day, you'll have almost $1,800 saved by the end of the year. Keep this up during four years of college and you'll have saved more than $7,000 by graduation. And that's before adding any interest your money will earn. Cost-saving choices you might consider to reach this goal are listed in Figure D.1.

figure D.1

POSSIBLE COST-SAVING CHOICES

The effect of the choices you make today can have a dramatic impact on your financial future. Compare the differences these few choices you can make now would mean to your future net worth. If you would make the lower-cost choices every month during your four years of college, and invest the savings in a mutual fund earning 6 percent compounded annually, you would double your money every 12 years.

FIRST CHOICE COST PER MONTH	ALTERNATE CHOICE COST PER MONTH	SAVINGS PER MONTH
Starbucks caffe latte $3.00 for 20 days = $60.00	Quick Trip's Cappuccino $.60 for 20 days = $12.00	$48.00
Fast-food lunch of burger, fries, and soft drink $4.00 for 20 days = $80.00	Lunch brought from home $2 for 20 days = $40.00	40.00
Evian bottled water $1.50 for 20 days = $30.00	Generic bottled water $.50 for 20 days = $10.00	20.00
CD = $15.00	Listen to your old CDs = $0.00	15.00
Banana Republic T-shirt = $34.00	Old Navy T-shirt = $10.00	24.00
	Total savings per month	$147.00
		× 48 months
	Total savings through 4 years of college	$7,056.00

Running a household is similar to running a small business. It takes the same careful record keeping, the same budget processes and forecasting, and the same control procedures. Sometimes it also creates the same need to borrow funds or rely on a credit card and become familiar with interest rates. The time you spend practicing budgeting techniques will benefit you throughout your life. You might start by going online to Mint.com. It will help you with your budgeting needs.

Step 4: Pay Off Your Debts The first thing to do with the money remaining after you pay your monthly bills is to pay off your debts, starting with those carrying the highest interest rates. Credit card debt may be costing you 18 percent or more a year. A survey of 100 campuses found 26 percent of college students said they had been charged a fee for a late payment. It's better to pay off a debt that costs 18 percent than put the money in a bank account that earns, say, 2 percent or less. Check credit card statements and other mailings carefully to make certain the charges are accurate.

Step 5: Start a Savings Plan It's important to save some money each month in a separate account for large purchases you're likely to make (such as a car or house). Then, when it comes time to make that purchase, you'll have the needed cash. Save at least enough for a significant down payment so that you can reduce the finance charges you'll pay to borrow the rest.

 The best way to save money is to *pay yourself first*. When you get your paycheck, first take out money for savings and then plan what to do with the rest. You can arrange with your bank or mutual fund to deduct a certain amount for savings every month. You'll be pleasantly surprised when the money starts accumulating and earning interest over time. With some discipline, you can eventually reach your goal of becoming a millionaire. It's not as difficult as you may think. Figure D.2 shows how $5,000 grows over various periods at different rates of return. If you start saving at age 40, you'll have 25 years in by the time you reach 65.

Step 6: Borrow Only to Buy Assets That Increase in Value or Generate Income Don't borrow money for ordinary expenses; you'll only get into more debt that way. If you have budgeted for emergencies, such as car repairs and health care costs, you should be able to stay financially secure. Most financial experts advise saving about six months of earnings for contingencies. Keep this money in highly liquid accounts, such as a bank account or money market fund.

> *It might take a little time to balance your income with your expenses to make sure you have money left to save and invest, but the effort is worth it. People who don't take this step can reach retirement without enough funds to live on. How could you cut back your expenses?*

	Annual Rate of Return			
TIME	**2%**	**5%**	**8%**	**11%**
5 years	$5,520	$ 6,381	$ 7,347	$ 8,425
10 years	6,095	8,144	10,795	14,197
15 years	6,729	10,395	15,861	23,923
20 years	7,430	13,266	23,305	40,312
25 years	8,203	16,932	34,242	67,927

figure D.2

HOW MONEY GROWS
This chart illustrates how $5,000 would grow at various rates of return. Recent savings account interest rates were very low (less than 2 percent), but in earlier years they've been over 5 percent.

Only the most unexpected of expenses should cause you to borrow. It is hard to wait until you have enough money to buy what you want, but learning to wait is a critical part of self-discipline. Of course, you can always try to produce more income by working overtime or by working on the side for extra revenue.

If you follow these six steps, not only will you have money for investment but you'll have developed most of the financial techniques needed to become financially secure. If you find it hard to live within a budget at first, remember the payoff is well worth the effort.

LEARNING goal 2

Explain how to build a financial base, including investing in real estate, saving money, and managing credit.

BUILDING YOUR FINANCIAL BASE

The path to success in a capitalist system is to have capital to invest, yet many students today graduate with debt.[9] As you've read, accumulating capital takes discipline and careful planning. With the money you save, however, you can become an entrepreneur, one of the fastest ways to wealth. As you read in this chapter's opening Profile, that often means living frugally.

Living frugally is extremely difficult for the average person. Most people are eager to spend their money on a new car, furniture, electronics, clothes, entertainment, and the like. They look for a fancy apartment with all the amenities. A capital-generating strategy may require forgoing most (though not all) of these purchases to accumulate investment money. It might mean living like a frugal college student, in a relatively inexpensive apartment furnished in hand-me-downs from parents, friends, Craigslist, and resale shops.

For five or six years, you can manage with the old sound system, a used car, and a few nice clothes. The strategy is sacrifice, not luxury. It's important not to feel burdened by this plan; instead, feel happy knowing your financial future will be more secure. That's the way the majority of millionaires got their money. If living frugally seems too restrictive for you, you can still save at least a little. It's better to save a smaller amount than not to save at all.

It's wise to plan your financial future with the same excitement and dedication you bring to other aspects of your life. If you get married, for example, it is important to discuss financial issues with your spouse. Conflicts over money are a major cause of divorce, so agreeing on a financial strategy before marriage is very important.[10]

A great strategy for couples is to try to live on one income and to save the other. The longer you wait to marry, the more likely that one of you can be earning enough to do that—as a college graduate. If the second spouse makes $25,000 a year after taxes, saving that income for five years quickly adds up to $125,000 (plus interest).

What do you do with the money you accumulate? Your first investment might be a low-priced home.[11] Why? The purpose of this investment is to lock in payments for your shelter at a fixed amount. Through the years, homeownership has been a wise investment, unlike renting.[12] However, many young people take huge risks by buying too much home for their income, something the millionaires in this chapter's opening Profile simply don't do. Furthermore, young people sometimes take out interest-only or other loans that are very risky, as recent headlines have shown. The rule of thumb "Don't buy a home that costs more than two and a half times your annual income" still stands.

Buy for the long term and stay within your means. What has happened to housing prices in your area over the last couple of years? Lower prices mean opportunity if the market gains strength.[13]

Real Estate: Historically, a Relatively Secure Investment

The real estate bust beginning in 2008 was a relatively uncommon occurrence. House prices had risen dramatically, causing a bubble that burst. Prices have fallen sharply, but history shows that home prices are likely to rise again and will continue to provide several investment benefits. First, a home is the one investment that you can live in. Second, once you buy a home, your mortgage payments are relatively fixed (though taxes and utilities may go up). As your income rises, mortgage payments get easier to make, but renters often find that rents go up at least as fast as income. On the other hand, the recent fall in home prices has made it more important than ever for you to check whether it is better to own or rent. How deeply particular cities were affected by the falling housing prices varies greatly from region to region.[14]

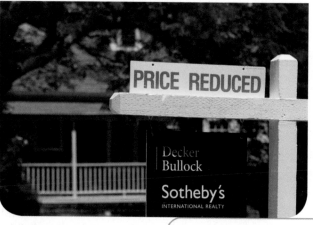

Buying a home has usually been a very good and safe investment. But sometimes housing prices can rise fast, as they did between 2000 and 2007, and then fall, as they've done since 2008. What has happened to housing prices in your area over the last few years?

Paying for a home has historically been a good way of forcing yourself to save. You must make the payments every month. Those payments are an investment that proves very rewarding over time for most people. A home is also a good asset to use when applying for a business loan.

Some couples have used the seed money accumulated from saving one income (in the strategy outlined above) to buy two attached homes so that they can live in one part and rent out the other. The rent they earn covers a good part of the payments for both homes, so the couple can live comfortably, yet inexpensively, while their investment in a home appreciates. In this way they accumulate capital, and as they grow older, they pull far ahead of their peers in terms of financial security. As capital accumulates and values rise, they can sell and buy an even larger apartment building or a single-family home. Many have made fortunes in real estate in just this way.

Once you understand the benefits of homeownership versus renting, you can decide whether those same principles apply to owning the premises where you set up your own business—or owning your own equipment, vehicles, and the like. Figure D.3 will give you some idea of how expensive a house you can afford, given your income. You can find current mortgage interest rates and mortgage calculators at Interest.com.

figure D.3

HOW MUCH HOUSE CAN YOU AFFORD?
Monthly mortgage payments—including interest, principal, real estate taxes, and insurance—generally shouldn't amount to more than 28 percent of monthly income. Here's how much people in various income categories can afford to pay for a home if they use a 30-year mortgage and make a 10 percent down payment. How do you think the changes in mortgage interest rates affect the average price of homes?

		Interest Rates			
INCOME	**MONTHLY PAYMENT**	**5%**	**6%**	**7%**	**15%**
$ 30,000	$ 700	$106,263	$ 98,303	$ 91,252	$56,870
50,000	1,167	180,291	167,081	155,376	98,606
80,000	1,867	287,213	266,056	247,308	155,916
100,000	2,333	361,240	334,832	311,433	198,013

Source: Federal Housing Finance Board.

Tax Deductions and Homeownership

Buying a home is likely to be the largest and perhaps the most important investment you'll make. It's nice to know that the federal government is willing to help you with it. Here's how: Interest on your home mortgage payments is tax-deductible. So are your real estate taxes. Since virtually all your mortgage payments during the first few years are applied to the interest on your loan, almost all the early payments are tax-deductible—a tremendous benefit. If your payments are $1,000 a month and your income is in a 25 percent tax bracket, during the early years of your mortgage the government will, in effect, give you credit for about $250 of your payment, lowering your real cost. This makes homeownership much more competitive with renting than it may appear.

There are three keys to getting the optimal return on a home or any real estate investment: location, location, and location. A home in the best part of town, near schools, shopping, and work, is usually a sound financial investment. Less expensive homes may appreciate in value more slowly than homes in the city or town center. It's usually better, from a financial viewpoint, to buy a smaller home in a great location than a large home in a not-so-great setting.

Where to Put Your Savings

What are some other good places to save your money? For a young person, one of the worst places to keep long-term investments is a bank or savings and loan. It is important to have savings equivalent to about six months of living expenses in the bank for emergencies, but the bank is not the best place to invest. Internet banks pay higher interest than your local bank, but even their rates are relatively low.

One of the best places to invest over time has been the stock market. The stock market does tend to go up and down, but over a longer period of time it has proved to be one of the best investments. About half of U.S. households own stock and mutual funds. Most financial experts believe the stock market will grow more slowly in the future than it has over the last 50 years, but the U.S. economy has always managed to rise up after a crisis like the stock market fall of recent years.

The future always looks gloomy during a financial crisis, but that doesn't mean you shouldn't take risks. Remember, the greater the risk, usually the greater the return. When stock prices are low, that's the time to *buy*. When stocks collapse, it's an opportunity to get into the stock market, not avoid it. The average investor buys when the market is high and sells when it's low. Clearly, that's not a good idea. It takes courage to buy when everyone else is selling. In the long run, however, this **contrarian approach** to investing is the way the rich get richer.

contrarian approach
Buying stock when everyone else is selling or vice versa.

Chapter 19 gave you a foundation for starting an investment program. That chapter also talked about bonds, but bonds have traditionally lagged behind stocks as a long-term investment.

Learning to Manage Credit

Credit cards are an important element in your personal financial system, even if you rarely use them.[15] First, you may have to own a credit card to buy certain goods or even rent a car, because some businesses require one for identification and to ensure payment. Second, you can use a credit card to keep track of purchases. A gasoline credit card gives you records of purchases over time for your income tax returns (if you drive for work) and financial planning purposes. Third, a credit card is more convenient than cash or checks. You can carry less cash and easily cancel a stolen card to protect your account. Not all credit cards are alike, however. You can decide which card is best for you by comparing them at CardRatings.com or CreditCards.com.[16]

College credit-card debt is on the rise. Half of college students have four or more cards and only 17 percent report regularly paying off their balance.[17] If you do use a credit card, pay the balance in full during the period when no interest is charged.[18] Finance charges on credit card purchases usually amount to 12 to 26 percent annually. Some credit card companies will reward you for paying on time.[19] If you finance a TV, home appliances, or other purchases with a credit card, you may end up spending much more than if you pay with cash. Not having to pay 18 percent or more in interest is as good as earning 18 percent tax-free. You may want to choose a card that pays you back in cash or offers credits toward the purchase of a car or frequent-flier miles. The value of these "givebacks" can be as high as 5 percent. Some cards have no annual fees; others have lower interest rates.

Credit card companies like First USA often encourage young people to apply for credit cards by giving away gifts for signing up. Why are such companies so willing to give you a credit card?

The danger of a credit card is the flip side of its convenience. It's too easy to buy things you wouldn't buy if you had to pay cash, or to pile up debts you can't repay. If you aren't the type who can stick to a financial plan or household budget, *it may be better not to have a credit card at all.*[20] Imagine a customer who has a $10,000 balance on his or her credit card with a 16 percent interest rate and pays the minimum 4 percent monthly payment. How long will it take to pay off the debt, and what would the cost for interest be? The answers: 14 years and nearly $5,000—and that's without using the card again to purchase so much as a candy bar. Prior to 2006, the minimum payment was 2 percent. The lower minimum payment may have been enticing for the short term, but over time that same $10,000 balance would have taken over 30 years to repay and cost over $18,000 in interest if only the 2 percent minimum was paid.

Some people would be better off with a *debit* card only. Debit cards can be set up so that you cannot spend more than you have in the bank, a great benefit for those who are not as careful with their spending as they should be.[21] Furthermore, there are no interest payments or annual fees.[22]

Of the debtors seeking help at the National Consumer Counseling Service, more than half were between 18 and 32. The Credit Card Act of 2009 created new consumer credit card protections and went into effect February 2010. The new law allows card issuers to increase interest rates for only a limited number of reasons and restricts increasing rates at all during the first year of a new card account. People must be at least 21 years old or get an adult to co-sign with them if they want new credit cards on their own.[23] The Consumer Financial Protection Bureau regulates financial products and services, including mortgages, credit cards, student loans and debt collection.[24] You would be wise to explore what is available to you.

progress assessment

- What are the six steps you can take to control your finances?
- What steps should a person follow to build capital?
- Why is real estate a good investment?

LEARNING goal **3**

Explain how buying the appropriate insurance can protect your financial base.

PROTECTING YOUR FINANCIAL BASE: BUYING INSURANCE

One of the last things young people think about is the idea that they may become sick, get injured, or die. It is not a pleasant thought, but the unexpected does happen every day. To protect your loved ones from the loss of your income, you should buy life insurance. Nearly a third of U.S. households have no life insurance coverage, the highest percentage in more than four decades.[25] This is one sign of how the financial pressures of today have affected families.

The simplest and least expensive form of life insurance is **term insurance.** It is pure insurance protection for a given number of years that typically costs less the younger you buy it (see Figure D.4). Every few years, you might have to renew the policy, and the premium can then rise. Check prices through a service like InsWeb.com or use one of Quicken's personal finance software packages.

How much insurance do you need? *Newsweek* posed this question: We just had our first baby; how much life insurance should we have? Answer: Seven times your family income plus $100,000 for college. Apportion your coverage so that a spouse earning 60 percent of the income carries 60 percent of the insurance.

Multiyear level-premium insurance guarantees that you'll pay the same premium for the life of the policy. Recently, 40 percent of new term policies guaranteed a set rate for 20 years or more. Some companies allow you to switch your term policy for a more expensive whole or universal life policy.

Whole life insurance combines pure insurance and savings, so you are buying both insurance and a savings plan. This may be a good idea for those people who have trouble saving money. A universal life policy lets you choose how much of your payment should go to insurance and how much to investments. The investments in such plans traditionally are very conservative but pay a steady interest rate.[26]

term insurance
Pure insurance protection for a given number of years.

whole life insurance
Life insurance that combines pure insurance and savings.

figure D.4

WHY BUY TERM INSURANCE?

INSURANCE NEEDS IN EARLY YEARS ARE HIGH	INSURANCE NEEDS DECLINE AS YOU GROW OLDER
1. Children are young and need money for education.	1. Children are grown.
2. Mortgage is high relative to income.	2. Mortgage is low or completely paid off.
3. Often there are auto payments and other bills to pay.	3. Debts are paid off.
4. Loss of income would be disastrous.	4. Insurance needs are few.
	5. Retirement income is needed.

Variable life insurance is a form of whole life insurance that invests the cash value of the policy in stocks or other high-yielding securities. Death benefits may thus vary, reflecting the performance of the investments.

Life insurance companies recognized people's desire to earn higher returns on their insurance (and to protect themselves against running out of money before they die) and began selling annuities. An **annuity** is a contract to make regular payments to a person for life or for a fixed period. With an annuity, you are guaranteed to have an income until you die.

There are two kinds of annuities: fixed and variable. *Fixed annuities* are investments that pay the policyholder a specified interest rate. They are not as popular as *variable annuities*, which provide investment choices identical to mutual funds. Such annuities are becoming more popular than term or whole life insurance. But buyers must be careful in selecting an insurance company and choosing the investments made with their money.

Consult a financial adviser who is not an insurance agent and who can help you make the wisest decision about insurance. You can also check out the insurance company through a rating service such as A. M. Best (www.ambest.com) or Moody's Investors Service (www.moodys.com).

Health Insurance

You may already have health insurance coverage through your employer. If not, you can buy it from a health insurance provider like Blue Cross/Blue Shield, a health maintenance organization (HMO), or a preferred provider organization (PPO). President Obama has promised to expand health insurance coverage, but those who already have it may not be affected. Clearly, it will be important to keep alert to changes in health insurance over the next few years.

For quick online help in picking a health insurance provider, eHealthInsurance.com can help you get affordable health insurance quotes and compare individual health insurance plans side by side so that you can find the best medical insurance plans for your needs and budget. You may be able to buy health insurance for less through a professional organization. One of the more popular alternatives to traditional health insurance is a health savings account (HSA), discussed in Bonus Chapter C. Be sure to do a careful search to find the best program for you and your family.

Your chances of becoming disabled at an early age are much higher than your chances of dying in an accident. It's dangerous financially not to have any health insurance. Hospital costs are simply too high to risk financial ruin by going uninsured. As mentioned in Bonus Chapter C, it's often a good idea to supplement health insurance policies with **disability insurance** that pays part of the cost of a long-term sickness or an accident. Call an insurance agent or check the Internet for possible costs of such insurance. The cost is relatively low to protect yourself from losing your income for an extended period.

Homeowner's or Renter's Insurance

You may be surprised how much it would cost to replace all the things you own. As you begin to accumulate possessions, you may want to have apartment or homeowner's insurance that covers their loss. Specify that you want *guaranteed replacement cost*. That means the insurance company will give you whatever it costs to buy all those things *new*. It costs a little more than a policy without guaranteed replacement, but you will get a lot more if you have a loss.

The other option is insurance that covers the *depreciated cost* of the items. A sofa you bought five years ago for $600 may be worth only $150 now. That current value is what your insurance would pay you, not the $700 or more to

variable life insurance
Whole life insurance that invests the cash value of the policy in stocks or other high-yielding securities.

annuity
A contract to make regular payments to a person for life or for a fixed period.

disability insurance
Insurance that pays part of the cost of a long-term sickness or an accident.

buy a brand-new sofa. If your computer is stolen, you might get only a couple hundred dollars rather than its replacement cost.

Most policies don't cover expensive items like engagement and wedding rings. You can buy a *rider* to your policy to cover them at a reasonable cost.

Other Insurance

Most states require drivers to have automobile insurance; if your state doesn't, it's a good idea to buy it anyway. Be sure to insure against losses from uninsured motorists. Consider accepting a large deductible to keep the premiums low, and pay for small damages yourself.

You'll also need liability insurance to protect yourself against being sued by someone you accidentally injure. Often you can get a discount by buying all your insurance (life, health, homeowner's, automobile) with one company. This is called an **umbrella policy.** Look for other discounts such as for safe driving, good grades, and more.

umbrella policy
A broadly based insurance policy that saves you money because you buy all your insurance from one company.

LEARNING goal 4

Outline a strategy for retiring with enough money to last a lifetime.

PLANNING YOUR RETIREMENT

It may seem a bit early to be planning your retirement; however, not doing so would be a big mistake.[27] Successful financial planning means long-range planning, and retirement is a critical phase of life.[28] What you do now could make a world of difference in your quality of life after age 65, or whenever you retire.

One purpose of planning your personal finances is to have enough money for retirement. If you plan to relax and travel when you retire, you need to begin saving now. What are your retirement goals, and what resources will you need to accomplish them?

Social Security

Social Security is the Old-Age, Survivors, and Disability Insurance Program established by the Social Security Act of 1935. It consists not of a fund of money but of a continuous flow of contributions in and payments out. The Social Security money you'll begin to receive when you retire will come directly from the Social Security taxes being paid by workers at that time. However, the number of people retiring and living longer is increasing dramatically, while the number paying into Social Security is declining.[29] Maintaining Social Security may thus require reducing benefits, encouraging people to retire later, limiting cost-of-living adjustments (COLAs) made to benefits over time, and increasing Social Security taxes.

Social Security will likely not provide you with ample funds for retirement.[30] Plan now to save your own funds for your nonworking years.[31] The government has established incentives to encourage you. Here are some specifics.

Individual Retirement Accounts (IRAs)

Traditionally, an **individual retirement account (IRA)** has been a tax-deferred investment plan that enables you (and your spouse, if you are married) to save part of your income for retirement. A traditional IRA allows people who qualify to deduct from their reported income the money they put into an account. **Tax-deferred contributions** are those for which you pay no current taxes, but the earnings gained in the IRA are taxed as income when they are withdrawn from your IRA after retirement.

Let's see why a traditional IRA is a good deal for an investor. The tremendous benefit is the fact that the invested money is not taxed. That means faster and higher returns for you. Say you put $5,000 into an IRA each year. (The maximum IRA contribution was $5,000 in 2011 and can increase each year in line with inflation. If you're 50 or older, you can make an additional $1,000 "catch-up" contribution.) Normally you'd pay taxes on that $5,000 when you receive it as income. But because you put it into an IRA, you won't. If you're in the 25 percent tax bracket, that means you'll save $1,250 in taxes! Put another way, the $5,000 you save costs you only $3,750—a huge bargain.

The earlier you start saving, the better—because your money has a chance to double and double again. If you save $5,000 a year for 35 years in an IRA and earn 10 percent a year, you'll accumulate savings of more than $1.5 million. If you start when you're just out of school, you'll be a millionaire by the time you're 55. All you have to do is save $5,000 a year and earn 10 percent. You may be wise to use a Roth IRA instead (see following).

If you increase your contribution to the maximum allowable each time it is raised, you can reach your million-dollar goal even earlier. The actual rate of return depends on the type of investments you choose. No one can predict future rates of return with certainty, and investments with higher rates of return also have higher risk. The actual rate of return on investments can vary widely over time (from the highest gain of 91 percent in 1983 to the lowest loss of –39 percent in 1974 and 2008), but the average annual gain for the S&P 500 between 1970 and 2008 was 9.7 percent. Some analysts expect it to be lower in the coming years, so you may need to save more to reach the same goals.

The earlier you start saving, the better. Consider this: If you were to start contributing $5,000 to an IRA earning 10 percent when you're 22 years old and do so for only five years, you'd have over $33,000 by the time you're 27. Even if you *never added another penny* to the IRA, by the time you're 65 you'd have almost $1.1 million. If you waited until you were 30 to start saving, you would

Social Security
The term used to describe the Old-Age, Survivors, and Disability Insurance Program established by the Social Security Act of 1935.

individual retirement account (IRA)
A tax-deferred investment plan that enables you (and your spouse, if you are married) to save part of your income for retirement; a traditional IRA allows people who qualify to deduct from their reported income the money they put into an account.

tax-deferred contributions
Retirement account deposits for which you pay no current taxes, but the earnings gained are taxed as regular income when they are withdrawn at retirement.

need to save $5,000 every year for 35 years to have the same nest egg. And what would you have if you started saving at 22 *and* continued nonstop every year until 65? More than $3 million! Can you see why investment advisers often say that an IRA is the best way to invest in your retirement?

A second kind of IRA is the **Roth IRA.** You don't get up-front deductions from your taxes as with a traditional IRA, but earnings grow tax-free and are tax-free when withdrawn. *This is usually the best deal for college-age students.* You can transfer money from a traditional IRA into a Roth IRA. You will have to pay taxes first, but the long-term benefits often make this exchange worthwhile if you believe your tax rate will be higher when you retire than it is now.

Both types of IRA have advantages and disadvantages, so ask a financial adviser which is best for you. You may decide to have both.

You can't take money from either type of IRA until you are 59½ years old without paying a 10 percent penalty. That's a benefit for you, because it can keep you from tapping into your IRA in an emergency or when you're tempted to make a large impulse purchase. But the money is there if a real need or emergency arises. The government now allows you to take out some funds to invest in an education or a first home. But check the rules; they change over time.

Your local bank, savings and loan, and credit union all have different types of IRAs. Insurance companies offer them too. If you're looking for a higher return (and more risk), you can put your IRA funds into U.S. and international stocks, bonds, mutual funds, exchange-traded funds, or precious metals. You can switch from fund to fund or from investment to investment. You can even open several different IRAs as long as the total doesn't exceed the government's limit. Consider contributing to an IRA through payroll deductions to ensure that you invest the money before you're tempted to spend it.

If the value of your retirement account plunges, you may have to defer your dream of an early retirement. If you have already started to save for your retirement, is your portfolio well diversified?

Roth IRA
An IRA where you don't get upfront deductions on your taxes as you would with a traditional IRA, but the earnings grow tax-free and are also tax-free when they are withdrawn.

Simple IRAs

Companies with 100 or fewer workers can provide them with a simple IRA. Employees can contribute a larger part of their income annually than with a regular IRA (up to $11,500 versus $5,000), and the company matches their contribution. This plan enables people to save much more money over time and can help small companies compete for available workers.

401(k) Plans

401(k) plan
A savings plan that allows you to deposit pretax dollars and whose earnings compound tax free until withdrawal, when the money is taxed at ordinary income tax rates.

A **401(k) plan** is an employer-sponsored savings plan that allows you to deposit a set amount of pretax dollars and collect compounded earnings tax-free until withdrawal, when the money is taxed at ordinary income tax rates. Such plans account for about half the private pension savings in the United States; 401(k)s at more than 220,000 companies now cover some 55 million workers. These or similar plans are the only pension many people have, but only about 70 percent of eligible employees make any contributions, and many companies are discontinuing their benefits.[32]

The plans have three benefits: (1) your contributions reduce your present taxable income, (2) tax is deferred on the earnings, and (3) 61 percent of employers will match your contributions, sometimes 50 cents on a dollar.[33] No investment will give you a better deal than an instant 50 percent return on your money. Not all companies have equally good programs, so be sure to check out what is available to you.[34]

You should deposit at least as much as your employer matches, often up to 15 percent of your salary.[35] You can usually select how the money in a 401(k) plan is invested: stocks, bonds, and in some cases real estate. Be careful not to invest all your money in the company where you work. It's always best to diversify your funds among different companies and among stocks, bonds, and real estate investment trusts.

Like the simple IRA, there is a simple 401(k) plan for those firms that employ 100 or fewer employees. Employees again are allowed to invest an amount (maximum of $16,500 in 2011) that is matched by the employer. This is a rather new program, but it should also prove popular among small businesses in attracting new workers.

Keogh Plans

Millions of small-business owners don't have the benefit of a corporate retirement system. Such people can contribute to an IRA, but the amount they can invest is limited. The alternative for all those doctors, lawyers, real estate agents, artists, writers, and other self-employed people is to establish their own Keogh plan. It's like an IRA for entrepreneurs. You can also look into simplified employee pension (SEP) plans, the best types of IRAs for sole proprietors.

The advantage of Keogh plans is that participants can invest up to $40,000 per year. Like traditional IRAs, Keogh funds aren't taxed until they are withdrawn, nor are the returns the funds earn. Thus, a person in the 25 percent tax bracket who invests $10,000 yearly in a Keogh saves $2,500 in taxes. That means, in essence, that the government is financing 25 percent of his or her retirement fund. As with an IRA, this is an excellent deal.

As with an IRA, there's a 10 percent penalty for early withdrawal. Also like an IRA, funds may be withdrawn in a lump sum or spread out over the years. However, the key decision is the one you make now—to begin early to put funds into an IRA, a Keogh plan, or both so that the "magic" of compounding can turn that money into a sizable retirement fund.

Financial Planners

If the idea of developing a comprehensive financial plan for yourself or your business seems overwhelming, relax; help is available from financial planners.[36] Be careful, though—anybody can claim to be a financial planner today. It's often best to find a certified financial planner (CFP), that is, a professional who has completed a curriculum on 106 financial topics and a 10-hour examination. In the United States today there are about 36,000 CFPs. Unfortunately, many so-called financial planners are simply insurance salespeople.

Your financial assets can protect your children and even your grandchildren far into the future, if you have taken the right steps through estate planning. What can you do now in order to make sure your assets are divided the way you would like them to be when you're gone?

In the past few years, there has been an explosion in the number of companies offering other businesses financial services, sometimes called one-stop financial centers or financial supermarkets because they provide a variety of financial services, ranging from banking service to mutual funds, insurance, tax assistance, stocks, bonds, and real estate. It pays to shop around for financial advice. Find someone who understands your business and is willing to spend some time with you.

Financial planning covers all aspects of investing, from life and health insurance all the way to retirement and death. Financial planners can advise you on the proper mix of IRAs, stocks, bonds, real estate, and so on.

Estate Planning

Your retirement may be far away, but it is never too early to begin thinking about estate planning, or making financial arrangements for those who will inherit from you. You may even help your parents or others to do such planning. An important first step is to select a guardian for your minor children. That person should have a genuine concern for your children as well as a parental style and moral beliefs you endorse.

Also ensure that you leave sufficient resources to rear your children, not only for living expenses but also for medical bills, college, and other major expenses. Often life insurance is a good way to ensure such a fund. Be sure to discuss all these issues with the guardian, and choose a contingent guardian in case the first choice is unable to perform the needed functions.

A second step is to prepare a **will**, a document that names the guardian for your children, states how you want your assets distributed, and names the executor for your estate. An **executor** assembles and values your estate, files income and other taxes, and distributes assets.

A third step is to prepare a durable power of attorney. This document gives an individual you name the power to take over your finances if you become incapacitated. A *durable power of attorney for health care* delegates power to a person you name to make health care decisions for you if you are unable to make such decisions yourself.

Other steps to follow are beyond the scope of this text. You may need to contact a financial planner/attorney to help you do the paperwork and planning to preserve and protect your investments for your children and spouse and others.[37] But it all begins with a strong financial base.

will
A document that names the guardian for your children, states how you want your assets distributed, and names the executor for your estate.

executor
A person who assembles and values your estate, files income and other taxes, and distributes assets.

progress assessment

- What are three advantages of using a credit card?
- What kind of life insurance is recommended for most people?
- What are the advantages of investing through an IRA? A Keogh account? A 401(k) account?
- What are the main steps in estate planning?

summary

Learning Goal 1. Outline the six steps for controlling your assets.
- **What are the six steps to managing personal assets?**
(1) Take an inventory of your financial assets by developing a balance sheet for yourself with the fundamental accounting equation: Assets = Liabilities + Owners' equity; (2) keep track of all your expenses; (3) prepare a budget; (4) pay off your debts; (5) start a savings plan (the best way is to pay yourself first); and (6) if you must borrow, borrow only for assets that can increase in value or generate income.

Learning Goal 2. Explain how to build a financial base, including investing in real estate, saving money, and managing credit.

- **How can I accumulate funds?**

First, find a job. Try to live as frugally as possible. Invest your savings to generate even more capital. One such investment is a duplex home where the renter helps the owner pay the mortgage.

- **Why is real estate such a good investment?**

First, a home is the one investment you can live in. Second, once you buy a home, the payments are relatively fixed (though taxes and utilities may go up). As your income rises, the house payments get easier to make, while rents tend to go up at least as fast as income.

- **How does the government help you buy real estate?**

The government allows you to deduct interest payments on the mortgage, which lets you buy more home for the money.

- **Where is the best place to keep savings?**

It is best, in the long run, to invest in stocks. Although they go up and down in value, in the long run stocks earn more than most other investments. Diversify among mutual funds and other investments.

- **What is a good way to handle credit cards?**

Pay the balance in full during the period when no interest is charged. Not having to pay 16 percent interest is as good as earning 16 percent tax-free. Often a debit card is better than a credit card because it limits your spending to the amount you have in the bank.

Learning Goal 3. Explain how buying the appropriate insurance can protect your financial base.

- **What is the role of insurance in protecting capital?**

Insurance protects you from loss. If you were to die, your heirs would lose the income you would have earned. You can buy life insurance to make up for some or all of that loss.

- **Why is term insurance preferred?**

Term insurance is pure insurance protection for a given number of years. You can buy much more term insurance than whole life insurance for the same amount of money.

- **Do I need other insurance?**

It is important to have health insurance to protect against large medical bills. You also need car insurance (get a high deductible) and liability insurance in case you injure someone. You should also have homeowner's or renter's insurance. Often an umbrella policy will provide all your insurance protection for a lower cost.

Learning Goal 4. Outline a strategy for retiring with enough money to last a lifetime.

- **Can I rely on Social Security to cover my retirement expenses?**

Social Security depends on payments from current workers to cover the needs of retired people. Fewer workers are paying into the system, so you cannot rely on it to cover all your retirement expenses.

- **What are the basics of saving for retirement?**

Supplement Social Security with savings plans of your own. Everyone should have an IRA or some other retirement account. A Roth IRA is especially good for young people because your money grows tax-free and is tax-free when you withdraw it. For entrepreneurs, a Keogh plan or simplified employee pension (SEP) plan is wise. If you work for someone else, check out the 401(k) plan. Find a financial adviser who can recommend the best savings plan and help you make other investments.

- **What are the basics of estate planning?**
  You need to choose a guardian for your children, prepare a will, and assign an executor for your estate. Sign a durable power of attorney to enable someone else to handle your finances if you are not capable. The same applies to a health durable power of attorney. Estate planning is complex and often calls for the aid of a financial planner/attorney, but the money is well spent to protect your assets.

key terms

401(k) plan D-14
annuity D-11
contrarian approach D-8
disability insurance D-11
executor D-16

individual retirement account (IRA) D-13
Roth IRA D-14
Social Security D-13
tax-deferred contributions D-13

term insurance D-10
umbrella policy D-12
variable life insurance D-11
whole life insurance D-10
will D-16

critical thinking

1. Have you given any thought to becoming an entrepreneur? Do the statistics in this bonus chapter about millionaires give you some courage to pursue such a venture?

2. Housing prices in many parts of the United States are falling. What is the situation where you live? Would you encourage a college graduate in your area to buy a home or rent?

3. What kinds of questions must a person ask before considering the purchase of a home?

4. What insurance coverage do you have? What type of insurance do you need to buy next?

developing workplace skills

1. Check your local paper or use an online realtor to gather information regarding the cost to rent a two-bedroom apartment and to buy a two-bedroom condominium in your area. Go to Dinkytown.net and use the site's "rent-versus-buy calculator" to compare these costs. Discuss your findings in small groups.

2. Talk with someone you know who has invested in a family home. What appreciation have they gained on the purchase price? (Or, conversely, how has the value depreciated?) What other benefits has the home brought? Draw up a list of the benefits and drawbacks of owning a home and real estate in general as an investment. Be prepared to give a one-minute presentation on what you learned.

3. Find out the cost of major medical/hospital treatments in your area. Ask some older friends or acquaintances about medical insurance and whether

they have ever gone without any. What types of insurance do they recommend? Discuss your results with the class.

4. The best time to start saving for the future is *now*. To prove this point to yourself, calculate how much you will have at age 65 if you begin saving $100 a month now, and $100 a month 10 years from now. Type "compound interest calculator" in a search engine and find an appropriate site to help you with the calculations.

5. Check out the benefits and drawbacks of both traditional and Roth IRAs. Be prepared to make a two-minute presentation about each and to discuss your findings in class.

taking it to the net

Purpose

To use online resources to make smart personal finance decisions.

Exercise

Use the calculators at Dinkytown.net to answer the following questions:

1. You need $5,000 for a trip to Europe in two years. How much would you have to deposit monthly in a savings account paying 1 percent in order to meet your goal?

2. Investing $1,000 at 6 percent for five years, what is the difference in purchasing power of your savings if inflation increases by 2 percent annually during that time? By 4 percent?

3. Starting today, how much would you need to save each month in order to become a millionaire before you retire?

4. You need a new car. What car can you afford if you have $1,500 for a down payment, can make monthly payments of $300, and get $1,000 for trading in your old clunker?

5. How much house can you afford if you earn $36,000 a year and have $10,000 savings for a down payment, a $6,000 car loan balance, and no credit card debts?

chapter notes

PROLOGUE

1. U.S. Department of Education Institute for Education Science, http://nces.ed.gov, accessed June 2011.
2. U.S. Census Bureau, www.census.gov, accessed June 2011.
3. Anne Kates Smith, "New Jobs, New Skills," *Kiplinger's Personal Finance,* November 2010.
4. Robert Rodriguez, "How Rude! Poor Etiquette on the Rise, Workplace Experts Say," *Sun-Journal* (Lewiston, ME), January 13, 2008.
5. Robert Half International, "Tech Etiquette," www.careerbuilder.com, accessed June 2011.
6. Rachel Farrell, "Social Media Can Kill Your Career—But Not The Way You Think," www.careerbuilder.com, accessed June 2011.

CHAPTER 1

1. Emily Glazer, "Fund Firms Cautiously Tweet Their Way into a New World," *The Wall Street Journal,* February 7, 2011.
2. Lewis D'Vorkin, "The Wealth List In a New Era," *Forbes,* March 28, 2011.
3. "The Numbers," *Barron's,* June 14, 2010.
4. John B. Taylor, "A Two-Track Plan to Restore Growth," *The Wall Street Journal,* January 28, 2011.
5. A.G. Lafley, "I Think of My Failures as a Gift," *Harvard Business Review,* April 2011.
6. Keith Naughton, "The Happiest Man in Detroit," *Bloomberg Businessweek,* February 7–February 13, 2011.
7. Daniel Burke, "The Happiness Business," *The Washington Post,* December 4, 2010.
8. Venkat Ramaswamy and Francis Gouilart, "Building the Co-Creative Enterprise," *Harvard Business Review,* October 2010.
9. Brendan Coffey, "Managing the Growing Risk of Environmental Liability," *Forbes,* March 28, 2011.
10. Robert M. Kimmitt and Matthew J. Slaughter, "Insourcing: The Secret to Job Growth," *The Wall Street Journal,* December 6, 2010.
11. Ibid.
12. Rob Johnson, "Learning from the Good Book," *The Wall Street Journal,* May 17, 2010.
13. Bruce Einhorn and Ruth David, "An IPO for India's Top Lender to the Poor," *Bloomberg Businessweek,* May 10–May 16, 2010.
14. John Cuneo, "10 Perks We Love," *Inc.,* June 2010.
15. Carolyn M. Brown, "Minority Female Firms Outpace All Others," *Black Enterprise,* January 2009.
16. Mike Cosgrove, "Debt, Tax Burdens Holding Back Growth," *Investor's Business Daily,* February 3, 2011.
17. David Wessel, "Channeling Milton Friedman," *The Wall Street Journal,* October 28, 2010.
18. Max H. Bazerman and Ann E. Tenbrunsel, "Ethical Breakdowns," *Harvard Business Review,* April 2011.
19. Alina Dizik, "Social Concerns Gain New Urgency," *The Wall Street Journal,* March 4, 2010.

20. Thomas G. Donlan, "The Real American Job," *Barron's,* August 16, 2010.
21. John Jannarone, "Retailers Struggle in Amazon Jungle," *The Wall Street Journal,* February 22, 2011.
22. Robert Hsu, "450 Million Chinese Internet Users Are a Big 2011 Trend," *Investors Place Asia,* January 3, 2011.
23. Scott Steinberg, "Protecting Your Business from Identity Theft," *The Costco Connection,* August 2010.
24. "Senior Services," *Entrepreneur,* January 2011.
25. "John Tozzi," "Home-Care Companies Brace for Regulation," *Bloomberg Businessweek,* March 21–March 27, 2011.
26. "*Entrepreneur Magazine*'s Emerging Entrepreneur of 2009," *Entrepreneur,* January 2010.
27. Annya M. Lott, "The Future of Work," *Black Enterprise,* August 2010.

CHAPTER 2

1. Bomi Lim, Sangim Han, and Kevin Cho, "Commerce Is Caught in a Crossfire at the DMZ," *Bloomberg Businessweek,* June 7–June 13, 2010.
2. Terry Miller, "The U.S. Loses Ground on Economic Freedom," *The Wall Street Journal,* January 12, 2011.
3. Steve Forbes, "Marx Would Be Impressed," *Forbes,* April 12, 2010.
4. Stephen Spruiell, "Mechanical Failure," *National Review,* July 19, 2010.
5. Alan Cohen, "A Sustainable Future," advertisement in *Fortune,* July 26, 2010.
6. Tamera Nielsen, "An Unlikely Life Aquatic," *Entrepreneur,* March 2010.
7. Jason Daley, "Green Fallout," *Entrepreneur,* August 2010.
8. Robert J. Samuelson, "America's Parent Trap," *The Washington Post,* August 9, 2010.
9. William W. Beach, "Greater Freedom Is the Answer to Our Economic Woes," *The Washington Times,* January 28, 2010.
10. Jonathan R. Laing, "Beyond Laissez-Faire," *Barron's,* February 28, 2011.
11. Thomas Heath, "How They Give," "*The Washington Post,*" November 21, 2010.
12. Amy C. Cosper, "Trash Talk," *Entrepreneur,* April, 2011.
13. John Meidl, "10 Questions," *Time,* December 27, 2009–January 3, 2010.
14. Dominic Barton, "Capitalism for the Long Term," *Harvard Business Review,* March 2011.
15. Gordon G. Chang, "Perils of State Capitalism," *National Review,* July 19, 2011.
16. Ibid.
17. Hernando de Soto, "Egypt's Economic Apartheid," *The Wall Street Journal,* February 3, 2011.
18. Bryan Walsh, "Down and Dirty," *Time,* March 21, 2011.
19. Matthew Barakat, "Better Burgers Are Sizzling," *St. Louis Post-Dispatch,* July 18, 2010.
20. Duane Stanford, "Nature's Gatorade," *Bloomberg Businessweek,* March 14–March 20, 2011.

21. Drake Bennet, "The Inequality Delusion," *Bloomberg Businessweek,* October 25–October 31, 2010.
22. Steven Mufson, "Ultimately We See Our Role as Catalysts," *The Washington Post,* November 21, 2010.
23. Caroline Winter, David Glovin and Jennifer Daniel, "The Great Hedge Fund Takedown," *Bloomberg Businessweek,* March 14–March 20, 2011.
24. Michael Porter and Mark R. Kramer, "Creating Shared Value," *Harvard Business Review,* January–February 2011.
25. Michael Knox Beran, "The Descent of Liberalism," *National Review,* April 5, 2010.
26. Linda Darling-Hammond, "They're Number One," *neatoday,* October/November 2010.
27. "The Keynesian Dead End," *The Wall Street Journal,* June 26–27, 2010.
28. George F. Will, "No Rational Exuberance," *Newsweek,* January 25, 2010.
29. Gene Epstein, "Deflation Demystified," *Barron's,* August 30, 2010.
30. Christopher Wood, "Don't Rule Out a Double Dip Recession," *The Wall Street Journal,* May 24, 2010.
31. Mark J. Perry, "The Truth about U.S. Manufacturing," *The Wall Street Journal,* February 25, 2011.
32. "The Obama Tax Trap," *The Wall Street Journal,* July 2, 2010.
33. Benjamin Bower, "Keynes Was a Better Economist than His Disciples Are," *The Wall Street Journal,* July 2, 2010.
34. Susan Lund and Richard Dobbs, "Myths about Interest Rates," *The Washington Post,* January 23, 2011.
35. Neil Irwin, "Bernanke Defends U.S. Policies," *The Washington Post,* February 19, 2011.

CHAPTER 3

1. Michael Bekins, "Taking Your Career on the Road," *The Wall Street Journal,* June 14, 2010.
2. "World Population Clock," U.S. Census Bureau, www.census.gov/ipc/www/popclockworld.html, accessed March 14, 2011; and WorldAtlas.com, accessed March 14, 2011.
3. "U.S. Trade Deficit Expands Even as Exports Accelerate," *New York Times,* February 11, 2011.
4. UPS.com, accessed March 11, 2011; Walmart.com, accessed March 11, 2011; and "The Beast in the Bush," *The Economist,* February 19, 2011.
5. NBA.com, accessed March 14, 2011.
6. "Bigger Abroad," *The Economist,* February 19, 2011.
7. World Bank, www.worldbank.org, accessed March 16, 2011; and World Trade Organization, www.wto.org, accessed March 16, 2011.
8. Andrew Malcolm, "Australia's Prime Minister Julia Gillard: 'There's a Reason the World Always Looks to America,'" *Los Angeles Times,* March 10, 2011.
9. "Time to Act on Free Trade," *The Washington Post,* March 14, 2011.
10. Jack Markowitz, "China's Idea of Free Trade Hardly Fair," *Pittsburgh Tribune-Review,* January 20, 2011; and Bill Lambrecht, "U.S. Accused of Letting China Flout Trade Law," *St. Louis Post Dispatch,* March 17, 2011.
11. Matthew J. Slaughter, "Comparative Advantage and American Jobs, *The Wall Street Journal,* January 26, 2011; and www.NetMBA.com, accessed March 14, 2011.
12. Steven Pearlstein and Dana Rodrik, "The Globalization Paradox," *The Washington Post,* March 13, 2011; and Clyde Prestowitz, "Why Isn't the iPhone Made in America?," *Foreign Policy,* March 8, 2011.
13. Cyndia Zwahlen, "Exporting Presents Opportunities and Challenges for Small Businesses," *Los Angeles Times,* February 21, 2011.
14. Courtney Rubin, "Obama Encourages Small Firms to Go Global," *Inc. Magazine,* March 15, 2010; and Martha White, "Thinking Small," *Slate,* December 6, 2010.
15. www.zeromillion.com, accessed March 14, 2011; and www.myprimetime.com, accessed March 20, 2011.
16. Fredrick Balfour and Michael Wei, "Selling Skin Cream to China's 'City Jade Men,'" *Bloomberg Businessweek,* January 9, 2011.
17. C. Fred Bergston, "How Best to Boost U.S. Exports," *The Washington Post,* February 3, 2010.
18. "U.S. Trade Deficit Expands Even as Exports Accelerate," *The New York Times,* February 11, 2011.
19. Keith Bradsher, "Inflation in China May Limit U.S. Trade Deficit," *The New York Times,* January 30, 2011.
20. Daniel Gross, "It's Time for More Companies to Stretch Globally," *The Washington Post,* August 29, 2010; and Michelle Jarboe, "President Obama to Hear About Tight Budgets, Taxes, and Trade from Cleveland-area Small Businesses," *The Plain Dealer,* February 11, 2011.
21. Mark Drajem, "Chinese Steel Drill-Pipe Exporters to Face U.S. Dumping Duties," *Bloomberg Businessweek,* February 7, 2011.
22. www.goldmarks.com, accessed March 15, 2011.
23. "Frederick's of Hollywood Announces International Expansion," *PR Newswire,* March 15, 2011.
24. Adam Wooten, "Local Export Assistance Remedies International Headaches," *Deseret News* (Salt Lake City), January 28, 2011; www.buyusa.gov, accessed March 15, 2011; and www.export.gov, accessed March 2011.
25. www.rockymountainchocolatefactory.com, accessed March 15, 2011.
26. Lan Ann Nguyen, "Home Cooking," *Forbes,* February 28, 2011; and Mike Eckel, "Living Loud in Hanoi," *The Seattle Times,* February 28, 2011.
27. www.yum.com, accessed March 16, 2011; and Vincent Mao, "China Demand Boosts Yum's Sales, Earnings," *Investors Business Daily,* February 4, 2011.
28. www.yum.com, accessed March 16, 2011; and Celia Hatton, "KFC's Finger-Lickin' Success in China," *CBS News,* March 6, 2011.
29. Alan R. Elliott "Jabil and TTM in Early Stage Chart Patterns," *Investors Business Daily,* March 2, 2011.
30. Elizabeth Woyke, "The Company Behind Your Laptop," *Forbes,* December 4, 2009; and www.flextronics.com, accessed March 16, 2011.
31. Jessica Beaton, "Shanghai Disneyland Budget: The Numbers Are In," *CNN International,* March 7, 2011; and "Shanghai Reveals New Disneyland Blueprints for First Time," *Forbes,* March 9, 2011.
32. "Marriott Joint-Venture a Sign of Things to Come," *Travelweekly,* March 15, 2011.
33. Rumman Ahmed, "Tata Tea, PepsiCo Explore Joint Venture," *The Wall Street Journal,* April 9, 2010; and www.pepsico.com, accessed March 15, 2011.
34. Sean D. Hamill, "How UPMC's Overseas Operation Blossomed in 14 Years," *Pittsburgh Post-Gazette,* May 30, 2010.
35. www.nestle.com, accessed March 16, 2011.
36. Veera Pandiyan, "Time to Ace the Race Card for Better Unity," *The Malaysian Star,* March 10, 2011.
37. Chrissie Thompson, "Lincoln Number 1 in Long-Term Quality, but Foreign Brands Still Better Overall," *Detroit*

Free Press, March 17, 2011; and Chris Woodyard, "Auto Exports from U.S. on Rise," *USA Today,* March 7, 2011.

38. Adam Wooten, "Wrong Flowers Can Mean Death for Global Business," *Deseret News* (Salt Lake City), February 4, 2011.

39. Jennifer Reingold, "Can P&G Make Money in Places Where People Earn $2 a Day?" *Fortune,* January 17, 2011; and www.procter&gamble.com, accessed March 20, 2011.

40. Hao Li, "Marc Chandler: In Defense of the Dollar," *International Business Times,* March 4, 2011.

41. Peter Coy, "On the Yuan, Be Careful What You Wish For," *Bloomberg Businessweek,* October 3, 2010.

42. "Cuba Cuts Hard Currency Peso to Par with Dollar," Associated Press, March 14, 2011; and Paul Abelsky, "Belarus Central Bank Says No Plans to Devalue Domestic Currency," *Bloomberg,* March 15, 2011.

43. www.wto.org, accessed March 20, 2011; and www.worldbank.org, accessed March 21, 2011.

44. Dionne Searcey, "Former Enforcer Sees Looming Fights," *The Wall Street Journal,* March 17, 2011; and "IBM to Pay $10M to Settle Foreign Bribery Case," *Accounting Today,* March 18, 2011.

45. "Bribery/Anti-Corruption: Introduction," *The Lawyer,* March 19, 2011; and www.oecd.org, accessed March 20, 2011.

46. Ian Fletcher, "In Praise of Mercantilism (or Why Economic History Isn't Boring)," *The Huffington Post,* March 19, 2011; and www.referenceforbusiness.com, accessed March 19, 2011.

47. Marc Lacey, "Dreaming of Cuban Profits in Post-Embargo World," *The New York Times,* March 28, 2010; and Sarah Stephens, "Like Oil and Water in the Gulf," *Los Angeles Times,* March 14, 2011.

48. Jennifer Liberto, "Newest Trade War: Obama vs. Congress," CNN Money.com, March 19 2011; and David Shepardson, "Obama Administration Urges Speedy Approval of Korea Trade Deal," *The Detroit News,* March 10, 2011.

49. www.wto.org, accessed March 21, 2011.

50. "WTO Rules in China's Favor in U.S. Trade Dispute," *Los Angeles Times,* March 11, 2011; and "A Win for China," *The Wall Street Journal,* March 17, 2011.

51. "Doha Round: U.S. Presses China, India, and Brazil," BBC Mobile, March 1, 2011; and "A Deadline for Doha," *The Economist,* January 27, 2011.

52. Riva Froymovich, "EU: Euro-Zone GDP Slows in H2 2010 as Expected," *The Wall Street Journal,* March 1, 2011.

53. Reinhardt Krause, "Euro Debt Too High; 'Haircuts' Inevitable?" *Investors Business Daily,* March 10, 2011.

54. Ian Talley, Charles Forelle, and Riva Froymovich, "IMF: EU Crisis Pact Important Step, Awaiting More Progress," *The Wall Street Journal,* March 17, 2011.

55. Matthew Dalton, "EU Agrees on Economic Overhaul," *The Wall Street Journal,* March 15, 2011.

56. "Unasur Fearful of Overlapping with the Andean Pack and Mercosur," *Merco Press,* June 16, 2010.

57. www.aseansec.org, accessed March 22, 2011; and www.finance.bantolo.net, accessed March 22, 2011.

58. www.ustr.gov/trade-agreements, accessed March 22, 2011.

59. Bill Ong Hing, "Mexico's Economy Is the Problem That Anti-Immigration Laws Won't Solve," *The Huffington Post,* February 28, 2011.

60. Sewell Chan, "U.S. Plans for Trade Are Stalled," *The New York Times,* February 28, 2011.

61. Tom Barkley, "U.S. Seeks Major Progress on Trans Pacific Trade Deal by November," *The Wall Street Journal,* March 14, 2011.

62. "The 9 Billion-People Question," *The Economist,* February 26, 2011.

63. Owen Fletcher, "Foreign Direct Investment in China Rises 17%," *The Wall Street Journal,* January 19, 2011.

64. Chinmei Sung and Jay Wang, "Foreign Investment in China Climbs for 13th Straight Month to $7.6 Billion," *Bloomberg,* September 14, 2010; and "Now No. 2, Could China Become No. 1?" *Time,* February 28, 2011.

65. www.mckinsey.com/mgi, accessed March 20, 2011.

66. Sung and Wang, "Foreign Investment in China Climbs for 13th Straight Month to $7.6 Billion."

67. Peter Coy, "If Demography Is Destiny, Then India Has the Edge," *Bloomberg Businessweek,* January 23, 2011.

68. Tim Gosling, "Multinationals Sensing Business Opportunities in Russia," *Business New Europe,* February 25, 2011.

69. Rachel Morarjee, "Foreign Investment in Russian Car Market Moves Up a Gear," *Business New Europe,* March 18, 2011; and Tim Higgins and Tommaso Ebhardt, "Deal Means Ford Will Build Cars in Russia," *Bloomberg News,* February 19, 2011.

70. Lyubov Pronina, "Dreams of an iPad Economy for Russia," *Bloomberg Businessweek,* February 13, 2011.

CHAPTER 4

1. Michael Elliott, "Was It Really So Bad?" *Time,* November 24, 2010.

2. Zachary Karabell, "The Big Bad Bankers, and Their Bonuses, Are Back," *Time,* January 22, 2011.

3. Joy Fitzgerald, "Seek Financial Disclosure," *The Boston Herald,* January 12, 2011; and Timothy R. Homan, "Economics Professors Will Consider Code of Ethics," *Bloomberg Businessweek,* January 1, 2011.

4. "Versions of the Golden Rule in 21 World Religions," Religious Tolerance, www.religioustolerance.org, accessed March 14, 2011.

5. P. M. Pursey, A. R. Heugens, Muel Kaptein, and J. (Hans) van Oosterhout, "Contracts to Communities: A Processual Model of Organizational Virtue," *Journal of Management Studies,* January 2008; and Martha Perego, "Focus on the Fundamentals," *Public Management,* January 1, 2009.

6. U.S. Census Bureau.

7. David Nagel, "Cognite 3.5 Moves to Android, Integrates Plagiarism Detection, *THE Journal,* February 15, 2011; and "Turn It In," www.turnitin.com, accessed March 14, 2011.

8. Kathy Gurchiek, "Ethics, Schmethics, U.S. Teens Say," *HR News,* February 1, 2008; and Cheating Culture, www.cheatingculture.com/academic-dishonesty, accessed March 14, 2011.

9. Kenneth Blanchard and Norman Vincent Peale, *The Power of Ethical Management* (New York: William Morrow, 1996).

10. Richard F. Stolz, "Taking the Lead," *Human Resource Executive,* May 16, 2007; Jeff Waller, "Creating Ethical Business Standards: Adopt a Modern Ethics Policy and Make It Public," *Alaska Business Monthly,* April 1, 2010; and John Allen, "Nature vs. Nurture: Company Culture Can Be Defined and Refined." *Houston Business Journal,* February 25, 2011.

11. Bob Sullivan, "Can't Cancel That Service? Blame 'Perverse Incentives,'" www.redtape.msnbc.com, posted May 13, 2008; and Peter R. Kensicki, "Code-Dependent: Creating a Companywide Ethics Policy Will Spur Professionalism and Success," *Best's Review,* January 1, 2010.

12. Eric Krell, "How to Conduct an Ethics Audit: An Ethics Audit Can Reveal Gaps in Your Ethics Policies and

Practices," *HRMagazine,* April 1, 2010; Michael Quint, "Cuomo Orders Ethics Training for Staff, Top Officials," *Bloomberg Businessweek,* January 3, 2011; Steve Karnowski, "New Food Safety Law Protects Whistleblowers," *Bloomberg Businessweek,* February 11, 2011; Ryan J. Donmoyer, "IRS Alters Rules to Pay Informants in More Cases," *Bloomberg Businessweek,* January 14, 2011; David S. Hilzenrath, "IRS Reverses Position, Which Could Benefit Whistleblowers," *The Washington Post,* January 15, 2011; Ben Sutherly, "Incentive Missing to Report Fraud," *Dayton Daily News,* February 6, 2011; Joe Davidson, "A Victory for Chambers Might Not be a Victory for Whistleblowers," *The Washington Post,* January 13, 2011; "In Fired Park Police Chief's Saga, a Happy Ending and a Warning," *The Washington Post,* January 20, 2011; David S. Hilzenrath, "SEC Names Head of New Whistleblower Office," *The Washington Post,* February 19, 2011; Joanne S. Barry, "Dodd-Frank Sleeper Leaves Confusion in Its Wake," *The CPA Journal,* January 1, 2011; "Guidelines Stress Whistleblower Protection," *Healthcare Risk Management,* January 1, 2011; Paul Sweeney, "Will New Regulations Deter Corporate Fraud?" *Financial Executive,* January 1, 2011; Robert Schmidt, "U.S. Regulators Struggle to Keep Up with Dodd-Frank," *Bloomberg Businessweek,* February 10, 2011; and Kay Bell, "Enron Whistleblower Gets $1 Million From the IRS," MSN, www.msn.com, March 18, 2011.

13. Miranda S. Spivack, "Johnson's Cases Renew Ethics-Reform Debate in Prince George's," *The Washington Post,* February 16, 2011.

14. "German Ex-Judge Becomes Daimler Integrity Chief," *Forbes,* February 15, 2011.

15. "Does Corporate Social Responsibility Matter?" *Gallup Management Journal,* January 28, 2010.

16. Kent Byus, Donald Deis, and Bo Ouyang, "Doing Well by Doing Good: Corporate Social Responsibility and Profitability," *SAM Advanced Management Journal,* January 1, 2010; "Juniper Networks Earns Ethics Inside Certification from the Ethisphere Institute," *Politics & Government Week,* February 17, 2011; and "Corporate Social Responsibility Can Enhance Customer Value," *States News Service,* February 15, 2011.

17. Gates Foundation, www.gatesfoundation.org, accessed March 14, 2011.

18. TNT, www.tnt.com, accessed March 15, 2011.

19. Patagonia, www.patagonia.com, accessed March 25, 2011.

20. Xerox, www.xerox.com, accessed March 17, 2011; and Suzanne Stevens, "Xerox Lends Exec to Hacienda CDC," *Portland Business Journal,* March 4, 2011.

21. Joshua Kucera, "Bottom Line on Corporate Giving," *U.S. News & World Report,* November 2010.

22. Samantha Marshall, "Incorporating the Cause; Gen Y Entrepreneurs Pair Profits with Philanthropy," *Crain's New York Business,* January 14, 2008; and "Generation Y: A Snapshot of People in Their Twenties," *The Chronicle of Philanthropy,* May 3, 2010.

23. "Juniper Networks Earns Ethics Inside Certification from the Ethisphere Institute."

24. "Executives Say Crowdsourcing Is Valuable to Corporate Social Responsibility Efforts," *Telecommunications Weekly,* February 23, 2011.

25. Clay Holtzman, "Venture Capital with a Conscience," *Washington Business Journal,* June 25, 2010.

26. Elliot Smith, "SAC's Trading Mimics Insider Dealings Identified by Prosecutors," *Bloomberg Businessweek,* February 11, 2011; Caroline Winter, David Glovin, and Jennifer Daniel, "A Guide to the Galleon Case," *Bloomberg Businessweek,* March 10, 2011; and Paul M. Barrett, Katherine Burton, and Saijel Kishan, "The Rajaratnam Conviction," *Bloomberg Businessweek,* May 11, 2011.

27. David Saxby, "What Makes a Satisfied Employee?" *Rural Telecommunications,* January 1, 2008; and Dennis Huspeni, "Human Resource Personnel Balance Process, Compassion," *Denver Business Journal,* March 19, 2010.

28. Bill Catlette and Richard Hadden, *Contented Cows Give Better Milk* (Contented Cow Partners, 2000); Bill Catlette and Richard Hadden, *Contented Cows Moove Faster* (R. Brent & Company, 2007); and Contented Cow Partners, www.contentedcows.com, accessed March 21, 2011.

29. Costco, www.costco, accessed March 20, 2011.

30. Association of Certified Fraud Examiners, www.acfe.com, accessed March 21, 2011.

31. American Solar Energy Society, www.ases.org, accessed March 19, 2011.

32. Tim Grant, "'Socially Responsible' Investing Joins Your Money with Your Ideals," *Pittsburgh Post-Gazette,* March 16, 2010; Social Funds, www.socialfunds.com, accessed March 19, 2011; and Social Investment Forum, www.socialinvest.org, accessed March 19, 2011.

33. www.ethisphere.com, accessed March 19, 2011.

34. Rainforest Action Network, www.ran.org, accessed March 19, 2011.

35. Price Waterhouse Coopers' 2011 Global CEO Survey, www.pwc.com, accessed March 19, 2011.

36. Ibid.

37. Eugenia Levenson, "Citizen Nike," *Fortune,* November 17, 2008.

38. Ibid.

39. Andrew Bast, "Going After Graft," *Newsweek,* November 1, 2010; and Ben Stier, "Too Big to Be Nailed," *Fortune,* April 19, 2010.

40. Organization of American States, www.oas.org, accessed March 19, 2011.

CHAPTER 5

1. www.sba.gov, accessed March 27, 2011; and www.score.org, accessed March 27, 2011.

2. Deborah McSweeney, "How to Decide Which Business Structure Fits Your Business Idea Best," *Business Insider,* March 25, 2011.

3. www.taxes.about.co, accessed March 27, 2011; and www.myownbusiness.org, accessed March 27, 2011.

4. Richard Gibson, "Help from the Inside," *The Wall Street Journal,* February 14, 2011.

5. Donald Marron, "Six Things to Remember about Taxes and Small Business," *Christian Science Monitor,* March 3, 2011.

6. Dimitra DeFotis, "Master Limited Partnerships: A Good Place to Get 6% Payouts," *Barron's,* March 7, 2011.

7. www.sunoco.com, accessed March 27, 2011.

8. Colleen Dibaise, Sarah E. Needleman, and Emily Maltby, "Married to the Job (And Each Other)," *The Wall Street Journal,* February 14, 2011.

9. www.smallbusiness.yahoo.com, accessed March 27, 2011,

10. Jonelle, Marte, "A New Haven in Corporate Bonds," *Smart Money Magazine,* March 4, 2011.

11. Jesse Westbrook, "The SEC's Plan to Pry Open Corporate Boards," *Bloomberg Businessweek,* August 29, 2010.

12. www.smallbusiness.yahoo.com, accessed March 28, 2011.

13. www.incorporate101.com, accessed March 28, 2011.

14. Michael J. De La Merced and Jeffrey Cane, "Confident Deal Makers Pulled Out Checkbooks in 2010," *The New York Times,* January 3, 2011.

15. Patrick Seitz, "Shifting from Public to Private," *Investors Business Daily,* March 14, 2011.

16. Andrea Murphy, "From LBO to IPO," *Forbes Magazine,* February 9, 2011.

17. www.sabmiller.com, accessed March 28, 2011.

18. Courtney Rubin, "Should You Consider Franchising?" *Inc.,* September 23, 2010.

19. www.franchise.org, accessed March 28, 2011.

20. Ned Smith, "Franchises Play Vital Role in U.S. Economy," *Business News Daily,* September 15, 2010.

21. Julie Jargon, "Subway Runs Past McDonald's Chain," *The Wall Street Journal,* March 8, 2011

22. Jason Daily, "A Senior Moment," *Entrepreneur,* January 25, 2011.

23. www.aboutmcdonald's.com, accessed March 29, 2011.

24. www.franchisetimes.com, accessed March 29, 2011.

25. Rosemary Black, "KFC Is Hot on Grilled Chicken but Customers Aren't Buying It," *The New York Daily News,* August 17, 2010; and Burt Helm, "At KFC, a Battle among the Chicken-Hearted," *Bloomberg Businessweek,* August 29, 2010.

26. Richard Gibson, "Franchisee v. Franchisor," *The Wall Street Journal,* February 4, 2011.

27. www.smallbiztrends.com, accessed March 29, 2011.

28. www.franchise.org, accessed March 29, 2011.

29. Nancy Weingartner, "Junior Executives," *Franchise Times,* March 28, 2011.

30. Issie Lapowsky, "How to Start a Home-Based Franchise," *Inc.,* May 13, 2010.

31. Mark Henricks, "Sponsored Section: Bricks or Clicks?" *Inc.,* February 1, 2010.

32. Ibid.

33. Jason Ankeny, "Social Climbers," *Entrepreneur,* January 2011.

34. www.franchisedirect.com, accessed March 29, 2011; www.franchise.org, accessed March 29, 2011; and www.mcdonalds.com, accessed March 29, 2011.

35. Kavita Kumar, "Build-A-Bear Stirs to New Life after the Long, Cold Recession," *St. Louis Post Dispatch,* March 20, 2011.

36. Eric Markowitz, "A Fresh Take on a Franchise Start-Up," *Inc.,* March 16, 2011.

37. www.franchisedirect.com, accessed March 29, 2011; and www.hrblock.com, accessed March 29, 2011.

38. www.usda.gov, accessed March 29, 2011.

39. Mark Day, "Can Worker-Owned Cooperatives Offer a Solution to Our Economic Woes?" *La Prensa San Diego,* February 11, 2011.

CHAPTER 6

1. Philipp Harper, "History's 10 Greatest Entrepreneurs," www.msnbc.com, accessed April 2011; and Andrew Beattie, "The 10 Greatest Entrepreneurs," www.investopedia.com, accessed April 2011.

2. Stefan Theil, "Golden Age," *Newsweek,* September 6, 2010; and Rebecca U. Cho, "The Time for Entrepreneurship Is Now," *Inland Valley Daily Bulletin,* February 20, 2011.

3. "The Forbes 400 Richest People in America," www.Forbes.com, accessed April 2011.

4. www.willnroses.com, accessed April 2011.

5. Venkatesan Vembu, "Entrepreneurs Aren't Born, They're Made," *DNA: Daily News & Analysis,* May 29, 2010; and

Jennifer, Wilson, "Four Myths of Entrepreneurship," *PT in Motion,* February 1, 2011.

6. Paul Davis, "Requirements for Business Success," *National Driller,* January 1, 2011; and Erik Calonius, "How to Think like Steve Jobs," *Fortune,* March 15, 2011.

7. www.rushcommunications.com, accessed April 2011.

8. www.anitaroddick.com, accessed April 2011.

9. Robert Celaschi, "Startup Savvy: A Little Planning Can See the Smallest Businesses through the Rough Times," *Boston Business Journal,* July 2, 2010; and Jennifer Wang, "Be Disruptive," *Entrepreneur,* January 2011.

10. Long Cheng, Zhong-Ming Wang, and Wei Zhang, "The Effects of Conflict on Team Decision Making," *Social Behavior and Personality,* March 1, 2011.

11. "Thinking Small," *The Kiplinger Letter,* July 20, 2010.

12. Emili Vesilind, "The Home Office Is Humming," *Entrepreneur,* June 2010.

13. Lesley Spencer Pyle, "Working from Home Doesn't Have to Be a Stigma," *Entrepreneur,* March 5, 2010; Bianca Male, "Working from Home Is Hard Work," *Entrepreneur,* February 26, 2010; and Jennifer Wang, "9 Pitfalls of Working from Home," www.entrepreneur.com, accessed April 2011.

14. Erick Schonfeld, "Forrester Forecast: Online Sales Will Grow to $250 Billion by 2014," www.techcrunch.com, accessed April 2011.

15. Kyle Swenson, "Sales for Dummies," *All Business,* www.allbusiness.com, accessed April 2011; and www.throwthings.com, accessed April 2011.

16. Gwen Moran, "The Sins of Website Design," *Entrepreneur Magazine,* January 2011.

17. Donald L. Ariail, Gregory R. Quinet, and Robert M. Thacker, "Creating and Fostering Sustainable Intrapreneurship: A Conversation with David Gutierrez," *Journal of Applied Management and Entrepreneurship,* April 1, 2010.

18. www.3m.com, accessed April 2011.

19. www.lockheedmartin.com, accessed April 2011.

20. James R. Edwards, Jr., "Securing the Blessings of Liberty," *Center for Immigration Studies,* March 2011.

21. Andrew Hanson and Shawn Rohlin, "The Effect of Location-Based Tax Incentives on Establishment Location and Employment across Industry Sectors," *Public Finance Review,* March 2011.

22. National Business Incubator Association, www.nbia.org, accessed April 2011.

23. Barbara Haislip, "Laid Off and Launching," *The Wall Street Journal,* February 14, 2011.

24. www.whitehouse.gov/issues/startup-america.

25. "White House Names Network for Teaching Entrepreneurship to Startup America Partnership," *U.S. Newswire,* January 31, 2011; and Jim Kuhnhenn, "Startups Get Lift from White House," *The Seattle Times,* February 1, 2011.

26. Small Business Administration, www.sba.gov, accessed April 2011; U.S. Census Bureau, www.census.gov, accessed April 2011; Vivien Lou Chen and Timothy R. Homan, "Small Business Is Hiring, but Very Carefully," *Bloomberg Businessweek,* January 6, 2011; and "Uncorking Enterprise," *The Economist,* February 26, 2011.

27. National Business Incubator Association, www.nbia.org, accessed April 2011.

28. Martin Willoughby, "Reality Is that Every Business Will Shut Down or Be Sold," *The Mississippi Business Journal,* March 22, 2010.

29. Deniz Ucbasaran, Paul Westhead, and Mike Wright, "Why Serial Entrepreneurs Don't Learn from Failure," *Harvard Business Review,* April 2011.

30. Emmett Dulaney, "Don't Underestimate Experience When Starting a Business," *The Herald Bulletin,* March 28, 2011.

31. Sarah E. Needleman, "Businesses Put Up for Sale Smack into Harsh Reality," *The Wall Street Journal,* October 14, 2010.

32. Ivy Hughes, "A Simple Plan," *Entrepreneur,* August 2010.

33. Dyan Machan, "Your Nearest and Dearest," *SmartMoney,* August 2010.

34. Joseph De Avila, "Microfinance Groups Think Big," *The Wall Street Journal,* July 6, 2010.

35. Mark Pinsky, "Help for Small Businesses: Loans Are Just the Start," *Bloomberg Businessweek,* October 25, 2010.

36. Pui-Wing Tam and Spencer E. Ante, "'Super Angels' Fly In to Aid Start-Ups," *The Wall Street Journal,* August 16, 2010; and Doree Shafrir, "Pennies from Heaven," *Newsweek,* November 29, 2010.

37. John Simons, "How to Get a Loan the Web 2.0 Way," *Black Enterprise,* December 2010.

38. Helen Coster, "Startup Juice," *Forbes,* August 9, 2010; Gwen Moran, "The Voice of Venture Capital," *Entrepreneur,* July 2010; and Pui-Wing Tam, "Casing Out Start-Ups Gets More Complicated," *The Wall Street Journal,* February 16, 2011.

39. Dan Primack, "Venture Capital Gets Disrupted (in a Good Way)," *Fortune,* March 7, 2011.

40. Marshall Eckblad, "The SBA Has a Deal for You," *The Wall Street Journal,* June 21, 2010.

41. April H. Lee, "Loan Program Helps Some Small U.S. Businesses Survive," *The Wall Street Journal,* April 11, 2011.

42. National Association of Small Business Investment Companies, www.nasbic.org, accessed April 2011.

43. Karen E. Klein, "The SBA's New Small Business Loan Program," *Bloomberg Businessweek,* February 17, 2011; and Kent Hoover, "House Panel Proposes $100M Cut to SBA Budget," *The Business Journal,* March 21, 2011.

44. Jennifer Heldt Powell, "Color Your Employees Happy," *The Boston Herald,* May 16, 2010; and David Beisel, "How to Find the Perfect Startup Job," *Fortune,* February 7, 2011.

45. Jonathan Blum, "The Financial Times, They Are A'changing," *Entrepreneur,* February 2011.

46. Benjamin K. Riley, "Three Legal Lessons for Startups," *Fortune,* February 17, 2011.

47. "SCORE Helps Create Jobs and Businesses as the Economy Recovers," *U.S. Newswire,* January 27, 2010.

48. "World Population Clock," U.S. Census Bureau, www.census.gov/ipc/www/popclockworld.html, accessed April 2011; and WorldAtlas.com, accessed April, 2011.

49. "Export Goal Is a Tall Order, but Some Minnesota Firms Will Give It a Shot," *Star Tribune* (Minneapolis, MN), May 18, 2010; Courtney Rubin, "Obama Encourages Small Firms to Go Global," *Inc.,* March 15, 2010; and Martha White, "Thinking Small," *Slate,* December 6, 2010.

CHAPTER 7

1. "A Company of 'Level Five' Leaders," *Inc.,* June 2010.

2. Alan Murray, "The End of Management," *The Wall Street Journal,* August 21, 2010.

3. Jeanne C. Meister and Karie Willyerd, "Mentoring Mill," *Harvard Business Review,* May 2010.

4. Leigh Buchanan, "Learning from the Best," *Inc.,* June 2010.

5. Steven Pearlstein, "The New Division of Labor: Adding Profits, Subtracting Workers," *The Washington Post,* July 20, 2010.

6. Tamara J. Erickson, "The Leaders We Need Now," *Harvard Business Review,* May 2010.

7. Jason Ankeny, "Green Idols," *Entrepreneur,* April 2011.

8. Mac Margolis, "Executives Wanted," *Newsweek,* June 14, 2010.

9. Geoff Colvin, "Ursula Burns," *Fortune,* May 3, 2010.

10. Johanna Neuman, "The Year of the (Business) Woman," *U.S. News and World Report,* Summer 2010.

11. Virginia Postrel, "Love and Money," *Entrepreneur,* February 2011.

12. John Mackey, "What Is It That Only I Can Do?" *Harvard Business Review,* January–February 2011.

13. Monica Langley and Sharon Terlep, "'I'm Not a Car Guy': On the Road with the New Man at GM's Wheel," *The Wall Street Journal,* January 8–9, 2011.

14. Robert H. Schaffer, "Mistakes Leaders Keep Making," *Harvard Business Review,* September 2010.

15. A. G. Lafley, "I Think of My Failures as a Gift," *Harvard Business Review,* April 2011.

16. Mark Whitehouse, "Elusive Economic Indicator: Quality of Life Gauge," *The Wall Street Journal,* January 10, 2011.

17. Jason Dean and Aaron Back, "China Growth Shows Contrast with U.S.," *The Wall Street Journal,* January 21, 2011.

18. Elie Ofek and Luc Wathieu, "Trends That Could Shake Up Your Business," *Harvard Business Review,* July–August 2010.

19. Stephen Bungay, "How to Make the Most of Your Company's Strategy," *Harvard Business Review,* January–February 2011.

20. Carl Icahn, "Why Blockbuster Failed," *Harvard Business Review,* April, 2011.

21. "Lessons from a Killer Quake," *Newsweek,* March 21, 2011.

22. William Pesek, "The Cataclysm This Time," *Bloomberg Businessweek,* March 21–March 27, 2011.

23. Jennifer Wang, "Business Models Illustrated," *Entrepreneur,* April 2010.

24. Peter S. Delisi, Dennis Moberg, and Ronald Danielson, "Why CIOs Are Last among Equals," *The Wall Street Journal,* May 24, 2010.

25. Lynda Gratton, "The End of the Middle Manager," *Harvard Business Review,* January–February 2011.

26. Ray Fisman, "In Defense of Middle Management," *The Washington Post,* October 17, 2010.

27. Boris Groysberg, L. Kevin Kelly and Bryan MacDonald, "The New Path to the C-Suite," *Harvard Business Review,* March 2011.

28. Lee Smith, "A Leadership Playbook," *Fortune,* March 21, 2011.

29. Rich Karlgaard, "Ten Tips: Great Restructuring Winners," *Forbes,* February 28, 2011.

30. Henry Mintzberg, "We're Overled and Undermanaged," *Businessweek,* August 17, 2009.

31. Martin Schoeller, "Can Ellen Kullman Make Dupont Great Again?" *Fortune,* May 3, 2010.

32. Steven Muffson, "Ultimately We See Our Role as Catalysts," *The Washington Post,* November 21, 2010.

33. Andrew Schwedel and Karen Harris, "After Easy Money: Managing In a New Era," *The Wall Street Journal,* May 14, 2010.

34. Christopher Meyer and Julia Kirby, "Leadership in the Age of Transparency," *Harvard Business Review,* April 2010.

35. Adam M. Grant, "The Hidden Advantages of Quiet Bosses," *Harvard Business Review,* December 2010.
36. Julian Birkinshaw, "Rethinking Management," *MIT Sloan Management Review,* Summer 2010.
37. Karl Taro Greenfeld, "Organized Chaos," *Bloomberg Businessweek,* April 26–May 6, 2010.
38. "First, People," *Inc.,* June 2010.
39. Tom Quinly, "Grooming the Next Generation of Leaders," *Harvard Business Review,* April 2011.

CHAPTER 8

1. Howard Schultz, "How Starbucks Got Its Mojo Back," *Newsweek,* March 21, 2011.
2. Adi Ignatius, "We Had to Own the Mistakes," *Harvard Business Review,* July–August 2010.
3. Howard Schultz, "When Latte Lost Its Luster," *The Wall Street Journal,* March 29, 2011.
4. Schultz, "How Starbucks Got Its Mojo Back."
5. Rana Foroohar, "How to Build Again," *Newsweek,* July 19, 2010.
6. "Nurturing a Spirit of Giving," *Inc.,* June 2010.
7. Alan Abelson, "Nuclear Nightmare," *Barron's,* March 21, 2011.
8. Damian Joseph, "Score Two for Sustainability," *Fast Company,* November 2010.
9. Virginia Postrel, "Love and Money," *Entrepreneur,* February 2011.
10. Dan Balz, "Obama's Team Moving Ahead Quickly to Prepare for 2012," *The Washington Post,* March 6, 2011.
11. Mark Sherman, "Walmart Faces Class-Action Lawsuit," *The Washington Times,* March 28, 2011.
12. Roger L. Martin, "The Effective Organization," *Harvard Business Review,* July–August 2010.
13. John Cloud and Oak Brook, "McDonald's Has a Chef?" *Time,* February 22, 2010.
14. Marcia W. Blenko, Michael C. Mankins, and Paul Rogers, "Strategies for a Changing World," *Harvard Business Review,* June 2010.
15. Joan E. Ricart, "How to Design a Winning Business Model," *Harvard Business Review,* January–February 2011.
16. Roger L. Martin, "How Hierarchy Can Hurt Strategy Execution," *Harvard Business Review,* July–August 2010.
17. Yun-Hee Kim, "New iPad Is Two-Edged Sword for Suppliers," *The Wall Street Journal,* March 4, 2011.
18. "How to Build Business Alliances," *Inc.,* June 2010.
19. Miles D. White, "The Four Ps of Global Business Expansion," *The Wall Street Journal,* November 12, 2010.
20. Jessica McKimmie, "Virtural Reality," *Inc.,* June 2010.
21. Robert M. Kimmit and Matthew J. Slaughter, "Insourcing: The Secret to Job Growth," *The Wall Street Journal,* December 6, 2010.
22. Paul Leinwand and Cesare Mainardi, "The Coherence Premium," *Harvard Business Review,* June 2010.
23. Pankaj Ghemawat, "Finding Your Strategy In the New Landscape," *Harvard Business Review,* March 2010.
24. Rich Karlgaard, "Ten Tips: Great Restructuring Winners," *Forbes,* February 28, 2011.
25. Michael S. Hopkins, "Putting the Science in Management Science," *MIT Sloan Management Review,* Summer 2010.
26. Pamela S. Shockley-Zalabak and Sherwyn P. Morreale, "Building High-Trust Organizations," *Leader to Leader,* Spring 2011.
27. Jeffrey Pfeffer, "How to Turn Around a Toxic Workplace," *Inc.,* June 2010.
28. Freek Vermeulen, Phanish Puranam, and Ranjay Gulati, "Change for Change's Sake," *Harvard Business Review,* June 2010.

CHAPTER 9

1. Michael S. Rosenwald, "Manufacturing Falls to 26-Year Low," *The Washington Post*, November 4, 2008.
2. Conor Dougherty, "Unemployment Rises in Every State," *The Wall Street Journal*, January 28, 2009.
3. Carmen M. Reinhart and Kenneth S. Rogoff, "What Other Financial Crises Tell Us," *The Wall Street Journal*, February 3, 2009.
4. Jonathan Wisman, Greg Hitt and Nafali Bendavid, "House Passes Stimulus Package," *The Wall Street Journal*, January 29, 2009.
5. Mark J. Perry, "The Truth about U.S. Manufacturing," *The Wall Street Journal*, February 25, 2011.
6. Thomas G. Donlan, "Manufacturing Jobs," *Barron's*, March 28, 2011.
7. Ibid.
8. Sam Williford, "U.S. Manufacturing Is Certainly Not What It Once Was," *The Wall Street Journal*, March 5–6, 2011.
9. Nick Leiber, "Suddenly, Made in USA Looks like a Strategy," *Bloomberg Businessweek*, March 28–April 3, 2011.
10. Robert M. Kimmit and Matthew J. Slaughter, "How to Jump Start U.S. Manufacturing," *The Washington Post*, August 13, 2010.
11. Mike Ramsey and Neal E. Boudette, "Japan Shortages Hit U.S. Units," *The Wall Street Journal*, March 30, 2011.
12. Keith Naughton, "The Happiest Man in Detroit," *Bloomberg Businessweek*, February 7–February 13, 2011.
13. Steven A. Melnyk, Edward D. Davis, Robert E. Spekman, and Joseph Sandor, "Outcome-Driven Supply Chains," *MIT Sloan Management Review*, Winter 2010.
14. Joe Light, "Manufacturing, Services Diverge on the Outlook," *The Wall Street Journal*, March 28, 2011.
15. Greg Bernas, "We're Listening and We Hear the Future," *Forbes*, March 28, 2011.
16. Nancy Trejos, "The Sewing Kit Checks Out, the Future Checks In," *The Washington Post*, March 20, 2011.
17. Virginia Postrel, "Love and Money," *Entrepreneur*, February 2010.
18. Brian Bremner, "Rise of the Machines (Again)," *Bloomberg Businessweek*, March 7–March 13, 2011.
19. Tom Mulier, "Nestlé's Recipe for Juggling Volatile Commodity Costs," *Bloomberg Businessweek*, March 21–March 27, 2011.
20. Lisa Brown, "Going Lean, But Not Mean," *St. Louis Post-Dispatch*, August 15, 2010.
21. Joan Muller, "The Bespoke Auto," *Forbes*, September 27, 2010.
22. Marilyn Much, "The Changing Face(book) of Internet Commerce," *Investor's Business Daily*, February 2, 2011.
23. John Jannarone, "Retailers Struggle In Amazon Jungle," *The Wall Street Journal*, February 22, 2011.
24. James R. Hagerty and Bob Tita, "Caterpillar Restarts Its Growth Engine—in the South," *The Wall Street Journal*, August 13, 2010.
25. Sudeep Reddy and Brian Blackstone, "Global Manufacturing Picks Up Pace," *The Wall Street Journal*, March 2, 2011.
26. Jim Efstathiou, Jr., and Kim Chapman, "The Great Shale Gas Rush," *Bloomberg Businessweek*, March 7–March 13, 2011.

27. David Simchi-Levi, "The 6 Forces Driving Supply Chain Design," *MIT Sloan Management Review*, Winter 2010.
28. Joe Gose, "Are Office Buildings Becoming Obsolete?" *Investor's Business Daily*, January 21, 2011.
29. James R. Hagerty, "Assembled Elsewhere," *The Wall Street Journal*, January 25, 2011.
30. Michael Schuman, "How Germany Became the China of Europe," *Time*, March 7, 2011.

CHAPTER 10

1. Rick Brimeyer, "Motivating Employees So That They Give a Rip," *Telegraph-Herald* (Dubuque), March 15, 2010.
2. Jamie Flinchbaugh, "Keys to Employee Engagement," *Assembly*, April 1, 2010; and Vineet Nayar, "Employee Happiness: Zappos vs. HCL, *Bloomberg Businessweek*, January 4, 2011.
3. Grace M. Endres, "The Human Resource Craze," *Organization Development Journal*, April 1, 2008; and "MetLife Study: Employee Loyalty Not Recession-Proof," *BusinessWire*, March 28, 2011.
4. Susan Adams, "In Praise of Praise," *Forbes*, www.forbes.com, accessed July 12, 2010; and Patricia Sellers, "How Dreamworks' CEO Builds a Happy Workforce," *Fortune*, March 15, 2011.
5. Michael Barone, "Message to Unions: Taylorism Died Long Ago," *Washington Examiner*, March 6, 2011.
6. Mike Hofman, "The Idea That Saved My Company," *Inc.*, October 2007; and Joie de Vivre Hotels, www.jdvhotels.com, accessed April 2011.
7. Luke Haywood, "Watch Your Workers Win," *Management Revue*, January 1, 2011; and "Motivation in Their Work Reduces Stress among IT Consultants," *Information Technology Newsweekly*, March 15, 2011.
8. Amanda Shantz and Gary Latham, "The Effect of Primed Goals on Employee Performance," *Human Resource Management*, March/April 2011.
9. Steve Schumacher, "Employee Evaluation," *Rock Products*, May 1, 2010.
10. Rachel Remley, "Retaining Top Talent," *Collector*, February 1, 2011.
11. Glenn G. Kautt, "Deep Rewards: If You Want to Motivate Your Clients and Staff, You Need to Develop the Framework for Moving Them in the Right Direction," *Financial Planning*, March 1, 2011.
12. David Nadler and Edward Lawler, "Motivation—a Diagnostic Approach," *Perspectives on Behavior in Organizations* (New York: McGraw-Hill, 1977).
13. Mohamed Hossam el-Din Hassan Khalifa and Quang Truong, "The Effects of Internal and External Equity on Components of Organizational Commitment," *International Journal of Management*, March 1 2011; and Rick Wartzman, "Yes, You Can Make Performance Reviews Worthwhile," *Bloomberg Businessweek*, April 8, 2011.
14. "Give Employees a Break and Keep Them Loyal," *The Dominion Post* (Morgantown, WV), March 12, 2011.
15. Wenzel Matiaske and Cerd Grozinger, "Introduction: Job Satisfaction Revisited," *Management Revue*, January 1, 2011.
16. Cameron Kauffman, "Employee Involvement: A New Blueprint for Success," *Journal of Accountancy*, May 1, 2010.
17. Sherri May, "Employees Disengaged? Try Out These Practices," *American Banker*, April 27, 2010.
18. "Mustang Sales Strong in March with More than 130% Increase over February," www.mustangdaily.com, accessed April 2011.

19. "Motivation: 4-to-1 Praise Ratio Works Wonders," *Capital*, February 27, 2011.
20. "The Global Star Search," *Fortune*, February 4, 2008; and Brian W. Swider, Wendy R. Boswell, and Ryan D. Zimmerman, "Examining the Job Search–Turnover Relationship," *Journal of Applied Psychology*, March 2011.
21. Dow Chemical Company, www.dow.com, accessed April 2011.
22. Michelle Kerr, "Champions for Change," *Risk & Insurance*, February 1, 2011.
23. Trish Chandler, "Employee Education, Development Prove Valuable to Businesses," *Business First*, January 14, 2011.
24. Lee Barney, "Speaking the Language of Generations X and Y," *Money Management Executive*, February 14, 2011; and Ronald J. Alsop, "Youth and Consequences," *Workforce Management*, February 1, 2011.
25. "Working with Millennials," *The Futurist*, March 1, 2011.
26. Patricia Quinn, "A Multigenerational Perspective on Employee Communications," *Risk Management*, January 1, 2010.
27. David Javitch, "Motivating Gen X, Gen Y Workers," *Entrepreneur*, www.entrepreneur.com, accessed July 12, 2010; and Lynee C. Lancaster, "Are You Ready for 76 Million Echo Boomers?" *Bottom Line Secrets*, September 15, 2010.
28. Megan L. Thomas, "Gen Y: No Jobs, Lots of Loans, Grim Future," www.msnbc.com, July 29, 2010; and Mark Scott, with Suzzanne Woollery, Chris Prentice, Moira Herbst, and Matt Robinson, "Gen Y's Empty Piggy Bank," *Bloomberg Businessweek*, July 19–July 25, 2010.
29. Jodi Glickman, "Leading Older Employees," *Bloomberg Businessweek*, April 5, 2011.
30. Rachel Reynolds, "Corporate Champions See Many Advantages in Diverse Work Force," *Business First*, February 2, 2011.

CHAPTER 11

1. Bill Taylor, "Why We (Shouldn't) Hate HR," *Harvard Business Review*, www.hbr.org, accessed June 2010.
2. Elisabeth Boone, "Human Resources Consulting," *Rough Notes*, February 1, 2011; Edward E. Lawler, III, Jay Jamrog, and John Boudreau, "Shining Light on HR Profession," *HRMagazine*, February 1, 2011; Benjamin Schneider and Karen B. Paul, "In the Company We Trust," *HRMagazine*, January 1, 2011; Leigh Buchanan, "Meet the Millennials," *Inc.*, September 2010; Joe Light, "Help Wanted," *The Wall Street Journal*, February 26, 2011; Robert Powell, "Working in Retirement," *The Wall Street Journal*, March 21, 2011; and Corrinne Hess, "Study: Women Hurt Most by Economic Downturn," *The Business Journal* (Milwaukee), April 28, 2011.
3. Roger Clegg, "At Age 50, Affirmative Action Looks Tired," *The Washington Times*, March 4, 2011.
4. Greg Stohr, "Wal-Mart vs. a Million Angry Women," *Bloomberg Businessweek*, November 22–November 28, 2010; Joan Biskupic, "High Court to Hear Wal-Mart's Appeal in Sex Bias Suit," *USA Today*, December 6, 2010; Richard Thompson Ford, "Everyday Discrimination," *Slate*, March 28, 2011; "Wal-Mart Sex Bias Case Hits Possible Court Block," *Boston Herald*, March 29, 2011; and Greg Stohr, "Wal-Mart Faces the Big Box of Class Actions," *Bloomberg Businessweek*, March 28–April 3, 1011.
5. "Myths and Stereotypes about Mental Disabilities Greatest Barrier to Employment," *States News Service*, March 15, 2011.

6. "ADA Violations at Hilton Hotels," *Paraplegia News,* March 1, 1011.

7. "AARP Lauds New Regulations That Will Help Protect Millions of Americans with Disabilities from Discrimination," *States News Service,* March 24, 2011; and Pat Murphy, "Employee with 'Episodic' Disability Can Sue, Rules 7th Circuit*," Lawyers USA,* January 4, 2011.

8. "Who's Disabled? Feds Expand the Definition," *The Wall Street Journal,* March 25, 2011; Stephanie Armour, "Workers with Epilepsy, Diabetes Gain under Obama Disability Rule," *Bloomberg Businessweek,* March 24, 2011; and Karen E. Klein, "Employers Gird for Disabilities Act Changes," *Bloomberg Businessweek,* April 27, 2011.

9. Susan M. Schaecher, "Nondisabled People Can't Pursue Claims that Testing Screens Out People with Disabilities," *HRMagazine,* January 1, 2011: Todd Shields, "Jewel-Osco Settles $3.2 Million Lawsuit Involving Employees with Disabilities," *Oak Leaves* (Oak Park, IL), January 20, 2011; and "Job Bias Claims Set New Record on Disability Surge," *Capital* (Annapolis), January 11, 2011.

10. James Dowd, "Experts Share Hiring Strategies—Finding, Keeping Best Workers Takes Effort," *The Commercial Appeal* (Memphis), April 6, 2011.

11. Steven E. F. Brown, "Survey: Social Networks Top Hiring Tool," *San Francisco Business Times,* June 30, 2010; and Susan Adams, "Expert Tips for Using LinkedIn," *Forbes,* www.forbes.com, accessed June 2011.

12. Kronos, www.kronos.com/hiring-software, accessed May 2011.

13. Jennifer Wang, "Unbeatable," *Entrepreneur,* February 2011.

14. Jim Rendon, "10 Things Human Resources Won't Say," *SmartMoney,* April 22, 2010.

15. Lexis Nexis, www.lexisnexis.com, accessed May 2011.

16. Rachel Farrell, "6 Cardinal Sins of Management," www.MSN.Careerbuilder.com, accessed May 2011.

17. Nancy Miller, "Temps, the New Normal?" *Barron's,* October 18, 2010; Nancy Lublin, "In Defense of Millennials," *Fast Company,* October 2010.

18. Randstad, www.us.randstad.com, accessed May 2011.

19. Matt Quinn, "Creative Employee Training Ideas," www.Inc.com, accessed May 2011.

20. U.S. Department of Labor, www.doleta.gov, accessed May 2011.

21. Red Cross, www.redcross.org, accessed May 2011.

22. GlobeSmart, www.globesmart.com, accessed May 2011.

23. Kasthuri V. Henry, "Grooming the Next Generation," *Strategic Finance,* January 1, 2011.

24. Diana Middleton, "Want to Know Which Training Works? Take This Course," *The Wall Street Journal,* www.wsj.com, accessed June 2011.

25. Alix Stuart, "Blazing Their Own Trails," *CFO,* September 2010.

26. McDonalds, www.mcdonalds.com, accessed June 2011.

27. Ivy Hughes, "Meet Your Mentor," *Entrepreneur,* September 2010; and Gwen Moran, "Meet Your Mentor," *Entrepreneur,* December 2010.

28. Dave Willmer, "8 Ways to Keep Your Best Workers on Board," *Computerworld,* June 21, 2010.

29. Motley Fool Staff, "Q-and-A with Nucor CEO Dan DiMicco," *The Motley Fool,* www.fool.com, January 10, 2011.

30. Josh Heck, "Study: Health Insurance Accounts for 8 Percent of Total Employee Compensation," *Wichita Business Journal,* June 9, 2010; and "Employee Compensation Averages $29.39 an Hour," *Charlotte Business Journal,* June 12, 2010.

31. Jessica Flint, "Analyze This," *Bloomberg Businessweek,* February 21–February 27, 2011; and Joe Mullich, "2011 Benefits Trends," *The Wall Street Journal,* April 5, 2011.

32. "100 Best Companies to Work For," *Fortune,* May, 2011.

33. Sarah E. Needleman, "Should a Business Offer Paid Maternity Leave?" *The Wall Street Journal,* July 6, 2010.

34. B. Checket-Hanks, "Employee Needs Comes First," *Air Conditioning, Heating & Refrigeration News,* January 31, 2011.

35. "Moving Work Forward," *States News Service,* February 1, 2011; and Katherin Reynolds Lewis, "Flexible Jobs = Happy Worker Bees?" *Fortune,* April 20, 2011.

36. Alix Stuart, "The Perils of Flextime," *CFO,* July/August 2010.

37. Rachel Kenshalo, "Evolving Office Technologies: Telecommuting, Conserving Energy and Resources," *Alaska Business Monthly,* February 1, 2010.

38. Shane Kite, "No Dress Code Required," *US Banker,* January 1, 2011.

39. Ben Horowitz, "Why Even Your Ultra-Hip Startup Team Needs Job Titles," *Fortune,* March 16, 2011.

CHAPTER 12

1. James Estrin, "Answers about the Nation's Labor Laws," *The New York Times,* April 4, 2011.

2. Sam Hananel, "Membership in Labor Unions Continues to Decline, *The Washington Times,* January 23, 2011.

3. Peter Whoriskey and Amy Gardner, "As Unions' Dynamic Shifts, So Does Fight," *The Washington Post,* February 28, 2011.

4. Drake Bennett, "Dispatch from a Divided State," *Bloomberg Businessweek,* March 20, 2011.

5. "Wisconsin and Wider," *The Economist,* February 26, 2011.

6. Mark Mix, "The Real Issue in Labor Battle," *Investors Business Daily,* March 8, 2011.

7. Nick Keppler, "Business Leaders Bristle at the Honoring of Labor History," *New Haven Advocate,* March 31, 2011.

8. Nadia Sussman, "Triangle Fire: In Search of Sweatshops," *The New York Times,* March 25, 2011.

9. Jon Healey, "How Hard Should It be to Form a Union?" *The Los Angeles Times,* March 30, 2011.

10. Valerie Van Kooten, "The Fire That Changed History," *The Des Moines Register,* March 23, 2011.

11. Joe DeMarco, "Unions Were Responsible for Child Labor Laws, 40-Hour Work Week," www.madison.com, March 22, 2011.

12. James Estrin, "Answers about the Nation's Labor Laws," *The New York Times,* March 24, 2011.

13. Sam Hananel, "Laborer's Move Boosts Hope for Unified Unions," *Associated Press,* August 14, 2010.

14. www.aflcio.org, accessed June 2011.

15. Mark Niquette, "Workers' Rights Battle Goes National at Pivotal Time for Labor," *Bloomberg Businessweek,* February 22, 2011.

16. Nina Easton, "Labor Unions: Flailing in D.C. and Making Enemies on Main Street," *Fortune,* March 21, 2011.

17. Robert Samuelson, "Is Organized Labor Obsolete?" *The Buffalo News,* March 4, 2011.

18. Niquette, "Workers' Rights Battle Goes National at Pivotal Time for Labor."

19. Joanna Weiss, "Unions Are Losing the PR Battle," *The Boston Globe,* February 27, 2011.

20. Ron Borgas, "NFL Talks Take a Backward Step," *The Boston Herald,* March 22, 2011.

21. Barb Kocera, "'Labor Law Still Matters,' NLRB Chair Says," *Workday Minnesota,* April 4, 2011; and www.nlrb.gov, accessed June 2011.

22. Antoinette Oliver, "Facebook Comments and the NLRB," *Pittsburgh Post Gazette,* April 4, 2011.

23. David Montgomery, "Feds May Sue Over Secret Ballot Vote," *Rapid City Journal,* March 18, 2011.

24. Robert Barro, "Unions vs. the Right-To-Work," *The Wall Street Journal,* February 28, 2011.

25. Susan Redden, "Debate Heats Up in State Capitol on Right-To-Work Issue," *The Joplin (Missouri) Times,* March 19, 2011.

26. Grant Schulte, "Anti-Union Mood Moves to Nebraska's Modest Unions," *The Seattle Times,* March 30, 2011.

27. www.dol.gov, accessed April 5, 2011; and Christopher Hinton, "American Flight Attendants Forbidden to Strike," *The Wall Street Journal,* March 25, 2011.

28. Sam Farmer, "NFL Labor Negotiations Mark 15th Day of Mediation," *The Los Angeles Times,* March 11, 2011.

29. "Entertainment Events Wins Arbitration Relating to Late Night Catechism," *Broadway World.Com,* March 17, 2011.

30. "Wade Davis' $12.6 Million Pre-Arbitration Contract with the Tampa Bay Rays," *Business Insider,* April 4, 2011; and Colin Fly, "Hart Secure with Brewers after Big Season," *USA Today,* March 29, 2011.

31. www.adr.org, accessed June 2011.

32. Terry Maxon, "APFA: American Airlines Is Losing Money, the Economy Is Bad and We're Not Going to Get a Release," *The Dallas Morning News,* March 24, 2011.

33. Ashby Jones, "A Season on the Brink? Judge Declines to Halt NFL Lockout," *The Wall Street Journal,* April 7, 2011.

34. Bill Saporito, "The Life of a $725,000 Scab," *Fortune,* March 20, 2011.

35. "A Union Education," *The Wall Street Journal,* March 1, 2011.

36. David Shephardson, "UAW Membership Up 6 Percent," *The Detroit News,* April 1, 2011.

37. Tom Krisher, "Auto Union Must Look Out for Companies Too," *Bloomberg Businessweek,* February 18, 2011.

38. Ezra Klein, "Does Big Labor Have Any Big Ideas?" *The Washington Post,* February 27, 2011; and www.aflcio.org, accessed June 2011.

39. www.dol.gov, accessed April 8, 2011; and www.bea.gov, accessed June 2011.

40. "Celebrity 100," *Forbes,* July 19, 2010.

41. Joann S. Lublin, "A Closer Look at Three Big Paydays," *The Wall Street Journal,* November 16, 2011.

42. Stephen Gandel, "CEO Pay Up, Average Worker Not So Much," *Time,* March 18, 2011.

43. Gary Strauss and Matt Krantz, "Stock Options Swell CEO Pay," *USA Today,* April 4, 2011.

44. Ibid.

45. Gretchen Morgenson, "Report Criticizes High Pay at Fannie and Freddie," *The New York Times,* March 31, 2011.

46. Connie Guglielmo, "HP Chief Executive Hurd Resigns after Sexual Harassment Probe," *Bloomberg Businessweek,* August 7, 2010.

47. Rana Foroohab, "Stuffing Their Pockets," *Newsweek,* September 13, 2010.

48. Todd Frankel, "Do Today's Rich Deserve What They Get? Maybe Not," *St. Louis Post Dispatch,* March 6, 2011.

49. "25 Highest Paid CEOs with MBAs," *Bloomberg Businessweek,* April 11, 2011.

50. Jason Clenfield and Ian Katz, "In Japan, Underpaid—And Loving It," *Bloomberg Businessweek,* July 11, 2010.

51. Elizabeth G. Olsen, "Wal-Mart's Gender Bias Case: What's at Stake?" *Fortune,* April 4, 2011.

52. Jenna Goudreau, "The 15 Jobs Where Women Earn More than Men," *Forbes,* March 14, 2011.

53. Lisa Quast, "Good News for Younger Women: There's a Smaller Wage Gap," *Forbes,* November 29, 2010.

54. Stephen Miller, "Despite Strides by U.S.Women, Wage Gap Remains," *Society for Human Resource Management Journal,* March 4, 2011.

55. www.americanprogress.org, accessed June 2011.

56. Katie Kiernan, "Responding to a Sex Harassment Claim," *New Hampshire Business Review,* January 28, 2011.

57. www.eeoc.gov/law, accessed April 10, 2011; and Alissa Figueroa, "Workplace Harassment: Same Sex Sexual Harassment Cases Are on the Rise," *The Christian Science Monitor,* July 21, 2010.

58. Oliver Staley, "Yale Probed by Education Department over Sex Harassment Claim," *Bloomberg Businessweek,* April 1, 2011.

59. Jessica Bennett, "Everything I Learned about Women I Learned from Reality TV," *Newsweek,* November 11, 2010.

60. www.workingmother.com, accessed June 2011.

61. Selena Maranjian, "The Companies Doing Best by Their Employees," *The Motley Fool,* April 7, 2011.

62. www.haemonetics.com, accessed June 2011.

63. Jason Daley, "A Senior Moment," *Entrepreneur,* January 25, 2011.

64. Pamela Vip, "Caring for an Elderly Loved One Can Take a Financial Toll," *St. Louis Post Dispatch,* April 3, 2011.

65. www.nih.gov, accessed June 2011.

66. www.dol.gov, accessed June 2011.

67. Jonathan Martin, "Medical-Pot Users Await High Court Decision on Workplace," *The Seattle Times,* February 28, 2011.

68. Andrew Denney, "Workplace Violence Decline," *Columbia Daily Tribune,* March 29, 2011.

69. Rich Cordivari, "Warning Signs of Workplace Violence," *The West Hartford News,* April 3, 2011.

70. Lisa Quast, "Workplace Violence—the 5 Most Important Tips Women Need to Know to Protect Themselves," *Forbes,* January 10, 2011.

CHAPTER 13

1. Emily Steel, "At Super Bowl, Many Ads Fail to Score," *The Wall Street Journal,* February 7, 2011.

2. Alden M. Hayashi, "Are You 'Pushing' in a 'Pull' World?" *MIT Sloan Management Review,* Spring 2010.

3. www.vehix.com, accessed April 2011.

4. Amy Chen, "How to Find Hidden Airfare Deals," *Money,* April 2011.

5. Susan Spano, "Top 10 Websites," *Entrepreneur,* May 2010.

6. Marilyn Much, "The Changing Face(book) of Internet Commerce," *Investor's Business Daily,* February 2, 2011.

7. Mikal E. Belicove, "A Community of One's Own," *Entrepreneur,* March 2010.

8. J. Bonasia, "The Art of Generating Wisdom from Crowds," *Investor's Business Daily,* April 26, 2010.

9. Lauren A. E. Schuker, "Double Feature: Dinner and a Movie," *The Wall Street Journal,* January 5, 2011.

10. Beth Comstock, "Unleashing the Power of Marketing," *Harvard Business Review,* October 2010.

11. Pamela Oldham, "Selling the Sales Team," *Deliver Magazine,* July 2010.

12. Pamela Oldham, "Shifting Loyalties," *Deliver Magazine,* July 2010.
13. Amy C. Cosper, "Go Gaga," *Entrepreneur,* February 2011.
14. Jennifer Wang, "Never Fly Coach Again," *Entrepreneur,* November 2010.
15. www.pharpro.com, accessed April 2011.
16. Bruce Einhorn, Stuart Bigg, and Caroline Winter, "More Car Jobs Shift to Mexico," *Bloomberg Businessweek,* June 28–July 4, 2010.
17. Sharon Terlep, "UAW Puts Preserving Jobs at Top of Agenda," *The Wall Street Journal,* March 30, 2011.
18. Jennie Yabroff, "No More Sacred Cows," *Newsweek,* January 11, 2010.
19. Nick Lieber, "Speed Dial: Getting Prices Right," *Bloomberg Businessweek,* May 31–June 8, 2010.
20. If you are interested in finding vegetarian restaurants, check out happycow.net before you go on a trip. You will find places to go, hours, and prices; *Budget Travel,* April 2010.
21. Marcia Layton Turner, "Business Gurus Wise Up," *Deliver Magazine,* October 2010.
22. Joseph Sternberg, "Now Comes the Global Revolution in Services," *The Wall Street Journal,* February 10, 2011.
23. Mikal E. Belicove, "Gentle Reminders," *Entrepreneur,* April 2011.
24. Joseph Checkler and Jeffrey A. Trachtenberg, "Bookseller Borders Begins a New Chapter . . . II," *The Wall Street Journal,* February 17, 2011.
25. Yuval Levin, "The Debt Dilemma," *Time,* April 4, 2011.
26. Erik K. Clemon, Paul F. Nunes, and Matt Reilly, "Six Strategies for Successful Niche Marketing," *The Wall Street Journal,* May 24, 2010.

CHAPTER 14

1. Lisa Lin, Tian Ling and Li Yanping, "Foreign Carmakers Try Brands Just for China," *Bloomberg Businessweek,* March 7–March 13, 2011.
2. "Don't Ruin Your Reputation," *Deliver Magazine,* July 2010.
3. Michelle Locke, "Minidesserts Provide Quick Fix for Snack Lovers," *The Washington Times,* March 25, 2011.
4. David Sharp, "L.L. Bean Puts Pressure on Rivals by Eliminating Shipping Charges," *The Washington Times,* March 25, 2011.
5. Richard McGill Murphy, "Eclectic Electrics," *Bloomberg Businessweek,* May 17–May 23, 2010.
6. Matthew Barakat, "Better Burgers Are Sizzling," *St. Louis Post-Dispatch,* July 18, 2010.
7. Paul Ziorbro, "Smoothie Hype Cools for Now," *The Wall Street Journal,* July 2, 2010.
8. James R. Hagerty, "Zippo Preps for a Post-Smoker World," *The Wall Street Journal,* March 8, 2011.
9. Catherine Bolgar, "A Giant Leap for the World of Business and Industry," *The Wall Street Journal,* March 21, 2011.
10. Jason Amaral, Edward G. Anderson Jr. and Geofrey G. Parker, "Putting It Together: How to Succeed in Distributed Product Development," *MIT Sloan Management Review,* Winter 2011.
11. Marc Gunther, "3 M's Innovation Revival," *Fortune,* September 27, 2010.
12. Sriram Dasu and Richard B. Chase, "Designing the Soft Side of Customer Service," *MIT Sloan Management Review,* Fall 2010.
13. Ellen Byron, "Whitens, Brightens and Confuses," *The Wall Street Journal,* February 23, 2011.
14. Matt Vilano, "The Secret Sauce Part II," *Entrepreneur,* April 2011.
15. Rebecca W. Hamilton, Joydeep Srivastava and Ajay Thomas Abraham, "When Should You Nickel-and-Dime Your Customers?" *MIT Sloan Management Review,* Fall 2010.
16. Barry Newman, "The Lighter Side of Counterfeiting Puts Zippo in a Fix," *The Wall Street Journal,* March 25, 2011.
17. Kurt Badenhausen, "The World's Most Valuable Brands, "*Forbes,* August 30, 2010.
18. Anne Kadet, "Chasing Lost Brands," *Smart Money,* November 2020.
19. Roben Farzad, "Tang Gets a Second Rocket Ride," *Bloomberg Businessweek,* April 26–May 2, 2010.
20. Joan Schneider and Julie Hall, "Why Most Product Launches Fail," *Harvard Business Review,* April 2011.
21. Walter S. Mosberg, "In and Out of Office: Putting iPads to Work," *The Wall Street Journal,* March 17, 2011.
22. John Donahoe, "How eBay Developed a Culture of Experimentation," *Harvard Business Review,* March 2011.
23. Kris Hudson and Alexandra Berzon, "Hoteliers Build on the Hipness Factor," *The Wall Street Journal,* February 22, 2011.
24. David C. Edelman, "Branding In the Digital Age," *Harvard Business Review,* December 2010.
25. Ari Levy and Joseph Gaiante, "Who Wants to Buy a Digital Elephant?" *Bloomberg Businessweek,* March 8, 2010.
26. Beth Kowitt, "When Less Is . . . Less?" *Fortune,* November 15, 2010.
27. Uzma Khan and Ravi Dhar, "Making the Price of Indulgence Right," *MIT Sloan Management Review,* Spring 2011.
28. Jay Palmer, "Pricing Power in the Grocery Aisle," *Barron's,* February 21, 2011.

CHAPTER 15

1. Robert Wright and John Reed, "Pressure Grows on Supply Chains," *Financial Times,* April 21, 2010; and William Pesek, "The Cataclysm This Time," *Bloomberg Businessweek,* March 21–March 27, 2011.
2. Damian Joseph, "Score Two for Sustainability," *Fast Company,* November 2010.
3. "Product Pipeline," *Fortune,* May 3, 2010.
4. Matthew Boyle, "Who's Really Stocking Your Grocer's Shelf," *Bloomberg Businessweek,* March 28–April 3, 2011.
5. Geoff Colvin, "The UPS Green Dream," *Fortune,* December 27, 2010.
6. David M. Katz, "The Shortest Distance to Cash," *CFO,* March 2010.
7. P. Fraser Johnson and Michiel R. Leenders, "Minding the Supply Savings Gap," *MIT Sloan Management Review,* Winter 2010.
8. Cotton Timberlake, "With Stores Nationwide, Macy's Goes Local," *Bloomberg Businessweek,* October 4–October 10, 2010; Marilyn Alva, "The Retaking of the Retail Trade, " *Investor's Business Daily,* February 28, 2011; and "Suburban Renewal," *Barron's,* February 21, 2011.
9. Jen Wieczner, "The Mall Goes High Tech," *Smart Money,* November 2010.
10. Jonathan Birchall, "Walmart Launches Same-Day Pickup," *Financial Times,* October 7, 2010.
11. Marisa Taylor, "Treasure Hunt," *Smart Money,* April 2011.
12. "An ATM That Dispenses Gold," *The Wall Street Journal,* May 14, 2010.

13. David Sharp, "L.L. Bean Puts Pressure on Rivals by Eliminating Shipping Charges," *The Washington Times*, March 25, 2011.

14. Russ Banham, "Managing the Strategic Supply Chain," *The Wall Street Journal*, April 27, 2010.

15. Hau L. Lee, "Don't Tweak Your Supply Chain—Rethink It End to End," *Harvard Business Review*, October 2010.

16. Moon Ihlwan and Kevin Cho, "Creative When No One's Looking," *Bloomberg Businessweek*, April 25, 2010.

17. Charles H. Fine, "Collaborate or Race? How to Design the Value Chain You Need," *MIT Sloan Management Review*, Winter 2010.

18. David Simchi-Levi, "The 6 Forces Driving Supply Chain Design," *MIT Sloan Management Review*, Winter 2010.

19. Mark Vandenbosch and Stephen Sapp, "Opportunism Knocks," *MIT Sloan Management Review*, Fall 2010.

20. Kathleen Kingsbury, "Prescription for a Turnaround," *Time*, February 15, 2010.

21. Peter Senge, "The Sustainable Supply Chain," *Harvard Business Review*, October 2010.

22. Todd W. Price, "Making Resource Management Work: Sustainability and the Supply Chain," *Harvard Business Review*, March 2011.

23. "XPorta," *Bloomberg Businessweek*, accessed online, April 12, 2011.

24. Mike Olson, "Reverse Logic," *Bloomberg Businessweek*, March 28–April 3, 2011.

25. "A Key Link in the Supply Chain," *Fortune*, September 6, 2010.

26. Jennifer Lawler, "The Logic of Thirds," *Entrepreneur*, March 2010.

27. Ibid.

28. Michael Gaynor, "Stand and Deliver," *Washingtonian*, December 2010.

29. Marc Gunter, "Union Pacific: 'Building America,'" *Fortune*, July 8, 2010.

30. "A Scan-tastic App Goes Mainstream," *Entrepreneur*, May 2010.

CHAPTER 16

1. "Does Return on Social Media Justify the Spending?" *Deliver Magazine*, July 2010.

2. Walter S. Mossberg, "iPad 2: Thin, Not Picture Perfect," *The Wall Street Journal*, March 10, 2011.

3. Brian Quinton, "Multiple Marketing Personalities," *Entrepreneur*, January 2011.

4. Leslie Dance, "It's All about Me," advertisement in *BtoB*, January 17, 2011.

5. Kate Maddox, "Motorola's New Solution," *BtoB*, January 17, 2011.

6. Felix Gillette, "Don Draper's Revenge," *Bloomberg Businessweek*, November 29–December 5, 2010.

7. Sharon Begley, "I Can't Think," *Newsweek*, March 7, 2011.

8. Marilyn Much, "The Changing Face(book) of Internet Commerce," *Investor's Business Daily*, February 2, 2011.

9. Denise Campbell, "What Is Your Social Media Strategy?" *Black Enterprise*, November 2010.

10. Peter Romeo, "Social Media 50," *Restaurant Business*, April 2011.

11. Gregory Unruh and Richard Ettenson, "Growing Green," *Harvard Business Review*, June 2010; and Jason Ankeny, "Green Idols," *Entrepreneur*, April 2011.

12. Sam Schechner and Emily Steel, "Super Bowl Promises Extra Kick for Ads," *The Wall Street Journal*, January 31, 2011.

13. Emily Steel, "At Super Bowl, Many Ads Fail to Score," *The Wall Street Journal*, February 7, 2011.

14. Sam Schechner and Emily Steel, "Demand Builds for TV Ad Time," *The Wall Street Journal*, April 25, 2011.

15. Edmund Lee, "Major Marketers Shift More Dollars toward Social Marketing," *Advertising Age*, April 11, 2011.

16. Jeff Bercovici, "This Space for Rent," *Forbes*, May 9, 2011.

17. J. Turner, A. Scheller-Wolf, and S. Tayur, "Scheduling of Dynamic In-Game Advertising," *Operations Research*, January–February 2011.

18. Matt Robinson, "As Seen on TV—And Sold at Your Local Store," *Bloomberg Businessweek*, July 26–August 1, 2010.

19. Jason Ankeny, "Building a Brand on a Budget," *Entrepreneur*, May 2011.

20. Ellen Byron, "In-Store Sales Begin at Home," *The Wall Street Journal*, April 25, 2011.

21. Reggie Bradford and David Rollo, "Marketing Flourishes via Social Media," *Advertising Age*, February 14, 2011.

22. "Does Return on Social Media Justify the Spending?"

23. www.garden.com, accessed April 2011.

24. Brian Truitt, "37 Ways Social Media Can Make Your Life Just a Little Easier," *USA Weekend*, March 25–27, 2011.

25. Christopher Hosford, "Direct in Reverse," *BtoB*, February 14, 2011.

26. www.vitamix.com, accessed April 2011.

27. Geoffrey A. Fowler, "Are You Talking to Me?" *The Wall Street Journal*, April 25, 2011.

28. www.pocarisweat.com, accessed March 2011.

29. www.performanceprobe.com, accessed April 2011.

30. www.masterfoods.com, accessed April 2011.

31. Joann Muller, "The Bespoke Auto," *Forbes*, September 27, 2010.

32. Neil Woodcock, Andrew Green, and Michael Starkey, "Social CRM as a Business Strategy," *Journal of Database Marketing & Customer Strategy Management*, March 2011; and Michael Bush, "What Is Social CRM?" *Advertising Age*, February 28, 2011.

33. Pamela Oldham, "Selling the Sales Team," *Deliver Magazine*, July 2010.

34. David H. Freedman, "On the Road with a Salesperson," *Inc.*, April 2010.

35. Kasey Welrum, "Sales Tips from the World's Toughest Customers," *Inc.*, April 2010.

36. Christopher Hosford, "Content Drives Sales Enablement," *BtoB*, May 2, 2011.

37. Suzanne Vranica, "Public Relations Learned the Hard Way," *The Wall Street Journal*, December 20, 2010.

38. Christopher Hosford, "Social Marketing Gaining Prominence in Companies' Plans," *BtoB*, April 4, 2011.

39. Kathryn Koegel, "On the Road to Mass Mobile Coupons: Printables and Paperless," *Advertising Age*, May 9, 2011.

CHAPTER 17

1. Bill Saporito, "Where the Jobs Are: The Right Spots in the Recovery," *Time*, January 14, 2011.

2. www.bls.gov/oco, accessed May 2011.

3. Ali Velshi, "Today's 'It' Jobs: Accounting and IT," *Money*, February 2011.

4. Jeffrey C. Thomson, "Let's Talk about the CPA," *Strategic Finance*, January 1, 2011.

5. www.imanet.org/certification, accessed May 2011.

6. Teresa Odie, "Hot Jobs: Accountants," *Philadelphia Inquirer Digital*, April 19, 2011.

7. "Choosing the Right Accountant for Your Business," *Inc.,* April 19, 2010.

8. www.aicpa.org, accessed May 2011;

9. Francine McKenna, "Why No Warnings? Investors Press Audit Regulator," *Forbes,* March 28, 2011.

10. Roger Parloff, "Sarbanes-Oxley Struck Down? Not Even Close," *Fortune Magazine,* June 28, 2010; and www.pacobus.org, accessed May 2011.

11. Joshua Zumbrun, "Fed Requests Comments on Proposals for Dodd-Frank Law," *Bloomberg Businessweek,* February 8, 2011; and Joshua Gallu, "Dodd-Frank May Cost $6.5 Billion and 5,000 Workers," *Bloomberg Businessweek,* February 14, 2011.

12. Matthew Furman, "Auditing Your Auditor," *CFO,* April 2010.

13. Brenden Sheehan, "Senate Questions Auditors' and SEC's Role in Financial Crisis," *Business Insider,* April 13, 2011.

14. Steve Eder, "Lehman Auditor May Bear the Brunt," *The Wall Street Journal,* March 14, 2011.

15. Jim McTague, "Auditors in the Doghouse," *Barron's,* March 21, 2011.

16. www.theiia.org/certification, accessed May 2011.

17. Henry Unger, "How Would You Change Our Tax System?" *The Atlanta Journal-Constitution,* April 18, 2011.

18. "Super Rich See Super Savings on Taxes," *Detroit Free Press,* April 17, 2011.

19. www.gasb.org, accessed May 2011; and "Factbox: Top Budgetary Threats to State, Local Governments," *Reuters,* April 21, 2011.

20. Elizabeth Heubeck, "Nonprofits Face Fierce Funding Climate," *Baltimore Business Journal,* March 11, 2011.

21. Ted Needleman, "Making the Next Step: Mid-Range Accounting Packages Offer More Capabilities for More Users," *Accounting Today,* February 1, 2011.

22. Jeffrey L. Wilson, "The Best Small Business Accounting Software," *PC Magazine,* May 13, 2010.

23. Dave McClure, "Changing with the Times: Entry-Level Accounting Packages in the Midst of Three Revolutions," *Accounting Today,* January 1, 2011.

24. Joseph M. Langmead and Jalai Soroosh, "Accounting for Financial Instruments: More Turmoil Ahead," *The CPA Journal,* February 1, 2011.

25. www.associatedcontent.com/article/7980907, accessed May 2011.

26. Ken King, "Financial Goals by the Numbers," *Sheboygan Press,* April 30, 2011.

27. Chris James, "Controlling Your Business Cash," *Dallas Business Journal,* July 28, 2010; and Jack G. Hardy, "Get Serious about Cash Flow," *The Miami Herald,* April 25, 2011.

28. Rich Smith, "Under Armour Fouls Out," *The Motley Fool,* April 26, 2011.

29. Sanjiv Mahajan, "Economy Up or Down—'Cash Is Always King,'" *Supply & Demand Chain Executive,* March 1, 2011.

30. Julie Briggs, Tracy Higginbotham, and Theresa Slater, "Here Are Some Tips for Trimming Expenses," *The Post-Standard* (Syracuse, NY), March 1, 2011.

31. www.bizfinance@about.com, accessed May 2011; and Mitchell Eichen, "Not All Cash Is Created Equal," *Forbes,* March 25, 2011.

32. Anand Chokkavelu, "How Cheap Is Nordstrom's Stock by the Numbers," *The Motley Fool,* May 2, 2011.

CHAPTER 18

1. Diane Richey, "Security and the CFO: Show Me the Money," *Security Magazine,* February 1, 2011.

2. David Skok, "Cash Is King: 8 Tips for Optimizing Your Startup Financial Strategy," *Fortune,* April 26, 2011.

3. Sewell Chan, "Financial Crisis Was Avoidable, Inquiry Finds," *The New York Times,* January 25, 2011.

4. Mark Modica, "'Government Motors' Is Still a Lemon," *The New York Post,* April 17, 2011; and David Welch, "For Investors the Shine Is Off the New GM," *Bloomberg Businessweek,* April 14, 2011.

5. Robert Samuelson, "Why TARP Has Been a Success Story," *The Washington Post,* March 27, 2011.

6. www.mccormick.com, accessed May 2011.

7. Jonathan Blum, "Smart Money," *Entrepreneur,* February 2011.

8. Kevin Garcia, "How to Undertake a Financial Restructuring," *Inc.,* April 30, 2011.

9. Trevor Clawson, "Are CFOs Getting It Right on Internal Auditing," *CFO World,* April 21, 2011.

10. Peter Millar, "Making FCPA Compliance Sustainable," *Business Finance Magazine,* May 2, 2011.

11. Martin Zwilling, "How to Predict Your Start-up's Financial Future," *Inc.,* April 8, 2011.

12. David M. Katz, "Luke Skywalker, Supply-Chain Hero," *CFO,* June 11, 2010.

13. Joe Keohane, "That Guy Who Called the Big One? Don't Listen to Him. Inside the Paradox of Forecasting," *The Boston Globe,* January 9, 2011.

14. Morey Stettner, "Accurate Budget Forecasts Rely on Full Team Efforts," *Investor's Business Daily,* April 11, 2011.

15. Martin Shenk, "Oil-Price Estimate for 2011 Increased by 8.5% by U.S. on Growing Fuel Demand," *Bloomberg Businessweek,* January 11, 2011; and "The 2011 Oil Shock," *The Economist,* March 3, 2011.

16. Lauren Cannon, "How to Pay Employees When You Can't Make Payroll," *Inc.,* April 1, 2011.

17. Robert Bovarnick, "Make Them Pay," *Forbes,* November 23, 2010.

18. Jason Notte, "MasterCard May Best Giant Visa on Swipe Fees," *The Street.com,* May 4, 2011; and "MasterCard IQ Tops Forecasts on Consumer Spending," *The Wall Street Journal,* April 3, 2011.

19. Kishore S. Swaminathan, "Taming the Data That Dominates Our Work Lives," *Fortune Magazine,* April 14, 2011.

20. Bea Quirk, "Find Financing Alternatives to Banks," *Atlanta Business Chronicle,* April 29, 2011.

21. "Paying Your Suppliers. What Kind of Payment Methods Will Your Suppliers Prefer?" *Entrepreneur,* May 6, 2011.

22. www.nifb.com/webinars/alternative-funding-sources, accessed May 2011.

23. Pamela Ostermiller, "Borrowing from the Family: Get It in Writing, Even from Mom," *Utah Business,* January 1, 2011.

24. "CFOs Say Cash Flow Is Top Concern and Financial Priority for 2011," *The Secured Lender,* January 1, 2011.

25. Bridget Riley, "Lending Picks Up," *San Francisco Business Times,* May 6, 2011; and Robb Mandelbaum, "Survey Says Small-Business Lending Is Surging," *The New York Times,* April 30, 2011.

26. Vincent Ryan, "Lien on Me," *CFO,* April 2010.

27. www.businessfinance.com/revolving-line-of-credit/htm, accessed May 2011; and Vincent Ryan, "Revolvers Return, with Some Twists," *CFO,* May 1, 2011.

28. www.gecapital.com, accessed May 2011.

29 Dyan Machan, "Borrowers Say They Got Good Deals When Investors Buy Their Receivables," *Smart Money,* March 2011.

30 Neil Berdiev, "The Post-Banking Loan," *Entrepreneur,* May 2010.

31 Karen E. Kline, "A Menu of Finance Options for Exporters," *Bloomberg Businessweek,* March 15, 2011.

32 Dyan Machan, "Are Small-Business Credit Cards a Plastic Trap?" *Smart Money,* May 4, 2011.

33 Ibid.

34 www.pfizer.com, accessed May 2011; and "Power of Incentives," *Investors Business Daily,* April 8, 2011.

35 Tim Mullaney, "Is Help on the Way for the Tech IPO Market?" *USA Today,* May 5, 2011.

36 Ben Worthen, "For Silicon Valley Start-Ups, Funding Boom Is Lopsided," *The Wall Street Journal,* May 6, 2011.

37 "Most Debt-Laden Companies in the S&P 500," www.cnbc.com, accessed May 2011.

38 Matthew Vincent, "Sales Soaring High Despite Regulatory Concerns," *Financial Times,* May 6, 2011; and Rory Lancman, "Wall Street's Sheriff Needs Many More Deputies," *Bloomberg Businessweek,* May 3, 2011.

39 Brooke Masters, "How Madoff Cast His Spell," *Financial Times,* May 4, 2011.

40 Sebastian Walsh, "Is Dodd-Frank Already Doomed to Fail?" *Financial News,* May 6, 2011; and Ben Protess, "Treasury Urges Small Banks to Embrace Dodd-Frank," *The New York Times,* May 2, 2011.

CHAPTER 19

1. Lynn Cowan, "Linkedin, Freescale Poised to IPO by End of Month," *Dow Jones Newswire,* May 10, 2011.

2. Roben Farzad, "Initial Private Offering," *Bloomberg Businessweek,* January 16, 2011.

3. Halah Touryalai, "Profit Shakes Up Goldman Sachs," *Forbes,* January 19, 2011.

4. Aaron Lucchetti, Gina Chon, and Jacob Bunge, "Nasdaq Looking for a Partner," *The Wall Street Journal,* February 26, 2011; and Chris Redman, "Are Bigger Stock Exchanges Better?" *Fortune Magazine,* March 21, 2011.

5. "Exchange Undergoes a Face-Lift," *The Washington Times,* April 11, 2011; and Michael Santoli, "Nasdaq and ICE Make Their Move," *Barron's,* April 4, 2011.

6. Nina Mehta, Lynn Thomasson, and Paul M. Barrett, "The Machines That Ate the Market," *Bloomberg Businessweek,* May 30, 2010; and David K. Randall, "New York Stock Exchange Sold," *Associated Press,* February 16, 2011.

7. Ibid.

8. www.nyse.com, accessed May 15, 2011.

9. Jonathan Weil, "NASDAQ Eating Machine Starving for NYSE Deal," *Bloomberg Businessweek,* April 27, 2011.

10. Nicole Perlroth, "NYSE: You Are Witnessing A 'Complete Crushing' of the NASDAQ," *Forbes,* May 10, 2011.

11. "Metalink's Shares to Be Delisted from NASDAQ," *PR Newswire,* April 18, 2011; and Emily Chasan, "Will Stock Split Really Change Citi's Shareholder Base," *The Wall Street Journal,* May 10, 2011.

12. Nathaniel Popper, "Galleon Billionaire Raj Rafaratnam Convicted in Insider Trading Case," *The Los Angeles Times,* May 11, 2011.

13. Aude Lagorce, "Africa Offers New Investment Opportunities," *St. Louis Post Dispatch,* July 11, 2011; and Richard (Rick) Mills, "Looking into Africa," *Resource Investor,* May 11, 2011.

14. Jennifer Schonberger, "Preferred Stocks," *Kiplinger's Personal Finance,* April 2011.

15. Carla Fried, "Bonds 101," *Money Magazine,* June 2010; and www.investopedia.com, accessed May 2011.

16. "Companies Considering Issuing 100-Year Bonds; Investors Should Steer Clear," *The Wall Street Journal,* August 23, 2010; and Katy Burne, "MIT Offers Century Bond," *The Wall Street Journal,* May 11, 2011.

17. "About Bond Ratings," *Charles Schwab On Investing,* Winter 2010.

18. Robert Frick, "Convertible Bonds," *Kiplinger's Personal Finance,* April 2011.

19. William Baldwin, "Six Ways to Inflation-Proof Your Bonds," *Forbes,* March 2, 2011.

20. Kevin Harlan, "The Changing Broker Scene Offers Options for Traders," *Investor's Business Daily,* April 25, 2011.

21. Theresa W. Carey, "Newest Trading Play: Screen Savings," *Barron's,* March 15, 2010; and Elizabeth Ody, "The Best of the Online Brokers," *Kiplinger's Personal Finance,* February 2011.

22. David Futrelle, "How Well Do You Know Risk?" *Money Magazine,* January–February 2011; and Elizabeth Ody, "5 Strategies to Lower Risk," *Kiplinger's Personal Finance,* January 2011.

23. "Yale May Not Have the Key: When Diversification Does Not Work," *The Economist,* March 12, 2011.

24. William Baldwin, "Capital Gains and Capital Losses: Rules for Investors," *Forbes,* March 25, 2011.

25. www.aboutmcdonalds/mcd/investors.html, accessed May 2011.

26. Dan Caplinger, "Why This Stock Is Not Doomed," *The Motley Fool,* May 10, 2011.

27. www.finance.yahoo.com, accessed May 2011.

28. Karen Gullo, "Goldman Sachs Accused by Marvell Founder of Margin Call Fraud," *Bloomberg Businessweek,* April 12, 2011.

29. James B. Stewart, "Municipal Bond Investors Can Collect Their Interest and Sleep Peacefully," *Smart Money,* April 2011.

30. "Why Junk Bond Rally Should Be Cheered—and Jeered," *Associated Press,* May 9, 2011; and Nicole Bullock, "Junk Bond Yields Hit Record Lows," *Financial Times,* May 10, 2011.

31. Mark Jewell, "Three Experts Debunk Mutual Fund Myths," *St. Louis Post Dispatch,* April 3, 2011.

32. John Waggoner, "USA Today's Fund All-Stars: 20 Top Performers," *USA Today,* May 13, 2011.

33. Elizabeth Ody, "Now You Can Buy Load Funds Commission-Free," *Kiplinger's Personal Finance,* May 2010; and Chris Barth, "How a Family Shopping Spree Can Help Your Mutual Fund Performance," *Forbes,* May 4, 2011.

34. Mark Jewell, "Investors Flee Managed Funds," *St. Louis Post Dispatch,* April 17, 2011.

35. Andrew Bary, "ETFs Everywhere," *Barron's,* November 18, 2010; Andrew Leckey, "The Numbers Don't Lie: ETFs Are a Growing Trend," *St. Louis Post Dispatch,* December 26, 2010; and Mark Jewell, "ETFs Are Coming of Age with Their Low-Cost Appeal," *St. Louis Post Dispatch,* January 2, 2011.

36. Robert Samuelson, "For the Young, There's a Silver Lining in the Housing Bust," *The Washington Post,* May 14, 2011.

37. Alex J. Pollock, "On Housing, There Will Be More Lean Years Ahead," *The Wall Street Journal,* May 12, 2011.

38. Ibid.

39. Gillian Tett, "TARP Shows that U.S. Can Break Political Deadlock," *Financial Times,* May 12, 2011.

CHAPTER 20

1. Curtis Arnold, "Best Credit Cards for 2010," *Bottom Line Personal,* March 15, 2010.
2. www.barterquest.com/, accessed April 2011.
3. Judy Holland, "Face Value," *Washingtonian,* October 2010.
4. Brady Dennis, "New $100 Bills Delayed by Errors In Production," *The Washington Post,* December 7, 2010.
5. Steve Forbes, "Memo to Merkel: Stop Killing the Euro," *Forbes,* April 25, 2011.
6. Andy Greenberg, "Crypto Currency," *Forbes,* May 9, 2011.
7. Bill Saporito, "The Swipe-Fee Free-for-All," *Time,* April 4, 2011.
8. Michael Santoli, "A Crowd Climbs Aboard QE2," *Barron's,* October 11, 2010; and "Quantitative Easing," editorial, *The Washington Post,* October 20, 2010.
9. Kelly Evans, "Overlooked Inflation Cue: Follow the Money," *The Wall Street Journal,* April 12, 2011.
10. David Von Drehle, "The Many Who Said No to Easy Money," *Time,* February 14, 2011.
11. Sudeep Reddy and Luca Di Leo," Opinions Are Split on Feb Policy Move," *The Wall Street Journal,* November 3, 2010.
12. Forbes, "Memo to Merkel."
13. www.federalreserveonline.gov, accessed April 2011.
14. "How the Fed Works," *Time,* January 4, 2010.
15. www.federalreserve.gov/monetarypolicy/reservereq, accessed April 2011.
16. Randall W. Forsyth, "Monetary Steroids," *Barron's,* October 25, 2010.
17. George Melloan, "The Fed Can Create Money, Not Confidence," *The Wall Street Journal,* August 24, 2010.
18. Laura Cohn, "Battle Royal: Credit vs. Debit," *Kiplinger's Personal Finance,* April 2010.
19. www.investorwords.com/955/commercial_bank, accessed April 2011.
20. http://legal-dictionary.thefreedictionary.com/Glass-Steagall+Act, accessed April, 2011.
21. Lynn Brenner, "The Little Banks That Can," *AARP,* July and August 2010.
22. Saporito, "The Swipe-Fee Free-for-All."
23. www.data.worldbank.org/, accessed April 2011.
24. Neil Irwin, "World Bank, IMF Leaders: Recovery Still a Shaky One," *The Washington Post,* April 17, 2011.
25. Howard Schneider, "IMF Chief Sees Recovery as a Work In Progress," *The Washington Post,* April 12, 2011.
26. Howard Schneider, "IMF Considers a Restocked 'Tool Kit,'" *The Washington Post,* July 2, 2010.
27. Bob Davis, "IMF Sees Rising Risks Slowing Pace of World Recovery," *The Wall Street Journal,* July 8, 2010; and Howard Schneider, "IMF Panel Seeks a New Consensus," *The Washington Post,* March 8, 2011.
28. Ian Talley and Sudeep Reddy, "IMF Shifts Stance on Capital Controls," *The Wall Street Journal,* April 6, 2011.

CHAPTER A

1. Lloyd Grove, "Geithner Says New Financial Crisis Coming," *Business Insider,* May 19, 2011; and Peter Ferrara, "How the Government Created a Financial Crisis," *Forbes,* May 19, 2011.
2. Michael Virtanen, "New York Court Reinstates Restaurant Worker's Product Liability Suit," *Insurance Journal,* May 13, 2011; and "NY Top Court Reinstates Product Liability Suit," *The Wall Street Journal,* May 10, 2011.
3. Carl Schramm, "Are We Thwarting Medical Innovations?" *Forbes,* March 8, 2011.

4. Robert Kelly, "Five Questions: Partner Says Fighting for the Little Guy Drives Law Firm," *St. Louis Post Dispatch,* May 13, 2011; and Ashby Jones, "Mississippi Jury Returns Largest Asbestos Verdict in U.S. History," *The Wall Street Journal,* May 6, 2011.
5. Jack Elliott Jr., "Sherwin Williams Appeals Mississippi Lead Paint Verdict," *Bloomberg Businessweek,* April 19, 2011.
6. Jeffrey Liker, "Toyota Recall Crisis: What Have We Learned?" *Harvard Business Review,* February 11, 2011; and Makiko Kitamura, Alan Ohneman, and Yuki Hagiwara, "Why Lexus Doesn't Lead the Pack in China," *Bloomberg Businessweek,* March 24, 2011.
7. Daniel Fisher, "NASA Report Makes Life Tougher for Lawyers Suing Toyota," *Forbes,* February 8, 2011.
8. Tom Randall, "Merck's Risky Bet on Research," *Bloomberg Businessweek,* May 1, 2011.
9. Sophia Pearson and Jeff Feeley, "Merck Vioxx Accord Spawns Pay-Day Scrap among Lawyers," *Bloomberg,* February 18, 2011.
10. Scott James, "Long Battle Against Guns Began with Son's Death," *The New York Times,* May 12, 2011.
11. Andrew M. Harris, "McDonald's Obesity Case Can't Proceed as Group Suit," *Bloomberg,* October 27, 2010.
12. Quentin Fottrell, "Will High Court Ruling Hurt Consumers?" *Smart Money,* May 18, 2011.
13. Reuven Brenner, "Google's Conundrum: Buy the Patents or Pay the Lawyers," *Forbes,* April 7, 2011.
14. John Tozzi and Susan Decker, "Patent Reform: High Stakes for Small Biz," *Bloomberg Businessweek,* October 3, 2010; and Toby Kusner, "The Patent Office Dilemma: How Congress Robs Peter to Pay Paul," *Forbes,* May 6, 2011.
15. Abigail Field, "The Supreme Court's 'Landmark' Ruling Didn't Really Change Much," *Daily Finance,* June 29, 2011; and Thomas Claburn, "Supreme Court Patent Ruling Avoids Tough Issues," *Information Week,* June 27, 2010.
16. www.islandpatent.com, accessed June 2011.
17. Brian Deagon, "Big Patent-Infringement Awards More Exception than Rule: Study," *Investor's Business Daily,* March 24, 2011; and Ben Dobbin, "New Look at Kodak Infringement Claim," *St. Louis Post Dispatch,* March 26, 2011.
18. Gregg Keizer, "Microsoft Downplays Impact of Possible Supreme Court Ruling," *Computerworld,* April 19, 2011.
19. Stephanie Bodoni, "Microsoft, Nokia, Challenge Apple's 'App Store' EU Trademark," *Bloomberg Businessweek,* May 13, 2011.
20. Alina Tugend, "Buyer, Be Aware the Law Is on Your Side," *The New York Times,* May 6, 2011.
21. Patricia Mertz Esswein, "What You Need to Know about Warranties," *Kiplinger's Personal Finance,* January 2011.
22. David J. Popeo, "The SEC's Misguided New Mission: Foreign Government Change Agent," *Forbes,* May 18, 2011.
23. "Did the Microsoft Case Change the World?" *The New York Times,* May 14, 2011; and Nick Eaton, "DOJ Will Let Microsoft Antitrust Oversight Expire in May," *Seattle Post Intelligencer,* April 28, 2011.
24. David Sarno, "Justice Department's Landmark Judgment Against Microsoft Will Expire," *The Los Angeles Times,* May 11, 2011.
25. Nina Mehta, "NYSE-NASDAQ Deal Seen as Producing Multiple Monopolies by Justice Lawyers," *Bloomberg,* May 18, 2011.
26. Ben Protess, "Treasury Urges Small Banks to Embrace Dodd-Frank," *The New York Times,* May 2, 2011; Phil Mattingly, "Dodd-Frank Consumer Bureau Changes Approval by U.S.

House Panel," *Bloomberg Businessweek,* May 22, 2011; and Ashby Jones, "Fine Print on Dodd-Frank, 'Sox on Steroids,' Slow to Arrive," *The Wall Street Journal,* May 2, 2011.

27. Michelle Singletary, "Bureau Drafts New Forms to Make Adjustable-Rate Mortgages 'True Costs' Clearer," *The Washington Post,* May 21, 2011.

28. Douglas A. McIntyre, Ashley C. Allen, Charles B. Stockdale, Michael B. Sauter, and Jonathan Berr, "The 10 States That Profit Most from Sin," *The Atlantic Monthly,* May 16, 2011.

29. John Merline, "Rich Pay Growing Share of Tax," *Investor's Business Daily,* April 27, 2011; and Peter Coy, "Taxation Without Complication," *Bloomberg Businessweek,* February 20, 2011.

30. Penelope Lemov, "States Look to Collect Internet Sales Taxes," *Governing,* May 19, 2011.

31. Janet Novack, "Has Amazon Lost the South and Tea Party in Internet Tax War?" *Forbes,* April 29, 2011.

32. Kyung M. Song, "Battle over Internet Sales Taxes Rekindles in Congress," *The Seattle Times,* May 21, 2011.

33. Angie Mohr, "5 Myths about Personal Bankruptcy," *San Francisco Chronicle,* May 5, 2011.

34. www.bankruptcyaction.com, accessed June 2011; and Les Christie, "Bankruptcy Can Save Your House from Foreclosure," CNN Money.com, July 24, 2010.

35. Paul M. Barrett, "A New Assault on Regulation Is Gathering Force—and It's Deploying a Constitutional Weapon," *Bloomberg Businessweek,* February 20, 2011.

36. Stephen Breyer, "Airline Deregulation Revisited," *Bloomberg Businessweek,* January 20, 2011.

37. Robert Samuelson, "Stuck in a Post-Crisis Gloom," *The Washington Post,* May 22, 2011; and Charles Gasparino, "More Useless Govt," *The New York Post,* May 22, 2011.

38. Paul Sperry, "Dodd-Frank Red Tape Will Kill 1,000 Small Banks," *Investor's Business Daily,* May 20, 2011; and Sam Batkins, "The Costs of Dodd-Frank? Even the Feds Don't Know," *The Hill,* May 18, 2011.

39. Robert Pear and David M. Herszenhorn, "Obama Hails Vote on Health Care as Answering 'the Call of History,'" *The New York Times,* March 21, 2010; and David Goldstein, "Sebelius Takes the Heat in Debate Over Health Care Reform," *The Kansas City Star,* May 21, 2011.

40. "U.S. House of Representatives Votes to Repeal President Obama's Health Care Bill," *The Herald Sun,* January 20, 2011.

CHAPTER B

1. Steve Lohr, "Harnessing the Deluge of Information," *International Herald Tribune,* April 25, 2011.

2. Doug Henschen, "SAP's Blockbuster BusinessObjects Upgrade," *InformationWeek,* March 14, 2011; David Raths, "Business Intelligence Efforts Get a Boost," *Healthcare Informatics,* January 1, 2011; and "Deloitte Announces Alliance Agreement with MicroStrategy to Deliver Business Intelligence and Analytic Solutions, *Computer Weekly News,* March 24, 2011.

3. "CEOs Give Technology Executives Power Tips," *The Wall Street Journal,* May 19, 2011; Shawn Banerji, "The Next Phase of CIO Leadership," *Baseline,* January 1, 2011; Susan Nunziata, "Executive Briefing: Analysis & Insights for the Busy CIO," *CIO Insight,* March 1, 2011; Robert L. Bailey, "Planning Your Information Career," *Information Management Journal,* January 1, 2011; and Chris Murphy, "Create," *InformationWeek,* March 14, 2011.

4. Maryanne MacDonald, "Put an End to Electronic Clutter," *The Commercial Appeal,* March 4, 2011.

5. "Data Mining for Business Intelligence," *Journal of Mathematics,* March 22, 2011; Doug Henschen, "HP's Murky Move Back into Data Warehousing," *InformationWeek,* February 28, 2011; and Chris Murphy, "Is Data Mining Free Speech?" *InformationWeek,* May 16, 2011.

6. Yahoo Pipes, pipes.yahoo.com, accessed June 2011.

7. Chris Anderson, "The Web Is Dead," *Wired,* September 2010.

8. Ed Arnold, "A Second Knock—Sposto Interactive CEO Hears Opportunity Calling Again with Idea for Extranet System," *The Commercial Appeal,* March 14, 2011.

9. Kurt Marko, "How Secure Is Your iPad?" *InformationWeek,* May 12, 2011.

10. Olga Kharif, "Brownnosing for Google Broadband," *Bloomberg Businessweek,* March 11, 2010.

11. Amy Schatz, "Obama Broadband Plan Faces Uncertain Future," *The Wall Street Journal,* February 10, 2011.

12. Stacey Higginbotham, "Broadband Caps: Maybe It's Not Just about TV," *Bloomberg Businessweek,* March 18, 2011; and Amy Schatz and Thomas Catan, "AT&T Deal Is Key Test for Obama," *The Wall Street Journal,* March 22, 2011.

13. Paul Korzeniowski, "Medical Robots Bring Docs to Patients," *Investor's Business Daily,* March 30, 2011.

14. Internet2, www.internet2.edu, accessed June 2011.

15. Douglas MacMillan, "With Friends Like This, Who Needs Facebook?" *Bloomberg Businessweek,* September 13–September 19, 2010; Ben Paynter, "Happy Hour," *Fast Company,* March 2010; and Victoria Barret "The Web's Big Upstart," *Forbes,* September 6, 2010.

16. Jason Daley, "Tearing Down the Walls," *Entrepreneur,* December 2010.

17. Sheila Riley, "Social Media Complicating Tech Field's Ethical Issues," *Investor's Business Daily,* March 31, 2011; and Jon Newberry "Social Media Create Regulatory Worries for Businesses," *Courier,* February 4, 2011.

18. Edward Gismatullin, "The Big Business of Sifting through Social Media Data," *Bloomberg Businessweek,* October 25–October 31, 2010; and Doug Henschen, "IT Meets Marketing," *InformationWeek,* April 11, 2011.

19. Tony Shaw, "Web 2.0 for Smarter Business," *Baseline,* March 1, 2011.

20. Reinhardt Krauss, "Mobile Pay Spurs Rush to Control Systems," *Investor's Business Daily,* March 30, 2011; Douglas MacMillan, "Turning Smartphones into Cash Registers," *Bloomberg Businessweek,* February 14–February 20, 2011; and Pete Barlas, "Mobile Payments Draw a Crowd," *Investor's Business Daily,* March 29, 2011.

21. Michael Green, "Better, Smarter, Faster: Web 3.0 and the Future of Learning," *American Society for Training and Development,* April 1, 2011.

22. K. Rupp and S. Selberherr, " The Economic Limit to Moore's Law," *Semiconductor Manufacturing,* February 2011.

23. Chris Murphy, "Innovation Atrophy," *InformationWeek,* May 30, 2011.

24. Doug Henschen, "They're Ready," *InformationWeek,* February 14, 2011.

25. Bob Evans, "Why CIOs Must Have a Tablet Strategy," *InformationWeek,* March 14, 2011; and Robert Cini, "Corporate Technology Experts May Have Some Issues with iPads," *South Florida Business Journal,* January 14, 2011.

26. Katie Hoffmann, "IBM Mainframes: Boring but Profitable," *Bloomberg Businessweek,* July 28–August 1, 2010.

27. John Agsalud, "Virtual Desktops Provide Lower Cost, Less Upkeep," *Honolulu Star,* February 22, 2011; and David Stodder, "APM for Virtualization," *InformationWeek,* March 14, 2011.

28. Kurt Eisele-Dyrli, "Expanding Computing with Virtual Desktops," *District Administration,* February 1, 2011.

29. Thomas Claburn, "Google Slows App Rollouts for Businesses," *InformationWeek,* March 28, 2011; Charles Babcock, "What's a Cloud Operating System?" *InformationWeek,* March 28, 2011; and Charles Babcock, "Lessons from FarmVille," *InformationWeek,* May 16, 2011.

30. April Wortham, "Cloud Experts Simplify a Complex Idea," *Houston Business Journal,* January 7, 2011.

31. Andrew Binstock, "Cloud Programming? Ready, Set . . . Yow," *InformationWeek,* March 26, 2011; and Charles Babcock, "VMware Tries Integrated Approach to Hybrid Cloud Management," *InformationWeek,* March 28, 2011.

32. Jon Newberry, "A Down-to-Earth Look at Cloud Computing," *Business Courier* (Cincinnati), February 4, 2011; M. O'Bannon, "Three Buzzwords That Really Changed the Profession," *CPA Practice Advisor,* April 1, 2011; Ashlee Vance, "The Power of the Cloud," *Bloomberg Businessweek,* March 7–March 13, 2011; Michal Lev-Ram, "Intel's Sunny Vision for the Cloud," *Fortune,* January 17, 2011; Mickey McManus, "The Madness of the Clouds," *Bloomberg Businessweek,* March 28, 2011; Joseph Galante, "Amazon.com Service Aims to Simplify Cloud Computing," *Bloomberg,* January 19, 2011; and Ashlee Vance, "The Cloud: Battle of the Tech Titans," *Bloomberg Businessweek,* March 3, 2011.

33. Thomas Claburn, "Google Gambles on Chromebooks as a Service," *InformationWeek,* May 30, 2011.

34. Mathew J. Schwartz, "Dropbox Accused of Misleading on Security," *InformationWeek,* May 30, 2011.

35. Gina Smith, "VMware Sercie Manages Cloud Apps," *InformationWeek,* May 30, 2011; Charles Babcock, "VMware Platform Takes It Deeper into Cloud," *InformationWeek,* April 25, 2011; Charles Babcock, "VMware's Hybrid Cloud Plan: All in the Family," *InformationWeek,* February 28, 2011.

36. Victoria Barret, "Free Software for Suits," *"Forbes,* February 2011; Aaron Ricadela and Cliff Edwards, "Apotheker Pushes HP into Cloud, Software," *Bloomberg Businessweek,* March 15, 2011; Kenneth J. Richard, "Enterprise Software," *InformationWeek,* March 28, 2011; Alexander Wolfe, "IT Pro Ranking," *InformationWeek,* April 11, 2011; and Doug Henschen, "Chatter.com," InformationWeek, February 14, 2011.

37. Andrew Conry-Murray, "Your Health? There's an App for That," *InformationWeek,* September 13, 2010; Christianna McCausland, "There's an App Maker for That," *Fast Company,* September 2010; and "Top 10 Mobile Apps for Business Collaboration," *InformationWeek,* April 19, 2011.

38. Marianne Kolbasuk McGee, "Ford Driving Health, Safety With Mobile Apps," *InformationWeek,* May 18, 2011.

39. Grant Moerschel, "4 Ways to Lower Mobility Risk," *InformationWeek,* January 31, 2011.

40. Christine Hall, "Dos and Don'ts of IT Security from Houston Experts," *Houston Business Journal,* January 7, 2011; and Erik Bataller, "Risk Avengers," *InformationWeek,* January 31, 2011.

41. Mike Smith, "Information Security," *Mortgage Technology,* March 1, 2011.

42. Mathew J. Schwartz, "Sony Reels from Massive Customer Data Breach," *InformationWeek,* May 16, 2011; and Daisuke Wakabayashi, "Accounts Hacked at Small Sony Unit," *The Wall Street Journal,* May 21, 2011.

43. "Study Reveals There Is a 'Golden Hour' for Phishing," *Credit Union Journal,* February 7, 2011; and Peter Svensson, "Banks, Card Issuers Warn of E-Mail Breach—Companies Expect Wave of Spam, 'Spear Phishing,'" *The Commerical Appeal,* April 5, 2011.

44. Matt Liebowitz, "Cybercrime Blotter: High Profile Hacks of 2011," *Security News Daily,* February 24, 2011; and Kelly Jackson Higgins, "Hack Highlights Vulnerability," *InformationWeek,* April 11, 2011.

45. Erik Bataller, "Cyber Partnerships," *InformationWeek,* March 28, 2011.

46. Platform for Privacy Preferences, www.w3.org/P3P, accessed June 2011.

47. Natasha Singer, "Drawing Some Boundaries around Data Mining," *International Herald Tribune,* May 2, 2011.

48. Alisa Gumbs, "How Tweet It Is," *Black Enterprise,* December 2010.

CHAPTER C

1. Leslie P. Norton, "In Japan's Turmoil, There's Fresh Logic in a Logistics Provider," *Barron's,* March 28, 2011.

2. Timothy W. Martin, Thomas M. Burton and Stephanie Simon, "Tornadoes Leave a Trail of Devastation," *The Wall Street Journal,* April 29, 2011.

3. Scott Steinberg, "Protecting Your Business from Identity Theft," *The Costco Connection,* August 2010; and Joan Goldwasser, "Top Gripe: ID Theft," *Kiplinger's Personal Finance,* June 2011.

4. Adrian Sainz and Matt Sedensky, "Memphis Nearing Flood Record," *The Washington Post,* May 10, 2011.

5. "Expecting the Unexpected," advertisement in *Bloomberg Businessweek,* March 7–March 13, 2011.

6. Karan Girotra and Serguei Netessine, "How to Build Risk into Your Business Model," *Harvard Business Review,* May 2011.

7. Adam Borison and Gregory Hamm, "How to Manage Risk (After Risk Management Has Failed)," *MIT Sloan Management Review,* Fall 2010.

8. Andy Pasztor and Peter Sanders, "Boeing Miscalculated Risks," *The Wall Street Journal,* April 6, 2011.

9. Figures are from *GEICO Direct,* Spring/Summer 2010.

10. Dinah Wisenberg Brin, "More Firms Insuring Selves," *The Wall Street Journal,* March 23, 2011.

11. M. P. McQueen, "Disaster Insurance: How Well Are You Covered?" *The Wall Street Journal,* March 26–27, 2011.

12. Joe Mullich, "Sustainability's Third Wave," *The Wall Street Journal,* April 22, 2011.

CHAPTER D

1. "The Billionaire Issue," *Forbes,* March 28, 2011.

2. "Thinking Your Way to Wealth," *AAA World,* July/August 2010.

3. E. S. Browning, "Retiring Boomers Find 401(K) Plans Fall Short," *The Wall Street Journal,* February 19–20, 2011.

4. Glenn Townes, "Living the Frugal Life," *Black Enterprise,* January 2010.

5. Glenn Townes, "Thrifty Family Living," *Black Enterprise,* March 2011.

6. Michelle Singletary, "Want to Be Rich? Stop Acting like It," *The Washington Post,* January 31, 2010.

7. Donna Rosato, "7 Secrets of Super Savers," *Money,* August 2010.
8. Jason Evers Roberson, "Lessons from Her Father," *Black Enterprise,* April 2010.
9. Janet Bodnar, "The College Debt Trap," *Kiplinger's Personal Finance,* December 2010.
10. Kimberly Lankford, "Tying the Knot," *Kiplinger's Personal Finance,* June 2010.
11. LaToya M. Smith, "There's No Place Like (a New) Home," *Black Enterprise,* October 2010.
12. James B. Stewart, "Does the Sacred Cow of Home Ownership Make Sense Financially?" *Smart Money,* May 2011.
13. Ali Veshi, "Buying a Home Now Is a No-Brainer," *Money,* December 2010.
14. Patricia Mertz Esswein, "Should You Buy or Rent?" *Kiplinger's Pesonal Finance,* April 2010.
15. J. D. Roth, "Credit Care," *Entrepreneur,* March 2011.
16. "Most Rewarding Cards If . . . " *Money,* May 2011.
17. Angela Wu, "College Credit," *Newsweek,* September 10, 2010.
18. Rosalind Resnick, "Keep Your Credit Clean," *Entrepreneur,* July 2010.
19. Joan Goldwasser, "Win Rewards for Paying Off Debt," *Kiplinger's Personal Finance,* February 2011.
20. Glenn Townes, "Ingredients for Success," *Black Enterprise,* January 2011.
21. Jeff Wuorio, "Debit Cards Are Great, But Not for Everything," *USA Weekend,* February 18, 2011.
22. Laura Cohn, "Battle Royal: Credit vs. Debt," *Kiplinger's Personal Finance,* April 2010.
23. Connie Prater, "What the New Credit Card Law Means to You," www.creditcard.com, accessed May 2011.
24. Anne Kates Smith, "Financial Reform and Your Wallet," *Kiplinger's Personal Finance,* September 2010.
25. Leslie Scism, "More Go without Life Insurance," *The Wall Street Journal,* August 30, 2010.
26. Kimberly Lankford, "Life (Insurance) Begins at 50," *Kiplinger's Personal Finance,* June 2011.
27. Mary Beth Franklin, "The New Look of Retirement," *Kiplinger's Personal Finance,* February 2011.
28. Dallas Salisbury, "Workers Are Waking Up to the New Normal," *The Wall Street Journal,* April 5, 2011.
29. Donna Rosato, "Don't Be Bummed Out, Boomer," *Money,* March 2011.
30. Robert J. Samuelson, "Social Security Is Middle-Class Welfare," *Newsweek,* March 14, 2011.
31. Rosalind Resnick, "A Better Plan for Not Working," *Entrepreneur,* June 2010.
32. Laura Cohn, "The Latest Blow: Shrinking Pensions," *Kiplinger's Personal Finance,* June 2010.
33. Hilery Z. Simpson, "How Does Your 401(k) Match," Bureau of Labor Statistics, May 26, 2010.
34. Penelope Wang, "Make the Best of a Bad 401(k)," *Money,* March 2010.
35. Ezra Klein, "The Great Risk Shift," *Newsweek,* December 8, 2010.
36. Christopher Condon, "The Quiet Force in Personal Finance," *Bloomberg Businessweek,* March 7–March 13, 2011.
37. Paul Sullivan, "More Money for the Kids," *Fortune,* February 7, 2011.

glossary

401(k) plan (p. D-14) A savings plan that allows you to deposit pretax dollars and whose earnings compound tax free until withdrawal, when the money is taxed at ordinary income tax rates.

absolute advantage (p. 62) The advantage that exists when a country has a monopoly on producing a specific product or is able to produce it more efficiently than all other countries.

accounting (p. 464) The recording, classifying, summarizing, and interpreting of financial events and transactions to provide management and other interested parties the information they need to make good decisions.

accounting cycle (p. 470) A six-step procedure that results in the preparation and analysis of the major financial statements.

accounts payable (p. 474) Current liabilities involving money owed to others for merchandise or services purchased on credit but not yet paid for.

acquisition (p. 131) One company's purchase of the property and obligations of another company.

administered distribution system (p. 421) A distribution system in which producers manage all of the marketing functions at the retail level.

administrative agencies (p. A-3) Federal or state institutions and other government organizations created by Congress or state legislatures with delegated power to pass rules and regulations within their mandated area of authority.

advertising (p. 438) Paid, nonpersonal communication through various media by organizations and individuals who are in some way identified in the advertising message.

affiliate marketing (p. 156) An Internet-based marketing strategy in which a business rewards individuals or other businesses (affiliates) for each visitor or customer the affiliate sends to its website.

affirmative action (p. 294) Employment activities designed to "right past wrongs" by increasing opportunities for minorities and women.

agency shop agreement (p. 331) Clause in a labor–management agreement that says employers may hire nonunion workers; employees are not required to join the union but must pay a union fee.

agents/brokers (p. 407) Marketing intermediaries who bring buyers and sellers together and assist in negotiating an exchange but don't take title to the goods.

American Federation of Labor (AFL) (p. 326) An organization of craft unions that championed fundamental labor issues; founded in 1886.

annual report (p. 466) A yearly statement of the financial condition, progress, and expectations of an organization.

annuity (p. D-11) A contract to make regular payments to a person for life or for a fixed period.

apprentice programs (p. 304) Training programs involving a period during which a learner works alongside an experienced employee to master the skills and procedures of a craft.

arbitration (p. 334) The agreement to bring in an impartial third party (a single arbitrator or a panel of arbitrators) to render a binding decision in a labor dispute.

assembly process (p. 240) That part of the production process that puts together components.

assets (p. 474) Economic resources (things of value) owned by a firm.

auditing (p. 468) The job of reviewing and evaluating the information used to prepare a company's financial statements.

autocratic leadership (p. 192) Leadership style that involves making managerial decisions without consulting others.

balance of payments (p. 65) The difference between money coming into a country (from exports) and money leaving the country (for imports) plus money flows from other factors such

Note: Terms and definitions printed in italics are considered business slang, or jargon.

as tourism, foreign aid, military expenditures, and foreign investment.

balance of trade (p. 64) The total value of a nation's exports compared to its imports over a particular period.

balance sheet (p. 473) Financial statement that reports a firm's financial condition at a specific time and is composed of three major accounts: assets, liabilities, and owners' equity.

ballyhooed *Talked about in an exaggerated way.*

banker's acceptance (p. 571) A promise that the bank will pay some specified amount at a particular time.

bankruptcy (p. A-15) The legal process by which a person, business, or government entity unable to meet financial obligations is relieved of those obligations by a court that divides any assets among creditors, allowing creditors to get at least part of their money and freeing the debtor to begin anew.

bargaining zone (p. 333) The range of options between the initial and final offer that each party will consider before negotiations dissolve or reach an impasse.

barter (p. 555) The direct trading of goods or services for other goods or services.

bear market *Situation where the stock market is declining in value and investors feel it will continue to decline.*

been there, done that *Prior experience.*

benchmarking (p. 221) Comparing an organization's practices, processes, and products against the world's best.

benefit segmentation (p. 368) Dividing the market by determining which benefits of the product to talk about.

blog (p. 454) An online diary (Web log) that looks like a Web page but is easier to create and update by posting text, photos, or links to other sites.

bond (p. 529) A corporate certificate indicating that a person has lent money to a firm.

bonds payable (p. 475) Long-term liabilities that represent money lent to the firm that must be paid back.

bookkeeping (p. 470) The recording of business transactions.

bottom line *The last line in a profit and loss statement; it refers to net profit or loss.*

brain drain (p. 42) The loss of the best and brightest people to other countries.

brainstorming (p. 187) Coming up with as many solutions to a problem as possible in a short period of time with no censoring of ideas.

brand (p. 387) A name, symbol, or design (or combination thereof) that identifies the goods or services of one seller or group of sellers and distinguishes them from the goods and services of competitors.

brand association (p. 389) The linking of a brand to other favorable images.

brand awareness (p. 389) How quickly or easily a given brand name comes to mind when a product category is mentioned.

brand equity (p. 389) The value of the brand name and associated symbols.

brand loyalty (p. 389) The degree to which customers are satisfied, like the brand, and are committed to further purchases.

brand manager (p. 390) A manager who has direct responsibility for one brand or one product line; called a product manager in some firms.

brand name (p. 358) A word, letter, or group of words or letters that differentiates one seller's goods and services from those of competitors.

breach of contract (p. A-10) When one party fails to follow the terms of a contract.

break-even analysis (p. 397) The process used to determine profitability at various levels of sales.

brightest days *The best of times for a person or organization.*

broadband technology (p. B-10) Technology that offers users a continuous connection to the Internet and allows them to send and receive mammoth files that include voice, video, and data much faster than ever before.

budget (p. 498) A financial plan that sets forth management's expectations, and, on the basis of those expectations, allocates the use of specific resources throughout the firm.

bull market *Situation where the stock market is increasing in value and investors feel it will continue to grow.*

bundling (p. 386) Grouping two or more products together and pricing them as a unit.

bureaucracy (p. 209) An organization with many layers of managers who set rules and regulations and oversee all decisions.

business (p. 4) Any activity that seeks to provide goods and services to others while operating at a profit.

business cycles (p. 49) The periodic rises and falls that occur in economies over time.

business environment (p. 11) The surrounding factors that either help or hinder the development of businesses.

business intelligence (BI) (p. B-3) Any of a variety of software applications that analyze an organization's raw data and take out useful insights from it.

business law (p. A-2) Rules, statutes, codes, and regulations that are established to provide a legal framework within which business may be conducted and that are enforceable by court action.

business plan (p. 163) A detailed written statement that describes the nature of the business, the target market, the advantages the business will have in relation to competition, and the resources and qualifications of the owner(s).

business-to-business (B2B) market (p. 365) All the individuals and organizations that want goods and services to use in producing other goods and services or to sell, rent, or supply goods to others.

buying stock on margin (p. 537) Purchasing stocks by borrowing some of the purchase cost from the brokerage firm.

cafeteria-style fringe benefits (p. 312) Fringe benefits plan that allows employees to choose the benefits they want up to a certain dollar amount.

cannibalize a business *One franchise pulls business away from another franchise, for example.*

capital budget (p. 498) A budget that highlights a firm's spending plans for major asset purchases that often require large sums of money.

capital expenditures (p. 503) Major investments in either tangible long-term assets such as land, buildings, and equipment or intangible assets such as patents, trademarks, and copyrights.

capital gains (p. 535) The positive difference between the purchase price of a stock and its sale price.

capitalism (p. 35) An economic system in which all or most of the factors of production and distribution are privately owned and operated for profit.

cash-and-carry wholesalers (p. 413) Wholesalers that serve mostly smaller retailers with a limited assortment of products.

cash budget (p. 498) A budget that estimates cash inflows and outflows during a particular period like a month or a quarter.

cash flow (p. 480) The difference between cash coming in and cash going out of a business.

cash flow forecast (p. 487) Forecast that predicts the cash inflows and outflows in future periods, usually months or quarters.

center stage *A very important position.*

centralized authority (p. 210) An organization structure in which decision-making authority is maintained at the top level of management at the company's headquarters.

certificate of deposit (CD) (p. 563) A time-deposit (savings) account that earns interest to be delivered at the end of the certificate's maturity date.

certification (p. 329) Formal process whereby a union is recognized by the National Labor Relations Board (NLRB) as the bargaining agent for a group of employees.

certified internal auditor (CIA) (p. 469) An accountant who has a bachelor's degree and two years of experience in internal auditing, and who has passed an exam administered by the Institute of Internal Auditors.

certified management accountant (CMA) (p. 466) A professional accountant who has met certain educational and experience requirements, passed a qualifying exam in the field, and been certified by the Institute of Certified Management Accountants.

certified public accountant (CPA) (p. 467) An accountant who passes a series of examinations established by the American Institute of Certified Public Accountants (AICPA).

chain of command (p. 209) The line of authority that moves from the top of a hierarchy to the lowest level.

channel of distribution (p. 406) A whole set of marketing intermediaries, such as agents, brokers, wholesalers, and retailers, that join together to transport and store goods in their path (or channel) from producers to consumers.

claim (p. C-7) A statement of loss that the insured sends to the insurance company to request payment.

climate change (p. 19) The movement of the temperature of the planet up or down over time.

climbed the ladder *Promoted to higher-level jobs.*

closed shop agreement (p. 331) Clause in a labor–management agreement that specified workers had to be members of a union before being hired (was outlawed by the Taft-Hartley Act in 1947).

cloud computing (p. B-14) A form of virtualization in which a company's data and applications are stored at offsite data centers that are accessed over the Internet (the cloud).

collective bargaining (p. 328) The process whereby union and management representatives form a labor–management agreement, or contract, for workers.

command economies (p. 43) Economic systems in which the government largely decides what goods and services will be produced, who will get them, and how the economy will grow.

commercial bank (p. 563) A profit-seeking organization that receives deposits from individuals and corporations in the form of checking and savings accounts and then uses some of these funds to make loans.

commercial finance companies (p. 507) Organizations that make short-term loans to borrowers who offer tangible assets as collateral.

commercialization (p. 393) Promoting a product to distributors and retailers to get wide distribution, and developing strong advertising and sales campaigns to generate and maintain interest in the product among distributors and consumers.

commercial paper (p. 508) Unsecured promissory notes of $100,000 and up that mature (come due) in 270 days or less.

common law (p. A-3) The body of law that comes from decisions handed down by judges; also referred to as unwritten law.

common market (p. 77) A regional group of countries that have a common external tariff, no internal tariffs, and a coordination of laws to facilitate exchange; also called a *trading bloc*. An example is the European Union.

common stock (p. 528) The most basic form of ownership in a firm; it confers voting rights and the right to share in the firm's profits through dividends, if offered by the firm's board of directors.

communism (p. 42) An economic and political system in which the government makes almost all economic decisions and owns almost all the major factors of production.

comparative advantage theory (p. 62) Theory that states that a country should sell to other countries those products that it produces most effectively and efficiently, and buy from other countries those products that it cannot produce as effectively or efficiently.

competition-based pricing (p. 397) A pricing strategy based on what all the other competitors are doing. The price can be set at, above, or below competitors' prices.

compliance-based ethics codes (p. 96) Ethical standards that emphasize preventing unlawful behavior by increasing control and by penalizing wrongdoers.

compressed workweek (p. 314) Work schedule that allows an employee to work a full number of hours per week but in fewer days.

computer-aided design (CAD) (p. 241) The use of computers in the design of products.

computer-aided manufacturing (CAM) (p. 241) The use of computers in the manufacturing of products.

computer-integrated manufacturing (CIM) (p. 241) The uniting of computer-aided design with computer-aided manufacturing.

concept testing (p. 392) Taking a product idea to consumers to test their reactions.

conceptual skills (p. 190) Skills that involve the ability to picture the organization as a whole and the relationship among its various parts.

conglomerate merger (p. 131) The joining of firms in completely unrelated industries.

Congress of Industrial Organizations (CIO) (p. 326) Union organization of unskilled workers; broke away from the American Federation of Labor (AFL) in 1935 and rejoined it in 1955.

consideration (p. A-9) Something of value; consideration is one of the requirements of a legal contract.

consumerism (p. A-13) A social movement that seeks to increase and strengthen the rights and powers of buyers in relation to sellers.

consumer market (p. 365) All the individuals or households that want goods and services for personal consumption or use.

consumer price index (CPI) (p. 48) Monthly statistics that measure the pace of inflation or deflation.

contingency planning (p. 186) The process of preparing alternative courses of action that may be used if the primary plans don't achieve the organization's objectives.

contingent workers (p. 302) Workers who do not have the expectation of regular, full-time employment.

continuous process (p. 240) A production process in which long production runs turn out finished goods over time.

contract (p. A-9) A legally enforceable agreement between two or more parties.

contract law (p. A-9) Set of laws that specify what constitutes a legally enforceable agreement.

contract manufacturing (p. 68) A foreign country's production of private-label goods to which a domestic company then attaches its brand name or trademark; part of the broad category of *outsourcing*.

contractual distribution system (p. 420) A distribution system in which members are bound to cooperate through contractual agreements.

contrarian approach (p. D-8) Buying stock when everyone else is selling or vice versa.

controlling (p. 183) A management function that involves establishing clear standards to determine whether or not an organization is progressing toward its goals and objectives, rewarding people for doing a good job, and taking corrective action if they are not.

convenience goods and services (p. 382) Products that the consumer wants to purchase frequently and with a minimum of effort.

conventional (C) corporation (p. 123) A state-chartered legal entity with authority to act and have liability separate from its owners.

cookies (p. B-21) Pieces of information, such as registration data or user preferences, sent by a website over the Internet to a Web browser that the browser software is expected to save and send back to the server whenever the user returns to that website.

cooking the books *Making accounting information look better than it actually is to outside observers and users of financial information of a company.*

cooling-off period (p. 335) When workers in a critical industry return to their jobs while the union and management continue negotiations.

cooperative (p. 140) A business owned and controlled by the people who use it—producers, consumers, or workers with similar needs who pool their resources for mutual gain.

copyright (p. A-7) A document that protects a creator's rights to materials such as books, articles, photos, and cartoons.

core competencies (p. 222) Those functions that the organization can do as well as or better than any other organization in the world.

core time (p. 313) In a flextime plan, the period when all employees are expected to be at their job stations.

corporate distribution system (p. 420) A distribution system in which all of the organizations in the channel of distribution are owned by one firm.

corporate philanthropy (p. 99) The dimension of social responsibility that includes charitable donations.

corporate policy (p. 99) The dimension of social responsibility that refers to the position a firm takes on social and political issues.

corporate responsibility (p. 99) The dimension of social responsibility that includes everything from hiring minority workers to making safe products.

corporate social initiatives (p. 99) Enhanced forms of corporate philanthropy directly related to the company's competencies.

corporate social responsibility (CSR) (p. 98) A business's concern for the welfare of society.

corporation (p. 116) A legal entity with authority to act and have liability separate from its owners.

cost of capital (p. 513) The rate of return a company must earn in order to meet the demands of its lenders and expectations of its equity holders.

cost of goods sold (or cost of goods manufactured) (p. 476) A measure of the cost of merchandise sold or cost of raw materials and supplies used for producing items for resale.

couch potatoes *People who sit and watch TV for hours at a time.*

countertrading (p. 74) A complex form of bartering in which several countries may be involved, each trading goods for goods or services for services.

counting on it *Expecting it.*

craft union (p. 326) An organization of skilled specialists in a particular craft or trade.

credit unions (p. 565) Nonprofit, member-owned financial cooperatives that offer the full variety of banking services to their members.

critical path (p. 252) In a PERT network, the sequence of tasks that takes the longest time to complete.

cross-functional self-managed teams (p. 218) Groups of employees from different departments who work together on a long-term basis.

current assets (p. 474) Items that can or will be converted into cash within one year.

customer relationship management (CRM) (p. 355) The process of learning as much as possible about customers and doing everything you can over time to satisfy them—or even exceed their expectations—with goods and services.

damages (p. A-10) The monetary settlement awarded to a person who is injured by a breach of contract.

database (p. 16) An electronic storage file for information.

data processing (DP) (p. B-2) Name for business technology in the 1970s; included technology that supported an existing business and was primarily used to improve the flow of financial information.

dealer (private-label) brands (p. 387) Products that don't carry the manufacturer's name but carry a distributor or retailer's name instead.

debenture bonds (p. 530) Bonds that are unsecured (i.e., not backed by any collateral such as equipment).

debit card (p. 570) An electronic funds transfer tool that serves the same function as checks: it withdraws funds from a checking account.

debt financing (p. 504) Funds raised through various forms of borrowing that must be repaid.

decentralized authority (p. 210) An organization structure in which decision-making authority is delegated to lower-level managers more familiar with local conditions than headquarters management could be.

decertification (p. 329) The process by which workers take away a union's right to represent them.

decision making (p. 187) Choosing among two or more alternatives.

deflation (p. 48) A situation in which prices are declining.

demand (p. 37) The quantity of products that people are willing to buy at different prices at a specific time.

demand deposit (p. 563) The technical name for a checking account; the money in a demand deposit can be withdrawn anytime on demand from the depositor.

demographic segmentation (p. 368) Dividing the market by age, income, and education level.

demography (p. 17) The statistical study of the human population with regard to its size, density, and other characteristics such as age, race, gender, and income.

departmentalization (p. 212) The dividing of organizational functions into separate units.

depreciation (p. 477) The systematic write-off of the cost of a tangible asset over its estimated useful life.

depression (p. 49) A severe recession, usually accompanied by deflation.

deregulation (p. A-17) Government withdrawal of certain laws and regulations that seem to hinder competition.

devaluation (p. 74) Lowering the value of a nation's currency relative to other currencies.

digital natives (p. 222) Young people who have grown up using the Internet and social networking.

direct marketing (p. 419) Any activity that directly links manufacturers or intermediaries with the ultimate consumer.

direct selling (p. 419) Selling to consumers in their homes or where they work.

disability insurance (p. D-11) Insurance that pays part of the cost of a long-term sickness or an accident.

discount rate (p. 559) The interest rate that the Fed charges for loans to member banks.

disinflation (p. 48) A situation in which price increases are slowing (the inflation rate is declining).

distributed product development (p. 379) Handing off various parts of your innovation process—often to companies in other countries

diversification (p. 534) Buying several different investment alternatives to spread the risk of investing.

dividends (p. 527) Part of a firm's profits that the firm may distribute to stockholders as either cash payments or additional shares of stock.

double-entry bookkeeping (p. 470) The practice of writing every business transaction in two places.

Dow Jones Industrial Average (the Dow) (p. 542) The average cost of 30 selected industrial stocks, used to give an indication of the direction (up or down) of the stock market over time.

drop shippers (p. 413) Wholesalers that solicit orders from retailers and other wholesalers and have the merchandise shipped directly from a producer to a buyer.

dumping (p. 66) Selling products in a foreign country at lower prices than those charged in the producing country.

e-commerce (p. 14) The buying and selling of goods over the Internet.

economic pie *The money available in the economy.*

economics (p. 30) The study of how society chooses to employ resources to produce goods and services and distribute them for consumption among various competing groups and individuals.

economies of scale (p. 206) The situation in which companies can reduce their production costs if they can purchase raw materials in bulk; the average cost of goods goes down as production levels increase.

electronic funds transfer (EFT) system (p. 569) A computerized system that electronically performs financial transactions such as making purchases, paying bills, and receiving paychecks.

electronic retailing (p. 417) Selling goods and services to ultimate customers (e.g., you and me) over the Internet.

e-mail snooped *When someone other than the addressee reads e-mail messages.*

embargo (p. 76) A complete ban on the import or export of a certain product, or the stopping of all trade with a particular country.

empowerment (p. 17) Giving frontline workers the responsibility, authority, freedom, training, and equipment they need to respond quickly to customer requests.

enabling (p. 194) Giving workers the education and tools they need to make decisions.

enterprise resource planning (ERP) (p. 247) A newer version of materials requirement planning (MRP) that combines the computerized functions of all the divisions and subsidiaries of the firm—such as finance, human resources, and order fulfillment—into a single integrated software program that uses a single database.

enterprise zones (p. 157) Specific geographic areas to which governments try to attract private business investment by offering lower taxes and other government support.

entrepreneur (p. 4) A person who risks time and money to start and manage a business.

entrepreneurial team (p. 152) A group of experienced people from different areas of business who join together to form a managerial team with the skills needed to develop, make, and market a new product.

entrepreneurship (p. 149) Accepting the risk of starting and running a business.

environmental scanning (p. 363) The process of identifying the factors that can affect marketing success.

equity financing (p. 504) Money raised from within the firm, from operations or through the sale of ownership in the firm (stock or venture capital).

equity theory (p. 272) The idea that employees try to maintain equity between inputs and outputs compared to others in similar positions.

ethics (p. 91) Standards of moral behavior, that is, behavior accepted by society as right versus wrong.

everyday low pricing (EDLP) (p. 398) Setting prices lower than competitors and then not having any special sales.

exchange rate (p. 74) The value of one nation's currency relative to the currencies of other countries.

exchange-traded funds (ETFs) (p. 540) Collections of stocks that are traded on exchanges but are traded more like individual stocks than like mutual funds.

exclusive distribution (p. 417) Distribution that sends products to only one retail outlet in a given geographic area.

executor (p. D-16) A person who assembles and values your estate, files income and other taxes, and distributes assets.

expectancy theory (p. 271) Victor Vroom's theory that the amount of effort employees exert on a specific task depends on their expectations of the outcome.

exporting (p. 61) Selling products to another country.

express warranties (p. A-9) Specific representations by the seller that buyers rely on regarding the goods they purchase.

external customers (p. 196) Dealers, who buy products to sell to others, and ultimate customers (or end users), who buy products for their own personal use.

extranet (p. B-9) A semiprivate network that uses Internet technology and allows more than one company to access the same information or allows people on different servers to collaborate.

extrinsic reward (p. 261) Something given to you by someone else as recognition for good work; extrinsic rewards include pay increases, praise, and promotions.

facility layout (p. 246) The physical arrangement of resources (including people) in the production process.

facility location (p. 244) The process of selecting a geographic location for a company's operations.

factoring (p. 508) The process of selling accounts receivable for cash.

factors of production (p. 9) The resources used to create wealth: land, labor, capital, entrepreneurship, and knowledge.

Federal Deposit Insurance Corporation (FDIC) (p. 568) An independent agency of the U.S. government that insures bank deposits.

finance (p. 494) The function in a business that acquires funds for the firm and manages those funds within the firm.

financial accounting (p. 466) Accounting information and analyses prepared for people outside the organization.

financial control (p. 499) A process in which a firm periodically compares its actual revenues, costs, and expenses with its budget.

financial management (p. 494) The job of managing a firm's resources so it can meet its goals and objectives.

financial managers (p. 494) Managers who examine financial data prepared by accountants and recommend strategies for improving the financial performance of the firm.

financial statement (p. 472) A summary of all the transactions that have occurred over a particular period.

fiscal policy (p. 50) The federal government's efforts to keep the economy stable by increasing or decreasing taxes or government spending.

fixed assets (p. 474) Assets that are relatively permanent, such as land, buildings, and equipment.

flat organization structure (p. 210) An organization structure that has few layers of management and a broad span of control.

flexible manufacturing (p. 242) Designing machines to do multiple tasks so that they can produce a variety of products.

flextime plan (p. 313) Work schedule that gives employees some freedom to choose when to work, as long as they work the required number of hours.

focus group (p. 362) A small group of people who meet under the direction of a discussion leader to communicate their opinions about an organization, its products, or other given issues.

foreign direct investment (FDI) (p. 70) The buying of permanent property and businesses in foreign nations.

foreign subsidiary (p. 70) A company owned in a foreign country by another company, called the *parent company*.

formal organization (p. 225) The structure that details lines of responsibility, authority, and position; that is, the structure shown on organization charts.

form utility (p. 239) The value producers add to materials in the creation of finished goods and services.

franchise (p. 133) The right to use a specific business's name and sell its products or services in a given territory.

franchise agreement (p. 133) An arrangement whereby someone with a good idea for a business sells the rights to use the business name and sell a product or service to others in a given territory.

franchisee (p. 133) A person who buys a franchise.

franchisor (p. 133) A company that develops a product concept and sells others the rights to make and sell the products.

free-for-all atmosphere *A situation where all order seems to be lost in conducting business.*

free-market economies (p. 43) Economic systems in which the market largely determines what goods and services get produced, who gets them, and how the economy grows.

free-rein leadership (p. 194) Leadership style that involves managers setting objectives and employees being relatively free to do whatever it takes to accomplish those objectives.

free trade (p. 62) The movement of goods and services among nations without political or economic barriers.

freight forwarder (p. 425) An organization that puts many small shipments together to create a single large shipment that can be transported cost-effectively to the final destination.

fringe benefits (p. 311) Benefits such as sick-leave pay, vacation pay, pension plans, and health plans that represent additional compensation to employees beyond base wages.

from scratch *From the beginning.*

fundamental accounting equation (p. 472) Assets = Liabilities + Owners' equity; this is the basis for the balance sheet.

Gantt chart (p. 252) Bar graph showing production managers what projects are being worked on and what stage they are in at any given time.

General Agreement on Tariffs and Trade (GATT) (p. 77) A 1948 agreement that established an international forum for negotiating mutual reductions in trade restrictions.

general partner (p. 119) An owner (partner) who has unlimited liability and is active in managing the firm.

general partnership (p. 119) A partnership in which all owners share in operating the business and in assuming liability for the business's debts.

generic goods (p. 388) Nonbranded products that usually sell at a sizable discount compared to national or private-label brands.

geographic segmentation (p. 367) Dividing the market by cities, counties, states, or regions.

get in on the dough *Take the opportunity to make some money.*

givebacks (p. 336) Concessions made by union members to management; gains from labor negotiations are given back to management to help employers remain competitive and thereby save jobs.

go for the gold *To work to be the very best (figuratively winning a gold medal).*

go out with me *Go with me to dinner or to a movie or some other entertainment.*

goals (p. 183) The broad, long-term accomplishments an organization wishes to attain.

goal-setting theory (p. 270) The idea that setting ambitious but attainable goals can motivate workers and improve performance if the goals are accepted, accompanied by feedback, and facilitated by organizational conditions.

gone off the deep end *Doing something risky, almost crazy—like jumping into the deep end of a swimming pool when you can't swim.*

goods (p. 4) Tangible products such as computers, food, clothing, cars, and appliances.

goofing off *Doing things at work not associated with the job, such as talking with others at the drinking fountain.*

government and not-for-profit accounting (p. 469) Accounting system for organizations whose purpose is not generating a profit but serving ratepayers, taxpayers, and others according to a duly approved budget.

greening (p. 19) The trend toward saving energy and producing products that cause less harm to the environment.

grievance (p. 333) A charge by employees that management is not abiding by the terms of the negotiated labor–management agreement.

gross domestic product (GDP) (p. 46) The total value of final goods and services produced in a country in a given year.

gross profit (or gross margin) (p. 477) How much a firm earned by buying (or making) and selling merchandise.

hand over the keys *Give access to others.*

hard copy *Copy printed on paper.*

Hawthorne effect (p. 262) The tendency for people to behave differently when they know they are being studied.

health maintenance organizations (HMOs) (p. C-9) Health care organizations that require members to choose from a restricted list of doctors.

health savings accounts (HSAs) (p. C-10) Tax-deferred savings accounts linked to low-cost, high-deductible health insurance policies.

heart *The most important part of something; the central force or idea.*

hierarchy (p. 208) A system in which one person is at the top of the organization and there is a ranked or sequential ordering from the top down of managers who are responsible to that person.

high–low pricing strategy (p. 398) Setting prices that are higher than EDLP stores, but having many special sales where the prices are lower than competitors'.

horizontal merger (p. 131) The joining of two firms in the same industry.

hot second *Immediately.*

human relations skills (p. 190) Skills that involve communication and motivation; they enable managers to work through and with people.

human resource management (HRM) (p. 290) The process of determining human resource needs and then recruiting, selecting, developing, motivating, evaluating, compensating, and scheduling employees to achieve organizational goals.

hygiene factors (p. 265) In Herzberg's theory of motivating factors, job factors that can cause dissatisfaction if missing but that do not necessarily motivate employees if increased.

identity theft (p. 16) The obtaining of individuals' personal information, such as Social Security and credit card numbers, for illegal purposes.

If it isn't broken, don't fix it *Don't risk making things worse by changing things that don't need to be changed.*

implied warranties (p. A-9) Guarantees legally imposed on the seller.

importing (p. 61) Buying products from another country.

import quota (p. 76) A limit on the number of products in certain categories that a nation can import.

inbound logistics (p. 424) The area of logistics that involves bringing raw materials, packaging, other goods and services, and information from suppliers to producers.

income statement (p. 476) The financial statement that shows a firm's profit after costs, expenses, and taxes; it summarizes all of the resources that have come into the firm (revenue), all the resources that have left the firm, expenses, and the resulting net income or net loss.

incubators (p. 158) Centers that offer new businesses low-cost offices with basic business services.

indenture terms (p. 510) The terms of agreement in a bond issue.

independent audit (p. 468) An evaluation and unbiased opinion about the accuracy of a company's financial statements.

individual retirement account (IRA) (p. D-13) A tax-deferred investment plan that enables you (and your spouse, if you are married) to save part of your income for retirement; a traditional IRA allows people who qualify to deduct from their reported income the money they put into an account.

industrial goods (p. 384) Products used in the production of other products. Sometimes called business goods or B2B goods.

industrial unions (p. 326) Labor organizations of unskilled and semiskilled workers in mass-production industries such as automobiles and mining.

inflation (p. 47) A general rise in the prices of goods and services over time.

infomercial (p. 442) A full-length TV program devoted exclusively to promoting goods or services.

informal organization (p. 225) The system that develops spontaneously as employees meet and form cliques, relationships, and lines of authority outside the formal organization; that is, the human side of the organization that does not appear on any organization chart.

information systems (IS) (p. B-2) Technology that helps companies do business; includes such tools as automated teller machines (ATMs) and voice mail.

information technology (IT) (p. B-2) Technology that helps companies change business by allowing them to use new methods.

information utility (p. 412) Adding value to products by opening two-way flows of information between marketing participants.

initial public offering (IPO) (p. 522) The first public offering of a corporation's stock.

injunction (p. 336) A court order directing someone to do something or to refrain from doing something.

insider trading (p. 101) An unethical activity in which insiders use private company information to further their own fortunes or those of their family and friends.

institutional investors (p. 523) Large organizations—such as pension funds, mutual funds, and insurance companies—that invest their own funds or the funds of others.

insurable interest (p. C-5) The possibility of the policyholder to suffer a loss.

insurable risk (p. C-5) A risk that the typical insurance company will cover.

insurance policy (p. C-6) A written contract between the insured and an insurance company that promises to pay for all or part of a loss.

intangible assets (p. 474) Long-term assets (e.g., patents, trademarks, copyrights) that have no real physical form but do have value.

integrated marketing communication (IMC) (p. 437) A technique that combines all the promotional tools into one comprehensive and unified promotional strategy.

integrity-based ethics codes (p. 96) Ethical standards that define the organization's guiding values, create an environment that supports ethically sound behavior, and stress a shared accountability among employees.

intensive distribution (p. 416) Distribution that puts products into as many retail outlets as possible.

interactive promotion (p. 442) Promotion process that allows marketers to go beyond a monologue, where sellers try to persuade buyers to buy things, to a dialogue in which buyers and sellers work together to create mutually beneficial exchange relationships.

interest (p. 529) The payment the issuer of the bond makes to the bondholders for use of the borrowed money.

intermittent process (p. 241) A production process in which the production run is short and the machines are changed frequently to make different products.

intermodal shipping (p. 426) The use of multiple modes of transportation to complete a single long-distance movement of freight.

internal customers (p. 196) Individuals and units within the firm that receive services from other individuals or units.

International Monetary Fund (IMF) (p. 572) Organization that assists the smooth flow of money among nations.

Internet2 (p. B-10) The private Internet system that links government supercomputer centers and a select group of universities; it runs more than 22,000 times faster than today's public infrastructure and supports heavy-duty applications.

intranet (p. B-9) A companywide network, closed to public access, that uses Internet-type technology.

intrapreneurs (p. 157) Creative people who work as entrepreneurs within corporations.

intrinsic reward (p. 261) The personal satisfaction you feel when you perform well and complete goals.

inverted organization (p. 223) An organization that has contact people at the top and the chief executive officer at the bottom of the organization chart.

investment bankers (p. 523) Specialists who assist in the issue and sale of new securities.

invisible hand (p. 33) A phrase coined by Adam Smith to describe the process that turns self-directed gain into social and economic benefits for all.

involuntary bankruptcy (p. A-15) Bankruptcy procedures filed by a debtor's creditors.

IOUs *Debt; abbreviation for "I owe you."*

ISO 14000 (p. 251) A collection of the best practices for managing an organization's impact on the environment.

ISO 9000 (p. 251) The common name given to quality management and assurance standards.

job analysis (p. 297) A study of what is done by employees who hold various job titles.

job description (p. 297) A summary of the objectives of a job, the type of work to be done, the responsibilities and duties, the working conditions, and the relationship of the job to other functions.

job enlargement (p. 274) A job enrichment strategy that involves combining a series of tasks into one challenging and interesting assignment.

job enrichment (p. 273) A motivational strategy that emphasizes motivating the worker through the job itself.

job rotation (p. 274) A job enrichment strategy that involves moving employees from one job to another.

job sharing (p. 315) An arrangement whereby two part-time employees share one full-time job.

job simulation (p. 305) The use of equipment that duplicates job conditions and tasks so that trainees can learn skills before attempting them on the job.

job specifications (p. 297) A written summary of the minimum qualifications required of workers to do a particular job.

joint venture (p. 70) A partnership in which two or more companies (often from different countries) join to undertake a major project.

journal (p. 470) The record book or computer program where accounting data are first entered.

judiciary (p. A-2) The branch of government chosen to oversee the legal system through the court system.

jumped headfirst *Began quickly and eagerly without hesitation.*

junk bonds (p. 538) High-risk, high-interest bonds.

just-in-time (JIT) inventory control (p. 249) A production process in which a minimum of inventory is kept on the premises and parts, supplies, and other needs are delivered just in time to go on the assembly line.

Keynesian economic theory (p. 50) The theory that a government policy of increasing spending and cutting taxes could stimulate the economy in a recession.

key player *Important participant.*

kick back and relax *To take a rest.*

Knights of Labor (p. 326) The first national labor union; formed in 1869.

knockoff brands (p. 388) Illegal copies of national brand-name goods.

know-how *A level of specific expertise.*

knowledge management (p. 195) Finding the right information, keeping the information in a readily accessible place, and making the information known to everyone in the firm.

latchkey kids *School-age children who come home to empty houses since all of the adults are at work.*

law of large numbers (p. C-7) Principle that if a large number of people are exposed to the same risk, a predictable number of losses will occur during a given period of time.

leading (p. 183) Creating a vision for the organization and guiding, training, coaching, and motivating others to work effectively to achieve the organization's goals and objectives.

lean manufacturing (p. 242) The production of goods using less of everything compared to mass production.

ledger (p. 470) A specialized accounting book or computer program in which information from accounting journals is accumulated into specific categories and posted so that managers can find all the information about one account in the same place.

letter of credit (p. 571) A promise by the bank to pay the seller a given amount if certain conditions are met.

level playing field *Treating everyone equally.*

leverage (p. 513) Raising needed funds through borrowing to increase a firm's rate of return.

leveraged buyout (LBO) (p. 131) An attempt by employees, management, or a group of investors to purchase an organization primarily through borrowing.

liabilities (p. 474) What the business owes to others (debts).

licensing (p. 66) A global strategy in which a firm (the licensor) allows a foreign company (the licensee) to produce its product in exchange for a fee (a royalty).

limited liability (p. 119) The responsibility of a business's owners for losses only up to the amount they invest; limited partners and shareholders have limited liability.

limited liability company (LLC) (p. 128) A company similar to an S corporation but without the special eligibility requirements.

limited liability partnership (LLP) (p. 119) A partnership that limits partners' risk of losing their personal assets to only their own acts and omissions and to the acts and omissions of people under their supervision.

limited partner (p. 119) An owner who invests money in the business but does not have any management responsibility or liability for losses beyond the investment.

limited partnership (p. 119) A partnership with one or more general partners and one or more limited partners.

line of credit (p. 507) A given amount of unsecured short-term funds a bank will lend to a business, provided the funds are readily available.

line organization (p. 215) An organization that has direct two-way lines of responsibility, authority, and communication running from the top to the bottom of the organization, with all people reporting to only one supervisor.

line personnel (p. 215) Employees who are part of the chain of command that is responsible for achieving organizational goals.

liquidity (p. 474) The ease with which an asset can be converted into cash.

lockout (p. 335) An attempt by management to put pressure on unions by temporarily closing the business.

logistics (p. 423) The marketing activity that involves planning, implementing, and controlling the physical flow of materials, final goods, and related information from points of origin to points of consumption to meet customer requirements at a profit.

long-term financing (p. 504) Funds needed for more than a year (usually 2 to 10 years).

long-term forecast (p. 498) Forecast that predicts revenues, costs, and expenses for a period longer than 1 year, and sometimes as far as 5 or 10 years into the future.

loss (p. 4) When a business's expenses are more than its revenues.

M-1 (p. 556) Money that can be accessed quickly and easily (coins and paper money, checks, traveler's checks, etc.).

M-2 (p. 556) Money included in M-1 plus money that may take a little more time to obtain (savings accounts, money market accounts, mutual funds, certificates of deposit, etc.).

M-3 (p. 556) M-2 plus big deposits like institutional money market funds.

Ma Bell *Telecommunication giant, AT&T.*

macroeconomics (p. 30) The part of economics study that looks at the operation of a nation's economy as a whole.

management (p. 181) The process used to accomplish organizational goals through planning, organizing, leading, and controlling people and other organizational resources.

management by objectives (MBO) (p. 270) Peter Drucker's system of goal setting and implementation; it involves a cycle of discussion, review, and evaluation of objectives among top and middle-level managers, supervisors, and employees.

management development (p. 306) The process of training and educating employees to become good managers and then monitoring the progress of their managerial skills over time.

managerial accounting (p. 465) Accounting used to provide information and analyses to managers within the organization to assist them in decision making.

manufacturers' brands (p. 387) The brand names of manufacturers that distribute products nationally.

market (p. 169) People with unsatisfied wants and needs who have both the resources and the willingness to buy.

marketing (p. 352) The activity, set of institutions, and processes for creating, communicating, delivering, and exchanging offerings that have value for customers, clients, partners, and society at large.

marketing concept (p. 355) A three-part business philosophy: (1) a customer orientation, (2) a service orientation, and (3) a profit orientation.

marketing intermediaries (p. 406) Organizations that assist in moving goods and services from producers to businesses (B2B) and from businesses to consumers (B2C).

marketing mix (p. 357) The ingredients that go into a marketing program: product, price, place, and promotion.

marketing research (p. 360) The analysis of markets to determine opportunities and challenges, and to find the information needed to make good decisions.

market price (p. 39) The price determined by supply and demand.

market segmentation (p. 366) The process of dividing the total market into groups whose members have similar characteristics.

marriage of software, hardware, etc. *Combination of various technologies.*

Maslow's hierarchy of needs (p. 263) Theory of motivation based on unmet human needs from basic physiological needs to safety, social, and esteem needs to self-actualization needs.

mass customization (p. 242) Tailoring products to meet the needs of individual customers.

mass marketing (p. 369) Developing products and promotions to please large groups of people.

master limited partnership (MLP) (p. 119) A partnership that looks much like a corporation (in that it acts like a corporation and is traded on a stock exchange) but is taxed like a partnership and thus avoids the corporate income tax.

materials handling (p. 424) The movement of goods within a warehouse, from warehouses to the factory floor, and from the factory floor to various workstations.

materials requirement planning (MRP) (p. 247) A computer-based operations management system that uses sales forecasts to make sure that needed parts and materials are available at the right time and place.

matrix organization (p. 216) An organization in which specialists from different parts of the organization are brought together to work on specific projects but still remain part of a line-and-staff structure.

maturity date (p. 529) The exact date the issuer of a bond must pay the principal to the bondholder.

measuring stick *Tool used to evaluate or compare something.*

mediation (p. 334) The use of a third party, called a mediator, who encourages both sides in a dispute to continue negotiating and often makes suggestions for resolving the dispute.

mentor (p. 307) An experienced employee who supervises, coaches, and guides lower-level employees by introducing them to the right people and generally being their organizational sponsor.

merchant wholesalers (p. 413) Independently owned firms that take title to the goods they handle.

merger (p. 131) The result of two firms forming one company.

Mickey D's *Nickname for McDonald's.*

microeconomics (p. 30) The part of economics study that looks at the behavior of people and organizations in particular markets.

micropreneurs (p. 152) Entrepreneurs willing to accept the risk of starting and managing the type of business that remains small, lets them do the kind of work they want to do, and offers them a balanced lifestyle.

middle management (p. 189) The level of management that includes general managers, division managers, and branch and plant managers who are responsible for tactical planning and controlling.

mine the knowledge *Make maximum use of the knowledge employees have.*

mission statement (p. 183) An outline of the fundamental purposes of an organization.

mixed economies (p. 44) Economic systems in which some allocation of resources is made by the market and some by the government.

monetary policy (p. 50) The management of the money supply and interest rates by the Federal Reserve Bank.

money (p. 555) Anything that people generally accept as payment for goods and services.

money supply (p. 556) The amount of money the Federal Reserve Bank makes available for people to buy goods and services.

monopolistic competition (p. 39) The degree of competition in which a large number of sellers produce very similar products that buyers nevertheless perceive as different.

monopoly (p. 40) A degree of competition in which only one seller controls the total supply of a product or service, and sets the price.

more than meets the eye *More than one can see with his or her own eyes; much is happening that is not visible.*

motivators (p. 265) In Herzberg's theory of motivating factors, job factors that cause employees to be productive and that give them satisfaction.

mouse-click away *Ease of doing something by using the computer or Internet.*

muddy the water *Making things even more difficult than they currently are.*

multinational corporation (p. 70) An organization that manufactures and markets products in many different countries and has multinational stock ownership and multinational management.

mutual fund (p. 539) An organization that buys stocks and bonds and then sells shares in those securities to the public.

mutual insurance company (p. C-7) A type of insurance company owned by its policyholders.

NASDAQ (p. 524) A nationwide electronic system that communicates over-the-counter trades to brokers.

national debt (p. 50) The sum of government deficits over time.

negligence (p. A-4) In tort law, behavior that causes unintentional harm or injury.

negotiable instruments (p. A-9) Forms of commercial paper (such as checks) that are transferable among businesses and individuals and represent a promise to pay a specified amount.

negotiated labor-management agreement (labor contract) (p. 330) Agreement that sets the tone and clarifies the terms under which management and labor agree to function over a period of time.

net income or net loss (p. 476) Revenue left over after all costs and expenses, including taxes, are paid.

network computing system (or client/server computing) (p. B-14) Computer systems that allow personal computers (clients) to obtain needed information from huge databases in a central computer (the server).

networking (pp. 219, 307) The process of establishing and maintaining contacts with key managers in one's own organization and other organizations and using those contacts to weave strong relationships that serve as informal development systems.

niche marketing (p. 368) The process of finding small but profitable market segments and designing or finding products for them.

nonbanks (p. 556) Financial organizations that accept no deposits but offer many of the services provided by regular banks (pension funds, insurance companies, commercial finance companies, consumer finance companies, and brokerage houses).

nonprofit organization (p. 7) An organization whose goals do not include making a personal profit for its owners or organizers.

North American Free Trade Agreement (NAFTA) (p. 79) Agreement that created a free-trade area among the United States, Canada, and Mexico.

notes payable (p. 475) Short-term or long-term liabilities that a business promises to repay by a certain date.

objectives (p. 184) Specific, short-term statements detailing how to achieve the organization's goals.

off-the-job training (p. 305) Training that occurs away from the workplace and consists of internal or external programs to develop any of a variety of skills or to foster personal development.

oligopoly (p. 39) A degree of competition in which just a few sellers dominate the market.

one-to-one marketing (p. 369) Developing a unique mix of goods and services for each individual customer.

online training (p. 305) Training programs in which employees complete classes via the Internet.

on-the-job training (p. 304) Training at the workplace that lets the employee learn by doing or by watching others for a while and then imitating them.

open-market operations (p. 559) The buying and selling of U.S. government bonds by the Fed with the goal of regulating the money supply.

open shop agreement (p. 332) Agreement in right-to-work states that gives workers the option to join or not join a union, if one exists in their workplace.

operating (or master) budget (p. 498) The budget that ties together the firm's other budgets and summarizes its proposed financial activities.

operating expenses (p. 477) Costs involved in operating a business, such as rent, utilities, and salaries.

operational planning (p. 186) The process of setting work standards and schedules necessary to implement the company's tactical objectives.

operations management (p. 238) A specialized area in management that converts or transforms resources (including human resources) into goods and services.

organizational (or corporate) culture (p. 224) Widely shared values within an organization that provide unity and cooperation to achieve common goals.

organization chart (p. 188) A visual device that shows relationships among people and divides the organization's work; it shows who is accountable for the completion of specific work and who reports to whom.

organizing (p. 182) A management function that includes designing the structure of the organization and creating conditions and systems in which everyone and everything work together to achieve the organization's goals and objectives.

orientation (p. 303) The activity that introduces new employees to the organization; to fellow employees; to their immediate supervisors; and to the policies, practices, and objectives of the firm.

other side of the tracks *The area where people with less money live.*

out of the office loop *Out of the line of communication that occurs in the workplace.*

outbound logistics (p. 424) The area of logistics that involves managing the flow of finished products and information to business buyers and ultimate consumers (people like you and me).

outsourcing (p. 7) Contracting with other companies (often in other countries) to do some or all of the functions of a firm, like its production or accounting tasks.

over-the-counter (OTC) market (p. 524) Exchange that provides a means to trade stocks not listed on the national exchanges.

owners' equity (p. 475) The amount of the business that belongs to the owners minus any liabilities owed by the business.

participative (democratic) leadership (p. 193) Leadership style that consists of managers and employees working together to make decisions.

partnership (p. 116) A legal form of business with two or more owners.

patent (p. A-6) A document that gives inventors exclusive rights to their inventions for 20 years.

pave the way *Process of making a task easier.*

peanut butter and jelly *Popular combination for sandwich; the two are seen as perfect complementary products.*

penetration strategy (p. 398) Strategy in which a product is priced low to attract many customers and discourage competition.

pension funds (p. 566) Amounts of money put aside by corporations, nonprofit organizations, or unions to cover part of the financial needs of members when they retire.

perks *Short for* perquisites; *compensation in addition to salary, such as day care or a company car.*

perfect competition (p. 39) The degree of competition in which there are many sellers in a market and none is large enough to dictate the price of a product.

performance appraisal (p. 308) An evaluation that measures employee performance against established standards in order to make decisions about promotions, compensation, training, or termination.

personal selling (p. 446) The face-to-face presentation and promotion of goods and services.

pick economy (p. 456) Customers who pick out their products from online outlets or who do online comparison shopping.

piece of the action   *A share in the opportunity.*

pink slip   *A notice that you've lost your job.*

pitch in   *To help as needed.*

place utility (p. 411)   Adding value to products by having them where people want them.

planning (p. 182)   A management function that includes anticipating trends and determining the best strategies and tactics to achieve organizational goals and objectives.

PMI (p. 187)   Listing all the pluses for a solution in one column, all the minuses in another, and the implications in a third column.

podcasting (p. 454)   A means of distributing audio and video programs via the Internet that lets users subscribe to a number of files, also known as feeds, and then hear or view the material at the time they choose.

possession utility (p. 412)   Doing whatever is necessary to transfer ownership from one party to another, including providing credit, delivery, installation, guarantees, and follow-up service.

poster child   *Best example.*

precedent (p. A-3)   Decisions judges have made in earlier cases that guide the handling of new cases.

preferred provider organizations (PPOs) (p. C-10)   Health care organizations similar to HMOs except that they allow members to choose their own physicians (for a fee).

preferred stock (p. 528)   Stock that gives its owners preference in the payment of dividends and an earlier claim on assets than common stockholders if the company is forced out of business and its assets sold.

premium (p. C-6)   The fee charged by an insurance company for an insurance policy.

price leadership (p. 397)   The strategy by which one or more dominant firms set the pricing practices that all competitors in an industry follow.

primary boycott (p. 335)   When a union encourages both its members and the general public not to buy the products of a firm involved in a labor dispute.

primary data (p. 361)   Data that you gather yourself (not from secondary sources such as books and magazines).

principle of motion economy (p. 262)   Theory developed by Frank and Lillian Gilbreth that every job can be broken down into a series of elementary motions.

private accountant (p. 466)   An accountant who works for a single firm, government agency, or nonprofit organization.

problem solving (p. 187)   The process of solving the everyday problems that occur. Problem solving is less formal than decision making and usually calls for quicker action.

process manufacturing (p. 240)   That part of the production process that physically or chemically changes materials.

producer price index (PPI) (p. 48)   An index that measures prices at the wholesale level.

product (p. 358)   Any physical good, service, or idea that satisfies a want or need plus anything that would enhance the product in the eyes of consumers, such as the brand name.

product analysis (p. 391)   Making cost estimates and sales forecasts to get a feeling for profitability of new-product ideas.

product differentiation (p. 382)   The creation of real or perceived product differences.

product liability (p. A-4)   Part of tort law that holds businesses liable for harm that results from the production, design, sale, or use of products they market.

product life cycle (p. 393)   A theoretical model of what happens to sales and profits for a product class over time; the four stages of the cycle are introduction, growth, maturity, and decline.

product line (p. 381)   A group of products that are physically similar or are intended for a similar market.

product mix (p. 382)   The combination of product lines offered by a manufacturer.

product placement (p. 441)   Putting products into TV shows and movies where they will be seen.

product screening (p. 391)   A process designed to reduce the number of new-product ideas being worked on at any one time.

production (p. 237)   The creation of finished goods and services using the factors of production: land, labor, capital, entrepreneurship, and knowledge.

production management (p. 237) The term used to describe all the activities managers do to help their firms create goods.

productivity (p. I5) The amount of output you generate given the amount of input (e.g., hours worked).

profit (p. 4) The amount of money a business earns above and beyond what it spends for salaries and other expenses.

program evaluation and review technique (PERT) (p. 252) A method for analyzing the tasks involved in completing a given project, estimating the time needed to complete each task, and identifying the minimum time needed to complete the total project.

program trading (p. 544) Giving instructions to computers to automatically sell if the price of a stock dips to a certain point to avoid potential losses.

promissory note (p. 505) A written contract with a promise to pay a supplier a specific sum of money at a definite time.

promotion (p. 359) All the techniques sellers use to inform people about and motivate them to buy their products or services.

promotion mix (p. 436) The combination of promotional tools an organization uses.

pros and cons *Arguments for and against something.*

prospect (p. 447) A person with the means to buy a product, the authority to buy, and the willingness to listen to a sales message.

prospecting (p. 447) Researching potential buyers and choosing those most likely to buy.

prospectus (p. 525) A condensed version of economic and financial information that a company must file with the SEC before issuing stock; the prospectus must be sent to prospective investors.

psychographic segmentation (p. 367) Dividing the market using the group's values, attitudes, and interests.

psychological pricing (p. 399) Pricing goods and services at price points that make the product appear less expensive than it is.

public accountant (p. 466) An accountant who provides accounting services to individuals or businesses on a fee basis.

public domain software (or freeware) (p. B-I6) Software that is free for the taking.

publicity (p. 45I) Any information about an individual, product, or organization that's distributed to the public through the media and that's not paid for or controlled by the seller.

public relations (PR) (p. 450) The management function that evaluates public attitudes, changes policies and procedures in response to the public's requests, and executes a program of action and information to earn public understanding and acceptance.

pull strategy (p. 455) Promotional strategy in which heavy advertising and sales promotion efforts are directed toward consumers so that they'll request the products from retailers.

pump up the profits *Making profits in a company appear larger than they actually are under recognized accounting rules.*

purchasing (p. 249) The function in a firm that searches for quality material resources, finds the best suppliers, and negotiates the best price for goods and services.

pure risk (p. C-3) The threat of loss with no chance for profit.

push strategy (p. 455) Promotional strategy in which the producer uses advertising, personal selling, sales promotion, and all other promotional tools to convince wholesalers and retailers to stock and sell merchandise.

qualifying (p. 447) In the selling process, making sure that people have a need for the product, the authority to buy, and the willingness to listen to a sales message.

quality (p. 249) Consistently producing what the customer wants while reducing errors before and after delivery to the customer.

quality of life (p. 6) The general well-being of a society in terms of its political freedom, natural environment, education, health care, safety, amount of leisure, and rewards that add to the satisfaction and joy that other goods and services provide.

quid pro quo *Latin phrase meaning "something given in return for something else."*

quite a stir *Something that causes a feeling of concern.*

rack jobbers (p. 413) Wholesalers that furnish racks or shelves full of merchandise to retailers, display products, and sell on consignment.

ratio analysis (p. 482) The assessment of a firm's financial condition using calculations and interpretations of financial ratios developed from the firm's financial statements.

real time (p. 220) The present moment or the actual time in which something takes place.

recession (p. 49) Two or more consecutive quarters of decline in the GDP.

recruitment (p. 298) The set of activities used to obtain a sufficient number of the right people at the right time.

reinforcement theory (p. 272) Theory that positive and negative reinforcers motivate a person to behave in certain ways.

relationship marketing (p. 369) Marketing strategy with the goal of keeping individual customers over time by offering them products that exactly meet their requirements.

reserve requirement (p. 559) A percentage of commercial banks' checking and savings accounts that must be physically kept in the bank.

resource development (p. 31) The study of how to increase resources and to create the conditions that will make better use of those resources.

restructuring (p. 223) Redesigning an organization so that it can more effectively and efficiently serve its customers.

retailer (p. 407) An organization that sells to ultimate consumers.

retained earnings (p. 475) The accumulated earnings from a firm's profitable operations that were reinvested in the business and not paid out to stockholders in dividends.

revenue (p. 4) The total amount of money a business takes in during a given period by selling goods and services.

reverse discrimination (p. 294) Discrimination against whites or males in hiring or promoting.

reverse logistics (p. 424) The area of logistics that involves bringing goods back to the manufacturer because of defects or for recycling materials.

revolving credit agreement (p. 507) A line of credit that is guaranteed but usually comes with a fee.

right-to-work laws (p. 332) Legislation that gives workers the right, under an open shop, to join or not join a union if it is present.

risk (p. 5) The chance an entrepreneur takes of losing time and money on a business that may not prove profitable.

risk (p. C-3) The chance of loss, the degree of probability of loss, and the amount of possible loss.

risk/return trade-off (p. 510) The principle that the greater the risk a lender takes in making a loan, the higher the interest rate required.

Roth IRA (p. D-14) An IRA where you don't get upfront deductions on your taxes as you would with a traditional IRA, but the earnings grow tax-free and are also tax-free when they are withdrawn.

rule of indemnity (p. C-7) Rule saying that an insured person or organization cannot collect more than the actual loss from an insurable risk.

rules-of-the-road orientation *Introduction to the proper procedures within an organization.*

sales promotion (p. 451) The promotional tool that stimulates consumer purchasing and dealer interest by means of short-term activities.

sampling (p. 453) A promotional tool in which a company lets consumers have a small sample of a product for no charge.

savings and loan association (S&L) (p. 564) A financial institution that accepts both savings and checking deposits and provides home mortgage loans.

Savings Association Insurance Fund (SAIF) (p. 569) The part of the FDIC that insures holders of accounts in savings and loan associations.

scientific management (p. 261) Studying workers to find the most efficient ways of doing things and then teaching people those techniques.

S corporation (p. 127) A unique government creation that looks like a corporation but is taxed like sole proprietorships and partnerships.

sea of information *Lots of information, often too much to process.*

secondary boycott (p. 335) An attempt by labor to convince others to stop doing business with a firm that is the subject of a primary boycott; prohibited by the Taft-Hartley Act.

secondary data (p. 361) Information that has already been compiled by others and published in journals and books or made available online.

secured bond (p. 511) A bond issued with some form of collateral.

secured loan (p. 506) A loan backed by collateral (something valuable, such as property).

Securities and Exchange Commission (SEC) (p. 525) Federal agency that has responsibility for regulating the various exchanges.

selection (p. 300) The process of gathering information and deciding who should be hired, under legal guidelines, for the best interests of the individual and the organization.

selective distribution (p. 417) Distribution that sends products to only a preferred group of retailers in an area.

self-insurance (p. C-4) The practice of setting aside money to cover routine claims and buying only "catastrophe" policies to cover big losses.

Service Corps of Retired Executives (SCORE) (p. 171) An SBA office with volunteers from industry, trade associations, and education who counsel small businesses at no cost (except for expenses).

services (p. 4) Intangible products (i.e., products that can't be held in your hand) such as education, health care, insurance, recreation, and travel and tourism.

service utility (p. 412) Adding value by providing fast, friendly service during and after the sale and by teaching customers how to best use products over time.

sexual harassment (p. 341) Unwelcome sexual advances, requests for sexual favors, and other conduct (verbal or physical) of a sexual nature that creates a hostile work environment.

shaky ground *Idea that possible problems lie ahead.*

shareware (p. B-16) Software that is copyrighted but distributed to potential customers free of charge.

Sherlock Holmes *A famous fictional detective who was particularly adept at uncovering information to solve very difficult mysteries.*

shoestring budget *A budget that implies the company is short on funds and only includes a minimal amount of financial expenditures (i.e., it's as thin as a shoestring).*

shopping goods and services (p. 382) Those products that the consumer buys only after comparing value, quality, price, and style from a variety of sellers.

shop stewards (p. 333) Union officials who work permanently in an organization and represent employee interests on a daily basis.

short-term financing (p. 504) Funds needed for a year or less.

short-term forecast (p. 497) Forecast that predicts revenues, costs, and expenses for a period of one year or less.

sift through mountains of information *Sort through large volumes of information.*

sin taxes *Taxes used to discourage the use of goods like liquor or cigarettes.*

sinking fund (p. 531) A reserve account in which the issuer of a bond periodically retires some part of the bond principal prior to maturity so that enough capital will be accumulated by the maturity date to pay off the bond.

Six Sigma quality (p. 250) A quality measure that allows only 3.4 defects per million opportunities.

skimming price strategy (p. 398) Strategy in which a new product is priced high to make optimum profit while there's little competition.

small business (p. 159) A business that is independently owned and operated, is not dominant in its field of operation, and meets certain standards of size (set by the Small Business Administration) in terms of employees or annual receipts.

Small Business Administration (SBA) (p. 168) A U.S. government agency that advises and assists small businesses by providing management training and financial advice and loans.

Small Business Investment Company (SBIC) Program (p. 168) A program through which private investment companies licensed by the Small Business Administration lend money to small businesses.

smart card (p. 570) An electronic funds transfer tool that is a combination credit card, debit card, phone card, driver's license card, and more.

smoking gun *An issue or other disclosure that could prove a person or organization has done something wrong.*

social audit (p. 104) A systematic evaluation of an organization's progress toward implementing socially responsible and responsive programs.

Social Security (p. D-13) The term used to describe the Old-Age, Survivors, and Disability Insurance Program established by the Social Security Act of 1935.

socialism (p. 41) An economic system based on the premise that some, if not most, basic businesses should be owned by the government so that profits can be more evenly distributed among the people.

sole proprietorship (p. 116) A business that is owned, and usually managed, by one person.

sovereign wealth funds (SWFs) (p. 70) Investment funds controlled by governments holding large stakes in foreign companies.

span of control (p. 210) The optimum number of subordinates a manager supervises or should supervise.

specialty goods and services (p. 382) Consumer products with unique characteristics and brand identity. Because these products are perceived as having no reasonable substitute, the consumer puts forth a special effort to purchase them.

speculative risk (p. C-3) A chance of either profit or loss.

squeezing franchisees' profits *Tightening or reducing profits.*

staffing (p. 190) A management function that includes hiring, motivating, and retaining the best people available to accomplish the company's objectives.

staff personnel (p. 216) Employees who advise and assist line personnel in meeting their goals.

stagflation (p. 48) A situation when the economy is slowing but prices are going up anyhow.

stakeholders (p. 6) All the people who stand to gain or lose by the policies and activities of a business and whose concerns the business needs to address.

standard of living (p. 5) The amount of goods and services people can buy with the money they have.

state-of-the-art *The most modern type available.*

statement of cash flows (p. 479) Financial statement that reports cash receipts and disbursements related to a firm's three major activities: operations, investments, and financing.

statistical process control (SPC) (p. 250) The process of taking statistical samples of product components at each stage of the production process and plotting those results on a graph. Any variances from quality standards are recognized and can be corrected if beyond the set standards.

statistical quality control (SQC) (p. 250) The process some managers use to continually monitor all phases of the production process to assure that quality is being built into the product from the beginning.

statutory law (p. A-2) State and federal constitutions, legislative enactments, treaties of the federal government, and ordinances—in short, written law.

staying afloat *Staying in business during tough times.*

stockbroker (p. 532) A registered representative who works as a market intermediary to buy and sell securities for clients.

stock certificate (p. 527) Evidence of stock ownership that specifies the name of the company, the number of shares it represents, and the type of stock being issued.

stock exchange (p. 523) An organization whose members can buy and sell (exchange) securities for companies and investors.

stock insurance company (p. C-7) A type of insurance company owned by stockholders.

stocks (p. 527) Shares of ownership in a company.

stock splits (p. 536) An action by a company that gives stockholders two or more shares of stock for each one they own.

strategic alliance (p. 70) A long-term partnership between two or more companies established to help each company build competitive market advantages.

strategic planning (p. 185) The process of determining the major goals of the organization and the policies and strategies for obtaining and using resources to achieve those goals.

strict product liability (p. A-5) Legal responsibility for harm or injury caused by a product regardless of fault.

strike (p. 335) A union strategy in which workers refuse to go to work; the purpose is to further workers' objectives after an impasse in collective bargaining.

strikebreakers (p. 336) Workers hired to do the jobs of striking workers until the labor dispute is resolved.

supervisory management (p. 189) Managers who are directly responsible for supervising workers and evaluating their daily performance.

supply (p. 37) The quantity of products that manufacturers or owners are willing to sell at different prices at a specific time.

supply chain (or value chain) (p. 421) The sequence of linked activities that must be performed by various organizations to move goods from the sources of raw materials to ultimate consumers.

supply-chain management (p. 421) The process of managing the movement of raw materials, parts, work in progress, finished goods, and related information through all the organizations involved in the supply chain; managing the return of such goods, if necessary; and recycling materials when appropriate.

SWOT analysis (p. 184) A planning tool used to analyze an organization's strengths, weaknesses, opportunities, and threats.

tactical planning (p. 186) The process of developing detailed, short-term statements about what is to be done, who is to do it, and how it is to be done.

tall organization structure (p. 210) An organizational structure in which the pyramidal organization chart would be quite tall because of the various levels of management.

target costing (p. 397) Designing a product so that it satisfies customers and meets the profit margins desired by the firm.

target marketing (p. 367) Marketing directed toward those groups (market segments) an organization decides it can serve profitably.

tariff (p. 76) A tax imposed on imports.

tax accountant (p. 469) An accountant trained in tax law and responsible for preparing tax returns or developing tax strategies.

tax-deferred contributions (p. D-13) Retirement account deposits for which you pay no current taxes, but the earnings gained are taxed as regular income when they are withdrawn at retirement.

taxes (p. A-14) How the government (federal, state, and local) raises money.

technical skills (p. 190) Skills that involve the ability to perform tasks in a specific discipline or department.

technology (p. 14) Everything from phones and copiers to computers, medical imaging devices, personal digital assistants, and the various software programs that make business processes more effective, efficient, and productive.

telecom *Short for telecommunications.*

telecommuting (p. 246) Working from home via computer and modem.

telemarketing (p. 418) The sale of goods and services by telephone.

telephone tag *To leave a telephone message when you attempt to return a message left for you.*

term insurance (p. D-10) Pure insurance protection for a given number of years.

term-loan agreement (p. 510) A promissory note that requires the borrower to repay the loan in specified installments.

test marketing (p. 358) The process of testing products among potential users.

thorny issue *An issue that can cause pain or difficulty (as a thorn on a rose bush may).*

through the grapevine *Informal information communication; stories told by one person to the next.*

time deposit (p. 563) The technical name for a savings account; the bank can require prior notice before the owner withdraws money from a time deposit.

time in the trenches *Working with the other employees and experiencing what they contend with as opposed to managing from an office and relying solely on reports about what is happening in the workplace.*

time-motion studies (p. 261) Studies, begun by Frederick Taylor, of which tasks must be performed to complete a job and the time needed to do each task.

time utility (p. 411) Adding value to products by making them available when they're needed.

to take a break *To slow down and do something besides work.*

top management (p. 188) Highest level of management, consisting of the president and other key company executives who develop strategic plans.

tort (p. A-4) A wrongful act that causes injury to another person's body, property, or reputation.

total fixed costs (p. 397) All the expenses that remain the same no matter how many products are made or sold.

total product offer (p. 380) Everything that consumers evaluate when deciding whether to buy something; also called a *value package*.

trade credit (p. 504) The practice of buying goods and services now and paying for them later.

trade deficit (p. 64) An unfavorable balance of trade; occurs when the value of a country's imports exceeds that of its exports.

trademark (p. 387) A brand that has exclusive legal protection for both its brand name and its design.

trade protectionism (p. 76) The use of government regulations to limit the import of goods and services.

trade surplus (p. 64) A favorable balance of trade; occurs when the value of a country's exports exceeds that of its imports.

training and development (p. 303) All attempts to improve productivity by increasing an employee's ability to perform. Training focuses on short-term skills, whereas development focuses on long-term abilities.

transparency (p. 192) The presentation of a company's facts and figures in a way that is clear and apparent to all stakeholders.

trial balance (p. 471) A summary of all the financial data in the account ledgers that ensures the figures are correct and balanced.

trial close (p. 448) A step in the selling process that consists of a question or statement that moves the selling process toward the actual close.

trigger-happy *Term that refers to people reacting too fast to the circumstances facing them in a difficult situation.*

turn a blind eye *Ignore something of importance.*

turn the work off *Stop working.*

umbrella policy (p. D-12) A broadly based insurance policy that saves you money because you buy all your insurance from one company.

unemployment rate (p. 47) The number of civilians at least 16 years old who are unemployed and tried to find a job within the prior four weeks.

Uniform Commercial Code (UCC) (p. A-8) A comprehensive commercial law, adopted by every state in the United States, that covers sales laws and other commercial laws.

uninsurable risk (p. C-5) A risk that no insurance company will cover.

union (p. 324) An employee organization that has the main goal of representing members in employee–management bargaining over job-related issues.

union security clause (p. 331) Provision in a negotiated labor–management agreement that stipulates that employees who benefit from a union must either officially join or at least pay dues to the union.

union shop agreement (p. 331) Clause in a labor–management agreement that says workers do not have to be members of a union to be hired, but must agree to join the union within a prescribed period.

unlimited liability (p. 118) The responsibility of business owners for all of the debts of the business.

unsecured bond (p. 511) A bond backed only by the reputation of the issuer; also called a debenture bond.

unsecured loan (p. 507) A loan that doesn't require any collateral.

unsought goods and services (p. 383) Products that consumers are unaware of, haven't necessarily thought of buying, or find that they need to solve an unexpected problem.

utility (p. 411) In economics, the want-satisfying ability, or value, that organizations add to goods or services when the products are made more useful or accessible to consumers than they were before.

value (p. 378) Good quality at a fair price. When consumers calculate the value of a product, they look at the benefits and then subtract the cost to see if the benefits exceed the costs.

variable costs (p. 397) Costs that change according to the level of production.

variable life insurance (p. D-11)   Whole life insurance that invests the cash value of the policy in stocks or other high-yielding securities.

venture capital (p. 512)   Money that is invested in new or emerging companies that are perceived as having great profit potential.

venture capitalists (p. 167)   Individuals or companies that invest in new businesses in exchange for partial ownership of those businesses.

vertical merger (p. 131)   The joining of two companies involved in different stages of related businesses.

vestibule training (p. 305)   Training done in schools where employees are taught on equipment similar to that used on the job.

viral marketing (p. 454)   The term now used to describe everything from paying customers to say positive things on the Internet to setting up multilevel selling schemes whereby consumers get commissions for directing friends to specific websites.

virtual corporation (p. 220)   A temporary networked organization made up of replaceable firms that join and leave as needed.

virtualization (p. B-14)   A process that allows networked computers to run multiple operating systems and programs through one central computer at the same time.

virtual private network (VPN) (p. B-9)   A private data network that creates secure connections, or "tunnels," over regular Internet lines.

virus (p. B-18)   A piece of programming code inserted into other programming to cause some unexpected and, for the victim, usually undesirable event.

vision (p. 183)   An encompassing explanation of why the organization exists and where it's trying to head.

volume (or usage) segmentation (p. 368)   Dividing the market by usage (volume of use).

voluntary bankruptcy (p. A-15)   Legal procedures initiated by a debtor.

walk out the door   *Leave the company; quit your job.*

watching over your shoulder   *Looking at everything you do.*

Web 2.0 (p. B-12)   The set of tools that allow people to build social and business connections, share information, and collaborate on projects online (including blogs, wikis, social networking sites and other online communities, and virtual worlds).

Web 3.0 (p. B-12)   A combination of technologies that adds intelligence and changes how people interact with the Web, and vice versa (consists of the semantic Web, mobile Web, and immersive Internet).

whistleblowers (p. 97)   Insiders who report illegal or unethical behavior.

whole life insurance (p. D-10)   Life insurance that stays in effect until age 100.

wholesaler (p. 407)   A marketing intermediary that sells to other organizations.

will (p. D-16)   A document that names the guardian for your children, states how you want your assets distributed, and names the executor for your estate.

word-of-mouth promotion (p. 453)   A promotional tool that involves people telling other people about products they've purchased.

World Bank (p. 572)   The bank primarily responsible for financing economic development; also known as the International Bank for Reconstruction and Development.

World Trade Organization (WTO) (p. 77)   The international organization that replaced the General Agreement on Tariffs and Trade, and was assigned the duty to mediate trade disputes among nations.

yellow-dog contract (p. 328)   A type of contract that required employees to agree as a condition of employment not to join a union; prohibited by the Norris-LaGuardia Act in 1932.

photo credits

name index

organization index

subject index

Q

Qualifying, 447
Quality
Baldrige Awards, 250, 310
as competitive advantage, 16
defined, 249
ISO 9000 standards, 251
perceived, 389
six sigma, 250
sustainability and, 381
Quality control
continuous improvement process, 250
at end of production, 249–250
Quality Digest, C-2
Quality of life, 6, 245
Quick ratio, 483

R

Race; *see* Diversity; Minorities
Rack jobbers, 413
Radio advertising, 440
Radio frequency identification (RFID), 386, 427, 570, B-5
Railroads, 407, 425
Ratio analysis
activity ratios, 485–486
defined, 482
leverage ratios, 483, 513
liquidity ratios
acid-test (quick) ratio, 483
current ratio, 482–483
purpose, 482
profitability ratios, 483–484
basic earnings per share, 484
diluted earnings per share, 484
return on equity, 484–485
return on sales, 484
Real estate; *see also* Mortgages
bubbles, D-7
investing in, D-6 to D-8
property taxes, A-14, D-8
Real time, 220
Realtors, 412
Recessions; *see also* Economic crisis
of 2008–
definition, 49
duration, 562
effects in retail, 210, 365
financial management, 502, 506, 514
Recognizing employees, 276–277
Recruitment, employee; *see also* Job searches
affirmative action and, 294
application forms, 301
background investigations, 301
challenges, 298–299
of contingent workers, 302–303
defined, 298
employment tests, 301
interviews, P-15 to P-16, P-23 to P-26
online services, 299, 300
physical exams, 302
selecting employees, 300–302
by small businesses, 299–300
sources, 299, 300
traits sought, P-25
trial periods, 302
Reference groups, 369
Regulations; *see also* Legal environment
consumer protection, 545, A-13
deregulation, 40, A-17 to A-19
effects on global markets, 75
financial services, 514, 545, A-13, A-18
on hamburgers, A-18

health care system, A-18 to A-19
packaging, 386
securities markets, 511–512, 525–526
support for, A-18, A-19
Reinforcement theory, 272
Reinsurance, C-1
Relationship marketing, 369
Religious differences, 73
Renter's insurance, D-11 to D-12
Research; *see* Marketing research; Product development
Reserve requirements, 559
Resignations, 317
Resource development, 31
Resource files, P-5
Resources; *see* Factors of production
Restrictions on trade; *see* Trade barriers
Restructuring
competing with, 17
for empowerment, 223–224
Résumés
cover letters, P-15, P-22 to P-23
key words, P-18 to P-19
posting on Internet, P-19 to P-21
sample, P-20, P-21
writing, P-15, P-18 to P-19
Retail industry; *see also* E-commerce
catalog companies, 419–420
cooperatives, 421
decentralized authority, 209
distribution strategies, 416–417
jobs in, 21
nonstore retailing, 417–420
number of stores in United States, 415
pop-up stores, 416
pricing strategies, 398
in recessions, 210, 365
salespersons, 449
supermarkets, 299, 415, 453
types of stores, 415–416
Retailers, 407, 413
Retained earnings, 475, 512
Retirement planning, D-12
defined-contribution plans, D-14 to D-15
401(k) plans, D-14 to D-15
IRAs, 563, 568, D-13 to D-14
Keogh plans, D-15
Social Security, 18, C-5, D-13
Retirements, 296, 317
Return on equity (ROE), 484–485
Return on investment (ROI), 396
Return on sales, 484
Returns, risk and, 510, 538
Revenue tariffs, 76
Revenues
defined, 4, 476
forecasting, 497–498
Reverse discrimination, 294
Reverse logistics, 424
Revolving credit agreements, 507
RFID; *see* Radio frequency identification
Right-to-work laws, 332
Risk
avoidance, C-4
defined, 5, C-3
insurable, C-5 to C-6
investment, 533–535, 538
matching profits and, 5
pure, C-3
reduction, C-3 to C-4
return on equity, 484–485
speculative, C-3
uninsurable, C-5

Risk management; *see also* Insurance
environmental risks, C-11
importance, C-2
options, C-3 to C-5
rapid change and, C-2 to C-3
Risk/return trade-off, 510, 538
Robinson-Patman Act of 1936, A-12
Rockefeller family, 512
ROE; *see* Return on equity
ROI; *see* Return on investment
Ronald McDonald Houses, 99
Roth IRAs, D-14
Royalties, 66
Rule of indemnity, C-7
Russia
barter trade, 555
corruption, 81
dumping disputes, 66
factors of production, 10
income tax rates, 42
as market, 81

S

S corporations, 127–128
S&Ls; *see* Savings and loan associations
SADC; *see* Southern African Development Community
Safety, 205
SAIF; *see* Savings Association Insurance Fund
Salaries, 311; *see also* Compensation
Sales; *see also* Personal selling
difference from revenues, 476
gross, 476
net, 476
return on, 484
Sales agents, 415
Sales law, A-8 to A-9
Sales promotion; *see also* Promotion
defined, 451
internal, 453
to marketing intermediaries, 453–454
sampling, 453
techniques, 451–453
Sales representatives; *see also* Personal selling
in retail stores, 449
sales promotion to, 453
Sales taxes, 41, A-14 to A-15
Sampling, 453
Sarbanes-Oxley Act, 96, 467, 468, A-13
Saudi Arabia
entrepreneurs, 173
flag, 73
franchises in, 73
imports, 63
Savings; *see also* Retirement planning
personal, D-5, D-8
rates of return, D-5
Savings accounts, 563
Savings and loan associations (S&Ls)
defined, 564
failures, 565
federal deposit insurance, 568–569
IRAs, D-14
as marketing intermediaries, 412
services, 564–565
Savings Association Insurance Fund (SAIF), 568, 569
SBA; *see* Small Business Administration
SBDCs; *see* Small Business Development Centers
SBIC; *see* Small Business Investment Company